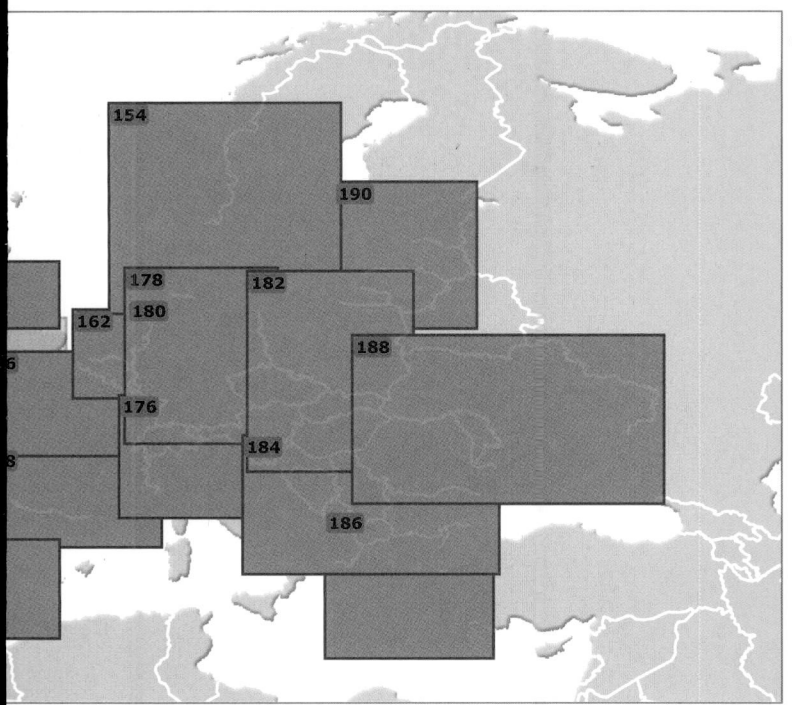

City plans

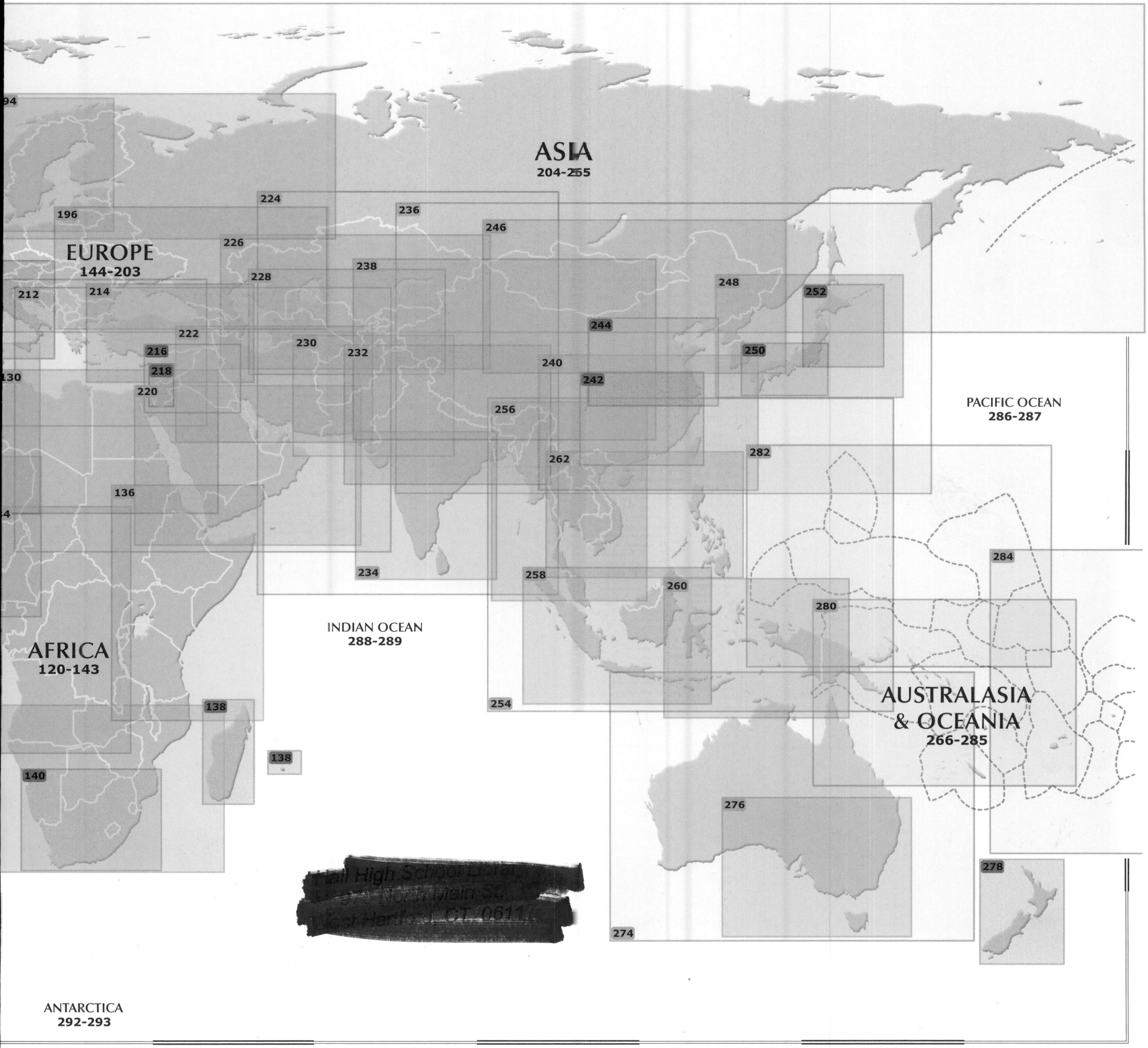

ASIA
204-255

EUROPE
144-203

PACIFIC OCEAN
286-287

AFRICA
120-143

INDIAN OCEAN
288-289

AUSTRALASIA
& OCEANIA
266-285

ANTARCTICA
292-293

ENCYCLOPÆDIA

Britannica®

WORLD
ATLAS

ENCYCLOPÆDIA

Britannica®

WORLD ATLAS

Published by Encyclopædia Britannica, Inc., 2011

www.britannica.com

www.britannica.co.uk

www.britannica.com.au

www.britannicaindia.com

www.britannica.co.kr

www.britannica.co.jp

First printing August 2010

ISBN: 978-1-61535-359-0

Colour reproduction by MDP Ltd., Wiltshire, UK

Printed and bound by Tien Wah Press, Singapore

ACKNOWLEDGEMENTS

Jonathan Metcalf (Publisher); Bryn Walls (Art Director);
David Roberts (Managing Editor); Simon Mumford (Senior Cartographic Editor);
Advanced Illustration, Congleton, UK, Encompass Graphics, Brighton,
UK, Lovell Johns Ltd., Long Hanborough, UK, Netmaps, Barcelona,
Spain (Digital Map Suppliers); Digital terrain data and continental
images created by Planetary Visions Ltd., Farnham, UK (Digital Terrain
Data); Paul Eames, Edward Merritt, John Plumer, Rob Stokes, Iorwerth
Watkins (Cartographers); Tony Chambers, John Dear, Ruth Hall, Andrew
Johnson, Belinda Kane, Lynn Neal, Ann Stephenson (Cartographic
Editors); T-Kartor, Sweden, Francesca Albini, Eleanor Arkwright, Renata
Dyntarova, Edward Heelas, Britta Hansesgaard (Indexing and Database);
Robert Dinwiddie (Editor); Nicola Liddiard, Yak El-Droubie (Designers);
Louise Thomas, Jenny Baskaya (Picture Research).

Flags courtesy of The Flag Institute, Cheshire, UK

The Encyclopædia Britannica World Atlas
was created and produced by Dorling Kindersley Limited

Introduction

The World at the beginning of the 21st Century would be a place of unimaginable change to our forefathers. Since 1900 the human population has undergone a fourfold growth coupled with an unparalleled development in the technology at our disposal. The last vestiges of the unknown World are gone, and previously hostile realms claimed for habitation. The advent of aviation technology and the growth of mass tourism have allowed people to travel farther and more frequently than ever before.

Allied to this, the rapid growth of global communication systems means that World events have become more accessible than ever before and their knock on effects quickly ripple across the whole planet. News broadcasts bring the far-flung corners of the world into everyone's lives, and with them, a view of the people and places that make up that region. The mysteries of the World that once fueled global exploration and the quest to discover the unknown are behind us; we inhabit a world of mass transportation, a world where even the most extreme regions have been mapped, a world with multifaceted view points on every event, a World of communication overload.

However, does this help us make sense of the World? It is increasingly important for us to have a clear vision of the World in which we live and such a deluge of information can leave us struggling to find some context and meaning. It has never been more important to own an atlas; the *Encyclopædia Britannica World Atlas* has been conceived to meet this need. At its core, like all atlases, it seeks to define where places are, to describe their main characteristics, and to locate them in relation to other places. By gathering a spectacular collection of satellite imagery and draping it with carefully selected and up-to-date geographic information this atlas filters the World's data into clear, meaningful and user-friendly maps.

The World works on different levels and so does the *Encyclopædia Britannica World Atlas*. Readers can learn about global issues of many kinds or they can probe in a little further for the continental context. Delving even further they can explore at regional, national or even sub-national level. The very best available satellite data has been used to create topography and bathymetry that reveal the breathtaking texture of landscapes and sea-floors. These bring out the context of the places and features selected to appear on top of them. The full-spread map areas purposefully overlap to emphasize the connectivity and interdependence of our World.

The *Encyclopædia Britannica World Atlas* not only allows you to travel around our planet without leaving your seat but perhaps more importantly, helps you to understand the World around you.

Contents

The atlas is organized by continent, moving eastwards from the International Date Line. The opening section describes the world's structure, systems and its main features. The Atlas of the World which follows, is a continent-by-continent guide to today's world, starting with a comprehensive insight into the physical, political and economic structure of each continent, followed by detailed maps of carefully selected geopolitical regions.

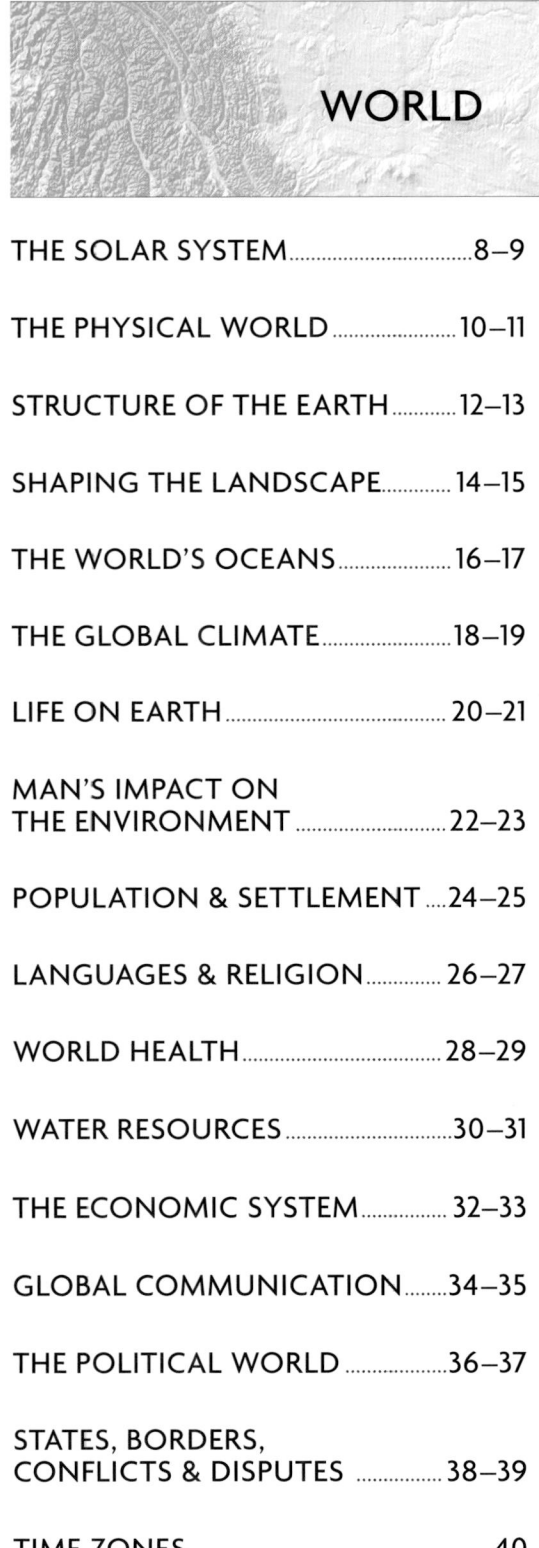

WORLD

NORTH AMERICA

SOUTH AMERICA

AFRICA

EUROPE

ASIA

AUSTRALASIA & OCEANIA

INDEX & GAZETTEER

Key to regional maps

Physical features

elevation

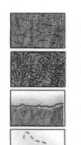

6000m / 19,686ft
4000m / 13,124ft
3000m / 9843ft
2000m / 6562ft
1000m / 3281ft
500m / 1640ft
250m / 820ft
100m / 328ft
sea level
below sea level

▲ elevation above sea level (mountain height)
▲ volcano
✕ pass
▼ elevation below sea level (depression depth)

sand desert
lava flow
coastline
reef
atoll

sea depth

sea level
-250m / -820ft
-500m / -1640ft
-1000m / -3281ft
-2000m / -6562ft
-3000m / -9843ft

▲ seamount / guyot symbol
▼ undersea spot depth

Drainage features

main river
secondary river
tertiary river
minor river
main seasonal river
secondary seasonal river
canal
waterfall
rapids
dam
perennial lake
seasonal lake
perennial salt lake
seasonal salt lake
reservoir
salt flat / salt pan
marsh / salt marsh
mangrove
wadi
○ spring / well / waterhole / oasis

Ice features

ice cap / sheet
ice shelf
glacier / snowfield
summer pack ice limit
winter pack ice limit

Graticule features

lines of latitude and longitude / Equator
Tropics / Polar circles
45° degrees of longitude / latitude

Communications

motorway / highway
motorway / highway (under construction)
major road
minor road
tunnel (road)
main line
minor line
tunnel (rail)
✈ international airport

Borders

full international border
undefined international border
disputed de facto border
disputed territorial claim border
indication of country extent (Pacific only)
indication of dependent territory extent (Pacific only)
demarcation / cease fire line
autonomous / federal region border
2nd order internal administrative border
3rd order internal administrative border

Miscellaneous features

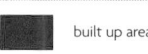 ancient wall
◇ site of interest
○ scientific station

Settlements

built up area

settlement population symbols

■ more than 5 million
◨ 1 million to 5 million
◉ 500,000 to 1 million
⊛ 100,000 to 500,000
⊕ 50,000 to 100,000
○ 10,000 to 50,000
○ fewer than 10,000

■●● country/dependent territory capital city
■ seat of government
■●● autonomous / federal region / 2nd order internal administrative center
■●● 3rd order internal administrative center

Typographic key

Physical features

landscape features ... *Namib Desert*
Massif Central
ANDES

headland .... *Nordkapp*

elevation / volcano / pass .... Mount Meru
4556 m

drainage features .... *Lake Geneva*

rivers / canals spring / well / waterhole / oasis / waterfall / rapids / dam .... *Mekong*

ice features .... *Vatnajökull*

Physical features (continued)

sea features .... *Golfe de Lion*
Andaman Sea
INDIAN OCEAN

undersea features ... *Barracuda Fracture Zone*

Regions

country .... **ARMENIA**

dependent territory with parent state ..... NIUE (to NZ)

autonomous / federal region .... MINAS GERAIS

2nd order internal administrative region .... MINSKAYA VOBLASTS'

3rd order internal administrative region .... Vaucluse

cultural region .... New England

Settlements

capital city .... **BEIJING**

dependent territory capital city .... FORT-DE-FRANCE

other settlements ... Chicago
Adana
Tizi Ozou
Yonezawa
Farnham

Miscellaneous

sites of interest / miscellaneous .... Valley of the Kings

Tropics / Polar circles .... *Antarctic Circle*

The Solar System

The Solar System consists of our local star, the Sun, and numerous objects that orbit the Sun – eight planets, five currently recognized dwarf planets, over 165 moons orbiting these planets and dwarf planets, and countless smaller bodies such as comets and asteroids. Including a vast outer region that is populated only by comets, the Solar System is about 9,300 billion miles (15,000 billion km) across. The much smaller region containing just the Sun and planets is about 7.5 billion miles (12 billion km) across. The Sun, which contributes over 99 percent of the mass of the entire Solar System, creates energy from nuclear reactions deep within its interior, providing the heat and light that make life on Earth possible.

THE MOON'S PHASES

As the Moon orbits Earth, the relative positions of Moon, Sun and Earth continuously change. Thus, the angle at which the Moon's sunlit face is seen by an observer on Earth varies in a cyclical fashion, producing the Moon's phases, as shown at right. Each cycle takes 29.5 days.

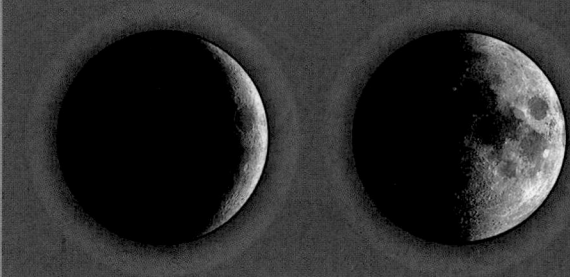

1. WAXING CRESCENT   2. FIRST QUARTER

The Earth and Moon's relative sizes are clear in this long-range image from space.

The Moon

Earth's only satellite, the Moon, is thought to have formed 4.5 billion years ago from a cloud of debris produced when a large asteroid hit the young Earth. The Moon is too small to have retained an atmosphere, and is therefore a lifeless, dusty and dead world. However, although the Moon has only about 1 percent of the mass of the Earth, its gravity exerts an important influence on Earth's oceans, manifest in the ebb and flow of the tides.

What is a Planet?

The International Astronomical Union defines a Solar System planet as a near-spherical object that orbits the Sun (and no other body) and has cleared the neighborhood around its orbit of other bodies. A dwarf planet is a planet that is not big enough to have cleared its orbital neighborhood. Extra-solar planets are objects orbiting stars other than the Sun.

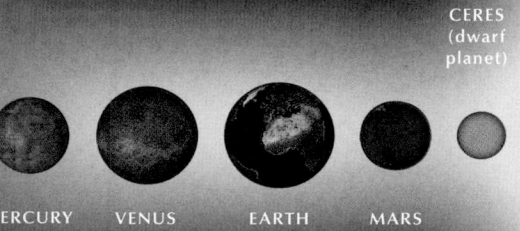

CERES
(dwarf planet)

MERCURY   VENUS   EARTH   MARS

JUPITER

The Sun

The Sun is a huge sphere of exceedingly hot plasma (ionized gas), consisting mainly of the elements hydrogen and helium. It formed about 4.6 billion years ago, when a swirling cloud of gas and dust began to contract under the influence of gravity. When the center of this cloud reached a critically high temperature, hydrogen nuclei started combining to form helium nuclei – a process called nuclear fusion – with the release of massive amounts of energy. This process continues to this day.

SOLAR ECLIPSE

A solar eclipse occurs when the Moon passes between Earth and the Sun, casting its shadow on Earth's surface. During a total eclipse (below), viewers along a strip of Earth's surface, called the area of totality, see the Sun totally blotted out for a short time, as the umbra (Moon's full shadow) sweeps over them. Outside this area is a larger one, where the Sun appears only partly obscured, as the penumbra (partial shadow) passes over.

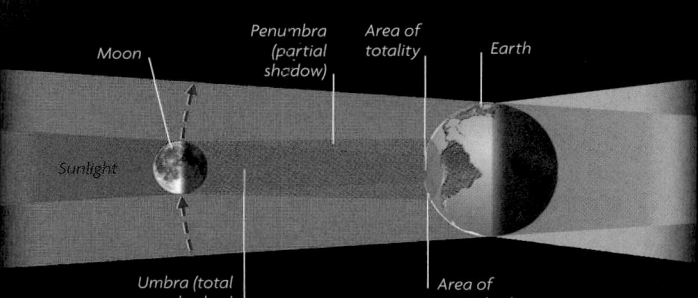

Moon

Penumbra (partial shadow)

Area of totality

Earth

Sunlight

Umbra (total shadow)

Area of partial eclipse

INSIDE THE SUN

The Sun has three internal layers. At its center is the core, where temperatures reach 27 million°F (15 million°C) and nuclear fusion occurs. The radiative zone is a slightly cooler region through which energy radiates away from the core. Further out, in the convective zone, plumes of hot plasma carry the energy towards the Sun's visible surface layer, called the photosphere. Once there, the energy escapes as light, heat and other forms of radiation.

Photosphere

Core

Radiative zone

Convective zone

Sunspots mark cooler areas of surface

Prominences are loops of gas arching above the photosphere

| | 3. WAXING GIBBOUS | 4. FULL MOON | 5. WANING GIBBOUS | 6. LAST QUARTER | 7. WANING CRESCENT | 8. NEW MOON |

PLANETS / DWARF PLANETS

	MERCURY	VENUS	EARTH	MARS	JUPITER	SATURN	URANUS	NEPTUNE	CERES	PLUTO	ERIS
DIAMETER	3029 miles (4875 km)	7521 miles (12,104 km)	7928 miles (12,756 km)	4213 miles (6780 km)	88,846 miles (142,984 km)	74,898 miles (120,536 km)	31,763 miles (51,118 km)	30,775 miles (49,528 km)	590 miles (950 km)	1432 miles (2304 km)	1429-1553 miles (2300-2500 km)
AVERAGE DISTANCE FROM THE SUN	36 mill. miles (57.9 mill. km)	67.2 mill. miles (108.2 mill. km)	93 mill. miles (149.6 mill. km)	141.6 mill. miles (227.9 mill. km)	483.6 mill. miles (778.3 mill. km)	889.8 mill. miles (1431 mill. km)	1788 mill. miles (2877 mill. km)	2795 mill. miles (4498 mill. km)	257 mill. miles (414 mill. km)	3675 mill. miles (5,915 mill. km)	6344 mill. miles (10,210 mill. km)
ROTATION PERIOD	58.6 days	243 days	23.93 hours	24.62 hours	9.93 hours	10.65 hours	17.24 hours	16.11 hours	9.1 hours	6.38 days	not known
ORBITAL PERIOD	88 days	224.7 days	365.26 days	687 days	11.86 years	29.37 years	84.1 years	164.9 years	4.6 years	248.6 years	557 years
SURFACE TEMPERATURE	-292°F to 806°F (-180°C to 430°C)	896°F (480°C)	-94°F to 131°F (-70°C to 55°C)	-184°F to 77 °F (-120°C to 25°C)	-160°F (-110°C)	-220°F (-140°C)	-320°F (-200°C)	-320°F (-200°C)	-161°F (-107°C)	-380°F (-230°C)	-405°F (-243°C)

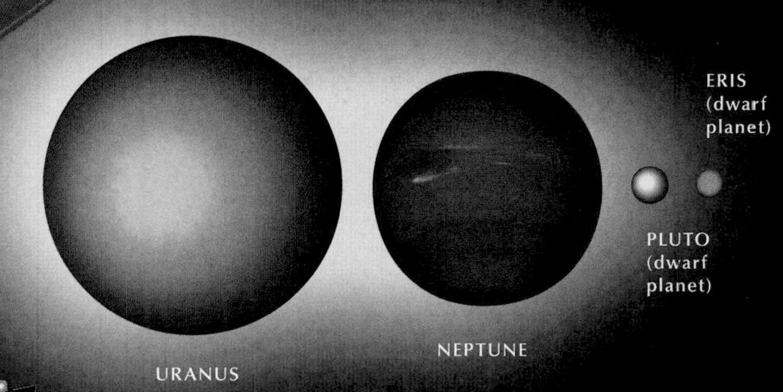

ERIS (dwarf planet)

PLUTO (dwarf planet)

URANUS NEPTUNE

SATURN

THE OUTER PLANETS

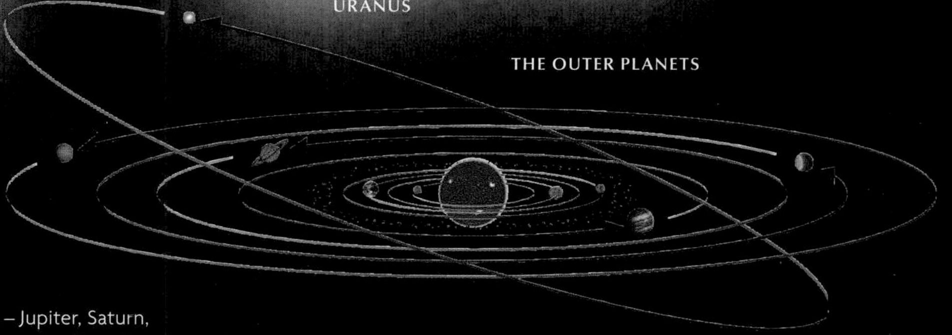

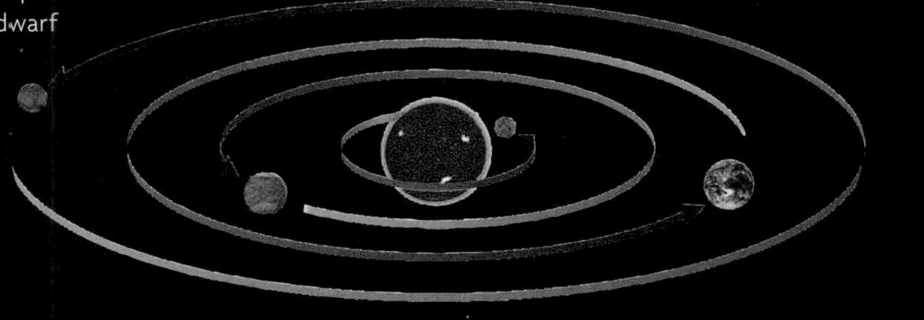

Orbits

All the Solar System's planets and dwarf planets orbit the Sun in the same direction and (apart from Pluto) roughly in the same plane. All the orbits have the shapes of ellipses (stretched circles). However in most cases, these ellipses are close to being circular: only Pluto and Eris have very elliptical orbits. Orbital period (the time it takes an object to orbit the Sun) increases with distance from the Sun. The more remote objects not only have further to travel with each orbit, they also move more slowly.

THE OUTER PLANETS
The four gigantic outer planets – Jupiter, Saturn, Uranus and Neptune – consist mainly of gas, liquid and ice. All have rings and many moons. The dwarf planet Pluto is made of rock and ice.

THE INNER PLANETS
The four planets closest to the Sun – Mercury, Venus, Earth and Mars – are composed mainly of rock and metal. They are much smaller than the outer planets, have few or no moons, and no rings.

THE INNER PLANETS

AVERAGE DISTANCE FROM THE SUN

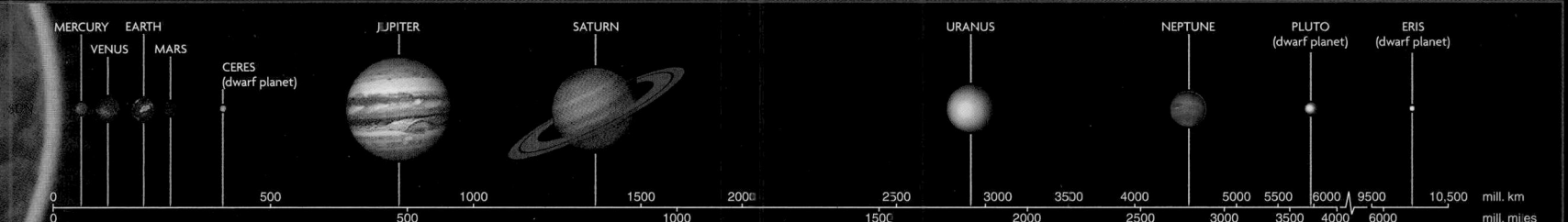

The Physical World

Earth's surface is constantly being transformed. Movements of the rigid tectonic plates that make up this surface are continuously, if slowly, shifting its landmasses around, while the land itself is constantly weathered and eroded by wind, water, and ice. Sometimes change is dramatic, the spectacular results of earthquakes or floods. More often it is a slow process lasting for millions of years. A physical map of the world represents a snapshot of Earth's ever-evolving architecture. The terrain maps below and at right show the planet's whole surface, including variations in ocean depth as well as the mountain-rippled texture of Earth's continents.

THE WORLD'S OCEANS
Earth's surface is dominated by water. The hemisphere shown here, centered around the southwest Pacific, is nearly all ocean, with the waters interrupted only by Antarctica, a part of South America, Australia, and the numerous islands of Australasia & Oceania, and southeast Asia.

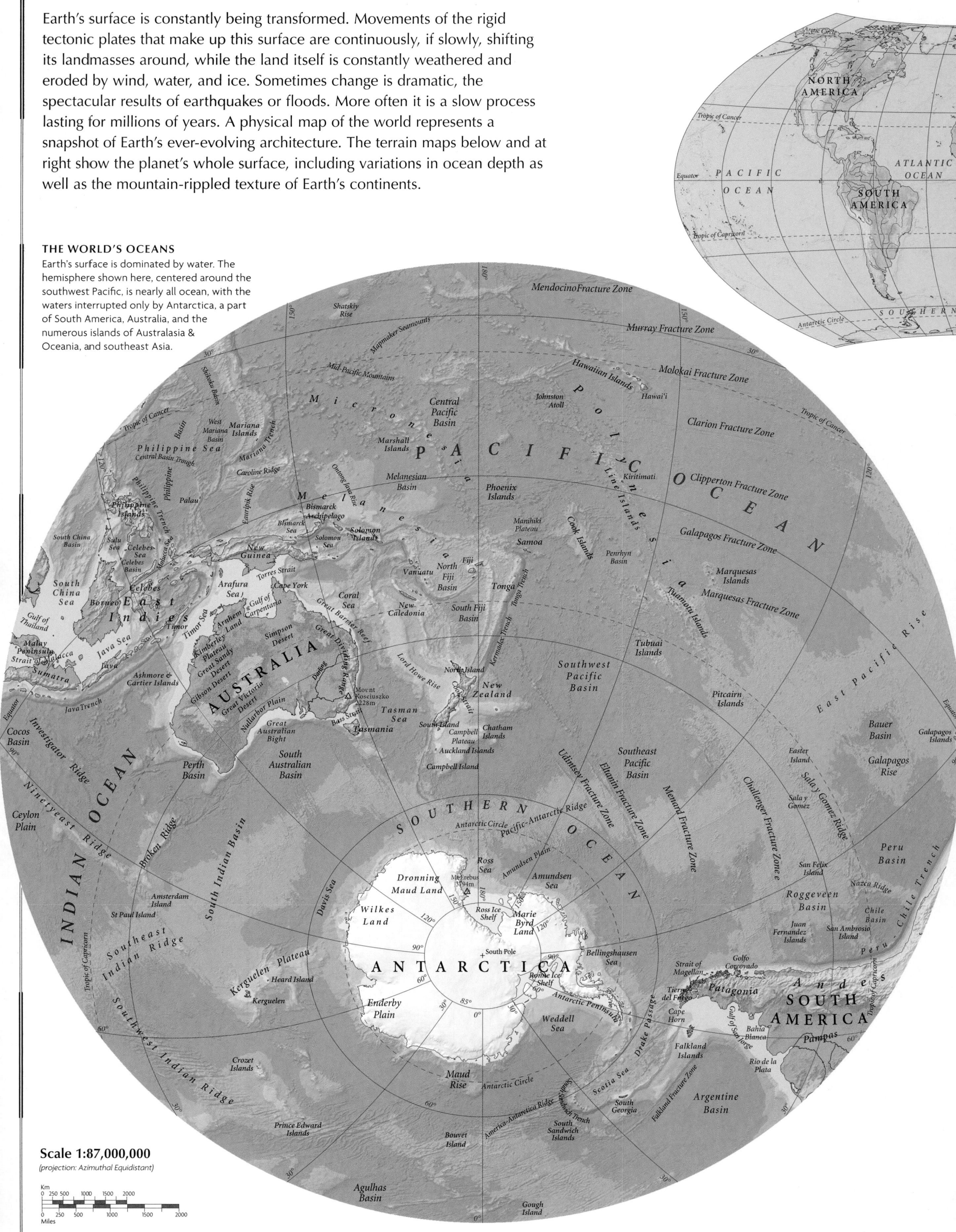

Scale 1:87,000,000
(projection: Azimuthal Equidistant)

Km
0 250 500   1000   1500   2000

0   250   500   1000   1500   2000
Miles

6000m
4000m
3000m
2000m
1000m
500m
250m
100m
Sea Level
-250m
-500m
-1000m

THE EARTH

DIAMETER AT EQUATOR: 7,926 miles (12,756 km)

DIAMETER FROM POLE TO POLE: 7,900 miles (12,714 km)

EQUATORIAL CIRCUMFERENCE: 24,901 miles (40,075 km)

MASS: 5988 million billion tons (tonnes)

VOLUME OF OCEANS: 324 million cu miles (1.36 billion cu km)

SURFACE AREA OF OCEANS, SEAS AND LAKES: 140 million sq miles (361 million sq km)

SURFACE AREA OF LAND: 57.5 million sq miles (149 million sq km)

SURFACE AREA OF LAND COVERED BY ICE: 6 million sq miles (15.6 million sq km)

SURFACE AREA COVERED BY MOUNTAINS: 12 million sq miles km (30 million sq)

SURFACE AREA COVERED BY DESERTS: 7.5 million sq miles (19 million sq km)

SURFACE AREA COVERED BY FORESTS: 17 million sq miles (44 million sq km)

MAXIMUM HEIGHT OF LAND: 29,035 ft (8,850 m) (Mt. Everest, Himalayas)

MAXIMUM DEPTH OF OCEANS: 35,827 ft (10,920 m) (Mariana Trench, Pacific Ocean)

THE WORLD'S LAND

Most of the world's land is concentrated in a hemisphere centered around Europe. This concentration was even greater before tectonic movement opened up the Atlantic, splitting the Americas from Europe and Africa, some 170 million years ago.

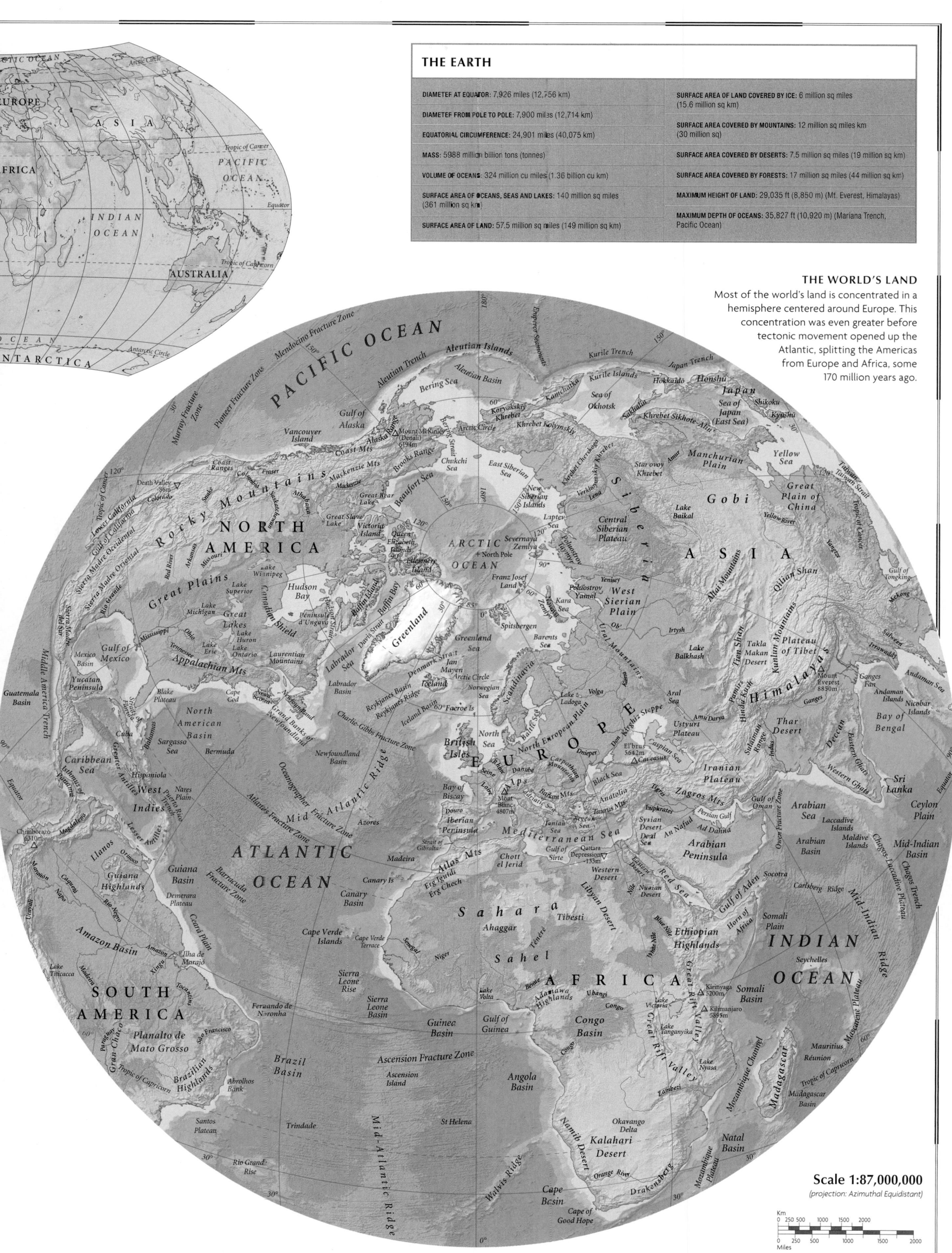

Scale 1:87,000,000

(projection: Azimuthal Equidistant)

Km
0 250 500 1000 1500 2000

Miles
0 250 500 1000 1500 2000

19,686ft

13,124ft

9843ft

6562ft

3281ft

1640ft

820ft

328ft

Sea Level

-820ft

-6562ft

-13,124ft

ARCTIC OCEAN
ASIA
INDIAN OCEAN
AUSTRALIA
ANTARCTICA
Arctic Circle
Tropic of Cancer
Tropic of Capricorn
Antarctic Circle
NORTH AMERICA
Rocky Mountains
Great Plains
Hudson Bay
Greenland
ARCTIC OCEAN
North Pole
SOUTH AMERICA
ATLANTIC OCEAN
Mid-Atlantic Ridge
Siberia
ASIA
Gobi
Sahara
Sahel
INDIAN OCEAN
Arabian Peninsula
Mediterranean Sea
Congo Basin
Kalahari Desert
Madagascar
Gulf of Mexico
Caribbean Sea
Amazon Basin
Planalto de Mato Grosso
Brazilian Highlands
Bering Sea
Sea of Okhotsk
Japan
Yellow Sea
Bay of Bengal
Arabian Sea
Red Sea
Black Sea
Caspian Sea
Mount Everest 8850m
Mount McKinley (Denali) 6194m
Mont Blanc 4807m
El'brus 5642m
Kilimanjaro 5895m
Chimborazo 6310m
DIAMETER AT EQUATOR: 7,926 miles (12,756 km)	**SURFACE AREA OF LAND COVERED BY ICE:** 6 million sq miles (15.6 million sq km)
DIAMETER FROM POLE TO POLE: 7,900 miles (12,714 km)	**SURFACE AREA COVERED BY MOUNTAINS:** 12 million sq miles km (30 million sq)
MASS: 5988 million billion tons (tonnes)	**SURFACE AREA COVERED BY DESERTS:** 7.5 million sq miles (19 million sq km)
VOLUME OF OCEANS: 324 million cu miles (1.36 billion cu km)	**SURFACE AREA COVERED BY FORESTS:** 17 million sq miles (44 million sq km)
SURFACE AREA OF OCEANS, SEAS AND LAKES: 140 million sq miles (361 million sq km)	**MAXIMUM HEIGHT OF LAND:** 29,035 ft (8,850 m) (Mt. Everest, Himalayas)
SURFACE AREA OF LAND: 57.5 million sq miles (149 million sq km)	**MAXIMUM DEPTH OF OCEANS:** 35,827 ft (10,920 m) (Mariana Trench, Pacific Ocean)

The Structure of the Earth

Earth is an almost perfect sphere consisting of a partly liquid core overlain by a deep, semisolid layer, called the mantle, and two types of surface crust, known as continental and oceanic crust. Our planet has constantly evolved since it formed some 4.5 billion years ago. Its continents are neither fixed nor stable. Over the course of history, gradual movements of rocky material within Earth's mantle, resulting from massive internal flows of heat, have caused the great slabs of material that make up the planet's surface, known as tectonic plates, to shift around. The plates have moved, collided, joined together, and sometimes split apart. These processes continue to mold Earth's surface, causing earthquakes and volcanic eruptions, and creating oceans, mountain ranges, rift valleys, deep ocean trenches, and island chains.

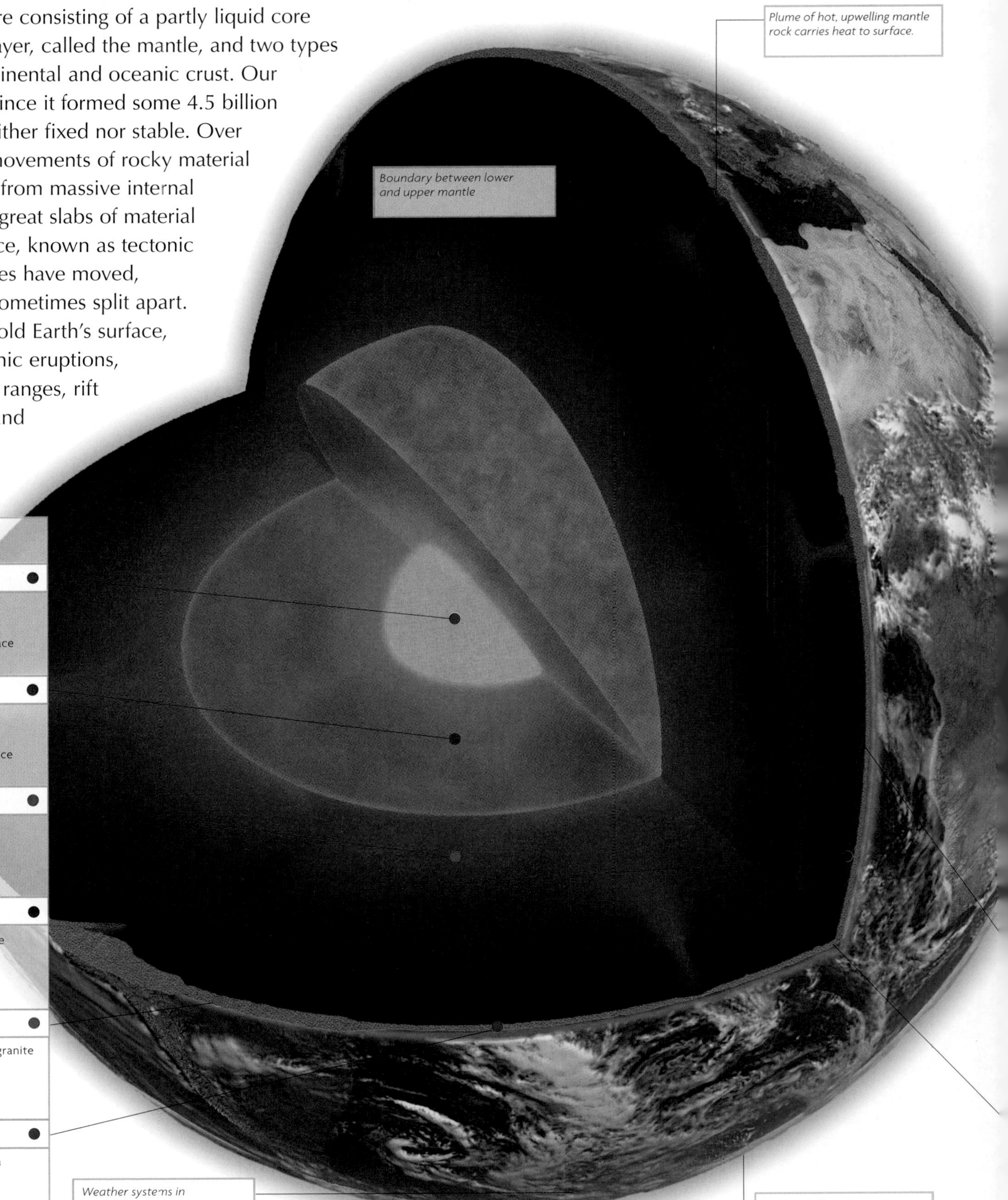

Plume of hot, upwelling mantle rock carries heat to surface.

Boundary between lower and upper mantle

Weather systems in lower atmosphere.

Ocean surface

EARTH FACTS & FIGURES

INNER CORE ●
COMPOSITION: Solid iron, with some nickel
DENSITY: 12 g/cm³
DEPTH: 3200–3963 miles (5150–6378 km) below surface
TEMPERATURE: 7200–8500°F (4000–4700°C)

OUTER CORE ●
COMPOSITION: Liquid iron and nickel
DENSITY: 10 g/cm³
DEPTH: 1907–3200 miles (2990–5150 km) below surface
TEMPERATURE: 6300–7200°F (3500–4000°C)

LOWER MANTLE ●
COMPOSITION: Semisolid high-density silicates
DENSITY: 5.5 g/cm³
DEPTH: 48–1907 miles (75–2990 km) below surface
TEMPERATURE: 1800–6300°F (1000–3500°C)

UPPER MANTLE ●
COMPOSITION: Semisolid rock, primarily peridotite
DENSITY: 3.5 g/cm³
DEPTH: 3–48 miles (5–75 km) below surface
TEMPERATURE: 1800°F (Less than 1000°C)

CONTINENTAL CRUST ●
COMPOSITION: Solid, relatively light rock such as granite
DENSITY: 2.7 g/cm³
DEPTH: 0–48 miles (0–75 km) below surface
TEMPERATURE: 1800°F (Less than 1000°C)

OCEANIC CRUST ●
COMPOSITION: Solid, relatively dense basaltic lava
DENSITY: 3 g/cm³
DEPTH: 2–7 miles (3–11 km) below surface
TEMPERATURE: 1800°F (Less than 1000°C)

FROM THE BIG BANG TO THE PRESENT DAY

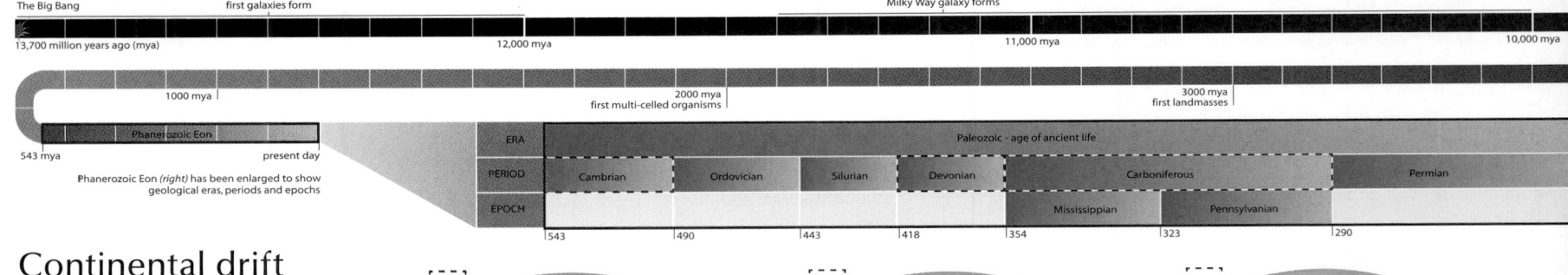

The Big Bang | first galaxies form | Milky Way galaxy forms

13,700 million years ago (mya) | 12,000 mya | 11,000 mya | 10,000 mya

1000 mya | 2000 mya first multi-celled organisms | 3000 mya first landmasses

Phanerozoic Eon | present day
543 mya
Phanerozoic Eon (right) has been enlarged to show geological eras, periods and epochs

ERA	Paleozoic - age of ancient life					
PERIOD	Cambrian	Ordovician	Silurian	Devonian	Carboniferous	Permian
EPOCH					Mississippian	Pennsylvanian	

543 | 490 | 443 | 418 | 354 | 323 | 290

Continental drift

Although Earth's tectonic plates move only a few inches (centimeters) each year, over hundreds of millions of years, its landmasses have moved many thousands of miles (kilometers), to create new continents, oceans, and mountain chains.

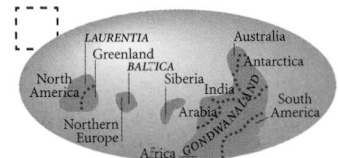
Cambrian 543–490 million years ago

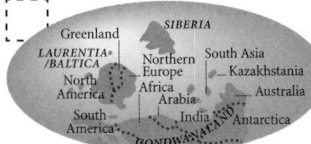
Devonian 418–354 million years ago

Carboniferous 354–290 million years ago

Dynamic Earth

Earth's surface is split up into several rigid, closely-fitting sections, called tectonic plates. Each of the plates contains some oceanic crust, and most also contain some continental crust. The plates constantly move relative to one another. Movements at different types of plate boundary produce various types of geological structure and activity.

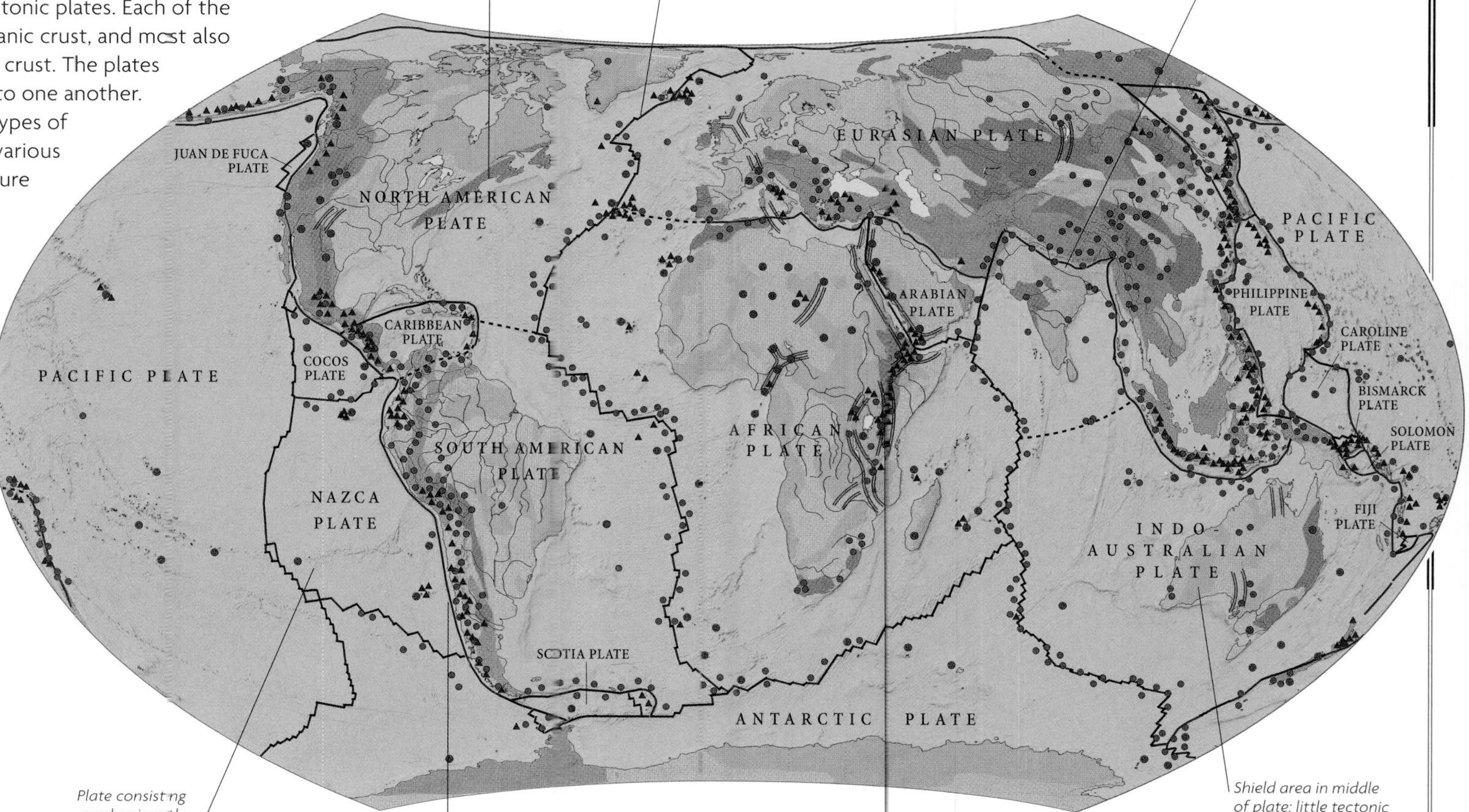

Tectonic Activity and Geological Regions

Plate Boundaries
— Convergent
— Divergent
— Transform
--- Uncertain

Tectonic Activity
▲ volcanic zone
● earthquake zone
● hot spot
— rift valley
Sedimentary cover
Mesozoic & Cenozoic volcanic rock
Cenozoic (65 mya – present)
Mesozoic (252 mya – 65 mya)
Paleozoic (543 mya – 252 mya)
pre-Cambrian Shields

Plate consisting partly of continental and partly of oceanic crust

Mid-ocean ridge (divergent plate boundary)

Zone of mountain-building

JUAN DE FUCA PLATE

NORTH AMERICAN PLATE

EURASIAN PLATE

PACIFIC PLATE

CARIBBEAN PLATE

COCOS PLATE

ARABIAN PLATE

PHILIPPINE PLATE

CAROLINE PLATE

BISMARCK PLATE

SOLOMON PLATE

PACIFIC PLATE

SOUTH AMERICAN PLATE

AFRICAN PLATE

NAZCA PLATE

FIJI PLATE

INDO-AUSTRALIAN PLATE

SCOTIA PLATE

ANTARCTIC PLATE

Plate consisting predominantly of oceanic crust

Convergent plate boundary, associated with high tectonic activity

Area of rifting, where continental crust is splitting apart

Shield area in middle of plate: little tectonic activity occurs here

EFFECTS AT PLATE BOUNDARIES

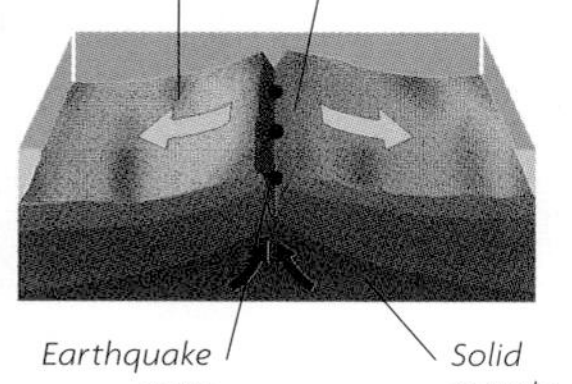

Ocean floor moves away from ridge | Magma pushed upward along center of ridge

Earthquake zone | Solid mantle

FORMATION OF A MID-OCEAN RIDGE

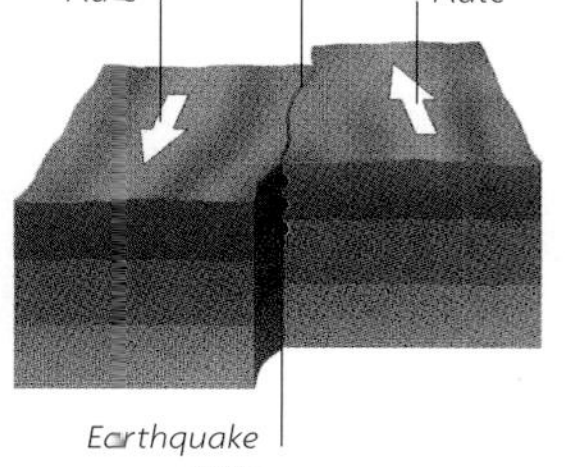

Plate | Fault line | Plate

Earthquake zone

SLIDING PLATES (TRANSFORM BOUNDARY)

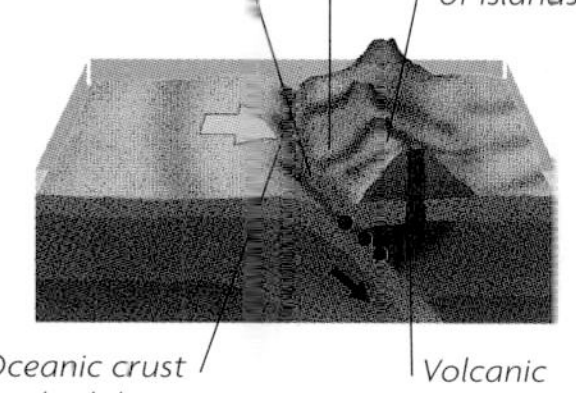

Overriding oceanic crust | Arc (chain) of islands | Ocean trench

Oceanic crust pushed down | Volcanic activity

FORMATION OF ISLAND ARC AND OCEAN TRENCH

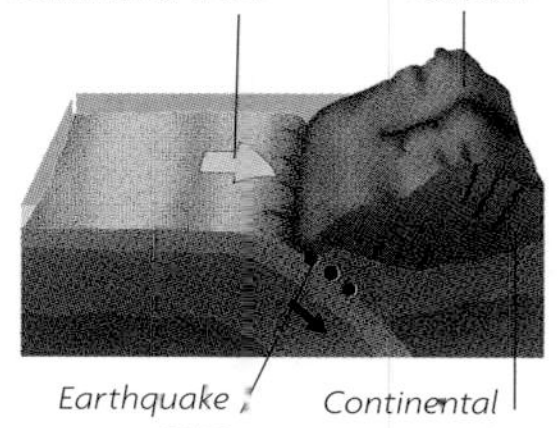

Oceanic crust forced under continental crust | Mountains thrust up by collision

Earthquake zone | Continental crust

SUBDUCTION OF OCEANIC CRUST UNDER CONTINENTAL CRUST

Plate buckles as it collides | Mountains thrust upward

Crust thickens in response to the impact | Earthquake zone

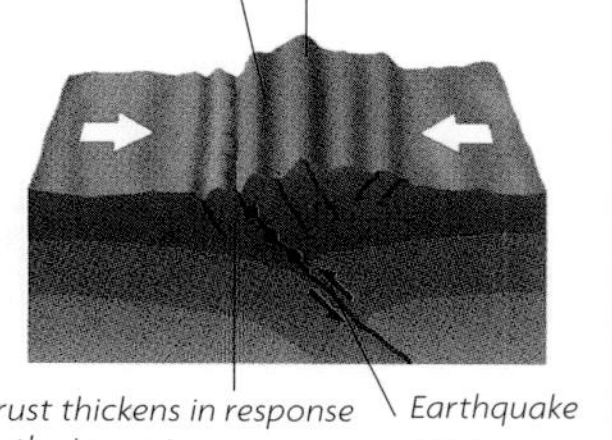

BLOCKS OF CONTINENTAL CRUST COLLIDE TO FORM MOUNTAINS

Boundary between upper mantle and crust

Sea floor made of oceanic crust

CONVECTION CURRENTS

Deep within Earth's core, temperatures may exceed 8100°F (4500°C). The heat from the core warms rocks in the mantle, which become semimolten and rise upward, displacing cooler rock below the solid oceanic and continental crust. This rock sinks and is warmed again by heat given off from the core. The process continues in a cyclical fashion, producing convection currents below the crust. These currents lead, in turn, to gradual movements of the tectonic plates over the planet's surface.

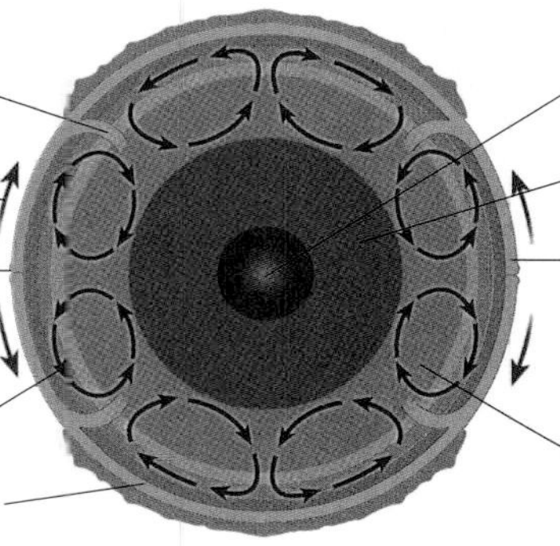

Subduction zone

Movement of plate

Mid-ocean ridge

Convection current

Continental crust

Inner core

Outer core

Oceanic crust

Mantle

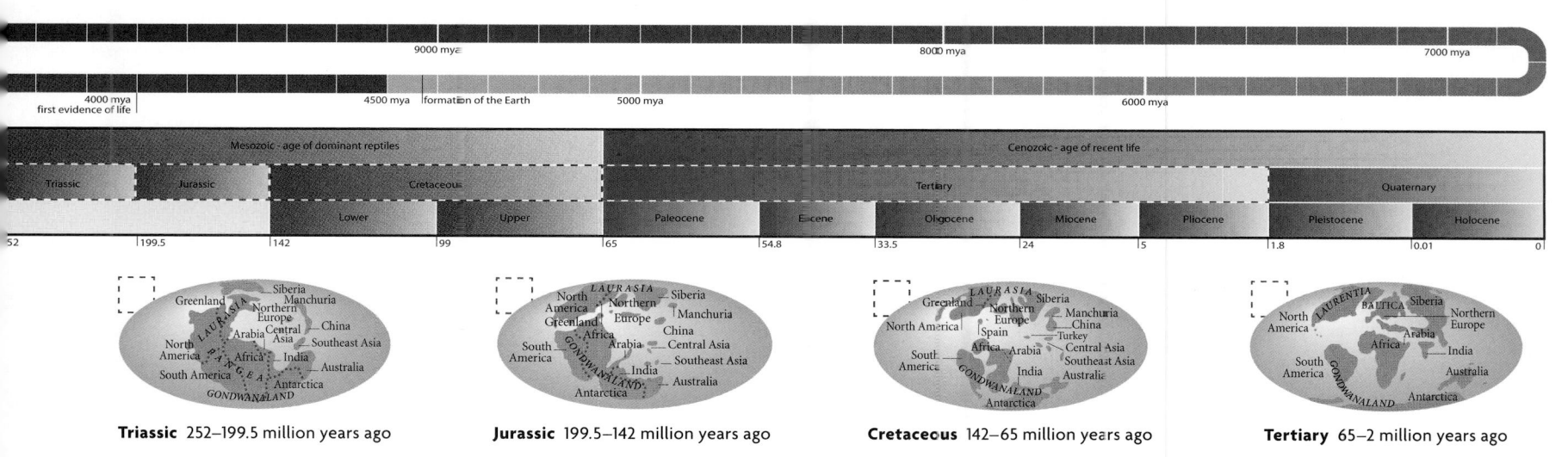

9000 mya | 8000 mya | 7000 mya

4000 mya first evidence of life | 4500 mya formation of the Earth | 5000 mya | 6000 mya

Mesozoic - age of dominant reptiles | Cenozoic - age of recent life

Triassic | Jurassic | Cretaceous | Tertiary | Quaternary

Lower | Upper | Paleocene | Eocene | Oligocene | Miocene | Pliocene | Pleistocene | Holocene

252 | 199.5 | 142 | 99 | 65 | 54.8 | 33.5 | 24 | 5 | 1.8 | 0.01 | 0

Triassic 252–199.5 million years ago

Jurassic 199.5–142 million years ago

Cretaceous 142–65 million years ago

Tertiary 65–2 million years ago

Shaping the Landscape

The basic material of Earth's surface is solid rock: valleys, deserts, soil, and sand are all evidence of the powerful agents of weathering, erosion and deposition that constantly transform Earth's landscapes. Water, whether flowing in rivers or grinding the ground in the form of glaciers, has the most clearly visible impact on Earth's surface. Also, wind can transport fragments of rock over huge distances and strip away protective layers of vegetation, exposing rock surfaces to the impact of extreme heat and cold. Many of the land-shaping effects of ice and water can be seen in northern regions such as Alaska *(below)*, while the effects of heat and wind are clearly visible in the Sahara *(far right)*.

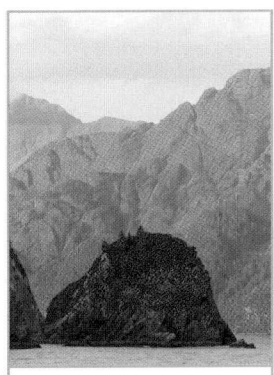

● FJORD
A valley carved by an ancient glacier and later flooded by the sea is called a fiord.

Ice and water

Some of the most obvious and striking features of Earth's surface are large flows and bodies of liquid water, such as rivers, lakes, and seas. In addition to these are landforms caused by the erosional or depositional power of flowing water, which include gullies, river valleys, and coastal features such as headlands and deltas. Ice also has had a major impact on Earth's appearance. Glaciers—rivers of ice formed by the compaction of snow—pick up and carry huge amounts of rocks and boulders as they pass over the landscape, eroding it as they do so. Glacially-sculpted landforms range from mountain *cirques* and U-shaped valleys to fiords and glacial lakes.

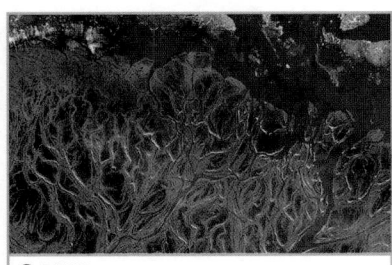

● DELTA
A delta, such as that of the Yukon River (above), is a roughly triangular or fan-shaped area of sediment deposited by a river at its mouth.

● PINGO
These blister-like mounds, seen in regions of Arctic tundra, are formed by the upward expansion of water as it freezes in the soil.

● TIDEWATER GLACIER
Glaciers of this type flow to the sea, where they calve (disgorge) icebergs. Like all glaciers, they erode huge amounts of rock from the landscape.

● LANDSLIDE
The freezing and later thawing of water, which occurs in a continuous cycle, can shatter and crumble rocks, eventually causing landslides.

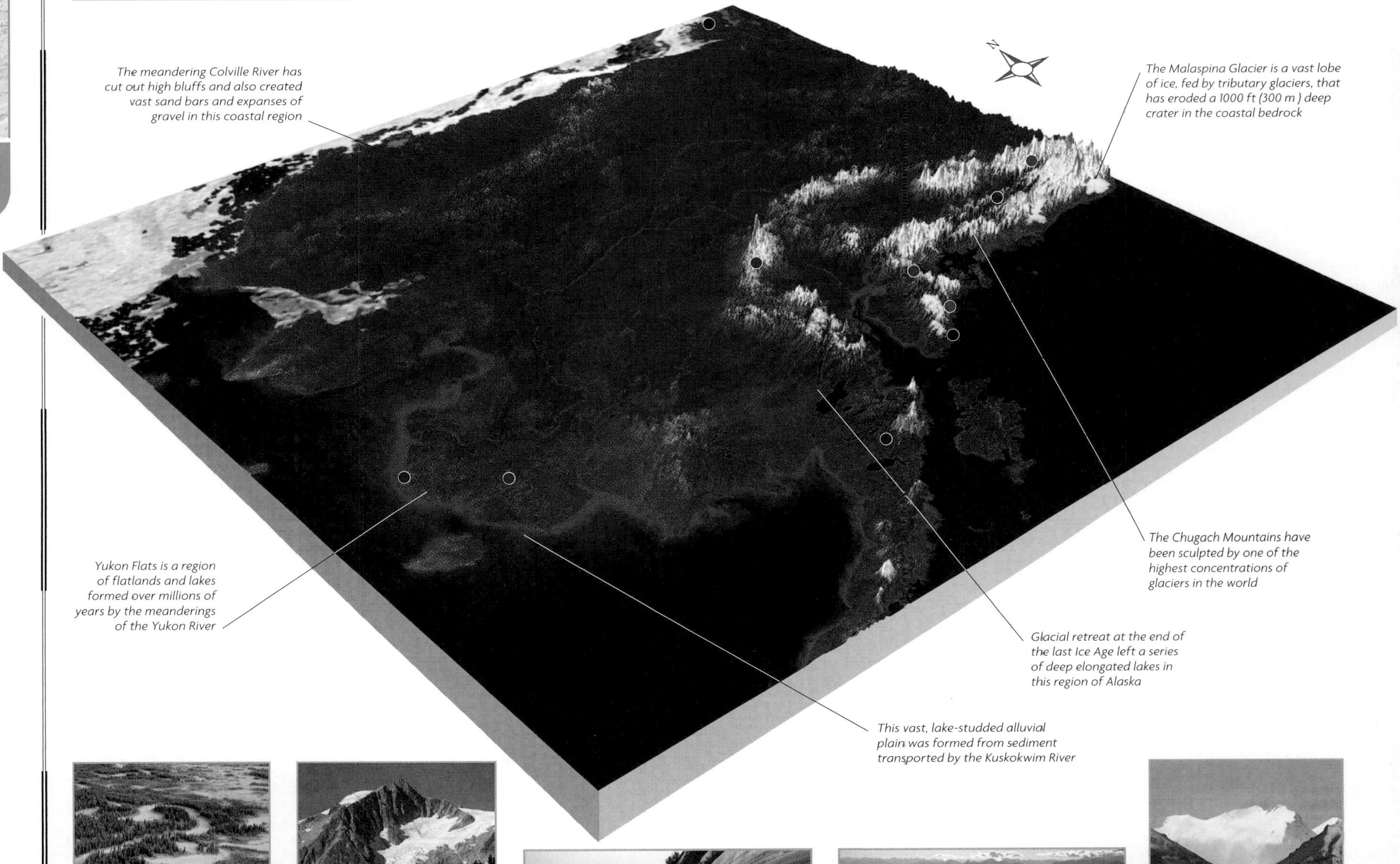

The meandering Colville River has cut out high bluffs and also created vast sand bars and expanses of gravel in this coastal region

The Malaspina Glacier is a vast lobe of ice, fed by tributary glaciers, that has eroded a 1000 ft (300 m) deep crater in the coastal bedrock

Yukon Flats is a region of flatlands and lakes formed over millions of years by the meanderings of the Yukon River

The Chugach Mountains have been sculpted by one of the highest concentrations of glaciers in the world

Glacial retreat at the end of the last Ice Age left a series of deep elongated lakes in this region of Alaska

This vast, lake-studded alluvial plain was formed from sediment transported by the Kuskokwim River

● MEANDERING RIVER
In their lower courses, some rivers carve out a series of looping bends called meanders.

● CIRQUE
A cirque is a hollow formed high on a mountain by glacial action. It may be ice-filled.

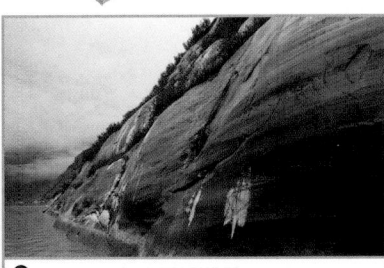

● POSTGLACIAL FEATURES
Glacially-polished cliffs like these are a tell-tale sign of ancient glacial action. Other signs include various forms of sculpted ridge and hummock.

● RIVER VALLEY
Over thousands of years, rivers erode uplands to form characteristic V-shaped valleys, with flat narrow floors and steeply-rising sides.

● GULLIES
Gullies are deep channels cut by rapidly flowing water, as here below Alaska's Mount Denali.

Heat and wind

Marked changes in temperature—rapid heating caused by fierce solar radiation during the day, followed by a sharp drop in temperature at night—cause rocks at the surface of hot deserts to continually expand and contract. This can eventually result in cracking and fissuring of the rocks, creating thermally-fractured desert landscapes. The world's deserts are also swept and scoured by strong winds. The finer particles of sand are shaped into surface ripples, dunes, or sand mountains, which can rise to a height of 650 ft (200 m). In other areas, the winds sweep away all the sand, leaving flat, gravelly areas called desert pavements.

DESERT LANDSCAPES

In desert areas, wind picks up loose sand and blasts it at the surface, creating a range of sculpted landforms from faceted rocks to large-scale features such as *yardangs*. Individually sculpted-rocks are called ventifacts. Where the sand abrasion is concentrated near the ground, it can turn these rocks into eccentrically-shaped "stone mushrooms." Other desert features are produced by thermal cracking and by winds continually redistributing the vast sand deposits.

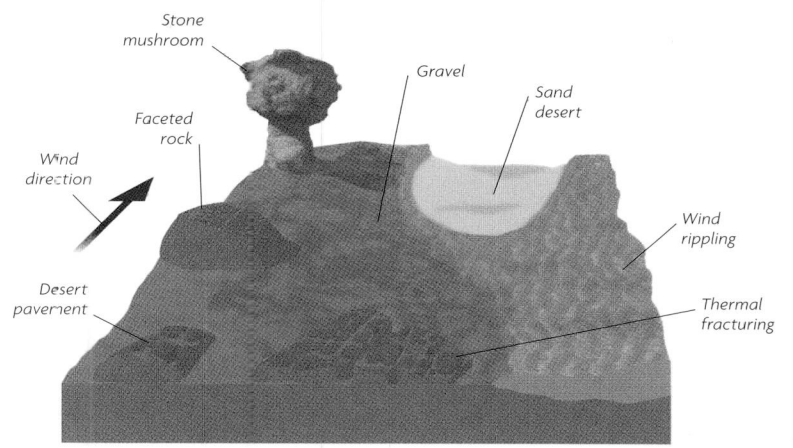

Stone mushroom · Gravel · Sand desert · Faceted rock · Wind direction · Wind rippling · Desert pavement · Thermal fracturing

FEATURES OF A DESERT SURFACE

● **DUST STORM**
A common phenomenon in some deserts, dust storms result from intense heating of the ground creating strong convection currents.

● **LOESS DEPOSIT**
A deposit of silt that has been transported over long distances by wind, then compacted. Loess is found in a few marginal areas of the Sahara.

● **YARDANG**
A yardang is a ridge of rock produced by wind erosion, usually in a desert. Large yardangs can be many miles long.

● **DESERT PAVEMENT**
Dark, gravelly surfaces like this result from wind removing all the sand from an area of desert.

Part of the Grand Erg Oriental, this region is a vast wind-sculpted sea of sand, much affected by sand storms

This area of complex dune morphology has resulted from two different types of dunes overlapping and coalescing

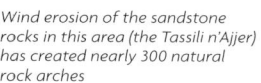

Wind erosion of the sandstone rocks in this area (the Tassili n'Ajjer) has created nearly 300 natural rock arches

The Tefedest is an impressive, sun-baked, wind-eroded, granite massif located in southern Algeria

This highland region, called the Ahaggar Mountains, has largely been blasted free of sand and is heavily eroded throughout

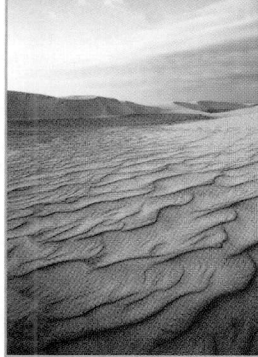

● **TRANSVERSE DUNES**
This series of parallel sand ridges lies at right angles to the prevailing wind direction.

● **VENTIFACT**
A ventifact is a rock that has been heavily sculpted and abraded by wind-driven sand.

● **CRACKED DESERT**
Intensely heated and dried-out desert areas often developed geometrically-patterned surface cracking.

● **WADI**
Wadis are dried out stream beds, found in some desert regions, that carry water only during occasional periods of heavy rain.

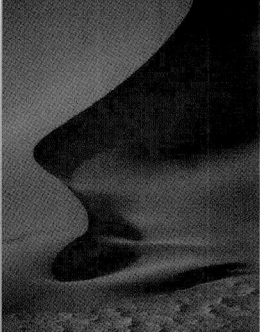

● **BARCHAN DUNE**
This arc-shaped type of dune migrates across the desert surface, blown by the wind.

The World's Oceans

Two-thirds of Earth's surface is covered by the five oceans: the Pacific, Atlantic, Indian, Southern (or Antarctic), and Arctic. The basins that form these oceans, and the ocean floor landscape, have formed over the past 200 million years through volcanic activity and gradual movements of the Earth's crust. Surrounding the continents are shallow flat regions called continental shelves. These shelves extend to the continental slope, which drops steeply to the ocean floor. There, vast submarine plateaus, known as abyssal plains, are interrupted by massive ridges, chains of seamounts, and deep ocean trenches.

Ocean currents

Surface currents are driven by winds and by the Earth's rotation. Together these cause large circular flows of water over the surface of the oceans, called gyres. Deep sea currents are driven by changes in the salinity or temperature of surface water. These changes cause the water to become denser and sink, forcing horizontal movements of deeper water.

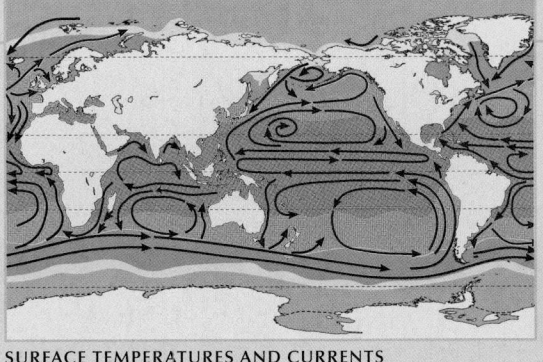

SURFACE TEMPERATURES AND CURRENTS

Surface temperature and currents

----- ice-shelf (below 32°F / 0°C)

▨ sea-ice* (average) below 28°F / -2°C

☐ sea-water 28–32°F / -2 to 0°C * sea-water freezes at 28.4°F / -1.9°C

▨ 32–50°F / 0–10°C

▨ 50–68°F / 10–20°C

▨ 68–86°F / 20–30°C

→ warm current

→ cold current

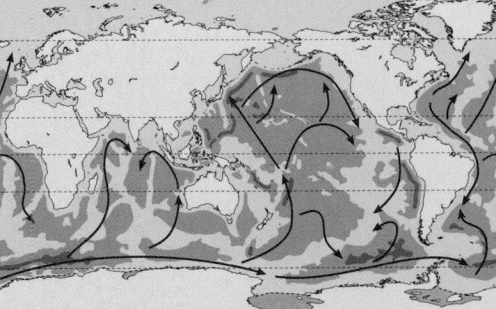

DEEP SEA TEMPERATURES AND CURRENTS

The ocean floor

The ages of seafloor rocks increase in parallel bands outward from central ocean ridges. At these ridges, new oceanic crust is continuously created from lava that erupts from below the seafloor and then cools to form solid rock. As this new crust forms, it gradually pushes older crust away from the ridge.

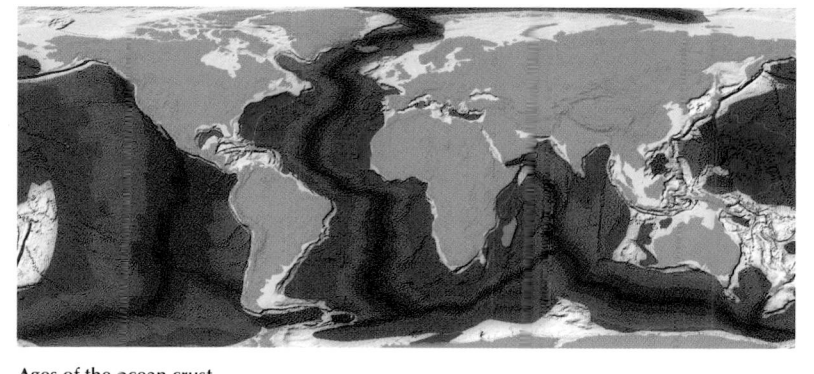

Ages of the ocean crust

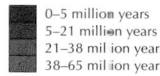

- 0–5 million years
- 5–21 million years
- 21–38 million years
- 38–65 million years
- 65–140 million years
- 140–190 million years
- continental shelf
- no data

Tides

Tides are caused by gravitational interactions between the Earth, Moon, and Sun. The strongest tides occur when the three bodies are aligned and the weakest when the Sun and Moon align at right angles.

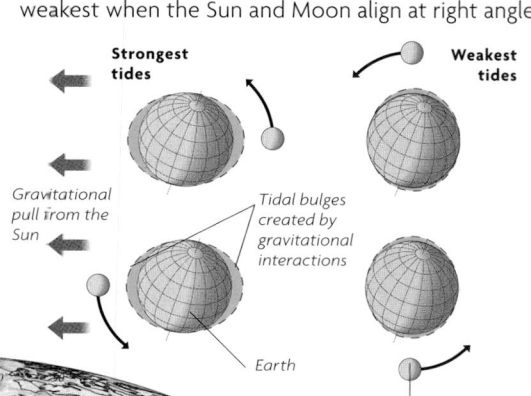

Strongest tides

Weakest tides

Gravitational pull from the Sun

Tidal bulges created by gravitational interactions

Earth

Moon

(Globe map with labels: ASIA, NORTH AMERICA, SOUTH AMERICA, AUSTRALIA, ANTARCTICA, PACIFIC OCEAN, SOUTHERN OCEAN, and numerous oceanographic features including Bering Sea, Gulf of Alaska, Kurile Trench, Aleutian Trench, Mendocino Fracture Zone, Murray Fracture Zone, Molokai Fracture Zone, Clarion Fracture Zone, Clipperton Fracture Zone, Galapagos Fracture Zone, Marquesas Fracture Zone, Tuamotu Fracture Zone, Austral Fracture Zone, Mendaña Fracture Zone, Agassiz Fracture Zone, Challenger Fracture Zone, Easter Fracture Zone, Middle America Trench, East Pacific Rise, Peru-Chile Trench, Northwest Pacific Basin, Central Pacific Basin, East Mariana Basin, West Mariana Basin, Melanesian Basin, Coral Sea, Tasman Sea, Southwest Pacific Basin, Wharton Basin, Perth Basin, South Australian Basin, South Indian Basin, Indian Ridge, etc.)

THE WORLD

17

Deep sea temperature and currents

- ice-shelf (below 32°F / 0°C)
- sea-water 28–32°F / -2 to 0°C (below 16,400 ft / 5000 m)
- sea-water 32–41°F / 0–5°C (below 13,120 ft / 4000 m)
- → primary currents
- → secondary currents

Sinking regions

Winter sea-ice cover

Deep southerly return flow

North Atlantic Drift

Subtropical recirculation

Gulf Stream

North Atlantic Heat Conveyor

The North Atlantic Heat Conveyor is a system of heat flows in the Atlantic that keeps western Europe relatively warm. Surface currents, notably the Gulf Stream and its extension, the North Atlantic Drift, carry warm water from the tropical Atlantic into the northeastern Atlantic. There, the heat they supply is released, warming Europe, while the water itself cools and sinks. This cold water then returns at depth toward the equator.

Temperature

0°C 5 10 15 20 25

32°F 41 50 59 68 77

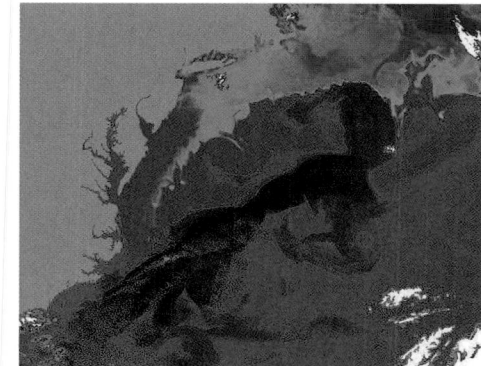

A key part of the North Atlantic Heat Conveyor is the warm Gulf Stream, visible as the dark red ribbon in this Atlantic sea-surface temperature map.

Global Climate

The climates of different regions on Earth are the typical long-term patterns of temperature and humidity in those regions. By contrast, weather consists of short-term variations in factors such as wind, rainfall, and sunshine. Climates are determined primarily by the Sun's variable heating of different parts of Earth's atmosphere and oceans, and by Earth's rotation. These factors drive the ocean currents and prevailing winds, which in turn redistribute heat energy and moisture between the equator and poles, and between sea and land. Most scientists think that major changes are currently occurring in global climate due to the effects of rising carbon dioxide levels in the atmosphere.

The atmosphere

Earth's atmosphere is a giant ocean of air that surrounds the planet. It extends to a height of about 625 miles (1000 km) but has no distinct upper boundary. The Sun's rays pass through the atmosphere and warm Earth's surface, causing the air to move and water to evaporate from the oceans.

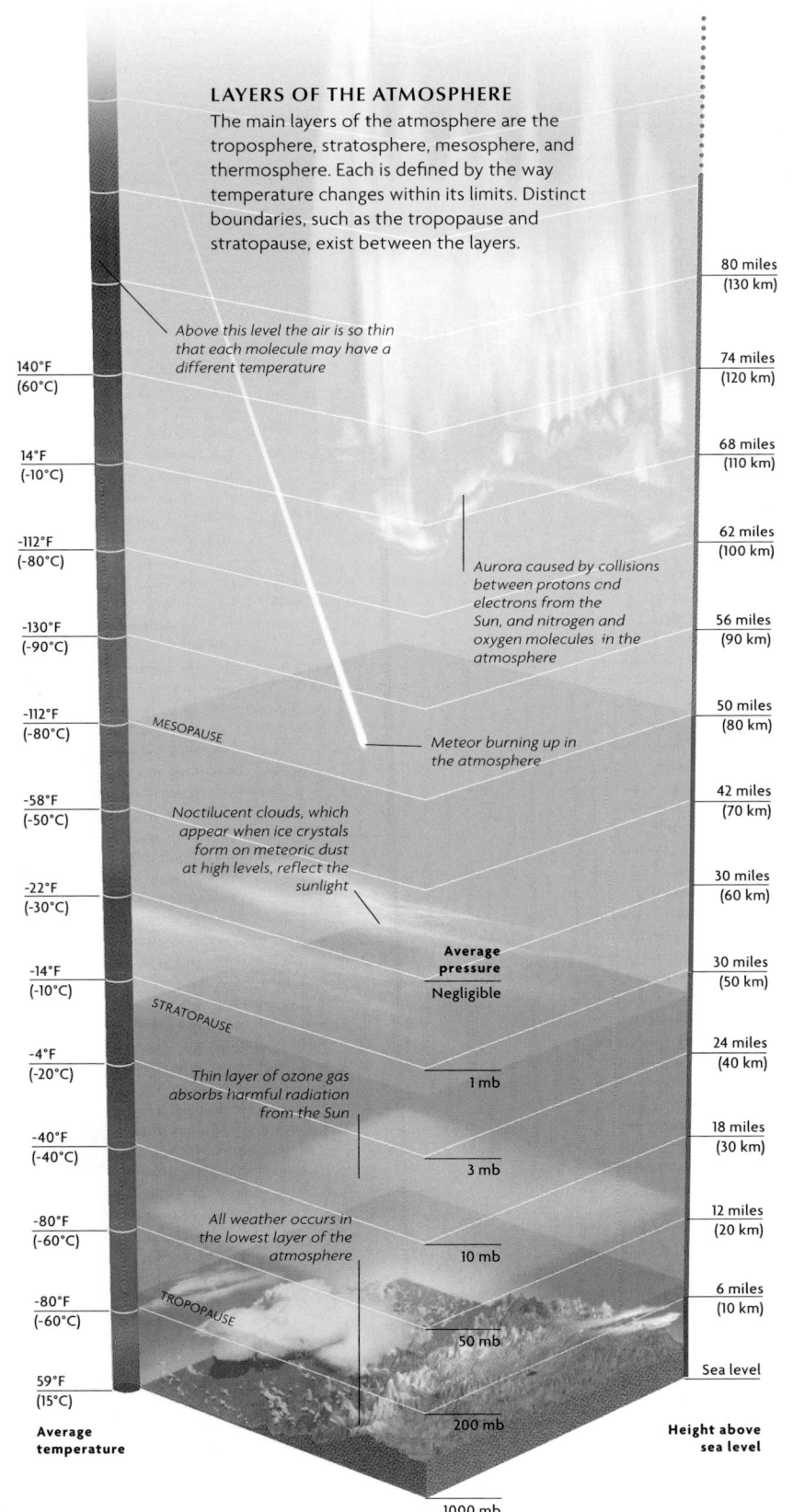

LAYERS OF THE ATMOSPHERE
The main layers of the atmosphere are the troposphere, stratosphere, mesosphere, and thermosphere. Each is defined by the way temperature changes within its limits. Distinct boundaries, such as the tropopause and stratopause, exist between the layers.

Above this level the air is so thin that each molecule may have a different temperature

MESOPAUSE

Aurora caused by collisions between protons and electrons from the Sun, and nitrogen and oxygen molecules in the atmosphere

Meteor burning up in the atmosphere

Noctilucent clouds, which appear when ice crystals form on meteoric dust at high levels, reflect the sunlight

STRATOPAUSE

Average pressure
Negligible

Thin layer of ozone gas absorbs harmful radiation from the Sun

1 mb

3 mb

All weather occurs in the lowest layer of the atmosphere

10 mb

TROPOPAUSE

50 mb

200 mb

1000 mb

Average temperature		Height above sea level
140°F (60°C)		80 miles (130 km)
14°F (-10°C)		74 miles (120 km)
-112°F (-80°C)		68 miles (110 km)
-130°F (-90°C)		62 miles (100 km)
-112°F (-80°C)		56 miles (90 km)
-58°F (-50°C)		50 miles (80 km)
-22°F (-30°C)		42 miles (70 km)
-14°F (-10°C)		30 miles (60 km)
-4°F (-20°C)		30 miles (50 km)
-40°F (-40°C)		24 miles (40 km)
-80°F (-60°C)		18 miles (30 km)
-80°F (-60°C)		12 miles (20 km)
59°F (15°C)		6 miles (10 km)
		Sea level

Global air circulation

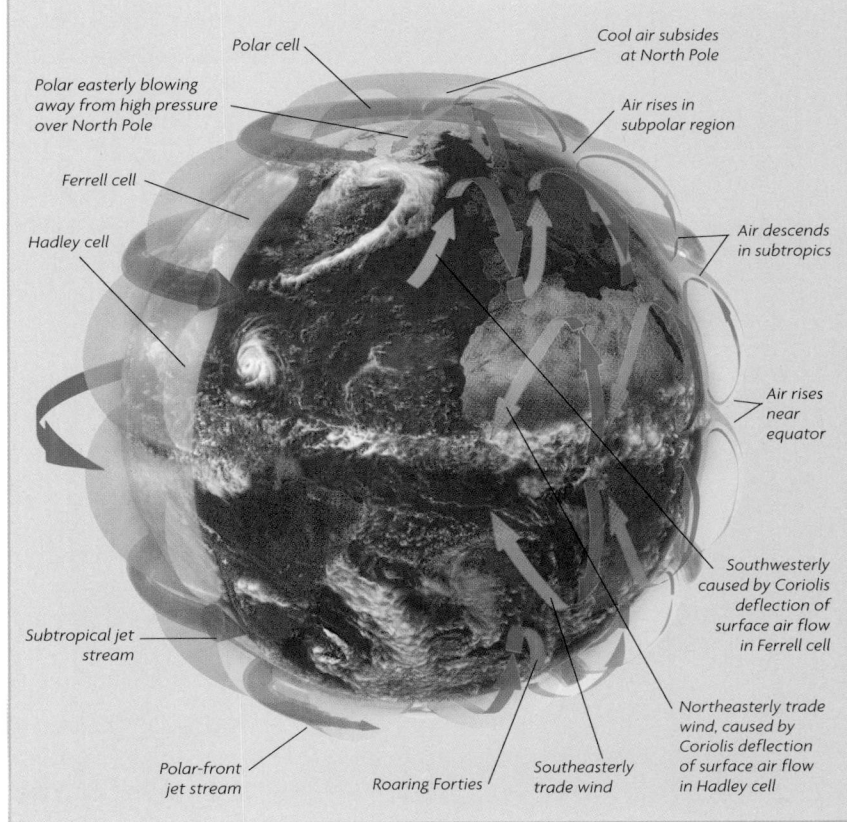

Cool air subsides at North Pole

Polar cell

Polar easterly blowing away from high pressure over North Pole

Air rises in subpolar region

Ferrell cell

Hadley cell

Air descends in subtropics

Air rises near equator

Southwesterly caused by Coriolis deflection of surface air flow in Ferrell cell

Northeasterly trade wind, caused by Coriolis deflection of surface air flow in Hadley cell

Subtropical jet stream

Polar-front jet stream

Roaring Forties

Southeasterly trade wind

Winds, currents, and climate

Earth has 12 climatic zones, ranging from ice-cap and tundra to temperate, arid (desert), and tropical zones. Each of these zones features a particular combination of temperature and humidity. The effects of prevailing winds, ocean currents of both the warm and cold variety, as well as latitude and altitude, all have an important influence on a region's climate. For example, the climate of western Europe is influenced by the effects of the warm North Atlantic Drift current.

● **THERMOSPHERE**
This layer extends from a height of 50 miles (80 km) upward. Its temperature increases rapidly above a height of 60 miles (90 km), due to absorption of highly energetic solar radiation.

● **MESOSPHERE**
The temperature of the lower part of this layer stays constant with height; but above 35 miles (55 km), it drops, reaching -112°F (80°C) at the mesopause.

● **STRATOSPHERE**
The temperature of the stratosphere is a fairly constant -76° F (-60°C) up to an altitude of about 12 miles (20 km), then increases, due to absorption of ultraviolet radiation.

● **TROPOSPHERE**
This layer extends from Earth's surface to a height of about 10 miles (16 km) at the equator and 5 miles (8 km) at the poles. Air temperature in this layer decreases with height.

Air moves within giant atmospheric cells called Hadley, Ferrell, and polar cells. These cells are caused by air being warmed and rising in some latitudes, such as near the equator, and sinking in other latitudes. This north-south circulation combined with the Coriolis effect *(below)* produces the prevailing surface winds.

THE CORIOLIS EFFECT

Air moving over Earth's surface is deflected in a clockwise direction in the northern hemisphere and counterclockwise in the south. Known as the Coriolis effect, and caused by Earth's spin, these deflections to the air movements produce winds such as the trade winds and westerlies.

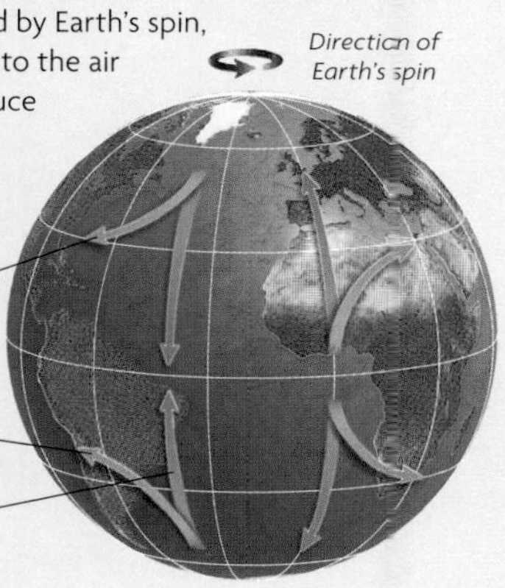

Direction of Earth's spin

Deflected clockwise

Deflected counterclockwise

Initial direction

Temperature and precipitation

The world divides by latitude into three major temperature zones: the warm tropics, the cold polar regions; and an intermediate temperate zone. In addition, temperature is strongly influenced by height above sea level. Precipitation patterns are related to factors such as solar heating, atmospheric pressure, winds, and topography. Most equatorial areas have high rainfall, caused by moist air being warmed and rising, then cooling to form rain clouds. In areas of the subtropics and near the poles, sinking air causes high pressure and low precipitation. In temperate regions rainfall is quite variable.

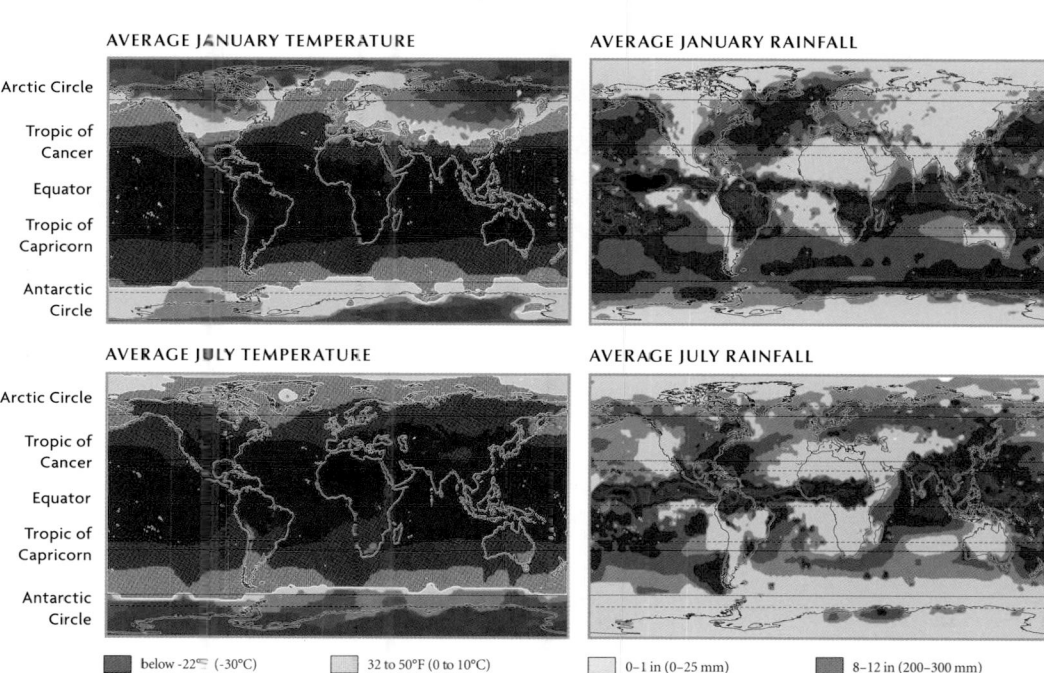

AVERAGE JANUARY TEMPERATURE

Arctic Circle
Tropic of Cancer
Equator
Tropic of Capricorn
Antarctic Circle

AVERAGE JANUARY RAINFALL

AVERAGE JULY TEMPERATURE

Arctic Circle
Tropic of Cancer
Equator
Tropic of Capricorn
Antarctic Circle

AVERAGE JULY RAINFALL

- below -22°F (-30°C)
- -22 to -4°F (-30 to -20°C)
- -4 to 14°F (-20 to -10°C)
- 14 to 32°F (-10 to 0°C)
- 32 to 50°F (0 to 10°C)
- 50 to 68°F (10 to 20°C)
- 68 to 86°F (20 to 30°C)
- above 86°F (30°C)

- 0–1 in (0–25 mm)
- 1–2 in (25–50 mm)
- 2–4 in (50–100 mm)
- 4–8 in (100–200 mm)
- 8–12 in (200–300 mm)
- 12–16 in (300–400 mm)
- 16–20 in (400–500 mm)
- above 20 in (500 mm)

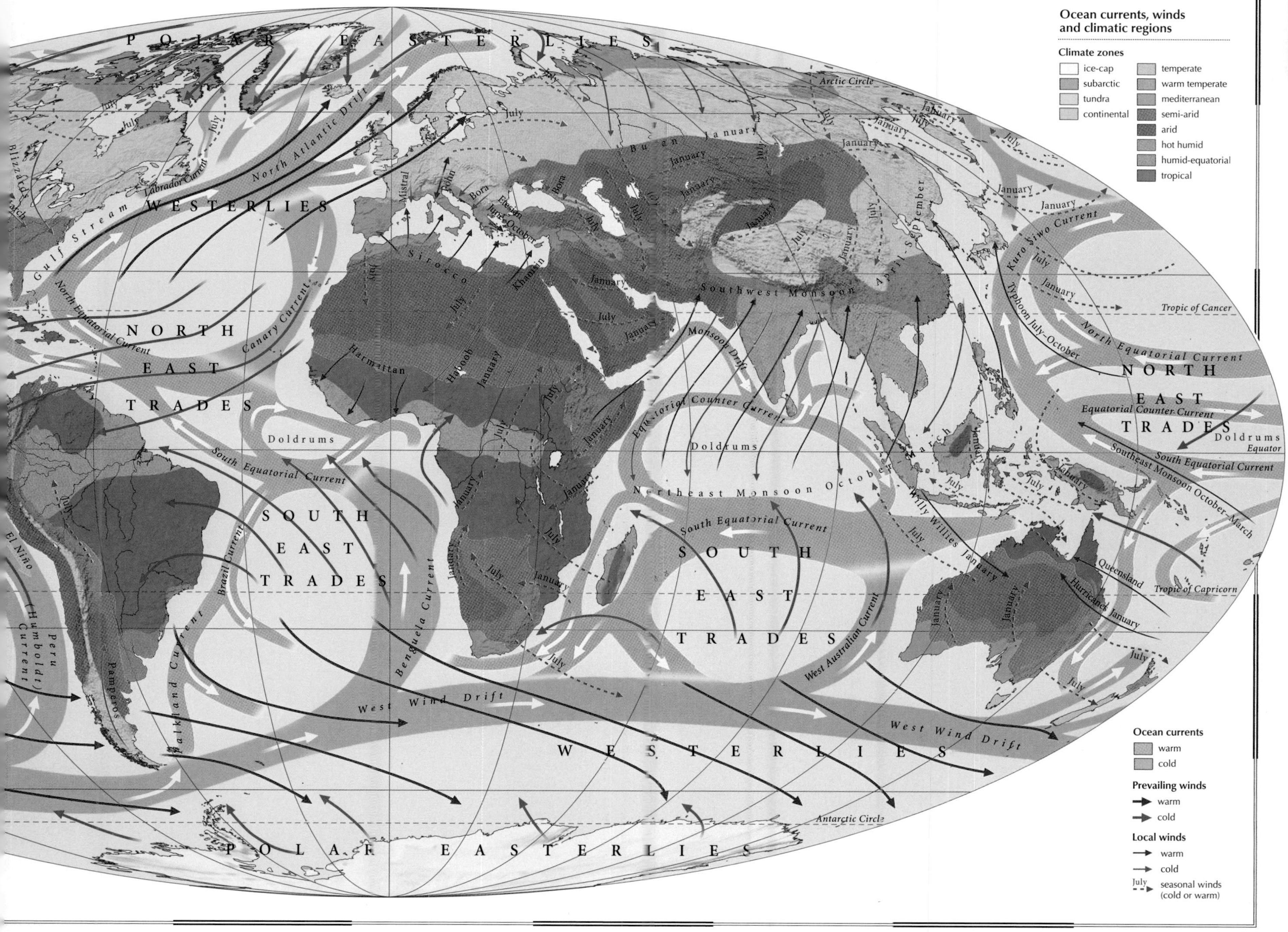

Ocean currents, winds and climatic regions

Climate zones

- ice-cap
- subarctic
- tundra
- continental
- temperate
- warm temperate
- mediterranean
- semi-arid
- arid
- hot humid
- humid-equatorial
- tropical

Ocean currents
- warm
- cold

Prevailing winds
→ warm
→ cold

Local winds
→ warm
→ cold
July seasonal winds (cold or warm)

POLAR EASTERLIES
WESTERLIES
NORTH EAST TRADES
Doldrums
SOUTH EAST TRADES
WESTERLIES
POLAR EASTERLIES

NORTH EAST TRADES
Equatorial Counter Current
Doldrums
Equator
SOUTH EAST TRADES

Arctic Circle
Tropic of Cancer
Tropic of Capricorn
Antarctic Circle

Gulf Stream
North Atlantic Drift
Labrador Current
North Equatorial Current
Canary Current
Brazil Current
Benguela Current
Falkland Current
Peru (Humboldt) Current
El Niño
Pampero
West Wind Drift
South Equatorial Current
Kuro Siwo Current
North Equatorial Current
Equatorial Counter Current
South Equatorial Current
West Australian Current
West Wind Drift
Typhoon July–October
Southwest Monsoon
Northeast Monsoon October
Southeast Monsoon October–March
Hurricanes January
Queensland
Willy Willies January
Mistral
Bora
Sirocco
Khamsin
Harmattan
Berg
Blizzard

Life on Earth

A unique combination of an oxygen-rich atmosphere and plentiful surface water is the key to life on Earth, where few areas have not been colonized by animals, plants, or smaller life-forms. An important determinant of the quantity of life in a region is its level of primary production—the amount of energy-rich substances made by organisms living there, mainly through the process of photosynthesis. On land, plants are the main organisms responsible for primary production; in water, algae fulfil this role. These primary producers supply food for animals. Primary production is affected by climatic, seasonal, and other local factors. On land, cold and aridity restrict the quantity of life in a region, whereas warmth and regular rainfall allow a greater diversity of species. In the oceans, production is mainly affected by sunlight levels, which reduce rapidly with depth, and by nutrient availability.

POLAR REGIONS
Ice restricts life in these regions to just a few species, such as polar bears in the Arctic.

Biogeographical regions

Earth's biogeographical regions, or biomes, are communities where certain species of plants and animals coexist within the constraints of particular climatic conditions. They range from tundra to various types of grassland, forest, desert, and marine biomes such as coral reefs. Factors like soil richness, altitude and human activities such as deforestation can affect the local distribution of living species in each biome.

TEMPERATE GRASSLAND
Also known as steppe or prairie, grassland of this type occurs mainly in the northern hemisphere and in South America (the Pampas).

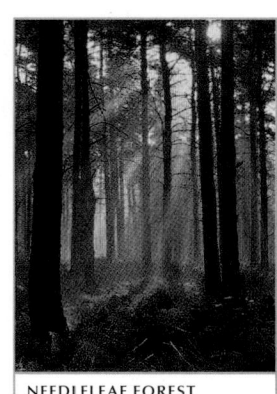

NEEDLELEAF FOREST
These vast forests of coniferous trees cover huge areas of Canada, Siberia, and Scandinavia.

TROPICAL GRASSLAND
This type of grassland is widespread in Africa and South America, supporting large numbers of grazing animals and their predators.

World biomes

- polar
- tundra
- needleleaf forest
- broadleaf forest
- temperate rainforest
- temperate grassland
- cold desert

Animal diversity

The number of animal species, and the range of genetic diversity within the populations of those species, determines the level of animal diversity within each country or other region of the world. The animals that are endemic to a region—that is, those found nowhere else on the planet—are also important in determining its level of animal diversity.

Number of animal species per country

- more than 2000
- 1000–1999
- 700–999
- 400–699
- 200–399
- 100–199
- 0–99
- data not available

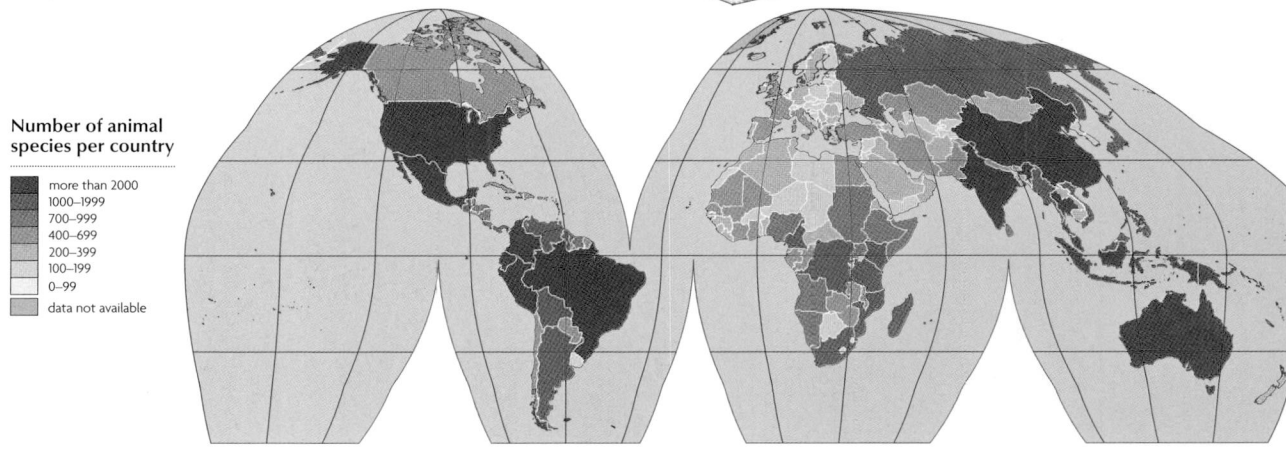

TUNDRA
With little soil and large areas of frozen ground, the tundra is largely treeless, though briefly clothed by small flowering plants in summer.

TEMPERATE RAIN FOREST
Occurring in mid-latitudes in areas of high rainfall, these forests may be predominantly coniferous or mixed with deciduous species.

CORAL REEFS
Occurring in clear tropical waters, coral reefs support an extraordinary diversity of species, especially fish and many types of invertebrate.

MOUNTAINS
In high mountain areas only a few hardy species of plant will grow above the tree-line.

TROPICAL RAINFOREST
Characterized by year-round warmth and high rainfall, tropical rainforests contain the highest diversity of plant and animal species on Earth.

World biomes
(continued)

- mediterranean
- hot desert
- tropical grassland
- dry woodland
- tropical rainforest
- mountain
- wetland

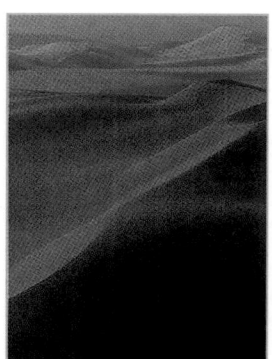

HOT DESERT
Only a few highly adapted species can survive in hot deserts, which occur mainly in the tropics.

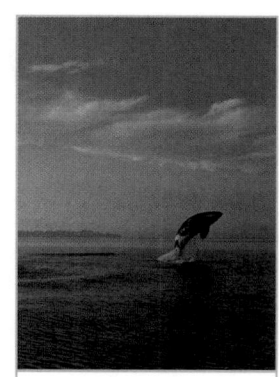

OPEN OCEAN
Earth's largest biome, the oceans are home to a vast diversity of fish, mammals, invertebrates, and algae.

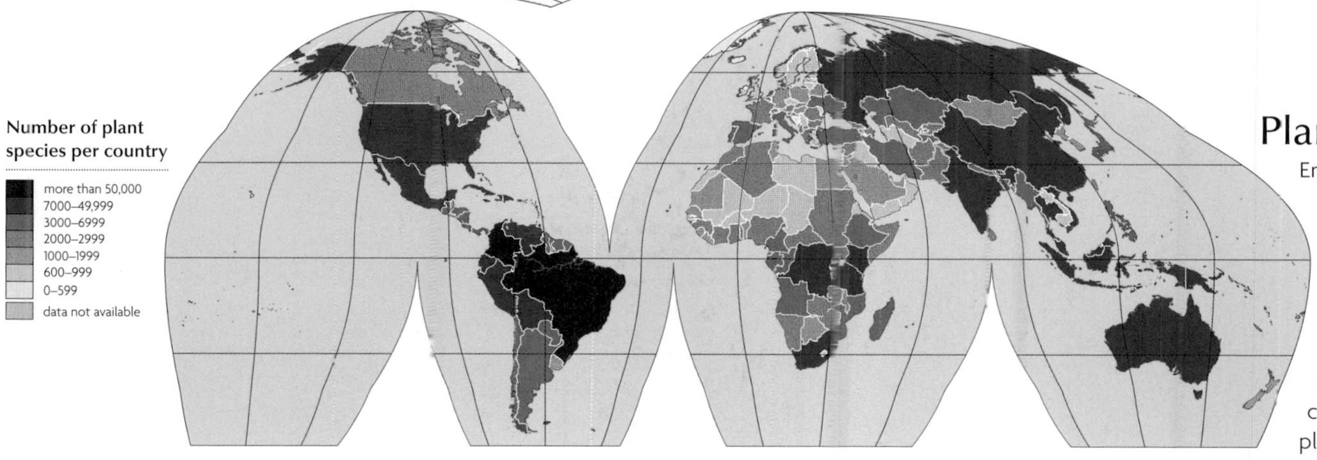

Number of plant species per country

- more than 50,000
- 7000–49,999
- 3000–6999
- 2000–2999
- 1000–1999
- 600–999
- 0–599
- data not available

Plant diversity

Environmental conditions, particularly climate, soil type, and the extent of competition with other living organisms, influence the development of plants into distinctive forms and thus also the extent of plant diversity. Human settlement and intervention has considerably reduced the diversity of plant species in many areas.

Man and the Environment

The impact of human activity on the environment has widened from being a matter of local concern (typically over the build-up of urban waste, industrial pollution, and smog) to affect whole ecosystems and, in recent decades, the global climate. Problems crossing national boundaries first became a major issue over acid rain, toxic waste dumping at sea, and chemical spillages polluting major rivers. Current concerns center on loss of biodiversity and vital habitat including wetlands and coral reefs, the felling and clearance of great tropical and temperate forests, overexploitation of scarce resources, the uncontrolled growth of cities and, above all, climate change.

OZONE HOLE
Man-made chlorofluorocarbons (CFCs), used in refrigeration and aerosols, damaged the ozone layer in the stratosphere which helps filter out the sun's harmful ultraviolet rays. When a seasonal ozone hole first appeared in 1985 over Antarctica, a shocked world agreed to phase out CFC use.

1980   1985

CO$_2$ emissions in 2003 (million tons)
- over 4000
- 1000–4000
- 500–1000
- 100–500
- 50–100
- 10–50
- 2–10
- 0–2
- no data

Kyoto Protocol
- ▲ countries that have reached targets
- ▼ countries that have not reached targets
- ● industrialized countries that have not ratified

Climate change

Global warming is happening much faster than Earth's normal long-term cycles of climate change. The consequences include unpredictable extreme weather and potential disruption of ocean currents. Melting ice-caps and glaciers, and warmer oceans, will raise average sea levels and threaten coastlines and cities. Food crops like wheat are highly vulnerable to changes in temperature and rainfall. Such changes can also have a dramatic affect on wildlife habitats.

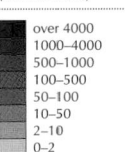

Projections
Direct measurements
Ice core data

Billions of tons of carbon dioxide

Years

Since 1800 the amount of CO$_2$ in the atmosphere has risen sharply. Urgent worldwide action to control emissions is vital to stabilize the level by the mid 21st century.

THE GREENHOUSE EFFECT
Some solar energy, reflected from the Earth's surface as infra red radiation, is reflected back as heat by "greenhouse gases" (mainly carbon dioxide and methane) in the atmosphere. Nearly all scientists now agree that an upsurge in emissions caused by humans burning fossil fuel has contributed to making the resultant warming effect a major problem.

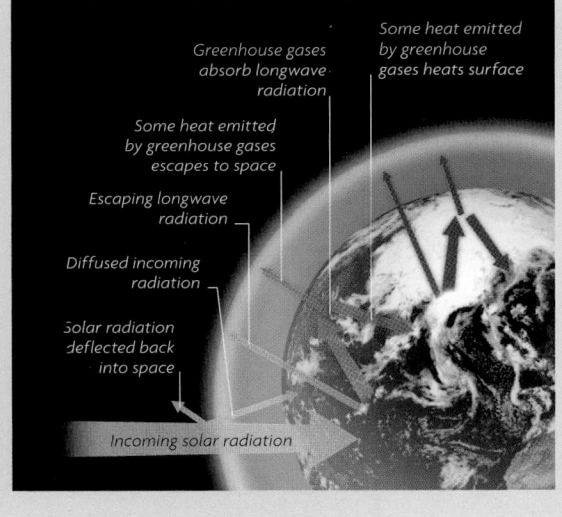

Greenhouse gases absorb longwave radiation

Some heat emitted by greenhouse gases heats surface

Some heat emitted by greenhouse gases escapes to space

Escaping longwave radiation

Diffused incoming radiation

Solar radiation deflected back into space

Incoming solar radiation

FOOD AND LAND USE
The world has about five billion hectares of agriculturally useful land, well under one hectare per person. The majority of this is pasture for grazing. Crops are grown on about 30 percent (and nearly a fifth of cropland is artificially irrigated). Mechanized farming encouraged vast single crop "monocultures," dependent on fertilizers and pesticides. North America's endless prairies of wheat and corn, huge soybean plantations, and southern cotton fields are mirrored in Ukraine (wheat), Brazil and Argentina (soya) and Uzbekistan (cotton). Elsewhere, scarce farmland can be squeezed by the housing needs of growing urban populations. Current interest in crop-derived "biofuels" means further pressure to grow food more productively on less land.

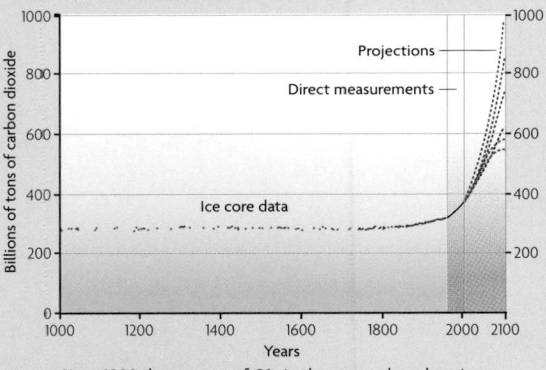

Intensive farming. Satellite photography picks up the greenhouses that now cover almost all the land in this Spanish coastal area southwest of Almeria.

1996   2000   2005

DEFORESTATION

At current rates of destruction, all tropical forests, and most old-growth temperate forest, will be gone by 2090. The Amazon rain forest is a valuable genetic resource, containing innumerable unique plants and animals, as well as acting as a crucial natural "sink" for absorbing climate-damaging carbon dioxide. Stemming the loss of these precious assets to logging and farming is one of the major environmental challenges of modern times.

Over 25,000 sq miles (60,000 sq km) of virgin rain forest are cleared annually by logging and agricultural activities, destroying an irreplaceable natural resource.

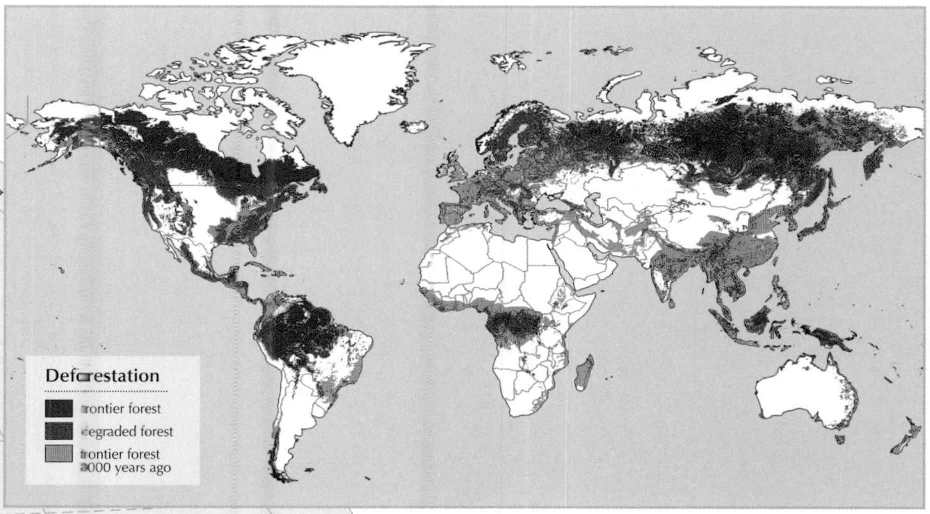

KAZAKHSTAN
MONGOLIA
GEORGIA
ARMENIA AZERB.
KYRG.
TURKMEN.
TAJ.
UZBEK.
SYRIA
LEBANON
AFGHANISTAN
PAKISTAN
IRAQ
IRAN
JORDAN
KUWAIT
BAHRAIN
QATAR
UAE
SAUDI ARABIA
OMAN
NEPAL
ERITREA
YEMEN
DJIBOUTI
ETHIOPIA
SOMALIA
KENYA
TANZANIA
MALAWI
MOZAMBIQUE
ZAMBIA
MADAGASCAR
COMOROS
SEYCHELLES
MAURITIUS
Réunion
(to France)
MALDIVES
SRI LANKA
NORTH KOREA
SOUTH KOREA
JAPAN
TAIWAN
MYANMAR (BURMA)
LAOS
VIETNAM
THAILAND
CAMBODIA
PHILIPPINES
BRUNEI
MALAYSIA
SINGAPORE
PALAU
INDONESIA
PAPUA NEW GUINEA
EAST TIMOR
NAURU
SOLOMON ISLANDS
VANUATU
TONGA
FIJI
AUSTRALIA
NEW ZEALAND

INDIAN OCEAN

PACIFIC OCEAN

Deforestation
- frontier forest
- degraded forest
- frontier forest 8000 years ago

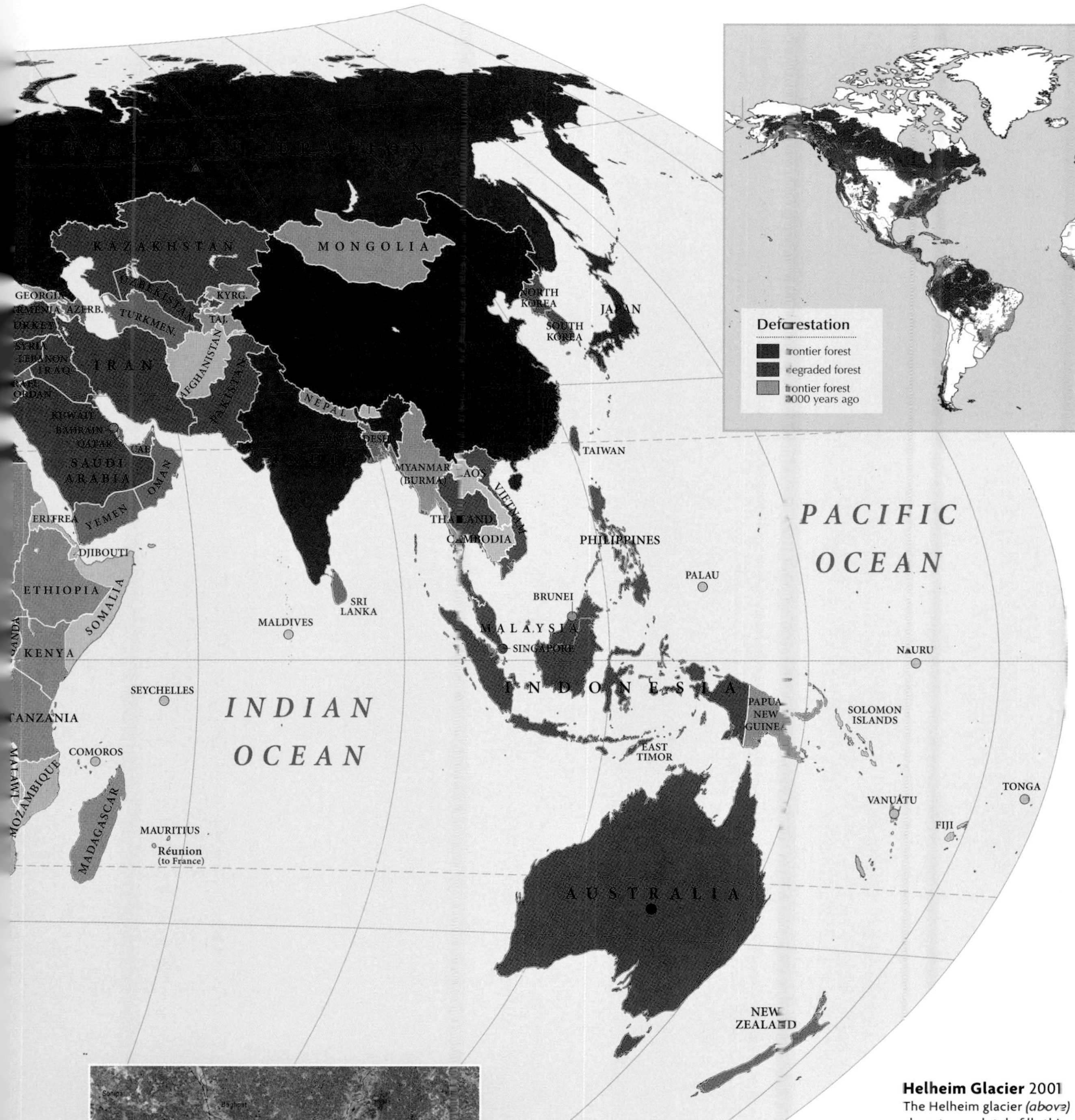

GLACIATION

The world's glaciers and ice sheets have been in retreat for decades, forming less new ice at high altitudes than they lose by melting lower down. The loss of ice from Greenland doubled between 1996 and 2005, with alarming implications for rising sea levels. Other dramatic evidence of global warming includes the rapid thinning of ice in the Himalayas, and the highly symbolic loss of the snowcap on Africa's Mount Kilimanjaro.

Helheim Glacier 2001
The Helheim glacier (above) almost completely fills this image, with the leading edge visible on the righthand side, and was in a relatively stable condition.

Helheim Glacier 2005
By 2005 (right) it had retreated by 2.5 miles (4 km).

Delhi 1971
In 1971 Delhi (above) occupied an area of about 190 sq miles (500 sq km).

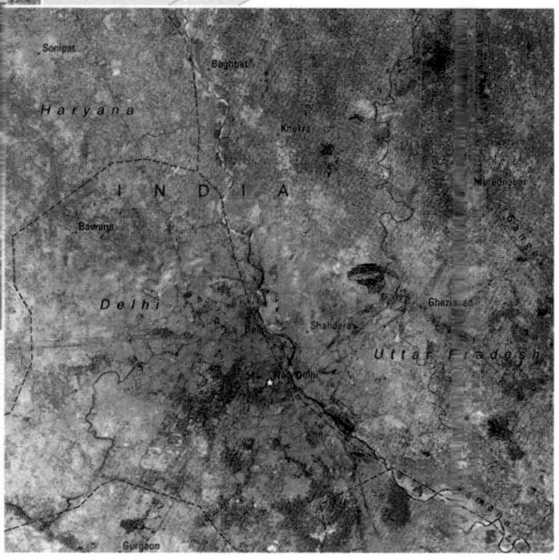

Delhi 1999
By 1999 (right) it had sprawled to cover 500 sq miles (1300 sq km). It vies with Mumbai in the southwest to be the sub-continent's most populous city, fast approaching 20 million people.

CITY GROWTH

The world in 2006 had five cities with populations over 20 million—Tokyo, Mexico City, Seoul, New York City, and São Paulo. The number of cities with populations between 10 and 20 million has reached 20 and continues to rise. The search for work, and the hope of escape from rural poverty, drives migration from rural to urban areas across the developing world. Urban dwellers now amount to more than half the world's population, and consume more resources than their rural counterparts.

Population and Settlement

Earth's human population is projected to rise from its current level of 6.5 billion to between 7.6 and 11 billion by the year 2050. The distribution of this population is very uneven and is dictated by climate, terrain, and by natural and economic resources. Most people live in coastal zones and along the valleys of great rivers such as the Ganges, Indus, Nile, and Yangtze. Deserts cover over 20 percent of Earth's surface but support less than 5 percent of its human population. Over half the world's population live in cities—most of them in Asia, Europe, and North America—as a result of mass migrations that have occurred from rural areas as people search for jobs. Many of these people live in so-called "megacities"—sprawling urban areas that have populations higher than 10 million.

Population density by country (population per sq mile)

over 2600	260-389	65–129
775-2599	195–259	26–64
390-774	130–194	0–25

Population density

A few regions, including Europe, India, and much of eastern Asia, have extremely high population densities. Within these areas, a few spots, such as Monaco and Hong Kong, have densities of over 12,900 per sq mile (5000 people per sq km). Other regions (mostly desert, mountain, ice cap, tundra, or thickly forested areas) have densities close to zero –examples include large areas of Australia, western China, Siberia, North Africa, Canada, Greenland, and much of the Amazon rain forest region.

NORTH AMERICA

World population World land area
9% 17.0%

EUROPE

World population World land area
14% 7.1%

Million-person cities

In the year 1900 there were fewer than 20 cities in the world with a population that exceeded one million. By 1950 there were 75 such cities, and by the year 2000 there were more than 300 such cities, 40 of them in China alone, with another 30 in India, 14 in Brazil, and 10 in Japan.

Population density (persons per sq mile)

520–2600
260–520
130–260
52–130
26–52
13–26
3–13
0–3

Million-cities in 1900

● Cities over 1 million in population

SOUTH AMERICA

World population World land area
5.5% 11.8%

Million-cities in 1950

ANTARCTICA

World population World land area
0.0% 8.9%

Million-cities in 2006

Tokyo urban sprawl

—— City boundary, 1860 —— City boundary, 1964

GREATER TOKYO

The Greater Tokyo Area is the most populous urban area in the world, with an estimated head count in 2006 of 35.5 million. It includes Tokyo City, which has a population of about 12 million, and adjoining cities such as Yokohama. This satellite photograph shows the Greater Tokyo Area today, and also the boundaries of Tokyo City in 1860 (red) and 1964 (yellow).

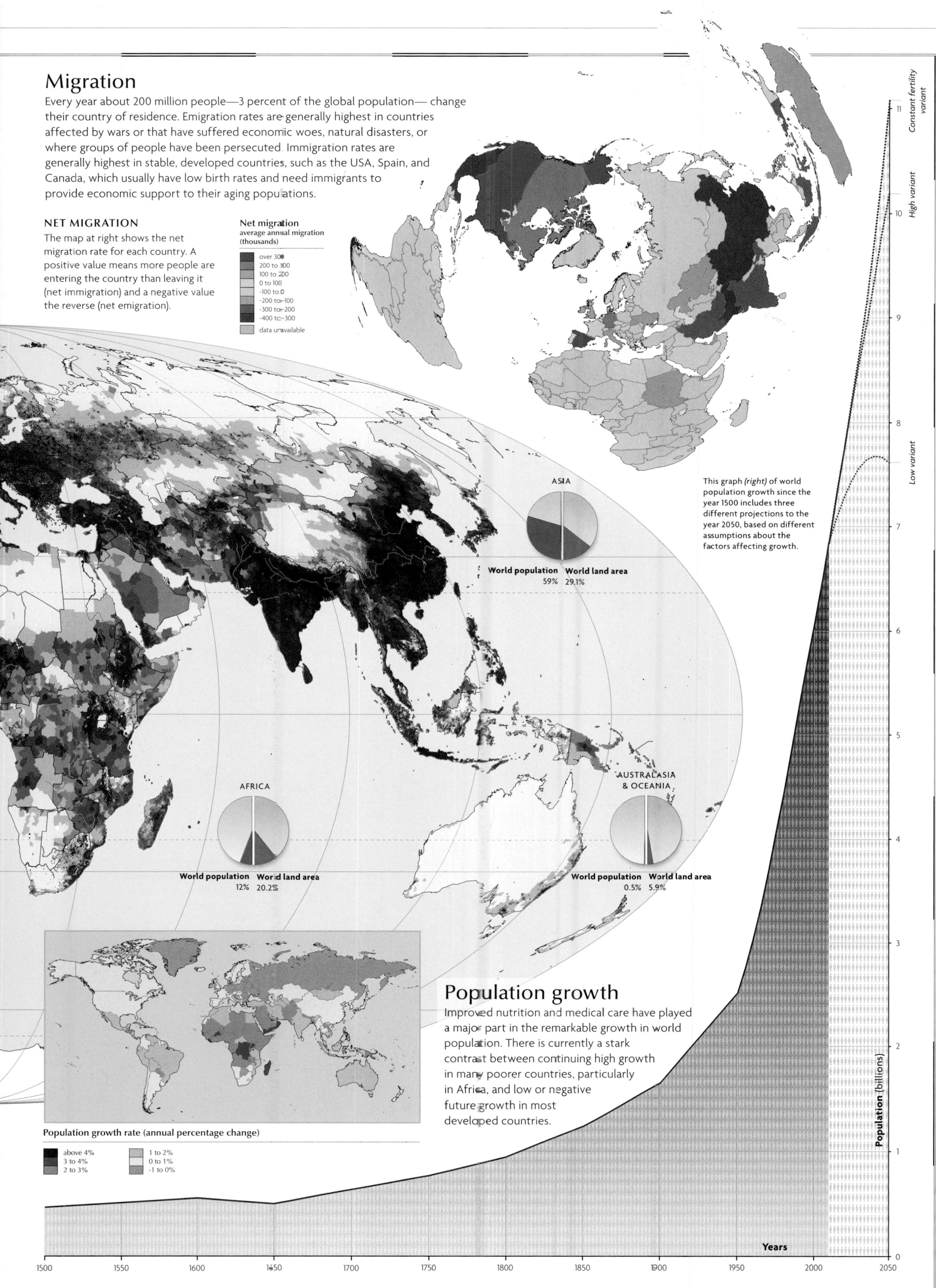

Migration

Every year about 200 million people—3 percent of the global population— change their country of residence. Emigration rates are generally highest in countries affected by wars or that have suffered economic woes, natural disasters, or where groups of people have been persecuted. Immigration rates are generally highest in stable, developed countries, such as the USA, Spain, and Canada, which usually have low birth rates and need immigrants to provide economic support to their aging populations.

NET MIGRATION

The map at right shows the net migration rate for each country. A positive value means more people are entering the country than leaving it (net immigration) and a negative value the reverse (net emigration).

Net migration
average annual migration (thousands)

- over 300
- 200 to 300
- 100 to 200
- 0 to 100
- -100 to 0
- -200 to -100
- -300 to -200
- -400 to -300
- data unavailable

ASIA

World population 59%   **World land area** 29.1%

This graph *(right)* of world population growth since the year 1500 includes three different projections to the year 2050, based on different assumptions about the factors affecting growth.

AFRICA

World population 12%   **World land area** 20.2%

AUSTRALASIA & OCEANIA

World population 0.5%   **World land area** 5.9%

Population growth

Improved nutrition and medical care have played a major part in the remarkable growth in world population. There is currently a stark contrast between continuing high growth in many poorer countries, particularly in Africa, and low or negative future growth in most developed countries.

Population growth rate (annual percentage change)

- above 4%
- 3 to 4%
- 2 to 3%
- 1 to 2%
- 0 to 1%
- -1 to 0%

Constant fertility variant

High variant

Low variant

Population (billions)

Years

1500 1550 1600 1650 1700 1750 1800 1850 1900 1950 2000 2050

Language

Over 6800 different languages exist throughout the world, each one with its own unique evolutionary history and cultural connotations. Most of these languages are spoken only by small groups of people in remote regions. Sadly these minority tongues are dying out—it is estimated that about a third will have disappeared by the year 2100. The relatively small number of widely-spoken languages have gained their current predominance and pattern of distribution through a variety of historical factors. Among these have been the economic, military, or technological success of certain peoples and cultures, differing population growth rates, and the effects of migrations and colonization.

The European Union (EU) embraces the diversity of its 27 countries and 23 official languages by providing a translation and interpretation service for the majority of its meetings and documentation. This costs around US$ 650 million per year, which equates to 1 percent of the EU budget.

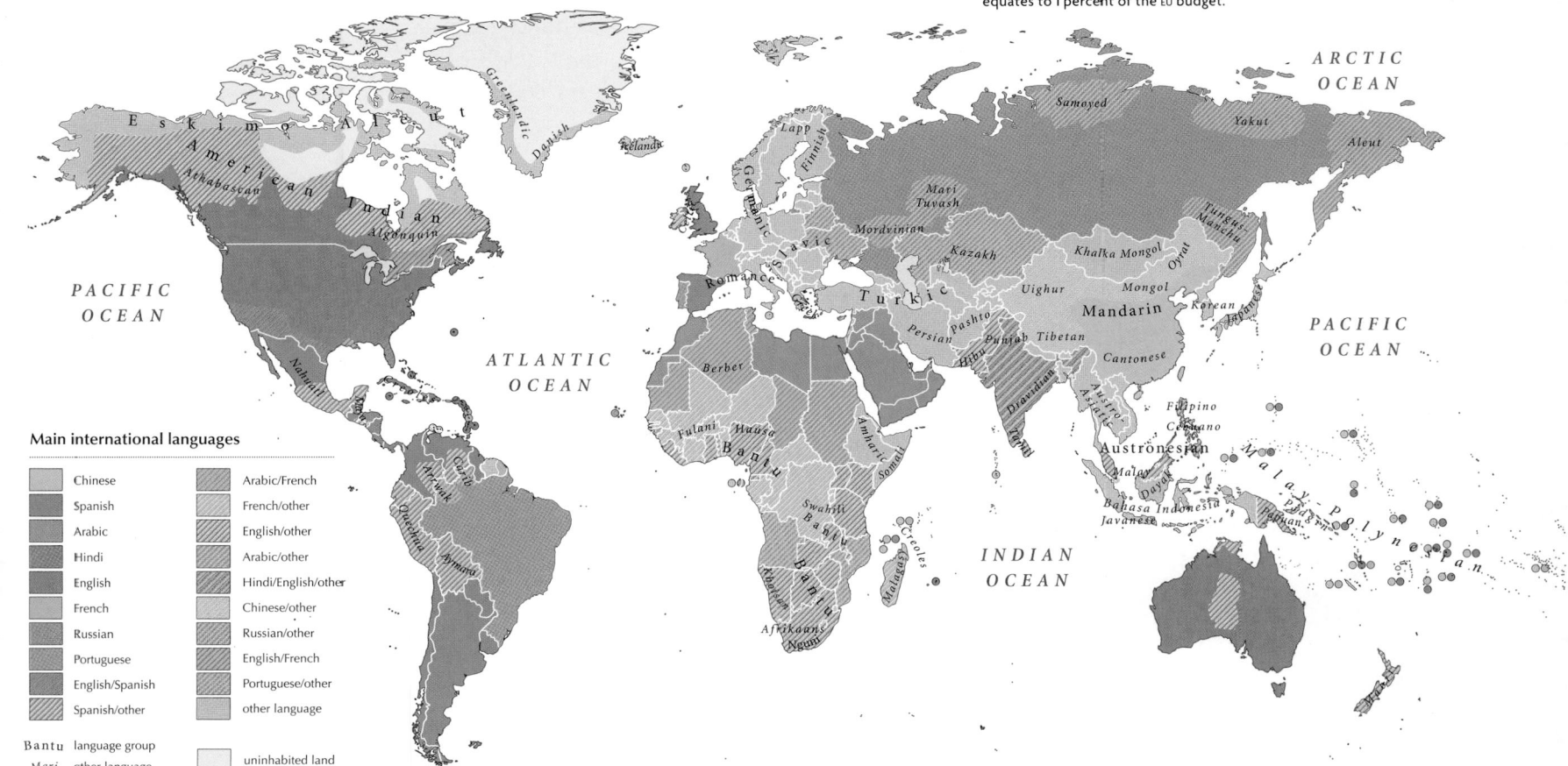

Main international languages

- Chinese
- Spanish
- Arabic
- Hindi
- English
- French
- Russian
- Portuguese
- English/Spanish
- Spanish/other
- Arabic/French
- French/other
- English/other
- Arabic/other
- Hindi/English/other
- Chinese/other
- Russian/other
- English/French
- Portuguese/other
- other language

Bantu language group
Mari other language

uninhabited land

The colonial powers

Colonialism between the 15th and 20th centuries had a major influence in establishing the world prevalence of various, mainly European, languages. Britain, for example, was the colonial power in Canada, the USA (until 1776), the Indian subcontinent, Australia, and parts of Africa and the Caribbean. Hence, English is still the main (or a major) language in these areas. The same applies to France and the French language in parts of Africa and southeast Asia, and to Spain and the Spanish language in much of Latin America. For similar reasons, Portuguese is the main language in Brazil and parts of Africa, and there are many Dutch speakers in Indonesia.

This dual language sign, written in both in Hindi and English, stands outside Shimla railway station in northern India. The sign reflects India's past—the British used Shimla as their summer capital during the colonial period.

TOP TEN LANGUAGES

About 45 percent of people speak one of just ten languages as their native tongue. Mandarin Chinese is spoken by far the largest number—a situation likely to persist, as minority language speakers in China are encouraged to switch to Mandarin. English usage is also increasing, as it is the most favored language on the internet and in business circles. Wherever English is not the mother tongue, it is often the second language.

THE TEN MOST SPOKEN LANGUAGES
(number of native speakers)

- Mandarin Chinese (1.1 billion)
- English (330 million)
- Spanish (300 million)
- Hindi/Urdu (250 million)
- Arabic (200 million)
- Bengali (185 million)
- Portuguese (160 million)
- Russian (160 million)
- Japanese (125 million)
- German (100 million)

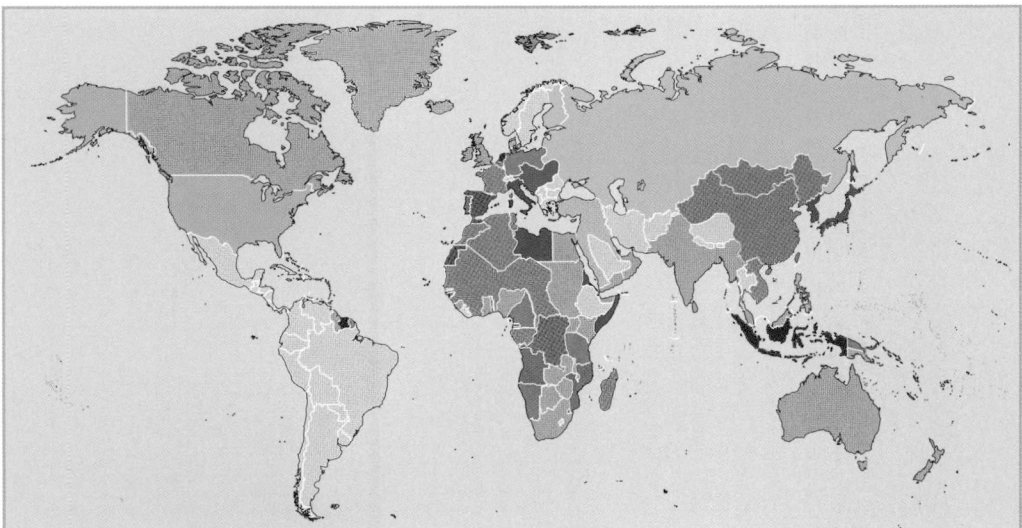

Colonial Empires in 1914

- Austro-Hungarian
- Belgian
- British
- Chinese
- Danish
- Dutch
- French
- German
- Italian
- Japanese
- Ottoman
- Portuguese
- Russian
- Spanish
- United States
- Independent
- Disputed

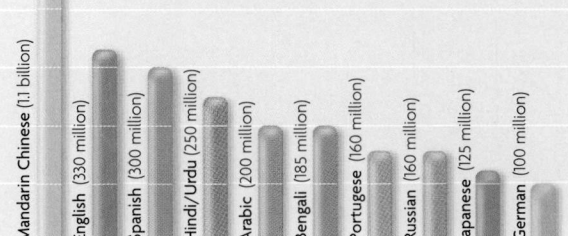
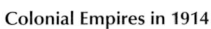
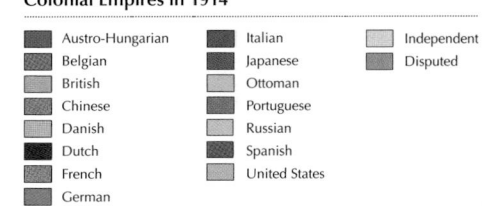

Religion

The spread of religion

By their nature, religions usually start off in small geographical areas and then spread. For Christianity and Islam, this spread was rapid and extensive. Buddhism diffused more slowly from around 500 BCE into a large part of Asia. The oldest religion, Hinduism, has always been concentrated in the Indian subcontinent, although its adherents in other parts of the world now number millions following migrations from India.

1ST– 7TH CENTURY

During this period, Christianity spread from its origins in the eastern Mediterranean, while Hinduism and forms of Buddhism spread in Asia. Islam became established in Arabia.

Rise and spread of the classical religions to 650 CE

- Buddhist heartland
- Chinese Confucianism/ Daoism and indigenous primal traditions
- Converted to Christianity by 600 CE
- Hinduism
- Islam under Muhammad
- Mahayana Buddhism
- Shintoism
- Zoroastrianism
- → spread of Buddhism
- → spread of Christianity
- → spread of Hinduism
- → dispersion of Jews, to 500 CE

7TH–16TH CENTURY

Islam later spread further through Asia and into parts of Africa and Europe. Christianity diffused through Europe and was then carried to many other parts of the world by colonialists and missionaries. Buddhism spread further in Asia.

World religions c.1500 CE

- Catholic Christianity
- area converted to Catholic Christianity
- Hinduism
- Islam
- Mahayana Buddhism and Confucianism, Daoism and Shinto
- Mahayana Buddhism and Confucianism, Daoism
- Russian Orthodoxy
- Theravada Buddhism
- Tibetan Buddhism
- Aztec Empire
- Inca Empire
- → spread of Catholicism
- → spread of Islam
- → spread of Protestantism
- → spread of Russian Orthodoxy

Each year millions of Muslims visit Mecca during the the Islamic pilgrimage known as the *Hajj*

About 83 percent of the world's population adheres to a religion. The remainder adopt irreligious stances such as atheism. In terms of broad similarities of belief, there are about 20 different religions in the world with more than 1 million adherents. However, the larger of these are split into several denominations, which differ in their exact beliefs and practices. Christianity, for example, includes three major groupings that have historically been in conflict—Roman Catholicism, Protestantism, and Orthodox Christianity—as well as hundreds of separate smaller groups. Many of the world's other main religious, such as Islam and Buddhism, are also subdivided.

RELIGION AROUND THE WORLD

About 72 percent of humanity adheres to one of five religions: Christianity, Islam, Hinduism, Buddhism, and Chinese traditional religion (which includes Daoism and Confucianism). Of the remainder, many are adherents of primal indigenous religions (a wide range of tribal or folk religions such as shamanism).

- Buddhist (0.36 billion)
- Judaism (15 million)
- Sikhism (23 million)
- Chinese traditional (0.36 billion)
- Christianity (1.9 billion)
- Primal indigenous (0.36 billion)
- Hindu (0.84 billion)
- Not religious (0.96 billion)
- Islam (1.06 billion)

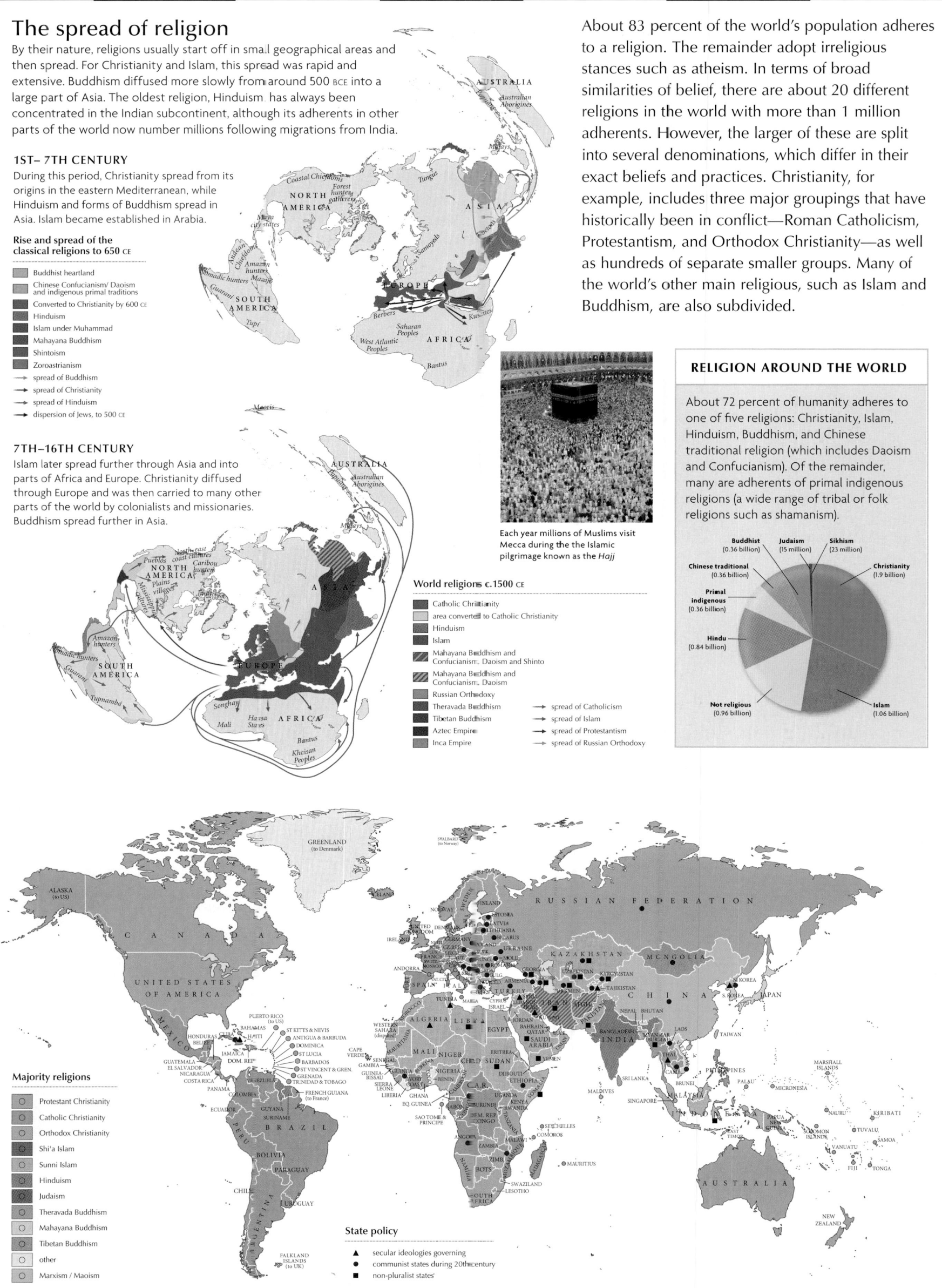

Majority religions

- Protestant Christianity
- Catholic Christianity
- Orthodox Christianity
- Shi'a Islam
- Sunni Islam
- Hinduism
- Judaism
- Theravada Buddhism
- Mahayana Buddhism
- Tibetan Buddhism
- other
- Marxism / Maoism

State policy

- ▲ secular ideologies governing
- ● communist states during 20th century
- ■ non-pluralist states

Health

On most health parameters, the countries of the world split into two distinct groups. The first of these encompass the richer, developed, countries, where medical care is good to excellent, infant mortality and the incidence of deadly infectious diseases is low, and life expectancy is high and rising. Some of the biggest health problems in these countries arise from overeating, while the two main causes of death are heart disease and cancer. The second region consists of the poorer developing countries, where medical care is much less adequate, infant mortality is high, many people are undernourished, and infectious diseases such as malaria are major killers. Life expectancy in these countries is much lower and in some cases is falling.

Life expectancy

Life expectancy has risen remarkably in developed countries over the past 50 years and has now topped 80 years in many of them. In contrast, life expectancy in many of the countries of sub-Saharan Africa has fallen well below 50, in large part due to the high prevalence of HIV/AIDS.

Many people in developed countries are now living for 15–20 years after retirement, putting greater pressure on welfare and health services.

Infant deaths and births

Infant mortality is still high in many developing nations, especially some African countries, due in part to stretched medical services. As well as lower infant mortality, the world's developed countries have much lower birth rates—greater female emancipation and easier access to contraceptives are two causative factors.

World infant mortality rates (deaths per 1000 live births)

| above 125 | 75–124 | 35–74 | 15–34 | below 15 |

Number of births (per 1000 people)

| above 40 | 30–39 | 20–29 | below 20 |

Nutrition

Two-thirds of the world's food is consumed in developed nations, many of which have a daily calorific intake far higher than is needed by their populations. By contrast, about 800 million people in the developing world do not have enough food to meet basic nutritional needs.

Daily calorie intake per capita

| above 3000 | 2500–2999 | 2000–2499 | below 2000 |

Life expectancy

| above 80 years |
| 75–80 years |
| 70–75 years |
| 60–70 years |
| 50–60 years |
| below 50 years |

United States of America: has an average life expectancy of about 78 years, with women living about 5 years longer than men.

Liberia: currently has one of the lowest life expectancies in West Africa, at less than 40 years, owing to factors such as high rates of infectious disease, recent conflict, and poverty.

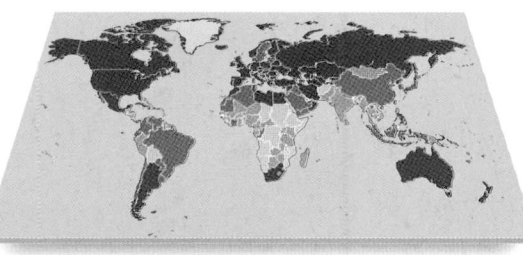

The extensive public healthcare system in Cuba provides for around 6 doctors per 1000 people, one of the highest ratios in the world.

Healthcare

An indicator of the strength of healthcare provision in a country is the number of doctors per 1000 population. Some communist and former communist countries such as Cuba and Russia score well in this regard. In general, healthcare provision is good or adequate in most of the world's richer countries but scanty throughout much of Africa and in parts of Asia and Latin America.

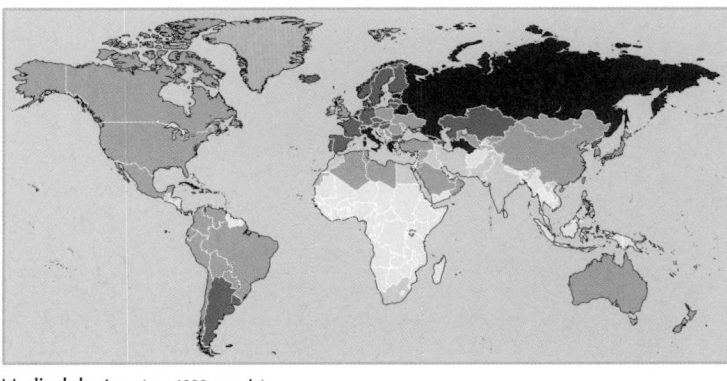

Medical doctors (per 1000 people)

| above 5 | 4–5 | 3–4 | 1–3 | 0.5–1 | below 0.5 | no data |

Smoking

Cigarette smoking—one of the most harmful activities to health—is common throughout much of the world. Smoking prevalence is generally highest in the richer, developed countries. However, awareness of the health risks has seen cigarette consumption in most of these countries stabilize or begin to fall. By contrast, more and more people, especially males, are taking up the habit in poorer developing countries.

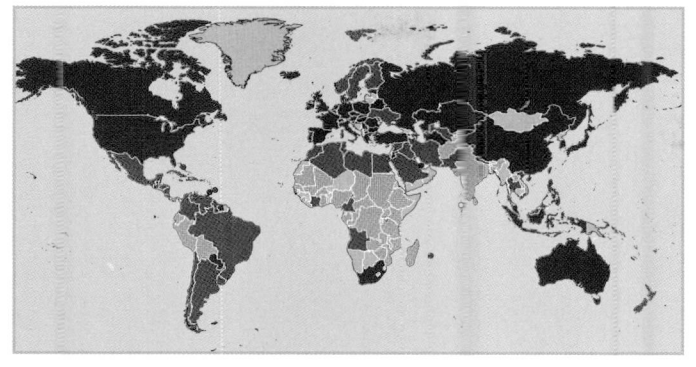

Annual cigarette consumption (per person)

- above 2500
- 1500–2499
- 500–1499
- 1–499
- no data

Communicable diseases

Despite advances in their treatment and prevention, infectious diseases remain a huge problem, especially in developing countries. Three of the most common and deadly are tuberculosis (TB), HIV/AIDS, and malaria. Of these, active TB affects about 15 million people (often as a complication of AIDS), with a particularly high prevalence in parts of Africa. HIV/AIDS has spread since 1981 to become a global pandemic. Malaria affects about 400 million people every year.

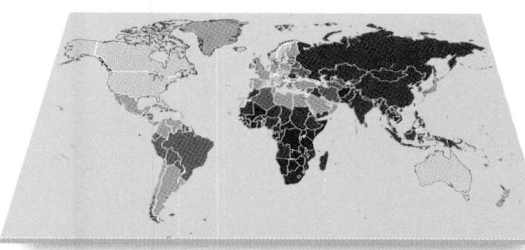

Estimated tuberculosis cases (per 100,000 per year)

- above 300
- 100–300
- 50–100
- 10–50
- below 10

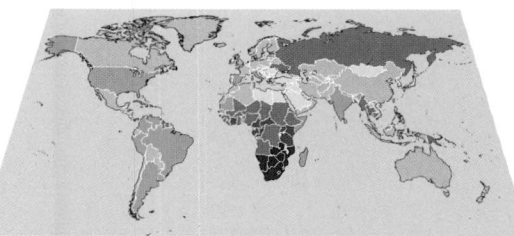

Adult (15-49) HIV prevalence rate (percent of population)

- 15–34
- 5–15
- 1–5
- 0.5–1
- 0.1–0.5
- below 0.1
- no data

Malaria cases (per 100,000 per year)

- above 25,000
- 10,000–25,000
- 1000–10,000
- 100–1000
- 10–100
- below 10
- low risk

RUSSIAN FEDERATION

KAZAKHSTAN

MONGOLIA

PACIFIC OCEAN

UZBEKISTAN

TURKMEN.

KYRG.

CHINA

NORTH KOREA

SOUTH KOREA

JAPAN

IRAN

PAKISTAN

NEPAL

BHUTAN

BANGLADESH

TAIWAN

INDIA

MYANMAR (BURMA)

LAOS

VIETNAM

THAILAND

PHILIPPINES

MICRONESIA

MARSHALL ISLANDS

CAMBODIA

PALAU

SRI LANKA

MALDIVES

BRUNEI

MALAYSIA

SINGAPORE

NAURU

INDONESIA

PAPUA NEW GUINE

SOLOMON ISLANDS

EAST TIMOR

VANUATU

SEYCHELLES

INDIAN OCEAN

COMOROS

TANZANIA

MAURITIUS

MADAGASCAR

MOZAMBIQUE

ZIMBABWE

AUSTRALIA

SWAZILAND

LESOTHO

NEW ZEALAND

Japan: has one of the world's highest life expectancies, at over 81 years—a fact commonly put down to the typical Japanese low-fat diet of rice, fish, and soy products.

Swaziland: currently has the lowest life expectancy in the world, at about 33 years, due to widespread HIV/AIDS.

Preventive medicine

Throughout the world, doctors recognize that the prevention of disease and disease transmission is just as important as the treatment of illness. Preventive medicine has many aspects and includes advice about diet and nutrition; education about the avoidance of health-threatening behaviors such as smoking, excess alcohol consumption, and unprotected sex; and the use of vaccines against diseases such as typhoid, polio and cholera. In developing countries, some of the main priorities in preventive medicine are the provision of pure water supplies and proper sanitation, as well as measures against malaria, including the use of antimalarial drugs and mosquito nets.

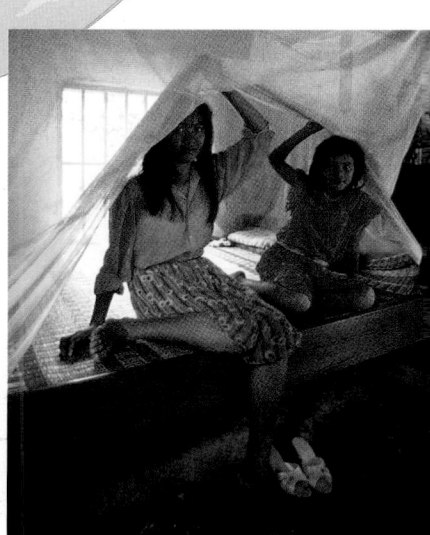

The use of mosquito nets greatly reduces the transmission of malaria and the risk of infection.

TOP TEN KILLER DISEASES, 2004

The world's biggest killer diseases fall into two main groups. One group, which includes HIV/AIDS, malaria, tuberculosis, and childhood diseases such as measles, mainly kills people in poor countries. The other group includes cardiovascular diseases and cancer, the big killers in rich countries.

- Cardiovascular diseases (heart disease and stroke) (16.7 million)
- Cancer (7.1 million)
- Respiratory infection (4 million)
- Other respiratory diseases (3.7 million)
- HIV/AIDS (2.9 million)
- Digestive diseases (1.9 million)
- Tuberculosis (1.5 million)
- Childhood cluster diseases (1.1 million)
- Diabetes (0.9 million)
- Malaria (0.9 million)

Water Resources

Water covers 71 percent of Earth's surface, but only 2.5 percent of this is fresh water, and two thirds of that is locked up in glaciers and polar ice sheets. Patterns of human settlement have developed around fresh water availability, but increasing numbers of people are now vulnerable to chronic shortage or interruptions in supply. Worldwide, fresh water consumption multiplied more than sixfold during the 20th century as populations increased and agriculture became more dependent on irrigation, much of it hugely wasteful because of evaporation and run-off. Industrial water demand also rose, as did use in the home, for washing, flushing, cooking, and gardening.

Amid the desert of Wadi Rum, Jordan, crops grow on circular patches of land irrigated with water from an underground aquifer.

Water withdrawal

Agriculture accounts for 70 percent of water consumption worldwide. Industry and domestic use each account for 15 percent. Excessive withdrawal of water affects the health of rivers and the needs of people. China's Yellow River now fails to reach the sea for most of the year.

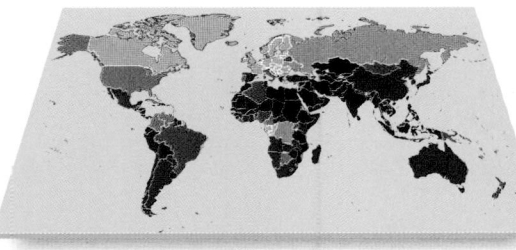

Percentage of freshwater withdrawal by agriculture

79–100 66–79 47–66 31–47 16–31 0–16

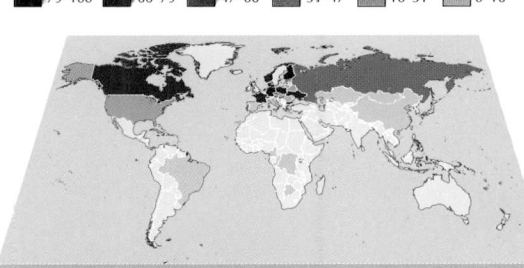

Percentage of freshwater withdrawal by industry

79–100 66–79 47–66 31–47 16–31 0–16

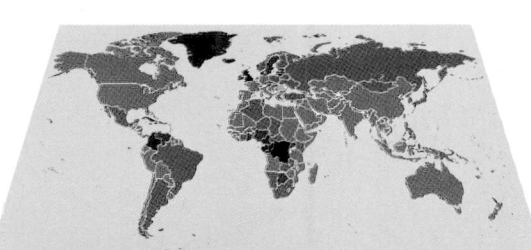

Percentage of freshwater withdrawal by domestic use

60–81 45–60 30–45 15–30 0–15 no data

Availability of fresh water
total renewable
(cubic yards/capita/per year)

- less than 1300 (water scarcity)
- 1300–2221 (water stress)
- 2222–3921 (insufficient water)
- 3922–12,999 (relatively sufficient)
- 13,000 or more (plentiful supplies)
- major drainage basin
- ▼ over 50% of water resource originating from outside country

Map labels: USA (Alaska), Yukon, Mackenzie, CANADA, Greenland (to Denmark), ICELAND, UNITED KINGDOM, IRELAND, St. Lawrence, UNITED STATES OF AMERICA, Colorado, Mississippi/Missouri, ATLANTIC OCEAN, FRANCE, PORTUGAL, SPAIN, Rio Grande, MOROCCO, ALGERIA, Hawai'i (to US), BAHAMAS, CUBA, WESTERN SAHARA (occupied by Morocco), MEXICO, JAMAICA, HAITI, DOMINICAN REPUBLIC, MAURITANIA, MALI, CAPE VERDE, SENEGAL, Niger, BELIZE, GUATEMALA, HONDURAS, ST KITTS & NEVIS, ANTIGUA & BARBUDA, GAMBIA, GUINEA-BISSAU, GUINEA, BURKINA, EL SALVADOR, NICARAGUA, BARBADOS, SIERRA LEONE, IVORY COAST, GHANA, BENIN, PACIFIC OCEAN, COSTA RICA, PANAMA, TRINIDAD & TOBAGO, VENEZUELA, GUYANA, SURINAME, French Guiana (to France), LIBERIA, TOGO, EQUATORIAL GUINEA, COLOMBIA, Orinoco, SAO TOME & PRINCIPE, ECUADOR, Amazon, BRAZIL, PERU, São Francisco, BOLIVIA, Paraná, PARAGUAY, CHILE, ARGENTINA, URUGUAY, ATLANTIC OCEAN, SOUTHERN OCEAN

Drought

The disruption of normal rainfall patterns can cause drought problems even in temperate zones, with consequences ranging from domestic water usage restrictions to low crop yields to forest fires. In regions of the developing world where monsoon rains fail, or water is perennially scarce, drought is a life or death issue. Parts of central and east Africa, for instance, have suffered severe and recurring droughts in recent decades, with disastrous results including destruction of livestock, desertification, famine, and mass migration.

In a severe drought, river beds may dry up (above left), leaving stranded fish to die, as here in Florida.

A Chinese farmer waters dry fields (above) in China's southern province of Guangdong. This picture was taken in May 2002, but the image is timeless; it could be August 2006 in Sichuan province, to the northwest of here—or almost any year in water-stressed northern China.

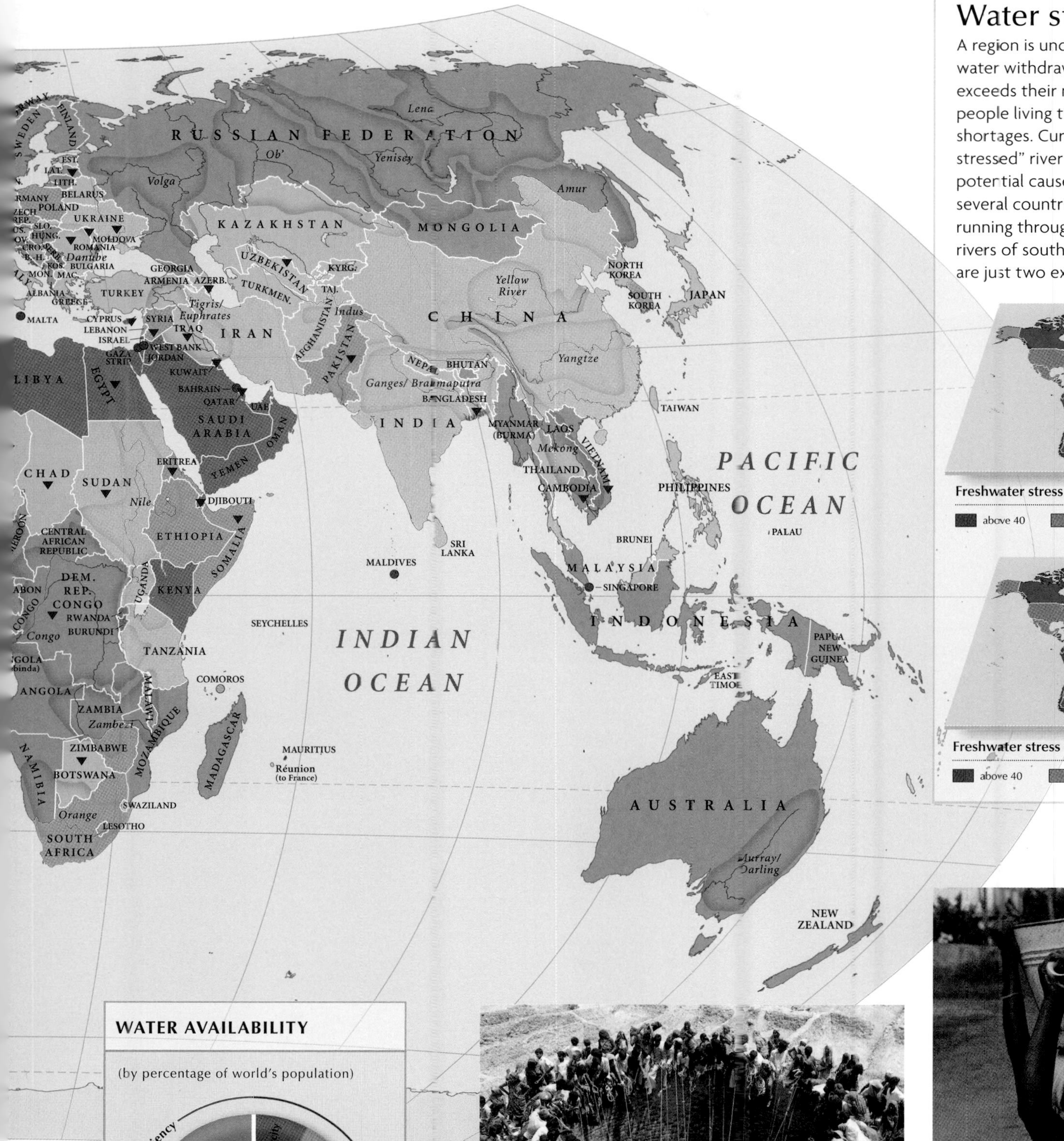

Water stress

A region is under "water stress" when the rate of water withdrawal from its rivers and aquifers exceeds their natural replenishment, so that people living there are subject to frequent shortages. Currently 1.7 billion people live in "highly stressed" river basins worldwide. This is a major potential cause of conflict, particularly when several countries share one river; the Euphrates, running through Turkey, Syria, and Iraq, or the rivers of southern China running south into Korea, are just two examples.

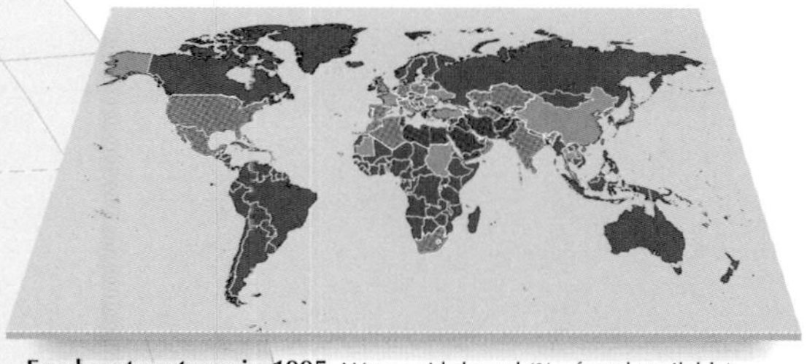

Freshwater stress in 1995 Water withdrawal (% of total available)

| above 40 | 20–40 | 10–20 | below 10 |

Freshwater stress in 2025 Water withdrawal (% of total available)

| above 40 | 20–40 | 10–20 | below 10 |

WATER AVAILABILITY

(by percentage of world's population)

relative sufficiency

insufficiency

Plentiful
16.3%

Water scarcity 18%

Water stress
24.5%

Relatively
sufficient
24.5%

Insufficient
16.7%

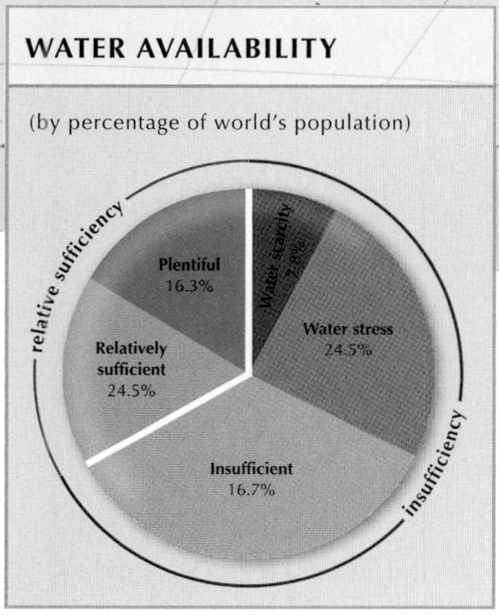

Clean drinking water

Sub-Saharan Africa is among the most deprived regions for lack of access to safe drinking water. Worldwide, this terrible health hazard affects over a billion people—at least 15 percent of the population. One of the agreed United Nations "millennium goals" for international development is to halve this proportion by 2015, by tackling chemical pollution from agriculture and industry, and by introducing essential purification facilities and local supply systems. In the industrialized world, people have come to expect clean drinking water on tap, even if they face rising prices for its treatment and supply.

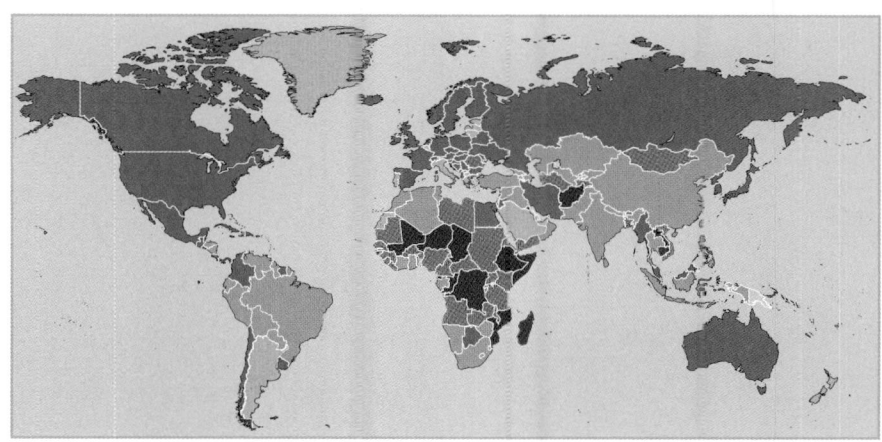

Mozambican children *(above)* fetch precious water in metal pans.

Gujarati villagers gather to draw water from a huge well *(above left)* in Natwarghad, western India. Many wells and village ponds ran dry in the severe drought of 2003, leaving local people to wait for irregular supplies brought in by state-run tankers.

**Access to safe
drinking water source**
(percentage of population)

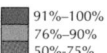 91%–100%
76%–90%
50%–75%

 below 50%
no data

Economic Systems

The world economy is now effectively a single global system based on "free market" capitalist principles. Few countries still cling, like North Korea, to the "command economy" formula developed in the former communist bloc, where centralized state plans set targets for investment and production. In the West, state ownership of companies has greatly diminished thanks to the wave of privatization in the last 25 years. Major companies move capital and raw materials around the globe to take advantage of different labor costs and skills. The World Trade Organization (WTO) promotes free trade, but many countries still use subsidies, and protect their markets with import tariffs or quotas, to favor their own producers.

Enormous volumes of trade pass through the world's stock markets making them key indicators of the strength of the global economy.

Balance of trade

Few countries earn from their exports exactly as much as they spend on imports. If the imbalance is persistently negative, it creates a potentially serious problem of indebtedness. The European Union's (EU) external trade is broadly in balance, but the US balance of trade has been in deficit since the 1970s, partly because it imports so many consumer goods. This deficit has recently spiralled to over US$ 800 billion a year.

Balance of trade
(million US$)

over 30,000	
10,000–29,000	
1000–9999	Surplus
0–999	
0–999	
1000–9999	
10,000–29,999	Deficit
over 30,000	
data unavailable	

TOP TEN GLOBAL COMPANIES (as of March, 2008)

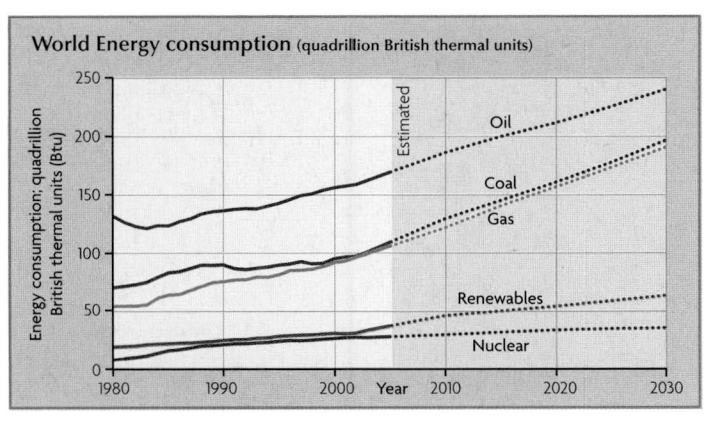

Market sector
- Oil and gas producers
- Banks
- General Industrials
- Telecommunications
- Computer software

Market value (US$ million) — Multinational corporation

Petro China (China), Exxon Mobil (US), General Electric (US), Gazprom (Russia), China Mobile (China), Microsoft (US), Ind. & Comm. Bank (China), Petrobas (Brazil), Royal Dutch Shell (Neth.), AT&T (US)

Energy

Countries with oil and gas to sell (notably in the Middle East and Russia) can charge high prices; trade in fuel was worth US$ 1.4 trillion in 2005. The US and others are turning back to nuclear power (despite safety fears) for generating electricity. China relies heavily on (polluting) coal. Renewable technologies promise much, but so far make relatively minor contributions.

World Energy consumption (quadrillion British thermal units)

Oil, Coal, Gas, Renewables, Nuclear
1980, 1990, 2000, Year, 2010, 2020, 2030

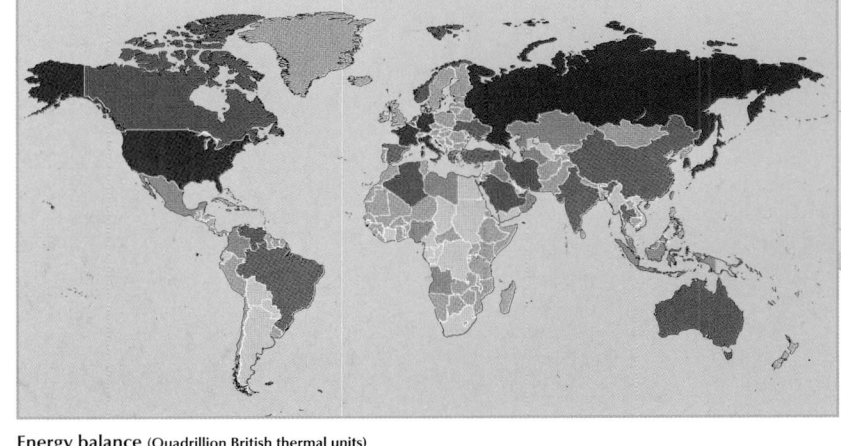

Energy balance (Quadrillion British thermal units)

net producer	10 and above	5 to 10	1 to 5	0 to 1		data unavailable
net consumer	0 to -1	-1 to -5	-5 to -10	-10 and below		

SOUTH AMERICA

New York

EUROPE

London

AFRICA

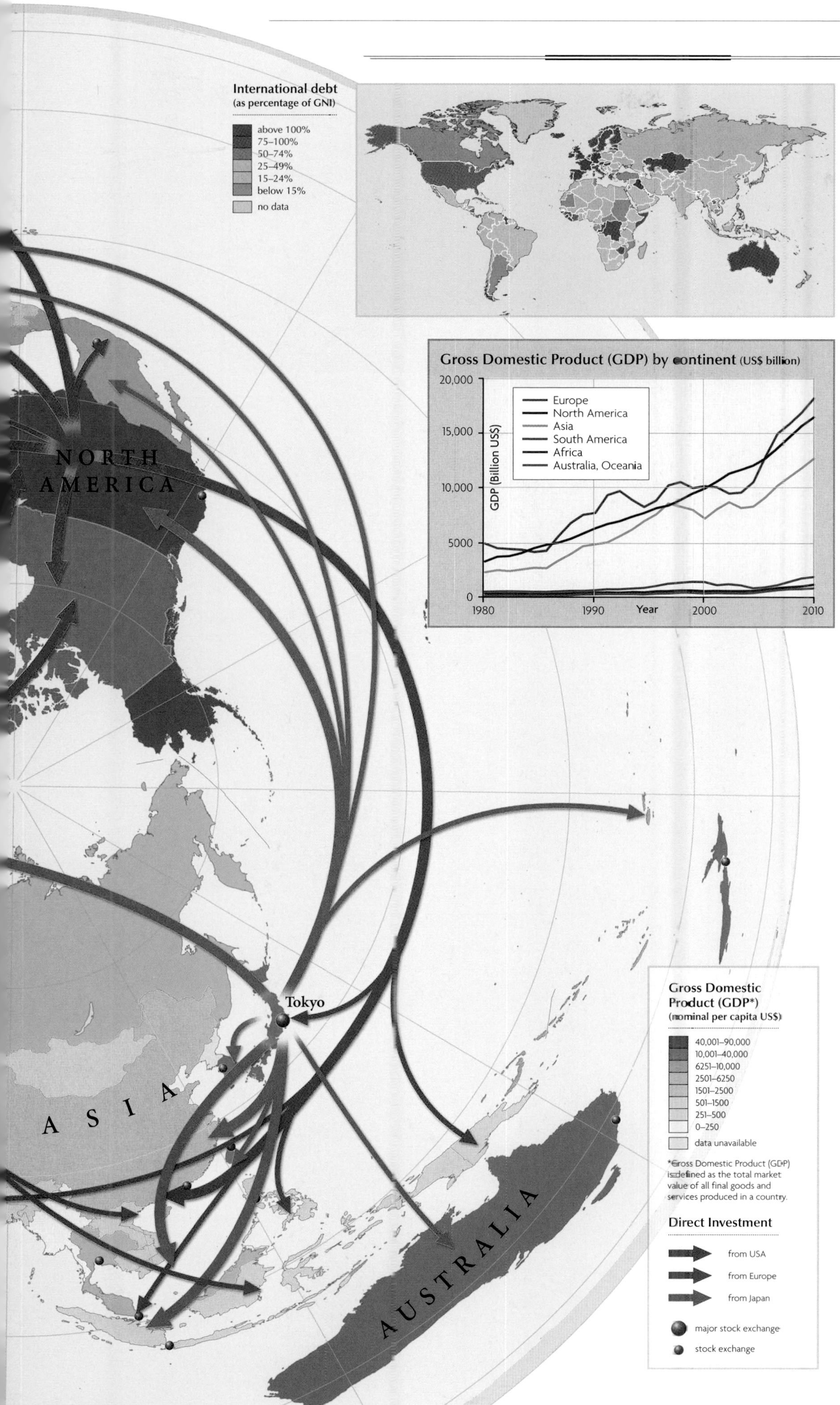

International debt

International debt
(as percentage of GNI)

- above 100%
- 75–100%
- 50–74%
- 25–49%
- 15–24%
- below 15%
- no data

Saddled with crippling debts from past borrowing, the world's poorest countries are still paying off US $100 million a day. This is despite recent successful campaigns to get some of their debts cancelled to allow them to use their limited resources for development. Most international debt, however, is owed by developed countries to one another. The US owes literally trillions of dollars, nearly a third of it's total debt, to Japan.

Gross Domestic Product (GDP) by continent (US$ billion)

- Europe
- North America
- Asia
- South America
- Africa
- Australia, Oceania

GDP (Billion US$)

20,000
15,000
10,000
5000

1980   1990   Year   2000   2010

Trade sector

World trade in merchandise tops US$ 10 trillion a year. The global pattern is uneven. Latin America, Africa, the Middle East, and Russia principally export "primary" goods (agricultural produce, mining and fuel). The "secondary" manufacturing sector includes iron and steel, machine tools, chemicals, clothing and textiles, cars and other consumer goods. The West still dominates the "tertiary" or non-merchandise sector, worth US$ 2.4 trillion, in services such as insurance and banking.

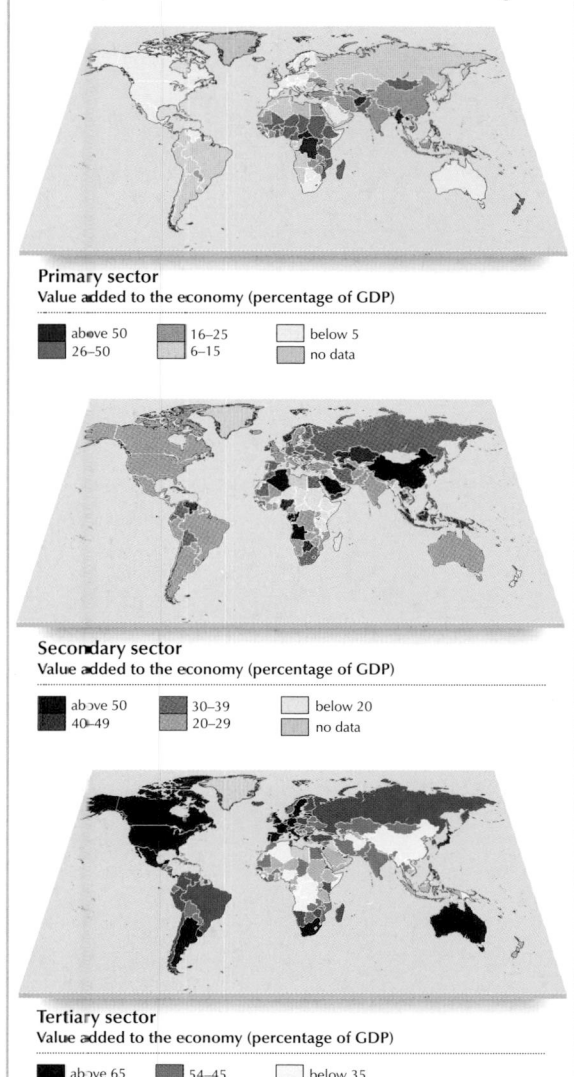

Primary sector
Value added to the economy (percentage of GDP)

- above 50
- 26–50
- 16–25
- 6–15
- below 5
- no data

Secondary sector
Value added to the economy (percentage of GDP)

- above 50
- 40–49
- 30–39
- 20–29
- below 20
- no data

Tertiary sector
Value added to the economy (percentage of GDP)

- above 65
- 55–64
- 54–45
- 35–44
- below 35
- no data

NORTH AMERICA

ASIA

Tokyo

AUSTRALIA

Gross Domestic Product (GDP*)
(nominal per capita US$)

- 40,001–90,000
- 10,001–40,000
- 6251–10,000
- 2501–6250
- 1501–2500
- 501–1500
- 251–500
- 0–250
- data unavailable

*Gross Domestic Product (GDP) is defined as the total market value of all final goods and services produced in a country.

Direct Investment

- from USA
- from Europe
- from Japan

- major stock exchange
- stock exchange

Average monthly salary
(US$)

- above 3000
- 2000–3000
- 1000–2000
- 500–1000
- 250–500
- below 250
- no data

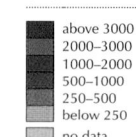

Labor

China's huge low-cost labor force promotes its conquest of world markets for manufactured goods. India's educated workforce attracts call centers and other service sector jobs, while the more economically developed countries's (MEDC) caring professions, and low-wage agriculture, draw in immigrant labor.

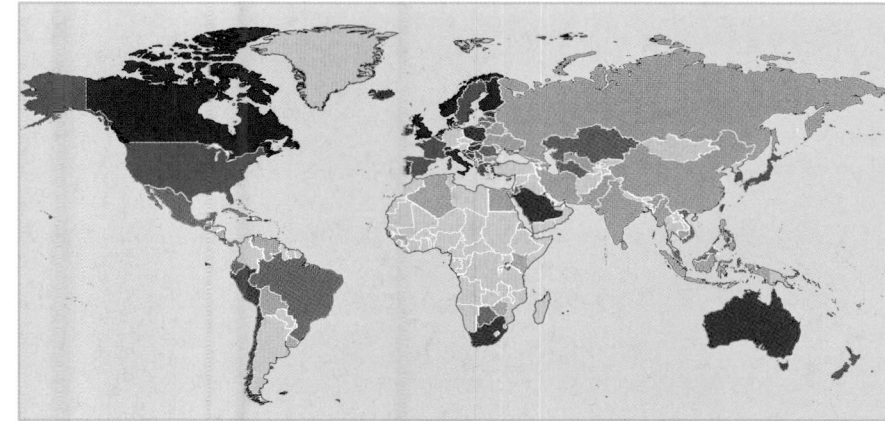

Travel

Mass travel is now a ubiquitous feature of all developed countries, and the provision of transport and tourism facilities one of the world's biggest industries, employing well over 100 million people. The travel explosion has come about, first, through major improvements in transportation technology; and second, as a result of increasing amounts of disposable income and leisure time in the world's wealthier countries. The main reasons for travel today include leisure pursuits and tourism (accounting for well over half of the total financial outlay), work and business, pilgrimage, migration, and visits to family and friends.

There are currently around 4.2 billion air travelers a year passing through over 1600 international and domestic airports. This figure is forecast to grow by 4 percent each year, leading to increased pressure on air traffic control and ground handling systems that, in many areas, are already close to maximum capacity.

Major modes of transportation

The major transport modes for people in the 21st century are road, rail, and air travel. The most popular air routes are highly concentrated within and between the USA, western Europe, and Asia. Major roads and railroads are more evenly spread, following the general distribution of the world's population.

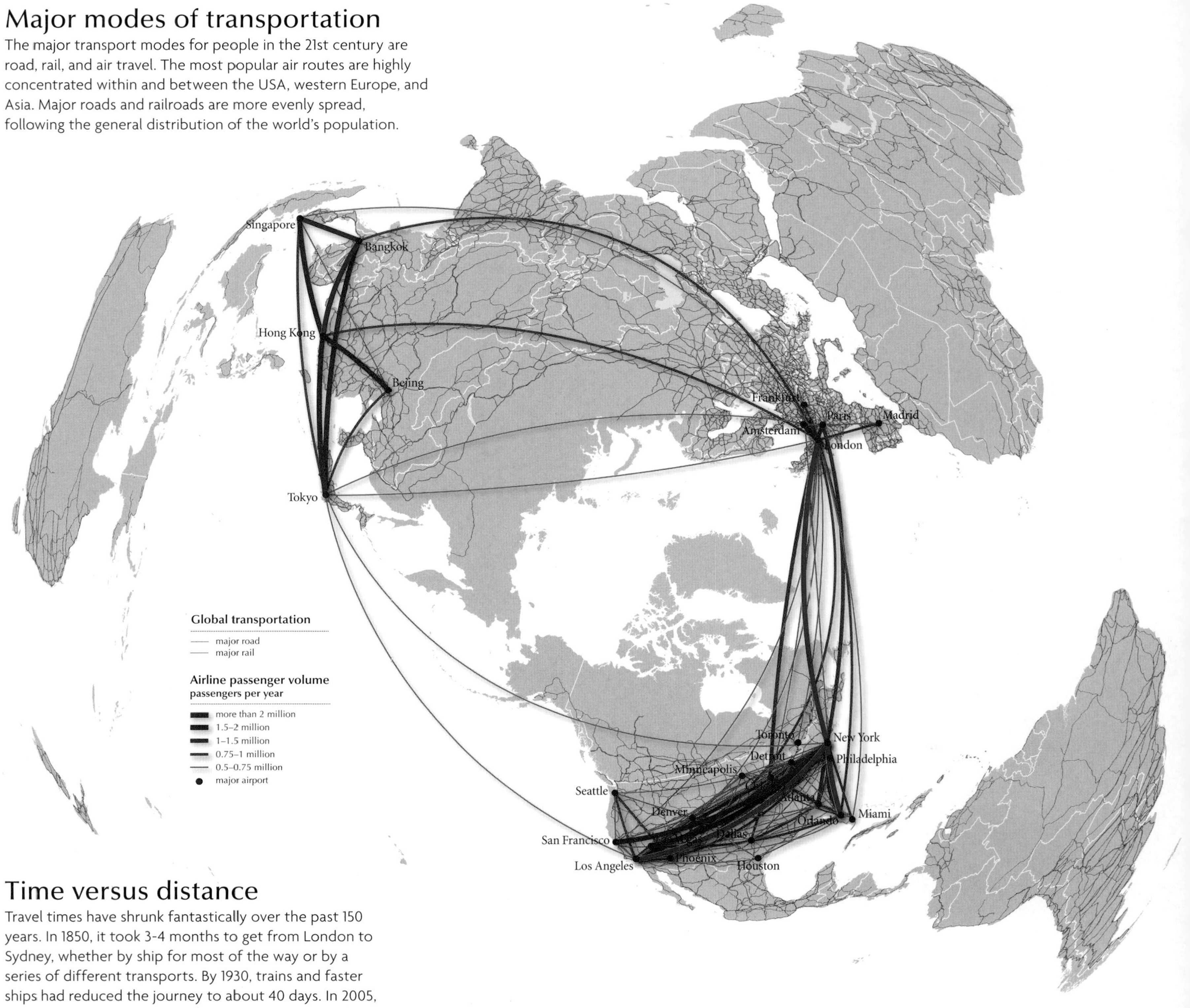

Global transportation
— major road
— major rail

Airline passenger volume
passengers per year

- more than 2 million
- 1.5–2 million
- 1–1.5 million
- 0.75–1 million
- 0.5–0.75 million
- ● major airport

Map labels: Singapore, Bangkok, Hong Kong, Beijing, Tokyo, Frankfurt, Paris, Madrid, Amsterdam, London, Toronto, New York, Detroit, Philadelphia, Minneapolis, Seattle, Atlanta, Denver, Miami, Orlando, San Francisco, Dallas, Los Angeles, Phoenix, Houston

Time versus distance

Travel times have shrunk fantastically over the past 150 years. In 1850, it took 3–4 months to get from London to Sydney, whether by ship for most of the way or by a series of different transports. By 1930, trains and faster ships had reduced the journey to about 40 days. In 2005, the trip took just 21 hours by air.

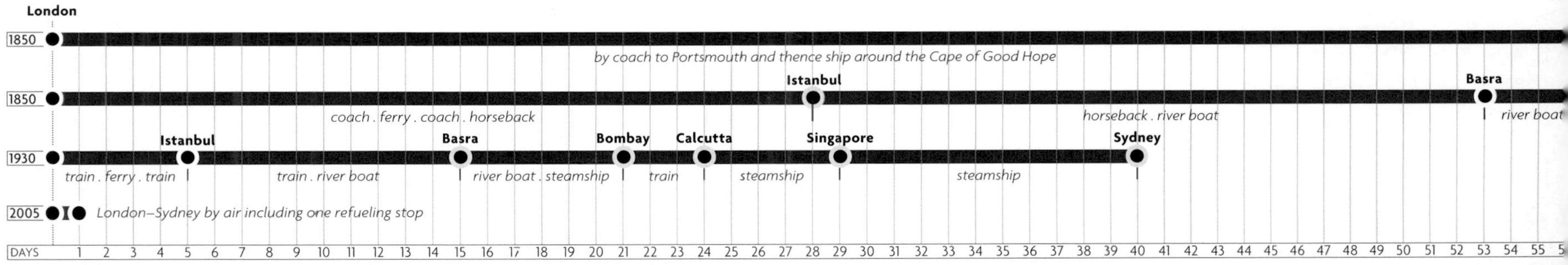

London

1850 — by coach to Portsmouth and thence ship around the Cape of Good Hope

1850 — Istanbul — coach . ferry . coach . horseback — horseback . river boat — Basra — river boat

1930 — Istanbul — train . ferry . train — train . river boat — Basra — river boat . steamship — Bombay — train — Calcutta — steamship — Singapore — steamship — Sydney

2005 ●I● London–Sydney by air including one refueling stop

DAYS 1 2 3 4 5 6 7 8 9 10 11 12 13 14 15 16 17 18 19 20 21 22 23 24 25 26 27 28 29 30 31 32 33 34 35 36 37 38 39 40 41 42 43 44 45 46 47 48 49 50 51 52 53 54 55 5

Media and Communications

Over the past 50 years, the term "media" has come to denote various means of communicating information between people at a distance. These include mass media—methods such as newspapers, radio, and television that can be used to rapidly disseminate information to large numbers of people—and two-way systems, such as telephones and e-mail. Currently, the communication systems undergoing the most rapid growth worldwide include mobile telephony and various Internet-based applications, such as web sites, blogs, and podcasting, which can be considered forms of mass media.

Internet usage

Internet usage has grown extremely rapidly since the early 1990s, largely as a result of the invention of the World Wide Web. Usage rates are highest in the USA (where about 80 percent of people were using the Internet in 2006), Australia, Japan, South Korea, and Finland. They are lowest in Africa, where on average less than 5 percent of the population were Internet users in 2006.

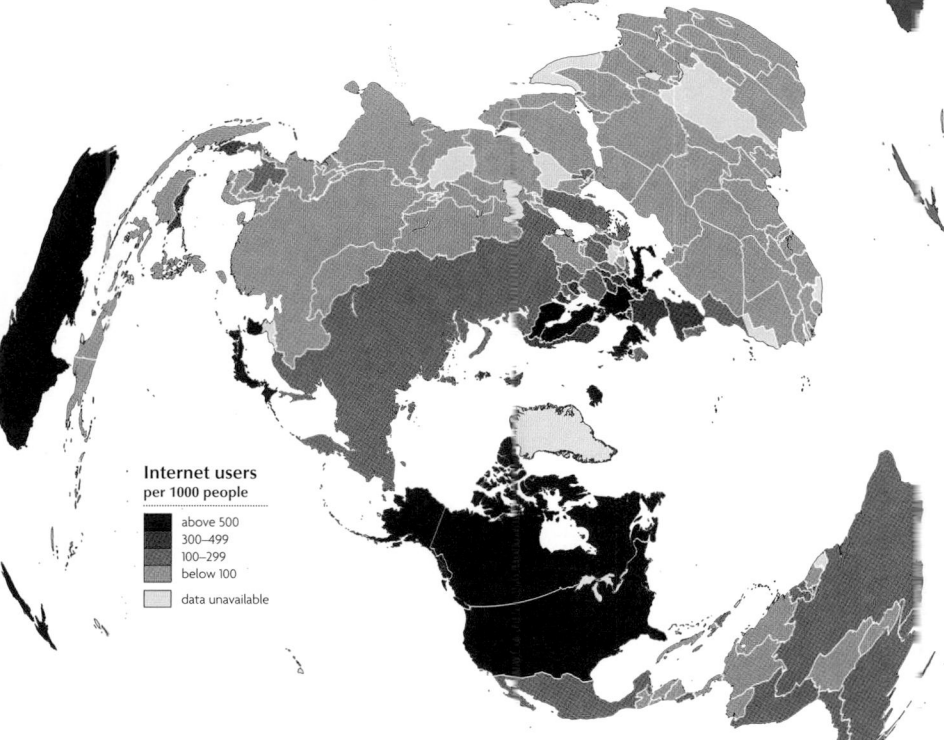

Internet users
per 1000 people
- above 500
- 300–499
- 100–299
- below 100
- data unavailable

The internet emerged in the early 1990s as a computer-based global communication system. Since then massive growth has seen user numbers increase to around 1.1 billion people, or roughly 17 percent of the world's population.

Mobile phone usage

By 2006, there were more than 2.5 billion mobile phone users worldwide. In some parts of Europe, such as Italy, almost everyone owns and uses a mobile—many possess more than one phone. In contrast, throughout much of Southern Asia and Africa, less than 10 percent of the population are users. As well as utilizing them as telephones, most users now employ the devices for the additional functions they offer, such as text messaging and e-mail.

Mobile phone users
per 1000 people
- above 900
- 700–899
- 500–699
- 300–499
- 100–299
- below 100
- data unavailable

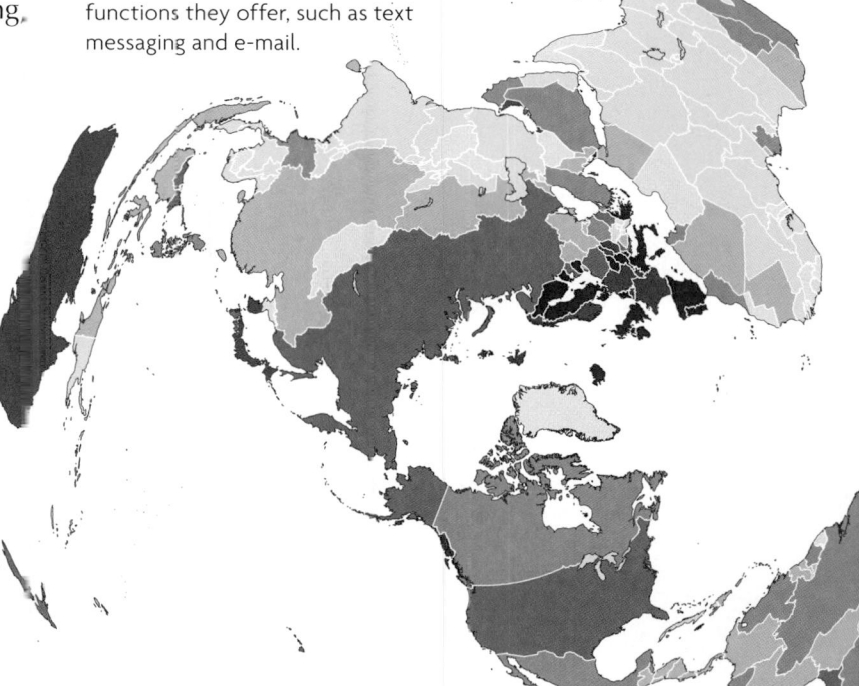

Satellite Communications

Modern communications satellites are used extensively for international telephony, for television and radio broadcasting, and to some extent for transmitting Internet data. Many of these satellites are deployed in clusters or arrays, often in geostationary orbits—that is, in positions that appear fixed to Earth-based observers.

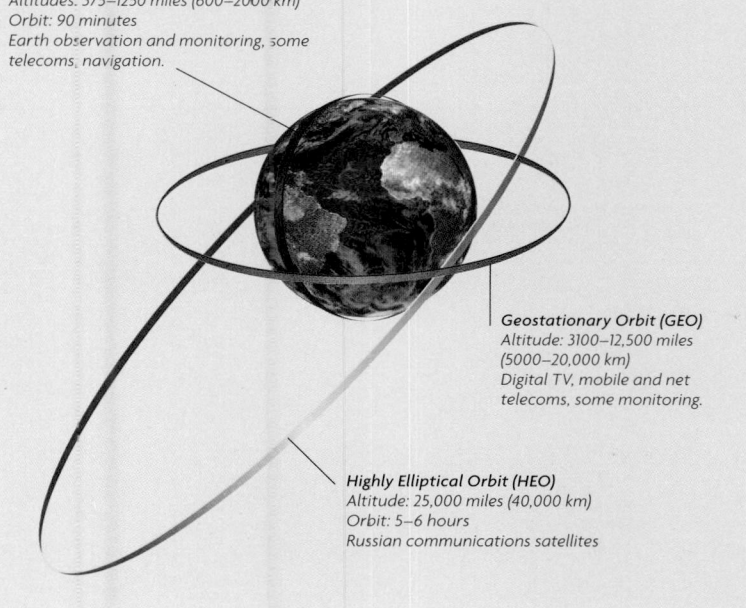

Low Earth Orbit (LEO)
Altitudes. 375–1250 miles (600–2000 km)
Orbit: 90 minutes
Earth observation and monitoring, some telecoms, navigation.

Geostationary Orbit (GEO)
Altitude: 3100–12,500 miles (5000–20,000 km)
Digital TV, mobile and net telecoms, some monitoring.

Highly Elliptical Orbit (HEO)
Altitude: 25,000 miles (40,000 km)
Orbit: 5–6 hours
Russian communications satellites

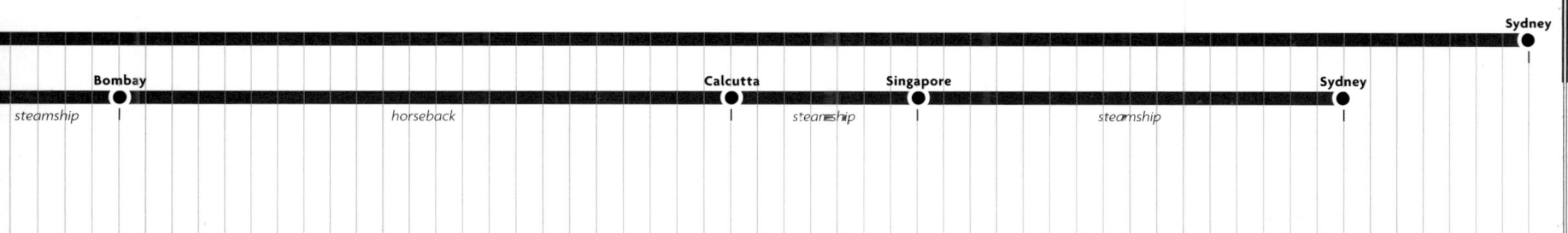

steamship | horseback | steamship | steamship | Sydney

Bombay | Calcutta | Singapore | Sydney

58 59 60 61 62 63 64 65 66 67 68 69 70 71 72 73 74 75 76 77 78 79 80 81 82 83 84 85 86 87 88 89 90 91 92 93 94 95 96 97 98 99 100 101 102 103 104 105 106 107 108 109 110 111 112 113 114 115

The Political World

Today's world map shows nearly 200 independent states, compared with about 80 after World War II. The transformation is mainly due to the withdrawal of European powers from huge colonial empires; their remaining overseas dependencies are tiny by comparison. The late 20th century also saw the collapse of communism, realignment in Europe, and fragmentation in former Yugoslavia. Globally, the Soviet Union's demise left the USA as the sole superpower, though with fast-growing China and India emerging as economic giants of the future. US security preoccupations switched to combating terrorism, while looming oil and other resource shortages, and environmental constraints, underlined the need for more effective international cooperation.

CONTINENTAL FACTFILE

	Total area: sq miles	Total area: sq km	Total population
North & Central America	9,358,340	24,238,000	516.8 million
South America	6,886,000	17,835,000	380.2 million
Africa	11,712,434	30,335,000	924.6 million
Europe	4,053,309	10,498,000	711.5 million
Asia	16,838,365	43,608,000	3978.2 million
Australia & Oceania	3,285,048	8,508,238	32.7 million

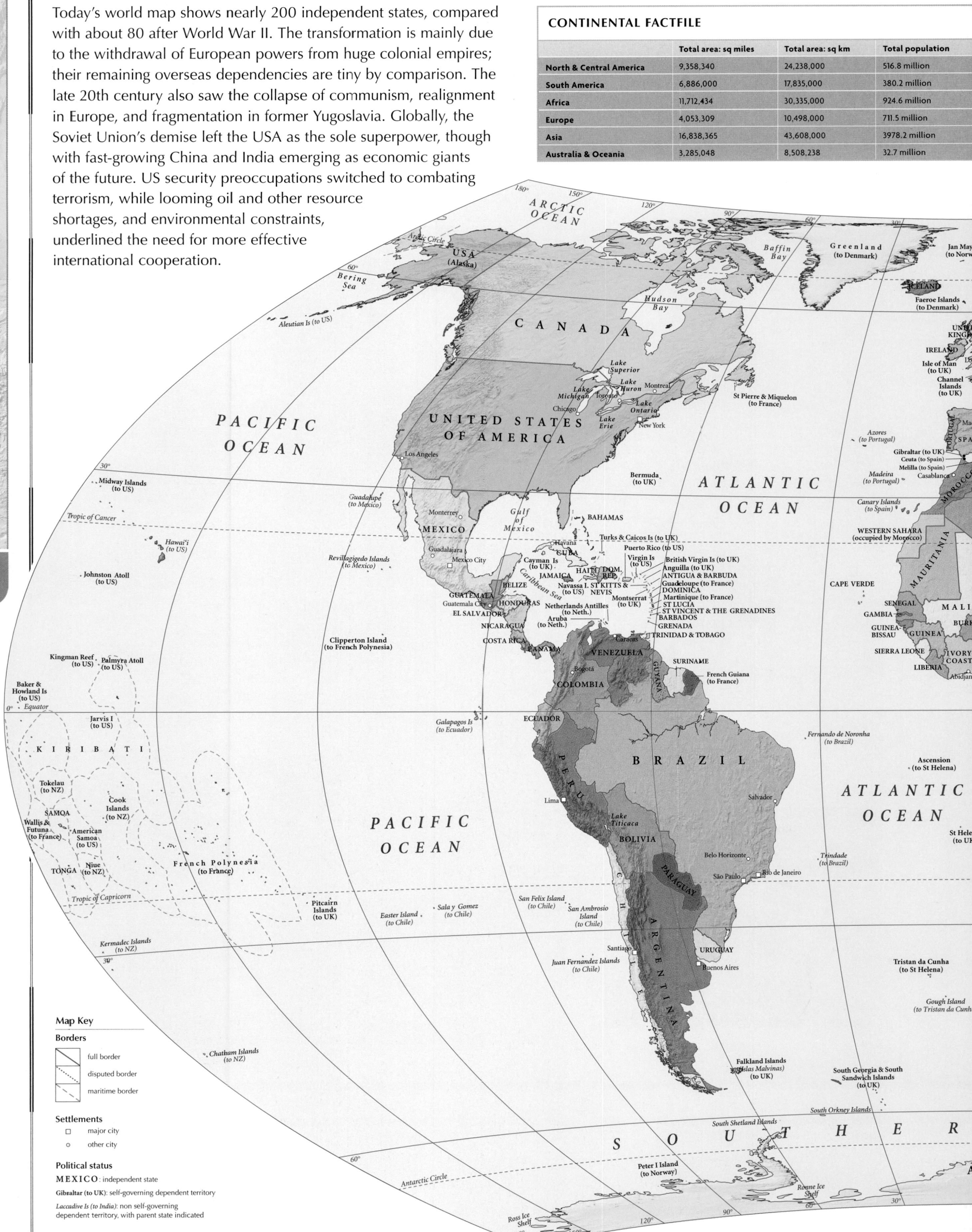

Map Key

Borders

- full border
- disputed border
- maritime border

Settlements

- □ major city
- ○ other city

Political status

MEXICO: independent state

Gibraltar (to UK): self-governing dependent territory

Laccadive Is (to India): non self-governing dependent territory, with parent state indicated

Countries	Largest country	Country with largest population
23	Canada 3,855,171 sq miles (9,984,670 sq km)	United States 301 million
12	Brazil 3,286,470 sq miles (8,511,965 sq km)	Brazil 188.9 million
53	Sudan 967,493 sq miles (2,505,810 sq km)	Nigeria 134.4 million
46	European Russia 1,527,341 sq miles (3,955,818 sq km)	European Russia 114 million
49	Asiatic Russia 5,065,394 sq miles (13,119,382 sq km)	China 1323.6 million
14	Australia 2,967,893 sq miles (7,686,850 sq km)	Australia 20.4 million

International borders

The world political map of today displays a complex pattern of boundaries that has evolved through history, and is still constantly changing as new countries emerge and disputes and territorial claims are slowly resolved. The map shows two main types of border. Full borders represent internationally agreed and recognized territorial boundaries. A disputed border is indicated where a *de facto* territorial boundary exists, which is not agreed or is still subject to arbitration.

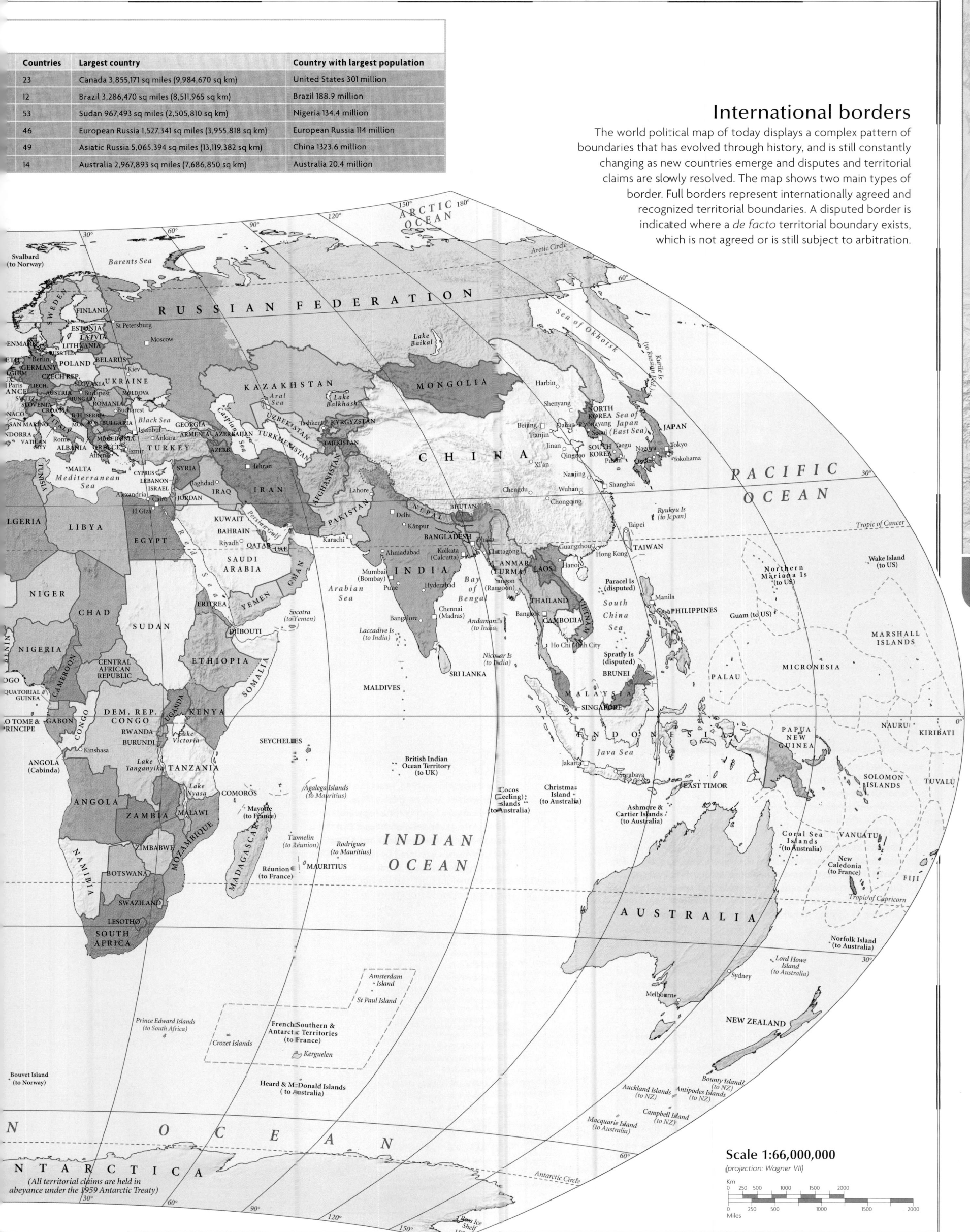

Scale 1:66,000,000

(projection: Wagner VII)

NORTH AMERICA

A
B
C
D
E
F
G
1
2
3
4
5
6
7
8
9
10
ARCTIC OCEAN
North Pole
Franz Josef Land
East Siberian Sea
Sea of Okhotsk
Chukchi Sea
Bering Strait
Bering Sea
Aleutian Basin
Bowers Ridge
Anadyrskiy Zaliv
St Lawrence Island
Nunivak Island
Norton Sound
Kuskokwim Bay
Bristol Bay
Aleutian Islands
Alaska Peninsula
PACIFIC PLATE
Gulf of Alaska
Patton Seamount
Dickins Seamount
Queen Charlotte Islands
Cobb Seamount
Vancouver Island
Cascadia Basin
JUAN DE FUCA PLATE
Gorda Ridge
San Francisco
Monterey Bay
Point Barrow
Beaufort Sea
Mackenzie Bay
Amundsen Gulf
McClure Strait
Parry Islands
Viscount Melville Sound
Victoria Island
Queen Elizabeth Islands
Ellesmere Island
Kap Morris Jesup
Nordostrundingen
Greenland Sea
Norwegian Sea
Greenland
King Christian X Land
King Frederik VIII Land
Iceland
Denmark Strait
Jones Sound
Lancaster Sound
Baffin Bay
Baffin Island
Gulf of Boothia
Queen Maud Gulf
Coronation Gulf
Great Slave Lake
Davis Strait
Foxe Basin
Foxe Channel
Cumberland Sound
Frobisher Bay
Hudson Strait
Labrador Sea
Southampton Island
Coats Island
Mansel Island
Roes Welcome Sound
Hudson Bay
Ungava Bay
Belcher Islands
James Bay
Gulf of St Lawrence
NORTH AMERICA
Lake Superior
Lake Michigan
Lake Huron
Lake Ontario
Lake Erie
Black Hills
Cape Cod
Long Island
Delaware Bay
Chesapeake Bay
Cape Hatteras
Cape Lookout
Blake Plateau
Blake-Bahama Ridge
Cape Canaveral
Lake Okeechobee
Tampa Bay
Apalachee Bay
Mississippi Fan
Galveston Bay
Sigsbee Escarpment
Gulf of Mexico
Mexico Basin
Campeche Bank
Straits of Florida
Yucatan Channel
Yucatan Basin
Bay of Campeche
Sonoran Desert
Gulf of California
Cabo San Lucas
Revillagigedo Islands
Islas Alijos
PACIFIC OCEAN
Mendocino Fracture Zone
Pioneer Fracture Zone
Murray Fracture Zone
Molokai Fracture Zone
Clarion Fracture Zone
Clipperton Fracture Zone
Mathematicians Seamounts
Clipperton Seamounts
Clipperton Island
Orozco Fracture Zone
East Pacific Rise
COCOS PLATE
PACIFIC PLATE
Siqueiros Fracture Zone
Albatross Plateau
Tehuantepec Ridge
Middle America Trench
Guatemala Basin
Cocos Ridge
Colón Ridge
Panama Basin
Gulf of Honduras
Nicaraguan Rise
Jamaica
Cayman Trench
CARIBBEAN PLATE
NORTH AMERICAN PLATE
Caribbean Sea
Colombian Basin
Peninsula de la Guajira
Gulf of Darién
Gulf of Panama
Península de Azuero
Hatteras Plain

North America is the world's third largest continent with
a total area of 9,358,340 sq miles (24,238,000 sq km)
including Greenland and the Caribbean islands.
It lies wholly within the Northern Hemisphere.

FACTFILE

N **Most Northerly Point:** Kap Morris Jesup, Greenland 83° 38' N
S **Most Southerly Point:** Peninsula de Azuero, Panama 7° 15' N
E **Most Easterly Point:** Nordøstrundingen, Greenland 12° 08' W
W **Most Westerly Point:** Attu, Aleutian Islands, USA 172° 30' E

Largest Lakes:
1. Lake Superior, Canada/USA 31,151 sq miles (83,270 sq km)
2. Lake Huron, Canada/USA 23,436 sq miles (60,700 sq km)
3. Lake Michigan, USA 22,402 sq miles (58,020 sq km)
4. Great Bear Lake, Canada 12,274 sq miles (31,790 sq km)
5. Great Slave Lake, Canada 10,981 sq miles (28,440 sq km)

Longest Rivers:
1. Mississippi-Missouri, USA 3710 miles (5969 km)
2. Mackenzie, Canada 2640 miles (4250 km)
3. Yukon, Canada/USA 1978 miles (3184 km)
4. St Lawrence/Great Lakes, Canada/USA 1900 miles (3058 km)
5. Rio Grande, Mexico/USA 1900 miles (3057 km)

Largest Islands:
1. Greenland 849,400 sq miles (2,200,000 sq km)
2. Baffin Island, Canada 183,800 sq miles (476,000 sq km)
3. Victoria Island, Canada 81,900 sq miles (212,000 sq km)
4. Ellesmere Island, Canada 75,700 sq miles (196,000 sq km)
5. Newfoundland, Canada 42,031 sq miles (108,860 sq km)

Highest Points:
1. Mount McKinley (Denali), USA 20,332 ft (6194 m)
2. Mount Logan, Canada 19,550 ft (5959 m)
3. Volcán Pico de Orizaba, Mexico 18,700 ft (5700 m)
4. Mount St Elias, USA 18,008 ft (5489 m)
5. Popocatépetl, Mexico 17,887 ft (5452 m)

Lowest Point:
▼ Death Valley, USA -282 ft (-86 m) below sea level

Highest recorded temperature:
● Death Valley, USA 135°F (57°C)

Lowest recorded temperature:
– Northice, Greenland -87°F (-66°C)

Wettest Place:
≋ Vancouver, Canada 183 in (4645 mm)

Driest Place:
– Death Valley, USA 2 in (50 mm)

Cross-section from San Francisco to Washington DC

line of cross-section

| 0 | 500 | 1000 Km |
| 0 | 500 | 1000 Miles |

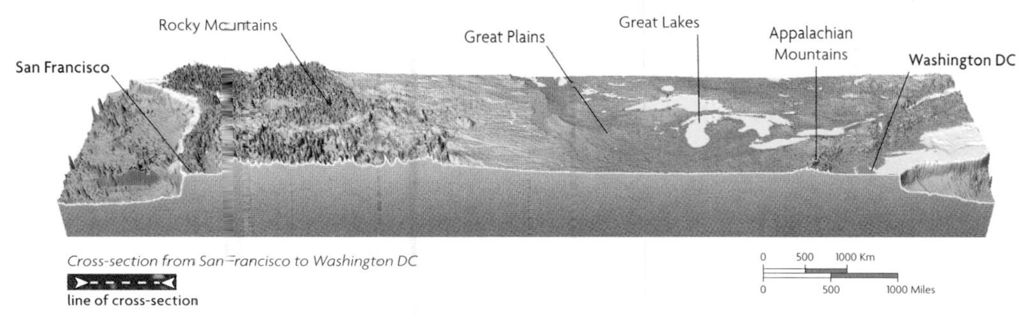

NORTH AMERICA

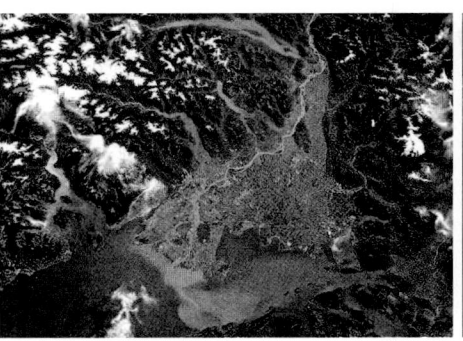

1 VANCOUVER, BRITISH COLUMBIA, CANADA
Canada's premier west coast city occupies the delta of the Fraser river, formed amongst the Coast Mountains.

2 MOUNT SAINT HELENS, WASHINGTON, USA
In 1980, this volcano's catastrophic eruption devastated 270 sq miles (700 sq km) of forest almost instantly.

3 GREAT SALT LAKE, UTAH, USA
A causeway carries a railway line, blocking circulation between the northern and southern parts, the water reddened by salt-loving bacteria in the more saline north.

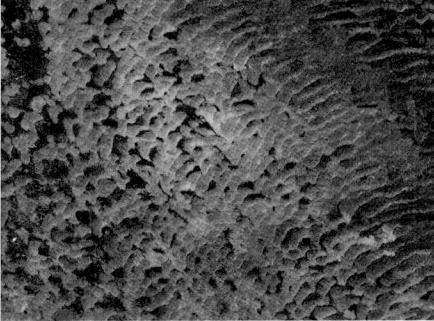

4 SAND HILLS, NEBRASKA, USA
Forming the largest sand sea in the Western Hemisphere, these hills are not classified as desert because today's relatively wet climate has allowed grasses to take hold.

9 LOS ANGELES AND LONG BEACH, CALIFORNIA, USA
Taken together, these west coast cities constitute the busiest sea port in the United States.

10 ISLA GUADALUPE, MEXICO
The volcanic island, 186 miles (300 km) off the west coast of Mexico, is a protected wildlife reserve.

11 GRAND CANYON, ARIZONA, USA
The 5250 ft (1600 m) deep canyon cuts through the Kaibab Plateau in this southwest-looking view.

12 DENVER, COLORADO, USA
Colorado's state capital nestles under the Rocky Mountains with the South Platte River running through its centre.

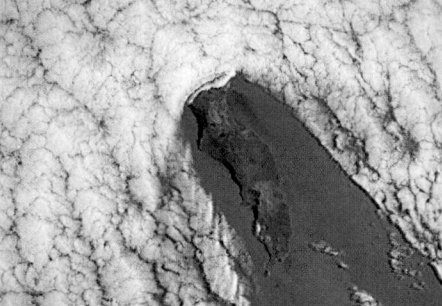

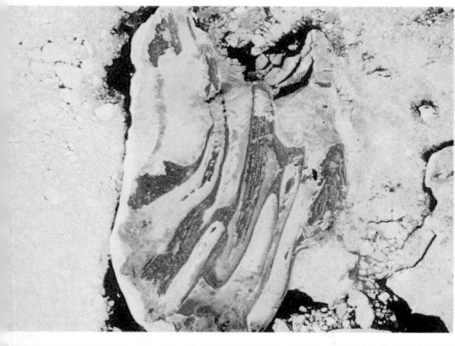

BELCHER ISLANDS, NUNAVUT, CANADA 5
These low-lying, treeless and sparsely-populated islands lie icebound in Hudson Bay for much of the year.

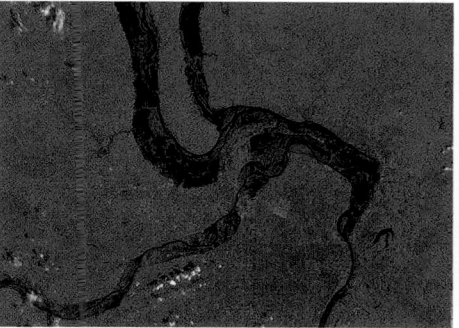

MISSISSIPPI, MISSOURI AND ILLINOIS RIVERS, USA 6
This Infrared image shows how these rivers burst their banks in many places after heavy rains in the summer of 1993, leading to the area's worst floods on record.

RÉSERVOIR MANICOUAGAN, QUÉBEC, CANADA 7
This unusual 62 mile (100 km) diameter, annular lake occupies the low ground between the rim and central uplift of an ancient meteorite crater.

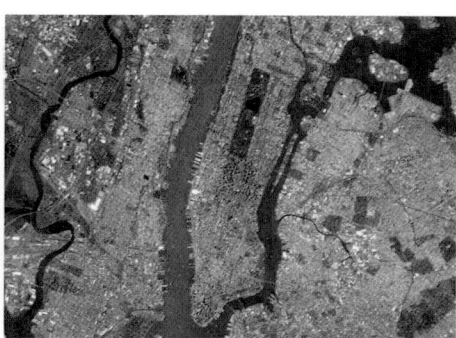

NEW YORK, USA 8
The largest city in the United States, with a population of over 8 million, it is also the country's main financial centre.

MISSISSIPPI RIVER DELTA, LOUISIANA, USA 13
This delta has developed a 'bird's foot' shape due to the shifting course of the river over the last 6000 years.

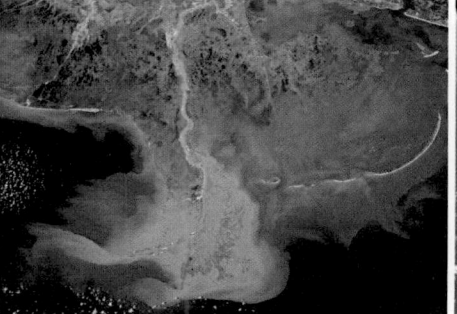

FLORIDA, USA 14
This low-lying, subtropical peninsula is home to thousands of lakes that have formed amongst its limestone 'karst' topography.

HAVANA, CUBA 15
Cuba's capital city is home to 2 million people and was founded by the Spanish in 1519 around a natural harbour.

BARRIER REEF, BELIZE 16
The world's second-longest barrier reef lies about 12 miles (20 km) off the coast of Belize.

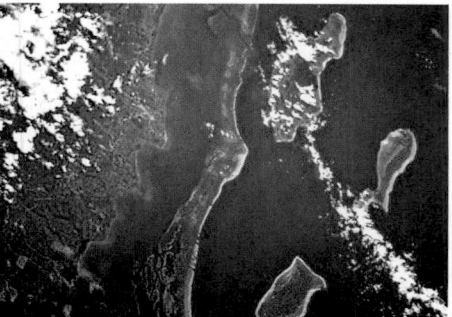

Canada

193
286
60

A
B
C
D
E
F
G
1
2
3
4
5
6
7
8
9
10
ARCTIC OCEAN
Beaufort Sea
Chukchi Sea
Bering Sea
Bering Strait
RUSSIAN FEDERATION
UNITED STATES OF AMERICA
Brooks Range
Alaska Range
Kuskokwim Mountains
Yukon River
Alaska Peninsula
Aleutian Range
Bristol Bay
Kodiak Island
Gulf of Alaska
PACIFIC OCEAN
Alexander Archipelago
Queen Charlotte Islands
Vancouver Island
YUKON TERRITORY
NORTHWEST TERRITORIES
BRITISH COLUMBIA
ALBERTA
SASKATCHEWAN
MANITOBA
Mackenzie Mountains
Selwyn Mountains
Coast Mountains
Rocky Mountains
CANADA
Great Bear Lake
Great Slave Lake
Lake Athabasca
Victoria Island
Banks Island
Melville Island
Prince Patrick Island
Parry Islands
Amundsen Gulf
Coronation Gulf
North Magnetic Pole (2005)
Whitehorse
Yellowknife
Edmonton
Calgary
Saskatoon
Regina
Prince George
Prince Rupert
Seattle
Spokane
Portland
Salem
MONTANA
IDAHO
OREGON
WASHINGTON
WYOMING
NEVADA
CALIFORNIA
NORTH DAKOTA
SOUTH DAKOTA
NEBRASKA
UNITED STATES
Vancouver
0 10 Km
0 10 Miles
North Vancouver
Burnaby
Coquitlam
Port Moody
Maple Ridge
New Westminster
Richmond
Surrey
Sea Island
Vancouver Intl Airport
Steveston
Port Kells
Langley
White Rock
Tsawwassen
Boundary Bay
Point Roberts
Blaine
Birch Bay
Lynden
Ferndale
Marietta
Bellingham
CANADA
USA
Strait of Georgia
Gulf Islands
Galiano Island
Mayne Island
Saturna Island
Salt Spring Island
Pender Islands
Waldron Island
Orcas Island
Lummi Island
Burrard Inlet
Horseshoe Bay
Bowen Island
Gambier Island
Anvil Island
Cypress Provincial Park
Mount Seymour Provincial Park
Coquitlam Lake
Pitt Lake
6000m
4000m
3000m
2000m
1000m
500m
250m
100m
Sea Level
-250m
-2000m
-4000m

Scale 1:14,815,000
(projection: Lambert Azimuthal Equal Area)

| 0 | 50 | 100 | 150 | 200 | 250 | 300 | 350 | 400 Km |
| 0 | 50 | 100 | 150 | 200 | 250 | 300 | 350 | 400 Miles |

Population

| ■ above 5 million | ▣ 1 million to 5 million | ◉ 500,000 to 1 million |
| ◎ 100,000 to 500,000 | ⊕ 50,000 to 100,000 | ○ 10,000 to 50,000 | ∘ below 10,000 |

Map of eastern Canada, Greenland, Iceland, and northeastern United States.

Major labels include:

GREENLAND (to Denmark) · Greenland Sea · ICELAND · REYKJAVÍK · Kong Christian IX Land · Kong Frederik IX Land · Kong Frederik VI Kyst · NUUK · Nunap Isua (Kap Farvel)

Baffin Bay · Baffin Island · Davis Strait · Labrador Sea · Cumberland Peninsula · Cumberland Sound · Hall Peninsula · Frobisher Bay · Iqaluit · Foxe Basin · Foxe Peninsula · Meta Incognita Peninsula · Resolution Island · Hudson Strait · Ungava Bay · Péninsule d'Ungava

NUNAVUT · Ellesmere Island · Devon Island · Lancaster Sound · Somerset Island · Prince Charles Island · Southampton Island · Coats Island · Mansel Island · Baker Lake · Rankin Inlet · Whale Cove · Eskimo Point · Arviat

Hudson Bay · James Bay · Belcher Islands · Sanikiluaq · Long Island · Akimiski Island

QUÉBEC · ONTARIO · NEWFOUNDLAND & LABRADOR · Laurentian Mountains · Churchill Falls · Labrador City · Gulf of St. Lawrence · Île d'Anticosti · Prince Edward Island · Charlottetown · NOVA SCOTIA · Halifax · Dartmouth · Sydney · NEW BRUNSWICK · Fredericton · St. John · Bay of Fundy · ST-PIERRE & MIQUELON (to France) · St. John's · Cape Race · Newfoundland · Corner Brook · Gander

ATLANTIC OCEAN · Limit of winter pack ice · Arctic Circle

MINNESOTA · WISCONSIN · MICHIGAN · IOWA · ILLINOIS · OHIO · NEW YORK · NEW JERSEY · RHODE ISLAND · MAINE · Winnipeg · Thunder Bay · Lake Superior · Lake Michigan · Lake Huron · Lake Erie · Lake Ontario · Minneapolis · Saint Paul · Madison · Milwaukee · Chicago · Detroit · Cleveland · Toledo · Toronto · Ottawa · Montréal · Québec · Boston · Providence · New York · Philadelphia · Halifax · Cape Cod · Gulf of Maine · Portland

NORTH AMERICA

51

295 · 290 · 61

| 19,686ft |
| 13,124ft |
| 9843ft |
| 6562ft |
| 3281ft |
| 1640ft |
| 820ft |
| 328ft |
| Sea Level |
| -820ft |
| -6562ft |
| -13,124ft |

Northern Canada

ARCTIC OCEAN

Beaufort Sea

Limit of permanent ice cap

Limit of summer pack ice

North Magnetic Pole (2005)

Sverdrup

Queen

Parry Is

Banks Island

Melville Island

Victoria Island

Prince of Wales Island

Amundsen Gulf

Viscount Melville Sound

Parry Channel

McClintock Channel

Dolphin and Union Strait

Coronation Gulf

Queen Maud Gulf

King William Island

USA ALASKA

YUKON TERRITORY

NORTHWEST TERRITORIES

CANADA

Mackenzie Mountains

Selwyn Mountains

Pelly Mountains

Brooks Range

Philip Smith Mountains

British Mountains

Richardson Mountains

Franklin Mountains

Great Bear Lake

Great Slave Lake

Yellowknife

Tuktoyaktuk Peninsula

Mackenzie Bay

Herschel Island

Prudhoe Bay

Cape Bathurst

Cape Parry

Cape Lyon

Cape Baring

Prince Albert Sound

Wollaston Peninsula

Collinson Peninsula

Cape Felix

Adelaide Peninsula

Boothia Peninsula

Cambridge Bay

Prince Patrick Island

Eglinton Island

Mackenzie King Island

Borden Island

Meighen Island

Ellef Ringnes Island

Bathurst Island

Emerald Isle

Dundas Peninsula

Prince Albert Peninsula

Stefansson Island

Minto Head

Kent Peninsula

Cape Krusenstern

Kugluktuk

Fort Good Hope

Norman Wells

Fort Franklin Deline

Fort Simpson

Horn Plateau

South Nahanni

North Nahanni

Nahanni Butte

Arctic Red River

Fort McPherson

Inuvik

Aklavik

Old Crow

Dawson

Faro

Ross River

Kaktovik

Camden Bay

Harrison Bay

Cape Halkett

Kuparuk River

Colville River

Porcupine

Eagle Plains

Wrigley

Tulita

Keith Arm

Smith Arm

Dease Arm

McVicar Arm

Takijuq Lake

Contwoyto Lake

Point Lake

MacKay Lake

Aylmer Lake

Clinton-Colden Lake

Artillery Lake

Aberdeen Lake

Schultz Lake

Garry Lake

Back

Dubawnt Lake

Tebesjuak Lake

MacAlpine Lake

Pelly Point

Gateshead Island

Washburn Lake

Zeta Lake

Tahiryuak Lake

Hadley Bay

Minto Inlet

Holman

Sachs Harbour

Cape Kellett

Prince of Wales Strait

Peel Point

Passage Point

Richard Collinson Inlet

Lowther Island

Russell Island

Cape John Dyer

Cape Richard Collinson

Cape Swinburne

Franklin Strait

Larsen Sound

Cape Alexander

Royal Geographical Society Islands

Jenny Lind Island

Melbourne Island

Whitebear Point

Bowes Point

Dease Strait

Byron Bay

Melville Sound

Sherard Bay

Sabine Peninsula

Cameron Island

Seymour Island

King Christian Island

Penny Strait

Hazen Strait

Byam Channel

Byam Martin Island

Hearne Point

Liddon Gulf

Cape Russell

McClure Strait

Cape Prince Alfred

Cape Wrottesley

Bernard Island

Meek Point

Dyer Bay

Mould Bay

Crozier Channel

Kellet Strait

Satellite Bay

Cape Leopold McClintock

Brock Island

Wilkins Strait

Ballantyne Strait

Prince Gustaf Adolf Sea

Lands End

Lougheed Island

Hassel Sound

Sverdrup Channel

Peary Channel

Bad Weather Cape

Limit of permanent ice cap

Demarcation Point

Warren Point

Liverpool Bay

Eskimo Lakes

Sitidgi Lake

Travaillant Lake

Colville Lake

Lac Belot

Lac Maunoir

Aubry Lake

Lac des Bois

Kilekale Lake

Mahony Lake

Hottah Lake

Rebesca Lake

Point Lake

Lac Grandin

Lac la Martre

Redrock Lake

Snare Lakes

Lac de Gras

Little Marten Lake

Lockhart Lake

Gordon Lake

Fletcher Lake

Walmsley Lake

Reliance

McLeod Bay

Wha Ti

Rae

Edzo

Birch Lake

Willow Lake

Mills Lake

Great Bear Lake

Bluenose Lake

Kugluktuk

Bathurst Inlet

Inulik Lake

Echo Bay

Camsell

Deline

294

83

54

6000m
4000m
3000m
2000m
1000m
500m
250m
100m
Sea Level
-250m
-2000m
-4000m

Scale 1:7,500,000
(projection: Lambert Conformal Conic)

| 0 25 50 75 100 125 150 175 200 Km |
| 0 25 50 75 100 125 150 175 200 Miles |

Population

- ■ above 5 million
- ◉ 100,000 to 500,000
- □ 1 million to 5 million
- ⊕ 50,000 to 100,000
- ◉ 500,000 to 1 million
- ⊙ 10,000 to 50,000
- ○ below 10,000

NORTH AMERICA

53

19,686ft
13,124ft
9843ft
6562ft
3281ft
1640ft
820ft
328ft
Sea Level
-820ft
-6562ft
-13,124ft

GREENLAND
(to Denmark)

AVANNAARSUA

TUNU

KITAA

KONG FREDERIK IX LAND

Knud Rasmussen Land

Qimusseriarsuaq

Baffin Bay

Davis Strait

Limit of summer pack ice

Limit of winter pack ice

Arctic Circle

Ellesmere Island

Axel Heiberg Island

Queen Elizabeth Islands

British Empire Range

Cape Columbia
Cape Discovery
Cape Bicknor
Alert Point
Cape Bourne
Cape Stallworthy
Alert
Hall Basin
Lake Hazen
Agassiz Ice Cap
North Geomagnetic Pole (2005)
Kane Basin
Eureka
Nansen Sound
Norwegian Bay
Bjorne Peninsula
Cornwall Island
Buckingham Island
Simmons Peninsula
Raanes Peninsula
Princess Marie Bay
Bache Peninsula
Buchanan Bay
Cape Herschel
Smith Sound
Qaanaaq
Savissivik
Innaanganeq
Kullorsuaq
Cape Dunsterville
Smith Bay
Clarence Head
Cape Norton Shaw
Grise Fiord
Coburg Island
Cape Storm
Jones Sound
Lady Ann Strait
Bear Bay
Cape Parker
Devon Island
Cape Sherard
Cape Warrander
Resolute
Barrow Strait
Lancaster Sound
Cape York
Cape Crawford
Cape Byam Martin
Cape Graham Moore
Bylot Island
Pond Inlet
Nova Zembla Island
Buchan Gulf
Cape Hunter
Cape Adair
Cape Raper
Cape Henry Kater
Clyde River
Home Bay
Kekertaluk Island
Upernavik
Qeqertarsuaq
Qeqertarsuup Tunua
Qaasuitsup
Sisimiut
Somerset Island
Prince Regent Inlet
Brodeur Peninsula
Admiralty Inlet
Arctic Bay
Borden Peninsula
Creswell Bay
McBean Bay
Gifford
Bernier Bay
Berlinguez Inlet
Neergaard Lake
Murray Maxwell Bay
Nina Bang Lake
Conn Lake
Bieler Lake
Barnes Ice Cap
Lake Gillian
Baffin Island
Cumberland Peninsula
Exeter Sound
Cape Dyer
Kargeeak Point
Qikiqtarjuaq
Broughton Island
Kingnait Fiord
Pangnirtung
Cumberland Sound
Nettilling Fiord
Lemieux Islands
Boothia Peninsula
Cape Palmerston
Cape Margaret
Krusenstern Lake
Boothia
Gulf of Boothia
Crown Prince Frederick Island
Fury and Hecla Strait
Cape Englefield
Igloolik
Jens Munk Island
Rowley Island
Bray Island
South Tweedsmuir Island
Baird Peninsula
Prince Charles Island
Air Force Island
Foxe Basin
Taverner Bay
Koukdjuak
Nettilling Lake
Amadjuak Lake
Cumberland Sound
Spicer Grinnell Lake
Mingo Lake
Hall Peninsula
Brevoort Island
Frobisher Bay
Meta Incognita Peninsula
Gabriel Strait
Resolution Island
Astronomical Society Islands
Taloyoak
Cape Kjer
Cape Chapman
Committee Bay
Simpson Peninsula
Pelly Bay
Hall Lake
Parry Bay
Matty Island
Lady Melville Lake
Wales Island
Melville Peninsula
Gjoa Haven
Rasmussen Basin
Mindham
Rae Isthmus
Lefroy Bay
CANADA
Franklin Lake
Brown Lake
Tehek Lake
Baker Lake
Peter Lake
Quoich
Armit Lake
Chesterfield Inlet
Wager Bay
White Island
Hansine Lake
Repulse Bay
Winter Island
Vansittart Island
Southampton Island
Roes Welcome Sound
Foxe Channel
Cape Bylot
Cape Comfort
Shukbuk Bay
Foxe Peninsula
Cape Dorchester
Finnie Bay
Bowman Bay
Cape Dominion
Markham Bay
Fair Ness
Amadjuak Lake
Salisbury Island
Mill Island
Seahorse Point
Native Bay
Coral Harbour
Nottingham Island
Evans Strait
Fisher Strait
Bay of Gods Mercy
Cape Kendall
Cape Low
Coats Island
Mansel Island
Cape Pembroke
Nuvuk Islands
Digges Islands
Charles Island
Hudson Strait
Sanuraq
Sangissujuaq
Quaqtaq
Diana Bay
Cap Hopes Advance
Whitley Bay
Ungava Bay
Akpatok Island
Button Islands
Cape Chidley
Killinek Island
Deception Bay
QUÉBEC
Péninsule d'Ungava
Lake Harbour
Big Island
Loks Land
Blunt Peninsula
Iqaluit
Angijak Island
Hoare Bay

Western Canada

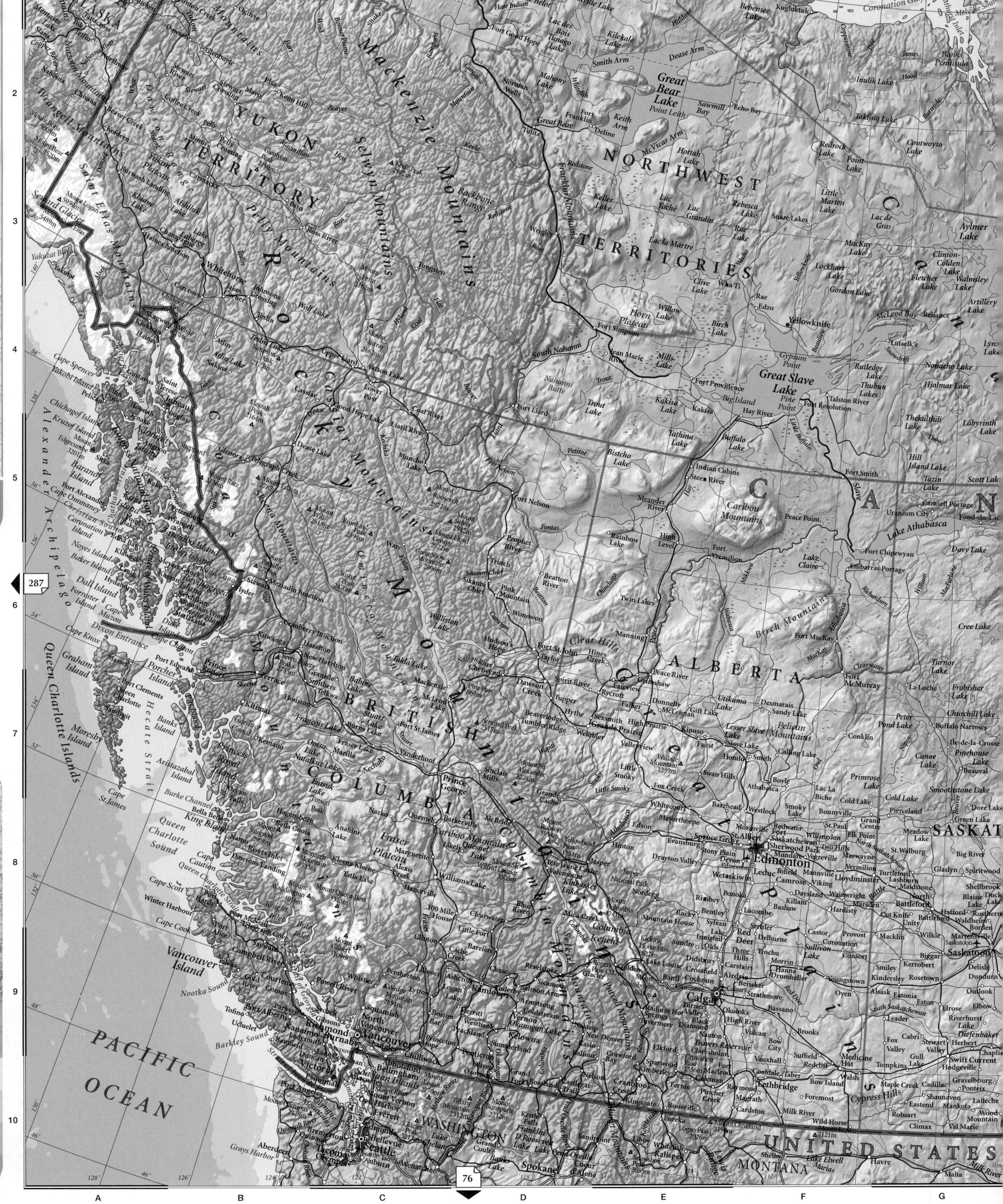
52
287
76
PACIFIC OCEAN
UNITED STATES
WASHINGTON
MONTANA
USA ALASKA
YUKON TERRITORY
NORTHWEST TERRITORIES
BRITISH COLUMBIA
ALBERTA
SASKAT
Victoria Island
Great Bear Lake
Great Slave Lake
Lake Athabasca
Mackenzie Mountains
Selwyn Mountains
Cassiar Mountains
Ogilvie Mountains
Pelly Mountains
Coast Mountains
Skeena Mountains
Omineca Mountains
Rocky Mountains
Columbia Mountains
Selkirk Mountains
Purcell Mountains
Saint Elias Mountains
Wrangell Mountains
Caribou Mountains
Birch Mountains
Backbone Range
Fraser Plateau
Horn Plateau
Great Plains
Queen Charlotte Islands
Queen Charlotte Sound
Hecate Strait
Dixon Entrance
Alexander Archipelago
Vancouver Island
Coronation Gulf
Dolphin and Union Strait
Whitehorse
Yellowknife
Fort Simpson
Fort Nelson
Prince George
Prince Rupert
Kamloops
Kelowna
Vancouver
Victoria
Seattle
Calgary
Edmonton
Red Deer
Lethbridge
Medicine Hat
Saskatoon
Fort McMurray
Grande Prairie
Dawson Creek
Fort St. John
Hay River
Fort Smith
Inuvik
Juneau

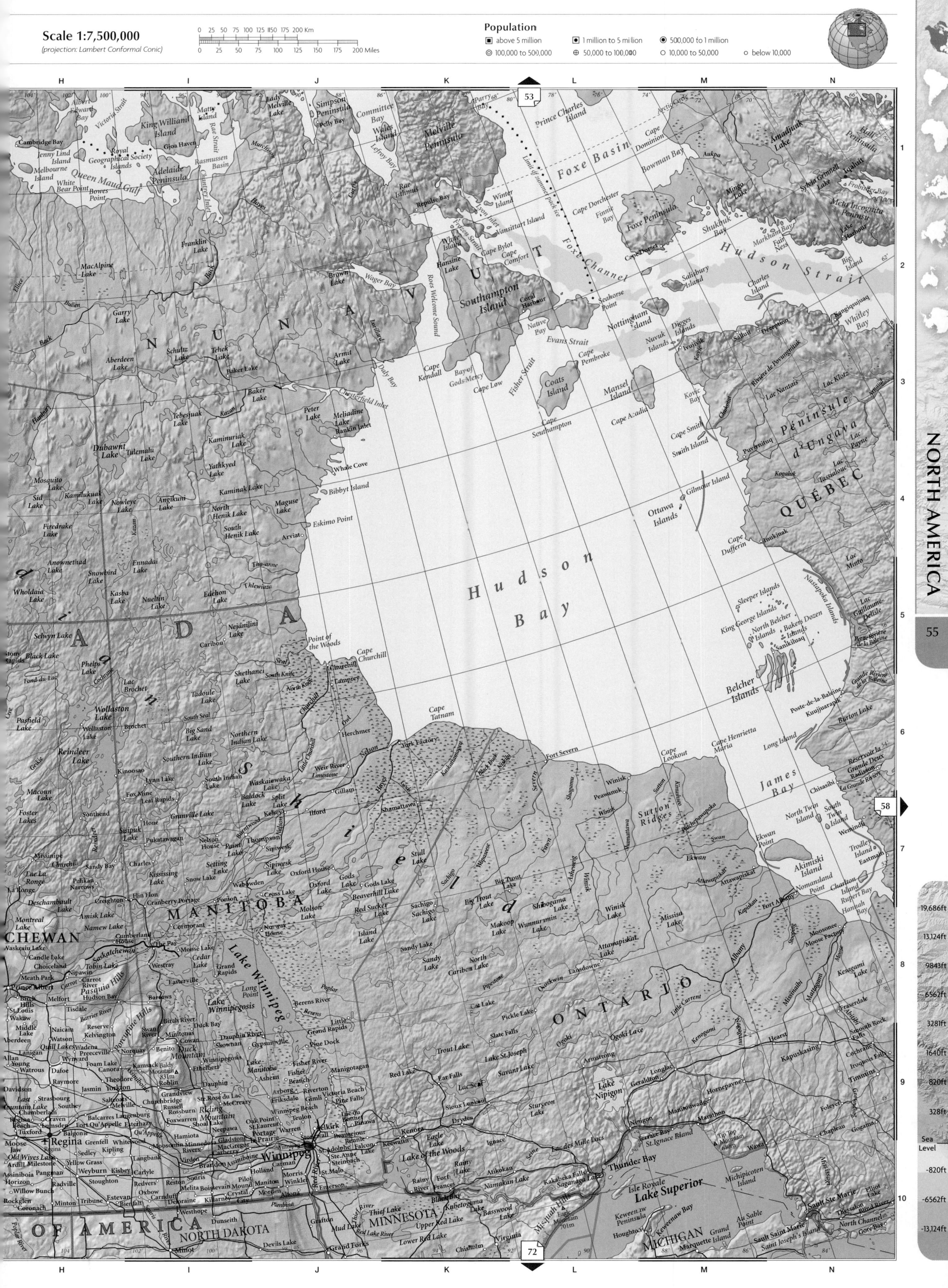

Scale 1:7,500,000
(projection: Lambert Conformal Conic)
0 25 50 75 100 125 150 175 200 Km
0 25 50 75 100 125 150 175 200 Miles
Population
above 5 million
1 million to 5 million
500,000 to 1 million
100,000 to 500,000
50,000 to 100,000
10,000 to 50,000
below 10,000
NORTH AMERICA
55
53
58
72
19,686ft
13,124ft
9843ft
6562ft
3281ft
1640ft
820ft
328ft
Sea Level
-820ft
-6562ft
-13,124ft
Hudson Bay
James Bay
Hudson Strait
Foxe Basin
Foxe Channel
Foxe Peninsula
Southampton Island
Coats Island
Mansel Island
Belcher Islands
Melville Peninsula
King William Island
Adelaide Peninsula
Queen Maud Gulf
Cambridge Bay
Gjoa Haven
Repulse Bay
Coral Harbour
Rankin Inlet
Chesterfield Inlet
Baker Lake
Whale Cove
Arviat
Churchill
Cape Churchill
York Factory
Fort Severn
Cape Henrietta Maria
Akimiski Island
Moosonee
Moose Factory
Péninsule d'Ungava
QUÉBEC
Nastapoka Islands
Sleeper Islands
King George Islands
Ottawa Islands
Nottingham Island
Salisbury Island
Mingo Lake
Amadjuak Lake
Hall Peninsula
Meta Incognita Peninsula
Frobisher Bay
Prince Charles Island
Bowman Bay
Cape Dorset
Vansittart Island
Wager Bay
Roes Welcome Sound
Evans Strait
Fisher Strait
Cape Low
Bay of Gods Mercy
N U N A V U T
C A N A D A
Canadian Shield
MANITOBA
ONTARIO
SASKATCHEWAN
Lake Winnipeg
Lake Winnipegosis
Lake Manitoba
Lake of the Woods
Lake Nipigon
Lake Superior
Isle Royale
Thunder Bay
Winnipeg
Regina
Brandon
Thompson
The Pas
Flin Flon
Prince Albert
Kenora
Sault Ste Marie
Timmins
Kapuskasing
Hearst
Wollaston Lake
Reindeer Lake
Southern Indian Lake
Dubawnt Lake
Nueltin Lake
Kasba Lake
Baker Lake
Red Lake
Sioux Lookout
Lac Seul
Trout Lake
Big Trout Lake
Sandy Lake
Attawapiskat
Fort Albany
Winisk
Sutton Ridges
UNITED STATES OF AMERICA
NORTH DAKOTA
MINNESOTA
MICHIGAN
Minot
Grand Forks
Devils Lake

Southwest Canada

PACIFIC OCEAN

BRITISH COLUMBIA

Vancouver Island

Queen Charlotte Sound

Queen Charlotte Strait

Strait of Georgia

Strait of Juan de Fuca

ROCKY MOUNTAINS

Columbia Mountains

Selkirk Mountains

Cariboo Mountains

Fraser Plateau

Coast Mountains

Skeena Mountains

Omineca Mountains

Clear Hills

WASHINGTON

UNITED STATES

USA ALASKA

Vancouver
Victoria
Seattle
Tacoma
Prince George
Kamloops
Kelowna
Prince Rupert
Nanaimo

Scale 1:3,750,000
(projection: Lambert Azimuthal Equal Area)

0 20 40 60 80 100 Km
0 20 40 60 80 100 Miles

Population
- ■ above 5 million
- ◉ 100,000 to 500,000
- ▣ 1 million to 5 million
- ⊕ 50,000 to 100,000
- ◉ 500,000 to 1 million
- ○ 10,000 to 50,000
- ○ below 10,000

19,686ft
13,124ft
9843ft
6562ft
3281ft
1640ft
820ft
328ft
Sea Level
-820ft
-6562ft
-13,124ft

CANADA

ALBERTA

SASKATCHEWAN

UNITED STATES OF AMERICA

MONTANA

IDAHO

Edmonton
Calgary
Saskatoon
Regina
Red Deer
Lethbridge
Medicine Hat
Moose Jaw
Prince Albert
North Battleford
Fort McMurray

Birch Mountains
Rocky Mountains
Cypress Hills
Purcell Mountains
Cabinet Mountains

Lesser Slave Lake
Peter Pond Lake
Churchill Lake
Cold Lake
Primrose Lake
Reindeer Lake
Lac La Ronge
Montreal Lake
Lake Diefenbaker
Last Mountain Lake
Old Wives Lake
Flathead Lake
Fort Peck Lake
Travers Reservoir
Hungry Horse Reservoir

Missouri River
Milk River
South Saskatchewan
North Saskatchewan
Battle
Red Deer
Clearwater

6000m
4000m
3000m
2000m
1000m
500m
250m
100m
Sea Level
-250m
-2000m
-4000m

Hudson Bay

C A N A D A

O N T A R I O

Canadian Shield

Lake Winnipeg

Lake Superior

Lake Michigan

Lake Huron

Lake Erie

Lake Ontario

UNITED STATES OF AMERICA

MINNESOTA
WISCONSIN
MICHIGAN
IOWA
ILLINOIS
INDIANA
OHIO
MISSOURI
NORTH DAKOTA
SOUTH DAKOTA
PENNSYLVANIA
NEW YORK

Winnipeg
Thunder Bay
Minneapolis
Saint Paul
Madison
Milwaukee
Chicago
Detroit
Toronto
Ottawa
Mississauga
Markham
Scarborough
Hamilton
Cleveland
Des Moines

Péninsule
Belcher Islands
Sleeper Islands
Akimiski Island
Coats Island
Mansel Island
Charles Island

Reservoir la Grande Deux
Reservoir Gouin

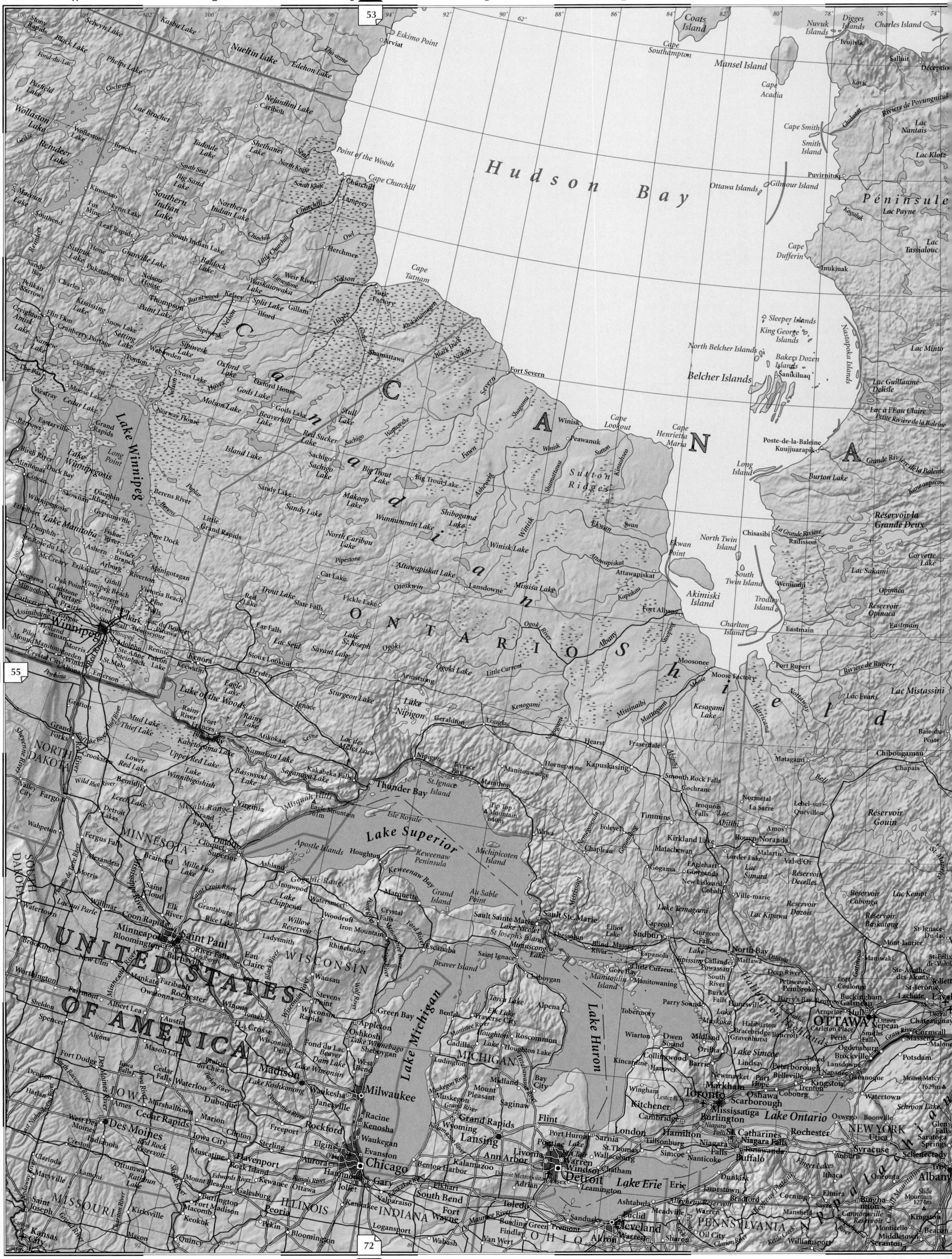

The United States of America

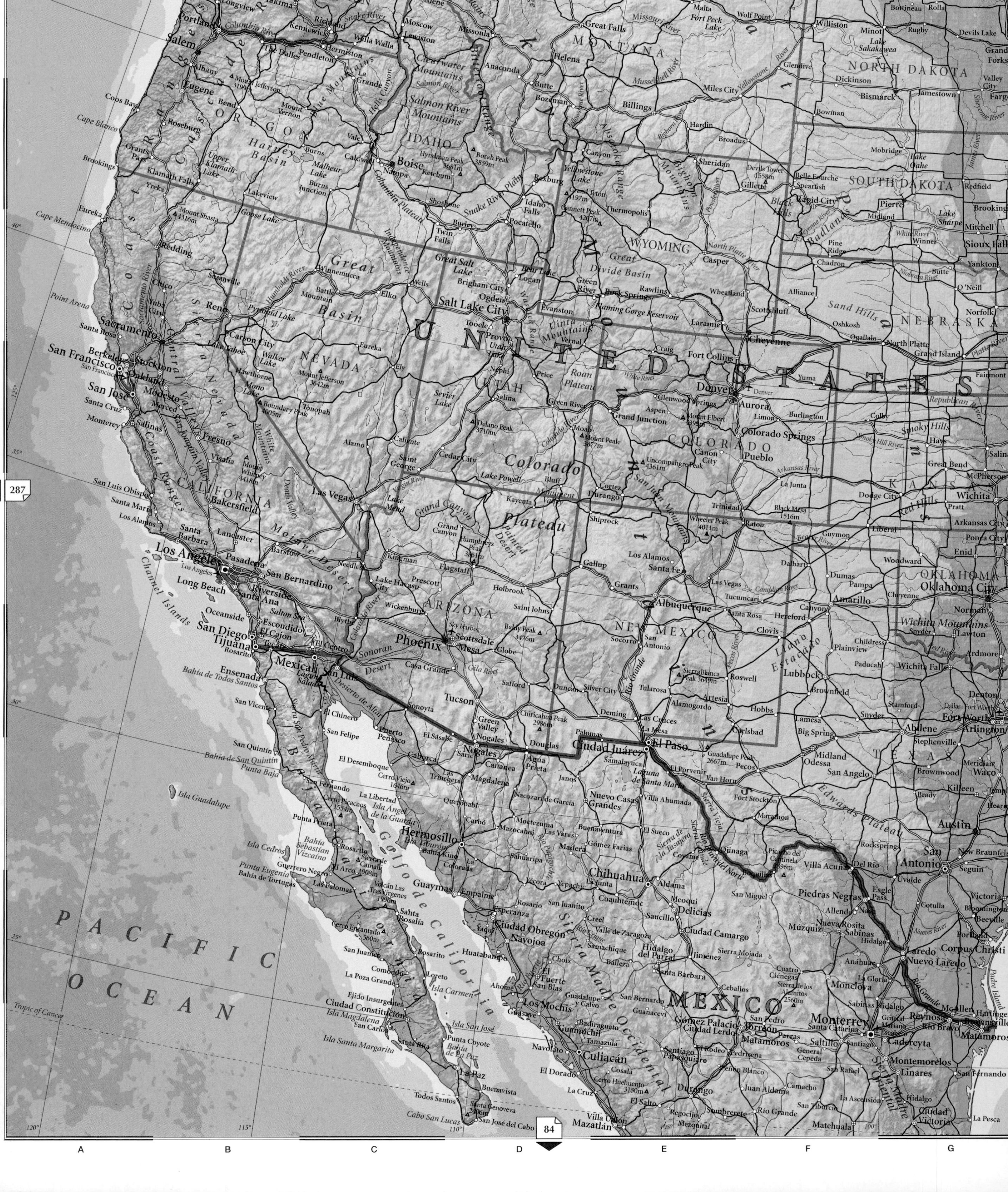

60

PACIFIC OCEAN

Tropic of Cancer

Sea Level

6000m
4000m
3000m
2000m
1000m
500m
250m
100m
Sea Level
-250m
-2000m
-4000m

Scale 1:10,250,000
(projection: Lambert Azimuthal Equal Area)

0 50 100 150 200 250 300 Km
0 50 100 150 200 250 300 Miles

Population
■ above 5 million
◉ 100,000 to 500,000
▣ 1 million to 5 million
⊕ 50,000 to 100,000
◎ 500,000 to 1 million
○ 10,000 to 50,000
· below 10,000

51

90

290

19,686ft
13,124ft
9843ft
6562ft
3281ft
1640ft
820ft
328ft
Sea Level
-820ft
-6562ft
-13,124ft

USA – Northeast States & Southeast Canada

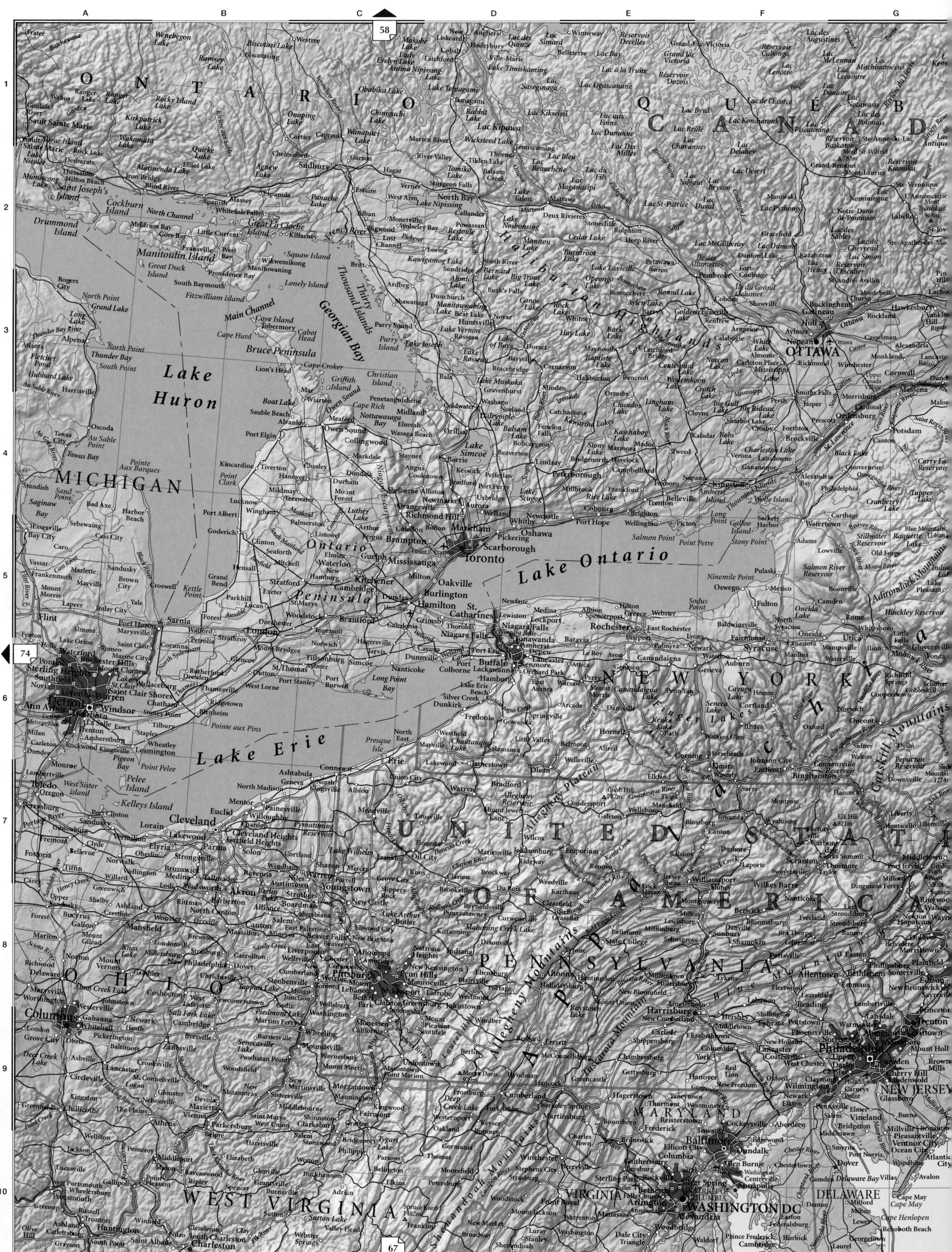

ONTARIO
QUÉBEC
CANADA
MICHIGAN
OHIO
PENNSYLVANIA
NEW YORK
WEST VIRGINIA
VIRGINIA
MARYLAND
DELAWARE
NEW JERSEY
UNITED STATES OF AMERICA
Lake Huron
Lake Erie
Lake Ontario
Georgian Bay
Bruce Peninsula
Manitoulin Island
Ontario Peninsula
Haliburton Highlands
Thousand Islands
Finger Lakes
Allegheny Plateau
Allegheny Mountains
Appalachian Mountains
Catskill Mountains
Adirondack Mountains
Blue Mountain
Tuscarora Mountain
Shenandoah Mountains
OTTAWA
WASHINGTON DC
Toronto
Montreal
Detroit
Windsor
Cleveland
Pittsburgh
Columbus
Buffalo
Rochester
Syracuse
Philadelphia
Baltimore
Harrisburg
Hamilton
London
Kingston
Sudbury
North Bay
Youngstown
Akron
Toledo
Erie
Scranton
Allentown
Binghamton
Utica
Wilmington
58
74
67

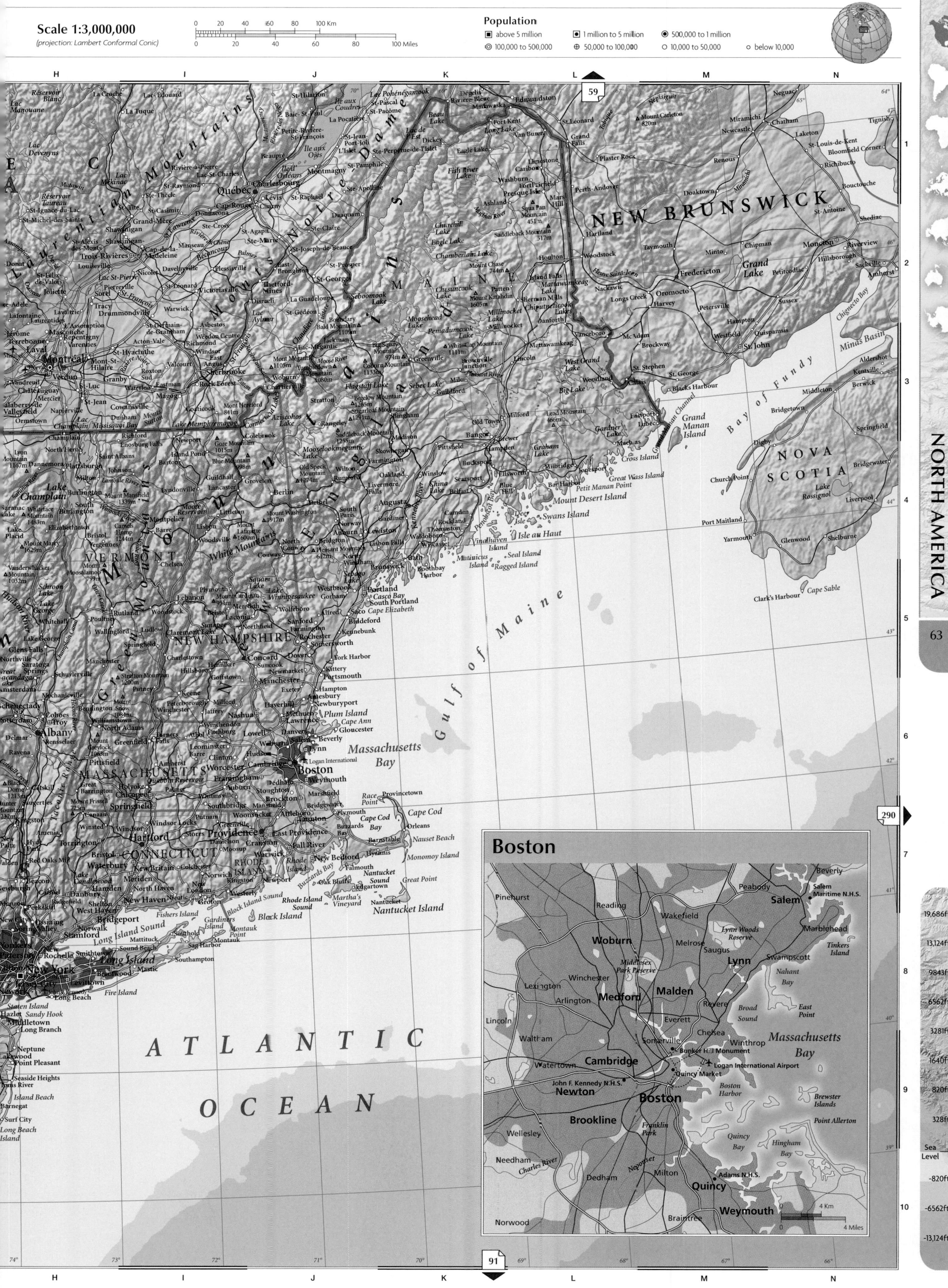

Scale 1:3,000,000
(projection: Lambert Conformal Conic)
0 20 40 60 80 100 Km
0 20 40 60 80 100 Miles
Population
above 5 million
1 million to 5 million
500,000 to 1 million
100,000 to 500,000
50,000 to 100,000
10,000 to 50,000
below 10,000
59
290
91
NORTH AMERICA
63
NEW BRUNSWICK
NOVA SCOTIA
MAINE
VERMONT
NEW HAMPSHIRE
MASSACHUSETTS
CONNECTICUT
RHODE ISLAND
Laurentian Mountains
Notre Dame Mountains
White Mountains
Green Mountains
Gulf of Maine
Bay of Fundy
Massachusetts Bay
Cape Cod Bay
Cape Cod
Nantucket Island
Martha's Vineyard
Block Island
Long Island
Long Island Sound
ATLANTIC OCEAN
Québec
Montreal
Trois-Rivières
Sherbrooke
Fredericton
Saint John
Moncton
Bangor
Augusta
Portland
Concord
Manchester
Boston
Providence
Hartford
New Haven
Bridgeport
Springfield
Worcester
Albany
New York
Burlington
Lake Champlain
Mount Washington 1917m
Mount Katahdin 1605m
Mount Desert Island
Grand Manan Island
Cape Sable
Boston
Beverly
Salem
Salem Maritime N.H.S.
Peabody
Marblehead
Tinkers Island
Wakefield
Reading
Pinehurst
Woburn
Lynn Woods Reserve
Melrose
Saugus
Lynn
Swampscott
Nahant Bay
Middlesex Fells Reserve
Winchester
Lexington
Arlington
Medford
Malden
Revere
Broad Sound
East Point
Massachusetts Bay
Everett
Lincoln
Waltham
Chelsea
Somerville
Winthrop
Bunker Hill Monument
Watertown
Cambridge
Logan International Airport
Quincy Market
John F. Kennedy N.H.S.
Newton
Boston
Boston Harbor
Brewster Islands
Brookline
Franklin Park
Point Allerton
Wellesley
Quincy Bay
Hingham Bay
Needham
Charles River
Dedham
Neponset
Milton
Adams N.H.S.
Quincy
Norwood
Braintree
Weymouth
4 Km
4 Miles
19,686ft
13,124ft
9843ft
6562ft
3281ft
1640ft
820ft
328ft
Sea Level
-820ft
-6562ft
-13,124ft

NORTH AMERICA

62

67

NEW YORK

UNITED STATES OF

PENNSYLVANIA

Appalachian Mountains

Allegheny Mountains

Catskill Mountains

Finger Lakes

Susquehanna River

WEST VIRGINIA

VIRGINIA

MARYLAND

NEW JERSEY

DELAWARE

DISTRICT OF COLUMBIA

WASHINGTON DC

Chesapeake Bay

Delaware Bay

Lake Erie

CANADA
USA

6000m
4000m
3000m
2000m
1000m
500m
250m
100m
Sea Level
-250m
-2000m
-4000m

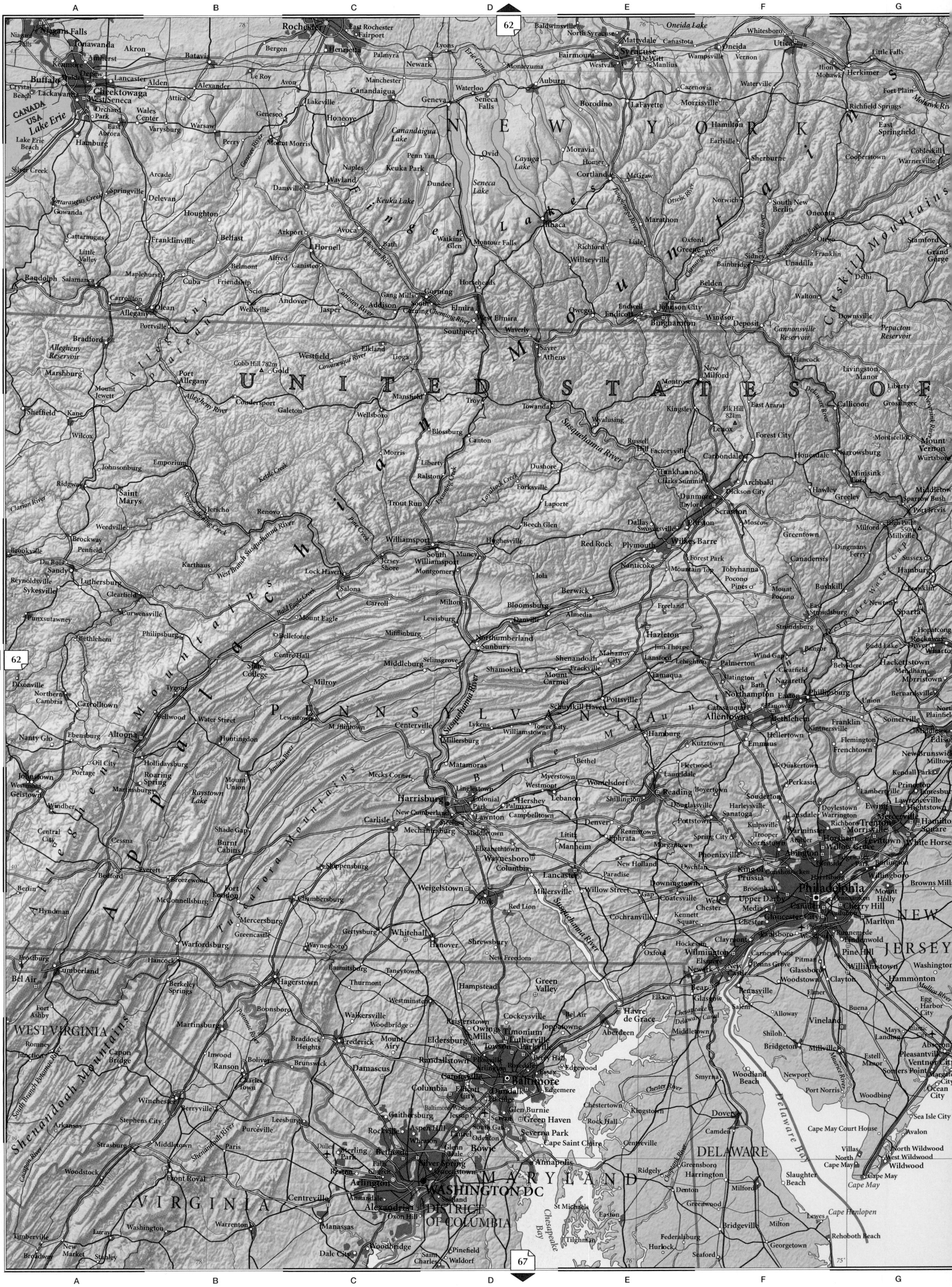

Scale 1:1,500,000
(projection: Lambert Conformal Conic)
0 10 20 30 40 50 Km
0 10 20 30 40 50 Miles
Population
above 5 million
1 million to 5 million
500,000 to 1 million
100,000 to 500,000
50,000 to 100,000
10,000 to 50,000
below 10,000
H
I
J
K
L
M
N
63
290
90
1
2
3
4
5
6
7
8
9
10
VERMONT
NEW HAMPSHIRE
MASSACHUSETTS
CONNECTICUT
RHODE ISLAND
AMERICA
Taconic Range
Gulf of Maine
Massachusetts Bay
Cape Cod Bay
Cape Cod
Buzzards Bay
Nantucket Sound
Nantucket Island
Martha's Vineyard
Rhode Island Sound
Block Island Sound
Block Island
Fishers Island
Long Island Sound
Fire Island
Sandy Hook
Island Beach
Long Beach Island
ATLANTIC OCEAN
Great Sacandaga Lake
Saratoga Springs
Amsterdam
Schenectady
Albany
Troy
Pittsfield
Springfield
Hartford
New Haven
Bridgeport
Stamford
Waterbury
Worcester
Boston
Lowell
Manchester
Nashua
Portsmouth
Providence
Fall River
New Bedford
Newport
New London
Provincetown
Nantucket
Montauk
Riverhead
Hampton Bays
Hempstead
Long Beach
New York
Newark
Paterson
Yonkers
Jersey City
Elizabeth
Perth Amboy
Asbury Park
Point Pleasant
Seaside Heights
Atlantic City
Brigantine
Martha's Vineyard
Hudson River
New York
Long Island Sound
Wallington
Fort Lee
Bronx
Rutherford
North Bergen
North Arlington
Kings Point
Rikers Island
East River
East Orange
Kearny
Union City
Manhattan
Central Park
Met. Museum of Art
La Guardia Airport
Whitestone
Empire State Building
Hoboken
Jackson Heights
Flushing
Newark
Newark Intl. Airport
Jersey City
Statue of Liberty
Maspeth
Queens
Elizabeth
Upper New York Bay
Prospect Heights
Woodhaven
Jamaica
Bayonne
Brooklyn
John F. Kennedy Intl. Airport
Sunset Park
Jamaica Bay
Fort Hamilton
Flatlands
Staten Island
Dongan Hills
Coney Island
Brighton Beach
Rockaway Beach
Oakwood
Lower New York Bay
Rockaway Point
Atlantic Ocean
0 5 10 Km
0 5 10 Miles
19,686ft
13,124ft
9843ft
6562ft
3281ft
1640ft
820ft
328ft
Sea Level
-820ft
-6562ft
-13,124ft

Scale 1:3,000,000
(projection: Lambert Conformal Conic)

0 20 40 60 80 100 Km
0 20 40 60 100 Miles

Population

- ■ above 5 million
- ◨ 1 million to 5 million
- ◉ 500,000 to 1 million
- ◎ 100,000 to 500,000
- ⊛ 50,000 to 100,000
- ⊙ 10,000 to 50,000
- ○ below 10,000

PENNSYLVANIA

WEST VIRGINIA

VIRGINIA

MARYLAND

DELAWARE

NEW JERSEY

NORTH CAROLINA

SOUTH CAROLINA

UNITED STATES OF AMERICA

Pittsburgh
Philadelphia
Baltimore
WASHINGTON DC
DISTRICT OF COLUMBIA
Richmond
Norfolk
Virginia Beach
Newport News
Hampton
Charlotte
Raleigh
Greensboro
Winston Salem
High Point
Durham
Columbia
Charleston
Savannah

Chesapeake Bay
Delaware Bay
Albemarle Sound
Pamlico Sound
Raleigh Bay
Onslow Bay
Long Bay

ATLANTIC OCEAN

Cape Hatteras
Cape Lookout
Cape Fear
Hatteras Island
Ocracoke Island
Roanoke Island
Assateague Island

BERMUDA (to UK)
HAMILTON
St George's Island
St Catherine Point
St George
St David's Island
Ireland Island North
Ireland Island South
Somerset Island
Gibbs Hill 73m
Kindley Field
Commissioner's Point
Harrington Sound
Great Sound
Little Sound
Spanish Point
Flatts Village
Tucker's Town

Scale 1:500,000
0 2.5 5 Km
0 2.5 5 Miles

ATLANTIC OCEAN

19,686ft
13,124ft
9843ft
6562ft
3281ft
1640ft
820ft
328ft
Sea Level
-820ft
-6562ft
-13,124ft

67

62

290

69

NORTH AMERICA

68

G u l f   o f   M e x i c o

ARKANSAS

TEXAS

LOUISIANA

MISSISSIPPI

U N I T E D   S T A T

New Orleans

Lake Pontchartrain

0   5 Km
0   5 Miles

Kenner
Metairie
New Orleans
Chalmette
Marrero

Scale 1:3,000,000
(projection: Lambert Conformal Conic)

0 20 40 60 80 100 Km
0 20 40 60 80 100 Miles

Population

- ■ above 5 million
- ◉ 100,000 to 500,000
- ■ 1 million to 5 million
- ⊕ 50,000 to 100,000
- ◉ 500,000 to 1 million
- ○ 10,000 to 50,000
- ○ below 10,000

Miami

Miramar · Ives Estates · Hallandale
Carol City · Norland · North Miami Beach
Golden Glades · North Miami · Miami Shores
Westview · West Little River · North Bay Village
Hialeah · Hialeah Park · Gladeview
Virginia Gardens · Brownsville
Miami International Airport ✈
Streetwater · West Miami · Miami
Florida Int'l University · Miami Beach
Westchester · Coral Gables · Virginia Key
Olympia Heights · Miami Seaquarium
Kendall · Key Biscayne · Key Biscayne
Weeks Air Museum · Pinecrest · Cape Florida
Richmond Heights
Westwood Lake · South Miami Heights · Perrine · Cutler Ridge
Goulds
Redland · Naranja · South Allapattah
Leisure City · Sands Key
Homestead · Elliot Key
Florida City

Atlantic Ocean

Biscayne Bay

0 5 Km
0 5 Miles

ALABAMA · GEORGIA · SOUTH CAROLINA · FLORIDA

ATLANTIC OCEAN

Montgomery · Columbus · Macon · Savannah · Jacksonville · Orlando · Tampa · Saint Petersburg · Miami · Fort Lauderdale · Hollywood

Lake Okeechobee · The Everglades · Big Cypress Swamp · Okefenokee Swamp

Straits of Florida · Florida Keys · Key West · Key Largo

19,686ft · 13,124ft · 9843ft · 6562ft · 3281ft · 1640ft · 820ft · 328ft · Sea Level · -820ft · -6562ft · -13,124ft

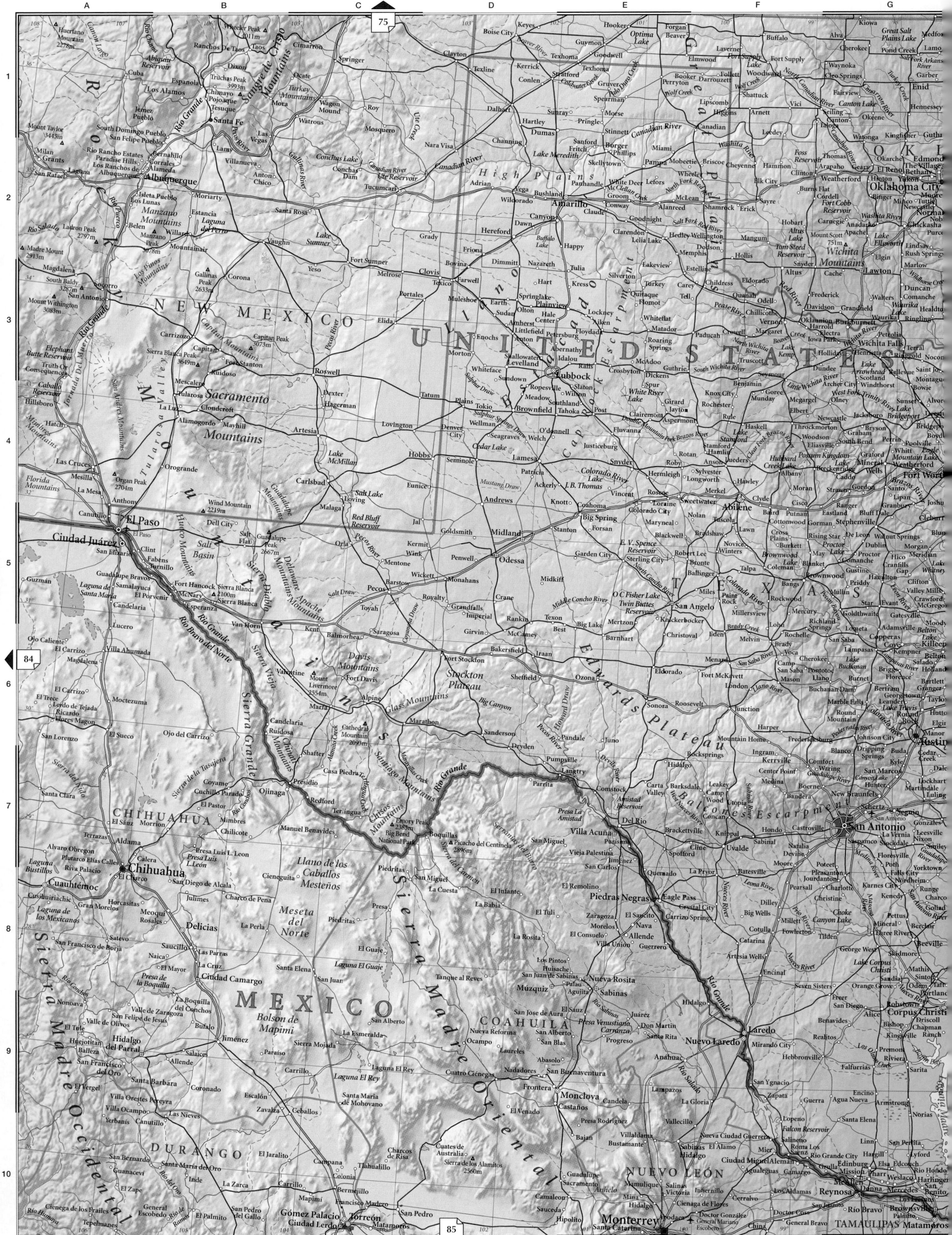

Scale 1:3,750,000
(projection: Lambert Conformal Conic)

0 20 40 60 80 100 Km
0 20 40 60 80 100 Miles

Population

■ above 5 million   ▣ 1 million to 5 million   ⊙ 500,000 to 1 million
◉ 100,000 to 500,000   ⊕ 50,000 to 100,000   ○ 10,000 to 50,000   ∘ below 10,000

MISSOURI

OZARK PLATEAU

Boston Mountains

ARKANSAS

Ouachita Mountains

OKLAHOMA

UNITED STATES OF AMERICA

TENNESSEE

Memphis

Little Rock

North Little Rock

Nashville

TEXAS

Dallas
Plano
Arlington
Garland

Tyler

Shreveport
Bossier City

Monroe

MISSISSIPPI

Jackson

ALABAMA

Meridian

Mobile

LOUISIANA

Beaumont

Houston
Pasadena
Galveston

Baton Rouge

New Orleans
Metairie
Kenner

College Station

Waco

Gulf of Mexico

Padre Island

Houston

Houston Intl. Airport

North Houston

Mount Houston

Lake Houston

Highlands

Channelview

George Bush Park

Bunker Hill Village

Antique Car Museum

Anheuser Busch Brewery

Jacinto City

Contemporary Arts Museum

Houston

Galena Park

Battleship Texas

Baytown

Bellaire West

Bellaire

Museum of Fine Arts

Zoo

Buffalo Bayou

Sugar Land

South Houston

Pasadena

La Porte

William P. Hobby Airport

Missouri City

Pearland

Johnson Space Ctr. & Space Center Houston

Seabrook

Clear Lake

Friendswood

Galveston Bay

19,686ft
13,124ft
9843ft
6562ft
3281ft
1640ft
820ft
328ft
Sea Level
-820ft
-6562ft
-13,124ft

USA – Great Lake States

Scale elevation key:
6000m
4000m
3000m
2000m
1000m
500m
250m
100m
Sea Level
-250m
-2000m
-4000m

Lake Superior

Lake Huron

Lake Michigan

Georgian Bay

CANADA

ONTARIO

MINNESOTA

WISCONSIN

MICHIGAN

Ontario Peninsula

Thirty Thousand Islands

Isle Royale

Michipicoten Island

Apostle Islands

Manitoulin Island

Lake Nipigon

Lake Nipissing

Lake Winnebago

Thunder Bay

Duluth

Milwaukee

Madison

Sudbury

Saginaw Bay

Green Bay

Grand Traverse Bay

Keweenaw Peninsula

Gogebic Range

Porcupine Mountains

Huron Mountains

Doorr Peninsula

Whitefish Bay

Straits of Mackinac

Sault Sainte Marie

Marquette

North Channel

Cabot Head

Bruce Peninsula

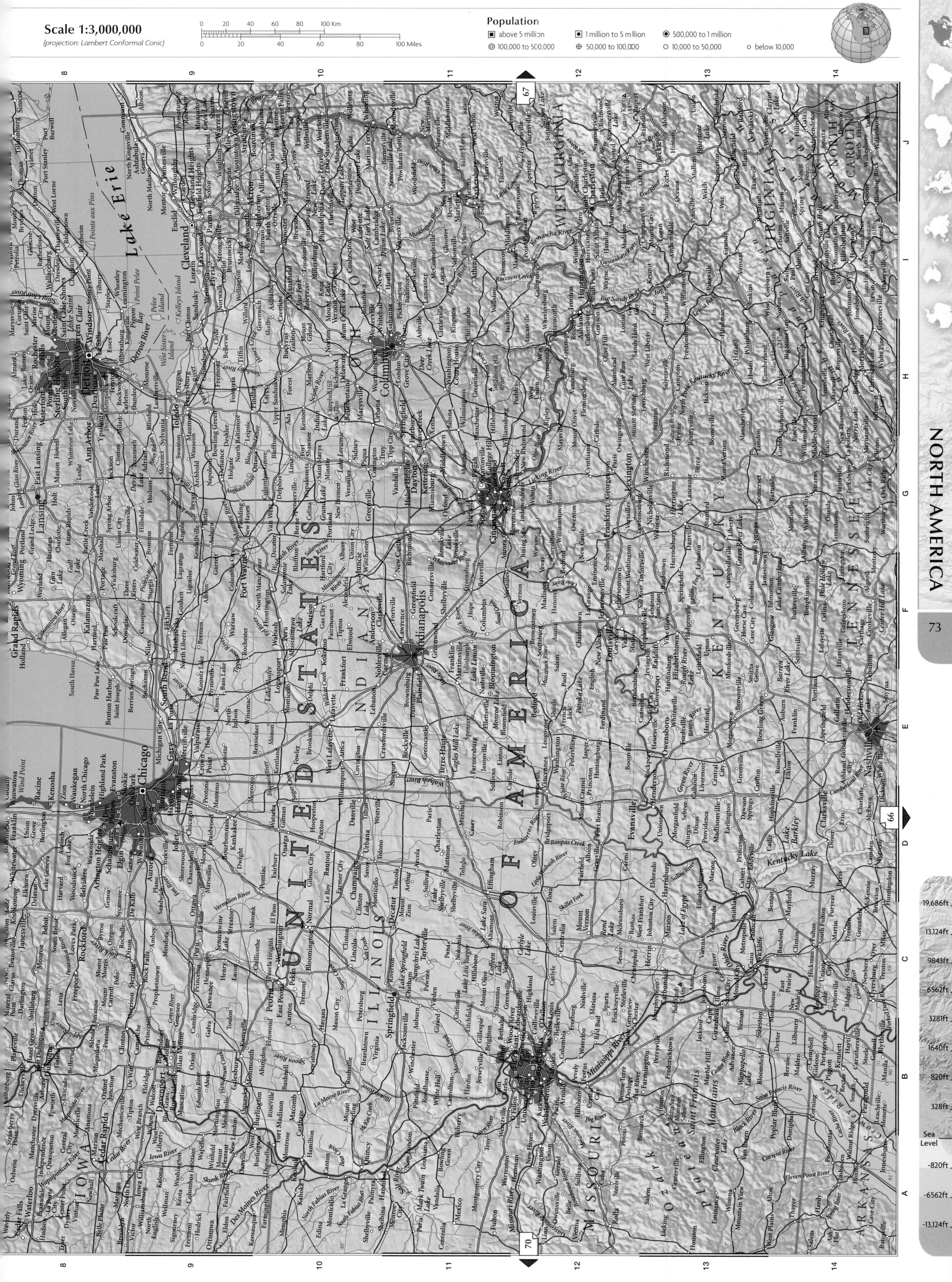

Scale 1:3,000,000
(projection: Lambert Conformal Conic)

Population
■ above 5 million ▣ 1 million to 5 million ◉ 500,000 to 1 million
◎ 100,000 to 500,000 ⊕ 50,000 to 100,000 ○ 10,000 to 50,000 ∘ below 10,000

0 20 40 60 80 100 Km
0 20 40 60 80 100 Miles

19,686ft
13,124ft
9843ft
6562ft
3281ft
1640ft
820ft
328ft
Sea Level
-820ft
-6562ft
-13,124ft

USA – Great Plains States

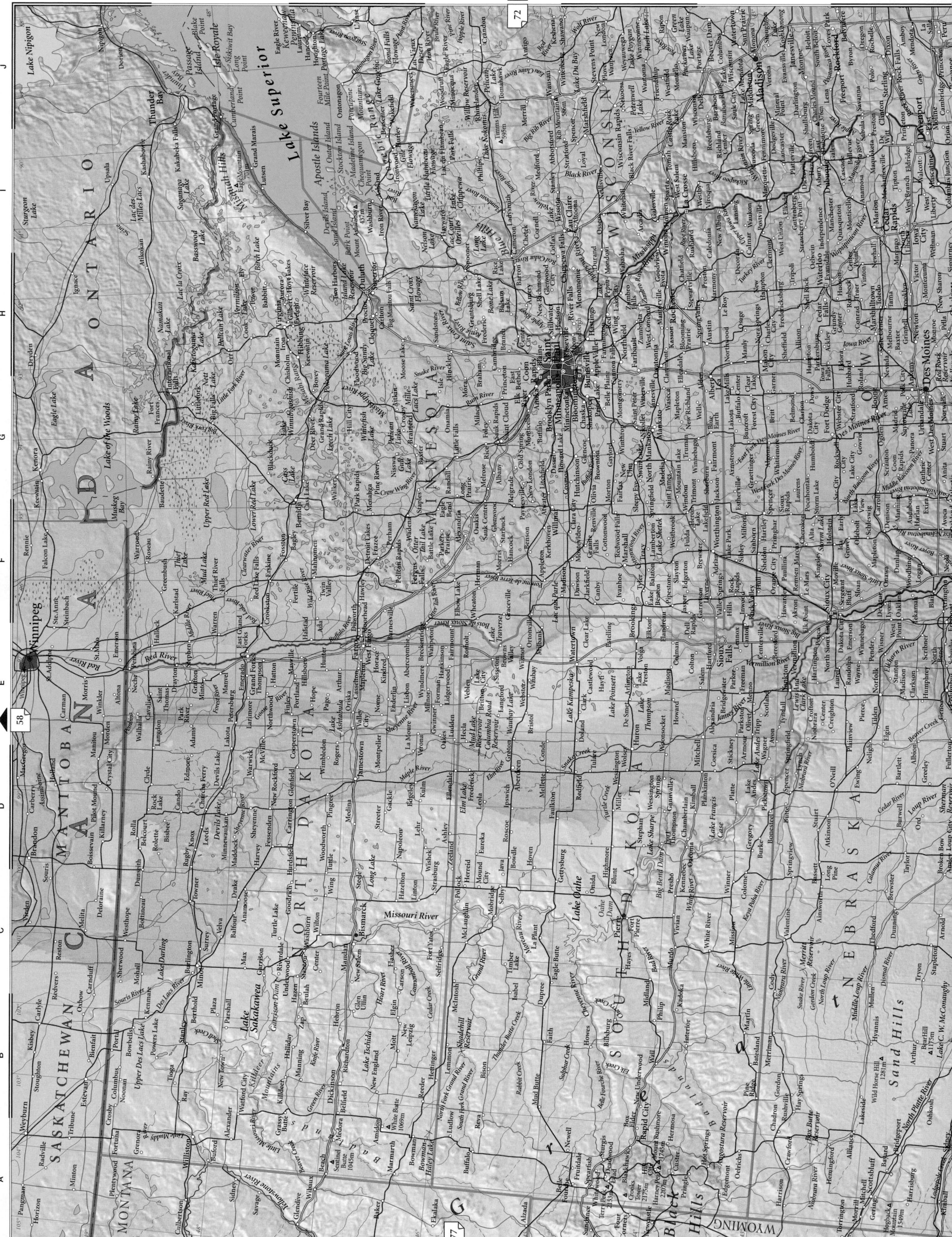

Lake Superior
Lake of the Woods
Lake Nipigon
Winnipeg
Duluth
Saint Paul
Minneapolis
Des Moines
Sioux Falls
Bismarck
Pierre
Rapid City
Madison
Rockford
Davenport
Cedar Rapids
Sioux City
Fargo
Grand Forks
Aberdeen
Lake Sakakawea
Lake Oahe
Missouri River
Red River
Sand Hills
Black Hills
Apostle Islands
CANADA
MANITOBA
ONTARIO
SASKATCHEWAN
MONTANA
WYOMING
NORTH DAKOTA
SOUTH DAKOTA
MINNESOTA
WISCONSIN
IOWA
NEBRASKA
6000m
4000m
3000m
2000m
1000m
500m
250m
100m
Sea Level
-250m
-2000m
-4000m
58
72
77

Scale 1:3,750,000
(projection: Lambert Conformal Conic)

0 20 40 60 80 100 Km
0 20 40 60 80 100 Miles

Population
■ above 5 million   ▣ 1 million to 5 million   ◉ 500,000 to 1 million
⊕ 100,000 to 500,000 ⊕ 50,000 to 100,000   ⊕ 10,000 to 50,000   ○ below 10,000

19,686ft
13,124ft
9843ft
6562ft
3281ft
1640ft
820ft
328ft
Sea Level
-820ft
-6562ft
-13,124ft

USA – Northwest States

A B C D E F G

1 2 3 4 5 6 7 8 9 10

56

287

78

PACIFIC OCEAN

BRITISH COLUMBIA

WASHINGTON

OREGON

CALIFORNIA

NEVADA

IDAHO

UNITED STATES

Vancouver Island

Coast Mountains

Olympic Mountains

Cascade Range

Coast Ranges

Columbia Basin

Blue Mountains

Harney Basin

Great Basin

Snake River Plateau

Salmon River Mountains

Clearwater Mountains

Bitterroot Range

Selkirk Mountains

Purcell Mountains

Cabinet Mountains

Klamath Mountains

Sierra Nevada

Columbia River

Snake River

Vancouver

Victoria

Seattle

Tacoma

Olympia

Spokane

Portland

Salem

Eugene

Bend

Boise

Medford

Redding

Yakima

Kamloops

Kelowna

Mount Rainier 4392m

Mount Hood 3424m

Mount Saint Helens 2549m

Mount Adams 3741m

Mount Shasta 4316m

Mount Olympus 2428m

6000m

4000m

3000m

2000m

1000m

500m

250m

100m

Sea Level

-250m

-2000m

-4000m

Scale 1:3,750,000
(projection: Lambert Conformal Conic)

0 20 40 60 80 100 Km
0 20 40 60 80 100 Miles

Population
- ■ above 5 million
- ▣ 1 million to 5 million
- ◉ 500,000 to 1 million
- ◎ 100,000 to 500,000
- ⊕ 50,000 to 100,000
- ○ 10,000 to 50,000
- ∘ below 10,000

19,686ft
13,124ft
9843ft
6562ft
3281ft
1640ft
820ft
328ft
Sea Level
-820ft
-6562ft
-13,124ft

CANADA

ALBERTA

SASKATCHEWAN

MANITOBA

Regina

Great Plains

MONTANA

NORTH DAKOTA

SOUTH DAKOTA

WYOMING

NEBRASKA

UTAH

COLORADO

UNITED STATES OF AMERICA

Rocky Mountains

Bighorn Mountains

Laramie Mountains

Wasatch Range

Uinta Mountains

Bighorn Basin

Great Divide Basin

Yellowstone National Park

Grand Teton 4197m

Gannett Peak 4207m

Fremont Peak 4189m

Kings Peak 4123m

Granite Peak 3901m

Great Salt Lake

Bonneville Salt Flats

Salt Lake City

Denver

Cheyenne

Casper

Billings

Great Falls

Helena

Bozeman

Butte

Pocatello

Idaho Falls

Rapid City

Black Hills

Badlands

Missouri River

Yellowstone River

Milk River

North Platte River

Snake River

Green River

Powder River

Lake Sakakawea

Fort Peck Lake

Lake Diefenbaker

Medicine Hat

Lethbridge

Williston

Dickinson

Bismarck

Miles City

Glasgow

Havre

Sheridan

Buffalo

Gillette

Riverton

Lander

Rock Springs

Evanston

Ogden

Provo

Fort Collins

Greeley

Boulder

Aurora

Lakewood

79

57

74

USA – Southwest States

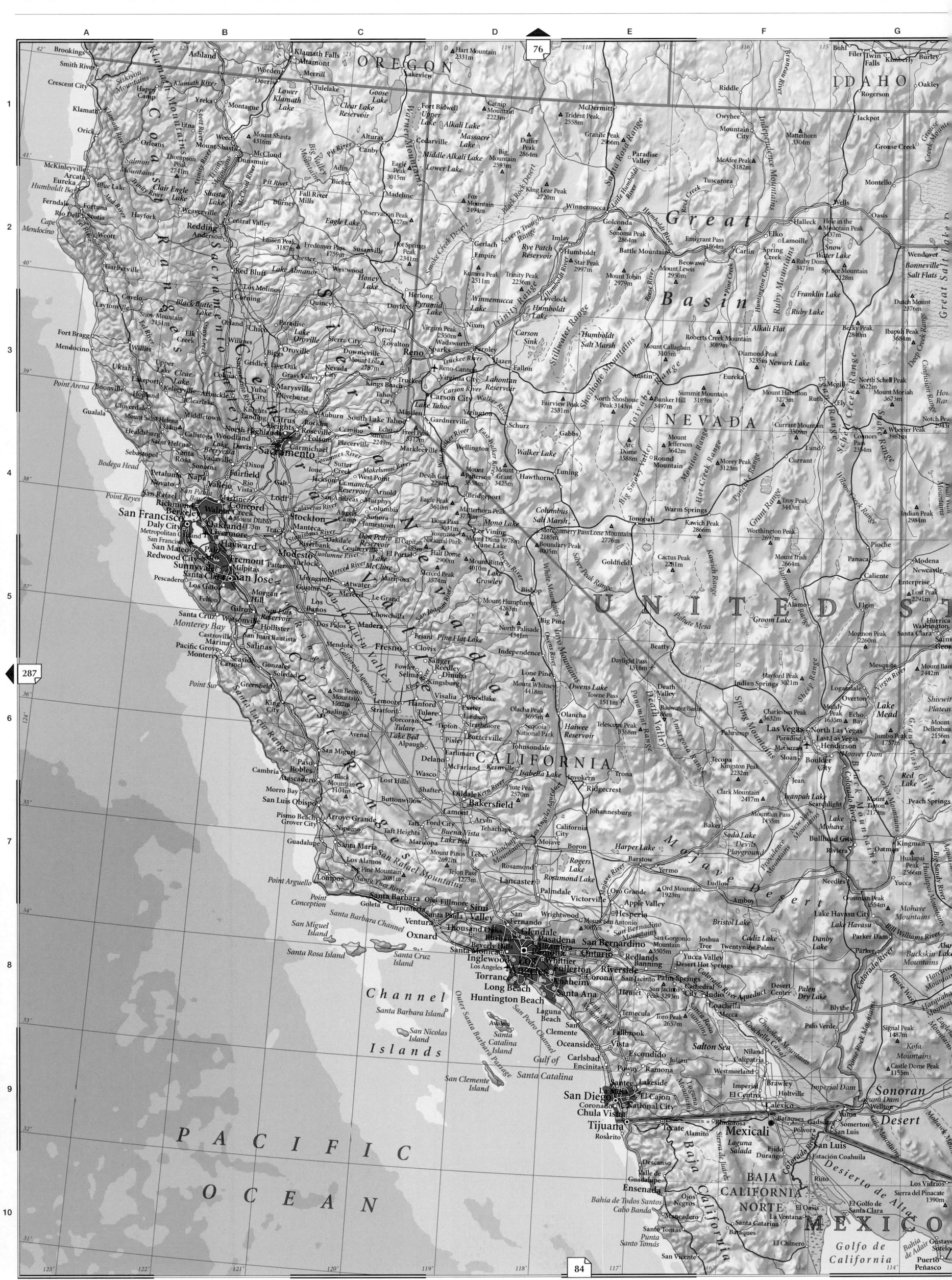
A
B
C
D
E
F
G
1
2
3
4
5
6
7
8
9
10
76
84
287
OREGON
IDAHO
NEVADA
CALIFORNIA
UNITED S
MEXICO
PACIFIC
OCEAN
Great Basin
Coast Ranges
Sacramento Valley
Sierra Nevada
Central Valley
Mojave Desert
Sonoran Desert
Channel Islands
Klamath Mountains
Salton Sea
Lake Tahoe
Lake Mead
Pyramid Lake
Mono Lake
BAJA CALIFORNIA NORTE
Golfo de California
Sacramento
San Francisco
Oakland
San Jose
Fresno
Bakersfield
Los Angeles
Long Beach
San Bernardino
Riverside
Santa Ana
San Diego
Tijuana
Mexicali
Ensenada
Reno
Carson City
Las Vegas
Stockton
Modesto
Santa Barbara
Oxnard
Monterey
Salinas
Redding
Eureka
Klamath Falls
Winnemucca
Elko
Tonopah
Barstow
Lancaster
Yuma
Henderson
Mount Whitney 4418m
Mount Shasta 4316m
Death Valley
Santa Catalina
Monterey Bay
Point Arena
Point Conception
Cape Mendocino
Santa Barbara Channel
6000m
4000m
3000m
2000m
1000m
500m
250m
100m
Sea Level
-250m
-2000m
-4000m

Scale 1:3,750,000
(projection: Lambert Conformal Conic)

0 20 40 60 80 100 Km
0 20 40 60 80 100 Miles

Population
■ above 5 million
■ 1 million to 5 million
◉ 500,000 to 1 million
◎ 100,000 to 500,000
⊕ 50,000 to 100,000
○ 10,000 to 50,000
○ below 10,000

77
75
70
85

19,686ft
13,124ft
9843ft
6562ft
3281ft
1640ft
820ft
328ft
Sea Level
-820ft
-6562ft
-13,124ft

WYOMING

UTAH

COLORADO

NEW MEXICO

ARIZONA

NEBRASKA

TEXAS

SONORA

CHIHUAHUA

UNITED STATES OF AMERICA

Great Salt Lake
Salt Lake City
Denver
Colorado Springs
Pueblo
Albuquerque
Santa Fe
Phoenix
Tucson
Flagstaff
Grand Junction
Cheyenne
El Paso
Ciudad Juárez
Las Cruces
Roswell
Carlsbad

ROCKY MOUNTAINS

Great Divide Basin

Sangre de Cristo Mountains

San Juan Mountains

Colorado Plateau

Grand Canyon

Mogollon Rim

USA – California

NEVADA
UNITED STATES OF AMERICA
Sierra Nevada
Central Valley
San Joaquin Valley
Diablo Range
Coast Range
Santa Lucia Range
Sacramento Valley
Lake Tahoe
Reno
Sacramento
San Francisco
San Jose
Oakland
Stockton
Modesto
Fresno
Monterey Bay
78
287
6000m
4000m
3000m
2000m
1000m
500m
250m
100m
Sea Level
-250m
-2000m
-4000m

Scale 1:1,875,000
(projection: Lambert Conformal Conic)

0 10 20 30 40 50 Km
0 10 20 30 40 50 Miles

Population
- ■ above 5 million
- ▣ 1 million to 5 million
- ◉ 500,000 to 1 million
- ⊙ 100,000 to 500,000
- ⊕ 50,000 to 100,000
- ○ 10,000 to 50,000
- ∘ below 10,000

Major regions and features:

CALIFORNIA

ARIZONA

MEXICO

BAJA CALIFORNIA NORTE

NEVADA

PACIFIC OCEAN

Mojave Desert

Sonoran Desert

Death Valley

Panamint Range

Amargosa Range

Argus Range

San Gabriel Mountains

San Rafael Mountains

Tehachapi Mountains

Bullion Mountains

Chocolate Mountains

Channel Islands

Santa Catalina Island

San Clemente Island

San Nicolas Island

Santa Cruz Island

Santa Rosa Island

San Miguel Island

Santa Barbara Island

Gulf of Santa Catalina

San Pedro Channel

Santa Barbara Channel

Outer Santa Barbara Passage

Colorado River

Salton Sea

Lake Mead

Lake Havasu

Major cities/places (selection):

Los Angeles

Las Vegas

North Las Vegas

Henderson

Boulder City

Bakersfield

Long Beach

Santa Monica

Pasadena

Glendale

Inglewood

Torrance

Anaheim

Santa Ana

Riverside

San Bernardino

Ontario

Fontana

Corona

Oceanside

Carlsbad

Escondido

San Diego

National City

Chula Vista

Tijuana

Mexicali

El Centro

Palm Springs

Santa Barbara

Ventura

Oxnard

Thousand Oaks

Simi Valley

Santa Clarita

Lancaster

Palmdale

Victorville

Barstow

Needles

Blythe

Yuma

Ensenada

Rosarito

Elevation scale (feet):

19,686ft

13,124ft

9843ft

6562ft

3281ft

1640ft

820ft

328ft

Sea Level

-820ft

-6562ft

-13,124ft

79

84

287

NORTH AMERICA

82

193

294

286

Hawai'i Inset (United States of America, Hawai'i)

UNITED STATES
OF AMERICA
HAWAI'I

PACIFIC
OCEAN

Scale 1:5,000,000

0 20 40 60 80 100 120 Km
0 20 40 60 80 100 120 Miles

Hawaiian Islands

Kaua'i
Hanalei Kilauea
Kahala Point
Lehua Island Kapa'a
Pu'uwai Lihu'e
'Ele'ele Kōloa
Ni'ihau Makahū'ena Point
Kawaihoa Point
Waimea
Kaunakakai
Kekaha

O'ahu
Kahuku
Kahuku Point
Ka'ena Point Hau'ula
Wahiawa
Wai'anae Pearl City
Makakilo City Honolulu
'Ewa Beach
Diamond Head
Pearl Harbor

Moloka'i
Kalaupapa
Kaunakakai
Pailolo Channel
Nākālele Point
Kalohi Channel
Lāna'i City Lahaina Pā'ia Kailua
Lāna'i Kīhei Haleakalā Hāna
Kaho'olawe Pu'u 'Ula'ula (Red Hill) 3055m
'Alalākeiki Channel
'Alenuihaha Channel

Maui

Upolu Point
Hawi Honoka'a Laupahoehoe
Waimea Wailea
Keāhole Point Mauna Kea 4205m
Kalaoa Pāpa'ikou
Kailua-Kona Kea'au Hilo
Kahaluu Kealakekua Mountain View
Captain Cook Mauna Loa 4169m Pāhoa
Kalalea Kīlauea Cape Kumukahi
Pāhala Caldera
Kaunā Point Apua Point
Ka Lae (South Point) Na'alehu

Hawai'i

Main Map

ARCTIC

Chukchi Sea

Wainwright
Icy Cape
Point Lay
Elok Lok River
Cape Lisburne
Point Hope
Point Hope
De Lon
Kukpowruk River
Noatak River
Mishequk Mountain 1350m
Kivalina
Noatak
Tututalak Mountain 1366m
Baird
Kiana
Noorvik
Selawik
Selawik Lake
Kotzebue Sound
Cape Espenberg
Kobuk River
Buckland
Goodhope Bay
Deering Candle
Shishmaref
Kiwalik
Kougarok Mountain 875m
Brooks
Wales Mountain 685m
Brevig Mission
Port Clarence
Teller
Kauwerak River
Seward Peninsula
Koyuk River Haycock
Koyuk
Council
Solomon
Nome Elim
Cape Nome
Golovin
Cape Darby
Shaktoolik
Unalakleet

Poluostrov Chukotskiy
Enurmino
Arctic Circle
Ulen
Lavrentiya
Little Diomede Island
Big Diomede Island
Cape Prince of Wales
Cape Rodney
Provideniya
Mys Chukotskiy

Kamenskoye
CHUKOTSKIY AVTONOMNYY OKRUG
Velikaya
Nagor'ye
Gora Ledyanaya 2562m
Koryakskoye Nagor'ye
KORYAKSKIY AVTONOMNYY OKRUG
Kor Tilichiki
Pakhachi
Olyutorskiy Zaliv
Mys Olyutorskiy
Khatyrka
Meynypil'gyno
Beringovskiy
Anadyrskiy Zaliv
Mys Navarin

RUSSIAN FEDERATION

Northwest Cape Gambell Savoonga
Southwest Cape
Saint Lawrence Island
Northeast Cape Camp Kulowiye
Southeast Cape

Norton Sound
Stuart Island
Pastol Bay
Saint Michael
Stebbins
Hamilton
Kotlik
Alakanuk
Sheldons Point
Emmonak
Scammon Bay
Mountain Village
Saint Marys
Pitkas Point Russian Mission
Hooper Bay Chevak Pilot Station
Marshall
Aropuk Lake
Newtok
Hazen Bay
Tanunak
Baird Inlet
Nightmute
Kipnuk
Mekoryuk
Nunivak Island
Baird Strait
Chefornak
Kwigillingok
Quinhagak
Roberts Mountain 510m

Grayling
Shageluk
Anvik
Paradise
Holy Cross
Russian Mission
Lower Kalskag
Kalskag
Tuluksak
Akiachak
Kasigluk
Bethel Napakiak
Napaskiak
Tuntutuliak
Oscarville
Eek River
Eek
Kuskokwim Bay

Bering Sea

Limit of winter pack ice

Hall Island Glory of Russia Cape
Saint Matthew Island Upright Cape
Pinnacle Island
Cape Mohican
Cape Mendenhall

Bristol Bay

Saint Paul Island Saint Paul
Pribilof Islands
Saint George Island Saint George

Cape Newenham
Goodnews
Platinum
Togiak
Twin Hills
Hagemeister Island

Port Moller

Alaska
Amak Island
Cold Bay
Port Moller
Pavlof Volcano
Unimak Island
Pogromni Volcano 2002m
Shishaldin Volcano 2856m
False Pass
Korovin Island
Sand Point
Belkofski
King Cove
Deer Island
Nelson Lagoon
Shumagin Islands
Unimak Pass
Akutan Island
Makushin Volcano 2036m
Akutan
Unalaska Island
Dutch Harbor
Umnak Island
Krenitzin Islands
Fox Islands
Nikolski
Sanak Islands
Paulof Harbor
Pauloff Harbor
Yigalda Island
Avatanak Island

Near Islands
Cape Wrangell
Attu Island Attu
Agattu Strait
Shemya Island
Agattu Island Krugloi Point
Cape Sabak

Aleutian Islands

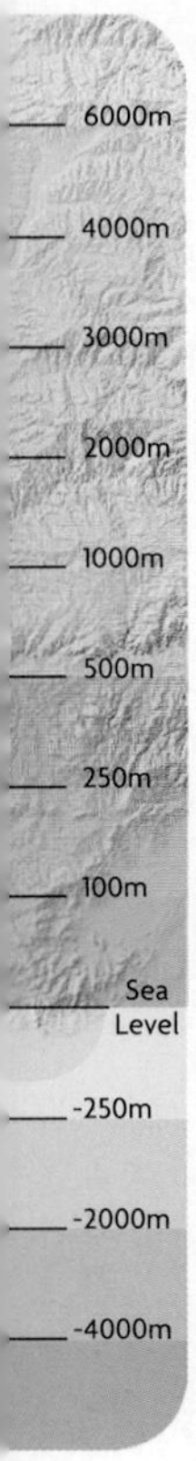

Kiska Island
Segula Island
Little Sitkin Island
Semisopochnoi Island
Vega Point
Rat Island
Amchikta Island
Anvil Peak 1221m
Rat Islands
Delarof Islands
Tanaga Volcano 1806m
Tanaga Island
Kanaga Volcano 1307m
Great Sitkin Island
Amchitka Pass
Garelot Island
Cape Kanaga
Sasmik Island
Adak Island
Kagalaska Island
Atka Island
Kagalaska
Atka
Korovin Volcano 1533m
Kanaton Ridge
Andreanof Islands
Amlia Island
Seguam Island
Seguam Pass
Amukta Island
Amukta Pass
Chagulak Island
Yunaska Island
Herbert Island
Carlisle Island
Islands of Four Mountains

Scale and relief legend:

6000m
4000m
3000m
2000m
1000m
500m
250m
100m
Sea Level
-250m
-2000m
-4000m

Scale 1:8,000,000
(projection: Lambert Conformal Conic)
0 25 50 75 100 125 150 175 200 Km
0 25 50 75 100 125 150 175 200 Miles
Population
above 5 million
1 million to 5 million
500,000 to 1 million
100,000 to 500,000
50,000 to 100,000
10,000 to 50,000
below 10,000
OCEAN
Beaufort Sea
Limit of summer pack ice
Amundsen Gulf
Dolphin and Union Strait
Cape Bathurst
Cape Parry
Cape Dalhousie
Liverpool Bay
Franklin Bay
NUNAVUT
Point Barrow
Barrow
Cape Halkett
Prudhoe Bay
Deadhorse
Kaktovik
Martin Point
Demarcation Point
Herschel Island
Mackenzie Bay
Tuktoyaktuk
Inuvik
Aklavik
Fort McPherson
Great Bear Lake
Brooks Range
Philip Smith Mountains
Davidson Mountains
British Mountains
Richardson Mountains
Endicott Mountains
Schwatka Mountains
Yukon Flats
Fort Yukon
Old Crow
Eagle Plain
NORTHWEST TERRITORIES
Fort Good Hope
Norman Wells
Mackenzie Mountains
Selwyn Mountains
UNITED STATES OF AMERICA
ALASKA
CANADA
YUKON TERRITORY
Ogilvie Mountains
Rocky Mountains
Fairbanks
College
North Pole
Dawson
Mayo
Keno Hill
Ross River
Pelly Mountains
Faro
Alaska Range
Mount McKinley (Denali) 6194m
Wrangell Mountains
Talkeetna Mountains
Chugach Mountains
Saint Elias Mountains
Mount Logan 5959m
Mount St Elias 5489m
Anchorage
Whitehorse
Watson Lake
Cassiar Mountains
Coast Mountains
Kenai Peninsula
Cook Inlet
Kodiak Island
Gulf of Alaska
Alexander Archipelago
Juneau
Chichagof Island
Baranof Island
Prince of Wales Island
Dixon Entrance
Prince Rupert
Graham Island
Queen Charlotte Islands
Hecate Strait
BRITISH COLUMBIA
PACIFIC OCEAN
294
287
54
19,686ft
13,124ft
9843ft
6562ft
3281ft
1640ft
820ft
328ft
Sea Level
-820ft
-6562ft
-13,124ft

Northern Mexico

UNITED STATES
ARIZONA
CALIFORNIA
SONORA
BAJA CALIFORNIA NORTE
BAJA CALIFORNIA SUR
SINALOA
Golfo de California
PACIFIC OCEAN
Tropic of Cancer
San Diego
Tijuana
Chula Vista
Mexicali
Yuma
San Luis
Ensenada
Tucson
Nogales
Hermosillo
Guaymas
Ciudad Obregón
Navojoa
Los Mochis
Culiacán
Santa Rosalía
Loreto
Ciudad Constitución
La Paz
San José del Cabo
Cabo San Lucas
Isla Guadalupe
Isla Cedros
Isla Ángel de la Guarda
Isla Tiburón
Isla Magdalena
Isla Santa Margarita
Islas Alijos
Bahía Sebastián Vizcaíno
Desierto de Altar
Sierra Madre Occidental
Douglas
Agua Prieta
Nuevo Casas Grandes
Lordsburg
Sierra Vista
Caborca
Magdalena
Empalme
Puerto Peñasco
San Felipe
San Quintín
Guerrero Negro
Mulegé
Todos Santos
78
287
6000m
4000m
3000m
2000m
1000m
500m
250m
100m
Sea Level
-250m
-2000m
-4000m

Scale 1:4,250,000
(projection: Lambert Conformal Conic)

0 20 40 60 80 100 Km
0 20 40 60 80 100 Miles

Population
- above 5 million
- 1 million to 5 million
- 500,000 to 1 million
- 100,000 to 500,000
- 50,000 to 100,000
- 10,000 to 50,000
- below 10,000

H I J K L M N

1 2 3 4 5 6 7 8 9 10

70

UNITED STATES OF AMERICA
NEW MEXICO
TEXAS
MEXICO
CHIHUAHUA
COAHUILA
NUEVO LEÓN
TAMAULIPAS
DURANGO
ZACATECAS
SAN LUIS POTOSÍ
NAYARIT
AGUASCALIENTES
JALISCO
GUANAJUATO
QUERÉTARO
HIDALGO
VERACRUZ-LLAVE
PUEBLA
Sierra Madre Occidental
Gulf of Mexico
Edwards Plateau
Balcones Escarpment
Rio Grande / Río Bravo del Norte
Tropic of Cancer

90

86

19,686ft
13,124ft
9843ft
6562ft
3281ft
1640ft
820ft
328ft
Sea Level
-820ft
-6562ft
-13,124ft

NORTH AMERICA

Southern Mexico
A B C D E F G
1 2 3 4 5 6 7 8 9 10
PACIFIC OCEAN
MEXICO
COAHUILA
NUEVO LEON
TAMAULIPAS
DURANGO
SINALOA
ZACATECAS
NAYARIT
AGUASCALIENTES
SAN LUIS POTOSI
JALISCO
GUANAJUATO
QUERETARO
HIDALGO
VERACRUZ-LLAVE
COLIMA
MICHOACAN
MEXICO
DISTRITO FEDERAL
TLAXCALA
MORELOS
PUEBLA
GUERRERO
Monterrey
Saltillo
Torreón
Gómez Palacio
Ciudad Lerdo
Durango
Mazatlán
Tepic
Zacatecas
Fresnillo
Aguascalientes
San Luis Potosí
Ciudad Victoria
Tampico
Ciudad Madero
Matamoros
Reynosa
Brownsville
McAllen
Guadalajara
Tlaquepaque
León
Guanajuato
Irapuato
Querétaro
Morelia
Colima
Manzanillo
Puerto Vallarta
Lázaro Cárdenas
Acapulco
Chilpancingo
Cuernavaca
Toluca
MEXICO (MEXICO CITY)
Pachuca
Puebla
Tlaxcala
Orizaba
Córdoba
Xalapa
Oaxaca
Tehuacán
Tuxpan
Poza Rica
Ciudad Mante
Ciudad Valles
Matehuala
Celaya
Salamanca
Uruapan
Zihuatanejo
Iguala
Taxco
Cuautla
Puerto Escondido
Padre Island
Tropic of Cancer
Islas Tres Marias
Isla María Madre
Isla María Magdalena
Isla María Cleofas
Bahía de Banderas
Cabo Corrientes
Laguna de Chapala
Laguna Madre
Laguna de Tamiahua
Sierra Madre Oriental
Sierra Madre del Sur
6000m
4000m
3000m
2000m
1000m
500m
250m
100m
Sea Level
-250m
-2000m
-4000m
70
287
287

Scale 1:4,250,000
(projection: Lambert Conformal Conic)

0 20 40 60 80 100 Km
0 20 40 60 80 100 Miles

Population
■ above 5 million   ▣ 1 million to 5 million   ◉ 500,000 to 1 million
◎ 100,000 to 500,000   ⊕ 50,000 to 100,000   ○ 10,000 to 50,000   ∘ below 10,000

Mexico City

Ciudad Adolfo
López Mateos

0 5 Km
0 5 Miles

Tlalnepantla
Basílica de Guadalupe
Valle de Aragón
Canal de la Compañía
Lago Nabor Carrillo
Naucalpan de Juárez
Gustavo A. Madero
Azcapotzalco
zoo
Parque San Juan de Aragón
Nezahualcoyotl
Catedral
Benito Juárez Airport
Venustiano Carranza
México (Mexico City)
Castillo de Chapultepec
Cuauhtémoc
Iztacalco
La Perla
Bosque de Chapultepec
Miguel Hidalgo
Benito Juárez
Iztapalapa
Las Aguilas
Parque Nacional Cerro de Estrella
San Bernabe Ocotepec
Coyoacán
Reserva Ecológica del Pedregal
Estadio Azteca
Álvaro Obregón
Pirámide de Cuicuilco
Parque de Xochimilco
Tlalpan
Xochimilco
Tlahuac

Gulf of Mexico

Tropic of Cancer

Cabo Catoche
Isla Contoy
Punta Yalkabul   San Felipe   Río Lagartos   El Cuyo   Isla Holbox   Laguna de Yalahau   Chiquilá   Isla Mujeres
Telchac Puerto   Dzilam de Bravo   Panabá
Chicxulub   Progreso   Conkal   Motul   Temax   Tizimín   Yucatan   X-Can   León Vicario   Cancún
Sisal   Hunucmá   Hoctún   Tunkas   Cenotillo   Espita   Kantunilkin   Puerto Juárez   Isla Cancún
Celestún   Mérida   Xocchel   Kantunil   Izamal   Dzitas   Piste   Chichén-Itzá   Valladolid   Chemax   Puerto Morelos   Punta Molas del Norte
San Rafael   Soluta   Tekit   Zavala   Sotuta   Yaxcaba   Chichimila   Coba   Playa del Carmen   Melas   Cozumel
Maxcanú   Muna   Sacalum   Teabo   Mani   Oxkutzcab   Peto   Tihosuco   Xel-Há   Akumal   Isla Cozumel
La Costa   Halacho   Calkini   Dzibalche   Ticul   Tekax   Tzucacab   Santa Rosa   San Ramon   Ruinas de Tulum   Muyil
Jaina   Hecelchakán   Xul   Bolónchén de Rejón   Becanchen   Filomeno Mata   Vigia Chico   Xmaben   Punta Allen   Bahía de la Ascensión
Campeche   Lerma   Chencoyi   Hope-chen   Polyuc   Chunhuhub   Xiatil   Felipe Carrillo Puerto
Seybaplaye   Sihochac   Arellano   Pich   Chencoh   Iturbide   Dzibalchen   Naranjal Poniente   Pelcacab   Punta Herrero
Champotón   Tixmal   Pustunich   Valle Hermoso   Chacchoben   Bahía del Espíritu Santo
Majahual
Reforma   Laguna Bacalar   Banco Chinchorro   Cayo Centro
Chekubul   Francisco Escárcega   Xpujil   Kohunlich   Laguna Milagros   Chetumal   Banco Chinchorro   Cayo Lobos
Sabancuy   Mamantel   El Corozal   Pucte   Corozal   Rocky Point   Boca Bacalar Chico
Isla del Carmen   Isla Aguada   Puerto Real   Candelaria   Tres Garantias   Tomas Garrido   Caledonia   Orange Walk   Ambergris Cay   San Pedro
Carmen   Laguna de Términos   Zacatal   Nuevo Coahuila   La Union   Indian Church   New River   Altun Ha   Turneffe Islands
Alvaro Obregon   Frontera   Palizada   Carmelita   Hill Bank   Belize   Belize City   Lighthouse Reef
Paraíso   Tikal   Xunantunich   Belize   Glovers Reef
San Joaquin   Jonuta   Balancán   Benque Viejo   San Ignacio   Middlesex
Comalcalco   Emiliano Zapata   Tenito Juárez   Flores   Ciudad Melchor de Mencos   Cayo   Dangriga   Stann Creek
Cunduacán   Jalpa   Astapilla   Petén   Lago Petén Itzá   Victoria Peak 1120m   Maya Mountains
Cárdenas   Villahermosa   Morelos   Tenosique   San Benito   Richardson Peak   Monkey River Town
Reforma   Catazaja   La Libertad   Dolores   San Luis   Toledo   Punta Gorda   Gulf of Honduras
Huimanguillo   Teapa   Salto de Agua   Palenque   Sayaxché   San Antonio   Modesto Mendez   Punta Manabique
Pichucalco   Ixtapangajoya   Itla   Bonampak   Yaxchilan   Sarstoon   Bahía de Amatique   Puerto Barrios   Cortés   Santa
Ostuacán   Tapijulapa   Ciudad   Santo Tomás de Castilla
Volcán El Chichónal 1064m   Tecpatan   Copainala   Puerto Cortés
Raudales   Simojovel   Sierra del Lacandón   Morales   San Pedro Sula
Presa Netzahualcóyotl   Apic-Pac   Pantelho   Ocosingo   Los Amates   El Progreso
San Cristóbal de Las Casas   Altamirano   Santa Cruz del Quiché   Cobán   Izabal   Quiriguá
Benito Juárez   Tuxtla   Chiapa de Corzo   Teopisca   Las Rosas   Alta Verapaz   Salama   Zacapa   Copán   Santa Bárbara

GULF of MEXICO

Bahía de Campeche

Yucatan
Peninsula

YUCATÁN

CAMPECHE

QUINTANA ROO

TABASCO

BELIZE
BELMOPAN

PETÉN

NORTH AMERICA

87

90

Punta del Morro
Punta Mancha
Punta Villa Rica
Punta Zempoala
Zempoala   Cardel
La Antigua
Veracruz   Boca del Río
Jamapa   Punta de Antón Lizardo   Antón Lizardo
Fortín   Ignacio de La Llave   Alvarado   Punta Roca Partida   Isla del Carmen
Acatlan   Joachin   Tlacotalpan   Laguna de Términos
Tierra Blanca   San Andrés Tuxtla   Sanchez Magallanes
Tres Valles   Catemaco   Tonala
Presa M. Alemán Azueta   Juan Díaz Covarrubias   Mata Espino   Comalcalco
San Felipe   Tuxtepec   Mata Limones   Soteapan   Jalpa   San Joaquin
Juan Rodríguez Clara   Acayucan   Cosoleacaque   Cunduacán
Valle Nacional   Abasolo del Valle   Sayula de Aleman   Minatitlan   Cárdenas   Villahermosa
Quiotepec   Yogope   Medias Aguas   Filisola   Zanapa   Reforma   Catazaja
Guelatao   Jesús Carranza   Chalchijapan   Huimanguillo   Pichucalco
Ixtlán de Juárez   Villa Alta   Santiago Chuapan   Suchilapan   Cuauhtémoc   Ostuacán
Totontepec   Zacatepec   Istmo de   Volcán El Chichónal
OAXACA   Cerro Zempoaltepec 3395m   Tehuantepec   Tecpatan   Raudales
Alpuebradas   Mitla   San Pedro Quiatoní   Matías Romero   San Miguel Chimalapa   Santo Domingo   Cintalapa   Tuxtla   Chiapa de Corzo
Ocotlán   Yaxe   Juquila Mixes   Lázaro Cárdenas   Cococuautla   Suchiapa   Teopisca
Totolapan   Zoquitlan   Union Hidalgo   CHIAPAS   Venustiano Carranza   Las Margaritas
Coatecas   Quiechapa   Ixtepec   Lxhuatan   Ixtapanatepec   Tzimol   Comitán   La Trinitaria
Miahuatlán   Ecatepec   Juchitán   Laguna Superior   Arriaga   Villa Flores   Francisco Sarabia
Salina Cruz   Laguna Inferior   Rincón   Chahuites   Villa Corzo   La Concordia
Santiago Astata   Mar Muerto   Paredon   Tonalá   Jaltenango   Presa de la Angostura
Huatulco   Tehuantepec   Sierra Madre   Barillas
Pochutla   Golfo de Tehuantepec   Puerto Arista   Tres Picos   Chisec   El Palmar
Puerto Ángel   Salina Cruz   El Manguito   Pijijiapan   Ciudad   Rabinal   Salamá   Sierra de las Minas   Gracias
Mapastepec   Cuauhtémoc   HUEHUETENANGO   QUICHÉ   Cobán   Represa El Chixoy
El Talismán   Comalapa   Sierra de los Cuchumatanes   San Cristóbal Verapaz   Victoria
Cerro Tres Cruces 2932m   Motozintla   Volcán Tacaná 4093m   GUATEMALA   Zacapa   Ruinas de Copán   HONDURAS
Tuzantan   Ixtahuacán   SAN   Chichicastenango   COMAYAGUA
Tapachula   Escuintla   MARCOS   Lago de Atitlán   Santiago   CIUDAD DE   San Luis   Esquipulas
Puerto Madero   San Marcos   Quezaltenango   Sololá   Atitlán   GUATEMALA   Jalapa   La Esperanza
Ciudad Hidalgo   Colomba   Totonicapán   GUATEMALA CITY   Jutiapa   Nueva Ocotepeque   INTIBUCA   San Antonio
Retalhuleu   Mazatenango   EL SALVADOR   LEMPIRA   La Paz
Tilapa   Champerico   Pueblo Nuevo Tiquisate   Escuintla   Chiquimulilla   Santa Ana

Golfo de Tehuantepec

Istmo de Tehuantepec

OAXACA

CHIAPAS

Sierra Madre

GUATEMALA

HONDURAS

EL SALVADOR

ALTA VERAPAZ

QUICHÉ

Gulf of Honduras

Punta Sal

CORTÉS   YORO

GUATEMALA:
ADMINISTRATIVE REGIONS:

① RETALHULEU
② QUEZALTENANGO
③ TOTONICAPÁN
④ SOLOLÁ
⑤ SUCHITEPÉQUEZ
⑥ ESCUINTLA
⑦ CHIMALTENANGO
⑧ SACATEPÉQUEZ
⑨ GUATEMALA
⑩ BAJA VERAPAZ
⑪ EL PROGRESSO
⑫ ZACAPA
⑬ CHIQUIMULA
⑭ JALAPA
⑮ SANTA ROSA
⑯ JUTIAPA

19,686ft
13,124ft
9843ft
6562ft
3281ft
1640ft
820ft
328ft
Sea Level
-820ft
-6562ft
-13,124ft

NORTH AMERICA

88

GUATEMALA:
ADMINISTRATIVE REGIONS:
① RETALHULEU   ⑨ GUATEMALA
② QUEZALTENANGO   ⑩ BAJA VERAPAZ
③ TOTONICAPÁN   ⑪ EL PROGRESO
④ SOLOLÁ   ⑫ ZACAPA
⑤ SUCHITEPÉQUEZ   ⑬ CHIQUIMULA
⑥ ESCUINTLA   ⑭ JALAPA
⑦ CHIMALTENANGO   ⑮ SANTA ROSA
⑧ SACATEPÉQUEZ   ⑯ JUTIAPA

EL SALVADOR:
ADMINISTRATIVE REGIONS:
① AHUACHAPÁN   ⑧ CABAÑAS
② SANTA ANA   ⑨ LA PAZ
③ SONSONATE   ⑩ SAN VICENTE
④ CHALATENANGO   ⑪ USULUTÁN
⑤ LA LIBERTAD   ⑫ SAN MIGUEL
⑥ SAN SALVADOR   ⑬ MORAZÁN
⑦ CUSCATLÁN   ⑭ LA UNIÓN

Guatemala City

Scale 1:4,250,000
(projection: Lambert Conformal Conic)

0 20 40 60 80 100 Km

0 20 40 60 80 100 Miles

Population
- ■ above 5 million
- ◉ 100,000 to 500,000
- ▣ 1 million to 5 mllion
- ⊕ 50,000 to 100,000
- ◉ 500,000 to 1 million
- ⊙ 10,000 to 50,000
- ○ below 10,000

90

102

90

Panama City

Sara Sotillo
San Miguelito
Santa Clara
Villa Caceres
Miraflores
Villa de Fuentes
Rio Abajo
Juan Díaz
Reparto Nuevo Panamá
Nuevo Paitilla
Clayton
Curundú
Pueblo Nuevo
El Cangrejo
Los Angeles
Coco del Mar
Parque Nacional Metropolitano
Lo Locería
Parque Omar Torrijos Herrera
San Francisco
Bahía de Panamá
Corozal
Iglesia del Carmen
Panamá (Panama City)
Bella Vista
Museo de las Ciencias Naturales
Aeropuerto de Paitilla
Aeropuerto Albrook
Calidonia
Bahía de Panamá
Altos de Diablo
Museo Reina Torres de Araúz
Pacific Ocean
Anacón
Canal de Panamá
Balboa
Palacio Presidencial
Santa Ana
Iglesia de San José

0 1 Km
0 1 Miles

JAMAICA

Montego Bay
Lucea
Grange Hill
South Negril Point
Savanna-La-Mar
Crab Pond Point
Black River
Great Pedro Bluff
Long Bay
Falmouth
The Cockit Country
Mount Denham 2256m
Christiana
Mandeville
Malvern 25m
May Pen
Lionel Town
Portland Point
Ocho Rios
Annotto Bay
Spanish Town
Old Harbour
Normah Manley
KINGSTON
Port Maria
Port Antonio
North East Point
Mountain Peak 2256m
Morant Bay
Jamaica Channel

Caribbean Sea

Laguna de Caratasca
Puerto Lempira
GRACIAS A DIOS
Cabo de Gracias a Dios
Río Coco
Boom
Laguna Bismuna
Arrecifes de la Media Luna
Arrecife Edinburgh
Cayo Muerto
Cayos Miskitos
Cayos Londres
Waspam
Río Wawa
Yablis
REGIÓN AUTÓNOMA
Dakura
San Luis
La Rosita
ATLÁNTICO
Río Bambana
Alamikamba
Wounta
NORTE
Makantaka
Prinzapolka
Cayos Guerrero
Barra de Río Grande
REGIÓN AUTÓNOMO
Kara
La Cruz de Río Grande
Cayos King
Cayos de Perlas
ATLÁNTICO SUR
Laguna de Perlas
Punta de Perlas
Punta Mosquito
Islas del Maíz
Río Escondido
El Rama
Kama
Bahía de Bluefields
Bluefields
El Bluff
Nueva Guinea
Río Punta Gorda
Monkey Point
Punta Gorda
El Castillo de La Concepción
San Juan del Norte
Río San Juan
Barra del Colorado
Río Colorado
HEREDIA
Itamira
Puerto Viejo
Puesada
Grecia
Volcán Poás 2704m
Volcán Barva 2906m
Volcán Irazú 3339m
SAN JOSÉ
San Ignacio
San Marcos
Cerro La Muerte 3491m
Quepos
Paraíso
CARTAGO
Turrialba
Bribri
Buabito
LIMÓN
Matina
Limón
Punta Mona
Dominical
PUNTARENAS
Cortés
Buenos Aires
Cerro Chirripó Grande 3819m
San Isidro
Cerro Kámuk 3554m
Changuinola
Bocas del Toro
Archipiélago de Bocas del Toro
Península Valiente
Coclé del Norte
Bahía de Coronado
Palmar Sur
Península de Osa
Golfo Dulce
San Vito
Volcán Barú 3475m
Boquete
Cerro Chorcha 2238m
COSTA RICA
Río Chiriquí
BOCAS DEL TORO
Golfito
La Concepción
David
CHIRIQUÍ
Volcán
Remedios
Puerto Armuelles
Isla Sevilla
Isla Parida
Golfo de Chiriquí
Punta Burica
Horconcitos
Cerro Santiago 2121m
Calobre
Santa Fe
VERAGUAS
Las Palmas
Soná
Santiago
Río de Jesús
Atalaya
Santa María
Guarumal
HERRERA
Macaracas
Las Tablas
Pedasí
Punta Mala
Isla de Coiba
Isla Cébaco
Cerro Hoya 1560m
Península LOS SANTOS
Tonosí

PANAMA

Golfo de Panamá

Archipiélago de San Blas
Portobelo
Santa Isabel
El Porvenir
Colón
Nuevo Chagres
Miguel de la Borda
Lago Gatún
Panama City
Chepo
PANAMÁ
Ailigandi
SAN BLAS
Punta Mosquito
Gulf of Darien
Cordillera de Santos
Serranía del Darién
Arboletes
Lorica
CÓRDOBA
La Chorra
Capira
Cerro Peña Blanca 1314m
El Valle
Cerro 1172m
COCLÉ
Penonomé
Antón
Aguadulce
Natá
Río Hato
Nueva Gorgona
Chame
Punta Chame
PANAMÁ (PANAMA CITY)
San Miguelito
Balboa
Bahía de Panamá
Archipiélago de las Perlas
San Carlos
Isla del Rey
Isla San José
Punta Garachiné
Punta Brava
Golfo de San Miguel
San Miguel
Garachiné
La Palma
DARIÉN
Río Chucunaque
Cerro Pirre 1200m
Puerto Obaldía
Adandi
Río Tuira
El Real
Cerro Tacarcuna 1875m
Turbo
Río Atrato
CHOCÓ
Jaqué
Jurado
Tierralta
Montería
COLOMBIA
ANTIOQUIA
Dabeiba
Frontino

19,686ft
13,124ft
9843ft
6562ft
3281ft
1640ft
820ft
328ft
Sea Level
-820ft
-6562ft
-13,124ft

UNITED STATES OF AMERICA

Saint Petersburg · Bradenton · Avon Park · Sebastian · Vero Beach
Sarasota · Arcadia · Fort Pierce · Jensen Beach · Stuart
Venice · Okeechobee · Hobe Sound
Port Charlotte · Punta Gorda · La Belle · Indiantown
Fort Myers · **FLORIDA** · Belle Glade · West Palm Beach · West End
Bonita Springs · Big Cypress Swamp · Lake Worth · Boynton Beach · Freeport · Eight Mile Rock
Naples · The Everglades · Boca Raton · Pompano Beach
Everglades City · Fort Lauderdale · Hollywood
Cape Romano · Hialeah · North Miami · Miami Beach
Cape Sable · Kendall · **Miami** · Homestead
Bimini Islands

Gulf of Mexico

Dry Tortugas · Marathon
Marquesas Keys · Key West · Florida Keys · Key Largo · Islamorada
Florida Bay

Straits of Florida

Grand Bahama Island · Great Sale Cay · Little Abaco · Coopers Town
Pelican Point · Marsh Harbour · Great Abaco · Cherokee Sound
Moores Island

Northwest Providence Channel
Berry Islands · Nicholls Town · Current · Eleuthera Island
Northeast Providence Channel

BAHAMAS
Adelaide · **NASSAU** · New Providence · Governor's Harbour
Androa Town · Behring Point · Rock Sound
Andros Island · Bannerman Town · Arthur's Town · Cat Island
Tongue of the Ocean · Exuma Sound
Kemp's Bay · Great Guana Cay · Exuma Cays · Cockburn Town · San Salvador
Cay Sal · Anguilla Cays · Columbus Point · Conception Island
Santaren Channel · Great Exuma Island · George Town · Little Exuma · Rum Cay
Nicholas Channel · Long Island · Clarence Town · Crooked Island Passage
Archipiélago de Sabana · Old Bahama Channel · Cape Verde · Deadman's Cay · Samana Cay
Archipiélago de Camagüey · Colonel Hill · Plana Cays · Mayaguana
Ragged Island Range · Acklins Island · Snug Corner · The Carlton · Mayaguana Passage
Salina Point · Southeast Point

La HABANA (HAVANA)
Mariel · Guanabacoa · Matanzas
Artemisa · Jovellanos
Minas de Matahambre · Güines · Santa Domingo
San Cristóbal · Güira de Melena · Jagüey Grande · Colón · Santa Clara
Pinar del Río · Consolación del Sur · Los Palacios · Cruces · Placetas
Península de Zapata · Aguada de Pasajeros · Cienfuegos · Cayo Fragoso
Golfo de Guanahacabibes · Cabo San Antonio · Cayo Coco
Nueva Gerona · Cayo Largo · Pico San Juan 1150m · Sancti Spíritus · Morón
Santa Fé · Trinidad · Ciego de Ávila
Isla de la Juventud · Archipiélago de los Canarreos · **CUBA**
Golfo de Ana María · Camagüey
Archipiélago de los Jardines de la Reina · Florida · Nuevitas
Vertientes · Puerto Padre · Great Inagua
Santa Cruz del Sur · Las Tunas · Gibara · Lake Rosa
San Pedro · Holguín · Cabo Lucrecia · Matthew Town
Golfo de Guacanayabo · Bayamo · Jiguaní · Cueto · Moa · Northeast Point
Manzanillo · Palma Soriano · Sierra del Cristal · Baracoa
Campechuela · La Maya · Maisí
Cabo Cruz · Pico Turquino 1944m · Santiago de Cuba · **Guantánamo** · Île de la Tortue
Sierra Maestra · Bahía de Guantánamo (to US)

Great Antilles

Windward Passage

HAITI
Port-de-Paix · Jean-Rabel · Gros-Morne · Gonaïves
Môle-St-Nicolas · St-Marc
Golfe de la Gonâve · Canal de St-Marc
Cap Dame Marie · Dame-Marie · Canal de la Gonâve
Jérémie · Corail · Île de la Gonâve · Léogâne
Massif de la Hotte · Petit Goâve
Chardonnières · Port Salut · Cayes · Jacmel
Pointe à Gravois · Île à Vache

CAYMAN ISLANDS (to UK)
Little Cayman · Cayman Brac
Owen Roberts · Bodden Town
GEORGE TOWN · Grand Cayman

JAMAICA
Sangster · Montego Bay · Port Maria
South Negril Point · Christiana · Port Antonio
Savanna-La-Mar · Mandeville · Spanish Town
Black River · May Pen · **KINGSTON** · Morant Bay
Blue Mountain Peak 2256m · Norman Manley
Portland Point

NAVASSA ISLAND (to US) · Jamaica Channel

ISLAS DE LA BAHÍA
Roatán · Isla de Guanaja
Isla de Roatán · Punta Caxinas
Balfate · Trujillo · Tupán · Triunfo
Río Aguán · Brus Laguna
San Esteban · Puerto Lempira
Gualaco · **HONDURAS** · Cabo de Gracias a Dios
GRACIAS A DIOS · Río Coco
Juticalpa · OLANCHO · Waspam
Bocay · Laguna Bismuna
Bonanza · Yablis · Dákura
La Rosita · San Luis · Tuapi
REGIÓN AUTÓNOMA · ATLÁNTICO NORTE · Puerto Cabezas
Jinotega · Wounta
Matagalpa · Prinzapolka
MATAGALPA · Río Grande de Matagalpa
Muelle de los Bueyes · La Sirena · Barra de Río Grande
BOACO · Kara
Boaco · Cayos King
CHONTALES · **NICARAGUA** · Cayos de Perlas · Islas del Maíz
Juigalpa · El Escondido · Bluefields
Muelle de los Bueyes · REGIÓN AUTÓNOMA · Monkey Point
Lago de Nicaragua · ATLÁNTICA SUR
Volcán Concepción · Río Punta Gorda · Punta Gorda
Rivas · Río San Juan · RÍO SAN JUAN
Isla de Ometepe · San Miguelito
San Carlos
El Castillo de la Concepción · San Juan del Norte
Los Chiles · Barra del Colorado
Upala · Puerto Viejo
GUANACASTE · ALAJUELA · HEREDIA · LIMÓN
Cañas · Quesada · Heredia
Puntarenas · Alajuela · **COSTA RICA** · Limón
SAN JOSÉ

Caribbean Sea

Arrecifes de la Media Luna
Cabo de Gracias a Dios · Arrecife Edinburgh
Cayo Muerto · Cayos Miskitos · Cayos Londres
Cayos Guerrero

COLOMBIA
Ríohacha · Dibulla
Santa Marta · Pajaro
Barranquilla · Ciénaga
Puerto Colombia · MAGDALENA · Pico Cristóbal Colón 5775m
Soledad · ATLÁNTICO
Cartagena · Valledupar

Jamaica inset

JAMAICA · Caribbean Sea
Montego Bay · Sangster · Falmouth · Discovery Bay
Lucea · Clark's Town · St Ann's Bay · Port Maria
Dolphin Head · The Cockpit Country · Browns Town · Ocho Rios
Negril · Birch Hill 545m · Grange Hill · Mount Denham 888m · Alexandria · Claremont · Don Christophers Point
Little London · Cambridge · Frankfield · Linstead · Annotto Bay · Buff Bay
Savanna-La-Mar · Christiana · Ewarton · Highgate · Port Antonio
Crab Pond Point · Maggotty · Mandeville · Spanish Town · Bog Walk · North East Point
Santa Cruz · May Pen · Blue Mountain Peak 2256m
Black River · Malvern 725m · Old Harbour · Portmore · **KINGSTON** · Golden Grove
Alligator Pond · Lionel Town · Port Royal · Yallahs Hill · Bath · Port Morant
Great Pedro Bluff · Long Bay · Portland Bight · Wreck Point · Morant Bay

Caribbean Sea · Portland Point

Scale 1:2,500,000
0 5 10 20 Km
0 5 10 20 Miles

Scale bar (elevation):
6000m · 4000m · 3000m · 2000m · 1000m · 500m · 250m · 100m · Sea Level · -250m · -2000m · -4000m

Scale 1:6,250,000
(projection: Lambert Conformal Conic)
0 25 50 75 100 125 150 175 200 Km
0 25 50 75 100 125 150 175 200 Miles
Population
above 5 million
1 million to 5 million
500,000 to 1 million
100,000 to 500,000
50,000 to 100,000
10,000 to 50,000
below 10,000
GUADELOUPE
(to France)
Guadeloupe Passage
Port-Louis
Grande Terre
Basse Terre
Pointe-à-Pitre
Ste-Anne
St-François
Capesterre-Belle-Eau
BASSE-TERRE
Canal des Saintes
Caribbean Sea
ATLANTIC OCEAN
Scale 1:2,500,000
DOMINICA
Portsmouth
Marigot
Castle Bruce
Rosalie
La Plaine
ROSEAU
Berekua
Martinique Passage
Scale 1:2,000,000
MARTINIQUE
(to France)
Martinique Passage
Grand' Rivière
Basse-Pointe
Ste-Marie
St-Pierre
le Robert
le Lamentin
FORT-DE-FRANCE
le François
Rivière-Pilote
Ste-Anne
Saint Lucia Channel
ST LUCIA
Pointe Du Cap
Gros Islet
CASTRIES
Dennery
Soufrière
Micoud
Vieux Fort
Saint Vincent Passage
BARBADOS
North Point
Speightstown
Holetown
Bathsheba
BRIDGETOWN
Oistins
The Crane
Grantley Adams
ST VINCENT & THE GRENADINES
Saint Vincent Passage
Fancy
Georgetown
Barrouallie
KINGSTOWN
Stubbs
GRENADA
Sauteurs
Victoria
Gouyave
Grenville
ST GEORGE'S
St David's
Grand Anse
Point Salines
ATLANTIC OCEAN
TURKS & CAICOS ISLANDS
(to UK)
Caicos Islands
Grand Caicos
East Caicos
South Caicos
Grand Turk Island
COCKBURN TOWN
Turks Islands
Mouchoir Passage
Tropic of Cancer
Hispaniola
DOMINICAN REPUBLIC
Monte Cristi
Cabo Isabela
Puerto Plata
Cap-Haïtien
Santiago
Cabo Francés Viejo
Bahía Escocesa
San Francisco de Macorís
Bahía de Samaná
La Vega
Pico Duarte 3175m
Cabo Engaño
Higüey
San Pedro de Macorís
La Romana
PORT-AU-PRINCE
SANTO DOMINGO
Barahona
Isla Saona
Pedernales
Isla Beata
Cabo Beata
Mona Passage
Isla Mona
PUERTO RICO
(to US)
SAN JUAN
Arecibo
Bayamón
Carolina
Caguas
Mayagüez
Ponce
Guayama
Aguadilla
Cabo Rojo
BRITISH VIRGIN ISLANDS
(to UK)
Anegada
ROAD TOWN
Tortola
CHARLOTTE AMALIE
VIRGIN ISLANDS
(to US)
St Croix
Christiansted
Frederiksted
Vieques
Culebra
Virgin Passage
Anegada Passage
Sombrero
(to Anguilla)
ANGUILLA
(to UK)
THE VALLEY
St-Martin (to France)
Philipsburg
Sint Maarten
(to Netherlands)
St-Barthélemy
(to France)
Saba
St Eustatius
NETHERLANDS ANTILLES
(to Netherlands)
BASSETERRE
ST KITTS & NEVIS
Nevis
Charlestown
ANTIGUA & BARBUDA
Codrington
Barbuda
Antigua
ST JOHN'S
Redonda
PLYMOUTH
MONTSERRAT
(to UK)
Guadeloupe Passage
la Désirade
GUADELOUPE
(to France)
Marie-Galante
Grand-Bourg
BASSE-TERRE
les Saintes
Dominica Passage
DOMINICA
ROSEAU
MARTINIQUE
(to France)
FORT-DE-FRANCE
St Lucia Channel
CASTRIES
ST LUCIA
BARBADOS
BRIDGETOWN
St Vincent Passage
KINGSTOWN
ST VINCENT & THE GRENADINES
Bequia
Mustique
Canouan
Union Island
Carriacou
The Grenadines
GRENADA
ST GEORGE'S
Leeward Islands
Lesser Antilles
Windward Islands
ATLANTIC OCEAN
PUERTO RICO
(to US)
ATLANTIC OCEAN
Caribbean Sea
Isla de Vieques
Isla de Culebra
Scale 1:2,500,000
TRINIDAD & TOBAGO
Caribbean Sea
Galera Point
PORT-OF-SPAIN
Arima
Sangre Grande
Chaguanas
Couva
Trinidad
Gulf of Paria
San Fernando
Point Fortin
Siparia
Rio Claro
Moruga
Galeota Point
The Serpent's Mouth
The Dragon's Mouth
VENEZUELA
Scale 1:2,500,000
Lesser Antilles
ARUBA
(to Netherlands)
ORANJESTAD
NETHERLANDS ANTILLES
(to Netherlands)
Curaçao
WILLEMSTAD
Bonaire
Kralendijk
Islas Las Aves
Islas Los Roques
Isla La Orchila
Isla Blanquilla
Islas Los Testigos
Tobago
Scarborough
Charlotteville
TRINIDAD & TOBAGO
PORT-OF-SPAIN
Punta Gallinas
Península de la Guajira
Golfo de Venezuela
Maracaibo
Coro
VENEZUELA
Isla La Tortuga
Isla de Margarita
NUEVA ESPARTA
La Asunción
Porlamar
Cumaná
Barcelona
CARACAS
Valencia
Maracay
Maturín
Gulf of Paria

290
102

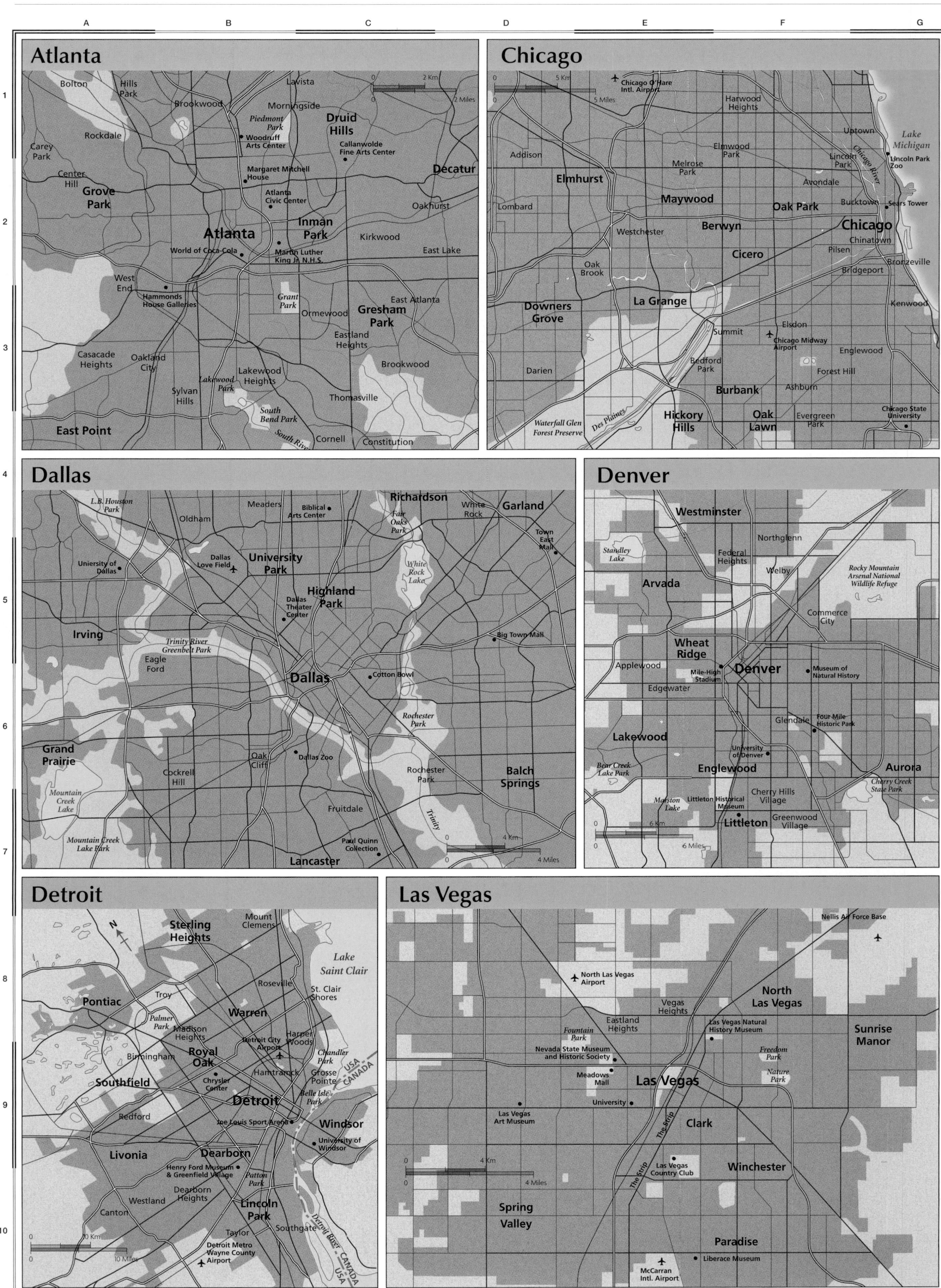

Atlanta

Bolton · Hills Park · Lavista · Brookwood · Morningside · Piedmont Park · Druid Hills · Woodruff Arts Center · Callanwolde Fine Arts Center · Rockdale · Carey Park · Center Hill · Grove Park · Margaret Mitchell House · Atlanta Civic Center · Decatur · Oakhurst · Atlanta · Inman Park · Kirkwood · East Lake · World of Coca-Cola · Martin Luther King Jr N.H.S. · West End · Hammonds House Galleries · Grant Park · Ormewood · Gresham Park · East Atlanta · Casacade Heights · Oakland City · Lakewood Park · Lakewood Heights · Eastland Heights · Brookwood · Sylvan Hills · Thomasville · East Point · South Bend Park · South River · Cornell · Constitution

0 2 Km
0 2 Miles

Chicago

Chicago O'Hare Intl. Airport · Harwood Heights · Uptown · Lake Michigan · Addison · Elmwood Park · Lincoln Park · Lincoln Park Zoo · Melrose Park · Avondale · Elmhurst · Maywood · Oak Park · Bucktown · Sears Tower · Lombard · Westchester · Berwyn · Chicago · Chinatown · Cicero · Pilsen · Bronzeville · Oak Brook · Bridgeport · Downers Grove · La Grange · Kenwood · Summit · Elsdon · Chicago Midway Airport · Englewood · Darien · Bedford Park · Forest Hill · Burbank · Ashburn · Chicago State University · Waterfall Glen Forest Preserve · Des Plaines · Hickory Hills · Oak Lawn · Evergreen Park

0 5 Km
0 5 Miles

Dallas

L.B. Houston Park · Meaders · Biblical Arts Center · Richardson · White Rock · Garland · Oldham · Fair Oaks Park · Town East Mall · University Park · Dallas Love Field · White Rock Lake · Uniersity of Dallas · Highland Park · Dallas Theater Center · Irving · Big Town Mall · Trinity River Greenbelt Park · Eagle Ford · Dallas · Cotton Bowl · Rochester Park · Grand Prairie · Oak Cliff · Dallas Zoo · Rochester Park · Balch Springs · Cockrell Hill · Mountain Creek Lake · Fruitdale · Trinity · Mountain Creek Lake Park · Paul Quinn Collection · Lancaster

0 4 Km
0 4 Miles

Denver

Westminster · Northglenn · Standley Lake · Federal Heights · Welby · Rocky Mountain Arsenal National Wildlife Refuge · Arvada · Commerce City · Wheat Ridge · Denver · Museum of Natural History · Applewood · Mile-High Stadium · Edgewater · Lakewood · Glendale · Four Mile Historic Park · Bear Creek Lake Park · University of Denver · Englewood · Aurora · Cherry Hills Village · Cherry Creek State Park · Marston Lake · Littleton Historical Museum · Greenwood Village · Littleton

0 6 Km
0 6 Miles

Detroit

Sterling Heights · Mount Clemens · Lake Saint Clair · Pontiac · Troy · Roseville · St. Clair Shores · Palmer Park · Madison Heights · Warren · Harper Woods · Birmingham · Detroit City Airport · Chandler Park · Grosse Pointe · Royal Oak · Hamtramck · Belle Isle Park · Southfield · Chrysler Center · Detroit · Windsor · Joe Louis Sport Arena · University of Windsor · Redford · Livonia · Dearborn · Henry Ford Museum & Greenfield Village · Patton Park · Dearborn Heights · Lincoln Park · Westland · Canton · Taylor · Southgate · USA CANADA · Detroit Metro Wayne County Airport · Detroit River

0 10 Km
0 10 Miles

Las Vegas

Nellis Air Force Base · North Las Vegas Airport · Vegas Heights · North Las Vegas · Eastland Heights · Las Vegas Natural History Museum · Sunrise Manor · Fountain Park · Nevada State Museum and Historic Society · Freedom Park · Meadows Mall · Las Vegas · Nature Park · University · Las Vegas Art Museum · The Strip · Clark · Las Vegas Country Club · Winchester · Spring Valley · Liberace Museum · Paradise · McCarran Intl. Airport

0 4 Km
0 4 Miles

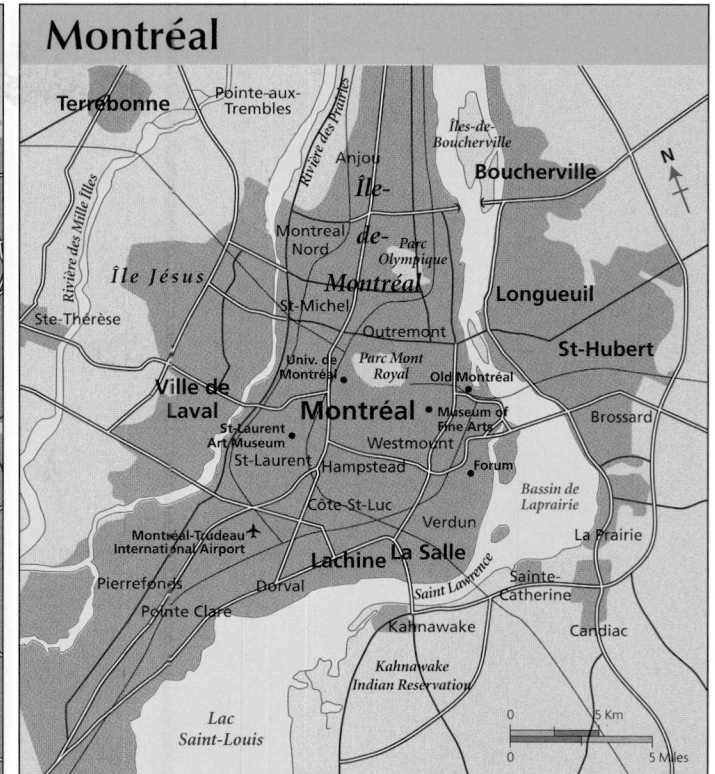

Los Angeles

Montréal

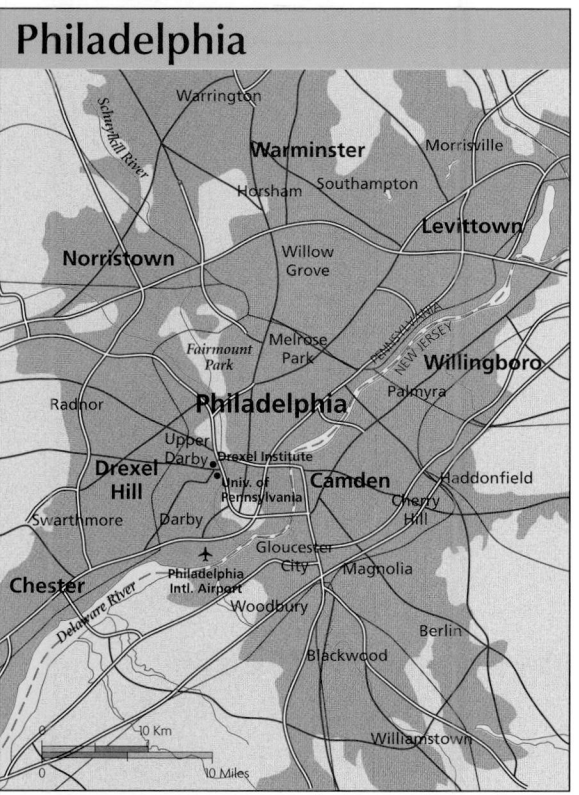

Philadelphia

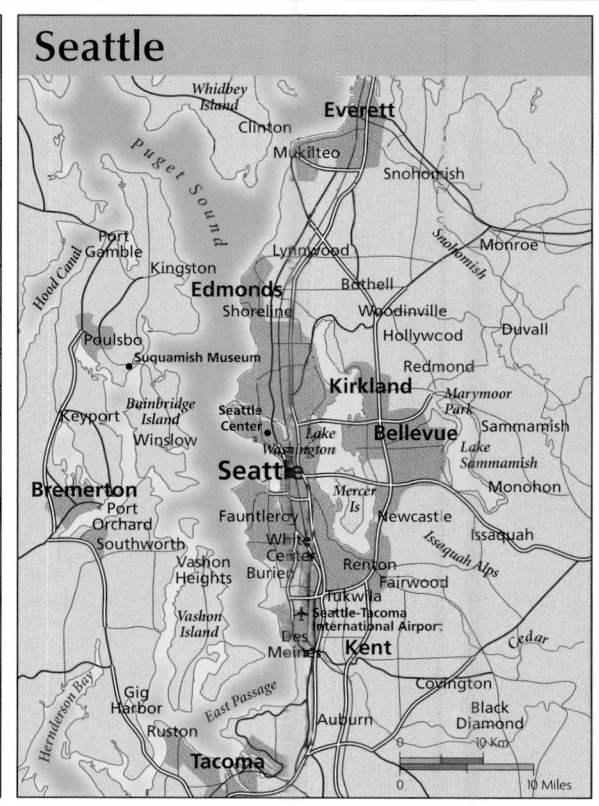

Seattle

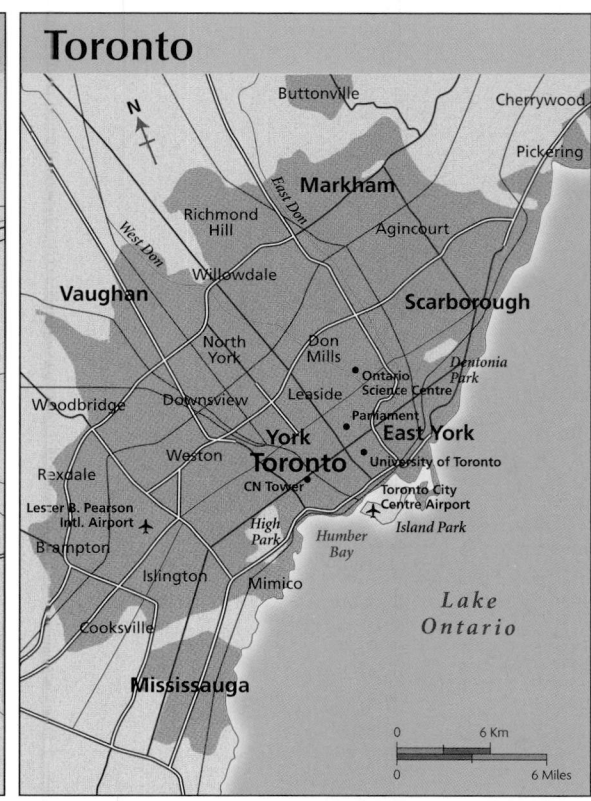

Toronto

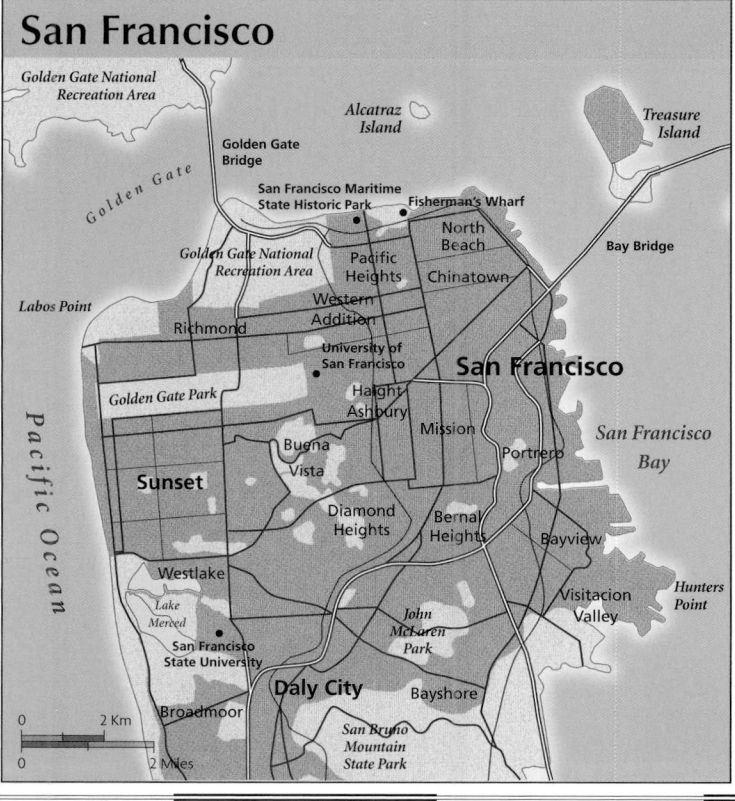

San Francisco

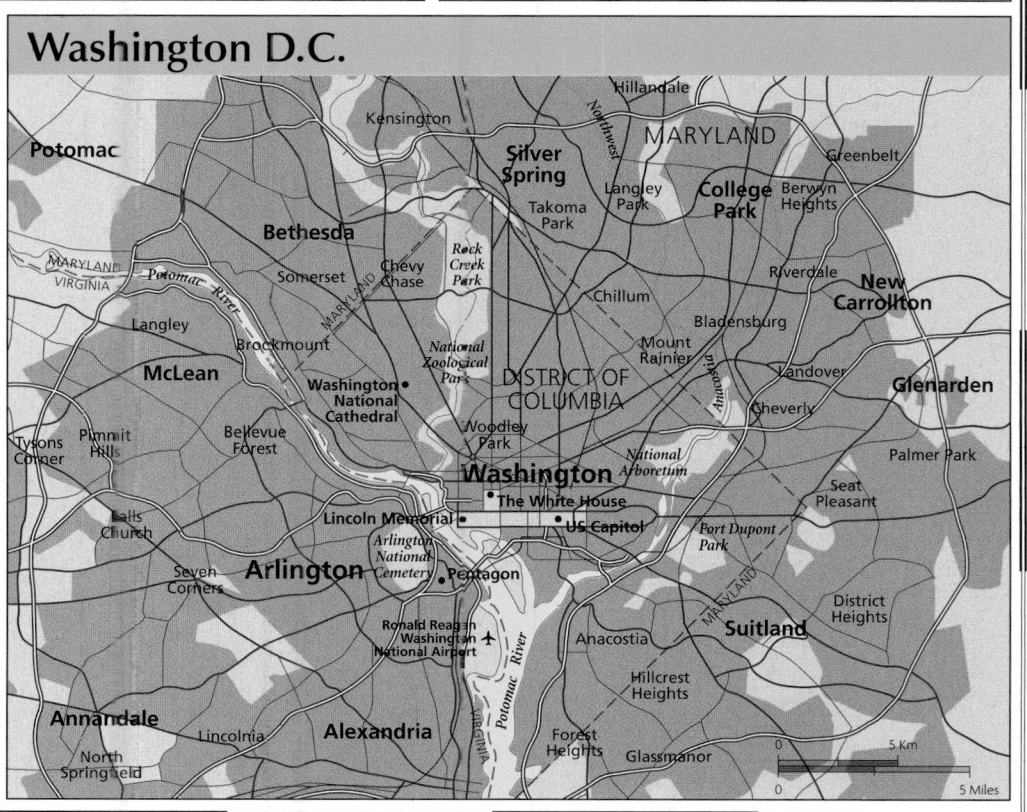

Washington D.C.

SOUTH AMERICA

South America reaches from the humid tropics down into the cold South Atlantic, with a total area of 6,886,000 sq miles (17,835,000 sq km). It comprises 12 separate countries, with the largest, Brazil, covering almost half the continent.

FACTFILE

N **Most Northerly Point:** Punta Gallinas, Colombia 12° 28′ N
S **Most Southerly Point:** Cape Horn, Chile 55° 59′ S
E **Most Easterly Point:** Ilhas Martin Vaz, Brazil 28° 51′ W
W **Most Westerly Point:** Galapagos Islands, Ecuador 92° 00′ W

Largest Lakes:
1 Lake Titicaca, Bolivia/Peru 3141 sq miles (8135 sq km)
2 Mirim Lagoon, Brazil/Uruguay 1158 sq miles (3000 sq km)
3 Lago Poopó, Bolivia 976 sq miles (2530 sq km)
4 Lago Buenos Aires, Argentina/Chile 864 sq miles (2240 sq km)
5 Laguna Mar Chiquita, Argentina 695 sq miles (1800 sq km)

Longest Rivers:
1 Amazon, Brazil/Colombia/Peru 4049 miles (6516 km)
2 Paraná, Argentina/Brazil/Paraguay 2920 miles (4700 km)
3 Madeira, Bolivia/Brazil 2100 miles (3379 km)
4 Purus, Brazil/Peru 2013 miles (3239 km)
5 São Francisco, Brazil 1802 miles (2900 km)

Largest Islands:
1 Tierra del Fuego, Argentina/Chile 18,302 sq miles (47,401 sq km)
2 Ilha de Marajo, Brazil 15,483 sq miles (40,100 sq km)
3 Isla de Chiloé, Chile 3241 sq miles (8394 sq km)
4 East Falkland, Falkland Islands 2550 sq miles (6605 sq km)
5 Isla Wellington, Chile 2145 sq miles (5556 sq km)

Highest Points:
1 Cerro Aconcagua, Argentina 22,831 ft (6959 m)
2 Cerro Ojos del Salado, Argentina/Chile 22,572 ft (6880 m)
3 Cerro Bonete, Argentina 22,546 ft (6872 m)
4 Monte Pissis, Argentina 22,224 ft (6774 m)
5 Cerro Mercedario, Argentina 22,211 ft (6768 m)

Lowest Point:
▼ Península Valdés -131 ft (-40 m) below sea level

Highest recorded temperature:
● Rivadavia, Argentina 120°F (49°C)

Lowest recorded temperature:
— Sarmiento, Argentina -27°F (-33°C)

Wettest Place:
≋ Quibdó, Colombia 354 in (8990 mm)

Driest Place:
⌣ Arica, Chile 0.03 in (0.8 mm)

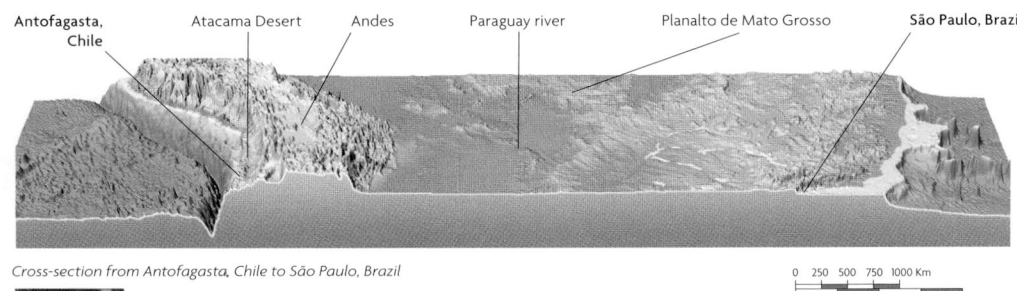

Antofagasta, Chile | Atacama Desert | Andes | Paraguay river | Planalto de Mato Grosso | São Paulo, Brazil

Cross-section from Antofagasta, Chile to São Paulo, Brazil

▷─◁─◁─◁
line of cross-section

0   250   500   750   1000 Km
0   250   500   750   1000 Miles

SOUTH AMERICA

H I J K L M N

Gulf of Mexico
Mississippi Fan
Sigsbee Escarpment
Apalachee Bay
Cape Canaveral
Lake Okeechobee
Straits of Florida
Great Bahama Bank
Bahamas
Hatteras Plain
Sargasso Sea
Nares Plain
Tropic of Cancer
Cape Verde Basin
Cape Verde Islands
West Indies
Puerto Rico Trench
Cuba
Yucatan Peninsula
Yucatan Basin
Greater Antilles
Cayman Trench
Cayman Trough
Windward Passage
Hispaniola
Puerto Rico
Jamaica
Leeward Islands
Nevis
Barbuda
Antigua
Guadeloupe
Dominica
Martinique
Saint Lucia
Barbados
Grenada
Tobago
Trinidad
NORTH AMERICAN PLATE
SOUTH AMERICAN PLATE
MID-ATLANTIC RIDGE
ATLANTIC OCEAN
Gambia Plain
Gulf of Honduras
Caribbean Sea
Lesser Antilles
Isla de Margarita
Grenada Basin
Windward Islands
Nicaraguan Rise
Mosquito Coast
Punta Gallinas
Peninsula de la Guajira
Aruba
Bonaire
Curaçao
Gulf of Venezuela
Lake Maracaibo
Cordillera de la Costa
Colombian Basin
Lake Nicaragua
Gulf of Fonseca
Middle America Trench
Gulf of Darien
Mosquito Gulf
Isthmus of Panama
Gulf of Panama
Guatemala Basin
Peninsula de Azuero
Colon Ridge
Panama Basin
Demerara Plain
Guiana Basin
African Plate
Doldrums Fracture Zone
Four North Fracture Zone
Saint Paul Fracture Zone
Equator
Llanos
Orinoco
Guiana Highlands
Serra Parima
Amazon Fan
Baía de Marajó
Ilha de Marajó
Baía de São Marcos
Ceará Plain
Atol das Rocas
Fernando de Noronha
Cabo de São Roque
Cabo Branco
Pernambuco Plain
Planalto da Borborema
Amazon Basin
Rio Negro
Represa de Tucuruí
SOUTH AMERICA
Chimborazo
Galapagos Islands
Gulf of Guayaquil
Punta Pariñas
Represa de Sobradinho
Baía de Todos os Santos
Brazil Basin
Chapada dos Parecis
Planalto do Mato Grosso
Abrolhos Bank
Ilhas Martin Vaz
Trindade Spur
Tropic of Capricorn
Lake Titicaca
Altiplano
Yungas
Peru Basin
Peru-Chile Trench
Mendaña Fracture Zone
SOUTH AMERICAN PLATE
NAZCA PLATE
PACIFIC OCEAN
Atacama Desert
Chile Basin
Nazca Ridge
Gran Chaco
Ilha de São Sebastião
Santos Plateau
Ilha de São Francisco
Rio Grande Rise
Islas de los Desventurados
Sala y Gomez Fracture Zone
Easter Island
East Pacific Rise
Roggeveen Basin
Juan Fernandez Islands
Pampas
Mesopotamia
Embalse del Rio Negro
Lagoa dos Patos
Mirim Lagoon
Río de la Plata
Argentine Basin
Bahía Blanca
Golfo San Matías
Península Valdés
Argentine Plain
Gulf of San Jorge
Bahía Grande
Isla de Chiloé
Golfo Corcovado
Isla Wellington
Strait of Magellan
Falkland Escarpment
Maurice Ewing Bank
Falkland Plateau
Falkland Islands
South Georgia
South Sandwich
Scotia Ridge
SCOTIA PLATE
Scotia Sea
Cape Horn
South Shetland Islands
South Orkney Islands
Weddell Sea
ANTARCTICA
NAZCA PLATE
ANTARCTIC PLATE
PACIFIC PLATE

1 2 3 4 5 6 7 8 9 10

N W E S

H I J K L M N

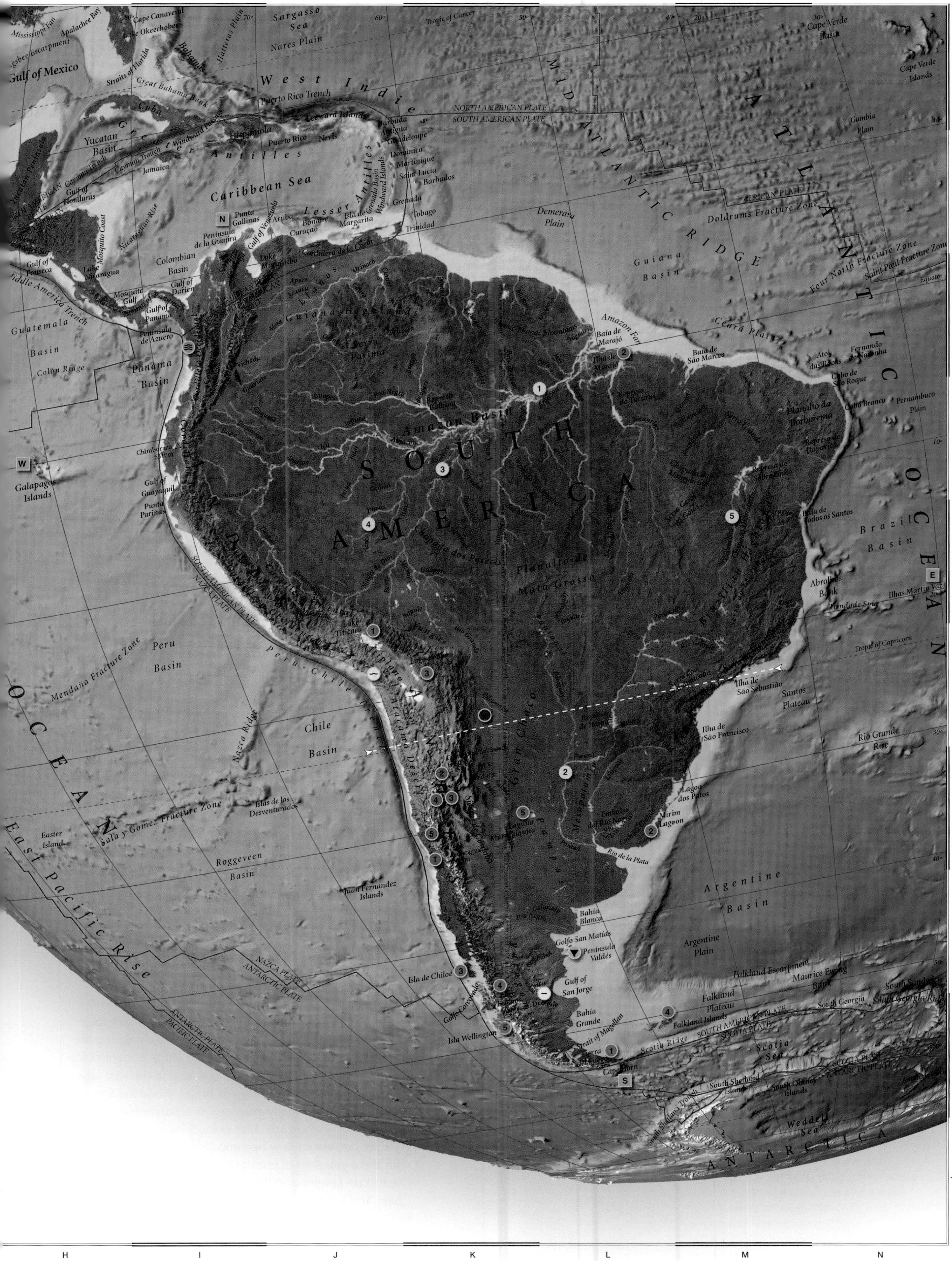

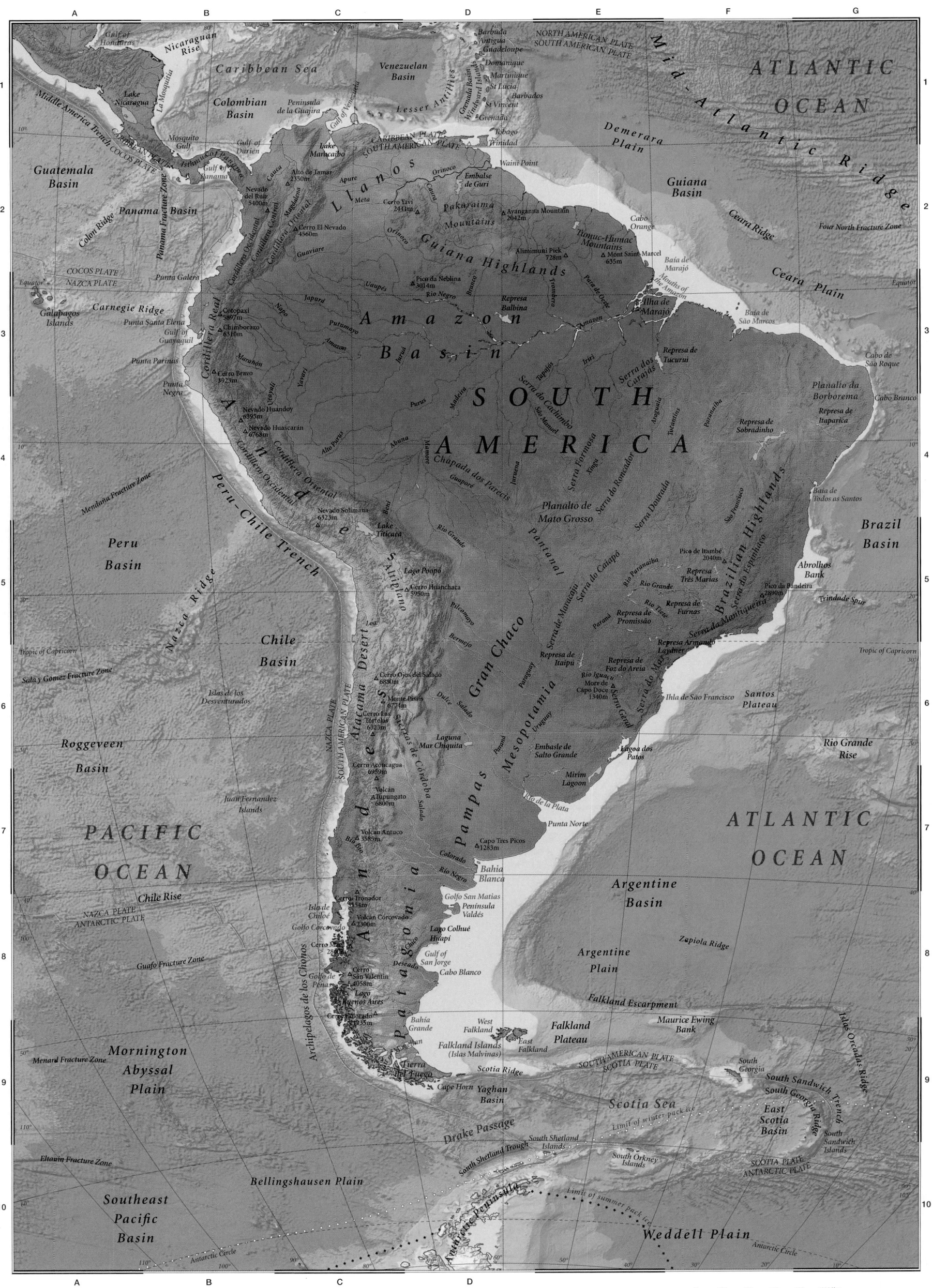

Scale 1:29,000,000

(projection: Lambert Azimuthal Equal Area)

Climate

The climate of South America is influenced by three principal factors: the seasonal shift of high pressure air masses over the tropics, cold ocean currents along the western coast, affecting temperature and precipitation, and the mountain barrier produced by by the Andes, which creates a rain shadow over much of the south.

Climate

- tundra
- cool continental
- warm humid
- semi-arid
- arid
- humid equatorial
- tropical

☀ daily hours of sunshine, January
☀ daily hours of sunshine, July
→ cold wind

Average Rainfall

January rainfall   *July rainfall*

Rainfall

- 0–1 in (0–25 mm)
- 1–2 in (25–50 mm)
- 2–4 in (50–100 mm)
- 4–8 in (100–200 mm)
- 8–12 in (200–300 mm)
- 12–16 in (300–400 mm)
- 16–20 in (400–500 mm)
- more than 20 in (500 mm)

Average Temperature

January temperature   *July temperature*

Temperature

- below -22°F (-30°C)
- -22 to -4°F (-30 to -20°C)
- -4 to 14°F (-20 to -10°C)
- 14 to 32°F (-10 to 0°C)
- 32 to 50°F (0 to 10°C)
- 50 to 68°F (10 to 20°C)
- 68 to 86°F (20 to 30°C)
- above 86°F (30°C)

Landuse

Many foods now common worldwide originated in South America. These include the potato, tomato, squash, and cassava. Today, large herds of beef cattle roam the temperate grasslands of the Pampas, supporting an extensive meat-packing trade in Argentina, Uruguay and Paraguay. Corn (maize) is grown as a staple crop across the continent and coffee is grown as a cash crop in Brazil and Colombia. Coca plants grown in Bolivia, Peru and Colombia provide most of the western world's cocaine. Fish and shellfish are caught off the western coast, especially anchovies off Peru, shrimps off Ecuador and sardines off Chile.

Environmental Issues

The Amazon Basin is one of the last great wilderness areas left on Earth. The tropical rainforests which grow there are a valuable genetic resource, containing innumerable unique plants and animals. The forests are increasingly under threat from new and expanding settlements and 'slash and burn' farming techniques, which clear land for the raising of beef cattle, causing land degradation and soil erosion.

Environmental Issues

- national parks
- tropical forest
- forest destroyed
- desert
- desertification
- polluted rivers
- marine pollution
- heavy marine pollution
- • poor urban air quality

Using the Land and Sea

- barren land
- cropland
- desert
- forest
- mountain region
- pasture
- • major conurbations
- cattle
- pigs
- sheep
- bananas
- corn (maize)
- citrus fruits
- cocoa
- cotton
- coffee
- fishing
- oil palms
- peanuts
- rubber
- shellfish
- soya beans
- sugar cane
- vineyards
- wheat

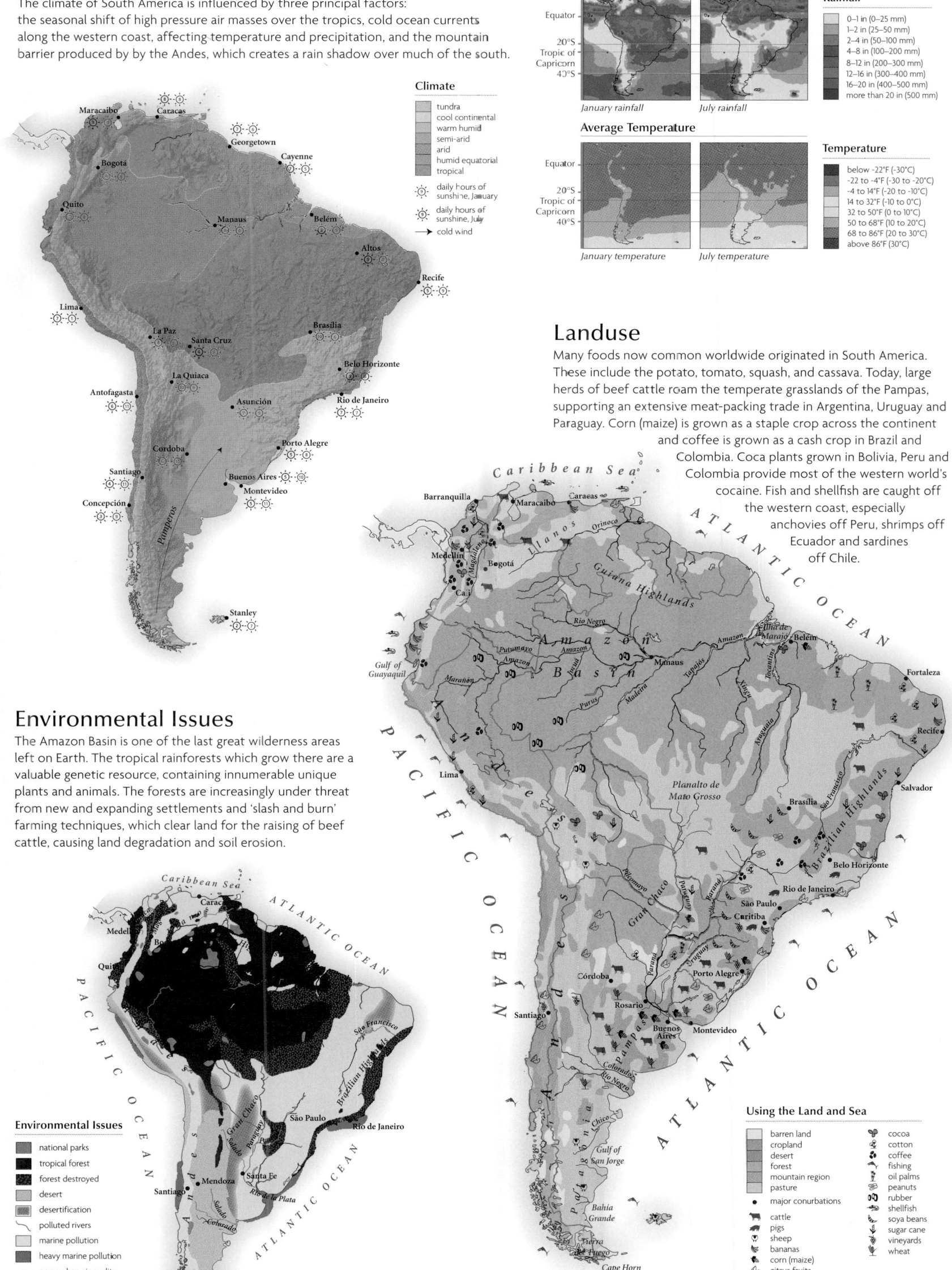

SOUTH AMERICA

1 SANTIAGO, CHILE
Chile's capital city was founded in 1541 by Pedro de Valdivia who chose the location because it had a Mediterranean climate and was easy to defend.

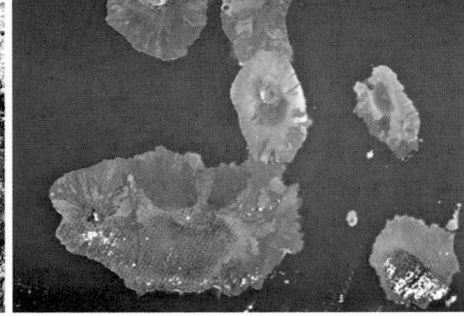

2 GALAPAGOS ISLANDS, ECUADOR
These islands are a collection of volcanoes rising from the ocean floor 621 miles (1000 km) west of the South American mainland.

3 SALAR DE UYUNI, BOLIVIA
Occupying a depression high up on the Altiplano between the volcanoes of the western Andes and the fold belts of the eastern Andes, this is the world's largest salt flat.

4 MACHU PICCHU, PERU
Perched precariously above the Urubamba valley, the lost Inca retreat was rediscovered in 1911 by Hiram Bingham, an American archaeologist.

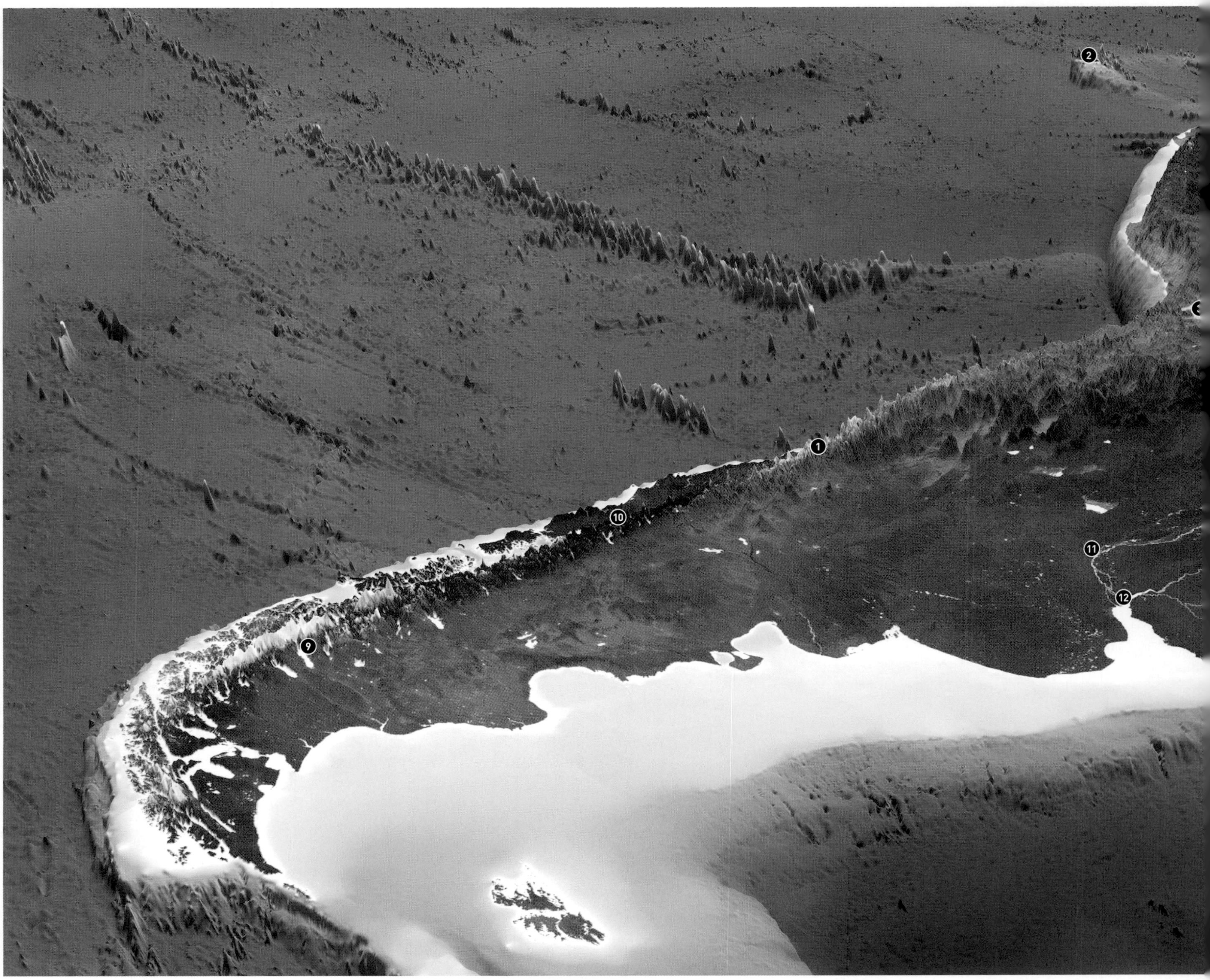

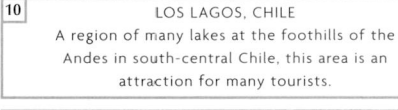

9 LAGO VIEDMA, ARGENTINA
Lago Viedma enjoys a milky-blue appearance due to the glacial sediment suspended in its waters.

10 LOS LAGOS, CHILE
A region of many lakes at the foothills of the Andes in south-central Chile, this area is an attraction for many tourists.

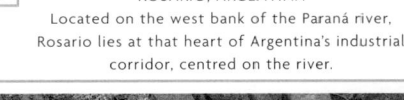

11 ROSARIO, ARGENTINA
Located on the west bank of the Paraná river, Rosario lies at that heart of Argentina's industrial corridor, centred on the river.

12 RIVER PLATE, ARGENTINA/URUGUAY
Fed by the Paraná and Uruguay rivers, this Atlantic Ocean inlet separates Argentina and Uruguay.

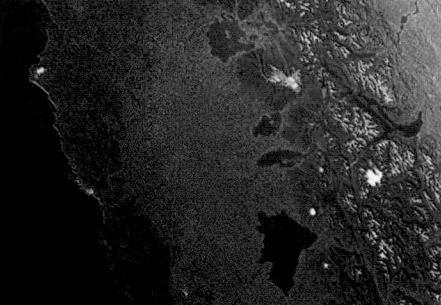

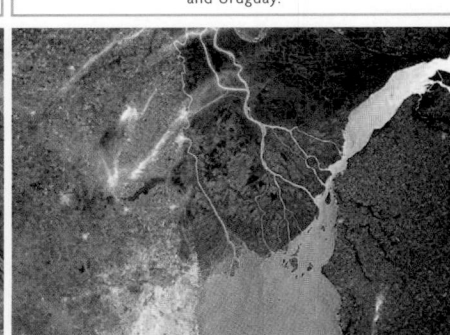

RONDÔNIA, BRAZIL 5
Pale strips of forest clearance can be seen along perpendicular tracks in this region of the Amazon Basin.

MARACAIBO, VENEZUELA 6
Maracaibo is the centre of Venezuela's oil industry and its second largest city with a population of 1.6 million.

AMAZON RIVER/RIO NEGRO, BRAZIL 7
The dark, plant debris-stained waters of the Rio Negro join the beige Amazon near the city of Manaus.

EMBALSE DE GURI, VENEZUELA 8
This enormous reservoir, on the Caroni river, was completed in 1986 and its hydroelectric plant was the first to produce more than 10 gigawatts of electricity.

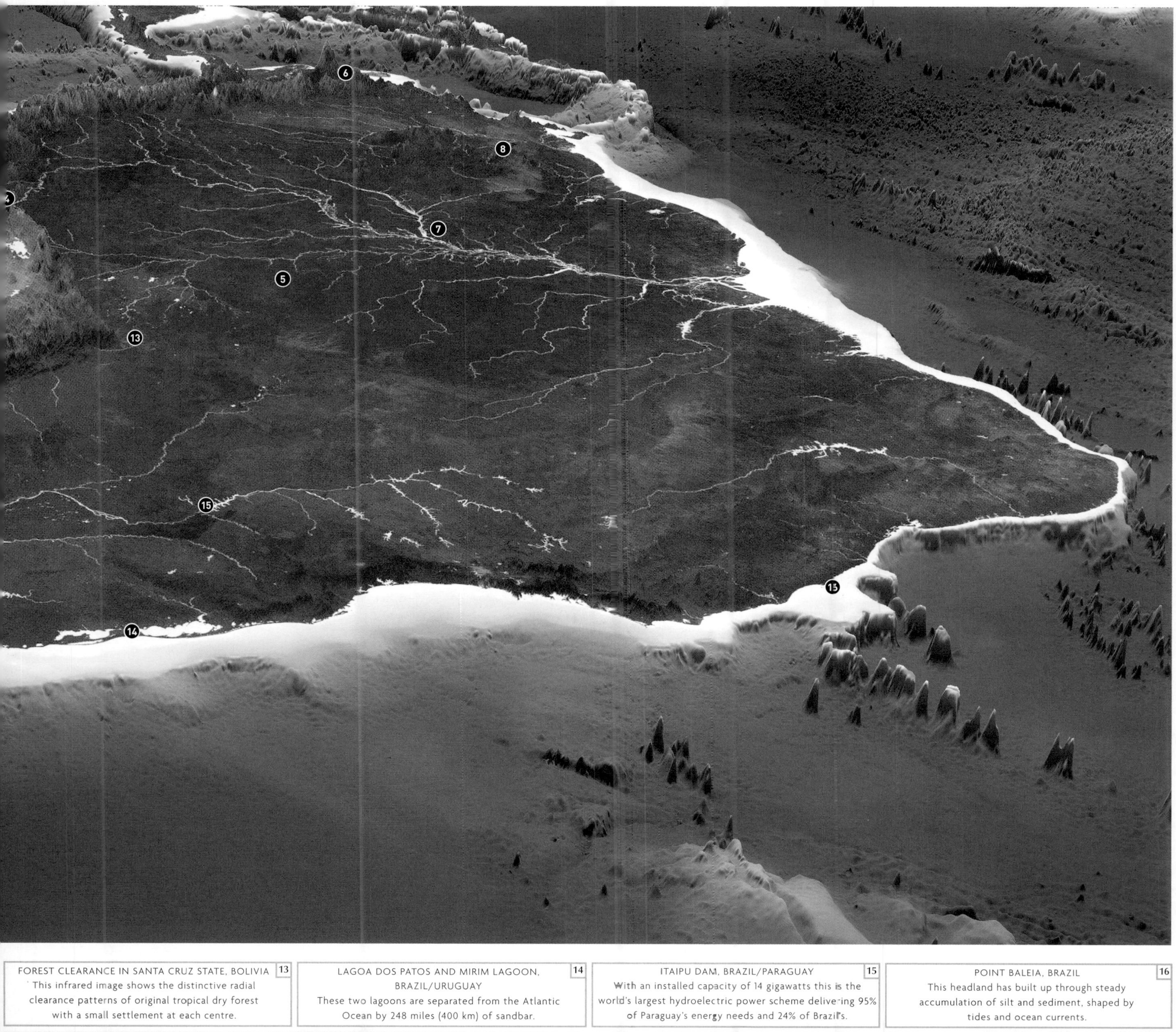

FOREST CLEARANCE IN SANTA CRUZ STATE, BOLIVIA 13
This infrared image shows the distinctive radial clearance patterns of original tropical dry forest with a small settlement at each centre.

LAGOA DOS PATOS AND MIRIM LAGOON, BRAZIL/URUGUAY 14
These two lagoons are separated from the Atlantic Ocean by 248 miles (400 km) of sandbar.

ITAIPU DAM, BRAZIL/PARAGUAY 15
With an installed capacity of 14 gigawatts this is the world's largest hydroelectric power scheme delivering 95% of Paraguay's energy needs and 24% of Brazil's.

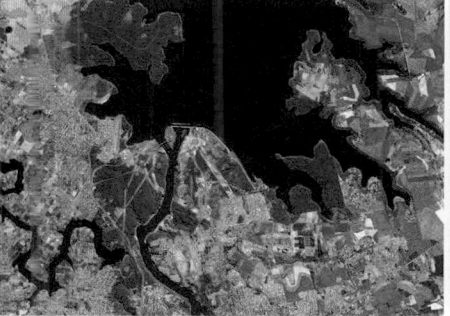

POINT BALEIA, BRAZIL 16
This headland has built up through steady accumulation of silt and sediment, shaped by tides and ocean currents.

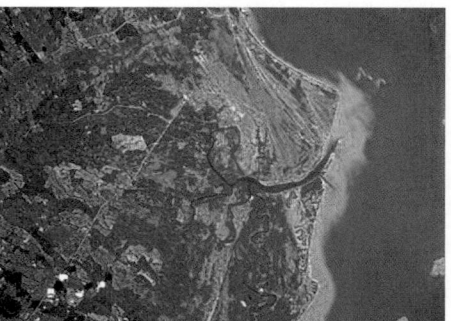

Northern South America

A
B
C
D
E
F
G
1
2
3
4
5
6
7
8
9
10
Caribbean Sea
PACIFIC OCEAN
ARUBA
(to Netherlands)
ORANJESTAD
NETHERLANDS ANTILLES
(to Netherlands)
Curaçao
WILLEMSTAD
Bonaire
Kralendijk
Punta Gallinas
Cabo de la Vela
Península de la Guajira
Golfo de Venezuela
Punto Fijo
Coro
FALCÓN
Maracaibo
Lago de Maracaibo
ZULIA
LARA
Barquisimeto
Valencia
Maracay
CARACAS
VARGAS
La Guaira
Los Teques
MIRANDA
CARABOBO
ARAGUA
COJEDES
San Carlos
YARACUY
San Felipe
Trujillo
TRUJILLO
Mérida
MÉRIDA
Barinas
BARINAS
PORTUGUESA
Guanare
GUÁRICO
San Fernando
Caicara del Orinoco
APURE
Puerto Ayacucho
AMAZONAS
San Cristóbal
TÁCHIRA
Cúcuta
NORTE DE SANTANDER
Riohacha
LA GUAJIRA
Santa Marta
Barranquilla
ATLÁNTICO
Soledad
Cartagena
Valledupar
CESAR
MAGDALENA
Sincelejo
SUCRE
Montería
CÓRDOBA
BOLÍVAR
PANAMA
Gulf of Darien
SAN BLAS
DARIÉN
Bucaramanga
Floridablanca
Barrancabermeja
SANTANDER
ANTIOQUIA
Medellín
Bello
Envigado
Quibdó
CHOCÓ
RISARALDA
Pereira
CALDAS
Manizales
QUINDÍO
Armenia
Ibagué
TOLIMA
BOGOTÁ
CUNDINAMARCA
BOYACÁ
Tunja
Yopal
CASANARE
ARAUCA
Arauca
Villavicencio
META
VICHADA
Puerto Carreño
Buenaventura
VALLE DEL CAUCA
Cali
Palmira
Tuluá
Neiva
HUILA
Popayán
CAUCA
NARIÑO
Pasto
Tumaco
Florencia
CAQUETÁ
PUTUMAYO
Mocoa
COLOMBIA
GUAVIARE
San José del Guaviare
GUAINÍA
Puerto Inírida
VAUPÉS
Mitú
AMAZONAS
Leticia
Tabatinga
Benjamin Constant
Tulcán
CARCHI
Ibarra
IMBABURA
PICHINCHA
QUITO
NAPO
SUCUMBÍOS
Nueva Loja (Lago Agrio)
ORELLANA
Puerto Francisco de Orellana (Coca)
ECUADOR
COTOPAXI
Latacunga
Ambato
TUNGURAHUA
Riobamba
CHIMBORAZO
BOLÍVAR
PASTAZA
MORONA SANTIAGO
CAÑAR
Cuenca
AZUAY
ZAMORA CHINCHIPE
Zamora
PERU
LORETO
Iquitos
Río Putumayo
Río Caquetá
Río Meta
Río Orinoco
Río Negro
Río Japurá
Río Içá
Amazon
Río Napo
Río Guaviare
Río Vaupés
Río Apaporis
Serra do Traíra
6000m
4000m
3000m
2000m
1000m
500m
250m
100m
Sea Level
-250m
-2000m
-4000m

90
287
104

Scale 1:6,500,000
(projection: Lambert Azimuthal Equal Area)

0 25 50 75 100 125 150 175 200 Km
0 25 50 75 100 125 150 175 200 Miles

Population
- above 5 million
- 1 million to 5 million
- 500,000 to 1 million
- 100,000 to 500,000
- 50,000 to 100,000
- 10,000 to 50,000
- below 10,000

Bogotá

Usaquén
Molinos
Canal de Guaymaral
Río Juan Amarillo
Monumento
Lara Bonita
Barrios
Unidos
Chapinero
Aeropuerto
Internacio
El Dorado
Engativá
Teusaquillo
Fontibón
Bogotá
Puente
Aranda
Museo
Nacional de
Colombia
Kennedy
Río Fucha
Los
Mártires
Catedral
La
Candelaria
Santa
Fe
Antonio
Nariño
San
Cristóbal
Tunjuelito
Rafael
Uribe
Km
1 Miles

ATLANTIC OCEAN

George F L Charles
CASTRIES
Mount Gimie
950m
ST LUCIA
Vieux Fort
Hewanorra
Saint Vincent Passage
St Vincent
KINGSTOWN
Arnos Vale
BARBADOS
BRIDGETOWN
Grantley
Adams
ST VINCENT &
THE GRENADINES
Bequia
Mustique
Canouan
Union Island
Carriacou
ST. GEORGE'S
GRENADA
Point Salines

Isla Blanquilla
Isla de Margarita
Islas los Testigos
NUEVA ESPARTA
Juangriego
Tobago
Charlotteville
Scarborough
Galera Point
Pampatar
La Asunción
Porlamar
Río Caribe
Boca de
Pozo
Punta de
Piedras
PORT-OF-SPAIN
Arima
Araya
Puerto
Cruz
Cumaná
Carúpano
Güiria
El Pilar
Irapa
Sangre Grande
Trinidad
Casanay
Puerta de
Gulf of Paria
Río Clara
TRINIDAD
& TOBAGO
Barcelona
SUCRE
San Antonio
Caripito
San Fernando
Point Fortin
Galeota Point
Araguá de Maturín
Caripe
Quiriquire
Rushville
Siparia
Guanta
Santa Rosa
Anaco
Aguasay
Punta
de Mata
Maturín
MONAGAS
Pedernales
Punta Baja
El Tigre
San Tomé
Temblador
San José de Guanipa
La Horqueta
Tucupita
DELTA AMACURO
Barrancas
ANZOÁTEGUI
Ciudad Guayana
Río Orinoco
Guasabones
Curiapo
Waini Point
Soledad
El Palmar
Waini
Ciudad Bolívar
El Rico
Upata
Port Kaituma
VENEZUELA
Mapire
Borbón
Arakaka
Matthews
Ridge
Banana River
Charity
Embalse
de Guri
Guasipati
El Callao
Guasipati
El Dorado
Tumeremo
Essequibo Islands
Spring Garden
Cerro Turagua
1838m
Las
Trincheras
Ciudad Piar
El Manteco
Kurácki
Aurora
Cuyuni River
Cuyuni River
Parika
GEORGETOWN
Georgetown
Cano Negro
Enachu Landing
Peters Mine
Bartica
New Amsterdam
Rose Hall
Canaima
BOLIVAR
Salto Angel
Cerro Venamo
1563m
Kamarang
Mazaruni River
Rockstone
Linden
Corriverton
WANICA
COMMEWIJNE
Nieuw Nickerie
Watergraafmeer
Totness
Groningen
Nieuw Amsterdam
Mana
Iles du Salut
Cerro Guaiquinima
2100m
Wangutima Mountain
GUYANA
Berbice River
NICKERIE
CORONIE
SARA
PARA
PARAMARIBO
Albina
St-Jean
Iracoubo
Sinnamary
Ile du Diable
Santa María
de Erebato
Caruana de Montaña
Mount Roraima
2810m
Issano
Apoera
Donderkamp
Kwakoegron
Brownsweg
Bergen Dal
Brokopondo
Citron
Apatou
St-Laurent
du Maroni
St-Élie
Kourou
Ténate
Roura
Cayenne
CAYENNE
Rémire
Matoury
Cabadisocana
Santa Elena de Uairén
Mount
Ayanganna
2042m
Orealla
Washabo
Kaaimanston
Pokigron
Hendrik Top
957m
SURINAME
BROKOPONDO
Poeketi
Grand-Santi
Cacao
Délices
Cerro
Guaiquinima
Délices
Bergi
Pointe Béhague
Baie de L'Oyapok
Cabo Orange
Sararina
Catisimina
Uaicás
Glendon
Mountains
Kurupukari
Kanuku Mountains
Saurwaunawa
Tafelberg
Boti-
Pasi
Djoemoe
FRENCH
GUIANA
(to France)
Saül
Montagnes
Bellevue de l'Inini
Cassiporé
Ounary
Oiapoque
Uonán
Normandia
Lethem
Apetina
SIPALIWINI
Aluminum Piek
Maripasoula
Mont Saint-Marcel
635m
Oiapoque
Calçoene
Boa Vista
Conceição do Mau
Urarkcera
Kuyuwini
Landing
New River
(Claimed by Suriname)
Appikale
Massif du Mitaraka
Trois
Sauts
Amapá
Horqueta Minas
Río Catrimani
RORAIMA
Caracaraí
Johi Village
Acarai Mountains
Tumuc Humác Mountains
(Claimed by Suriname)
AMAPÁ
Sierra
de Unturán
Missão Catrimani
São Luís
Sete Ilhas
Río Demini
Sierra
Tapirapecó
Catrimani
Río Uraricoera
Serra do Jatapú
Río Anauá
Río Jari
Río Negro
Tapurucuará
Boiaçu
Planalto
Maracanaquará
Monte Dourado
Ilha Grande
de Gurupá
Río Branco
Río Itapu
Represa
Balbina
Río Nhamundá
Río Trombetas
Macapá
Equator
BRAZIL
AMAZONAS
Barcelos
Carvoeiro
Moura
Novo Airão
Oriximiná
Óbidos
Alenquer
Porto de Moz
PARA
Amazon
Santarém
Portel
Río Negro
Río Solimões
Manacapuru
Manaus
Eduardo
Gomes
Caldeirão
Itacoatiara
Parintins
Urucará
Amazon
Basin
Tefé
Alvarães
Godajás
Beruri
Iranduba
Manaquiri
Careiro
Autazes
Rurópolis Presidente
Río Solimões
Río Purús
Ghari
Cáreiro
Itaituba
Pimenta
Río Tapajós
Altamira
Río Xingu

SOUTH AMERICA

19,686ft
13,124ft
9843ft
6562ft
3281ft
1640ft
820ft
328ft
Sea
Level
-820ft
-6562ft
-13,124ft

Scale 1:2,000,000
(projection: Lambert Conformal Conic)

0 10 20 30 40 50 60 70 80 Km
0 10 20 30 40 50 60 70 80 Miles

Population
■ above 5 million   ■ 1 million to 5 million   ◎ 500,000 to 1 million
◎ 100,000 to 500,000   ⊕ 50,000 to 100,000   ○ 10,000 to 50,000   ○ below 10,000

109

291

Rio de Janeiro

Olinda
Mesquita
Coelho
da Rocha
Duque de Caxias

Nilópolis
São João de Meriti
Rio de Janeiro
Guadalupe
Cordovil
Ilha do Governador
Galeão
Cocotá
Galeão

Bangu
Magalhães
Rocha
Miranda
Olaria
Ramos
Ilha do Governador

Padre Miguel
Inhaúme
Benfica
Baía de Guanabara

Praça Seca
Engenho Novo
São Cristóvão
Museu Nacional
Gâmboa

Taquara
Pechincha
Engenho Novo
Vila Isabel
Rio de Janeiro
Catedral Metropolitana
Santos Dumont

Neves

Niterói

Jacarepaguá
Gruta Paulo e Virginia
Monumento Cristo Redentor
Tijuca
Botafogo
Pão de Açúcar (Sugarloaf Mt.)

Lagoa de Jacarepaguá
Parque Nacional da Tijuca
Gávea
Lagoa Rodrigo de Freitas
Copacabana

Barra de Tijuca
Niemeyer
Ipanema
Tijucamar

Atlantic Ocean

0   2 Km
0   2 Miles

ATLANTIC

OCEAN

Tropic of Capricorn

19,686ft
13,124ft
9843ft
6562ft
3281ft
1640ft
820ft
328ft
Sea Level
-820ft
-6562ft
-13,124ft

Central South America

PACIFIC OCEAN

PERU
BOLIVIA
CHILE
ARGENTINA
PARAGUAY

LA PAZ
ORURO
SUCRE
POTOSÍ
CHUQUISACA
TARIJA
SANTA CRUZ
ALTO PARAGUAY
BOQUERÓN
PRESIDENTE HAYES
ASUNCIÓN
CHACO
FORMOSA
JUJUY
SALTA
TUCUMÁN
CATAMARCA
SANTIAGO DEL ESTERO
LA RIOJA
SAN JUAN
CÓRDOBA
SANTA FE
ENTRE RÍOS
SAN LUIS
MENDOZA
LA PAMPA
BUENOS AIRES
TARAPACÁ
ANTOFAGASTA
ATACAMA
COQUIMBO
VALPARAÍSO
SANTIAGO

Gran Chaco
Puna de Atacama
Salar de Uyuni
Salar de Atacama

Tacna
Iquique
Arica
Tocopilla
Calama
Antofagasta
Chañaral
Caldera
Copiapó
La Serena
Coquimbo
Valparaíso
Viña del Mar
Rancagua
Talca
Cochabamba
Oruro
Potosí
Tarija
Yacuiba
San Salvador de Jujuy
Salta
San Miguel de Tucumán
Santiago del Estero
San Fernando del Valle de Catamarca
La Rioja
San Juan
Mendoza
Godoy Cruz
San Luis
San Rafael
Córdoba
Río Cuarto
Villa María
Rosario
Santa Fe
Paraná
Resistencia
Corrientes
Formosa
Asunción
Buenos Aires
Avellaneda
La Plata

Tropic of Capricorn

6000m
4000m
3000m
2000m
1000m
500m
250m
100m
Sea Level
-250m
-2000m
-4000m

Scale 1:6,500,000
(projection: Lambert Azimuthal Equal Area)

0 25 50 75 100 125 150 175 200 Km
0 25 50 75 100 125 150 175 200 Miles

Population
- ■ above 5 million
- ▣ 1 million to 5 million
- ◉ 500,000 to 1 million
- ◎ 100,000 to 500,000
- ⊕ 50,000 to 100,000
- ○ 10,000 to 50,000
- ∘ below 10,000

109

BRAZIL

Pantanal

MATO GROSSO DO SUL

Campo Grande
Aquidauana
Coxim
Dourados
Bela Vista
Pedro Juan Caballero

GOIÁS
Rio Verde
Jataí
Itumbiara
Anhanguera
Araguari
Uberlândia
Uberaba
Araxá

MINAS GERAIS
Belo Horizonte
Divinópolis
Piripora
Diamantina
Curvelo
Sete Lagoas
Betim
Itabira
Ipatinga
Ouro Preto
Barbacena
São João del Rei
Juiz de Fora
Governador Valadares

SÃO PAULO
São José do Rio Preto
Araçatuba
Marília
Bauru
Araraquara
Ribeirão Preto
São Carlos
Rio Claro
Limeira
Piracicaba
Campinas
Jundiaí
São Paulo
Osasco
São Bernardo do Campo
Santos
São Vicente
Sorocaba
Presidente Prudente

RIO DE JANEIRO
Rio de Janeiro
Nova Iguaçu
Niterói
São Gonçalo
Volta Redonda
Petrópolis
Teresópolis
Nova Friburgo
Macaé
Campos

PARANÁ
Londrina
Maringá
Apucarana
Curitiba
Ponta Grossa
Paranaguá
Foz do Iguaçu
Cascavel
Guarapuava
União da Vitória
Guaíra

SANTA CATARINA
Joinville
Blumenau
Itajaí
Florianópolis
Criciúma
Tubarão
Laguna
Lages
Chapecó
Caçador

RIO GRANDE DO SUL
Porto Alegre
Canoas
Novo Hamburgo
Caxias do Sul
Passo Fundo
Santa Maria
Pelotas
Rio Grande
Bagé
Santana do Livramento
Santa Cruz do Sul
Gravataí
Uruguaiana

URUGUAY
MONTEVIDEO
Rivera
Tacuarembó
Melo
Maldonado
Punta del Este
Rocha

Ciudad del Este
Encarnación
Posadas
MISIONES
ITAPUA
ALTO PARANÁ
CAAGUAZÚ
CANINDEYÚ

ATLANTIC OCEAN

Tropic of Capricorn

Ilha de Santa Catarina
Ilha de São Francisco
Ilha de São Sebastião
Ilha Grande
Ilha Comprida

Rio de la Plata
Lagoa dos Patos
Lagoa Mirim

Buenos Aires

Tigre
Las Conchas
San Isidro
Vicente López
San Miguel
General San Martín
San Justo
Morón
Moreno
Merlo
Belgrano
Palermo
Floresta
Hippodrome
Teatro Colón
Cathedral
Plaza de Mayo
Zoo
Sáenz Peña
Avellaneda
Lanús
Lomas de Zamora
Quilmes
Berazategui
Mariano Acosta
Villa Madero
Villa Alsina
Pontevedra
González Catán
Almirante Brown
Aeropuerto Internacional de Ezeiza
Rio de la Plata

0 10 Km
0 10 Miles

291

19,686ft
13,124ft
9843ft
6562ft
3281ft
1640ft
820ft
328ft
Sea Level
-820ft
-6562ft
-13,124ft

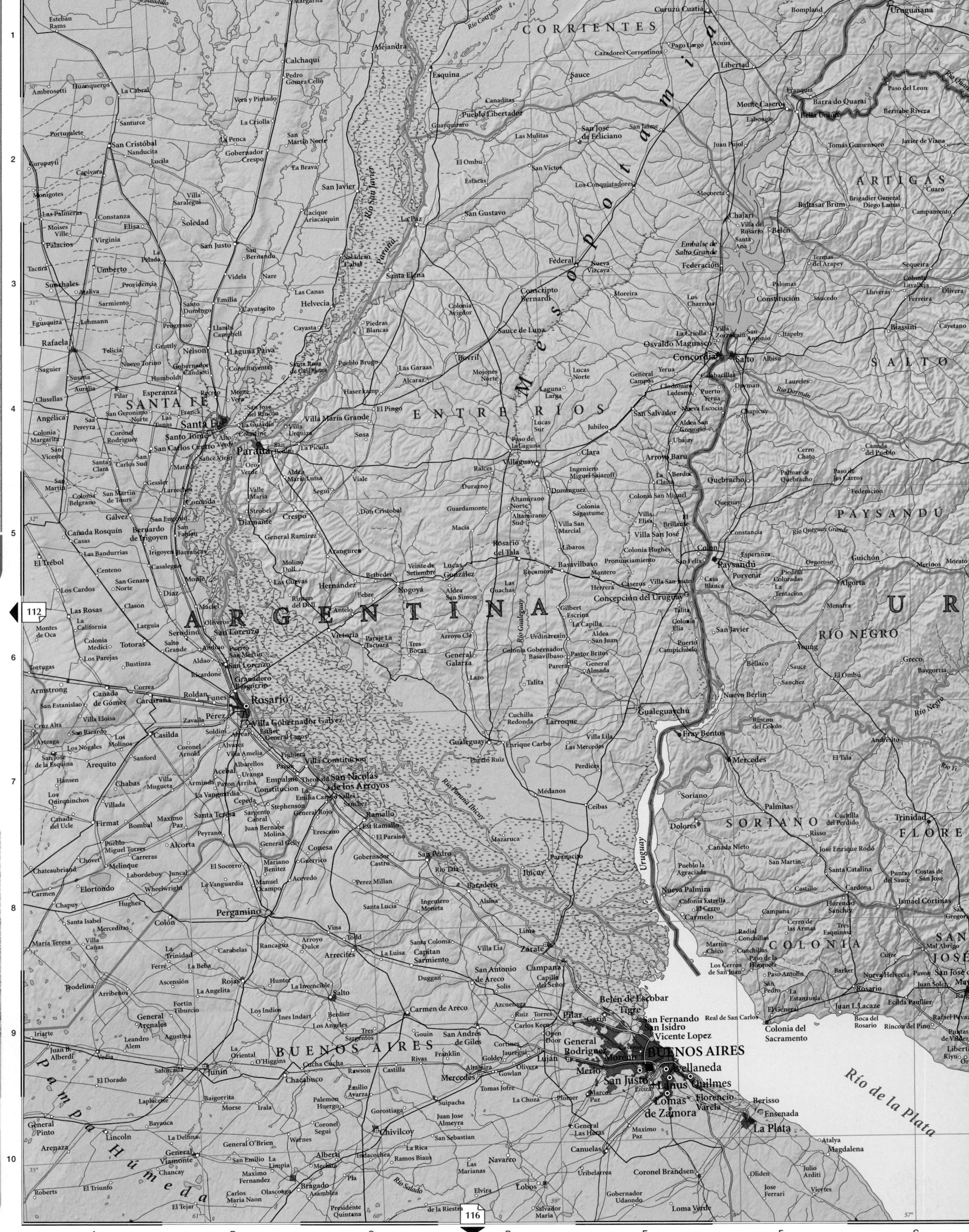

SOUTH AMERICA

6000m
4000m
3000m
2000m
1000m
500m
250m
100m
Sea Level
-250m
-2000m
-4000m

112

112

116

Scale 1:2,000,000
(projection: Lambert Conformal Conic)

0 10 20 30 40 50 60 70 80 Km
0 10 20 30 40 50 60 70 80 Miles

Population

■ above 5 million   ■ 1 million to 5 million   ◉ 500,000 to 1 million
◎ 100,000 to 500,000   ⊕ 50,000 to 100,000   ○ 10,000 to 50,000   ∘ below 10,000

113

291

116

19,686ft
13,124ft
9843ft
6562ft
3281ft
1640ft
820ft
328ft
Sea Level
-820ft
-6562ft
-13,124ft

BRAZIL

RIO GRANDE DO SUL

Serra das Encantadas

U R U G U A Y

RIVERA
TACUAREMBÓ
DURAZNO
CERRO LARGO
TREINTA Y TRES
FLORIDA
LAVALLEJA
ROCHA
CANELONES
MALDONADO

MONTEVIDEO

Santa Maria
Silveira Martins
Agudo
Candelaria
Santa Cruz do Sul
Passo do Sobrado
General Camara
Triunfo
São Jerónimo
Charqueadas
Arroio dos Ratos
Minas do Leao
Butia
Mariana Pimentel
Quiteria
Cerro Grande
Dom Feliciano
Camaquã

Magrete
Jacaquy
Rio Ibicui
Loreto
São Vicente do Sul
Caçequy
Restinga Seca
Tres Vendas
Ferreira
Formigueiro
Cachoeira do Sul
Rio Pardo
Cordilheira
Capane
Barro Vermelho
Pantano Grande
Capivarita
Encruzilhada do Sul

Plano Alto
Passo Novo
Ibirapuitã
Quarai
Artigas
Pintado Grande
Rosário do Sul
Itaqui
São Gabriel
Vaccacahye
Pampeiro
Dom Pedrito
Santana da Boa Vista
Rio Camaquã
Pedras Altas

Masoller
Rivera
Santana do Livramento
Palomas
Tranqueras
Zanja Honda
Punta de Corrales
Cerro Pelado del Este
Cerrillada
Minas de Corrales
Arroyo Blanco
Vichadero
Abrojal
Caraguata
Zanja Honda
Acegua
Isidoro Noblia
Cuchilla Caraguata
Mata Isabel
Cruz de Piedra
Paso del Centurión
Rio Jaguarão
Bagé
Candiota
Pinheiro Machado
Piratini
Canguçu
São Lourenço do Sul
Boqueirão
Pacheca
Pedreiras
Pelotas
Capao do Leao
Cerrito
Quilombo
Cerrito Alegre

Lagoa dos Patos

Mataojo
Quintana
Arboleda
Tambores
Piedra Sola
Tacuarembó
Los Rosanos
Curtina
Clara
Blanquillo
Las Arenas
Las Toscas
Larrayos
Achar
Peralta
Cuchilla de Peralta
Banado de Medina
Buena Vista
La Pedrera
Melo
Quilombo
Arroio Grande
Quinta
Rio Grande
São José do Norte
Estreito
Cassino

Fraile Muerto
Toledo
Cerro de las Cuentas
Arbolito
Uruguay
Jaguarão
Rio Branco
Tahim

Mirim Lagoon

Embalse del Rio Negro
Cardose
San Gregorio de Polanco
La Paloma
Yerbal
Tupambaé
Placido Rosas
Rincon
Vergara
Arrozal Treinta y Tres

Carlos Reyles
Ombues de Oribe
Sarandí del Yí
Cerro Chato
Mendizabal
Maria Sanz
Julio
Treinta y Tres
Enrique Martínez
General
Cebollatí
Arrozal Victoria

Durazno
Capilla del Sauce
Polanco del Yí
José Batlle y Ordoñez
Nico Pérez
Valentines
Villa Sara
Maria Albina
José Pedro Varela
Zapican
La Coronilla

Sarandí Grande
Alejandro Gallinal
Reboledo
Illescas
Piraraja
Rio Cebollatí
Lascano
Maria Isabel
Santa Victoria do Palmar
Diez y Ocho de Julio
Chuí
Chuy

Florida
Pintado
La Cruz
Mascala
Los Talas
Velázquez
La Coronilla

25 de Mayo
Mendoza Chico
Fray Marcos
Casupá
Bolivar
Aigua
Castillos
Cardal
Chamizo
San Ramón
Paralle
Maria Serrana
La Barra
Cabo Polonio

ATLANTIC OCEAN

Independencia
San Antonio
San Bautista
Tala
Solis
Minas
Rocha
La Paloma
Rodríguez
25 de Agosto
Santa Lucia
Santa Rosa
Migues
Montes
Solis de Mataojo
San Carlos
La Barra
Las Piedras
Toledo
Pando
San Jacinto
La Querencia
Tapia
San Ramón
Piedras de Afilar
Gregorio Aznarez
Nueva Carrara
Pan de Azucar
Maldonado
Piriápolis
Punta del Este

Lagoa Mangueira

Southern South America

BRAZIL
RIO GRANDE DO SUL
URUGUAY
MONTEVIDEO
BUENOS AIRES
Río de la Plata
ATLANTIC OCEAN
PACIFIC OCEAN
ARGENTINA
CHILE
SANTIAGO
Córdoba
CÓRDOBA
Rosario
Mendoza
MENDOZA
San Juan
SAN JUAN
San Luis
SAN LUIS
La Rioja
LA RIOJA
CATAMARCA
Santiago del Estero
SANTIAGO DEL ESTERO
SANTA FE
ENTRE RÍOS
CORRIENTES
Corrientes
Paraná
Santa Fe
La Plata
Mar del Plata
Bahía Blanca
Santa Rosa
LA PAMPA
NEUQUÉN
Neuquén
RÍO NEGRO
Valparaíso
Viña del Mar
Rancagua
Talca
MAULE
BÍO BÍO
Concepción
Talcahuano
Temuco
ARAUCANÍA
Valdivia
Osorno
Puerto Montt
LOS LAGOS
COQUIMBO
Coquimbo
La Serena
ATACAMA
VALPARAÍSO
Golfo San Matías
Viedma
A n d e s
P a m p a s
Sierras de Córdoba
112
291
287
6000m
4000m
3000m
2000m
1000m
500m
250m
100m
Sea Level
-250m
-2000m
-4000m

Scale 1:6,500,000
(projection: Lambert Azimuthal Equal Area)

0 25 50 75 100 125 150 175 200 Km
0 25 50 75 100 125 150 175 200 Miles

Population
- ■ above 5 million
- ⊡ 1 million to 5 million
- ◉ 500,000 to 1 million
- ◎ 100,000 to 500,000
- ⊕ 50,000 to 100,000
- ○ 10,000 to 50,000
- ○ below 10,000

Montevideo

Joaquín Suárez
Ciudad de la Costa
A. del Toledo
Aeropuerto de Carrasco
Toledo
Villa García
Flor de Maroñas
Villa Española
Las Piedras
La Paz
Aeródromo Melilla
Bakwin
Ciudad Vieja
Santiago Vázquez
Cerro
Kel
Caputro
Terminal Marítima
Montevideo
Punta de Lobos
Punta Brava
Pajas Blancas
Delta del Tigre
Punta Yeguas
Punta Carretas
Rio de la Plata

0 5 Km
0 5 Miles

FALKLAND ISLANDS
(Islas Malvinas)
(to UK)

Cape Dolphin
Cape Bougainville
Macbride Head
Cape Carysfort
Volunteer Point
Berkeley Sound
STANLEY
Port Louis
Bluff Cove
Pebble Island
North Falkland Sound
Port San Carlos
San Carlos Settlement
Darwin
Goose Green
Lively Island
Motley Island
Driftwood Point
Keppel Island
Saunders Island
Carcass Island
South Jason Island
Westpoint Island
Hill Cove Settlement
Roy Cove Settlement
Passage Island
New Island
North Island
Beaver Settlement
Weddell Island
Port Stephens Settlement
Cape Meredith
Cape Orford
Barren Island
Sea Lion Islands
Eagle Passage
Porpoise Point
Speedwell Island
Arch Islands
George Island

Jason Islands
Steeple Jason
Grand Jason

Scale 1:3,000,000
0 10 20 30 40 50 60 Km
0 10 20 30 40 50 60 Miles

FALKLAND ISLANDS
(Islas Malvinas)
(to UK)

Cape Dolphin
West Falkland
STANLEY
Bluff Cove
East Falkland
Keppel Island
King George Bay
Jason Islands
Weddell Island
Cape Meredith

ATLANTIC OCEAN

Península Valdés
Salinas Grandes
Punta Delgada
Golfo San José
Golfo Nuevo
Puerto Lobos
Puerto Madryn
Trelew
Rawson
Gaiman
Dolavon
Bahía Vera
Bahía Camarones
Camarones
Cabo Blanco
Puerto Deseado
Punta Pozos
Bahía de los Nodales
CHUBUT
Golfo San Jorge
Comodoro Rivadavia
Rada Tilly
Caleta Olivia
Pico Truncado
Puerto San Julián
Gran Bajo
Gran Bajo de San Julián
SANTA CRUZ
Río Chico
Río Santa Cruz
Río Coig
Río Gallegos
Bahía Grande
Punta Bustamante
Punta Dungeness
Punta Delgada
Río Grande
TIERRA DEL FUEGO
Bahía San Sebastián
Punta Arenas
Río Gallegos
Estrecho de Magallanes
Strait of Magellan
Cabo de Hornos
Estrecho de le Maire
Isla de los Estados

ANDES

AISEN
MAGALLANES
Golfo de Penas
Archipiélago de los Chonos
Isla Chiloé
Canal Moraleda
Isla Wellington
Península Tres Montes
Golfo Corcovado
Golfo Trinidad
Golfo Madre de Dios
Archipiélago Reina Adelaida
Isla Santa Inés
Isla Desolación
Cabo Froward
Isla Santa Inés
Isla Clarence
Isla Dawson
Isla Wollaston
Isla Lennox
Isla Nueva
Isla Navarino
Lago Fagnano
Lago Buenos Aires

SOUTH AMERICA

117

19,686ft
13,124ft
9843ft
6562ft
3281ft
1640ft
820ft
328ft
Sea Level
-820ft
-6562ft
-13,124ft

Central Chile & Argentina

Scale 1:2,600,000
(projection: Lambert Conformal Conic)

0 10 20 30 40 50 Km
0 10 20 30 40 50 Miles

Easter Island (Isla de Pascua) (to Chile)

Punta San Juan
Cabo Norte
Punta Rosalia
Playa de Anakena
Maunga Terevaka 506m
Bahía de La Perouse
Cabo O'Higgins
Ahu Riki
Maunga Pukatikei 370m
Cabo Roggewein
Motu Tautara
Maunga Pokatikei
Mataveri
Vaihu
Punta Akahanga
Rano Raraku
Hanga Roa
Ahu Vinapu
Punta Baja
Orongo
Motu Nui
Cabo Sur

Scale 1:500,000
0 2.5 5 Km
0 2.5 5 Miles

PACIFIC OCEAN

PACIFIC OCEAN

CHILE
ARGENTINA

A n d e s

Regions / Provinces
SAN JUAN
COQUIMBO
VALPARAÍSO
SANTIAGO
LIBERTADOR
MENDOZA
MAULE
BÍO BÍO
ARAUCANÍA
NEUQUÉN
LA PAMPA

Selected place names
Santiago
Valparaíso
Viña del Mar
San Antonio
San Felipe
Rancagua
Curicó
Talca
Linares
Chillán
Concepción
Talcahuano
Los Ángeles
Temuco
Mendoza
Godoy Cruz
San Juan
San Rafael
General Alvear
Cerro Aconcagua 6959m
Volcán Tupungato 6800m
Cerro Mercedario 6769m

Elevation scale
6000m
4000m
3000m
2000m
1000m
500m
250m
100m
Sea Level
-250m
-2000m
-4000m

Brazília

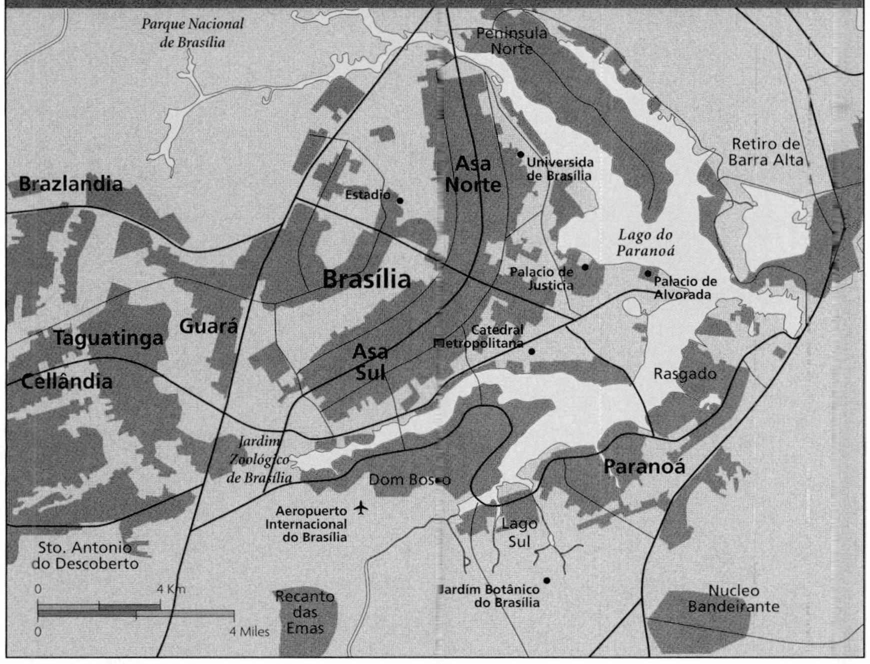

Parque Nacional de Brasília
Península Norte
Brazlandia
Asa Norte
Universida de Brasília
Estádio
Retiro de Barra Alta
Lago do Paranoá
Brasília
Palacio de Justicia
Palacio de Alvorada
Taguatinga
Guará
Asa Sul
Catedral Metropolitana
Rasgado
Cellândia
Jardim Zoológico de Brasília
Dom Bosco
Paranoá
Aeroporto Internacional do Brasília
Sto. Antonio do Descoberto
Lago Sul
Recanto das Emas
Jardim Botánico do Brasilia
Nucleo Bandeirante
0 4 Km
0 4 Miles

Caracas

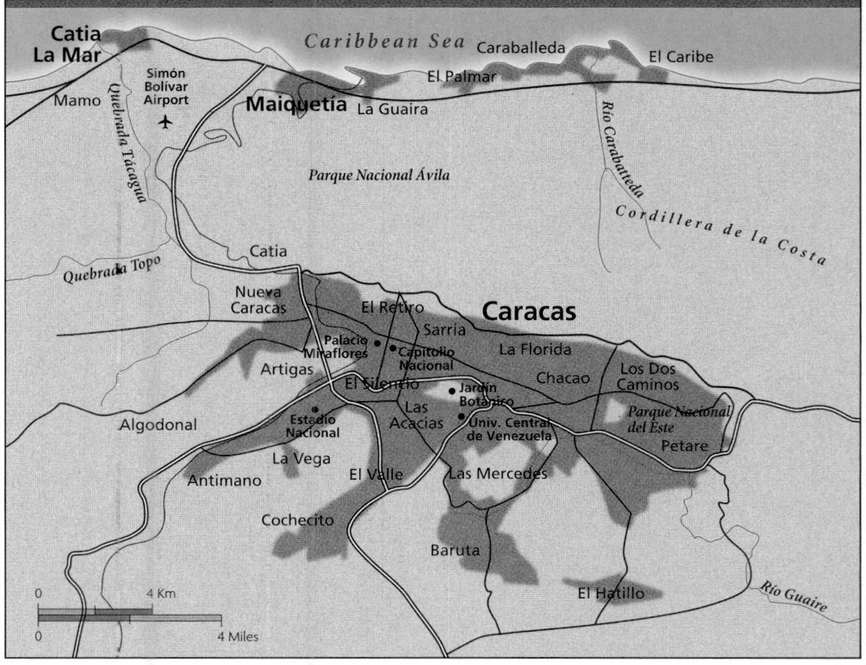

Caribbean Sea
Catia La Mar
Simón Bolívar Airport
Caraballeda
El Caribe
Mamo
El Palmar
Maiquetía
La Guaira
Catia
Parque Nacional Ávila
Río Carabelleda
Cordillera de la Costa
Quebrada Topo
Quebrada Tácagua
Nueva Caracas
El Retiro
Sarria
Caracas
Palacio Miraflores
Capitolio Nacional
La Florida
Los Dos Caminos
Artigas
El Silencio
Jardin Botánico
Chacao
Algodonal
Las Acacias
Univ. Central de Venezuela
Parque Nacional del Este
Petare
Estadio Nacional
La Vega
Antimano
El Valle
Las Mercedes
Cochecito
Baruta
El Hatillo
Río Guaire
0 4 Km
0 4 Miles

Havana

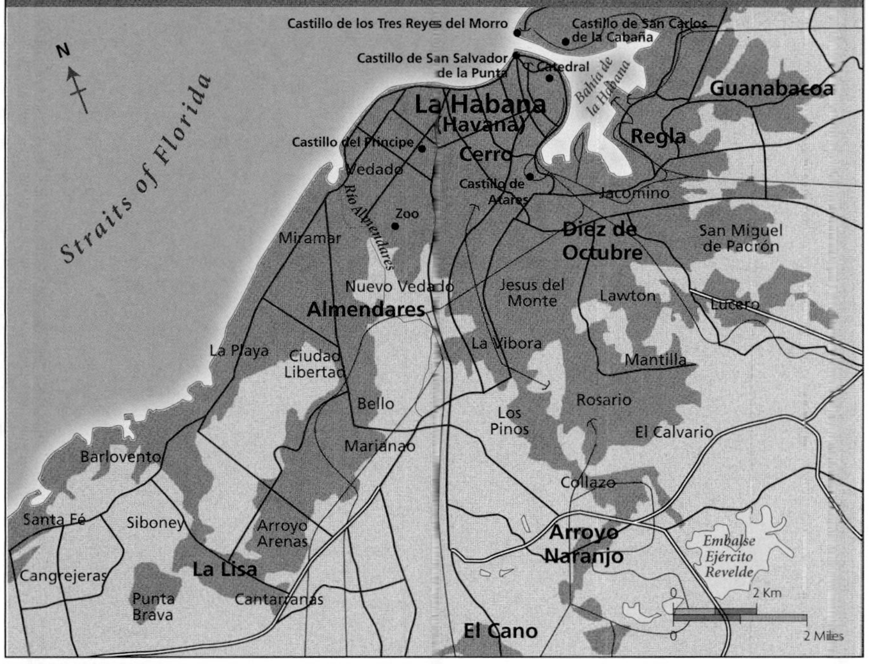

N
Castillo de los Tres Reyes del Morro
Castillo de San Carlos de la Cabaña
Castillo de San Salvador de la Punta
Catedral
La Habana (Havana)
Guanabacoa
Castillo del Príncipe
Bahía de la Habana
Vedado
Regla
Cerro
Straits of Florida
Castillo de Atares
Jacomino
Río Almendares
Zoo
Diez de Octubre
San Miguel de Padron
Miramar
Nuevo Vedado
Jesus del Monte
Lawton
Lucero
Almendares
La Playa
Ciudad Libertad
La Vibora
Mantilla
Barlovento
Bello
Rosario
El Calvario
Santa Fé
Siboney
Marianao
Los Pinos
Collazo
Cangrejeras
Arroyo Arenas
Arroyo Naranjo
Embalse Ejército Revelde
Punta Brava
La Lisa
Cantaranas
El Cano
0 2 Km
0 2 Miles

Quito

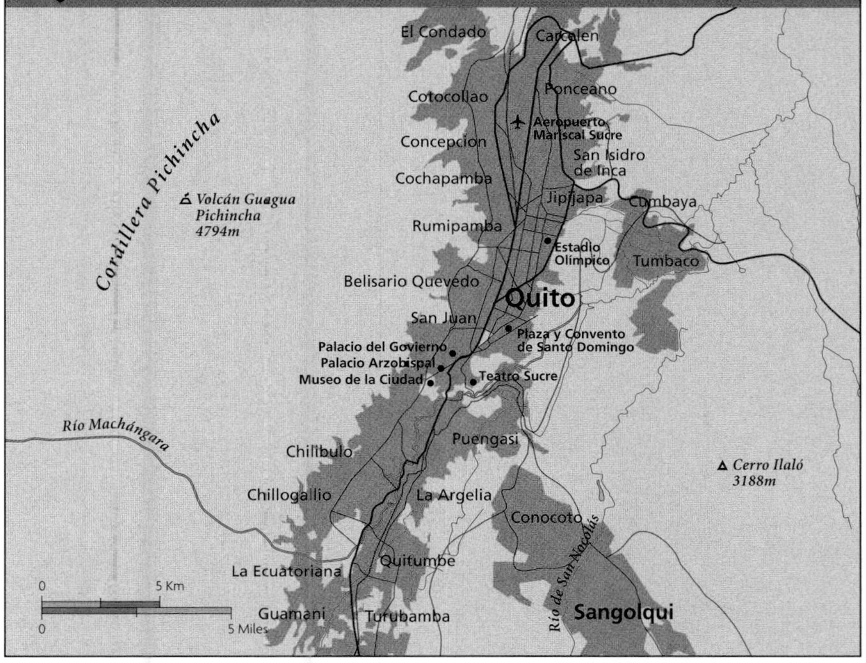

El Condado
Carcelen
Cotocollao
Ponceano
Aeropuerto Mariscal Sucre
Concepcion
San Isidro de Inca
Cordillera Pichincha
Cochapamba
Jipijapa
Cumbaya
Volcán Guagua Pichincha 4794m
Rumipamba
Estadio Olimpico
Tumbaco
Belisario Quevedo
Quito
San Juan
Plaza y Convento de Santo Domingo
Palacio del Govierno
Palacio Arzobispal
Teatro Sucre
Museo de la Ciudad
Río Machángara
Chillbulo
Puengasi
Cerro Ilaló 3188m
Chillogallio
La Argelia
La Ecuatoriana
Conocoto
Quitumbe
Río de San Nicolás
Guamani
Torubamba
Sangolqui
0 5 Km
0 5 Miles

Santiago

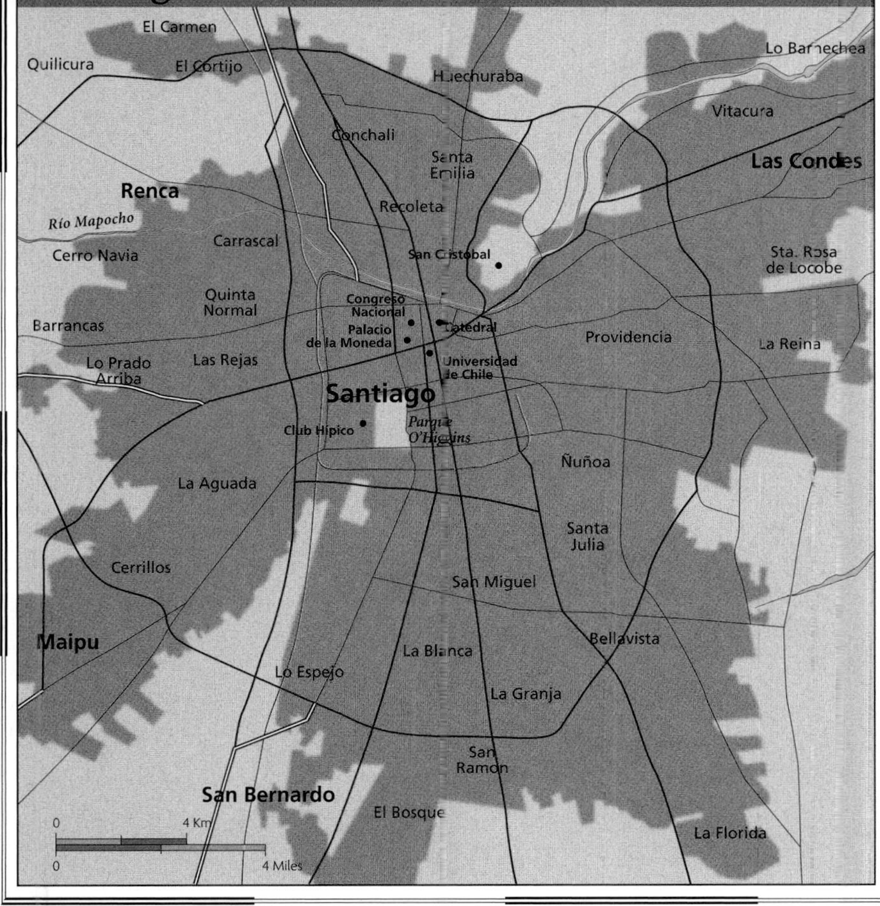

El Carmen
Quilicura
Lo Barnechea
El Cortijo
Huechuraba
Vitacura
Conchali
Las Condes
Renca
Santa Emilia
Recoleta
Río Mapocho
Carrascal
San Cristobal
Cerro Navia
Sta. Rosa de Locobe
Quinta Normal
Congreso Nacional
Catedral
Barrancas
Palacio de la Moneda
Providencia
La Reina
Lo Prado Arriba
Las Rejas
Universidad de Chile
Santiago
Club Hipico
Parque O'Higgins
La Aguada
Ñuñoa
Cerrillos
Santa Julia
Maipu
San Miguel
Bellavista
La Blanca
La Granja
Lo Espejo
San Ramon
San Bernardo
El Bosque
La Florida
0 4 Km
0 4 Miles

São Paulo

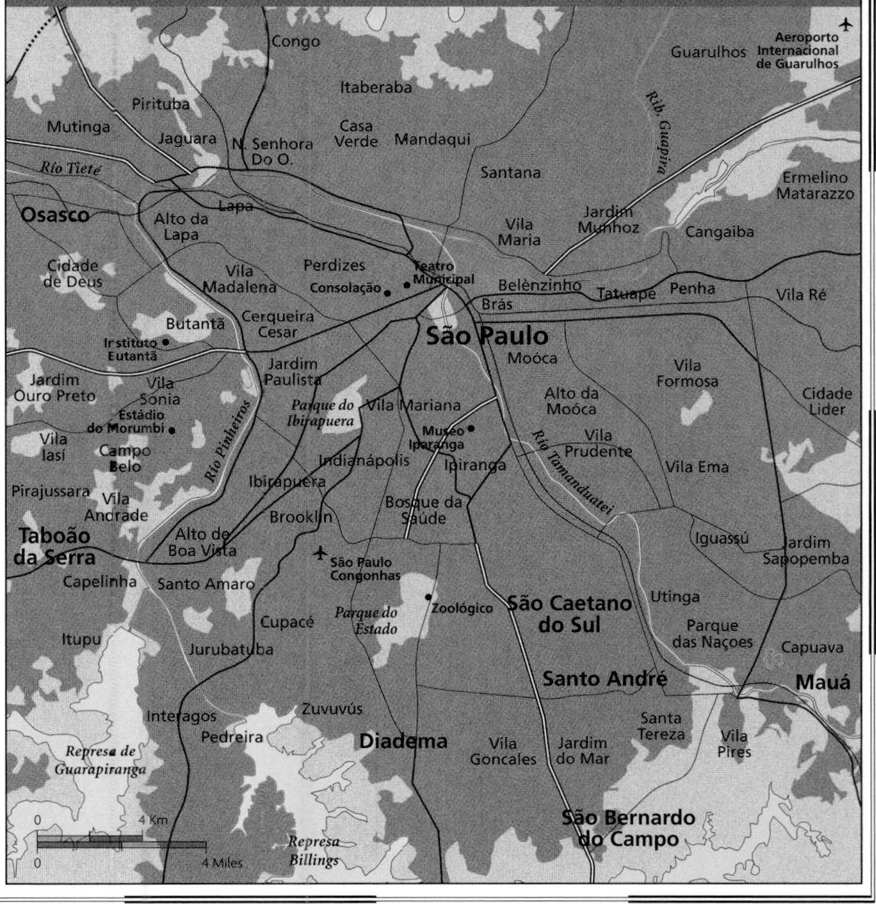

Congo
Guarulhos
Aeroporto Internacional de Guarulhos
Itaberaba
Mutinga
Pirituba
Casa Verde
Rib. Guapira
Jaguara
Mandaqui
Río Tiete
N. Senhora Do O.
Santana
Ermelino Matarazzo
Osasco
Alto da Lapa
Lapa
Vila Maria
Jardim Michhoz
Cangaiba
Cidade de Deus
Vila Madalena
Perdizes
Teatro Municipal
Belênzinho
Tatuape
Penha
Vila Ré
Butantã
Consolação
Brás
Instituto Eutantã
Cerqueira Cesar
São Paulo
Mooca
Jardim Paulista
Alto da Mooca
Vila Formosa
Jardim Ouro Preto
Vila Sonia
Parque do Ibirapuera
Vila Mariana
Vila Prudente
Cidade Lider
Vila Iasi
Estádio do Morumbi
Museu Ipiranga
Campo Belo
Indianápolis
Ipiranga
Vila Ema
Pirajussara
Ibirapuera
Brooklin
Bosque da Saúde
Taboão da Serra
Vila Andrade
Alto de Boa Vista
Iguassú
Jardim Sapopemba
São Paulo Congonhas
Capelinha
Santo Amaro
Zoológico
São Caetano do Sul
Utinga
Itupu
Cupacé
Parque do Estado
Capuava
Jurubatuba
Parque das Naçoes
Interlagos
Pedreira
Zuvuvús
Santo André
Mauá
Represa de Guarapiranga
Diadema
Vila Goncales
Jardim do Mar
Santa Tereza
Vila Pires
Represa Billings
São Bernardo do Campo
0 4 Km
0 4 Miles

19.686ft
13,124ft
9843ft
6562ft
3281ft
1640ft
820ft
328ft
Sea Level
-820ft
-6562ft
-13,124ft

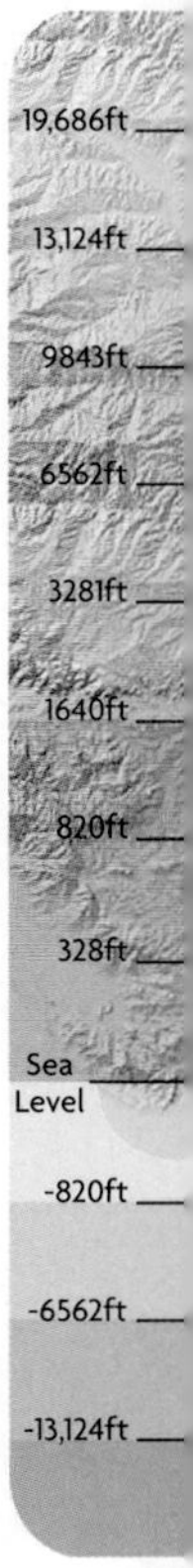

AFRICA

Africa is the world's second largest continent with a total area of 11,712,434 sq miles (30,335,000 sq km). It has 53 separate countries, including Madagascar in the Indian Ocean. It straddles the equator and is the only continent to stretch from the northern to southern temperate zones.

FACTFILE

N **Most Northerly Point:** Jalta, Tunisia 37° 31′ N
S **Most Southerly Point:** Cape Agulhas, South Africa 34° 52′ S
E **Most Easterly Point:** Raas Xaafuun, Somalia 51° 24′ E
W **Most Westerly Point:** Santo Antão, Cape Verde, 25° 11′ W

Largest Lakes:
1. Lake Victoria, Kenya/Tanzania/Uganda 26,828 sq miles (69,484 sq km)
2. Lake Tanganyika, Dem. Rep. Congo/Tanzania 12,703 sq miles (32,900 sq km)
3. Lake Nyasa, Malawi/Mozambique/Tanzania 11,600 sq miles (30,044 sq km)
4. Lake Turkana, Ethiopia/Kenya 2473 sq miles (6405 sq km)
5. Lake Albert, Dem. Rep. Congo/Uganda 2046 sq miles (5299 sq km)

Longest Rivers:
1. Nile, NE Africa 4160 miles (6695 km)
2. Congo, Angola/Congo/Dem. Rep. Congo 2900 miles (4667 km)
3. Niger, W Africa 2589 miles (4167 km)
4. Zambezi, Southern Africa 1673 miles (2693 km)
5. Ubangi-Uele, C Africa 1429 miles (2300 km)

Largest Islands:
1. Madagascar, 229,300 sq miles (594,000 sq km)
2. Réunion, 970 sq miles (2535 sq km)
3. Tenerife, Canary Islands 785 sq miles (2034 sq km)
4. Isla de Bioco, Equatorial Guinea 779 sq miles (2017 sq km)
5. Mauritius, 709 sq miles (1836 sq km)

Highest Points:
1. Kilimanjaro, Tanzania 19,340 ft (5895 m)
2. Kirinyaga, Kenya 17,058 ft (5199 m)
3. Mount Stanley, Dem. Rep. Congo/Uganda 16,762 ft (5109 m)
4. Mount Speke, Uganda 16,043 ft (4890 m)
5. Mount Baker, Uganda 15,892 ft (4844 m)

Lowest Point:
▼ Lac 'Assal, Djibouti -512 ft (-156 m) below sea level

Highest recorded temperature:
● Al'Aziziyah, Libya 136°F (58°C)

Lowest recorded temperature:
— Ifrane, Morocco -11°F (-24°C)

Wettest Place:
≋ Cape Debundsha, Cameroon 405 in (10,290 mm)

Driest Place:
— Wadi Halfa, Sudan <0.1 in (<2.5 mm)

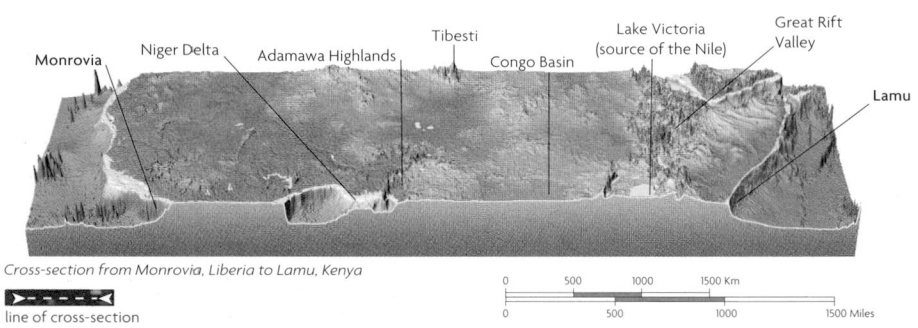

Monrovia · Niger Delta · Adamawa Highlands · Tibesti · Congo Basin · Lake Victoria (source of the Nile) · Great Rift Valley · Lamu

Cross-section from Monrovia, Liberia to Lamu, Kenya

line of cross-section

| 0 | 500 | 1000 | 1500 Km |
| 0 | 500 | 1000 | 1500 Miles |

H I J K L M N

1 2 3 4 5 6 7 8 9 10

Sardinia
Balearic Islands
Tyrrhenian Sea
Strait of Gibraltar
Mediterranean Sea
Ionian Sea
Ionian Basin
Aegean Sea
Sea of Crete
Hellenic Trough
Cyprus
Malta
Atlas Mountains
Saharan Atlas
Grand Erg Occidental
Chott el Jerid
Gulf of Sirte
Grand Erg Oriental
Al Jabal al Akhḑar
Qattara Depression
Nile Fan
Suez Canal
Sinai
Dead Sea
Syrian Desert
An Nafud
Euphrates
Persian Gulf
Arabian Peninsula
Tropic of Cancer
Plateau du Tademaït
SAHARA
Great Sand Sea
Western Desert
Libyan Desert
Eastern Desert
Erg Chech
Tassili-n-Ajjer
Idhān Murzuq
Ahaggar
Tanezrouft
Lake Nasser
Nubian Desert
Red Sea
Ar Rubʿ al Khālī
Adrar des Ifôghas
Ténéré du Tafassâsset
Tibesti
Grand Erg de Bilma
Azaouâd
Massif de l'Aïr
Ténéré
Ouadi Howa
Ouadi Haouach
Gulf of Aden
Horn of Africa
Sahel
Lake Chad
Jos Plateau
Niger Delta
Niger Fan
Gulf of Guinea
Isla de Bioco
Príncipe
São Tomé
Guinea Basin
Somali Basin
Somali Plain
Equator
INDIAN OCEAN
Lake Victoria
Providence Atoll
Pemba
Zanzibar
Lake Tanganyika
Congo Canyon
Congo Fan
Comoro Islands
Comoro Basin
Mozambique Channel
Angola Basin
ATLANTIC OCEAN
Saint Helena
Madagascar Basin
Madagascar Plateau
Kalahari Desert
Natal Basin
Natal Valley
Mozambique Plateau
Orange Fan
Tristan da Cunha
Gough Island
Cape Basin
Cape of Good Hope
Southwest Indian Ridge
Crozet Islands
Prince Edward Islands
Crozet Plateau

H I J K L M N

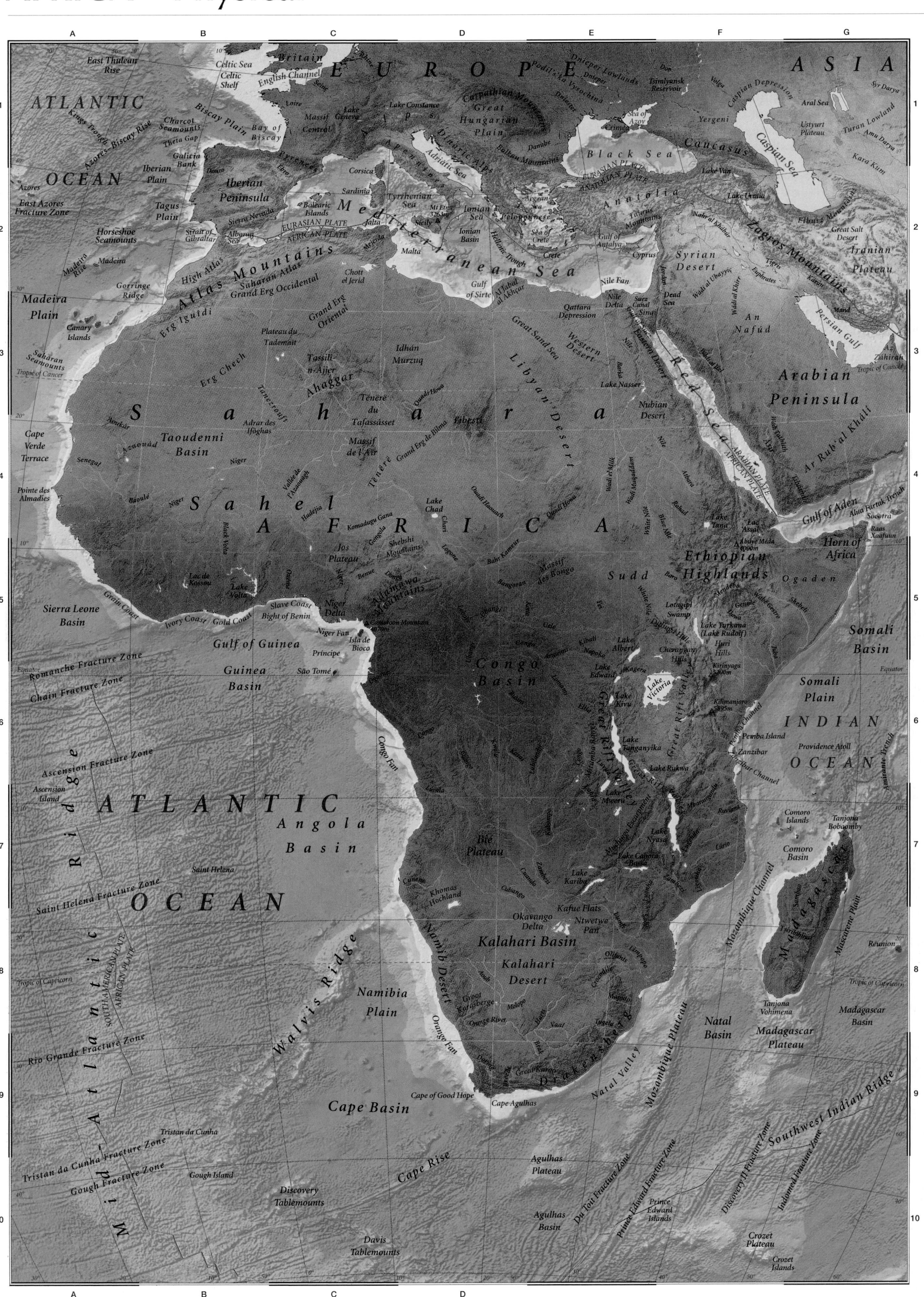

Scale 1:35,000,000
(projection: Lambert Azimuthal Equal Area)

0   250   500   750   1000   1250 Km
0   250   500   750   1000   1250 Miles

Climate

The climates of Africa range from mediterranean to arid, dry savannah and humid equatorial. In East Africa, where snow settles at the summit of volcanoes such as Kilimanjaro, climate is also modified by altitude. The winds of the Sahara export millions of tons of dust a year both northward and eastward.

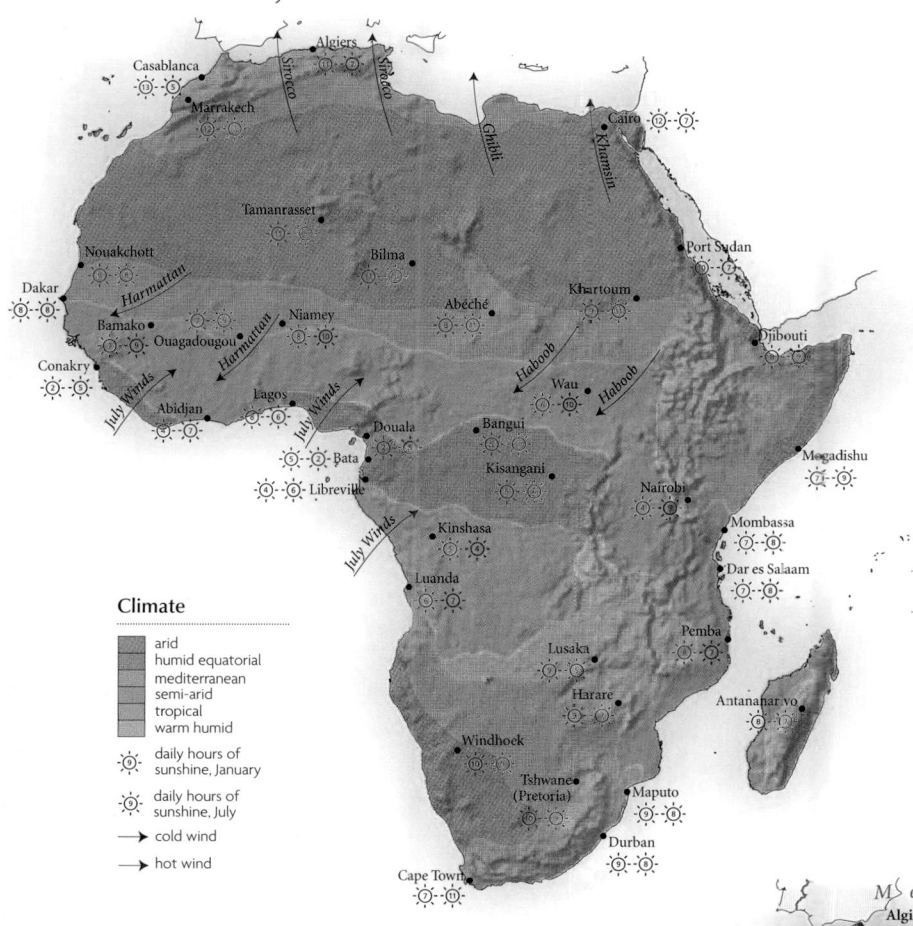

Average Rainfall

January rainfall

July rainfall

Rainfall
- 0–1 in (0–25 mm)
- 1–2 in (25–50 mm)
- 2–4 in (50–100 mm)
- 4–8 in (100–200 mm)
- 8–12 in (200–300 mm)
- 12–16 in (300–400 mm)
- 16–20 in (400–500 mm)
- more than 20 in (500 mm)

Average Temperature

January temperature

July temperature

Temperature
- below -22°F (-30°C)
- -22 to -4°F (-30 to -20°C)
- -4 to 14°F (-20 to -10°C)
- 14 to 32°F (-10 to 0°C)
- 32 to 50°F (0 to 10°C)
- 50 to 68°F (10 to 20°C)
- 68 to 86°F (20 to 30°C)
- above 86°F (30°C)

Climate
- arid
- humid equatorial
- mediterranean
- semi-arid
- tropical
- warm humid
- ☼ daily hours of sunshine, January
- ☼ daily hours of sunshine, July
- → cold wind
- → hot wind

Landuse

Some of Africa's most productive agricultural land is found in the eastern volcanic uplands, where fertile soils support a wide range of valuable export crops including vegetables, tea, and coffee. The most widely-grown grain is corn and peanuts (groundnuts) are particularly important in West Africa. Without intensive irrigation, cultivation is not possible in desert regions and unreliable rainfall in other areas limits crop production. Pastoral herding is most commonly found in these marginal lands. Substantial local fishing industries are found along coasts and in vast lakes such as Lake Nyasa and Lake Victoria.

Environmental issues

One of Africa's most serious environmental problems occurs in marginal areas such as the Sahel where scrub and forest clearance, often for cooking fuel, combined with overgrazing, are causing desertification. Game reserves in southern and eastern Africa have helped to preserve many endangered animals, although the needs of growing populations have led to conflict over land use, and poaching is a serious problem.

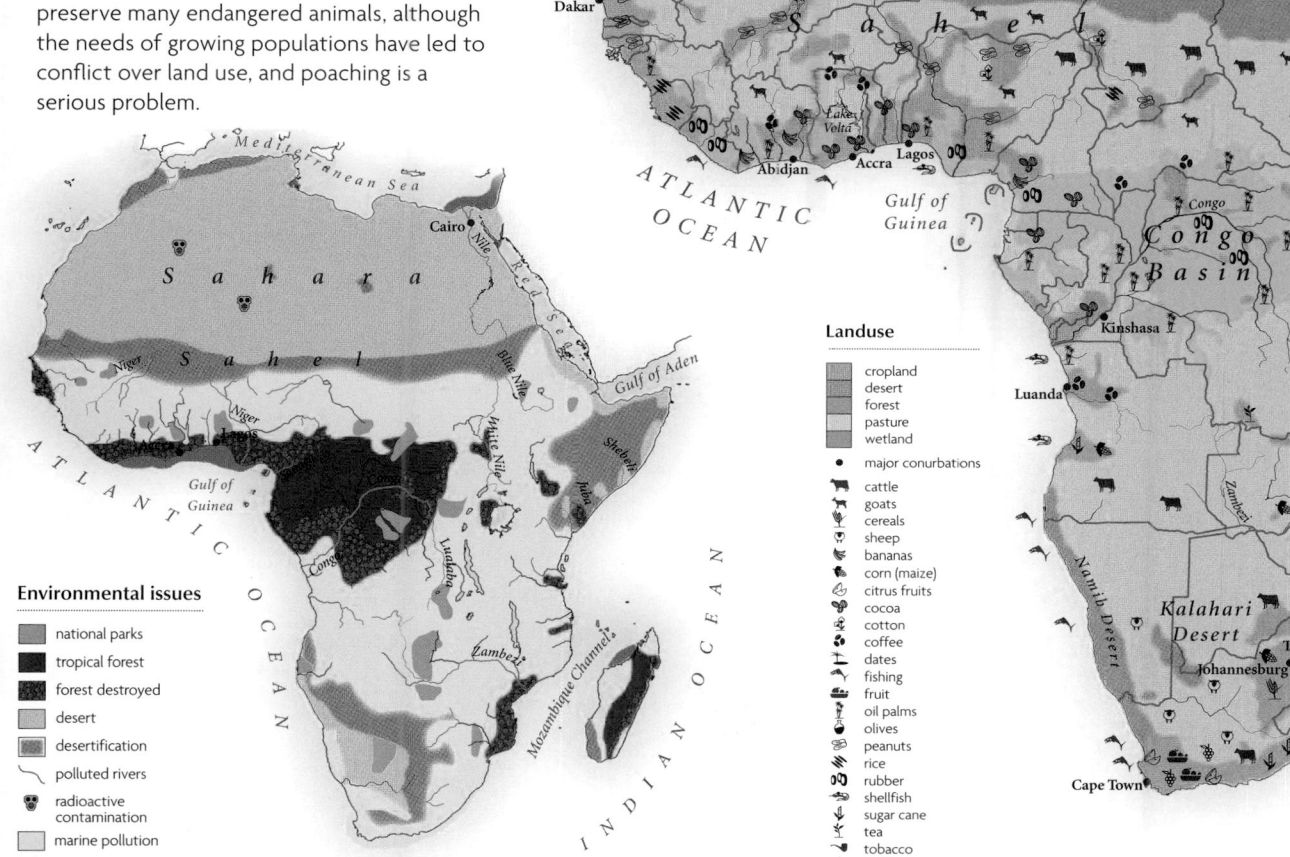

Landuse
- cropland
- desert
- forest
- pasture
- wetland
- • major conurbations
- cattle
- goats
- cereals
- sheep
- bananas
- corn (maize)
- citrus fruits
- cocoa
- cotton
- coffee
- dates
- fishing
- fruit
- oil palms
- olives
- peanuts
- rice
- rubber
- shellfish
- sugar cane
- tea
- tobacco
- vineyards
- wheat

Environmental issues
- national parks
- tropical forest
- forest destroyed
- desert
- desertification
- polluted rivers
- radioactive contamination
- marine pollution
- heavy marine pollution
- • poor urban air quality

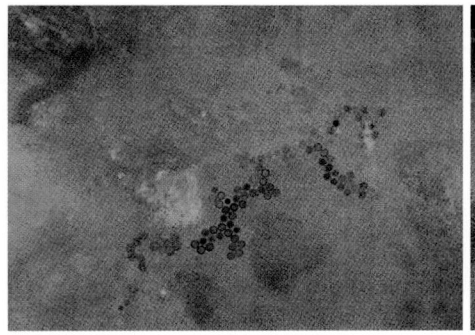

1 AL KHUFRAH, LIBYA
The circular irrigation patterns at this oasis have developed through the use of sprinkler units sweeping around a central point.

2 ERG DU DJOURAB, CHAD
Looking southwest, the pale area, just south of the darker Tibesti mountains on the right and the Ennedi plateau on the left, shows a desert sandstorm in motion.

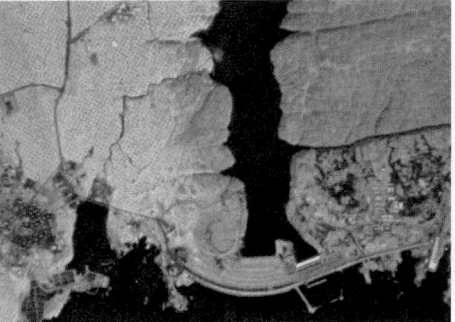

3 ASWAN HIGH DAM, EGYPT
Completed in 1970 the dam controls flooding along the lower stretches of the Nile river.

4 KHARTOUM, SUDAN
The capital of Sudan lies at the junction of the Blue Nile, flowing from the east, and the broad White Nile, flowing from the south.

9 LAKE FAGUIBINE, MALI
Part of the Niger river's 'inland delta', a region of lakes, creeks and backwaters near Tombouctou.

10 TASSILI-N-AJJER, ALGERIA
These sand dunes, one of a variety found in the Sahara, overlie the darker sandstone bedrock of the Tassili-n-Ajjer plateau.

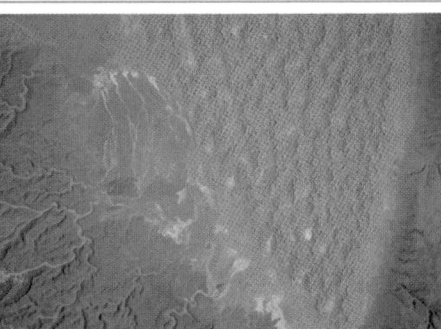

11 NIGER DELTA, NIGERIA
At this point lies the vast, low-lying region through which the waters of the Niger river drain into the Gulf of Guinea.

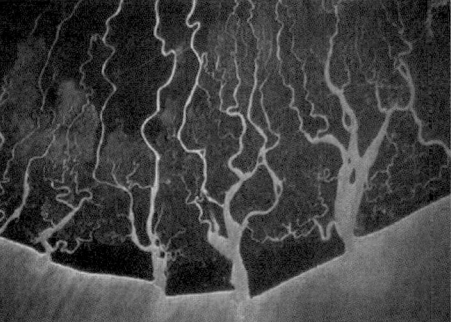

12 CONGO/UBANGI RIVERS, DR CONGO
The confluence of these two rivers lies at the heart of the Congo Basin.

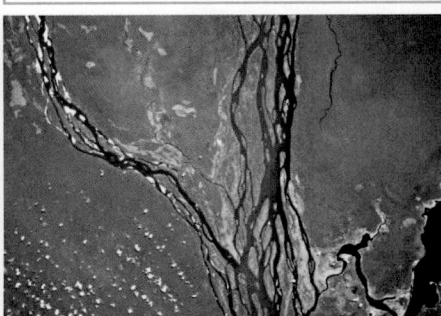

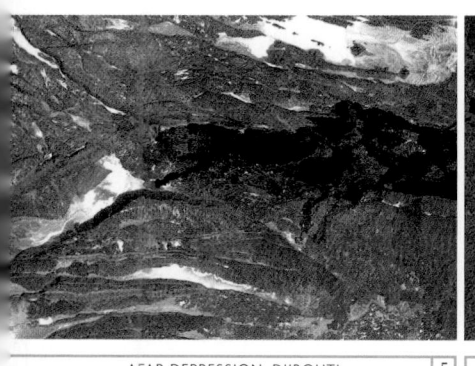

AFAR DEPRESSION, DJIBOUTI [5]
This low point is located at the junction of three tectonic plates - the Gulf of Aden to the east, the Red Sea to the north and the Great Rift Valley to the south.

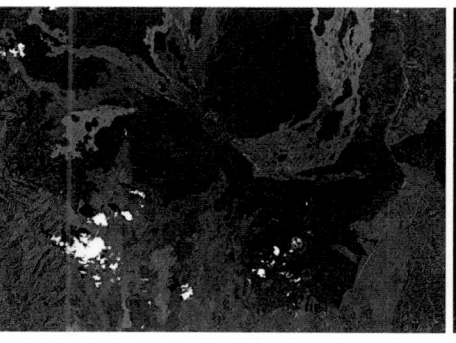

NYIRAGONGO AND NYAMURAGIRA VOLCANOES, [6]
DR CONGO
These two volcanoes, lying to the west of the Great Rift Valley, last erupted in 2002 and 2001 respectively.

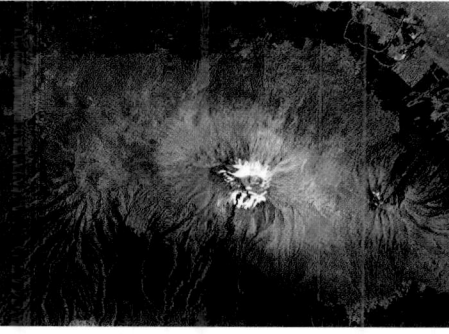

KILIMANJARO, TANZANIA [7]
An extinct volcano, its great height modifies the local climate, forcing moist air streams from the Indian Ocean to rise, inducing rain and, higher up, snow.

BETSIBOKA RIVER, MADAGASCAR [8]
The waters of Madagascar's second longest river are red with sediment as it carries eroded topsoil from the interior and deposits it at it's mouth on the Indian Ocean.

MALEBO POOL, CONGO/DR CONGO [13]
A lake in the lower reaches of the Congo river, it hosts two capital cities on its banks, Brazzaville, Congo to the north and Kinshasa, DR Congo to the south.

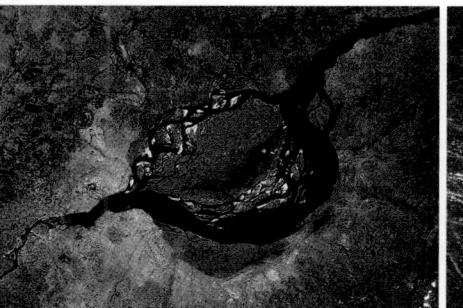

ZAMBEZI RIVER, ZAMBIA [14]
Seasonal flooding of the river and its tributaries turned the Mulonga and Liuwa plains on the Zambia-Angola border into a vast wetland in April 2004

BEIRA, MOZAMBIQUE [15]
This port and beach resort lies on the north side of the mouth of the Pungoé river.

CAPE TOWN, SOUTH AFRICA [16]
South Africa's third largest city with a population of 2.9 million, it is also the seat of the country's parliament.

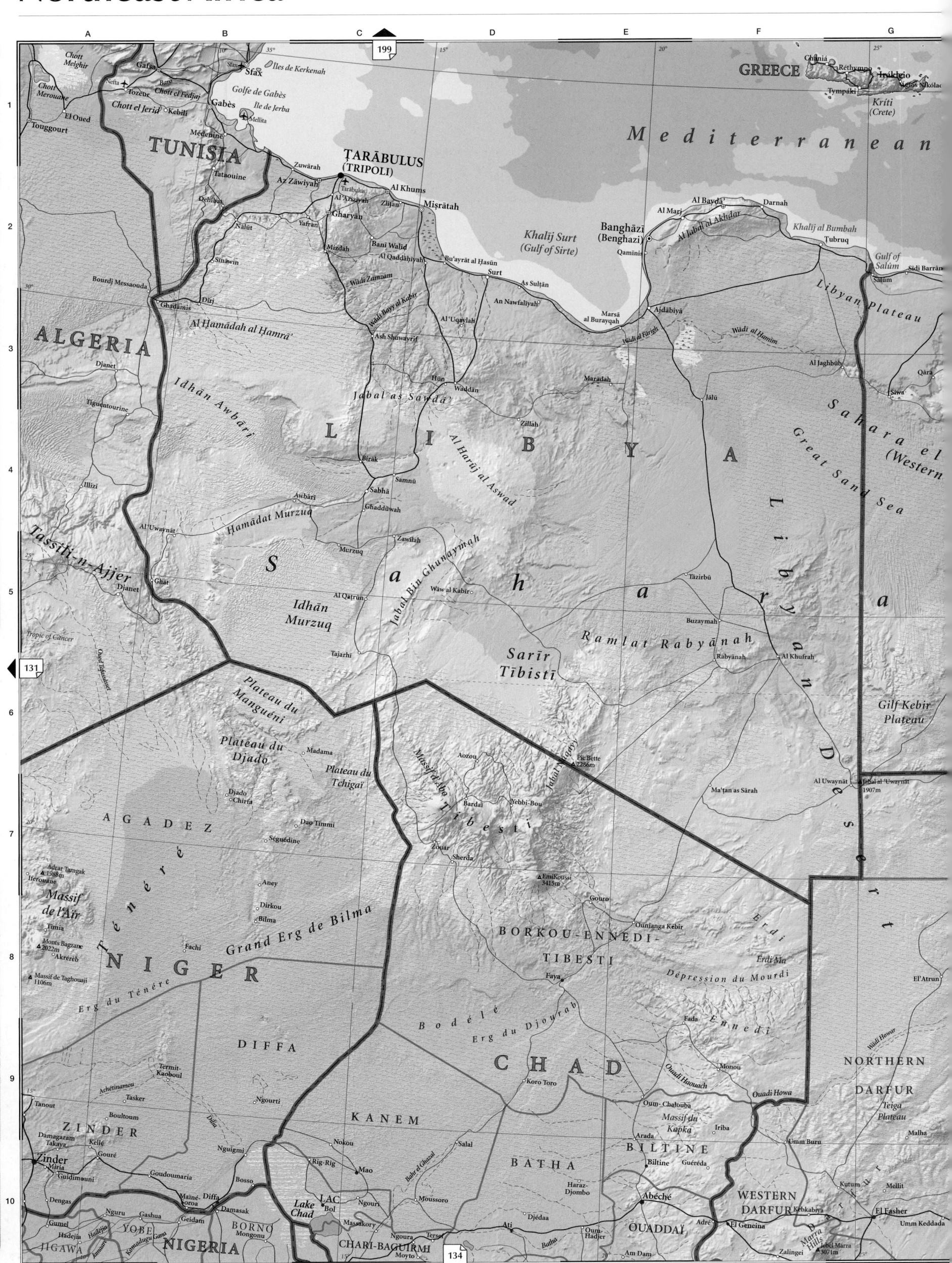

199

134

Map labels

GREECE

Chaniá
Réthymno
Iráklejo
Týmpaki
Ríos Nikólao
Kríti
(Crete)

Mediterranean

Chott Melghir
Chott Merouane
El Oued
Touggourt
Netta
Tozeur
Kebili
Gafsa
Gabès
Stax
Sfax
Iles de Kerkenah
Golfe de Gabès
Ile de Jerba
Mellita

TUNISIA
Tataouine
Medenine
Dehibat

Zuwārah
Az Zāwiyah
Ţarābulus
**ŢARĀBULUS
(TRIPOLI)**
Al 'Azīzīyah
Gharyān
Yafran
Nalut
Mizdah
Bani Walīd
Sīnāwin
Al Qaddāhīyah
Wādī Zamzam
Zlīţan
Al Khums
Mişrātah
Bu'ayrāt al Ḥasūn
Surt
*Khalīj Surt
(Gulf of Sirte)*
As Sulţān
An Nawfalīyah
Al 'Uqaylah
Marsā al Burayqah
Ajdābiyā
Wādī al Fārigh

Al Marj
**Banghāzī
(Benghazi)**
Qamīnis
Al Jabal al Akhdar
Al Bayḍā'
Darnah
Tubruq
Khalīj al Bumbah
Gulf of Salūm
Sidi Barrāni
Salūm

Bourdj Messaouda
Ghadāmis
Dirj
Al Ḥamādah al Ḥamrā'

ALGERIA
Djanet
Tiguentourine
Illizi

Idhān Awbārī

L I B Y A

Jabal as Sawdā'
Hūn
Waddān
Maradah
Ash Shuwayrif
Zīllah
Wādī Bayy al Kabīr

Al Ḥarūj al Aswad

Birāk
Samnū
Sabhā
Awbārī
Ghaddūwah
Zawīlah
Murzuq

Ḥamādat Murzuq

Al 'Uwaynāt

S a h a r a

*Idhān
Murzuq*
Al Qaţrūn
Wāw al Kabīr
Jabal Bin Ghunaymah

Tāzirbū
Buzaymah
Ramlat Rabyānah
Rabyānah
Al Khufrah

*Sarīr
Tībistī*

Tajarhī

*Sahara el
(Western)*

Great Sand Sea

Al Jaghbūb
Jālū
Qāra
Siwa

Libyan Plateau

*Gilf Kebir
Plateau*

Libyan Desert

AGADEZ

*Plateau du
Manguéni*

*Plateau du
Djado*
Madama
*Plateau du
Tchigaï*
Djado
Chirfa
Dao Timmi
Séguédine

Massif du Tibesti
Aozou
Bardaï
Yebbi-Bou
Jabal Nūqay
Pic Bette
2286m

Ma'tan as Sārah
Al Uwaynāt
Jabal al 'Uwaynāt
1907m

Adrar Tamgak
1988m
Iferouane
*Massif
de l'Aïr*
Monts Bagzane
2022m
Akréréb
Tunia
Massif de Taghouaji
1106m

Aney
Dirkou
Bilma
Zouar
Sherda
▲EmiKoussi
3415m
Gouro
Ounianga Kebir
Erdi
Erdi Ma
Brdi

Ténéré

N I G E R

Grand Erg de Bilma

Fachi

Erg du Ténéré

**BORKOU-ENNEDI-
TIBESTI**
Faya
Dépression du Mourdi
Fada
Ennedi
Wādī Howar

Bodélé
Erg du Djourab

**NORTHERN
DARFUR**
*Teiga
Plateau*
Iriba
Umm Buru

DIFFA
Termit-Kaoboul
Achétinamou
Tasker
Tanout
Ngourti

Koro Toro
Monou
Ouadi Haouach
Arada
Ouadi Howa
Malha

ZINDER
Damagaram
Takaya
Kellé
Gouré
Boultoum
Diffa
N'guigmi
Bosso
Nokou
Salal
KANEM
Mao
Bahr el Ghazal
CHAD
Oum-Chalouba
Fada
BILTINE
Biltine
Guéréda
Kebkabiya
Mellit
El Fasher
Umm Keddada

Zinder
Miria
Goudoumaria
Maïné-Soroa
Diffa
Bol
LAC
Lake
Chad
Ngouri
Massakory
Ngoura
Nokou
Rig-Rig
BATHA
Haraz-Djombo
Ati
OUADDAÏ
Abéché
Adré
**WESTERN
DARFUR**
El Geneina
*Marra
Hills*
Jebel Marra
3071m
Zalingei
Umm Buru
Kutum

Tanout
Gumel
Hadejia
JIGAWA
YOBE
Nguru
Gashua
Geidam
Damasak
BORNO
Mongonu
NIGERIA
CHARI-BAGUIRMI
Moyto
Bokoro
Am Dam
Sea Level

Scale 1:8,000,000
(projection: Lambert Azimuthal Equal Area)

0 25 50 75 100 125 150 175 200 Km
0 25 50 75 100 125 150 175 200 Miles

Population
- ■ above 5 million
- ■ 1 million to 5 million
- ● 500,000 to 1 million
- ◎ 100,000 to 500,000
- ⊕ 50,000 to 100,000
- ○ 10,000 to 50,000
- ○ below 10,000

19,686ft
13,124ft
9843ft
6562ft
3281ft
1640ft
820ft
328ft
Sea Level
-820ft
-6562ft
-13,124ft

TURKISH REPUBLIC OF NORTHERN CYPRUS
(recognized only by Turkey)
NICOSIA
CYPRUS
Páfos
Lárnaka
Lemesós (Limassol)
Kárpathos
Sea

Al Ládhiqíyah (Latakia)
Hamāh
Tartūs
Tripoli
LEBANON
BEYROUTH (BEIRUT)
DIMASHQ (DAMASCUS)
Hims (Homs)
SYRIA
Syrian Desert
Al Jazīrah
Tikrīt
Kermānshāh (Bākhtarān)
KERMANSHAH
IRAN
Tigris
Euphrates
BAGHDĀD
IRAQ
Al Hillah
Al Kūt
An Najaf
Karbalā
Ba'qūbah
Al Fallūjah

ISRAEL
Tel Aviv-Yafo
Holon
Ashdod
JERUSALEM
Gaza Strip
Be'ér Sheva
El 'Arīsh
Hefa (Haifa)
Nahariyya
West Bank
AMMĀN
Az Zarqā'
JORDAN
Ma'dabā
Al Karak
Dead Sea

Nile Delta
Dumyât (Damietta)
Port Said
Rashid (Rosetta)
Kafr el Sheikh
Alexandria
El 'Alamein
Matrûh
Damanhûr
Tanta
Zagazig
El Mansûra
Isma'iliya
Benha
CAIRO
El Gîza
Helwân
Suez
Suez Canal
Gulf of Suez
Sinai
Abu Zenima
Gebel Musa 2285m
El Tûr
Râs Gharib
Hurghada
Bûr Safâga
Quseir
Marsa 'Alam
Berenice
Ras Banâs

EGYPT
Gharbiya Desert
Qasr Farâfra
Bawiti
El Faiyûm
Beni Suef
El Fashn
Beni Mazâr
El Minya
Mallawi
Dairût
Asyût
Tahta
Sohâg
Girga
Akhmîm
Qena
Luxor
Valley of the Kings
Isna
Idfu
Kôm Ombo
Aswân
Aswân High Dam
Lake Nasser
El Khârga
Baris
Abu Simbel

SAUDI ARABIA
Tabûk
TABUK
Al Bi'r
An Nafûd
Hā'il
HĀ'IL
Buraydah
AL QASĪM
Najd
Al Madīnah (Medina)
AL MADINAH
MAKKAH
Makkah (Mecca)
JIDDAH (JEDDA)
At Tā'if
King Abdul Aziz
Yanbu 'al Bahr
Rābigh
Al Lith
Al Qunfudhah
ASIR
Khamīs Mushayt
Abha
NAJRĀN
Najrān

Red Sea
RED SEA

SUDAN
NORTHERN
Laqiya Arba'in
Dongola
Argo
Delgo
Akasha
Wadi Halfa
Nubian Desert
NORTHERN KORDOFAN
Western Kordofan
El Obeid
Sodiri
Wad Banda
Hamrat esh Sheikh
RIVER NILE
Atbara
Ed Damer
Berber
Shendi
Port Sudan
Suakin
Tokar
KHARTOUM
Omdurman
KHARTOUM
Khartoum North
Wad Medani
GEZIRA
WHITE NILE
Kosti
Sennar
El Manaqil
Rabak
Singa
SINNAR
KASSALA
Kassala
Gedaref
GEDAREF

ERITREA
ASMARA
Massawa
Keren
Mendefera
Dahlak Archipelago

ETHIOPIA
TIGRAY
AMHARA
AFAR
Mek'ele
Aksum
Adwa
Gonder

YEMEN
SAN'A (SANA)
Al Hudaydah (Hodeida)
Ta'izz

DJIBOUTI

290

290

AFRICA

6000m
4000m
3000m
2000m
1000m
500m
250m
100m
Sea Level
-250m
-2000m
-4000m

A · B · C · D · E · F · G

PORTUGAL

SPAIN

Sines
Córdoba
Jaén
Sevilla
Huelva
Jerez de la Frontera
Granada
Málaga
Cádiz
Costa del Sol
Marbella
Algeciras
GIBRALTAR (to UK)
Ceuta (to Spain)
Tanger
Larache
Melilla (to Spain)
Cap des Trois Fourches
Tétouan
Chefchaouen
Al-Hoceima
Nador
Oujda

RABAT
Salé
Kénitra
Casablanca
Mohammedia
Meknès
Fès
Taza
El-Jadida
Khenifra
Khouribga
Safi
Beni-Mellal
Er-Rachidia
MOROCCO
Marrakech
Essaouira
Ouarzazate
Erfoud
Béchar
Agadir
Taroudannt
Anti Atlas
Haut Atlas
Hamada du Guir
Sidi-Ifni
Tiznit
Tata
Hamada du Dra
Guelmime
Draa
Tan-Tan
Hamada Tounassine
Tarfaya

ATLANTIC OCEAN

Madeira (to Portugal)
Porto Santo
Funchal
Ilhas Desertas

La Palma
Santa Cruz de la Palma
Tenerife
Santa Cruz de Tenerife
Gomera
Lanzarote
Arrecife
Fuerteventura
Puerto del Rosario
Las Palmas de Gran Canaria
Hierro
Islas Canarias (Canary Islands) (to Spain)
Gran Canaria
Cap Juby

LAÂYOUNE
Saguia al Hamra
Smara
Boujdour
Bou Craa
WESTERN SAHARA (occupied by Morocco)

ALGE RIA

Tindouf
Sebkha de Tindouf
El Mahbas
El Eglab
'Erg Iguidi
Yetti
'Ain Ben Tili
Galat-Zemmour
Bir Mogrein
Chegga

Tropic of Cancer

Ad Dakhla
Sebkhet Aghzoumal
TIRIS
ZEMMOUR
'Ayoûn 'Abd el Malek
Kâghet
El Hank
El Mreïti
'Erg Ahmar
'Erg Chech

Cap Barbas
Adrar Souttouf
Aousard
Zouérat
F'dérik
El Hammâmi
Taoudenni
Aghouinit
Tourine
Toûajil
Bir Gandouz
Techla
Char
Malqteïr
'Erg Atouila

Nouâdhibou
Lagouira
Ras Nouâdhibou
Dakhlet Nouâdhibou
Boû Lanouâr
Choûm
Ouarâne
'El Mraÿer
'El Guettâra
'Erg I-n-Sâkâne

DAKHLET NOUÂDHIBOU
INCHIRI
Et Tidra
Atâr
Ouâdane
ADRAR
'Erg Atouila
'Erîgât
TOMBOUCTOU
Araouane

Bennichâb
Akjoujt
Oujeft
Chinguetti
El Mreyyé

Nouâmghâr
Ras Timirist
Boû Rjeïmât
MAURITANIA
Rachid
Tidjikja
Tichît
HODH
ECH CHARGUI
Boû Djébéha

NOUAKCHOTT
Idini
TRARZA
TAGANT
Aoukâr
Moudjéria
Boumdeïd
Oualâta
Araouane
MALI
Oudeïka
Bamba

Tiguent
Boutilimit
Magta' Lahjar
Kiffa
'Ayoûn el 'Atroûs
Néma
Lac Faguibine
Tombouctou
Gourma-Rharous

Mederdra
Rkiz
BRAKNA
Aleg
Guérou
Tâmchekket
Timbedgha
Goundam
Diré
Lac Garou
Lac Niangay

Saint Louis
Rosso
Dagana
Richard Toll
Lac de Guier
Podor
Bogué
Bababé
Kaédi
Mônguel
Kiffa
Kankossa
Fintrâne
Kobenni
Bassikounou
Nampala
Lac Aougoundou

Kébémer
Louga
Dara
Linguère
Ranérou
Matam
Maghama
ASSABA
HODH EL GHARBI
'Adel Bagrou
MOPTI
Youvarou

DAKAR
Pointe des Almadies
Thiès
Rufisque
Mbour
Diourbel
Mbaké
Bambey
SENEGAL
Vélingara
GUIDIMAKA
GORGOL
Sélibabi
Bakel
Yélimané
Mbout
KAYES
Nioro
KOULIKORO
SEGOU

AFRICA

Scale 1:8,000,000
(projection: Lambert Azimuthal Equal Area)

0 25 50 75 100 125 150 175 200 Km
0 25 50 75 100 125 150 175 200 Miles

Population
- ■ above 5 million
- ◉ 1 million to 5 million
- ◉ 500,000 to 1 million
- ◉ 100,000 to 500,000
- ⊕ 50,000 to 100,000
- ○ 10,000 to 50,000
- ○ below 10,000

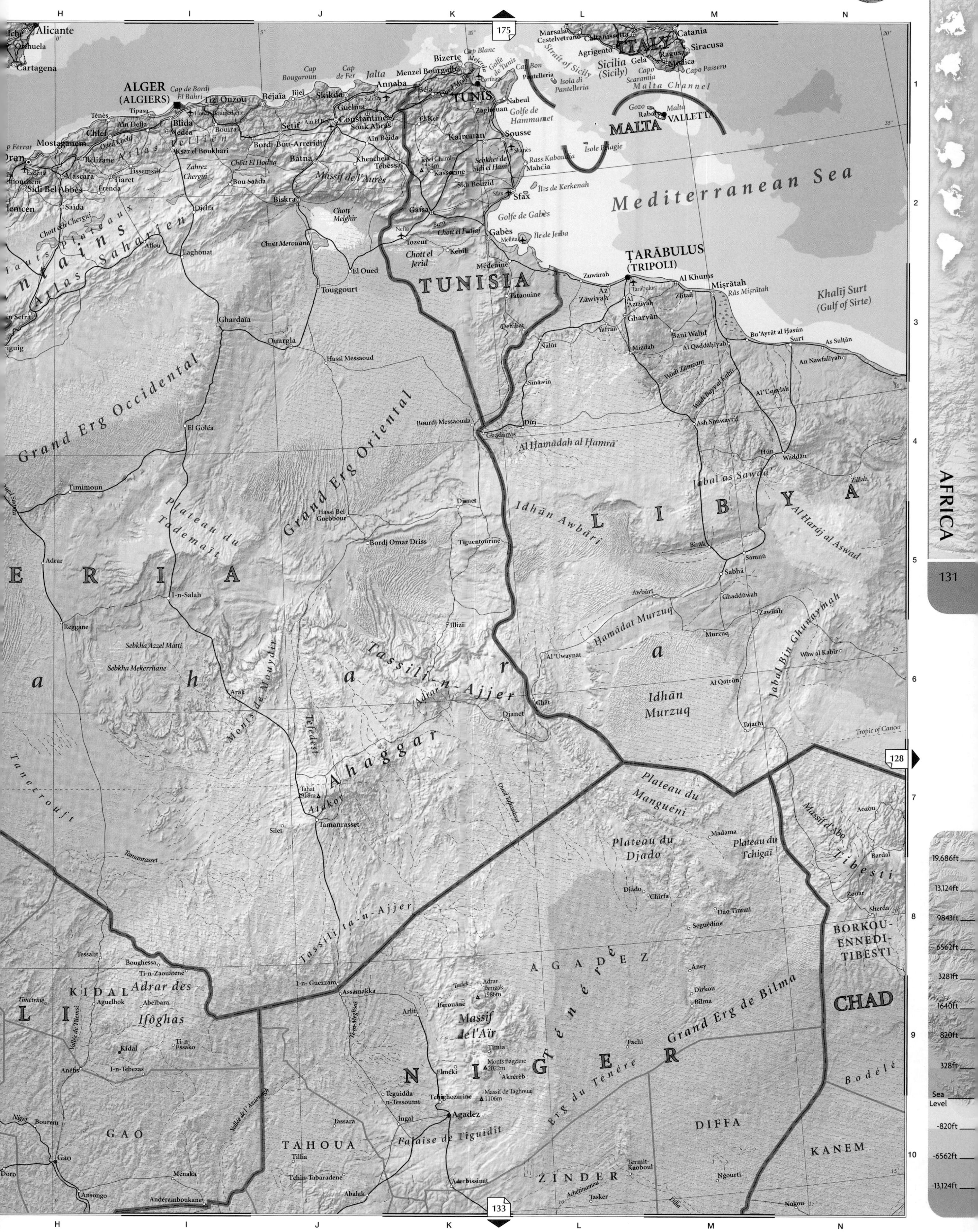

175

128

133

Mediterranean Sea

Alicante
Orihuela
Cartagena
Ichi
p Ferrat
Oran
Mostaganem
Relizane
Mascara
Sidi Bel Abbès
Saïda
Tlemcen
Aïn Sefra
Béchar
Iguig

ALGER (ALGIERS)
Cap de Bordj El Bahri
Tipasa
Ténès
Chlef
Aïn Defla
Blida
Médéa
Bouira
Ksar el Boukhari
Tizi Ouzou
Béjaïa
Jijel
Skikda
Sétif
Aïn El Fal
Bordj-Bou-Arreridj
Bou Saâda
Batna
Khenchela
Aïn Beïda
Biskra
Djelfa
Aflou
Laghouat
Ghardaïa
Ouargla
Touggourt
El Oued
Hassi Messaoud
El Goléa
Timimoun
Adrar
Reggane
I-n-Salah
Arák

Constantine
Guelma
Souk Ahras
Tébessa
Annaba
Béja
Jendouba
Le Kef
Kairouan
Sousse
Mahdia
Sfax
Gabès
Médenine
Tataouine
Dehibat

TUNIS
Bizerte
Menzel Bourguiba
Nabeul
Zaghouan
Kasserine
Sidi Bouzid
Gafsa
Tozeur
Nefta
Kebili
Zuwārah

TUNISIA

Massif de l'Atrès
Chott El Hodna
Chott Melghir
Chott el Fejaj
Chott el Jerid
Chott Merouane

Golfe de Tunis
Cap Bon
Golfe de Hammamet
Golfe de Gabès
Île de Jerba
Îles de Kerkenah

ITALY
MALTA
VALLETTA
Sicilia (Sicily)
Catania
Siracusa
Marsala
Agrigento
Gela
Ragusa
Modica
Capo Passero
Pantelleria
Malta Channel
Gozo
Strait of Sicily

ṬARĀBULUS (TRIPOLI)
Az Zāwiyah
Al Khums
Mişrātah
Zlitan
Gharyān
Banī Walīd
Al Qaddāhiyah
Mizdah
Surt
As Sultān
An Nawfaliyah
Al 'Uqaylah
Ash Shuwayrif
Hūn
Waddān
Zillah
Birāk
Samnū
Sabhā
Ghaddūwah
Awbārī
Murzuq
Zawilah
Tajarhī
Al Qatrūn

LIBYA

Khalīj Surt (Gulf of Sirte)

Al Ḥamādah al Ḥamrā'
Jabal as Sawdā'
Al Ḥarūj al Aswad
Jabal Bin Ghunaymah
Wāw al Kabīr
Idhān Awbārī
Idhān Murzuq
Ḥamādat Murzuq
Wadi Zamzam

Ghadāmis
Dirj
Nālūt
Sināwin
Yafran
'Al 'Uwaynāt
Ghat

Ahaggar
Tassili-n-Ajjer
Adrar-n-Ajjer
Djanet
Illizi
Tiguentourine
Bordj Omar Driss
Hassi Bel Guebbour
Bourdj Messaouda
Plateau du Tademaït
Grand Erg Oriental
Grand Erg Occidental

Monts de Moydir
Teledest
Atakor
Tahat 2918m
Silet
Tamanrasset

Sebkha Azzel Matti
Sebkha Mekerrhane
Tanezrouft

Tropic of Cancer

Plateau du Manguéni
Plateau du Djado
Plateau du Tchigaï
Djado
Chirfa
Madama
Aozou
Bardaï
Zouar
Sherda
Dao Timmi
Séguédine

Tibesti
BORKOU-ENNEDI-TIBESTI
CHAD

NIGER
AGADEZ
Arlit
Iferouâne
Massif de l'Aïr
Monts Bagzane 2022m
Akrérèb
Agadez
Ingal
Teguidda-n-Tessoumt
Tchirozérine
Massif de Taghouaji 1106m
Elméki
Abalak
Tabelot
Dirkou
Bilma
Aney
Fachi
Grand Erg de Bilma
Erg du Ténère
Ténéré

Adrar Tamgak 1988m

ZINDER
DIFFA
KANEM
Termit-Kaoboul
Ngourti
Bodélé

MALI
KIDAL
Adrar des Ifôghas
Tessalit
Boughessa
Ti-n-Zaouâtene
Aguelhok
Abeïbara
Kidal
Anefis
I-n-Tebezas
Timétrine
Vallée de Tilemsi
Ti-n-Essako
I-n-Guezzam
Assamakka
Tin-Zaouâtene

GAO
Bourem
Gao
Ansongo
Ménaka
Andéramboukane
Doro

TAHOUA
Tillia
Tassara
Tchin-Tabaradene
Aderbissinat

Massif de l'Aïr

Faillaise de Tiguidit

19,686ft
13,124ft
9843ft
6562ft
3281ft
1640ft
820ft
328ft
Sea Level
-820ft
-6562ft
-13,124ft

West Africa

130

290

MAURITANIA

TIRIS ZEMMOUR

ADRAR

INCHIRI

TRARZA

BRAKNA

TAGANT

HODH ECH CHARGUI

HODH EL GHARBI

ASSABA

GORGOL

GUIDIMAKA

TOMBOUCTOU

'Erg Atouila

'Erg I-n-Sâkâne

'Erîgât

Azaouâd

El Mreyyé

Aoukâr

Sahel

MALI

KAYES

KOULIKORO

SÉGOU

MOPTI

SENEGAL

GAMBIA

BANJUL

DAKAR

NOUAKCHOTT

NOUÂDHIBOU

GUINEA-BISSAU

BISSAU

GUINEA

Fouta Djallou

CONAKRY

SIERRA LEONE

FREETOWN

LIBERIA

MONROVIA

IVORY COAST

YAMOUSSOUKRO

Abidjan

BURKINA

OUAGADOUGOU

BOBO-DIOULASSO

SIKASSO

BAMAKO

GHANA

KUMASI

ATLANTIC OCEAN

Cape Palmas

Cape Three Points

Cities and towns
Cap Barbas, Bir-Gandouz, Nouâdhibou, Lagouira, Râs Nouâdhibou, Dakhlet Nouâdhibou, Bou Lanouâr, Techla, Aghouinit, Touâjil, Tourine, Choûm, Chár, Atâr, Chinguetti, Ouadâne, El Mráyer, El Guettâra, Laoudenni

Nouâmghâr, Râs Timiris, Bennichâb, Akjoujt, Boû Rjeimât, Aoujeft, Moudjéria, Rachid, Tidjikja, Tichit, Araouane, Boû Djébéha

Nouakchott, Idini, Boutilimit, Magta' Lahjar, Aleg, Bogué, Bababé, Kaédi, Monguel, Mbout, Kiffa, Kankossa, Kobenni, 'Ayoûn el 'Atroûs, Tintane, Timbedgha, Amourj, Bassikounou, 'Adel Bagrou, Nema, Oualâta, Goundam, Timbouctou, Gourma-Rharous, Bamba

Rosso, Dagana, Richard Toll, Podor, Saint Louis, Louga, Kébémèr, Dara, Linguère, Ranérou, Matam, Maghama, Sélibabi, Yélimané, Nioro, Balé, Nara, Nampala, Niafunké, Youvarou, Diré, Lac Faguibine

Mékhé, Tivaouane, Thiès, Youba, Vélingara, Kaffrine, Kidira, Kayes, Sandaré, Diéma, Sokolo, Niono, Ténenkou, Mopti, Sévaré, Bandiagara, Koro, Konna, Djibo

Pointe des Almadies, Mbaké, Diourbel, Fatick, Kaolack, Mbour, Joal-Fadiout, Sédhiou, Goudiri, Bakel, Ambidédi, Matam, Dhaming, Sadiola, Kéniéba, Bafoulabé, Kita, Koutiala, Yorosso, San, Bobo

Brikama, Basse Santa Su, Vélingara, Kolda, Médina Gounas, Tambacounda, Dialakoto, Saraya, Kédougou, Mali, Kangaba, Bougouni, Kolondiéba, Orodara, Banfora

Bignona, Ziguinchor, Cacheu, Bissorã, Farim, Gabú, Boké, Kindia, Dubréka, Forécariah, Port Loko, Makeni, Koidu, Kabala, Faranah, Kissidougou, Guéckédou, Macenta, Nzérékoré, Odienné, Boundiali, Korhogo, Ferkessédougou, Kong, Bouna

Conakry, Kambia, Pendembu, Magburaka, Lunsar, Bo, Kenema, Moyamba, Shenge, Bonthe, Mattru, Pujehun, Sulima, Robertsport, Tubmanburg, Kakata, Harbel, Marshall, Buchanan, Zwedru, Tai, River Cess, Greenville, Grand Cess, Plibo, Harper, Tabou

Danané, Man, Duékoué, Guiglo, Gagnoa, Divo, Lakota, Soubré, San-Pédro, Sassandra, Grand-Lahou, Grand-Bassam, Aboisso, Half Assini, Axim, Sekondi-Takoradi

Scale bars (left margin)
6000m, 4000m, 3000m, 2000m, 1000m, 500m, 250m, 100m, Sea Level, -250m, -2000m, -4000m

CAPE VERDE (inset)
Santo Antão, Ilhas de Barlavento, Pombas, Mindelo, São Vicente, Ribeira Brava, São Nicolau, Pedra Lume, Amílcar Cabral, Sal, Boa Vista, ATLANTIC OCEAN, Tarrafal, Fogo, Maio, São Filipe, Santiago, PRAIA, Ilhas de Sotavento
Scale 1:8,000,000 0 50 100 Km 0 50 100 Miles

ASCENSION ISLAND (to Saint Helena) (inset)
North Point, Sisters Peak, Porpoise Point, North East Bay, Clarence Bay, The Peak, South East Point, South West Bay, GEORGETOWN, Wideawake Airfield, Portland Point, Mars Bay, South Point, Pillar Bay, ATLANTIC OCEAN
Scale 1:750,000 0 5 10 Km 0 5 10 Miles

TRISTAN DA CUNHA (to Saint Helena) (inset)
ATLANTIC OCEAN, Big Point, Rookery Point, Anchorstock Point, EDINBURGH, Sandy Point, Queen Mary's Peak 2060m, Lyon Point, Longbluff, Cave Point, Stonyhill Point, Stonybeach Bay
Scale 1:750,000 0 5 10 Km 0 5 10 Miles

SAINT HELENA (to UK) (inset)
Sugar Loaf Point, Flagstaff Bay, JAMESTOWN, Horse Pasture Point, The Haystack, Longwood, Egg Island, Diana's Peak, Gill Point, South West Point, Long Range Point, Speery Island, Castle Rock Point, ATLANTIC OCEAN
Scale 1:750,000 0 5 10 Km 0 5 10 Miles

Central Africa

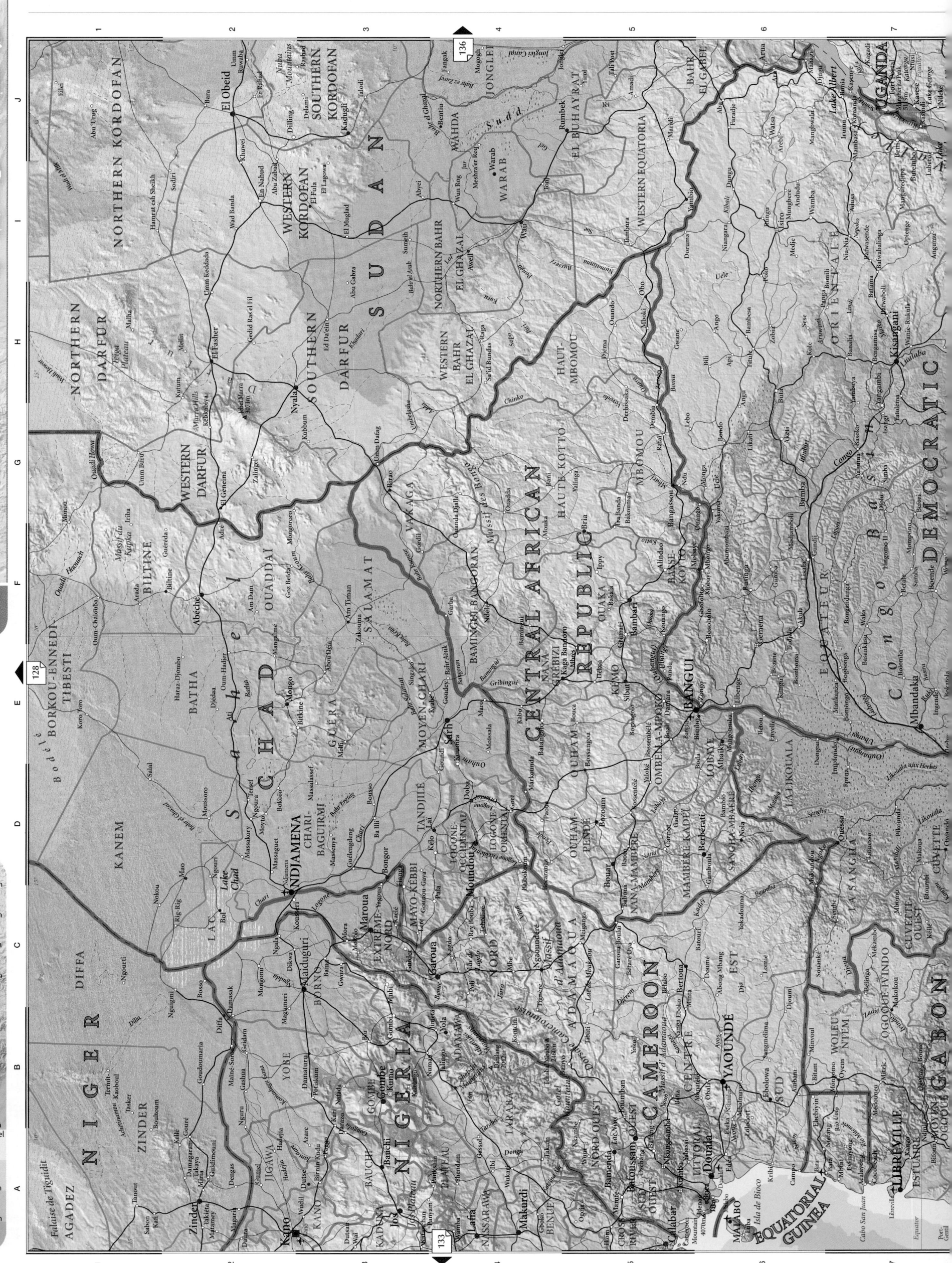
SUDAN
CHAD
NIGER
NIGERIA
CAMEROON
CENTRAL AFRICAN REPUBLIC
DEMOCRATIC
GABON
EQUATORIAL GUINEA
UGANDA
NDJAMENA
BANGUI
YAOUNDE
LIBREVILLE
Kano
Maiduguri
Zinder
El Obeid
El Fasher
Nyala
Abéché
Douala
Garoua
Maroua
Sarh
Moundou
Berbérati
Kisangani
Mbandaka
Malabo
NORTHERN DARFUR
WESTERN DARFUR
SOUTHERN DARFUR
NORTHERN KORDOFAN
WESTERN KORDOFAN
SOUTHERN KORDOFAN
BORKOU-ENNEDI-TIBESTI
KANEM
BATHA
OUADDAI
SALAMAT
GUERA
MOYEN-CHARI
Lake Chad
Lake Albert
Isla de Bioco
Congo
Ubangi
6000m
4000m
3000m
2000m
1000m
500m
250m
100m
Sea Level
-250m
-2000m
-4000m

AFRICA

Scale 1:8,000,000
(projection: Lambert Azimuthal Equal Area)

0 25 50 75 100 125 150 175 200 Km
0 25 50 75 100 125 150 175 200 Miles

Population
- ■ above 5 million
- ▣ 1 million to 5 million
- ◉ 500,000 to 1 million
- ◎ 100,000 to 500,000
- ⊕ 50,000 to 100,000
- ○ 10,000 to 50,000
- ∘ below 10,000

Countries and regions

REPUBLIC OF CONGO
CONGO
RWANDA
BURUNDI
TANZANIA
ZAMBIA
ZIMBABWE
NAMIBIA
ANGOLA
CABINDA (to Angola)

NORD-KIVU
SUD-KIVU
MANIEMA
KATANGA
KASAI ORIENTAL
KASAI OCCIDENTAL
BANDUNDU
BAS-CONGO
UIGE
BENGO
MALANJE
LUNDA NORTE
LUNDA SUL
MOXICO
CUANDO CUBANGO
NORTH WESTERN
COPPERBELT
LUAPULA
NORTHERN
CENTRAL
EASTERN
SOUTHERN
WESTERN
HUAMBO
BENGUELA
HUILA
NAMIBE
CUNENE
KUANZA NORTE
KUANZA SUL
MASHONALAND CENTRAL
MASHONALAND WEST
MATABELELAND NORTH
MIDLANDS
OKAVANGO
CAPRIVI STRIP
OHANGWENA
OSHANA
OTJIKOTO

Cities

BUJUMBURA
KIGALI
KINSHASA
BRAZZAVILLE
LUANDA
LUBUMBASHI
LUSAKA
HARARE
Mbuji-Mayi
Kananga
Kigoma
Kindu
Kolwezi
Kipushi
Solwezi
Kitwe
Ndola
Lobito
Benguela
Lubango
Namibe
Malanje
Livingstone
Kabwe
Kafue
Pointe-Noire
Matadi
Boma
Cabinda

Physical features

ATLANTIC OCEAN
Lake Tanganyika
Lake Mweru
Lake Bangweulu
Congo
Zambezi
Cuango
Cuanza
Kwango
Kasai
Plateau do Bié
Huíla Plateau
Mulonga Plain
Liuwa Plain
Monts Kundelungu
Monts Mitumba
Albufeira de Cahora Bassa

Elevation

19,686ft
13,124ft
9843ft
6562ft
3281ft
1640ft
820ft
328ft
Sea Level
-820ft
-6562ft
-13,124ft

137
138
291

East Africa

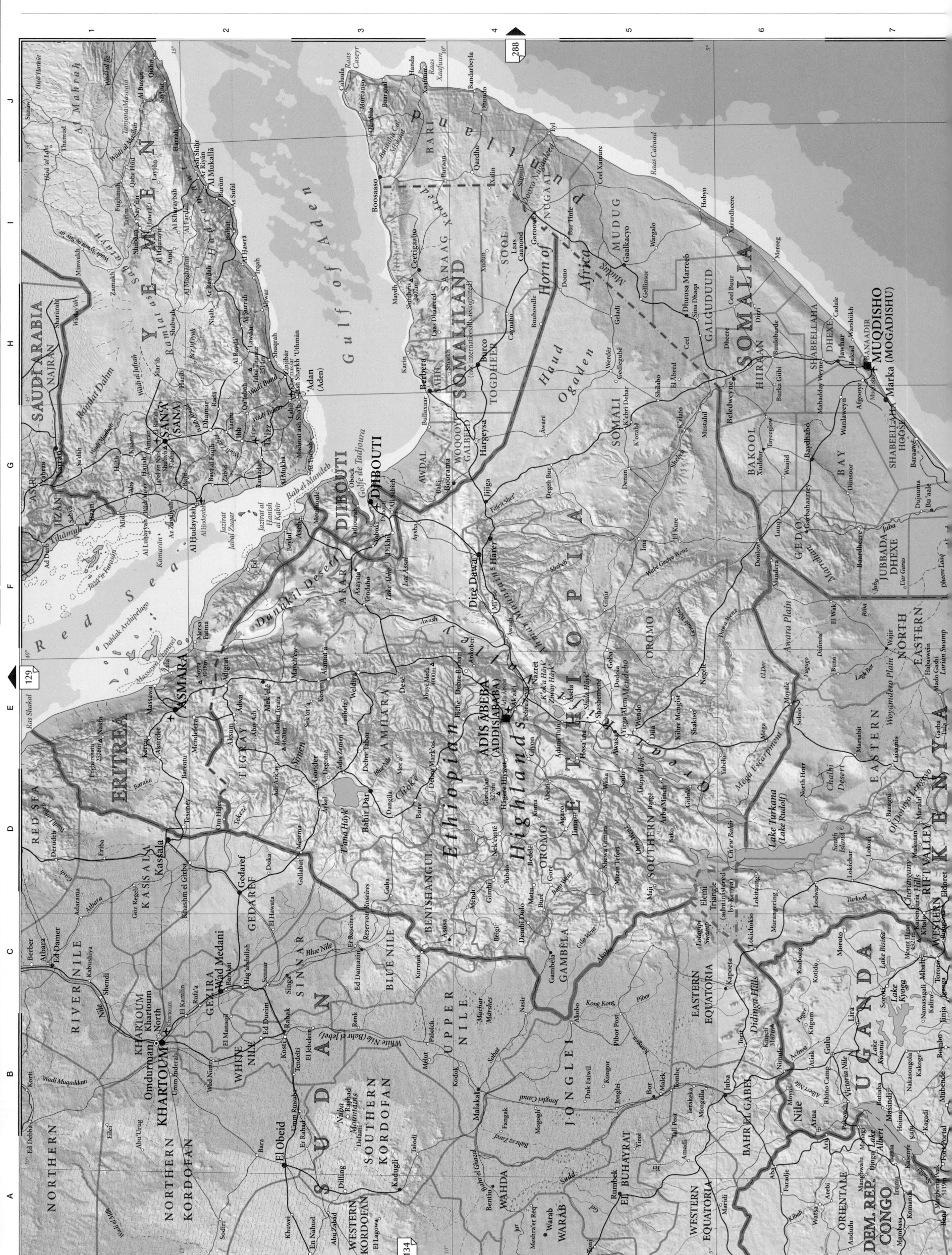
SAUDI ARABIA
NAJRAN
YEMEN
ṢAN'Ā' (SANA)
'Adan (Aden)
Red Sea
Gulf of Aden
Bab el Mandeb
Golfe de Tadjoura
ERITREA
ASMARA
Dahlak Archipelago
DJIBOUTI
Danakil Desert
AFAR
SOMALILAND (not internationally recognized)
Hargeysa
Berbera
Boosaaso
Horn of Africa
SOMALIA
MUQDISHO (MOGADISHU)
Marka
Haud
Ogaden
ETHIOPIA
Ethiopian Highlands
ĀDĪS ĀBEBA (ADDIS ABABA)
Dirē Dawa
Harer
T'ana Hāyk'
Bahir Dar
Gonder
Simēn
Āwasa
SUDAN
KHARTOUM
Khartoum North
Omdurman
Wad Medani
Kassala
Gedaref
El Obeid
Blue Nile
White Nile (Bahr el Jebel)
Nuba Mountains
Sudd
Jonglei Canal
Machar Marshes
Juba
Malakal
Elemi Triangle (administered by Kenya)
Lake Turkana (Lake Rudolf)
Chalbi Desert
KENYA
NORTH EASTERN
EASTERN
RIFT VALLEY
UGANDA
Lake Kyoga
Lake Albert
DEM. REP. CONGO
6000m
4000m
3000m
2000m
1000m
500m
250m
100m
Sea Level
-250m
-2000m
-4000m
129
134
288

Scale 1:8,000,000

(projection: Lambert Azimuthal Equal Area)

0 25 50 75 100 125 150 175 200 Km

0 25 50 75 100 125 150 175 200 Miles

Population

■ above 5 million   ■ 1 million to 5 million   ◉ 500,000 to 1 million

◎ 100,000 to 500,000   ⊕ 50,000 to 100,000   ○ 10,000 to 50,000   ○ below 10,000

SEYCHELLES

Inner Islands

Scale 1:2,000,000

Ile Aride
Cerf Island   Les Sœurs
Cousine   Grand Seur
Cousin   Félicité
   Marianne
La Digue
Frégate

Mamelles
Silhouette   Ile au Cerf
North Point   Ile aux Recifs
Sainte Anne
VICTORIA   Ile Thérèse
Morne Seychellois   Cascade
Pointe Lazare   Anse Boileau
Quatre Bornes
Mount Dauban
450m   Pointe Police

Ile du Nord

INDIAN OCEAN

RÉUNION
(to France)

Scale 1:2,000,000

ST-DENIS
Ste-Marie
Ste-Suzanne
Le Port   St-André
St-Paul   La Plaine-des-Palmistes
Salazie   St-Benoit
Cilaos   Piton de la Fournaise
St-Gilles-les-Bains   2631m
Pointe des
Aigrettes   Trois-Bassins
St-Louis   Ste-Rose
St-Leu   Piton des Neiges
St-Pierre   3069m
St-Joseph   St-Philippe
Pointe au Sel   St-Etienne
Pointe de la Table

INDIAN OCEAN

MAURITIUS

Scale 1:2,000,000

Round Island
Flat Island
Gunner's Quoin
Triolet
Pamplemousses
Rivière du Rempart
PORT LOUIS   Centre de Flacq
Beau Bassin   Rose Hill
Quatre Bornes
Rose Belle   Mahebourg
Mont du Rempart   Nouvelle France
Curepipe
Tamarin   Rivière Noire
Rivière Noire   Souillac
Pointe aux Sables   Grand Port
Canonniers Point
Le D'Ambre

INDIAN OCEAN

SEYCHELLES

Farquhar Group

Providence Atoll

Cosmoledo Group

Aldabra Group
Assumption Island
Astove Island

Nosy Glorieuses

COMOROS

Comoro Islands
Grande Comore
MORONI
Le Karthala   Moutsamoudou   Anjouan
2361m   Dembeni
Mohéli

MAYOTTE
(to France)
MAMOUDZOU
Pamandzi

INDIAN OCEAN

Mozambique Channel

MADAGASCAR

ANTSIRANANA
Ambilobe
Tsaratanana
2876m

Mahajanga

Mainland

Kismaayo
JUBBADA HOOSE
Buur Gaabo
Ngangerabeli Plain
Pate Island
Lamu
Kipini
Malindi
Mombasa
Kilifi

COAST

KENYA

NAIROBI
CENTRAL
Nakuru
Nyeri
Thika
Machakos

Lake Victoria
KAMPALA
Entebbe
Kisumu
NYANZA

RWANDA
KIGALI

BURUNDI
BUJUMBURA

Lake Tanganyika

KIGOMA

TANZANIA

TABORA
MWANZA
Shinyanga
SHINYANGA
Singida
SINGIDA
DODOMA
MANYARA
ARUSHA
Arusha
Moshi
KILIMANJARO
Kilimanjaro
5895m
TANGA
Tanga
Pangani
PWANI
DAR ES SALAAM
Zanzibar
ZANZIBAR WEST
ZANZIBAR SOUTH
PEMBA NORTH
Chake Chake
PEMBA SOUTH
Mafia
MOROGORO
Morogoro
IRINGA
Iringa
MBEYA
Mbeya

Lake Nyasa

MALAWI
LILONGWE
CENTRAL
Blantyre
SOUTHERN

ZAMBIA
EASTERN
CENTRAL
LUSAKA
Kabwe

LINDI
MTWARA
Mtwara
Lindi
RUVUMA
Songea

NIASSA
Lichinga

CABO DELGADO
Pemba

MOZAMBIQUE
NAMPULA
Nampula

ZAMBÉZIA

ZIMBABWE
MASHONALAND
CENTRAL
MANICA

TETE

Lake Kariba

Elevation scale

19,686ft
13,124ft
9843ft
6562ft
3281ft
1640ft
820ft
328ft
Sea Level
-820ft
-6562ft
-13,124ft

Southern Africa

135
291
292

ATLANTIC OCEAN

ANGOLA

NAMIBIA

BOTSWANA

ZAMBIA

SOUTH AFRICA

LESOTHO

Countries, regions and major features

Planalto do Bié · BENGUELA · HUAMBO · BIÉ · MOXICO · HUÍLA · CUNENE · CUANDO CUBANGO · NAMIBE · Huila Plateau · Ovamboland · OHANGWENA · OMUSATI · OSHANA · OTJIKOTO · OKAVANGO · Caprivi Strip · CAPRIVI · NORTH WESTERN · WESTERN · SOUTHERN · COPPERBELT · CENTRAL · Lake Kariba · MATABELELAND NORTH · MATABELELAND SOUTH · ZIM · KUNENE · Etosha Pan · Damaraland · OTJOZONDJUPA · Okavango Delta · NORTH-WEST · GHANZI · CENTRAL · ERONGO · KHOMAS · OMAHEKE · Kalahari Desert · KGALAGADI · KWENENG · SOUTHERN · SOUTH EAST · KGATLENG · LIMPOPO (NORTHERN) · HARDAP · Namaqualand · KARAS · NORTH-WEST · FREE STATE · NORTHERN CAPE · Great Karoo · Little Karoo · WESTERN CAPE · EASTERN CAPE

Selected cities and towns

Lobito · Benguela · Lubango · Namibe · Tombua · Huambo · Kuito · Menongue · LUSAKA · Livingstone · Victoria Falls · Bulawayo · Francistown · Maun · Ghanzi · WINDHOEK · Swakopmund · Walvis Bay · Lüderitz · Keetmanshoop · GABORONE · TSHWANE (PRETORIA) · Johannesburg · Soweto · Germiston · Kimberley · BLOEMFONTEIN · MASERU · Upington · Port Nolloth · Springbok · Beaufort West · CAPE TOWN · Simon's Town · George · Mosselbaai · Port Elizabeth · East London · Grahamstown · Umtata

Tropic of Capricorn

Cape of Good Hope · Cape Agulhas · Cape Columbine · Danger Point · Quoin Point

Elevation scale

6000m · 4000m · 3000m · 2000m · 1000m · 500m · 250m · 100m · Sea Level · -250m · -2000m · -4000m

SOUTH AFRICA: CAPITAL CITIES
TSHWANE (PRETORIA) – administrative capital
CAPE TOWN – legislative capital
BLOEMFONTEIN – judicial capital

Scale 1:8,000,000
(projection: Lambert Azimuthal Equal Area)

0 25 50 75 100 125 150 175 200 Km
0 25 50 75 100 125 150 175 200 Miles

Population
- ■ above 5 million
- ■ 1 million to 5 million
- ● 500,000 to 1 million
- ◎ 100,000 to 500,000
- ■ 50,000 to 100,000
- ○ 10,000 to 50,000
- ○ below 10,000

COMOROS

MAYOTTE (to France)

Comoro Islands

Moutsamudou Mohéli Anjouan MAMOUDZOU

Mozambique Channel

Mahajanga

MADAGASCAR

ANTSIRANANA

Antsiranana

Nosy Be

Ambanja

MAHAJANGA

Mahajanga

ANTANANARIVO

Antananarivo

Toamasina

TOAMASINA

Fianarantsoa

FIANARANTSOA

Toliara

TOLIARA

Tropic of Capricorn

INDIAN OCEAN

Mozambique major labels:

LILONGWE

MALAWI

Blantyre

NAMPULA

Nampula

CABO DELGADO

Pemba

NIASSA

TETE

Tete

ZAMBEZIA

Quelimane

MOZAMBIQUE

SOFALA

Beira

Chimoio

MANICA

HARARE

Chitungwiza

Mutare

BABWE (ZIMBABWE)

MANICALAND

MASHONALAND

MASVINGO

MIDLANDS

Beitbridge

INHAMBANE

GAZA

Inhambane

Xai-Xai

MAPUTO

MAPUTO

Matola

MBABANE

SWAZILAND

Manzini

MPUMALANGA

Nelspruit

KWAZULU/NATAL

Pietermaritzburg

Durban

EASTERN CAPE

INDIAN OCEAN

Cape St. Lucia

Mozambique Channel

Comoros inset:

Scale 1:4,500,000

0 20 40 60 80 Km
0 20 40 60 80 Miles

Grande Comore

Mitsamiouli

Karthala 2361m

MORONI

Koimbani

Mbéni

Mohéli

Fomboni

Anjouan

Moutsamoudou

Mutsamudu

MAYOTTE (to France)

MAMOUDZOU

Comoro Islands

Mozambique Channel

INDIAN OCEAN

Madagascar scale inset:

Scale 1:8,000,000

0 25 50 75 100 125 150 Km
0 25 50 75 100 125 150 Miles

Elevation legend:
19,686ft
13,124ft
9843ft
6562ft
3281ft
1640ft
820ft
328ft
Sea Level
-820ft
-6562ft
-13,124ft

SOUTH AFRICA: CAPITAL CITIES

TSHWANE (PRETORIA) – administrative capital
CAPE TOWN – legislative capital
BLOEMFONTEIN – judicial capital

Scale 1:4,650,000
(projection: Lambert Azimuthal Equal Area)

0 20 40 60 80 100 Km
0 20 40 60 80 100 Miles

Population
■ above 5 million
■ 1 million to 5 million
◉ 500,000 to 1 million
◎ 100,000 to 500,000
⊕ 50,000 to 100,000
○ 10,000 to 50,000
○ below 10,000

ZIMBABWE

MOZAMBIQUE

INHAMBANE

GAZA

BOTSWANA

LIMPOPO
(NORTHERN)

MPUMALANGA

GAUTENG

FREE STATE

KWAZULU-NATAL

EASTERN CAPE

SWAZILAND

LESOTHO

INDIAN OCEAN

GABORONE
TSHWANE (PRETORIA)
Johannesburg
MBABANE
Matola · MAPUTO
BLOEMFONTEIN
MASERU
Pietermaritzburg
Durban
Port Elizabeth
East London

Tropic of Capricorn

AFRICA

141

139
288
293

19,686ft
13,124ft
9843ft
6562ft
3281ft
1640ft
820ft
328ft
Sea Level
-820ft
-6562ft
-13,124ft

A B C D E F G

Algiers

1

Mediterranean Sea

L'Ermitage
Cap de Bordj

Grande Mosquée
Bab El Oued
Bordj El Bahri

Alger (Algiers)

Kasbah
El Biar
Chéraga
Palais du Gouvernement
Ben Aknoun
Agha

2

Hussein-Dey

Musée des Beaux Arts
Birmandreis
Bordj El Kiffan

Cité Olympique
Kouba

Draria
Birkhadem

Dar El Beïda

El Harrach

3

Oued Smar
Algiers Airport

Douera

Oued Harrach

Baraki

0   3 Km
0   3 Miles

Cairo

Abu Al Ghayt
Bahtîm
El Matariya
Cairo International Airport

1

Nile
Shubra Al Amiriya

Warrâq el Hadr
El Zeitûn
Masr el Gedida (Heliopolis)

Shubra Al Khaymah
Mâdinet Nasr

Warrâq el'Arab

Imbâbah

2

Aguza
Bûlâq
El Ezbekîya

Egyptian Antiquities Museum
Âbdin
Cairo

El Dûqqî
Central Government Building
The Citadel

Garden City

Zoological Gardens
Masr el Qadima

El Gîza

3

El Basâlin

Cheops
Sphinx
Nile
El Ma'âdi

Pyramids of Giza

0   3 Km
0   3 Miles

Cape Town

Atlantic Ocean
Table Bay

4

Granger Bay
Paarden Eiland

Mouille Point
Ben Schoeman Dock

Fort Wynyard
South Africa Maritime Museum

5

Green Point
Duncan Dock

Foreshore
Salt River

Three Anchor Bay
Cape Town

Three Anchor Bay
De Waterkant
Central
Woodstock

Sea Point
Signal Hill
Malay Quarter
Castle

Schotsche Kloof

6

Botanical Gardens
Houses of Parliament

Tamboerskloof
Zonnebloem

Bantry Bay
Vredehoek
Devils Peak Estate

Clifton
Gardens Toine

Lions Head

Clifton Bay

7

0   1 Km
0   1 Miles

Casablanca

Atlantic Ocean

El Hank
Mosquée Hassan II
Aïn Harrounda

Old Medina

5

Aïn Diab
Marchée Centrale
Aïn Sebaa

Essoukour Assawda
Hay Mohammadi

Casablanca

Anfa
Palais du Roi
Sidi Moumen Ahl Ahl Loughlam

Casablanca Airport
El Maarif
El Fida Drissia
Moulay Rachid

Mohamed V
Sidi Othmane

Notre Dame de Lourdes
Ben Msick

6

Aïn Clock Sidi Maarouf

Sbata Salmia

L'Oasis

7

0   3 Km
0   3 Miles

Dakar

Industrial Zone

Grand Dakar
Belgravia

Fass
Colobane

8

Gouye Salane
Darou Kipp

Point E

Medina
Gibraltar
Dakar-Marine

Fann Hok
Grande Mosquée

Claudel
Abattoirs

9

Rebeus
Dakar
Pointe de Dakar

Théâtre Daniel Sorano
Palais Présidentiel

Musée Dakar

Atlantic Ocean
Le Plateau

Pointe Bernard

10

0   1 Km
0   1 Miles

Harare

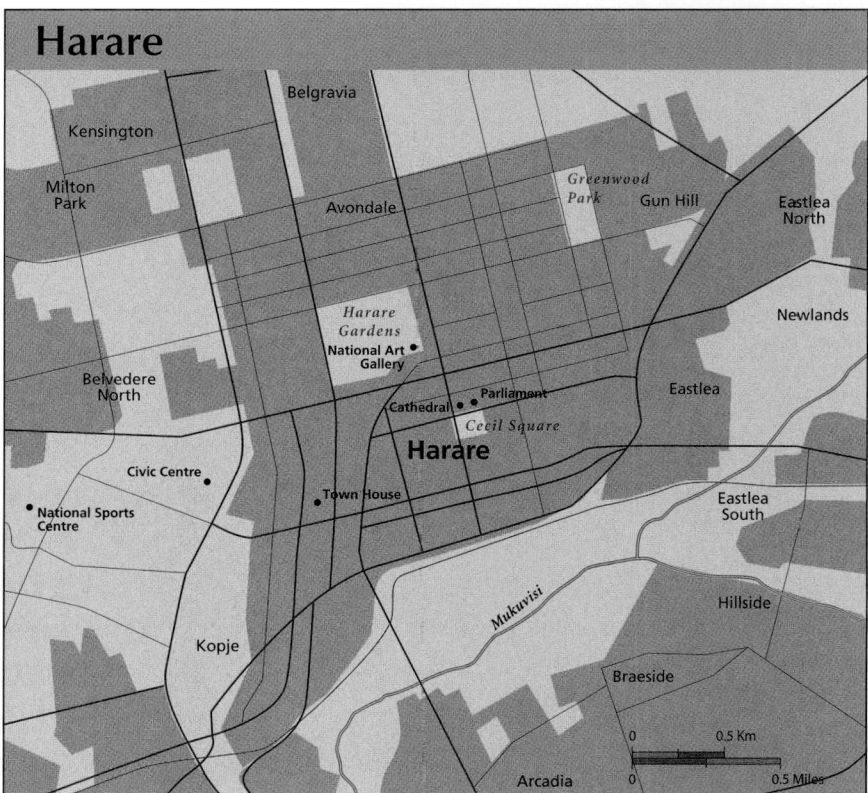

Kensington
Belgravia

Milton Park

8

Avondale
Greenwood Park
Gun Hill
Eastlea North

Harare Gardens
Newlands

National Art Gallery

Belvedere North
Cathedral
Parliament
Eastlea

9

Cecil Square
Harare

Civic Centre

National Sports Centre
Town House
Eastlea South

Kopje

Mukuvisi
Hillside

10

Braeside

Arcadia

0   0.5 Km
0   0.5 Miles

A B C D E F G

Johannesburg

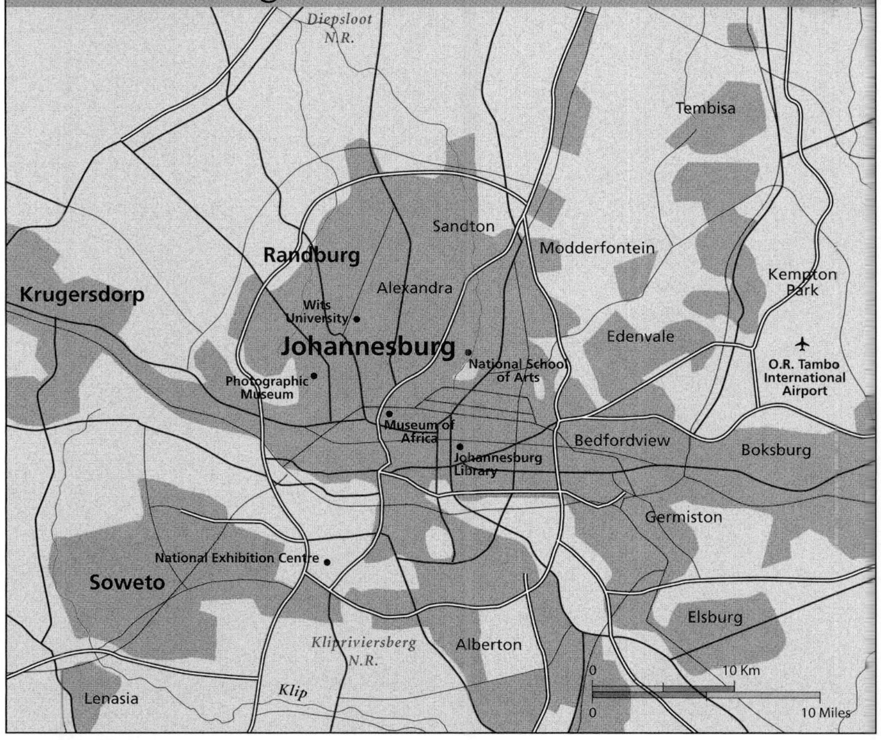

Diepsloot N.R.
Tembisa
Sandton
Modderfontein
Randburg
Alexandra
Kempton Park
Krugersdorp
Wits University
Johannesburg
National School of Arts
Edenvale
O.R. Tambo International Airport
Photographic Museum
Museum of Africa
Johannesburg Library
Bedfordview
Boksburg
Germiston
National Exhibition Centre
Soweto
Elsburg
Kliprivriersberg N.R.
Alberton
Klip
Lenasia

0 — 10 Km
0 — 10 Miles

Kinshasa

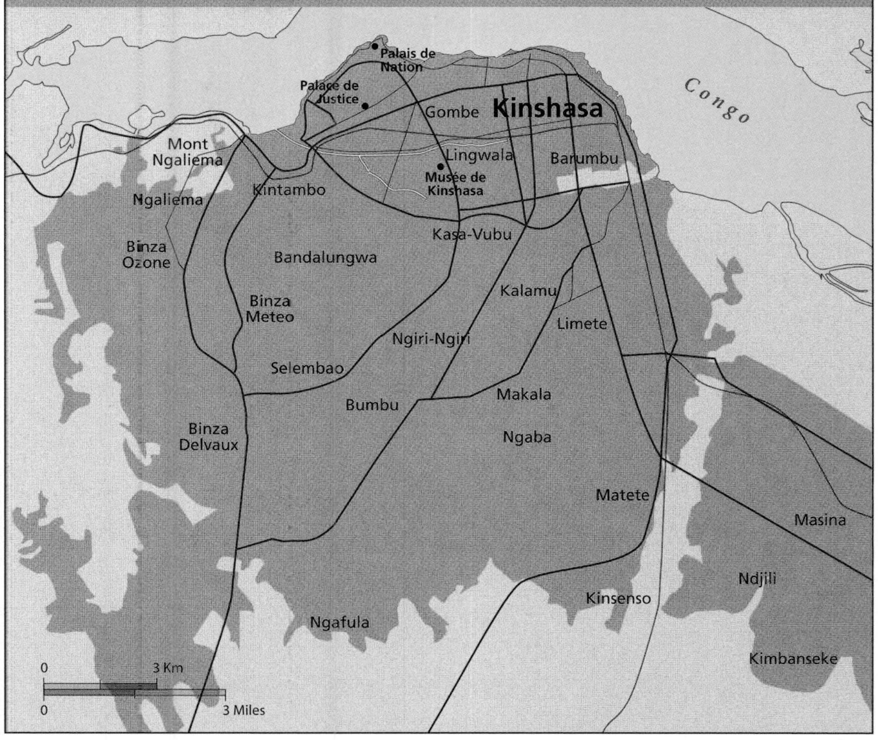

Palais de Nation
Palace de Justice
Gombe
Kinshasa
Mont Ngaliema
Lingwala
Barumbu
Ngaliema
Kintambo
Musée de Kinshasa
Binza Ozone
Kasa-Vubu
Bandalungwa
Kalamu
Binza Meteo
Ngiri-Ngiri
Limete
Selembao
Bumbu
Makala
Binza Delvaux
Ngaba
Matete
Masina
Kinsenso
Ngafula
Ndjili
Kimbanseke
Congo

0 — 3 Km
0 — 3 Miles

Lagos

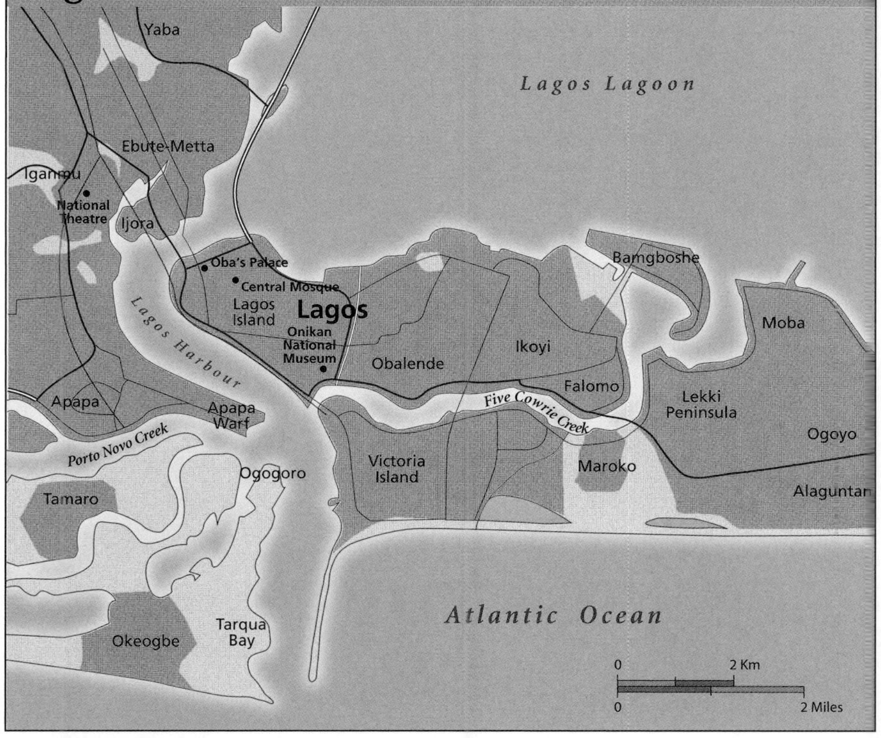

Yaba
Lagos Lagoon
Ebute-Metta
Iganmu
National Theatre
Ijora
Oba's Palace
Bamgboshe
Central Mosque
Lagos Island
Lagos
Apapa
Onikan National Museum
Moba
Apapa Warf
Obalende
Ikoyi
Lagos Harbour
Falomo
Porto Novo Creek
Five Cowrie Creek
Lekki Peninsula
Ogogoro
Tamaro
Victoria Island
Maroko
Ogoyo
Okeogbe
Tarqua Bay
Alaguntan
Atlantic Ocean

0 — 2 Km
0 — 2 Miles

Nairobi

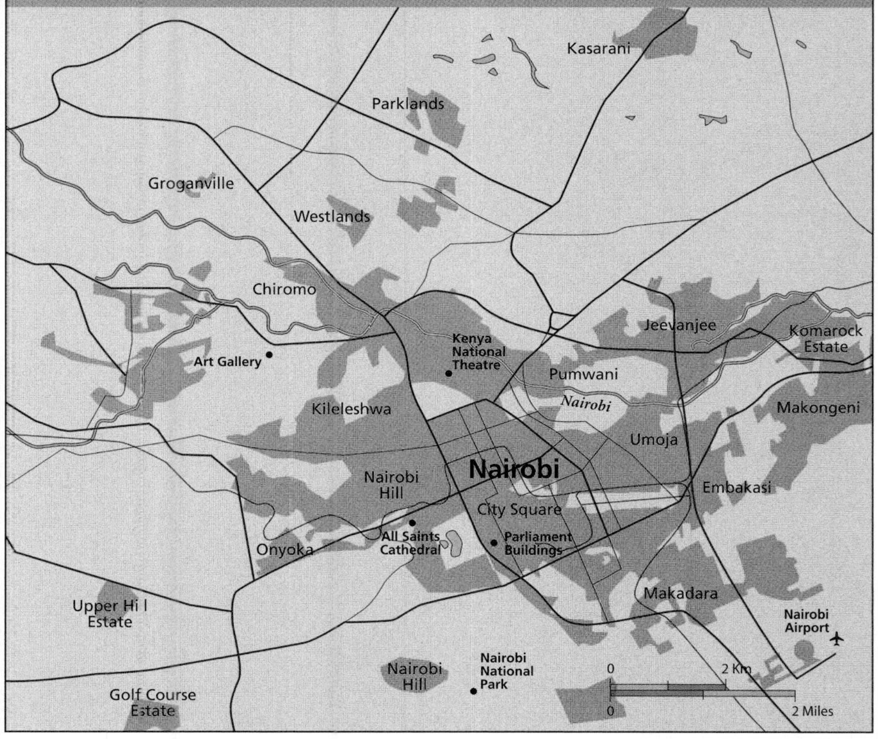

Kasarani
Parklands
Groganville
Westlands
Chiromo
Jeevanjee
Komarock Estate
Art Gallery
Kenya National Theatre
Pumwani
Makongeni
Kileleshwa
Nairobi
Umoja
Nairobi Hill
Nairobi
Embakasi
Onyoka
City Square
All Saints Cathedral
Parliament Buildings
Makadara
Upper Hi l Estate
Nairobi Airport
Nairobi Hill
Nairobi National Park
Golf Course Estate

0 — 2 Km
0 — 2 Miles

Tripoli

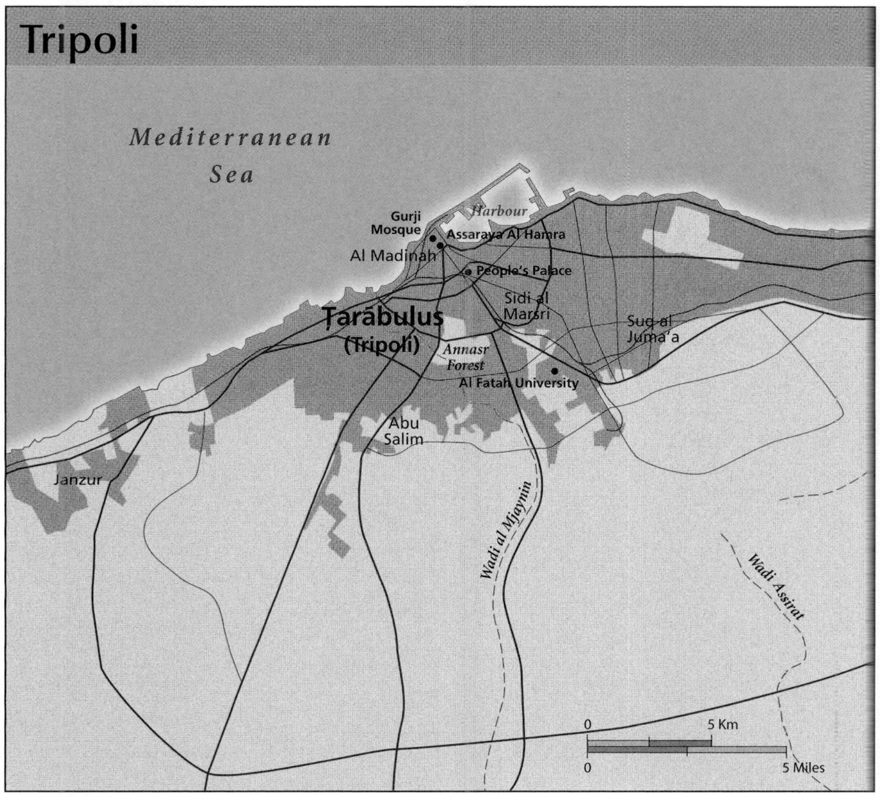

Mediterranean Sea
Harbour
Gurji Mosque
Assaraya Al Hamra
Al Madinah
People's Palace
Tarābulus (Tripoli)
Sidi al Mansri
Suq al Juma'a
Annasr Forest
Al Fatah University
Abu Salim
Janzur
Wadi al Mejrnin
Wadi Assrat

0 — 5 Km
0 — 5 Miles

Tunis

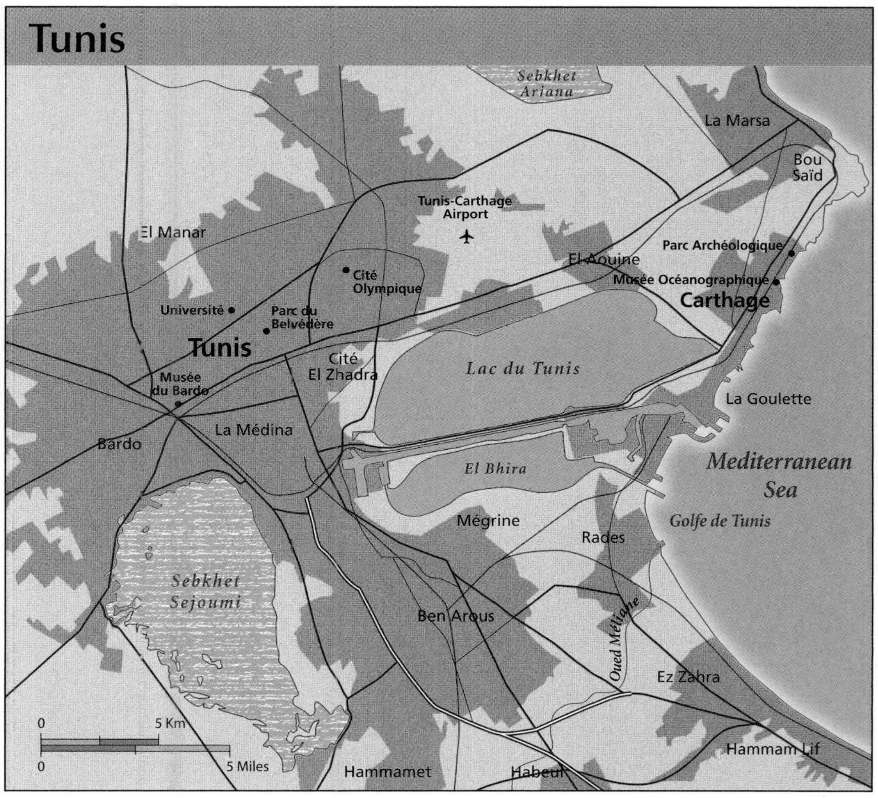

Sebkhet Ariana
La Marsa
Bou Saïd
Tunis-Carthage Airport
El Manar
Parc Archéologique
Cité Olympique
El Aouine
Musée Océanographique
Université
Parc du Belvédère
Carthage
Tunis
Cité El Zhadra
Musée du Bardo
Lac du Tunis
Bardo
La Médina
La Goulette
El Bhira
Mégrine
Rades
Mediterranean Sea
Sebkhet Sejoumi
Golfe de Tunis
Ben Arous
Oued Mél iache
Ez Zahra
Hammamet
Habeul
Hammam Lif

0 — 5 Km
0 — 5 Miles

AFRICA

143

EUROPE

ARCTIC OCEAN
North Pole
Ellesmere Island
Greenland
King Frederik VIII Land
King Christian IX Land
Greenland Sea
NORTH AMERICAN PLATE
EURASIAN PLATE
Spitsbergen
Franz Josef Land
Ostrov Rudol'fa
Severnaya Zemlya
Laptev Sea
Kara Sea
Mys Flissingskiy
Ostrov Severnyy
Novaya Zemlya
Barents Sea
Bjørnøya
Barents Trough
North Cape
Nordkinn
Tromsøflaket
Fugløya Bank
Baydaratskaya Guba
Kara Strait
Murmansk Rise
Ostrov Kolguyev
Poluostrov Kanin
White Sea
Onega Bay
Jan Mayen Fracture Zone
Jan Mayen
Jan Mayen Ridge
Denmark Strait
Kolbeinsey Ridge
Arctic Circle
Iceland Plateau
Bjargtangar
Iceland
Vatnajökull
Norwegian Sea
Norwegian Basin
Vøring Plateau
Vesterålen
Lofoten
Træna Bank
Reykjanes Ridge
Faeroe-Iceland Ridge
Faeroe Islands
Iceland Basin
Bill Baileys Bank
Faeroe-Shetland Trough
Shetland Islands
Viking Bank
Hatton Ridge
Rockall Rise
Outer Hebrides
Orkney Islands
Norwegian Trench
Feni Ridge
Rockall Trough
North Channel
British Isles
Ireland
Irish Sea
Britain
North Sea
Jutland Bank
Skagerrak
Kattegat
Great Fisher Bank
Dogger Bank
Jylland
Gulf of Bothnia
Åland
Gulf of Finland
Gulf of Riga
Gotland
Baltic Sea
Frisian Islands
North European Plain
Porcupine Plain
Celtic Sea
Celtic Shelf
St. George's Channel
Bristol Channel
Land's End
English Channel
Channel Islands
Strait of Dover
E U R O P E
ATLANTIC OCEAN
Charcot Seamounts
Azores-Biscay Rise
Biscay Plain
Bay of Biscay
Galicia Bank
Iberian Plain
Iberian Peninsula
Gulf of Lion
Ligurian Sea
Corsica
Strait of Bonifacio
Sardinia
Adriatic Sea
Corno Grande 2912m
Adriatic Basin
Tyrrhenian Sea
Tyrrhenian Basin
Gulf of Taranto
Strait of Otranto
Sea of Azov
Black Sea
Sea of Marmara
Aegean Sea
Myrtoan Sea
Sea of Crete
Tagus Plain
Gorringe Bank
Cape Saint Vincent
Punta de Tarifa
Horseshoe Seamounts
Ampere Seamount
Strait of Gibraltar
Alboran Sea
Gulf of Valencia
Balearic Islands
Algerian Basin
EURASIAN PLATE
AFRICAN PLATE
Mediterranean Sea
Ionian Sea
Ionian Basin
Sicily
Malta
Mediterranean Ridge
Seine Plain
Seine Seamount
Madeira
Tell Atlas
Atlas Mountains
Middle Atlas
High Atlas
Saharan Atlas
Dacia Seamount
Agadir Canyon
Chott el Jerid
Gulf of Sirte
Levantine Basin
Cyprus Basin
Nile Fan
Suez Canal
Canary Islands
Grand Erg Occidental
Grand Erg Oriental
Qattara Depression -133m
Western Desert
Libyan Desert
Erg Iguidi
Erg Chech
A F R I C A
S A H A R A
Red Sea

Europe is the world's second smallest continent with a total area of 4,053,309 sq miles (10,498,000 sq km). It comprises 46 separate countries, including Turkey and the Russian Federation, although the greater parts of these nations lie in Asia.

FACTFILE

N   **Most Northerly Point:** Ostrov Rudol'fa, Russian Federation 81° 47′ N

S   **Most Southerly Point:** Gávdos, Greece 34° 51′ N

E   **Most Easterly Point:** Mys Flissingskiy, Novaya Zemlya, Russian Federation 69° 03′ E

W   **Most Westerly Point:** Bjargtangar, Iceland 24° 33′ W

Largest Lakes:
1. Lake Ladoga, Russian Federation 7100 sq miles (18,390 sq km)
2. Lake Onega, Russian Federation 3819 sq miles (9891 sq km)
3. Vänern, Sweden 2141 sq miles (5545 sq km)
4. Lake Peipus, Estonia/Russian Federation 1372 sq miles (3555 sq km)
5. Vättern, Sweden 737 sq miles (1910 sq km)

Longest Rivers:
1. Volga, Russian Federation 2265 miles (3645 km)
2. Danube, C Europe 1771 miles (2850 km)
3. Dnieper, Belarus/Russian Federation/Ukraine 1421 miles (2287 km)
4. Don, Russian Federation 1162 miles (1870 km)
5. Pechora, Russian Federation 1124 miles (1809 km)

Largest Islands:
1. Britain, 88,700 sq miles (229,800 sq km)
2. Iceland, 39,315 sq miles (101,826 sq km)
3. Ireland, 31,521 sq miles (81,638 sq km)
4. Ostrov Severny, Novaya Zemlya, Russian Federation 18,177 sq miles (47,079 sq km)
5. Spitsbergen, Svalbard 15,051 sq miles (38,981 sq km)

Highest Points:
1. El'brus, Russian Federation 18,510 ft (5642 m)
2. Dykhtau, Russian Federation 17,077 ft (5205 m)
3. Koshtantau, Russian Federation 16,903 ft (5152 m)
4. Jangitau, Georgia/Russian Federation 16,598 ft (5059 m)
5. Pushkin Peak, Georgia/Russian Federation 16,512 ft (5033 m)

Lowest Point:
▼ Caspian Depression, Russian Federation -92 ft (-28 m) below sea level

Highest recorded temperature:
● Seville, Spain 122°F (50°C)

Lowest recorded temperature:
○ Ust' Shchugor, Russian Federation -67°F (-55°C)

Wettest Place:
◉ Crkvice, Bosnia and Herzegovina 183 in (4648 mm)

Driest Place:
○ Astrakhan', Russian Federation 6.4 in (162.5 mm)

Caspian Sea

Syrian Desert

An Nafud

Arabian

Ad Dahna

Persian Gulf

Ar Rub' al Khali

Peninsula

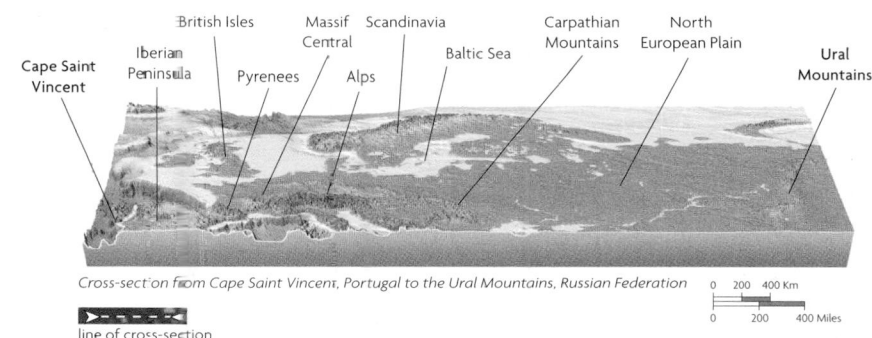

Cape Saint Vincent   Iberian Peninsula   British Isles   Pyrenees   Massif Central   Alps   Scandinavia   Baltic Sea   Carpathian Mountains   North European Plain   Ural Mountains

Cross-section from Cape Saint Vincent, Portugal to the Ural Mountains, Russian Federation

0   200   400 Km

0   200   400 Miles

▷▷▷▷◁ line of cross-section

Political

The political boundaries of Europe have changed many times, especially during the 20th century in the aftermath of two world wars, the break-up of the empires of Austria-Hungary, Nazi Germany, and, toward the end of the century, the collapse of communism in eastern Europe. The fragmentation of Yugoslavia has again altered the political map of Europe, highlighting a trend towards nationalism and devolution. In contrast, economic federalism is growing. In 1958, the formation of the European Economic Community (now the European Union or EU) started a move toward economic and political union and increasing internal migration. This process is still ongoing and the accession of Bulgaria and Romania in January 2007 brought the number of EU member states to twenty seven. Of these, fifteen have joined the Eurozone by adopting the Euro as their official currency.

Population
- ■ above 5 million
- ■ 1 million to 5 million
- ◉ 500,000 to 1 million
- ◉ 100,000 to 500,000
- ⊕ 50,000 to 100,000
- ○ 10,000 to 50,000
- ● Country capital

Borders
- full international border

Scale 1:17,250,000
(projection: Lambert Azimuthal Equal Area)

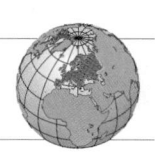

Languages

There are three main European language groups: Germanic languages predominate in central and northern Europe; Romance languages in western and Mediterranean Europe and Romania; while Slavic languages are spoken in eastern Europe and the Russian Federation. Isolated pockets of local languages, such as Basque and Gaelic, persist and frequently provide a focus for national identity.

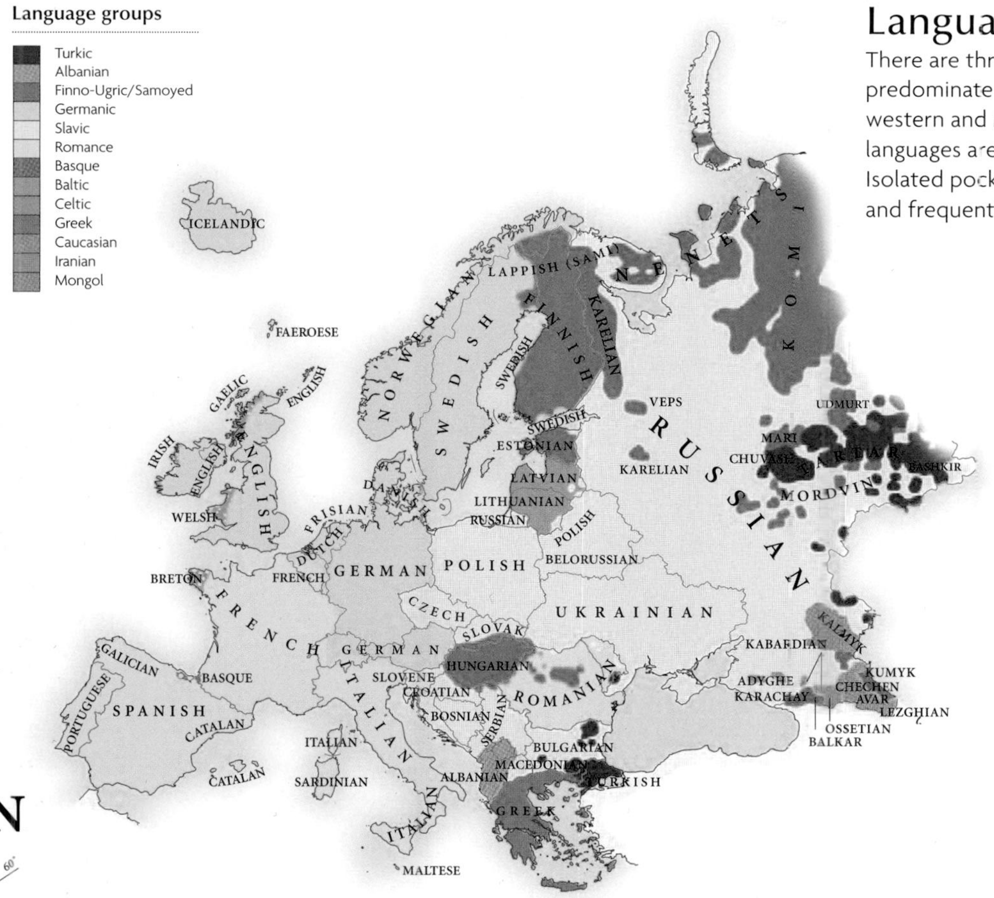

Language groups

- Turkic
- Albanian
- Finno-Ugric/Samoyed
- Germanic
- Slavic
- Romance
- Basque
- Baltic
- Celtic
- Greek
- Caucasian
- Iranian
- Mongol

Population

Europe is a densely populated, urbanized continent; in Belgium over 90% of people live in urban areas. The highest population densities are found in an area stretching east from southern Britain and northern France, into Germany. The northern fringes are only sparsely populated.

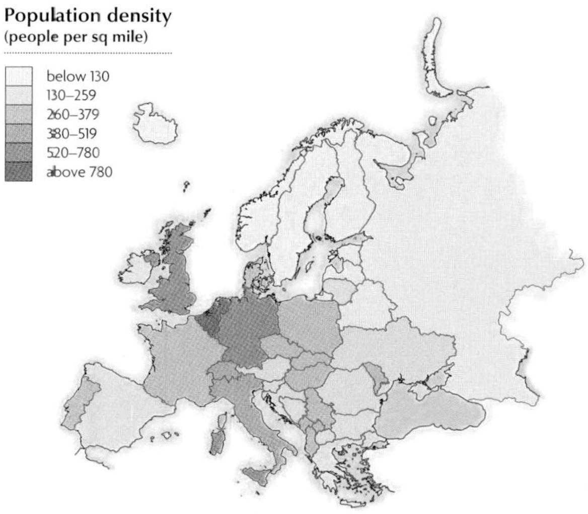

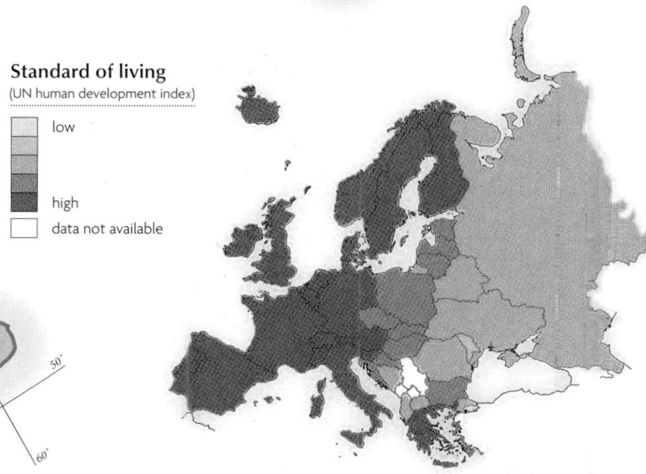

Population density
(people per sq mile)

- below 130
- 130–259
- 260–379
- 380–519
- 520–780
- above 780

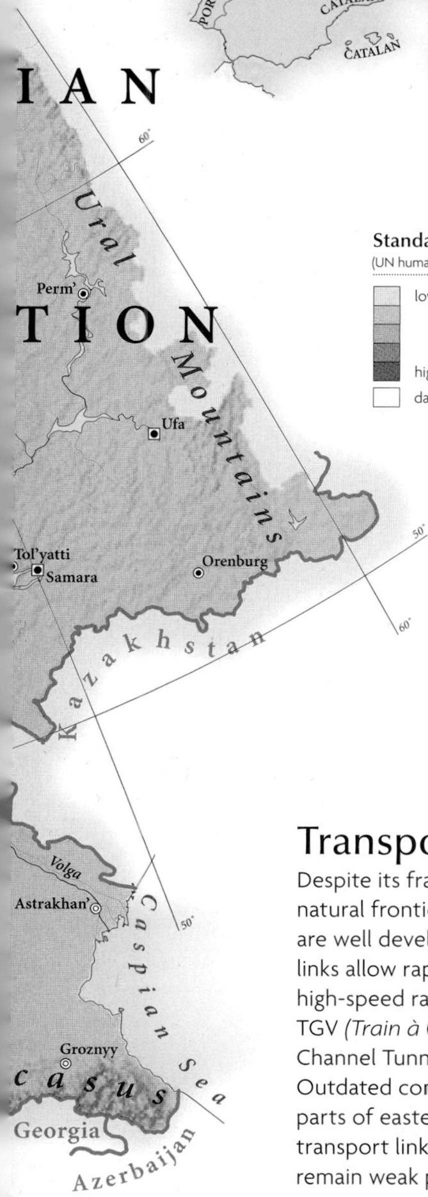

Standard of living

Living standards in western Europe are among the highest in the world, although there is a growing sector of homeless, jobless people. Eastern Europeans have lower overall standards of living—a legacy of stagnated economies.

Standard of living
(UN human development index)

- low
- high
- data not available

Transportation

Despite its fragmented geography and many natural frontiers, communications in Europe are well developed. Extensive motorway links allow rapid road transportation, while high-speed rail connections like France's TGV *(Train à Grande Vitesse)*, and the Channel Tunnel have improved rail travel. Outdated communication infrastructures in parts of eastern Europe, and insufficient transport links across the Alps, however, remain weak parts of the network.

Transportation

- major roads and motorways
- major railroads
- international borders
- transport intersections
- major international airports
- major ports

Scale 1:22,500,000
(projection: Lambert Conformal Conic)

| 0 | 200 | 400 | 600 | 800 | 1000 Km |

| 0 | 200 | 400 | 600 | 800 | 1000 Miles |

Climate

Europe experiences few extremes in either rainfall or temperature, with the exception of the far north and south. Along the west coast, the warm currents of the North Atlantic Drift moderate temperatures. Although east–west air movement is relatively unimpeded by relief, the Alpine Uplands halt the progress of north–south air masses, protecting most of the Mediterranean from cold, north winds.

Average Rainfall

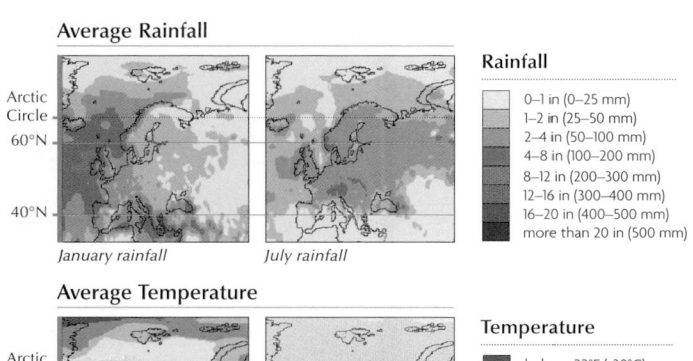

January rainfall   July rainfall

Rainfall

	0–1 in (0–25 mm)
	1–2 in (25–50 mm)
	2–4 in (50–100 mm)
	4–8 in (100–200 mm)
	8–12 in (200–300 mm)
	12–16 in (300–400 mm)
	16–20 in (400–500 mm)
	more than 20 in (500 mm)

Average Temperature

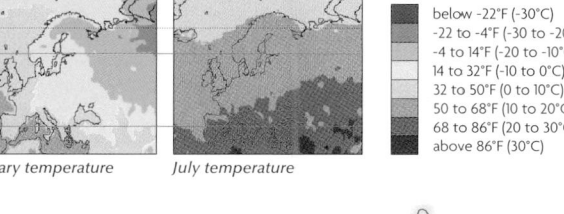

January temperature   July temperature

Temperature

	below -22°F (-30°C)
	-22 to -4°F (-30 to -20°C)
	-4 to 14°F (-20 to -10°C)
	14 to 32°F (-10 to 0°C)
	32 to 50°F (0 to 10°C)
	50 to 68°F (10 to 20°C)
	68 to 86°F (20 to 30°C)
	above 86°F (30°C)

Climate

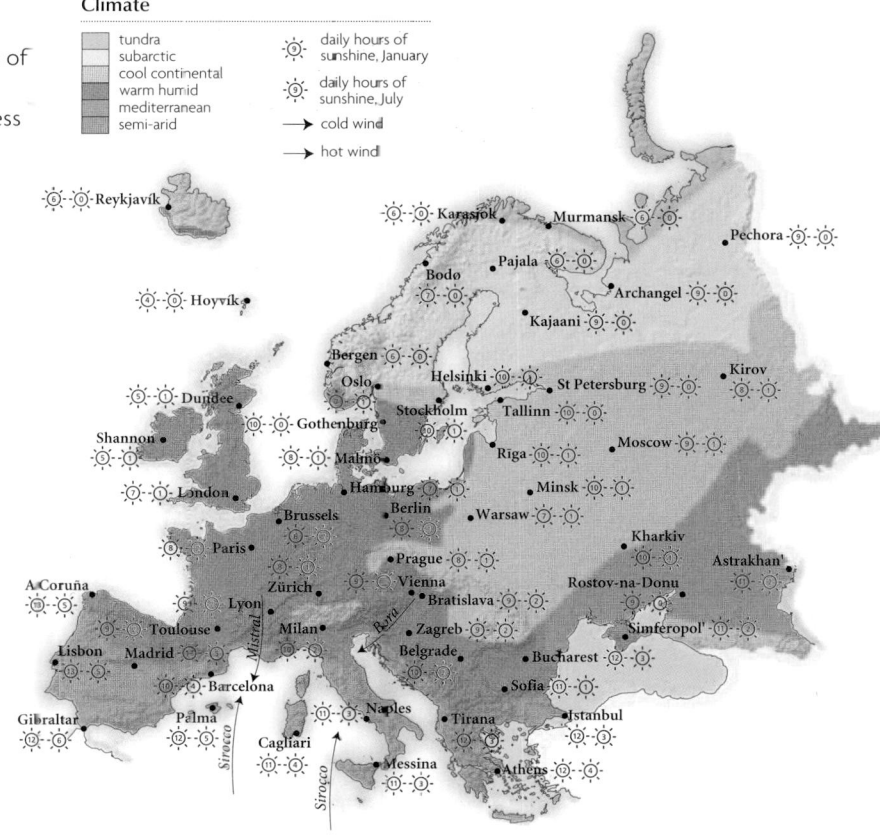

	tundra	☼	daily hours of sunshine, January
	subarctic		
	cool continental	☼	daily hours of sunshine, July
	warm humid		
	mediterranean	→	cold wind
	semi-arid	→	hot wind

Environmental issues

The partially enclosed waters of the Baltic and Mediterranean seas have become heavily polluted, while the Barents Sea is contaminated with spent nuclear fuel from Russia's navy. Acid rain, caused by emissions from factories and power stations, is actively destroying northern forests. As a result, pressure is growing to safeguard Europe's natural environment and prevent further deterioration.

Environmental issues

	national parks		marine pollution
	acid rain		heavy marine pollution
	polluted rivers	•	poor urban air quality
	radioactive contamination		

Landuse

Europe's swelling urban population and the outward expansion of many cities has created acute competition for land. Despite this, European resourcefulness has maximized land potential, and over half of Europe's land is still used for a wide variety of agricultural purposes. Land in northern Europe is used for cattle-rearing, pasture, and arable crops. Towards the Mediterranean, the mild climate allows the growing of grapes for wine; olives, sunflowers, tobacco and citrus fruits. EU subsidies, however, have resulted in massive overproduction and a land "set-aside" policy has been introduced.

Using the land and sea

	cropland		citrus fruits
	forest		cotton
	ice cap		fishing
	mountain region		fodder
	pasture		fruit
	tundra		olive oil
	wetland		potatoes
•	major conurbations		rice
	cattle		root crops
	goats		roses
	pigs		shellfish
	poultry		sunflowers
	reindeer		timber
	sheep		tobacco
	cereals		vineyards

EUROPE

1 VATNAJÖKULL, ICELAND
Europe's largest ice cap is located in the
southeast of this Atlantic island.

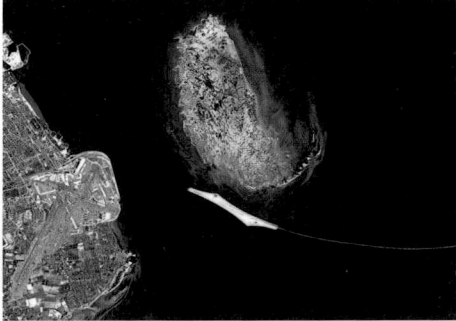

2 ORESUND LINK, DENMARK/SWEDEN
This link was opened to traffic in 2000, joining the
Danish capital, Copenhagen, with the Swedish town of
Malmo across the waters of the Oresund Strait.

3 BALSFJORD, NORWAY
Fjords were cut into Norway's west coast by glaciers
during the last ice age but as the ice retreated rising
sea-levels flooded the valleys left behind.

4 PRAGUE, CZECH REPUBLIC
In August 2002 some parts of the capital
were still under water after the worst
floods in living memory.

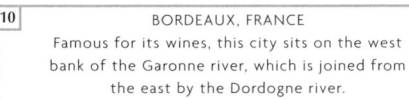

9 GIBRALTAR
A British colony since 1713, this rocky
promontory commands a strategic position at
the southern end of the Iberian Peninsula.

10 BORDEAUX, FRANCE
Famous for its wines, this city sits on the west
bank of the Garonne river, which is joined from
the east by the Dordogne river.

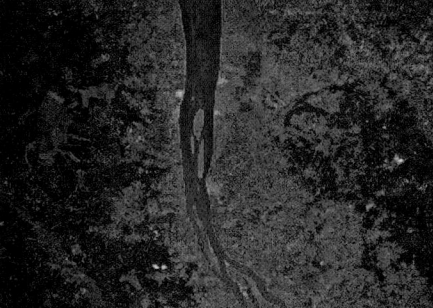

11 SOUTH FLEVOLAND, NETHERLANDS
This polder was reclaimed from the sea in
the early 1970s and is now home to extensive
farmland and small towns.

12 RHINE, GERMANY
The Rhine has been straightened in places, such
as here, just south of Mannheim,
to ease navigation.

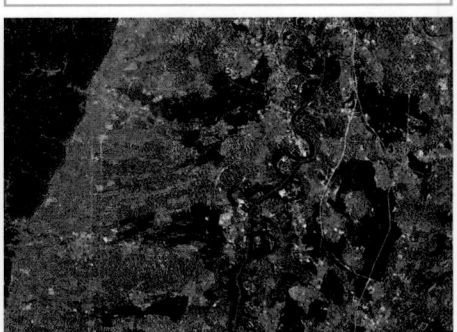

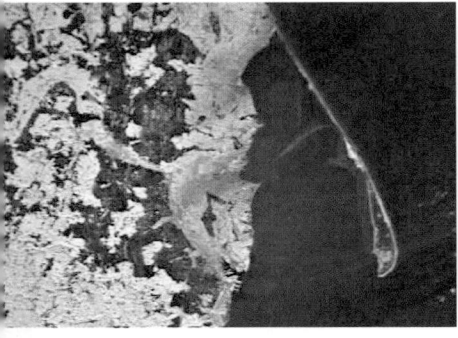

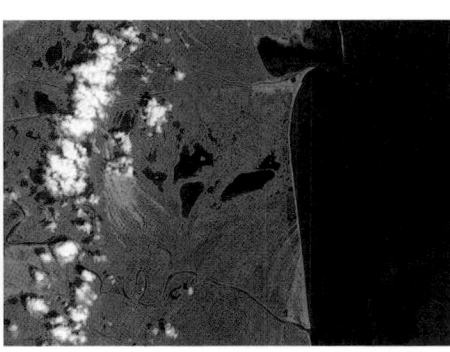

HEL PENINSULA, POLAND 5
The long spit of this peninsula encloses Puck Bay and shelters the important port of Gdynia.

TALLINN, ESTONIA 6
The capital and main port of Estonia has become a popular tourist destination in recent years.

LAKE VODLOZERO, RUSSIAN FEDERATION 7
The lake lies within a national park, which protects one of the most untouched wilderness areas in Europe and encompasses plains, taiga forests and wetlands.

DANUBE DELTA, ROMANIA 8
The Danube river splits into several channels as it flows into the Black Sea, forming one of Europe's most important wetland ecosystems.

VENICE, ITALY 13
Occupying the largest island in a sheltered lagoon at the north end of the Adriatic, this city was founded in 452 CE and grew rich on an extensive trading network.

ISTRA PENINSULA, CROATIA 14
This triangular peninsula marks the northern extent of Croatia's Dalmatian coastline.

MOUNT ETNA, SICILY, ITALY 15
This combination of visible and thermal images shows the volcano erupting in July 2001 and clearly indicates the major lava flows.

KEFALLONIÁ, GREECE 16
The largest of the Ionian Islands off Greece's west coast, Kefalloniá is mountainous with relatively high rainfall.

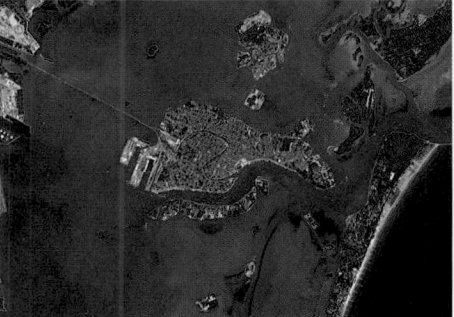

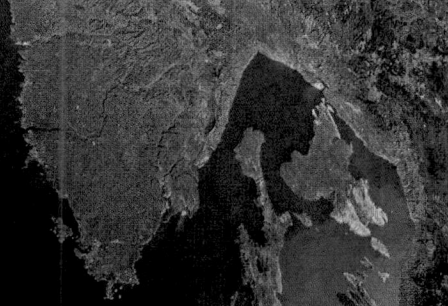

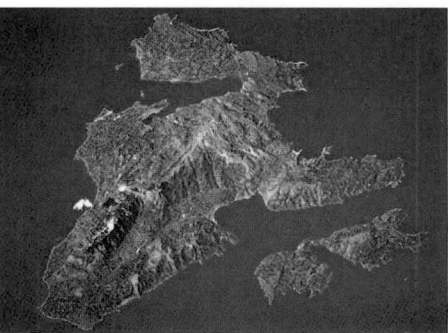

Scandinavia, Finland & Iceland

ARCTIC OCEAN

Barents Sea

RUSSIAN FEDERATION

Greenland Sea

Norwegian Sea

ATLANTIC OCEAN

Denmark Strait

ICELAND

REYKJAVÍK

Scale 1:4,900,000

0 20 40 60 80 100 Km
0   20   40   60   80 100 Miles

SVALBARD
(to Norway)

LONGYEARBYEN

Scale 1:8,000,000

0 20 40 60 80 100 Km
0   20   40   60   80 100 Miles

6000m
4000m
3000m
2000m
1000m
500m
250m
100m
Sea Level
-250m
-2000m
-4000m

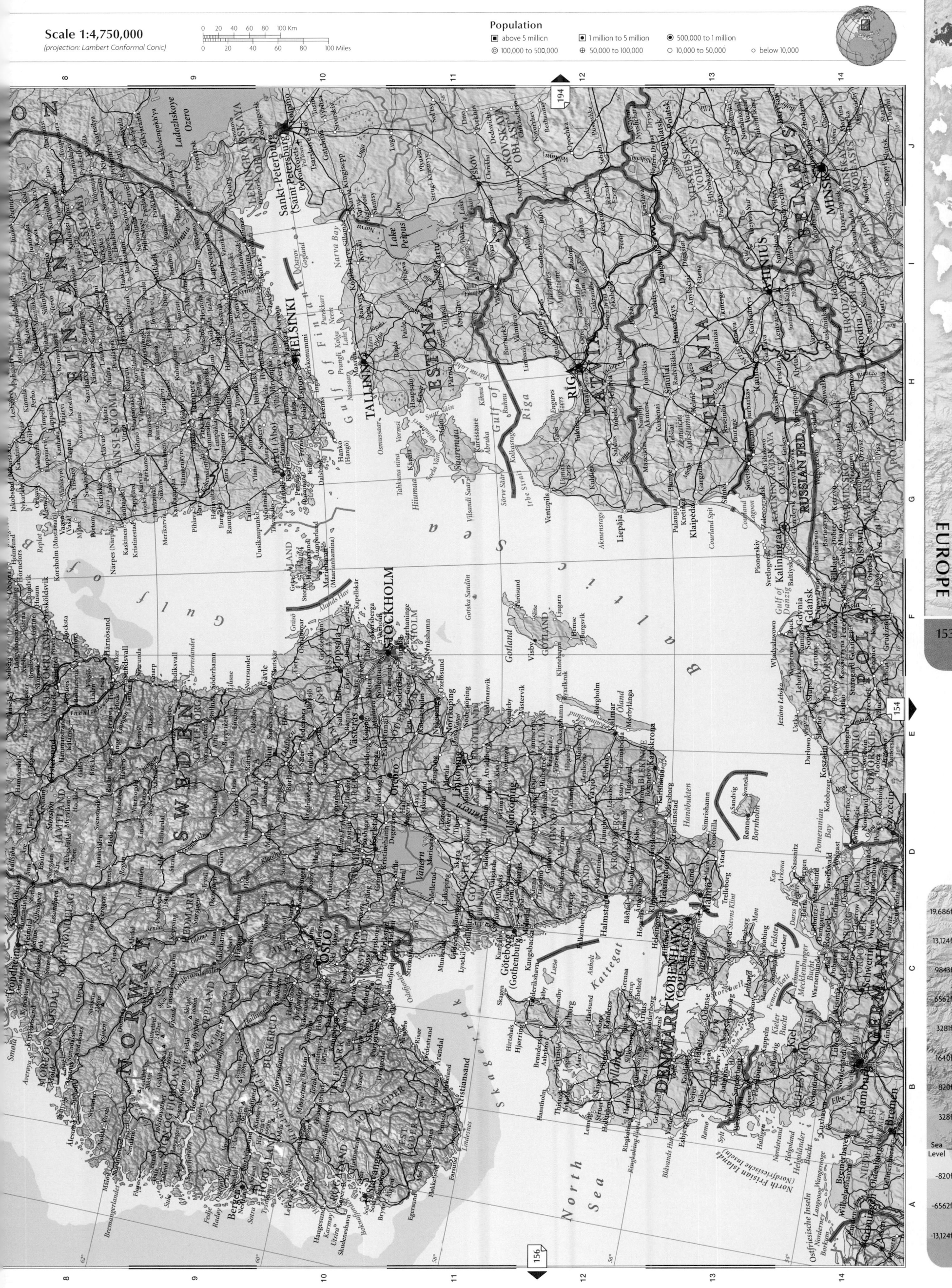
Scale 1:4,750,000
(projection: Lambert Conformal Conic)
0 20 40 60 80 100 Km
0 20 40 60 80 100 Miles
Population
above 5 million
1 million to 5 million
500,000 to 1 million
100,000 to 500,000
50,000 to 100,000
10,000 to 50,000
below 10,000
NORWAY
SWEDEN
FINLAND
ESTONIA
LATVIA
LITHUANIA
BELARUS
POLAND
DENMARK
GERMANY
RUSSIAN FED.
OSLO
STOCKHOLM
HELSINKI
TALLINN
RIGA
VILNIUS
MINSK
KØBENHAVN (COPENHAGEN)
Sankt-Peterburg (Saint Petersburg)
North Sea
Skagerrak
Kattegat
Baltic Sea
Gulf of Bothnia
Gulf of Finland
Gulf of Riga
19,686ft
13,124ft
9843ft
6562ft
3281ft
1640ft
820ft
328ft
Sea Level
-820ft
-6562ft
-13,124ft
EUROPE
153

Southern Scandinavia

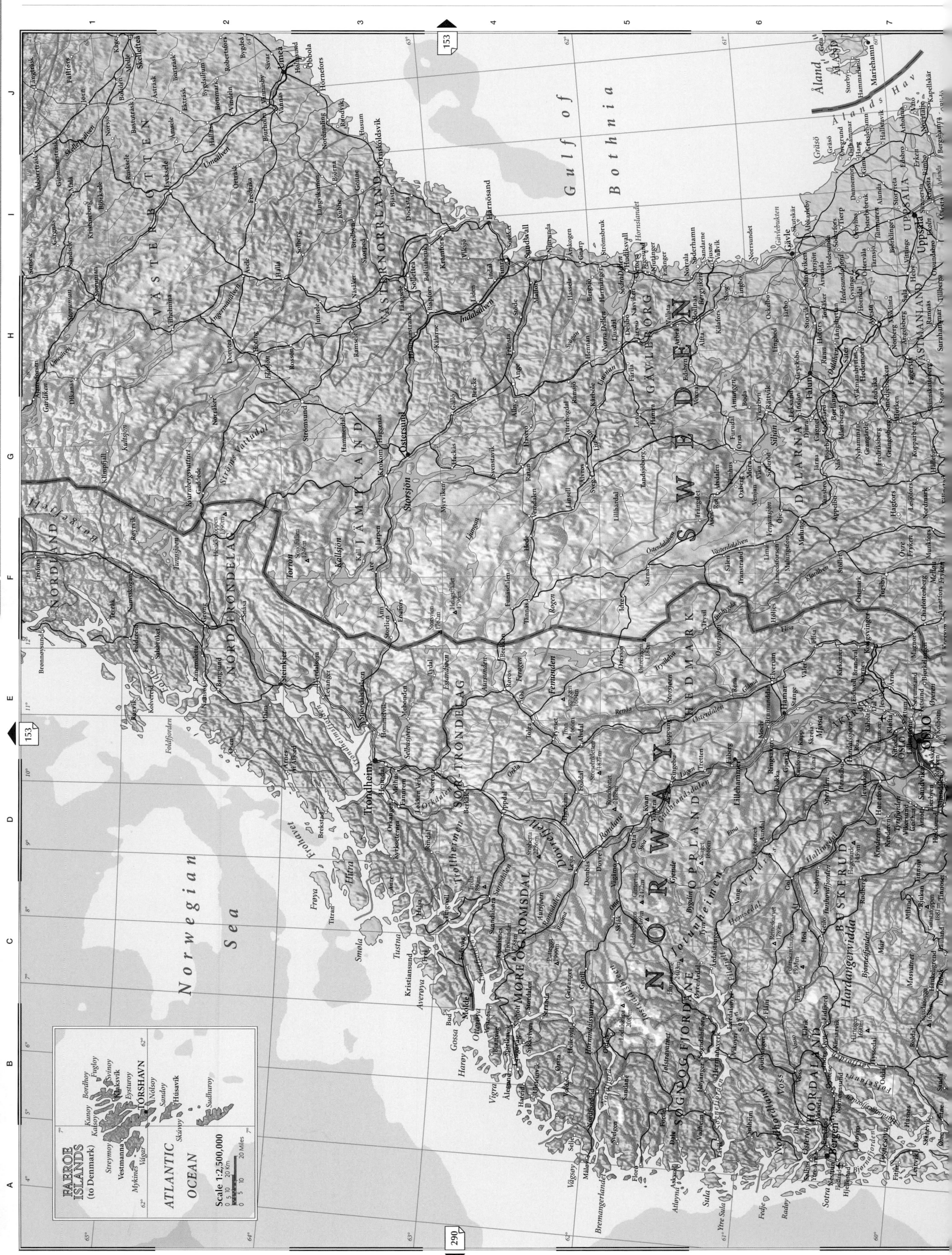

Gulf of Bothnia
Norwegian Sea
SWEDEN
NORWAY
VÄSTERBOTTEN
VÄSTERNORRLAND
JÄMTLAND
GÄVLEBORG
DALARNA
UPPSALA
VÄSTMANLAND
NORDLAND
NORD-TRØNDELAG
SØR-TRØNDELAG
MØRE OG ROMSDAL
HEDMARK
OPPLAND
AKERSHUS
BUSKERUD
HORDALAND
SOGN OG FJORDANE
Åland
Ålands Hav
Umeå
Östersund
Storsjön
Siljan
Sundsvall
Härnösand
Gävle
Uppsala
Falun
Trondheim
Lillehammer
Hamar
OSLO
Bergen
Ålesund
Molde
Kristiansund
Smøla
Hitra
Frøya
Trondheimsfjorden
Sognefjorden
Hardangervidda
Jotunheimen
Dovrefjell
FAEROE ISLANDS (to Denmark)
TÓRSHAVN
ATLANTIC OCEAN
Scale 1:2,500,000
6000m
4000m
3000m
2000m
1000m
500m
250m
100m
Sea Level
-250m
-2000m
-4000m
EUROPE
153
290

Northern Britain & Ireland

A B C D E F G

156

157

157

ATLANTIC

OCEAN

Sea of the Hebrides

Inner Hebrides

Highland

SCOTLAND

Firth of Lorn

Jura

Islay

North Channel

Firth of Clyde

Ayrshire

Dumfries

Isle of Arran

Mull of Kintyre

Malin Head

DONEGAL

Donegal Bay

UNITED

NORTHERN IRELAND

Lough Neagh

Belfast

Londonderry

Sperrin Mountains

Strangford Lough

Ards Peninsula

ISLE OF MAN
(to UK)

DOUGLAS

Ramsey

Peel

MAYO

SLIGO

LEITRIM

ROSCOMMON

LONGFORD

CAVAN

MONAGHAN

LOUTH

WEST MEATH

MEATH

Dundalk Bay

Irish

Sea

Connaught

GALWAY

OFFALY

KILDARE

IRELAND

DUBLIN

Dublin Bay

Dún Laoghaire

Anglesey

Holyhead

6000m
4000m
3000m
2000m
1000m
500m
250m
100m
Sea Level
-250m
-2000m
-4000m

A B C D E F G

157

Scale 1:2,750,000
(projection: Lambert Conformal Conic)

0 10 20 30 40 50 60 70 80 Km
0 10 20 30 40 50 60 70 80 Miles

Population
- ■ above 5 million
- ■ 1 million to 5 million
- ◉ 500,000 to 1 million
- ◎ 100,000 to 500,000
- ⊕ 50,000 to 100,000
- ○ 10,000 to 50,000
- ○ below 10,000

19,686ft
13,124ft
9843ft
6562ft
3281ft
1640ft
820ft
328ft
Sea
Level
-820ft
-6562ft
-13,124ft

North Sea

Baltic Sea

Kattegat

Skagerrak

DENMARK

GERMANY

POLAND

Gotland

Öland

Bornholm

STOCKHOLM

KØBENHAVN (COPENHAGEN)

Hamburg

Göteborg (Gothenburg)

Malmö

Örebro

Linköping

Norrköping

Ålborg

Århus

Odense

Kiel

Rostock

Schwerin

Gdynia

Gdańsk

Pomeranian Bay

Gulf of Danzig

SKÅNE

BLEKINGE

KRONOBERG

KALMAR

ÖSTERGÖTLAND

VÄSTRA GÖTALAND

VÄRMLAND

SÖDERMANLAND

VÄSTMANLAND

NORDJYLLAND

MIDTJYLLAND

SYDDANMARK

SJÆLLAND

FYN

SCHLESWIG-HOLSTEIN

MECKLENBURG-VORPOMMERN

NIEDERSACHSEN

ZACHODNIO-POMORSKIE

POMORSKIE

155

290

290

EUROPE

UNITED KINGDOM

North Sea

ATLANTIC OCEAN

Shetland Islands

Herma Ness
Unst
Fetlar
Yell
Out Skerries
Yell Sound
Whalsay
Hillswick
Sullom Voe
Bressay
Lerwick
St Magnus Bay
Papa Stour
Scalloway
West Burra
Foula
Fitful Head
Sumburgh Head

Fair Isle

Orkney Islands

Papa Westray
The North
North Ronaldsay
Westray
Rousay
Sanday
Mainland
Eday
Stronsay
Hoy
Kirkwall
Burray
St Margaret's Hope
South Ronaldsay
Pentland Firth
Stromness
Dunnet Head
Duncansby Head
John o'Groats
Ness Head
Wick

Scotland

Kinnaird Head
Fraserburgh
Peterhead
Buchan Ness
Aberdeen
Girdle Ness
Stonehaven
Montrose
Arbroath
Carnoustie
Firth of Tay
St Andrews
Fife Ness
Dundee
North Berwick
St Abb's Head
Eyemouth
Berwick-upon-Tweed
Holy Island

Newcastle upon Tyne
Tynemouth
South Shields
Blyth
Morpeth
Alnwick
The Cheviot

Edinburgh
Firth of Forth
Haddington
Dunfermline
Kirkcaldy
Falkirk
Stirling
Glasgow
Paisley
East Kilbride
Kilmarnock
Ayr
Troon
Irvine
Firth of Clyde
Campbeltown
Ailsa Craig
Ballantrae

Isle of Lewis
Port of Ness
Butt of Lewis
Broad Bay
Stornoway
Carloway
Tarbert
Loch Roag
Scarp
Taransay
Pabbay
South Harris
The Little Minch
Lochmaddy
Monach Islands
North Uist
Benbecula
South Uist
Lochboisdale
Eriskay
Barra
Barra Head

Outer Hebrides

Sula Sgeir
North Rona
Sule Skerry
Stack Skerry

St Kilda

Inner Hebrides

Isle of Skye
Portree
Broadford
Rum
Canna
Eigg
Muck
Coll
Tiree
Iona
Mull
Colonsay
Jura
Islay
Port Ellen
Gigha Island

Mull of Kintyre

Cape Wrath
Loch Eriboll
Durness
Tongue
Strathy Point
Thurso
Halladale
Bettyhill
Ben Klibreck
Ben Hope
Ben Loyal
Helmsdale
Brora
Golspie
Dornoch
Dornoch Firth
Tarbat Ness
Cromarty
Beauly
Inverness
Loch Ness
Fort Augustus
Ben Nevis
Fort William
Mallaig
Loch Linnhe
Oban
Lochgilphead
Inveraray
Loch Fyne

North Channel

Rathlin Island
Ballycastle
Malin Head
Inishtrahull
Tory Island
Bloody Foreland
Dunfanaghy
Gweedore
Sheep Haven

-4000m
-2000m
-250m
Sea Level
100m
250m
500m
1000m
2000m
3000m
4000m
6000m

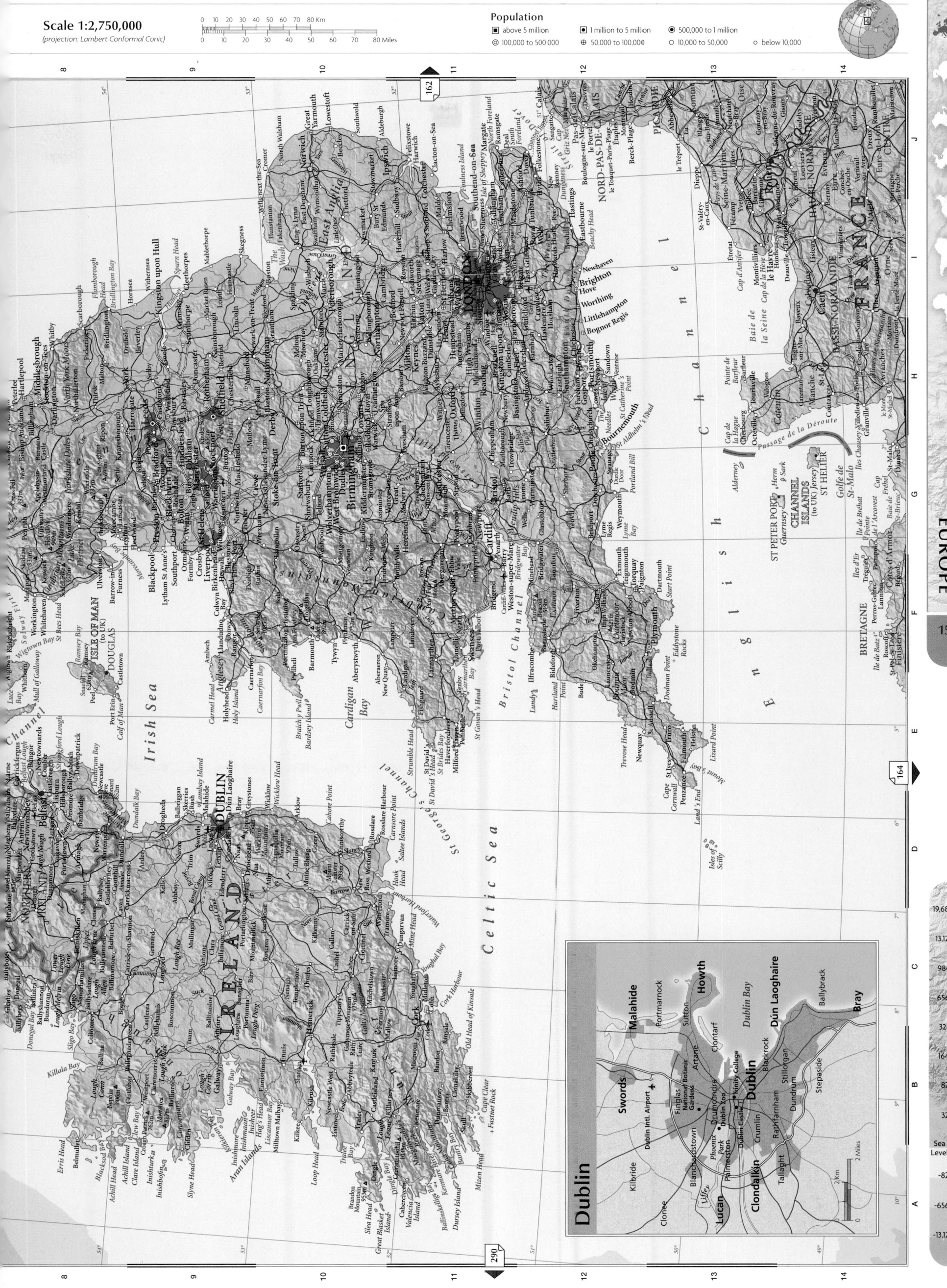

Scale 1:2,750,000
(projection: Lambert Conformal Conic)
0 10 20 30 40 50 60 70 80 Km
0 10 20 30 40 50 60 70 80 Miles
Population
above 5 million
1 million to 5 million
500,000 to 1 million
100,000 to 500 000
50,000 to 100,000
10,000 to 50,000
below 10,000
IRELAND
DUBLIN
Belfast
NORTHERN IRELAND
Irish Sea
ISLE OF MAN (to UK)
DOUGLAS
Celtic Sea
St George's Channel
Cardigan Bay
WALES
ENGLAND
LONDON
Birmingham
Manchester
Liverpool
Leeds
Sheffield
Bristol
Cardiff
Bristol Channel
English Channel
CHANNEL ISLANDS (to UK)
ST PETER PORT
ST HELIER
FRANCE
BRETAGNE
BASSE-NORMANDIE
HAUTE-NORMANDIE
NORD-PAS-DE-CALAIS
PICARDIE
Dublin
Swords
Malahide
Howth
Dublin Bay
Dún Laoghaire
Bray
Lucan
Clondalkin
Tallaght
EUROPE
19,686ft
13,124ft
9843ft
6562ft
3281ft
1640ft
820ft
328ft
Sea Level
-820ft
-6562ft
-13,124ft

162
164
290

Northern Britain & Ireland

ATLANTIC OCEAN
Inner Hebrides
Sea of the Hebrides
Highland
Argyll
Jura
Islay
Colonsay
Coll
Tiree
Mull
Mingulay
Barra Head
Firth of Lorn
Sound of Jura
Firth of Clyde
Isle of Arran
Stirlingshire
Ayrshire
Dumfries
North Channel
Rathlin Island
Giants Causeway
Ailsa Craig
Mull of Kintyre
Mull of Galloway
Malin Head
Inishtrahull
Tory Island
Bloody Foreland
Inishowen
Lough Foyle
Lough Swilly
Donegal Bay
DONEGAL
Londonderry
Coleraine
Belfast
Belfast Lough
Lough Neagh
NORTHERN IRELAND
UNITED
Lower Lough Erne
Upper Lough Erne
Enniskillen
Armagh
Newry
Mourne Mountains
Dundalk Bay
Carlingford Lough
Strangford Lough
Ards Peninsula
ISLE OF MAN (to UK)
DOUGLAS
Point of Ayre
Calf of Man
SLIGO
LEITRIM
MONAGHAN
CAVAN
LOUTH
MEATH
MAYO
ROSCOMMON
LONGFORD
WEST MEATH
GALWAY
OFFALY
KILDARE
Connaught
IRELAND
DUBLIN
Dublin Bay
Dún Laoghaire
Lambay Island
Wicklow Mountains
Slieve Bloom Mountains
Lough Ree
Lough Derg
Irish Sea
Anglesey
Holyhead
Holy Island
Europe
158

Scale 1:1,300,000
(projection: Lambert Conformal Conic)
0 10 20 30 40 50 Km
0 10 20 30 40 50 Miles
Population
above 5 million
1 million to 5 million
500,000 to 1 million
100,000 to 500,000
50,000 to 100,000
10,000 to 50,000
below 10,000
H I J K L M N
156
161
162
EUROPE
159
North Sea
Edinburgh
Dundee
Arbroath
Montrose
St Andrews
Firth of Forth
Dunfermline
Kirkcaldy
Dunbar
Berwick-upon-Tweed
Holy Island
Farne Islands
Lunan Bay
Fife Ness
Isle of May
Bass Rock
St. Abb's Head
Angus
Perthshire
Fife
Southern Uplands
Borders
Cheviot Hills
Northumberland
Dumfries and Galloway
Solway Firth
KINGDOM
Newcastle upon Tyne
Sunderland
South Shields
Hartlepool
Middlesbrough
Stockton-on-Tees
Darlington
Durham
Carlisle
Cumbria
Lake District
Workington
Whitehaven
Penrith
Kendal
Barrow-in-Furness
Isle of Walney
Morecambe Bay
Lancaster
Blackpool
Preston
Lancashire
Southport
Liverpool
Liverpool Bay
Manchester
Yorkshire Dales
North York Moors
Yorkshire
Scarborough
Whitby
Bridlington
Flamborough Head
Bridlington Bay
York
Harrogate
Leeds
Bradford
Kingston upon Hull
Grimsby
Cleethorpes
Spurn Head
Scunthorpe
Sheffield
Doncaster
Lincolnshire
Lincoln
Nottinghamshire
Mansfield
Chesterfield
Peak District
Derbyshire
Cheshire
Great Ormes Head
Point of Ayr
WALES
ENGLAND
Pennines
Ness Point
Robin Hood's Bay
Tees Bay
Druridge Bay
Filey Bay
Skegness
19,686ft
13,124ft
9843ft
6562ft
3281ft
1640ft
820ft
328ft
Sea Level
-820ft
-6562ft
-13,124ft

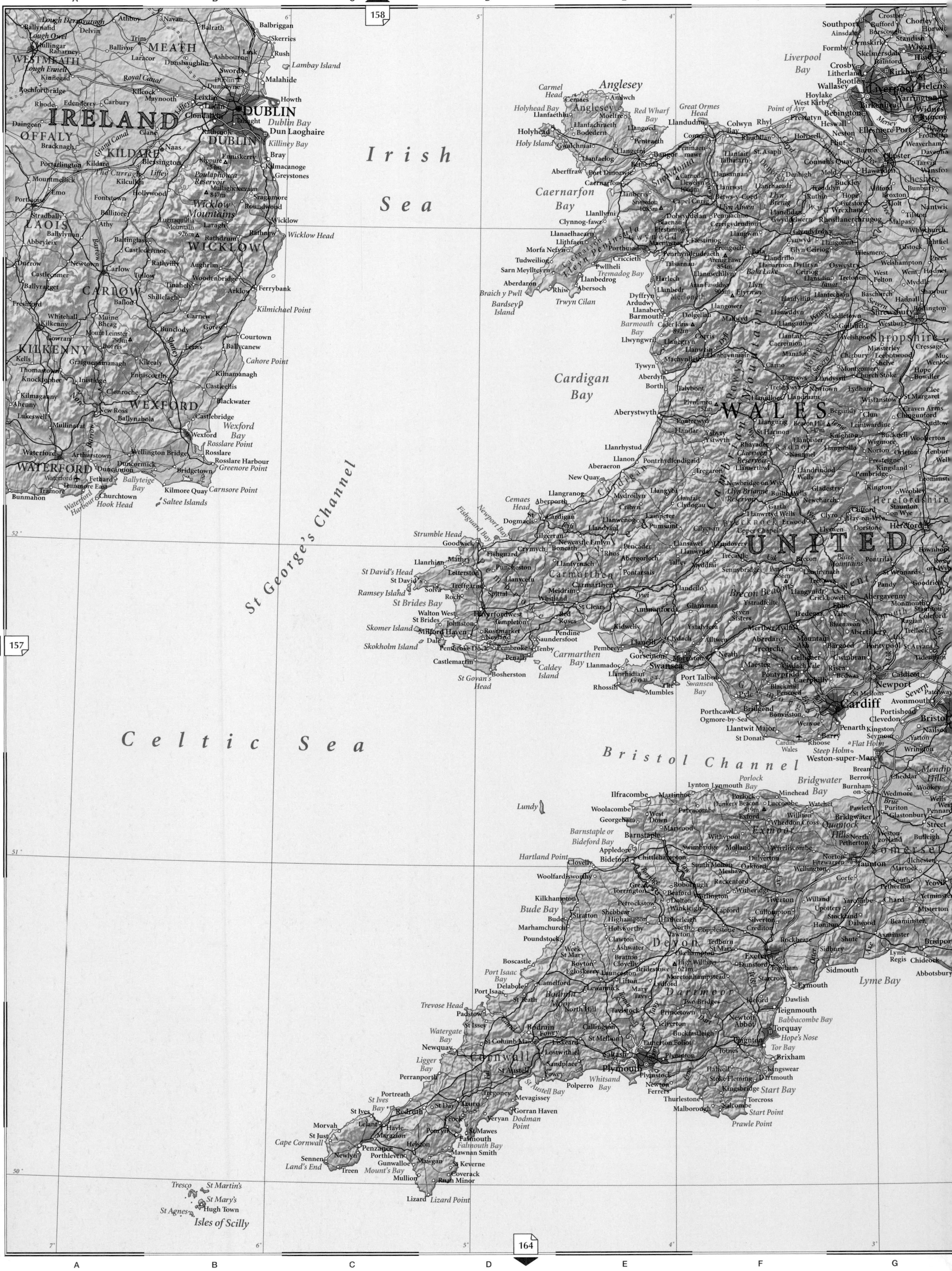

158

157

164

Seas and Water Bodies
Irish Sea

St George's Channel

Celtic Sea

Bristol Channel

Cardigan Bay

Caernarfon Bay

Carmarthen Bay

Swansea Bay

Bridgwater Bay

Lyme Bay

Dublin Bay

Killiney Bay

Wexford Bay

Lundy

Major Regions
IRELAND

WALES

UNITED

Counties / Regions
WESTMEATH

MEATH

OFFALY

KILDARE

LAOIS

CARLOW

KILKENNY

KELLS

WEXFORD

WATERFORD

WICKLOW

Shropshire

Herefordshire

Cheshire

Somerset

Devon

Cornwall

Major Cities
DUBLIN

Dun Laoghaire

Liverpool

Cardiff

Bristol

Plymouth

Swansea

Newport

Weston-super-Mare

Exeter

Torquay

Land's End

Lizard Point

Start Point

Isles of Scilly

St Mary's

Hugh Town

Tresco

St Martin's

St Agnes

Elevation Scale
6000m
4000m
3000m
2000m
1000m
500m
250m
100m
Sea Level
-250m
-2000m
-4000m

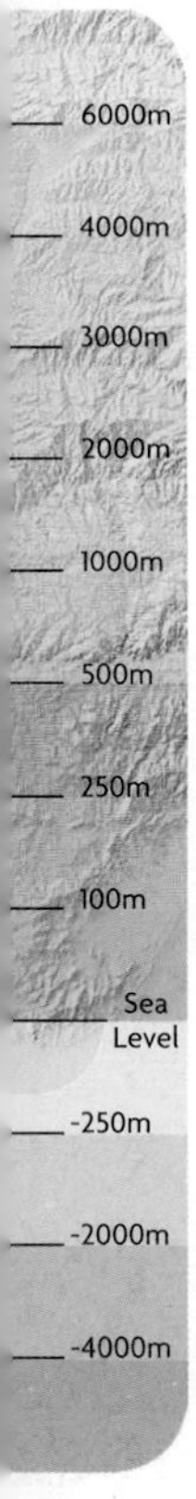

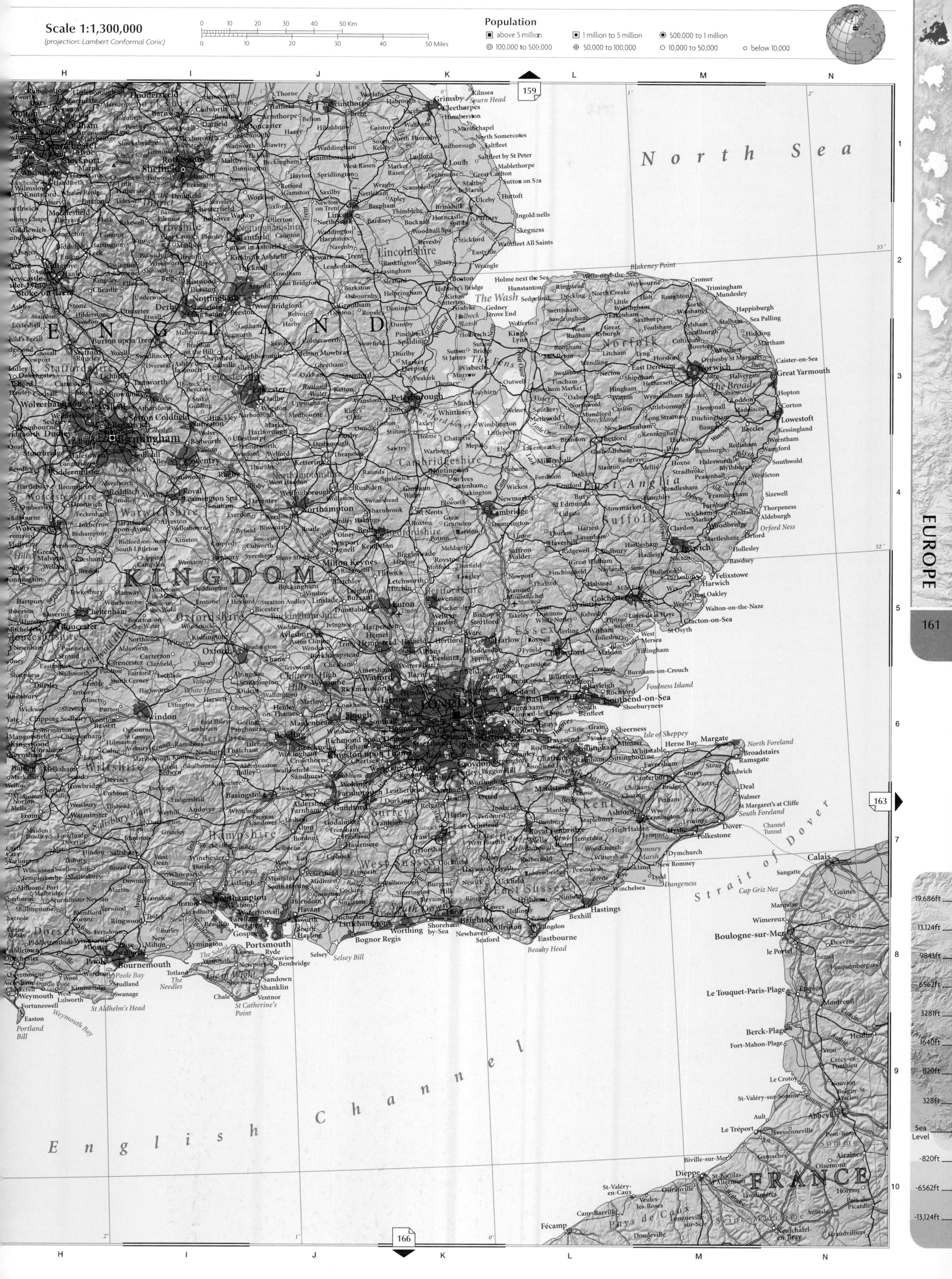

Scale 1:1,300,000
(projection: Lambert Conformal Conic)

0 10 20 30 40 50 Km
0   10   20   30   40   50 Miles

Population

■ above 5 million   ■ 1 million to 5 million   ● 500,000 to 1 million
◎ 100,000 to 500,000   ⊕ 50,000 to 100,000   ○ 10,000 to 50,000   ○ below 10,000

North Sea

ENGLAND

KINGDOM

English Channel

Strait of Dover

FRANCE

19,686ft
13,124ft
9843ft
6562ft
3281ft
1640ft
820ft
328ft
Sea
Level
-820ft
-6562ft
-13,124ft

The Low Countries

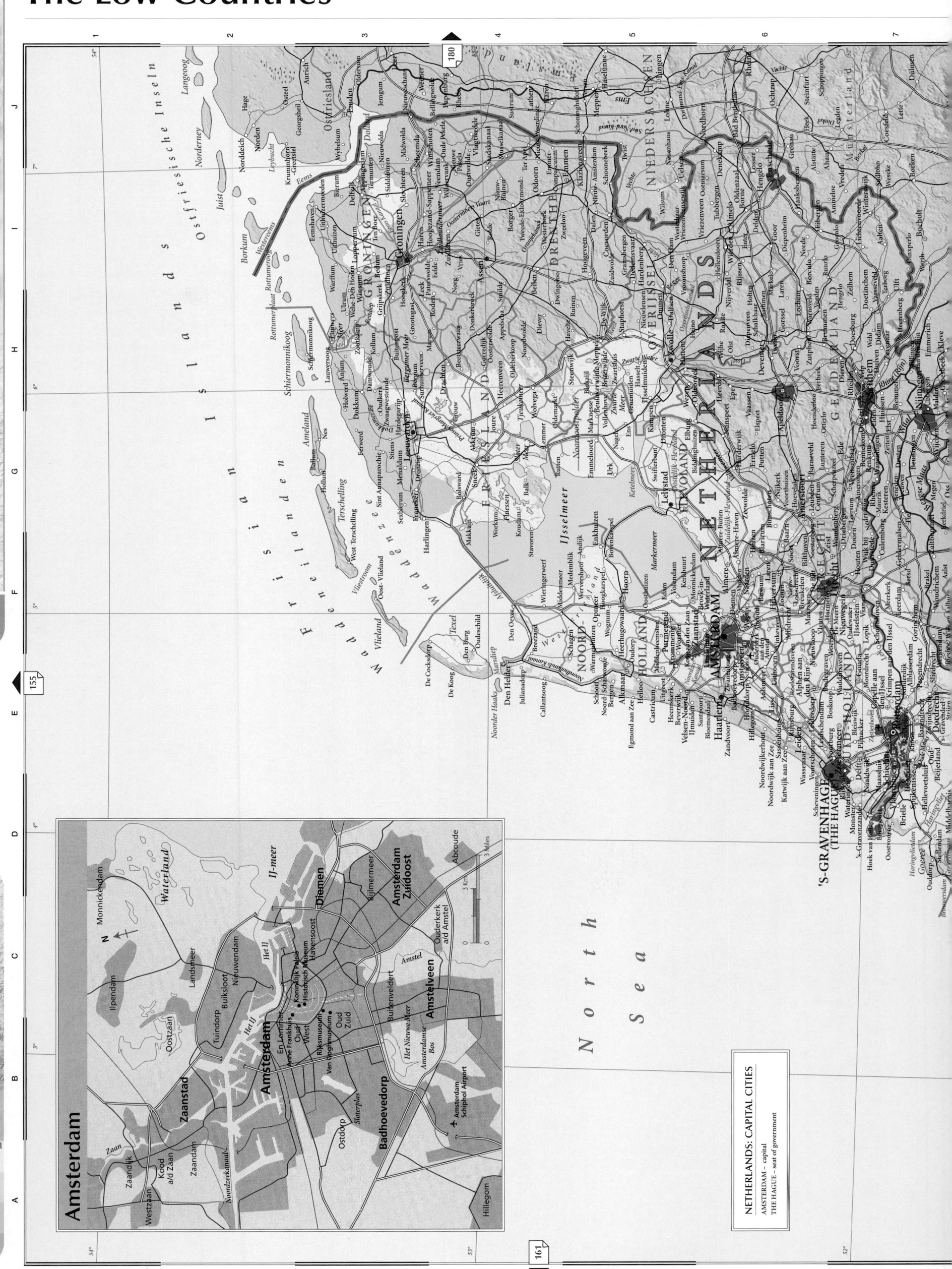

Amsterdam
Monnickendam
Ilpendam
Waterland
Zaandijk
Westzaan
Kood a/d Zaan
Oostzaan
Zaanstad
Zaandam
Landsmeer
Tuindorp
Buiksloot
Nieuwendam
Noordzeekanaal
Het IJ
Amsterdam
IJ-meer
En Lommer
Anne Frankhuis
Oud West
Koninklijk Paleis
Historisch Museum
Havensoost
Diemen
Rijksmuseum
Van Goghmuseum
Oud Zuid
Ostdorp
Sloterplas
Bijlmermeer
Badhoevedorp
Buitenveldert
Amsterdam Zuidoost
Het Nieuwe Meer
Amstel
Amsterdamse Bos
Amstelveen
Ouderkerk a/d Amstel
Abcoude
Amsterdam Schiphol Airport
Hillegom
North Sea
Frisian Islands
Waddeneilanden
Waddenzee
Ostfriesische Inseln
IJsselmeer
Markermeer
NETHERLANDS
AMSTERDAM
'S-GRAVENHAGE (THE HAGUE)
Haarlem
Groningen
Leeuwarden
Zwolle
Arnhem
Nijmegen
Rotterdam
Utrecht
Enschede
Apeldoorn
Lelystad
Assen
NIEDERSACHSEN
Ostfriesland
GRONINGEN
FRIESLAND
DRENTHE
OVERIJSSEL
GELDERLAND
FLEVOLAND
NOORD-HOLLAND
ZUID-HOLLAND
UTRECHT
Texel
Vlieland
Terschelling
Ameland
Schiermonnikoog
Borkum
Juist
Norderney
Langeoog
NETHERLANDS: CAPITAL CITIES
AMSTERDAM – capital
THE HAGUE – seat of government

155
161
180

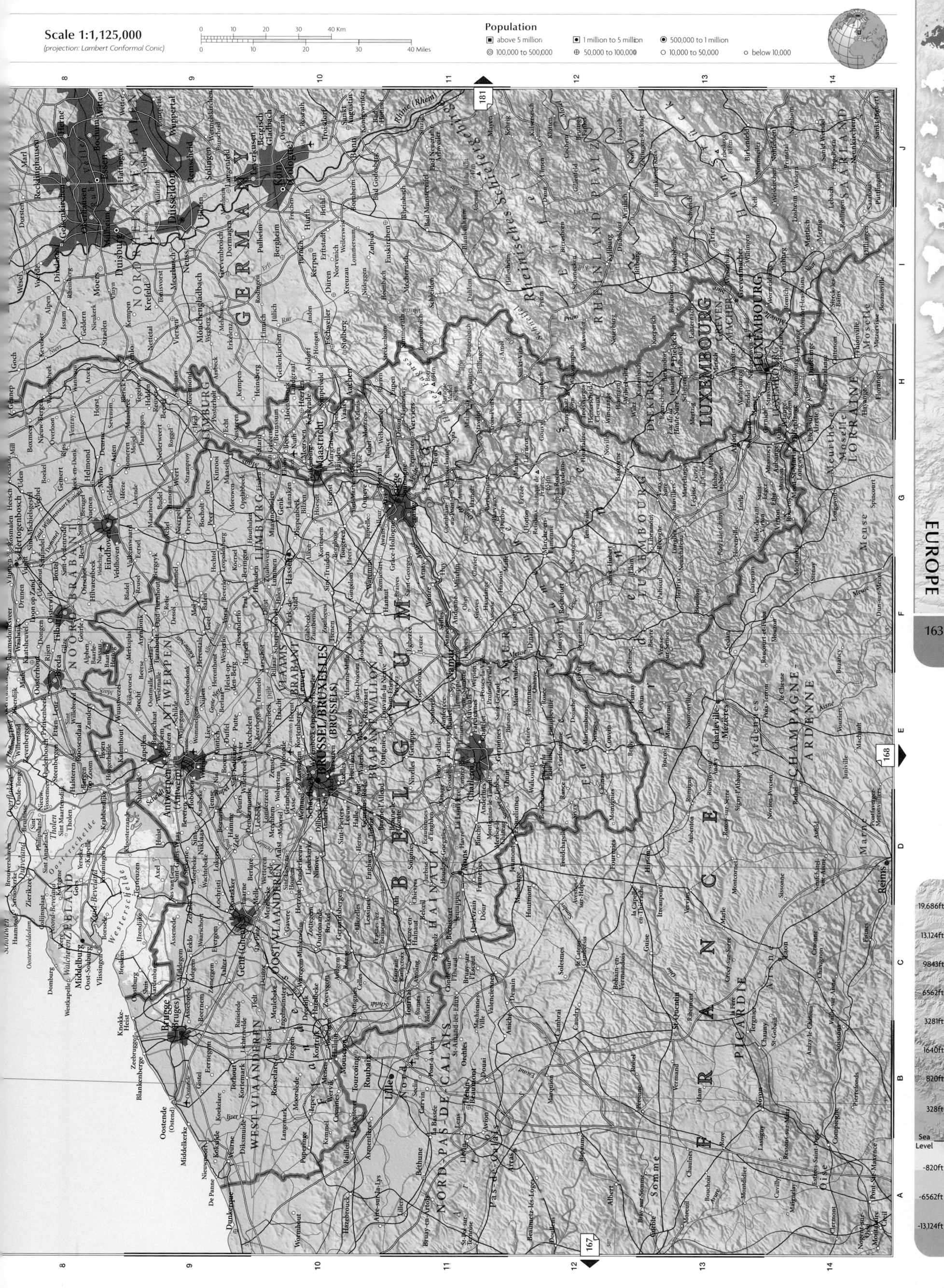

Scale 1:1,125,000
(projection: Lambert Conformal Conic)
0 10 20 30 40 Km
0 10 20 30 40 Miles
Population
above 5 million
1 million to 5 million
500,000 to 1 million
100,000 to 500,000
50,000 to 100,000
10,000 to 50,000
below 10,000
EUROPE
163
19,686ft
13,124ft
9843ft
6562ft
3281ft
1640ft
820ft
328ft
Sea Level
-820ft
-6562ft
-13,124ft
181
168
167
BELGIUM
FRANCE
GERMANY
LUXEMBOURG
BRUSSEL/BRUXELLES (BRUSSELS)
Antwerpen (Antwerp)
Gent (Ghent)
Brugge (Bruges)
Liège
Charleroi
Namur
Maastricht
Eindhoven
Köln (Cologne)
Düsseldorf
Lille
Reims

France

160

UNITED
KINGDOM

ATLANTIC

OCEAN

English Channel

CHANNEL ISLANDS
(to UK)

ST PETER PORT
ST HELIER

Guernsey
Herm
Sark
Jersey
Alderney

Cap de
la Hague
Cherbourg
Octeville

BASSE-NORMANDIE

le Havre
Baie de la Seine

Caen

BRETAGNE

Brest
Quimper
Lorient

Rennes

Le Mans

PAYS DE LA LOIRE

Nantes

Angers

Tours

POITOU-
CHARENTES

la Rochelle

Niort
Poitiers

Bay of

Biscay

Bordeaux

AQUITAINE

Angoulême

Périgueux

Paris

Seine

Forêt de
St-Germain

Montmorency

Aéroport
Charles de Gaulle

St-Denis
Drancy
Aulnay-
sous-Bois

Tremblay-
en-France

Argenteuil
Asnières
Enghien

Aubervilliers

St-Germain-
en-Laye

Nanterre
Montmartre
Sacré-
Cœur
Arc de Triomphe
Tour Eiffel
Paris

Le Raincy
Lagny

Marly-
le-Roi
Rueil
Malmaison
Boulogne-
Billancourt
Musée du Louvre
Bastille
Notre-Dame

Montreuil
Vincennes

Marne-la-Vallée

château
de Versailles
Meudon

Versailles

Vitry-sur-
Seine
Orly

Créteil

Champigny-
sur-Marne

Trappes

Sceaux

Chevreuse
Palaiseau

Antony

Aéroport
d'Orly

Brie-
Comte-Robert

Orsay

Mortgeron

0   5 Km
0   5 Miles

6000m
4000m
3000m
2000m
1000m
500m
250m
100m
Sea
Level
-250m
-2000m
-4000m

A Coruña
(La Coruña)

Costa Verde

Oviedo
Gijón (Xixón)
Santander

Donostia-
San Sebastián

GALICIA

CORDILLERA CANTÁBRICA

CANTABRIA

PAÍS VASCO

Bilbao

Pamplona
(Iruña)

Ourense
Orense

León

CASTILLA Y LEÓN

Burgos

LA RIOJA

Logroño

S P A I N

PORTUGAL

Valladolid

Zamora

Palencia

Soria

ARAGÓN

Zaragoza

170

290

Scale 1:3,250,000
(projection: Lambert Conformal Conic)
0 20 40 60 80 100 Km
0 20 40 60 80 100 Miles
Population
above 5 million
1 million to 5 million
500,000 to 1 million
100,000 to 500,000
50,000 to 100,000
10,000 to 50,000
below 10,000
H I J K L M N
1 2 3 4 5 6 7 8 9 10
181
177
198
EUROPE
165
19,686ft
13,124ft
9843ft
6562ft
3281ft
1640ft
820ft
328ft
Sea Level
-820ft
-6562ft
-13,124ft
BELGIUM
BRUSSEL/BRUXELLES (BRUSSELS)
LUXEMBOURG
GERMANY
SWITZERLAND
AUSTRIA
LIECHTENSTEIN
MONACO
ANDORRA
PARIS
Frankfurt am Main
Stuttgart
München (Munich)
Strasbourg
Dijon
Lyon
Genève (Geneva)
BERN
Milano (Milan)
Torino (Turin)
Genova (Genoa)
Marseille
Nice
Toulouse
Montpellier
Grenoble
Clermont-Ferrand
Limoges
Reims
Nancy
Metz
Besançon
Zürich
Innsbruck
Verona
Bologna
Firenze (Florence)
Livorno
Perpignan
Corse (Corsica)
Ajaccio
Bastia
Ligurian Sea
Mediterranean Sea
Tyrrhenian Sea
Golfe du Lion
Golfo di Genova
Lake Constance
Lake Geneva
Isola d'Elba

EUROPE

166

165

161

168

UNITED KINGDOM

English Channel

Bay of Biscay

Biscay

CHANNEL ISLANDS
(to UK)

Guernsey
ST PETER PORT
Herm
Sark
Jersey
ST HELIER

Golfe de St-Malo

Les Sept Îles
Alderney

Cap de la Hague
Pointe de Barfleur
Cotentin

Baie de la Seine

Cap d'Antifer
Cap de la Hève

HAUTE-NORMANDIE
Rouen
le Havre

BASSE-NORMANDIE
Caen
Calvados
Orne

BRETAGNE
Rennes
Ille-et-Vilaine
Côtes d'Armor
Morbihan
Finistère
Quimper

PAYS DE LA LOIRE
Nantes
Angers
Loire-Atlantique
Maine-et-Loire
Vendée
la Roche-sur-Yon

Le Mans
Sarthe
Mayenne
Maine

Tours
Indre-et-Loire
Loir-et-Cher

Orléans

CENTRE

ÎLE-DE-FRANCE
Versailles
Chartres

Eure-et-Loir

Poitiers
POITOU-CHARENTES

la Rochelle
Charente-Maritime

Île de Ré
Île d'Oléron
Île de Noirmoutier
Île d'Yeu
Belle Île
Île de Groix

Sea Level
6000m
4000m
3000m
2000m
1000m
500m
250m
100m
Sea Level
-250m
-2000m
-4000m

Scale 1:1,750,000
(projection: Lambert Conformal Conic)

| 0 | 10 | 20 | 30 | 40 | 50 Km |
| 0 | 10 | 20 | 30 | 40 | 50 Miles |

Population

- ■ above 5 million
- ▣ 1 million to 5 million
- ◉ 500,000 to 1 million
- ⊙ 100,000 to 500,000
- ⊕ 50,000 to 100,000
- ○ 10,000 to 50,000
- ∘ below 10,000

EUROPE

167

176

19,686ft
13,124ft
9843ft
6562ft
3281ft
1640ft
820ft
328ft
Sea Level
-820ft
-6562ft
-13,124ft

BELGIUM
GERMANY
LUXEMBOURG
FRANCE
SWITZERLAND

BRUSSEL/BRUXELLES (BRUSSELS)
Köln (Cologne)
Düsseldorf
Luxembourg
Paris
Reims
Nancy
Strasbourg
Dijon
Besançon
Bern
Genève (Geneva)

PICARDIE
CHAMPAGNE-ARDENNE
LORRAINE
ALSACE
BOURGOGNE
FRANCHE-COMTÉ
AUVERGNE
RHÔNE-ALPES

Southern France & the Pyrenees

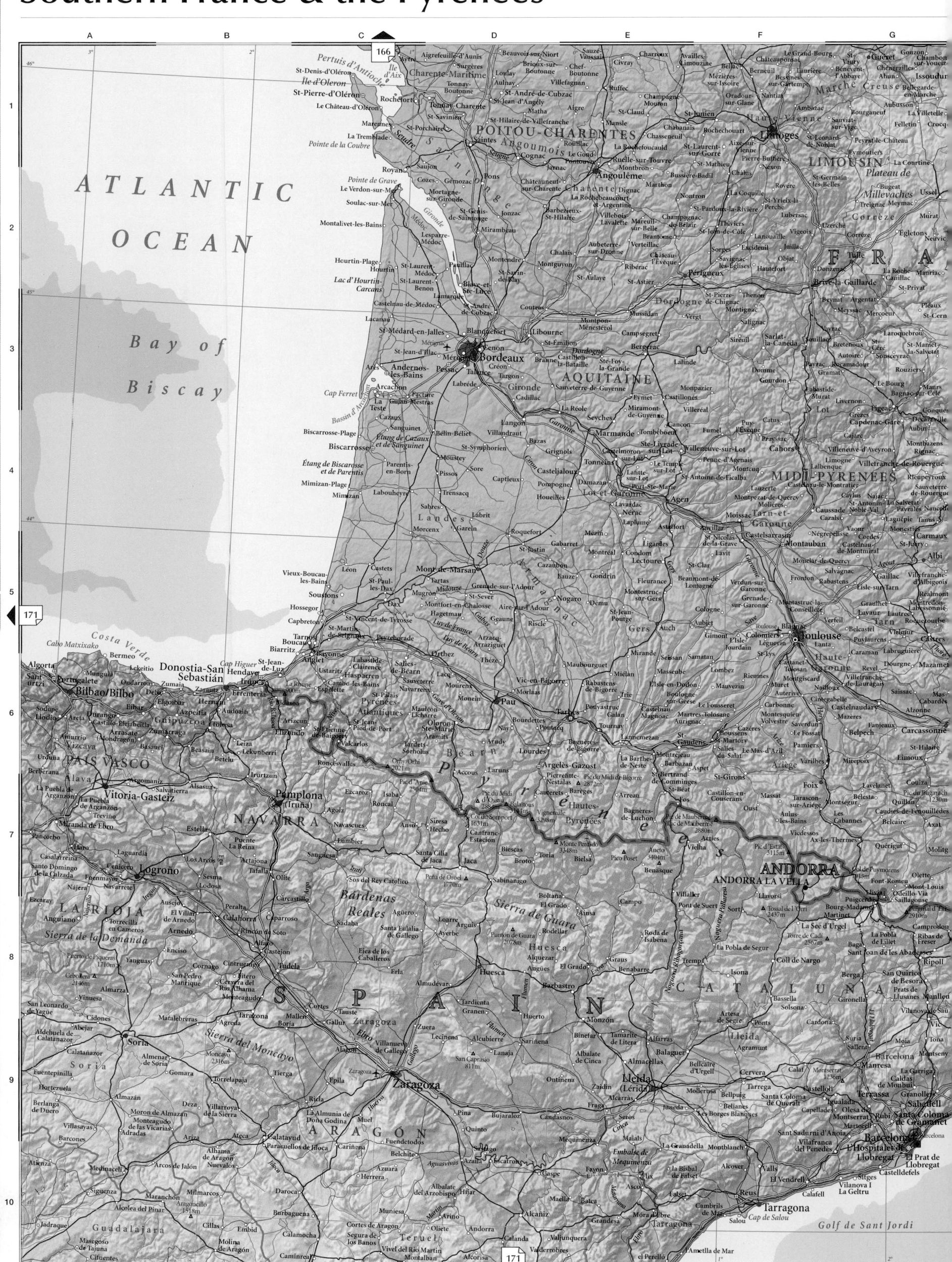
ATLANTIC OCEAN
Bay of Biscay
Golf de Sant Jordi
Costa Verde
POITOU-CHARENTES
AQUITAINE
LIMOUSIN
MIDI-PYRENEES
FRANCE
PAIS VASCO
NAVARRA
LA RIOJA
ARAGÓN
CATALUNA
ANDORRA
ANDORRA LA VELLA
SPAIN
Pyrénées
Bordeaux
Limoges
Angoulême
Périgueux
Toulouse
Pau
Tarbes
Agen
Montauban
Bayonne
Biarritz
Donostia-San Sebastián
Bilbao/Bilbo
Vitoria-Gasteiz
Pamplona (Iruña)
Logroño
Zaragoza
Huesca
Lleida (Lérida)
Barcelona
Tarragona
Soria
Landes
Gironde
Dordogne
Garonne
Sierra de Guara
Sierra del Moncayo
Bárdenas Reales
166
171
171
A B C D E F G
1 2 3 4 5 6 7 8 9 10
6000m
4000m
3000m
2000m
1000m
500m
250m
100m
Sea Level
-250m
-2000m
-4000m
EUROPE

Scale 1:1,750,000
(projection: Lambert Conformal Conic)
0 10 20 30 40 50 Km
0 10 20 30 40 50 Miles
Population
above 5 million
1 million to 5 million
500,000 to 1 million
100,000 to 500,000
50,000 to 100,000
10,000 to 50,000
below 10,000
H I J K L M N
167
174
198
EUROPE
169
19,686ft
13,124ft
9843ft
6562ft
3281ft
1640ft
820ft
328ft
Sea Level
-820ft
-6562ft
-13,124ft
Mediterranean Sea
Golfe du Lion
Ligurian Sea
Golfo di Genova
Côte d'Azur
Costa Brava
ITALY
MONACO
AUVERGNE
Massif Central
RHÔNE-ALPES
PROVENCE-ALPES-CÔTE D'AZUR
LANGUEDOC-ROUSSILLON
Clermont-Ferrand
St-Étienne
Lyon
Villeurbanne
Grenoble
Chambéry
Annecy
Valence
Avignon
Nîmes
Montpellier
Marseille
Toulon
Aix-en-Provence
Nice
Cannes
Antibes
Monaco
Torino (Turin)
Perpignan
Girona
Figueres
Béziers
Narbonne
Sète
Arles
Orange
Montélimar
Le Puy
Rodez
Mende
Sanremo
Savoie
Haute-Savoie
Vercors
Maritime Alps
Camargue
Mont Blanc
Matterhorn
Monts du Cantal
Monts Dore
Ardèche
Drôme
Vaucluse
Var
Hautes-Alpes
Isère
Bouches-du-Rhône
Hérault
Gard
Lozère
Aveyron
Cap d'Agde
Cap de Creus
Cap Croisette
Cap Camarat
Îles d'Hyères

Southern Iberia

ATLANTIC OCEAN
PORTUGAL
PORTO
Porto (Oporto)
Vila Nova de Gaia
Matosinhos
VILA REAL
BRAGANÇA
AVEIRO
VISEU
GUARDA
COIMBRA
CASTELO BRANCO
LEIRIA
SANTARÉM
PORTALEGRE
LISBOA
LISBOA (LISBON)
Setúbal
SETÚBAL
ÉVORA
Évora
BEJA
Beja
FARO
Faro
Badajoz
Cáceres
Mérida
Salamanca
CASTILLA-LEÓN
EXTREMADURA
Sevilla
Córdoba
Huelva
Cádiz
Jeréz de la Frontera
Málaga
Algeciras
Gibraltar
GIBRALTAR (to UK)
Strait of Gibraltar
Golfo de Cádiz
Costa de la Luz
Tanger
Ceuta (to Spain)
MOROCCO
Cabo da Roca
Cabo de São Vicente
Cabo Espichel
Tagus
Guadiana
Guadalquivir
Sierra Morena
AZORES (to Portugal)
Ponta Delgada
Angra do Heroísmo
Horta
Scale 1:6,500,000
170
290
130

EUROPE

Scale 1:1,900,000
(projection: Lambert Conformal Conic)
0 10 20 30 40 50 Km
0 10 20 30 40 50 Miles
Population
above 5 million
1 million to 5 million
500,000 to 1 million
100,000 to 500,000
50,000 to 100,000
10,000 to 50,000
below 10,000
171
175
131
EUROPE
173
19,686ft
13,124ft
9843ft
6562ft
3281ft
1640ft
820ft
328ft
Sea Level
-820ft
-6562ft
-13,124ft
Madrid
Móstoles
Getafe
Toledo
Guadalajara
Cuenca
Teruel
Castellón
Valencia
Albacete
Ciudad Real
Alicante (Alacant)
Elche (Elx)
Murcia
Cartagena
Jaén
Granada
Almería
Tarragona
Puertollano
Linares
Lorca
ARAGÓN
CATALUÑA
PAÍS VALENCIANO
CASTILLA-LA MANCHA
MURCIA
MADRID
Golfo de Valencia
Golf de Sant Jordi
Golfo de Mazarrón
Golfo de Almería
Costa del Azahar
Costa Blanca
Mediterranean Sea
Alboran Sea
Isla de Alborán
Islas Baleares (Balearic Islands)
ILLES BALEARES
Ibiza
Formentera
Islas Columbretes
Sierra Nevada
Sierra de los Filabres
Sierra de Segura
Sierra de Alcaraz
Sistema Ibérico
La Mancha
Campo de Montiel
Cabo de Gata
Cabo de Palos
Cabo de La Nao
Cabo de San Antonio
ALGERIA
Oran
Mostaganem
Relizane
Chlef

The Italian Peninsula
6000m
4000m
3000m
2000m
1000m
500m
250m
100m
Sea Level
-250m
-2000m
-4000m

Scale 1:3,000,000
(projection: Lambert Conformal Conic)

0 20 40 60 80 100 Km
0 20 40 60 80 100 Miles

Population
■ above 5 million
▣ 1 million to 5 million
◉ 500,000 to 1 million
⊚ 100,000 to 500,000
⊕ 50,000 to 100,000
○ 10,000 to 50,000
○ below 10,000

186
171
131

175

Inset: MALTA

MALTA

Gozo

Victoria
Ras San
Dimitri
Ras il-
Wardija

Mgarr

Comino
(Kemmuna)

Mellieha
Naxxar
St Julian's
Sliema

San Pawl il-Bahar

Rabat
Mdina
Malta

VALLETTA
Paola
Zabbar
Birzebbuga
Marsaxlokk
Bay

Il-Kullana

Mediterranean Sea

Scale 1:900,000

Seas and regions
Adriatic Sea
Strait of Otranto
Ionian Sea
Tyrrhenian Sea
Mediterranean Sea
Golfo di Taranto
Malta Channel
Strait of Sicily

Countries and regions
MONTENEGRO
NERETVA
ALGERIA
TUNISIA
MALTA
ABRUZZO
CAMPANIA
PUGLIA
BASILICATA
CALABRIA
SICILIA (Sicily)
Sardegna (Sardinia)
CORSE

Major cities
VATICAN CITY
ROMA (ROME)
NAPOLI (NAPLES)
Bari
Palermo
Catania
Siracusa
Cagliari
Ajaccio
TUNIS
Reggio di Calabria
Messina
Taranto
Brindisi
Lecce
Foggia
Potenza
Cosenza
Catanzaro
Crotone
Trapani
Marsala

Elevation scale
19,686ft
13,124ft
9843ft
6562ft
3281ft
1640ft
820ft
328ft
Sea Level
-820ft
-6562ft
-13,124ft

The Alpine States & Northern Italy

Scale 1:2,100,000
(projection: Lambert Conformal Conic)
0 10 20 30 40 50 60 70 80 Km
0 10 20 30 40 50 60 70 80 Miles
Population
above 5 million
1 million to 5 million
500,000 to 1 million
100,000 to 500,000
50,000 to 100,000
10,000 to 50,000
below 10,000
CZECH REPUBLIC
AUSTRIA
SLOVAKIA
HUNGARY
SLOVENIA
CROATIA
BOSNIA & HERZEGOVINA
SAN MARINO
Adriatic Sea
Gulf of Venice
Gulf of Trieste
WIEN (VIENNA)
BRATISLAVA
LJUBLJANA
ZAGREB
München (Munich)
Salzburg
Linz
Graz
Klagenfurt
Innsbruck
Trieste
Venezia (Venice)
Rijeka
Split
Zadar
Ancona
Rimini
Ravenna
Ferrara
Padova (Padua)
Vicenza
Perugia
Győr
Sopron
Szombathely
Veszprém
Székesfehérvár
Pécs
Banja Luka
Zenica
Mostar
Bohemian Forest
Hohe Tauern
Karawanken
Balaton
Bakony
Dinaric Alps
Apennines
183
184
175
EUROPE
19,686ft
13,124ft
9843ft
6562ft
3281ft
1640ft
820ft
328ft
Sea Level
-820ft
-6562ft
-13,124ft

Germany

North Sea
Baltic Sea
Kattegat
DENMARK
SWEDEN
POLAND
NETHERLANDS
KØBENHAVN (COPENHAGEN)
BERLIN
Hamburg
Bremen
Hannover
Kiel
Lübeck
Rostock
Szczecin
Magdeburg
Potsdam
Malmö
Århus
Odense
SCHLESWIG-HOLSTEIN
MECKLENBURG-VORPOMMERN
NIEDERSACHSEN
BRANDENBURG
SACHSEN-ANHALT
NORDRHEIN-WESTFALEN
Jylland
Sjælland
Fyn
Rügen
Bornholm
Fehmarn
Pomeranian Bay
Helgoländer Bucht
Ostfriesische Inseln
North Frisian Islands (Nordfriesische Inseln)
6000m
4000m
3000m
2000m
1000m
500m
250m
100m
Sea Level
-250m
-2000m
-4000m
155
182
163

Scale 1:2,250,000
(projection: Lambert Conformal Conic)

0 10 20 30 40 50 60 70 80 Km
0 10 20 30 40 50 60 70 80 Miles

Population

■ above 5 million	■ 1 million to 5 million	◉ 500,000 to 1 million
◎ 100,000 to 500,000	⊕ 50,000 to 100,000	○ 10,000 to 50,000	o below 10,000

GERMANY

CZECH REPUBLIC

AUSTRIA

FRANCE

SWITZERLAND

ITALY

BELGIUM

LUXEMBOURG

PRAGUE

München

Stuttgart

Nürnberg

Erfurt

19,686ft
13,124ft
9843ft
6562ft
3281ft
1640ft
820ft
328ft
Sea
Level
-820ft
-6562ft
-13,124ft

Rhineland & Hamburg

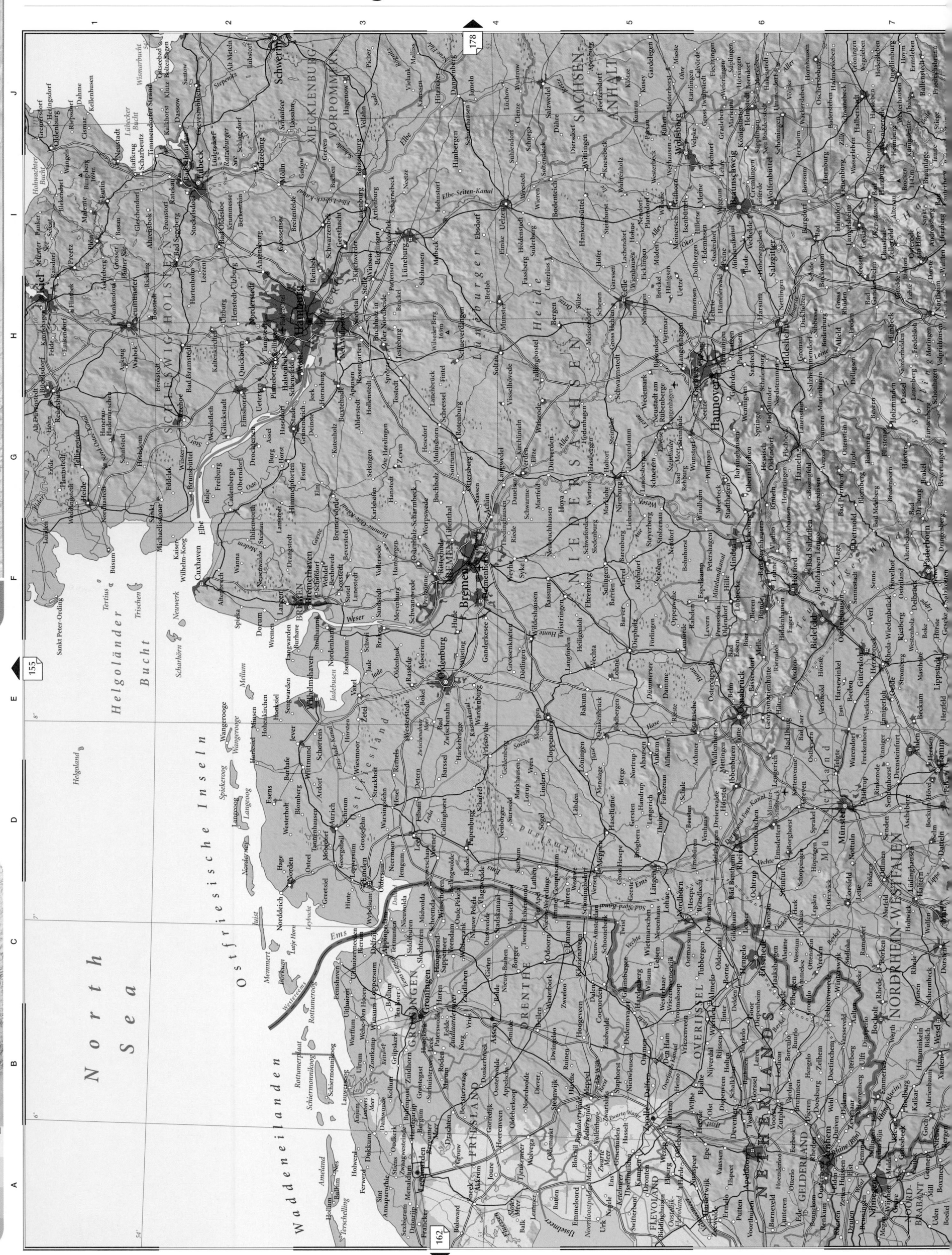
North Sea
Helgoländer Bucht
Ostfriesische Inseln
Waddeneilanden
SCHLESWIG-HOLSTEIN
MECKLENBURG-VORPOMMERN
NIEDERSACHSEN
SACHSEN-ANHALT
NORDRHEIN-WESTFALEN
NETHERLANDS
GRONINGEN
FRIESLAND
DRENTHE
OVERIJSSEL
GELDERLAND
FLEVOLAND
Hamburg
Bremen
Hannover
Kiel
Lübeck
Schwerin
Oldenburg
Osnabrück
Münster
Bielefeld
Braunschweig
Groningen
Lüneburger Heide
155
162
178

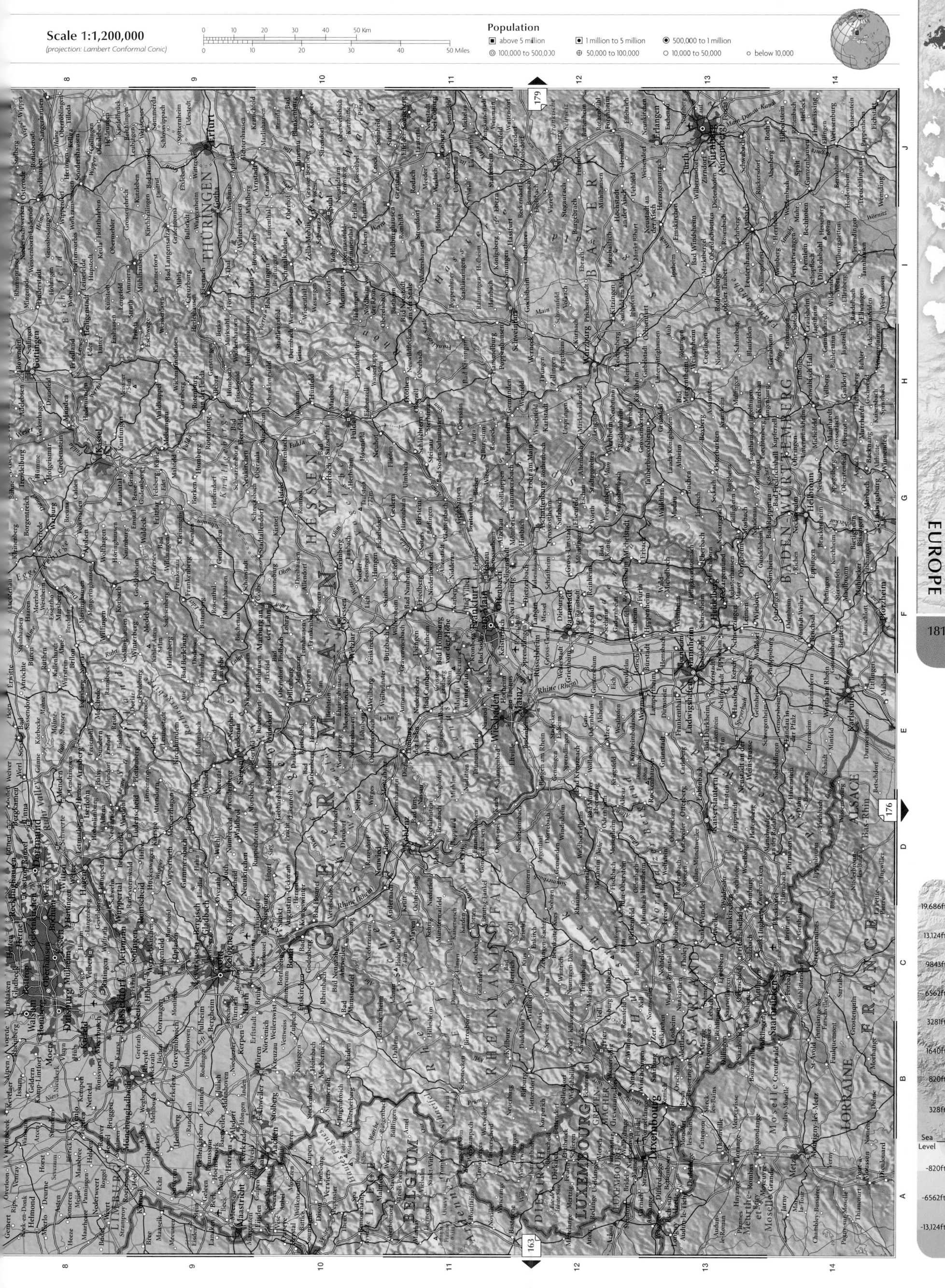

Scale 1:1,200,000
(projection: Lambert Conformal Conic)
0 10 20 30 40 50 Km
0 10 20 30 40 50 Miles
Population
above 5 million
1 million to 5 million
500,000 to 1 million
100,000 to 500,000
50,000 to 100,000
10,000 to 50,000
below 10,000
GERMANY
THÜRINGEN
HESSEN
BAYERN
BADEN-WÜRTTEMBERG
RHEINLAND-PFALZ
SAARLAND
LUXEMBOURG
BELGIUM
FRANCE
LORRAINE
ALSACE
Bas-Rhin
Frankfurt am Main
Köln (Cologne)
Düsseldorf
Dortmund
Essen
Kassel
Erfurt
Würzburg
Nürnberg (Nürnberg)
Mannheim
Heidelberg
Karlsruhe
Saarbrücken
Luxembourg
Wiesbaden
Mainz
Darmstadt
Koblenz
Bonn
Aachen
Maastricht
Metz
163
176
179
EUROPE
181
19,686ft
13,124ft
9843ft
6562ft
3281ft
1640ft
820ft
328ft
Sea Level
-820ft
-6562ft
-13,124ft

Countries

LATVIA

LITHUANIA

RUSSIAN FEDERATION

BELARUS

POLAND

GERMANY

DENMARK

SWEDEN

Seas and Water Bodies

BALTIC SEA

Gulf of Danzig

Kattegat

Pomeranian Bay

Mecklenburger Bucht

Courland Lagoon

Major Cities

KØBENHAVN (COPENHAGEN)

WARSZAWA (WARSAW)

Kaliningrad

Gdańsk

Gdynia

Szczecin

Poznań

Wrocław

Łódź

Lublin

Białystok

Brest

Kaunas

Klaipėda

Šiauliai

Panevėžys

Liepāja

Malmö

Kalmar

Schwerin

Elevation Scale

6000m
4000m
3000m
2000m
1000m
500m
250m
100m
Sea Level
−250m
−2000m
−4000m

Regions (Poland voivodeships)

POMORSKIE

ZACHODNIO-POMORSKIE

KUJAWSKO-POMORSKIE

WARMIŃSKO-MAZURSKIE

PODLASKIE

MAZOWIECKIE

WIELKOPOLSKIE

LUBUSKIE

DOLNOŚLĄSKIE

OPOLSKIE

ŁÓDZKIE

LUBELSKIE

ŚWIĘTOKRZYSKIE

Other Labels

ŻEMAITIJA

AUKŠTUMAS

SUWAŁKI

BORNHOLM

ÖLAND

SKÅNE

BLEKINGE

KRONOBERG

VORPOMMERN

MECKLENBURG

BRANDENBURG

KALININGRADSKAYA OBLAST

191
155
178

Scale 1:2,750,000
(projection: Lambert Conformal Conic)

0 10 20 30 40 50 60 70 80 Km

0 10 20 30 40 50 60 70 80 Miles

Population

- ■ above 5 million
- ▣ 1 million to 5 million
- ◉ 500,000 to 1 million
- ◎ 100,000 to 500,000
- ⊕ 50,000 to 100,000
- ○ 10,000 to 50,000
- ∘ below 10,000

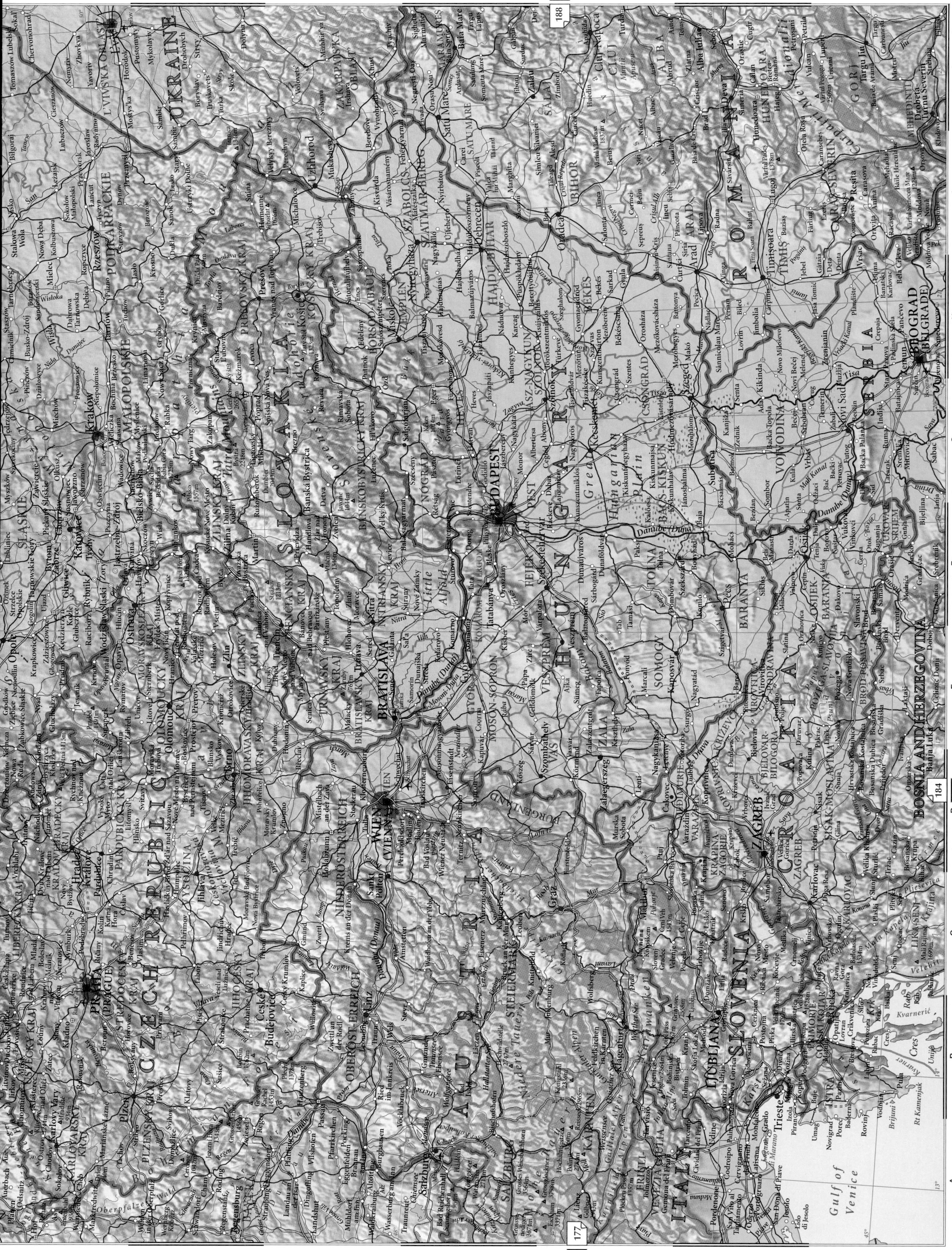

19,686ft
13,124ft
9843ft
6562ft
3281ft
1640ft
820ft
328ft
Sea Level
-820ft
-6562ft
-13,124ft

UKRAINE

CZECH REPUBLIC

PRAHA (PRAGUE)

SLOVAKIA

BRATISLAVA

WIEN (VIENNA)

AUSTRIA

HUNGARY

BUDAPEST

ROMANIA

SLOVENIA

LJUBLJANA

CROATIA

ZAGREB

BOSNIA AND HERZEGOVINA

SERBIA

BEOGRAD (BELGRADE)

ITALY

Gulf of Venice

Southeast Europe

EUROPE

184

Countries and regions

SLOVENIA · LJUBLJANA
CROATIA · ZAGREB
BOSNIA & HERZEGOVINA · SARAJEVO
FEDERACIJA BOSNA I HERCEGOVINA
REPUBLIKA SRPSKA
SERBIA
MONTENEGRO · PODGORICA
KOSOVO (full independence not yet recognized) · PRISHTINË (PRISTINA)
ALBANIA · TIRANE (TIRANA) · Durrës
MAC(EDONIA) · SKOPJE
HUNGARY · Great Hungarian Plain · VOJVODINA
ITALY · CALABRIA · PUGLIA · BASILICATA · CAMPANIA · MOLISE · ABRUZZO
Napoli (Naples) · Bari · Taranto · Pescara
ZELGRAD (BELGRADE) · Novi Sad · Zemun

Seas

Adriatic Sea
Tyrrhenian Sea
Strait of Otranto
Golfo di Taranto
Golfo di Napoli
Golfo di Manfredonia

Selected cities and towns

Trieste · Rijeka · Zadar · Split · Dubrovnik · Mostar · Zenica · Tuzla · Banja Luka
Karlovac · Sisak · Osijek · Subotica · Sombor · Pécs · Kaposvár · Szeged · Arad
Timisoara · Zrenjanin · Pancevo · Smederevo · Kragujevac · Kraljevo · Novi Pazar
Nikšić · Cetinje · Kotor · Budva · Bar · Ulcin · Shkodër · Lezhë · Elbasan · Berat · Vlorë · Fier · Korçë
Skopje · Tetovo · Gostivar · Prizren · Peć · Mitrovica
Foggia · Manfredonia · Barletta · Andria · Brindisi · Lecce · Potenza · Matera · Cosenza
Campobasso · Isernia · Benevento · Salerno · Avellino

Kérkyra (Corfu)
DYTIKI MAKEDONIA
IPEIROS
Lake Scutari · Lake Ohrid · Lake Prespa

6000m
4000m
3000m
2000m
1000m
500m
250m
100m
Sea Level
-250m
-2000m
-4000m

Scale 1:2,500,000
(projection: Lambert Conformal Conic)

0 10 20 30 40 50 Km
0 10 20 30 40 50 Miles

Population
■ above 5 million
■ 1 million to 5 million
◉ 500,000 to 1 million
◎ 100,000 to 500,000
⊕ 50,000 to 100,000
○ 10,000 to 50,000
○ below 10,000

EUROPE

19,686ft
13,124ft
9843ft
6562ft
3281ft
1640ft
820ft
328ft
Sea Level
-820ft
-6562ft
-13,124ft

Romania, Moldova & Ukraine

A
B
C
D
E
F
G
1
2
3
4
5
6
7
8
9
10
WARSZAWA (WARSAW)
POLAND
BELARUS
SLOVAKIA
HUNGARY
MOLDOVA
ROMANIA
SERBIA
BULGARIA
BEOGRAD (BELGRADE)
BUCUREȘTI (BUCHAREST)
CHIȘINĂU
Łódź
Kraków
Lublin
Kielce
Rzeszów
Brest
Pinsk
Lviv
Rivne
Luts'k
Ternopil'
Zhytomyr
Vinnytsya
Khmel'nyts'kyy
Ivano-Frankivs'k
Chernivtsi
Uzhhorod
Košice
Prešov
Miskolc
Debrecen
Nyíregyháza
Szeged
Oradea
Arad
Timișoara
Cluj-Napoca
Satu Mare
Baia Mare
Suceava
Botoșani
Iași
Bacău
Brașov
Sibiu
Craiova
Pitești
Ploiești
Galați
Brăila
Constanța
Tulcea
Ruse
Dobrich
Tiraspol
Bălți
LVIVS'KA OBLAST'
VOLYNS'KA OBLAST'
RIVNENS'KA OBLAST'
ZHYTOMYRS'KA OBLAST'
KHMEL'NYTS'KA OBLAST'
VINNYTS'KA OBLAST'
TERNOPIL'S'KA OBLAST'
IVANO-FRANKIVS'KA OBLAST'
CHERNIVETS'KA OBLAST'
ZAKARPATS'KA OBLAST'
BRESTSKAYA VOBLASTS'
HOMYEL'SKAYA VOBLASTS'
LUBELSKIE
MAZOWIECKIE
ŁÓDZKIE
ŚWIĘTOKRZYSKIE
MAŁOPOLSKIE
PODKARPACKIE
TRANSNISTRIA
Pripet Marshes
Podil's'ka Vysochyna
Carpații Meridionali
6000m
4000m
3000m
2000m
1000m
500m
250m
100m
Sea Level
-250m
-2000m
-4000m

191
183
185

Scale 1:2,500,000
(projection: Lambert Conformal Conic)

0 10 20 30 40 50 Km
0 10 20 30 40 50 Miles

Population
■ above 5 million
□ 1 million to 5 million
◉ 500,000 to 1 million
⊚ 100,000 to 500,000
⊕ 50,000 to 100,000
○ 10,000 to 50,000
○ below 10,000

188

214

187

19,686ft
13,124ft
9843ft
6562ft
3281ft
1640ft
820ft
328ft
Sea Level
-820ft
-6562ft
-13,124ft

MOLDOVA
UKRAINE
ROMANIA
BULGARIA
TURKEY
GREECE
MACEDONIA

Black Sea
Marmara Denizi (Sea of Marmara)
Thracian Sea
Aegean Sea

BUCUREȘTI (BUCHAREST)
SOFIA
ISTANBUL
Thessaloníki
Constanța
Varna
Burgas
Plovdiv
Bursa

Carpathian Mountains
Danube (Dunărea)
Balkan Mountains
Rhodope Mountains
Delta Dunării

Greece

Athens

Acharnés
Kifisiá
Nea Liosia
Nea Ionia
Halandri
Patissia
Olympiako Stadio
Peristeri
Athína (Athens)
Arheol. Moussio
Likavitas
Zografos
Egaleo
Parthenon
Távros
Agora
Akropoli
Panathinaiko Stadio
Viron
Imitos
Kalithea
Nea Smirni
Ilioupoli
Paleo Faliro
Falirou
Kalamaki
Peiraías (Piraeus)
Nikea
Nea Alexandria
Argiroupoli
Voula
Varkiza
Aspropyrgos
Oros Egaleo
Oros Imitos
Pikermi
Spáta
Peania
Eleftherios Venizelos Intl. Airport
Saronikós Kólpos

0 4 Km
0 4 Miles

Adriatic Sea
Ionian Sea
Mediterranean Sea
Strait of Otranto
Golfo di Taranto
Golfo di Manfredonia

ITALY
PUGLIA
BASILICATA
CALABRIA
Foggia
Bari
Taranto
Brindisi
Lecce
Manfredonia
Barletta
Potenza
Catanzaro
Cosenza
Reggio di Calabria
Crotone

ALBANIA
TIRANË (TIRANA)
Durrës
Shkodër
Vlorë
Berat
Fier
Korçë
Gjirokastër
KOSOVO
SKOPJE
MACEDONIA
Bitola
Ohrid
Lake Ohrid
Lake Prespa

Kérkyra (Corfu)
Lefkáda
Kefalloniá
Zákynthos
IÓNIOI NÍSOI
Ítháki
Ioánnina
Lárisa
Vólos
Pátra
Tripoli
PELOPÓNNISOS
STEREÁ ELLÁS
THESSALÍ
ÍPEIROS
DYTIKÍ MAKEDONÍA
KENTRIKÍ MAKEDONÍA
Kalamáta
Olympia
Kórinthos
Árgos
Kyparissiakós Kólpos
Messiniakós Kólpos
Lakoníkós Kólpos
Kythira

Scale 1:2,500,000
(projection: Lambert Conformal Conic)
0 10 20 30 40 50 Km
0 10 20 30 40 50 Miles
Population
above 5 million
1 million to 5 million
500,000 to 1 million
100,000 to 500,000
50,000 to 100,000
10,000 to 50,000
below 10,000
H
I
J
K
L
M
N
185
214
129
EUROPE
187
19,686ft
13,124ft
9843ft
6562ft
3281ft
1640ft
820ft
328ft
Sea Level
-820ft
-6562ft
-13,124ft
Black Sea
BULGARIA
TURKEY
Rhodope Mountains
Thracian Sea
Aegean Sea
Marmara Denizi
(Sea of Marmara)
Mediterranean Sea
Kritikó Pélagos
(Sea of Crete)
Mirtóo Pélagos
Aegean Islands
Kykládes
(Cyclades)
Dodekánisa
Karpáthio Pélagos
Anatolia
İstanbul
İzmir
Bursa
Edirne
Plovdiv
Khaskovo
Tekirdağ
Çanakkale
Balıkesir
Manisa
Aydın
Denizli
Muğla
Kütahya
Eskişehir
Uşak
Burdur
Adapazarı
İzmit
ATHINA
(ATHENS)
Peiraias
(Piraeus)
Irákleio
Alexandroúpoli
Komotiní
Xánthi
Kavála
Thásos
Samothráki
Límnos
Lésvos
(Lesbos)
Chíos
Sámos
Ikaría
Kos
Ródos (Rhodes)
Kárpathos
Kríti (Crete)
Évvoia
(Euboea)
Ándros
Tínos
Sýros
Mýkonos
Náxos
Páros
Amorgós
Santoríni
Mílos
Kýthira
Skýros
Vóreies Sporádes
VÓREION AIGAÍON
NÓTION AIGAÍON
KRÍTI
ATTIKÍ
Gökçeada
Bozcaada
Çanakkale Boğazı
(Dardanelles)
İstanbul Boğazı
(Bosporus)
Saros Körfezi
Edremit Körfezi
Kuşadası Körfezi
Stenó Kasou
Stenó Karpathou

Romania, Moldova & Ukraine

A
B
C
D
E
F
G
1
2
3
4
5
6
7
8
9
10
191
183
185
POLAND
WARSZAWA (WARSAW)
BELARUS
Brest
BRESTSKAYA VOBLASTS'
HOMYEL'SKAYA VOBLASTS'
Pripet Marshes
Łódź
Kraków
Lublin
Rzeszów
Kielce
ŁÓDZKIE
MAZOWIECKIE
LUBELSKIE
ŚWIĘTOKRZYSKIE
MAŁOPOLSKIE
PODKARPACKIE
SLOVAKIA
Prešov
Košice
Miskolc
HUNGARY
Debrecen
Nyíregyháza
Szeged
L'VIVS'KA OBLAST'
L'viv
Ternopil'
Luts'k
Rivne
Zhytomyr
Vinnytsya
Khmel'nyts'kyy
Ivano-Frankivs'k
Uzhhorod
Chernivtsi
VOLYNS'KA OBLAST'
RIVNENS'KA OBLAST'
ZHYTOMYRS'KA OBLAST'
TERNOPIL'S'KA OBLAST'
KHMEL'NYTS'KA OBLAST'
VINNYTS'KA OBLAST'
IVANO-FRANKIVS'KA OBLAST'
ZAKARPATS'KA OBLAST'
CHERNIVETS'KA OBLAST'
Podil's'ka Vysochyna
Carpathian Mountains
MOLDOVA
CHIŞINĂU
Bălţi
Tiraspol
TRANSNISTRIA
ROMANIA
BUCUREŞTI (BUCHAREST)
Cluj-Napoca
Oradea
Satu Mare
Baia Mare
Suceava
Botoşani
Iaşi
Bacău
Galaţi
Brăila
Constanţa
Tulcea
Ploieşti
Braşov
Sibiu
Timişoara
Arad
Craiova
Piteşti
Târgu Mureş
Drobeta-Turnu Severin
Transylvanian Alps
SERBIA
BEOGRAD (BELGRADE)
BULGARIA
Ruse
Dobrich
Danube
Dnister
Prut
Siret

Scale 1:3,000,000
(projection: Lambert Conformal Conic)

0 20 40 60 80 100 Km
0 20 40 60 80 100 Miles

Population

■ above 5 million   ■ 1 million to 5 mill on   ◉ 500,000 to 1 million

◎ 100,000 to 500,000   ⊕ 50,000 to 100,000   ○ 10,000 to 50,000   ○ below 10,000

196

214

196

19,686ft
13,124ft
9843ft
6562ft
3281ft
1640ft
820ft
328ft
Sea
Level
-820ft
-6562ft
-13,124ft

RUSSIAN FEDERATION

U K R A I N E

ORLOVSKAYA OBLAST'

LIPETSKAYA OBLAST'

KURSKAYA OBLAST'

BELGORODSKAYA OBLAST'

VORONEZHSKAYA OBLAST'

CHERNIHIVS'KA OBLAST'

SUMS'KA OBLAST'

KHARKIVS'KA OBLAST'

LUHANS'KA OBLAST'

POLTAVS'KA OBLAST'

CHERKAS'KA OBLAST'

DNIPROPETROVS'KA OBLAST'

DONETS'KA OBLAST'

KIROVOHRADS'KA OBLAST'

MYKOLAYIVS'KA OBLAST'

ZAPORIZ'KA OBLAST'

ODES'KA OBLAST'

KHERSONS'KA OBLAST'

KRASNODARSKIY KRAY

Black Sea

Sea of Azov

Gulf of Taganrog

Black Sea Lowland

KRYMS'KYY PIVOSTRIV

RESPUBLIKA KRYM

Voronezh

Kursk

Belgorod

Sumy

Kharkiv

Luhans'k

Donets'k

Rostov-na-Donu

KYYIV (KIEV)

Poltava

Dnipropetrovs'k

Zaporizhzhya

Mariupol'

Mykolayiv

Kherson

Odesa

Simferopol'

Sevastopol'

Krasnodar

The Baltic States & Belarus

6000m
4000m
3000m
2000m
1000m
500m
250m
100m
Sea Level
-250m
-2000m
-4000m
FINLAND
ESTONIA
LATVIA
RUSSIAN FEDERATION
HELSINKI
TALLINN
RĪGA
Sankt-Peterburg (Saint Petersburg)
Ladozhskoye Ozero
Lake Peipus
Gulf of Finland
Gulf of Riga
Gulf of Bothnia
Baltic Sea
Ålands Hav
Irbe Strait
Narva Bay
Hiiumaa
Saaremaa
Gotland
Åland
Tartu
Pärnu
Narva
Pskov
Velikiy Novgorod
Liepāja
Ventspils
Klaipėda
Šiauliai
Jelgava
Daugavpils
Turku (Åbo)
Espoo
Vantaa
Kotka
Vyborg
Kronshtadt
Ostrov Gogland
Ozero Il'men'
153
194

Scale 1:2,750,000
(projection: Lambert Conformal Conic)

0 10 20 30 40 50 60 70 80 Km
0 10 20 30 40 50 60 70 80 Miles

Population

■ above 5 million
■ 1 million to 5 million
◉ 500,000 to 1 million
⊕ 100,000 to 500,000
⊕ 50,000 to 100,000
○ 10,000 to 50,000
○ below 10,000

19,686ft
13,124ft
9843ft
6562ft
3281ft
1640ft
820ft
328ft
Sea Level
-820ft
-6562ft
-13,124ft

The Russian Federation

THE RUSSIAN FEDERATION:
ADMINISTRATIVE REGIONS

The administrative area names in European Russia
have been omitted west of the Ural Mountains.
Please refer to pages 194-195 and 196-197 where
these areas are shown at a larger scale.

Scale 1:17,500,000
(projection: Lambert Conformal Conic)

| 0 | 100 | 200 | 300 | 400 | 500 Km |
| 0 | 100 | 200 | 300 | 400 | 500 Miles |

Population

◼ above 5 million   ▣ 1 million to 5 million   ⊙ 500,000 to 1 million

◎ 100,000 to 500,000   ⊡ 50,000 to 100,000   ○ 10,000 to 50,000   ∘ below 10,000

19,686ft
13,124ft
9843ft
6562ft
3281ft
1640ft
820ft
328ft
Sea Level
-820ft
-6562ft
-13,124ft

O C E A N

Ostrov Shmidta
Ostrov Komsomolets
Severnaya Zemlya

Poluostrov Taymyr

More Laptevykh

Novosibirskiye Ostrova

Vostochno-Sibirskoye More

Chukchi Sea

ALASKA
UNITED STATES OF AMERICA

Bering Strait

Bering Sea

Srednesibirskoye Ploskogor'ye

S I B I R

RESPUBLIKA SAKHA (YAKUTIYA)

Verkhoyanskiy Khrebet

Khrebet Cherskogo

MAGADANSKAYA OBLAST

Okhotskoye More (Sea of Okhotsk)

Magadan

Petropavlovsk-Kamchatskiy

KAMCHATSKAYA OBLAST

Yakutsk

F E D E R A T I O N

EVENKIYSKY AVTONOMNYY OKRUG

IRKUTSKAYA OBLAST

KHABAROVSKIY KRAY

SAKHALINSKAYA OBLAST'

Ostrov Sakhalin

Kuril'skiye Ostrova

Bratsk

Irkutsk Ulan-Ude

RESPUBLIKA BURYATIYA

CHITINSKAYA OBLAST'

AMURSKAYA OBLAST'

Blagoveshchensk

Komsomol'sk-na-Amure

Khabarovsk

Yuzhno-Sakhalinsk

Chita

ULAANBAATAR (ULAN BATOR)

M O N G O L I A

Vladivostok

JAPAN

Sapporo
Hakodate

Sendai

PACIFIC OCEAN

C H I N A

BEIJING

Shenyang

Changchun

Harbin

NORTH KOREA

PYONGYANG

SOUTH KOREA

SEOUL (SEOUL)

Sea of Japan (East Sea)

TOKYO
Yokohama

Nagoya

Bo Hai

Norwegian Sea

N O R W A Y

S W E D E N

FINLAND

LAPPLAND

NORRBOTTEN

VÄSTERBOTTEN

VÄSTERNORRLAND

GÄVLEBORG

UPPSALA

STOCKHOLM

LÄNSI-SUOMI

ITÄ-SUOMI

OULU

ETELÄ-SUOMI

HELSINKI

Gulf of Finland

TALLINN

ESTONIA

LATVIA

RIGA

LITHUANIA

KALININGRAD

Baltic Sea

Gulf of Riga

B a r e n

Murmansk

MURMANSKAYA OBLAST'

Kol'skiy Poluostrov

Beloye More (White Sea)

RESPUBLIKA KARELIYA

R U S S I A N

Petrozavodsk

Onezhskoye Ozero

ARKHANGEL'SKAYA

Arkhangel'sk (Archangel)

Severodvinsk

Ladozhskoye Ozero

Sankt-Peterburg (Saint Petersburg)

LENINGRADSKAYA OBLAST'

VOLOGODSKAYA OBLAST'

Cherepovets

Vologda

Lake Peipus

Velikiy Novgorod

NOVGORODSKAYA OBLAST'

Pskov

PSKOVSKAYA OBLAST'

TVERSKAYA OBLAST'

Tver'

YAROSLAVSKAYA OBLAST'

Yaroslavl'

Rybinsk

Kostroma

IVANOVSKAYA OBLAST'

VLADIMIRSKAYA OBLAST'

Vladimir

BELARUS

6000m
4000m
3000m
2000m
1000m
500m
250m
100m
Sea Level
-250m
-2000m
-4000m

295

153

191

Scale 1:5,750,000
(projection: Lambert Conformal Conic)
0 25 50 75 100 125 150 175 200 Km
0 25 50 75 100 125 150 175 200 Miles
Population
above 5 million
1 million to 5 million
500,000 to 1 million
100,000 to 500,000
50,000 to 100,000
10,000 to 50,000
below 10,000
EUROPE
195
Novaya Zemlya
Ostrov Mezhdusharskiy
Proliv Karskiye Vorota
Ostrov Vaygach
Pechorskoye More
Ostrov Kolguyev
Ostrov Dolgiy
Pechorskaya Guba
Baydaratskaya Guba
Poluostrov Yamal
Yugorskiy Poluostrov
Khrebet Pay-Khoy
Obskaya Guba
Tazovskaya Guba
Pomorskiy Proliv
Kanin Nos
Kanin Kamen'
Poluostrov Kanin
Cheshskaya Guba
Mezenskaya Guba
Limit of winter pack ice
Arctic Circle
NENETSKIY AVTONOMNYY OKRUG
YAMALO-NENETSKIY AVTONOMNYY OKRUG
KHANTY-MANSIYSKIY AVTONOMNYY OKRUG
Bol'shezemel'skaya Tundra
Malozemel'skaya Tundra
Timanskiy Kryazh
Gryada Chernysheva
Polyarnyy Ural
Ural'skiye Gory
Severnyy Ural
Sredniy Ural
Zapadno-Sibirskaya Ravnina
Sibirskiye Uvaly
Severnyye Uvaly
RESPUBLIKA KOMI
RUSSIAN FEDERATION
Nar'yan-Mar
Vorkuta
Inta
Pechora
Ukhta
Salekhard
Labytnangi
Khanty-Mansiysk
Syktyvkar
Kotlas
Kirov
Perm'
Izhevsk
Yekaterinburg
Chelyabinsk
Tyumen'
Kurgan
Nizhniy Novgorod
Cheboksary
Yoshkar-Ola
Nizhniy Tagil
PERMSKAYA OBLAST'
SVERDLOVSKAYA OBLAST'
TYUMENSKAYA OBLAST'
KURGANSKAYA OBLAST'
CHELYABINSKAYA OBLAST'
KIROVSKAYA OBLAST'
KOSTROMSKAYA OBLAST'
NIZHEGORODSKAYA OBLAST'
UDMURTSKAYA RESPUBLIKA
RESPUBLIKA MARIY EL
RESPUBLIKA TATARSTAN
RESPUBLIKA BASHKORTOSTAN
Pechora
Ob'
19,686ft
13,124ft
9843ft
6562ft
3281ft
1640ft
820ft
328ft
Sea Level
-820ft
-6562ft
-13,124ft

Scale 1:5,750,000
(projection: Lambert Conformal Conic)

0 25 50 75 100 125 150 175 200 Km

0 25 50 75 100 125 150 175 200 Miles

Population

◼ above 5 million   ◼ 1 million to 5 million   ⬤ 500,000 to 1 million

◎ 100,000 to 500,000   ⊙ 50,000 to 100,000   ◯ 10,000 to 50,000   ∘ below 10,000

195

222

226

19,686ft

13,124ft

9843ft

6562ft

3281ft

1640ft

820ft

328ft

Sea
Level

-820ft

-6562ft

-13,124ft

The Mediterranean

ATLANTIC OCEAN
Bay of Biscay
English Channel
Mediterranean Sea
Tyrrhenian Sea
Ligurian Sea
Golfe du Lion
Golfo de Valencia
Malta Channel
Strait of Sicily
UNITED KINGDOM
LONDON
NETHERLANDS
BELGIUM
BRUXELLES (BRUSSEL)
GERMANY
LUXEMBOURG
PARIS
FRANCE
SWITZ.
BERN
LIECHTENSTEIN
AUSTRIA
CZECH
SLOVENIA
LJUBLJANA
ITALY
ROMA (ROME)
VATICAN CITY
SAN MARINO
MONACO
ANDORRA
SPAIN
MADRID
PORTUGAL
LISBOA (LISBON)
GIBRALTAR (to UK)
MOROCCO
RABAT
ALGERIA
ALGER (ALGIERS)
TUNISIA
TUNIS
MALTA
VALLETTA
TARĀBULUS (TRIPOLI)
Islas Baleares (Balearic Islands)
Mallorca (Majorca)
Menorca (Minorca)
Ibiza
Formentera
Corse (Corsica)
Sardegna (Sardinia)
Sicilia (Sicily)
CHANNEL ISLANDS (to UK)
Barcelona
Valencia
Alicante
Málaga
Sevilla (Seville)
Córdoba
Granada
Zaragoza
Bilbao
Porto (Oporto)
Marseille
Lyon
Toulouse
Bordeaux
Nantes
Milano (Milan)
Torino (Turin)
Genova (Genoa)
Napoli (Naples)
Palermo
Cagliari
Casablanca
Marrakech
Oran
Constantine
Haut Atlas
Atlas Saharien
Hauts Plateaux
Grand Erg Occidental
Grand Erg Oriental
Plateau du Tademaït
Hamada du Dra
Erg Iguidi
Erg Chech
Al Hamādah al Hamrā'
Idhān Awbārī
157
290
131
6000m
4000m
3000m
2000m
1000m
500m
250m
100m
Sea Level
-250m
-2000m
-4000m

Scale 1:8,750,000
(projection: Lambert Conformal Conic)

0 25 50 75 100 125 150 175 200 Km
0 25 50 75 100 125 150 175 200 Miles

Population

▣ above 5 million	▣ 1 million to 5 million	⦿ 500,000 to 1 million
◎ 100,000 to 500,000	⊕ 50,000 to 100,000	○ 10,000 to 50,000
○ below 10,000		

H I J K L M N

196

POLAND
WARSZAWA (WARSAW)
BELARUS
UKRAINE
KYYIV (KIEV)
RUSSIAN FEDERATION
MOLDOVA
CHIŞINĂU
SLOVAKIA
HUNGARY
BUDAPEST
ROMANIA
BUCUREŞTI (BUCHAREST)
CROATIA
ZAGREB
BOSNIA AND HERZEGOVINA
SARAJEVO
SERBIA
BEOGRAD (BELGRADE)
MONTENEGRO
PODGORICA
KOSOVO
PRISHTINË (PRISTINA)
MACEDONIA
SKOPJE
ALBANIA
TIRANË (TIRANA)
BULGARIA
SOFIYA (SOFIA)
GREECE
ATHÍNA (ATHENS)
TURKEY
ANKARA
İstanbul
GEORGIA
SYRIA
DIMASHQ (DAMASCUS)
LEBANON
BEYROUTH (BEIRUT)
CYPRUS
NICOSIA
TURKISH REPUBLIC OF NORTHERN CYPRUS (recognised only by Turkey)
ISRAEL
JERUSALEM
JORDAN
'AMMAN
IRAQ
SAUDI ARABIA
EGYPT
CAIRO
LIBYA

Black Sea
Sea of Azov
Aegean Sea
Ionian Sea
Mediterranean Sea
Red Sea
Kríti (Crete)
Ródos (Rhodes)

1 2 3 4 5 6 7 8 9 10

216

129

H I J K L M N

19,686ft
13,124ft
9843ft
6562ft
3281ft
1640ft
820ft
328ft
Sea Level
-820ft
-6562ft
-13,124ft

Barcelona

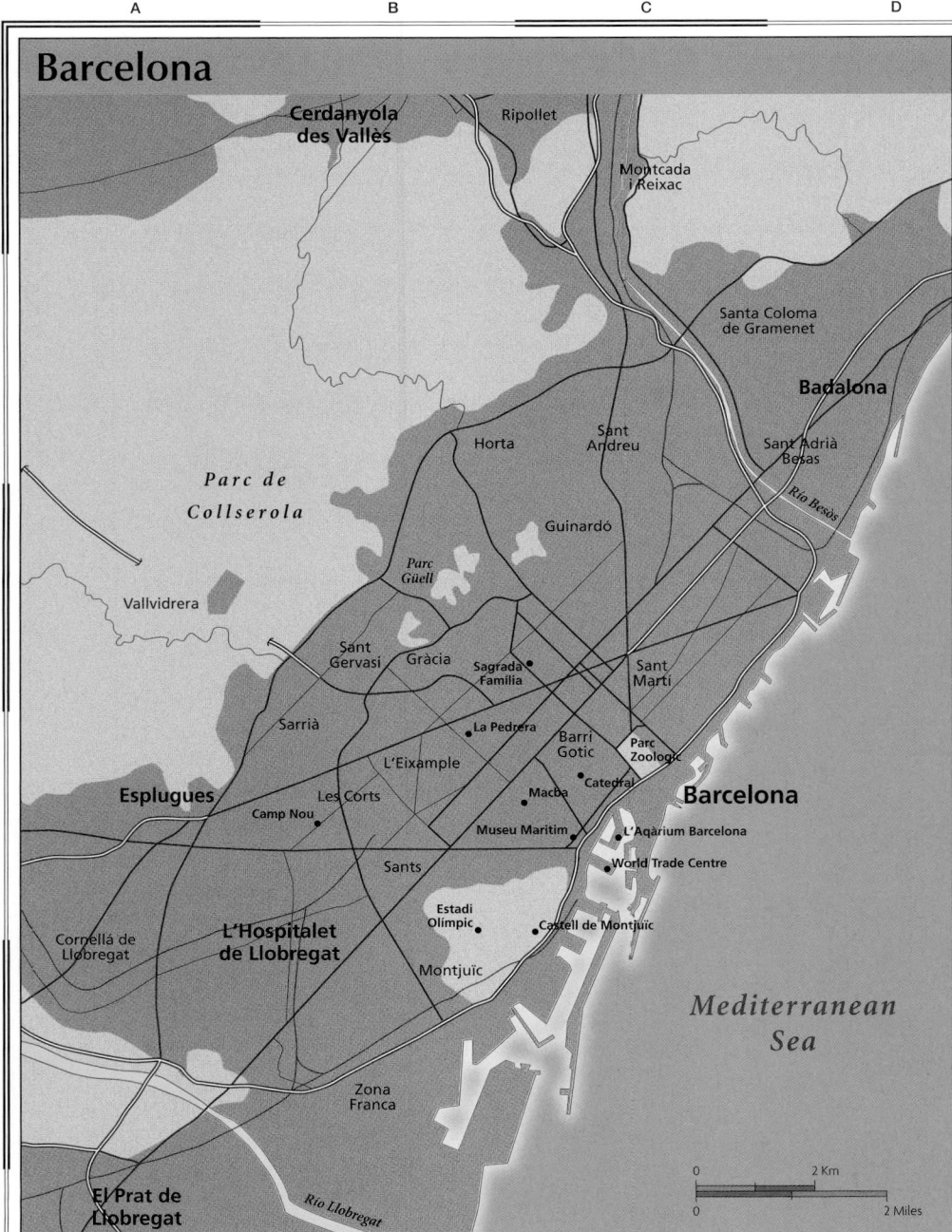

Cerdanyola
des Vallès
Ripollet
Montcada
i Reixac
Santa Coloma
de Gramenet
Badalona
Horta
Sant Andreu
Sant Adrià
Besòs
Parc de
Collserola
Guinardó
Rio Besòs
Parc
Güell
Vallvidrera
Sant Gervasi
Gràcia
Sagrada
Família
Sant
Martí
Sarrià
La Pedrera
Barri
Gòtic
Parc
Zoologic
L'Eixample
Esplugues
Les Corts
Macba
Catedral
Barcelona
Camp Nou
Museu Maritim
L'Aqàrium Barcelona
Sants
World Trade Centre
Cornellá de
Llobregat
L'Hospitalet
de Llobregat
Estadi
Olímpic
Castell de Montjuïc
Montjuïc
Mediterranean
Sea
Zona
Franca
El Prat de
Llobregat
Rio Llobregat
0   2 Km
0   2 Miles

Belgrade

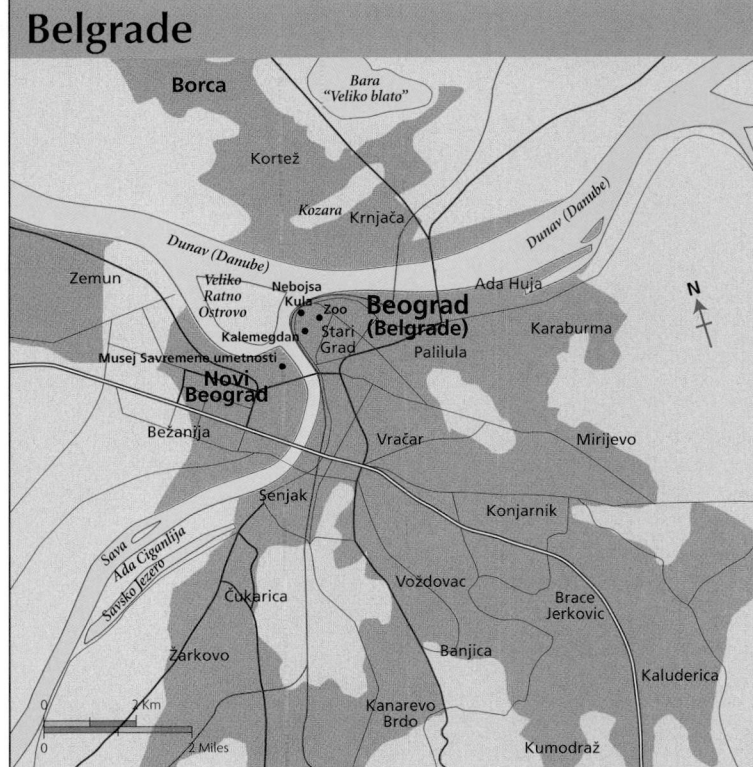

Borca
Bara
"Veliko blato"
Kortež
Kozara
Krnjača
Dunav (Danube)
Dunav (Danube)
Zemun
Veliko
Ratno
Ostrovo
Nebojsa
Kula
Zoo
Beograd
(Belgrade)
Ada Huja
Kalemegdan
Stari
Grad
Karaburma
Musej Savremene umetnosti
Novi
Beograd
Palilula
Bežanija
Vračar
Mirijevo
Šenjak
Sava
Ada Ciganlija
Savsko Jezero
Čukarica
Voždovac
Konjarnik
Žarkovo
Brace
Jerkovic
Banjica
Kaluderica
0   2 Km
Kanarevo
Brdo
0   2 Miles
Kumodraž

Bucharest

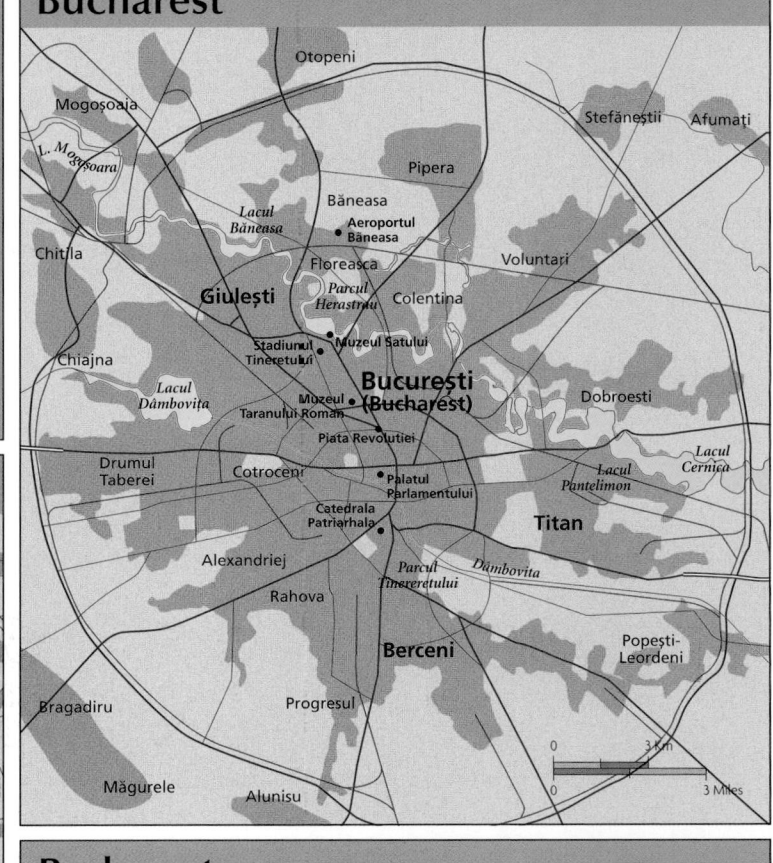

Otopeni
Mogoşoaia
Ştefăneştii
Afumaţi
L. Mogoşoara
Pipera
Băneasa
Lacul
Băneasa
Aeroportul
Băneasa
Chitila
Floreasca
Voluntari
Giuleşti
Parcul
Herastrau
Colentina
Chiajna
Stadiunul
Tineretului
Muzeul Satului
Lacul
Dâmbovita
Bucureşti
(Bucharest)
Muzeul
Taranului Roman
Dobroesti
Lacul
Cernica
Piata Revolutiei
Drumul
Taberei
Cotroceni
Palatul
Parlamentului
Lacul
Pantelimon
Alexandriej
Catedrala
Patriarhala
Parcul
Tineretului
Titan
Rahova
Parcul
Tineretului
Dâmbovita
Berceni
Popeşti-
Leordeni
Bragadiru
Progresul
Măgurele
Alunisu
0   3 Km
0   3 Miles

Berlin

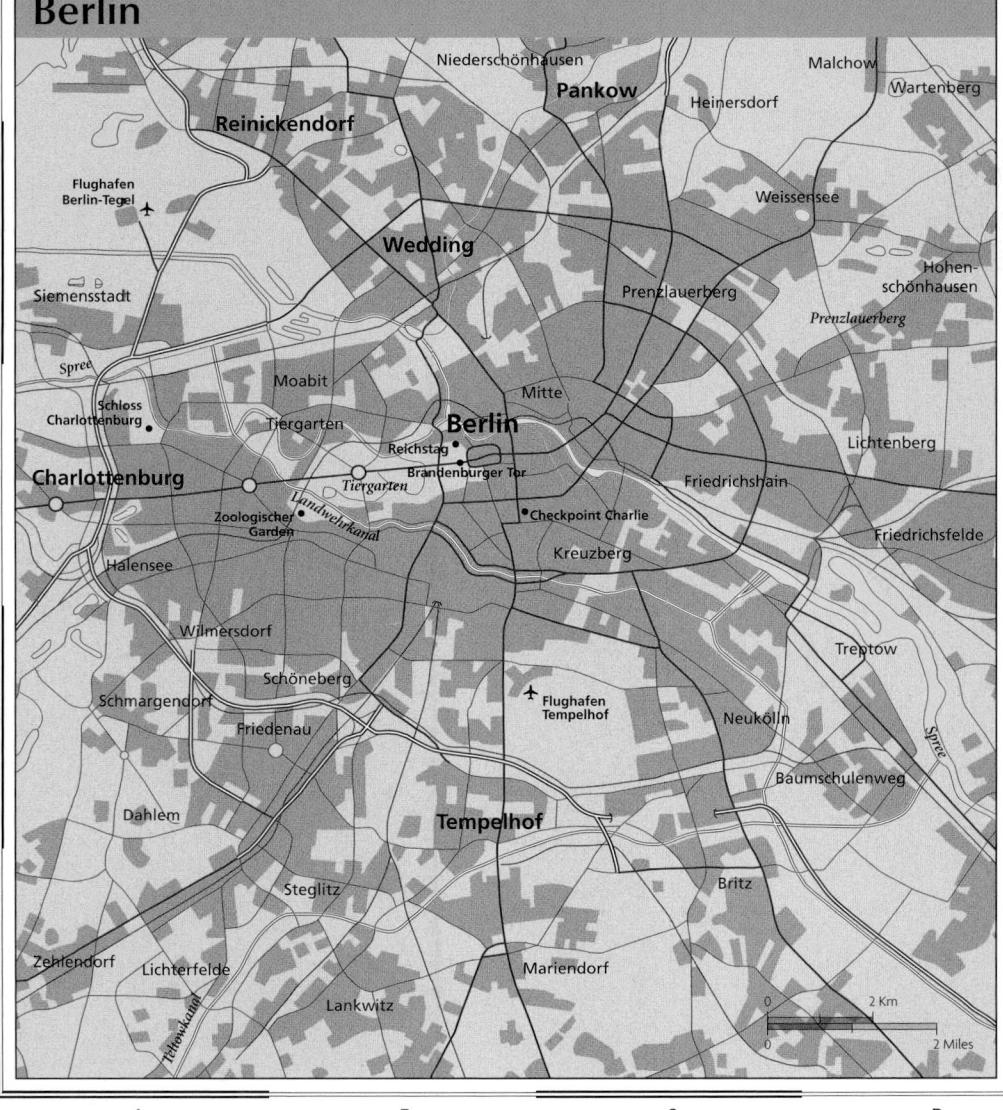

Niederschönhausen
Malchow
Reinickendorf
Pankow
Wartenberg
Heinersdorf
Flughafen
Berlin-Tegel
Weissensee
Siemensstadt
Wedding
Hohen
schönhausen
Spree
Prenzlauerberg
Prenzlauerberg
Moabit
Schloss
Charlottenburg
Mitte
Tiergarten
Berlin
Lichtenberg
Charlottenburg
Reichstag
Tiergarten
Brandenburger Tor
Friedrichshain
Friedrichsfelde
Zoologischer
Garden
Checkpoint Charlie
Halensee
Kreuzberg
Wilmersdorf
Schöneberg
Treptow
Spree
Schmargendorf
Friedenau
Flughafen
Tempelhof
Neukölln
Dahlem
Baumschulenweg
Tempelhof
Zehlendorf
Lichterfelde
Britz
Steglitz
Lankwitz
Mariendorf
0   2 Km
0   2 Miles

Budapest

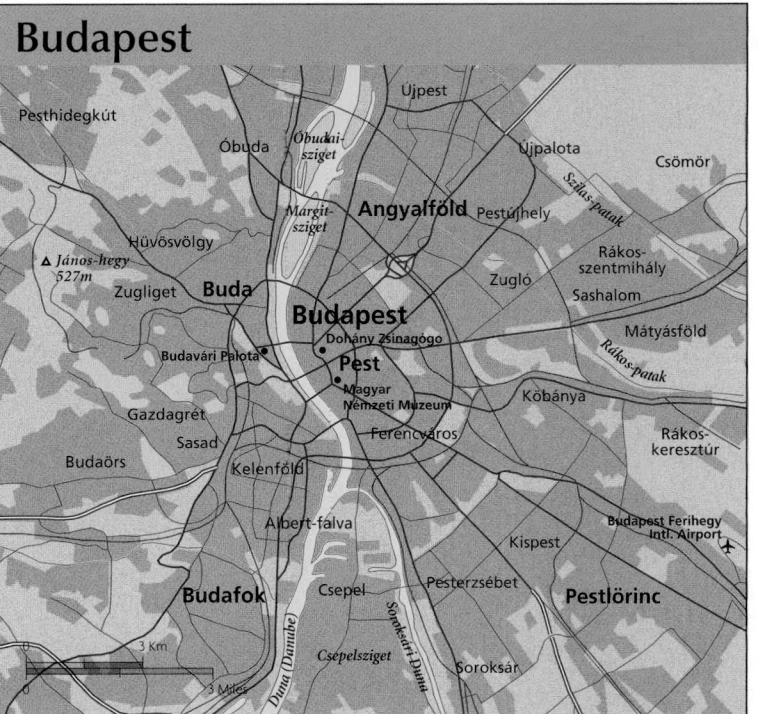

Újpest
Pesthidegkút
Óbudai-
sziget
Újpalota
Csömör
Óbuda
Pestújhely
Margit-
sziget
Angyalföld
Hüvösvölgy
Szilas-patak
Rákos-
szentmihály
János-hegy
527m
Zugliget
Buda
Zugló
Sashalom
Budapest
Mátyásföld
Budavári Palota
Dohány Zsinagóga
Pest
Rákos-patak
Magyar
Nemzeti Múzeum
Kőbánya
Gazdagrét
Rákos-
keresztúr
Sasad
Ferencváros
Budaörs
Kelenföld
Budapest Ferihegy
Intl. Airport
Albert-falva
Kispest
Budafok
Csepel
Pesterzsébet
Pestlörinc
0   3 Km
Csépel-sziget
Soroksári Duna
Dunav (Danube)
Soroksár
0   3 Miles

H I J K L M N

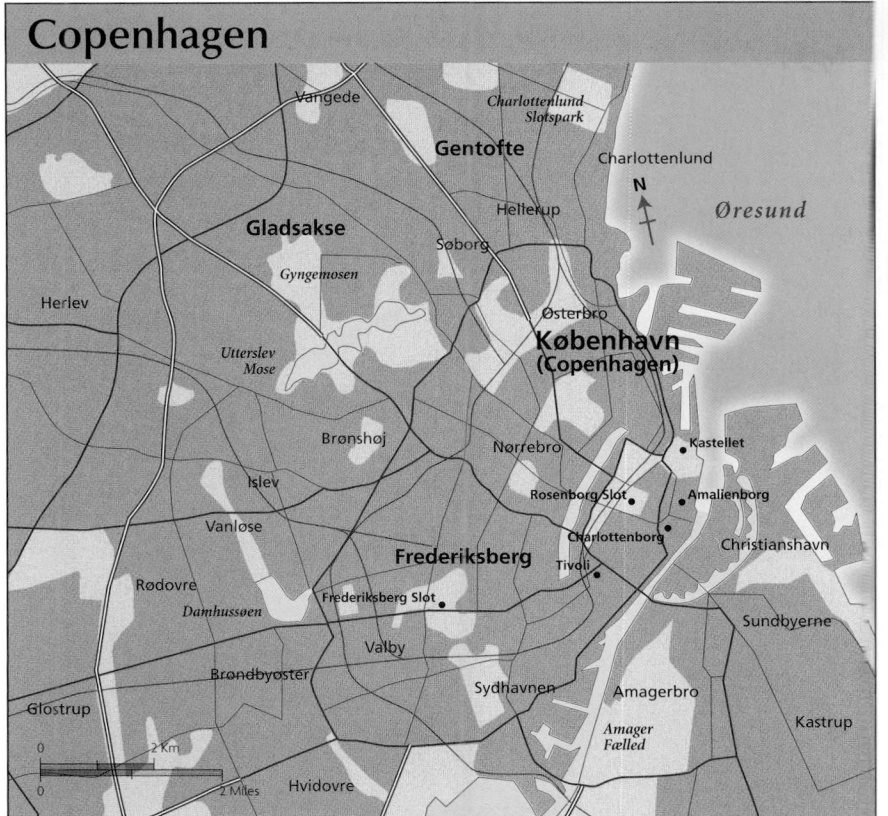
Copenhagen
Vangede
Charlottenlund Slotspark
Gentofte
Charlottenlund
N
Øresund
Hellerup
Gladsakse
Søborg
Gyngemosen
Herlev
Østerbro
København
(Copenhagen)
Utterslev Mose
Brønshøj
Nørrebro
Kastellet
Islev
Rosenborg Slot
Amalienborg
Vanløse
Charlottenborg
Christianshavn
Frederiksberg
Tivoli
Rødovre
Frederiksberg Slot
Damhussøen
Sundbyerne
Valby
Brøndbyøster
Sydhavnen
Amagerbro
Glostrup
Amager Fælled
Kastrup
0 2 Km
0 2 Miles
Hvidovre

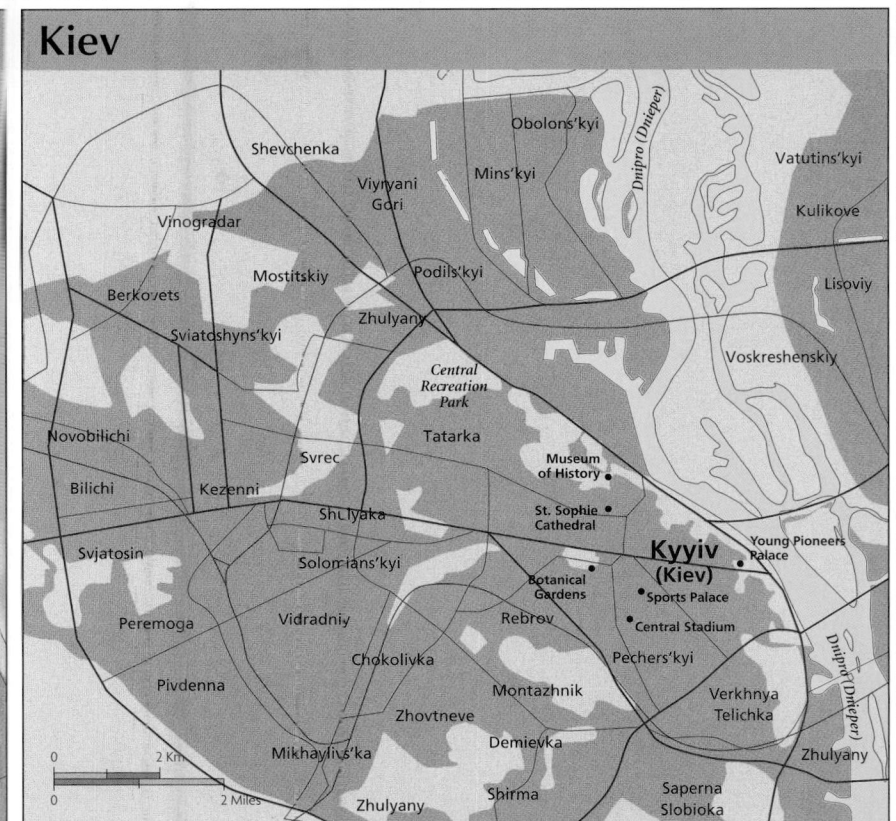
Kiev
Obolons'kyi
Dnipro (Dnieper)
Shevchenka
Mins'kyi
Vatutins'kyi
Viyryani Gori
Kulikove
Vinogradar
Podil's'kyi
Mostitskiy
Lisoviy
Berkovets
Zhulyany
Sviatoshyns'kyi
Voskreshenskiy
Central Recreation Park
Tatarka
Novobilichi
Svrec
Museum of History
Bilichi
Kezenni
Shulyaka
St. Sophie Cathedral
Kyyiv
(Kiev)
Young Pioneers Palace
Svjatosin
Solomians'kyi
Botanical Gardens
Sports Palace
Peremoga
Vidradniy
Rebrov
Central Stadium
Chokolivka
Pechers'kyi
Dnipro (Dnieper)
Pivdenna
Montazhnik
Verkhnya Telichka
Zhovtneve
Demievka
Mikhaylivs'ka
Zhulyany
0 2 Km
0 2 Miles
Zhulyany
Shirma
Saperna Slobioka

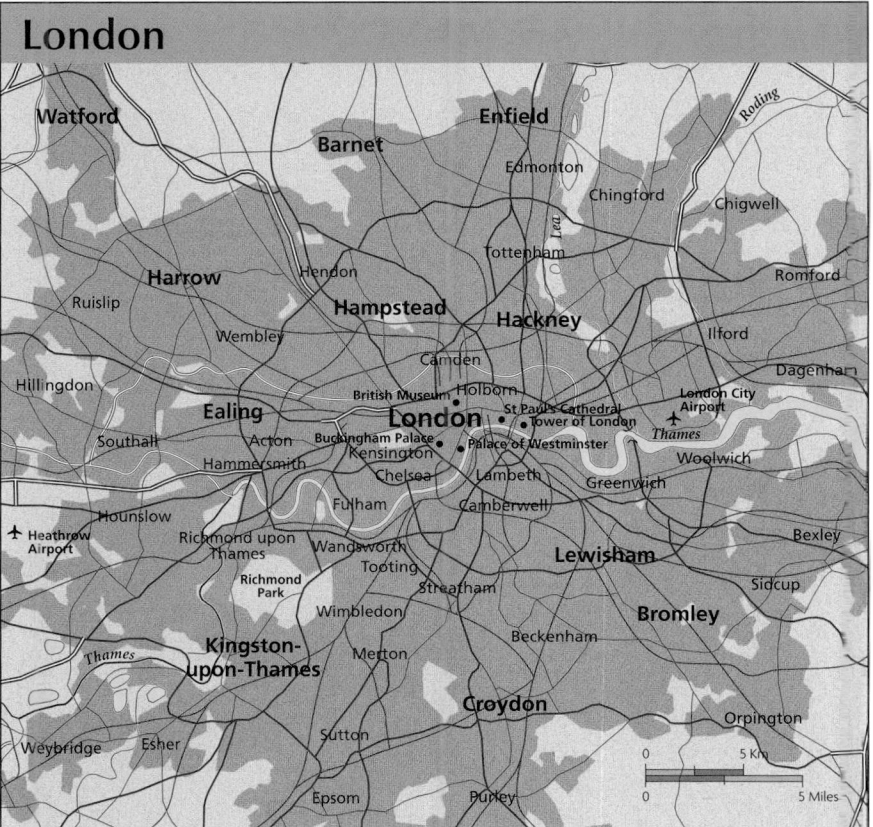
London
Watford
Enfield
Roding
Barnet
Edmonton
Chingford
Chigwell
Lea
Tottenham
Harrow
Hendon
Romford
Ruislip
Hampstead
Hackney
Wembley
Ilford
Camden
Dagenham
Hillingdon
Holborn
British Museum
London City Airport
Ealing
London
St Paul's Cathedral
Tower of London
Southall
Acton
Buckingham Palace
Thames
Kensington
Palace of Westminster
Hammersmith
Chelsea
Lambeth
Woolwich
Greenwich
Fulham
Camberwell
Hounslow
Heathrow Airport
Richmond upon Thames
Wandsworth
Bexley
Tooting
Lewisham
Richmond Park
Sidcup
Streatham
Wimbledon
Bromley
Thames
Kingston-upon-Thames
Beckenham
Merton
Croydon
Orpington
Weybridge
Esher
Sutton
0 5 Km
0 5 Miles
Epsom
Purley

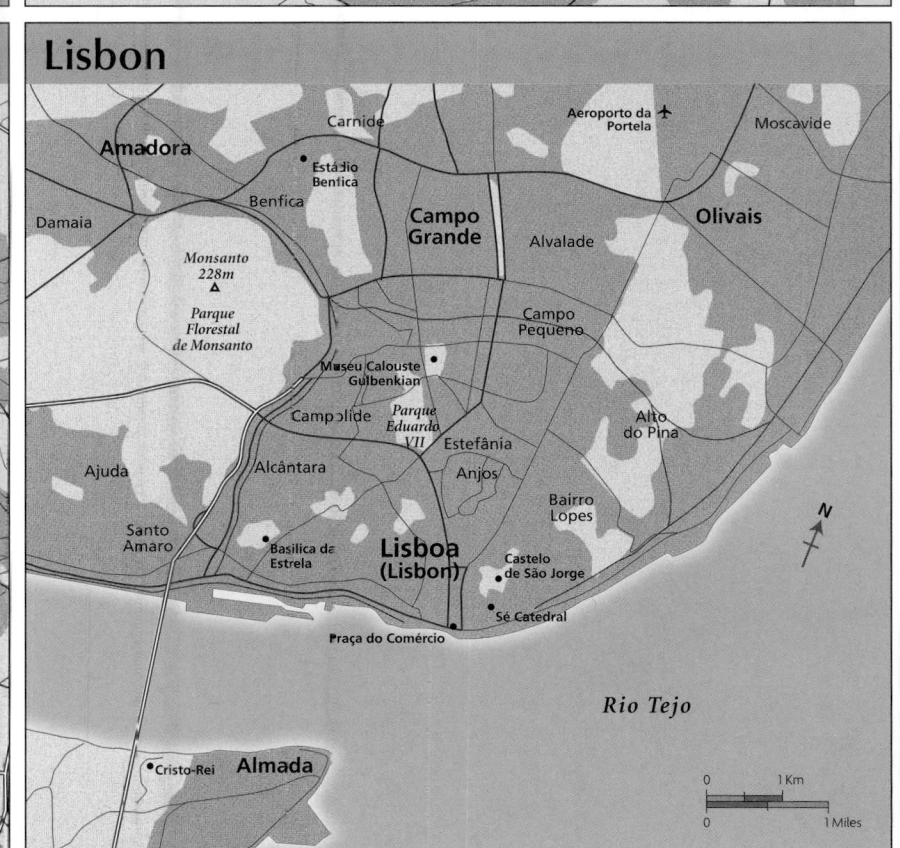
Lisbon
Carnide
Aeroporto da Portela
Moscavide
Amadora
Estádio Benfica
Benfica
Damaia
Campo Grande
Olivais
Alvalade
Monsanto 228m
Parque Florestal de Monsanto
Campo Pequeno
Museu Calouste Gulbenkian
Campolide
Parque Eduardo VII
Alto do Pina
Estefânia
Ajuda
Alcântara
Anjos
Bairro Lopes
N
Santo Amaro
Basilica da Estrela
Lisboa
(Lisbon)
Castelo de São Jorge
Sé Catedral
Praça do Comércio
Rio Tejo
Cristo-Rei
Almada
0 1 Km
0 1 Miles

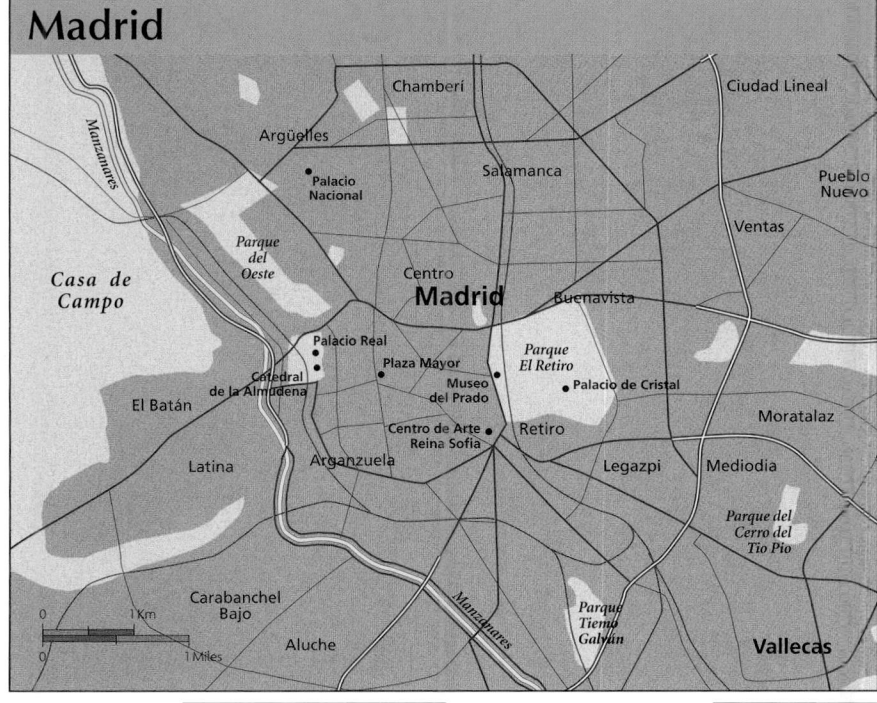
Madrid
Chamberí
Ciudad Lineal
Argüelles
Manzanares
Palacio Nacional
Salamanca
Pueblo Nuevo
Ventas
Parque del Oeste
Casa de Campo
Centro
Madrid
Buenavista
Palacio Real
Parque El Retiro
Catedral de la Almudena
Plaza Mayor
Museo del Prado
Palacio de Cristal
El Batán
Moratalaz
Centro de Arte Reina Sofia
Retiro
Latina
Arganzuela
Legazpi
Mediodia
Parque del Cerro del Tío Pío
Carabanchel Bajo
Manzanares
Parque Tierno Galván
0 1 Km
0 1 Miles
Aluche
Vallecas

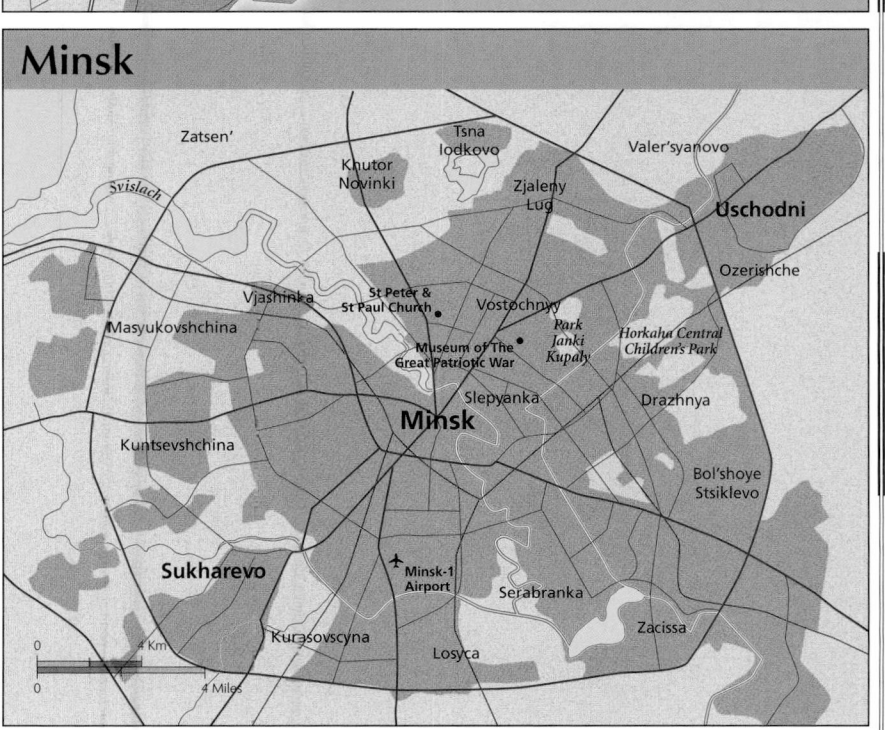
Minsk
Zatsen'
Tsna Iodkovo
Valer'syanovo
Khutor Novinki
Svislach
Zjaleny Lug
Uschodni
Ozerishche
Vjashinka
St Peter & St Paul Church
Vostochny
Masyukovshchina
Museum of The Great Patriotic War
Park Janki Kupaly
Horkaha Central Children's Park
Slepyanka
Drazhnya
Minsk
Kuntsevshchina
Bol'shoye Stsiklevo
Sukharevo
Minsk-1 Airport
Serabranka
Zacissa
Kurasovscyna
Losyca
0 4 Km
0 4 Miles

1 2 3 4 5 6 7 8 9 10

H I J K L M N

Moscow

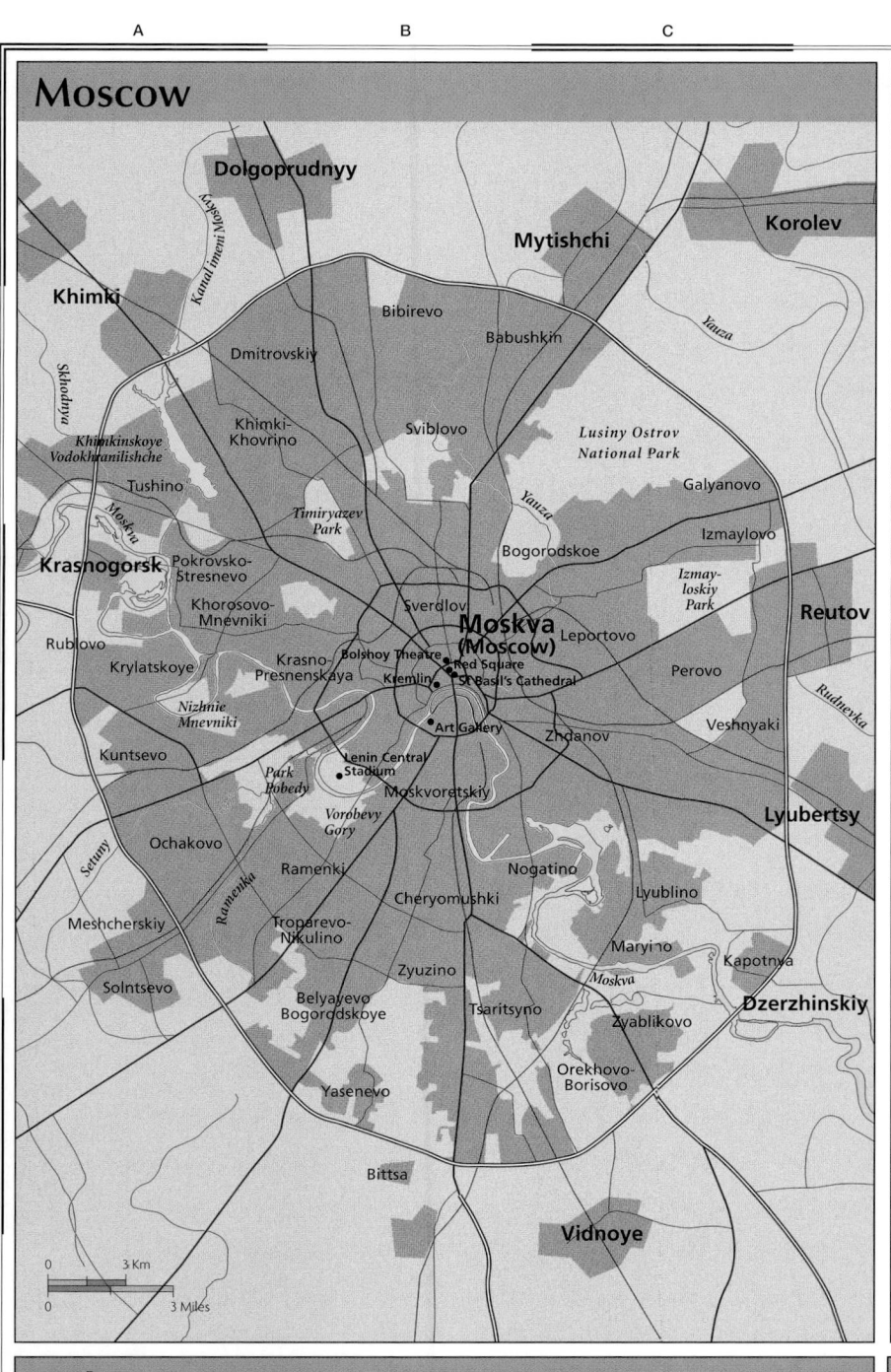

Dolgoprudnyy

Khimki

Mytishchi

Korolev

Bibirevo

Babushkin

Dmitrovskiy

Khimki-Khovrino

Sviblovo

Lusiny Ostrov National Park

Galyanovo

Khimkinskoye Vodokhranilishche

Tushino

Timiryazev Park

Yauza

Izmaylovo

Krasnogorsk

Pokrovsko-Stresnevo

Bogorodskoe

Izmayloskiy Park

Reutov

Rublovo

Khorosovo-Mnevniki

Sverdlov

Leportovo

Krylatskoye

Krasno-Presnenskaya

Bolshoy Theatre

Kremlin

Moskva (Moscow)

Red Square

St Basil's Cathedral

Perovo

Veshnyaki

Rudnerka

Nizhnie Mnevniki

Art Gallery

Zhdanov

Kuntsevo

Lenin Central Stadium

Park Pobedy

Moskvoretskiy

Ochakovo

Vorobevy Gory

Ramenki

Cheryomushki

Nogatino

Lyublino

Meshcherskiy

Troparevo-Nikulino

Zyuzino

Maryino

Moskva

Kapotnya

Solntsevo

Belyayevo Bogorodskoye

Tsaritsyno

Zyablikovo

Dzerzhinskiy

Yasenevo

Orekhovo-Borisovo

Bittsa

Vidnoye

3 Km / 3 Miles

Munich

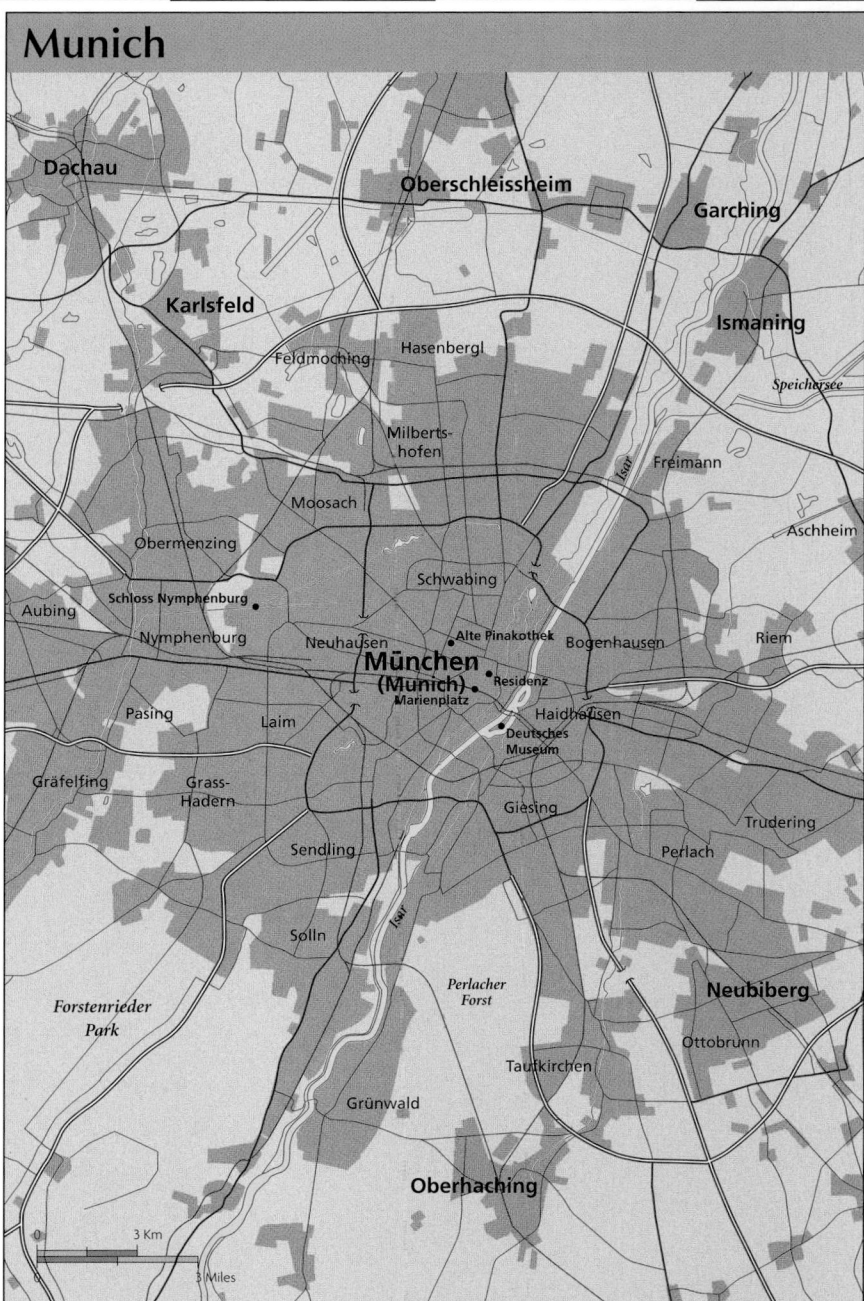

Dachau

Oberschleissheim

Garching

Karlsfeld

Feldmoching

Hasenbergl

Ismaning

Milberts-hofen

Speichersee

Moosach

Freimann

Obermenzing

Schwabing

Aschheim

Aubing

Schloss Nymphenburg

Alte Pinakothek

Bogenhausen

Riem

Nymphenburg

Neuhausen

München (Munich)

Residenz

Pasing

Marienplatz

Haidhausen

Laim

Deutsches Museum

Gräfelfing

Grass-Hadern

Giesing

Trudering

Sendling

Perlach

Spöln

Isar

Forstenrieder Park

Perlacher Forst

Neubiberg

Tautkirchen

Ottobrunn

Grünwald

Oberhaching

3 Km / 3 Miles

Oslo

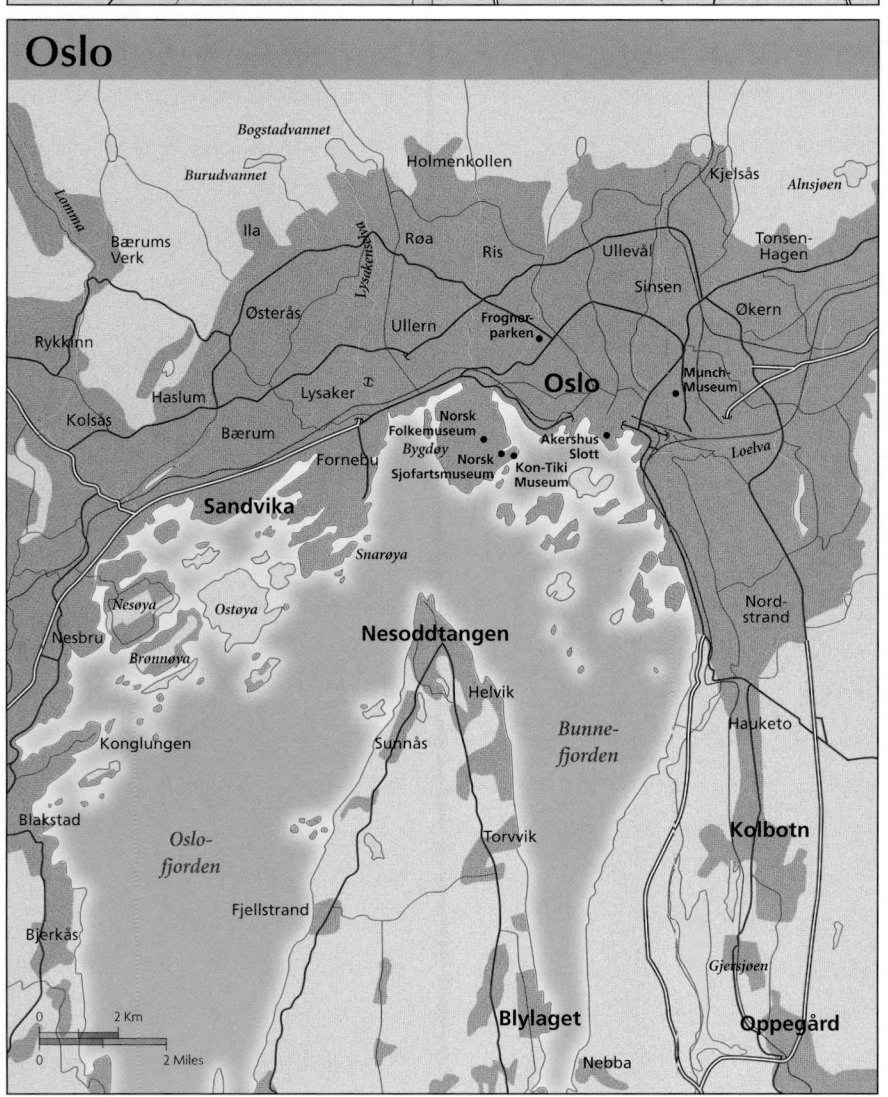

Bogstadvannet

Holmenkollen

Kjelsås

Alnsjøen

Burudvannet

Ila

Røa

Ris

Ullevål

Tonsen-Hagen

Bærums Verk

Østerås

Sinsen

Lomma

Ullern

Frogner-parken

Økern

Rykkinn

Lysaker

Oslo

Munch-Museum

Haslum

Norsk Folkemuseum

Akershus Slott

Kolsås

Bærum

Bygdøy

Norsk Sjofartsmuseum

Kon-Tiki Museum

Loelva

Forneby

Sandvika

Snarøya

Nordstrand

Nesøya

Ostøya

Nesoddtangen

Helvik

Nesbru

Brønnøya

Bunne-fjorden

Hauketo

Konglungen

Sunnås

Oslo-fjorden

Blakstad

Torvvik

Kolbotn

Bjerkås

Fjellstrand

Gjersjøen

Fjellstrand

Blylaget

Oppegård

Nebba

2 Km / 2 Miles

Prague

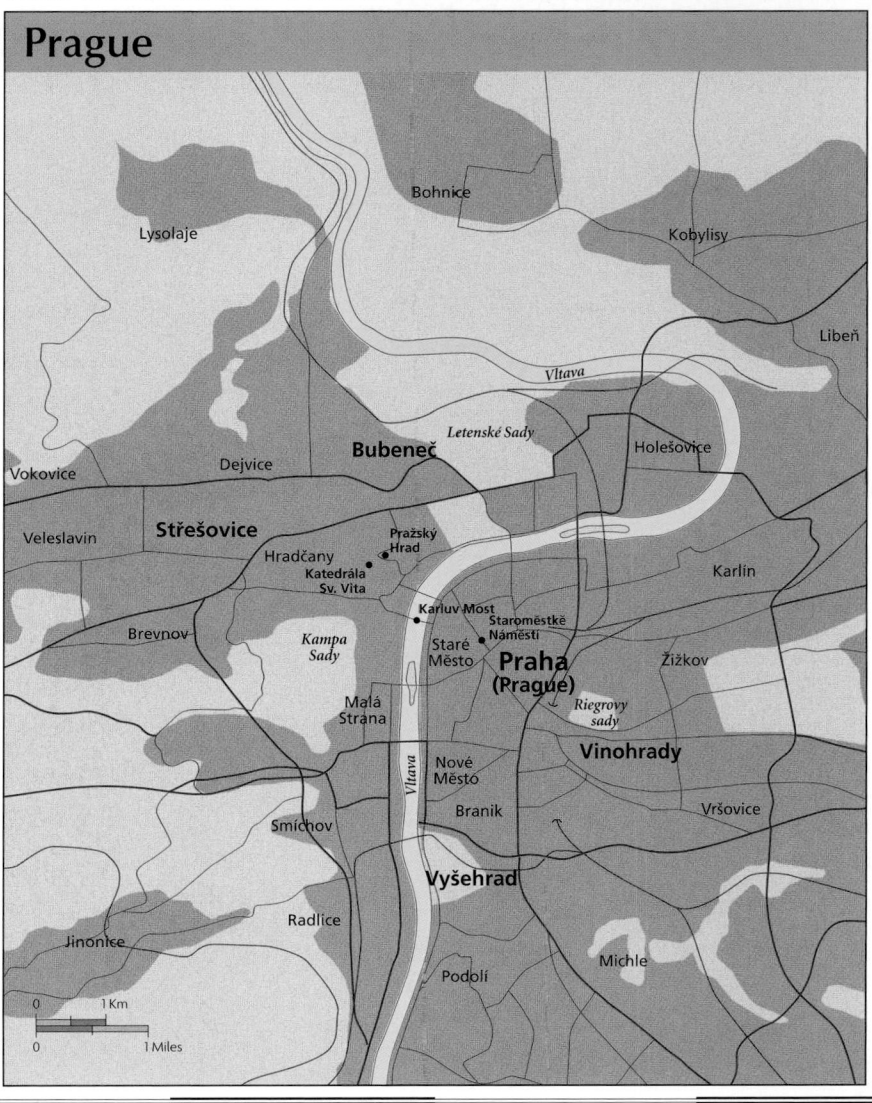

Bohnice

Lysolaje

Kobylisy

Vltava

Vokovice

Letenské Sady

Libeň

Dejvice

Bubeneč

Holešovice

Veleslavin

Střešovice

Pražský Hrad

Karlin

Hradčany

Katedrála Sv. Vita

Brevnov

Karluv Most

Staroměstké

Kampa Sady

Staré Město

Náměstí

Žižkov

Malá Strana

Praha (Prague)

Riegrovy sady

Nové Město

Vinohrady

Smíchov

Branik

Vršovice

Jinonice

Radlice

Vyšehrad

Michle

Podolí

1 Km / 1 Miles

Rome

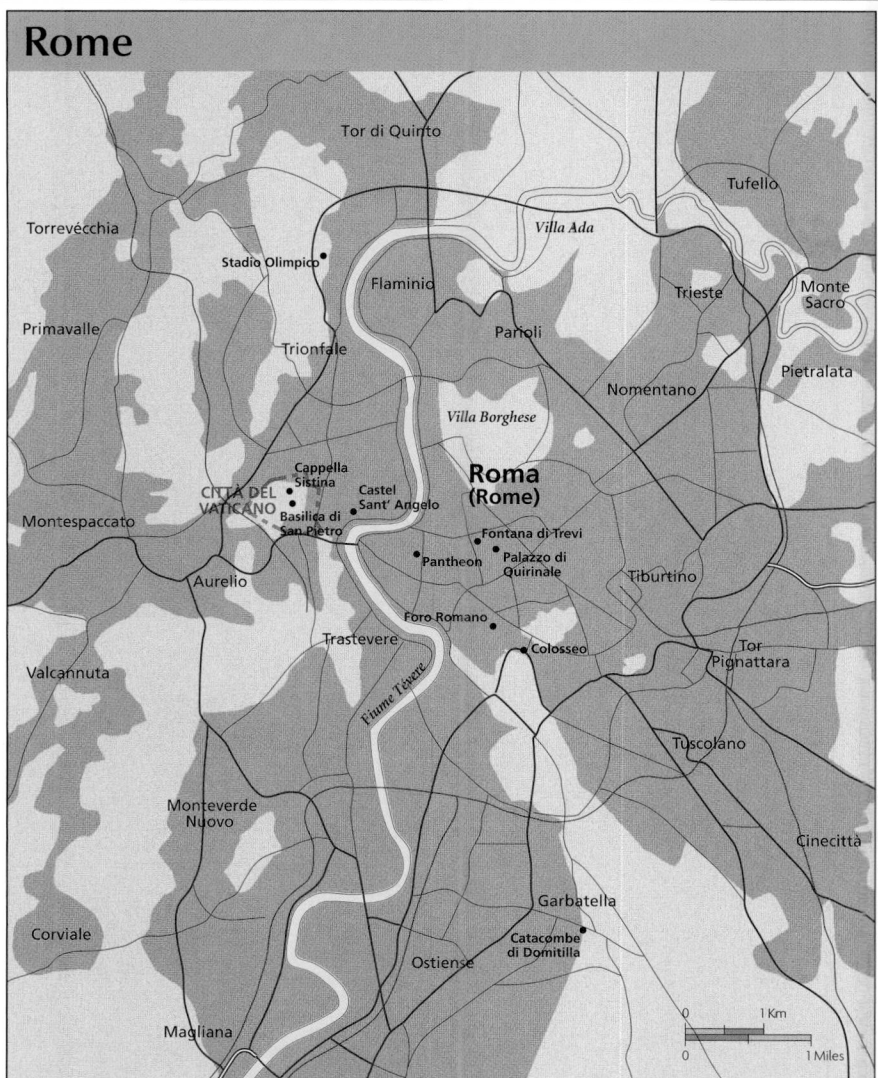

Torrevécchia · Tor di Quinto · Villa Ada · Tufello · Monte Sacro · Primavalle · Flaminio · Stadio Olimpico · Trieste · Pietralata · Trionfale · Parioli · Nomentano · Villa Borghese · Montespaccato · Cappella Sistina · CITTÀ DEL VATICANO · Roma (Rome) · Castel Sant' Angelo · Basilica di San Pietro · Fontana di Trevi · Palazzo di Quirinale · Aurelio · Pantheon · Tiburtino · Foro Romano · Trastevere · Fiume Tevere · Colosseo · Tor Pignattara · Valcannuta · Tuscolano · Monteverde Nuovo · Garbatella · Cinecittà · Corviale · Ostiense · Catacombe di Domitilla · Magliana

0   1 Km
0   1 Miles

St Petersburg

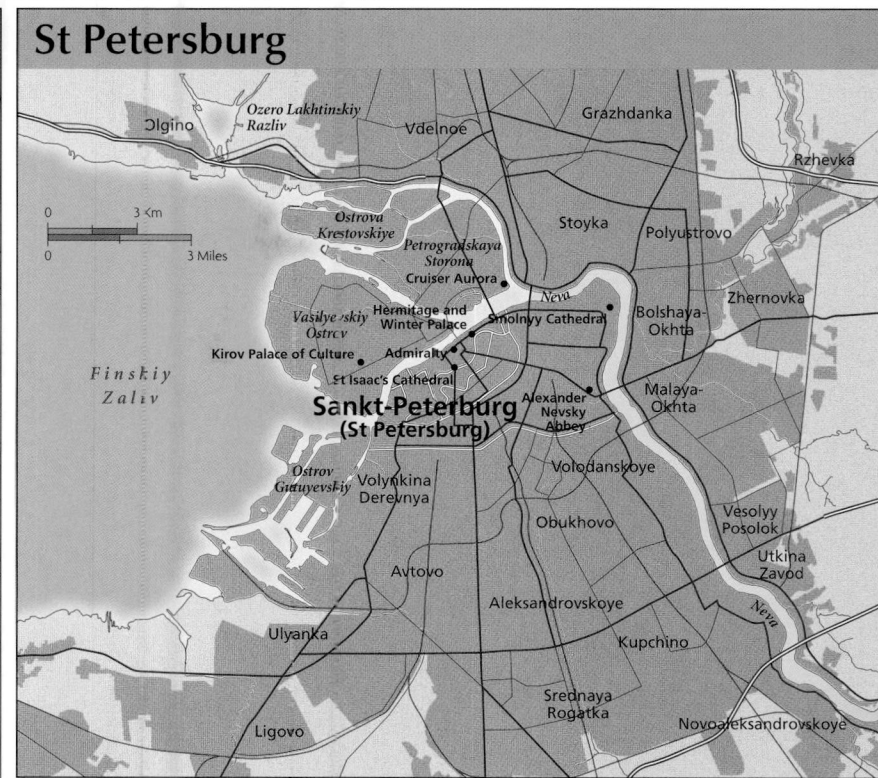

Ozero Lakhtinskiy Razliv · Olgino · Vdelnoe · Grázhdanka · Rzhevká · Ostrova Krestovskiye · Stoyka · Polyustrovo · Petrogradskaya Storona · Cruiser Aurora · Zhernovka · Vasílyevskiy Óstrov · Hermitage and Winter Palace · Smolnyy Cathedral · Neva · Bolshaya-Okhta · Kirov Palace of Culture · Admiralty · Finskiy Zaliv · St Isaac's Cathedral · Sankt-Peterburg (St Petersburg) · Alexander Nevsky Abbey · Malaya-Okhta · Ostrov Golodayevskiy · Volynkina Derevnya · Volodanskoye · Vésolyy Posolok · Avtovo · Obukhovo · Utkina Zavod · Ulyanka · Neva · Aleksandrovskoye · Kupchino · Ligovo · Srednaya Rogatka · Novoaleksandrovskoye

0   3 Km
0   3 Miles

Sofia

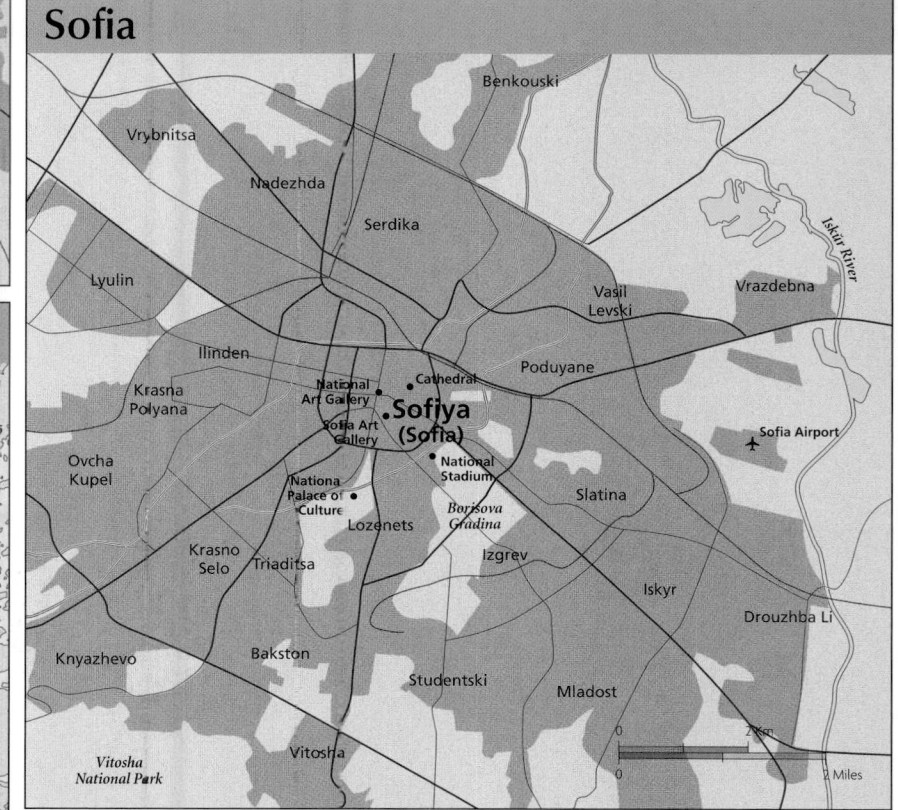

Benkouski · Vrybnitsa · Nadezhda · Serdika · Lyulin · Iskir River · Vasil Levski · Vrazdebna · Ilinden · Krasna Polyana · National Art Gallery · Cathedral · Poduyane · Sofia Art Gallery · Sofiya (Sofia) · Sofia Airport · Ovcha Kupel · National Palace of Culture · National Stadium · Slatina · Krasno Selo · Lozenets · Borisova Gradina · Izgrev · Iskyr · Drouzhba Li · Knyazhevo · Triaditsa · Bakston · Studentski · Mladost · Vitosha National Park · Vitosha

0   2 Km
0   2 Miles

Stockholm

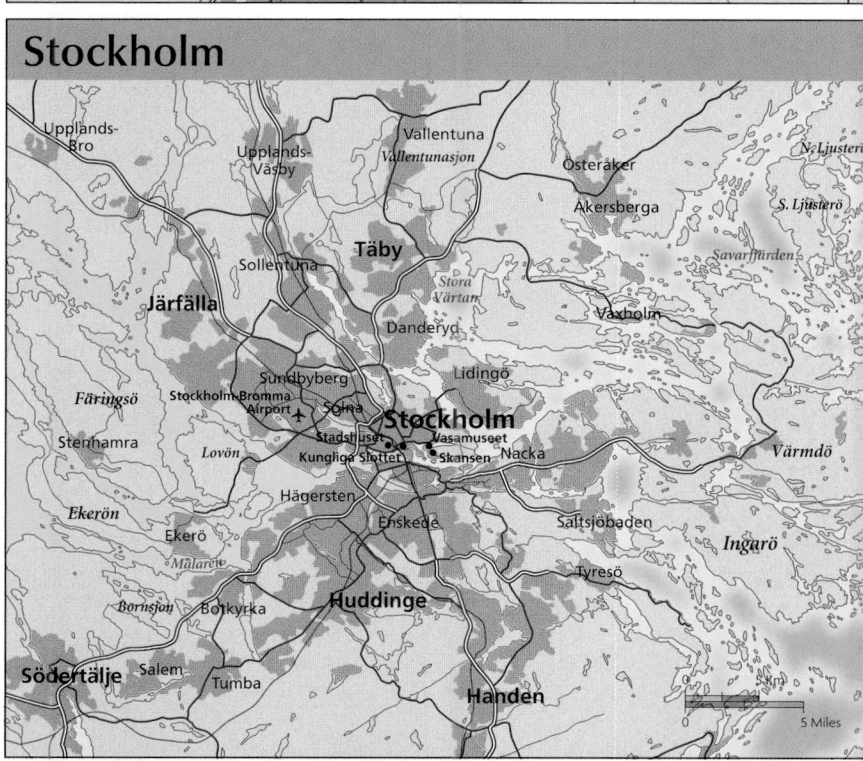

Upplands-Bro · Upplands-Väsby · Vallentuna · Vallentunasjön · Österåker · N. Ljusterö · Täby · S. Ljusterö · Järfälla · Sollentuna · Akersberga · Savarfjärden · Fåringsö · Danderyd · Vaxholm · Stenhamra · Sundbyberg · Stockholm Bromma Airport · Solna · Stockholm · Lidingö · Värmdö · Stora Värtan · Stadshuset · Vasamuseet · Lovön · Kungliga Slottet · Skansen · Nacka · Ekerön · Hägersten · Ingarö · Ekerö · Enskede · Saltsjöbaden · Mälare · Tyresö · Bornsjön · Botkyrka · Huddinge · Södertälje · Salem · Tumba · Handen

0   5 Miles

Warsaw

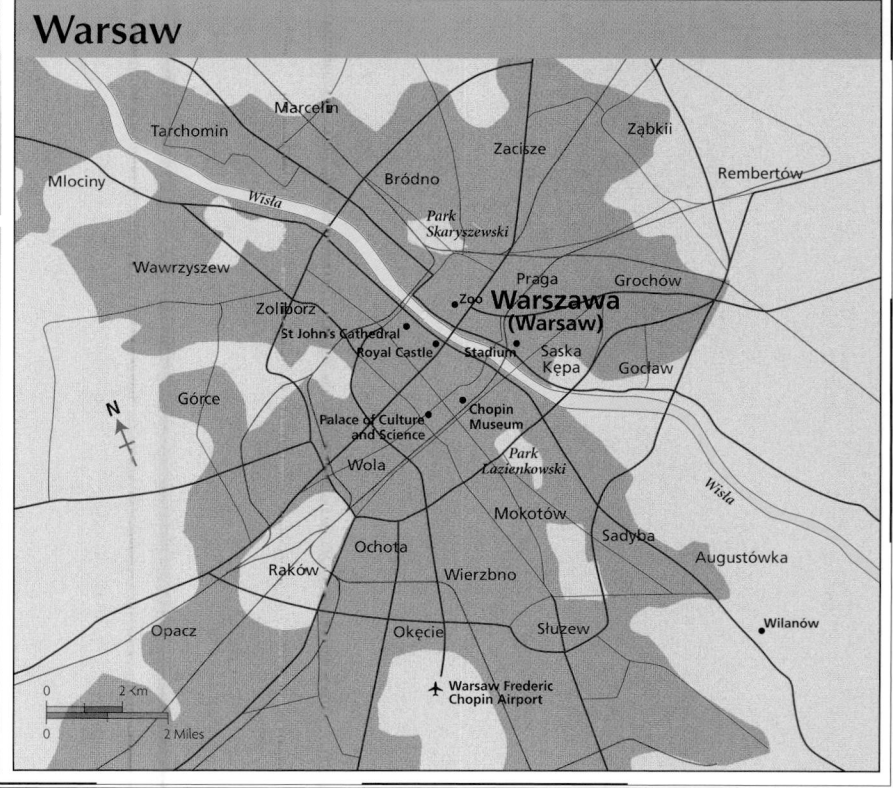

Marcelin · Tarchomin · Zacisze · Ząbki · Mlociny · Wisla · Bródno · Rembertów · Wawrzyszew · Park Skaryszewski · Praga · Grochów · Zoliborz · Zoo · Warszawa (Warsaw) · St John's Cathedral · Royal Castle · Stadium · Saska Kępa · Górce · Saska · Palace of Culture and Science · Chopin Museum · Godaw · Wola · Park Lazienkowski · Wisla · Mokotów · Ochota · Sadyba · Raków · Wierzbno · Augustówka · Opacz · Okęcie · Służew · Wilanów · Warsaw Frederic Chopin Airport

N

0   2 Km
0   2 Miles

Zagreb

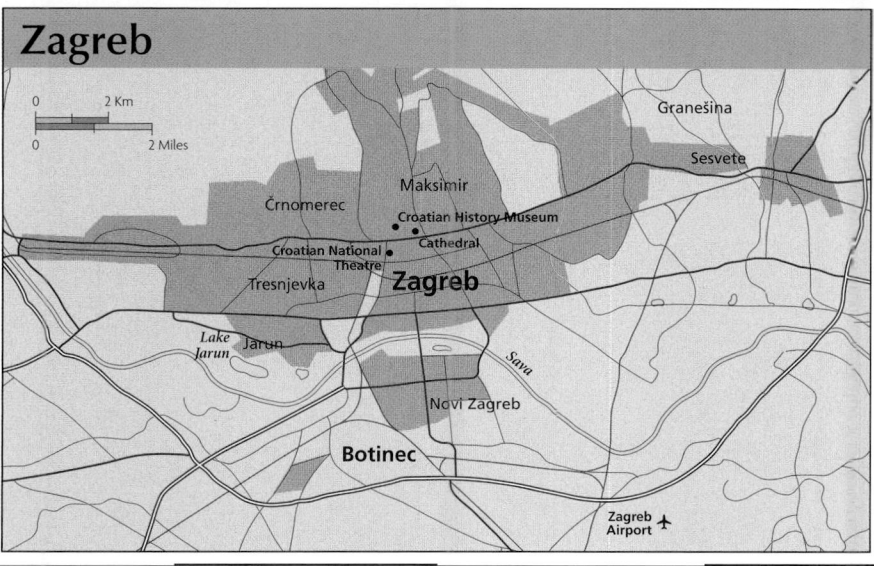

Granešina · Sesvete · Maksimir · Crnomerec · Croatian History Museum · Croatian National Theatre · Cathedral · Tresnjevka · Zagreb · Lake Jarun · Jarun · Sava · Novi Zagreb · Botinec · Zagreb Airport

0   2 Km
0   2 Miles

ASIA

Asia is the world's largest continent with a total area of 16,838,365 sq miles (43,608,000 sq km). It comprises 49 separate countries, including 97% of Turkey and 72% of the Russian Federation. Almost 60% of the world's population lives in Asia.

FACTFILE

N **Most Northerly Point:** Mys Articesku, Russia 81° 12′ N
S **Most Southerly Point:** Pulau Pamana, Indonesia 11° S
E **Most Easterly Point:** Mys Dezhneva, Russia 169° 40′ W
W **Most Westerly Point:** Bozca Adası, Turkey 26° 2′ E

Largest Lakes:
1 Caspian Sea, Asia/Europe 143,243 sq miles (371,000 sq km)
2 Lake Baikal, Russian Federation 11,776 sq miles (30,500 sq km)
3 Lake Balkhash, Kazakhstan/China 7115 sq miles (18,428 sq km)
4 Aral Sea, Kazakhstan/Uzbekistan 6625 sq miles (17,160 sq km)
5 Tonlé Sap, Cambodia 3861 sq miles (10,000 sq km)

Longest Rivers:
1 Yangtze, China 3915 miles (6299 km)
2 Yellow River, China 3395 miles (5464 km)
3 Mekong, SE Asia 2749 miles (4425 km)
4 Lena, Russian Federation 2734 miles (4400 km)
5 Yenisey, Russian Federation 2541 miles (4090 km)

Largest Islands:
1 Borneo, Brunie/Indonesia/Malaysia 292,222 sq miles (757,050 sq km)
2 Sumatra, Indonesia 202,300 sq miles (524,000 sq km)
3 Honshu, Japan 88,800 sq miles (230,000 sq km)
4 Sulawesi, Indonesia 73,057 sq miles (189,218 sq km)
5 Java, Indonesia 53,589 sq miles (138,794 sq km)

Highest Points:
1 Mount Everest, China/Nepal 29,035 ft (8850 m)
2 K2, China/Pakistan 28,253 ft (8611 m)
3 Kangchenjunga I, India/Nepal 28,210 ft (8598 m)
4 Lhotse, Nepal 27,939 ft (8516 m)
5 Makalu I, China/Nepal 27,767 ft (8463 m)

Lowest Point:
▼ Dead Sea, Israel/Jordan -1286 ft (-392 m) below sea level

Highest recorded temperature:
● Tirat Tsvi, Israel 129°F (54°C)

Lowest recorded temperature:
– Verkhoyansk, Russian Federation -90°F (-68°C)

Wettest Place:
☰ Cherrapunji, India 450 in (11,430 mm)

Driest Place:
– Aden, Yemen 1.8 in (46 mm)

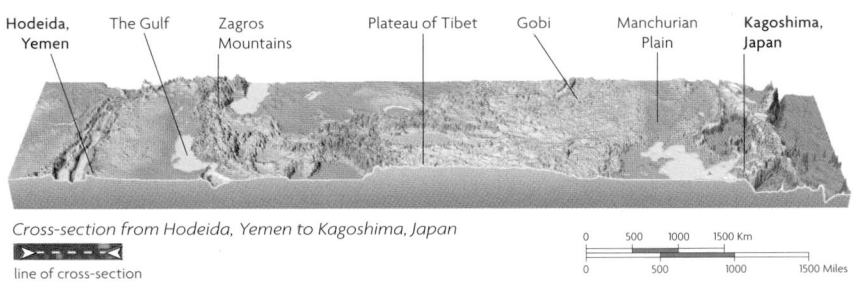

Cross-section from Hodeida, Yemen to Kagoshima, Japan

▷ – ◁ – ◁
line of cross-section

0   500   1000   1500 Km
0   500   1000   1500 Miles

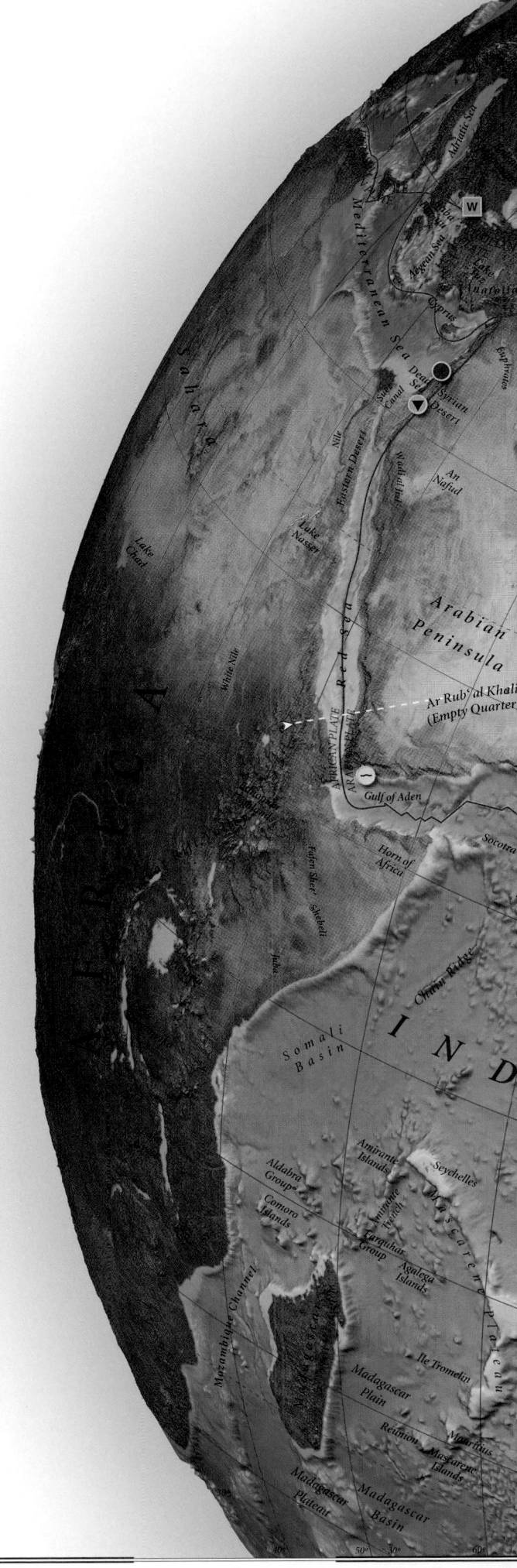

H I J K L M N

ARCTIC OCEAN
North Pole
NORTH AMERICAN PLATE
EURASIAN PLATE
Norwegian Sea
North Sea
Gulf of Bothnia
Baltic Sea
Gulf of Finland
White Sea
North Cape
Barents Sea
Franz Josef Land
Novaya Zemlya
Kara Sea
Severnaya Zemlya
Mys Chelyuskin
Laptev Sea
New Siberian Islands
East Siberian Sea
Long Strait
Bering Strait
Bering Sea
EUROPE
Ural Mountains
West Siberian Plain
North Siberian Lowland
Black Sea
Caspian Depression
Caspian Sea
Ustyurt Plateau
Aral Sea
Kirghiz Steppe
Turan Lowland
Lake Balkhash
Lake Zaysan
Altai Mountains
Lake Baikal
Sea of Okhotsk
ASIA
Dzungaria
Plateau of Mongolia
Gobi
Hulun Nur
Manchurian Plain
Great Salt Desert
Zagros Mountains
Iranian Plateau
Tarim Basin
Takla Makan Desert
Lop Nur
Hindu Kush
Altun Shan
Kunlun Mountains
Plateau of Tibet
Ordos Desert
Bo Hai
Korea Bay
Sea of Japan (East Sea)
PACIFIC OCEAN
Persian Gulf
Strait of Hormuz
Gulf of Oman
Central Makran Range
Rigestan
Punjab Plains
Thar Desert
Yellow Sea
Cheju-do
Korea Strait
East China Sea
Gulf of Kachchh
INDO-AUSTRALIAN PLATE
ARABIAN PLATE
IRANIAN PLATE
Vindhya Range
Satpura Range
Gulf of Khambhat
Ajanta Range
Deccan
Owen Fracture Zone
Arabian Sea
Arabian Basin
Mouths of the Ganges
Taiwan Strait
Ryukyu Islands
Tropic of Cancer
Hainan Strait
Gulf of Tongking
Hainan
Luzon Strait
Philippine Sea
Bay of Bengal
Laccadive Islands
Malabar Coast
Coromandel Coast
Cape Comorin
Gulf of Mannar
Sri Lanka
Gulf of Martaban
Andaman Islands
Andaman Sea
Gulf of Thailand
Mouths of the Mekong
South China Sea
South China Basin
Mindoro
Panay
Negros
Palawan
Sulu Sea
Philippine Basin
Samar
Mindanao
Palau
Maldives
INDIAN OCEAN
Nicobar Islands
Sunda Shelf
Natuna Islands
Anambas Islands
Strait of Malacca
Celebes Sea
Ceylon Plain
Chagos Bank
Chagos Trench
Nikitin Seamount
Greater Sunda Islands
East Indies
Pulau Bangka
Molucca Sea
Halmahera
New Guinea Trench
Equator
Mid-Indian Basin
Cocos Basin
Java Sea
Banda Sea
Buru
Seram
Sunda Trough
Java Trench
Bali
Flores Sea
Lesser Sunda Islands
Sumba
Timor
Timor Trough
Arafura Sea
Torres Strait
Cocos Islands
Christmas Island
Investigator Ridge
Ninetyeast Ridge
Mid-Indian Ridge
Tropic of Capricorn

H I J K L M N

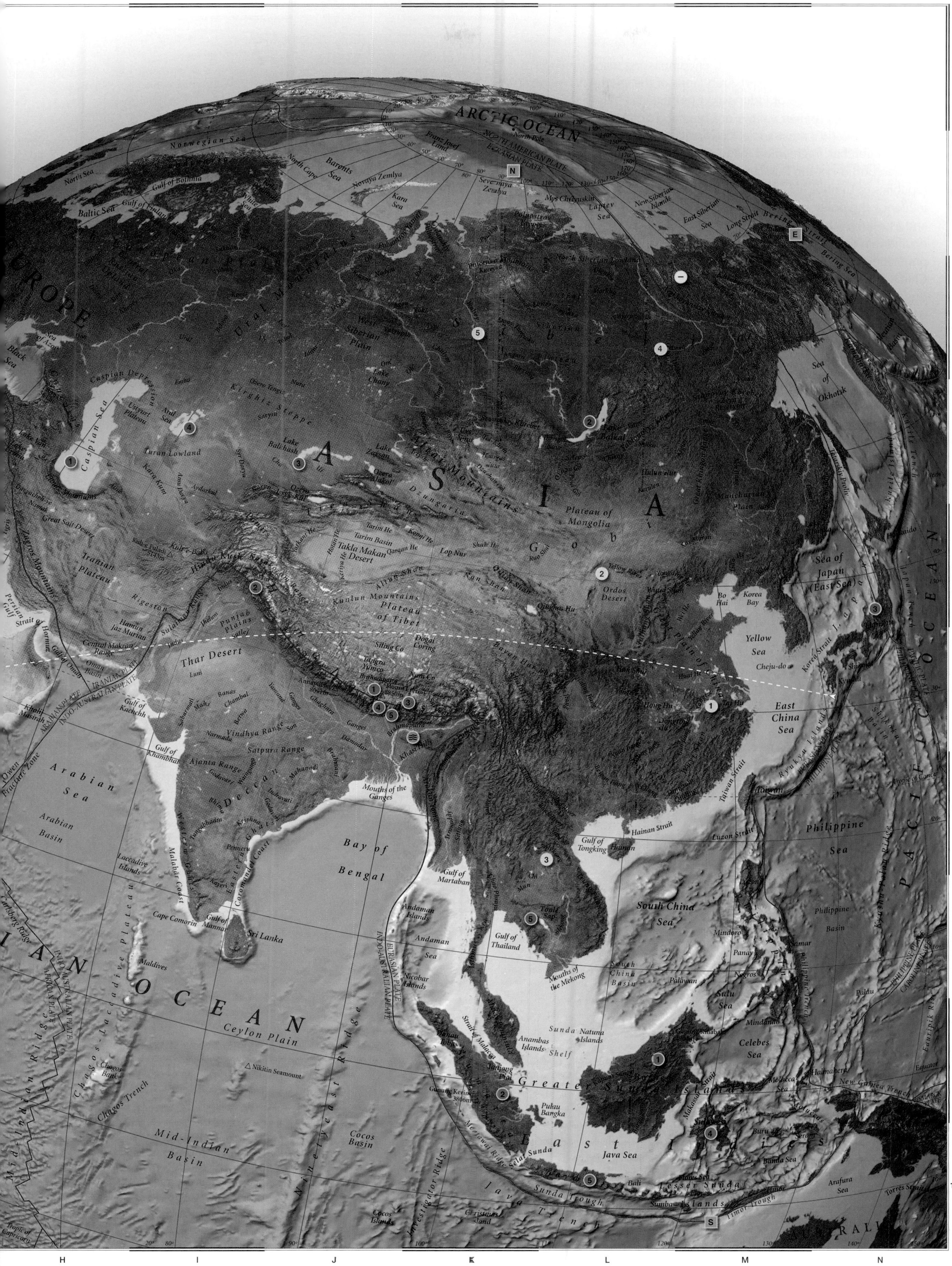

Scale 1:47,500,000
(projection: Gall Stereographic)

| 0 | 500 | 1000 | 1500 Km |
| 0 | 500 | 1000 | 1500 Miles |

Climate

The climate of Asia exhibits marked differences from region to region, with freezing polar conditions in the north, hot and cold deserts in central regions and subtropical conditions throughout the south. Much of this variation can be attributed to enormous mountain barriers and internal depressions found across the continent. Monsoon winds, which reverse semi-annually, cause alternate wet and dry seasons across southern Asia. These air masses moving north from the ocean are stripped of their moisture over the Himalayas causing arid conditions across the Plateau of Tibet. Both the south and east are susceptible to tropical cyclones or typhoons.

Average Rainfall

January rainfall

July rainfall

Rainfall

	0–1 in (0–25 mm)
	1–2 in (25–50 mm)
	2–4 in (50–100 mm)
	4–8 in (100–200 mm)
	8–12 in (200–300 mm)
	12–16 in (300–400 mm)
	16–20 in (400–500 mm)
	more than 20 in (500 mm)

Average Temperature

January temperature

July temperature

Temperature

	below -22°F (-30°C)
	-22 to -4°F (-30 to -20°C)
	-4 to 14°F (-20 to -10°C)
	14 to 32°F (-10 to 0°C)
	32 to 50°F (0 to 10°C)
	50 to 68°F (10 to 20°C)
	68 to 86°F (20 to 30°C)
	above 86°F (30°C)

Climate

	tundra
	subarctic
	cool continental
	warm humid
	mediterranean
	semi-arid
	arid
	humid equatorial
	tropical

☼	daily hours of sunshine, January
☼	daily hours of sunshine, July
→	cyclone
⇒	typhoon
→	cold/dry monsoon
→	warm/wet monsoon
→	cold wind

Using the land and sea

	cropland
	desert
	forest
	mountain region
	pasture
	tundra
	wetland

⬤	major conurbations		

	cattle		fruit
	pigs		jute
	goats		peanuts
	sheep		rice
	coconuts		rubber
	corn (maize)		shellfish
	cotton		soya beans
	dates		sugar beet
	fishing		

	sugar cane
	tea
	timber
	wheat

Environmental issues

The transformation of Uzbekistan by the former Soviet Union into the world's fifth largest producer of cotton led to the diversion of several major rivers for irrigation. Starved of this water, the Aral Sea diminished in volume by over 75% since 1960, irreversibly altering the ecology of the area. Heavy industries in eastern China have polluted coastal waters, rivers and urban air, while in Myanmar (Burma), Malaysia and Indonesia, ancient hardwood rainforests are felled faster than they can regenerate.

Environmental issues

	tropical forest
	forest destroyed
	desert
	desertification
	acid rain

	polluted rivers
	marine pollution
	heavy marine pollution
☢	radioactive contamination
⬤	poor urban air quality

Landuse

Vast areas of Asia remain uncultivated as a result of unsuitable climatic and soil conditions. In favourable areas such as river deltas, farming is intensive. Rice is the staple crop of most Asian countries, grown in paddy fields on waterlogged alluvial plains and terraced hillsides, and often irrigated for higher yields. Across the black earth region of the Eurasian steppe in southern Siberia and Kazakhstan, wheat farming is the dominant activity. Cash crops, like tea in Sri Lanka and dates in the Arabian Peninsula, are grown for export, and provide valuable income. The sovereignty of the rich fishing grounds in the South China Sea is disputed by China, Malaysia, Taiwan, the Philippines and Vietnam, because of potential oil reserves.

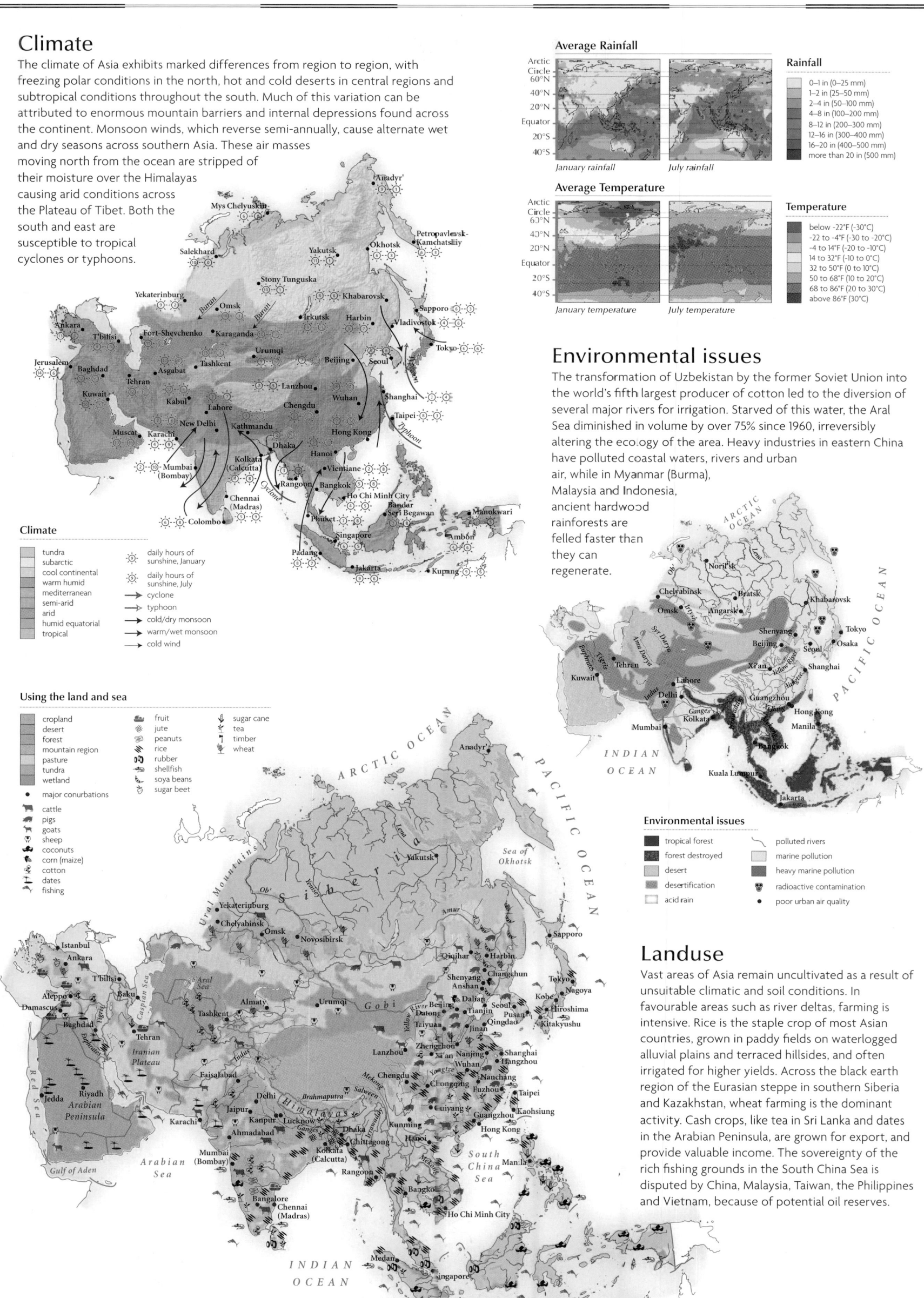

ASIA

1 BOSPORUS, TURKEY
The Bosporus provides the only outlet for the Black Sea, linking it with the Sea of Marmara to the south and then with the Mediterranean Sea via the Dardanelles.

2 MOUNT ARARAT, TURKEY
Said to be the resting place for Noah's Ark, this extinct volcanic massif lies in the far east of Turkey.

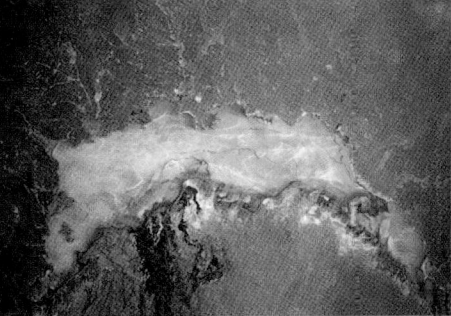

3 LAKE BALKHASH, KAZAKHSTAN
Still covered in winter ice in this image, this lakes lies in a dry desert region and has no outlet.

4 OZERO ISSYK-KUL', KYRGYZSTAN
Against the dry slopes of the Tien Shan mountains to the south this lake appears bright blue.

9 KUWAIT'S OILFIELDS, KUWAIT
The dark plumes are smoke rising from the 700 wells set alight by Iraqi forces during the Gulf War of 1991.

10 PALM ISLAND, UNITED ARAB EMIRATES
This luxury housing development and tourist resort, one mile (1.6 km) off the seafront of Dubai, is built from sediments dredged from the nearby port of Jebel Ali.

11 MALDIVES
The Maldives consist of 1300 coral formations in 19 atolls and stretch over 1491 miles (2400 km).

12 KARACHI, PAKISTAN
Pakistan's main seaport and former capital lies to the northwest of the delta of the Indus river.

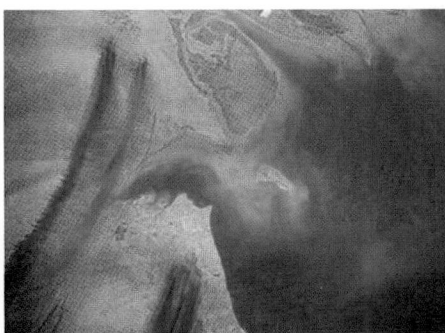

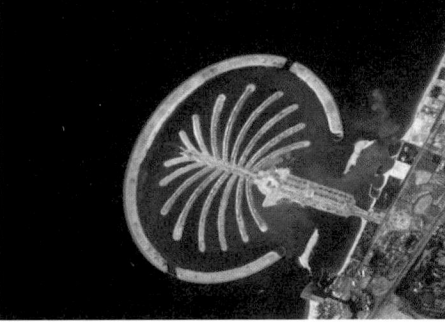

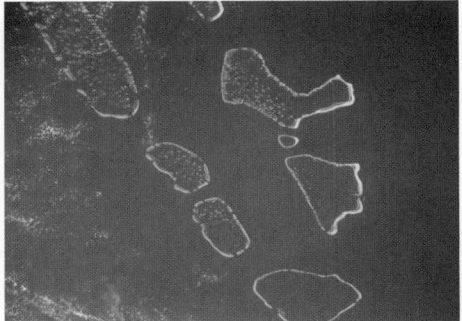

THREE GORGES DAM, CHINA 5
Seen here during its construction in 2000, the world's largest dam is designed to tame the Yangtze river which has regularly flooded.

BEIJING, CHINA 6
China's ancient capital was laid out on a grid pattern centred on the Forbidden City and its streets are picked out in this winter image by snowfall.

MOUNT FUJI, JAPAN 7
The steep, symmetrical, snow-capped volcano last erupted in 1707.

VULKAN KLYUCHEVSKAYA SOPKA, RUSSIAN FEDERATION 8
The Kamchatka Peninsula's highest and most active volcano last erupted in 1994.

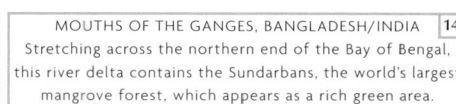

MOUNT EVEREST, CHINA/NEPAL 13
The world's highest mountain at 29,035 ft (8850 m) straddles the border between China and Nepal.

MOUTHS OF THE GANGES, BANGLADESH/INDIA 14
Stretching across the northern end of the Bay of Bengal, this river delta contains the Sundarbans, the world's largest mangrove forest, which appears as a rich green area.

MEKONG DELTA, VIETNAM 15
The Mekong river flows over 2494 miles (4000 km) from the Plateau of Tibet before crossing Vietnam to reach the South China Sea.

HONG KONG, CHINA 16
Handed back to China by the British in 1997, this city remains east Asia's trade and finance center.

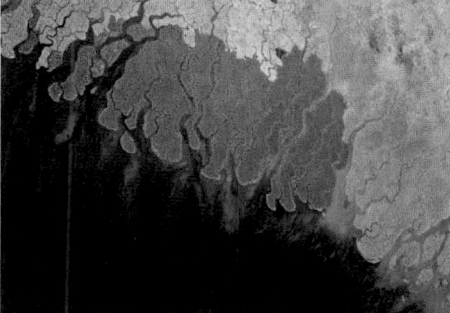

Southwest Asia

RUSSIAN FEDERATION

Black Sea

GEORGIA
T'BILISI

TURKEY
ANKARA

ARMENIA
YEREVAN

Mediterranean Sea

CYPRUS
NICOSIA

SYRIA
Halab (Aleppo)

LEBANON
BEYROUTH (BEIRUT)

DIMASHQ (DAMASCUS)

IRAQ
BAGHDAD

ISRAEL
JERUSALEM
Tel Aviv-Yafo

JORDAN
AMMAN

Syrian Desert

EGYPT
CAIRO
El Giza
Alexandria

Nile Delta

Suez Canal

Sinai

Red Sea

SAUDI ARABIA
Makkah (Mecca)
JIDDAH (JEDDA)
Al Madīnah (Medina)

LIBYA
SAHARA
Libyan Desert

CHAD

SUDAN
KHARTOUM
Omdurman

Nubian Desert

Lake Nasser

ERITREA
ASMARA

ETHIOPIA
Ethiopian Highlands

DJIBOUTI

SAN'A' (SANA)

6000m
4000m
3000m
2000m
1000m
500m
250m
100m
Sea Level
-250m
-2000m
-4000m

Scale 1:11,750,000
(projection: Lambert Azimuthal Equal Area)
0 50 100 150 200 250 300 Km
0 50 100 150 200 250 300 Miles
Population
above 5 million
1 million to 5 million
500,000 to 1 million
100,000 to 500,000
50,000 to 100,000
10,000 to 50,000
below 10,000
H
I
J
K
L
M
N
226
232
288
KAZAKHSTAN
UZBEKISTAN
TURKMENISTAN
KYRGYZSTAN
TAJIKISTAN
AZERBAIJAN
CHINA
AFGHANISTAN
PAKISTAN
INDIA
IRAN
KUWAIT
BAHRAIN
QATAR
UNITED ARAB EMIRATES
OMAN
YEMEN
SOMALIA
SOMALILAND
(not internationally recognized)
Caspian Sea
Persian Gulf
Gulf of Oman
Arabian Sea
Gulf of Aden
Gulf of Kachchh
Gulf of Khambhat
Strait of Hormuz
Makran Coast
Ustyurt Plateau
Kyzyl Kum
Turan Lowland
Garagum
Kopetdag Gershi
Koppeh Dāgh
Reshteh-ye Kūhhā-ye Alborz
Dasht-e Kavīr
Dasht-e Lūt
Iranian Plateau
Zagros Mountains
Hindu Kush
Karakoram Range
Tien Shan
Sulaiman Range
Central Brahui Range
Siahan Range
Central Makran Range
Chagai Hills
Thar Desert
Rann of Kachchh
Tropic of Cancer
Mouths of the Indus
Kāthiāwār Peninsula
Ar Rub' al Khālī (Empty Quarter)
Arabian Peninsula
Jabal Tuwayq
Ad Dahnā
Ramlat Al Wahibah
Ramlat as Sab'atayn
Hadramawt
Al Mahrah
Zufār
Jiddat al Harāsīs
Suquṭrā (Socotra)
BAKI (BAKU)
TEHRĀN
KĀBOL (KABUL)
ISLĀMĀBĀD
TOSHKENT (TASHKENT)
BISHKEK
DUSHANBE
AŞGABAT
AL KUWAYT (KUWAIT)
AL MANĀMAH (MANAMA)
AD DAWHAH (DOHA)
ABŪ ZABY (ABU DHABI)
MASQAT (MUSCAT)
AR RIYĀD (RIYADH)
Mashhad
Esfahān
Shīrāz
Tabrīz
Qom
Kermān
Zāhedān
Bandar-e 'Abbās
Ahvāz
Herāt
Kandahār
Mazār-e Sharīf
Quetta
Karāchi
Hyderābād
Lahore
Faisalābād
Rāwalpindi
Peshāwar
Multān
Amritsar
Srinagar
Ahmadābād
Vadodara
Surat
Rājkot
Jodhpur
Samarqand
Buxoro
Dubayy (Dubai)
Ash Shāriqah
Salālah
Al Mukallā
ASIA
Riyadh
Ar Riyād (Riyadh)
Ad Dir'iyah
Al Marooj
Al Mursalat
Al Hamra
King Khaled Intl. Airport
Al Roudah Park
Al Rawabi Park
Al Quds
Al Ulayah
Zoo
Al Murabba
Al Malaz
Al Amir Fahad Park
Al Noor
Dhrata Badiah
Al Masmak Fortress
Al Nasiriyah Gate
Al Hamrah Palace
Main Juma'a Mosque
King Abdul Aziz Manakh Park
Hijrat Laban
Al Madinah As Sinaiiyah
Yamamah
Al Masanya
Al Dar Al Baida
Jiza
Nammar
0 3 Km
0 3 Miles
19,686ft
13,124ft
9843ft
6562ft
3281ft
1640ft
820ft
328ft
Sea Level
-820ft
-6562ft
-13,124ft

6000m
4000m
3000m
2000m
1000m
500m
250m
100m
Sea Level
-250m
-2000m
-4000m

189

187

129

A B C D E F G

UKRAINE

Sea of Azov

ROMANIA

BUCUREŞTI
(BUCHAREST)

Black Sea

BULGARIA

REPUBLIKA KRYM

Novorossiysk

İSTANBUL

İstanbul Boğazı
(Bosporus)

TEKİRDAĞ

EDİRNE

Marmara Denizi
(Sea of Marmara)

KOCAELİ

ZONGULDAK

KASTAMONU

SİNOP

SAMSUN

ORDU

KIRKLARELİ

ÇANAKKALE

BURSA

BİLECİK

SAKARYA

BOLU

ÇANKIRI

AMASYA

TOKAT

BALIKESİR

KÜTAHYA

ESKİŞEHİR

ANKARA

KIRIKKALE

KIRŞEHİR

YOZGAT

SİVAS

Aegean Islands

MANİSA

İZMİR

UŞAK

AFYON

NEVŞEHİR

KAYSERİ

AYDIN

DENİZLİ

İSPARTA

BURDUR

KONYA

AKSARAY

NİĞDE

KAHRAMANMARAŞ

MUĞLA

Ródos
(Rhodes)

ANTALYA

Antalya
Körfezi

KARAMAN

ADANA

MERSİN

GAZİANTEP

KİLİS

İskenderun
Körfezi

HALAB
(Aleppo)

Kríti

Mediterranean Sea

TURKISH REPUBLIC OF
NORTHERN CYPRUS
(recognised only by Turkey)

CYPRUS

NICOSIA

Lemesós (Limassol)

İDLİB

HAMÂH

LEBANON

BEYROUTH
(BEIRUT)

DİMASHQ
(DAMASCUS)

DİMASHQ

Scale 1:4,300,000
(projection: Lambert Conformal Conic)
0 20 40 60 80 100 Km
0 20 40 60 80 100 Miles
Population
above 5 million
1 million to 5 million
500,000 to 1 million
100,000 to 500,000
50,000 to 100,000
10,000 to 50,000
below 10,000
H I J K L M N
1 2 3 4 5 6 7 8 9 10
197
228
217
RUSSIAN FEDERATION
KRASNODARSKIY KRAY
STAVROPOL'SKIY KRAY
RESPUBLIKA KALMYKIYA
Caspian Depression
Stavropol'skaya Vozvyshennost'
Nogayskaya Step
CHECHENSKAYA RESPUBLIKA
INGUSHSKAYA RESPUBLIKA
KABARDINO-BALKARSKAYA RESPUBLIKA
KARACHAYEVO-CHERKESSKAYA RESPUBLIKA
RESPUBLIKA SEVERNAYA OSETIYA-ALANIYA
RESPUBLIKA DAGESTAN
RESPUBLIKA ADYGEYA
Caspian Sea
KAZAKHSTAN
Plato Mangyshlak
Krasnodar
Stavropol'
Maykop
Cherkessk
Nevinnomyssk
Pyatigorsk
Kislovodsk
Nal'chik
Vladikavkaz
Groznyy
Makhachkala
Derbent
Sochi
Aktau
Fort-Shevchenko
GEORGIA
ABKHAZIA
ADJARA
South Ossetia
Sokhumi
K'ut'aisi
Bat'umi
P'ot'i
T'BILISI
Rust'avi
Gori
ARMENIA
YEREVAN
Gyumri
Vanadzor
Sevana Lich
AZERBAIJAN
BAKI (Baku)
Sumqayit
Gäncä
Mingäçevir
Naxçivan
AZERB.
Xankändi
Lankäran
Abşeron Yarımadası
TURKEY
Trabzon
Rize
Giresun
Erzurum
Erzincan
Kars
Ardahan
Artvin
Bayburt
Ağrı
Iğdır
Muş
Bitlis
Van
Van Gölü
Bingöl
Tunceli
Elazığ
Malatya
Diyarbakır
Batman
Siirt
Mardin
Şanlıurfa
Adıyaman
Hakkâri
Şırnak
Toros Dağları
IRAN
Tabriz
Ardabil
Orūmīyeh
Daryācheh-ye Orūmīyeh
Rasht
Qazvin
Zanjān
Hamadān
Sanandaj
Kermānshāh (Bākhtarān)
Khorramābād
Arāk
Borūjerd
Malāyer
ĀZARBĀYJĀN-E SHARQĪ
ĀZARBĀYJĀN-E GHARBĪ
KORDESTĀN
KERMĀNSHĀH
LORESTĀN
HAMADĀN
MARKAZĪ
ZANJĀN
GĪLĀN
ĪLĀM
Reshteh-ye Kūhhā-ye Alborz (Elburz Mountains)
Zagros Mountains
IRAQ
BAGHDĀD
Al Mawşil (Mosul)
Arbīl
Kirkūk
As Sulaymānīyah
Tikrīt
Sāmarrā'
Ar Ramādī
Al Fallūjah
SYRIA
Al Ḩasakah
Ar Raqqah
Dayr az Zawr
Al Jazīrah
Tudmur (Palmyra)
Euphrates
Tigris
Aras
Kura
ASIA
19,686ft
13,124ft
9843ft
6562ft
3281ft
1640ft
820ft
328ft
Sea Level
-820ft
-6562ft
-13,124ft

The Near East

A
B
C
D
E
F
G
214
199
220
TURKEY
Karaman
KARAMAN
Toros Dağları
Adana
ADANA
Mersin
MERSİN
Tarsus
Osmaniye
OSMANİYE
Kahramanmaraş
Gaziantep
GAZİANTEP
Kilis
KİLİS
Şanlıurfa
ŞANLIURFA
Mardin
MARDİN
Nusaybin
Viranşehir
Birecik
Suruç
Ceylanpınar
Kızıltepe
İskenderun
İskenderun Körfezi
HATAY
Antakya
Samandağı
Anamur
Aydıncık
Silifke
Erdemli
Deli Burnu
Akıncı Burnu
TURKISH REPUBLIC OF NORTHERN CYPRUS
(recognized only by Turkey)
Zafer Burnu (Rizokárpason)
Dipkarpaz (Rizokárpason)
Girne (Kerýneia)
NICOSIA
Gazimağusa Körfezi (Kólpos Ammóchostos)
Gazimağusa (Ammóchostos, Famagusta)
Agia Nápa
Lárnaka
Lemesós (Limassol)
Akrotíri Gkréko
Sovereign Base Area (to UK)
Kólpos Akrotírion
CYPRUS
Mediterranean Sea
SYRIA
Halab (Aleppo)
HALAB
Idlib
IDLIB
Al Lādhiqīyah (Latakia)
AL LĀDHIQĪYAH
Jablah
Bāniyās
Ḥamāh
HAMĀH
Ṭarṭūs
TARTUS
Ḥimş (Homs)
Salamīyah
Manbij
Al Bāb
Buḥayrat al Asad
Ar Raqqah
AR RAQQAH
Al Ḥasakah
AL ḤASAKAH
Al Qāmishlī
Ash Shadādah
Dayr az Zawr
DAYR AZ ZAWR
Al Mayādīn
Abū Kamāl
Tudmur (Palmyra)
ḤIMŞ
Jabal Abū Rajbah
Fayḍat
Al Qaryatayn
Ar Rutbah
Turayf
Jabal ʻUnayzah 940m
Syrian Desert
Al Ḥamad
Al Ḥarrah
Wādī as Sirḥān
LEBANON
BEYROUTH (BEIRUT)
Tripoli
Baalbek
Zahlé
Şaïda
Soûr
Lac de Qaraoun
Mount Hermon 2814m
DIMASHQ (DAMASCUS)
DIMASHQ
AL QUNAYṬIRAH
DAR'Ā
Dar'ā
AS SUWAYDĀ'
As Suwaydā'
Jabal al 'Arab
ISRAEL
Hefa (Haifa)
HAIFA
NORTHERN
Nazerat (Nazareth)
Lake Tiberias (Sea of Galilee)
Tel Aviv-Yafo
TEL AVIV
Petah Tiqwa
Ramat Gan
Bat Yam
Holon
Netanya
Hadera
Ashdod
Ashqelon
JERUSALEM
Bethlehem
Jericho
West Bank
Gaza Strip
Gaza
Khān Yūnis
Rafah
Be'er Sheva
SOUTHERN
HaNegev
Dead Sea
El'Arish
Elat
Gulf of Aqaba
JORDAN
Irbid
IRBID
Jarash
Al Mafraq
AL MAFRAQ
Az Zarqā'
AZ ZARQĀ'
'AMMĀN
'AMMĀN
Mādabā
MĀDABĀ
Al Karak
AL KARAK
Aṭ Ṭafīlah
AṬ ṬAFĪLAH
Ma'ān
MA'ĀN
Al 'Aqabah
AL 'AQABAH
Ṭuwayyil ash Shīhāq
Jabal Ramm 1754m
Al Quwayrah
Al Mudawwarah
Jabal Mubārak 1727m
EGYPT
Sinai
Haql
Jabal al Lawz 2580m
Al Bad'
Gebel Mûsa 2285m
SAUDI
AL JAWF
Sakākah
Al Jawf
At Tubayq
TABŪK
Al Bi'r
Bi'r Fajr
Al Qurayyāt
6000m
4000m
3000m
2000m
1000m
500m
250m
100m
Sea Level
-250m
-2000m
-4000m
1
2
3
4
5
6
7
8
9
10

Scale 1:3,000,000
(projection: Lambert Conformal Conic)
0 20 40 60 80 100 Km
0 20 40 60 80 100 Miles
Population
above 5 million
1 million to 5 million
500,000 to 1 million
100,000 to 500,000
50,000 to 100,000
10,000 to 50,000
below 10,000
H I J K L M N
1 2 3 4 5 6 7 8 9 10
215
222
221
ASIA
217
19,686ft
13,124ft
9843ft
6562ft
3281ft
1640ft
820ft
328ft
Sea Level
-820ft
-6562ft
-13,124ft
ŞIRNAK
Cizre
Tigris
Hakkâri
HAKKÂRI
Yüksekova
Orūmīyeh
Daryācheh-ye Orūmīyeh
Bonāb
Marāgheh
ĀZARBĀYJĀN-E SHARQĪ
Fowman
Langarūd
GĪLĀN
Reshteh-ye Kūhhā-ye Alborz (Elburz Mountains)
Zanjān
ZANJĀN
Qazvīn
QAZVĪN
Soltānīyeh
Qeydār
Abhar
Tākestān
Āb Garm
Āvaj
Zākhō
Al Mālikiyah
Al 'Amādiyah
Great Zab
Mangīsh
Harki
Mari Milā
Khayrūzūk
Nāqadeh
Pīrānshahr
Mahābād
Mīāndowāb
ĀZARBĀYJĀN-E GHARBĪ
Būkān
Sümēl
Dahūk
Ākrē
Tall Kūshik
Tall Zāhir
Tall 'Uwaynāt
Rāyat
Rawāndiz
Bēkhma
Tall Ḩuqnah
Eski Mosul
Tall Kayf
Bardarash
Rashwān
Shaqlāwa
Darband
Rānya
Qala Diza
Saqqez
Khān as Sūr
Jabal Sinjār
Sinjār
Tall 'Afar
Al Mawşil (Mosul)
Eski Kalak
Arbīl
Tall ash Sha'īr
Al Fatsī
Ḩammām al 'Alīl
Tall Ḩassūnah
Gūwēr
Koi Sanjaq
Bingird
Dokan
Bāneh
Bījār
Al Ba'āj
Al Bādī
Jawan
Dibaga
Kānī Sulaymān
Altin Köprü
Taqtaq
Little Zab
Siyāh Gūz
Chwārta
Gormak
KORDESTĀN
Tall 'Abṭah
Tall 'Azbah
Makhmūr
Dargazayn
Jazīrah
Al Ḩadr
Ash Sharqāţ
Khānūqah
Bāba Gurgur
Qizil Yār
Chamchamāl
Kirkūk
Qara Anjīr
Kutabān
Shākh-i Bāranān
As Sulaymānīyah
Arbat
Marwān
Qara Gol
Khurmal
Zarēn
Ḩalabja
Sanandaj
Qorveh
Kabūd Rāhang
Razan
Nowbarān
I R A N
Ḩawījah
Ash Shakk
Tāza Khurmātū
Sadd Darband-i Khān
Pāveh
Hamadān
HAMADĀN
Al Fatḩah
Dāqūq
Kōrmōr
Khān Zūr
La'li Khān
Umm al Ţūz
Bayjī
Abū Rajāsh
Jabal Ḩamrīn
Ţūz Khurmātū
Sonqor
Tūysarkān
MARKAZĪ
Malḩāt
Bi'r Hazim
Sulaymān Beg
Kifrī
Sarqalā
Hawshqurah
Kangāvar
Malāyer
Tikrit
Şārīhah
Qaşr-e Shīrīn
Sar-e Pol-e Ẕahāb
KERMĀNSHĀH
Kermānshāh (Bākhtarān)
Nahāvand
Arāk
Rāwah
Hawbayn al Gharbīyah
'Ānah
Ān Nāhīyah
Umayqah
Ad Dawr
Mukayshīfah
Buḩayrat Shārī
Chāy Khānah
Amīn Ḩabīb
Khānaqīn
Naqnah
Tūreh
Al Fuḩaymī
Shahimah
Tārtasah
Sāmarrā'
Al 'Uzaym
As Sa'dīyah
Sarāy
Naft Khāneh
Eslāmābād
Borūjerd
Ālūs
Bardasah
Buḩayrat ath Tharthār
Tigris
Balad
Al Muqdādīyah
Ad Dujayl
Abū Ḩassawiyah
Al Khāliş
Makātū
Mandalī
Īlām
Do Rūd
Alīgūdarz
Marwānīyah
Wādī Ḩawrān
Al Baghdādī
Sahilīyah
Zāzīyah
Khān al Mashāhidah
Ba'qūbah
Balad Rūz
Kir Kush
Qazāniyah
Khorramābād
Maskhān
Hīt
Qaşr 'Amīj
'Ayn Zāzūh
'Aqabah
Euphrates
Sumayr al Muḩammad
Shaykh Ḩātim
Al Kāzimīyah
BAGHDĀD
Tursāq
Ḩāshimah
Kānī Sakht
Zurbāţīyah
Shandrūkh
Amīrābād
Mehrān
Darreh Shahr
LORESTĀN
Muḩammadiyah
Ar Ramādī
Al Fallūjah
Abū al Jīr
Buḩayrat Ḩabbānīyah
Khān Āzād
Badrah
ĪLĀM
R A Q
Abū Farūkh
Al Maḩmūdīyah
Sarābādī
Fallāḩ
Al 'Azīzīyah
Al Karmashiyah
Dehlorān
Daryācheh-ye Sadd-e Dez
Buḩayrat ar Razāzah
Al Iskandarīyah
Aş Şuwayrah
Sayyid 'Abid
Wādī al Ghadaf
Wādī Abū Jahal
Ar Raḩḩālīyah
Imām Ibn Hāshim
Al Musayyib
Muḩammad
'Alī
Hawr ash Shuwayjah
Shaykh 'Abid
Salmān Bin 'Arāzah
Andīmeshk
Dezfūl
Wādī Tibal
Qaşr Darwīshāh
Karbalā'
Babylon
Al Maḩāwīl
Al Ḩillah
An Nu'mānīyah
Shaykh Sa'd
Al Kūt
'Alī al Gharbī
Manzilīyah
Kawayt
Al Mardah
Al Hindīyah
Hawr as Sa'diyah
Qal'at Aḩmad
Qal'at Ḩusayh
Shūsh
Shushtar
Ukhaydhir
Ḩasan Ibn Ḩassūn
Najm al Ḩassūn
Al Hāshimīyah
'Abid 'Alī
Muwaffaqīyah
Mīr Ḩājī Khalīl
Al Ḩayy
Hawr ad Dujaylah
Ḩāmid Amīn
Shaykh Najm
Shaykh Fāris
Masjed Soleymān
Sha'īb Abū Ghār
Al Habbārīyah
Bi'r al Islām
Khān al Musallā
Wādī al Milh
Al Daghgharah
'Afak
Al 'Abd Allāh
Tarād al Kahf
Rūd-e Karkheh
At Taqţaqānah
'Athiyah
Al Kūfah
Ad Dīwānīyah
Tabrīr
Qal'at Sukkar
Hawr Umm al Baqar
Al 'Amārah
Hawr Umm Sawān
222
An Nukhayb
An Najaf
Abū Şukhayr
Ash Shāmīyah
Ar Rifā'ī
Al Maymūnah
Hawr al Ḩawīzah
Sūsangerd
KHUZESTĀN
Fayşalīyah
Qal'at Majnūnah
Al Kharrar
Askar
'Abtar
Al Makmin
Khān ar Ruḩbah
Qādisīyah
Ash Shanāfīyah
An Naşr
Qal'at Şāliḩ
Al Laşaf
Imām 'Abd Allāh
Ar Rumaythah
Shaţţ al Gharrāf
Kassārah
Ahvāz
Judayyidat Ḩāmir
Bi'r an Nişf
'Alī al Ḩassūnī
Ḩajjama
Ash Shaţrah
Hawr Ghamūkah
Rāshid
Nahrash
Kārūn
Bā'ij al Mahdī
Chamcham
Birkat Ḩāmid
As Samāwah
Al Baţḩā'
An Nāşirīyah
Al Qurnah
Al Barīt
Khāra'ib 'Abd al Karīm
Ghanūn as Sa'ūdī
Al Chabā'ish
Shanāwah
Al Ḩammām
Abū Qabr
Zahrat al Baţn
Abū Sudayrah
Thaqb Abū at Tubrah
Irjal ash Shaykhīyah
Ar Rijāb
'Ayn Ḩamūd
Sūq ash Shuyūkh
Tall al Laḩm
Hawr al Ḩammār
Ash Shāfī
Ad Dayr
Al Hārithah
Al Başrah (Basra)
Khorramshahr
Bandar-e Māhshahr
Al Ma'ānīyah
Abū Jasrah
Al Quşayr
Jalībah
Ar Raţāwī
Al Ţūbah
Abū al Khaşīb
Ābādān
Şaḩrā' al Ḩijārah
As Salmān
Ḩaddānīyah
Jalīb Shahāb
Ash Shāmīyah
Az Zubayr
Aş Şībah
Shaţţ al 'Arab
Al Lifīyah
Al 'Athāmīn
366m
Al Jil
Ar Ruḑaymah
Ghadīr Abū Raqrāq
Makhfar Al Buşayyah
Rumaylah
Şafwān
Umm Qaşr
Al Ḩajārah
Ash Shubrūm
Takhādīd
Thaqb al Ḩajj
Al Qash'ānīyah
Ar Rawḑatayn
Khawr 'Abd Allāh
Al Faw
Jazīrat Būbīyān
Sha'īb al Gharībīyah
'Uqlat aţ Ţudhaybah
KUWAIT
Jūn al Kuwayt
Faylakah
AL KUWAYT (KUWAIT)
Persian Gulf
Al Labbah
Rafḩah
Ar Rukhaymīyah
Al Ahţīyah
Al Ḩāniyah
Ad Dibdibah
Al Jahrā'
Al Kuwayt
Al Aḩmadī
Al Fuḩayḩīl
Bi'r Jurayb
Aţ Ţawal
As Sālimī
'Adhfā'
Nişab
Wādī al Bāţin
Aş Şubayḩīyah
Al Khīrān
ARABIA
AL ḨUDŪD ASH SHAMĀLĪYAH
Al Wafrā'
Al Arţāwīyah
Ra's al Khafjī
Ḩafar al Bāţin
Kurdistan
Kūhhā-ye Zāgros
Zagros Mountains

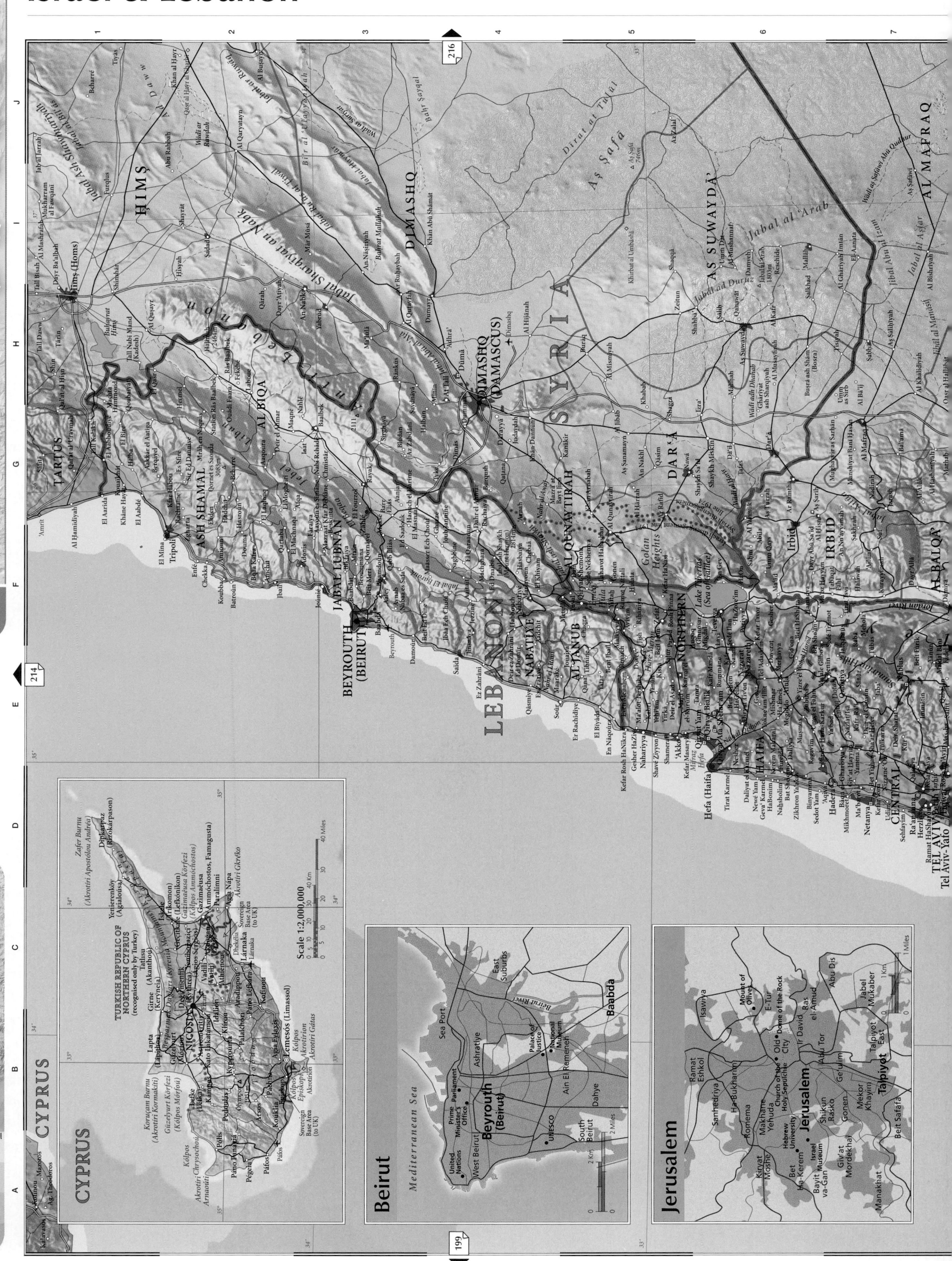

218

Scale 1:2,000,000

Beirut

Jerusalem

CYPRUS

Elevation

6000m
4000m
3000m
2000m
1000m
500m
250m
100m
Sea Level
-250m
-2000m
-4000m

Scale 1:1,500,000
(projection: Lambert Conformal Conic)

| | 0 | 10 | 20 | 30 | 40 | 50 Km |
| | 0 | 10 | 20 | 30 | 40 | 50 Miles |

Population

■ above 5 million ■ 1 million to 5 million ● 500,000 to 1 million
◉ 100,000 to 500,000 ⊕ 50,000 to 100,000 ○ 10,000 to 50,000 ∘ below 10,000

SAUDI ARABIA

AL JAWF

AZ-ZARQA'

AMMAN

JORDAN

Jibāl al 'Adhriyāt

Ma'ān

TABŪK

SAUDI ARABIA

AL KARAK

AT TAFĪLAH

Dead Sea

AL 'AQABAH

ISRAEL

JERUSALEM

West Bank

Gaza Strip
(Final status of Gaza Strip and
West Bank to be determined)

Mediterranean Sea

SOUTHERN

HaNegev

EGYPT

Gebel el Tih

Sinai

Gulf of Aqaba

19,686ft
13,124ft
9843ft
6562ft
3281ft
1640ft
820ft
328ft
Sea Level
-820ft
-6562ft
-13,124ft

Countries & regions: EGYPT, SAHARA, LIBYAN Plateau, SINAI, ISRAEL, JORDAN, IRAQ, KUWAIT, SAUDI ARABIA, SUDAN, NORTHERN KORDOFAN, SOUTHERN KORDOFAN, WHITE NILE, BLUE NILE, SINNAR, GEZIRA, KASSALA, GEDAREF, RIVER NILE, NORTHERN, ERITREA, ETHIOPIA, AMHARA, TIGRAY, OROMO, BENISHANGUL, AFAR, SOMALI, DJIBOUTI, SOMALILAND (not internationally recognized), YEMEN, NAJRAN, ASIR, AL BAHAH, MAKKAH, AL MADINAH, HAIL, AL QASIM, AR RIYAD, AL JAWF, TABUK, AL HUDUD ASH SHAMALIYAH

Water bodies: Red Sea, RED SEA, Gulf of Suez, Gulf of Aqaba, Lake Nasser, Nile, Blue Nile, White Nile, Bab el Mandeb, Golfe de Tadjoura, Gulf, Suez Canal

Deserts: Sahara el Gharbiya (Western Desert), Sahara el Sharqiya (Eastern Desert), Nubian Desert, Syrian Desert, An Nafud, Al Harrah, Ramlat as Sab'atayn, Ramlat Dahm, Najd, Arabian Peninsula

Cities & towns (Egypt/Sudan): CAIRO, El Giza, Helwan, Alexandria, Damanhur, Tanta, Kafr el Sheikh, Rashid (Rosetta), Dumyat (Damietta), Port Said, El Mansura, Zagazig, Benha, Shibin el Kôm, El Faiyûm, Beni Suef, Beni Mazar, El Minya, Mallawi, Asyut, Dairût, Abnûb, Sohâg, Girga, Qena, Luxor, Valley of the Kings, Isna, Idfu, Kôm Ombo, Aswân, Aswan High Dam, Marsa 'Alam, Quseir, Bûr Safâga, Hurghada, Gharib, Ghârib, Ras Gharib, El Tûr, Sharm el Sheikh, Suez, El 'Arish, Gaza, Gaza Strip, Abu Simbel, El Kharga, The Great Oasis, Qasr Farâfra, Baris, Mût, Abû Balâs, El Qasr, Qara, El 'Alamein, Ras el-Kanâyis, Qâ'ir, Monkhafad el Qattâra (Qattara Depression)

Sudan: KHARTOUM, Omdurman, Khartoum North, Wad Medani, El Obeid, Kosti, Rabak, Sennar, Singa, Ed Damazin, Gedaref, Kassala, Atbara, Ed Damer, Berber, Shendi, Dongola, Merowe, Karima, Abu Hamed, Wadi Halfa, Port Sudan, Suakin, Tokar, Haiya, Sinkat, Halaib, Muhammad Qol, Dunqunab, Dongola, El Khandaq, Ed Debba, Korti

Saudi Arabia: AR RIYAD (RIYADH), JIDDAH (JEDDA), Makkah (Mecca), Al Madinah (Medina), Ta'if, Tabuk, Ha'il, Buraydah, 'Unayzah, Yanbu' al Bahr, Rabigh, Al Lith, Al Qunfudhah, Al Birk, Abha, Khamis Mushayt, Jizan, Najran, Sabya, Sa'dah, Hafar al Batin, Al Khari, Layla, As Sulayyil

Yemen/Eritrea/Ethiopia: SAN'A' (SANA), Al Hudaydah (Hodeida), Aden ('Adan), Ta'izz, Ibb, Dhamar, Rada', Zabid, ASMARA, Massawa, Keren, Mek'ele, Gonder, Bahir Dar, Debre Mark'os, Debre Tabor, Lalibela, Adwa, Aksum, DJIBOUTI, Berbera

Elevation scale: 6000m, 4000m, 3000m, 2000m, 1000m, 500m, 250m, 100m, Sea Level, -250m, -2000m, -4000m

Scale 1:8,000,000
(projection: Lambert Conformal Conic)
0 25 50 75 100 125 150 175 200 Km
0 25 50 75 100 125 150 175 200 Miles
Population
above 5 million
1 million to 5 million
500,000 to 1 million
100,000 to 500,000
50,000 to 100,000
10,000 to 50,000
below 10,000
H I J K L M N
224
IRAN
AFGHANISTAN
PAKISTAN
BALUCHISTAN
KHORĀSĀN-E JANŪBĪ
NĪMRŪZ
HELMAND
KANDAHAR
Quetta
Karāchi
Esfahān
Yazd
Kermān
Shīrāz
Zāhedān
Bandar-e 'Abbās
HORMOZGĀN
SĪSTĀN VA BALŪCHESTĀN
FĀRS
BŪSHEHR
KHŪZESTĀN
Ahvāz
Basrah
AL KUWAYT (KUWAIT)
Bandar-e Būshehr
Persian Gulf
BAHRAIN
AL MANĀMAH (MANAMA)
QATAR
AD DAWHAH (DOHA)
ABŪ ZABĪ (ABU DHABI)
Dubayy (Dubai)
Ash Shāriqah
Ra's al Khaymah
Al Fujayrah
UNITED ARAB EMIRATES
Strait of Hormuz
Makran Coast
Gulf of Oman
MASQAṬ (MUSCAT)
OMAN
Tropic of Cancer
ARABIA
ASH SHARQĪYAH
Ar Rub 'al Khālī (Empty Quarter)
Jazīrat Maşīrah
Arabian Sea
Jiddat al Ḥarāsīs
Jabal al Qamar
Al Mahrah
Ḥaḍramawt
Al Mukallā
Gulf of Aden
Suquṭrā (Socotra)
SOMALIA
SANAAG
BARI
234
288
Dubai
Persian Gulf
Sharjah
Al Hamriya
Muhaisnah North
Sharjah International Airport
Al Baraha
Al Nasr Square
Dubai International Airport
Al Twar
Art Centre
Dubayy (Dubai)
Al Rigga
Dubai Creek
Jaddat
Trade Centre
Zoo
Al Garhoud
Nadd Al Hamar
The Palm Jumeirah
Burj Al Arab Hotel
Al Wasl
Al Quoz
0 5 Km
0 5 Miles
ASIA
221
19,686ft
13,124ft
9843ft
6562ft
3281ft
1640ft
820ft
328ft
Sea Level
-820ft
-6562ft
-13,124ft

South & Central Asia

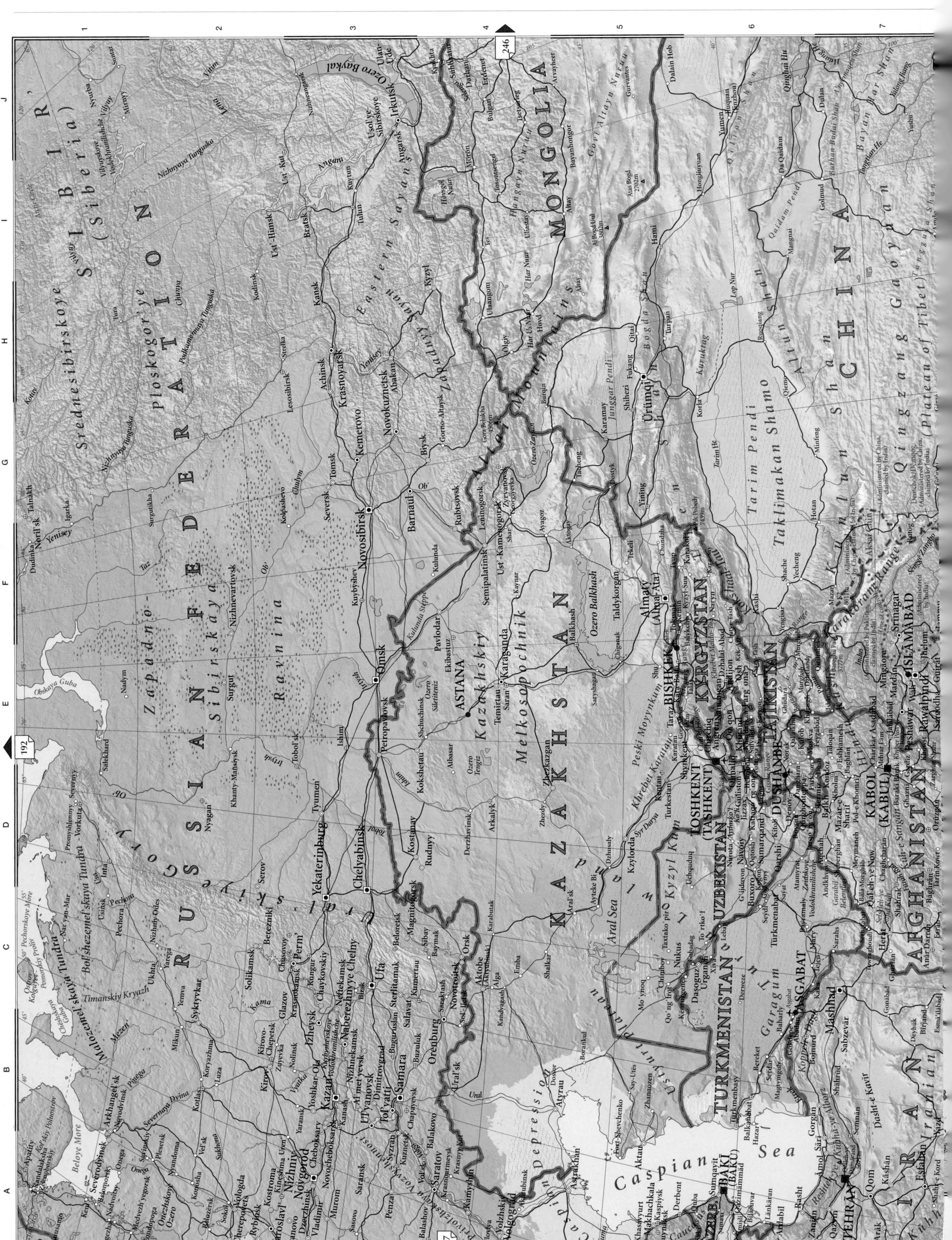
RUSSIAN FEDERATION
KAZAKHSTAN
MONGOLIA
CHINA
UZBEKISTAN
TURKMENISTAN
KYRGYZSTAN
TAJIKISTAN
AFGHANISTAN
IRAN
ASTANA
BISHKEK
DUSHANBE
TOSHKENT (TASHKENT)
ASGABAT
KABUL
ISLAMABAD
TEHRAN
BAKI (BAKU)
Caspian Sea
Aral Sea
Ozero Baykal
Ozero Balkhash
Zapadno-Sibirskaya Ravnina
Sredne-sibirskoye Ploskogor'ye
Ural'skiye Gory
Tarim Pendi
Taklimakan Shamo
Kazakhskiy Melkosopochnik
Qingzang Gaoyuan (Plateau of Tibet)
246
192
197
6000m
4000m
3000m
2000m
1000m
500m
250m
100m
Sea Level
-250m
-2000m
-4000m

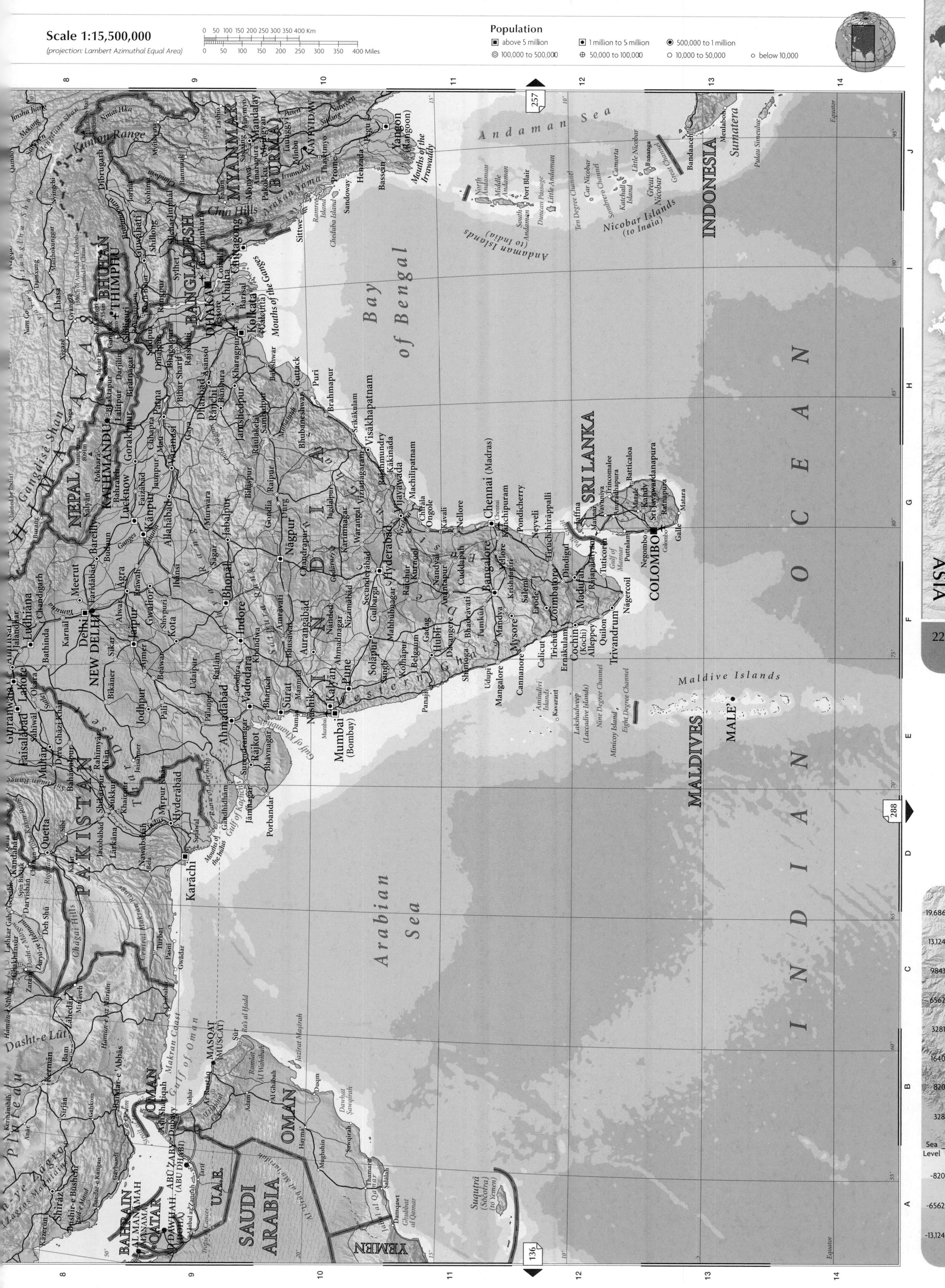

Scale 1:15,500,000
(projection: Lambert Azimuthal Equal Area)

0 50 100 150 200 250 300 350 400 Km
0 50 100 150 200 250 300 350 400 Miles

Population

■ above 5 million ▣ 1 million to 5 million ◉ 500,000 to 1 million
◎ 100,000 to 500,000 ⊡ 50,000 to 100,000 ○ 10,000 to 50,000 ∘ below 10,000

Andaman Sea

Bay
of Bengal

INDIAN
OCEAN

Arabian
Sea

I N D I A

PAKISTAN

NEPAL

BHUTAN
THIMPHU

BANGLADESH
DHAKA

MYANMAR
(BURMA)

SRI LANKA
COLOMBO

MALDIVES
MALE'

INDONESIA
Sumatera

OMAN
MASQAT
(MUSCAT)

SAUDI
ARABIA

U.A.E.
ABU ZABY
(ABU DHABI)

QATAR

BAHRAIN

YEMEN

NEW DELHI
Delhi

Mumbai
(Bombay)

Kolkata

Chennai (Madras)

Bangalore

Hyderabad

Karāchi

Maldive Islands

Nicobar Islands
(to India)

Andaman Islands
(to India)

19,686ft
13,124ft
9843ft
6562ft
3281ft
1640ft
820ft
328ft
Sea
Level
-820ft
-6562ft
-13,124ft

Kazakhstan

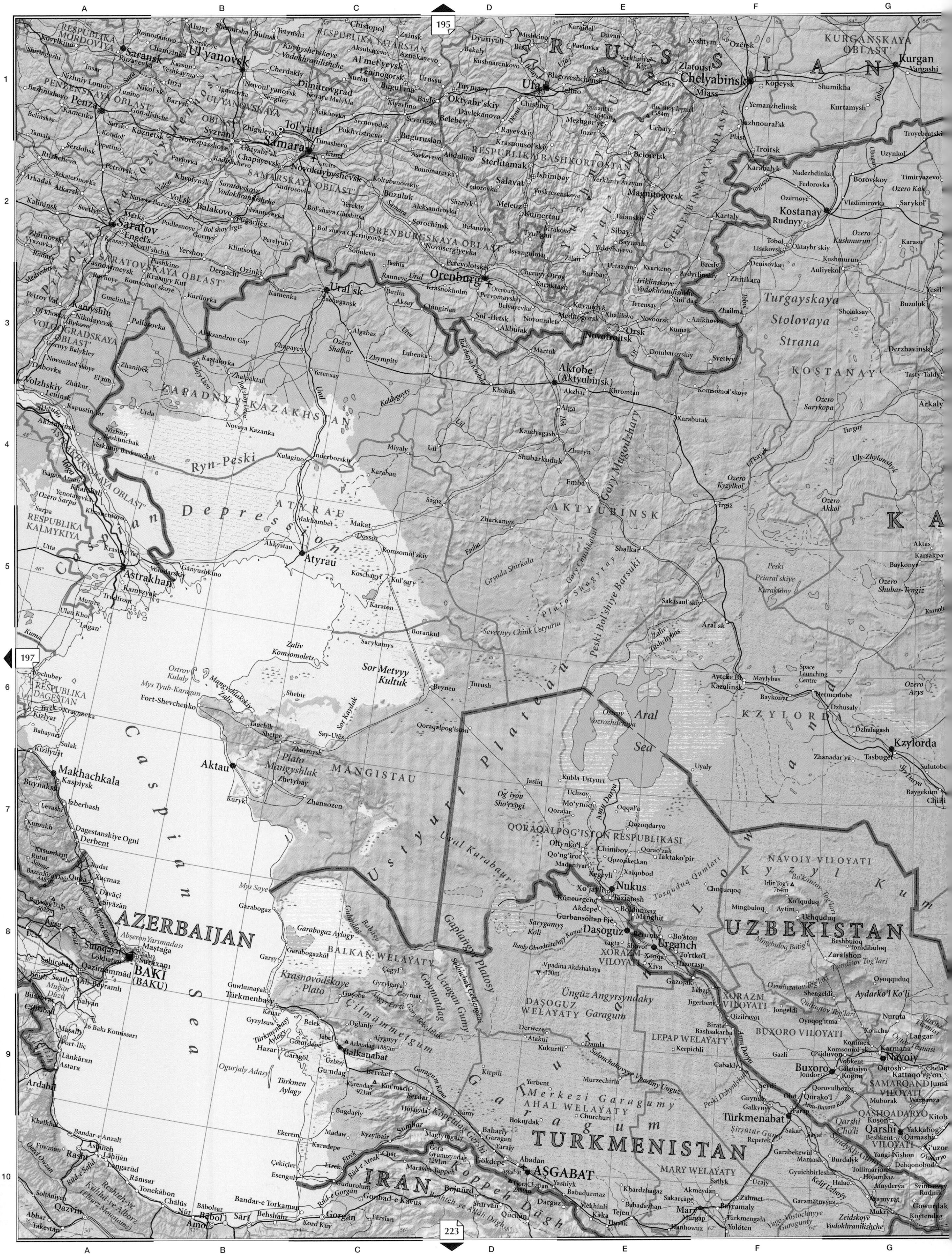

195

197

223

RUSSIAN

RESPUBLIKA MORDOVIYA

PENZENSKAYA OBLAST'

Penza

RESPUBLIKA KATARSTAN

RESPUBLIKA BASHKORTOSTAN

Ufa

Chelyabinsk

KURGANSKAYA OBLAST'

Kurgan

Ul'yanovsk

Dimitrovgrad

Tol'yatti

Samara

Novokuybyshevsk

Saratov

'Engel's

SARATOVSKAYA OBLAST'

VOLGOGRADSKAYA OBLAST'

Ural'sk

Orenburg

ORENBURGSKAYA OBLAST'

Orsk

Novotroitsk

Aktobe
(Aktyubinsk)

ZAPADNYY KAZAKHSTAN

Kostanay
Rudnyy

Turgayskaya Stolovaya Strana

KOSTANAY

Derzhavinsk

Ryn-Peski

Caspian Depression

ATYRAU

AKTYUBINSK

Gory Mugodzhary

KA

Astrakhan

RESPUBLIKA KALMYKIYA

RESPUBLIKA DAGESTAN

Makhachkala

Atyrau

Makat

Dossor

Turgay

KZYLORDA

Space Launching Centre

Kazalinsk

Baykonyr

Sor Metvyy Kultuk

Beyneu

Fort-Shevchenko

Aktau

Plato Mangyshlak

MANGISTAU

Ustyurt Plateau

Qoraqalpog'iston

Aral Sea

Ostrov Vozrozhdeniya

Nukus

Kzylorda

Chiili

Low land

AZERBAIJAN

BAKI
(BAKU)

Sumqayıt

Caspian Sea

BALKAN WELAYATY

QORAQALPOG'ISTON RESPUBLIKASI

Daşoguz

Urganch
XORAZM VILOYATI
Xiva

UZBEKISTAN

Kyzylkum

NAVOIY VILOYATI

Buxoro

Navoiy

SAMARQAND VILOYATI

Garagum

DAŞOGUZ WELAYATY

AHAL WELAYATY

Türkmenabat

XORAZM VILOYATI

LEPAP WELAYATY

BUXORO VILOYATI

QASHQADARYO VILOYATI

Qarshi

TURKMENISTAN

Aşgabat

IRAN

MARY WELAYATY

Mary

Central Asia

226
215
223
Atyrau
ATYRAU
Kul'sary
Karaton
Borankul
Sarykamys
Zaliv Komsomolets
Ostrov Kulaly
Sor Mertvyy Kultuk
Sor Kaydak
Beyneu
Turush
Shebir
Port-Shevchenko
Say-Utes
Shetpe
Zharmysh
Aktau
Plato Mangyshlak
Zhetybay
Zhanaozen
Kuryk
MANGISTAU
Ustyurt Plateau
Gryada Shirkala
Shalkar
AKTYUBINSK
Severnyy Chink Ustyurta
Sakasaul'skiy
Aral'sk
Zaliv Tushchybas
Peski Priaral'skiye Karakumy
K A Z A
Ozero Shubar-Tengiz
Ayteke Bi
Kazalinsk
Baykonyr
Dermentobe
Syr Darya
Dzhusaly
Dzhalagash
Kzylorda
Tasbuget
Zhanadar'ya
KYZLORDA
Aral Sea
Ostrov Vozrozhdeniya
Qoraqalpog'iston
Kubla-Ustyurt
Jasliq
Uchsoy
Mo'ynoq
Amu Darya
Oqqal'a
Qorajar
QORAQALPOG'ISTON RESPUBLIKASI
Qozoqdaryo
Oltynko'l
Chimboy
Qorao'zak
Taxtako'pir
Qo'ng'irot
Qozonketkan
Kegeyli
Xalqobod
Shumanay
Nukus
Xo'jayli
Taxiatosh
Köneürgenç
Boldumsaz
Akdepe
Gubadag
Gurbansoltan Eje
Daşoguz
Tagta
Urganch
Xiva
Hazorasp
Pitnak
Beruniy
Bo'ston
Türtkül
Mang'it
Chuqurqoq
Tosquduq Qumlari
Turan Lowland
UZBEKISTAN
Kyzyl
NAVOIY VILOYATI
Mingbuloq
Uchquduq
Aytim
Beshbuloq
Tomdibuloq
Zarafshon
Sarygamyş Köli
DAŞOGUZ WELAÝATY
Vpadina Akdzhakaya -130m
Üngüz Angyrsyndaky Garagum
Gazojak
Lebap
Tuproqqal'a
Jigerbent
Qizilravot
Birata
Bashsakarba
BUXORO VILOYATI
G'ijduvon
Romiton
Vobkent
Buxoro
Kogon
Navoiy
Karmana
Mys Soye
Garabogaz
Garabogazköl
Garabogaz Aylagy
Garşy
Krasnovodskoye Plato
Guwlumaýak
Türkmenbaşy
Gyzylsuw
Kenar
Belek
Oglanly
Jebel
Arlandag 1880m
Balkanabat
Hazar
Garagöl
Uzboy
BALKAN WELAÝATY
Gumdag
Kürendag 971m
Bereket
Çilmämmetgum
Ogurjaly Adasy
Türkmen Aylagy
Caspian Sea
Derweze
Atakui
Kukurtli
Damla
Kerpichli
Kirpili
Merkezi Garagumy
Murzechirla
Yerbent
TURKMENISTAN
Garagum
Bokurdak
Churchuri
Serdar
Hojagala
Bugdaýly
Bamy
Baharly
Garaboyaz
Madaw
Karadepe
Kyzylbair
Gora Gyunuzyndag 1291m
Könekesir
Garagan
Gökdepe
Abadan
AHAL WELAÝATY
Aşgabat
Gora Chapan 2889m
Çekiçler
Esenguly
Gudurolum
Etrek
Köpetdag
Kopet Dagh
LEBAP WELAÝATY
Türkmenabat
Sakar
Sayat
Repetek
Sandykly Gumy
MARY WELAÝATY
Mary
Bayramaly
Murgap
Tejen
Sarahs
Serhetabat
Yolöten
Saýat
Yugo-Vostochnyye Garagumy
Garabil Belentligi
Bandar-e Torkaman
Gorgān
Bābol
Sārī
Āmol
Behshahr
GOLESTĀN
Gonbad-e Kāvūs
MĀZANDARĀN
Bojnūrd
Shīrvān
Qūchān
KHORĀSĀN-E SHEMĀLĪ
Reshteh-ye Kūhhā-ye Alborz (Elburz Mountains)
Shāhrūd
Dāmghān
Semnān
SEMNĀN
Mashhad
Neyshābūr
Sabzevār
Kashaf Rūd
I R A N
Dasht-e Kavīr
Kāshmar
Torbat-e Heydarīyeh
Torbat-e Jām
KHORĀSĀN-E RAZAVĪ
Kavīr-e Namak
Tāybād
Gonābād
Ferdows
Qā'en
Ṭabas
YAZD
EṢFAHĀN
Anarak
Jandaq
Nā'in
Herāt
HERĀT
Eslām Qal'eh
Kūhestān
Ghūrīān
Zendeh Jān
Namakzar
Selseleh-ye Safīd Kūh
Qal'eh-ye Now
Qādes
BĀDGHĪS
AFGH
Meymaneh
FĀRYĀB
Andkhvoy
Dowlatābād
Bālā Morghāb
Chaghcharān
GHOWR
Shahrak
Qal'eh Shahr
Kūh-e Chehel Abdālān
A
B
C
D
E
F
G
1
2
3
4
5
6
7
8
9
10
6000m
4000m
3000m
2000m
1000m
500m
250m
100m
Sea Level
-250m
-2000m
-4000m

Scale 1:4,750,000
(projection: Lambert Conformal Conic)
0 20 40 60 80 100 Km
0 20 40 60 80 100 Miles
Population
above 5 million
1 million to 5 million
500,000 to 1 million
100,000 to 500,000
50,000 to 100,000
10,000 to 50,000
below 10,000
227
231
238
ASIA
229
19,686ft
13,124ft
9843ft
6562ft
3281ft
1640ft
820ft
328ft
Sea Level
-820ft
-6562ft
-13,124ft
KARAGANDA
Zhezkazgan
Satpayev
Baykonyr
Karsakpay
Aktas
Atasu
Koktas
Moyynty
Balkhash
Konyrat
Gul'shat
Sayak
Aktogay
VOSTOCHNYY KAZAKHSTAN
Ozero Sasykkol'
Urdzhar
Taskesken
Zhanaortalyk
Gory Agat 464m
Akkense
KHSTAN
Ozero Karakoyyn
Ozero Arys
Betpak-Dala
Saryshagan
Tasaral
Ozero Balkhash
Karaoy
Peski Saryyesik-Atyrau
ALMATY
Ushtobe
Taldykorgan
Karabulak
Tekeli
Balpyk Bi
Lepsy
Matay
Aksu
Sarkand
Dzhansugurov
Kabanbay
Ozero Alakol'
Üch-Aral
Koshkarkol'
Kopbirlik
Mynaral
Chiganak
Burubaytal
Akkol'
Bakanas
Peski Taukum
Chu-Iliyskiye Gory
Step' Zhusandala
Balkhakty
Aynabulak
Saryozek
Rudnichnyy
Kugaly
Konyrolen
Khorgos
Koktal
Zharkent
Huocheng
Sayram Hu
Wenquan
Dzhungarskiy Alatau
Kapchagayskoye Vodokhranilishche
Kapchagay
Shengel'dy
Zhetigen
Malovodnoye
Talgar
Yesik
Chilik
Charyn
Chundzha
Kol'zhat
Almaty (Alma-Ata)
Boralday
Uzunagach
Fabrichnyy
Otar
Zhalanash
Tuyuk
Kegen
Khrebet Ketmen
Narynkol
Tekes
Ravnina Dar'yalyktakyr
Zhuantobe
Sulutobe
Bakyrly
Baygekum
Chiili
Zhanakorgan
Syr Darya
Suzak
Peski Moyynkum
ZHAMBYL
Karaboget
Moyynkum
Khantau
Chokpar
Shu
Sholakkorgan
Saudakent
Uyuk
Khrebet Karatau
Kentau
Zhanatas
Akkol'
Turkestan
Staroikan
Karatau
YUZHNYY
Shayan
Kum
Shaulder
Taraz
Koksaray
Temirlanovka
KAZAKHSTAN
Karabulak
Arys
Shymkent
Lenger
Bairkum
Step' Nardara
BISHKEK
Kara-Balta
Tokmak
Kant
Kemin
Merke
Kulan
Oytal
Kaindy
Sokuluk
Chuy
Korday
Tatti
Kirghiz Range
CHUYSKAYA OBLAST'
Bordunskiy
Kungei Ala Tau
Ak-Tyuz
Grigor'yevka
Cholpon-Ata
Kuturgu
Tyup
Chok-Tal
Novovoznesenovka
Dzhergalan
Taldy-Suu
Ozero Issyk-Kul'
Karakol
Balykchy
Orto-Tokoy
Kadzhi-Say
Ak-Terek
Kyzyl-Suu
ISSYK-KUL'SKAYA OBLAST'
Barskoon
Enil'chek
Khrebet Terskey Ala-Too
Tien Shan
Pik Khan Tengri/ Hantengri Feng 6995m
Pik Pobedy/ Tomür Feng 7439m
Talas
Pokrovka
Kyzyl-Adyr
Klyuchevka
Leninpol'
Chat-Bazar
Khrebet Talasskiy Alatau
Gora Manas 4482m
TALASSKAYA OBLAST'
Toktogul
Toktogul'skoye Vodokhranilishche
Susamyr
Tyugel'-Say
Chaek
Kochkorka
Cholpon
Sary-Bulak
KYRGYZSTAN
Khrebet Moldo-Too
Naryn
Kazarman
Kek-Dzhar
Karakol
Kara-Say
Ak-Shyyrak
Bedel Pass 4741m
Kokshaal-Tau
NARYNSKAYA OBLAST'
Dostuk
At-Bashy
Chatyr-Tashi
Kosh-Dëbë
Gora Ak-Tash 4718m
Ozero Chatyr-Köl
Torugart Pass 3752m
Kek-Aygyr
Kara-Köl
Dzhalal-Abad
DZHALAL-ABADSKAYA OBLAST'
Ferganskiy Khrebet
Kara-Kul'
Tash-Kumyr
Mayluu-Suu
Chatkal Range
Korgon-Dëbë
Dzhany-Bazar
Terek-Say
Ala-Buka
Sumsar
Kosonsoy
Kek-Tash
Kok-Yangak
Chirchiq
Saryagash
TOSHKENT (TASHKENT)
TOSHKENT VILOYATI
Iskandar
Ghazalkent
Yangiobod
Angren
Yangiyo'l
To'ytepa
Chardara
Chardarinskoye Vodokhranilishche
Aydarko'l Ko'li
Darvoza
Zhetysay
Sirdaryo
Olmaliq
Ohangaron
Chinoz
SIRDARYO VILOYATI
Kuramin Range
Namangan
NAMANGAN VILOYATI
Uchqo'rg'on
ANDIJON VILOYATI
Andijon
Shahrixon
Fergana Valley
Marg'ilon
Farg'ona
FARG'ONA VILOYATI
Quqon
Quvasoy
Asaka
Osh
Uzgen
Bek-Dzhar
Gul'cha
OSHSKAYA OBLAST'
Kara-Kul'dzha
Taldy-Suu
Oy-Tal
Kek-Art
Eski-Nookat
Kyzyl-Kiya
Sopu-Korgon
Adrasmon
Besharik
Taboshar
Obanbori Qayroqqum
Khujand
Guliston
Gagarin
Yangiyer
Xovos
Paxtakor
Jizzax
JIZZAX VILOYATI
Nurota
Forish
Do'stlik
Yangiqishloq
Langar
Nurota Tizmasi
Oqtov Tizmasi
Qo'shrabot
Qo'ytosh
Zarbdor
Ishtixon
Chelak
G'allaorol
Kattaqo'rg'on
Oqtosh
Juma
Ingichka
Samarqand
SAMARQAND VILOYATI
Urgut
Panjakent
QASHQADARYO VILOYATI
Kitob
Shahrisabz
Yakkabog'
Qarshi
Beshkent
Qamashi
Yangi-Nishon
G'uzor
Dehqonobod
Derbent
Boysun
SURXONDARYO VILOYATI
Sayrob
Sherobod
Sho'rchi
Qumqo'rg'on
Denov
Sariosiyo
Qarluq
Tursunzoda
Xufar
Qo'rg'ontepa
Jarqo'rg'on
Köytendag
Gowurdak
Termiz
Qarqin
Shur Tappeh
Kalininobod
Vakhsh
Kolkhozobod
Farkhor
Moskva
Panj
Shahrtuz
Dusti
Amu Darya
Zarafshon
Turkestan Range
Qatorkŭhi Zarafshon
Gissar Range
Ayni
Anzob
Pastigav
Shahriston
Isfana
Zomin
Savat
Oroteppa
Ghafurov
Kanibodom
Isfara
Batken
BATKENSKAYA OBLAST'
Sulyukta
Khaydarkan
Vorukh
Frunze
Vodil
Alai Range
Karamyk
Daroot-Korgon
Zaalayskiy Khrebet
Lenin Peak 7134m
Jirgatol
Pildon
Tojikobod
Gharm
Navobod
Komsomolobod
TAJIKISTAN
DUSHANBE
Obigarm
Pichandar
Hisor
Kofarnihon
Norak
Yovon
Danghara
Dahana
Kulob
Vahdat
Tavildara
Khingov
Qullai Revolyutsiya 6974m
Bunay
Vanj
Kalaikhum
Qatorkŭhi Yazgulom
Leningrad
Dashtijum
Qatorkŭhi Darvoz
Bartang
Rushon
Qatorkŭhi Rushon
Ghund
Shazud
Dzhelondy
Khorugh
Barsem
Qatorkŭhi Shughnon
Qatorkŭhi Shokhdara
Qatorkŭhi Alichuri Shimoli
Qatorkŭhi Alichuri Janubi
Alichur
Murghob
Kŭli Sarez
Uzbel Shankou 4655m
Qarakŭl
Sarykol Range
Rangkul
Tokhtamish
Qizilrabot
Murgab
Langar
Vrang
Ishkoshim
Nicholas Range
Little Pamir
Khandud
Kilik Pass 4827m
Mintaka Pass 4709m
Khunjerab Pass 4700m
Baroghil Pass 3777m
Ulugqat
Kashi
Artux
Shule
Shufu
Yopurga
Jiashi
Bachu
Sanchakou
Yarkant He
Yengisar
Akto
Kongur Shan 7649m
Muztagata 7509m
Yarkant He
Shache
Zepu
Yecheng
Pishan
Taxkorgan
Kokyar
Akmeqit
XINJIANG UYGUR ZIZHIQU
Tarim Pendi
Taklimakan Shamo
Markit
CHINA
Aksu
Aksu He
Wensu
Wushi
Akqi
Kalpin
Sugun
Baykurt
Kunlun Shan
Mazar
Xaidulla
Dahongliutan
Karakax He
Aksai Chin (Administered by China, claimed by India)
Karakoram Pass 5575m
Rimo Muztāgh
Siachen Muztāgh
Karakoram Range
Gasherbrum 8068m
K2 8611m
(Administered by China, claimed by India)
Hunza
Dastegil Sar 7885m
Rakaposhi 7788m
Gilgit
PAKISTAN
Indus
Astor
Nanga Parbat 8126m
(Administered by Pakistan, claimed by India)
(line of control)
Kargil
Ladakh Range
Zanskar Range
JAMMU AND KASHMIR
Srinagar
Sopur
Baramula
Gulmarg
Anantnag
Nun Kun 7135m
(Administered by India)
Pir Panjal Range
Kishtwar
Chenab
Muzaffarabad
Lake Wular
Shyok
Bangong Co
Pamzal
Hindu Kush
Tirich Mir 7708m
Chitral
Drosh
Lawarai Pass 3118m
Babusar Pass 4173m
NORTH-WEST FRONTIER PROVINCE
Mingaora
Kamdeysh
Barikowt
NURESTAN
KONAR
Asmar
Asadabad
Jalalabad
NANGARHAR
Achin
Khyber Pass 1080m
Peshawar
Charsadda
Nowshera
Mardan
Tarbela Reservoir
Attock City
Fatehjang
Hazro
Wah
Haripur
Murree
Abbottabad
Mansehra
Battagram
Havelian
ISLAMABAD
Rawalpindi
Kahuta
Kohat
Parachinar
Tangi
Mazar-e Sharif
Balkh
JOWZJAN
BALKH
Sheberghan
Aqchah
Kholm
KONDOZ
Kondoz
Khanabad
Taloqan
Farkhar
TAKHAR
Eshkamesh
BADAKHSHAN
Feyzabad
Eshkashem
Aybak
Baghlan
Pol-e Khomri
BAGHLAN
Andarab
SAMANGAN
Tokzar
Sar-e Pol
SAR-E POL
Lar Gerd
Tagow Bay
Chiras
Marghi
Quil-Qala
PANJSHIR
Bazarak
KAPISA
Mahmud-e Raqi
LAGHMAN
Charikar
PARVAN
ANISTAN
BAMIAN
Bamian
Kuh-e Baba
KABOL (KABUL)
Bagrami
Gardan Diwal
Band-e Bayan
Meydan Shahr
Paghman
VARDAK
Panjab
DAIKONDI
Tagab
LOWGAR
Pol-e Alam
Baraki Barak
Ali Khel
Hasan Khel
PAKTIA
Gardiz
Ghazni
GHAZNI
Nili
Sharan
Mehtar Lam
Darya-ye Kabul

Afghanistan & Pakistan

TURKMENISTAN
UZBEKISTAN
DUSHANBE
ASGABAT
AHAL WELAÝATY
LEBAP WELAÝATY
MARY WELAÝATY
Koppeh Dagh
GOLESTĀN
KHORĀSĀN-E SHEMĀLĪ
Gorgān
Mashhad
SEMNĀN
Dasht-e Kavīr
KHORĀSĀN-E RAŽAVĪ
Garagum Kanaly
Yugo-Vostochnyye Garagumy
Garabil Belentligi
JOWZJĀN
BALKH
Mazār-e Sharīf
KONDOZ
SAMANGĀN
FĀRYĀB
SAR-E POL
BĀDGHĪS
Qal'eh-ye Now
Selseleh-ye Band-e Torkestān
AFGHANISTAN
BĀMIĀN
PARVĀN
Herāt
HERĀT
Selseleh-ye Safīd Kūh
GHOWR
Band-e Bayān
DĀIKONDĪ
VARDAK
GHAZNĪ
Kūh-e Chehel Abdālān
Kūh-e Sangān
IRAN
YAZD
Iranian Plateau
KHORĀSĀN-E JANŪBĪ
Dasht-e Lūt
FARAH
Dasht-e Khāsh
ORŪZGĀN
ZĀBOL
PAKTĪKĀ
Kandahār
KANDAHĀR
Toba Kākar Range
Dasht-e Mārgow
NĪMRŪZ
HELMAND
Rīgestān
Quetta
Kermān
KERMĀN
Zāhedān
Dasht-e Gowd-e Zereh
Chāgai Hills
Dasht-i Tāhlāb
PAKISTAN
SĪSTĀN VA BALŪCHESTĀN
BALUCHISTAN
Central Brahui Range
HORMOZGĀN
Bandar-e Abbās
Strait of Hormuz
OMAN
U.A.E.
Makrān
Siāhān Range
Central Makrān Range
Kirthar Range
SIND
Makran Coast
Gulf of Oman
Hyderābād
Karāchi
MASQAT (MUSCAT)
Arabian Sea
Mouths of the Indus
6000m
4000m
3000m
2000m
1000m
500m
250m
100m
Sea Level
-250m
-2000m
-4000m

Scale 1:5,250,000
(projection: Lambert Conformal Conic)
0 25 50 75 100 125 150 175 200 Km
0 25 50 75 100 125 150 175 200 Miles
Population
above 5 million
1 million to 5 million
500,000 to 1 million
100,000 to 500,000
50,000 to 100,000
10,000 to 50,000
below 10,000
238
233
234
ASIA
TAJIKISTAN
Pamirs
Taklimakan Shamo
XINJIANG UYGUR ZIZHIQU
Kunlun Shan
Hindu Kush
Karakoram Range
CHINA
Qingzang Gaoyuan (Plateau of Tibet)
XIZANG ZIZHIQU (TIBET)
Gangdisê Shan
HIMALAYAS
JAMMU AND KASHMIR (Administered by India)
(Line of Control)
Aksai Chin
NORTH-WEST FRONTIER PROVINCE
PUNJAB
HIMACHAL PRADESH
UTTARAKHAND
HARYANA
RĀJASTHĀN
UTTAR PRADESH
MADHYA PRADESH
GUJARĀT
NEPAL
FAR WESTERN
MID WESTERN
INDIA
Thar Desert
Vindhya Range
Aravalli Range
Rann of Kachchh
ISLĀMĀBĀD
Rawalpindi
Peshāwar
Lahore
Faisalābād
Multān
Gujrānwāla
Srīnagar
Jammu
Amritsar
Ludhiāna
Chandigarh
Shimla
Dehra Dūn
Delhi
NEW DELHI
Meerut
Ghāziābād
Āgra
Jaipur
Lucknow
Kānpur
Gwalior
Bhopāl
Jodhpur
Ajmer
Kota
Udaipur
Bīkaner
Bareilly
Allahābād
K2 8611m
Nanga Parbat 8126m
Tirich Mir 7708m
Nanda Devi 7817m
Tropic of Cancer
19,686ft
13,124ft
9843ft
6562ft
3281ft
1640ft
820ft
328ft
Sea Level
-820ft
-6562ft
-13,124ft

Northern India, Nepal & Bangladesh

A B C D E F G
1 2 3 4 5 6 7 8 9 10
229
230
234
AFGHANISTAN
PAKISTAN
KĀBOL (KABUL)
ISLĀMĀBĀD
Rawalpindi
Peshāwar
Lahore
Faisalābād
Gujrānwala
Multān
Quetta
Hyderābād
Karāchi
Sukkur
Bahāwalpur
Srinagar
JAMMU AND KASHMIR
XINJIANG UYGUR
Aksai Chin
HIMĀCHAL PRADESH
PUNJAB
HARYĀNA
UTTARAKHAND
FAR WESTERN
UTTAR PRADESH
DELHI
NEW DELHI
Delhi
Chandigarh
Ludhiāna
Amritsar
Shimla
Dehra Dūn
Meerut
Āgra
Lucknow
Kānpur
Allahābād
Bareilly
Gwalior
Jhānsi
RĀJASTHĀN
Jaipur
Jodhpur
Bīkāner
Ajmer
Kota
Udaipur
Thar Desert
SIND
BALUCHISTĀN
NORTH WEST FRONTIER PROVINCE
GUJARĀT
Ahmadābād
Vadodara
Sūrat
Rājkot
Kāthiāwār Peninsula
Gulf of Kachchh
Gulf of Khambhāt
Rann of Kachchh
Tropic of Cancer
Mouths of the Indus
MADHYA PRADESH
Bhopāl
Indore
Jabalpur
Ujjain
MAHĀRĀSHTRA
Nāgpur
Mumbai (Bombay)
Pune
Nāshik
Aurangābād
DAMĀN AND DIU
DĀDRA AND NAGAR HAVELI
ANDHRA PRADESH
Raipur
Arabian Sea
Hindu Kush
Karakoram Range
Ladakh Range
Zaskar Range
Sulaimān Range
Toba Kākar Range
Central Brahui Range
Kīrthar Range
Arāvalli Range
Vindhya Range
Sātpura Range
Ajanta Range
Indus
Chenāb
Jhelum
Sutlej
Yamuna
Ganges
Narmada
Chambal
K2 8611m
Nanga Parbat 8126m
Rakaposhi 7788m
Tirich Mir 7708m
Nanda Devi 7817m
6000m
4000m
3000m
2000m
1000m
500m
250m
100m
Sea Level
-250m
-2000m
-4000m

Scale 1:6,250,000
(projection: Lambert Conformal Conic)

0 25 50 75 100 125 150 175 200 Km
0 25 50 75 100 125 150 175 200 Miles

Population
- ■ above 5 million
- ◉ 100,000 to 500,000
- ■ 1 million to 5 million
- ⊕ 50,000 to 100,000
- ◉ 500,000 to 1 million
- ○ 10,000 to 50,000
- ◦ below 10,000

256

19,686ft
13,124ft
9843ft
6562ft
3281ft
1640ft
820ft
328ft
Sea
Level
-820ft
-6562ft
-13,124ft

Southern India & Sri Lanka

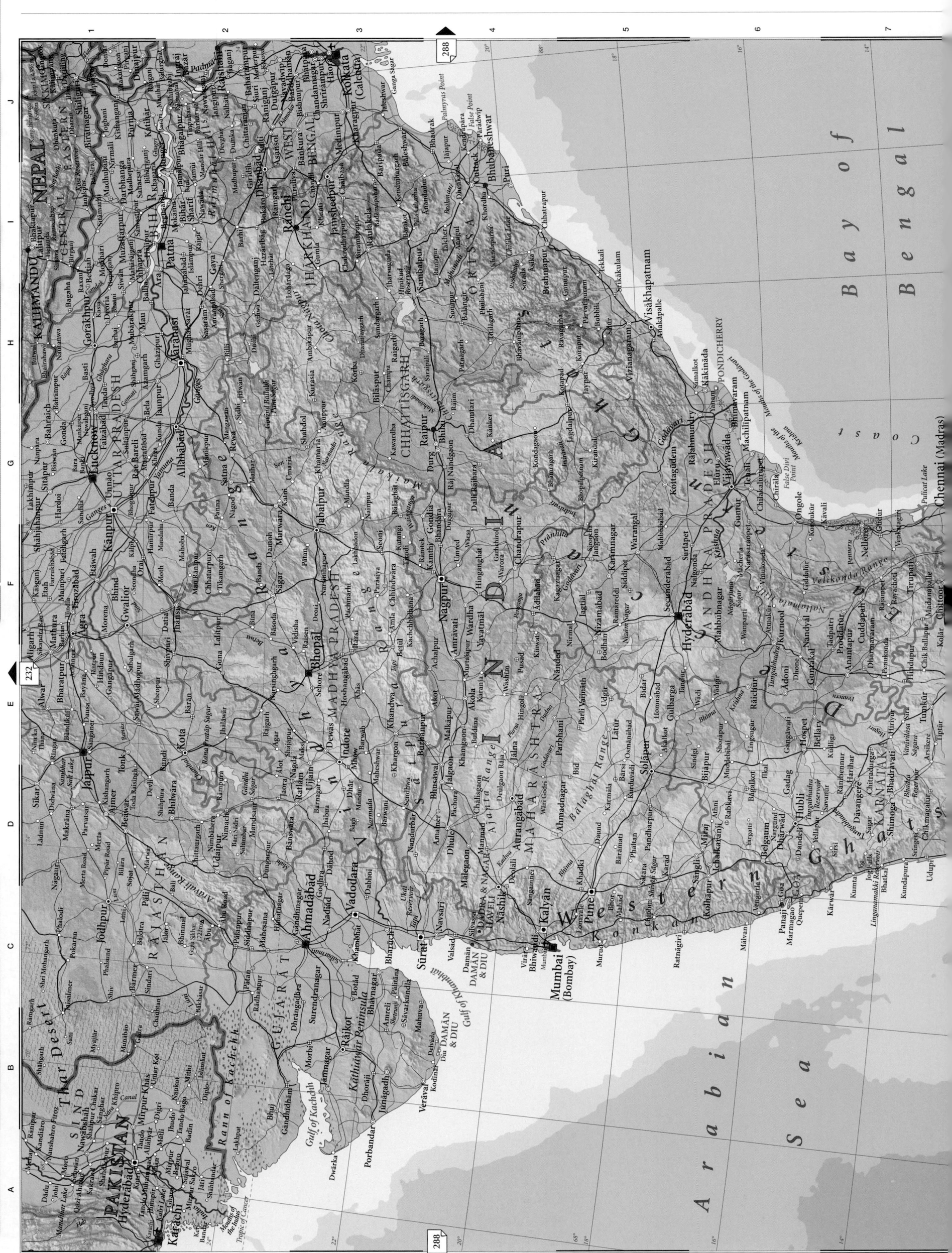

Bay of Bengal
Arabian Sea
INDIA
NEPAL
PAKISTAN
Kathmandu
Kolkata (Calcutta)
Mumbai (Bombay)
Chennai (Madras)
Hyderābād
Nagpur
Bhopāl
Ahmadābād
Karāchi
Visākhapatnam
Pune
Sūrat
Vadodara
Jaipur
Lucknow
Kānpur
Patna
Rānchi
Raipur
Indore
Jabalpur
MADHYA PRADESH
UTTAR PRADESH
MAHARASHTRA
ANDHRA PRADESH
CHHATTĪSGARH
JHĀRKHAND
ORISSA
WEST BENGAL
BIHAR
RĀJASTHĀN
GUJARĀT
KARNĀTAKA
SIND
Thar Desert
Rann of Kachchh
Gulf of Kachchh
Gulf of Khambhāt
Kāthiāwār Peninsula
Western Ghats
Eastern Ghats
Deccan
Vindhya Range
Sātpura Range
Tropic of Cancer
DAMĀN & DIU
DĀDRA & NAGAR HAVELI
PONDICHERRY
232
288
6000m
4000m
3000m
2000m
1000m
500m
250m
100m
Sea Level
-250m
-2000m
-4000m

ASIA

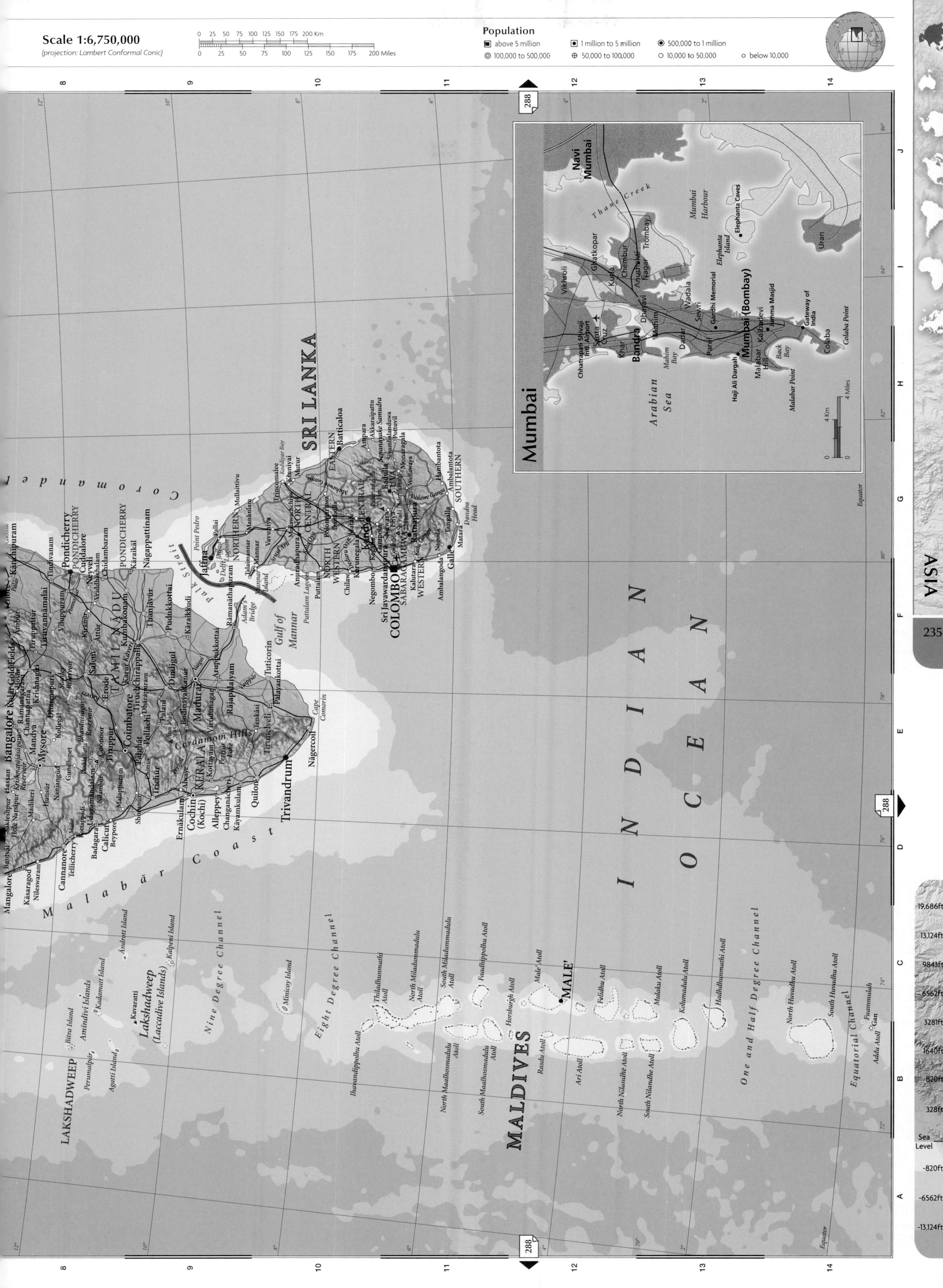

LAKSHADWEEP
Lakshadweep (Laccadive Islands)
Amindivi Islands
Bitra Island
Kadamatt Island
Perumalpar
Agatti Island
Andrott Island
Kavaratti
Kalpeni Island
Minicoy Island
Malabar Coast
Coromandel
Nine Degree Channel
Eight Degree Channel
One and Half Degree Channel
Equatorial Channel
Bangalore
Mysore
Mangalore
Cannanore
Tellicherry
Calicut
Coimbatore
TAMIL NADU
KERALA
PONDICHERRY
Pondicherry
Cuddalore
Kanchipuram
Thanjavur
Nagappattinam
Tiruchchirappalli
Dindigul
Madurai
Ernakulam
Cochin (Kochi)
Alleppey
Quilon
Trivandrum
Tuticorin
Nagercoil
Cape Comorin
Gulf of Mannar
Palk Strait
Adam's Bridge
Point Pedro
Jaffna
SRI LANKA
NORTHERN
NORTH CENTRAL
NORTH WESTERN
CENTRAL
EASTERN
SABARAGAMUWA
WESTERN
SOUTHERN
UVA
Trincomalee
Anuradhapura
Batticaloa
Kandy
Negombo
Sri Jayawardanapura
COLOMBO
Ratnapura
Badulla
Kalutara
Galle
Matara
Hambantota
Dondra Head
MALDIVES
MALE'
Male' Atoll
Ari Atoll
Ihavandippolhu Atoll
Thiladhunmathi Atoll
North Miladummadulu Atoll
South Miladummadulu Atoll
North Maalhosmadulu Atoll
South Maalhosmadulu Atoll
Faadhippolhu Atoll
Horsburgh Atoll
Rasdu Atoll
Felidhu Atoll
North Nilandhe Atoll
South Nilandhe Atoll
Mulaku Atoll
Kolumadulu Atoll
Hadhdhunmathi Atoll
North Huvadhu Atoll
South Huvadhu Atoll
Fuammulah
Gan
Addu Atoll
Equator
INDIAN OCEAN
288
Mumbai
Vikhroli
Chhatrapati Shivaji Intl. Airport
Santa Cruz
Ghatkopar
Navi Mumbai
Thane Creek
Khar
Kurla
Chembur
Bandra
Anushakti Nagar
Trombay
Dharavi
Arabian Sea
Mahim
Mahim Bay
Dadar
Wadala
Mumbai Harbour
Sewri
Parel
Gandhi Memorial
Elephanta Island
Elephanta Caves
Haji Ali Dargah
Mumbai (Bombay)
Malabar Hill
Kalbadevi
Jumma Masjid
Back Bay
Malabar Point
Gateway of India
Uran
Colaba
Colaba Point
0 4 Km
0 4 Miles
Scale 1:6,750,000
(projection: Lambert Conformal Conic)
0 25 50 75 100 125 150 175 200 Km
0 25 50 75 100 125 150 175 200 Miles
Population
above 5 million
1 million to 5 million
500,000 to 1 million
100,000 to 500,000
50,000 to 100,000
10,000 to 50,000
below 10,000
19,686ft
13,124ft
9843ft
6562ft
3281ft
1640ft
820ft
328ft
Sea Level
-820ft
-6562ft
-13,124ft
ASIA

192

ASIA

236

231

Scale bar:
6000m
4000m
3000m
2000m
1000m
500m
250m
100m
Sea Level
-250m
-2000m
-4000m

Countries and regions:

RUSSIAN

KAZAKHSTAN

MONGOLIA

ULAANBAATAR (ULAN BATOR)

KYRGYZSTAN

BISHKEK

XINJIANG UYGUR ZIZHIQU

Tarim Pendi

Taklimakan Shamo

C H I N A

Qingzang Gaoyuan (Plateau of Tibet)

XIZANG ZIZHIQU (TIBET)

QINGHAI

GANSU

NINGXIA

SHAANXI

SICHUAN

CHONGQING

GUIZHOU

YUNNAN

GUANGXI ZHUANGZU ZIZHIQU

HAINAN

Hainan Dao

JAMMU AND KASHMIR

HIMACHAL PRADESH

PUNJAB

HARYANA

UTTARAKHAND

UTTAR PRADESH

RAJASTHAN

MADHYA PRADESH

MAHARASHTRA

ANDHRA PRADESH

ORISSA

JHARKHAND

WEST BENGAL

BIHAR

CHHATTISGARH

I N D I A

NEPAL

KATHMANDU

BHUTAN

THIMPHU

BANGLADESH

DHAKA

MYANMAR (BURMA)

NAYPYIDAW

YANGON (RANGOON)

THAILAND

LAOS

VIANGCHAN (VIENTIANE)

HANOI

Cities and towns (selection):

Omsk, Novosibirsk, Tomsk, Achinsk, Krasnoyarsk, Kansk, Ust'-Ilimsk, Bratsk, Ust'-Kut, Petropavlovsk, Kostanay, Rudny, Kokshetau, Shchuchinsk, Kemerovo, Leninsk-Kuznetskiy, Kiselevsk, Berdsk, Barnaul, Novokuznetsk, Abakan, Minusinsk, Tayshet, Zima, Tulun, Cheremkhovo, Angarsk, Irkutsk, Usol'ye-Sibirskoye, ASTANA, Temirtau, Karaganda, Abay, Saran, Semipalatinsk, Ust'-Kamenogorsk, Leninogorsk, Gorno-Altaysk, Mezhdurechensk, Abaza, Ulan-Ude, Selenginsk, Zhezkazgan, Balkhash, Konyrat, Ayagoz, Zaysan, Darhan, Sühbaatar, Kyakhta, BISHKEK, Almaty, Taldykorgan, Tekeli, Yining, Ürümqi, Qitai, Turpan, Hami, ULAANBAATAR, Erdenet, Bulgan, Hovd, Uliastay, Bayanhongor, Altay, Dalandzadgad, Saynshand, Baotou, Ordos, Wuhai, Yinchuan, Lanzhou, Xining, Xianyang, Xi'an, Baoji, Hanzhong, Chengdu, Chongqing, Kunming, Guiyang, Guilin, Nanning, Haikou, Srinagar, Jammu, Gujranwala, Lahore, Amritsar, Ludhiana, Chandigarh, Shimla, Delhi, NEW DELHI, Meerut, Bareilly, Lucknow, Kanpur, Jaipur, Gwalior, Agra, Bhopal, Jabalpur, Nagpur, Raipur, Hyderabad, Visakhapatnam, KATHMANDU, Patna, Varanasi, Allahabad, Gaya, Dhanbad, Ranchi, Jamshedpur, Asansol, DHAKA, Kolkata, Chittagong, Khulna, Guwahati, Shillong, Imphal, Aizawl, Mandalay, YANGON, Bay of Bengal, Gulf of Tongking, Đà Nẵng

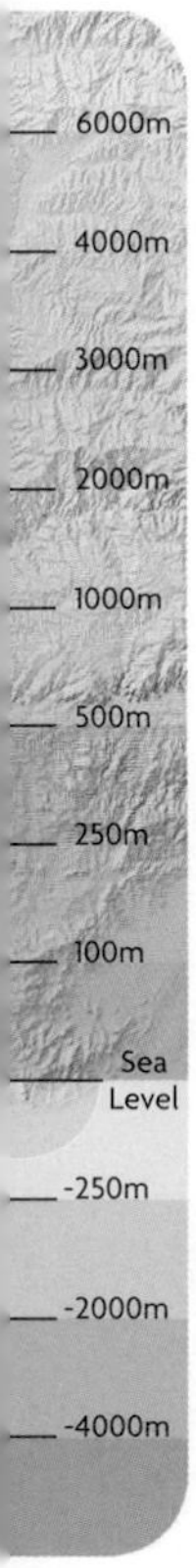

Scale 1:14,500,000
(projection: Lambert Azimuthal Equal Area)

0 50 100 150 200 250 300 350 400 Km
0 50 100 150 200 250 300 400 Miles

Population
■ above 5 million
◉ 100,000 to 500,000
▣ 1 million to 5 million
⊚ 50,000 to 100,000
◉ 500,000 to 1 million
⊙ 10,000 to 50,000
○ below 10,000

19,686ft
13,124ft
9843ft
6562ft
3281ft
1640ft
820ft
328ft
Sea Level
-820ft
-6562ft
-13,124ft

193
263
286

FEDERATION

Bodaybo
Neryungri
Stanovoy Khrebet
Khrebet Dzhugdzhur
Olyokma
Tynda
Nikolayevsk-na-Amure
Petropavlovsk-Kamchatskiy
Yablonovyy Khrebet
Chita
Mogocha
Skovorodino
Never
Zeyskoye Vodokhranilishche
Shimanovsk
Pervyy Kuril'skiy Proliv
Ostrov Paramushir
Karymskoye
Olovyannaya
Krasnokamensk
Shilka
Svobodnyy
Novyy Urgal
Komsomol'sk-na-Amure
Ostrov Sakhalin
Sea of Okhotsk
Nogliki
Onon Gol
Labyrinth
Manzhouli
Hailar
Argun
Jagdaqi
Blagoveshchensk
Berezovyy
Ostrov Urup
Menengiyn Tal
Baruun-Urt
Hulun Nur
Zalantun
Yichun
Obluch'ye
Birobidzhan
Khabarovsk
Tatarskiy Proliv
Ostrov Iturup
(Administered by Russian Federation, claimed by Japan)
Kerulen
Choybalsan
Qiqihar
Hegang
Amur
Khor
Bikin
Dal'negorsk
Kuril'skiye Ostrova (Kuril Islands)
Dzamin-Üüd
Erenhot
HEILONGJIANG
Daqing
Harbin
Suihua
Shangzhi
Jiamusi
Jixi
Dal'nerechensk
Ussuriysk
Yuzhno-Sakhalinsk
La Pérouse Strait
Rebun-tō
Wakkanai
MONGOL ZIZHIQU
Ulanhot
Hulingol
Baicheng
JILIN
Changchun
Jilin
Mudanjiang
Lake Khanka
Spassk-Dal'niy
Vladivostok
Nakhodka
Rishiri-tō
Okushiri-tō
Nayoro
Asahikawa
Abashiri
Kitami
Nemuro
Kushiro
Bayan Ul
Tongliao
Siping
Liaoyuan
Dunhua
Yanji
Hunchun
Najin
Ch'ŏngjin
Sapporo
Otaru
Tomakomai
Chitose
Obihiro
Hokkaidō
Muroran
Hakodate
Xilinhot
Linxi
Chifeng
Fuxin
Tieling
Baishan
Hyesan
Kanggye
Kimch'aek
Tsugaru-kaikyō
Aomori
Hachinohe
Baochang
Beipiao
Shenyang
Fushun
LIAONING
Anshan
Namsan-ni
Hamhŭng
Hirosaki
Noshiro
Kuji
Miyako
Hohhot
Chaoyang
Jinzhou
Haicheng
Dandong
Sinŭiju
Hŭich'ŏn
Chŏngju
NORTH KOREA
Wŏnsan
Akita
Kobe
Iwate
Morioka
Kesennuma
Zhangjiakou
Chengde
Jinxhou
Baoding
Tangshan
Qinhuangdao
P'YŎNGYANG
Namp'o
Sariwŏn
Sea of Japan (East Sea)
Sekata
Shinjo
Ishinomaki
Datong
BEIJING SHI
BEIJING (PEKING)
Beijing
Tianjin
TIANJIN SHI
Dalian
Bo Hai
Korea Bay
Haeju
Kaesŏng
SŎUL
Inch'ŏn
Suwŏn
Wŏnju
Sokch'o
Kangnŭng
Tonghae
JAPAN
Niigata
Jōetsu
Sado
Yamagata
Fukushima
Kōriyama
Iwaki
Hitachi
Taiyuan
Shijiazhuang
Cangzhou
SHANXI
Handan
Dezhou
Binzhou
Yantai
Ongjin
Chŏnan
Andong
P'ohang
Oki-shotō
Matsue
Tottori
Takaoka
Toyama
Nagano
Komatsu
Matsumoto
Maebashi
Utsunomiya
Mito
Honshū
TŌKYŌ
Jinzhong
Xingtai
Jinan
SHANDONG
Zibo
Weifang
Qingdao
SOUTH KOREA
Taejŏn
Chŏnju
Taegu
Ulsan
Gōtsu
Okayama
Gifu
Nagoya
Hamamatsu
Yokohama
Chiba
Haneda
Sagami-nada
Changzhi
Anyang
Kaifeng
Zaozhuang
Lianyungang
Kunsan
Namwŏn
Kwangju
Pusan
Kōbe
Hiroshima
Kyōto
Ōsaka
Ise
Nii-jima
Ō-shima
Mikura-jima
Sanmenxia
Luoyang
Zhengzhou
Xuzhou
JIANGSU
Mokp'o
Cheju-haehyŏp
Sunch'ŏn
Kokura
Yamaguchi
Hōfu
Kitakyūshū
Kurume
Shikoku
Kōchi
Kii-suidō
Tanabe
Owase
Pingdingshan
HENAN
Nanyang
Xinyang
Bengbu
Great Plain of China
Hefei
ANHUI
Wuhu
Wuxi
Nanjing
SHANGHAI SHI
Cheju-do
Fukuoka
Saseho
Nagasaki
Ōita
Nakamura
Nobeoka
Hachijō-jima
Laohekou
Xiangfan
Suizhou
HUBEI
Wuhan
Huangshi
Anqing
Jiujiang
Nanchang
Hangzhou
Jiaxing
Shanghai
Yatsushiro
Kumamoto
Kagoshima
Miyazaki
Miyakonojō
Yichang
Yueyang
Dongting Hu
Nanchang
Jingdezhen
Shangrao
ZHEJIANG
Jinhua
Taizhou
Yaku-Shima
Tanega-Shima
Changsha
Loudi
Xiangtan
JIANGXI
Ji'an
East China Sea
Wenzhou
Nansei-shotō (Ryukyu Islands)
Naze
Amami-Ō-shima
Shaoyang
Hengyang
HUNAN
Quanzhou
Chenzhou
Nanping
FUJIAN
Fuzhou
Yong'an
Matsu Tao (to Taiwan)
Chilung
Senkaku-shotō (Claimed by China, Japan and Taiwan)
Ishigaki-jima
Miyako-jima
An'nan-guntō
Amami-guntō
Okinawa
Naha
Ogasawara-shotō
Hezhou
Shaoguan
Ganzhou
Longyan
Zhangzhou
Quanzhou
Xiamen
Chiang Kai-shek
Chinmen Tao (to Taiwan)
T'AIPEI
Taiwan Strait
T'aichung
Iriomote-jima
Sakishima-shotō
PACIFIC OCEAN
GUANGDONG
Chaozhou
Shantou
T'ainan
Chiai
Taiwan
TAIWAN
Tropic of Cancer
Zhaoqing
Foshan
Guangzhou
Kaohsiung
Kaohsiung
Jiangmen
Xi Jiang
Hong Kong
Macau
Chep Lap Kok
Luzon Strait
South China Sea
Babuyan Islands
Babuyan Channel
Philippine Sea
Paracel Islands (disputed)
Laoag
Baguio
Tuguegarao
Ilagan
Dagupan
Cabanatuan
Angeles
Luzon
Quezon City
MANILA
PHILIPPINES

Shanghai inset:
Baoshan
Gucun
Miaphang
Gaojing
Wujiao Chang
Yangpu
Kailu Xincun
Huangpu Jiang
Dachang
Pengpu
Zhabei
Jiangwan
Hongkou Stadium
Lu Xun Tomb
Gaohang
Zhengnu
Putuo
Yichuan
Hongkou
Tilan Qiao
Huangshan Xincun
Jinquiao
Shanghai
Shanghai University
Pudong
Jiaodong University
Jing'an
Temple of the Jade Buddha
Huangpu
People's Square
Shanghai Museum
Yanguiadu
Zhangjiang
Changning
Beixinjing
Sun Yat Sen's Former Residence
Dapu
Nanshi
Muamu
Humau Zhen
Hongqiao
Xujiahui
Luwan
Huangpu Jiang
Zhoujiadu
Yugiao
Beicai
Wusong Jiang
Qibao Zhen
Changhua
Longhua
Sanlin
Liuliqiao
Cache
Yichuan

ASIA

238

KAZAKHSTAN

Karaganda · Karagandy

Ozero Balkhash

Betpak-Dala

Peski Moyynkum

ALMATY

BISHKEK

KYRGYZSTAN

Almaty · Alma-Ata

Taldykorgan

Shymkent

TOSHKENT (TASHKENT)

UZBEK.

DUSHANBE

TAJIKISTAN

Tien Shan

Ürümqi

Junggar Pendi
Gurbantüngüt Shamo

RUSS. FED.

XINJIANG UYGUR ZIZHIQU

C H I N A

Tarim Pendi

Taklimakan Shamo

Lop Nur

K u n l u n S h a n

Altun Shan

AFGHANISTAN

PAKISTAN

Karakoram Range

Aksai Chin

Islamabad

Srinagar

JAMMU AND KASHMIR

Peshawar
Rawalpindi

Lahore
Amritsar

PUNJAB

Multan

HIMACHAL PRADESH

Chandigarh
Ludhiana
Shimla

HARYANA

NEW DELHI
DELHI

UTTAR PRADESH

RAJASTHAN

INDIA

Jaipur

Agra

Kanpur · Lucknow

UTTARAKHAND

Q i n g z a n g   P l a t e a u

Tangula

XIZANG ZIZHIQU (TIBET)

NEPAL

KATHMANDU

H I M A L A Y A

THIMPHU
BHUTAN

Lhasa

Sea Level
6000m
4000m
3000m
2000m
1000m
500m
250m
100m
−250m
−2000m
−4000m

Scale 1:7,750,000
(projection: Lambert Conformal Conic)
0 25 50 75 100 125 150 175 200 Km
0 25 50 75 100 125 150 175 200 Miles
Population
above 5 million
1 million to 5 million
500,000 to 1 million
100,000 to 500,000
50,000 to 100,000
10,000 to 50,000
below 10,000
H
I
J
K
L
M
N
1
2
3
4
5
6
7
8
9
10
246
244
256
ASIA
239
19,686ft
13,124ft
9843ft
6562ft
3281ft
1640ft
820ft
328ft
Sea Level
-820ft
-6562ft
-13,124ft
ULAANBAATAR
(ULAN BATOR)
MONGOLIA
GOBI
NEI MONGOL ZIZHIQU
DORNOD
HENTIY
SÜHBAATAR
DORNOGOVI
DUNDGOVI
ÖMNÖGOVI
ÖVÖRHANGAY
BAYANHONGOR
GOVI-ALTAY
DZAVHAN
ARHANGAY
HÖVSGÖL
BULGAN
TÖV
Nei Mongol Gaoyuan
Badain Jaran Shamo
Tengger Shamo
Mu Us Shamo
Qilian Shan
QINGHAI
Qinghai Hu
Qaidam Pendi
Burhan Budai Shan
Bayan Har Shan
Gaoyuan of Tibet
GANSU
NINGXIA
SHAANXI
SHANXI
HENAN
HUBEI
HUNAN
SICHUAN
GUIZHOU
YUNNAN
Sichuan Pendi
Qin Ling
Daba Shan
Micang Shan
Hengduan Shan
Nyainqêntanglha Shan
ARUNACHAL PRADESH
(Administered by India, claimed by China)
ASSAM
KACHIN STATE
MYANMAR (BURMA)
CHONGQING SHI
Lanzhou
Xining
Yinchuan
Baotou
Hohhot
Datong
Taiyuan
Shijiazhuang
Zhengzhou
Luoyang
Xi'an
Chengdu
Chongqing
Guiyang
Mianyang
Nanchong
Leshan
Zigong
Zunyi
Hami
Jiayuguan
Jining
Zhangjiakou
Erenhot
Xilinhot
Hanzhong
Baoji
Panzhihua
Dibrugarh

ASIA

240

233

246

256

Scale legend:
6000m
4000m
3000m
2000m
1000m
500m
250m
100m
Sea Level
-250m
-2000m
-4000m

Major regions and countries

QINGHAI — Qinghai Hu, Qingzang Gaoyuan (Plateau of Tibet), Xining, Lanzhou

GANSU — Xianyang, Xi'an, SHAANXI, Luoyang

XIZANG ZIZHIQU (Tibet)

INDIA — ARUNACHAL PRADESH (Administered by India, claimed by China)

SICHUAN — Chengdu, Mianyang, Deyang, Leshan, Zigong, Chongqing (CHONGQING), HUBEI, Yichang

MYANMAR (BURMA) — KACHIN STATE, SHAN STATE, KAYAH STATE, Myitkyina, Lashio

YUNNAN — Kunming, Dali, Dongchuan, Panzhihua, Xichang, Gejiu

GUIZHOU — Guiyang, Zunyi, Anshun, Duyun

HUNAN — Changsha, Huaihua, Shaoyang, Hengyang

GUANGXI ZHUANGZU ZIZHIQU — Nanning, Liuzhou, Guilin, Wuzhou

VIETNAM — HANOI, Hai Phong, Hong Gai, Thanh Hoa, Vinh

LAOS — VIANGCHAN (VIENTIANE), Louangphabang

THAILAND — Chiang Mai, Lampang

CHINA

HAINAN — Hainan Dao, Haikou, Sanya, Wenchang

Gulf of Tongking

Qiongzhou Haixia

Weizhou Dao

Scale 1:7,000,000

(projection: Lambert Conformal Conic)

0 25 50 75 100 125 150 175 200 Km

0 25 50 75 100 125 150 175 200 Miles

Population

■ above 5 million   ■ 1 million to 5 million   ◉ 500,000 to 1 million

◎ 100,000 to 500,000   ⊕ 50,000 to 100,000   ○ 10,000 to 50,000   ○ below 10,000

ASIA

241

Yangtze River Valley

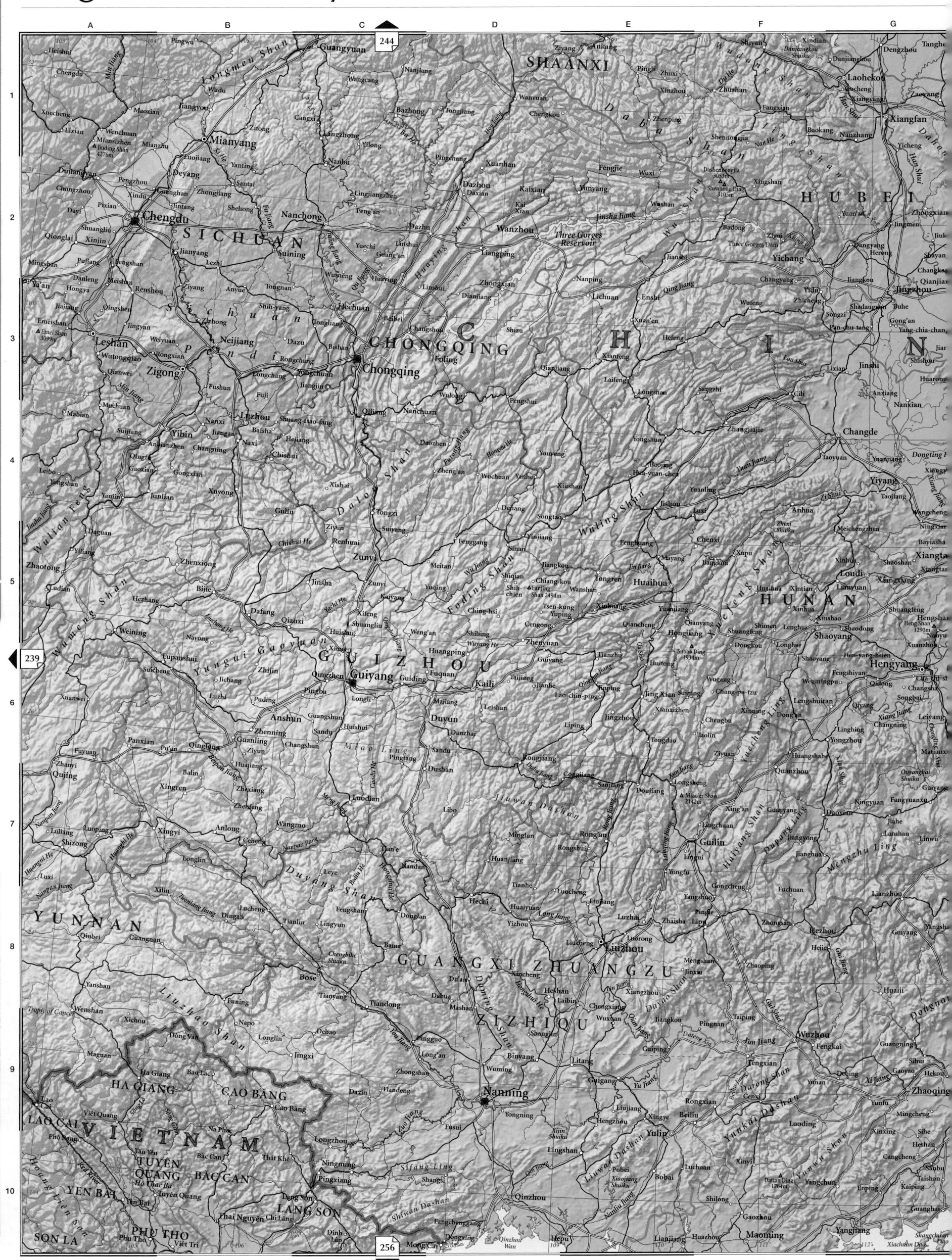

A
B
C
D
E
F
G
1
2
3
4
5
6
7
8
9
10
244
239
256
SHAANXI
SICHUAN
CHONGQING
CHINA
HUBEI
HUNAN
GUIZHOU
YUNNAN
GUANGXI ZHUANGZU ZIZHIQU
VIETNAM
Chengdu
Chongqing
Guiyang
Nanning
Mianyang
Nanchong
Leshan
Zigong
Yibin
Luzhou
Neijiang
Guangyuan
Dazhou
Wanzhou
Yichang
Xiangfan
Changde
Hengyang
Guilin
Liuzhou
Wuzhou
Yulin
Zhaoqing
Zunyi
Anshun
Kaili
Duyun
Qujing
Bose
Hechi
Qinzhou
Maoming
Shaoyang
Jishou
Huaihua
Three Gorges Reservoir
Longmen Shan
Daba Shan
Wuling Shan
Dalou Shan
Miao Ling
Sichuan Pendi
Yungui Gaoyuan
Wumeng Shan
Duyang Shan
Liuzhao Shan
Xuefeng Shan
Yuecheng Ling
Mengzhu Ling
Dayao Shan
Yunkai Dashan
Shiwan Dashan
HA GIANG
CAO BANG
LAO CAI
TUYEN QUANG
BAC CAN
YEN BAI
LANG SON
PHU THO
SON LA
6000m
4000m
3000m
2000m
1000m
500m
250m
100m
Sea Level
-250m
-2000m
-4000m

Scale 1:3,750,000
(projection: Lambert Conformal Conic)
0 20 40 60 80 100 Km
0 20 40 60 80 100 Miles
Population
above 5 million
1 million to 5 million
500,000 to 1 million
100,000 to 500,000
50,000 to 100,000
10,000 to 50,000
below 10,000
ASIA
243
245
263
286
19,686ft
13,124ft
9843ft
6562ft
3281ft
1640ft
820ft
328ft
Sea Level
-820ft
-6562ft
-13,124ft
HENAN
ANHUI
JIANGSU
SHANGHAI SHI
ZHEJIANG
JIANGXI
FUJIAN
GUANGDONG
TAIWAN
East China Sea
South China Sea
Taiwan Strait
Bashi Channel
Pescadores Channel
Tropic of Cancer
(Taiwan administered separately from China)
Nanjing
Hefei
Wuhan
Shanghai
Hangzhou
Ningbo
Nanchang
Changsha
Fuzhou
Xiamen
Shantou
Guangzhou
Kowloon (Julong)
Hong Kong (Xianggang)
Macau (Aomen)
T'AIPEI
T'aichung
T'ainan
Kaohsiung
Wenzhou
Jinhua
Jingdezhen
Ganzhou
Shaoguan
Zhangzhou
Quanzhou
Suzhou
Wuxi
Changzhou
Wuhu
Anqing
Jiujiang
Huangshan
Shangrao
Taizhou
Huzhou
Jiaxing
Shaoxing
Yangzhou
Nantong
Zhuhai
Shenzhen
Dongguan
Foshan
Meizhou
Longyan
Sanming
Nanping
Putian
Chaozhou
Jieyang
Hualien
Chilung
Hsinchu
Chiai
Makung

Yellow River Valley

A
B
C
D
E
F
G
1
2
3
4
5
6
7
8
9
10
246
239
242
NEI MONGOL ZIZHIQU
(INNER MONGOLIA)
Bayan Obo
Bailingmiao
Haliut
Ulan Hua
Lang Shan
Wuyuan
Ulansuhai Nur
Xishanzui
Yin Shan
Baotou
Hohhot
Donghe
Shulinzhao
Salaqi
Qasq
Huang He (Yellow River)
Togtoh
Horinger
Liangcheng
Zhuozi
Daqing Shan
Wuchuan
Guyang
Chasu-chi
Tamsag Muchang
Bayan Mod
Badain Jaran Shamo
Xamba
Linhe
Dengkou
Bayan Gol
Xar Burd
Yabrai Shan
Ulan Buh Shamo
Jartai Yanchi
Suhait
Wuhai (Haibowan)
Xinzhao Shan 2515m
Zhuozi Shan 2148m
Wuda
Ordos
Altan Xiret
Qingshuihe
Xuejiawan
Ehen Hudag
Zhoujianjing
Xiqu
Dongzhen
Shitanjing
Shizuishan
Shizuishan
Rujigou
Pingluo
Taole
Ulan
Mu Us Shadi
Hotong Qagan Nur
Bag Nur
Hongjian Nur
Shenmu
Xiasifen
Jinchang
Hexibao
Minqin
Bayan Hot
Helan Shan
Xincheng
Yinchuan
Dabqig
Yongchang
Tengger Shamo
Yongning
Yinchuan
Qingtongxia
Lingwu
Wuzhong
Ciyaopu
Caijialiang
Oljoq
Yulin
Wuwei
Lenglong Ling 4843m
Haomen
Gulang
Bingcaowan
Yingpanshui
Gantang
Qingtongxia Shuiku
Majiatan
Yanchi
Hengshan
Guandi Shan 2831m
Fenhe Shuiku
Gujiao
Taiyuan
SHAN
Tianzhu
Jingtai
Zhongwei
Zhongning
Hui'anpu
Dashuikeng
Dingbian
Jingbian
Mizhi
Zizhou
Suide
Liulin
Lishi
Qingxu
Wenshui
Fenyang
Xiaoyi
Jiexiu
Weiyuan
QINGHAI
Xining
Ping'anyi
Ledu
Huzhu
Huang He (Yellow River)
NINGXIA
Baiyu Shan
Huangtu Gaoyuan
Zichang
Qingjian
Yanchuan
Yongdeng
Hongshan Xia
Baiyin
Tongxin
Yuwang
Liwangbu
Hongde
Huanxian
Wuqi
Yan'an
Minhe
Gaolan
Jingyuan
Haiyuan
Maojing
Huachi
Nangdoi
Hualong
Lanzhou
Guochengyi
Donghaiba
Hozhou
Gando
Yongjing
Yuzhong
Gangouyi
Shenjiahe Shuiku
Qingcheng
Hongtong
Linfen
Jainca
Xunhua
Linxia
GANSU
Dongxiangzu
Dingxi
Huining
Xiji
Guyuan
Pengyang
Qingyang
Heshui
Fuxian
Yichuan
Jixian
Xiahe
Hezheng
Guanghe
Kangle
Lintao
Jingning
Longde
Migang Shan 2942m
Pingliang
Jingyuan
Malian He
Ningxian
Huangling
Luochuan
Jishan
Xinjiang
Quwo
Yicheng
Houma
Hezuo
Weiyuan
Longxi
Tongwei
Zhuanglang
Huating
Chongxing
Zhangjiachuan
Jingchuan
Changwu
Zhengning
Hancheng
Hejin
Wanrong
Wenxi
Yangcheng
Li Shan 2322m
Luqu
Lintan
Zhangxian
Wenfengzhen
Qin'an
Lingtai
Tongchuan
Heyang
Linyi
Yuncheng
Xiaxian
Jiyuan
Wushan
Qingshui
Jone
Gangu
SHAANXI
Pucheng
Fuping
Dali
Zhongtiao Shan
Ruicheng
Sanmenxia
Yima
Yanshi
Luoyang
Minxian
Lujing
Tianshui
Beidao
Sanyuan
Jingyang
Huayin
Tongguan
Lingbao
Tewo
Lazikou
Lixian
Baoji
Fengxian
Qishan
Qianxian
Fufeng
Xianyang
Xi'an
Weinan
Lintong
Lantian
Huxian
Zhouzhi
Wei He
Dangchang
Xihe
Liangdang
Fengxian
Taibai Shan 3767m
Shouyang Shan 2720m
Qin Ling
Luonan
Songxian
HE
Zhugqu
Zolgê
Huixian
Chengxian
Shangzhou
Danfeng
Laojun Shan 2192m
Funiu Shan
Waqên
Jiuzhaigou
Nanping
Zhongzhai
Longnan
Kangxian
Lüeyang
Shanyang
Zhen'an
Nanzhao
Min Shan
Hongyuan
Wenxian
Mianxian
Chenggu
Yangxian
Hanzhong
Shiquan
Xixia
Nexiang
Zhenping
Nanyang
Songpan
Bikou
Nanzheng
Xixiang
Xichuan
Yunxi
Qingchuan
Ningqiang
Xunyang
Xunxian
Den Xian
Dengzhou
Heishui
Pingwu
Guangyuan
Zhenba
Ziyang
Ankang
Shiyan
Danjiangkou
Danjiangkou Shuiku
Chengdu
Min Jiang
Longmen Shan
SHAANXI
Nanjiang
Wangcang
Pingli
Zhuxi
Wudang Shan
Laohekou
Gucheng
Xiangyang
Wudu
Jiangyou
SICHUAN
Xinzhou
Zhushan
Fangxian
Maoxian
Wanyuan
Chengkou
Daba Shan
Zhenping
Xiangfan
Xuecheng
Wenchuan
Zitong
Cangxi
Bazhong
Tongjiang
Baokang
Nanzhang
Lixian
Miansizhen
Jiuding Shan 4276m
Mianzhu
Mianyang
Langzhong
Yilong
Shennongjia
Yicheng
Luojiang
Yanting
Nanbu
Pingchang
Xuanhan
Fengjie
Wuxi
Dashennongjia 3053m
Xingshan
Guanxian
Deyang
Pengzhou
Santai
Dachuan
Daxian
Kaixian
Yunyang
Shennong Ding 3105m
HUBEI
Chongzhou
Dayi
Pixian
Xindu
Guanghan
Zhongjiang
Jintang
Shehong
Peng'an
Lingjiangzhen
Wushan
6000m
4000m
3000m
2000m
1000m
500m
250m
100m
Sea Level
-250m
-2000m
-4000m

ASIA

Scale 1:3,750,000
(projection: Lambert Conformal Conic)

0 20 40 60 80 100 Km
0 20 40 60 80 100 Miles

Population
- ■ above 5 million
- ◘ 1 million to 5 million
- ◉ 500,000 to 1 million
- ◎ 100,000 to 500,000
- ⊚ 50,000 to 100,000
- ○ 10,000 to 50,000
- ∘ below 10,000

247

248

243

19,686ft
13,124ft
9843ft
6562ft
3281ft
1640ft
820ft
328ft
Sea Level
-820ft
-6562ft
-13,124ft

LIAONING

Fushun, Shenyang, Fuxin, Beipiao, Chaoyang, Jinzhou, Liaoyang, Anshan, Haicheng, Benxi, Yingkou, Huludao, Qinhuangdao, Tangshan

BEIJING SHI, BEIJING (PEKING)

TIANJIN SHI, Tianjin

HEBEI

Datong, Zhangjiakou, Xuanhua, Baoding, Shijiazhuang, Yangquan, Handan, Cangzhou, Hengshui, Xingtai

Bo Hai, Bohai Wan, Bohai Haixia, Laizhou Wan, Liaodong Wan, Korea Bay, Yellow Sea

Dalian, Lüshun, Yantai, Weihai, Penglai, Longkou

SHANDONG, Shandong Bandao

Jinan, Zibo, Qingzhou, Weifang, Qingdao, Dongying, Binzhou, Linyi, Jining, Zaozhuang, Tai'an, Dezhou, Liaocheng

Huang He (Yellow River), Huanghe Kou

HENAN

Zhengzhou, Kaifeng, Xinxiang, Anyang, Xuchang, Pingdingshan, Luohe, Zhoukou, Shangqiu, Zhumadian

JIANGSU

Xuzhou, Lianyungang, Huai'an, Yancheng, Yangzhou, Taizhou, Nantong, Nanjing, Zhenjiang, Changzhou, Wuxi, Suzhou

ANHUI

Bengbu, Huainan, Hefei, Fuyang, Wuhu, Ma'anshan

SHANGHAI SHI, Shanghai

Tai Hu, Hongze Hu, Gaoyou Hu, Weishan Hu, Nanyang Hu

SHAN XI

Jining, Zhenjiang

Northeast China

ASIA

246

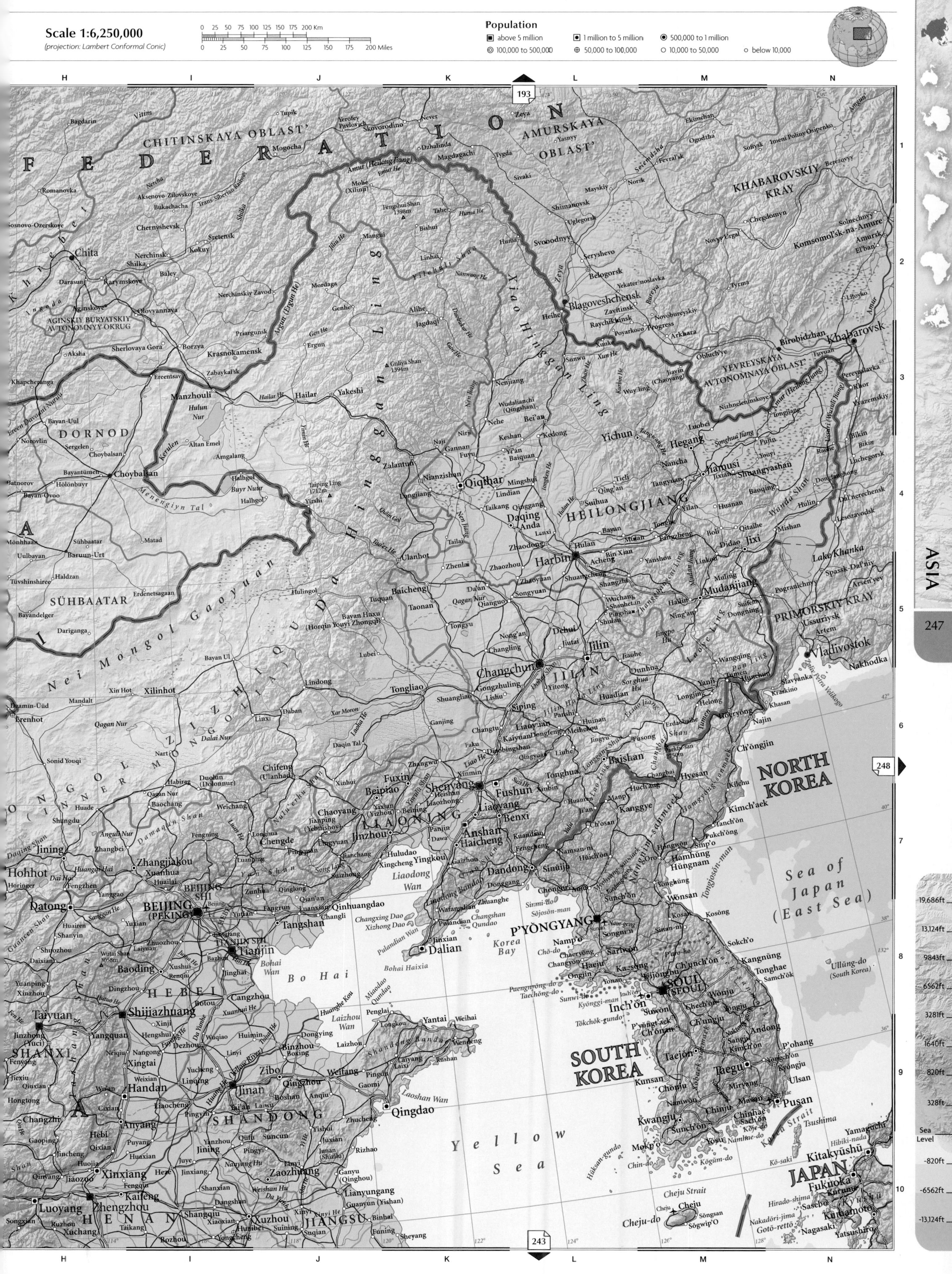

Scale 1:6,250,000
(projection: Lambert Conformal Conic)
0 25 50 75 100 125 150 175 200 Km
0 25 50 75 100 125 150 175 200 Miles
Population
above 5 million
1 million to 5 million
500,000 to 1 million
100,000 to 500,000
50,000 to 100,000
10,000 to 50,000
below 10,000
H
I
J
K
L
M
N
193
248
243
1
2
3
4
5
6
7
8
9
10
FEDERATION
CHITINSKAYA OBLAST'
AMURSKAYA OBLAST'
KHABAROVSKIY KRAY
AGINSKIY BURYATSKIY AVTONOMNYY OKRUG
YEVREYSKAYA AVTONOMNAYA OBLAST'
PRIMORSKIY KRAY
DORNOD
SÜHBAATAR
Nei Mongol Gaoyuan
HEILONGJIANG
JILIN
LIAONING
HEBEI
SHANXI
SHANDONG
HENAN
JIANGSU
NORTH KOREA
SOUTH KOREA
JAPAN
Sea of Japan (East Sea)
Yellow Sea
Bo Hai
Korea Bay
Liaodong Wan
Laizhou Wan
Bohai Haixia
Laoshan Wan
Cheju Strait
Korea Strait
Chita
Choybalsan
Manzhouli
Hailar
Blagoveshchensk
Khabarovsk
Birobidzhan
Komsomol'sk-na-Amure
Vladivostok
Nakhodka
Ussuriysk
Qiqihar
Daqing
Harbin
Jiamusi
Mudanjiang
Jixi
Changchun
Jilin
Siping
Shenyang
Fushun
Anshan
Dalian
Dandong
Jinzhou
Chifeng
Xilinhot
BEIJING (PEKING)
Tianjin
Tangshan
Qinhuangdao
Zhangjiakou
Datong
Hohhot
Baoding
Shijiazhuang
Taiyuan
Handan
Jinan
Zibo
Qingdao
Yantai
Weifang
Zhengzhou
Kaifeng
Luoyang
Xuzhou
Lianyungang
P'YŎNGYANG
Hamhŭng
Ch'ŏngjin
SŎUL (SEOUL)
Inch'ŏn
Taejŏn
Taegu
Kwangju
Pusan
Ulsan
Cheju
Fukuoka
Kitakyūshū
Nagasaki
ASIA
247
19,686ft
13,124ft
9843ft
6562ft
3281ft
1640ft
820ft
328ft
Sea Level
-820ft
-6562ft
-13,124ft

NEIMONGGOL ZIZHIQU (INNER MONGOLIA)

C H I N A

J I L I N

L I A O N I N G

RUSSIAN FEDERATION

PRIMORSKIY KRAY

Changchun

Jilin

Fushun

Shenyang

Anshan

Liaoyang

Haicheng

Yingkou

Gaizhou

Benxi

Liaodong Wan

Dandong

Sinŭiju

Chŏngju

P'YŎNGYANG

NORTH KOREA

Hamhŭng

Hŭngnam

Wŏnsan

Korea Bay

Namp'o

Sariwŏn

Haeju

Kaesŏng

Inch'ŏn

SŎUL (SEOUL)

Suwŏn

Yellow Sea

SOUTH KOREA

Taejŏn

Chŏnju

Kwangju

Mokp'o

Sunch'ŏn

Yŏsu

Taegu

P'ohang

Ulsan

Pusan

Sea of Japan (East Sea)

Vladivostok

Nakhodka

Ch'ŏngjin

Kimch'aek

Ullŭng-do

Kangnŭng

Tonghae

Samch'ŏk

Cheju-Strait

Cheju

Chejudo

Sŏgwip'o

East China Sea

J A P A N

Tsushima

Korea Strait

Kitakyūshū

Fukuoka

Shimonoseki

Hiroshima

Okayama

Kōbe

Ōsaka

Kyōto

Nagoya

Shikoku

Kyūshū

Kumamoto

Kagoshima

Miyazaki

Nagasaki

Philippine Sea

247

245

286

Scale 1:5,000,000
(projection: Lambert Conformal Conic)
0 20 40 60 80 100 Km
0 20 40 60 80 100 Miles
Population
above 5 million
1 million to 5 million
500,000 to 1 million
100,000 to 500,000
50,000 to 100,000
10,000 to 50,000
below 10,000
193
286
Ostrov Sakhalin
Korsakov
Zaliv Aniva
Mys Aniva
La Perouse Strait
Sea of Okhotsk
Ostrov Simushir
Ostrova Chernyy Brat'ya
Ostrov Urup
Kuril'skiye Ostrova
Kurile Islands
Kuril'sk
Ostrov Iturup
(Administered by Russian Federation, claimed by Japan)
Ostrov Kunashir
Yuzhno-kuril'sk
Ostrov Shikotan
Ostrov Zelënyy
Rebun-tō
Rishiri-tō
Wakkanai
Sōya-misaki
Hokkaidō
Sapporo
Otaru
Asahikawa
Kitami
Abashiri
Shiretoko-misaki
Nemuro
Kushiro
Obihiro
Tomakomai
Muroran
Hakodate
Erimo-misaki
Okushiri-tō
Tsugaru-kaikyō
Aomori
Hachinohe
Hirosaki
Akita
Morioka
Miyako
Kamaishi
Sakata
Yamagata
Sendai
Ishinomaki
Niigata
Sado
Fukushima
Kōriyama
Iwaki
Mito
Hitachi
Utsunomiya
Maebashi
Takasaki
Chiba
TOKYO
Kawasaki
Yokohama
Yokosuka
Shizuoka
Kakegawa
Irō-zaki
Ō-shima
Miyake-jima
Mikura-jima
Hachijō-jima
Aoga-shima
Izu-shotō
PACIFIC OCEAN
Seoul
Bukhansan National Park
Koyang
Tongdaenun-ga
Kangbuk-gu
Nowon-gu
Songbuk-gu
Unp'yong-gu
Chongno-gu
Namyangju
Chungnang-gu
Royal Tombs
Kyongboukkung Palace
Chung-gu
Tongdaemun-gu
Sejong Cultural Centre
Sodaemun-gu
Korea House
Kwangjin
Hangang (Han)
Toksungung Palace
Namsan Park
Songdon-gu
Kangdong-gu
Gimpo Airport
Map'o-gu
Seoul Tower
Sŏul (Seoul)
Yong San-gu
Korea Exhibition Centre
Olympic Stadium
Yangso-gu
Yongdungpo-gu
Kangnam-gu
Tongjak-gu
Songpa-gu
Socho-gu
Kuro-gu
Kwanak-gu
Seoul National Museum of Contemporary Art
Kumch'on-gu
Kwanchon
3 Km
3 Miles
ASIA
249
19,686ft
13,124ft
9843ft
6562ft
3281ft
1640ft
820ft
328ft
Sea Level
-820ft
-6562ft
-13,124ft

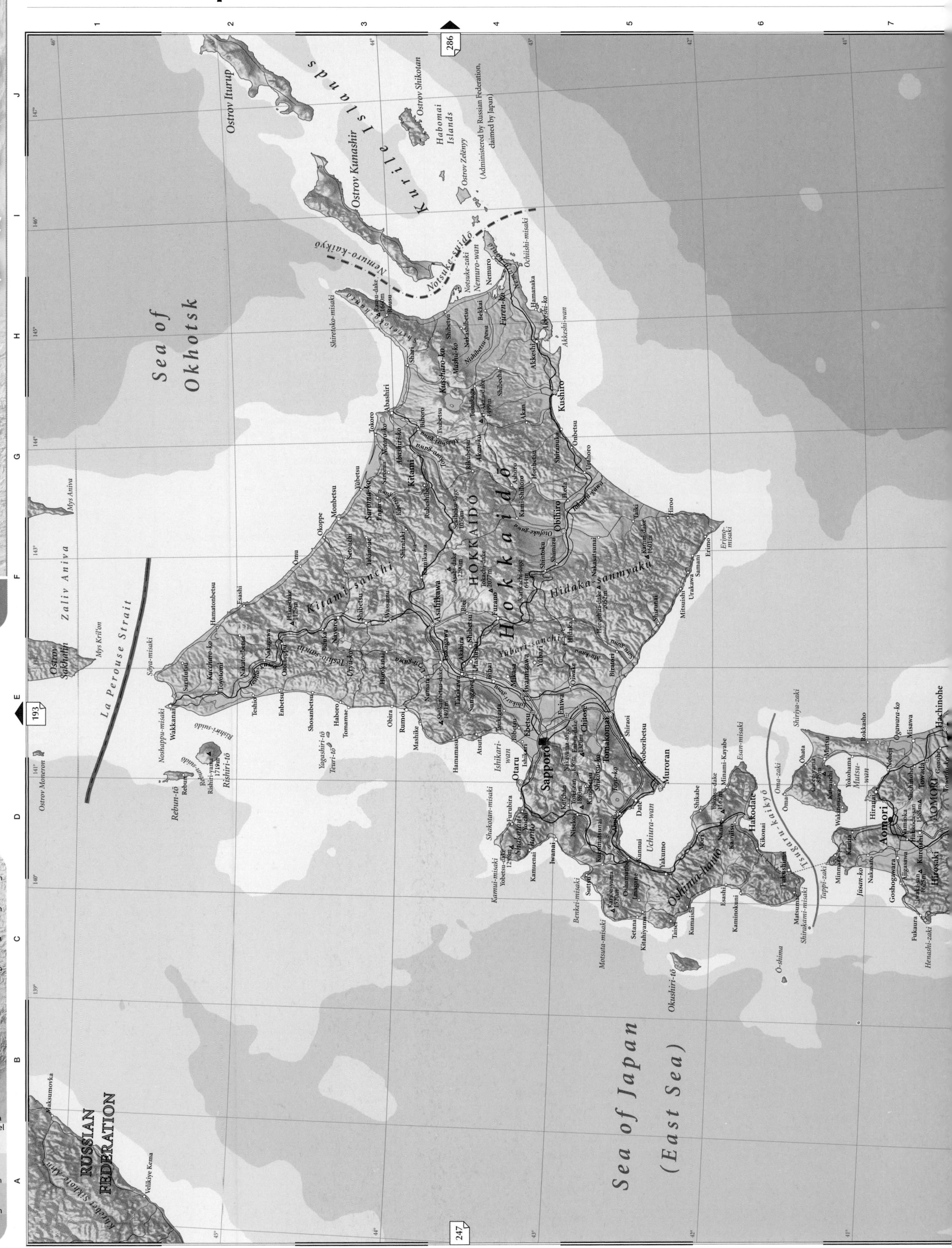

Sea of Okhotsk

Sea of Japan (East Sea)

RUSSIAN FEDERATION

HOKKAIDO

Kurile Islands

Ostrov Iturup

Ostrov Kunashir

Ostrov Shikotan

Habomai Islands

Ostrov Zelёnyy

(Administered by Russian Federation, claimed by Japan)

Nemuro-kaikyō

Notsuke-suidō

Ostrov Sakhalin

Ostrov Moneron

Zaliv Aniva

Mys Krilon

Mys Aniva

La Perouse Strait

Sapporo

Hakodate

Kushiro

Nemuro

Obihiro

Otaru

Muroran

Tomakomai

Kitami

AOMORI

Aomori

Hachinohe

Hidaka-sanmyaku

Kitami-sanchi

Teshio-sanchi

Yūbari-sanchi

Tsugaru-kaikyō

Oshima-hantō

6000m
4000m
3000m
2000m
1000m
500m
250m
100m
Sea Level
-250m
-2000m
-4000m

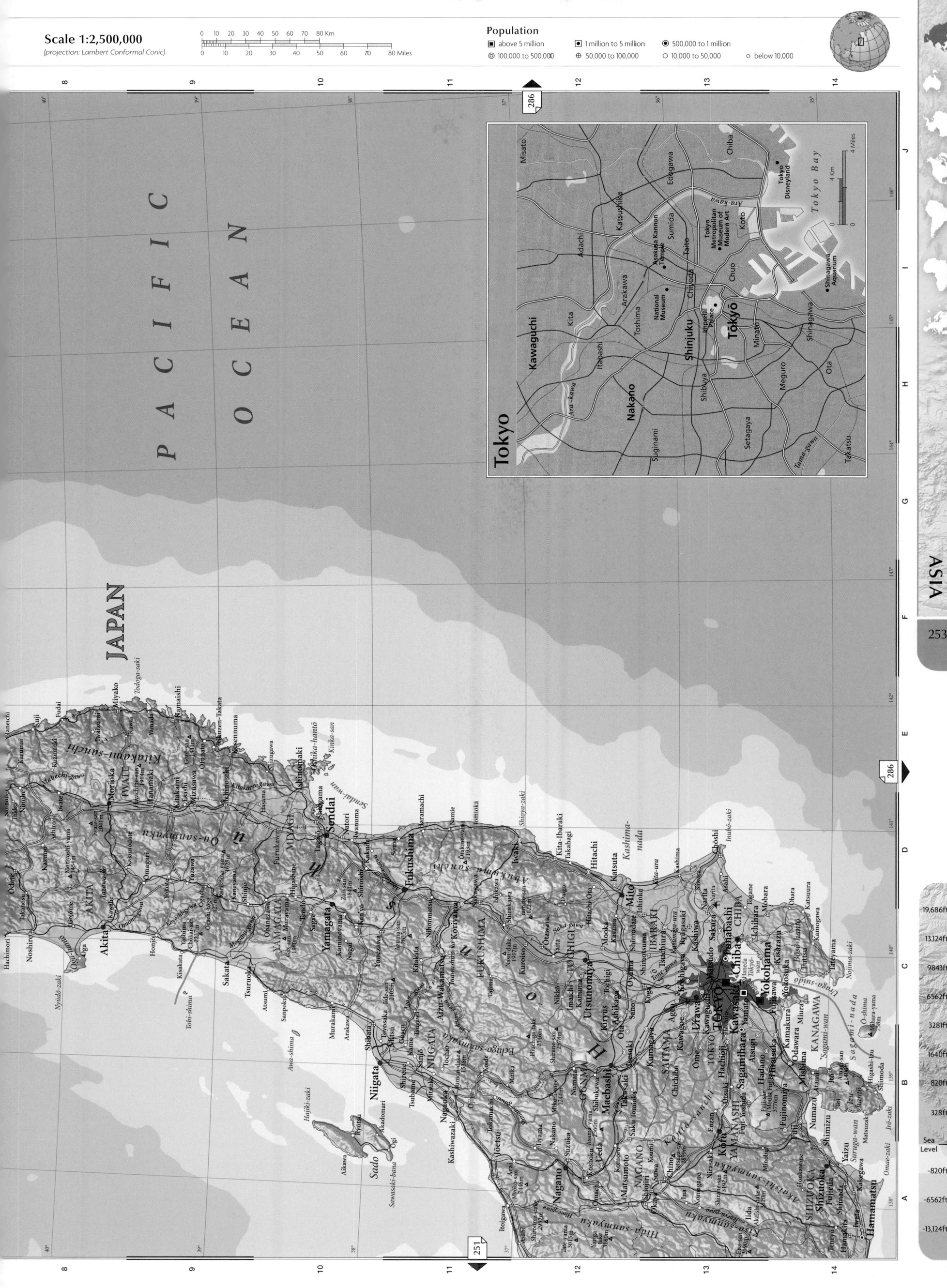

Scale 1:2,500,000
(projection: Lambert Conformal Conic)

0 10 20 30 40 50 60 70 80 Km

0 10 20 30 40 50 60 70 80 Miles

Population

■ above 5 million ▣ 1 million to 5 million ◉ 500,000 to 1 million

◎ 100,000 to 500,000 ⊕ 50,000 to 100,000 ○ 10,000 to 50,000 ○ below 10,000

Tokyo

Misato
Kawaguchi
Kita
Adachi
Itabashi
Arakawa
Toshima
Katsushika
Edogawa
Chiba
Ara-kawa
Sumida
Asakusa Kannon Temple
Taito
Koto
Tokyo Disneyland
Tokyo Bay
4 Miles
4 Km
Nakano
Nerima
National Museum
Tokyo Metropolitan Museum of Modern Art
Shinjuku
Imperial Palace
Tōkyō
Chiyoda
Chuo
Minato
Shinagawa Aquarium
Shibuya
Suginami
Setagaya
Meguro
Ota
Tama-gawa
Takatsu

JAPAN

PACIFIC OCEAN

286

286

251

Niigata
Sendai
Akita
Yamagata
Fukushima
Morioka
Utsunomiya
Maebashi
Nagano
Kōfu
Shizuoka
Hamamatsu
Yokohama
TŌKYŌ
Kawasaki
Chiba

ASIA

253

19,686ft
13,124ft
9843ft
6562ft
3281ft
1646ft
820ft
328ft
Sea Level
-820ft
-6562ft
-13,124ft

Southeast Asia

ASIA

254

234

Himalayas Xigaze Gyangze Lhasa Nangxian Mainling Rawu

Mount Everest 8850m Gangtok Kangri Lhünze Cona Administered by India, claimed by China Sadiya Dibrugarh

THIMPHU **BHUTAN** Itanagar Brahmaputra

CHINA

Zigong Neijiang **Chongqing** Zhangjiajie Yueyang Changde Jiujiang Jingdezhen Lanxi Jinhua
Yibin Luzhou Zunyi Tongren Yiyang Xiangtan Zhuzhou Nanchang Quzhou Shangrao
Xichang Zhaotong Bijie Huaihua Loudi Liling Pingxiang Fuzhou Yingtan
Panzhihua Dongchuan Quijing Anshun **Guiyang** Kaili Jingzhou Shaoyang Hengyang Jian Yong'an Nanping
Dali Weishan Qinglong Duyun Quanzhou Longyan Zhangzhou
Kunming Xingyi Aulong Dushan Guilin Daoxian Shaoguan Meizhou Chaozhou Xiamen
Yuxi Shizong Hechi Longchuan Jieyang Chenghai
Gejiu Mengzi **Nanning** Liuzhou Hezhou Wuzhou **Guangzhou** Foshan Dongguan Shantou Kaohsiung
Wenshan Funing Jingxi Binyang Yulin Lingshan Zhaoqing Jiangmen Zhuhai Kowloon T'ainan
Lijiang Qinzhou Beihai Maoming Zhanjiang **Hong Kong** (Xianggang) Macau (Aomen)

Ha Dong Hong Gai **Cam Pha** Xuwen
HÀ NỘI **Hai Phong** Haikou Qionghai **Homan Dao** Sanya

Nam Dinh **Gulf of Tongking** Dongfang

Bay of Bengal

MYANMAR (**BURMA**) **NAYPYIDAW**
Mandalay Myingyan Taunggyi Keng Tung
Pakokku Minbu Lashio
Prome Thayetmyo Chiang Mai Louangphabang
Pegu Thaton Moulmein Kyaikkami **LAOS** Tuong Duong Vinh
Yangon (Rangoon) **VIANGCHAN** (VIENTIANE) Nam Dou
Bassein Henzada Nakhon Sawan Khon Kaen Roi Et
Gulf of Martaban Phitsanulok Nakhon Ratchasima Ratchathani Huế
Tavoy **THAILAND** Ubon Pakxé Đà Nẵng **VIETNAM**
Khao Laem Reservoir **KRUNG THEP** (BANGKOK) Champasak
Mergui Phetchaburi Chuŏr Phnum Dângrêk Pleiku Quang Ngai
Mali Kyun Rayong Bătdâmbâng Tônle Sap **CAMBODIA** Kon Tum Quy Nhon
Andaman Islands (to India) Letsôk-aw Kyun **PHNUM PENH** (PHNOM PENH) Đà Lat Nha Trang Tuy Hoa
Kâmpóng Cham Biên Hoa Cam Ranh
Zadetkyi Kyun Kâmpóng Saôm Châu Đôc **Hồ Chí Minh** Vũng Tàu
Lanbi Kyun Rach Gia My Tho Cần Thơ
Ko Phangan Ko Samui Ca Mau **SOUTH CHINA SEA**
Sichon **Mouths of the Mekong** **PARACEL ISLANDS** (disputed)
Nakhon Si Thammarat **SPRATLY ISLANDS** (disputed)
Trung Song Ko Phuket Phuket Songkhla
Hat Yai Kota Bharu Kuala Terengganu
George Town Kota Kinabalu
Taiping Ipoh Kuantan **BRUNEI** **BANDAR SERI BEGAWAN** Sandakan
Langsa Miri Tawau
Strait of Malacca **MALAYSIA**
Medan Klang **KUALA LUMPUR** **PUTRAJAYA** Sibu Bintulu **Borneo**
Pematangsiantar Melaka Kuching Samarinda
Muar Batu Pahat Johor Bahru
SINGAPORE **SINGAPORE** Singkawang **Kalimantan**
Pekanbaru Pontianak Balikpapan Palu
Sumatera Rengat Parepare
Padang Jambi Sampit Banjarmasin
INDO Kangean
INDIAN OCEAN Palembang
Bengkulu **Greater Sunda Islands** **Java Sea** Makassar
Bandar Lampung
JAKARTA Cirebon Semarang **Surabaya** **Flores Sea**
Bogor Tegal Surakarta Bali
Sukabumi Bandung Yogyakarta **Jawa** (Java) Denpasar Sumbawa
Mataram Lombok **Nusa Tenggara** Pulau Sumba

INDIA Kolkata Chittagong
BANGLADESH **DHAKA**
Khulna Barisal Cox's Bazar
Mouths of the Ganges

Scale:
6000m 4000m 3000m 2000m 1000m 500m 250m 100m Sea Level -250m -2000m -4000m

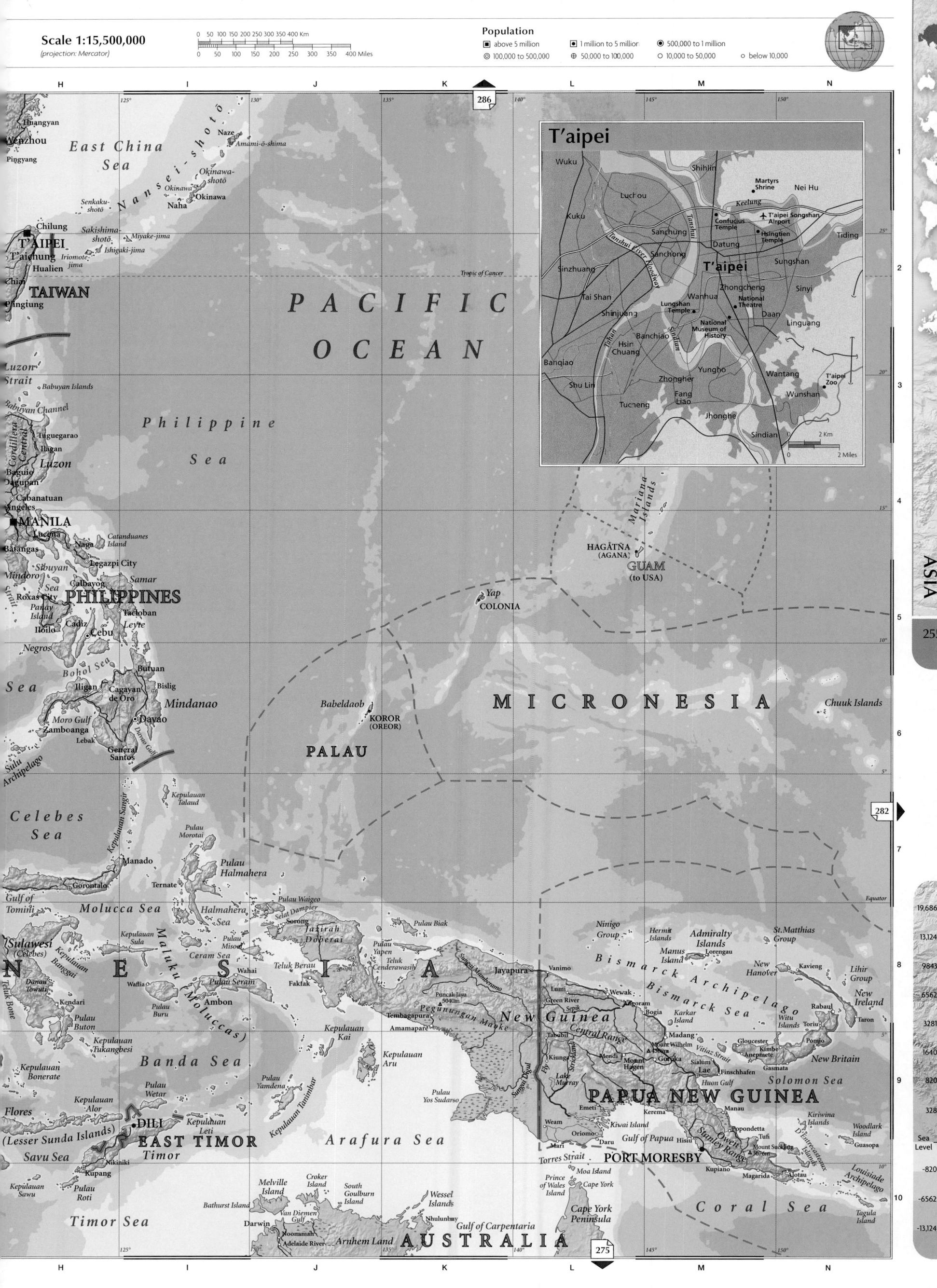

Scale 1:15,500,000
(projection: Mercator)

0 50 100 150 200 250 300 350 400 Km
0 50 100 150 200 250 300 350 400 Miles

Population
■ above 5 million ▪ 1 million to 5 million ◉ 500,000 to 1 million
◎ 100,000 to 500,000 ⊕ 50,000 to 100,000 ⊙ 10,000 to 50,000 ○ below 10,000

T'aipei

Wuku Shihlin
Luctou Martyrs Nei Hu
Shrine
Kuku
Confucius T'aipei Songshan
Temple Airport
Sanchung Hsingtien Tiding
Datung Temple Sungshan
Sinzhuang Tanshui Zhongcheng Sinyi
Tai Shan Wanhua National Daan Linguang
Shinjuang Lungshan Theatre
Temple
Banqiao National Museum Yungho Wantang
Hsin of History
Chuang Zhongher T'aipei
Shu Lin Zoo
Fang
Tucheng Liao Wunshan
Jhonghe
Sindian

0 2 Km
0 2 Miles

East China Sea
Hnangyan
Wenzhou
Piggyang
Nansei-shotō
Naze
Amami-ō-shima
Okinawa-shotō
Okinawa
Okinawa
Naha

Chilung
Sakishima-
shotō Miyake-jima
T'AIPEI
T'aichung Iriomote-jima
Hualien Ishigaki-jima
Chiai Tropic of Cancer
TAIWAN
Pingtung

PACIFIC
OCEAN

Luzon
Strait
Babuyan Islands
Babuyan Channel
Cordillera
Central
Tuguegarao
Ilagan
Baguio
Dagupan
Cabanatuan
Angeles
MANILA
Lucena
Batangas
Naga
Mindoro
Sibuyan
Sea
Calbayog
Roxas City
Panay
Island
Iloilo Cadiz Cebu
Negros
Bohol Sea
Iligan Butuan
Cagayan Bislig
de Oro
Mindanao
Davao
Moro Gulf
Zamboanga
Lebak
General
Santos
Sulu
Archipelago

Philippine

Sea

Catanduanes
Island
Legazpi City
Samar
Leyte
Tacloban

PHILIPPINES

Sea

Yap
COLONIA

HAGÅTÑA
(AGANA)
GUAM
(to USA)

Mariana
Islands

MICRONESIA

Chuuk Islands

Babeldaob
KOROR
(OREOR)

PALAU

Celebes
Sea

Kepulauan
Talaud

Kepulauan
Sangir
Pulau
Morotai

Manado
Gorontalo Pulau
Halmahera
Ternate

Gulf of
Tomini

Molucca Sea

Halmahera
Sea

Selat Dampier
Pulau Waigeo
Sorong
Jazirah
Doberai
Pulau
Misool

Pulau Biak
Pulau
Yapen
Teluk
Cenderawasih
Jayapura

Ninigo
Group
Hermit
Islands
Admiralty
Islands
Manus
Island Lorengau
St.Matthias
Group

New
Hanover

Kavieng
Lihir
Group

New
Ireland

NESIA

Sulawesi
(Celebes)

Kepulauan
Banggai

Danau
Towuti
Teluk Bone
Kendari

Pulau
Buton

Maluku
(Moluccas)

Kepulauan
Sula

Ceram Sea

Wahai
Pulau Seram
Ambon

Pulau
Buru

Teluk Berau
Fakfak

Puncak Jaya
5040m
Tembagapura
Amamapare

Pegunungan Maoke

Sungai Mamberamo

New Guinea

Central Range

Vanimo

Lumi
Green River
Sepik
Aitape
Wewak
Bogia

Bismarck

Karkar
Island

Madang

Mount Wilhelm
4509m
Mount
Hagen
Goroka
Sialum
Lae
Finschhafen
Huon Gulf

Bismarck Archipelago

Bismarck Sea

Witu
Islands
Toriu

Gloucester
Kimbe
Anepmete

Rabaul
Taron

New Britain

Gasmata

Pomio

Banda Sea

Kepulauan
Kai

Kepulauan
Aru

Kepulauan
Tukangbesi

Kepulauan
Bonerate

Pulau
Wetar

Kepulauan
Alor

Pulau
Yamdena

Pulau
Tanimbar

Tabubil
Kiunga
Fly
Lake
Murray

Strickland

Sungai Digul

Pulau
Yos Sudarso

Mendi

PAPUA NEW GUINEA

Manau

Solomon Sea

Kiriwina
Islands

Woodlark
Island
Guasopa

Flores

Kepulauan
Sawu

Pulau
Roti

DILI

EAST TIMOR

Timor

Nikiniki
Kupang

Savu Sea
(Lesser Sunda Islands)

Kepulauan
Leti

Arafura Sea

Weam
Mari

Emeti
Oriomo
Daru

Kiwai Island
Torres Strait

Moa Island
Prince
of Wales
Island

Cape York

PORT MORESBY

Owen
Stanley
Range

Kerema
Gulf of Papua
Hisiu

Kupiano

Popondetta
Tufi

Magarida

D'Entrecasteaux
Islands

Mount Suckling
3676m

Kupiano

Alotau

Louisiade
Archipelago

Tagula
Island

Timor Sea

Melville
Island

Croker
Island
South
Goulburn
Island

Wessel
Islands

Cape York
Peninsula

Coral Sea

Kepulauan
Sawu
Pulau
Sawu
Bathurst Island
Van Diemen
Gulf
Darwin
Nhulunbuy
Noomamah
Adelaide River
Arnhem Land
Gulf of Carpentaria

AUSTRALIA

Equator

19,686ft
13,124ft
9843ft
6562ft
3281ft
1640ft
820ft
328ft
Sea
Level
-820ft
-6562ft
-13,124ft

Mainland Southeast Asia

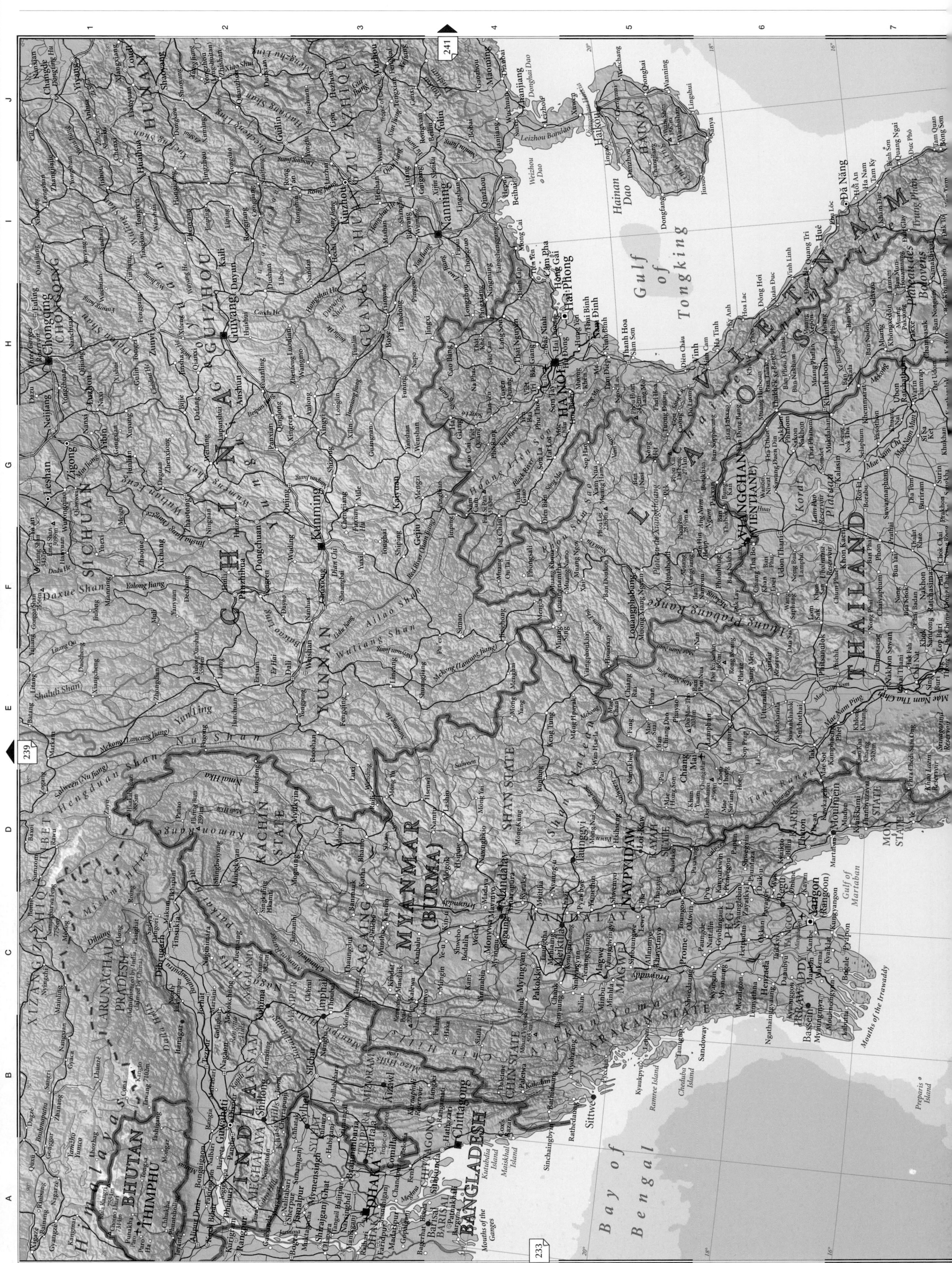
CHINA
MYANMAR (BURMA)
THAILAND
LAOS
VIETNAM
BHUTAN
BANGLADESH
INDIA
XIZANG ZIZHIQU (TIBET)
SICHUAN
YUNNAN
GUIZHOU
HUNAN
GUANGXI ZHUANGZU ZIZHIQU
HAINAN
KACHIN STATE
SAGAING
SHAN STATE
MANDALAY
KAYAH STATE
KAREN
MON STATE
PEGU
IRRAWADDY
ARAKAN STATE
CHIN STATE
MAGWE
ARUNACHAL PRADESH
Chongqing
Kunming
Guiyang
Nanning
HANOI
Hai Phong
VIANGCHAN (VIENTIANE)
NAYPYIDAW
Mandalay
Yangon (Rangoon)
DHAKA
THIMPHU
Chittagong
Đà Nẵng
Haikou
Bay of Bengal
Gulf of Tongking
Gulf of Martaban
Hainan Dao
Mouths of the Ganges
Mouths of the Irrawaddy
Himalayas
239
241
233
6000m
4000m
3000m
2000m
1000m
500m
250m
100m
Sea Level
-250m
-2000m
-4000m

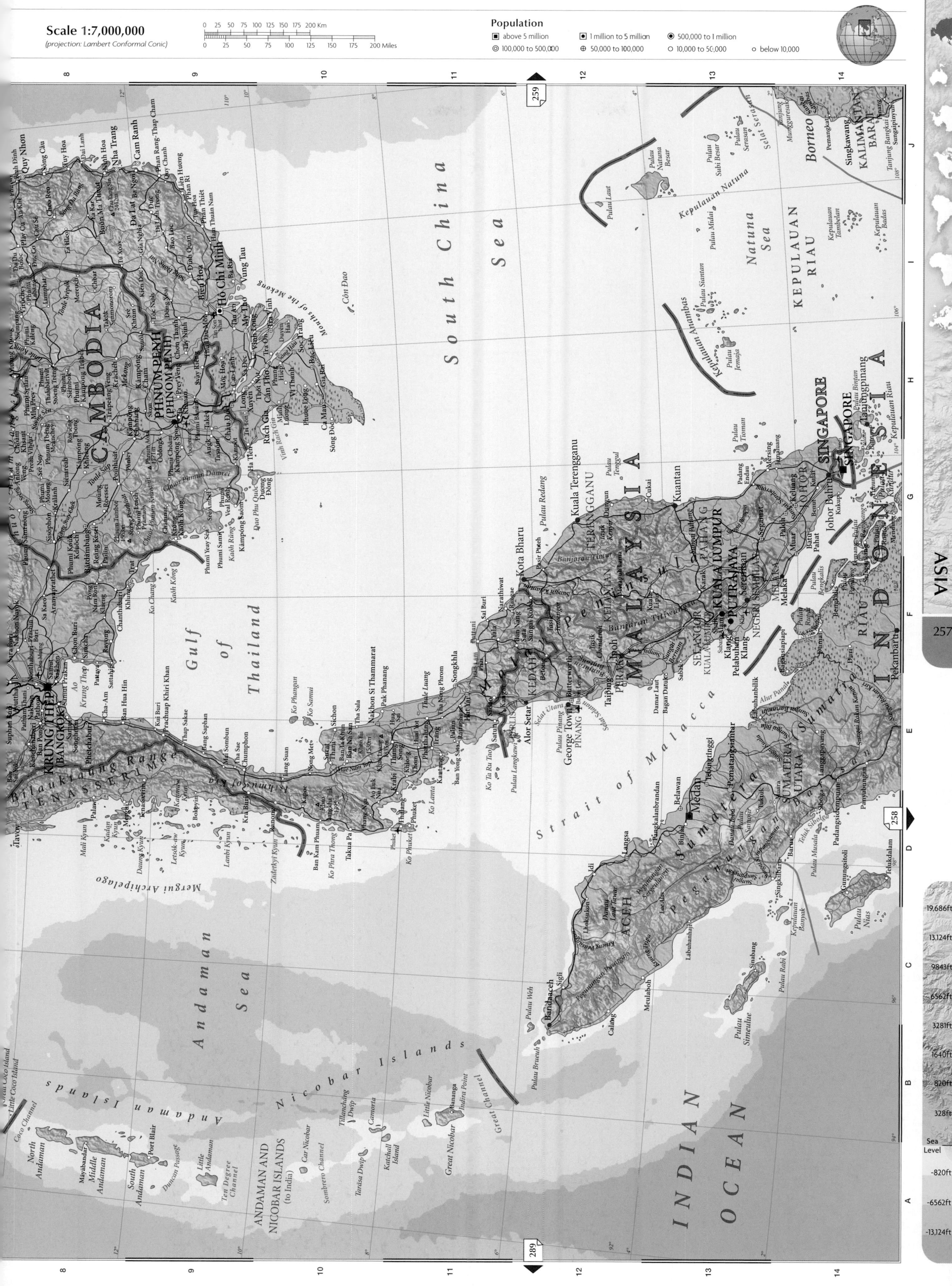

Scale 1:7,000,000

(projection: Lambert Conformal Conic)

0 25 50 75 100 125 150 175 200 Km

0 25 50 75 100 125 150 175 200 Miles

Population

■ above 5 million   ■ 1 million to 5 million   ● 500,000 to 1 million
◉ 100,000 to 500,000   ⊕ 50,000 to 100,000   ○ 10,000 to 50,000   ○ below 10,000

19,686ft
13,124ft
9843ft
6562ft
3281ft
1640ft
820ft
328ft
Sea Level
-820ft
-6562ft
-13,124ft

South China Sea

CAMBODIA

PHNUM PENH (PHNOM PENH)

Hô Chi Minh

Gulf of Thailand

KRUNG THEP (BANGKOK)

TENASSERIM RANGE

Bilauktaung Range

Andaman Sea

Mergui Archipelago

ANDAMAN AND NICOBAR ISLANDS (to India)

North Andaman
Middle Andaman
South Andaman
Little Andaman

Nicobar Islands

Great Nicobar

Strait of Malacca

MALAYSIA

KUALA LUMPUR
PUTRAJAYA

SINGAPORE

INDONESIA

Borneo

KALIMANTAN BARAT

KEPULAUAN RIAU

Natuna Sea

Pulau Natuna Besar

Kepulauan Natuna

Kepulauan Anambas

SUMATERA

SUMATERA UTARA

ACEH

Bandaaceh

Medan

Pematangsiantar

Pegunungan Barisan

INDIAN OCEAN

Pulau Nias

Pulau Simeulue

259
258
289

Singapore

Andaman Sea

THAILAND

George Town
PINANG

Taiping
Ipoh
PERAK

Medan

KUALA LUMPUR
PUTRAJAYA
Seremban

SUMATERA UTARA

Pekanbaru

SINGAPORE
Johor Bahru
SINGAPORE

Bukittinggi
Padangpanjang
Padang

Jambi

SUMATERA BARAT

SUMATERA SELATAN

Palembang

Bengkulu
BENGKULU

Bandarlampung
LAMPUNG

INDIAN OCEAN

JAKARTA
Serang
Tangerang
Bandung
BANTEN
JAWA BARAT

SOUTH CHINA SEA

KEPULAUAN RIAU
Tanjungpinang

Pangkalpinang
BANGKA-BELITUNG
Tanjungpandan

Greater

Natuna Sea

Singapore (inset)

Ang Mo Kio
Upper Peirce Reservoir
Central Catchment Nature Reserve
Bukit Timah Nature Reserve
MacRitchie Reservoir
Buangkok
Tampines
Jurong East
Toa Payoh
Bukit Timah
Raffles Park
Tan Tock Seng
Bedok
Clementi
University of Singapore
Kandang Kerbau
National Stadium
Queenstown
National Museum
Cathedral
City Hall
Raffles Hotel
Pasir Panjang
Singapore
Marina South
Buona Vista
Telok Blangah
Cable Car
Pulau Brani
Sentosa Island
Keppel Harbour
South China Sea
Straits of Singapore
Pulau Bukum
Pulau Tembakul
Pulau Sakijang Bendera

Christmas Island
(to Australia)

Scale 1:7,000,000
(projection: Mercator)
0 25 50 75 100 125 150 175 200 Km
0 25 50 75 100 125 150 175 200 Miles
Population
above 5 million
1 million to 5 million
500,000 to 1 million
100,000 to 500,000
50,000 to 100,000
10,000 to 50,000
below 10,000
H I J K L M N
1 2 3 4 5 6 7 8 9 10
110° 112° 114° 116° 118° 120° 122°
263
260
274
CHINA SEA
Sulu Sea
Mindanao
PHILIPPINES
Moro Gulf
Zamboanga
Sulu Archipelago
Celebes Sea
MALAYSIA
SABAH
Kota Kinabalu
Sandakan
Tawau
Labuan
BANDAR SERI BEGAWAN
BRUNEI
Miri
SARAWAK
Bintulu
Sibu
Kuching
Borneo
Kapuas Mountains
KALIMANTAN TIMUR
KALIMANTAN BARAT
Kalimantan
KALIMANTAN TENGAH
KALIMANTAN SELATAN
Pontianak
Singkawang
Samarinda
Balikpapan
Tarakan
Banjarmasin
Martapura
Pangkalanbuun
Ketapang
INDONESIA
Makassar Strait
Gulf of Tomini
GORONTALO
Gorontalo
Palu
SULAWESI TENGAH
SULAWESI BARAT
Sulawesi (Celebes)
SULAWESI SELATAN
SULAWESI TENGGARA
Makassar
Parepare
Kendari
Teluk Bone
Teluk Tolo
Flores Sea
Sunda Islands
Java Sea
Jawa (Java)
Semarang
JAWA TENGAH
Yogyakarta
YOGYAKARTA
Surabaya
Malang
JAWA TIMUR
Cirebon
Cilacap
Pulau Madura
Bali Sea
BALI
Denpasar
NUSA TENGGARA BARAT
Mataram
Sumbawa
Flores
Nusa Tenggara (Lesser Sunda Islands)
NUSA TENGGARA TIMUR
Pulau Sumba
Waingapu
Savu Sea
19,686ft
13,124ft
9843ft
6562ft
3281ft
1640ft
820ft
328ft
Sea Level
-820ft
-6562ft
-13,124ft

ASIA

260

259

263

274

Map labels (selected):

PHILIPPINES

Mindanao

Celebes Sea

MALAYSIA

SABAH

LABUAN

Labuan

BANDAR SERI BEGAWAN

BRUNEI

SARAWAK

KALIMANTAN TIMUR

Borneo

Kalimantan

Samarinda

Balikpapan

KALIMANTAN TENGAH

KALIMANTAN SELATAN

Banjarmasin

Makassar Strait

Molucca Sea

Manado

SULAWESI UTARA

GORONTALO

Gorontalo

MALUKU UTARA

Ternate

Pulau Halmahera

Halmahera Sea

SULAWESI TENGAH

Sulawesi (Celebes)

SULAWESI BARAT

Palu

Ceram Sea

MALUKU

Ambon

SULAWESI SELATAN

SULAWESI TENGGARA

Kendari

Banda Sea

INDONES

Makassar

Bali Sea

Flores Sea

Jawa (Java)

Bali

Denpasar

Mataram

NUSA TENGGARA BARAT

Sumbawa

Flores

Nusa Tenggara (Lesser Sunda Islands)

NUSA TENGGARA TIMUR

Savu Sea

Sumba

Kupang

DILI

EAST TIMOR

Timor Sea

INDIAN OCEAN

Elevation scale:

6000m
4000m
3000m
2000m
1000m
500m
250m
100m
Sea Level
-250m
-2000m
-4000m

Scale 1:7,000,000
(projection: Mercator)

0 25 50 75 100 125 150 175 200 Km

0 25 50 75 100 125 150 175 200 Miles

Population

■ above 5 million ▪ 1 million to 5 million ◉ 500,000 to 1 million
◎ 100,000 to 500,000 ⊕ 50,000 to 100,000 ○ 10,000 to 50,000 ○ below 10,000

282

275

280

P A C I F I C   O C E A N

Kepulauan Asia

Kepulauan Mapia *Pulau Bras*
Pulau Pegun

Kepulauan Ayu

Equator

Selat Halilo

Pulau Gebe
Kacepi

Kable Bet
Pulau Gag

Kabarei *Pulau Waigeo*
Urbinasopon
Lamtuu *Mercator*
Beon *Pulau*
Pulau *Gam*
Todlo *Selat Dampier*
Pulau *Sorong* *Makbon* *Sausapor* *Warmandi*
Hebera *Asbaken* *Kuwain*
Pulau *Segun* *Mega* *Klamano* *Gunung Kwoka*
Kofiau *Saileen* *Gasim* *Teminabuan* *Pegunungan Tamrau* *2652m*
Atkri *Konda* *Rawas* *Sau Korem*
Tip *Pulau Misool* *Baru* *Harmu* *Andoi* *Tanjung Saweba*
Kapocol *Kepulauan* *Inanwatan* *Mugoi* *Oransbari*
Segaf *Valse Pisang* *Tomu* *Ransiki* *Mumi*

Manokwari

Kepulauan Boo

Teluk Warong *Teluk Berau*
Wahai *Kobi* *Hoti* *Kepulauan* *Pisang* *Rumbati* *Koagas* *Andamata*
Seram *Bolifar* *Sonar* *Babo*
Wasul *Benu* *Haya* *Werr* *Tarak*
Haya *Waru* *Mawang* *Pulau Karas* *Mas*
Undur *Kilwo* *Pulau Manawoka* *Kelassi* *Obomei*
Kepulauan Banda *Namlea* *Ibonua*
Pulau Gorong *Pulau Kasiui* *Sopinusa*
Pulau Manuk *Gulir* *Watubela* *Obomei*
Nusawulan *Manggawitu* *Pulau Adi*

IRIAN JAYA BARAT

Jazirah Doberai
Gunung Meha *294m*

Teluk Bintuni
Semenanjung Bomberai
Jazirah Bomberai

Tanjung Weduar

Kepulauan Kai

C A S

I A

Remoon
Pulau Kur
Kepulauan *Wair*
Tayandu *Watlu* *Pulau* *Kai Kecil*
Pulau *Kai Besar*
Weduar

Pulau Gorong *Modowi*
Kokwari *Wariko* *Kurai*
Kaimana

Yapa Kopra
Aiduna *Wanapiri*
Uta
Kokenau
Timika

Pulau Warilau *Warilau*
Pulau Lutu
Kumzai
Dobo *Komfane*
Wamar *Pulau* *Pulau Jursian*
Ngoni *Wokam* *Namalau*
Taberfane *Pulau* *Kobroor*

Kepulauan Aru

Meyu
Yar
Pulau *Warjangan* *Workai*
Baimun

Tanjung Ngabordamlu
Kepulauan Jin

Pulau Molu
Pulau Fordate
Larat *Pulau Larat*

Pulau Yamdena
Pulau Wuliaru
Koreare
Amdassa
Manuwui *Yatoke* *Saumlaki*
Pulau Babar
Amplawas *Eliase*
Kepulauan *Tanjung*
Babar *Aro Usu* *Pulau Selaru*

A r a f u r a   S e a

Van Daalen

P A P U A
(IRIAN JAYA)

Rouffaer Reserves

Pegunungan Van Rees

Danau *Enarotali* *Paniai*
Puncak Jaya *5040m*
Tembagapura

Pegunungan Maoke

Pegunungan Jayawijaya
Sudirman

Amamapare

Teluk Flaming
Agats

Biwarlaut

Sungai Digul

Tusirah
Ki-sak
Abemaree
Muting
Bupul

Pulau Yos Sudarso
Kladar
Wamal *Alotip*
Komoran
Tanjung Vals *Wan*
Pulau Komoran

Kondombait
Weam
Morehead
Mari

Kerik
Erambu
Sota *Sasaramkar*
Merauke

Wanula *Island*
Emeti
Anggai
Balimo

WESTERN

GUINEA

Kikori

Jayapura

Yos Sudarso
Wutung *Vanimo*
Danau *Sentani*

SANDAUN

New   Guinea

PAPUA *EAST SEPIK*

Van Daalen

Central Range

ENGA
Porgera *Wabag*
Ok Tedi *Tari* *Mount Hagen*

NEW

Lake Murray
Mount Bosavi *2800m*

SOUTHERN
HIGHLANDS

GULF

Kukipi

Kiwai Island
Daru
Parama Island
Oriomo
Sibidiri

T o r r e s   S t r a i t

Badu Island *Moa Island*

Prince of Wales *Cape York*
Island

Kepulauan Tanimbar

Croker Island
Bathurst *Coburg Peninsula* *Marchinbar Island*
Island *South Goulburn Island* *Wessel Islands*
Melville *Island* *Elcho* *Island*
Van Diemen *Gulf* *Island*

Beagle Gulf *Nhulunbuy*

Darwin *Noonamah* *Cooinda* *Jabiru*

A U S T R A L I A
Arnhem
Land
Adelaide River *Mount Evelyn* *386m*
Fika River
Bulman

Gulf   of   Carpentaria

Weipa

Cape
York
Peninsula

Cape York

Endeavour Strait

C o r a l
S e a

Great Barrier Reef

19,686ft

13,124ft

9843ft

6562ft

3281ft

1640ft

820ft

328ft

Sea
Level

-820ft

-6562ft

-13,124ft

South China Sea & the Philippines

CHINA
YUNNAN
MYANMAR (BURMA)
SHAN STATE
Shan Plateau
LAOS
THAILAND
CAMBODIA
VIETNAM
MALAYSIA
INDONESIA
ACEH
GUANGXI ZHUANGZU ZIZHIQU
HAINAN
Hainan Dao
PARACEL ISLANDS (disputed)
Amphitrite Group
Crescent Group
Passu Keah
Triton Island
Spratly Island
Gulf of Tongking
Gulf of Thailand
South China Sea
Tropic of Cancer
Nanning
HA NOI
Hai Phong
Haikou
VIANGCHAN (VIENTIANE)
KRUNG THEP (BANGKOK)
PHNUM PENH (PHNOM PENH)
Hô Chi Minh
Da Nâng
Moulmein
Tavoy
George Town
Kota Bharu
Kuala Terengganu
Ipoh
Alor Setar
Louangphabang
Chiang Mai
Hat Yai
Songkhla
Nakhon Si Thammarat
Nha Trang
Cam Ranh
Quy Nhon
Huê
Mekong
Plateau de Xiangkhoang
Plateau des Bolovens
Korat Plateau
Tônlé Sap
Mergui Archipelago
TENASSERIM
Ko Phuket
Ko Samui
Ko Phangan
Ko Chang
Pulau Langkawi
Pulau Tenggul
Pulau Redang
Pulau Laut
Pulau Natuna Besar
Côn Dao
Mouths of the Mekong
Weizhou Dao
Donghai Dao
Leizhou Bandao
Qiongzhou Haixia
Xiachuan Dao
Ao Krung Thep
240
258
288
6000m
4000m
3000m
2000m
1000m
500m
250m
100m
Sea Level
-250m
-2000m
-4000m
A
B
C
D
E
F
G
1
2
3
4
5
6
7
8
9
10

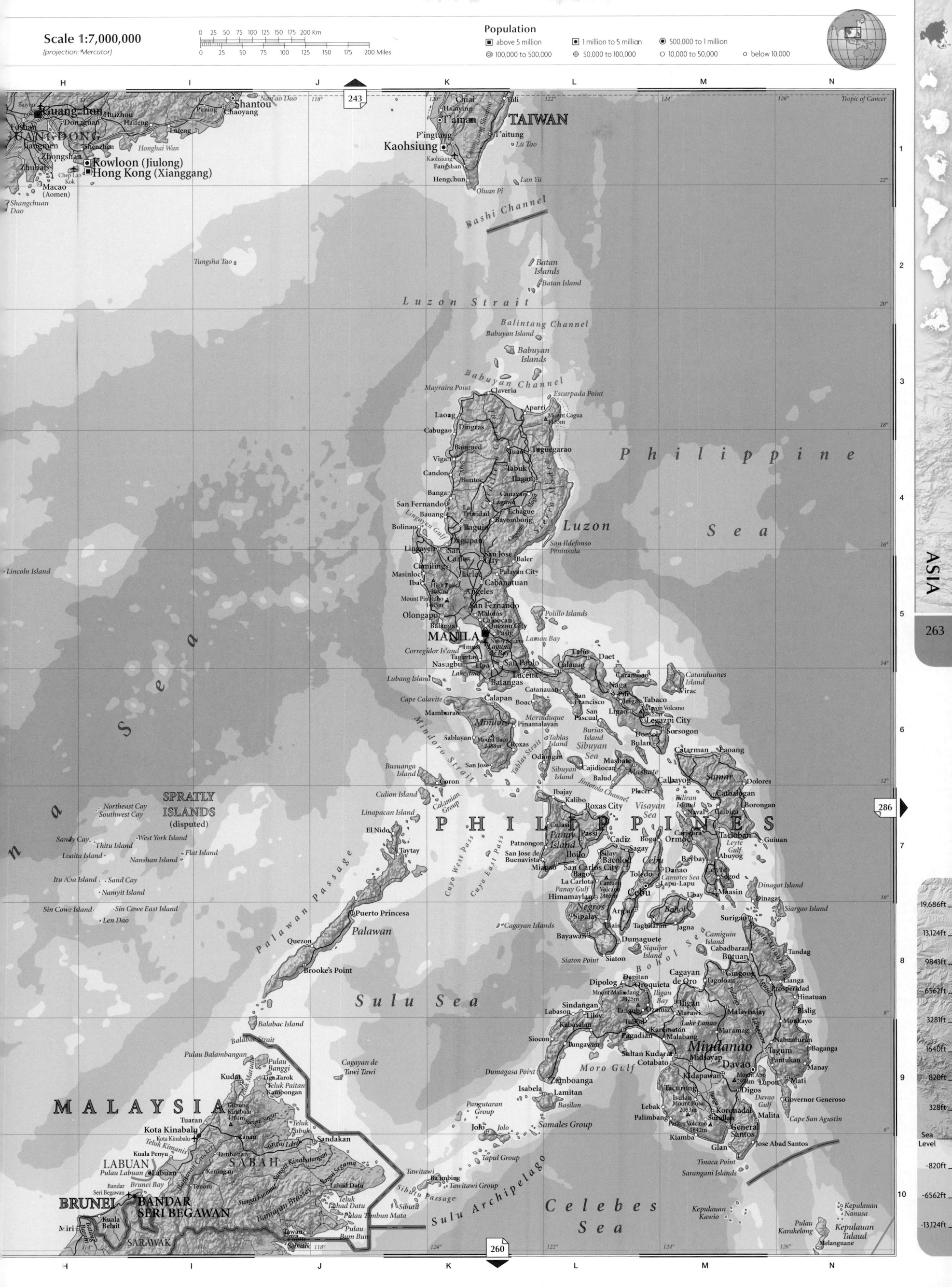

ASIA – Cities

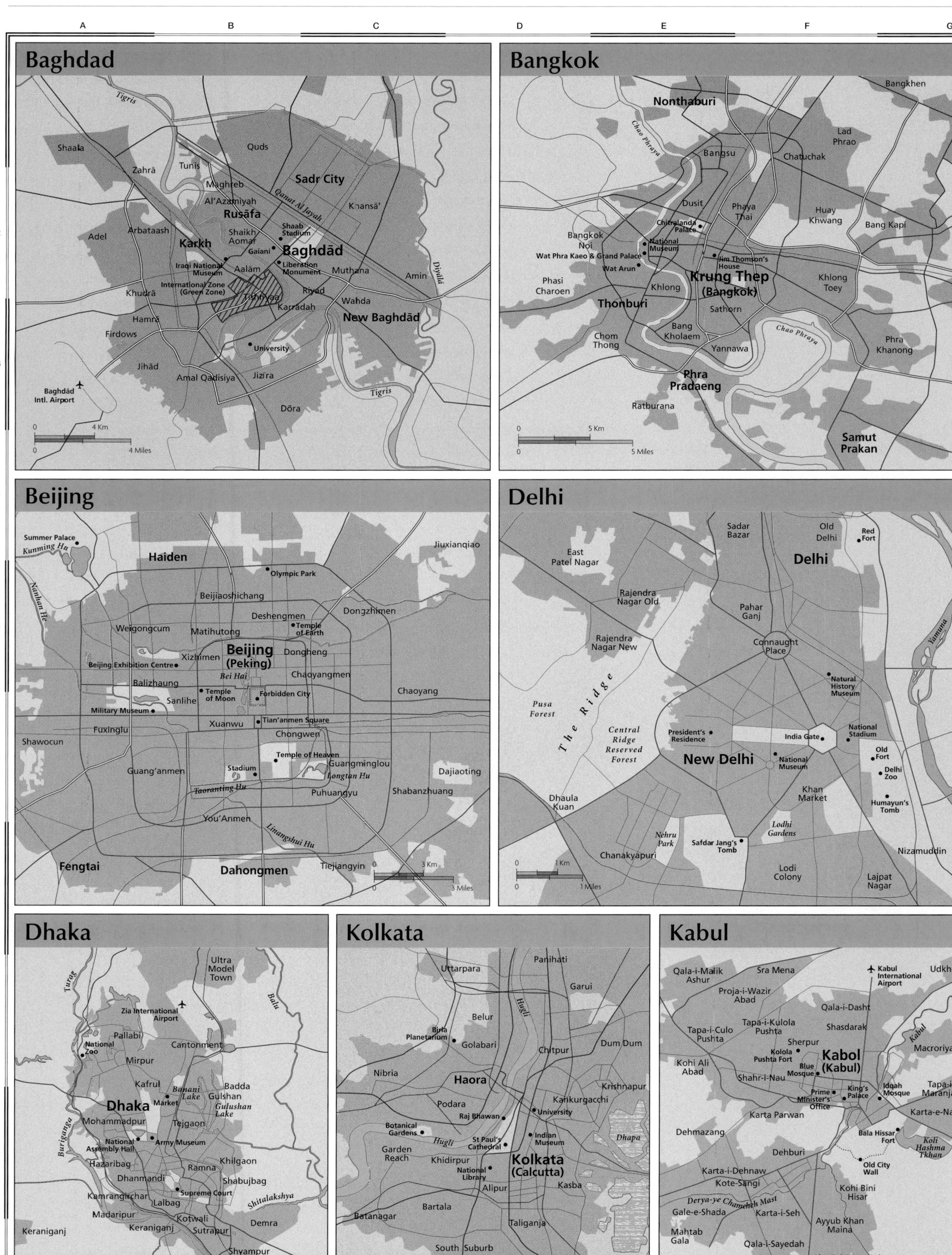

Baghdad
Sadr City
Baghdād
Karkh
Rusāfa
New Baghdād
Baghdād Intl. Airport
Bangkok
Krung Thep (Bangkok)
Nonthaburi
Thonburi
Samut Prakan
Beijing
Beijing (Peking)
Forbidden City
Tian'anmen Square
Temple of Heaven
Delhi
New Delhi
Connaught Place
India Gate
Dhaka
Zia International Airport
Kolkata
Kolkata (Calcutta)
Haora
Kabul
Kabol (Kabul)
Kabul International Airport

Hong Kong

Islamabad

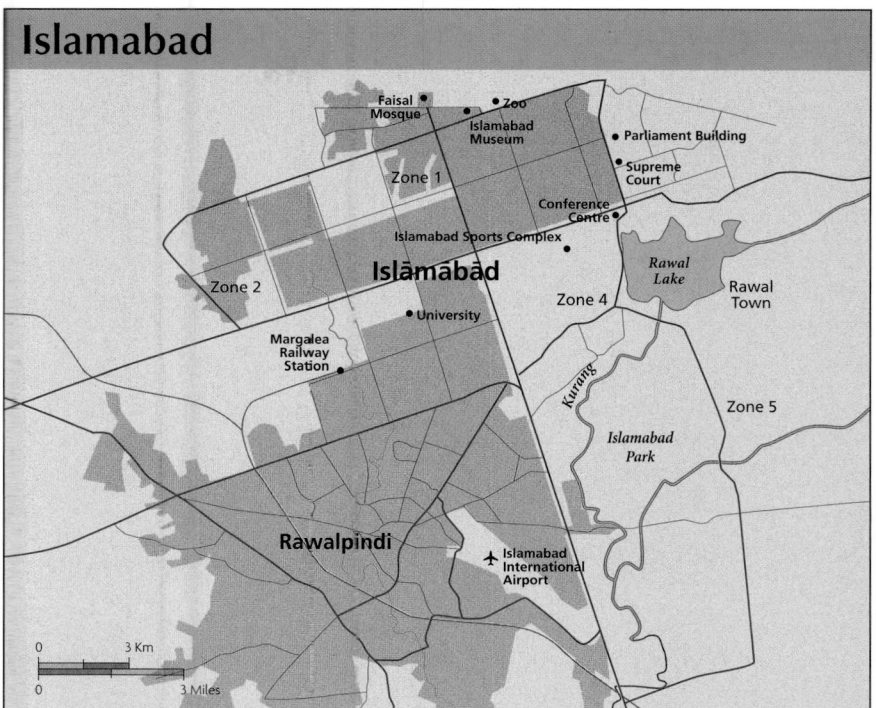

Istanbul

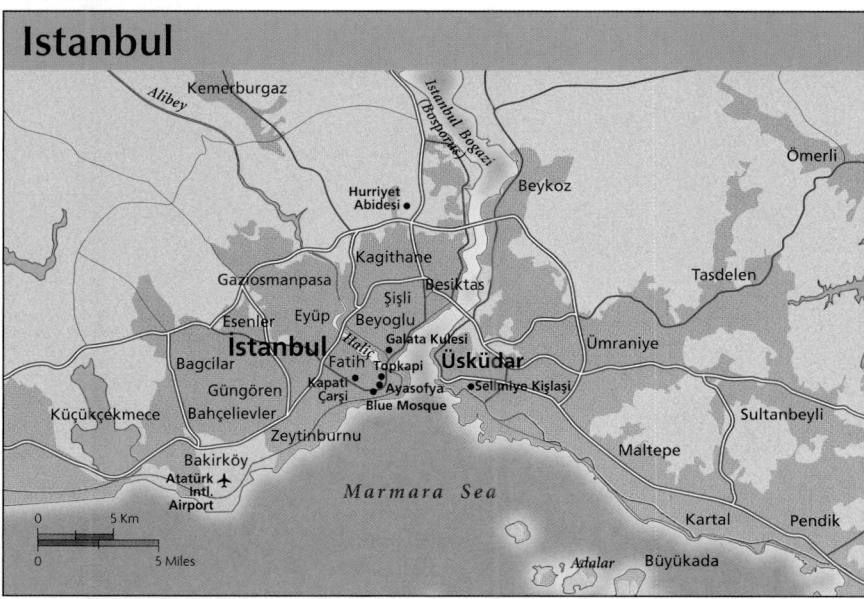

Jakarta

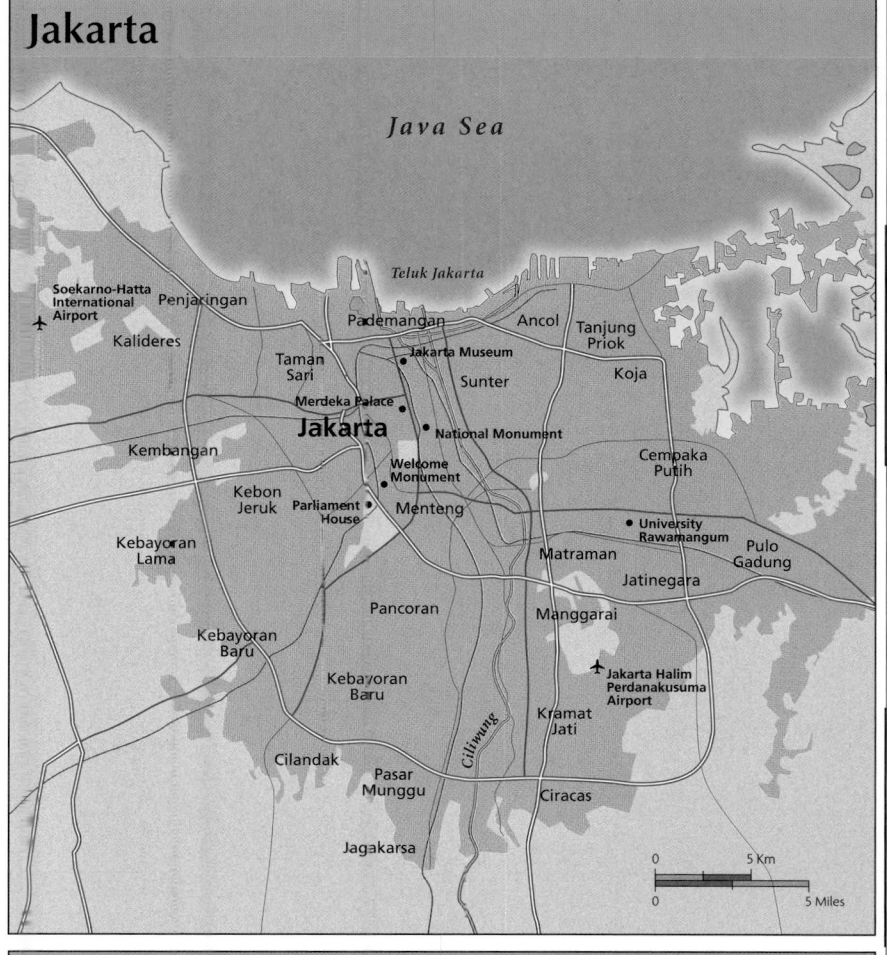

Kuala Lumpur

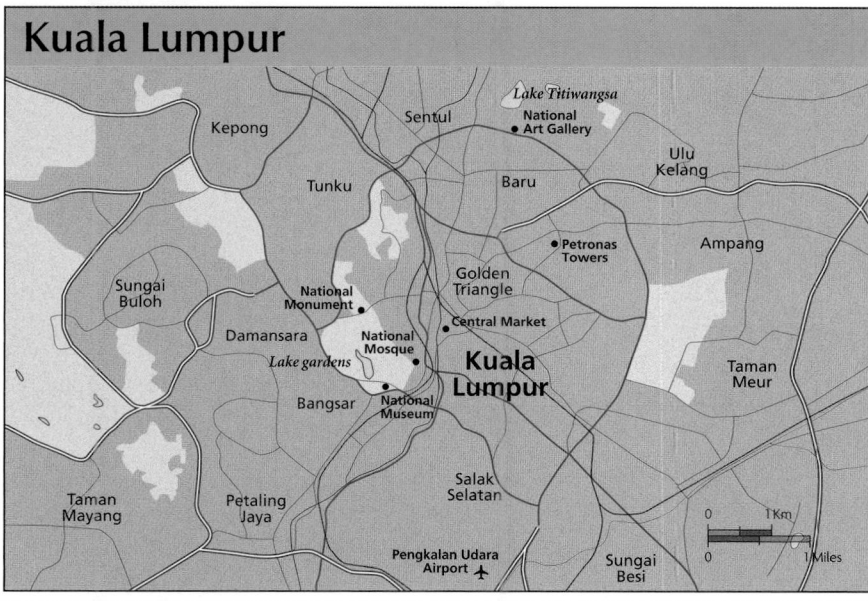

Manila

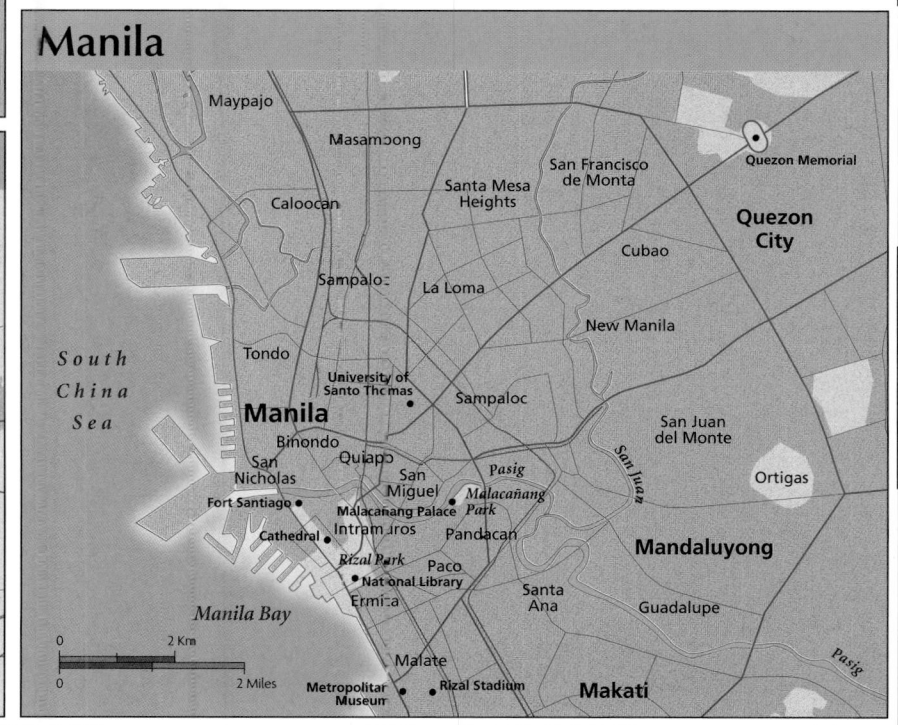

Ulan Bator

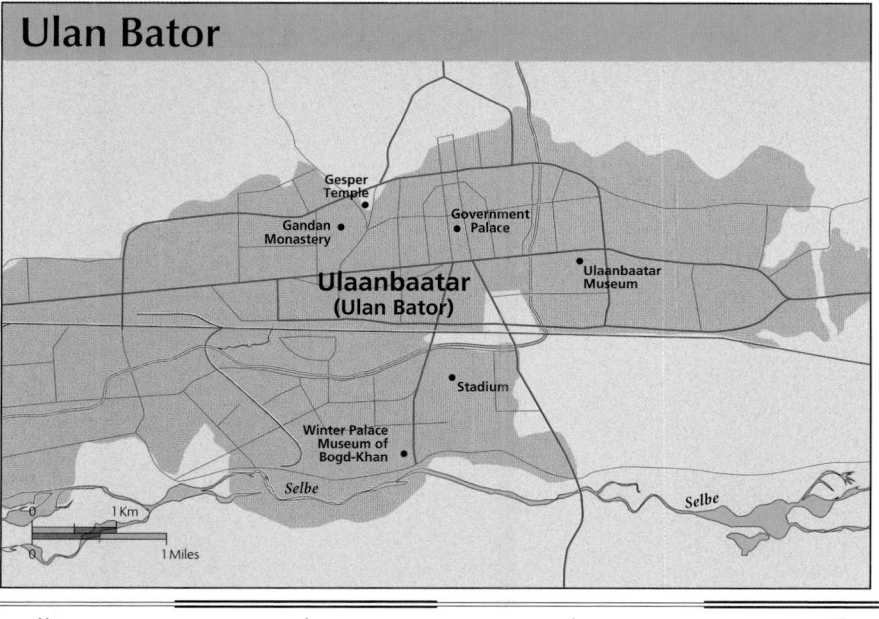

ASIA

265

Australasia and Oceania with a total land area of 3,285,048 sq miles (8,508,238 sq km), takes in 14 countries including the continent of Australia, New Zealand, Papua New Guinea, and many island groups scattered across the Pacific Ocean.

FACTFILE

N **Most Northerly Point:** Eastern Island, Midway Islands 28° 15′ N
S **Most Southerly Point:** Macquarie Island, New Zealand 54° 30′ S
E **Most Easterly Point:** Clipperton Island, 109° 12′ W
W **Most Westerly Point:** Cape Inscription, Australia 112° 57′ E

Largest Lakes:
1 Lake Eyre, Australia 3430 sq miles (8884 sq km)
2 Lake Torrens, Australia 2200 sq miles (5698 sq km)
3 Lake Gairdner, Australia 1679 sq miles (4349 sq km)
4 Lake Mackay, Australia 1349 sq miles (3494 sq km)
5 Lake Argyle, Australia 800 sq miles (2072 sq km)

Longest Rivers:
1 Murray-Darling, Australia 2330 miles (3750 km)
2 Cooper Creek, Australia 880 miles (1420 km)
3 Warburton-Georgina, Australia 870 miles (1400 km)
4 Sepik, Indonesia/Papua New Guinea 700 miles (1126 km)
5 Fly, Indonesia/Papua New Guinea 652 miles (1050 km)

Largest Islands:
1 New Guinea, 312,000 sq miles (808,000 sq km)
2 South Island, New Zealand 56,308 sq miles (145,836 sq km)
3 North Island, New Zealand 43,082 sq miles (111,583 sq km)
4 Tasmania, Australia 24,911 sq miles (64,519 sq km)
5 New Britain, Papua New Guinea 13,570 sq miles (35,145 sq km)

Highest Points:
1 Mount Wilhelm, Papua New Guinea 14,793 ft (4509 m)
2 Mount Giluwe, Papua New Guinea 14,331 ft (4368 m)
3 Mount Herbert, Papua New Guinea 13,999 ft (4267 m)
4 Mount Bangeta, Papua New Guinea 13,520 ft (4121 m)
5 Mount Victoria, Papua New Guinea 13,248 ft (4038 m)

Lowest Point:
▼ Lake Eyre, Australia -53 ft (-16 m) below sea level

Highest recorded temperature:
● Bourke, Australia 128°F (53°C)

Lowest recorded temperature:
– Canberra, Australia -8°F (-22°C)

Wettest Place:
≋ Bellenden Ker, Australia 443 in (11,251 mm)

Driest Place:
– Mulka Bore, Australia 4.05 in (102.8 mm)

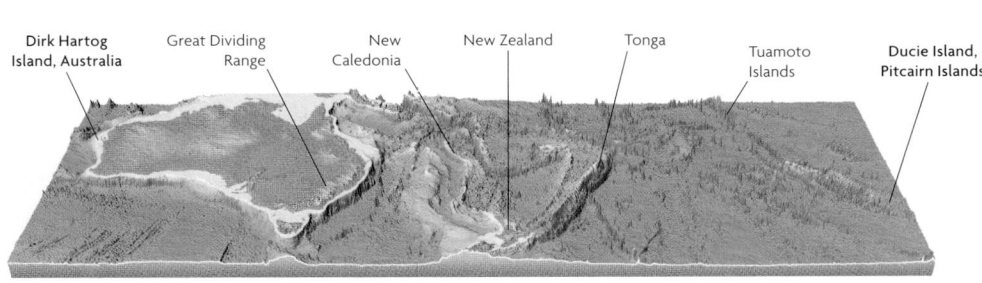

Cross-section from Dirk Hartog Island, Australia to Ducie Island, Pitcairn Islands

▷▷–▪–▪–◁
line of cross-section

0   500   1000 1500 Km
0   500   1000   1500 Miles

H   I   J   K   L   M   N

150°   160°   170°   180°   170°   160°   150°   140°

PACIFIC

OCEAN

Midway Islands

Murray Fracture Zone

Mapmaker Seamounts

Mid-Pacific Seamounts

Wake Island

Hawaiian Islands

Hawaiian Ridge

Necker Ridge

Molokai Fracture Zone

Tropic of Cancer

Johnston Atoll   Schjetman Reef

Hawai'i   Mauna Kea 4205m

East Mariana Basin

M i c r o n e s i a

Marshall Islands

Marshall Seamounts

Central Pacific Basin

Clarion Fracture Zone

Christmas Ridge

E

Nauru   Banaba   Tungaru

Melanesian Basin

Phoenix Islands

Kiritimati

Clipperton Fracture Zone

Solomon Islands

Guadalcanal   Malaita

Santa Cruz Islands

Tuvalu

M e l a n e s i a

P o l y n e s i a

Galapagos Fracture Zone   Equator   0°

North New Hebrides Trench   Espiritu Santo

PACIFIC PLATE

FIJI PLATE

Robbie Ridge

Northern Cook Islands

Manihiki Plateau

Marquesas Islands   Hiva Oa

Line Islands

Iles Loyaute

Vanuatu   North Fiji Basin   Fiji

Tanna   Viti Levu   Vanua Levu

Samoa   Savaii   Upolu

Samoa Basin

Penrhyn Basin

Tuamotu Ridge

Tuamotu Archipelago

Tiki Basin

New Caledonia   New Hebrides Trench

Capricorn Tablemount

Southern Cook Islands

Rarotonga

Society Islands

Society Ridge   Tahiti

Cook Fracture Zone   South Fiji Basin   Lau Basin   Tonga   Tonga Trench

Tuamotu Fracture Zone

Lord Howe Seamounts

New Caledonia Basin   Norfolk Ridge

Norfolk Island

Austral Islands

Iles Gambier

Austral Fracture Zone

Three Kings Rise   Kermadec Ridge   Kermadec Trench   Louisville Ridge

Pitcairn Island   Ducie Island   Henderson Island

Tropic of Capricorn

Lord Howe Rise   West Norfolk Ridge

Bay of Plenty

New Zealand

South Island   Taraki (Mount Cook) 3754m

Chatham Rise   Chatham Islands

Southwest Pacific Basin

East Pacific Rise

NAZCA PLATE

South West Cape   Bounty Trough

Campbell Plateau

Agassiz Fracture Zone

Macquarie Ridge

Macquarie Island

S

Eltanin Fracture Zone

Udintsev Fracture Zone

PACIFIC PLATE   ANTARCTIC PLATE

SOUTHERN OCEAN

ANTARCTICA

Pacific-Antarctic Ridge

Antarctic Circle

130°   140°   150°   160°   170°   180°   170°   160°   150°

1   2   3   4   5   6   7   8   9   10

Political

Vast expanses of ocean separate this geographically fragmented realm, characterized more by each country's isolation than by any political unity. Australia's and New Zealand's traditional ties with the United Kingdom, as members of the Commonwealth, are now being called into question as Australasian and Oceanian nations are increasingly looking to forge new relationships with neighboring Asian countries like Japan. External influences have featured strongly in the politics of the Pacific Islands; the various territories of Micronesia were largely under US control until the late 1980s, and France, New Zealand, the USA and the UK still have territories under colonial rule in Polynesia. Nuclear weapons-testing by Western superpowers was widespread during the Cold War period, but has now been discontinued.

Population
- above 5 million
- 1 million to 5 million
- 500,000 to 1 million
- 100,000 to 500,000
- 50,000 to 100,000
- 10,000 to 50,000
- below 10,000
- Country capital
- State capital

Borders
- full international border
- indication of maritime country extent
- indication of maritime dependent territory extent
- state border

Communications
- major roads
- major railroads

Scale 1:32,000,000
(projection: Lambert Azimuthal Equal Area)

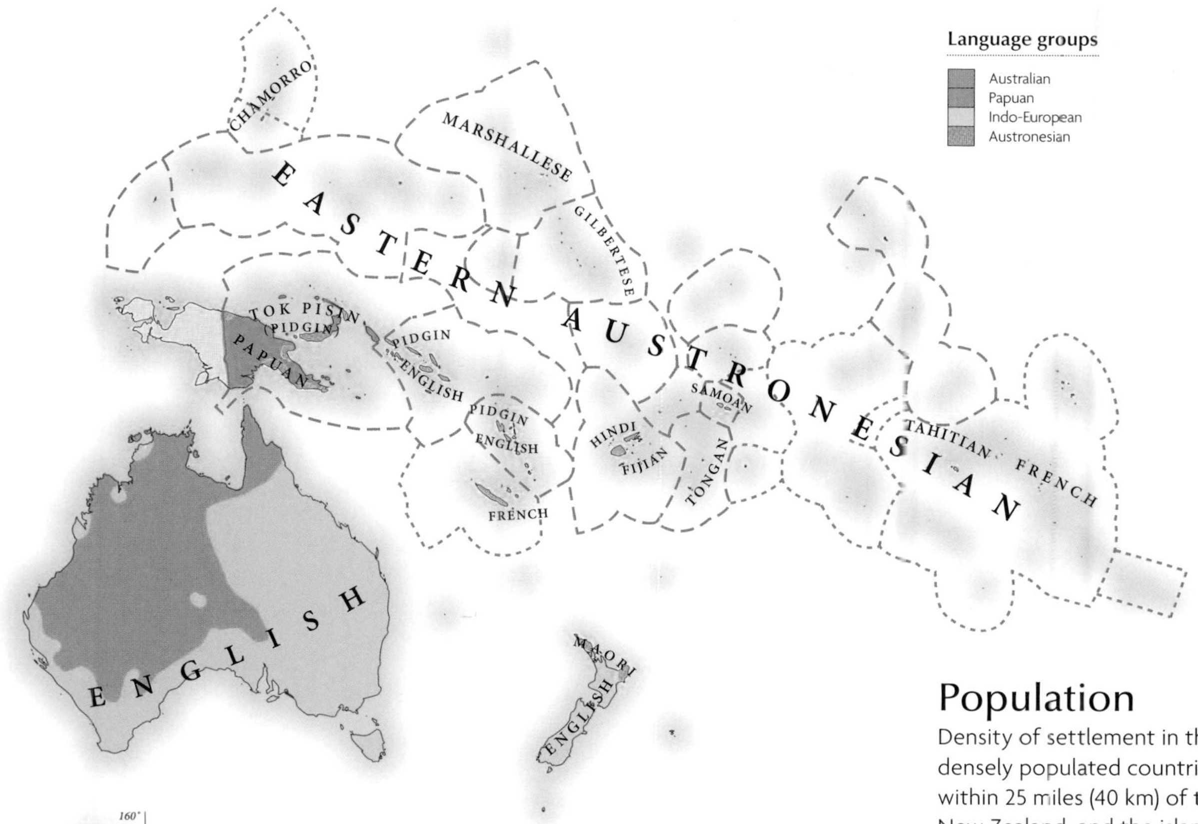

269

Language groups

- Australian
- Papuan
- Indo-European
- Austronesian

(Map labels) CHAMORRO · MARSHALLESE · GILBERTESE · EASTERN AUSTRONESIAN · TOK PISIN (PIDGIN) · PAPUAN · PIDGIN ENGLISH · PIDGIN ENGLISH · HINDI · FIJIAN · SAMOAN · TONGAN · TAHITIAN · FRENCH · FRENCH · ENGLISH · MAORI · ENGLISH

Languages

English is spoken throughout Australia and New Zealand. In Australia, English has been superimposed on a mosaic of Aboriginal languages. In New Zealand, the indigenous language, Maori, is the official language besides English. In Papua New Guinea, Melanesian Pidgin has become a *lingua franca* alongside several hundred indigenous languages. Across the region, the indigenous languages can be grouped into (1) the Aboriginal languages of Australia, (2) the Papuan languages spoken mostly inland in Papua New Guinea, and (3) the widely dispersed Austronesian, which includes coastal languages of Papua New Guinea, New Zealand Maori, and languages of Oceania.

Population

Density of settlement in the region is generally low. Australia is one of the least densely populated countries on Earth with over 80% of its population living within 25 miles (40 km) of the coast – mostly in the southeast of the country. New Zealand, and the island groups of Melanesia, Micronesia and Polynesia, are much more densely populated, although many of the smaller islands remain uninhabited.

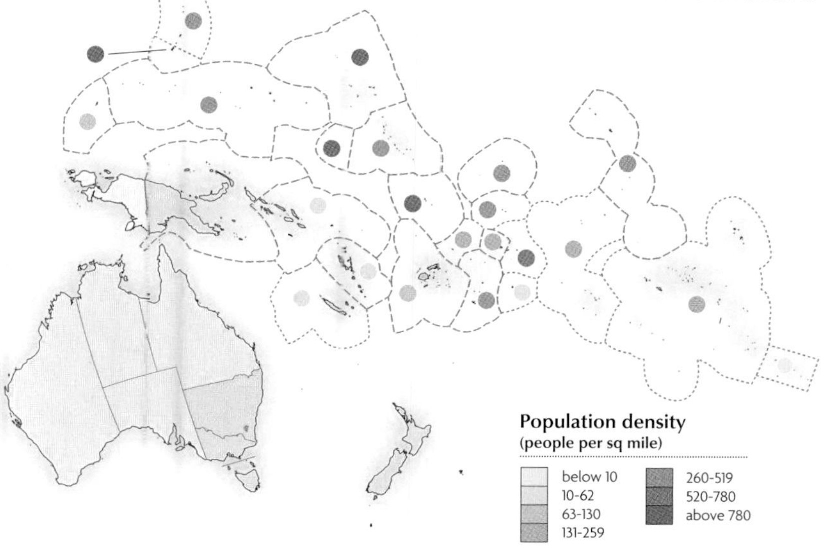

Population density
(people per sq mile)

- below 10
- 10-62
- 63-130
- 131-259
- 260-519
- 520-780
- above 780

(Map labels, left) Kingman Reef (to US) · Palmyra Atoll (to US) · Teraina · Tabuarean · KIRIBATI · Kiritimati · Jarvis Island (to US) · Malden Island · Starbuck Island · Line Islands · Equator · Northern Cook Islands · Penrhyn · Manihiki · Millennium Island · Flint Island · Marquesas Islands · Cook Islands (to NZ) · Tuamotu Islands · Society Islands · PAPEETE · Tahiti · Southern Cook Islands · AVARUA · Rarotonga · French Polynesia (to France) · Iles Australes · Mururoa · Tropic of Capricorn · Iles Gambier · Pitcairn Islands (to UK) · Pitcairn Island · OCEAN

Standard of living

In marked contrast to its neighbor, Australia, with one of the world's highest life expectancies and standards of living, Papua New Guinea is one of the world's least developed countries. In addition, high population growth and urbanization rates throughout the Pacific islands contribute to overcrowding. The Aboriginal and Maori people of Australia and New Zealand have been isolated for many years. Recently, their traditional land ownership rights have begun to be legally recognized in an effort to ease their social and economic isolation, and to improve living standards.

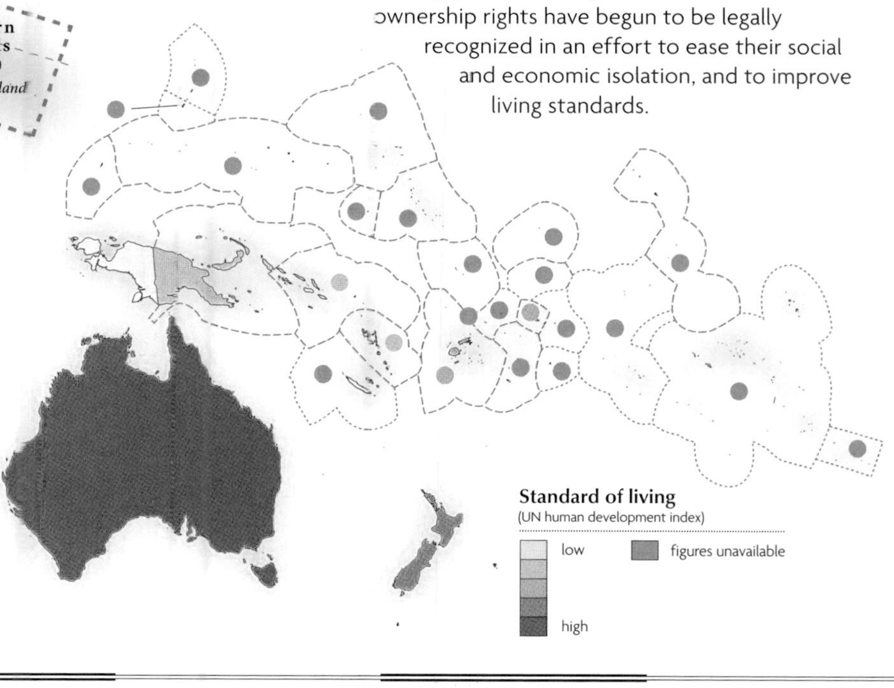

Standard of living
(UN human development index)

- low
- high
- figures unavailable

Transportation

While sea travel remains of paramount importance throughout the continent, well-developed regional and international air travel has reduced the region's global isolation. Internal air travel is particularly important in Australia, where distances are great and road systems are poorly developed or in some areas nonexistent. Australia's rail system, still operating on three different guages, a legacy of its piecemeal development, is being upgraded, particularly in the north-south links.

AUSTRALASIA & OCEANIA

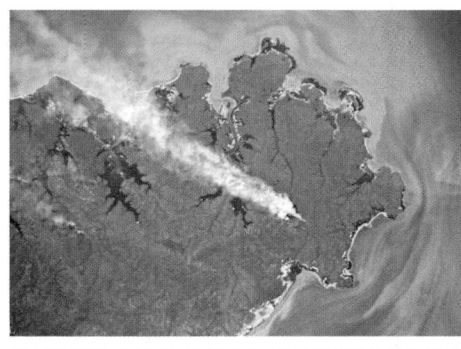

1 MELVILLE ISLAND, NORTHERN TERRITORY, AUSTRALIA
Lying off Australia's north coast, the island is sparsely populated consisting of sandy soils and mangrove swamps.

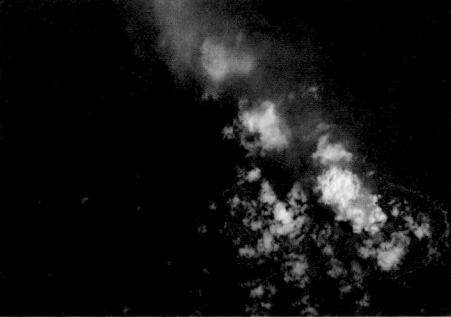

2 ANATAHAN, NORTHERN MARIANA ISLANDS
The volcano or Anatahan is one of 12 in the Mariana Islands and erupted on a large scale in April 2005.

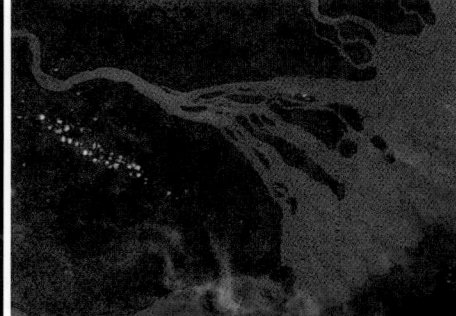

3 FLY RIVER, PAPUA NEW GUINEA
Flowing down from New Guinea's Central Range, the river carries a heavy load of sediment which it deposits in the Gulf of Papua, sometimes forming new islands.

4 RABAUL VOLCANO, NEW BRITAIN, PAPUA NEW GUINEA
After erupting in 1994, this image shows how the highest particles blew west causing condensation of water vapour over a wide area.

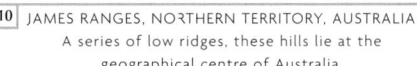

9 ULURU/AYERS ROCK, NORTHERN TERRITORY, AUSTRALIA
This enormous sandstone rock occupies Australia's heart, both physically and emotionally.

10 JAMES RANGES, NORTHERN TERRITORY, AUSTRALIA
A series of low ridges, these hills lie at the geographical centre of Australia.

11 LAKE EYRE, SOUTH AUSTRALIA, AUSTRALIA
This great salt lake consists of north and south sections, joined by a narrow channel, Lake Eyre South being the smaller, elongated saltflat at the bottom of the image.

12 NEWCASTLE, NEW SOUTH WALES, AUSTRALIA
The industrial seaport of Newcastle lies on the south bank of Hunter river.

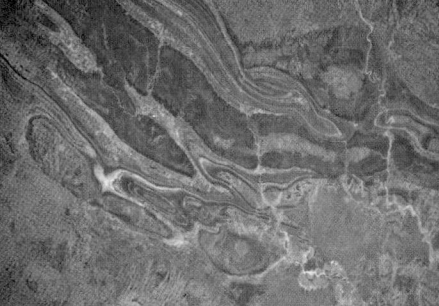

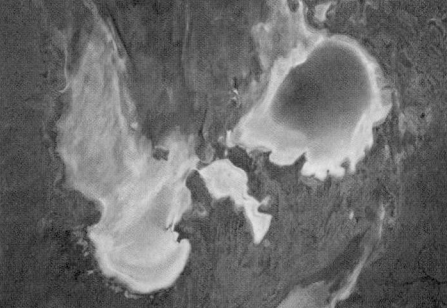

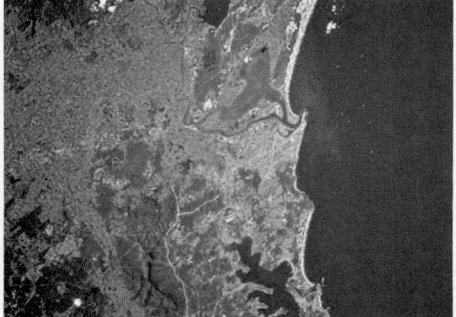

Climate

Surrounded by water, the climate of most areas is profoundly affected by the moderating effects of the oceans. Australia, however, is the exception. Its dry continental interior remains isolated from the ocean; temperatures soar during the day, and droughts are common. The coastal regions, where most people live, are cooler and wetter. The numerous islands scattered across the Pacific are generally hot and humid, subject to the different air circulation patterns and ocean currents that affect the area, including the El Niño ocean current anomaly, which produces extreme aridity.

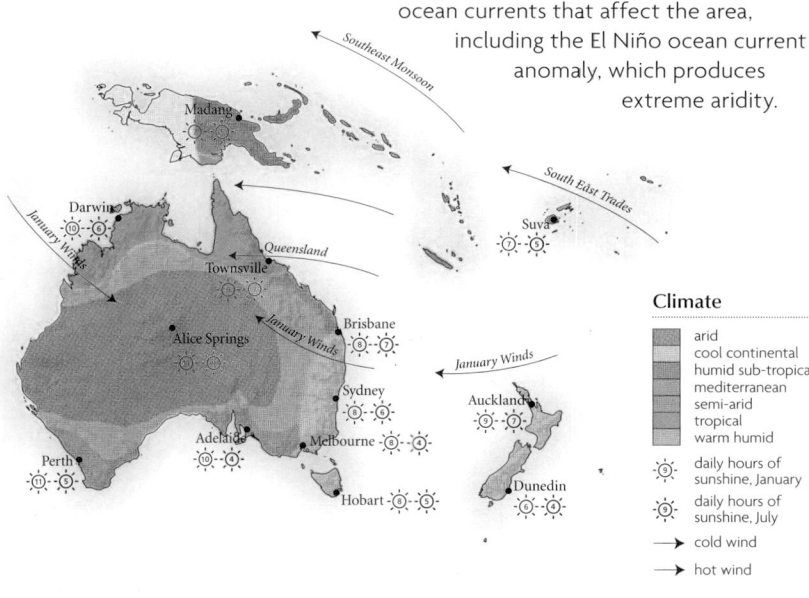

Climate

- arid
- cool continental
- humid sub-tropical
- mediterranean
- semi-arid
- tropical
- warm humid
- ☼ daily hours of sunshine, January
- ☼ daily hours of sunshine, July
- → cold wind
- → hot wind

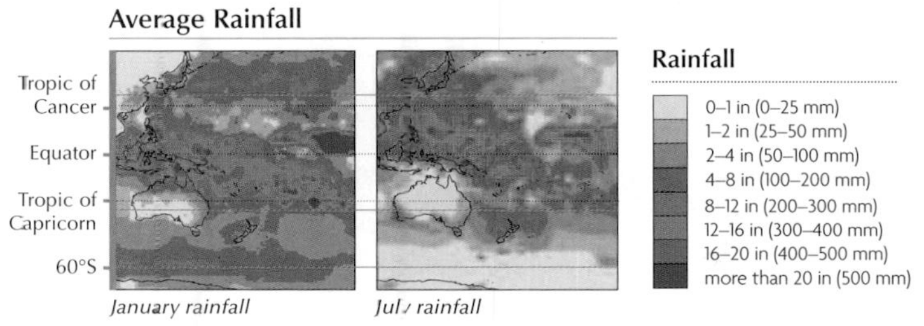

Average Rainfall

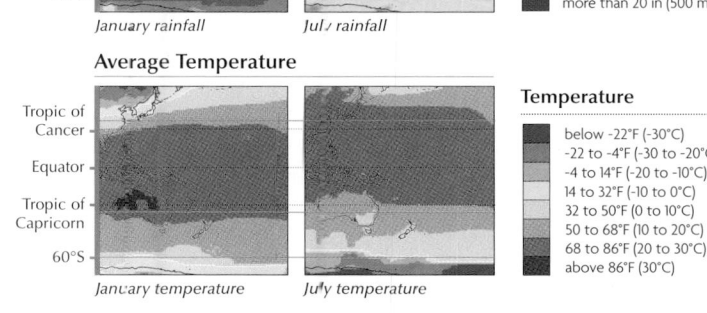

January rainfall   *July rainfall*

Rainfall

- 0–1 in (0–25 mm)
- 1–2 in (25–50 mm)
- 2–4 in (50–100 mm)
- 4–8 in (100–200 mm)
- 8–12 in (200–300 mm)
- 12–16 in (300–400 mm)
- 16–20 in (400–500 mm)
- more than 20 in (500 mm)

Average Temperature

January temperature   *July temperature*

Temperature

- below -22°F (-30°C)
- -22 to -4°F (-30 to -20°C)
- -4 to 14°F (-20 to -10°C)
- 14 to 32°F (-10 to 0°C)
- 32 to 50°F (0 to 10°C)
- 50 to 68°F (10 to 20°C)
- 68 to 86°F (20 to 30°C)
- above 86°F (30°C)

Environmental issues

The prospect of rising sea levels poses a threat to many low-lying islands in the Pacific. Nuclear weapons-testing, once common throughout the region, was finally discontinued in 1996. Australia's ecological balance has been irreversibly altered by the introduction of alien species. Although it has the world's largest underground water reserve, the Great Artesian Basin, the availability of fresh water in Australia remains critical. Periodic droughts combined with over-grazing lead to desertification and increase the risk of devastating bush fires, and occasional flash floods.

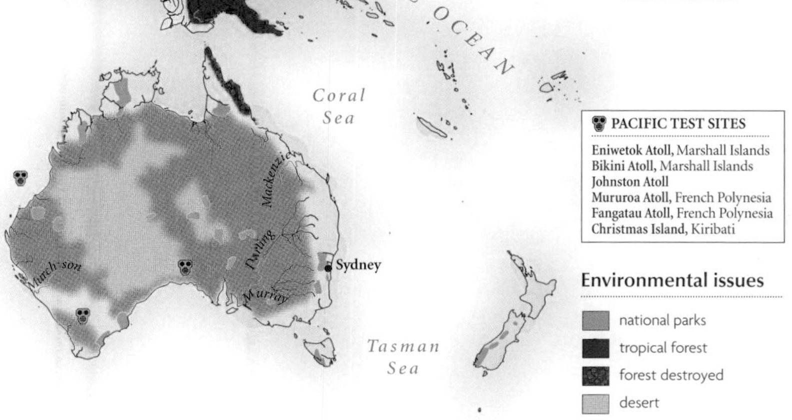

PACIFIC TEST SITES
Eniwetok Atoll, Marshall Islands
Bikini Atoll, Marshall Islands
Johnston Atoll
Mururoa Atoll, French Polynesia
Fangatau Atoll, French Polynesia
Christmas Island, Kiribati

Environmental issues

- national parks
- tropical forest
- forest destroyed
- desert
- desertification
- polluted rivers
- ☢ radioactive contamination
- marine pollution
- heavy marine pollution
- • poor urban air quality

Landuse

Much of the region's industry is resource-based: sheep farming for wool and meat in Australia and New Zealand; mining in Australia and Papua New Guinea and fishing throughout the Pacific islands. Manufacturing is mainly limited to the large coastal cities in Australia and New Zealand, like Sydney, Adelaide, Melbourne, Brisbane, Perth, and Auckland, although small-scale enterprises operate in the Pacific islands, concentrating on processing of fish and foods. Tourism continues to provide revenue to the area—in Fiji it accounts for 15 percent of GNP.

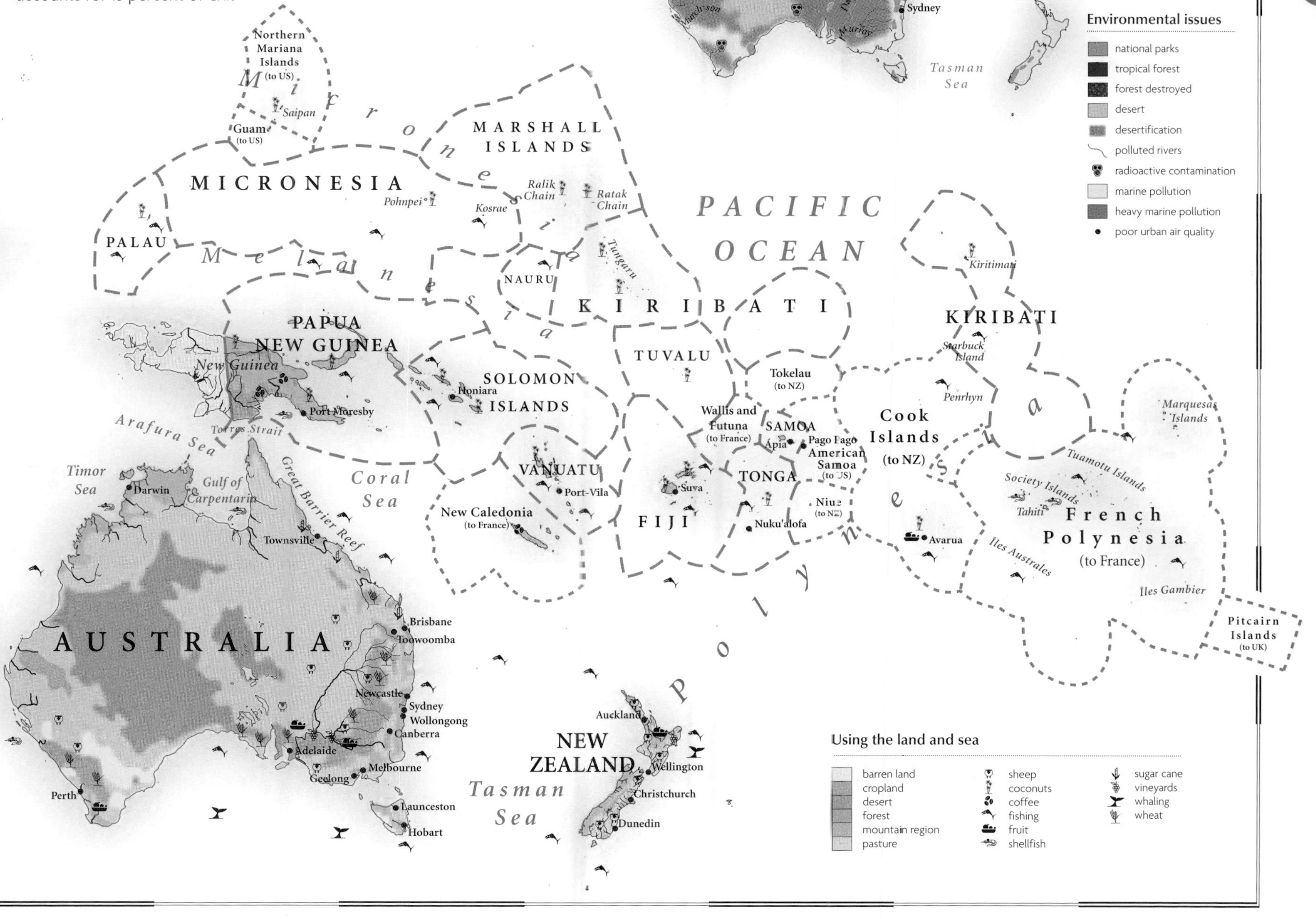

Using the land and sea

- barren land
- cropland
- desert
- forest
- mountain region
- pasture
- sheep
- coconuts
- coffee
- fishing
- fruit
- shellfish
- sugar cane
- vineyards
- whaling
- wheat

AUSTRALASIA & OCEANIA

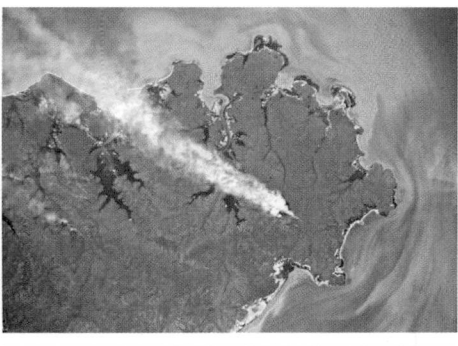

1 MELVILLE ISLAND, NORTHERN TERRITORY, AUSTRALIA
Lying off Australia's north coast, the island is sparsely populated consisting of sandy soils and mangrove swamps.

2 ANATAHAN, NORTHERN MARIANA ISLANDS
The volcano on Anatahan is one of 12 in the Mariana Islands and erupted on a large scale in April 2005.

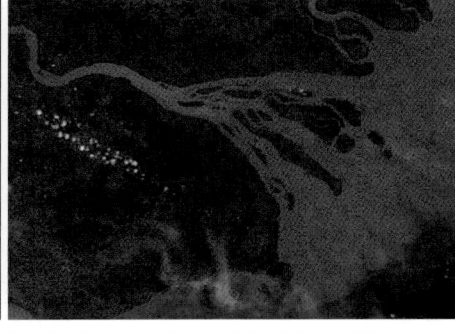

3 FLY RIVER, PAPUA NEW GUINEA
Flowing down from New Guinea's Central Range, the river carries a heavy load of sediment which it deposits in the Gulf of Papua, sometimes forming new islands.

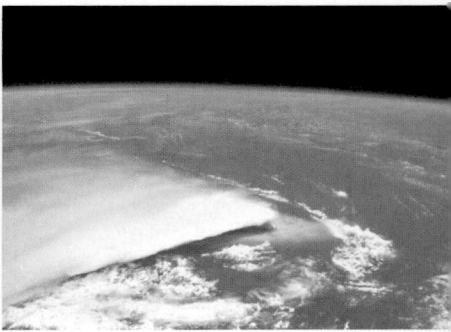

4 RABAUL VOLCANO, NEW BRITAIN, PAPUA NEW GUINEA
After erupting in 1994, this image shows how the highest particles blew west causing condensation of water vapour over a wide area.

9 ULURU/AYERS ROCK, NORTHERN TERRITORY, AUSTRALIA
This enormous sandstone rock occupies Australia's heart, both physically and emotionally.

10 JAMES RANGES, NORTHERN TERRITORY, AUSTRALIA
A series of low ridges, these hills lie at the geographical centre of Australia.

11 LAKE EYRE, SOUTH AUSTRALIA, AUSTRALIA
This great salt lake consists of north and south sections, joined by a narrow channel, Lake Eyre South being the smaller, elongated saltflat at the bottom of the image.

12 NEWCASTLE, NEW SOUTH WALES, AUSTRALIA
The industrial seaport of Newcastle lies on the south bank of Hunter river.

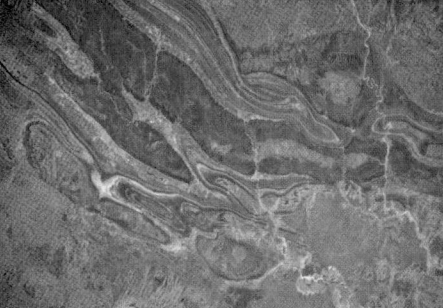

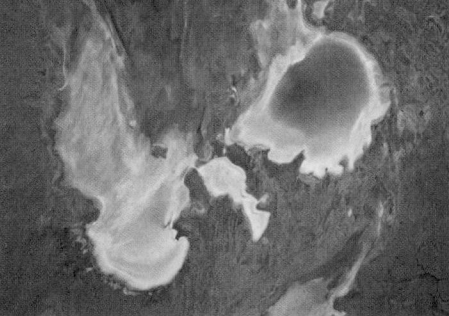

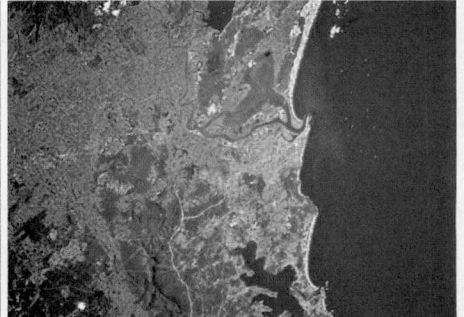

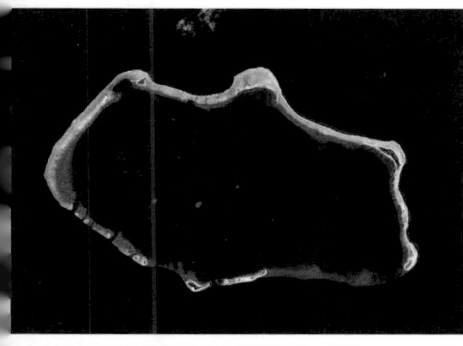

BIKINI ATOLL, MARSHALL ISLANDS `5`
This atoll was the site of 23 atomic bomb tests in the 1940s and 1950s, involving the intentional sinking of at least 13 naval vessels in the shallow lagoon.

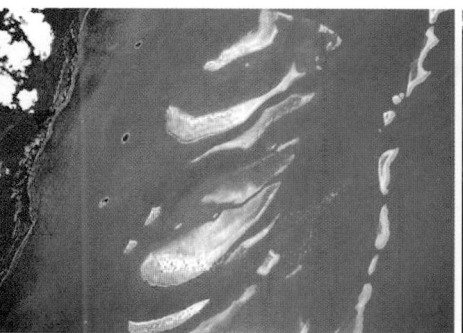

GREAT BARRIER REEF, QUEENSLAND, AUSTRALIA `6`
The world's largest reef system is made up of 3000 individual reefs and 900 islands and stretches for 1600 miles (2600 km).

AM3RYM, VANUATU `7`
Mount Marum, a 4166ft (1270 m) volcanc, erupted in April 2004 producing an extensive plume of ash.

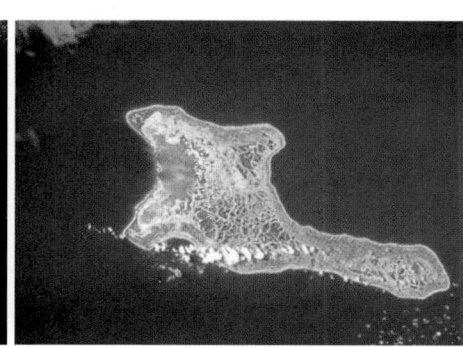

KIRITIMATI, KIRIBATI `8`
Kiritimati is the largest atoll in the Pacific Ocean, its interior lagoon filled in with coral growth.

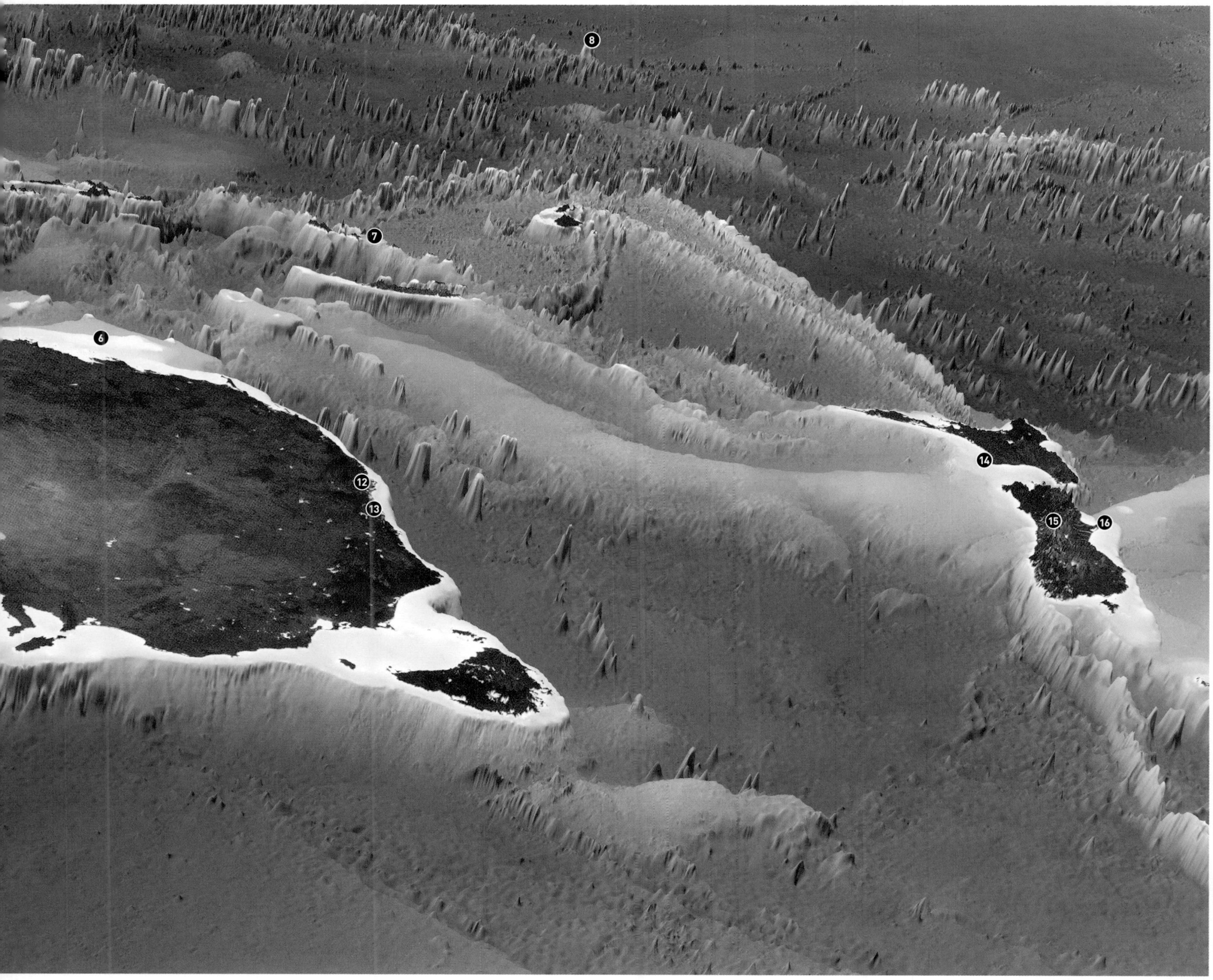

SYDNEY, NEW SOUTH WALES, AUSTRALIA `13`
Expanding outwards from the inlet of Port Jackson, Australia's largest city was founded in 1788.

MOUNT TARANAKI, NORTH ISLAND, NEW ZEALAND `14`
This dormant 8261 ft (2518 m) volcano is one of the most symmetrical in the world.

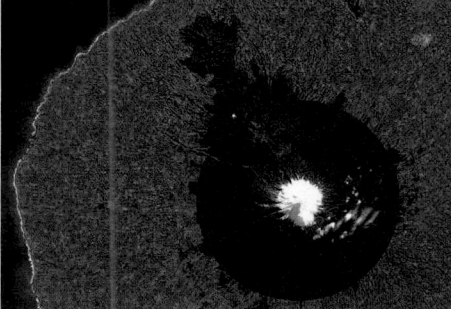

AORAKI/MOUNT COOK, SOUTH ISLAND, NEW ZEALAND `15`
New Zealand's highest peak rises 12,238 ft (374² m) and is surrounded by permanent ice fields.

BANKS PENINSULA, SOUTH ISLAND, NEW ZEALAND `16`
With a circular drainage pattern typical of eroded volcanoes, this is the only recognisably volcanic feature on New Zealand's South Island.

Australia

Perth

6000m
4000m
3000m
2000m
1000m
500m
250m
100m
Sea Level
-250m
-2000m
-4000m

Scale 1:13,000,000
(projection: Lambert Conformal Conic)

0 50 100 150 200 250 300 350 400 Km
0 50 100 150 200 250 300 350 400 Miles

Population

■ above 5 million   ▣ 1 million to 5 million   ◉ 500,000 to 1 million
◉ 100,000 to 500,000   ◉ 50,000 to 100,000   ○ 10,000 to 50,000   ○ below 10,000

Arafura Sea

PAPUA NEW GUINEA

New Guinea

Torres Strait

PORT MORESBY

Gulf of Papua

Solomon Sea

Solomon Islands

SOLOMON ISLANDS

HONIARA
Guadalcanal

Coral Sea

CORAL SEA ISLANDS
(to Australia)

Gulf of Carpentaria

Cape York Peninsula

Arnhem Land

QUEENSLAND

Great Artesian Basin

Simpson Desert

Lake Eyre Basin

AUSTRALIA

NEW CALEDONIA
(to France)

PACIFIC OCEAN

Tropic of Capricorn

Brisbane

Gold Coast
Surfers Paradise

NEW SOUTH WALES

Sydney

Newcastle

CANBERRA
AUSTRALIAN CAPITAL TERRITORY

Adelaide

VICTORIA

Melbourne

Bass Strait

TASMANIA

Hobart

Lord Howe Island
(to Australia)

280
286
293

19,686ft
13,124ft
9843ft
6562ft
3281ft
1640ft
820ft
328ft
Sea Level
-820ft
-6562ft
-13,124ft

Brisbane

Brisbane Airport

Everton Park

Toombul

Wynnum

The Gap

Red Hill

Lutwyche

Clayfield

Newstead

Hawthorne

Manly

Tingalpa

Brisbane

Botanical Gardens

Queensland Art Gallery

Indooroopilly

Woolloongabba

Greenslopes

Carina Heights

Belmont

Corinda

Mount Gravatt

Burbank

Tingalpa Reservoir

Cherms de

Myrtletown

Chams de

274

Elevation scale
6000m
4000m
3000m
2000m
1000m
500m
250m
100m
Sea Level
-250m
-2000m
-4000m

A B C D 274 E F G

1
Gibson Desert
NORTHERN TERRITORY
Simpson Desert
Kata Tjuta (Mount Olga) 1069m
Yulara
Uluru (Ayers Rock) 867m
Kulgera Roadhouse
Finke
Eyre Creek
Warburton Range
Tomkinson Ranges
Mann Ranges
Musgrave Ranges
Mount Morris 1288m
Mount Woodroffe 1514m
Pukatja
Marryat
Abminga
Pedirka
Lake Griselda
Clifton Hills
Pandie Pandie
Lake Etamunbanie
Warburton
Mount Davies 1058m
Mount Kintore 1070m
Fregon
Hamilton Creek
Alberga Creek
Macumba River
Lake Eyre Basin
Lake Throssell

2
WESTERN AUSTRALIA
Great Victoria Desert
Mount Illbалee 917m
Mimili
Chandler
Marla
Everard Ranges
North Branch Neales
South Branch Neales
Oodnadatta
AUSTRAL
Sturt Stony
Lake Yeo
Birksgate Range
Mount Sir Thomas 772m
Iltur
Cadney Homestead
Evelyn Creek
Arckaringa Creek
Algebuckina Bridge
Lake Eyre North
Tirari Desert
Strzelecki
Rason Lake
Wanna Lakes
Serpentine Lakes
Lake Meramangye
Emu Junction
SOUTH
Coober Pedy
Poatnoura
Loot Creek
Curdimurka
Lake Eyre South
Marree
Frome Creek
Lake Gregory
Lake Blanche
Mount Fitton
Lake Minigwal
Jubilee Lake
Forrest Lakes
Wyola Lake
Lake Dey-Dey
Lake Maurice
Wilkinsons Lakes
Lake Anthony
Half Moon Lake
Wirrida
Gina
Mirikata
Billa Kalina
AUSTRALIA
Olympic Dam
Roxby Downs
Andamooka
Lyndhurst
Leigh Creek
Copley
Arkaroola
Freeling Heights 914m

3
Lake Minigwal
AUSTRALIA
Maralinga
Ooldea
Watson
Mungala
Wynbring
Lyons
Tarcoola
Lake Younghusband
Glendambo
Woomera
Wirraminna
Pernatty Lagoon
Parachilna
Lake Frome
Frome Downs
Cutnamona

4
Kitchener
Rawlinna
Loongana
Reid
Hughes
Cook
Nullarbor
Yalata
Head of Bight
Coorabie
Bookabie
Koonibba
Ceduna
Lake Everard
Lake Acraman
Low Hill
Lake Macfarlane
Quorn
Nullarbor Plain
Eucla
Wilson Bluff
Cape Adieu
Cape Bell
Point Bell
Penong
Smoky Bay
Gairdner
Lake Gairdner
Port Augusta
Wilmington
Orroroo
Carrieton
Hampton Tableland
Madura
Cocklebiddy
Red Rocks Point
Fowlers Bay
Nuyts Archipelago
Wirrulla
Poochera
Minnipa
Bucklebog
Iron Knob
Iron Baron
Port Pirie
Melrose
Peterborough

5
Caiguna
Point Dover
Streaky Bay
Point Westall
Streaky Bay
Port Kenny
Kyancutta
Cape Blanche
Cape Radstock
Anxious Bay
Flinders Island
Lock
Mount Wedge
Elliston
Sheringa
Karkoo
Murdinga
Cleve
Cowell
Eyre Peninsula
Port Broughton
Snowtown
Wallaroo
Kadina
Clare
Balaklava
Robertstown
Morgan
Balladonia
Point Culver
Investigator Group
Cummins
Port Neill
Moonta
Maitland

6
Tower Peak 594m
Cape Arid
Cape Pasley
Archipelago of the Recherche
South East Isles
Great Australian Bight
Coffin Bay Peninsula
Point Whidbey
Coffin Bay
Port Lincoln
Cape Carnot
West Point
Sir Joseph Banks Group
Thistle Island
Gambier Islands
Cape Spencer
Spencer Gulf
Yorke Peninsula
Yorketown
Stenhouse Bay
Minlaton
Ardrossan
Port Victoria
Saint Vincent
Gulf
Elizabeth
Adelaide
Mount Barker
Murray Bridge
Menangle
Investigator Strait
Kingscote
Parndana
Penneshaw
Kangaroo Island
Cape Borda
Cape de Couedic
Cape Gantheaume
Cape Hart
Encounter Bay
Victor Harbor
Goolwa
Lake Alexandrina
Younghusband Peninsula
Lacepede Bay

Melbourne

A B C D

7
Melbourne Airport
Tullamarine
Broadmeadows
Thomastown
Plenty
Maribyrnong River
Keilor
Fawkner
Bundoora
Greensborough
Brimbank Park
St Albans
Pascoe Vale
Heidelberg

8
Essendon
Coburg
Ivanhoe
Maribyrnong
Brunswick
Yarra River
Bullen Park
Doncaster
Ardeer
Footscray
Ascot Vale
Royal Park
University of Melbourne
Carlton
Yarra Bend Park
Nunawading
Brooklyn
Docklands
Melbourne
Kew
Box Hill

9
Newport
Port Melbourne
National Gallery
Royal Botanic Gardens
South Yarra
Camberwell
Glen Iris
Hobsons Bay
Albert Park
Malvern
Altona
Williamstown
St Kilda
Caulfield
Mount Waverley

10
Point Cook
Port Phillip Bay
Brighton
Sandringham
Oakleigh
Clayton
Moorabbin

0 5 Km
0 5 Miles

Sydney

D E F G

7
Ku-ring-gai National Park
Castle Hill
Pennant Hills
Pymble
Dee Why
Blacktown
Marsfield
Chatswood
Manly

8
Parramatta
Parramatta River
Ryde
Mosman
North Head
South Head
Prospect Reservoir
Homebush Bay
Olympic Park
Abbotsford
Sydney Harbour Bridge
Fairfield
Regents Park
Sydney Opera House
Sydney
Bossley Park
Burwood
Bondi
Canterbury
Redfern
Randwick

9
Liverpool
Bankstown
Hurstville
Maroubra
Kingsford Smith Intl. Airport
Georges River
La Perouse
Tasman Sea

10
Sutherland
Botany Bay
Kurnell
Cape Banks
Botany Bay National Park
Cronulla
Bate Bay
Port Hacking

0 5 Km
0 5 Miles

293

A B C D E F G

Scale 1:6,500,000
(projection: Lambert Conformal Conic)

0 25 50 75 100 125 150 175 200 Km
0 25 50 75 100 125 150 175 200 Miles

Population
- ▣ above 5 million
- ▣ 1 million to 5 million
- ◉ 500,000 to 1 million
- ◎ 100,000 to 500,000
- ⊕ 50,000 to 100,000
- ⊙ 10,000 to 50,000
- ○ below 10,000

AUSTRALASIA & OCEANIA

QUEENSLAND

NEW SOUTH WALES

VICTORIA

Tasmania

TASMANIA

Bass Strait

Tasman Sea

Brisbane
Sydney
CANBERRA
AUSTRALIAN CAPITAL TERRITORY
JERVIS BAY TERRITORY
Melbourne
Hobart
Newcastle
Wollongong
Geelong
Ballarat

Murray River
Darling River
Cooper Creek
Lake Yamma Yamma
Fraser Island
King Island
Flinders Island

19,686ft
13,124ft
9843ft
6562ft
3281ft
1640ft
820ft
328ft
Sea Level
-820ft
-6562ft
-13,124ft

Papua New Guinea & Melanesia

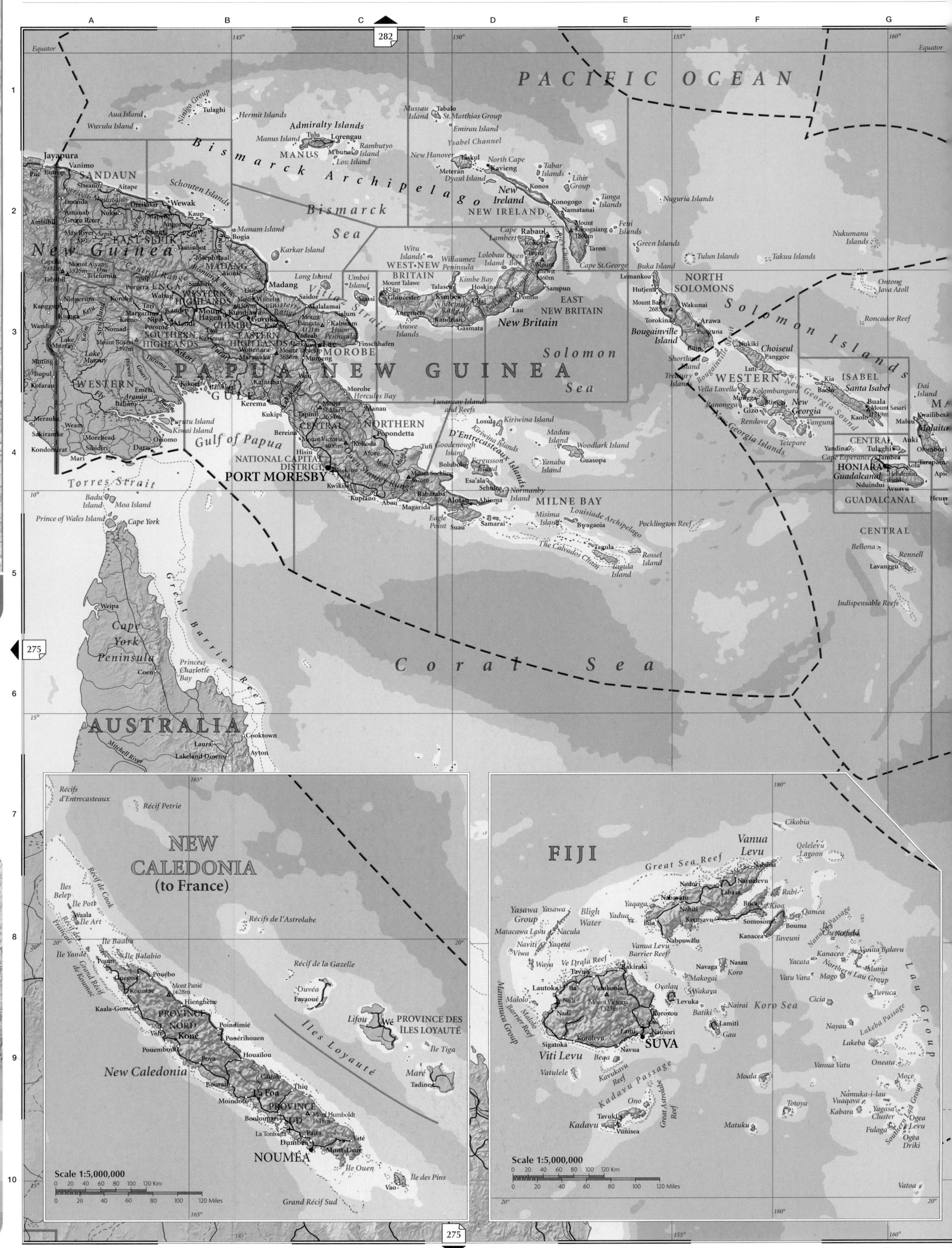

275

AUSTRALASIA & OCEANIA

Scale 1:5,000,000

NEW CALEDONIA (to France)

FIJI

Scale 1:10,100,000
(projection: Mercator)

0 50 100 150 200 250 300 Km
0 50 100 150 200 250 300 Miles

Population
■ above 5 million
◉ 100,000 to 500,000
▣ 1 million to 5 million
⊕ 50,000 to 100,000
◉ 500,000 to 1 million
○ 10,000 to 50,000
○ below 10,000

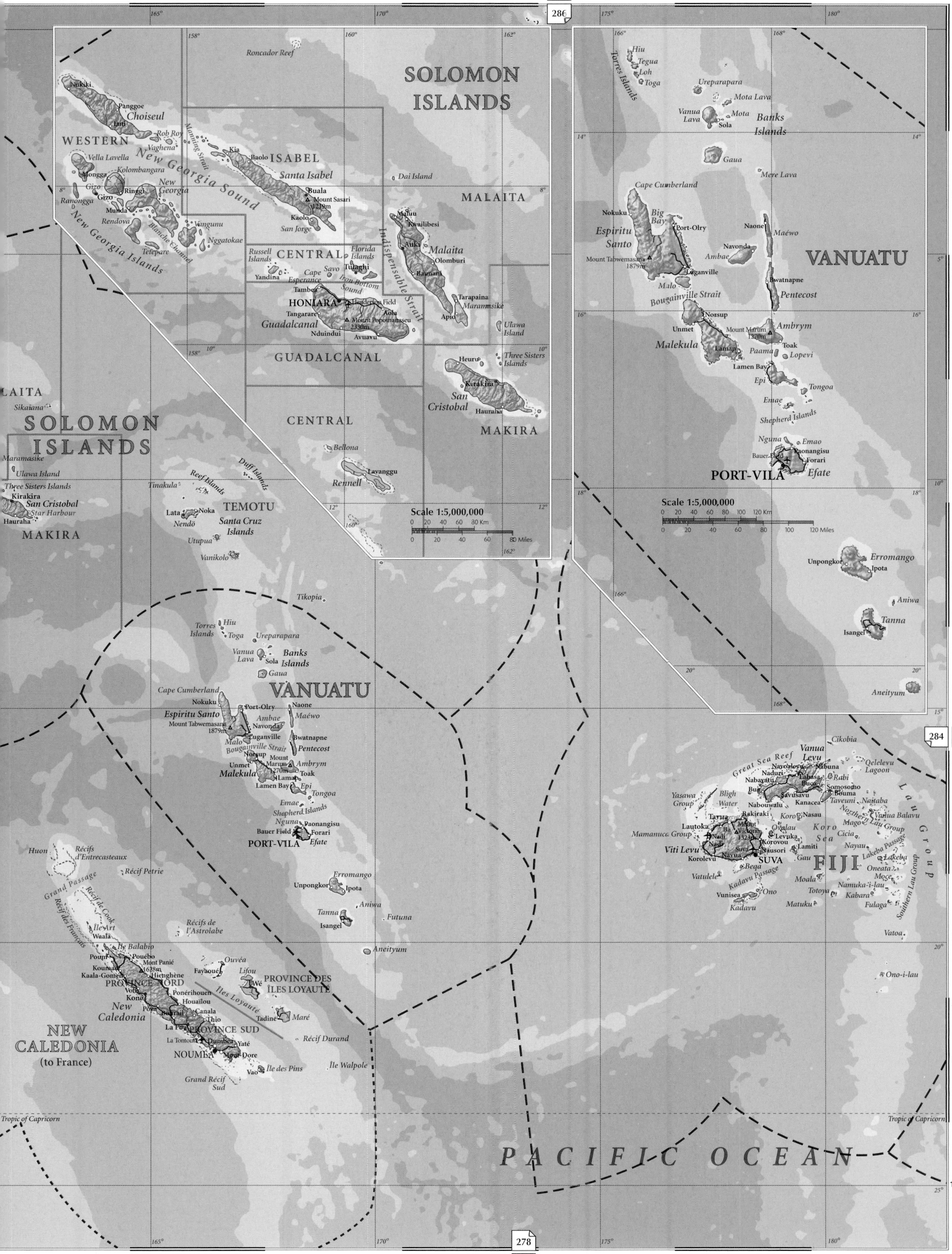

SOLOMON ISLANDS

Roncador Reef
Nukiki
Panggoe
Luti
Choiseul
WESTERN
Vella Lavella
Vaghena
Mongga
Kolombangara
Gizo
Ringgi
New
Georgia
Munda
Rendova
Ranongga
Blanche Channel
Tetepare
Vangunu
Nggatokae
New Georgia Islands
New Georgia Sound
Manning Strait
Kia
Baolo
ISABEL
Santa Isabel
Buala
Kaolo
San Jorge
Mount Sasari
1219m
Dai Island
MALAITA
Malu'u
Kwailibesi
Auki
Malaita
Olomburi
Kaolo
CENTRAL
Russell Islands
Yandina
Florida Islands
Savo
Tulaghi
Cape Esperance
Tambea
Iron Bottom Sound
Indispensable Strait
Tarapaina
Marammsike
HONIARA
Tangarare
Henderson Field
Mount Popomanaseu
2330m
GUADALCANAL
Nduindui
Avuavu
Heuru
Kirakira
Three Sisters Islands
Ulawa Island
San Cristobal
Hauraha
MAKIRA
CENTRAL
Bellona
Lavanggu
Rennell
TEMOTU
Reef Islands
Duff Islands
Tinakula
Lata
Noka
Nendö
Santa Cruz Islands
Utupua
Vanikolo

Scale 1:5,000,000
0 20 40 60 80 Km
0 20 40 60 80 Miles

VANUATU

Hiu
Tegua
Loh
Toga
Torres Islands
Ureparapara
Mota Lava
Vanua Lava
Sola
Mota
Banks Islands
Gaua
Mere Lava
Cape Cumberland
Nokuku
Big Bay
Port-Olry
Espiritu Santo
Naone
Maéwo
Mount Tabwemasana
1879m
Ambae
Navonda
Luganville
Malo
Norsup
Bougainville Strait
Pentecost
Unmet
Mount Marum
1270m
Ambrym
Malekula
Lamap
Paama
Toak
Lopevi
Lamen Bay
Epi
Emae
Tongoa
Shepherd Islands
Nguna
Emao
Paonangisu
Bauer Field
Forari
PORT-VILA
Efate
Unpongkor
Erromango
Ipota
Aniwa
Tanna
Isangel
Aneityum

Scale 1:5,000,000
0 20 40 60 80 100 120 Km
0 20 40 60 80 100 120 Miles

SOLOMON ISLANDS
LAITA
Sikaiana
Maramasike
Ulawa Island
Three Sisters Islands
Kirakira
San Cristobal
Star Harbour
Hauraha
MAKIRA

VANUATU
Hiu
Torres Islands
Toga
Ureparapara
Vanua Lava
Sola
Banks Islands
Gaua
Cape Cumberland
Nokuku
Port-Olry
Espiritu Santo
Naone
Mount Tabwemasana
1879m
Ambae
Maéwo
Navonda
Luganville
Malo
Bougainville Strait
Pentecost
Norsup
Bwatnapne
Unmet
Mount Marum
1270m
Ambrym
Malekula
Lamap
Toak
Lamen Bay
Epi
Emae
Tongoa
Shepherd Islands
Nguna
Paonangisu
Bauer Field
Forari
PORT-VILA
Efate
Unpongkor
Erromango
Ipota
Tanna
Aniwa
Futuna
Isangel
Aneityum

FIJI
Cikobia
Great Sea Reef
Vanua Levu
Qelelevu Lagoon
Nayouevu
Labasa
Rabi
Naduri
Buca
Bouma
Nabavatu
Savusavu
Taveuni
Vanua Balavu
Yasawa Group
Bligh Water
Rakiraki
Koro
Nasau
Nacula
Northern Lau Group
Mago
Cicia
Lautoka
Ba
Vatia
Ovalau
Levuka
Nayau
Lakeba
Mamanuca Group
Nadi
Korovou
Lamiti
Lakeba Passage
Viti Levu
Korolevu
Sausori
SUVA
Koro Sea
Oneata
Navua
Bequ
Moala
Namuka-i-lau
Vatulele
Kadavu Passage
Ono
Kabara
Vunisea
Totoya
Southern Lau Group
Kadavu
Matuku
Fulaga
Vatoa
Ono-i-lau
Lau Group

NEW CALEDONIA
(to France)
Récifs d'Entrecasteaux
Récif Petrie
Grand Passage
Récifs du Cook
Récif les François
Ile Art
Waala
Ile Balabio
Poum
Pouebo
Ouvéa
Lifou
Koumac
Mont Panié
1628m
Hienghene
Fayaoué
Wé
PROVINCE DES ÎLES LOYAUTÉ
Kaala-Gomen
Voh
PROVINCE NORD
Ponérihouen
Ponérihouen
Houailou
New Caledonia
Kone
Poya
Bourail
Canala
Thio
Tadine
Maré
La Foa
PROVINCE SUD
Récif Durand
La Tontouta
Dumbéa
Yaté
NOUMÉA
Mont Dore
Vao
Ile des Pins
Grand Récif Sud
Ile Walpole

Tropic of Capricorn

PACIFIC OCEAN

19,686ft
13,124ft
9843ft
6562ft
3281ft
1640ft
820ft
328ft
Sea Level
-820ft
-6562ft
-13,124ft

286
284
278

Polynesia

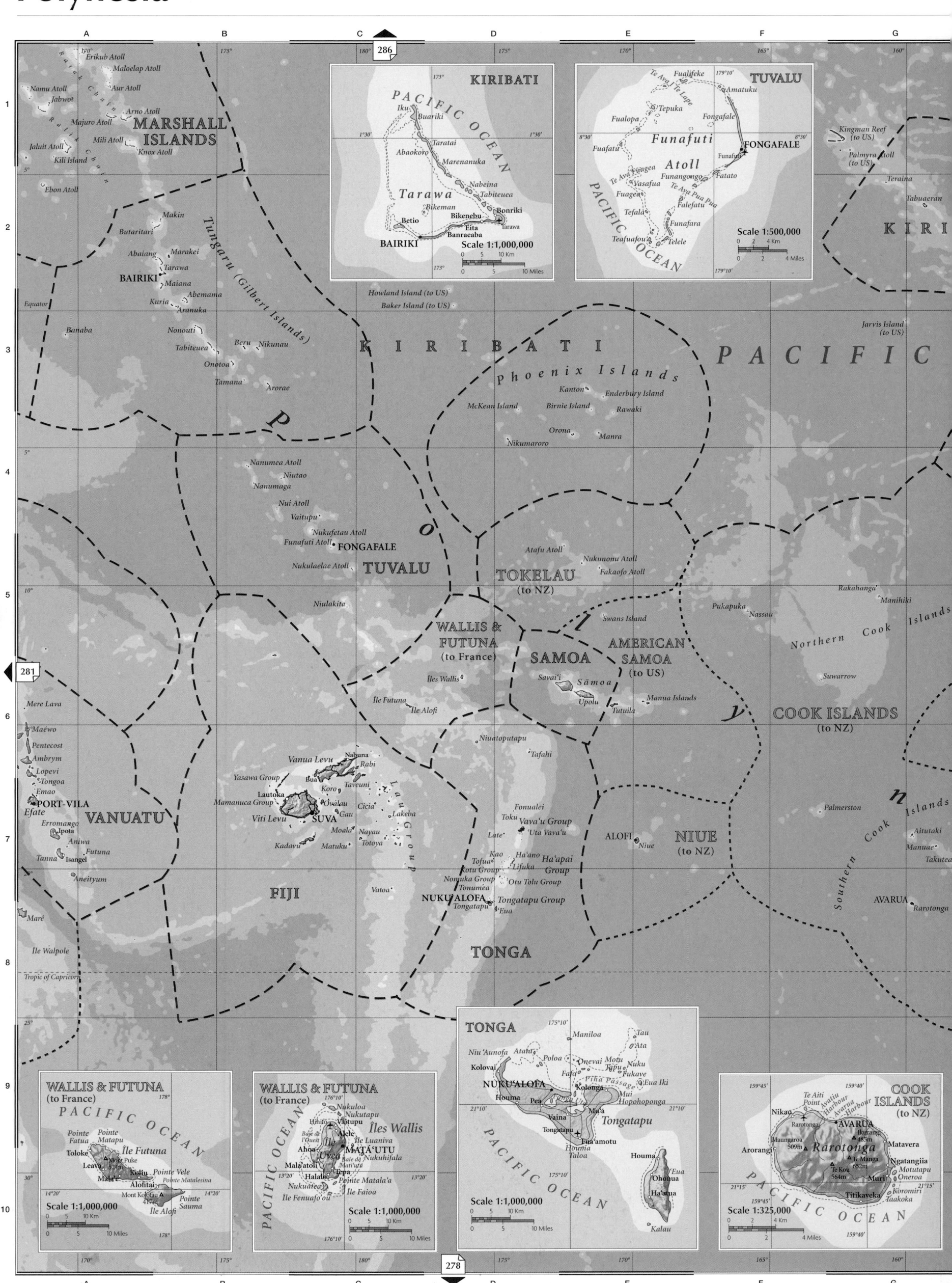
MARSHALL ISLANDS
KIRIBATI
TUVALU
TOKELAU (to NZ)
WALLIS & FUTUNA (to France)
SAMOA
AMERICAN SAMOA (to US)
COOK ISLANDS (to NZ)
NIUE (to NZ)
TONGA
FIJI
VANUATU
PACIFIC
Phoenix Islands
Tungaru (Gilbert Islands)
BAIRIKI
FONGAFALE
SUVA
PORT-VILA
NUKU'ALOFA
ALOFI
AVARUA
Scale 1:1,000,000
Scale 1:500,000
Scale 1:325,000
PACIFIC OCEAN

Scale 1:15,500,000
(projection: Mercator)

0 50 100 150 200 250-300 350 400 Km
0 50 100 150 200 250 300 350 400 Miles

Population

■ above 5 million   ▣ 1 million to 5 million   ◉ 500,000 to 1 million
◎ 100,000 to 500,000   ▫ 50,000 to 100,000   ○ 10,000 to 50,000   ∘ below 10,000

287

Samoa inset (Scale 1:3,000,000)

Savai'i
SAMOA
Faleálupo Sātoa Fagamálo
Cape Puava Silisili Tuasivi
Fálelima 1858m Pu'apu'a Salelologa
Sala'ilua Satupaiteau
Cape Taga
Asuisui APIA Upolu
Fagaloa Bay
Apolima Strait Feleolo Fito
Matautu 1113m Poutasi Ti'avea
Lotofaga Salani
Safata Bay

AMERICAN SAMOA
(to US)
Manua Islands
Olosega
Ofu Ta'ū
PAGO PAGO Luma
Cape Matatula
Cape Aunu'u Island
Taputapu Steps Point
Tutuila

Sāmoa

PACIFIC OCEAN

Scale 1:3,000,000
0 20 40 Km
0 20 40 Miles

Kiribati inset (Scale 1:1,175,000)

KIRIBATI
PACIFIC OCEAN
Northwest Point Cape Manning
London Banana Northeast Point
Cook Island Saint Motulu Lagoon
Paris Stanley
Bay
Poland Kiritimati Bay of Wrecks
(Christmas Island)
South Vaskess
West Joe's Hill
Point Bay Isles Lagoon 12m Aeon
Point
Azur Lagoon Pelican
Lagoon
South East Point

Scale 1:1,175,000
0 5 10 Km
0 5 10 Miles

Equator

French Polynesia (Tahiti) inset (Scale 1:1,000,000)

Baie d'Opunohu
Baie de Cook
Papetoai Pointe Aroa
Mont Matotea Paopao Pointe Vénus
714m Mahina Papenoo
Moorea Afareaitu PAPEETE Pirea Tarei
Mont Tohiea Faaa Faaa
Haapiti 1207m Faaa Hitiaa
Pointe Nuuper Mont Aorai
Punaauia 2066m
Pointe Nuuroa Mont Orohena
2241m Tahiti Faaone
Paea Taravao
Mont Teturfua Isthme de Taravao
1799m Baie de
FRENCH POLYNESIA Taravao
(to France) Afaahiti
Maraa Teohatu Tautira
Îles du Mataiea Vairao
Vent Papara Presqu'île
Récif Tepeae de Tautapu
Pointe Maraa Teahupoo Mont Ronui
1332m

PACIFIC OCEAN

Scale 1:1,000,000
0 5 10 Km
0 5 10 Miles

Main map

OCEAN

Line Islands

Kiritimati
(Christmas Island)

Malden Island
Starbuck Island
Penrhyn
Vostok Island Millennium Island
Flint Island

Îles Marquises
Hatutu Eiao
Nuku Hiva Ua Huka
Taiohae
Ua Pu Hiva Oa
Atuona
Tahuata Motane
Fatu Hiva Omoa

Îles Tuamotu

Îles du Roi Georges Îles
Ahe Manihi Îles du Désappointement
Mataiva Tikehau Takapoto Tepoto
Rangiroa Takaroa Tikei Napuka Pukapuka
Îles Palliser
Makatea Toau Aratika
Niau Kauehi Takume
Îles Sous le Vent Fakarava Raraka Raroia Fangatau
Motu One Tupai Faaite Katiu Fakahina
Bora-Bora Fare Tahanea Makemo
Manuae Maupiti Tuahu Huahine Marutea Nihiru Tehuata
Maupihaa Raiatea Tetiaroa Anaa Marutea Tauere Tatakoto
Maiao Moorea Mehetia Haraiki Hikueru Amanu
PAPEETE Reitoru Marokau Pukarua
Mitiaro Tahiti Ravahere Hao Akiaki Reao
Mauke Îles du Vent Nengonengo Vahitahi
Archipel de la Société Manuhangi Paraoa Vairaatea
Hereheretue Ahunui Pinaki

PACIFIC
OCEAN

FRENCH POLYNESIA
(to France)

Mangaia Maria
Rimatara Rurutu Vanavana Tureia Groupe Actéon
Mangareva Tenarara Marutea
Tubuai Tematangi Mururoa Maria
Îles Australes Fangataufa Îles Gambier
Mangareva Temoe
Raevavae

PITCAIRN ISLANDS
(to UK)

Tropic of Capricorn
Oeno Island Henderson Island
Ducie Island
Pitcairn Island

Rapa Iti
Marotiri

Niue inset (Scale 1:1,000,000)

NIUE (to NZ)
Hikutavake Toi Mutalau
Makefu Tuapa Lakepa
Makapu Alofi Bay
Point ALOFI Niue Liku
Halagigie Hamm
Point Tamakautoga
Avatele Hakupu
Tepa Point Mata Point
PACIFIC OCEAN

Scale 1:1,000,000
0 5 10 Km
0 5 10 Miles

Pitcairn Islands inset (Scale 1:125,000)

PITCAIRN ISLANDS
(to UK)
Young's Rock
Bounty Bay
ADAMSTOWN Adam's Rock
Pitcairn Island
Point St Paul's
Christian Point
PACIFIC OCEAN

Scale 1:125,000
0 0.5 1 Km
0 0.5 1 Miles

Elevation scale

19,686ft
13,124ft
9843ft
6562ft
3281ft
1640ft
820ft
328ft
Sea Level
-820ft
-6562ft
-13,124ft

Pacific Ocean

RUSSIAN FEDERATION
KAZAKHSTAN
MONGOLIA
ASIA
CHINA
Lake Baikal
Vladivostok
Sea of Okhotsk
Kamchatka Peninsula
Petropavlovsk-Kamchatskiy
Bering Sea
Aleutian Basin
Aleutian Islands
Aleutian Trench
Gulf of Anadyr
Anadyr
Magadan
UNITED STATES OF AMERICA (ALASKA)
Kurile Islands
Kurile Trench
Hokkaido
Sea of Japan (East Sea)
Japan Basin
JAPAN
NORTH KOREA
SOUTH KOREA
Dalian
Qingdao
Lianyungang
Yellow Sea
Shanghai
East China Sea
Tokyo
Japan Trench
Izu Trench
Bonin Trench
Fuzhou
Taiwan Strait
TAIWAN
Kaohsiung
Guangzhou
Hong Kong
Hai Phong
Haiphong
Gulf of Tongking
MYANMAR (BURMA)
LAOS
THAILAND
VIETNAM
CAMBODIA
Bangkok
Da Nang
Ho Chi Minh
Gulf of Thailand
Andaman Sea
Andaman Islands
Nicobar Islands
Luzon
Luzon Strait
Manila
PHILIPPINES
Palawan
Sulu Sea
Davao
Mindanao
South China Sea
Philippine Sea
Philippine Trench
Philippine Basin
Kyushu-Palau Ridge
West Mariana Basin
Mariana Islands
Mariana Trench
Challenger Deep
Northern Mariana Islands (to US)
Guam (to US)
Northwest Pacific Basin
Shatskiy Rise
Emperor Seamounts
Mid-Pacific Mountains
Magellan Seamounts
East Mariana Basin
Wake Island (to US)
Marcus Island (to Japan)
Midway Islands (to US)
Hawaiian Islands
Hawaiian Ridge
Honolulu
Johnston Atoll (to US)
PACIFIC
MARSHALL ISLANDS
Bikini Atoll
Enewetak
Micronesia
MICRONESIA
Caroline Islands
Caroline Ridge
PALAU
West Caroline Basin
East Caroline Basin
Melanesian Basin
NAURU
Central Pacific Basin
KIRIBATI
Kingman Reef (to US)
Palmyra Atoll (to US)
Baker & Howland Islands (to US)
Jarvis Island (to US)
Phoenix Islands
TUVALU
Tokelau (to NZ)
Cook Islands (to NZ)
Manihiki Plateau
SAMOA
American Samoa (to US)
Wallis & Futuna (to France)
Samoa Basin
TONGA
Tonga Trench
Lau Basin
FIJI
North Fiji Basin
South Fiji Basin
Kermadec Islands (to NZ)
Kermadec Trench
Louisville Ridge
VANUATU
New Hebrides Trench
New Caledonia (to France)
Coral Sea
Coral Sea Basin
Coral Sea Islands (to Australia)
SOLOMON ISLANDS
Solomon Sea
PAPUA NEW GUINEA
Port Moresby
New Britain
New Ireland
Bismarck Sea
New Guinea Trench
Arafura Sea
Timor Sea
Timor Trench
EAST TIMOR
Banda Sea
Celebes Sea
Celebes
INDONESIA
Borneo
Sumatra
Java Sea
Java
Jakarta
Surabaya
Java Trench
Makassar Strait
Moluccas
Ceram
BRUNEI
MALAYSIA
Kuantan
Kota Kinabalu
Kuching
SINGAPORE
Sunda Shelf
Cocos Basin
Investigator Ridge
Wharton Basin
INDIAN OCEAN
North Australian Basin
Exmouth Plateau
Cuvier Basin
Perth Basin
Naturaliste Plateau
Diamantina Fracture Zone
Broken Ridge
Ninetyeast Ridge
AUSTRALIA
Gulf of Carpentaria
Great Barrier Reef
Queensland Plateau
Brisbane
Sydney
Melbourne
Great Australian Bight
Kangaroo Island
South Australian Plain
Bass Strait
King Island
Tasmania
Hobart
East Tasman Plateau
Tasman Sea
Tasman Basin
Tasman Plateau
Tasman Fracture Zone
Lord Howe Island (to Australia)
Lord Howe Rise
Norfolk Island (to Australia)
Norfolk Ridge
New Caledonia Basin
Challenger Plateau
NEW ZEALAND
North Island
South Island
Auckland
Wellington
Dunedin
Chatham Rise
Chatham Islands
Bounty Trough
Bounty Islands (to NZ)
Antipodes Islands (to NZ)
Campbell Plateau
Campbell Island (to NZ)
Auckland Islands (to NZ)
Macquarie Island (to Australia)
Macquarie Ridge
Southeast Indian Ridge
South Indian Basin
Heard & McDonald Islands (to Australia)
Kerguelen Plateau
Banzare Seamounts
SOUTHERN OCEAN
Pacific-Antarctic Ridge
Balleny Islands
Scott Island (to NZ)
ANTARCTICA
Antarctic Circle
Arctic Circle
Tropic of Capricorn
Equator
Sea Level
-250m
-2000m
-4000m

Scale 1:62,500,000
(projection: Robinson)

0 500 1000 1500 2000 Km
0 500 1000 1500 2000 Miles

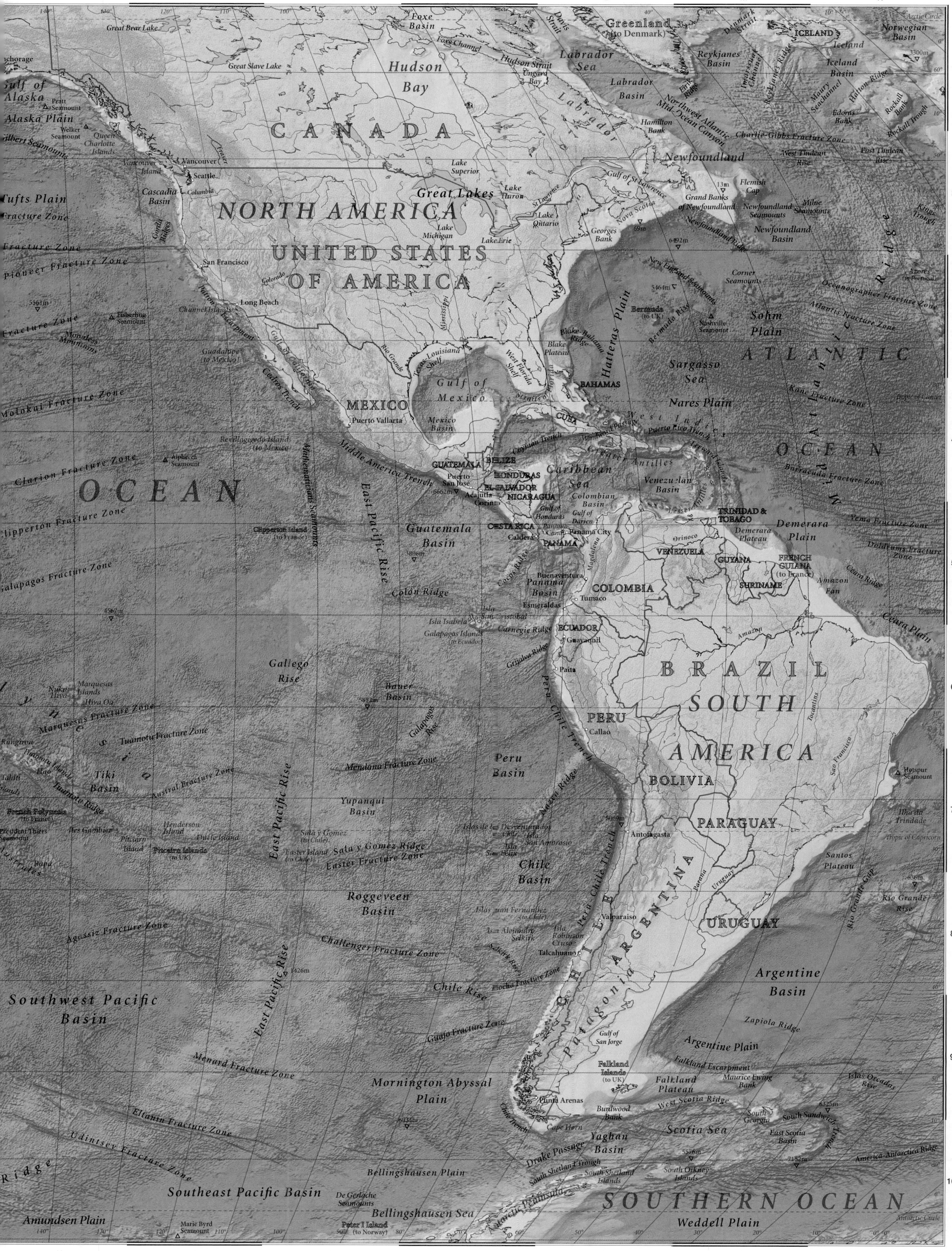

Sea Level
-820ft
-6562ft
-13,124ft

North America / Atlantic

Great Bear Lake
Great Slave Lake
Hudson Bay
Foxe Basin
Foxe Channel
Hudson Strait
Ungava Bay
Labrador Sea
Greenland (to Denmark)
ICELAND
Iceland
Norwegian Basin
Denmark Strait
Arctic Circle
Reykjanes Basin
Iceland Basin
Northwest Atlantic Mid-Ocean Canyon
Reykjanes Ridge
Maury Seachannel
Edoras Bank
Rockall Bank
Rockall Trough
Labrador Basin
Hamilton Bank
Charlie-Gibbs Fracture Zone
East Thulean Rise
West Thulean Rise

Anchorage
Gulf of Alaska
Alaska Plain
Pratt Seamount
Welker Seamount
Gilbert Seamounts
Queen Charlotte Islands
Vancouver Island
Vancouver
Seattle
Columbia
Cascadia Basin
Tufts Plain
Fracture Zone
Pioneer Fracture Zone
Molokai Fracture Zone
Clarion Fracture Zone
Clipperton Fracture Zone
Galapagos Fracture Zone

CANADA
NORTH AMERICA
UNITED STATES OF AMERICA

Lake Superior
Great Lakes
Lake Huron
Lake Michigan
Lake Ontario
Lake Erie
St Lawrence
Gulf of St Lawrence
Nova Scotia
Georges Bank
Grand Banks of Newfoundland
Newfoundland
Flemish Cap
Milne Seamounts
Newfoundland Seamounts
Newfoundland Basin
New England Seamounts
Corner Seamounts
Oceanographer Fracture Zone
Atlantis Fracture Zone
Azores (to Portugal)

San Francisco
Long Beach
Channel Islands
Murray Escarpment
Gorda Fracture Zone
Mendocino Mountains
Fieberling Seamount

Colorado
Mississippi
Rio Grande
Gulf of California
Guadalupe (to Mexico)
Cedros Trench
Texas-Louisiana Shelf
West Florida Shelf
Gulf of Mexico
MEXICO
Puerto Vallarta
Mexico Basin
Revillagigedo Island (to Mexico)
Alijos Seamount
Mathematicians Seamounts
Middle America Trench
East Pacific Rise
Clipperton Island (to France)

Blake Plateau
Blake-Bahama Ridge
Bermuda (to UK)
Bermuda Rise
Nashville Seamount
Sohm Plain
Sargasso Sea
Hatteras Plain
Nares Plain
ATLANTIC OCEAN
Kane Fracture Zone
Tropic of Cancer

BAHAMAS
CUBA
West Indies
Puerto Rico Trench
Cayman Trench
Greater Antilles
Lesser Antilles
Caribbean Sea
Venezuelan Basin
Barracuda Fracture Zone
Vema Fracture Zone
Doldrums Fracture Zone
Ceara Ridge
Ceara Plain

GUATEMALA
BELIZE
HONDURAS
EL SALVADOR
NICARAGUA
COSTA RICA
PANAMA
Puerto San José
Acajutla
Corinto
Caldera
Panama City
Gulf of Honduras
Gulf of Darién
Colombian Basin
TRINIDAD & TOBAGO
Demerara Plateau
Demerara Plain
GUYANA
SURINAME
FRENCH GUIANA (to France)
VENEZUELA
Orinoco
Amazon Fan

Guatemala Basin
Cocos Ridge
Colón Ridge
Panama Basin
Buenaventura
COLOMBIA
Tumaco
Esmeraldas
ECUADOR
Guayaquil
Carnegie Ridge
Galapagos Islands (to Ecuador)
Isla Isabela
Galapagos Rise
Grijalva Ridge
Paita

Pacific / South America

OCEAN
Gallego Rise
Bauer Basin
Marquesas Islands
Nuku Hiva
Hiva Oa
Marquesas Fracture Zone
Tuamotu Fracture Zone
Rangiroa
Tahiti
French Polynesia (to France)
Tuamotu Ridge
Iles Gambier
Austral Fracture Zone
Tiki Basin
Henderson Island
Pitcairn Island
Pitcairn Islands (to UK)
Ducie Island
President Thiers Seamount
Australes
Rapa

Yupanqui Basin
Mendana Fracture Zone
Peru Basin
Sala y Gomez (to Chile)
Easter Island (to Chile)
Sala y Gomez Ridge
Easter Fracture Zone
Roggeveen Basin
Islas de los Desventurados
Isla San Ambrosio
Isla San Félix

East Pacific Rise
Nazca Ridge
PERU
Callao
Antofagasta
Valparaíso
Islas Juan Fernández (to Chile)
Isla Alejandro Selkirk
Isla Robinson Crusoe
Talcahuano
Chile Basin
Chile Rise
Mocha Fracture Zone

BRAZIL
SOUTH AMERICA
BOLIVIA
PARAGUAY
ARGENTINA
URUGUAY
CHILE
São Francisco
Tropic of Capricorn
Hotspur Seamount
Ilha da Trindade
Santos Plateau
Rio Grande Rise
Argentine Basin
Zapiola Ridge
Argentine Plain
Gulf of San Jorge
Patagonia
Falkland Islands (to UK)
Falkland Escarpment
Falkland Plateau
Maurice Ewing Bank
Islas Orcadas Rise

Challenger Fracture Zone
Guajo Fracture Zone
Menard Fracture Zone
Southwest Pacific Basin
Agassiz Fracture Zone
Eltanin Fracture Zone
Udintsev Fracture Zone
Mornington Abyssal Plain
Southeast Pacific Basin
De Gerlache Seamounts
Bellingshausen Plain
Bellingshausen Sea
Amundsen Plain
Marie Byrd Seamount
Peter I Island (to Norway)
Antarctic Peninsula
South Shetland Trough
South Shetland Islands
South Orkney Islands
SOUTHERN OCEAN
Weddell Plain
Antarctic Circle

Punta Arenas
Cape Horn
Drake Passage
Yaghan Basin
Scotia Sea
West Scotia Ridge
Burdwood Bank
South Georgia
East Scotia Basin
South Sandwich
America-Antarctica Ridge

Indian Ocean

Sea Level
-250m
-2000m
-4000m

RUSSIAN FEDERATION

ASIA

CHINA

MONGOLIA

KAZAKHSTAN

EUROPE

FINLAND

SWEDEN

POLAND
BELARUS
UKRAINE
ROMANIA
BULGARIA
MOLDOVA
HUNGARY
SLOVAKIA
CZECH REPUBLIC
GERMANY
AUSTRIA
SLOVENIA
CROATIA
BOZ. & HERZ.
SERBIA
MONTENEGRO KOS.
MACEDONIA
ALBANIA
GREECE
ESTONIA
LATVIA
LITHUANIA
RUSS. FED.
DENMARK

TURKEY
SYRIA
LEBANON
ISRAEL
JORDAN
IRAQ
KUWAIT
SAUDI ARABIA
YEMEN
OMAN
U.A.E.
QATAR
BAHRAIN
IRAN
AFGHANISTAN
PAKISTAN
TURKMENISTAN
UZBEKISTAN
TAJIKISTAN
KYRGYZSTAN
GEORGIA
ARMENIA
AZERBAIJAN

INDIA
NEPAL
BHUTAN
BANGLADESH
MYANMAR (BURMA)
THAILAND
LAOS
CAMBODIA
VIETNAM
MALAYSIA
SINGAPORE
BRUNEI
PHILIPPINES
TAIWAN

NORTH KOREA
SOUTH KOREA
JAPAN

SRI LANKA
MALDIVES

LIBYA
EGYPT
SUDAN
CHAD
CENTRAL AFRICAN REPUBLIC
DEMOCRATIC
AFRICA
ERITREA
DJIBOUTI
ETHIOPIA
SOMALIA
KENYA

Barents Sea
Kara Sea
Laptev Sea
Caspian Sea
Black Sea
Mediterranean Sea
Red Sea
Dead Sea
Aral Sea
Lake Baikal
Lake Balkhash
Lake Zaysan
Lake Tana
Lake Turkana
Lake Albert

Persian Gulf
Gulf of Oman
Gulf of Aden
Arabian Sea
Arabian Basin
Bay of Bengal
Ganges Fan
Andaman Sea
Andaman Basin
South China Sea
South China Basin
East China Sea
Yellow Sea
Gulf of Thailand
Gulf of Tongking
Celebes Sea
Sulu Sea
Philippine Sea
Philippine Basin
Philippine Trench
Sunda Trench
Carlsberg Ridge
Laccadive Plateau
Somali

Lena
Yangtze
Yellow River
Volga
Tigris
Euphrates
Nile
White Nile
Blue Nile
Ganges
Indus
Syr Darya
Amu Darya
Mekong
Irrawaddy
Salween

Arctic Circle
Tropic of Cancer

Scale 1:32,000,000
(projection: Robinson)

0 200 400 600 800 1000 1200 Km
0 200 400 600 800 1000 1200 Miles

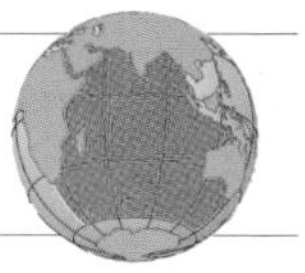

INDIAN OCEAN

SOUTHERN OCEAN

AUSTRALIA

INDONESIA

MADAGASCAR

Sea Level
-820ft
-6562ft
-13,124ft

Sumatra
Sunda Shelf
Java Sea
Java
Bali
Lombok Basin
Banda Sea
Celebes
Madura
Flores Sea
Savu Sea
Timor Sea
Timor
East Timor
Timor Trough
Sahul Shelf
Broome
Port Hedland
Rowley Shelf
Rowley Shoals
Exmouth Plateau
North Australian Basin
Gascoyne Plain
Cuvier Plateau
Cuvier Basin
Wallaby Plateau
Perth Basin
Geraldton
Fremantle
Bunbury
Albany

Great Australian Bight
South Australian Basin

South Indian Basin

Java Trench
Java Ridge
Roo Rise
Christmas Island
Venning Meinesz Seamounts
Cocos Islands
Cocos Basin
Wharton Basin
Investigator Ridge
East Indian Ridge

Ninetyeast Ridge

Osborn Plateau

Broken Ridge
Diamantina Fracture Zone
Naturaliste Fracture Zone
Naturaliste Plateau
Batavia Seamount
Golden Draak Seamount
Ob Trench
Amsterdam Island
St Paul Island
Amsterdam Fracture Zone

Southeast Indian Ridge

Mid-Indian Basin
Ceylon Plain
Chagos Trench
Chagos Archipelago
British Indian Ocean Territory (to UK)
Diego Garcia

Mid-Indian Ridge

Chagos Fracture Zone
Vema Fracture Zone
Argo Fracture Zone
Marie Celeste Fracture Zone
Egeria Fracture Zone
Rodrigues (to Mauritius)

Seychelles
Amirante Islands
Amirante Basin
Amirante Trench
Amirante Ridge
Seychelles Bank
Saya de Malha Bank
Nazareth Bank
Cargados Carajos Bank
MAURITIUS
Mascarene Plateau
Mascarene Basin
Mascarene Plain
Mascarene Islands
Réunion (to France)
Farquhar Group
Aldabra Group

COMOROS
Mayotte (to France)
Comoro Basin
Mozambique Channel
Davie Ridge
Bassas da India
Île Europa
Jaguar Seamount

Madagascar Basin
Madagascar Plateau
Walters Shoal

Mozambique Plateau
Mozambique Escarpment

Crozet Basin
Crozet Plateau
Crozet Islands
Del Cano Rise
Ob Tablemount
Prince Edward Islands (to South Africa)
Prince Edward Fracture Zone
Indomed Fracture Zone

Southwest Indian Ridge

Atlantic-Indian Ridge
Atlantic-Indian Basin

Enderby Plain

Kerguelen Plateau
Kerguelen (to France)
French Southern & Antarctic Territories (to France)
Heard & McDonald Islands (to Aust.)
Banzare Seamounts

Natal Basin
Natal Valley
Transkei Basin
Agulhas Plateau
Agulhas Basin
Africana Seamount

SOUTH AFRICA
Cape Town
Cape of Good Hope
Cape Agulhas
Mossel Bay
Port Elizabeth
East London
Durban
Drakensberg
LESOTHO
SWAZILAND
Maputo
BOTSWANA
ZIMBABWE
Limpopo
Orange River
Zambezi
ZAMBIA
MALAWI
Lake Nyasa
MOZAMBIQUE
Beira
Quelimane
Nacala
Pemba
TANZANIA
Dar es Salaam
Mafia
Zanzibar
Pemba
Tanga
Mombasa
Lake Tanganyika
Lake Rukwa
Lake Malawi
BURUNDI
RWANDA
Lake Kivu
Lake Victoria
REPUBLIC OF CONGO

Tropic of Capricorn

Atlantic Ocean

Sea Level
−250m
−2000m
−4000m

ARCTIC OCEAN

ATLANTIC OCEAN

NORTH AMERICA

CANADA

UNITED STATES OF AMERICA

EUROPE

AFRICA

Greenland (to Denmark)

Barents Sea

Norwegian Sea

Greenland Sea

Baffin Bay

Hudson Bay

Labrador Sea

Gulf of Mexico

Caribbean Sea

Sargasso Sea

Mediterranean Sea

Sahara

FINLAND · SWEDEN · NORWAY · ICELAND · UNITED KINGDOM · IRELAND · FRANCE · SPAIN · PORTUGAL · ITALY · GERMANY · POLAND · ESTONIA · LATVIA · LITHUANIA · BELARUS · UKRAINE · ROMANIA · HUNGARY · AUSTRIA · SWITZ. · CZECH REPUBLIC · SLOVAKIA · SLOVENIA · CROATIA · BOS. & HERZ. · SERBIA · MONTENEGRO · KOS. · ALBANIA · MACEDONIA · GREECE · DENMARK · NETH. · BELGIUM

MOROCCO · ALGERIA · LIBYA · TUNISIA · MAURITANIA · MALI · NIGER · CHAD · SENEGAL · GAMBIA · GUINEA-BISSAU · GUINEA · SIERRA LEONE · LIBERIA · IVORY COAST · GHANA · TOGO · BENIN · NIGERIA · CAMEROON · EQUATORIAL GUINEA · CONGO · CENTRAL AFRICAN REPUBLIC · CAPE VERDE · Western Sahara (occupied by Morocco)

MEXICO · GUATEMALA · BELIZE · HONDURAS · EL SALVADOR · NICARAGUA · COSTA RICA · PANAMA · COLOMBIA · VENEZUELA · GUYANA · SURINAME · FRENCH GUIANA · CUBA · JAMAICA · HAITI · DOMINICAN REPUBLIC · BAHAMAS · BARBADOS · TRINIDAD & TOBAGO

Mid-Atlantic Ridge · Charlie-Gibbs Fracture Zone · Oceanographer Fracture Zone · Atlantis Fracture Zone · Kane Fracture Zone · Vema Fracture Zone · Romanche Fracture Zone · Chain Fracture Zone

Scale 1:34,400,000
(projection: Robinson)

0 200 400 600 800 1000 1200 Km
0 200 400 600 800 1000 1200 Miles

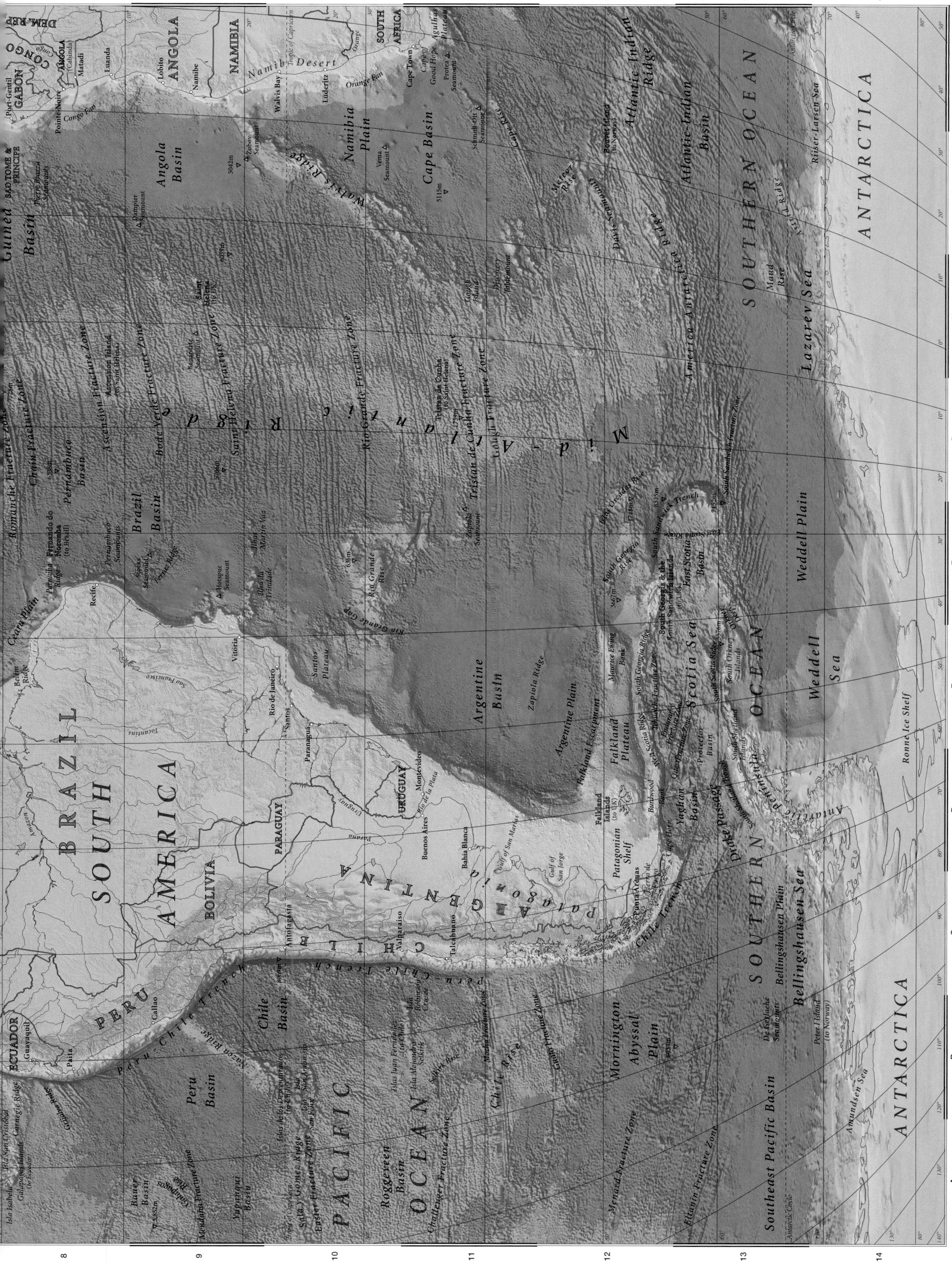

DEM. REP. CONGO
GABON
Port-Gentil
Pointe-Noire
Congo Fan
Matadi
Cabinda
ANGOLA
Luanda
Lobito
Namibe
NAMIBIA
Walvis Bay
Lüderitz
Namib Desert
Tropic of Capricorn
Orange Fan
SOUTH AFRICA
Cape Town
Cape of Good Hope
Agulhas Plateau

GABRIEL
GUINEA Basin
SÃO TOMÉ & PRÍNCIPE
Pierre Bouzu Seamounts
Angola Basin
9042m
Zubov Seamount
Dampier Seamount
Namibia Plain
Vema Seamount
Cape Basin
5115m
Schmidt-Ott Seamount
Protea Seamount
Meteor Rise
Agulhas Basin
Atlantic-Indian Ridge
Atlantic-Indian Basin
SOUTHERN OCEAN
ANTARCTICA
Maud Rise
Lazarev Sea
Riiser-Larsen Sea

Walvis Ridge
Saint Helena
Bode Verde Fracture Zone
Ascension Fracture Zone
Chain Fracture Zone
Romanche Fracture Zone
Ascension Island (to Saint Helena)
Bode Verde
Discovery Seamounts
Gough Island
Georgia Seamount
Discovery Tablemount

BRAZIL
SOUTH AMERICA
PERU
Belém
Recife
Amazon
Tocantins
São Francisco
Ceará Plain
Brazil Basin
Pernambuco Basin
Pernambuco Seamounts
Spiess Seamount
Fernando de Noronha (to Brazil)
Trindade Ridge
Hotspur Seamount
Ilha da Trindad
Vitória
Rio de Janeiro
Santos
Santos Plateau

Mid-Atlantic Ridge
Saint Helena Fracture Zone
Rio Grande Fracture Zone
Tristan da Cunha Fracture Zone
Cardno Fracture Zone
Rio Grande Rise
Rio Grande Gap
Tristan da Cunha (to Saint Helena)
Zapiola Seamount
Zapiola Ridge

PARAGUAY
URUGUAY
ARGENTINA
BOLIVIA
Paraguay
Montevideo
Río de la Plata
Buenos Aires
Bahía Blanca
Gulf of San Matías
Gulf of San Jorge
Patagonia
Patagonian Shelf

Argentine Basin
Argentine Plain
Falkland Escarpment
Falkland Plateau
Maurice Ewing Bank
Falkland Islands (to UK)
Burdwood Bank
Yaghan Basin
Protector Basin
Scotia Sea
South Georgia Ridge
South Georgia & the South Sandwich Islands
South Georgia
East Scotia Basin
South Sandwich Trench
South Sandwich Islands
South Orkney Islands
South Shetland Islands

CHILE
Valparaíso
Talcahuano
Punta Arenas
Tierra del Fuego
Cape Horn
Drake Passage
Antarctic Peninsula
SOUTHERN OCEAN
Bellingshausen Plain
Bellingshausen Sea
Peter I Island (to Norway)
De Gerlache Seamounts
Weddell Sea
Weddell Plain
Ronne Ice Shelf
ANTARCTICA
Amundsen Sea

PACIFIC OCEAN
ECUADOR
Guayaquil
Paita
Callao
Peru Basin
Chile Basin
Nazca Ridge
Roggeveen Basin
Nazca Fracture Zone
Mendaña Fracture Zone
Mornington Abyssal Plain
Chile Rise
Chile Trench
Peru-Chile Trench
Southeast Pacific Basin
Eltanin Fracture Zone
Galápagos Islands (to Ecuador)
Carnegie Ridge
Bauer Basin
Isla San Cristóbal
Isla Isabela
Islas Juan Fernández (to Chile)
Isla San Félix
Isla Alejandro Selkirk
Juan Fernández Ridge
Challenger Fracture Zone

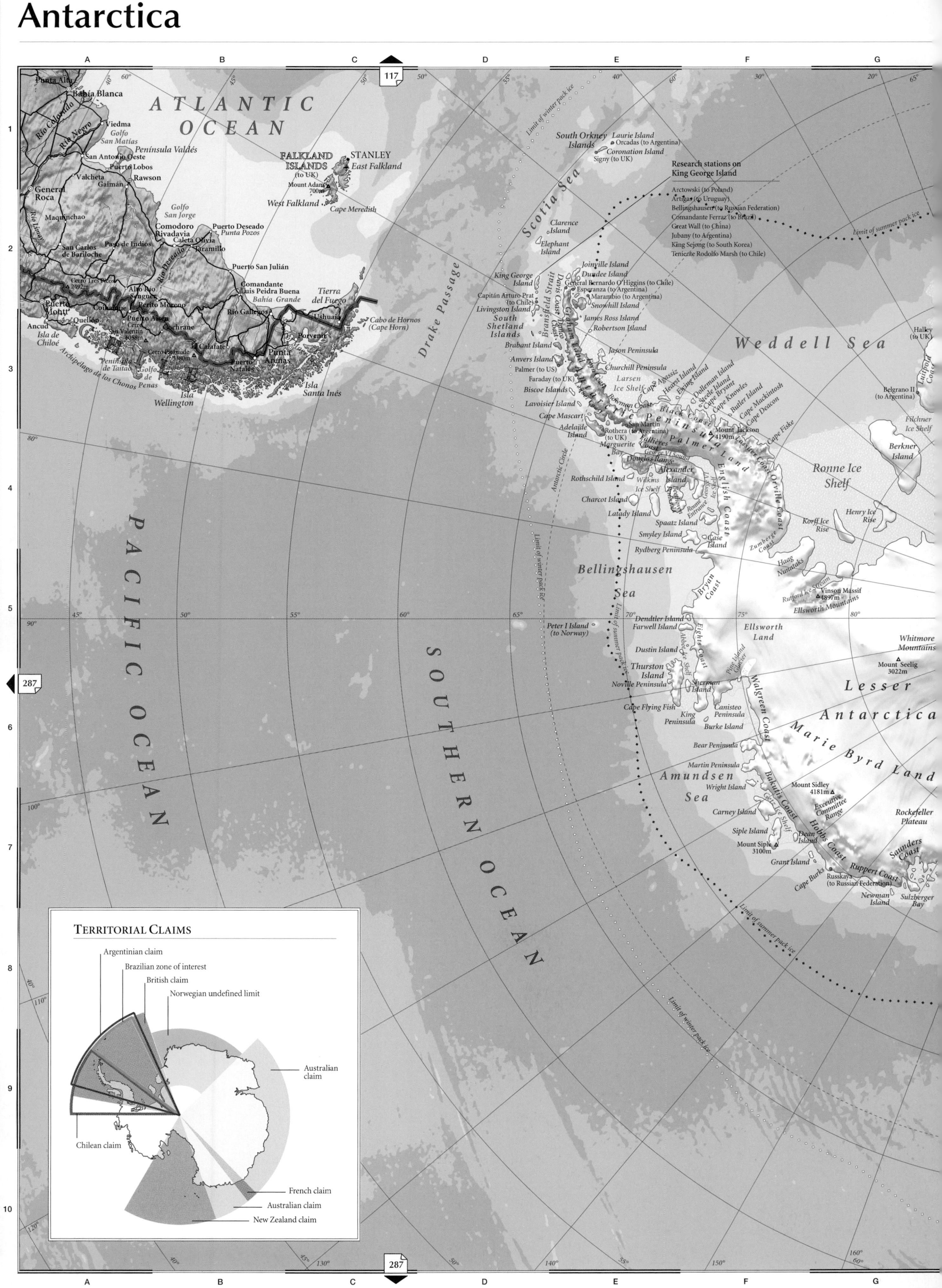

Antarctica

117

287

ATLANTIC OCEAN

Punta Alta
Bahía Blanca
Río Colorado
Viedma
Río Negro
Golfo San Matías
Península Valdés
San Antonio Oeste
Puerto Lobos
Valcheta
Gaimán
Rawson
General Roca
Maquinchao
Golfo San Jorge
San Carlos de Bariloche
Paso de Indios
Comodoro Rivadavia
Caleta Olivia
Jaramillo
Puerto Deseado
Punta Pozos
Cerro Tres Picos 2492m
Alto Río Senguer
Río Deseado
Perito Moreno
Puerto San Julián
Comandante Luis Piedra Buena
Puerto Montt
Coihaique
Ancud
Isla de Chiloé
Quellón
Cerro San Valentín 3058m
Puerto Aisén
Cochrane
Río Gallegos
Bahía Grande
Tierra del Fuego
Ushuaia
Archipiélago de los Chonos
Península de Taitao
Golfo de Penas
Cerro Lautaro 3380m
Calafate
Puerto Natales
Punta Arenas
Porvenir
Cabo de Hornos (Cape Horn)
Isla Wellington
Isla Santa Inés

FALKLAND ISLANDS (to UK)
STANLEY
East Falkland
Mount Adam 700m
West Falkland
Cape Meredith

PACIFIC OCEAN

SOUTHERN OCEAN

Drake Passage

Scotia Sea

Limit of winter pack ice

South Orkney Islands
Laurie Island
Orcadas (to Argentina)
Coronation Island
Signy (to UK)

Clarence Island
Elephant Island

King George Island
Capitán Arturo Prat (to Chile)
Livingston Island
South Shetland Islands
Brabant Island
Anvers Island
Palmer (to US)
Faraday (to UK)
Biscoe Islands
Lavoisier Island
Cape Mascart
Adelaide Island
Rothera (to UK)
Marguerite Bay
Rothschild Island
Charcot Island
Latady Island
Spaatz Island
Smyley Island
Rydberg Peninsula
Alexander Island
Wilkins Ice Shelf
Ronne Entrance

Research stations on King George Island
Arctowski (to Poland)
Artigas (to Uruguay)
Bellingshausen (to Russian Federation)
Comandante Ferraz (to Brazil)
Great Wall (to China)
Jubany (to Argentina)
King Sejong (to South Korea)
Teniente Rodolfo Marsh (to Chile)

Joinville Island
Dundee Island
General Bernardo O'Higgins (to Chile)
Esperanza (to Argentina)
Marambio (to Argentina)
Snowhill Island
James Ross Island
Robertson Island
Jason Peninsula
Churchill Peninsula
Larsen Ice Shelf
Cape Agassiz
Heaver Island
Eyring Island
Steele Island
Cape Bryant
Cape Knowles
Butler Island
Cape Mackintosh
Cape Deacon
Cape Fiske
San Martín
Mount Jackson 4190m

Bransfield Strait

Antarctic Peninsula
Palmer Land
English Coast
Black Coast
Orville Coast

Weddell Sea
Halley (to UK)
Belgrano II (to Argentina)
Filchner Ice Shelf
Berkner Island

Ronne Ice Shelf
Korff Ice Rise
Henry Ice Rise
Haag Nunataks

Antarctic Circle

Peter I Island (to Norway)

Limit of summer pack ice

Dendtler Island
Farwell Island
Dustin Island
Thurston Island
Noville Peninsula
Cape Flying Fish
King Peninsula
Burke Island
Bear Peninsula
Martin Peninsula
Carney Island
Siple Island
Mount Siple 3100m
Grant Island
Cape Burks

Bellingshausen Sea

Bryan Coast
Eights Coast
Abbot Ice Shelf
Sherman Island
Canisteo Peninsula
Walgreen Coast
Hobbs Coast
Bakutis Coast
Getz Ice Shelf
Dean Island
Russkaya (to Russian Federation)
Newman Island
Sulzberger Bay

Amundsen Sea

Ellsworth Land
Vinson Massif 4897m
Ellsworth Mountains

Lesser Antarctica
Whitmore Mountains
Mount Seelig 3022m
Mount Sidley 4181m
Executive Committee Range

Marie Byrd Land
Rockefeller Plateau
Saunders Coast
Ruppert Coast

TERRITORIAL CLAIMS

Argentinian claim
Brazilian zone of interest
British claim
Norwegian undefined limit
Australian claim
Chilean claim
French claim
Australian claim
New Zealand claim

6000m
4000m
3000m
2000m
1000m
500m
250m
100m
Sea Level
-250m
-2000m
-4000m

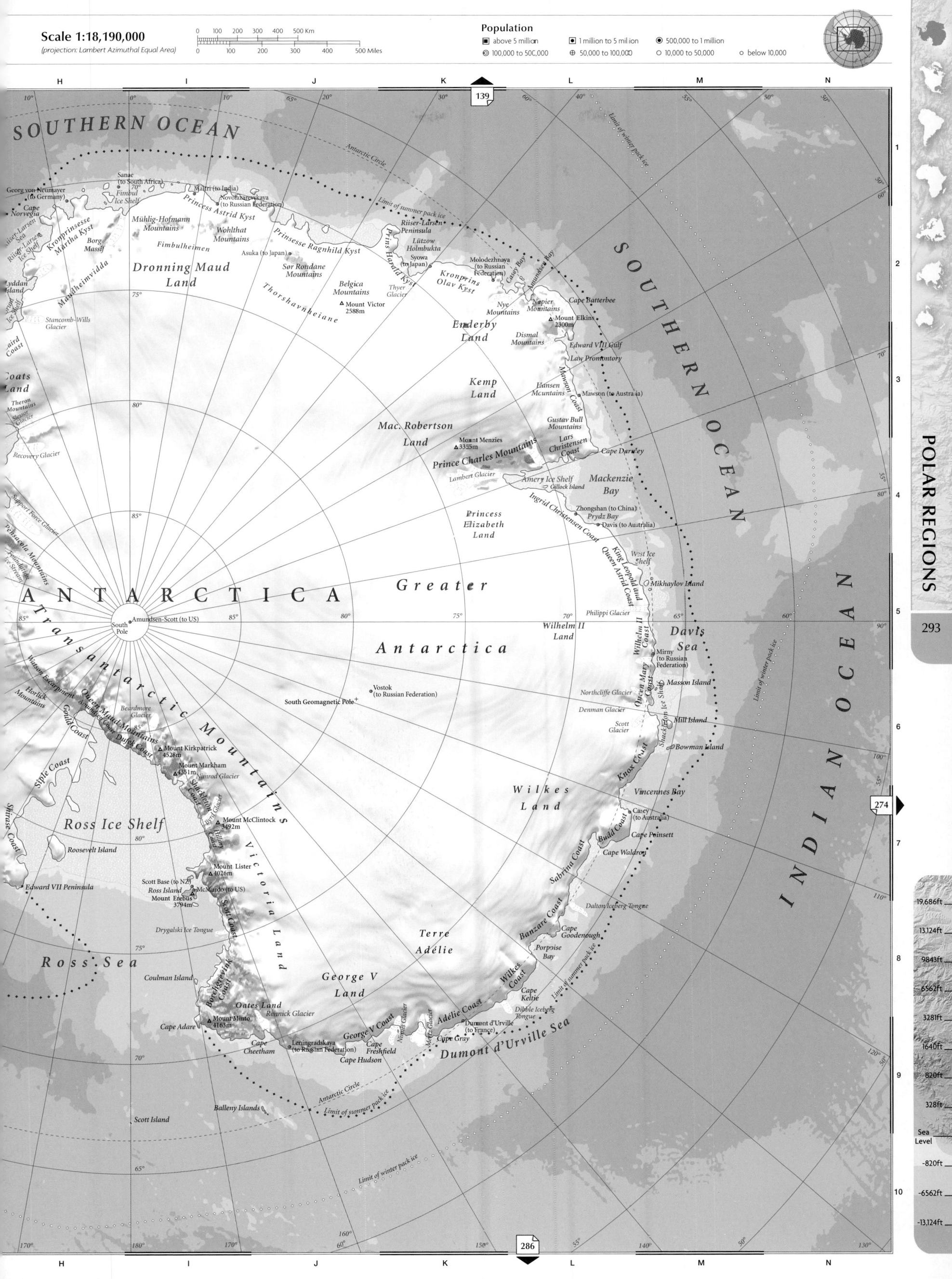

Scale 1:18,190,000
(projection: Lambert Azimuthal Equal Area)

0 100 200 300 400 500 Km
0 100 200 300 400 500 Miles

Population
- ■ above 5 million
- ▣ 100,000 to 500,000
- ■ 1 million to 5 million
- ⊕ 50,000 to 100,000
- ◉ 500,000 to 1 million
- ⊙ 10,000 to 50,000
- ○ below 10,000

139

286

274

SOUTHERN OCEAN

SOUTHERN OCEAN

INDIAN OCEAN

Antarctic Circle

Limit of winter pack ice

Limit of summer pack ice

Georg von Neumayer (to Germany)
Cape Norvegia
Riiser-Larsen Ice Shelf
Eyddan Island
Mannefallknausane
Maudheimvidda
Borg Massif
Kronprinsesse Märtha Kyst
Mühlig-Hofmann Mountains
Wohlthat Mountains
Fimbulheimen
Sanae (to South Africa)
Fimbul Ice Shelf
Maitri (to India)
Novolazarevskaya (to Russian Federation)
Princess Astrid Kyst
Prinsesse Ragnhild Kyst
Prins Harald Kyst
Asuka (to Japan)
Sør Rondane Mountains
Belgica Mountains
▲ Mount Victor 2588m
Thyer Glacier
Thorshavnheiane

Dronning Maud Land

Riiser-Larsen Peninsula
Lützow Holmbukta
Syowa (to Japan)
Molodezhnaya (to Russian Federation)
Kronprins Olav Kyst
Nye Mountains
Napier Mountains
▲ Mount Elkins 2300m
Cape Batterbee
Casey Bay
Amundsen Bay

Enderby Land

Dismal Mountains
Edward VIII Gulf
Law Promontory
Hansen Mountains
Mawson (to Australia)

Kemp Land

Gustav Bull Mountains
Mawson Coast

Mac. Robertson Land

Mount Menzies ▲ 3355m
Lars Christensen Coast
Cape Darnley
Prince Charles Mountains
Lambert Glacier
Amery Ice Shelf
Gillock Island

Mackenzie Bay

Ingrid Christensen Coast
Zhongshan (to China)
Prydz Bay
Davis (to Australia)

Princess Elizabeth Land

Coats Land
Theron Mountains
Slessor Glacier
Stancomb-Wills Glacier
Baird Coast
Recovery Glacier
Support Force Glacier
Pensacola Mountains
Foundation Ice Stream

Greater

ANTARCTICA

South Pole
Amundsen-Scott (to US)

Antarctica

West Ice Shelf
Mikhaylov Island
Philippi Glacier
Wilhelm II Land
Wilhelm II Coast

Davis Sea

King Leopold and Queen Astrid Coast
Mirny (to Russian Federation)
Masson Island
Northcliffe Glacier
Queen Mary Coast
Mill Island
Denman Glacier
Shackleton Ice Shelf
Scott Glacier
Knox Coast
Bowman Island

Vostok (to Russian Federation)
South Geomagnetic Pole

Wilkes Land

Vincennes Bay
Casey (to Australia)
Cape Poinsett
Budd Coast
Cape Waldron

Transantarctic Mountains

Wilson Hills
Horlick Mountains
Gould Coast
Siple Coast
Shirase Coast

Ross Ice Shelf

Roosevelt Island

Edward VII Peninsula

Queen Maud Mountains
Beardmore Glacier
Shackleton Coast
Dufek Coast
Nimrod Glacier
▲ Mount Kirkpatrick 4528m
Mount Markham ▲ 4351m
Shackleton Glacier
Byrd Glacier
Beardmore Glacier
▲ Mount McClintock 3492m
Mulock Glacier

Victoria Land

Mount Lister ▲ 4026m
Scott Base (to NZ)
Ross Island
McMurdo (to US)
Mount Erebus 3794m
Drygalski Ice Tongue

Ross Sea

Coulman Island
Borchgrevink Coast
Oates Land
Rennick Glacier
▲ Mount Minto 4163m
Cape Adare
Cape Cheetham
Leningradskaya (to Russian Federation)
Cape Freshfield
Cape Hudson
George V Coast

Oates Land

George V Land

Terre Adélie

Sabrina Coast
Banzare Coast
Cape Goodenough
Porpoise Bay
Wilkes Coast
Cape Keltie
Adélie Coast
Dibble Iceberg Tongue
Adélie Coast
Dumont d'Urville (to France)
Cape Gray
Ninnis Glacier
Mertz Glacier
Dalton Iceberg Tongue

Dumont d'Urville Sea

Balleny Islands
Scott Island

19,686ft
13,124ft
9843ft
6562ft
3281ft
1640ft
820ft
328ft
Sea Level
-820ft
-6562ft
-13,124ft

H I J K L M N

193

286

6000m
4000m
3000m
2000m
1000m
500m
250m
100m
Sea
Level
-250m
-2000m
-4000m

Scale 1:18,190,000

0   100 200 300 400 500 Km

0   100   200   300   400   500 Miles

(projection: Lambert Azimuthal Equal Area)

Population

☐ above 5 million   ☑ 1 million to 5 million   ◉ 500,000 to 1 million

◍ 100,000 to 500,000   ⊕ 50,000 to 100,000   ○ 10,000 to 50,000   ○ below 10,000

194

290

51

19,686ft

13,124ft

9843ft

6562ft

3281ft

1640ft

820ft

328ft

Sea Level

-820ft

-6562ft

-13,124ft

Geographical comparisons

Largest countries

Russian Federation	6,592,735 sq miles	(17,075,200 sq km)
Canada	3,851,788 sq miles	(9,976,140 sq km)
USA	3,717,792 sq miles	(9,629,091 sq km)
China	3,705,386 sq miles	(9,596,960 sq km)
Brazil	3,286,470 sq miles	(8,511,965 sq km)
Australia	2,967,893 sq miles	(7,686,850 sq km)
India	1,269,339 sq miles	(3,287,590 sq km)
Argentina	1,068,296 sq miles	(2,766,890 sq km)
Kazakhstan	1,049,150 sq miles	(2,717,300 sq km)
Sudan	967,493 sq miles	(2,505,815 sq km)

Smallest countries

Vatican City	0.17 sq miles	(0.44 sq km)
Monaco	0.75 sq miles	(1.95 sq km)
Nauru	8.2 sq miles	(21.2 sq km)
Tuvalu	10 sq miles	(26 sq km)
San Marino	24 sq miles	(61 sq km)
Liechtenstein	62 sq miles	(160 sq km)
Marshall Islands	70 sq miles	(181 sq km)
St. Kitts & Nevis	101 sq miles	(261 sq km)
Maldives	116 sq miles	(300 sq km)
Malta	124 sq miles	(320 sq km)

Largest islands

	To the nearest 1000 – or 100,000 for the largest	
Greenland	849,400 sq miles	(2,200,000 sq km)
New Guinea	312,000 sq miles	(808,000 sq km)
Borneo	292,222 sq miles	(757,050 sq km)
Madagascar	229,300 sq miles	(594,000 sq km)
Sumatra	202,300 sq miles	(524,000 sq km)
Baffin Island	183,800 sq miles	(476,000 sq km)
Honshu	88,800 sq miles	(230,000 sq km)
Britain	88,700 sq miles	(229,800 sq km)
Victoria Island	81,900 sq miles	(212,000 sq km)
Ellesmere Island	75,700 sq miles	(196,000 sq km)

Richest countries

	GNI per capita, in US$
Luxembourg	56,230
Norway	52,030
Liechtenstein	50,000
Switzerland	48,230
USA	41,400
Denmark	40,650
Iceland	38,620
Japan	37,810
Sweden	35,770
Ireland	34,280

Poorest countries

	GNI per capita, in US$
Burundi	90
Ethiopia	110
Liberia	110
Congo, Dem. Rep.	120
Somalia	120
Guinea-Bissau	160
Malawi	170
Eritrea	180
Sierra Leone	200
Rwanda	220
Afghanistan	222
Niger	230

Most populous countries

China	1,315,800,000
India	1,103,400,000
USA	298,200,000
Indonesia	222,800,000
Brazil	186,400,000
Cameroon	163,000,000
Pakistan	157,900,000
Russian Federation	143,200,000
Bangladesh	141,800,000
Nigeria	131,500,000

Least populous countries

Vatican City	921
Tuvalu	11,636
Nauru	13,048
Palau	20,303
San Marino	28,880
Monaco	32,409
Liechtenstein	33,717
St Kitts & Nevis	38,958
Marshall Islands	59,071
Antigua & Barbuda	68,722
Dominica	69,029
Andorra	70,549

Most densely populated countries

Monaco	43,212 people per sq mile	(16,620 per sq km)
Singapore	18,220 people per sq mile	(7049 per sq km)
Vatican City	5418 people per sq mile	(2093 per sq km)
Malta	3242 people per sq mile	(1256 per sq km)
Maldives	2836 people per sq mile	(1097 per sq km)
Bangladesh	2743 people per sq mile	(1059 per sq km)
Bahrain	2663 people per sq mile	(1030 per sq km)
Taiwan	1838 people per sq mile	(710 per sq km)
Mauritius	1671 people per sq mile	(645 per sq km)
Barbados	1627 people per sq mile	(628 per sq km)

Most sparsely populated countries

Mongolia	4 people per sq mile	(2 per sq km)
Namibia	6 people per sq mile	(2 per sq km)
Australia	7 people per sq mile	(3 per sq km)
Mauritania	8 people per sq mile	(3 per sq km)
Suriname	8 people per sq mile	(3 per sq km)
Botswana	8 people per sq mile	(3 per sq km)
Iceland	8 people per sq mile	(3 per sq km)
Canada	9 people per sq mile	(4 per sq km)
Libya	9 people per sq mile	(4 per sq km)
Guyana	10 people per sq mile	(4 per sq km)

Most widely spoken languages

1. Chinese (Mandarin)	6. Arabic
2. English	7. Bengali
3. Hindi	8. Portuguese
4. Spanish	9. Malay-Indonesian
5. Russian	10. French

Largest conurbations

	Population
Tokyo	34,200,000
Mexico City	22,800,000
Seoul	22,300,000
New York	21,900,000
São Paulo	20,200,000
Mumbai	19,850,000
Delhi	19,700,000
Shanghai	18,150,000
Los Angeles	18,000,000
Osaka	16,800,000
Jakarta	16,550,000
Kolkata	15,650,000
Cairo	15,600,000
Manila	14,950,000
Karachi	14,300,000
Moscow	13,750,000
Buenos Aires	13,450,000
Dacca	13,250,000
Rio de Janeiro	12,150,000
Beijing	12,100,000
London	12,000,000
Tehran	11,850,000
Istanbul	11,500,000
Lagos	11,100,000
Shenzhen	10,700,000

Countries with the most land borders

14: China	(Afghanistan, Bhutan, India, Kazakhstan, Kyrgyzstan, Laos, Mongolia, Myanmar, Nepal, North Korea, Pakistan, Russian Federation, Tajikistan, Vietnam)
14: Russian Federation	(Azerbaijan, Belarus, China, Estonia, Finland, Georgia, Kazakhstan, Latvia, Lithuania, Mongolia, North Korea, Norway, Poland, Ukraine)
10: Brazil	(Argentina, Bolivia, Colombia, French Guiana, Guyana, Paraguay, Peru, Suriname, Uruguay, Venezuela)
9: Congo, Dem. Rep.	(Angola, Burundi, Central African Republic, Congo, Rwanda, Sudan, Tanzania, Uganda, Zambia)
9: Germany	(Austria, Belgium, Czech Republic, Denmark, France, Luxembourg, Netherlands, Poland, Switzerland)
9: Sudan	(Central African Republic, Chad, Dem. Rep.Congo, Egypt, Eritrea, Ethiopia, Kenya, Libya, Uganda)
8: Austria	(Czech Republic, Germany, Hungary, Italy, Liechtenstein, Slovakia, Slovenia, Switzerland)
8: France	(Andorra, Belgium, Germany, Italy, Luxembourg, Monaco, Spain, Switzerland)
8: Tanzania	(Burundi, Dem. Rep.Congo, Kenya, Malawi, Mozambique, Rwanda, Uganda, Zambia)
8: Turkey	(Armenia, Azerbaijan, Bulgaria, Georgia, Greece, Iran, Iraq, Syria)
8: Zambia	(Angola, Botswana, Dem. Rep.Congo, Malawi, Mozambique, Namibia, Tanzania, Zimbabwe)

Longest rivers

Nile (NE Africa)	4160 miles	(6695 km)
Amazon (South America)	4049 miles	(6516 km)
Yangtze (China)	3915 miles	(6299 km)
Mississippi/Missouri (USA)	3710 miles	(5969 km)
Ob'-Irtysh (Russian Federation)	3461 miles	(5570 km)
Yellow River (China)	3395 miles	(5464 km)
Congo (Central Africa)	2900 miles	(4667 km)
Mekong (Southeast Asia)	2749 miles	(4425 km)
Lena (Russian Federation)	2734 miles	(4400 km)
Mackenzie (Canada)	2640 miles	(4250 km)
Yenisey (Russian Federation)	2541 miles	(4090km)

Highest mountains

	Height above sea level	
Everest	29,035 ft	(8850 m)
K2	28,253 ft	(8611 m)
Kanchenjunga I	28,210 ft	(8598 m)
Makalu I	27,767 ft	(8463 m)
Cho Oyu	26,907 ft	(8201 m)
Dhaulagiri I	26,796 ft	(8167 m)
Manaslu I	26,783 ft	(8163 m)
Nanga Parbat I	26,661 ft	(8126 m)
Annapurna I	26,547 ft	(8091 m)
Gasherbrum I	26,471 ft	(8068 m)

Largest bodies of inland water

	With area and depth	
Caspian Sea	143,243 sq miles (371,000 sq km)	3215 ft (980 m)
Lake Superior	31,151 sq miles (83,270 sq km)	1289 ft (393 m)
Lake Victoria	26,828 sq miles (69,484 sq km)	328 ft (100 m)
Lake Huron	23,436 sq miles (60,700 sq km)	751 ft (229 m)
Lake Michigan	22,402 sq miles (58,020 sq km)	922 ft (281 m)
Lake Tanganyika	12,703 sq miles (32,900 sq km)	4700 ft (1435 m)
Great Bear Lake	12,274 sq miles (31,790 sq km)	1047 ft (319 m)
Lake Baikal	11,776 sq miles (30,500 sq km)	5712 ft (1741 m)
Great Slave Lake	10,981 sq miles (28,440 sq km)	459 ft (140 m)
Lake Erie	9,915 sq miles (25,680 sq km)	197 ft (60 m)

Deepest ocean features

Challenger Deep, Mariana Trench (Pacific)	36,201 ft	(11,034 m)
Vityaz III Depth, Tonga Trench (Pacific)	35,704 ft	(10,882 m)
Vityaz Depth, Kurile-Kamchatka Trench (Pacific)	34,588 ft	(10,542 m)
Cape Johnson Deep, Philippine Trench (Pacific)	34,441 ft	(10,497 m)
Kermadec Trench (Pacific)	32,964 ft	(10,047 m)
Ramapo Deep, Japan Trench (Pacific)	32,758 ft	(9984 m)
Milwaukee Deep, Puerto Rico Trench (Atlantic)	30,185 ft	(9200 m)
Argo Deep, Torres Trench (Pacific)	30,070 ft	**(9165 m)**
Meteor Depth, South Sandwich Trench (Atlantic)	30,000 ft	(9144 m)
Planet Deep, New Britain Trench (Pacific)	29,988 ft	(9140 m)

Greatest waterfalls

	Mean flow of water	
Boyoma (Congo, Dem. Rep.)	600,400 cu. ft/sec	(17,000 cu.m/sec)
Khône (Laos/Cambodia)	410,000 cu. ft/sec	(11,600 cu.m/sec)
Niagara (USA/Canada)	195,000 cu. ft/sec	(5500 cu.m/sec)
Grande (Uruguay)	160,000 cu. ft/sec	(4500 cu.m/sec)
Paulo Afonso (Brazil)	100,000 cu. ft/sec	(2800 cu.m/sec)
Urubupunga (Brazil)	97,000 cu. ft/sec	(2750 cu.m/sec)
Iguaçu (Argentina/Brazil)	62,000 cu. ft/sec	(1700 cu.m/sec)
Maribondo (Brazil)	53,000 cu. ft/sec	(1500 cu.m/sec)
Victoria (Zimbabwe)	39,000 cu. ft/sec	(1100 cu.m/sec)
Kabalega (Uganda)	42,000 cu. ft/sec	(1200 cu.m/sec)
Churchill (Canada)	35,000 cu. ft/sec	(1000 cu.m/sec)
Cauvery (India)	33,000 cu. ft/sec	(900 cu.m/sec)

Highest waterfalls

	* indicates that the total height is a single leap	
Angel (Venezuela)	3212 ft	(979 m)
Tugela (South Africa)	3110 ft	(948 m)
Utigard (Norway)	2625 ft	(800 m)
Mongefossen (Norway)	2539 ft	(774 m)
Mtarazi (Zimbabwe)	2500 ft	(762 m)
Yosemite (USA)	2425 ft	(739 m)
Ostre Mardola Foss (Norway)	2156 ft	(657 m)
Tyssestrengane (Norway)	2119 ft	(646 m)
*Cuquenan (Venezuela)	2001 ft	(610 m)
Sutherland (New Zealand)	1903 ft	(580 m)
*Kjellfossen (Norway)	1841 ft	(561 m)

Largest deserts

NB – Most of Antarctica is a polar desert, with only 50mm of precipitation annually

Sahara	3,450,000 sq miles	(9,065,000 sq km)
Gobi	500,000 sq miles	(1,295,000 sq km)
Ar Rub al Khali	289,600 sq miles	(750,000 sq km)
Great Victorian	249,800 sq miles	(647,000 sq km)
Sonoran	120,000 sq miles	(311,000 sq km)
Kalahari	120,000 sq miles	(310,800 sq km)
Kara Kum	115,800 sq miles	(300,000 sq km)
Takla Makan	100,400 sq miles	(260,000 sq km)
Namib	52,100 sq miles	(135,000 sq km)
Thar	33,670 sq miles	(130,000 sq km)

Hottest inhabited places

Djibouti (Djibouti)	86° F	(30 °C)
Timbouctou (Mali)	84.7° F	(29.3 °C)
Tirunelveli (India)		
Tuticorin (India)		
Nellore (India)	84.5° F	(29.2 °C)
Santa Marta (Colombia)		
Aden (Yemen)	84° F	(28.9 °C)
Madurai (India)		
Niamey (Niger)		
Hodeida (Yemen)	83.8° F	(28.8 °C)
Ouagadougou (Burkina)		
Thanjavur (India)		
Tiruchchirappalli (India)		

Driest inhabited places

Aswân (Egypt)	0.02 in	(0.5 mm)
Luxor (Egypt)	0.03 in	(0.7 mm)
Arica (Chile)	0.04 in	(1.1 mm)
Ica (Peru)	0.1 in	(2.3 mm)
Antofagasta (Chile)	0.2 in	(4.9 mm)
El Minya (Egypt)	0.2 in	(5.1 mm)
Asyût (Egypt)	0.2 in	(5.2 mm)
Callao (Peru)	0.5 in	(12.0 mm)
Trujillo (Peru)	0.55 in	(14.0 mm)
El Faiyûm (Egypt)	0.8 in	(19.0 mm)

Wettest inhabited places

Buenaventura (Colombia)	265 in	(6743 mm)
Monrovia (Liberia)	202 in	(5131 mm)
Pago Pago (American Samoa)	196 in	(4990 mm)
Moulmein (Myanmar)	191 in	(4852 mm)
Lae (Papua New Guinea)	183 in	(4645 mm)
Baguio (Luzon Island, Philippines)	180 in	(4573 mm)
Sylhet (Bangladesh)	176 in	(4457 mm)
Padang (Sumatra, Indonesia)	166 in	(4225 mm)
Bogor (Java, Indonesia)	166 in	(4225 mm)
Conakry (Guinea)	171 in	(4341 mm)

Countries of the World

There are currently 195 independent countries in the world – more than at any previous time – and 59 dependencies. Antarctica is the only land area on Earth that is not officially part of, and does not belong to, any single country.

In 1950, the world comprised 82 countries. In the decades following, many more states came into being as they achieved independence from their former colonial rulers. Most recent additions were caused by the breakup of the former Soviet Union in 1991, and the former Yugoslavia in 1992, which swelled the ranks of independent states. In February 2008, Kosovo became the latest country to be formed by controversially declaring independence from Serbia.

Country factfile key

Formation Date of independence / date current borders were established

Population Total population / population density – based on total *land* area / percentage of urban-based population

Languages An asterisk (*) denotes the official language(s)

Calorie consumption Average number of calories consumed daily per person

AFGHANISTAN
Central Asia

Official name Islamic State of Afghanistan
Formation 1919 / 1919
Capital Kabul
Population 29.9 million / 119 people per sq mile (46 people per sq km) / 22%
Total area 250,000 sq miles (647,500 sq km)
Languages Pashtu*, Tajik, Dari, Farsi, Uzbek, Turkmen
Religions Sunni Muslim 84%, Shi'a Muslim 15%, Other 1%
Ethnic mix Pashtun 38%, Tajik 25%, Hazara 19%, Uzbek and Turkmen 15%, Other 3%
Government Transitional regime
Currency New afghani = 100 puls
Literacy rate 36%
Calorie consumption 1539 calories

ALBANIA
Southeast Europe

Official name Republic of Albania
Formation 1912 / 1921
Capital Tirana
Population 3.1 million / 293 people per sq mile (113 people per sq km) / 42%
Total area 11,100 sq miles (28,748 sq km)
Languages Albanian*, Greek
Religions Sunni Muslim 70%, Orthodox Christian 20%, Roman Catholic 10%
Ethnic mix Albanian 93%, Greek 5%, Other 2%
Government Parliamentary system
Currency Lek = 100 qindarka (qintars)
Literacy rate 99%
Calorie consumption 2848 calories

ALGERIA
North Africa

Official name People's Democratic Republic of Algeria
Formation 1962 / 1962
Capital Algiers
Population 32.9 million / 36 people per sq mile (14 people per sq km) / 60%
Total area 919,590 sq miles (2,381,740 sq km)
Languages Arabic, Tamazight (Kabyle, Shawia, Tamashek), French
Religions Sunni Muslim 99%, Christian and Jewish 1%
Ethnic mix Arab 75%, Berber 24%, European and Jewish 1%
Government Presidential system
Currency Algerian dinar = 100 centimes
Literacy rate 70%
Calorie consumption 3022 calories

ANDORRA
Southwest Europe

Official name Principality of Andorra
Formation 1278 / 1278
Capital Andorra la Vella
Population 70,549 / 392 people per sq mile (152 people per sq km) / 63%
Total area 181 sq miles (468 sq km)
Languages Spanish, Catalan, French, Portuguese
Religions Roman Catholic 94%, Other 6%
Ethnic mix Spanish 46%, Andorran 28%, Other 18%, French 8%
Government Parliamentary system
Currency Euro = 100 cents
Literacy rate 99%
Calorie consumption Not available

ANGOLA
Southern Africa

Official name Republic of Angola
Formation 1975 / 1975
Capital Luanda
Population 15.9 million / 33 people per sq mile (13 people per sq km) / 34%
Total area 481,351 sq miles (1,246,700 sq km)
Languages Portuguese*, Umbundu, Kimbundu, Kikongo
Religions Roman Catholic 50%, Other 30%, Protestant 20%
Ethnic mix Ovimbundu 37%, Other 25%, Kimbundu 25%, Bakongo 13%
Government Presidential system
Currency Readjusted kwanza = 100 lwei
Literacy rate 67%
Calorie consumption 2083 calories

ANTIGUA & BARBUDA
West Indies

Official name Antigua and Barbuda
Formation 1981 / 1981
Capital St. John's
Population 68,722 / 404 people per sq mile (156 people per sq km) / 37%
Total area 170 sq miles (442 sq km)
Languages English, English patois
Religions Anglican 45%, Other Protestant 42%, Roman Catholic 10%, Other 2%, Rastafarian 1%
Ethnic mix Black African 95%, Other 5%
Government Parliamentary system
Currency Eastern Caribbean dollar = 100 cents
Literacy rate 86%
Calorie consumption 2349 calories

ARGENTINA
South America

Official name Republic of Argentina
Formation 1816 / 1816
Capital Buenos Aires
Population 38.7 million / 37 people per sq mile (14 people per sq km) / 90%
Total area 1,068,296 sq miles (2,766,890 sq km)
Languages Spanish*, Italian, Amerindian languages
Religions Roman Catholic 90%, Other 6%, Protestant 2%, Jewish 2%
Ethnic mix Indo-European 83%, Mestizo 14%, Jewish 2%, Amerindian 1%
Government Presidential system
Currency new Argentine peso = 100 centavos
Literacy rate 97%
Calorie consumption 2992 calories

ARMENIA
Southwest Asia

Official name Republic of Armenia
Formation 1991 / 1991
Capital Yerevan
Population 3 million / 261 people per sq mile (101 people per sq km) / 70%
Total area 11,506 sq miles (29,800 sq km)
Languages Armenian*, Azeri, Russian
Religions Armenian Apostolic Church (Orthodox) 94%, Other 6%
Ethnic mix Armenian 93%, Azeri 3%, Other 2%, Russian 2%
Government Presidential system
Currency Dram = 100 luma
Literacy rate 99%
Calorie consumption 2268 calories

AUSTRALIA
Australasia & Oceania

Official name Commonwealth of Australia
Formation 1901 / 1901
Capital Canberra
Population 20.2 million / 7 people per sq mile (3 people per sq km) / 85%
Total area 2,967,893 sq miles (7,686,850 sq km)
Languages English*, Italian, Cantonese, Greek, Arabic, Vietnamese, Aboriginal languages
Religions Roman Catholic 26%, Anglican 24%, Other 23%, Nonreligious 13%, United Church 8%, Other Protestant 6%
Ethnic mix European 92%, Asian 5%, Aboriginal and other 3%
Government Parliamentary system
Currency Australian dollar = 100 cents
Literacy rate 99%
Calorie consumption 3054 calories

AUSTRIA
Central Europe

Official name Republic of Austria
Formation 1918 / 1919
Capital Vienna
Population 8.2 million / 257 people per sq mile (99 people per sq km) / 65%
Total area 32,378 sq miles (83,858 sq km)
Languages German*, Croatian, Slovenian, Hungarian (Magyar)
Religions Roman Catholic 78%, Nonreligious 9%, Other (including Jewish and Muslim) 8%, Protestant 5%
Ethnic mix Austrian 93%, Croat, Slovene, and Hungarian 6%, Other 1%
Government Parliamentary system
Currency Euro = 100 cents
Literacy rate 99%
Calorie consumption 3673 calories

AZERBAIJAN
Southwest Asia

Official name Republic of Azerbaijan
Formation 1991 / 1991
Capital Baku
Population 8.4 million / 251 people per sq mile (97 people per sq km) / 57%
Total area 33,436 sq miles (86,600 sq km)
Languages Azeri, Russian
Religions Shi'a Muslim 68%, Sunni Muslim 26%, Russian Orthodox 3%, Armenian Apostolic Church (Orthodox) 2%, Other 1%
Ethnic mix Azeri 90%, Dagestani 3%, Russian 3%, Other 2%, Armenian 2%
Government Presidential system
Currency Manat = 100 gopik
Literacy rate 99%
Calorie consumption 2575 calories

BAHAMAS
West Indies

Official name Commonwealth of the Bahamas
Formation 1973 / 1973
Capital Nassau
Population 323,000 / 84 people per sq mile (32 people per sq km) / 89%
Total area 5382 sq miles (13,940 sq km)
Languages English*, English Creole, French Creole
Religions Baptist 32%, Anglican 20%, Roman Catholic 19%, Other 17%, Methodist 6%, Church of God 6%
Ethnic mix Black African 85%, Other 15%
Government Parliamentary system
Currency Bahamian dollar = 100 cents
Literacy rate 96%
Calorie consumption 2755 calories

BAHRAIN
Southwest Asia

Official name Kingdom of Bahrain
Formation 1971 / 1971
Capital Manama
Population 727,000 / 2663 people per sq mile (1030 people per sq km) / 97%
Total area 239 sq miles (620 sq km)
Languages Arabic*
Religions Muslim (mainly Shi'a) 99%, Other 1%
Ethnic mix Bahraini 70%, Iranian, Indian, and Pakistani 24%, Other Arab 4%, European 2%
Government Monarchy
Currency Bahraini dinar = 1000 fils
Literacy rate 88%
Calorie consumption Not available

BANGLADESH
South Asia

Official name People's Republic of Bangladesh
Formation 1971 / 1971
Capital Dhaka
Population 142 million / 2743 people per sq mile (1059 people per sq km) / 25%
Total area 55,598 sq miles (144,000 sq km)
Languages Bengali*, Urdu, Chakma, Marma (Magh), Garo, Khasi, Santhali, Tripuri, Mro
Religions Muslim (mainly Sunni) 87%, Hindu 12%, Other 1%
Ethnic mix Bengali 98%, Other 2%
Government Parliamentary system
Currency Taka = 100 poisha
Literacy rate 41%
Calorie consumption 2205 calories

BARBADOS
West Indies

Official name Barbados
Formation 1966 / 1966
Capital Bridgetown
Population 270,000 / 1627 people per sq mile (628 people per sq km) / 50%
Total area 166 sq miles (430 sq km)
Languages English*, Bajan (Barbadian English)
Religions Anglican 40%, Other 24%, Nonreligious 17%, Pentecostal 8%, Methodist 7%, Roman Catholic 4%
Ethnic mix Black African 90%, Other 10%
Government Parliamentary system
Currency Barbados dollar = 100 cents
Literacy rate 99%
Calorie consumption 3091 calories

BELARUS
Eastern Europe

Official name Republic of Belarus
Formation 1991 / 1991
Capital Minsk
Population 9.8 million / 122 people per sq mile (47 people per sq km) / 71%
Total area 80,154 sq miles (207,600 sq km)
Languages Belarussian*, Russian
Religions Orthodox Christian 60%, Other 32%, Roman Catholic 8%
Ethnic mix Belarussian 78%, Russian 13%, Polish 4%, Ukrainian 3%, Other 2%
Government Presidential system
Currency Belarussian rouble = 100 kopeks
Literacy rate 99%
Calorie consumption 3000 calories

BELGIUM
Northwest Europe

Official name Kingdom of Belgium
Formation 1830 / 1919
Capital Brussels
Population 10.4 million / 821 people per sq mile (317 people per sq km) / 97%
Total area 11,780 sq miles (30,510 sq km)
Languages Dutch*, French*, German
Religions Roman Catholic 88%, Other 10%, Muslim 2%
Ethnic mix Fleming 58%, Walloon 33%, Other 6%, Italian 2%, Moroccan 1%
Government Parliamentary system
Currency Euro = 100 cents
Literacy rate 99%
Calorie consumption 3584 calories

BELIZE
Central America

Official name Belize
Formation 1981 / 1981
Capital Belmopan
Population 270,000 / 31 people per sq mile (12 people per sq km) / 54%
Total area 8867 sq miles (22,966 sq km)
Languages English*, English Creole, Spanish, Mayan, Garifuna (Carib)
Religions Roman Catholic 62%, Other 13%, Anglican 12%, Methodist 6%, Mennonite 4%, Seventh-day Adventist 3%
Ethnic mix Mestizo 44%, Creole 30%, Maya 11%, Garifuna 7%, Other 4%, Asian Indian 4%
Government Parliamentary system
Currency Belizean dollar = 100 cents
Literacy rate 77%
Calorie consumption 2869 calories

BENIN
West Africa

Official name Republic of Benin
Formation 1960 / 1960
Capital Porto-Novo
Population 8.4 million / 197 people per sq mile (76 people per sq km) / 42%
Total area 43,483 sq miles (112,620 sq km)
Languages French*, Fon, Bariba, Yoruba, Adja, Houeda, Somba
Religions Voodoo 50%, Muslim 30%, Christian 20%
Ethnic mix Fon 47%, Other 31%, Adja 12%, Bariba 10%
Government Presidential system
Currency CFA franc = 100 centimes
Literacy rate 34%
Calorie consumption 2548 calories

BHUTAN
Southeast Asia

Official name Kingdom of Bhutan
Formation 1656 / 1865
Capital Thimphu
Population 2.2 million / 121 people per sq mile (47 people per sq km) / 7%
Total area 18,147 sq miles (47,000 sq km)
Languages Dzongkha*, Nepali, Assamese
Religions Mahayana Buddhist 70%, Hindu 24%, Other 6%
Ethnic mix Bhute 50%, Other 25%, Nepalese 25%
Government Monarchy
Currency Ngultrum = 100 chetrum
Literacy rate 47%
Calorie consumption Not available

BOLIVIA
South America

Official name Republic of Bolivia
Formation 1825 /1938
Capital La Paz (administrative); Sucre (judicial)
Population 9.2 million / 22 people per sq mile (8 people per sq km) / 63%
Total area 424,162 sq miles (1,098,580 sq km)
Languages Aymara*, Quechua*, Spanish*
Religions Roman Catholic 93%, Other 7%
Ethnic mix Quechua 37%, Aymara 32%, Mixed race 13%, European 10%, Other 8%
Government Presidential system
Currency Boliviano = 100 centavos
Literacy rate 87%
Calorie consumption 2235 calories

BOSNIA & HERZEGOVINA
Southeast Europe

Official name Bosnia and Herzegovina
Formation 1992 / 1992
Capital Sarajevo
Population 3.9 million / 198 people per sq mile (76 people per sq km) / 43%
Total area 19,741 sq miles (51,129 sq km)
Languages Serbo-Croat*
Religions Muslim (mainly Sunni) 40%, Orthodox Christian 31%, Roman Catholic 15%, Other 10%, Protestant 4%
Ethnic mix Bosniak 48%, Serb 38%, Croat 14%
Government Parliamentary system
Currency Marka = 100 pfeninga
Literacy rate 95%
Calorie consumption 2894 calories

BOTSWANA
Southern Africa

Official name Republic of Botswana
Formation 1966 / 1966
Capital Gaborone
Population 1.8 million / 8 people per sq mile (3 people per sq km) / 50%
Total area 231,803 sq miles (600,370 sq km)
Languages English*, Setswana, Shona, San, Khoikhoi, isiNdebele
Religions Traditional beliefs 50%, Christian (mainly Protestant) 30%, Other (including Muslim) 20%
Ethnic mix Tswana 98%, Other 2%
Government Presidential system
Currency Pula = 100 thebe
Literacy rate 79%
Calorie consumption 2151 calories

BRAZIL
South America

Official name Federative Republic of Brazil
Formation 1822 / 1828
Capital Brasilia
Population 186 million / 57 people per sq mile (22 people per sq km) / 81%
Total area 3,286,470 sq miles (8,511,965 sq km)
Languages Portuguese*, German, Italian, Spanish, Polish, Japanese, Amerindian languages
Religions Roman Catholic 74%, Protestant 15%, Atheist 7%, Other 4%
Ethnic mix Black 53%, Mixed race 40%, White 6%, Other 1%
Government Presidential system
Currency Real = 100 centavos
Literacy rate 88%
Calorie consumption 3049 calories

BRUNEI
Southeast Asia

Official name Sultanate of Brunei
Formation 1984 / 1984
Capital Bandar Seri Begawan
Population 374,000 / 184 people per sq mile (71 people per sq km) / 72%
Total area 2228 sq miles (5770 sq km)
Languages Malay*, English, Chinese
Religions Muslim (mainly Sunni) 66%, Buddhist 14%, Other 10%, Christian 10%
Ethnic mix Malay 67%, Chinese 16%, Other 11%, Indigenous 6%
Government Monarchy
Currency Brunei dollar = 100 cents
Literacy rate 93%
Calorie consumption 2855 calories

BULGARIA
Southeast Europe

Official name Republic of Bulgaria
Formation 1908 / 1947
Capital Sofia
Population 7.7 million / 180 people per sq mile (70 people per sq km) / 70%
Total area 42,822 sq miles (110,910 sq km)
Languages Bulgarian*, Turkish, Romani
Religions Orthodox Christian 83%, Muslim 12%, Other 4%, Roman Catholic 1%
Ethnic mix Bulgarian 84%, Turkish 9%, Roma 5%, Other 2%
Government Parliamentary system
Currency Lev = 100 stotinki
Literacy rate 98%
Calorie consumption 2848 calories

BURKINA
West Africa

Official name Burkina Faso
Formation 1960 / 1960
Capital Ouagadougou
Population 13.2 million / 125 people per sq mile (48 people per sq km) / 19%
Total area 105,869 sq miles (274,200 sq km)
Languages French*, Mossi, Fulani, Tuareg, Dyula, Songhai
Religions Muslim 55%, Traditional beliefs 35%, Roman Catholic 9%, Other Christian 1%
Ethnic mix Other 50%, Mossi 50%
Government Presidential system
Currency CFA franc = 100 centimes
Literacy rate 13%
Calorie consumption 2462 calories

BURUNDI
Central Africa

Official name Republic of Burundi
Formation 1962 / 1962
Capital Bujumbura
Population 7.5 million / 757 people per sq mile (292 people per sq km) / 9%
Total area 10,745 sq miles (27,830 sq km)
Languages Kirundi*, French*, Kiswahili
Religions Christian 60%, Traditional beliefs 39%, Muslim 1%
Ethnic mix Hutu 85%, Tutsi 14%, Twa 1%
Government Presidential system
Currency Burundi franc = 100 centimes
Literacy rate 59%
Calorie consumption 1649 calories

CAMBODIA
Southeast Asia

Official name Kingdom of Cambodia
Formation 1953 / 1953
Capital Phnom Penh
Population 14.1 million / 207 people per sq mile (80 people per sq km) / 16%
Total area 69,900 sq miles (181,040 sq km)
Languages Khmer*, French, Chinese, Vietnamese, Cham
Religions Buddhist 93%, Muslim 6%, Christian 1%
Ethnic mix Khmer 90%, Other 5%, Vietnamese 4%, Chinese 1%
Government Parliamentary system
Currency Riel = 100 sen
Literacy rate 74%
Calorie consumption 2046 calories

CAMEROON
Central Africa

Official name Republic of Cameroon
Formation 1960 / 1961
Capital Yaoundé
Population 16.3 million / 907 people per sq mile (350 people per sq km) / 49%
Total area 183,567 sq miles (475,400 sq km)
Languages English*, French*, Bamileke, Fang, Fulani
Religions Roman Catholic 35%, Traditional beliefs 25%, Muslim 22%, Protestant 18%
Ethnic mix Cameroon highlanders 31%, Other 21%, Equatorial Bantu 19%, Kirdi 11%, Fulani 10%, Northwestern Bantu 8%
Government Presidential system
Currency CFA franc = 100 centimes
Literacy rate 68%
Calorie consumption 2273 calories

CANADA
North America

Official name Canada
Formation 1867 / 1949
Capital Ottawa
Population 32.3 million / 9 people per sq mile (4 people per sq km) / 77%
Total area 3,717,792 sq miles (9,984,670 sq km)
Languages English*, French*, Chinese, Italian, German, Ukrainian, Inuktitut, Cree
Religions Roman Catholic 44%, Protestant 29%, Other and nonreligious 27%
Ethnic mix British origin 44%, French origin 25%, Other European 20%, Other 11%
Government Parliamentary system
Currency Canadian dollar = 100 cents
Literacy rate 99%
Calorie consumption 3589 calories

CAPE VERDE
Atlantic Ocean

Official name Republic of Cape Verde
Formation 1975
Capital Praia
Population 507,000 / 326 people per sq mile (126 people per sq km) / 62%
Total area 1557 sq miles (4033 sq km)
Languages Portuguese*, Portuguese Creole
Religions Roman Catholic 97%, Other 2%, Protestant (Church of the Nazarene) 1%
Ethnic mix Mestizo 60%, African 30%, Other 10%
Government Mixed presidential–parliamentary system
Currency Cape Verde escudo = 100 centavos
Literacy rate 76%
Calorie consumption 3243 calories

CENTRAL AFRICAN REPUBLIC
Central Africa

Official name Central African Republic
Formation 1960 / 1960
Capital Bangui
Population 4 million / 17 people per sq mile (6 people per sq km) / 41%
Total area 240,534 sq miles (622,984 sq km)
Languages Sango, Banda, Gbaya, French
Religions Traditional beliefs 60%, Christian (mainly Roman Catholic) 35%, Muslim 5%
Ethnic mix Baya 34%, Banda 27%, Mandjia 21%, Sara 10%, Other 8%
Government Presidential system
Currency CFA franc = 100 centimes
Literacy rate 49%
Calorie consumption 1980 calories

CHAD
Central Africa

Official name Republic of Chad
Formation 1960 / 1960
Capital N'Djamena
Population 9.7 million / 20 people per sq mile (8 people per sq km) / 24%
Total area 495,752 sq miles (1,284,000 sq km)
Languages French, Sara, Arabic, Maba
Religions Muslim 55%, Traditional beliefs 35%, Christian 10%
Ethnic mix Nomads (Tuareg and Toubou) 38%, Sara 30%, Other 17%, Arab 15%
Government Presidential system
Currency CFA franc = 100 centimes
Literacy rate 26%
Calorie consumption 2114 calories

CHILE
South America

Official name Republic of Chile
Formation 1818 / 1883
Capital Santiago
Population 16.3 million / 56 people per sq mile (22 people per sq km) / 86%
Total area 292,258 sq miles (756,950 sq km)
Languages Spanish*, Amerindian languages
Religions Roman Catholic 80%, Other and nonreligious 20%
Ethnic mix Mixed race and European 90%, Amerindian 10%
Government Presidential system
Currency Chilean peso = 100 centavos
Literacy rate 96%
Calorie consumption 2863 calories

CHINA
East Asia

Official name People's Republic of China
Formation 960 / 1999
Capital Beijing
Population 1.32 billion / 365 people per sq mile (141 people per sq km) / 32%
Total area 3,705,386 sq miles (9,596,960 sq km)
Languages Mandarin*, Wu, Cantonese, Hsiang, Min, Hakka, Kan
Religions Nonreligious 59%, Traditional beliefs 20%, Other 13%, Buddhist 6%, Muslim 2%
Ethnic mix Han 92%, Other 6%, Hui 1%, Zhuang 1%
Government One-party state
Currency Renminbi (known as yuan) = 10 jiao
Literacy rate 91%
Calorie consumption 2951 calories

COLOMBIA
South America

Official name Republic of Colombia
Formation 1819 / 1903
Capital Bogotá
Population 45.6 million / 114 people per sq mile (44 people per sq km) / 74%
Total area 439,733 sq miles (1,138,910 sq km)
Languages Spanish*, Wayuu, Páez, and other Amerindian languages
Religions Roman Catholic 95%, Other 5%
Ethnic mix Mestizo 58%, White 20%, European–African 14%, African 4%, African–Amerindian 3%, Amerindian 1%
Government Presidential system
Currency Colombian peso = 100 centavos
Literacy rate 94%
Calorie consumption 2585 calories

COMOROS
Indian Ocean

Official name Union of the Comoros
Formation 1975 / 1975
Capital Moroni
Population 798,000 / 927 people per sq mile (358 people per sq km) / 33%
Total area 838 sq miles (2170 sq km)
Languages Arabic*, Comoran, French
Religions Muslim (mainly Sunni) 98%, Other 1%, Roman Catholic 1%
Ethnic mix Comoran 97%, Other 3%
Government Presidential system
Currency Comoros franc = 100 centimes
Literacy rate 56%
Calorie consumption 1754 calories

CONGO
Central Africa

Official name Republic of the Congo
Formation 1960 / 1960
Capital Brazzaville
Population 4 million / 30 people per sq mile (12 people per sq km) / 63%
Total area 132,046 sq miles (342,000 sq km)
Languages French*, Kongo, Teke, Lingala
Religions Traditional beliefs 50%, Roman Catholic 25%, Protestant 23%, Muslim 2%
Ethnic mix Bakongo 48%, Sangha 20%, Teke 17%, Mbochi 12%, Other 3%
Government Presidential system
Currency CFA franc = 100 centimes
Literacy rate 83%
Calorie consumption 2162 calories

CONGO, DEM. REP.
Central Africa

Official name Democratic Republic of the Congo
Formation 1960 / 1960
Capital Kinshasa
Population 57.5 million / 66 people per sq mile (25 people per sq km) / 30%
Total area 905,563 sq miles (2,345,410 sq km)
Languages French*, Kiswahili, Tshiluba, Kikongo, Lingala
Religions Roman Catholic 50%, Protestant 20%, Traditional beliefs and other 10%, Muslim 10%, Kimbanguist 10%
Ethnic mix Other 55%, Bantu and Hamitic 45%
Government Transitional regime
Currency Congolese franc = 100 centimes
Literacy rate 65%
Calorie consumption 1599 calories

COSTA RICA
Central America

Official name Republic of Costa Rica
Formation 1838 / 1838
Capital San José
Population 4.3 million / 218 people per sq mile (84 people per sq km) / 52%
Total area 19,730 sq miles (51,100 sq km)
Languages Spanish*, English Creole, Bribri, Cabecar
Religions Roman Catholic 76%, Other (including Protestant) 24%
Ethnic mix Mestizo and European 96%, Black 2%, Chinese 1%, Amerindian 1%
Government Presidential system
Currency Costa Rican colón = 100 centimos
Literacy rate 96%
Calorie consumption 2876 calories

CROATIA
Southeast Europe

Official name Republic of Croatia
Formation 1991 / 1991
Capital Zagreb
Population 4.6 million / 211 people per sq mile (81 people per sq km) / 58%
Total area 21,831 sq miles (56,542 sq km)
Languages Croatian*
Religions Roman Catholic 88%, Other 7%, Orthodox Christian 4%, Muslim 1%
Ethnic mix Croat 90%, Other 5%, Serb 4%, Bosniak 1%
Government Parliamentary system
Currency Kuna = 100 lipas
Literacy rate 98%
Calorie consumption 2799 calories

CUBA
West Indies

Official name Republic of Cuba
Formation 1902 / 1902
Capital Havana
Population 11.3 million / 264 people per sq mile (102 people per sq km) / 75%
Total area 42,803 sq miles (110,860 sq km)
Languages Spanish*
Religions Nonreligious 49%, Roman Catholic 40%, Atheist 6%, Other 4%, Protestant 1%
Ethnic mix White 66%, European–African 22%, Black 12%
Government One-party state
Currency Cuban peso = 100 centavos
Literacy rate 97%
Calorie consumption 3152 calories

CYPRUS
Southeast Europe

Official name Republic of Cyprus
Formation 1960 / 1960
Capital Nicosia
Population 835,000 / 234 people per sq mile (90 people per sq km) / 57%
Total area 3571 sq miles (9250 sq km)
Languages Greek, Turkish
Religions Orthodox Christian 78%, Muslim 18%, Other 4%
Ethnic mix Greek 85%, Turkish 12%, Other 3%
Government Presidential system
Currency Cyprus pound (Turkish lira in TRNC) = 100 cents (Cyprus pound); 100 kurus (Turkish lira)
Literacy rate 97%
Calorie consumption 3255 calories

CZECH REPUBLIC
Central Europe

Official name Czech Republic
Formation 1993 / 1993
Capital Prague
Population 10.2 million / 335 people per sq mile (129 people per sq km) / 75%
Total area 30,450 sq miles (78,866 sq km)
Languages Czech*, Slovak, Hungarian (Magyar)
Religions Roman Catholic 39%, Atheist 38%, Other 18%, Protestant 3%, Hussite 2%
Ethnic mix Czech 81%, Moravian 13%, Slovak 6%
Government Parliamentary system
Currency Czech koruna = 100 haleru
Literacy rate 99%
Calorie consumption 3171 calories

DENMARK
Northern Europe

Official name Kingdom of Denmark
Formation AD 950 / 1945
Capital Copenhagen
Population 5.4 million / 330 people per sq mile (127 people per sq km) / 85%
Total area 16,639 sq miles (43,094 sq km)
Languages Danish*
Religions Evangelical Lutheran 89%, Other 10%, Roman Catholic 1%
Ethnic mix Danish 96%, Other (including Scandinavian and Turkish) 3%, Faeroese and Inuit 1%
Government Parliamentary system
Currency Danish krone = 100 øre
Literacy rate 99%
Calorie consumption 3439 calories

DJIBOUTI
East Africa

Official name Republic of Djibouti
Formation 1977 / 1977
Capital Djibouti
Population 793,000 / 89 people per sq mile (34 people per sq km) / 83%
Total area 8494 sq miles (22,000 sq km)
Languages French*, Arabic*, Somali, Afar
Religions Muslim (mainly Sunni) 94%, Christian 6%
Ethnic mix Issa 60%, Afar 35%, Other 5%
Government Presidential system
Currency Djibouti franc = 100 centimes
Literacy rate 66%
Calorie consumption 2220 calories

DOMINICA
West Indies

Official name Commonwealth of Dominica
Formation 1978 / 1978
Capital Roseau
Population 69,029 / 238 people per sq mile (92 people per sq km) / 71%
Total area 291 sq miles (754 sq km)
Languages English*, French Creole
Religions Roman Catholic 77%, Protestant 15%, Other 8%
Ethnic mix Black 91%, Mixed race 6%, Carib 2%, Other 1%
Government Parliamentary system
Currency Eastern Caribbean dollar = 100 cents
Literacy rate 88%
Calorie consumption 2763 calories

DOMINICAN REPUBLIC
West Indies

Official name Dominican Republic
Formation 1865 / 1865
Capital Santo Domingo
Population 8.9 million / 476 people per sq mile (184 people per sq km) / 65%
Total area 18,679 sq miles (48,380 sq km)
Languages Spanish*, French Creole
Religions Roman Catholic 92%, Other and nonreligious 8%
Ethnic mix Mixed race 75%, White 15%, Black 10%
Government Presidential system
Currency Dominican Republic peso = 100 centavos
Literacy rate 88%
Calorie consumption 2347 calories

EAST TIMOR
Southeast Asia

Official name Democratic Republic of Timor-Leste
Formation 2002 / 2002
Capital Dili
Population 947,000 / 168 people per sq mile (65 people per sq km) / 8%
Total area 5756 sq miles (14,874 sq km)
Languages Tetum (Portuguese/Austronesian), Bahasa Indonesia, and Portuguese
Religions Roman Catholic 95%, Other (including Muslim and Protestant) 5%
Ethnic mix Papuan groups approx 85%, Indonesian approx 13%, Chinese 2%
Government Parliamentary system
Currency US dollar = 100 cents
Literacy rate 59%
Calorie consumption 2806 calories

ECUADOR
South America

Official name Republic of Ecuador
Formation 1830 / 1941
Capital Quito
Population 13.2 million / 123 people per sq mile (48 people per sq km) / 65%
Total area 109,483 sq miles (283,560 sq km)
Languages Spanish*, Quechua*, other Amerindian languages
Religions Roman Catholic 93%, Protestant, Jewish, and other 7%
Ethnic mix Mestizo 55%, Amerindian 25%, White 10%, Black 10%
Government Presidential system
Currency US dollar = 100 cents
Literacy rate 91%
Calorie consumption 2754 calories

EGYPT
North Africa

Official name Arab Republic of Egypt
Formation 1936 / 1982
Capital Cairo
Population 74 million / 193 people per sq mile (74 people per sq km) / 45%
Total area 386,660 sq miles (1,001,450 sq km)
Languages Arabic*, French, English, Berber
Religions Muslim (mainly Sunni) 94%, Coptic Christian and other 6%
Ethnic mix Eastern Hamitic 90%, Nubian, Armenian, and Greek 10%
Government Presidential system
Currency Egyptian pound = 100 piastres
Literacy rate 56%
Calorie consumption 3338 calories

EL SALVADOR
Central America

Official name Republic of El Salvador
Formation 1841 / 1841
Capital San Salvador
Population 6.9 million / 862 people per sq mile (333 people per sq km) / 47%
Total area 8124 sq miles (21,040 sq km)
Languages Spanish*
Religions Roman Catholic 80%, Evangelical 18%, Other 2%
Ethnic mix Mestizo 94%, Amerindian 5%, White 1%
Government Presidential system
Currency Salvadorean colón & US dollar = 100 centavos (colón); 100 cents (US dollar)
Literacy rate 80%
Calorie consumption 2584 calories

EQUATORIAL GUINEA
Central Africa

Official name Republic of Equatorial Guinea
Formation 1968 / 1968
Capital Malabo
Population 504,000 / 47 people per sq mile (18 people per sq km) / 48%
Total area 10,830 sq miles (28,051 sq km)
Languages Spanish*, Fang, Bubi
Religions Roman Catholic 90%, Other 10%
Ethnic mix Fang 85%, Other 11%, Bubi 4%
Government Presidential system
Currency CFA franc = 100 centimes
Literacy rate 84%
Calorie consumption Not available

ERITREA
East Africa

Official name State of Eritrea
Formation 1993 / 2002
Capital Asmara
Population 4.4 million / 97 people per sq mile (37 people per sq km) / 19%
Total area 46,842 sq miles (121,320 sq km)
Languages Arabic*, Tigrinya*, English, Tigre, Afar, Bilen, Kunama, Nara, Saho, Hadareb
Religions Christian 45%, Muslim 45%, Other 10%
Ethnic mix Tigray 50%, Tigray and Kunama 40%, Afar 4%, Other 3%, Saho 3%
Government Transitional regime
Currency Nakfa = 100 cents
Literacy rate 57%
Calorie consumption 1513 calories

ESTONIA
Northeast Europe

Official name Republic of Estonia
Formation 1991 / 1991
Capital Tallinn
Population 1.3 million / 75 people per sq mile (29 people per sq km) / 69%
Total area 17,462 sq miles (45,226 sq km)
Languages Estonian*, Russian
Religions Evangelical Lutheran 56%, Orthodox Christian 25%, Other 19%
Ethnic mix Estonian 62%, Russian 30%, Other 8%
Government Parliamentary system
Currency Kroon = 100 senti
Literacy rate 99%
Calorie consumption 3002 calories

ETHIOPIA
East Africa

Official name Federal Democratic Republic of Ethiopia
Formation 1896 / 2002
Capital Addis Ababa
Population 77.4 million / 181 people per sq mile (70 people per sq km) / 18%
Total area 435,184 sq miles (1,127,127 sq km)
Languages Amharic*, Tigrinya, Galla, Sidamo, Somali, English, Arabic
Religions Orthodox Christian 40%, Muslim 40%, Traditional beliefs 15%, Other 5%
Ethnic mix Oromo 40%, Amhara 25%, Other 14%, Sidamo 9%, Berta 6%, Somali 6%
Government Parliamentary system
Currency Ethiopian birr = 100 cents
Literacy rate 42%
Calorie consumption 1857 calories

FIJI
Australasia & Oceania

Official name Republic of the Fiji Islands
Formation 1970 / 1970
Capital Suva
Population 848,000 / 120 people per sq mile (46 people per sq km) / 49%
Total area 7054 sq miles (18,270 sq km)
Languages English*, Fijian*, Hindi, Urdu, Tamil, Telugu
Religions Hindu 38%, Methodist 37%, Roman Catholic 9%, Other 8%, Muslim 8%
Ethnic mix Melanesian 48%, Indian 46%, Other 6%
Government Parliamentary system
Currency Fiji dollar = 100 cents
Literacy rate 93%
Calorie consumption 2894 calories

FINLAND
Northern Europe

Official name Republic of Finland
Formation 1917 / 1947
Capital Helsinki
Population 5.2 million / 44 people per sq mile (17 people per sq km) / 67%
Total area 130,127 sq miles (337,030 sq km)
Languages Finnish*, Swedish*, Sámi
Religions Evangelical Lutheran 89%, Orthodox Christian 1%, Roman Catholic 1%, Other 9%
Ethnic mix Finnish 93%, Other (including Sámi) 7%
Government Parliamentary system
Currency Euro = 100 cents
Literacy rate 99%
Calorie consumption 3100 calories

FRANCE
Western Europe

Official name French Republic
Formation 987 / 1919
Capital Paris
Population 60.5 million / 285 people per sq mile (110 people per sq km) / 76%
Total area 211,208 sq miles (547,030 sq km)
Languages French*, Provençal, German, Breton, Catalan, Basque
Religions Roman Catholic 88%, Muslim 8%, Protestant 2%, Buddhist 1%, Jewish 1%
Ethnic mix French 90%, North African (mainly Algerian) 6%, German (Alsace) 2%, Breton 1%, Other (including Corsicans) 1%
Government Mixed presidential–parliamentary system
Currency Euro = 100 cents
Literacy rate 99%
Calorie consumption 3654 calories

GABON
Central Africa

Official name Gabonese Republic
Formation 1960 / 1960
Capital Libreville
Population 1.4 million / 14 people per sq mile (5 people per sq km) / 81%
Total area 103,346 sq miles (267,667 sq km)
Languages French*,Fang, Punu, Sira, Nzebi, Mpongwe
Religions Christian (mainly Roman Catholic) 55%, Traditional beliefs 40%, Other 4%, Muslim 1%
Ethnic mix Fang 35%, Other Bantu 29%, Eshira 25%, European and other African 9%, French 2%
Government Presidential system
Currency CFA franc = 100 centimes
Literacy rate 71%
Calorie consumption 2637 calories

GAMBIA
West Africa

Official name Republic of the Gambia
Formation 1965 / 1965
Capital Banjul
Population 1.5 million / 389 people per sq mile (150 people per sq km) / 33%
Total area 4363 sq miles (11,300 sq km)
Languages English*, Mandinka, Fulani, Wolof, Jola, Soninke
Religions Sunni Muslim 90%, Christian 9%, Traditional beliefs 1%
Ethnic mix Mandinka 42%, Fulani 18%, Wolof 16%, Jola 10%, Serahuli 9%, Other 5%
Government Presidential system
Currency Dalasi = 100 butut
Literacy rate 38%
Calorie consumption 2273 calories

GEORGIA
Southwest Asia

Official name Georgia
Formation 1991 / 1991
Capital Tbilisi
Population 4.5 million / 167 people per sq mile (65 people per sq km) / 61%
Total area 26,911 sq miles (69,700 sq km)
Languages Georgian*, Russian, Azeri, Armenian, Mingrelian, Ossetian, Abkhazian
Religions Georgian Orthodox 65%, Muslim 11%, Russian Orthodox 10%, Armenian Orthodox 8%, Other 6%
Ethnic mix Georgian 70%, Armenian 8%, Russian 6%, Azeri 6%, Ossetian 3%, Other 7%
Government Presidential system
Currency Lari = 100 tetri
Literacy rate 99%
Calorie consumption 2354 calories

GERMANY
Northern Europe

Official name Federal Republic of Germany
Formation 1871 / 1990
Capital Berlin
Population 82.7 million / 613 people per sq mile (237 people per sq km) / 88%
Total area 137,846 sq miles (357,021 sq km)
Languages German*, Turkish
Religions Protestant 34%, Roman Catholic 33%, Other 30%, Muslim 3%
Ethnic mix German 92%, Other 3%, Other European 3%, Turkish 2%
Government Parliamentary system
Currency Euro = 100 cents
Literacy rate 99%
Calorie consumption 3496 calories

GHANA
West Africa

Official name Republic of Ghana
Formation 1957 / 1957
Capital Accra
Population 22.1 million / 249 people per sq mile (96 people per sq km) / 38%
Total area 92,100 sq miles (238,540 sq km)
Languages Twi, Fanti, Ewe, Ga, Adangbe, Gurma, Dagomba (Dagbani)
Religions Christian 69%, Muslim 16%, Traditional beliefs 9%, Other 6%
Ethnic mix Ashanti and Fanti 52%, Moshi-Dagomba 16%, Ewe 12%, Other 11%, Ga and Ga-adanbe 8%, Yoruba 1%
Government Presidential system
Currency Cedi = 100 psewas
Literacy rate 54%
Calorie consumption 2667 calories

GREECE
Southeast Europe

Official name Hellenic Republic
Formation 1829 / 1947
Capital Athens
Population 11.1 million / 220 people per sq mile (85 people per sq km) / 60%
Total area 50,942 sq miles (131,940 sq km)
Languages Greek*, Turkish, Macedonian, Albanian
Religions Orthodox Christian 98%, Other 1%, Muslim 1%
Ethnic mix Greek 90%, Macedonian 2%, Albanian 1%, Turkish 1%, Other 6%
Government Parliamentary system
Currency Euro = 100 cents
Literacy rate 91%
Calorie consumption 3721 calories

GRENADA
West Indies

Official name Grenada
Formation 1974 / 1974
Capital St. George's
Population 89,502 / 683 people per sq mile (263 people per sq km) / 38%
Total area 131 sq miles (340 sq km)
Languages English*, English Creole
Religions Roman Catholic 68%, Anglican 17%, Other 15%
Ethnic mix Black African 82%, Mulatto (mixed race) 13%, East Indian 3%, Other 2%
Government Parliamentary system
Currency Eastern Caribbean dollar = 100 cents
Literacy rate 96%
Calorie consumption 2932 calories

GUATEMALA
Central America

Official name Republic of Guatemala
Formation 1838 / 1838
Capital Guatemala City
Population 12.6 million / 301 people per sq mile (116 people per sq km) / 40%
Total area 42,042 sq miles (108,890 sq km)
Languages Spanish*, Quiché, Mam, Cakchiquel, Kekchí
Religions Roman Catholic 65%, Protestant 33%, Other and nonreligious 2%
Ethnic mix Amerindian 60%, Mestizo 30%, Other 10%
Government Presidential system
Currency Quetzal = 100 centavos
Literacy rate 69%
Calorie consumption 2219 calories

GUINEA
West Africa

Official name Republic of Guinea
Formation 1958 / 1958
Capital Conakry
Population 9.4 million / 99 people per sq mile (38 people per sq km) / 33%
Total area 94,925 sq miles (245,857 sq km)
Languages French*, Fulani, Malinke, Soussou
Religions Muslim 65%, Traditional beliefs 33%, Christian 2%
Ethnic mix Fulani 30%, Malinke 30%, Soussou 15%, Kissi 10%, Other tribes 10%, Other 5%
Government Presidential system
Currency Guinea franc = 100 centimes
Literacy rate 41%
Calorie consumption 2409 calories

GUINEA-BISSAU
West Africa

Official name Republic of Guinea-Bissau
Formation 1974 / 1974
Capital Bissau
Population 1.6 million / 147 people per sq mile (57 people per sq km) / 24%
Total area 13,946 sq miles (36,120 sq km)
Languages Portuguese*, Balante, Fulani, Malinke, Portuguese Creole
Religions Traditional beliefs 52%, Muslim 40%, Christian 8%
Ethnic mix Other tribes 31%, Balante 25%, Fula 20%, Mandinka 12%, Mandyako 11%, Other 1%
Government Presidential system
Currency CFA franc = 100 centimes
Literacy rate 40%
Calorie consumption 2024 calories

GUYANA
South America

Official name Cooperative Republic of Guyana
Formation 1966 / 1966
Capital Georgetown
Population 751,000 / 10 people per sq mile (4 people per sq km) / 38%
Total area 83,000 sq miles (214,970 sq km)
Languages English*, Hindi, Tamil, Amerindian languages, English Creole
Religions Christian 57%, Hindu 33%, Muslim 9%, Other 1%
Ethnic mix East Indian 52%, Black African 38%, Other 4%, Amerindian 4%, European and Chinese 2%
Government Presidential system
Currency Guyanese dollar = 100 cents
Literacy rate 97%
Calorie consumption 2692 calories

HAITI
West Indies

Official name Republic of Haiti
Formation 1804 / 1844
Capital Port-au-Prince
Population 8.5 million / 799 people per sq mile (308 people per sq km) / 36%
Total area 10,714 sq miles (27,750 sq km)
Languages French Creole*, French*
Religions Roman Catholic 80%, Protestant 16%, Other (including Voodoo) 3%, Nonreligious 1%
Ethnic mix Black African 95%, Mulatto (mixed race) and European 5%
Government Transitional regime
Currency Gourde = 100 centimes
Literacy rate 52%
Calorie consumption 2086 calories

HONDURAS
Central America

Official name Republic of Honduras
Formation 1838 / 1838
Capital Tegucigalpa
Population 7.2 million / 167 people per sq mile (64 people per sq km) / 53%
Total area 43,278 sq miles (112,090 sq km)
Languages Spanish*, Garifuna (Carib), English Creole
Religions Roman Catholic 97%, Protestant 3%
Ethnic mix Mestizo 90%, Black African 5%, Amerindian 4%, White 1%
Government Presidential system
Currency Lempira = 100 centavos
Literacy rate 80%
Calorie consumption 2356 calories

HUNGARY
Central Europe

Official name Republic of Hungary
Formation 1918 / 1947
Capital Budapest
Population 10.1 million / 283 people per sq mile (109 people per sq km) / 64%
Total area 35,919 sq miles (93,030 sq km)
Languages Hungarian (Magyar)*
Religions Roman Catholic 52%, Calvinist 16%, Other 15%, Nonreligious 14%, Lutheran 3%
Ethnic mix Magyar 90%, Other 7%, Roma 2%, German 1%
Government Parliamentary system
Currency Forint = 100 fillér
Literacy rate 99%
Calorie consumption 3483 calories

ICELAND
Northwest Europe

Official name Republic of Iceland
Formation 1944 / 1944
Capital Reykjavík
Population 295,000 / 8 people per sq mile (3 people per sq km) / 93%
Total area 39,768 sq miles (103,000 sq km)
Languages Icelandic*
Religions Evangelical Lutheran 93%, Nonreligious 6%, Other (mostly Christian) 1%
Ethnic mix Icelandic 94%, Other 5%, Danish 1%
Government Parliamentary system
Currency Icelandic króna = 100 aurar
Literacy rate 99%
Calorie consumption 3249 calories

INDIA
South Asia

Official name Republic of India
Formation 1947 / 1947
Capital New Delhi
Population 1.1 billion / 961 people per sq mile (371 people per sq km) / 28%
Total area 1,269,338 sq miles (3,287,590 sq km)
Languages Hindi*, English*, Bengali, Marathi, Telugu, Tamil, Bihari, Gujarati, Kanarese, Urdu
Religions Hindu 83%, Muslim 11%, Christian 2%, Sikh 2%, Other 1%, Buddhist 1%
Ethnic mix Indo-Aryan 72%, Dravidian 25%, Mongoloid and other 3%
Government Parliamentary system
Currency Indian rupee = 100 paise
Literacy rate 61%
Calorie consumption 2459 calories

INDONESIA
Southeast Asia

Official name Republic of Indonesia
Formation 1949 / 1999
Capital Jakarta
Population 223 million / 321 people per sq mile (124 people per sq km) / 41%
Total area 741,096 sq miles (1,919,440 sq km)
Languages Bahasa Indonesia*, Javanese, Sundanese, Madurese, Dutch
Religions Sunni Muslim 87%, Protestant 6%, Roman Catholic 3%, Hindu 2%, Other 1%, Buddhist 1%
Ethnic mix Javanese 45%, Sundanese 14%, Coastal Malays 8%, Madurese 8%, Other 25%
Government Presidential system
Currency Rupiah = 100 sen
Literacy rate 88%
Calorie consumption 2904 calories

IRAN
Southwest Asia

Official name Islamic Republic of Iran
Formation 1502 / 1990
Capital Tehran
Population 69.5 million / 110 people per sq mile (42 people per sq km) / 62%
Total area 636,293 sq miles (1,648,000 sq km)
Languages Farsi*, Azeri, Luri, Gilaki, Mazanderani, Kurdish, Turkmen, Arabic, Baluchi
Religions Shi'a Muslim 93%, Sunni Muslim 6%, Other 1%
Ethnic mix Persian 35%, Azari 16%, Other 16%, Kurdish 13%, Luri 7%, Gilaki 5%, Mazandarani 5%, Afghan 3%
Government Islamic theocracy
Currency Iranian rial = 100 dinars
Literacy rate 77%
Calorie consumption 3085 calories

IRAQ
Southwest Asia

Official name Republic of Iraq
Formation 1932 / 1990
Capital Baghdad
Population 28.8 million / 171 people per sq mile (66 people per sq km) / 77%
Total area 168,753 sq miles (437,072 sq km)
Languages Arabic*, Kurdish, Turkic languages, Armenian, Assyrian
Religions Shi'a Muslim 60%, Sunni Muslim 35%, Other (including Christian) 5%
Ethnic mix Arab 80%, Kurdish 15%, Turkmen 3%, Other 2%
Government Transitional regime
Currency New Iraqi dinar = 1000 fils
Literacy rate 40%
Calorie consumption 2197 calories

IRELAND
Northwest Europe

Official name Ireland
Formation 1922 / 1922
Capital Dublin
Population 4.1 million / 154 people per sq mile (60 people per sq km) / 59%
Total area 27,135 sq miles (70,280 sq km)
Languages English*, Irish Gaelic*
Religions Roman Catholic 88%, Other and nonreligious 9%, Anglican 3%
Ethnic mix Irish 93%, Other 4%, British 3%
Government Parliamentary system
Currency Euro = 100 cents
Literacy rate 99%
Calorie consumption 3656 calories

ISRAEL
Southwest Asia

Official name State of Israel
Formation 1948 / 1994
Capital Jerusalem (not internationally recognized)
Population 6.7 million / 854 people per sq mile (330 people per sq km) / 91%
Total area 8019 sq miles (20,770 sq km)
Languages Hebrew*, Arabic, Yiddish, German, Russian, Polish, Romanian, Persian
Religions Jewish 80%, Muslim (mainly Sunni) 16%, Druze and other 2%, Christian 2%
Ethnic mix Jewish 80%, Other (mostly Arab) 20%
Government Parliamentary system
Currency Shekel = 100 agorot
Literacy rate 97%
Calorie consumption 3666 calories

ITALY
Southern Europe

Official name Italian Republic
Formation 1861 / 1947
Capital Rome
Population 58.1 million / 512 people per sq mile (198 people per sq km) / 67%
Total area 116,305 sq miles (301,230 sq km)
Languages Italian*, German, French, Rhaeto-Romanic, Sardinian
Religions Roman Catholic 85%, Other and nonreligious 13%, Muslim 2%
Ethnic mix Italian 94%, Other 4%, Sardinian 2%
Government Parliamentary system
Currency Euro = 100 cents
Literacy rate 99%
Calorie consumption 3671 calories

IVORY COAST
West Africa

Official name Republic of Côte d'Ivoire
Formation 1960 / 1960
Capital Yamoussoukro
Population 18.2 million / 148 people per sq mile (57 people per sq km) / 46%
Total area 124,502 sq miles (322,460 sq km)
Languages French*, Akan, Kru, Voltaic
Religions Muslim 38%, Traditional beliefs 25%, Roman Catholic 25%, Protestant 6%, Other 6%
Ethnic mix Baoulé 23%, Other 19%, Bété 18%, Senufo 15%, Agni-Ashanti 14%, Mandinka 11%
Government Presidential system
Currency CFA franc = 100 centimes
Literacy rate 48%
Calorie consumption 2631 calories

JAMAICA
West Indies

Official name Jamaica
Formation 1962 / 1962
Capital Kingston
Population 2.7 million / 646 people per sq mile (249 people per sq km) / 56%
Total area 4243 sq miles (10,990 sq km)
Languages English*, English Creole
Religions Other and nonreligious 45%, Other Protestant 20%, Church of God 18%, Baptist 10%, Anglican 7%
Ethnic mix Black African 75%, Mulatto (mixed race) 13%, European and Chinese 11%, East Indian 1%
Government Parliamentary system
Currency Jamaican dollar = 100 cents
Literacy rate 88%
Calorie consumption 2685 calories

JAPAN
East Asia

Official name Japan
Formation 1590 / 1972
Capital Tokyo
Population 128 million / 881 people per sq mile (340 people per sq km) / 79%
Total area 145,882 sq miles (377,835 sq km)
Languages Japanese, Korean, Chinese
Religions Shinto and Buddhist 76%, Buddhist 16%, Other (including Christian) 8%
Ethnic mix Japanese 99%, Other (mainly Korean) 1%
Government Parliamentary system
Currency Yen = 100 sen
Literacy rate 99%
Calorie consumption 2761 calories

JORDAN
Southwest Asia

Official name Hashemite Kingdom of Jordan
Formation 1946 / 1967
Capital Amman
Population 5.6 million / 163 people per sq mile (63 people per sq km) / 74%
Total area 35,637 sq miles (92,300 sq km)
Languages Arabic*
Religions Muslim (mainly Sunni) 92%, Other (mostly Christian) 8%
Ethnic mix Arab 98%, Circassian 1%, Armenian 1%
Government Monarchy
Currency Jordanian dinar = 1000 fils
Literacy rate 90%
Calorie consumption 2673 calories

KAZAKHSTAN
Central Asia

Official name Republic of Kazakhstan
Formation 1991 / 1991
Capital Astana
Population 14.8 million / 14 people per sq mile (5 people per sq km) / 56%
Total area 1,049,150 sq miles (2,717,300 sq km)
Languages Kazakh*, Russian*, Ukrainian, Tatar, German, Uzbek, Uighur
Religions Muslim (mainly Sunni) 47%, Orthodox Christian 44%, Other 9%
Ethnic mix Kazakh 53%, Russian 30%, Other 9%, Ukrainian 4%, Tatar 2%, German 2%
Government Presidential system
Currency Tenge = 100 tiyn
Literacy rate 99%
Calorie consumption 2677 calories

KENYA
East Africa

Official name Republic of Kenya
Formation 1963 / 1963
Capital Nairobi
Population 34.3 million / 157 people per sq mile (60 people per sq km) / 42%
Total area 224,961 sq miles (582,650 sq km)
Languages Kiswahili*, English*, Kikuyu, Luo, Kalenjin, Kamba
Religions Christian 60%, Traditional beliefs 25%, Other 9%, Muslim 6%
Ethnic mix Other 30%, Kikuyu 21%, Luhya 14%, Luo 13%, Kalenjin 11%, Kamba 11%
Government Presidential system
Currency Kenya shilling = 100 cents
Literacy rate 74%
Calorie consumption 2090 calories

KIRIBATI
Australasia & Oceania

Official name Republic of Kiribati
Formation 1979 / 1979
Capital Bairiki (Tarawa Atoll)
Population 103,092 / 376 people per sq mile (145 people per sq km) / 36%
Total area 277 sq miles (717 sq km)
Languages English*, Kiribati
Religions Roman Catholic 53%, Kiribati Protestant Church 39%, Other 8%
Ethnic mix Micronesian 96%, Other 4%
Government Nonparty system
Currency Australian dollar = 100 cents
Literacy rate 99%
Calorie consumption 2859 calories

KOSOVO (not yet fully recognized)
Southeast Europe

Official name Republic of Kosovo
Formation 2008 / 2008
Capital Pristina
Population 2.1 million / 499 people per sq mile (193 people per sq km) / 40%
Total area 4212 sq miles (10,908 sq km)
Languages Albanian*, Serbian*, Bosniak, Gorani, Roma, Turkish
Religions Muslim 92%, Roman Catholic 4%, Orthodox Christian 4%
Ethnic mix Albanian 92%, Serb 4%, Bosniak and Gorani 2%, Turkish 1%, Roma 1%
Government Parliamentary system
Currency Euro = 100 cents
Literacy rate 92%
Calorie consumption Not available

KUWAIT
Southwest Asia

Official name State of Kuwait
Formation 1961 / 1961
Capital Kuwait City
Population 2.7 million / 392 people per sq mile (152 people per sq km) / 98%
Total area 6880 sq miles (17,820 sq km)
Languages Arabic*, English
Religions Sunni Muslim 45%, Shi'a Muslim 40%, Christian, Hindu, and other 15%
Ethnic mix Kuwaiti 45%, Other Arab 35%, South Asian 9%, Other 7%, Iranian 4%
Government Monarchy
Currency Kuwaiti dinar = 1000 fils
Literacy rate 83%
Calorie consumption 3010 calories

KYRGYZSTAN
Central Asia

Official name Kyrgyz Republic
Formation 1991 / 1991
Capital Bishkek
Population 5.3 million / 69 people per sq mile (27 people per sq km) / 33%
Total area 76,641 sq miles (198,500 sq km)
Languages Kyrgyz*, Russian*, Uzbek, Tatar, Ukrainian
Religions Muslim (mainly Sunni) 70%, Orthodox Christian 30%
Ethnic mix Kyrgyz 57%, Russian 19%, Uzbek 13%, Other 7%, Tatar 2%, Ukrainian 2%
Government Presidential system
Currency Som = 100 tyyn
Literacy rate 99%
Calorie consumption 2999 calories

LAOS
Southeast Asia

Official name Lao People's Democratic Republic
Formation 1953 / 1953
Capital Vientiane
Population 5.9 million / 66 people per sq mile (26 people per sq km) / 24%
Total area 91,428 sq miles (236,800 sq km)
Languages Lao*, Mon-Khmer, Yao, Vietnamese, Chinese, French
Religions Buddhist 85%, Other (including animist) 15%
Ethnic mix Lao Loum 66%, Lao Theung 30%, Other 2%, Lao Soung 2%
Government One-party state
Currency New kip = 100 at
Literacy rate 69%
Calorie consumption 2312 calories

LATVIA
Northeast Europe

Official name Republic of Latvia
Formation 1991 / 1991
Capital Riga
Population 2.3 million / 92 people per sq mile (36 people per sq km) / 69%
Total area 24,938 sq miles (64,589 sq km)
Languages Latvian*, Russian
Religions Lutheran 55%, Roman Catholic 24%, Other 12%, Orthodox Christian 9%
Ethnic mix Latvian 57%, Russian 32%, Belarussian 4%, Ukrainian 3%, Polish 2%, Other 2%
Government Parliamentary system
Currency Lats = 100 santims
Literacy rate 99%
Calorie consumption 2938 calories

LEBANON
Southwest Asia

Official name Republic of Lebanon
Formation 1941 / 1941
Capital Beirut
Population 3.6 million / 911 people per sq mile (352 people per sq km) / 90%
Total area 4015 sq miles (10,400 sq km)
Languages Arabic*, French, Armenian, Assyrian
Religions Muslim 70%, Christian 30%
Ethnic mix Arab 94%, Armenian 4%, Other 2%
Government Parliamentary system
Currency Lebanese pound = 100 piastres
Literacy rate 87%
Calorie consumption 3196 calories

LESOTHO
Southern Africa

Official name Kingdom of Lesotho
Formation 1966 / 1966
Capital Maseru
Population 1.8 million / 154 people per sq mile (59 people per sq km) / 28%
Total area 11,720 sq miles (30,355 sq km)
Languages English*, Sesotho*, isiZulu
Religions Christian 90%, Traditional beliefs 10%
Ethnic mix Sotho 97%, European and Asian 3%
Government Parliamentary system
Currency Loti = 100 lisente
Literacy rate 81%
Calorie consumption 2638 calories

LIBERIA
West Africa

Official name Republic of Liberia
Formation 1847 / 1847
Capital Monrovia
Population 3.3 million / 89 people per sq mile (34 people per sq km) / 45%
Total area 43,000 sq miles (111,370 sq km)
Languages English*, Kpelle, Vai, Bassa, Kru, Grebo, Kissi, Gola, Loma
Religions Christian 68%, Traditional beliefs 18%, Muslim 14%
Ethnic mix Indigenous tribes (16 main groups) 95%, Americo-Liberians 5%
Government Transitional regime
Currency Liberian dollar = 100 cents
Literacy rate 58%
Calorie consumption 1900 calories

LIBYA
North Africa

Official name Great Socialist People's Libyan Arab Jamahariyah
Formation 1951 / 1951
Capital Tripoli
Population 5.9 million / 9 people per sq mile (3 people per sq km) / 88%
Total area 679,358 sq miles (1,759,540 sq km)
Languages Arabic*, Tuareg
Religions Muslim (mainly Sunni) 97%, Other 3%
Ethnic mix Arab and Berber 95%, Other 5%
Government One-party state
Currency Libyan dinar = 1000 dirhams
Literacy rate 82%
Calorie consumption 3320 calories

LIECHTENSTEIN
Central Europe

Official name Principality of Liechtenstein
Formation 1719 / 1719
Capital Vaduz
Population 33,717 / 544 people per sq mile (211 people per sq km) / 21%
Total area 62 sq miles (160 sq km)
Languages German*, Alemannish dialect, Italian
Religions Roman Catholic 81%, Other 12%, Protestant 7%
Ethnic mix Liechtensteiner 62%, Foreign residents 38%
Government Parliamentary system
Currency Swiss franc = 100 rappen/centimes
Literacy rate 99%
Calorie consumption Not available

LITHUANIA
Northeast Europe

Official name Republic of Lithuania
Formation 1991 / 1991
Capital Vilnius
Population 3.4 million / 135 people per sq mile (52 people per sq km) / 68%
Total area 25,174 sq miles (65,200 sq km)
Languages Lithuanian*, Russian
Religions Roman Catholic 83%, Other 12%, Protestant 5%
Ethnic mix Lithuanian 80%, Russian 9%, Polish 7%, Other 2%, Belarussian 2%
Government Parliamentary system
Currency Litas (euro is also legal tender) = 100 centu
Literacy rate 99%
Calorie consumption 3324 calories

LUXEMBOURG
Northwest Europe

Official name Grand Duchy of Luxembourg
Formation 1867 / 1867
Capital Luxembourg-Ville
Population 465,000 / 466 people per sq mile (180 people per sq km) / 92%
Total area 998 sq miles (2586 sq km)
Languages Luxembourgish*, German*, French*
Religions Roman Catholic 97%, Protestant, Orthodox Christian, and Jewish 3%
Ethnic mix Luxembourger 73%, Foreign residents 27%
Government Parliamentary system
Currency Euro = 100 cents
Literacy rate 99%
Calorie consumption 3701 calories

MACEDONIA
Southeast Europe

Official name Republic of Macedonia
Formation 1991 / 1991
Capital Skopje
Population 2 million / 201 people per sq mile (78 people per sq km) / 62%
Total area 9781 sq miles (25,333 sq km)
Languages Macedonian, Albanian, Serbo-Croat
Religions Orthodox Christian 59%, Muslim 26%, Other 10%, Roman Catholic 4%, Protestant 1%
Ethnic mix Macedonian 64%, Albanian 25%, Turkish 4%, Roma 3%, Other 2%, Serb 2%
Government Mixed presidential–parliamentary system
Currency Macedonian denar = 100 deni
Literacy rate 96%
Calorie consumption 2655 calories

MADAGASCAR
Indian Ocean

Official name Republic of Madagascar
Formation 1960 / 1960
Capital Antananarivo
Population 18.6 million / 83 people per sq mile (32 people per sq km) / 30%
Total area 226,656 sq miles (587,040 sq km)
Languages Malagasy*, French*
Religions Traditional beliefs 52%, Christian (mainly Roman Catholic) 41%, Muslim 7%
Ethnic mix Other Malay 46%, Merina 26%, Betsimisaraka 15%, Betsileo 12%, Other 1%
Government Presidential system
Currency Ariary = 5 iraimbilanja
Literacy rate 71%
Calorie consumption 2005 calories

MALAWI
Southern Africa

Official name Republic of Malawi
Formation 1964 / 1964
Capital Lilongwe
Population 12.9 million / 355 people per sq mile (137 people per sq km) / 25%
Total area 45,745 sq miles (118,480 sq km)
Languages English*, Chewa*, Lomwe, Yao, Ngoni
Religions Protestant 55%, Roman Catholic 20%, Muslim 20%, Traditional beliefs 5%
Ethnic mix Bantu 99%, Other 1%
Government Presidential system
Currency Malawi kwacha = 100 tambala
Literacy rate 64%
Calorie consumption 2155 calories

MALAYSIA
Southeast Asia

Official name Federation of Malaysia
Formation 1963 / 1965
Capital Kuala Lumpur; Putrajaya (administrative)
Population 25.3 million / 199 people per sq mile (77 people per sq km) / 57%
Total area 127,316 sq miles (329,750 sq km)
Languages Malay*, Chinese*, Bahasa Malaysia, Tamil, English
Religions Muslim (mainly Sunni) 53%, Buddhist 19%, Chinese faiths 12%, Other 7%, Christian 7%, Traditional beliefs 2%
Ethnic mix Malay 48%, Chinese 29%, Indigenous tribes 12%, Indian 6%, Other 5%
Government Parliamentary system
Currency Ringgit = 100 sen
Literacy rate 89%
Calorie consumption 2881 calories

MALDIVES
Indian Ocean

Official name Republic of Maldives
Formation 1965 / 1965
Capital Male'
Population 329,000 / 2836 people per sq mile (1097 people per sq km) / 30%
Total area 116 sq miles (300 sq km)
Languages Dhivehi (Maldivian)*, Sinhala, Tamil, Arabic
Religions Sunni Muslim 100%
Ethnic mix Arab–Sinhalese–Malay 100%
Government Nonparty system
Currency Rufiyaa = 100 lari
Literacy rate 97%
Calorie consumption 2548 calories

MALI
West Africa

Official name Republic of Mali
Formation 1960 / 1960
Capital Bamako
Population 13.5 million / 29 people per sq mile (11 people per sq km) / 30%
Total area 478,764 sq miles (1,240,000 sq km)
Languages French*, Bambara, Fulani, Senufo, Soninke
Religions Muslim (mainly Sunni) 80%, Traditional beliefs 18%, Christian 1%, Other 1%
Ethnic mix Bambara 32%, Other 26%, Fulani 14%, Senufu 12%, Soninka 9%, Tuareg 7%
Government Presidential system
Currency CFA franc = 100 centimes
Literacy rate 19%
Calorie consumption 2174 calories

MALTA
Southern Europe

Official name Republic of Malta
Formation 1964 / 1964
Capital Valletta
Population 402,000 / 3242 people per sq mile (1256 people per sq km) / 91%
Total area 122 sq miles (316 sq km)
Languages Maltese*, English
Religions Roman Catholic 98%, Other and nonreligious 2%
Ethnic mix Maltese 96%, Other 4%
Government Parliamentary system
Currency Maltese lira = 100 cents
Literacy rate 88%
Calorie consumption 3587 calories

MARSHALL ISLANDS
Australasia & Oceania

Official name Republic of the Marshall Islands
Formation 1986 / 1986
Capital Majuro
Population 59,071 / 844 people per sq mile (326 people per sq km) / 69%
Total area 70 sq miles (181 sq km)
Languages Marshallese*, English*, Japanese, German
Religions Protestant 90%, Roman Catholic 8%, Other 2%
Ethnic mix Micronesian 97%, Other 3%
Government Presidential system
Currency US dollar = 100 cents
Literacy rate 91%
Calorie consumption Not available

MAURITANIA
West Africa

Official name Islamic Republic of Mauritania
Formation 1960 / 1960
Capital Nouakchott
Population 3.1 million / 8 people per sq mile (3 people per sq km) / 58%
Total area 397,953 sq miles (1,030,700 sq km)
Languages French*, Hassaniyah Arabic, Wolof
Religions Sunni Muslim 100%
Ethnic mix Maure 81%, Wolof 7%, Tukolor 5%, Other 4%, Soninka 3%
Government Transitional regime
Currency Ouguiya = 5 khoums
Literacy rate 51%
Calorie consumption 2772 calories

MAURITIUS
Indian Ocean

Official name Republic of Mauritius
Formation 1968 / 1968
Capital Port Louis
Population 1.2 million / 1671 people per sq mile (645 people per sq km) / 41%
Total area 718 sq miles (1860 sq km)
Languages English*, French Creole, Hindi, Urdu, Tamil, Chinese, French
Religions Hindu 52%, Roman Catholic 26%, Muslim 17%, Other 3%, Protestant 2%
Ethnic mix Indo-Mauritian 68%, Creole 27%, Sino-Mauritian 3%, Franco-Mauritian 2%
Government Parliamentary system
Currency Mauritian rupee = 100 cents
Literacy rate 84%
Calorie consumption 2955 calories

MEXICO
North America

Official name United Mexican States
Formation 1836 / 1848
Capital Mexico City
Population 107 million / 145 people per sq mile (56 people per sq km) / 74%
Total area 761,602 sq miles (1,972,550 sq km)
Languages Spanish*, Nahuatl, Mayan, Zapotec, Mixtec, Otomi, Totonac, Tzotzil, Tzeltal
Religions Roman Catholic 88%, Other 7%, Protestant 5%
Ethnic mix Mestizo 60%, Amerindian 30%, European 9%, Other 1%
Government Presidential system
Currency Mexican peso = 100 centavos
Literacy rate 90%
Calorie consumption 3145 calories

MICRONESIA
Australasia & Oceania

Official name Federated States of Micronesia
Formation 1986 / 1986
Capital Palikir (Pohnpei Island)
Population 108,105 / 399 people per sq mile (154 people per sq km) / 28%
Total area 271 sq miles (702 sq km)
Languages Trukese, Pohnpeian, Mortlockese, Kosraean, English
Religions Roman Catholic 50%, Protestant 48%, Other 2%
Ethnic mix Micronesian 100%
Government Nonparty system
Currency US dollar = 100 cents
Literacy rate 81%
Calorie consumption Not available

MOLDOVA
Southeast Europe

Official name Republic of Moldova
Formation 1991 / 1991
Capital Chisinau
Population 4.2 million / 323 people per sq mile (125 people per sq km) / 46%
Total area 13,067 sq miles (33,843 sq km)
Languages Moldovan*, Ukrainian, Russian
Religions Orthodox Christian 98%, Jewish 2%
Ethnic mix Moldovan 65%, Ukrainian 14%, Russian 13%, Other 4%, Gagauz 4%
Government Parliamentary system
Currency Moldovan leu = 100 bani
Literacy rate 96%
Calorie consumption 2806 calories

MONACO
Southern Europe

Official name Principality of Monaco
Formation 1861 / 1861
Capital Monaco-Ville
Population 32,409 / 43212 people per sq mile (16620 people per sq km) / 100%
Total area 0.75 sq miles (1.95 sq km)
Languages French*, Italian, Monégasque, English
Religions Roman Catholic 89%, Protestant 6%, Other 5%
Ethnic mix French 47%, Other 20%, Monégasque 17%, Italian 16%
Government Monarchy
Currency Euro = 100 cents
Literacy rate 99%
Calorie consumption Not available

MONGOLIA
East Asia

Official name Mongolia
Formation 1924 / 1924
Capital Ulan Bator
Population 2.6 million / 4 people per sq mile (2 people per sq km) / 64%
Total area 604,247 sq miles (1,565,000 sq km)
Languages Khalkha Mongolian*, Kazakh, Chinese, Russian
Religions Tibetan Buddhist 96%, Muslim 4%
Ethnic mix Mongol 90%, Kazakh 4%, Other 2%, Chinese 2%, Russian 2%
Government Mixed presidential–parliamentary system
Currency Tugrik (tögrög) = 100 möngö
Literacy rate 98%
Calorie consumption 2249 calories

MONTENEGRO
Europe

Official name Republic of Montenegro
Formation 2006 / 2006
Capital Podgorica
Population 620,145 / 116 people per sq mile (45 people per sq km) / 62%
Total area 5,332 sq miles (13,812 sq km)
Languages Montenegrin, Serbian, Albanian
Religions Orthodox Christian 74%, Muslim 18%, Roman Catholic 4%, Other 4%
Ethnic mix Montenegrin 43%, Serb 32%, Bosniak 8%, Albanian 5%, Other 12%
Government Parliamentary system
Currency Euro = 100 cents
Literacy rate 98%
Calorie consumption Not available

MOROCCO
North Africa

Official name Kingdom of Morocco
Formation 1956 / 1956
Capital Rabat
Population 31.5 million / 183 people per sq mile (71 people per sq km) / 56%
Total area 172,316 sq miles (446,300 sq km)
Languages Arabic*, Tamazight (Berber), French, Spanish
Religions Muslim (mainly Sunni) 99%, Other (mostly Christian) 1%
Ethnic mix Arab 70%, Berber 29%, European 1%
Government Monarchy
Currency Moroccan dirham = 100 centimes
Literacy rate 51%
Calorie consumption 3052 calories

MOZAMBIQUE
Southern Africa

Official name Republic of Mozambique
Formation 1975 / 1975
Capital Maputo
Population 19.8 million / 65 people per sq mile (25 people per sq km) / 40%
Total area 309,494 sq miles (801,590 sq km)
Languages Portuguese*, Makua, Xitsonga, Sena, Lomwe
Religions Traditional beliefs 56%, Christian 30%, Muslim 14%
Ethnic mix Makua Lomwe 47%, Tsonga 23%, Malawi 12%, Shona 11%, Yao 4%, Other 3%
Government Presidential system
Currency Metical = 100 centavos
Literacy rate 47%
Calorie consumption 2079 calories

MYANMAR (BURMA)
Southeast Asia

Official name Union of Myanmar
Formation 1948 / 1948
Capital Rangoon (Yangon), Pyinmana
Population 50.5 million / 199 people per sq mile (77 people per sq km) / 28%
Total area 261,969 sq miles (678,500 sq km)
Languages Burmese*, Shan, Karen, Rakhine, Chin, Yangbye, Kachin, Mon
Religions Buddhist 87%, Christian 6%, Muslim 4%, Other 2%, Hindu 1%
Ethnic mix Burman (Bamah) 68%, Other 13%, Shan 9%, Karen 6%, Rakhine 4%
Government Military-based regime
Currency Kyat = 100 pyas
Literacy rate 90%
Calorie consumption 2937 calories

NAMIBIA
Southern Africa

Official name Republic of Namibia
Formation 1990 / 1994
Capital Windhoek
Population 2 million / 6 people per sq mile (2 people per sq km) / 31%
Total area 318,694 sq miles (825,418 sq km)
Languages English*, Ovambo, Kavango, Bergdama, German, Afrikaans
Religions Christian 90%, Traditional beliefs 10%
Ethnic mix Ovambo 50%, Other tribes 16%, Kavango 9%, Other 9%, Damara 8%, Herero 8%
Government Presidential system
Currency Namibian dollar = 100 cents
Literacy rate 85%
Calorie consumption 2278 calories

NAURU
Australasia & Oceania

Official name Republic of Nauru
Formation 1968 / 1968
Capital None
Population 13,048 / 1611 people per sq mile (621 people per sq km) / 100%
Total area 8.1 sq miles (21 sq km)
Languages Nauruan*, Kiribati, Chinese, Tuvaluan, English
Religions Nauruan Congregational Church 60%, Roman Catholic 35%, Other 5%
Ethnic mix Nauruan 62%, Other Pacific islanders 25%, Chinese and Vietnamese 8%, European 5%
Government Parliamentary system
Currency Australian dollar = 100 cents
Literacy rate 95%
Calorie consumption Not available

NEPAL
South Asia

Official name Kingdom of Nepal
Formation 1769 / 1769
Capital Kathmandu
Population 27.1 million / 513 people per sq mile (198 people per sq km) / 12%
Total area 54,363 sq miles (140,800 sq km)
Languages Nepali*, Maithili, Bhojpuri
Religions Hindu 90%, Buddhist 5%, Muslim 3%, Other (including Christian) 2%
Ethnic mix Nepalese 52%, Other 19%, Maithili 11%, Tibeto-Burmese 10%, Bhojpuri 8%
Government Monarchy
Currency Nepalese rupee = 100 paise
Literacy rate 49%
Calorie consumption 2453 calories

NETHERLANDS
Northwest Europe

Official name Kingdom of the Netherlands
Formation 1648 / 1839
Capital Amsterdam; The Hague (administrative)
Population 16.3 million / 1245 people per sq mile (481 people per sq km) / 89%
Total area 16,033 sq miles (41,526 sq km)
Languages Dutch*, Frisian
Religions Roman Catholic 36%, Other 34%, Protestant 27%, Muslim 3%
Ethnic mix Dutch 82%, Other 12%, Surinamese 2%, Turkish 2%, Moroccan 2%
Government Parliamentary system
Currency Euro = 100 cents
Literacy rate 99%
Calorie consumption 3362 calories

NEW ZEALAND
Australasia & Oceania

Official name New Zealand
Formation 1947 / 1947
Capital Wellington
Population 4 million / 39 people per sq mile (15 people per sq km) / 86%
Total area 103,737 sq miles (268,680 sq km)
Languages English*, Maori
Religions Anglican 24%, Other 22%, Presbyterian 18%, Nonreligious 16%, Roman Catholic 15%, Methodist 5%
Ethnic mix European 77%, Maori 12%, Other immigrant 6%, Pacific islanders 5%
Government Parliamentary system
Currency New Zealand dollar = 100 cents
Literacy rate 99%
Calorie consumption 3219 calories

NICARAGUA
Central America

Official name Republic of Nicaragua
Formation 1838 / 1838
Capital Managua
Population 5.5 million / 120 people per sq mile (46 people per sq km) / 65%
Total area 49,998 sq miles (129,494 sq km)
Languages Spanish*, English Creole, Miskito
Religions Roman Catholic 80%, Protestant Evangelical 17%, Other 3%
Ethnic mix Mestizo 69%, White 14%, Black 8% Amerindian 5%, Zambo 4%
Government Presidential system
Currency Córdoba oro = 100 centavos
Literacy rate 77%
Calorie consumption 2298 calories

NIGER
West Africa

Official name Republic of Niger
Formation 1960 / 1960
Capital Niamey
Population 14 million / 29 people per sq mile (11 people per sq km) / 21%
Total area 489,188 sq miles (1,267,000 sq km)
Languages French*, Hausa, Djerma, Fulani, Tuareg, Teda
Religions Muslim 85%, Traditional beliefs 14%, Other (including Christian) 1%
Ethnic mix Hausa 54%, Djerma and Songhai 21%, Fulani 10%, Tuareg 9%, Other 6%
Government Presidential system
Currency CFA franc = 100 centimes
Literacy rate 14%
Calorie consumption 2130 calories

NIGERIA
West Africa

Official name Federal Republic of Nigeria
Formation 1960 / 1961
Capital Abuja
Population 132 million / 374 people per sq mile (144 people per sq km) / 44%
Total area 356,667 sq miles (923,768 sq km)
Languages English*, Hausa, Yoruba, Ibo
Religions Muslim 50%, Christian 40%, Traditional beliefs 10%
Ethnic mix Other 29%, Hausa 21%, Yoruba 21%, Ibo 18%, Fulani 11%
Government Presidential system
Currency Naira = 100 kobo
Literacy rate 67%
Calorie consumption 2726 calories

NORTH KOREA
East Asia

Official name Democratic People's Republic of Korea
Formation 1948 / 1953
Capital Pyongyang
Population 22.5 million / 484 people per sq mile (187 people per sq km) / 60%
Total area 46,540 sq miles (120,540 sq km)
Languages Korean*
Religions Atheist 100%
Ethnic mix Korean 100%
Government One-party state
Currency North Korean won = 100 chon
Literacy rate 99%
Calorie consumption 2142 calories

NORWAY
Northern Europe

Official name Kingdom of Norway
Formation 1905 / 1905
Capital Oslo
Population 4.6 million / 39 people per sq mile (15 people per sq km) / 76%
Total area 125,181 sq miles (324,220 sq km)
Languages Norwegian* (Bokmål "book language" and Nynorsk "new Norsk"), Sámi
Religions Evangelical Lutheran 89%, Other and nonreligious 10%, Roman Catholic 1%
Ethnic mix Norwegian 93%, Other 6%, Sámi 1%
Government Parliamentary system
Currency Norwegian krone = 100 øre
Literacy rate 99%
Calorie consumption 3484 calories

OMAN
Southwest Asia

Official name Sultanate of Oman
Formation 1951 / 1951
Capital Muscat
Population 2.6 million / 32 people per sq mile (12 people per sq km) / 84%
Total area 82,031 sq miles (212,460 sq km)
Languages Arabic*, Baluchi, Farsi, Hindi, Punjabi
Religions Ibadi Muslim 75%, Other Muslim and Hindu 25%
Ethnic mix Arab 88%, Baluchi 4%, Persian 3%, Indian and Pakistani 3%, African 2%
Government Monarchy
Currency Omani rial = 1000 baizas
Literacy rate 74%
Calorie consumption Not available

PAKISTAN
South Asia

Official name Islamic Republic of Pakistan
Formation 1947 / 1971
Capital Islamabad
Population 158 million / 531 people per sq mile (205 people per sq km) / 37%
Total area 310,401 sq miles (803,940 sq km)
Languages Urdu*, Baluchi, Brahui, Pashtu, Punjabi, Sindhi
Religions Sunni Muslim 77%, Shi'a Muslim 20%, Hindu 2%, Christian 1%
Ethnic mix Punjabi 56%, Pathan (Pashtun) 15%, Sindhi 14%, Mohajir 7%, Other 4%, Baluchi 4%
Government Presidential system
Currency Pakistani rupee = 100 paisa
Literacy rate 49%
Calorie consumption 2419 calories

PALAU
Australasia & Oceania

Official name Republic of Palau
Formation 1994 / 1994
Capital Koror
Population 20,303 / 104 people per sq mile (40 people per sq km) / 70%
Total area 177 sq miles (458 sq km)
Languages Palauan, English, Japanese, Angaur, Tobi, Sonsorolese
Religions Christian 66%, Modekngei 34%
Ethnic mix Micronesian 87%, Filipino 8%, Chinese and other Asian 5%
Government Nonparty system
Currency US dollar = 100 cents
Literacy rate 98%
Calorie consumption Not available

PANAMA
Central America

Official name Republic of Panama
Formation 1903 / 1903
Capital Panama City
Population 3.2 million / 109 people per sq mile (42 people per sq km) / 56%
Total area 30,193 sq miles (78,200 sq km)
Languages Spanish*, English Creole, Amerindian languages, Chibchan languages
Religions Roman Catholic 86%, Other 8%, Protestant 6%
Ethnic mix Mestizo 60%, White 14%, Black 12%, Amerindian 8%, Asian 4%, Other 2%
Government Presidential system
Currency Balboa = 100 centesimos
Literacy rate 92%
Calorie consumption 2272 calories

PAPUA NEW GUINEA
Australasia & Oceania

Official name Independent State of Papua New Guinea
Formation 1975 / 1975
Capital Port Moresby
Population 5.9 million / 34 people per sq mile (13 people per sq km) / 17%
Total area 178,703 sq miles (462,840 sq km)
Languages Pidgin English*, Papuan*, English, Motu, 750 (est.) native languages
Religions Protestant 60%, Roman Catholic 37%, Other 3%
Ethnic mix Melanesian and mixed race 100%
Government Parliamentary system
Currency Kina = 100 toeas
Literacy rate 57%
Calorie consumption 2193 calories

PARAGUAY
South America

Official name Republic of Paraguay
Formation 1811 / 1938
Capital Asunción
Population 6.2 million / 40 people per sq mile (16 people per sq km) / 56%
Total area 157,046 sq miles (406,750 sq km)
Languages Guaraní*, Spanish*, German
Religions Roman Catholic 96%, Protestant (including Mennonite) 4%
Ethnic mix Mestizo 90%, Other 8%, Amerindian 2%
Government Presidential system
Currency Guaraní = 100 centimos
Literacy rate 92%
Calorie consumption 2565 calories

PERU
South America

Official name Republic of Peru
Formation 1824 / 1941
Capital Lima
Population 28 million / 57 people per sq mile (22 people per sq km) / 73%
Total area 496,223 sq miles (1,285,200 sq km)
Languages Spanish*, Quechua*, Aymara*
Religions Roman Catholic 95%, Other 5%
Ethnic mix Amerindian 50%, Mestizo 40%, White 7%, Other 3%
Government Presidential system
Currency New sol = 100 centimos
Literacy rate 88%
Calorie consumption 2571 calories

PHILIPPINES
Southwest Asia

Official name Republic of the Philippines
Formation 1946 / 1946
Capital Manila
Population 83.1 million / 722 people per sq mile (279 people per sq km) / 59%
Total area 115,830 sq miles (300,000 sq km)
Languages Filipino*, English*, Tagalog, Cebuano, Ilocano, Hiligaynon, many other local languages
Religions Roman Catholic 83%, Protestant 9%, Muslim 5%, Other (including Buddhist) 3%
Ethnic mix Malay 95%, Other 3%, Chinese 2%
Government Presidential system
Currency Philippine peso = 100 centavos
Literacy rate 93%
Calorie consumption 2379 calories

POLAND
Northern Europe

Official name Republic of Poland
Formation 1918 / 1945
Capital Warsaw
Population 38.5 million / 328 people per sq mile (126 people per sq km) / 66%
Total area 120,728 sq miles (312,685 sq km)
Languages Polish*
Religions Roman Catholic 93%, Other and nonreligious 5%, Orthodox Christian 2%
Ethnic mix Polish 97%, Other 2%, Silesian 1%
Government Parliamentary system
Currency Zloty = 100 groszy
Literacy rate 99%
Calorie consumption 3374 calories

PORTUGAL
Southwest Europe

Official name Republic of Portugal
Formation 1139 / 1640
Capital Lisbon
Population 10.5 million / 296 people per sq mile (114 people per sq km) / 64%
Total area 35,672 sq miles (92,391 sq km)
Languages Portuguese
Religions Roman Catholic 97%, Other 2%, Protestant 1%
Ethnic mix Portuguese 98%, African and other 2%
Government Parliamentary system
Currency Euro = 100 cents
Literacy rate 93%
Calorie consumption 3741 calories

QATAR
Southwest Asia

Official name State of Qatar
Formation 1971 / 1971
Capital Doha
Population 813,000 / 191 people per sq mile (74 people per sq km) / 93%
Total area 4416 sq miles (11,437 sq km)
Languages Arabic*
Religions Muslim (mainly Sunni) 95%, Other 5%
Ethnic mix Arab 40%, Indian 18%, Pakistani 18%, Other 14%, Iranian 10%
Government Monarchy
Currency Qatar riyal = 100 dirhams
Literacy rate 89%
Calorie consumption Not available

ROMANIA
Southest Europe

Official name Romania
Formation 1878 / 1947
Capital Bucharest
Population 21.7 million / 244 people per sq mile (94 people per sq km) / 56%
Total area 91,699 sq miles (237,500 sq km)
Languages Romanian*, Hungarian (Magyar), Romani, German
Religions Romanian Orthodox 87%, Roman Catholic 5%, Protestant 4%, Other 2%, Greek Orthodox 1%, Greek Catholic (Uniate) 1%
Ethnic mix Romanian 89%, Magyar 7%, Roma 3%, Other 1%
Government Presidential system
Currency Romanian leu = 100 bani
Literacy rate 97%
Calorie consumption 3455 calories

RUSSIAN FEDERATION
Europe / Asia

Official name Russian Federation
Formation 1480 / 1991
Capital Moscow
Population 143 million / 22 people per sq mile (8 people per sq km) / 78%
Total area 6,592,735 sq miles (17,075,200 sq km)
Languages Russian*, Tatar, Ukrainian, Chavash, various other national languages
Religions Orthodox Christian 75%, Other 15%, Muslim 10%
Ethnic mix Russian 82%, Other 10%, Tatar 4%, Ukrainian 3%, Chavash 1%
Government Presidential system
Currency Russian rouble = 100 kopeks
Literacy rate 99%
Calorie consumption 3072 calories

RWANDA
Central Africa

Official name Republic of Rwanda
Formation 1962 / 1962
Capital Kigali
Population 9 million / 934 people per sq mile (361 people per sq km) / 6%
Total area 10,169 sq miles (26,338 sq km)
Languages Kinyarwanda*, French*, Kiswahili, English
Religions Roman Catholic 56%, Traditional beliefs 25%, Muslim 10%, Protestant 9%
Ethnic mix Hutu 90%, Tutsi 9%, Other (including Twa) 1%
Government Presidential system
Currency Rwanda franc = 100 centimes
Literacy rate 64%
Calorie consumption 2084 calories

SAINT KITTS & NEVIS
West Indies

Official name Federation of Saint Christopher and Nevis
Formation 1983 / 1983
Capital Basseterre
Population 38,958 / 280 people per sq mile (108 people per sq km) / 34%
Total area 101 sq miles (261 sq km)
Languages English*, English Creole
Religions Anglican 33%, Methodist 29%, Other 22%, Moravian 9%, Roman Catholic 7%
Ethnic mix Black 94%, Mixed race 3%, Other and Amerindian 2%, White 1%
Government Parliamentary system
Currency Eastern Caribbean dollar = 100 cents
Literacy rate 98%
Calorie consumption 2609 calories

SAINT LUCIA
West Indies

Official name Saint Lucia
Formation 1979 / 1979
Capital Castries
Population 166,312 / 705 people per sq mile (273 people per sq km) / 38%
Total area 239 sq miles (620 sq km)
Languages English*, French Creole
Religions Roman Catholic 90%, Other 10%
Ethnic mix Black 90%, Mulatto (mixed race) 6%, Asian 3%, White 1%
Government Parliamentary system
Currency Eastern Caribbean dollar = 100 cents
Literacy rate 90%
Calorie consumption 2988 calories

SAINT VINCENT & THE GRENADINES
West Indies

Official name Saint Vincent and the Grenadines
Formation 1979 / 1979
Capital Kingstown
Population 117,534 / 897 people per sq mile (346 people per sq km) / 55%
Total area 150 sq miles (389 sq km)
Languages English*, English Creole
Religions Anglican 47%, Methodist 28%, Roman Catholic 13%, Other 12%
Ethnic mix Black 66%, Mulatto (mixed race) 19%, Asian 6%, Other 5%, White 4%
Government Parliamentary system
Currency Eastern Caribbean dollar = 100 cents
Literacy rate 88%
Calorie consumption 2599 calories

SAMOA
Australasia & Oceania

Official name Independent State of Samoa
Formation 1962 / 1962
Capital Apia
Population 185,000 / 169 people per sq mile (65 people per sq km) / 22%
Total area 1104 sq miles (2860 sq km)
Languages Samoan*, English*
Religions Christian 99%, Other 1%
Ethnic mix Polynesian 90%, Euronesian 9%, Other 1%
Government Parliamentary system
Currency Tala = 100 sene
Literacy rate 99%
Calorie consumption 2945 calories

SAN MARINO
Southern Europe

Official name Republic of San Marino
Formation 1631 / 1631
Capital San Marino
Population 28,880 / 1203 people per sq mile (473 people per sq km) / 94%
Total area 23.6 sq miles (61 sq km)
Languages Italian*
Religions Roman Catholic 93%, Other and nonreligious 7%
Ethnic mix Sammarinese 80%, Italian 19%, Other 1%
Government Parliamentary system
Currency Euro = 100 cents
Literacy rate 99%
Calorie consumption Not available

SÃO TOMÉ & PRÍNCIPE
West Africa

Official name Democratic Republic of São Tomé and Príncipe
Formation 1975 / 1975
Capital São Tomé
Population 187,410 / 505 people per sq mile (195 people per sq km) / 47%
Total area 386 sq miles (1001 sq km)
Languages Portuguese*, Portuguese Creole
Religions Roman Catholic 84%, Other 16%
Ethnic mix Black 90%, Portuguese and Creole 10%
Government Presidential system
Currency Dobra = 100 centimos
Literacy rate 83%
Calorie consumption 2460 calories

SAUDI ARABIA
Souhwest Asia

Official name Kingdom of Saudi Arabia
Formation 1932 / 1932
Capital Riyadh; Jiddah (administrative)
Population 24.6 million / 30 people per sq mile (12 people per sq km) / 86%
Total area 756,981 sq miles (1,960,582 sq km)
Languages Arabic*
Religions Sunni Muslim 85%, Shi'a Muslim 15%
Ethnic mix Arab 90%, Afro-Asian 10%
Government Monarchy
Currency Saudi riyal = 100 halalat
Literacy rate 79%
Calorie consumption 2844 calories

SENEGAL
West Africa

Official name Republic of Senegal
Formation 1960 / 1960
Capital Dakar
Population 11.7 million / 157 people per sq mile (61 people per sq km) / 47%
Total area 75,749 sq miles (196,190 sq km)
Languages French*, Diola, Mandinka, Malinke, Pulaar, Serer, Soninke, Wolof
Religions Sunni Muslim 90%, Christian (mainly Roman Catholic) 5%, Traditional beliefs 5%
Ethnic mix Wolof 43%, Toucouleur 24%, Serer 15%, Other 11%, Diola 4%, Malinke 3%
Government Presidential system
Currency CFA franc = 100 centimes
Literacy rate 39%
Calorie consumption 2279 calories

SERBIA
Europe

Official name Republic of Serbia
Formation 2006 / 2006
Capital Belgrade
Population 9.7 million / 290 people per sq mile (112 people per sq km) / 52%
Total area 34,116 sq miles (88,361 sq km)
Languages Serbo-Croat*, Albanian, Hungarian
Religions Orthodox Christian 85%, Muslim 6%, Other 6%, Roman Catholic 3%
Ethnic mix Serb 83%, Hungarian 4%, Bosniac 2%, Rom 1%, Yugoslav 1%, Croat 1%, Montenegrin 1%, Other 7%
Government Parliamentary system
Currency Dinar (Serbia) = 100 para
Literacy rate 98%
Calorie consumption Not available

SEYCHELLES
Indian Ocean

Official name Republic of Seychelles
Formation 1976 / 1976
Capital Victoria
Population 81,188 / 781 people per sq mile (301 people per sq km) / 64%
Total area 176 sq miles (455 sq km)
Languages French Creole*, English, French
Religions Roman Catholic 90%, Anglican 8%, Other (including Muslim) 2%
Ethnic mix Creole 89%, Indian 5%, Other 4%, Chinese 2%
Government Presidential system
Currency Seychelles rupee = 100 cents
Literacy rate 92%
Calorie consumption 2465 calories

SIERRA LEONE
West Africa

Official name Republic of Sierra Leone
Formation 1961 / 1961
Capital Freetown
Population 5.5 million / 199 people per sq mile (77 people per sq km) / 37%
Total area 27,698 sq miles (71,740 sq km)
Languages English*, Mende, Temne, Krio
Religions Muslim 30%, Traditional beliefs 30%, Other 30%, Christian 10%
Ethnic mix Mende 35%, Temne 32%, Other 21%, Limba 8%, Kuranko 4%
Government Presidential system
Currency Leone = 100 cents
Literacy rate 30%
Calorie consumption 1936 calories

SINGAPORE
Southeast Asia

Official name Republic of Singapore
Formation 1965 / 1965
Capital Singapore
Population 4.3 million / 18220 people per sq mile (7049 people per sq km) / 100%
Total area 250 sq miles (648 sq km)
Languages English*, Malay*, Mandarin*, Tamil*
Religions Buddhist 55%, Taoist 22%, Muslim 16%, Hindu, Christian, and Sikh 7%
Ethnic mix Chinese 77%, Malay 14%, Indian 8%, Other 1%
Government Parliamentary system
Currency Singapore dollar = 100 cents
Literacy rate 93%
Calorie consumption Not available

SLOVAKIA
Central Europe

Official name Slovak Republic
Formation 1993 / 1993
Capital Bratislava
Population 5.4 million / 285 people per sq mile (110 people per sq km) / 57%
Total area 18,859 sq miles (48,845 sq km)
Languages Slovak*, Hungarian (Magyar), Czech
Religions Roman Catholic 60%, Other 18%, Atheist 10%, Protestant 8%, Orthodox Christian 4%
Ethnic mix Slovak 85%, Magyar 11%, Other 2%, Roma 1%, Czech 1%
Government Parliamentary system
Currency Slovak koruna = 100 halierov
Literacy rate 99%
Calorie consumption 2889 calories

SLOVENIA
Central Europe

Official name Republic of Slovenia
Formation 1991 / 1991
Capital Ljubljana
Population 2 million / 256 people per sq mile (99 people per sq km) / 50%
Total area 7820 sq miles (20,253 sq km)
Languages Slovene*, Serbo-Croat
Religions Roman Catholic 96%, Other 3%, Muslim 1%
Ethnic mix Slovene 83%, Other 12%, Serb 2%, Croat 2%, Bosniak 1%
Government Parliamentary system
Currency Tolar = 100 stotinov
Literacy rate 99%
Calorie consumption 3001 calories

SOLOMON ISLANDS
Australasia & Oceania

Official name Solomon Islands
Formation 1978 / 1978
Capital Honiara
Population 478,000 / 44 people per sq mile (17 people per sq km) / 20%
Total area 10,985 sq miles (28,450 sq km)
Languages English*, Melanesian Pidgin, Pidgin English
Religions Anglican 34%, Roman Catholic 19%, Methodist 11%, Seventh-day Adventist 10%, South Seas Evangelical Church 17%, Other 9%
Ethnic mix Melanesian 94%, Polynesian 4%, Other 2%
Government Parliamentary system
Currency Solomon Islands dollar = 100 cents
Literacy rate 77%
Calorie consumption 2265 calories

SOMALIA
East Africa

Official name Somalia
Formation 1960 / 1960
Capital Mogadishu
Population 8.2 million / 34 people per sq mile (13 people per sq km) / 28%
Total area 246,199 sq miles (637,657 sq km)
Languages Somali*, Arabic*, English, Italian
Religions Sunni Muslim 98%, Christian 2%
Ethnic mix Somali 85%, Other 15%
Government Transitional regime
Currency Somali shilling = 100 centesimi
Literacy rate 24%
Calorie consumption 1628 calories

SOUTH AFRICA
Southern Africa

Official name Republic of South Africa
Formation 1934 / 1994
Capital Pretoria; Cape Town; Bloemfontein
Population 47.4 million / 101 people per sq mile (39 people per sq km) / 55%
Total area 471,008 sq miles (1,219,912 sq km)
Languages English, isiZulu, isiXhosa, Afrikaans, Sepedi, Setswana, Sesotho, Xitsonga, siSwati, Tshivenda, isiNdebele
Religions Christian 68%, Traditional beliefs and animist 29%, Muslim 2%, Hindu 1%
Ethnic mix Black 79%, White 10%, Colored 9%, Asian 2%
Government Presidential system
Currency Rand = 100 cents
Literacy rate 82%
Calorie consumption 2956 calories

SOUTH KOREA
East Asia

Official name Republic of Korea
Formation 1948 / 1953
Capital Seoul
Population 47.8 million / 1254 people per sq mile (484 people per sq km) / 82%
Total area 38,023 sq miles (98,480 sq km)
Languages Korean*
Religions Mahayana Buddhist 47%, Protestant 38%, Roman Catholic 11%, Confucianist 3%, Other 1%
Ethnic mix Korean 100%
Government Presidential system
Currency South Korean won = 100 chon
Literacy rate 98%
Calorie consumption 3058 calories

SPAIN
Southeast Europe

Official name Kingdom of Spain
Formation 1492 / 1713
Capital Madrid
Population 43.1 million / 224 people per sq mile (86 people per sq km) / 78%
Total area 194,896 sq miles (504,782 sq km)
Languages Spanish*, Catalan*, Galician*, Basque*
Religions Roman Catholic 96%, Other 4%
Ethnic mix Castilian Spanish 72%, Catalan 17%, Galician 6%, Basque 2%, Other 2%, Roma 1%
Government Parliamentary system
Currency Euro = 100 cents
Literacy rate 98%
Calorie consumption 3371 calories

SRI LANKA
South Asia

Official name Democratic Socialist Republic of Sri Lanka
Formation 1948 / 1948
Capital Colombo
Population 20.7 million / 828 people per sq mile (320 people per sq km) / 24%
Total area 25,332 sq miles (65,610 sq km)
Languages Sinhala, Tamil, Sinhala-Tamil, English
Religions Buddhist 69%, Hindu 15%, Muslim 8%, Christian 8%
Ethnic mix Sinhalese 74%, Tamil 18%, Moor 7%, Burgher, Malay, and Veddha 1%
Government Mixed presidential–parliamentary system
Currency Sri Lanka rupee = 100 cents
Literacy rate 90%
Calorie consumption 2385 calories

SUDAN
East Africa

Official name Republic of the Sudan
Formation 1956 / 1956
Capital Khartoum
Population 36.2 million / 37 people per sq mile (14 people per sq km) / 36%
Total area 967,493 sq miles (2,505,810 sq km)
Languages Arabic*, Dinka, Nuer, Nubian, Beja, Zande, Bari, Fur, Shilluk, Lotuko
Religions Muslim (mainly Sunni) 70%, Traditional beliefs 20%, Christian 9%, Other 1%
Ethnic mix Other Black 52%, Arab 40%, Dinka and Beja 7%, Other 1%
Government Presidential system
Currency Sudanese pound or dinar = 100 piastres
Literacy rate 59%
Calorie consumption 2228 calories

SURINAME
South America

Official name Republic of Suriname
Formation 1975 / 1975
Capital Paramaribo
Population 499,000 / 8 people per sq mile (3 people per sq km) / 74%
Total area 63,039 sq miles (163,270 sq km)
Languages Dutch* Sranan (Creole), Javanese, Sarnami Hindi, Saramaccan, Chinese, Carib
Religions Hindu 27%, Protestant 25%, Roman Catholic 23%, Muslim 20%, Traditional beliefs 5%
Ethnic mix Creole 34%, South Asian 34%, Javanese 18%, Black 9%, Other 5%
Government Parliamentary system
Currency Suriname dollar (guilder until 2004) = 100 cents
Literacy rate 88%
Calorie consumption 2652 calories

SWAZILAND
Southern Africa

Official name Kingdom of Swaziland
Formation 1968 / 1968
Capital Mbabane
Population 1 million / 151 people per sq mile (58 people per sq km) / 26%
Total area 6704 sq miles (17,363 sq km)
Languages English*, siSwati*, isiZulu, Xitsonga
Religions Christian 60%, Traditional beliefs 40%
Ethnic mix Swazi 97%, Other 3%
Government Monarchy
Currency Lilangeni = 100 cents
Literacy rate 79%
Calorie consumption 2322 calories

SWEDEN
Northern Europe

Official name Kingdom of Sweden
Formation 1523 / 1905
Capital Stockholm
Population 9 million / 57 people per sq mile (22 people per sq km) / 83%
Total area 173,731 sq miles (449,964 sq km)
Languages Swedish*, Finnish, Sámi
Religions Evangelical Lutheran 82%, Other 13%, Roman Catholic 2%, Muslim 2%, Orthodox Christian 1%
Ethnic mix Swedish 88%, Foreign-born or first-generation immigrant 10%, Finnish and Sámi 2%
Government Parliamentary system
Currency Swedish krona = 100 öre
Literacy rate 99%
Calorie consumption 3185 calories

SWITZERLAND
Central Europe

Official name Swiss Confederation
Formation 1291 / 1857
Capital Bern
Population 7.3 million / 475 people per sq mile (184 people per sq km) / 68%
Total area 15,942 sq miles (41,290 sq km)
Languages German*, French*, Italian*, Romansch*, Swiss-German
Religions Roman Catholic 46%, Protestant 40%, Other and nonreligious 12%, Muslim 2%
Ethnic mix German 65%, French 18%, Italian 10%, Other 6%, Romansch 1%
Government Parliamentary system
Currency Swiss franc = 100 rappen/centimes
Literacy rate 99%
Calorie consumption 3526 calories

SYRIA
Southwest Asia

Official name Syrian Arab Republic
Formation 1941 / 1967
Capital Damascus
Population 19 million / 267 people per sq mile (103 people per sq km) / 55%
Total area 71,498 sq miles (184,180 sq km)
Languages Arabic*, French, Kurdish, Armenian, Circassian, Turkic languages, Assyrian, Aramaic
Religions Sunni Muslim 74%, Other Muslim 16%, Christian 10%
Ethnic mix Arab 89%, Kurdish 6%, Other 3%, Armenian, Turkmen, and Circassian 2%
Government One-party state
Currency Syrian pound = 100 piasters
Literacy rate 83%
Calorie consumption 3038 calories

TAIWAN
East Asia

Official name Republic of China (ROC)
Formation 1949 / 1949
Capital Taipei
Population 22.9 million / 1838 people per sq mile (710 people per sq km) / 69%
Total area 13,892 sq miles (35,980 sq km)
Languages Amoy Chinese, Mandarin Chinese, Hakka Chinese
Religions Buddhist, Confucianist, and Taoist 93%, Christian 5%, Other 2%
Ethnic mix Han (pre-20th-century migration) 84%, Han (20th-century migration) 14%, Aboriginal 2%
Government Presidential system
Currency Taiwan dollar = 100 cents
Literacy rate 97%
Calorie consumption Not available

TAJIKISTAN
Central Asia

Official name Republic of Tajikistan
Formation 1991 / 1991
Capital Dushanbe
Population 6.5 million / 118 people per sq mile (45 people per sq km) / 28%
Total area 55,251 sq miles (143,100 sq km)
Languages Tajik*, Uzbek, Russian
Religions Sunni Muslim 80%, Other 15%, Shi'a Muslim 5%
Ethnic mix Tajik 62%, Uzbek 24%, Russian 8%, Other 4%, Tatar 1%, Kyrgyz 1%
Government Presidential system
Currency Somoni = 100 diram
Literacy rate 99%
Calorie consumption 1828 calories

TANZANIA
East Africa

Official name United Republic of Tanzania
Formation 1964 / 1964
Capital Dodoma
Population 38.3 million / 112 people per sq mile (43 people per sq km) / 33%
Total area 364,898 sq miles (945,087 sq km)
Languages English*, Kiswahili*, Sukuma, Chagga, Nyamwezi, Hehe, Makonde, Yao, Sandawe
Religions Muslim 33%, Christian 33%, Traditional beliefs 30%, Other 4%
Ethnic mix Native African (over 120 tribes) 99%, European and Asian 1%
Government Presidential system
Currency Tanzanian shilling = 100 cents
Literacy rate 69%
Calorie consumption 1975 calories

THAILAND
Southeastern Asia

Official name Kingdom of Thailand
Formation 1238 / 1907
Capital Bangkok
Population 64.2 million / 325 people per sq mile (126 people per sq km) / 22%
Total area 198,455 sq miles (514,000 sq km)
Languages Thai*, Chinese, Malay, Khmer, Mon, Karen, Miao
Religions Buddhist 95%, Muslim 4%, Other (including Christian) 1%
Ethnic mix Thai 83%, Chinese 12%, Malay 3%, Khmer and Other 2%
Government Parliamentary system
Currency Baht = 100 stang
Literacy rate 93%
Calorie consumption 2467 calories

TOGO
Western Africa

Official name Republic of Togo
Formation 1960 / 1960
Capital Lomé
Population 6.1 million / 290 people per sq mile (112 people per sq km) / 33%
Total area 21,924 sq miles (56,785 sq km)
Languages French*, Ewe, Kabye, Gurma
Religions Traditional beliefs 50%, Christian 35%, Muslim 15%
Ethnic mix Ewe 46%, Kabye 27%, Other African 26%, European 1%
Government Presidential system
Currency CFA franc = 100 centimes
Literacy rate 53%
Calorie consumption 2345 calories

TONGA
Australasia & Oceania

Official name Kingdom of Tonga
Formation 1970 / 1970
Capital Nuku'alofa
Population 112,422 / 404 people per sq mile (156 people per sq km) / 43%
Total area 289 sq miles (748 sq km)
Languages Tongan*, English
Religions Free Wesleyan 41%, Roman Catholic 16%, Church of Jesus Christ of Latter-day Saints 14%, Free Church of Tonga 12%, Other 17%
Ethnic mix Polynesian 99%, Other 1%
Government Monarchy
Currency Pa'anga (Tongan dollar) = 100 seniti
Literacy rate 99%
Calorie consumption Not available

TRINIDAD & TOBAGO
West Indies

Official name Republic of Trinidad and Tobago
Formation 1962 / 1962
Capital Port-of-Spain
Population 1.3 million / 656 people per sq mile (253 people per sq km) / 74%
Total area 1980 sq miles (5128 sq km)
Languages English*, English Creole, Hindi, French, Spanish
Religions Christian 60%, Hindu 24%, Other and nonreligious 9%, Muslim 7%
Ethnic mix East Indian 40%, Black 40%, Mixed race 19%, White and Chinese 1%
Government Parliamentary system
Currency Trinidad and Tobago dollar = 100 cents
Literacy rate 99%
Calorie consumption 2732 calories

TUNISIA
North Africa

Official name Republic of Tunisia
Formation 1956 / 1956
Capital Tunis
Population 10.1 million / 168 people per sq mile (65 people per sq km) / 74%
Total area 63,169 sq miles (163,610 sq km)
Languages Arabic*, French
Religions Muslim (mainly Sunni) 98%, Christian 1%, Jewish 1%
Ethnic mix Arab and Berber 98%, Jewish 1%, European 1%
Government Presidential system
Currency Tunisian dinar = 1000 millimes
Literacy rate 74%
Calorie consumption 3238 calories

TURKEY
Asia / Europe

Official name Republic of Turkey
Formation 1923 / 1939
Capital Ankara
Population 73.2 million / 246 people per sq mile (95 people per sq km) / 75%
Total area 301,382 sq miles (780,580 sq km)
Languages Turkish*, Kurdish, Arabic, Circassian, Armenian, Greek, Georgian, Ladino
Religions Muslim (mainly Sunni) 99%, Other 1%
Ethnic mix Turkish 70%, Kurdish 20%, Other 8%, Arab 2%
Government Parliamentary system
Currency new Turkish lira = 100 kurus
Literacy rate 88%
Calorie consumption 3357 calories

TURKMENISTAN
Central Asia

Official name Turkmenistan
Formation 1991 / 1991
Capital Ashgabat
Population 4.8 million / 25 people per sq mile (10 people per sq km) / 45%
Total area 188,455 sq miles (488,100 sq km)
Languages Turkmen*, Uzbek, Russian, Kazakh, Tatar
Religions Sunni Muslim 87%, Orthodox Christian 11%, Other 2%
Ethnic mix Turkmen 77%, Uzbek 9%, Russian 7%, Other 4%, Kazakh 2%, Tatar 1%
Government One-party state
Currency Manat = 100 tenga
Literacy rate 99%
Calorie consumption 2742 calories

TUVALU
Australasia & Oceania

Official name Tuvalu
Formation 1978 / 1978
Capital Fongafale, on Funafuti Atoll
Population 11,636 / 1164 people per sq mile (448 people per sq km) / 45%
Total area 10 sq miles (26 sq km)
Languages Tuvaluan, Kiribati, English
Religions Church of Tuvalu 97%, Other 1%, Baha'i 1%, Seventh-day Adventist 1%
Ethnic mix Polynesian 96%, Other 4%
Government Nonparty system
Currency Australian dollar and Tuvaluan dollar = 100 cents
Literacy rate 98%
Calorie consumption Not available

UGANDA
East Africa

Official name Republic of Uganda
Formation 1962 / 1962
Capital Kampala
Population 28.8 million / 374 people per sq mile (144 people per sq km) / 45%
Total area 91,135 sq miles (236,040 sq km)
Languages English*, Luganda, Nkole, Chiga, Lango, Acholi, Teso, Lugbara
Religions Roman Catholic 38%, Protestant 33%, Traditional beliefs 13%, Muslim (mainly Sunni) 8%, Other 8%
Ethnic mix Bantu tribes 50%, Other 45%, Sudanese 5%
Government Nonparty system
Currency New Uganda shilling = 100 cents
Literacy rate 69%
Calorie consumption 2410 calories

UKRAINE
Eastern Europe

Official name Ukraine
Formation 1991 / 1991
Capital Kiev
Population 46.5 million / 199 people per sq mile (77 people per sq km) / 68%
Total area 223,089 sq miles (603,700 sq km)
Languages Ukrainian*, Russian, Tatar
Religions Christian (mainly Orthodox) 95%, Other 4%, Jewish 1%
Ethnic mix Ukrainian 73%, Russian 22%, Other 4%, Jewish 1%
Government Presidential system
Currency Hryvna = 100 kopiykas
Literacy rate 99%
Calorie consumption 3054 calories

UNITED ARAB EMIRATES
Southwest Asia

Official name United Arab Emirates
Formation 1971 / 1972
Capital Abu Dhabi
Population 4.5 million / 139 people per sq mile (54 people per sq km) / 86%
Total area 32,000 sq miles (82,880 sq km)
Languages Arabic*, Farsi, Indian and Pakistani languages, English
Religions Muslim (mainly Sunni) 96%, Christian, Hindu, and other 4%
Ethnic mix Asian 60%, Emirian 25%, Other Arab 12%, European 3%
Government Monarchy
Currency UAE dirham = 100 fils
Literacy rate 77%
Calorie consumption 3225 calories

UNITED KINGDOM
Northwest Europe

Official name United Kingdom of Great Britain and Northern Ireland
Formation 1707 / 1922
Capital London
Population 59.7 million / 640 people per sq mile (247 people per sq km) / 90%
Total area 94,525 sq miles (244,820 sq km)
Languages English*, Welsh, Scottish Gaelic
Religions Anglican 45%, Roman Catholic 9%, Presbyterian 4%, Other 42%
Ethnic mix English 80%, Scottish 9%, West Indian, Asian, and other 5%, Northern Irish 3%, Welsh 3%
Government Parliamentary system
Currency Pound sterling = 100 pence
Literacy rate 99%
Calorie consumption 3412 calories

UNITED STATES
North America

Official name United States of America
Formation 1776 / 1959
Capital Washington D.C.
Population 298 million / 84 people per sq mile (33 people per sq km) / 77%
Total area 3,717,792 sq miles (9,626,091 sq km)
Languages English*, Spanish, Chinese, French, German, Tagalog, Vietnamese, Italian, Korean, Russian, Polish
Religions Protestant 52%, Roman Catholic 25%, Muslim 2%, Jewish 2%, Other 19%
Ethnic mix White 69%, Hispanic 13%, Black American/African 13%, Asian 4%, Native American 1%
Government Presidential system
Currency US dollar = 100 cents
Literacy rate 99%
Calorie consumption 3774 calories

URUGUAY
South America

Official name Eastern Republic of Uruguay
Formation 1828 / 1828
Capital Montevideo
Population 3.5 million / 52 people per sq mile (20 people per sq km) / 91%
Total area 68,039 sq miles (176,220 sq km)
Languages Spanish*
Religions Roman Catholic 66%, Other and nonreligious 30%, Jewish 2%, Protestant 2%
Ethnic mix White 90%, Mestizo 6%, Black 4%
Government Presidential system
Currency Uruguayan peso = 100 centésimos
Literacy rate 98%
Calorie consumption 2828 calories

UZBEKISTAN
Central Asia

Official name Republic of Uzbekistan
Formation 1991 / 1991
Capital Tashkent
Population 26.6 million / 154 people per sq mile (59 people per sq km) / 37%
Total area 172,741 sq miles (447,400 sq km)
Languages Uzbek*, Russian, Tajik, Kazakh
Religions Sunni Muslim 88%, Orthodox Christian 9%, Other 3%
Ethnic mix Uzbek 71%, Other 12%, Russian 8%, Tajik 5%, Kazakh 4%
Government Presidential system
Currency Som = 100 tiyin
Literacy rate 99%
Calorie consumption 2241 calories

VANUATU
Australasia & Oceania

Official name Republic of Vanuatu
Formation 1980 / 1980
Capital Port Vila
Population 211,000 / 45 people per sq mile (17 people per sq km) / 20%
Total area 4710 sq miles (12,200 sq km)
Languages Bislama* (Melanesian pidgin), English*, French*, other indigenous languages
Religions Presbyterian 37%, Other 19%, Anglican 15%, Roman Catholic 15%, Traditional beliefs 8%, Seventh-day Adventist 6%
Ethnic mix Melanesian 94%, Other 3%, Polynesian 3%
Government Parliamentary system
Currency Vatu = 100 centimes
Literacy rate 74%
Calorie consumption 2587 calories

VATICAN CITY
Southern Europe

Official name State of the Vatican City
Formation 1929 / 1929
Capital Vatican City
Population 921 / 5418 people per sq mile (2093 people per sq km) / 100%
Total area 0.17 sq miles (0.44 sq km)
Languages Italian*, Latin*
Religions Roman Catholic 100%
Ethnic mix The current pope is German. Cardinals are from many nationalities, but Italians form the largest group. Most of the resident lay persons are Italian.
Government Papal state
Currency Euro = 100 cents
Literacy rate 99%
Calorie consumption Not available

VENEZUELA
South America

Official name Bolivarian Republic of Venezuela
Formation 1830 / 1830
Capital Caracas
Population 26.7 million / 78 people per sq mile (30 people per sq km) / 87%
Total area 352,143 sq miles (912,050 sq km)
Languages Spanish*, Amerindian languages
Religions Roman Catholic 89%, Protestant and other 11%
Ethnic mix Mestizo 69%, White 20%, Black 9%, Amerindian 2%
Government Presidential system
Currency Bolivar = 100 centimos
Literacy rate 93%
Calorie consumption 2336 calories

VIETNAM
Southeast Asia

Official name Socialist Republic of Vietnam
Formation 1976 / 1976
Capital Hanoi
Population 84.2 million / 670 people per sq mile (259 people per sq km) / 20%
Total area 127,243 sq miles (329,560 sq km)
Languages Vietnamese*, Chinese, Thai, Khmer, Muong, Nung, Miao, Yao, Jarai
Religions Buddhist 55%, Other and nonreligious 38%, Christian (mainly Roman Catholic) 7%
Ethnic mix Vietnamese 88%, Other 6%, Chinese 4%, Thai 2%
Government One-party state
Currency Dông = 10 hao = 100 xu
Literacy rate 90%
Calorie consumption 2566 calories

YEMEN
Southwest Asia

Official name Republic of Yemen
Formation 1990 / 1990
Capital Sana
Population 21 million / 97 people per sq mile (37 people per sq km) / 25%
Total area 203,849 sq miles (527,970 sq km)
Languages Arabic*
Religions Sunni Muslim 55%, Shi'a Muslim 42%, Christian, Hindu, and Jewish 3%
Ethnic mix Arab 95%, Afro-Arab 3%, Indian, Somali, and European 2%
Government Presidential system
Currency Yemeni rial = 100 sene
Literacy rate 49%
Calorie consumption 2038 calories

ZAMBIA
Southern Africa

Official name Republic of Zambia
Formation 1964 / 1964
Capital Lusaka
Population 11.7 million / 41 people per sq mile (16 people per sq km) / 37%
Total area 290,584 sq miles (752,614 sq km)
Languages English*, Bemba, Tonga, Nyanja, Lozi, Lala-Bisa, Nsenga
Religions Christian 63%, Traditional beliefs 36%, Muslim and Hindu 1%
Ethnic mix Bemba 34%, Other African 26%, Tonga 16%, Nyanja 14%, Lozi 9%, European 1%
Government Presidential system
Currency Zambian kwacha = 100 ngwee
Literacy rate 68%
Calorie consumption 1927 calories

ZIMBABWE
Southern Africa

Official name Republic of Zimbabwe
Formation 1980 / 1980
Capital Harare
Population 13 million / 87 people per sq mile (34 people per sq km) / 35%
Total area 150,803 sq miles (390,580 sq km)
Languages English*, Shona, isiNdebele
Religions Syncretic (Christian/traditional beliefs) 50%, Christian 25%, Traditional beliefs 24%, Other (including Muslim) 1%
Ethnic mix Shona 71%, Ndebele 16%, Other African 11%, White 1%, Asian 1%
Government Presidential system
Currency Zimbabwe dollar = 100 cents
Literacy rate 90%
Calorie consumption 1943 calories

Geographical names

The following glossary lists geographical terms occurring on the maps and in main-entry names in the Index-Gazetteer. These terms may precede, follow or be run together with the proper element of the name; where they precede it the term is reversed for indexing purposes - thus Poluostrov Yamal is indexed as Yamal, Poluostrov.

Key

Geographical term
Language, Term

A

Å *Danish, Norwegian*, River
Āb *Persian*, River
Adrar *Berber*, Mountains
Agía, Ágios *Greek*, Saint
Air *Indonesian*, River
Ákra *Greek*, Cape, point
Alpen *German*, Alps
Alt- *German*, Old
Altiplanicie *Spanish*, Plateau
Älve(en) *Swedish*, River
-ån *Swedish*, River
Anse *French*, Bay
'Aqabat *Arabic*, Pass
Archipiélago *Spanish*, Archipelago
Arcipelago *Italian*, Archipelago
Arquipélago *Portuguese*, Archipelago
Arrecife(s) *Spanish*, Reef(s)
Aru *Tamil*, River
Augstiene *Latvian*, Upland
Aukštuma *Lithuanian*, Upland
Aust- *Norwegian*, Eastern
Avtonomnyy Okrug *Russian*, Autonomous district
Āw *Kurdish*, River
'Ayn *Arabic*, Spring, well
'Ayoûn *Arabic*, Wells

B

Baelt *Danish*, Strait
Bahía *Spanish*, Bay
Baḩr *Arabic*, River
Baía *Portuguese*, Bay
Baie *French*, Bay
Bañado *Spanish*, Marshy land
Bandao *Chinese*, Peninsula
Banjaran *Malay*, Mountain range
Barajı *Turkish*, Dam
Barragem *Portuguese*, Reservoir
Bassin *French*, Basin
Batang *Malay*, Stream
Beinn, Ben *Gaelic*, Mountain
-berg *Afrikaans, Norwegian*, Mountain
Besar *Indonesian, Malay*, Big
Birkat, Birket *Arabic*, Lake, well,
Boğazi *Turkish*, Lake
Boka *Serbo-Croatian*, Bay
Bol'sh-aya, -iye, -oy, -oye *Russian*, Big
Botigh(i) *Uzbek*, Depression basin
-bre(en) *Norwegian*, Glacier
Bredning *Danish*, Bay
Bucht *German*, Bay
Bugt(en) *Danish*, Bay
Buḩayrat *Arabic*, Lake, reservoir
Buḩeirat *Arabic*, Lake
Bukit *Malay*, Mountain
-bukta *Norwegian*, Bay
bukten *Swedish*, Bay
Bulag *Mongolian*, Spring
Bulak *Uighur*, Spring
Burnu *Turkish*, Cape, point
Buuraha *Somali*, Mountains

C

Cabo *Portuguese*, Cape
Caka *Tibetan*, Salt lake
Canal *Spanish*, Channel
Cap *French*, Cape
Capo *Italian*, Cape, headland
Cascada *Portuguese*, Waterfall
Cayo(s) *Spanish*, Islet(s), rock(s)
Cerro *Spanish*, Mountain
Chaîne *French*, Mountain range
Chapada *Portuguese*, Hills, upland
Chau *Cantonese*, Island
Chāy *Turkish*, River
Chhâk *Cambodian*, Bay
Chhu *Tibetan*, River
-chŏsuji *Korean*, Reservoir
Chott *Arabic*, Depression, salt lake
Chŭli *Uzbek*, Grassland, steppe
Ch'ün-tao *Chinese*, Island group
Chuŏr Phnum *Cambodian*, Mountains
Ciudad *Spanish*, City, town
Co *Tibetan*, Lake
Colline(s) *French*, Hill(s)
Cordillera *Spanish*, Mountain range
Costa *Spanish*, Coast
Côte *French*, Coast
Coxilha *Portuguese*, Mountains
Cuchilla *Spanish*, Mountains

D

Daban *Mongolian, Uighur*, Pass
Daği *Azerbaijani, Turkish*, Mountain
Dağlari *Azerbaijani, Turkish*, Mountains
-dake *Japanese*, Peak
-dal(en) *Norwegian*, Valley
Danau *Indonesian*, Lake
Dao *Chinese*, Island
Đao *Vietnamese*, Island
Daryā *Persian*, River
Daryācheh *Persian*, Lake
Dasht *Persian*, Desert, plain
Dawḩat *Arabic*, Bay
Denizi *Turkish*, Sea
Dere *Turkish*, Stream
Desierto *Spanish*, Desert
Dili *Azerbaijani*, Spit
-do *Korean*, Island
Dooxo *Somali*, Valley
Düzü *Azerbaijani*, Steppe
-dwīp *Bengali*, Island

E

-eilanden *Dutch*, Islands
Embalse *Spanish*, Reservoir
Ensenada *Spanish*, Bay
Erg *Arabic*, Dunes
Estany *Catalan*, Lake
Estero *Spanish*, Inlet
Estrecho *Spanish*, Strait
Étang *French*, Lagoon, lake
-ey *Icelandic*, Island
Ezero *Bulgarian, Macedonian*, Lake
Ezers *Latvian*, Lake

F

Feng *Chinese*, Peak
Fjord *Danish*, Fjord
-fjord(en) *Danish, Norwegian, Swedish*, fjord
-fjørdhur *Faeroese*, Fjord
Fleuve *French*, River
Fliegu *Maltese*, Channel
-fljór *Icelandic*, River
-flói *Icelandic*, Bay
Forêt *French*, Forest

G

-gan *Japanese*, Rock
-gang *Korean*, River
Ganga *Hindi, Nepali, Sinhala*, River
Gaoyuan *Chinese*, Plateau
Garagumy *Turkmen*, Sands
-gawa *Japanese*, River
Gebel *Arabic*, Mountain
-gebirge *German*, Mountain range
Ghadīr *Arabic*, Well
Ghubbat *Arabic*, Bay
Gjiri *Albanian*, Bay
Gol *Mongolian*, River
Golfe *French*, Gulf
Golfo *Italian, Spanish*, Gulf
Göl(ü) *Turkish*, Lake
Golyam, -a *Bulgarian*, Big
Gora *Russian, Serbo-Croatian*, Mountain
Góra *Polish*, mountain
Gory *Russian*, Mountain
Gryada *Russian*, ridge
Guba *Russian*, Bay
-gundo *Korean*, island group
Gunung *Malay*, Mountain

H

Ḩadd *Arabic*, Spit
-haehyŏp *Korean*, Strait
Haff *German*, Lagoon
Hai *Chinese*, Bay, lake, sea
Haixia *Chinese*, Strait
Hamada *Arabic*, Plateau
Ḩammādat *Arabic*, Plateau
Hāmūn *Persian*, Lake
-hantō *Japanese*, Peninsula
Har, Haré *Hebrew*, Mountain
Ḩarrat *Arabic*, Lava-field
Hav(et) *Danish, Swedish*, Sea
Hawr *Arabic*, Lake
Hāyk' *Amharic*, Lake
He *Chinese*, River
-hegység *Hungarian*, Mountain range
Heide *German*, Heath, moorland
Helodrano *Malagasy*, Bay
Higashi- *Japanese*, East(ern)
Ḩişā' *Arabic*, Well
Hka *Burmese*, River
-ho *Korean*, Lake
Hô *Korean*, Reservoir
Ḩolot *Hebrew*, Dunes
Hora *Belarussian, Czech*, Mountain
Hrada *Belarussian*, Mountain, ridge
Hsi *Chinese*, River
Hu *Chinese*, Lake
Huk *Danish*, Point

I

Île(s) *French*, Island(s)
Ilha(s) *Portuguese*, Island(s)
Ilhéu(s) *Portuguese*, Islet(s)
Imeni *Russian*, In the name of
Inish- *Gaelic*, Island
Insel(n) *German*, Island(s)
Irmağı, Irmak *Turkish*, River
Isla(s) *Spanish*, Island(s)
Isola (Isole) *Italian*, Island(s)

J

Jabal *Arabic*, Mountain
Jāl *Arabic*, Ridge
-järv *Estonian*, Lake
-järvi *Finnish*, Lake
Jazā'ir *Arabic*, Islands
Jazīrat *Arabic*, Island
Jazīreh *Persian*, Island
Jebel *Arabic*, Mountain
Jezero *Serbo-Croatian*, Lake
Jezioro *Polish*, Lake
Jiang *Chinese*, River
-jima *Japanese*, Island
Jižní *Czech*, Southern
-jõgi *Estonian*, River
-joki *Finnish*, River
-jökull *Icelandic*, Glacier
Jūn *Arabic*, Bay
Juzur *Arabic*, Islands

K

Kaikyō *Japanese*, Strait
-kaise *Lappish*, Mountain
Kali *Nepali*, River
Kalnas *Lithuanian*, Mountain
Kalns *Latvian*, Mountain
Kang *Chinese*, Harbor
Kangri *Tibetan*, Mountain(s)
Kaôh *Cambodian*, Island
Kapp *Norwegian*, Cape
Káto *Greek*, Lower
Kavīr *Persian*, Desert
K'edi *Georgian*, Mountain range
Kediet *Arabic*, Mountain
Kepi *Albanian*, Cape, point
Kepulauan *Indonesian, Malay*, Island group
Khalīg, Khalīj *Arabic*, Gulf
Khawr *Arabic*, Inlet
Khola *Nepali*, River
Khrebet *Russian*, Mountain range
Ko *Thai*, Island
-ko *Japanese*, Inlet, lake
Kólpos *Greek*, Bay
-kopf *German*, Peak
Körfäzi *Azerbaijani*, Bay
Körfezi *Turkish*, Bay
Kõrgustik *Estonian*, Upland
Kosa *Russian, Ukrainian*, Spit
Koshi *Nepali*, River
Kou *Chinese*, Rivermouth
Kowtal *Persian*, Pass
Kray *Russian*, Region, territory
Kryazh *Russian*, Ridge
Kuduk *Uighur*, Well
Kūh(hā) *Persian*, Mountain(s)
-kul' *Russian*, Lake
Kŭl(i) *Tajik, Uzbek*, Lake
-kundo *Korean*, Island group
-kysten *Norwegian*, Coast
Kyun *Burmese*, Island

L

Laaq *Somali*, Watercourse
Lac *French*, Lake
Lacul *Romanian*, Lake
Lagh *Somali*, Stream
Lago *Italian, Portuguese, Spanish*, Lake
Lagoa *Portuguese*, Lagoon
Laguna *Italian, Spanish*, Lagoon, lake
Laht *Estonian*, Bay
Laut *Indonesian*, Bay
Lembalemba *Malagasy*, Plateau
Lerr *Armenian*, Mountain
Lerrnashght'a *Armenian*, Mountain range
Les *Czech*, Forest
Lich *Armenian*, Lake
Liehtao *Chinese*, Island group
Liqeni *Albanian*, Lake
Límni *Greek*, Lake
Ling *Chinese*, Mountain range
Llano *Spanish*, Plain, prairie
Lumi *Albanian*, River
Lyman *Ukrainian*, Estuary

M

Madīnat *Arabic*, City, town
Mae Nam *Thai*, River
-mägi *Estonian*, Hill
Maja *Albanian*, Mountain
Mal *Albanian*, Mountains
Mal-aya, -oye, -yy, *Russian*, Small
-man *Korean*, Bay
Mar *Spanish*, Lake
Marios *Lithuanian*, Lake
Massif *French*, Mountains
Meer *German*, Lake
-meer *Dutch*, Lake
Melkosopochnik *Russian*, Plain
-meri *Estonian*, Sea
Mifraz *Hebrew*, Bay
Minami- *Japanese*, South(ern)
-misaki *Japanese*, Cape, point
Monkhafad *Arabic*, Depression
Montagne(s) *French*, Mountain(s)
Montañas *Spanish*, Mountains
Mont(s) *French*, Mountain(s)
Monte *Italian, Portuguese*, Mountain
More *Russian*, Sea
Mörön *Mongolian*, River
Mys *Russian*, Cape, point

N

-nada *Japanese*, Open stretch of water
Nagor'ye *Russian*, Upland
Naḩal *Hebrew*, River
Nahr *Arabic*, River
Nam *Laotian*, River
Namakzār *Persian*, Salt desert
Né-a, -on, -os *Greek*, New
Nedre- *Norwegian*, Lower
-neem *Estonian*, Cape, point
Nehri *Turkish*, River
-nes *Norwegian*, Cape, point
Nevado *Spanish*, Mountain (snow-capped)
Nieder- *German*, Lower
Nishi- *Japanese*, West(ern)
-nísi *Greek*, Island
Nisoi *Greek*, Islands
Nizhn-eye, -iy, -iye, -yaya *Russian*, Lower
Nizmennost' *Russian*, Lowland, plain
Nord *Danish, French, German*, North
Norte *Portuguese, Spanish*, North
Nos *Bulgarian*, Point, spit
Nosy *Malagasy*, Island
Nov-a, -i, *Bulgarian, Serbo-Croatian*, New
Nov-aya, -o, -oye, -yy, -yye *Russian*, New
Now-a, -e, -y *Polish*, New
Nur *Mongolian*, Lake
Nuruu *Mongolian*, Mountains
Nuur *Mongolian*, Lake
Nyzovyna *Ukrainian*, Lowland, plain

O

-ø *Danish*, Island
Ober- *German*, Upper
Oblast' *Russian*, Province
Órmos *Greek*, Bay
Orol(i) *Uzbek*, Island
Øster- *Norwegian*, Eastern
Ostrov(a) *Russian*, Island(s)
Otok *Serbo-Croatian*, Island
Oued *Arabic*, Watercourse
-oy *Faeroese*, Island
-øy(a) *Norwegian*, Island
Oya *Sinhala*, River
Ozero *Russian, Ukrainian*, Lake

P

Passo *Italian*, Pass
Pegunungan *Indonesian, Malay*, Mountain range
Pélagos *Greek*, Sea
Pendi *Chinese*, Basin
Penisola *Italian*, Peninsula
Pertuis *French*, Strait
Peski *Russian*, Sands
Phanom *Thai*, Mountain
Phou *Laotian*, Mountain
Pi *Chinese*, Point
Pic *Catalan, French*, Peak
Pico *Portuguese, Spanish*, Peak
-piggen *Danish*, Peak
Pik *Russian*, Peak
Pivostriv *Ukrainian*, Peninsula
Planalto *Portuguese*, Plateau
Planina, Planini *Bulgarian, Macedonian, Serbo-Croatian*, Mountain range
Plato *Russian*, Plateau
Ploskogor'ye *Russian*, Upland
Poluostrov *Russian*, Peninsula
Ponta *Portuguese*, Point
Porthmós *Greek*, Strait
Pótamos *Greek*, River
Presa *Spanish*, Dam
Prokhod *Bulgarian*, Pass
Proliv *Russian*, Strait
Pulau *Indonesian, Malay*, Island
Pulu *Malay*, Island
Punta *Spanish*, Point
Pushcha *Belorussian*, Forest
Puszcza *Polish*, Forest

Q

Qā' *Arabic*, Depression
Qalamat *Arabic*, Well
Qatorkŭh(i) *Tajik*, Mountain
Qiuling *Chinese*, Hills
Qolleh *Persian*, Mountain
Qu *Tibetan*, Stream
Quan *Chinese*, Well
Qulla(i) *Tajik*, Peak
Qundao *Chinese*, Island group

R

Raas *Somali*, Cape
-rags *Latvian*, Cape
Ramlat *Arabic*, Sands
Ra's *Arabic*, Cape, headland, point
Ravnina *Bulgarian, Russian*, Plain
Récif *French*, Reef
Recife *Portuguese*, Reef
Reka *Bulgarian*, River
Represa (Rep.) *Portuguese, Spanish*, Reservoir
Reshteh *Persian*, Mountain range
Respublika *Russian*, Republic, first-order administrative division
Respublika(si) *Uzbek*, Republic, first-order administrative division
-retsugan *Japanese*, Chain of rocks
-rettō *Japanese*, Island chain
Riacho *Spanish*, Stream
Riban' *Malagasy*, Mountains
Rio *Portuguese*, River
Río *Spanish*, River
Riu *Catalan*, River
Rivier *Dutch*, River
Rivière *French*, River
Rowd *Pashtu*, River
Rt *Serbo-Croatian*, Point
Rūd *Persian*, River
Rūdkhāneh *Persian*, River
Rudohorie *Slovak*, Mountains
Ruisseau *French*, Stream

S

-saar *Estonian*, Island
-saari *Finnish*, Island
Sabkhat *Arabic*, Salt marsh
Sāgar(a) *Hindi*, Lake, reservoir
Şaḩrā' *Arabic*, Desert
Saint, Sainte *French*, Saint
Salar *Spanish*, Salt-pan
Salto *Portuguese, Spanish*, Waterfall
Samudra *Sinhala*, Reservoir
-san *Japanese, Korean*, Mountain
-sanchi *Japanese*, Mountains
-sandur *Icelandic*, Beach
Sankt *German, Swedish*, Saint
-sanmaek *Korean*, Mountain range
-sanmyaku *Japanese*, Mountain range
San, Santa, Santo *Italian, Portuguese, Spanish*, Saint
São *Portuguese*, Saint
Sarir *Arabic*, Desert
Sebkha, Sebkhet *Arabic*, Depression, salt marsh
Sedlo *Czech*, Pass
See *German*, Lake
Selat *Indonesian*, Strait
Selatan *Indonesian*, Southern
-selkä *Finnish*, Lake, ridge
Selseleh *Persian*, Mountain range
Serra *Portuguese*, Mountain
Serranía *Spanish*, Mountain
-seto *Japanese*, Channel, strait
Sever-naya, -noye, -nyy, -o *Russian*, Northern
Sha'īb *Arabic*, Watercourse
Shākh *Kurdish*, Mountain
Shamo *Chinese*, Desert
Shan *Chinese*, Mountain(s)
Shankou *Chinese*, Pass
Shanmo *Chinese*, Mountain range
Shaţţ *Arabic*, Distributary
Shet' *Amharic*, River
Shi *Chinese*, Municipality
-shima *Japanese*, Island
Shiqqat *Arabic*, Depression
-shotō *Japanese*, Group of islands
Shuiku *Chinese*, Reservoir
Shŭrkhog(i) *Uzbek*, Salt marsh
Sierra *Spanish*, Mountains
Sint *Dutch*, Saint
-sjø(en) *Norwegian*, Lake
-sjön *Swedish*, Lake
Solonchak *Russian*, Salt lake
Solonchakovyye Vpadiny *Russian*, Salt basin, wetlands
Son *Vietnamese*, Mountain
Sông *Vietnamese*, River
Sør- *Norwegian*, Southern
-spitze *German*, Peak
Star-á, -é *Czech*, Old
Star-aya, -oye, -yy, -yye *Russian*, Old
Stenó *Greek*, Strait
Step' *Russian*, Steppe
Štít *Slovak*, Peak
Stœng *Cambodian*, River
Stolovaya Strana *Russian*, Plateau
Stredné *Slovak*, Middle
Střední *Czech*, Middle
Stretto *Italian*, Strait
Su Anbari *Azerbaijani*, Reservoir
-suidō *Japanese*, Channel, strait
Sund *Swedish*, Sound, strait
Sungai *Indonesian, Malay*, River
Suu *Turkish*, River

T

Tal *Mongolian*, Plain
Tandavan' *Malagasy*, Mountain range
Tangorombohitr' *Malagasy*, Mountain massif
Tanjung *Indonesian, Malay*, Cape, point
Tao *Chinese*, Island
Ţaraq *Arabic*, Hills
Tassili *Berber*, Mountain, plateau
Tau *Russian*, Mountain(s)
Taungdan *Burmese*, Mountain range
Techníti Límni *Greek*, Reservoir
Tekojärvi *Finnish*, Reservoir
Teluk *Indonesian, Malay*, Bay
Tengah *Indonesian*, Middle
Terara *Amharic*, Mountain
Timur *Indonesian*, Eastern
-tind(an) *Norwegian*, Peak
Tizma(si) *Uzbek*, Mountain range, ridge
-tō *Japanese*, island
Tog *Somali*, Valley
-tōge *Japanese*, pass
Togh(i) *Uzbek*, mountain
Tônlé *Cambodian*, Lake
Top *Dutch*, Peak
-tunturi *Finnish*, Mountain
Ţurāq *Arabic*, hills
Tur'at *Arabic*, Channel

U

Udde(n) *Swedish*, Cape, point
'Uqlat *Arabic*, Well
Utara *Indonesian*, Northern
Uul *Mongolian*, Mountains

V

Väin *Estonian*, Strait
Vallée *French*, Valley
-vatn *Icelandic*, Lake
-vatnet *Norwegian*, Lake
Velayat *Turkmen*, Province
-vesi *Finnish*, Lake
Vestre- *Norwegian*, Western
-vidda *Norwegian*, Plateau
-vík *Icelandic*, Bay
-viken *Swedish*, Bay, inlet
Vinh *Vietnamese*, Bay
Víztárloló *Hungarian*, Reservoir
Vodaskhovishcha *Belarussian*, Reservoir
Vodokhranilishche (Vdkhr.) *Russian*, Reservoir
Vodoskhovyshche (Vdskh.) *Ukrainian*, Reservoir
Volcán *Spanish*, Volcano
Vostochn-o, yy *Russian*, Eastern
Vozvyshennost' *Russian*, Upland, plateau
Vozyera *Belarussian*, Lake
Vpadina *Russian*, Depression
Vrchovina *Czech*, Mountains
Vrha *Macedonian*, Peak
Vychodné *Slovak*, Eastern
Vysochyna *Ukrainian*, Upland
Vysočina *Czech*, Upland

W

Waadi *Somali*, Watercourse
Wādī *Arabic* Watercourse
Wāḩat, Wâhat *Arabic*, Oasis
Wald *German*, Forest
Wan *Chinese*, Bay
Way *Indonesian*, River
Webi *Somali*, River
Wenz *Amharic*, River
Wiloyat(i) *Uzbek*, Province
Wyżyna *Polish*, Upland
Wzgórza *Polish*, Upland
Wzvyshsha *Belarussian*, Upland

X

Xé *Laotian*, River
Xi *Chinese*, Stream

Y

-yama *Japanese*, Mountain
Yanchi *Chinese*, Salt lake
Yang *Chinese*, Bay
Yanhu *Chinese*, Salt lake
Yarımadası *Azerbaijani, Turkish*, Peninsula
Yaylası *Turkish*, Plateau
Yazovir *Bulgarian*, Reservoir
Yoma *Burmese*, Mountains
Ytre- *Norwegian*, Outer
Yü *Chinese*, Island
Yunhe *Chinese*, Canal
Yuzhn-o, -yy *Russian*, Southern

Z

-zaki *Japanese*, Cape, point
Zaliv *Bulgarian, Russian*, Bay
-zan *Japanese*, Mountain
Zangbo *Tibetan*, River
Zapadn-aya, -o, -yy *Russian*, Western
Západné *Slovak*, Western
Západní *Czech*, Western
Zatoka *Polish, Ukrainian*, Bay
-zee *Dutch*, Sea
Zemlya *Russian*, Earth, land
Zizhiqu *Chinese*, Autonomous region

INDEX

THIS INDEX LISTS all the placenames and features shown on the regional and continental maps in this Atlas. Placenames are referenced to the largest scale map on which they appear. The policy followed throughout the Atlas is to use the local spelling or local name at regional level; commonly-used English language names may occasionally be added (in parentheses) where this is an aid to identification e.g. Firenze (Florence). English names, where they exist, have been used for all international features e.g. oceans and country names; they are also used on the continental maps and in the introductory World section; these are then fully cross-referenced to the local names found on the regional maps. The index also contains commonly-found alternative names and variant spellings, which are also fully cross-referenced.

All main entry names are those of settlements unless otherwise indicated by the use of italicized definitions or representative symbols, which are keyed at the foot of each page.

GLOSSARY OF ABBREVIATIONS

This glossary provides a comprehensive guide to the abbreviations used in this Atlas, and in the Index.

A
abbrev. abbreviated
AD Anno Domini
Afr. Afrikaans
Alb. Albanian
Amh. Amharic
anc. ancient
approx. approximately
Ar. Arabic
Arm. Armenian
ASEAN Association of South East Asian Nations
ASSR Autonomous Soviet Socialist Republic
Aust. Australian
Az. Azerbaijani
Azerb. Azerbaijan

B
Basq. Basque
BC before Christ
Bel. Belarussian
Ben. Bengali
Ber. Berber
B-H Bosnia-Herzegovina
bn billion (one thousand million)
BP British Petroleum
Bret. Breton
Brit. British
Bul. Bulgarian
Bur. Burmese

C
C central
C. Cape
°C degrees Centigrade
CACM Central America Common Market
Cam. Cambodian
Cant. Cantonese
CAR Central African Republic
Cast. Castilian
Cat. Catalan
CEEAC Central America Common Market
Chin. Chinese
CIS Commonwealth of Independent States
cm centimetre(s)
Cro. Croat
Cz. Czech
Czech Rep. Czech Republic

D
Dan. Danish
Div. Divehi
Dom. Rep. Dominican Republic
Dut. Dutch

E
E east
EC see EU
EEC see EU
ECOWAS Economic Community of West African States
ECU European Currency Unit
EMS European Monetary System
Eng. English
est estimated
Est. Estonian
EU European Union (previously European Community [EC], European Economic Community [EEC])

F
°F degrees Fahrenheit
Faer. Faeroese
Fij. Fijian
Fin. Finnish
Fr. French
Fris. Frisian
ft foot/feet
FYROM Former Yugoslav Republic of Macedonia

G
g gram(s)
Gael. Gaelic
Gal. Galician
GDP Gross Domestic Product (the total value of goods and services produced by a country excluding income from foreign countries)
Geor. Georgian
Ger. German
Gk Greek
GNP Gross National Product (the total value of goods and services produced by a country)

H
Heb. Hebrew
HEP hydro-electric power
Hind. Hindi
hist. historical
Hung. Hungarian

I
I. Island
Icel. Icelandic
in inch(es)
In. Inuit (Eskimo)
Ind. Indonesian
Intl International
Ir. Irish
Is Islands
It. Italian

J
Jap. Japanese

K
Kaz. Kazakh
kg kilogram(s)
Kir. Kirghiz
km kilometre(s)
km² square kilometre (singular)
Kor. Korean
Kurd. Kurdish

L
L. Lake
LAIA Latin American Integration Association
Lao. Laotian
Lapp. Lappish
Lat. Latin
Latv. Latvian
Liech. Liechtenstein
Lith. Lithuanian
Lux. Luxembourg

M
m million/metre(s)
Mac. Macedonian
Maced. Macedonia
Mal. Malay
Malg. Malagasy
Malt. Maltese
mi. mile(s)
Mong. Mongolian
Mt. Mountain
Mts Mountains

N
N north
NAFTA North American Free Trade Agreement
Nep. Nepali
Neth. Netherlands
Nic. Nicaraguan
Nor. Norwegian
NZ New Zealand

P
Pash. Pashtu
PNG Papua New Guinea
Pol. Polish
Poly. Polynesian
Port. Portuguese
prev. previously

R
Rep. Republic
Res. Reservoir
Rmsch Romansch
Rom. Romanian
Rus. Russian
Russ. Fed. Russian Federation

S
S south
SADC Southern Africa Development Community
SCr. Serbo-Croatian
Sinh. Sinhala
Slvk Slovak
Slvn. Slovene
Som. Somali
Sp. Spanish
St., St Saint
Strs Straits
Swa. Swahili
Swe. Swedish
Switz. Switzerland

T
Taj. Tajik
Th. Thai
Thai. Thailand
Tib. Tibetan
Turk. Turkish
Turkm. Turkmenistan

U
UAE United Arab Emirates
Uigh. Uighur
UK United Kingdom
Ukr. Ukrainian
UN United Nations
Urd. Urdu
US/USA United States of America
USSR Union of Soviet Socialist Republics
Uzb. Uzbek

V
var. variant
Vdkhr. Vodokhranilishche (Russian for reservoir)
Vdskh. Vodoskhovyshche (Ukrainian for reservoir)
Vtn. Vietnamese

W
W west
Wel. Welsh

Y
Yugo. Yugoslavia

◆ Country
● Country Capital
◇ Dependent Territory
○ Dependent Territory Capital
◈ Administrative Regions
✕ International Airport
▲ Mountain
▲ Mountain Range
☼ Volcano
♦ River
◎ Lake
◙ Reservoir

Ájluokta - Alfredo Chavez

INDEX

Ájluokta *see* Drag
221 J4 **'Ajmān** *var.* Ajman, 'Ujmān. 'Ajmān, NE United Arab Emirates 25°36′N 55°42′E
232 D6 **Ajmer** *var.* Ajmere. Rājasthān, N India 26°29′N 74°40′E
79 H9 **Ajo** Arizona, SW USA 32°22′N 112°51′W
170 G1 **Ajo, Cabo de** *headland* N Spain 43°31′N 03°36′W
79 H10 **Ajo Range** ▲▲ Arizona, SW USA
85 H8 **Ajoya** Sinaloa, Mexico 24°05′N 106°22′W
86 E7 **Ajuchitlàn del Progreso** Guerrero, Mexico 18°09′N 100°29′W
228 B6 **Ajyguýy** *Rus.* Adzhikui. Balkan Welaýaty, W Turkmenistan 39°46′N 53°57′E
Akaba *see* Al 'Aqabah
252 E4 **Akabira** Hokkaidō, NE Japan 43°30′N 142°04′E
290 F4 **Akademik Kurchatov Fracture Zone** *tectonic feature* N Atlantic Ocean
253 B10 **Akadomari** Niigata, Sado, C Japan 37°54′N 138°24′E
137 A9 **Akagera** *var.* Kagera. ≈ Rwanda/Tanzania *see also* Kagera
118 B2 **Akahanga, Punta** *headland* Easter Island, Chile, E Pacific Ocean
251 K4 **Akaishi-dake** ▲ Honshū, S Japan 35°26′N 138°09′E
251 K4 **Akaishi-sanmyaku** ▲▲ Honshū, S Japan
136 E4 **Āk'ak'i** Oromīya, C Ethiopia 08°50′N 38°51′E
234 E5 **Akalkot** Mahārāshtra, W India 17°36′N 76°10′E
Akamagaseki *see* Shimonoseki
252 G4 **Akan** Hokkaidō, NE Japan 43°09′N 144°08′E
252 G4 **Akan-ko** ◎ Hokkaidō, NE Japan
Akanthoú *see* Tatlısu
278 F10 **Akaroa** Canterbury, South Island, New Zealand 43°48′S 172°58′E
129 I7 **Akasha** Northern, N Sudan 21°03′N 30°46′E
251 H5 **Akashi** *var.* Akasi. Hyōgo, Honshū, SW Japan 34°39′N 135°00′E
216 G4 **'Akāsh, Wādī** *var.* Wādī 'Ukash. *dry watercourse* W Iraq
Akasi *see* Akashi
152 G5 **Äkäsjokisuu** Lappi, N Finland 67°28′N 23°44′E
215 J4 **Akbaba Dağı** ▲ Armenia/Turkey 41°04′N 43°28′E
171 M9 **Akbou** Algeria
Akbük Limanı *see* Güllük Körfezi
197 L4 **Akbulak** Orenburgskaya Oblast', W Russian Federation 51°01′N 55°35′E
215 H5 **Akçaabat** Trabzon, NE Turkey 41°00′N 39°36′E
214 D4 **Akçakoca** Düzce, NW Turkey 41°05′N 31°08′E
187 M7 **Akçay** ≈ Turkey
Akchakaya, Vpadina *see* Akdzhakaya, Vpadina
132 C1 **Akchâr** *desert* W Mauritania
227 J5 **Akchatau** *Kaz.* Aqshataū. Karaganda, C Kazakhstan 47°59′N 74°02′E
187 K5 **Akdag** ▲ İzmir, Turkey 38°33′N 26°30′E
214 G6 **Akdağlar** ▲▲ C Turkey
187 N8 **Ak Dağları** ▲▲ SW Turkey
214 F6 **Akdağmadeni** Yozgat, C Turkey 39°40′N 35°52′E
228 E4 **Akdepe** *prev.* Ak-Tepe, Leninsk, *Turkm.* Lenin. Daşoguz Welaýat, N Turkmenistan 42°10′N 59°17′E
Ak-Dere *see* Byala
218 C2 **Akdoğan** *Gk.* Lýsi. C Cyprus 35°06′N 33°42′E
192 G8 **Ak-Dovurak** Respublika Tyva, S Russian Federation 51°09′N 90°36′E
228 D5 **Akdzhakaya, Vpadina** *var.* Vpadina Akchakaya. *depression* N Turkmenistan
260 G3 **Akelamo** Pulau Halmahera, E Indonesia 01°27′N 128°39′E
159 J4 **Akeld** N England, United Kingdom 55°33′N 2°04′E
Aken *see* Aachen
Akermanceaster *see* Bath
155 I8 **Åkersberga** Stockholm, C Sweden 59°28′N 18°19′E
154 E7 **Akershus** ◐ *county* S Norway
134 G6 **Aketi** Orientale, N Dem. Rep. Congo 02°44′N 23°46′E
228 B5 **Akgyr Erezi** *Rus.* Gryada Akkyr. *hill range* NW Turkmenistan
Akhalskiy Velayat *see* Ahal Welaýaty
215 J4 **Akhalts'ikhe** SW Georgia 41°39′N 43°04′E
Akhangaran *see* Ohangaron
Akharnaí *see* Acharnés
128 F2 **Akhḍar, Al Jabal al** *hill range* NE Libya
Akhelóös *see* Achelóos
83 I8 **Akhiok** Kodiak Island, Alaska, USA 56°57′N 154°12′W
214 B6 **Akhisar** Manisa, W Turkey 38°54′N 27°50′E
129 I5 **Akhmīm** *var.* Akhmîm; *anc.* Panopolis. C Egypt 26°35′N 31°48′E
232 D3 **Akhnūr** Jammu and Kashmir, NW India 32°53′N 74°46′E
197 I6 **Akhtuba** ≈ SW Russian Federation
197 I6 **Akhtubinsk** Astrakhanskaya Oblast', SW Russian Federation 48°17′N 46°14′E
Akhtyrka *see* Okhtyrka
250 G6 **Aki** Kōchi, Shikoku, SW Japan 33°30′N 133°53′E
82 G6 **Akiachak** Alaska, USA 60°54′N 161°25′W
82 G6 **Akiak** Alaska, USA 60°54′N 161°12′W
285 K7 **Akiaki** *atoll* Îles Tuamotu, E French Polynesia
58 F5 **Akimiski Island** *island* Nunavut, C Canada
214 F8 **Akıncı Burnu** *headland* S Turkey 36°21′N 35°47′E
Akıncılar *see* Selçuk
189 K7 **Akinovka** Zaporiz'ka Oblast', S Ukraine
Åkirkeby *see* Aakirkeby
253 C8 **Akita** Akita, Honshū, C Japan 39°44′N 140°06′E
253 D8 **Akita** *off.* Akita-ken. ◐ *prefecture* Honshū, C Japan
132 C2 **Akjoujt** *prev.* Fort-Repoux. Inchiri, W Mauritania 19°42′N 14°28′W
152 F5 **Akka** *Lapp.* Áhkká. ▲ N Sweden 67°33′N 17°27′E
152 F5 **Akkajaure** ◎ N Sweden
Akkala *see* Oqqal'a
235 G10 **Akkaraipattu** Eastern Province, E Sri Lanka 07°13′N 81°51′E
140 E10 **Akkedisberg** ▲ Western Cape, South Africa 34°25′S 19°43′E
227 H6 **Akkense** *Kaz.* Aqkengse. Karaganda, C Kazakhstan 46°39′N 68°06′E
Akkerman *see* Bilhorod-Dnistrovs'kyy
197 M4 **Akkermanovka** Orenburgskaya Oblast', W Russian Federation 51°11′N 58°03′E
252 H4 **Akkeshi** Hokkaidō, NE Japan 43°03′N 144°49′E
252 H4 **Akkeshi-ko** ◎ Hokkaidō, NE Japan
252 H4 **Akkeshi-wan** *bay* NW Pacific Ocean
218 E5 **Akko** *Eng.* Acre, *Fr.* Saint-Jean-d'Acre, *Bibl.* Accho, Ptolemaïs. Northern, N Israel 32°55′N 35°04′E
227 I3 **Akkol'** *Kaz.* Aqköl; *prev.* Alekseyevka, *Kaz.* Alekseevka. Akmola, C Kazakhstan 51°58′N 70°58′E
227 J6 **Akkol'** *Kaz.* Aqköl. Almaty, SE Kazakhstan 45°01′N 75°38′E
227 I7 **Akkol'** *Kaz.* Aqköl. Zhambyl, C Kazakhstan 43°25′N 70°47′E
226 G5 **Akkol', Ozero** *prev.* Ozero Zhaman-Akkol. ◎ C Kazakhstan
162 G4 **Akkrum** Friesland, N Netherlands 53°01′N 05°52′E
227 K3 **Akku** *Kaz.* Aqqū; *prev.* Lebyazh'ye. Pavlodar, NE Kazakhstan 51°29′N 77°48′E
226 B5 **Akkystau** *Kaz.* Aqqystaū. Atyrau, SW Kazakhstan 47°17′N 51°03′E
52 B6 **Aklavik** Northwest Territories, NW Canada 68°15′N 135°02′W
190 B6 **Akmenrags** *prev.* Akmeņrags. *headland* W Latvia 56°49′N 21°03′E
Akmeņrags *see* Akmenrags
238 C6 **Akmeqit** Xinjiang Uygur Zizhiqu, NW China 37°10′N 76°59′E
228 F7 **Akmeydan** Mary Welaýaty, C Turkmenistan 37°50′N 62°08′E
227 H3 **Akmola** *off.* Akmolinskaya Oblast', *Kaz.* Aqmola Oblysy; *prev.* Tselinogradskaya Oblast. ◐ *province* C Kazakhstan
Akmola *see* Astana
Akmolinsk *see* Astana
Akmolinskaya Oblast' *see* Akmola
Aknavásár *see* Târgu Ocna
190 E7 **Aknīste** Jēkabpils, S Latvia 56°09′N 25°43′E
250 G4 **Akō** Hyōgo, Honshū, SW Japan 34°44′N 134°22′E
136 B5 **Akobo** Jonglei, SE Sudan 07°50′N 33°05′E
136 C5 **Akobo** *var.* Ākobowenz. ≈ Ethiopia/Sudan
Ākobowenz *see* Akobo
234 E4 **Akola** Mahārāshtra, C India 20°44′N 77°00′E
136 E2 **Ak'ordat** *var.* Agordat, Akurdet. C Eritrea 15°33′N 38°01′E
133 H8 **Akosombo Dam** *dam* SE Ghana
234 E4 **Akot** Mahārāshtra, C India 20°45′N 77°00′E
132 F8 **Akoupé** SE Ivory Coast 06°19′N 03°54′W
59 I2 **Akpatok Island** *island* Nunavut, E Canada
238 D4 **Akqi** Xinjiang Uygur Zizhiqu, NW China 40°51′N 78°20′E
216 D2 **Akrād, Jabal al** ▲▲ N Syria
Akragas *see* Agrigento
152 B3 **Akranes** Vesturland, W Iceland 64°19′N 22°01′W
217 I1 **Ākrē** *Ar.* 'Aqrah. Dahūk, N Iraq 36°46′N 43°52′E
155 A8 **Åkrehamn** Rogaland, S Norway 59°15′N 15°13′E
133 K3 **Akrérèb** Agadez, C Niger 17°45′N 09°01′E
186 F8 **Akrítas, Akrotírio** *headland* S Greece 36°43′N 21°52′E
79 N2 **Akron** Colorado, C USA 40°09′N 103°12′W
74 E6 **Akron** Iowa, C USA 42°49′N 96°33′W
64 B1 **Akron** New York, USA 43°01′N 78°30′W
73 I9 **Akron** Ohio, N USA 41°05′N 81°31′W
Akrotiri *see* Akrotírion
Akrotiri Bay *see* Akrotírion, Kólpos
218 B3 **Akrotírion** *var.* Akrotiri. *UK air base* S Cyprus 34°36′N 32°57′E
218 B3 **Akrotírion, Kólpos** *var.* Akrotiri Bay. *bay* S Cyprus
218 B3 **Akrotiri Sovereign Base Area** *UK military installation* S Cyprus
238 C6 **Aksai Chin** *Chin.* Aksayqin. *disputed region* China/India
Aksaj *see* Aksay
214 E6 **Aksaray** Aksaray, C Turkey 38°23′N 33°50′E
214 E6 **Aksaray** ◐ *province* C Turkey
195 M3 **Aksarka** Yamalo-Nenetskiy Avtonomnyy Okrug, Russian Federation
226 C3 **Aksay** *var.* Aksaj, *Kaz.* Aqsay. Zapadnyy Kazakhstan, NW Kazakhstan 51°11′N 53°00′E
197 H6 **Aksay** Volgogradskaya Oblast', SW Russian Federation 47°59′N 43°54′E
229 L5 **Ak-say** *var.* Toxkan He. ≈ China/Kyrgyzstan
Aksay/Aksay Kazakzu Zizhixian *see* Boluozhuanjing/Hongliuwan
Aksayqin *see* Aksai Chin
238 D7 **Aksayqin Hu** ◎ NW China
214 D6 **Akşehir** Konya, W Turkey 38°22′N 31°24′E
214 D6 **Akşehir Gölü** ◎ C Turkey
214 D7 **Akseki** Antalya, SW Turkey 37°03′N 31°46′E
193 J8 **Aksenovo-Zilovskoye** Chitinskaya Oblast', S Russian Federation 53°01′N 117°26′E
193 I8 **Aksha** Chitinskaya Oblast', S Russian Federation 50°16′N 113°22′E
227 L5 **Akshatau, Khrebet** ▲▲ E Kazakhstan
229 N4 **Ak-Shyyrak** Issyk-Kul'skaya Oblast', E Kyrgyzstan 41°46′N 78°34′E
Akstafa *see* Ağstafa
238 D4 **Aksu** Xinjiang Uygur Zizhiqu, NW China 41°17′N 80°15′E
227 I3 **Aksu** *Kaz.* Aqsū. Akmola, N Kazakhstan 52°31′N 72°00′E
227 L6 **Aksu** *Kaz.* Aqsū. Almaty, SE Kazakhstan 45°31′N 79°28′E
227 J3 **Aksu** *var.* Jermak, *Kaz.* Ermak; *prev.* Yermak. Pavlodar, NE Kazakhstan 52°03′N 76°55′E
227 L6 **Aksu** *Kaz.* Aqsū. ≈ SE Kazakhstan
227 M4 **Aksuat** *Kaz.* Aqsūat. Vostochnyy Kazakhstan, SE Kazakhstan 48°16′N 83°39′E
227 M5 **Aksuat** *Kaz.* Aqsūat. Vostochnyy Kazakhstan, E Kazakhstan 47°48′N 82°51′E
197 J2 **Aksubayevo** Respublika Tatarstan, W Russian Federation 54°52′N 50°50′E
238 D4 **Aksu He** *Rus.* Sary-Dzhaz. ≈ China/Kyrgyzstan *see also* Sary-Dzhaz
136 E2 **Āksum** Tigray, N Ethiopia 14°06′N 38°42′E
226 G5 **Aktas** *Kaz.* Aqtas. Karaganda, C Kazakhstan 48°03′N 66°21′E
Aktash *see* Oqtosh
229 L5 **Ak-Tash, Gora** ▲ C Kyrgyzstan 40°53′N 74°39′E
227 I4 **Aktau** *Kaz.* Aqtaū. Karaganda, C Kazakhstan 50°13′N 73°06′E
226 B7 **Aktau** *Kaz.* Aqtaū; *prev.* Shevchenko. Mangistau, W Kazakhstan 43°37′N 51°14′E
Aktau, Khrebet *see* Oqtogh, Qatorkŭhi. SW Tajikistan
Aktau, Khrebet *see* Oqtov Tizmasi, C Uzbekistan
Akte *see* Ágion Óros
Ak-Tepe *see* Akdepe
229 M4 **Ak-Terek** Issyk-Kul'skaya Oblast', E Kyrgyzstan 42°14′N 77°46′E
Aktí *see* Ágion Óros
Aktjubinsk/Aktyubinsk *see* Aktobe
238 C5 **Akto** Xinjiang Uygur Zizhiqu, NW China 39°07′N 75°43′E
226 D4 **Aktobe** *Kaz.* Aqtöbe; *prev.* Aktjubinsk, Aktyubinsk. Aktyubinsk, NW Kazakhstan 50°18′N 57°10′E
227 L5 **Aktogay** *Kaz.* Aqtoghay. Vostochnyy Kazakhstan, E Kazakhstan 46°56′N 79°40′E
227 J5 **Aktogay** *Kaz.* Aqtoghay. Zhezkazgan, C Kazakhstan 47°46′N 74°06′E
191 G11 **Aktsyabrski** *Rus.* Oktyabr'skiy; *prev.* Karpilovka. Homyel'skaya Voblasts', SE Belarus 52°38′N 28°53′E
226 E4 **Aktyubinsk** *off.* Aktyubinskaya Oblast', *Kaz.* Aqtöbe Oblysy. ◐ *province* W Kazakhstan
Aktyubinsk *see* Aktobe
229 L4 **Ak-Tyuz** *var.* Aktyuz. Chuyskaya Oblast', N Kyrgyzstan 42°50′N 76°05′E
134 F6 **Akula** Equateur, NW Dem. Rep. Congo 02°21′N 20°13′E
87 N5 **Akumal** Quintana Roo, Mexico
250 C8 **Akune** Kagoshima, Kyūshū, SW Japan 32°00′N 130°12′E
82 F9 **Akun Island** *island* Aleutian Islands, Alaska, USA
Akurdet *see* Ak'ordat
133 J7 **Akure** Ondo, SW Nigeria 07°18′N 05°13′E
152 C2 **Akureyri** Nordhurland Eystra, N Iceland 65°40′N 18°07′W
82 F9 **Akutan** Akutan Island, Alaska, USA 54°08′N 165°47′W
82 F9 **Akutan Island** *island* Aleutian Islands, Alaska, USA
133 K8 **Akwa Ibom** ◐ *state* SE Nigeria
Akyab *see* Sittwe
197 M4 **Ak"yar** Respublika Bashkortostan, W Russian Federation 51°51′N 58°13′E
226 E4 **Akzhar** *prev.* Novorossiyskiy, Novorossiyskoye. Aktyubinsk, NW Kazakhstan 50°14′N 57°57′E
227 M5 **Akzhar** *Kaz.* Aqzhar. Vostochnyy Kazakhstan, E Kazakhstan 47°36′N 83°38′E
154 C6 **Ål** Buskerud, S Norway 60°37′N 08°33′E
191 H11 **Ala** *Rus.* Ola. ≈ SE Belarus
69 H1 **Alabama** *off.* State of Alabama, *also known as* Camellia State, Heart of Dixie, The Cotton State, Yellowhammer State. ◐ *state* S USA
61 J8 **Alabama River** ≈ Alabama, S USA
66 D9 **Alabaster** Alabama, S USA 33°14′N 86°49′W
217 K7 **Al 'Abd Allāh** *var.* Al Abdullah. Al Qādisīyah, S Iraq 32°06′N 45°08′E
217 L9 **Al Abṭīyah** *well* S Iraq
229 J5 **Ala-Buka** Dzhalal-Abadskaya Oblast', W Kyrgyzstan 41°22′N 71°27′E
275 K1 **Alabule** ≈ C Papua New Guinea
214 F5 **Alaca** Çorum, N Turkey 40°10′N 34°52′E
214 F4 **Alaçam** Samsun, N Turkey 41°36′N 35°35′E
Alacant *see* Alicante
69 L4 **Alachua** Florida, SE USA 29°48′N 82°29′W
215 J6 **Aladağlar** ▲▲ W Turkey
214 F7 **Ala Dağları** ▲▲ C Turkey
172 F1 **Alaejos** Castilla y León, Spain 41°19′N 5°13′W
246 D3 **Alag-Erdene** *var.* Manhan. Hövsgöl, N Mongolia 50°05′N 100°01′E
215 K3 **Alagir** Respublika Severnaya Osetiya, SW Russian Federation 43°02′N 44°10′E
176 D6 **Alagna Valsesia** Valle d'Aosta, NW Italy 45°51′N 07°50′E
165 I7 **Alagnon** ≈ C France
110 G7 **Alagoa** Minas Gerais, Brazil 22°10′S 44°38′W
108 I6 **Alagoas** *off.* Estado de Alagoas. ◐ *state* E Brazil
109 H8 **Alagoinhas** Bahia, E Brazil 12°09′S 38°21′W
171 I3 **Alagón** Aragón, NE Spain 41°46′N 01°07′W
170 E5 **Alagón** ≈ W Spain
172 E3 **Alagón** ≈ Extremadura, Spain
153 G8 **Alahärmä** Länsi-Suomi, W Finland 63°15′N 22°50′E
al Ahdar *see* Al Akhḍar
Álaheaieatnu *see* Altaelva
217 M10 **Al Aḥmadī** *var.* Ahmadi. E Kuwait 29°02′N 48°01′E
Al Ain *see* Al 'Ayn
171 M5 **Alaior** *prev.* Alayor. Menorca, Spain, W Mediterranean Sea 39°56′N 04°08′E
229 K6 **Alai Range** *Rus.* Alayskiy Khrebet. ▲▲ Kyrgyzstan/Tajikistan
Alais *see* Alès
221 K6 **Al 'Ajā'iz** E Oman 19°33′N 57°12′E
221 K6 **Al 'Ajā'iz** *oasis* SE Oman
153 H8 **Alajärvi** Länsi-Suomi, W Finland 63°00′N 23°50′E
190 F4 **Alajõe** Ida-Virumaa, NE Estonia 59°00′N 27°26′E
89 H8 **Alajuela** Alajuela, C Costa Rica 10°00′N 84°12′W
88 G7 **Alajuela** *off.* Provincia de Alajuela. ◐ *province* N Costa Rica
82 G6 **Alakanuk** Alaska, USA 62°41′N 164°37′W
220 D2 **Al Akhḍar** *var.* al Ahdar. Tabūk, NW Saudi Arabia 28°04′N 37°13′E
Alaköl *see* Alakol', Ozero
227 L5 **Alakol', Ozero** *Kaz.* Alaköl. ◎ SE Kazakhstan
194 E4 **Alakurtti** Murmanskaya Oblast', NW Russian Federation 66°57′N 30°27′E
82 C2 **Alalākeiki Channel** *var.* Alalakeiki Channel. *channel* Hawaii, USA, C Pacific Ocean
129 H3 **Al 'Alamayn** *var.* El 'Alamein. N Egypt 30°50′N 28°57′E
218 G7 **Al Ālūk** Jordan 32°10′N 35°55′E
217 I1 **Al 'Amādīyah** Dahūk, N Iraq 37°09′N 43°27′E
282 E3 **Alamagan** *island* C Northern Mariana Islands
217 L7 **Al 'Amārah** *var.* Amara. Maysān, E Iraq 31°51′N 47°10′E
136 E3 **Ālamat'ā** Tigray, N Ethiopia 12°22′N 39°32′E
110 B9 **Alambari** São Paulo, Brazil 23°33′S 47°53′W
81 D8 **Alameda** California, USA 35°14′N 119°0′W
80 B3 **Alameda** California, USA 37°46′N 122°15′W
79 L7 **Alameda** New Mexico, SW USA 35°09′N 106°37′W
199 K9 **'Alam el Rûm, Râs** *headland* N Egypt 31°21′N 27°23′E
Alamícamba *see* Alamikamba
89 H5 **Alamikamba** *var.* Alamícamba. Región Autónoma Atlántico Norte, NE Nicaragua 13°26′N 84°09′W
172 G5 **Alamillo** Castilla-La Manacha, Spain 38°41′N 4°47′W
219 G9 **Al Āmirīyah** Jordan 31°34′N 36°05′E
84 B1 **Alamito** Baja California Norte, NE Mexico
84 E4 **Alamito** Sonora, Mexico 29°12′N 110°52′W
70 C6 **Alamito Creek** ≈ Texas, SW USA
86 D1 **Alamitos, Sierra de los** ▲ NE Mexico 26°15′N 102°14′W
86 G5 **Álamo** Veracruz-Llave, C Mexico 20°55′N 97°41′W
78 F5 **Alamo** Nevada, W USA 37°21′N 115°08′W
66 B6 **Alamo** Tennessee, S USA 35°47′N 89°09′W
79 L9 **Alamogordo** New Mexico, SW USA 32°52′N 105°57′W
81 J12 **Alamo Lake** ⊠ Arizona, SW USA
84 F5 **Alamos** Sonora, NW Mexico 26°59′N 108°53′W
79 L5 **Alamosa** Colorado, C USA 37°25′N 105°51′W
153 G10 **Åland** *var.* Aland Islands, *Fin.* Ahvenanmaa. ◐ *province* SW Finland
153 G10 **Åland** *var.* Aland Islands, *Fin.* Ahvenanmaa. *island group* SW Finland
Aland Islands *see* Åland
Aland Sea *see* Ålands Hav
154 J7 **Ålands Hav** *var.* Aland Sea. *strait* Baltic Sea/Gulf of Bothnia
172 E5 **Alange** Extremadura, Spain 38°47′N 6°15′W
89 I9 **Alanje** Chiriquí, SW Panama 08°26′N 82°33′W
70 E2 **Alanreed** Texas, SW USA 35°12′N 100°45′W
214 D8 **Alanya** Antalya, S Turkey 36°32′N 32°02′E
69 K3 **Alapaha River** ≈ Florida/Georgia, SE USA
195 M9 **Alapayevsk** Sverdlovskaya Oblast', C Russian Federation 57°48′N 61°50′E
219 E14 **Al 'Aqabah** *var.* Akaba, Aqaba, 'Aqaba; *anc.* Aelana, Elath. Al 'Aqabah, SW Jordan 29°32′N 35°00′E
219 E14 **Al Aqabah** Jordan 29°31′N 35°00′E
216 B9 **Al 'Aqabah** *off.* Muḥāfaẓat Al 'Aqabah. ◐ *governorate* SW Jordan
Al 'Arabīyah as Su'ūdīyah *see* Saudi Arabia
al Araïch *see* Larache
172 F2 **Alaraz** Castilla y León, Spain 40°45′N 5°17′W
171 H6 **Alarcón** Castilla-La Mancha, C Spain 39°32′N 02°05′W
173 J4 **Alarcón, Embalse de** ⊠ Castilla-La Manacha, Spain
171 H5 **Alarcón, Embalse de** ⊠ C Spain
216 D2 **Al 'Arīmah** *Fr.* Arime. Ḥalab, N Syria 36°27′N 37°41′E
129 J3 **Al 'Arīsh** *var.* El 'Arîsh. NE Egypt 33°00′N 31°00′E
217 N10 **Al Arṭāwīyah** SE Kuwait 28°32′N 48°06′E
220 G3 **Al Arṭāwīyah** Ar Riyāḍ, N Saudi Arabia 26°34′N 45°20′E
260 B8 **Alas** Sumbawa, S Indonesia 08°27′S 117°04′E
Alasca, Golfo de *see* Alaska, Gulf of
214 B6 **Alaşehir** Manisa, W Turkey 38°19′N 28°30′E
216 G4 **Al 'Ashārah** *var.* Ashara. Dayr az Zawr, E Syria 34°51′N 40°36′E
Al Ashkhara *see* Al Ashkharah
221 L5 **Al Ashkharah** *var.* Al Ashkhara. NE Oman 21°47′N 59°30′E
Al 'Aṣimah *see* 'Ammān
83 I4 **Alaska** *off.* State of Alaska, *also known as* Land of the Midnight Sun, The Last Frontier, Seward's Folly; *prev.* Russian America. ◐ *state* NW USA
83 K7 **Alaska, Gulf of** *var.* Golfo de Alasca. *gulf* Canada/USA
83 H8 **Alaska Peninsula** *peninsula* Alaska, USA
287 H1 **Alaska Plain** N Pacific Ocean
83 I5 **Alaska Range** ▲▲ Alaska, USA
258 C3 **Alas, Lae** ≈ Sumatera, NW Indonesia
Al-Asnam *see* Chlef
260 B8 **Alas, Selat** *strait* Nusa Tenggara, C Indonesia
176 D9 **Alassio** Liguria, NW Italy 44°01′N 08°12′E
215 N5 **Älät** *Rus.* Alyat; *prev.* Alyaty-Pristan'. SE Azerbaijan 39°57′N 49°24′E
Alat *see* Olot
217 I8 **Al 'Athāmīn** An Najaf, S Iraq 30°27′N 43°41′E
83 I4 **Alatna River** ≈ Alaska, USA
175 F8 **Alatri** Lazio, C Italy 41°43′N 13°21′E
Alattio *see* Alta
197 I2 **Alatyr'** Chuvashskaya Respublika, W Russian Federation 54°50′N 46°28′E
104 C2 **Alausí** Chimborazo, C Ecuador 02°11′S 78°52′W
171 H2 **Álava** *Basq.* Araba. ◐ *province* País Vasco, N Spain
215 K4 **Alaverdi** N Armenia 41°06′N 44°37′E
Alavo *see* Alavus
152 I7 **Ala-Vuokki** Oulu, E Finland 64°46′N 29°29′E
153 H8 **Alavus** *Swe.* Alavo. Länsi-Suomi, W Finland 62°33′N 23°38′E
Al 'Awābī *see* Awābī
217 H4 **Al 'Awānī** Al Anbār, W Iraq 34°28′N 41°43′E
128 G7 **Al Awaynāt** SE Libya 21°46′N 24°51′E
Al Awaynāt *see* Al 'Uwaynāt
277 H5 **Alawoona** South Australia 34°45′S 140°28′E
Alaykel'/Alay-Kuu *see* Këk-Art
221 J4 **Al 'Ayn** *var.* Al Ain. Abū Ẓaby, E United Arab Emirates 24°13′N 55°44′E
221 J4 **Al 'Ayn** *var.* Al Ain. ✈ Abū Ẓaby, E United Arab Emirates 24°16′N 55°31′E
219 F10 **Al Aynā** Jordan 30°58′N 35°46′E
219 F10 **Al 'Aynā** Al Karak, W Jordan 30°59′N 35°43′E
219 F11 **Al 'Ayn al Bayḍā'** Jordan
219 F11 **Al 'Ayn al Bayḍā'** Aṭ ṭafīlah, C Jordan
Alayor *see* Alaior
Alayskiy Khrebet *see* Alai Range
193 L3 **Alazeya** ≈ NE Russian Federation
217 K6 **Al 'Azīzīyah** *var.* Aziziya. Wāsiṭ, E Iraq 32°54′N 45°05′E
128 C2 **Al 'Azīzīyah** NW Libya 32°32′N 13°01′E
219 I8 **Al Azraq al Janūbī** Az Zarqā', N Jordan 31°49′N 36°48′E
219 I8 **Al Azraq ash Shamālī** Jordan 31°52′N 36°49′E
176 D8 **Alba** *anc.* Alba Pompeia. Piemonte, NW Italy 44°42′N 08°02′E
71 I4 **Alba** Texas, SW USA 32°47′N 95°37′W
188 C7 **Alba** ◐ *county* W Romania
217 H2 **Al Ba'āj** Nīnawá, N Iraq 36°02′N 41°43′E
216 D2 **Al Bāb** Ḥalab, N Syria 36°24′N 37°32′E
188 C7 **Albac** *Hung.* Fehérvölgy; *prev.* Álbák. Alba, SW Romania 46°27′N 22°58′E
171 H6 **Albacete** Castilla-La Mancha, C Spain 39°N 01°52′W
173 J5 **Albacete** ◐ *province* Castilla-La Mancha, C Spain
220 C2 **Al Bad'** Tabūk, NW Saudi Arabia 28°28′N 35°00′E
170 E4 **Alba de Tormes** Castilla-León, N Spain 40°50′N 05°30′W
217 H2 **Al Bādī** Nīnawá, N Iraq 35°57′N 41°37′E
221 J4 **Al Badī'ah** ✈ (Abū Ẓaby) Abū Ẓaby, C United Arab Emirates 24°27′N 54°39′E
221 J5 **Al Badī'ah** *var.* Al Bedei'ah. *spring/well* C United Arab Emirates 23°44′N 53°50′E
155 D10 **Ålbæk** Nordjylland, N Denmark 57°33′N 10°24′E
217 H5 **Al Baghdādī** *var.* Khān al Baghdādī. Al Anbār, SW Iraq 33°60′N 42°50′E
Al Bāha *see* Al Bāḥah
220 E6 **Al Bāḥah** *var.* Al Bāha. Al BāḤah, SW Saudi Arabia 20°01′N 41°29′E
220 E6 **Al Bāḥah** *var.* Minṭaqat al Bāḥah. ◐ *province* W Saudi Arabia
Al Baḥrayn *see* Bahrain
171 I6 **Albaida** País Valenciano, E Spain 38°51′N 00°31′W
218 H7 **Al Bā'ij** Jordan 32°22′N 36°21′E
188 C8 **Alba Iulia** *Ger.* Weissenburg, *Hung.* Gyulafehérvár; *prev.* Bălgrad, Karlsburg, Károly-Fehérvár. Alba, W Romania 46°06′N 23°33′E
Álbák *see* Albac
168 E9 **Albalate de Cinca** Aragón, Spain 41°43′N 0°09′E
173 L1 **Albalate del Arzobispo** Aragón, Spain 41°07′N 0°31′W
218 F7 **Al Balqā'** *off.* Muḥāfaẓat al Balqā', *var.* Balqā'. ◐ *governorate* NW Jordan
62 C2 **Alban** Ontario, S Canada 46°07′N 80°37′W
165 H8 **Alban** Tarn, S France 43°52′N 02°30′E
173 H7 **Albanchez de Ubeda** Andalucía, Spain 37°47′N 3°28′W
59 H6 **Albanel, Lac** ◎ Québec, SE Canada
184 E8 **Albania** *off.* Republic of Albania, *Alb.* Republika e Shqipqërisë, Shqipëria; *prev.* People's Socialist Republic of Albania. ◆ *republic* SE Europe
Albania *see* Aubagne
274 D8 **Albany** Western Australia 35°03′S 117°54′E
69 J3 **Albany** Georgia, SE USA 31°35′N 84°09′W
73 F10 **Albany** Indiana, N USA 40°18′N 85°14′W
66 F5 **Albany** Kentucky, S USA 36°42′N 85°08′W
74 G4 **Albany** Minnesota, N USA 45°39′N 94°33′W
75 G8 **Albany** Missouri, C USA 40°15′N 94°15′W
65 H2 **Albany** *state capital* New York, NE USA 42°39′N 73°45′W
76 B6 **Albany** Oregon, NW USA 44°38′N 123°06′W
70 F4 **Albany** Texas, SW USA 32°44′N 99°18′W
58 E6 **Albany** ≈ Ontario, S Canada
Alba Pompeia *see* Alba
Alba Regia *see* Székesfehérvár
114 B7 **Albarellos** Santa Fe, Argentina 33°14′S 60°38′W
216 D4 **Al Bāridah** *var.* Bāridah. Ḥimṣ, C Syria 34°15′N 37°39′E
217 H7 **Al Barīt** Al Anbār, S Iraq 31°16′N 42°28′E
171 I5 **Albarracín** Aragón, NE Spain 40°24′N 01°25′W
87 H8 **Albarradas** Oaxaca, Mexico 16°55′N 96°20′W
217 M8 **Al Baṣrah** *Eng.* Basra, *hist.* Busra, Bussora. Al Baṣrah, SE Iraq 30°30′N 47°50′E
217 K8 **Al Baṭḥā'** Dhī Qār, SE Iraq 31°06′N 45°54′E
230 A10 **Al Bāṭinah** *var.* Batinah. *coastal region* N Oman
42 D10 **Albatross Plateau** *undersea feature* E Pacific Ocean 10°00′N 103°00′W
Al Batrūn *see* Batroûn
128 F2 **Al Bayḍā'** *var.* Beida. NE Libya 32°46′N 21°43′E
220 G9 **Al Bayḍā'** *var.* Al Beida. SW Yemen 13°58′N 45°38′E
Al Bedei'ah *see* Al Badī'ah
Al Beida *see* Al Bayḍā'
67 J6 **Albemarle** *var.* Albermarle. North Carolina, SE USA 35°21′N 80°12′W
Albemarle Island *see* Isabela, Isla
67 M6 **Albemarle Sound** *inlet* W Atlantic Ocean
176 D9 **Albenga** Liguria, NW Italy 44°04′N 08°13′E
169 L1 **Albens** Rhône-Alpes, France 45°47′N 5°57′E
172 G2 **Alberche** ≈ C Spain
165 I10 **Albères, Chaîne des** *var.* les Albères, Montes Albères. ▲▲ France/Spain
Albères, Montes *see* Albères, Chaîne des
276 E1 **Alberga Creek** *seasonal river* South Australia
172 B2 **Albergaria-a-Velha** Aveiro, N Portugal 40°42′N 08°28′W
171 I6 **Alberic** País Valenciano, E Spain 39°07′N 00°31′W
Albermarle *see* Albemarle
175 I9 **Alberobello** Puglia, SE Italy 40°47′N 17°14′E
165 H2 **Albert** Somme, N France 50°N 02°38′E
54 F7 **Alberta** ◐ *province* SW Canada
52 G7 **Albert Edward Bay** *coastal sea feature* Victoria Island, Nunavut, NW Canada
Albert Edward Nyanza *see* Edward, Lake
114 C10 **Alberti** Buenos Aires, E Argentina 35°03′S 60°15′W
110 D7 **Albertina** Minas Gerais, Brazil 22°12′S 46°37′W
183 G11 **Albertirsa** Pest, C Hungary 47°15′N 19°36′E
163 F9 **Albertkanaal** *canal* N Belgium
134 J7 **Albert, Lake** *var.* Albert Nyanza, Lac Mobutu Sese Seko. ◎ Uganda/Dem. Rep. Congo
74 G6 **Albert Lea** Minnesota, N USA 43°39′N 93°22′W
136 B6 **Albert Nile** ≈ NW Uganda
Albert Nyanza *see* Albert, Lake
141 J4 **Alberton** Gauteng, South Africa 26°14′S 28°08′E
169 L1 **Albertville** Savoie, E France 45°41′N 06°24′E
66 E8 **Albertville** Alabama, S USA 34°16′N 86°12′W
Albertville *see* Kalemie
165 H8 **Albi** *anc.* Albiga. Tarn, S France 43°55′N 02°09′E
75 H8 **Albia** Iowa, C USA 41°01′N 92°48′W
Albiga *see* Albi
103 M5 **Albina** Marowijne, NE Suriname 05°29′N 54°08′W
135 B14 **Albina, Ponta** *headland* SW Angola 15°52′S 11°45′E
73 D12 **Albion** Illinois, N USA 38°22′N 88°03′W
73 F9 **Albion** Indiana, N USA 41°23′N 85°26′W
74 E7 **Albion** Nebraska, C USA 41°41′N 98°00′W
62 E5 **Albion** New York, NE USA 43°13′N 78°09′W
62 C7 **Albion** Pennsylvania, NE USA 41°52′N 80°18′W
218 G2 **Al Biqa** ◐ *governorate* Lebanon
Al Biqā' *see* El Beqaa
220 D2 **Al Bi'r** *var.* Bi'r Ibn Hirmās. Tabūk, NW Saudi Arabia 28°52′N 36°16′E
220 E7 **Al Birk** Makkah, SW Saudi Arabia 18°13′N 41°36′E
218 I7 **Al Bishrīyah** Al Mafraq, N Jordan
114 F4 **Albisu** Salto, Uruguay 31°20′S 57°48′W
220 G5 **Al Biyāḍ** *desert* C Saudi Arabia
162 E7 **Alblasserdam** Zuid-Holland, SW Netherlands 51°52′N 04°40′E
173 M2 **Albocàcer** Valenciana, Spain 40°21′N 0°01′E
Albocácer *see* Albocàsser
171 J5 **Albocàsser** *Cast.* Albocácer. País Valenciano, E Spain 40°21′N 00°01′E
Albona *see* Labin
170 G10 **Alborán, Isla de** *island* S Spain
Alborán, Mar de *see* Alboran Sea
170 G10 **Alboran Sea** *Sp.* Mar de Alborán. *sea* SW Mediterranean Sea
173 K4 **Alborea** Castilla-La Manacha, Spain 39°17′N 1°23′W
Ålborg *see* Aalborg
155 E11 **Ålborg Bugt** *var.* Aalborg Bugt. *bay* N Denmark
Ålborg-Nørresundby *see* Aalborg
222 F3 **Alborz, Reshteh-ye Kūhhā-ye** *Eng.* Elburz Mountains. ▲▲ N Iran
171 H8 **Albox** Andalucía, S Spain 37°22′N 02°08′W
179 D12 **Albstadt** Baden-Württemberg, SW Germany 48°13′N 09°01′E
172 B8 **Albufeira** Beja, S Portugal 37°05′N 08°15′W
216 G4 **Ālbū Gharz, Sabkhat** ◎ W Iraq
173 K7 **Albujón** Murcia, Spain 37°43′N 1°03′W
170 G9 **Albuñol** Andalucía, S Spain 36°48′N 03°11′W
79 L7 **Albuquerque** New Mexico, SW USA 35°05′N 106°38′W
221 J4 **Al Buraymī** *var.* Buraimi. N Oman 24°16′N 55°48′E
221 J4 **Al Buraymī** *var.* Buraimi. *spring/well* Oman/United Arab Emirates 24°27′N 55°33′E
Al Burayqah *see* Marsá al Burayqah
Alburgum *see* Aalborg
170 D6 **Alburquerque** Extremadura, W Spain 39°12′N 07°00′W
277 J6 **Albury** New South Wales, SE Australia 36°03′S 146°53′E
277 J6 **Albury-Wodonga** New South Wales/Victoria, SE Australia 36°04′S 146°58′E
218 J2 **Al Buṣayn** Syria 34°09′N 37°39′E
221 I8 **Al Buzūn** SE Yemen 15°40′N 50°53′E
154 G4 **Alby** Västernorrland, C Sweden 62°30′N 15°25′E
Albyn, Glen *see* Mor, Glen
172 B6 **Alcácer do Sal** Setúbal, W Portugal 38°22′N 08°29′W
172 C6 **Alcàçovas** Évora, Portugal 38°24′N 8°09′W
Alcalá de Chisvert/Alcalá de Chivert *see* Alcalá de Xivert
170 E8 **Alcalá de Guadaira** Andalucía, S Spain 37°20′N 05°50′W
170 G5 **Alcalá de Henares** *Ar.* Alkal'a; *anc.* Complutum. Madrid, C Spain 40°28′N 03°22′W
173 L2 **Alcalà de la Selva** Aragón, Spain 40°22′N 0°42′W
170 E9 **Alcalá de los Gazules** Andalucía, S Spain 36°29′N 05°43′W
173 M2 **Alcalá de Xivert** *var.* Alcalá de Chisvert, *Cast.* Alcalá de Chivert. País Valenciano, E Spain 40°19′N 00°13′E
170 G8 **Alcalá La Real** Andalucía, S Spain 37°28′N 03°55′W
175 E12 **Alcamo** Sicilia, Italy, C Mediterranean Sea 37°58′N 12°58′E
171 I3 **Alcanadre** ≈ NE Spain
171 J4 **Alcanar** Cataluña, NE Spain 40°33′N 00°28′E
170 E3 **Alcañices** Castilla-León, N Spain 41°41′N 06°21′W
171 I4 **Alcañiz** Aragón, NE Spain 41°03′N 00°09′W
170 D5 **Alcántara** Extremadura, W Spain 39°42′N 06°54′W
170 E5 **Alcántara, Embalse de** ⊠ W Spain
171 I7 **Alcantarilla** Murcia, SE Spain 37°59′N 01°12′W
172 G6 **Alcaracejos** Andalucía, Spain 38°23′N 4°58′W
114 C4 **Alcaraz** Entre Ríos, Argentina 31°28′S 59°36′W
171 H7 **Alcaraz** Castilla-La Mancha, C Spain 38°40′N 02°29′W
171 H7 **Alcaraz, Sierra de** ▲▲ C Spain
173 J5 **Alcaraz, Sierra de** ▲▲ Castilla-La Manacha, Spain
172 C3 **Alcaria** Castelo Branco, Portugal 40°12′N 7°31′W
172 B4 **Alcaria** Leiria, Portugal 39°34′N 8°47′W
170 D7 **Alcarrache** ≈ SW Spain
171 J3 **Alcarràs** Cataluña, NE Spain 41°34′N 00°31′E
173 I2 **Alcarria, Pàramos de la** *upland* Castilla-La Manacha, Spain
170 F8 **Alcaudete** Andalucía, S Spain 37°35′N 04°05′W
172 G3 **Alcaudete de la Jaya** Castilla-La Manacha, Spain 39°47′N 4°52′W
Alcázar *see* Ksar-el-Kebir
170 G6 **Alcázar de San Juan** *anc.* Alce. Castilla-La Mancha, C Spain 39°24′N 03°12′W
Alcazarquivir *see* Ksar-el-Kebir
Alce *see* Alcázar de San Juan
105 A9 **Alcebo, Volcán** ⛰ Galapagos Islands, Ecuador, E Pacific Ocean 0°25′S 91°06′W
217 L8 **Al Chabā'ish** *var.* Al Kaba'ish. Dhī Qār, SE Iraq 30°58′N 47°02′E
189 M5 **Alchevs'k** *prev.* Kommunarsk, Voroshilovsk. Luhans'ka Oblast', E Ukraine 48°29′N 38°52′E
Alcira *see* Alzira
66 G6 **Alcoa** Tennessee, S USA 35°47′N 83°58′W
172 B4 **Alcobaça** Leiria, C Portugal 39°32′N 08°59′W
170 G5 **Alcobendas** Madrid, C Spain 40°32′N 03°38′W
173 I2 **Alcocer** Castilla-La Manacha, Spain 40°28′N 2°36′W
Alcoi *see* Alcoy
172 G7 **Alcolea** Andalucía, Spain 37°56′N 4°40′W
171 H4 **Alcolea del Pinar** Castilla-La Mancha, C Spain 41°02′N 02°28′W
170 D7 **Alconchel** Extremadura, W Spain 38°31′N 07°04′W
173 L3 **Alcora** Valenciana, Spain 40°04′N 0°12′W
Alcora *see* L'Alcora
170 G5 **Alcorcón** Madrid, C Spain 40°20′N 03°52′W
171 I4 **Alcorisa** Aragón, NE Spain 40°53′N 00°23′W
114 B7 **Alcorta** Santa Fe, C Argentina 33°32′S 61°07′W
172 C7 **Alcoutim** Faro, S Portugal 37°28′N 07°29′W
77 L8 **Alcova** Wyoming, C USA 42°33′N 106°40′W
168 F10 **Alcover** Cataluña, Spain 41°16′N 1°10′E
171 I7 **Alcoy** *Cat.* Alcoi. País Valenciano, E Spain 38°42′N 00°29′W
168 D9 **Alcubierre** Aragón, Spain 41°48′N 0°27′W
171 L5 **Alcúdia** Mallorca, Spain, W Mediterranean Sea 39°51′N 03°06′E
171 L5 **Alcúdia, Badia d'** *bay* Mallorca, Spain, W Mediterranean Sea
289 C8 **Aldabra Group** *island group* SW Seychelles
217 J6 **Al Daghghārah** Bābil, C Iraq 32°10′N 44°57′E
85 H4 **Aldama** Chihuahua, N Mexico 28°50′N 105°52′W
86 G3 **Aldama** Tamaulipas, C Mexico 22°54′N 98°05′W
193 J7 **Aldan** Respublika Sakha (Yakutiya), NE Russian Federation 58°31′N 125°15′E
193 K6 **Aldan** ≈ NE Russian Federation
114 B6 **Aldao** Santa Fe, Argentina 32°43′S 60°49′W
Aldar *see* Aldarhaan
al Dar al Baida *see* Rabat
239 I1 **Aldarhaan** *var.* Aldar. Dzavhan, W Mongolia 47°43′N 96°36′E
159 M8 **Aldbrough** N England, United Kingdom 53°50′N 00°08′W
161 M4 **Alde** ≈ United Kingdom
172 G3 **Aldea del Fresno** Madrid, Spain 40°19′N 4°12′W
114 B5 **Aldea María Luisa** Entre Ríos, Argentina 31°53′S 60°23′W
114 E4 **Aldea San Gregorio** Entre Ríos, Argentina 31°43′S 58°16′W
114 E6 **Aldea San Juan** Entre Ríos, Argentina 32°42′S 58°46′W
114 D5 **Aldea San Simón** Entre Ríos, Argentina 32°25′S 59°31′W
161 M4 **Aldeburgh** E England, United Kingdom 52°12′N 01°36′E
171 H3 **Aldehuela de Calatañazor** Castilla-León, N Spain 41°42′N 02°46′W
Aldeia Nova *see* Aldeia Nova de São Bento
172 C7 **Aldeia Nova de São Bento** *var.* Aldeia Nova. Beja, S Portugal 37°55′N 07°24′W
74 G6 **Alden** Minnesota, N USA 43°40′N 93°34′W
64 B1 **Alden** New York, USA 42°54′N 78°30′W
181 B9 **Aldenhoven** Nordrhein-Westfalen, Germany 6°17′N 50°54′E
161 J6 **Aldermaston** United Kingdom 51°23′N 1°09′W
278 H4 **Aldermen Islands, The** *island group* N New Zealand
166 B3 **Alderney** *island* Channel Islands
161 J7 **Aldershot** S England, United Kingdom 51°15′N 00°47′W
67 I4 **Alderson** West Virginia, NE USA 37°43′N 80°38′W
160 G2 **Aldford** W England, United Kingdom 53°08′N 02°53′W
159 I10 **Aldford** W England, United Kingdom 53°08′N 02°53′W
Al Dhaid *see* Adh Dhayd
161 I5 **Aldsworth** United Kingdom 51°47′N 1°46′W
73 B9 **Aledo** Illinois, N USA 41°12′N 90°45′W
132 C3 **Aleg** Brakna, SW Mauritania 17°03′N 13°53′W
170 C9 **Alegranza** *island* Islas Canarias, Spain, NE Atlantic Ocean
79 K8 **Alegres Mountain** ▲ New Mexico, SW USA 34°09′N 108°11′W
115 I1 **Alegrete** Rio Grande do Sul, S Brazil 29°46′S 55°46′W
172 D4 **Alegrete** Portalegre, Portugal 39°14′N 7°19′W
115 L4 **Alegrias** Rio Grande do Sul, Brazil 31°50′S 53°25′W
114 C1 **Alejandra** Santa Fe, C Argentina 29°54′S 59°50′W
115 I8 **Alejandro Gallinal** Florida, Uruguay 33°49′S 55°33′W
287 K8 **Alejandro Selkirk, Isla** *island* Islas Juan Fernández, Chile, E Pacific Ocean
194 E8 **Alekhovshchina** Leningradskaya Oblast', NW Russian Federation 60°22′N 33°57′E
83 H7 **Aleknagik** Alaska, USA 59°16′N 158°37′W
Aleksandriya *see* Oleksandriya
Aleksandropol' *see* Gyumri
196 G1 **Aleksandrov** Vladimirskaya Oblast', W Russian Federation 56°24′N 38°42′E
184 G5 **Aleksandrovac** Serbia, C Serbia 43°28′N 21°05′E
197 J5 **Aleksandrov Gay** Saratovskaya Oblast', W Russian Federation 50°08′N 48°34′E
197 L3 **Aleksandrovka** Orenburgskaya Oblast', W Russian Federation 52°47′N 54°14′E
Aleksandrovka *see* Oleksandrivka
185 J5 **Aleksandrovo** Lovech, N Bulgaria 43°16′N 24°53′E
195 K8 **Aleksandrovsk** Permskaya Oblast', NW Russian Federation 59°12′N 57°27′E
Aleksandrovsk *see* Zaporizhzhya
197 H8 **Aleksandrovskoye** Stavropol'skiy Kray, SW Russian Federation 44°43′N 42°56′E
193 L7 **Aleksandrovsk-Sakhalinskiy** Ostrov Sakhalin, Sakhalinskaya Oblast', SE Russian Federation 50°55′N 142°12′E
182 F5 **Aleksandrów Kujawski** Kujawskio-pormorskie, C Poland 52°52′N 18°40′E
182 F6 **Aleksandrów Łódzki** Łódzkie, C Poland 51°49′N 19°19′E
Alekseevka *see* Akkol', Akmola, Kazakhstan
Alekseevka *see* Terekty
227 H2 **Alekseyevka** *Kaz.* Alekseevka. Akmola, N Kazakhstan 53°32′N 69°30′E
196 G5 **Alekseyevka** Belgorodskaya, W Russian Federation 50°35′N 38°41′E
197 K3 **Alekseyevka** Samarskaya Oblast', W Russian Federation 52°37′N 51°20′E
Alekseyevka *see* Akkol', Akmola, Kazakhstan
Alekseyevka *see* Terekty, Vostochnyy Kazakhstan, Kazakhstan
193 I7 **Alekseyevsk** Irkutskaya Oblast', C Russian Federation 57°46′N 108°07′E
197 J2 **Alekseyevskoye** Respublika Tatarstan, W Russian Federation 55°18′N 50°11′E
196 F2 **Aleksin** Tul'skaya Oblast', W Russian Federation 54°30′N 37°08′E
185 H5 **Aleksinac** Serbia, SE Serbia 43°33′N 21°43′E
284 C9 **Alele** Île Uvea, E Wallis and Futuna 13°14′S 176°09′W
155 H11 **Ålem** Kalmar, S Sweden 56°57′N 16°25′E
187 M2 **Alemdar** İstanbul, NW Turkey 41°03′N 29°14′E
111 J6 **Alem Parahyba** Minas Gerais, Brazil 21°52′S 42°41′W
164 G3 **Alençon** Orne, N France 48°26′N 00°04′E
107 J2 **Alenquer** Pará, NE Brazil 01°58′S 54°45′W
82 D2 **'Alenuihaha Channel** *var.* Alenuihaha Channel. *channel* Hawai'i, USA, C Pacific Ocean
Alep/Aleppo *see* Ḥalab
175 C8 **Aléria** Corse, France, C Mediterranean Sea 42°06′N 09°29′E
295 J6 **Alert** Ellesmere Island, Nunavut, N Canada 82°28′N 62°13′W
53 H1 **Alert Point** *headland* Nunavut, N Canada
165 I8 **Alès** *prev.* Alais. Gard, S France 44°08′N 04°05′E
188 B6 **Aleşd** *Hung.* Élesd. Bihor, SW Romania 47°03′N 22°22′E
176 E7 **Alessandria** *Fr.* Alexandrie. Piemonte, N Italy 44°54′N 08°37′E
Ålestrup *see* Aalestrup
154 B4 **Ålesund** Møre og Romsdal, S Norway 62°28′N 06°11′E
174 B3 **Aletschhorn** ▲ SW Switzerland 46°33′N 08°01′E
294 C6 **Aleutian Basin** *undersea feature* Bering Sea 57°00′N 177°00′E
82 D10 **Aleutian Islands** *island group* Alaska, USA
83 H8 **Aleutian Range** ▲▲ Alaska, USA
42 A3 **Aleutian Trench** *undersea feature* S Bering Sea 57°00′N 177°00′W
193 L6 **Alevina, Mys** *cape* E Russian Federation
74 A2 **Alexander** North Dakota, N USA 47°48′N 103°38′W
83 L8 **Alexander Archipelago** *island group* Alaska, USA
Alexanderbaai *see* Alexander Bay
140 C6 **Alexander Bay** *Afr.* Alexanderbaai. Northern Cape, W South Africa 28°40′S 16°30′E
52 G7 **Alexander, Cape** *headland* Nunavut, N Canada
69 H1 **Alexander City** Alabama, S USA 32°56′N 85°57′W
292 F4 **Alexander Island** *island* Antarctica
Alexander Range *see* Kirghiz Range
277 J7 **Alexandra** Victoria, SE Australia 37°12′S 145°43′E
278 C11 **Alexandra** Otago, South Island, New Zealand 45°15′S 169°25′E
186 G3 **Alexándreia** *var.* Alexándria. Kentrikí Makedonía, N Greece 40°38′N 22°27′E
Alexandretta *see* İskenderun
Alexandretta, Gulf of *see* İskenderun Körfezi
62 G3 **Alexandria** Ontario, SE Canada 45°19′N 74°37′W
129 H3 **Alexandria** *Ar.* Al Iskandarīyah. N Egypt 31°07′N 29°51′E
90 E8 **Alexandria** C Jamaica 18°18′N 77°21′W
188 D10 **Alexandria** Teleorman, S Romania 43°58′N 25°18′E
158 G3 **Alexandria** United Kingdom 55°59′N 4°36′W
73 F10 **Alexandria** Indiana, N USA 40°15′N 85°40′W
66 F3 **Alexandria** Kentucky, S USA 38°59′N 84°22′W
68 C3 **Alexandria** Louisiana, S USA 31°19′N 92°27′W
74 F4 **Alexandria** Minnesota, N USA 45°54′N 95°22′W
74 E6 **Alexandria** South Dakota, N USA 43°39′N 97°46′W
64 C10 **Alexandria** Virginia, NE USA 38°49′N 77°06′W
Alexándria *see* Alexándreia
62 F4 **Alexandria Bay** New York, NE USA 44°20′N 75°54′W
Alexandrie *see* Alessandria
276 G6 **Alexandrina, Lake** ◎ South Australia
187 J2 **Alexandroúpoli** *var.* Alexandroúpolis, *Turk.* Dedeagaç, Dedeagach. Anatolikí Makedonía kai Thráki, NE Greece 40°52′N 25°53′E
Alexandroúpolis *see* Alexandroúpoli
56 D6 **Alexis Creek** British Columbia, SW Canada 52°06′N 123°25′W
192 F8 **Aleysk** Altayskiy Kray, S Russian Federation 52°32′N 82°46′E
217 I5 **Al Fallūjah** *var.* Falluja. Al Anbār, C Iraq 33°21′N 43°46′E
173 K2 **Alfambra** Aragón, Spain 40°33′N 1°02′W
171 I5 **Alfambra** ≈ E Spain
Al Faqa *see* Faq'
221 H8 **Al Farḍah** C Yemen 14°51′N 48°33′E
172 A5 **Alfarim** Setúbal, Portugal 38°28′N 9°10′W
171 H3 **Alfaro** La Rioja, N Spain 42°13′N 01°45′W
171 J3 **Alfarràs** Cataluña, NE Spain 41°50′N 00°34′E
Al Fāshir *see* El Fasher
129 I4 **Al Fashn** *var.* El Fashn. C Egypt 28°49′N 30°54′E
185 L4 **Alfatar** Silistra, NE Bulgaria 43°56′N 27°17′E
217 I3 **Al Fatḥah** Ṣalāḥ ad Dīn, C Iraq 35°06′N 43°34′E
217 H2 **Al Fatsī** Nīnawá, N Iraq 36°04′N 42°39′E
221 H2 **Al Fāw** *var.* Fao. Al Baṣrah, SE Iraq 29°55′N 48°26′E
129 I3 **Al Fayyūm** *var.* El Faiyûm. N Egypt 29°19′N 30°50′E
El Faiyûm *see* Al Fayyūm
186 F7 **Alfeiós** *prev.* Alfiós; *anc.* Alpheius, Alpheus. ≈ S Greece
180 H7 **Alfeld** Niedersachsen, C Germany 51°58′N 09°49′E
110 E5 **Alfenas** Minas Gerais, Brazil 21°26′S 45°57′W
180 E5 **Alfhausen** Niedersachsen, Germany 7°57′N 52°30′E
Alfiós *see* Alfeiós
Alföld *see* Great Hungarian Plain
63 J5 **Alfred** Maine, NE USA 43°29′N 70°44′W
64 B2 **Alfred** New York, NE USA 42°15′N 77°47′W
111 L4 **Alfredo Chavez** Espírito Santo, Brazil 20°38′S 40°45′W

◆ Country
● Country Capital
◇ Dependent Territory
○ Dependent Territory Capital
◐ Administrative Regions
✈ International Airport
▲ Mountain
▲▲ Mountain Range
⛰ Volcano
≈ River
◎ Lake
⊠ Reservoir

◆ Country   ◇ Dependent Territory   ◉ Administrative Regions   ▲ Mountain   ▲ Volcano   ◎ Lake
● Country Capital   ○ Dependent Territory Capital   ✈ International Airport   ▲ Mountain Range   ♒ River   ⬤ Reservoir

◆ Country　　◇ Dependent Territory　　✕ Administrative Regions　　▲ Mountain　　⊚ Lake
● Country Capital　　○ Dependent Territory Capital　　✕ International Airport　　▲ Mountain Range　　≈ River　　◼ Reservoir

Ban Lam Phai - Bat'umi

257 F11 **Ban Lam Phai** Songkhla, SW Thailand 06°43′N 100°57′E
Ban Mae Sot *see* Mae Sot
Ban Mae Suai *see* Mae Suai
Ban Mak Khaeng *see* Udon Thani
256 C3 **Banmauk** Sagaing, N Myanmar (Burma) 24°26′N 95°54′E
243 K6 **Banmian** Fujian, SE China 26°03′N 118°08′E
Banmo *see* Bhamo
256 H7 **Ban Mun-Houamuang** S Laos 15°11′N 106°44′E
158 D7 **Bann** ≈ United Kingdom
157 D8 **Bann** *var.* Lower Bann, Upper Bann. ≈ N Northern Ireland, United Kingdom
256 H7 **Ban Nadou** Salavan, S Laos 15°51′N 105°38′E
256 H7 **Ban Nakala** Savannakhét, S Laos 16°14′N 105°09′E
256 F6 **Ban Nakha** Viangchan, C Laos 18°13′N 102°29′E
256 H6 **Ban Nakham** Khammouan, S Laos 17°10′N 105°25′E
166 A7 **Bannalec** Bretagne, France 47°56′N 3°42′W
256 F6 **Ban Namoun** Xaignabouli, N Laos 18°40′N 101°34′E
257 F12 **Ban Nang Sata** Yala, SW Thailand 06°15′N 101°13′E
257 E10 **Ban Na San** Surat Thani, SW Thailand 08°53′N 99°17′E
256 G5 **Ban Nasi** Xiangkhoang, N Laos 19°37′N 103°33′E
90 F2 **Bannerman Town** Eleuthera Island, C Bahamas 24°38′N 76°09′W
81 F11 **Banning** California, W USA 33°55′N 116°52′W
Banningville *see* Bandundu
159 H3 **Bannockburn** United Kingdom 56°05′N 3°53′W
256 H7 **Ban Nongsim** Champasak, S Laos 14°45′N 106°00′E
231 H4 **Bannu** *prev.* Edwardesabad. North-West Frontier Province, NW Pakistan 33°00′N 70°36′E
Bañolas *see* Banyoles
169 H8 **Bañoles** Cataluña, Spain 42°07′N 2°46′E
169 K5 **Banon** Provence-Alpes-Côte d'Azur, France 44°02′N 5°38′E
104 C2 **Baños** Tungurahua, C Ecuador 01°26′S 78°24′W
172 E2 **Baños** Extremadura, Spain 40°19′N 5°51′W
Bánovce *see* Bánovce nad Bebravou
183 F10 **Bánovce nad Bebravou** *var.* Bánovce, *Hung.* Bán. Trenčiansky Kraj, W Slovakia 48°43′N 18°15′E
184 E4 **Banovići** ◈ Federacija Bosna I Hercegovina, E Bosnia and Herzegovina
Banow *see* Andarāb
Ban Pak Phanang *see* Pak Phanang
256 E6 **Ban Pan Nua** Lampang, NW Thailand 18°51′N 99°57′E
256 F7 **Ban Phai** Khon Kaen, E Thailand 16°00′N 102°42′E
256 H6 **Ban Phou A Douk** Khammouan, C Laos 17°12′N 106°07′E
256 F6 **Ban Phu** Uthai Thani, W Thailand
257 E8 **Ban Pong** Ratchaburi, W Thailand 13°49′N 99°53′E
284 D2 **Banraeaba** Tarawa, W Kiribati 01°20′N 173°02′E
257 E8 **Ban Sai Yok** Kanchanaburi, W Thailand 14°24′N 98°54′E
Ban Sattahip/Ban Sattahipp *see* Sattahip
Ban Sichon *see* Sichon
Ban Si Racha *see* Siracha
183 F10 **Banská Bystrica** *Ger.* Neusohl, *Hung.* Besztercebánya. Banskobystricky Kraj, C Slovakia 48°46′N 19°08′E
183 F10 **Banskobystrický Kraj** ◈ *region* C Slovakia
256 G6 **Ban Sôppheung** Bolikhamxai, C Laos 18°33′N 104°18′E
Ban Sop Prap *see* Sop Prap
161 K6 **Banstead** United Kingdom 51°19′N 0°10′W
232 D8 **Bānswāra** Rājasthān, N India 23°32′N 74°28′E
245 K9 **Bantaji** Jiangsu, E China 32°41′N 118°35′E
257 E10 **Ban Ta Khun** Surat Thani, SW Thailand 08°53′N 98°52′E
Ban Takua Pa *see* Takua Pa
256 H6 **Ban Talak** Khammouan, C Laos 17°33′N 105°40′E
133 I7 **Bantè** W Benin 08°25′N 01°58′E
258 F8 **Banten** *off.* Propinsi Banten. ◈ *province* W Indonesia
Propinsi Banten *see* Banten
256 G6 **Ban Thabôk** Bolikhamxai, C Laos 18°21′N 103°12′E
Bantoel *see* Bantul
256 H7 **Ban Tôp** Savannakhét, S Laos 16°07′N 106°07′E
157 B11 **Bantry** *Ir.* Beanntraí. Cork, SW Ireland 51°41′N 09°27′W
157 A11 **Bantry Bay** *Ir.* Bá Bheanntraí. *bay* SW Ireland
259 H9 **Bantul** *prev.* Bantoel. Jawa, C Indonesia 07°56′S 110°21′E
235 D8 **Bantvāl** *var.* Bantwāl. Karnātaka, E India 12°57′N 75°04′E
Bantwāl *see* Bantvāl
185 M6 **Banya** Burgas, E Bulgaria 42°46′N 27°49′E
258 B4 **Banyak, Kepulauan** *prev.* Kepulauan Banjak. *island group* NW Indonesia
171 J4 **Banya, La** *headland* E Spain 40°34′N 00°37′E
134 B5 **Banyo** Adamaoua, NW Cameroon 06°47′N 11°50′E
171 L3 **Banyoles** *var.* Bañolas. Cataluña, NE Spain 42°07′N 02°46′E
257 E11 **Ban Yong Sata** Trang, SW Thailand 07°09′N 99°42′E
169 H7 **Banyuls-sur-Mer** Languedoc-Roussillon, France 42°29′N 3°08′E
259 J9 **Banyuwangi** *var.* Banjuwangi; *prev.* Banjoewangi. Jawa, S Indonesia 08°12′S 114°22′E
293 L8 **Banzare Coast** *physical region* Antarctica
289 F13 **Banzare Seamounts** *undersea feature* S Indian Ocean
Banzart *see* Bizerte
245 I1 **Baochang** *var.* Taibus Qi. Nei Mongol Zizhiqu, N China 41°55′N 115°22′E
245 J3 **Baodi** Tianjin Shi, NE China 39°43′N 117°18′E
245 I4 **Baoding** *var.* Pao-ting; *prev.* Tsingyuan. Hebei, E China 38°47′N 115°30′E
Baoebaoe *see* Baubau
Baoi, Oileán *see* Dursey Island
244 D8 **Baoji** *var.* Pao-chi, Paoki. Shaanxi, C China 34°23′N 107°16′E
242 E4 **Baojing** Hunan, C China 28°43′N 109°37′E
242 F1 **Baokang** Hubei, China 31°31′N 111°10′E
242 B9 **Bao Lac** Cao Bang, N Vietnam 22°57′N 105°40′E
281 I1 **Baolo** Santa Isabel, N Solomon Islands 07°41′S 158°47′E
257 I9 **Bao Lôc** Lâm Đông, S Vietnam 11°33′N 107°48′E
247 N4 **Baoqing** Heilongjiang, NE China 46°15′N 132°12′E
Baoqing *see* Shaoyang
134 D5 **Baoro** Nana-Mambéré, W Central African Republic 05°40′N 16°00′E
240 B6 **Baoshan** *var.* Pao-shan. Yunnan, SW China 25°05′N 99°07′E
244 F2 **Baotou** *var.* Pao-t'ou, Paotow. Nei Mongol Zizhiqu, N China 40°38′N 109°59′E
132 E6 **Baoulé** ≈ S Mali
132 E5 **Baoulé** ≈ W Mali
Bao Yèn *see* Phô Rang
245 L8 **Baoying** Jiangsu, China 33°08′N 119°12′E
165 I2 **Bapaume** Pas-de-Calais, N France 50°06′N 02°50′E
62 E3 **Baptiste Lake** ◎ Ontario, SE Canada
Bapu *see* Meigu
218 E7 **Bāqa el-Gharbīya** Israel 32°24′N 35°02′E
Baqanas *see* Bakanas
Baqbaqty *see* Bakbakty
239 H8 **Baqên** *var.* Dartang. Xizang Zizhiqu, W China 31°50′N 94°08′E
216 B9 **Bāqir, Jabal** ▲▲ S Jordan
243 I5 **Baqiu** Jiangxi, SE China 27°33′N 115°10′E
217 J5 **Ba'qūbah** *var.* Qubba. Diyālá, C Iraq 33°45′N 44°40′E
112 B4 **Baquedano** Antofagasta, N Chile 23°20′S 69°50′W
Baquerizo Moreno *see* Puerto Baquerizo Moreno
184 E7 **Bar** *It.* Antivari. S Montenegro 42°02′N 19°09′E
188 F4 **Bar** Vinnyts'ka Oblast', C Ukraine 49°05′N 27°40′E
136 A2 **Bara** Northern Kordofan, C Sudan 13°42′N 30°21′E
136 G7 **Baraawe** *It.* Brava. Shabeellaha Hoose, S Somalia 01°10′N 43°59′E
232 G6 **Bāra Banki** Uttar Pradesh, N India 26°56′N 81°11′E
192 F7 **Barabinsk** Novosibirskaya Oblast', C Russian Federation 55°19′N 78°01′E
72 C7 **Baraboo** Wisconsin, N USA 43°27′N 89°45′W
72 C7 **Baraboo Range** *hill range* Wisconsin, N USA
Baracaldo *see* San Vicente de Barakaldo
90 F5 **Baracoa** Guantánamo, E Cuba 20°23′N 74°31′W
114 D8 **Baradero** Buenos Aires, E Argentina 33°50′S 59°30′W
277 K3 **Baradine** New South Wales, SE Australia 30°55′S 149°03′E
Baraf Daja Islands *see* Damar, Kepulauan
234 H4 **Baragarh** *var.* Bargarh. Orissa, E India 21°25′N 83°35′E
136 D7 **Baragoi** Rift Valley, W Kenya 01°39′N 36°46′E
91 H6 **Barahona** SW Dominican Republic 18°13′N 71°07′W
233 L7 **Barail Range** ▲▲ NE India
136 D1 **Baraka** *var.* Baraka, *Ar.* Khawr Barakah. *seasonal river* Eritrea/Sudan
Baraka *see* Baraka
136 C2 **Barakat** Gezira, C Sudan 14°18′N 33°32′E
Barakī *see* Barakī Barak
230 G4 **Barakī Barak** *var.* Barakī, Baraki Rajan. Lowgar, E Afghanistan 33°58′N 68°58′E
Baraki Rajan *see* Barakī Barak
141 H8 **Barakke** Eastern Cape, South Africa 32°23′S 24°51′E
234 I3 **Bārākot** Orissa, E India 21°35′N 85°00′E
Baram *see* Baram, Batang
103 J4 **Barama River** ≈ N Guyana
234 D5 **Bārāmati** Mahārāshtra, W India 18°12′N 74°39′E
259 J3 **Baram, Batang** *var.* Baram, Barram. ≈ East Malaysia
232 D2 **Bāramūla** Jammu and Kashmir, NW India 34°15′N 74°24′E
191 H9 **Baran'** Vitsyebskaya Voblasts', NE Belarus 54°29′N 30°18′E
232 E7 **Bārān** Rājasthān, N India 25°08′N 76°32′E
217 K3 **Barānān, Shākh-i** ▲▲ E Iraq
191 E10 **Baranavichy** *Pol.* Baranowicze, *Rus.* Baranovichi. Brestskaya Voblasts', SW Belarus 53°08′N 26°02′E
195 L9 **Baranchinskiy** Sverdlovskaya Oblast', Russian Federation
193 M3 **Baranikha** Chukotskiy Avtonomnyy Okrug, NE Russian Federation 68°29′N 168°13′E
188 F3 **Baranivka** Zhytomyrs'ka Oblast', N Ukraine 50°16′N 27°40′E
83 L7 **Baranof Island** *island* Alexander Archipelago, Alaska, USA
Baranovichi/Baranowicze *see* Baranavichy
183 H8 **Baranów Sandomierski** Podkarpackie, SE Poland 50°28′N 21°31′E
183 F13 **Baranya** *off.* Baranya Megye. ◈ *county* S Hungary
Baranya Megye *see* Baranya
111 H3 **Barão de Cocais** Minas Gerais, Brazil 19°56′S 43°28′W
115 N2 **Barão do Triunfo** Rio Grande do Sul, Brazil 30°23′S 51°44′W
168 G4 **Baraqueville** Midi-Pyrénées, France 44°17′N 2°26′E
233 J7 **Barāri** Bihār, NE India 25°31′N 87°23′E
68 E5 **Barataria Bay** *bay* Louisiana, S USA
Barat Daya, Kepulauan *see* Damar, Kepulauan
102 C6 **Baraya** Huila, C Colombia 03°11′N 75°04′W
111 H5 **Barbacena** Minas Gerais, SE Brazil 21°13′S 43°47′W
102 A7 **Barbacoas** Nariño, SW Colombia 01°38′N 78°08′W
102 F3 **Barbacoas** Aragua, N Venezuela 09°29′N 66°58′W
91 K3 **Barbados** ◆ *commonwealth republic* SE West Indies
95 K2 **Barbados** *island* Barbados
171 K7 **Barbaria, Cap de** *var.* Cabo de Berberia. *headland* Formentera, E Spain 38°39′N 01°24′E
185 M8 **Barbaros** Tekirdağ, NW Turkey 40°55′N 27°28′E
130 B7 **Barbas, Cap** *headland* S Western Sahara 22°14′N 16°45′W
171 J3 **Barbastro** Aragón, NE Spain 42°02′N 00°07′E
172 E10 **Barbate** Andalucía, Spain 36°11′N 5°55′W
170 E9 **Barbate** ≈ SW Spain
170 E9 **Barbate de Franco** Andalucía, S Spain 36°11′N 05°55′W
168 E6 **Barbazan** Midi-Pyrénées, France 43°02′N 0°37′E
139 H6 **Barberton** Mpumalanga, NE South Africa 25°48′S 31°03′E
73 I10 **Barberton** Ohio, N USA 41°02′N 81°37′W
168 D2 **Barbezieux-St-Hilaire** Charente, W France 45°28′N 00°09′W
159 J7 **Barbon** United Kingdom 54°13′N 2°34′W
102 C5 **Barbosa** Boyaca, C Colombia 05°57′N 73°37′W
66 G5 **Barbourville** Kentucky, S USA 36°52′N 83°54′W
91 M6 **Barbuda** *island* N Antigua and Barbuda
275 J5 **Barcaldine** Queensland, E Australia 23°33′S 145°21′E
Barcarozsnyó *see* Râşnov
170 D7 **Barcarrota** Extremadura, W Spain 38°31′N 06°51′W
Barcău *see* Berettyó
Barce *see* Al Marj
175 G12 **Barcellona** *var.* Barcellona Pozzo di Gotto. Sicilia, Italy, C Mediterranean Sea 38°10′N 15°15′E
Barcellona Pozzo di Gotto *see* Barcellona
171 K4 **Barcelona** *anc.* Barcino, Barcinona. Cataluña, E Spain 41°25′N 02°10′E
103 H3 **Barcelona** Anzoátegui, NE Venezuela 10°08′N 64°43′W
171 K3 **Barcelona** ◈ *province* Cataluña, NE Spain
168 G9 **Barcelona** ✈ Cataluña, E Spain 41°25′N 02°10′E
165 K7 **Barcelonnette** Alpes-de-Haute-Provence, SE France 44°24′N 06°37′E
106 F2 **Barcelos** Amazonas, N Brazil 0°59′S 62°58′W
170 C3 **Barcelos** Braga, N Portugal 41°32′N 08°37′W
182 E5 **Barcin** *Ger.* Bartschin. Kujawski-pomorskie, C Poland 52°51′N 17°55′E
Barcino/Barcinona *see* Barcelona
168 A10 **Barcones** Castilla y León, Spain 41°17′N 2°49′W
Barcoo *see* Cooper Creek
172 C1 **Barcos** Viseu, Portugal 41°07′N 7°36′W
183 E13 **Barcs** Somogy, SW Hungary 45°58′N 17°26′E
81 H14 **Bard** California, USA 32°47′N 114°33′W
215 L5 **Bärdä** *Rus.* Barda. C Azerbaijan 40°25′N 47°07′E
Barda *see* Bärdä
118 G10 **Barda del Medio** Río Negro, Argentina 38°43′S 68°10′W
133 N1 **Bardaï** Borkou-Ennedi-Tibesti, N Chad 21°21′N 16°56′E
217 I2 **Bardaraşh** Dahūk, N Iraq 36°32′N 43°36′E
217 H4 **Bardasah** Al Anbār, SW Iraq 34°02′N 42°28′E
118 E6 **Bardas Blancas** Mendoza, Argentina 35°52′S 69°48′W
233 J8 **Barddhamān** West Bengal, NE India 23°10′N 88°03′E
183 H9 **Bardejov** *Ger.* Bartfeld, *Hung.* Bártfa. Presovský Kraj, E Slovakia 49°17′N 21°18′E
171 I3 **Bárdenas Reales** *physical region* N Spain
Bardera/Bardere *see* Baardheere
Bardesīr *see* Bardsīr
152 C2 **Bárdharbunga** ▲ C Iceland 64°39′N 17°30′W
Bardhë, Drini i *see* Beli Drim
176 F8 **Bardi** Emilia-Romagna, C Italy 44°39′N 09°44′E
Bardina, Gora *see* Bardin Seamount
289 D9 **Bardin Seamount** *var.* Gora Bardina. *undersea feature* SW Indian Ocean 13°56′S 53°38′E
159 M10 **Bardney** United Kingdom 53°13′N 0°19′W
176 C7 **Bardonecchia** Piemonte, W Italy 45°04′N 06°40′E
159 J6 **Bardon Mill** United Kingdom 54°58′N 2°20′W
180 I3 **Bardowick** Niedersachsen, Germany 10°23′N 53°18′E
160 D3 **Bardsey Island** *island* NW Wales, United Kingdom
223 H7 **Bardsīr** *var.* Bardesīr, Mashīz. Kermān, C Iran 29°58′N 56°29′E
66 E4 **Bardstown** Kentucky, S USA 37°49′N 85°29′W
Barduli *see* Barletta
66 C5 **Bardwell** Kentucky, S USA 36°52′N 89°01′W
168 E7 **Baréges** Midi-Pyrénées, France 42°54′N 0°04′E
232 F5 **Bareilly** *var.* Bareli. Uttar Pradesh, N India 28°20′N 79°24′E
Bareli *see* Bareilly
Baren *see* Jiashi
180 F5 **Barenburg** Niedersachsen, Germany 8°48′N 52°37′E
162 E7 **Barendrecht** Zuid-Holland, SW Netherlands 51°52′N 04°31′E
164 G2 **Barentin** Seine-Maritime, N France 49°33′N 00°57′E
152 A5 **Barentsburg** Spitsbergen, W Svalbard 78°01′N 14°19′E
Barentsevo More/Barents Havet *see* Barents Sea
152 B5 **Barentsøya** *island* E Svalbard
295 I4 **Barents Plain** *undersea feature* N Barents Sea
195 H1 **Barents Sea** *Nor.* Barents Havet, *Rus.* Barentsevo More. *sea* Arctic Ocean
295 K3 **Barents Trough** *undersea feature* SW Barents Sea 75°00′N 29°00′E
136 D2 **Barentu** W Eritrea 15°08′N 37°35′E
164 F2 **Barfleur** Manche, N France 49°41′N 01°18′W
164 F2 **Barfleur, Pointe de** *headland* N France 49°46′N 01°09′W
Barfrush/Barfurush *see* Bābol
238 D8 **Barga** Xizang Zizhiqu, W China 30°51′N 81°20′E
Bargarh *see* Baragarh
170 G5 **Bargas** Castilla-La Mancha, C Spain 39°56′N 04°00′W
136 D5 **Bargē** Southern Nationalities, S Ethiopia 06°11′N 37°04′E
176 C8 **Barge** Piemonte, NE Italy 44°49′N 07°21′E
160 F6 **Bargoed** United Kingdom 51°41′N 3°14′W
233 K9 **Barguna** Barisal, S Bangladesh 22°09′N 90°07′E
Bărguşad *see* Vorotan
193 I8 **Barguzin** Respublika Buryatiya, S Russian Federation 53°37′N 109°47′E
233 H6 **Barhaj** Uttar Pradesh, N India 26°16′N 83°44′E
277 I6 **Barham** New South Wales, SE Australia 35°39′S 144°09′E
232 F6 **Barhan** Uttar Pradesh, N India 27°21′N 78°11′E
63 L4 **Bar Harbor** Mount Desert Island, Maine, NE USA 44°23′N 68°14′W
233 J7 **Barharwa** Jhārkhand, NE India 24°52′N 87°47′E
233 I7 **Barhi** Jhārkhand, N India 24°19′N 85°25′E
175 I9 **Bari** *var.* Bari delle Puglie; *anc.* Barium. Puglia, SE Italy 41°06′N 16°52′E
136 J4 **Bari** *Off.* Gobolka Bari. ◈ *region* NE Somalia
257 I9 **Ba Ria** *var.* Châu Thanh. Ba Ria-Vung Tau, S Vietnam 10°30′N 107°10′E
Bāridah *see* Al Bāridah
Bari delle Puglie *see* Bari
Bari, Gobolka *see* Bari
171 N10 **Barika** Algeria
Barikot *see* Barīkowṯ
231 I3 **Barīkowṯ** *var.* Barikot. Konar, NE Afghanistan 35°18′N 71°36′E
88 B3 **Barillas** *var.* Santa Cruz Barillas. Huehuetenango, NW Guatemala 15°50′N 91°20′W
102 E4 **Barinas** Barinas, W Venezuela 08°36′N 70°15′W
102 E4 **Barinas** *off.* Estado Barinas; *prev.* Zamora. ◈ *state* C Venezuela
Barinas, Estado *see* Barinas
52 D7 **Baring, Cape** *headland* Northwest Territories, N Canada
102 E3 **Barinitas** Barinas, NW Venezuela 08°45′N 70°26′W
234 J3 **Bāripada** Orissa, E India 21°56′N 86°43′E
110 A7 **Bariri** São Paulo, S Brazil 22°04′S 48°46′W
129 I5 **Bârîs** *var.* Bâris. S Egypt 24°28′N 30°39′E
232 D7 **Bari Sādri** Rājasthān, N India 24°25′N 74°28′E
233 K8 **Barisal** Barisal, S Bangladesh 22°41′N 90°20′E
233 K8 **Barisal** ◈ *division* S Bangladesh
258 D4 **Barisan, Pegunungan** ▲▲ Sumatera, W Indonesia
259 K6 **Barito, Sungai** ≈ Borneo, C Indonesia
Barium *see* Bari
169 J4 **Barjac** Languedoc-Roussillon, France 44°18′N 4°21′E
Bårjås *see* Porjus
Barka *see* Al Marj
239 K8 **Barkam** Sichuan, C China 31°56′N 102°22′E
190 F6 **Barkava** Madona, C Latvia 56°43′N 26°34′E
114 F9 **Barker** Colonia, Uruguay 34°16′S 57°27′W
56 E5 **Barkerville** British Columbia, SW Canada 53°06′N 121°35′W
62 E3 **Bark Lake** ◎ Ontario, SE Canada
66 C5 **Barkley, Lake** ▣ Kentucky/Tennessee, S USA
56 C9 **Barkley Sound** *inlet* British Columbia, W Canada
141 I7 **Barkly East** *Afr.* Barkly-Oos. Eastern Cape, SE South Africa 30°58′S 27°35′E
Barkly-Oos *see* Barkly East
141 I8 **Barkly Pass** *pass* Eastern Cape, South Africa
275 H3 **Barkly Tableland** *plateau* Northern Territory/Queensland, N Australia
Barkly-Wes *see* Barkly West
140 G6 **Barkly West** *Afr.* Barkly-Wes. Northern Cape, N South Africa 28°32′S 24°32′E
239 H3 **Barkol** *var.* Barkol Kazak Zizhixian. Xinjiang Uygur Zizhiqu, NW China 43°37′N 93°01′E
239 H3 **Barkol Hu** ◎ NW China
Barkol Kazak Zizhixian *see* Barkol
72 B3 **Bark Point** *headland* Wisconsin, N USA 46°53′N 91°11′W
70 F7 **Barksdale** Texas, SW USA 29°43′N 100°03′W
161 J2 **Barkston** United Kingdom 52°57′N 0°36′W
Bar Kunar *see* Asmār
188 F8 **Bârlad** *prev.* Bîrlad. Vaslui, E Romania 46°12′N 27°39′E
188 F7 **Bârlad** *prev.* Bîrlad. ≈ E Romania
132 B9 **Barlavento, Ilhas de** *var.* Windward Islands. *island group* N Cape Verde
165 J3 **Bar-le-Duc** *var.* Bar-sur-Ornain. Meuse, NE France 48°46′N 05°10′E
274 D6 **Barlee, Lake** ◎ Western Australia
274 D5 **Barlee Range** ▲▲ Western Australia
175 H9 **Barletta** *anc.* Barduli. Puglia, SE Italy 41°20′N 16°17′E
182 C5 **Barlinek** *Ger.* Berlinchen. Zachodnio-pomorskie, NW Poland 53°N 15°11′E
75 G12 **Barling** Arkansas, C USA 35°19′N 94°18′W
261 I5 **Barma** Papua, E Indonesia 01°55′S 132°57′E
277 K5 **Barmedman** New South Wales, SE Australia 34°09′S 147°21′E
Barmen-Elberfeld *see* Wuppertal
232 C6 **Bārmer** Rājasthān, NW India 25°43′N 71°25′E
277 H5 **Barmera** South Australia 34°14′S 140°26′E
160 E3 **Barmouth** NW Wales, United Kingdom 52°44′N 04°04′W
160 E3 **Barmouth Bay** *bay* NW Wales, United Kingdom
232 D8 **Barnagar** Madhya Pradesh, C India 23°01′N 75°28′E
232 E4 **Barnāla** Punjab, NW India 30°26′N 75°33′E
159 J7 **Barnard Castle** N England, United Kingdom 54°35′N 01°55′W
277 J4 **Barnato** New South Wales, SE Australia 31°39′S 145°01′E
192 F8 **Barnaul** Altayskiy Kray, C Russian Federation 53°21′N 83°45′E
177 K4 **Bärnbach** Steiermark, SE Austria 47°05′N 15°07′E
65 H8 **Barnegat** New Jersey, NE USA 39°43′N 74°12′W
65 H8 **Barnegat Pines** New Jersey, NE USA 39°53′N 74°12′W
53 K7 **Barnes Icecap** *Ice feature* Nunavut, NE Canada
66 F9 **Barnesville** Georgia, SE USA 33°03′N 84°09′W
74 F3 **Barnesville** Minnesota, N USA 46°39′N 96°25′W
73 J11 **Barnesville** Ohio, N USA 39°59′N 81°10′W
161 K6 **Barnet** United Kingdom 51°39′N 0°12′W
162 G6 **Barneveld** *var.* Barnveld. Gelderland, C Netherlands 52°08′N 05°34′E
70 E6 **Barnhart** Texas, SW USA 31°07′N 101°09′W
71 H1 **Barnsdall** Oklahoma, C USA 36°33′N 96°09′W
159 K9 **Barnsley** N England, United Kingdom 53°34′N 01°28′W
65 N4 **Barnstable** Massachusetts, NE USA 41°42′N 70°17′W
160 E7 **Barnstaple** SW England, United Kingdom 51°05′N 04°04′W
Barnveld *see* Barneveld
67 I9 **Barnwell** South Carolina, SE USA 33°14′N 81°21′W
133 J7 **Baro** Niger, C Nigeria 08°35′N 06°28′E
121 L5 **Baro** *var.* Baro Wenz. ≈ Ethiopia/Sudan
Baro *see* Baro Wenz
141 H8 **Baroda** Eastern Cape, South Africa 32°00′S 25°31′E
Baroda *see* Vadodara
140 G9 **Baroe** Eastern Cape, South Africa 33°13′S 24°34′E
231 I2 **Baroghil Pass** *var.* Kowtal-e Barowghīl. *pass* Afghanistan/Pakistan
191 J10 **Baron'ki** *Rus.* Boron'ki. Mahilyowskaya Voblasts', E Belarus 53°09′N 32°08′E
276 G5 **Barossa Valley** *valley* South Australia
Baroui *see* Salisbury
136 D5 **Baro Wenz** *var.* Baro, Nahr Barū. ≈ Ethiopia/Sudan
Baro Wenz *see* Baro
Barowghīl, Kowtal-e *see* Baroghil Pass
233 K6 **Barpeta** Assam, NE India 26°19′N 91°05′E
72 H6 **Barques, Pointe Aux** *headland* Michigan, N USA 44°04′N 82°57′W
102 E3 **Barquisimeto** Lara, NW Venezuela 10°03′N 69°18′W
167 M6 **Barr** Alsace, France 48°24′N 7°27′E
158 G5 **Barr** United Kingdom 55°12′N 4°42′W
108 E7 **Barra** Bahia, E Brazil 11°06′S 43°15′W
172 B2 **Barra** Aveiro, Portugal 40°38′N 8°45′W
156 D5 **Barra** *island* NW Scotland, United Kingdom
277 L3 **Barraba** New South Wales, SE Australia 30°24′S 150°37′E
110 A7 **Barra Bonita** São Paulo, S Brazil 22°30′S 48°35′W
290 E6 **Barracuda Fracture Zone** *var.* Fifteen Twenty Fracture Zone. *tectonic feature* SW Atlantic Ocean
172 C4 **Barrada** Santarém, Portugal 39°25′N 8°04′W
115 H10 **Barra de Carrasco** Canelones, Uruguay 34°53′S 56°02′W
111 L5 **Barra de Itabapoana** Rio de Janeiro, Brazil 21°24′S 41°00′W
89 H7 **Barra del Colorado** Limón, NE Costa Rica 10°44′N 83°35′W
89 H5 **Barra de Río Grande** Región Autónoma Atlántico Sur, E Nicaragua 12°56′N 83°30′W
111 J6 **Barra de São Francisco** Rio de Janeiro, Brazil 21°58′S 42°42′W
111 L1 **Barra de S. Francisco** Esperíto Santo, Brazil 18°42′S 40°54′W
135 C11 **Barra do Cuanza** Luanda, NW Angola 09°12′S 13°08′E
111 H7 **Barra do Piraí** Rio de Janeiro, SE Brazil 22°30′S 43°47′W
116 H2 **Barra do Quaraí** Rio Grande do Sul, SE Brazil 31°03′S 58°10′W
107 H5 **Barra do São Manuel** Pará, N Brazil 07°12′S 58°03′W
139 J5 **Barra Falsa, Ponta da** *headland* S Mozambique 22°57′S 35°36′E
156 C5 **Barra Head** *headland* NW Scotland, United Kingdom 56°46′N 07°37′W
111 I3 **Barra Longa** Minas Gerais, Brazil 20°17′S 43°03′W
Barram *see* Baram, Batang
110 G7 **Barra Mansa** Rio de Janeiro, SE Brazil 22°25′S 44°03′W
104 C7 **Barranca** Lima, W Peru 10°46′S 77°46′W
102 C4 **Barrancabermeja** Santander, N Colombia 07°01′N 73°51′W
102 D2 **Barrancas** La Guajira, N Colombia 10°59′N 72°46′W
102 E3 **Barrancas** Barinas, NW Venezuela 08°47′N 70°07′W
103 I3 **Barrancas** Monagas, NE Venezuela 08°45′N 62°12′W
102 C3 **Barranco de Loba** Bolívar, N Colombia 08°56′N 74°07′W
170 D7 **Barrancos** Beja, S Portugal 38°08′N 06°59′W
111 N1 **Barra Nova** Espírito Santo, Brazil 18°54′S 39°46′W
112 G6 **Barranqueras** Chaco, N Argentina 27°29′S 58°54′W
102 C2 **Barranquilla** Atlántico, N Colombia 10°59′N 74°48′W
139 J5 **Barra, Ponta da** *headland* S Mozambique 23°46′S 35°33′E
171 H6 **Barrax** Castilla-La Mancha, C Spain 39°04′N 02°12′W
65 K2 **Barre** Massachusetts, NE USA 42°24′N 72°06′W
63 I4 **Barre** Vermont, NE USA 44°09′N 72°25′W
118 E1 **Barreal** San Juan, Argentina 31°38′S 69°28′W
109 E8 **Barreiras** Bahia, E Brazil 12°09′S 44°58′W
172 A5 **Barreiro** Setúbal, W Portugal 38°40′N 09°05′W
218 G3 **Barr Eliâs** Lebanon 33°46′N 35°54′E
169 L5 **Barrème** Provence-Alpes-Côte d'Azur, France 43°57′N 6°22′E
117 H12 **Barren Island** *island* S Falkland Islands
66 E5 **Barren River Lake** ▣ Kentucky, S USA
85 M7 **Barretal** Tamaulipas, Mexico 24°05′N 99°07′W
110 A4 **Barretos** São Paulo, S Brazil 20°33′S 48°33′W
158 G5 **Barrgrennan** SW Scotland, United Kingdom 55°03′N 04°42′W
57 I4 **Barrhead** Alberta, SW Canada 54°10′N 114°22′W
158 G3 **Barrhead** United Kingdom 55°47′N 4°23′W
158 G5 **Barrhill** United Kingdom 55°06′N 4°46′W
62 D4 **Barrie** Ontario, S Canada 44°22′N 79°42′W
180 F5 **Barrien** Niedersachsen, Germany 8°43′N 52°40′E
56 F7 **Barrière** British Columbia, SW Canada 51°10′N 120°06′W
277 H4 **Barrier Range** *hill range* New South Wales, SE Australia
88 E2 **Barrier Reef** *reef* E Belize
55 H8 **Barrier River** ≈ Saskatchewan, S Canada
282 B2 **Barrigada** C Guam 13°27′N 144°48′E
65 L4 **Barrington** Rhode Island, USA 41°44′N 71°19′W
Barrington Island *see* Santa Fe, Isla
277 L4 **Barrington Tops** ▲ New South Wales, SE Australia 32°06′S 151°18′E
277 J2 **Barringun** New South Wales, SE Australia 29°02′S 145°45′E
110 A5 **Barrinha** São Paulo, Brazil 21°12′S 48°09′W
109 B9 **Barro Alto** Goiás, S Brazil 15°07′S 48°56′W
108 F5 **Barro Duro** Piauí, NE Brazil 05°49′S 42°30′W
72 A5 **Barron** Wisconsin, N USA 45°24′N 91°50′W
62 E3 **Barron** ≈ Ontario, SE Canada
113 I7 **Barros Cassal** Rio Grande do Sul, S Brazil 29°12′S 52°33′W
111 H5 **Barroso** Minas Gerais, Brazil 21°11′S 43°58′W
118 E4 **Barroso, Río** ≈ Región Metropolitana, Chile
91 L3 **Barrouallie** Saint Vincent, W Saint Vincent and the Grenadines 13°14′N 61°17′W
115 L2 **Barro Vermelho** Rio Grande do Sul, Brazil 30°11′S 53°11′W
83 H2 **Barrow** Alaska, USA 71°17′N 156°47′W
160 A4 **Barrow** *Ir.* An Bhearú. ≈ SE Ireland
275 H4 **Barrow Creek Roadhouse** Northern Territory, N Australia 21°30′S 133°52′E
159 I8 **Barrow-in-Furness** NW England, United Kingdom 54°07′N 03°14′W
274 C4 **Barrow Island** *island* Western Australia
83 H1 **Barrow, Point** *headland* Alaska, USA 71°23′N 156°28′W
55 I8 **Barrows** Manitoba, S Canada 52°49′N 101°36′W
53 H5 **Barrow Strait** *Waterway* Nunavut, NW Canada
160 F6 **Barry** S Wales, United Kingdom 51°24′N 03°18′W
62 E3 **Barry's Bay** Ontario, SE Canada 45°30′N 77°41′W
195 H8 **Barsakel'mes, Ostrov** *island* SW Kazakhstan
Baršć Łužyca *see* Forst
229 K8 **Barsem** S Tajikistan 37°36′N 71°43′E
227 K5 **Barshatas** Vostochnyy Kazakhstan, E Kazakhstan 48°13′N 78°33′E
234 D5 **Bārsi** Mahārāshtra, W India 18°14′N 75°42′E
180 G6 **Barsinghausen** Niedersachsen, C Germany 53°19′N 09°30′E
229 M4 **Barskoon** Issyk-Kul'skaya Oblast', E Kyrgyzstan 42°07′N 77°34′E
180 D4 **Barssel** Niedersachsen, NW Germany 53°10′N 07°46′E
80 D5 **Barstow** California, USA 36°49′N 119°58′W
81 F10 **Barstow** California, W USA 34°52′N 117°00′W
70 C5 **Barstow** Texas, SW USA 31°27′N 103°23′W
165 J4 **Bar-sur-Aube** Aube, NE France 48°13′N 04°43′E
Bar-sur-Ornain *see* Bar-le-Duc
165 J4 **Bar-sur-Seine** Aube, N France 48°06′N 04°22′E
229 K7 **Bartang** S Tajikistan 38°06′N 71°48′E
229 K7 **Bartang** ≈ SE Tajikistan
Bartenstein *see* Bartoszyce
Bártfa/Bartfeld *see* Bardejov
178 H4 **Barth** Mecklenburg-Vorpommern, NE Germany 54°21′N 12°43′E
68 D1 **Bartholomew, Bayou** ≈ Arkansas/Louisiana, S USA
103 K5 **Bartica** N Guyana 06°24′N 58°36′W
214 E4 **Bartın** Bartın, NW Turkey 41°37′N 32°20′E
214 E4 **Bartın** ◈ *province* NW Turkey
275 J3 **Bartle Frere** ▲ Queensland, E Australia 17°15′S 145°43′E
75 F11 **Bartlesville** Oklahoma, C USA 36°44′N 95°59′W
74 D7 **Bartlett** Nebraska, C USA 41°51′N 98°32′W
66 B6 **Bartlett** Tennessee, S USA 35°12′N 89°52′W
70 G6 **Bartlett** Texas, SW USA 30°47′N 97°25′W
79 I8 **Bartlett Reservoir** ▣ Arizona, SW USA
181 I8 **Bartolfelde** Niedersachsen, Germany 10°27′N 51°36′E
159 K7 **Barton** United Kingdom 54°28′N 1°39′W
63 I4 **Barton** Vermont, NE USA 44°44′N 72°09′W
159 M9 **Barton upon Humber** United Kingdom 53°40′N 0°26′W
182 H3 **Bartoszyce** *Ger.* Bartenstein. Warmińsko-mazurskie, NE Poland 54°16′N 20°49′E
69 L7 **Bartow** Florida, SE USA 27°54′N 81°50′W
Bartschin *see* Barcin
261 I5 **Baru** Papua, E Indonesia 01°44′S 132°16′E
110 C9 **Barueri** São Paulo, Brazil 23°31′S 46°53′W
258 D4 **Barumun, Sungai** ≈ Sumatera, W Indonesia
Barū, Nahr *see* Baro Wenz
259 J9 **Barung, Nusa** *island* S Indonesia
258 C4 **Barus** Sumatera, NW Indonesia 02°02′N 98°20′E
239 J2 **Baruunbayan-Ulaan** *var.* Höövör. Övörhangay, C Mongolia 45°10′N 101°19′E
Baruunsuu *see* Tsogttsetsiy
239 M1 **Baruun-Urt** Sühbaatar, E Mongolia 46°40′N 113°17′E
89 I9 **Barú, Volcán** *var.* Volcán de Chiriquí. ✶ W Panama 08°49′N 82°32′W
163 G11 **Barvaux** Luxembourg, SE Belgium 50°21′N 05°30′E
89 H8 **Barva, Volcán** ✶ NW Costa Rica 10°07′N 84°08′W
180 F5 **Barver** Niedersachsen, Germany 8°36′N 52°37′E
189 L4 **Barvinkove** Kharkivs'ka Oblast', E Ukraine 48°54′N 37°03′E
232 E8 **Barwāh** Madhya Pradesh, C India 22°17′N 76°01′E
Bärwalde Neumark *see* Mieszkowice
232 D9 **Barwāni** Madhya Pradesh, C India 22°02′N 74°56′E
277 J3 **Barwon River** ≈ New South Wales, SE Australia
191 G9 **Barysaw** *Rus.* Borisov. Minskaya Voblasts', NE Belarus 54°14′N 28°30′E
197 I3 **Barysh** Ul'yanovskaya Oblast', W Russian Federation 53°32′N 47°06′E
189 H3 **Baryshivka** Kyyivs'ka Oblast', N Ukraine 50°21′N 31°21′E
134 E7 **Basankusu** Equateur, NW Dem. Rep. Congo 01°12′N 19°50′E
188 G7 **Basarabeasca** *Rus.* Bessarabka. SE Moldova 46°22′N 28°56′E
188 F10 **Basarabi** Constanța, SW Romania 44°10′N 28°26′E
84 G4 **Basaseachic** Chihuahua, NW Mexico 28°18′N 108°13′W
168 A6 **Basauri** Pais Vasco, Spain 43°01′N 2°24′W
114 D5 **Basavilbaso** Entre Ríos, E Argentina 32°23′S 58°55′W
169 H8 **Bàscara** Cataluña, Spain 42°10′N 2°55′E
160 G3 **Baschurch** W England, United Kingdom 52°48′N 02°55′W
135 C9 **Bas-Congo** *off.* Région du Bas-Congo; *prev.* Bas-Zaïre. ◈ *region* SW Dem. Rep. Congo
176 D3 **Basel** *Eng.* Basle, *Fr.* Bâle. Basel-Stadt, NW Switzerland 47°33′N 07°36′E
174 B2 **Basel** *Eng.* Basle, *Fr.* Bâle. ◈ *canton* NW Switzerland
169 J2 **Bas-en-Basset** Auvergne, France 45°18′N 4°06′E
223 I9 **Bashākerd, Kūhhā-ye** ▲▲ SE Iran
57 J6 **Bashaw** Alberta, SW Canada 52°40′N 112°53′W
228 F9 **Bashbedeng** Mary Welaýaty, S Turkmenistan 35°44′N 63°07′E
138 G9 **Bashee** ≈ S South Africa
263 L2 **Bashi Channel** *Chin.* Pa-shih Hai-hsia. *channel* Philippines/Taiwan
Bashkiria *see* Bashkortostan, Respublika
197 L2 **Bashkortostan, Respublika** *prev.* Bashkiria. ◈ *autonomous republic* W Russian Federation
197 H3 **Bashmakovo** Penzenskaya Oblast', W Russian Federation 53°13′N 43°00′E
228 F6 **Bashsakarba** Lebap Welaýaty, NE Turkmenistan 40°25′N 62°16′E
189 I6 **Bashtanka** Mykolayivs'ka Oblast', S Ukraine 47°24′N 32°27′E
243 I2 **Ba Shui** ≈ Hubei, China
263 L9 **Basilan** *island* Sulu Archipelago, SW Philippines
161 L6 **Basildon** United Kingdom 51°34′N 0°28′E
68 C4 **Basile** Louisiana, S USA 30°29′N 92°36′W
175 H10 **Basilicata** ◈ *region* S Italy
77 K6 **Basin** Wyoming, C USA 44°22′N 108°02′W
161 J7 **Basingstoke** S England, United Kingdom 51°16′N 01°08′W
223 I6 **Başīrān** Khorāsān-e Janūbī, E Iran 31°57′N 59°07′E
184 B3 **Baška** *It.* Bescanuova. Primorje-Gorski Kotar, NW Croatia 44°58′N 14°46′E
215 K7 **Başkale** Van, SE Turkey 38°03′N 43°59′E
62 G1 **Baskatong, Réservoir** ▣ Québec, SE Canada
215 H6 **Baskil** Elazığ, E Turkey 38°38′N 38°47′E
Basle *see* Basel
159 K10 **Baslow** United Kingdom 53°14′N 1°37′W
232 F8 **Bāsoda** Madhya Pradesh, C India 23°54′N 77°58′E
134 G7 **Basoko** Orientale, N Dem. Rep. Congo 01°14′N 23°26′E
Basque Country, The *see* País Vasco
Basra *see* Al Başrah
165 K3 **Bas-Rhin** ◈ *department* NE France
Bassam *see* Grand-Bassam
57 J7 **Bassano** Alberta, SW Canada 50°48′N 112°28′W
177 H6 **Bassano del Grappa** Veneto, NE Italy 45°45′N 11°45′E
133 H6 **Bassar** *var.* Bassari. NW Togo 09°15′N 00°47′E
Bassari *see* Bassar
289 B10 **Bassas da India** *island group* W Madagascar
176 C4 **Bassecourt** Jura, W Switzerland 47°20′N 07°16′E
256 C6 **Bassein** *var.* Bassein. Ayeyarwady, SW Myanmar (Burma) 16°46′N 94°45′E
Bassein *see* Bassein
134 F5 **Basse-Kotto** ◈ *prefecture* S Central African Republic
171 K3 **Bassella** Cataluña, NE Spain 42°01′N 01°17′E
180 G4 **Bassen** Niedersachsen, Germany 9°05′N 53°03′E
164 G3 **Basse-Normandie** *Eng.* Lower Normandy. ◈ *region* N France
159 I6 **Bassenthwaite Lake** ◎ United Kingdom
91 M1 **Basse-Pointe** N Martinique 14°52′N 61°07′W
132 B5 **Basse Santa Su** E Gambia 13°18′N 14°10′W
Basse-Saxe *see* Niedersachsen
91 J2 **Basse-Terre** ○ (Guadeloupe) Basse Terre, SW Guadeloupe 16°08′N 61°40′W
91 L6 **Basseterre** ● (Saint Kitts and Nevis) Saint Kitts, Saint Kitts and Nevis 17°16′N 62°45′W
91 J2 **Basse Terre** *island* W Guadeloupe
74 D6 **Bassett** Nebraska, C USA 42°34′N 99°32′W
67 J5 **Bassett** Virginia, NE USA 36°45′N 79°59′W
79 J9 **Bassett Peak** ▲ Arizona, SW USA 32°30′N 110°16′W
132 F4 **Bassikounou** Hodh ech Chargui, SE Mauritania 15°55′N 05°59′W
133 I7 **Bassila** W Benin 08°25′N 01°58′E
Bass, Îlots de *see* Marotiri
159 L10 **Bassingham** United Kingdom 53°07′N 0°38′W
80 E5 **Bass Lake** California, USA 37°19′N 119°34′W
73 E9 **Bass Lake** Indiana, N USA 41°12′N 86°35′W
159 I3 **Bass Rock** *island* E Scotland, United Kingdom
277 J8 **Bass Strait** *strait* SE Australia
180 F4 **Bassum** Niedersachsen, NW Germany 52°52′N 08°44′E
72 B2 **Basswood Lake** ◎ Canada/USA
155 F11 **Båstad** Skåne, S Sweden 56°25′N 12°50′E
217 K2 **Basṭah** As Sulaymānīyah, E Iraq 36°20′N 45°14′E
140 E8 **Basterberge** ▲▲ Northern Cape, South Africa
181 I11 **Bastheim** Bayern, Germany 10°12′N 50°24′E
233 H6 **Basti** Uttar Pradesh, N India 26°48′N 82°44′E
174 C7 **Bastia** Corse, France, C Mediterranean Sea 42°42′N 09°27′E
163 G12 **Bastogne** Luxembourg, SE Belgium 50°N 05°43′E
68 C1 **Bastrop** Louisiana, S USA 32°46′N 91°54′W
70 G7 **Bastrop** Texas, SW USA 30°07′N 97°21′W
154 J1 **Bastuträsk** Västerbotten, N Sweden 64°47′N 20°05′E
191 F11 **Bastyn'** *Rus.* Bostyn'. Brestskaya Voblasts', SW Belarus 52°23′N 26°45′E
Basuo *see* Dongfang
Basutoland *see* Lesotho
191 I9 **Basya** ≈ E Belarus
189 L5 **Basyl'kivka** Dnipropetrovs'ka Oblast', E Ukraine 48°12′N 36°00′E
Bas-Zaïre *see* Bas-Congo
134 A7 **Bata** NW Equatorial Guinea 01°51′N 09°48′E
134 A6 **Bata** ✈ S Equatorial Guinea 01°55′N 09°48′E
Batae Coritanorum *see* Leicester
193 K5 **Batagay** Respublika Sakha (Yakutiya), NE Russian Federation 67°36′N 134°44′E
193 J5 **Batagay-Alyta** Respublika Sakha (Yakutiya), NE Russian Federation 67°48′N 130°15′E
184 F3 **Batajnica** Vojvodina, N Serbia 44°55′N 20°17′E
214 E7 **Bataklık Gölü** ◎ S Turkey
185 J7 **Batak, Yazovir** ▣ SW Bulgaria
232 E3 **Batāla** Punjab, N India 31°48′N 75°12′E
172 B3 **Batalha** Leiria, C Portugal 39°40′N 08°50′W
134 H7 **Batama** Orientale, NE Dem. Rep. Congo 0°54′N 26°25′E
193 J6 **Batamay** Respublika Sakha (Yakutiya), NE Russian Federation 63°28′N 129°33′E
258 F4 **Batam, Pulau** *island* Kepulauan Riau, W Indonesia
245 L8 **Batan** Jiangsu, E China 34°09′N 120°04′E
240 B4 **Batang** *var.* Bazhong. Sichuan, C China 30°04′N 99°10′E
259 H8 **Batang** Jawa, C Indonesia 06°55′S 109°42′E
134 E4 **Batangafo** Ouham, NW Central African Republic 07°19′N 18°22′E
263 K6 **Batangas** *off.* Batangas City. Luzon, N Philippines 13°47′N 121°03′E
Batangas City *see* Batangas
Bătania *see* Battonya
263 L2 **Batan Island** *island group* N Philippines
263 L2 **Batan Islands** *island group* N Philippines
84 C1 **Bataques** Baja California Norte, NW Mexico 32°33′N 115°04′W
84 B2 **Bataques** Baja California Norte, NW Mexico
110 B4 **Batatais** São Paulo, S Brazil 20°54′S 47°37′W
64 B1 **Batavia** New York, NE USA 43°00′N 78°11′W
Batavia *see* Jakarta
289 H10 **Batavia Seamount** *undersea feature* E Indian Ocean 27°42′S 100°36′E
196 G7 **Bataysk** Rostovskaya Oblast', SW Russian Federation 47°10′N 39°46′E
62 A1 **Batchawana** ≈ Ontario, S Canada
72 G4 **Batchawana Bay** Ontario, S Canada 46°55′N 84°36′W
257 G8 **Bătdâmbâng** *prev.* Battambang. Bătdâmbâng, NW Cambodia 13°06′N 103°13′E
168 E10 **Batea** Cataluña, Spain 41°06′N 0°19′E
135 C9 **Batéké, Plateaux** *plateau* S Congo
277 L6 **Batemans Bay** New South Wales, SE Australia 35°45′S 150°09′E
67 I8 **Batesburg** South Carolina, SE USA 33°54′N 81°33′W
74 B6 **Batesland** South Dakota, N USA 43°05′N 102°07′W
75 I12 **Batesville** Arkansas, C USA 35°45′N 91°39′W
73 F11 **Batesville** Indiana, N USA 39°18′N 85°13′W
66 B7 **Batesville** Mississippi, S USA 34°18′N 89°56′W
70 F8 **Batesville** Texas, SW USA 28°56′N 99°38′W
190 H3 **Batetskiy** Novgorodskaya Oblast', Russian Federation
90 G8 **Bath** E Jamaica 17°57′N 76°22′W
161 H6 **Bath** *hist.* Akermanceaster; *anc.* Aquae Calidae, Aquae Solis. SW England, United Kingdom 51°23′N 02°22′W
63 K5 **Bath** Maine, NE USA 43°54′N 69°49′W
64 C2 **Bath** New York, NE USA 42°20′N 77°16′W
Bath *see* Berkeley Springs
134 E2 **Batha** *off.* Préfecture du Batha. ◈ *prefecture* C Chad
134 E2 **Batha** *seasonal river* C Chad
Batha, Préfecture du *see* Batha
221 K5 **Baṭhā', Wādī al** *dry watercourse* NE Oman
159 H3 **Bathgate** United Kingdom 55°54′N 3°38′W
232 D4 **Bathinda** Punjab, NW India 30°14′N 74°54′E
162 H6 **Bathmen** Overijssel, E Netherlands 52°15′N 06°16′E
141 H4 **Bathobatho** North-West, South Africa 26°12′S 25°28′E
91 L3 **Bathsheba** E Barbados 13°13′N 59°31′W
277 K5 **Bathurst** New South Wales, SE Australia 33°32′S 149°35′E
59 J7 **Bathurst** New Brunswick, SE Canada 47°37′N 65°40′W
Bathurst *see* Banjul
52 C6 **Bathurst, Cape** *headland* Northwest Territories, NW Canada 70°33′N 128°00′W
295 H9 **Bathurst Inlet** Nunavut, N Canada 66°23′N 107°00′W
52 E8 **Bathurst Inlet** *inlet* Nunavut, N Canada
274 F2 **Bathurst Island** *island* Northern Territory, N Australia
295 I8 **Bathurst Island** *island* Parry Islands, Nunavut, N Canada
132 G6 **Batié** SW Burkina 09°53′N 02°53′W
280 F9 **Batiki** *prev.* Mbatiki. *island* C Fiji
Batinah *see* Al Bāṭinah
217 L9 **Bāṭin, Wādī al** *dry watercourse* SW Asia
219 F10 **Batīr** Jordan 31°15′N 35°42′E
63 I1 **Batiscan** ≈ Québec, SE Canada
214 D7 **Batı Toroslar** ▲▲ SW Turkey
Batjan *see* Bacan, Pulau
229 J6 **Batken** Batenskaya Oblast', SW Kyrgyzstan 40°03′N 70°50′E
229 J6 **Batken** Batkenskaya Oblast', Uzbekistan 40°06′N 71°00′E
Batken Oblasty *see* Batkenskaya Oblast'
229 J6 **Batkenskaya Oblast'** *Kir.* Batken Oblasty. ◈ *province* SW Kyrgyzstan
159 K9 **Batley** United Kingdom 53°42′N 1°37′W
Batlle y Ordóñez *see* José Batlle y Ordóñez
277 K6 **Batlow** New South Wales, SE Australia 35°32′S 148°09′E
215 I7 **Batman** *var.* İluh. Batman, SE Turkey 37°52′N 41°06′E
215 I7 **Batman** ◈ *province* SE Turkey
131 J2 **Batna** NE Algeria 35°34′N 06°10′E
219 G14 **Baṭn al Ghūl** Jordan
239 M1 **Batnorov** *var.* Dundbürd. Hentiy, E Mongolia 47°55′N 111°37′E
Batoe *see* Batu, Kepulauan
239 J2 **Bat-Öldziy** *var.* Övt. Övörhangay, C Mongolia 46°50′N 102°15′E
Bat-Öldziyt *see* Dzaamar
68 D4 **Baton Rouge** *state capital* Louisiana, S USA 30°28′N 91°09′W
134 C5 **Batouri** Est, E Cameroon 04°26′N 14°27′E
219 F13 **Batrā', Jibāl al** ▲▲ S Jordan
218 F2 **Batroûn** *var.* Al Batrūn. N Lebanon 34°15′N 35°42′E
218 F2 **Batroûn** Lebanon 34°15′N 35°39′E
Batsch *see* Bač
Batsevichi *see* Batsevichy
191 H10 **Batsevichy** *Rus.* Batsevichi. Mahilyowskaya Voblasts', E Belarus 53°24′N 29°14′E
152 I3 **Båtsfjord** Finnmark, N Norway 70°37′N 29°42′E
218 E6 **Bat Shelomo** Israel 32°35′N 35°00′E
Batshireet *see* Hentiy
239 K1 **Batsümber** *var.* Mandal. Töv, C Mongolia 48°24′N 106°47′E
Battambang *see* Bătdâmbâng
181 F9 **Battenberg** Hessen, Germany 8°39′N 51°01′E
293 L2 **Batterbee, Cape** *headland* Antarctica
235 G10 **Batticaloa** Eastern Province, E Sri Lanka 07°44′N 81°43′E
163 G11 **Battice** Liège, E Belgium 50°39′N 05°50′E
184 B9 **Battipaglia** Campania, S Italy 40°36′N 14°59′E
57 J6 **Battle** ≈ Alberta/Saskatchewan, SW Canada
Battle Born State *see* Nevada
73 F8 **Battle Creek** Michigan, N USA 42°20′N 85°10′W
75 H11 **Battlefield** Missouri, C USA 37°07′N 93°22′W
57 L5 **Battleford** Saskatchewan, S Canada 52°45′N 108°20′W
74 F4 **Battle Lake** Minnesota, N USA 46°16′N 95°42′W
78 E2 **Battle Mountain** Nevada, W USA 40°37′N 116°55′W
80 J1 **Battle Mountain** ▲ Nevada, USA 40°41′N 117°08′W
183 H13 **Battonya** *Rom.* Bătania. Békés, SE Hungary 46°16′N 21°00′E
239 J1 **Battsengel** *var.* Jargalant. Arhangay, C Mongolia 47°46′N 101°56′E
260 E7 **Batuata, Pulau** *island* C Indonesia
118 C6 **Batuco** Maule, Chile 35°19′S 71°59′W
260 D4 **Batudaka, Pulau** *island* N Indonesia
258 C5 **Batu, Kepulauan** *prev.* Batoe. *island group* W Indonesia
215 I4 **Bat'umi** W Georgia 41°39′N 41°38′E

◆ Country
● Country Capital
◇ Dependent Territory
○ Dependent Territory Capital
◈ Administrative Regions
✈ International Airport
▲ Mountain
▲▲ Mountain Range
✶ Volcano
≈ River
◎ Lake
▣ Reservoir

Batu Pahat – Bellenz

INDEX

317

258 E4 **Batu Pahat** *prev.* Bandar Penggaram. Johor, Peninsular Malaysia 01°51′N 102°56′E
260 D5 **Baturebe** Sulawesi, N Indonesia 01°43′S 121°43′E
190 J7 **Baturino** Smolenskaya Oblast', Russian Federation
192 F7 **Baturino** Tomskaya Oblast', C Russian Federation 57°46′N 85°08′E
189 I2 **Baturyn** Chernihivs'ka Oblast', N Ukraine 51°20′N 32°54′E
219 D8 **Bat Yam** Tel Aviv, C Israel 32°01′N 34°45′E
197 I2 **Batyrevo** Chuvashskaya Respublika, W Russian Federation 55°04′N 47°34′E
Batys Qazaqstan Oblysy *see* Zapadnyy Kazakhstan
164 D3 **Batz, Île de** *island* NW France
259 H4 **Bau** Sarawak, East Malaysia 01°25′N 110°10′E
263 K4 **Bauang** Luzon, N Philippines 16°33′N 120°19′E
260 E6 **Baubau** *var.* Baoebaoe. Pulau Buton, C Indonesia 05°30′S 122°37′E
133 L6 **Bauchi** Bauchi, NE Nigeria 10°18′N 09°46′E
133 L6 **Bauchi** ◈ *state* C Nigeria
166 A7 **Baud** Morbihan, NW France 47°52′N 02°59′W
74 G2 **Baudette** Minnesota, N USA 48°42′N 94°36′W
287 J6 **Bauer Basin** *undersea feature* E Pacific Ocean 10°00′S 101°45′W
281 M4 **Bauer Field** *var.* Port Vila. ✈ (Port-Vila) Éfaté, C Vanuatu 17°42′S 168°21′E
166 E8 **Baugé** Pays de la Loire, France 47°10′N 0°16′W
167 H9 **Baugy** Centre, France 47°05′N 2°44′E
59 L5 **Bauld, Cape** *headland* Newfoundland and Labrador, E Canada 51°35′N 55°22′W
53 H3 **Baumann Fiord** *coastal sea feature* Nunavut, N Canada
165 K4 **Baume-les-Dames** Doubs, E France 47°22′N 06°20′E
181 J12 **Baunach** Bayern, Germany 10°51′N 49°59′E
281 J2 **Baunani** Malaita, N Solomon Islands 09°06′S 160°52′E
181 G8 **Baunatal** Hessen, C Germany 51°15′N 09°25′E
175 C10 **Baunei** Sardegna, Italy, C Mediterranean Sea 40°04′N 09°36′E
106 E8 **Baures, Río** ≈ N Bolivia
113 K3 **Bauru** São Paulo, S Brazil 22°19′S 49°07′W
181 F14 **Bauschlott** Baden-Württemberg, Germany 8°43′N 48°58′E
Baushar *see* Bawshar
190 D7 **Bauska** *Ger.* Bauske. Bauska, S Latvia 56°25′N 24°11′E
Bauske *see* Bauska
179 I8 **Bautzen** *Lus.* Budyšin. Sachsen, E Germany 51°11′N 14°29′E
227 I8 **Bauyrzhan Momyshuly** *Kaz.* Baūyrzhan Momyshuly; *prev.* Burnoye. Zhambyl, S Kazakhstan 42°36′N 70°46′E
Bauzanum *see* Bolzano
Bavaria *see* Bayern
177 H3 **Bavarian Alps** *Ger.* Bayrische Alpen. ▲▲ Austria/Germany
140 G9 **Baviaanskloofberge** ▲▲ Eastern Cape, South Africa
84 F3 **Baviácora** Sonora, Mexico
Bavière *see* Bayern
84 F3 **Bavispe** Sonora, Mexico 30°28′N 108°56′W
84 F3 **Bavispe, Río** ≈ NW Mexico
197 K2 **Bavly** Respublika Tatarstan, W Russian Federation 54°20′N 53°21′E
259 H6 **Bawal, Pulau** *island* N Indonesia
259 J6 **Bawan** Borneo, C Indonesia 01°36′S 113°55′E
277 J7 **Baw Baw, Mount** ▲ Victoria, SE Australia 37°49′S 146°16′E
161 M5 **Bawdsey** United Kingdom 52°01′N 1°26′E
261 J5 **Bawe** Papua, E Indonesia 02°56′S 134°39′E
259 J8 **Bawean, Pulau** *island* S Indonesia
259 I8 **Bawen** Jawa, S Indonesia 07°14′S 110°26′E
129 H4 **Bawîṭi** *var.* Bawîṭi. N Egypt 28°19′N 28°53′E
Bawîṭi *see* Bawîṭi
133 H6 **Bawku** N Ghana 11°00′N 00°12′W
256 D5 **Bawlakè** Kayah State, C Myanmar (Burma) 19°10′N 97°19′E
258 C5 **Bawo Ofuloa** Pulau Tanahmasa, W Indonesia 0°10′S 98°24′E
221 K4 **Bawshar** *var.* Baushar. NE Oman 23°32′N 58°24′E
161 J1 **Bawtry** N England, United Kingdom 53°26′N 01°03′W
159 L9 **Bawtry** N England, United Kingdom 53°26′N 01°03′W
238 G5 **Baxkorgan** Xinjiang Uygur Zizhiqu, W China 39°05′N 90°00′E
69 L2 **Baxley** Georgia, SE USA 31°46′N 82°21′W
239 I9 **Baxoi** *var.* Baima. Xizang Zizhiqu, W China 30°01′N 96°53′E
80 E1 **Baxter** California, USA 39°13′N 120°47′W
74 H7 **Baxter** Iowa, C USA 41°49′N 93°09′W
74 G3 **Baxter** Minnesota, N USA 46°21′N 94°18′W
75 G11 **Baxter Springs** Kansas, C USA 37°01′N 94°45′W
136 G7 **Bay** *off.* Gobolka Bay. ◈ *region* SW Somalia
Bay *see* Baicheng
90 E5 **Bayamo** Granma, E Cuba 20°21′N 76°38′W
91 I7 **Bayamón** E Puerto Rico 18°24′N 66°09′W
247 L4 **Bayan** Heilongjiang, NE China 46°05′N 127°24′E
260 B8 **Bayan** *prev.* Bajan. Pulau Lombok, C Indonesia 08°16′S 116°28′E
239 L1 **Bayan** *var.* Maanĭt. Töv, C Mongolia 47°14′N 107°34′E
Bayan *see* Hölönbuyr, Dornod, Mongolia
Bayan *see* Ihhet, Dornogovĭ, Mongolia
Bayan *see* Bayan-Uul, Govĭ-Altay, Mongolia
Bayan *see* Bayanhutag, Hentiy, Mongolia
Bayan *see* Bürentogtoh, Hövsgol, Mongolia
232 E6 **Bayāna** Rājasthān, N India 26°55′N 77°18′E
230 F3 **Bāyān, Band-e** ▲▲ C Afghanistan
239 I2 **Bayanbulag** Bayanhongor, C Mongolia 46°46′N 98°07′E
Bayanbulag *see* Ömnödelger
238 E3 **Bayanbulak** Xinjiang Uygur Zizhiqu, W China 43°05′N 84°05′E
239 K1 **Bayanchandmanĭ** *var.* Ihsüüj. Töv, C Mongolia 48°12′N 106°23′E
239 K3 **Bayandalay** *var.* Dalay. Ömnögovĭ, S Mongolia 43°27′N 103°30′E
239 M2 **Bayandelger** *var.* Shireet. Sühbaatar, SE Mongolia 45°33′N 112°19′E
246 D2 **Bayandzürh** *var.* Altraga. Hövsgöl, N Mongolia 50°08′N 98°54′E
244 D2 **Bayan Gol** Nei Mongol Zizhiqu, N China 40°18′N 106°59′E
Bayan Gol *see* Dengkou, China
Bayangol *see* Bugat, Mongolia
239 J3 **Bayangovĭ** *var.* Örgön. Bayanhongor, C Mongolia 44°43′N 100°23′E
239 J7 **Bayan Har Shan** *var.* Bayan Khar. ▲▲ C China
239 I1 **Bayanhayrhan** *var.* Altanbulag. Dzavhan, N Mongolia 49°16′N 96°22′E
239 J2 **Bayanhongor** Bayanhongor, C Mongolia 46°08′N 100°42′E
239 J2 **Bayanhongor** ◈ *province* C Mongolia
244 C4 **Bayan Hot** *var.* Alxa Zuoqi. Nei Mongol Zizhiqu, N China 38°49′N 105°40′E
239 L1 **Bayanhutag** *var.* Bayan. Hentiy, C Mongolia 47°13′N 110°57′E
247 K5 **Bayan Huxu** *var.* Horqin Zuoyi Zhongqi. Nei Mongol Zizhiqu, N China 45°02′N 121°28′E
Bayan Khar *see* Bayan Har Shan
258 D2 **Bayan Lepas** ✈ (George Town) Pinang, Peninsular Malaysia 05°18′N 100°15′E
239 J3 **Bayanlig** *var.* Hatansuudal. Bayanhongor, C Mongolia 44°34′N 100°41′E
244 C2 **Bayan Mod** Nei Mongol Zizhiqu, N China 40°45′N 104°29′E
239 L1 **Bayanmönh** *var.* Ulaan-Ereg. Hentiy, E Mongolia 46°50′N 109°39′E
Bayan Nuru *see* Xar Burd
238 G1 **Bayannuur** *var.* Tsul-Ulaan. Bayan-Ölgiy, W Mongolia 48°51′N 91°13′E
244 F1 **Bayan Obo** *prev.* Bayan Obo. Nei Mongol Zizhiqu, N China 41°45′N 109°58′E
Bayan Obo *see* Bayan Obo
89 L9 **Bayano, Lago** ◎ E Panama
238 G1 **Bayan-Ölgiy** ◈ *province* NW Mongolia
239 I3 **Bayan-Öndör** *var.* Bulgan. Bayanhongor, C Mongolia 44°48′N 98°39′E
239 K2 **Bayan-Öndör** *var.* Bumbat. Övörhangay, C Mongolia 46°30′N 104°08′E
239 K1 **Bayan-Önjüül** *var.* Ihhayrhan. Töv, C Mongolia 46°57′N 105°51′E
239 M1 **Bayan-Ovoo** *var.* Javhlant. Hentiy, E Mongolia 47°46′N 112°06′E
239 J2 **Bayan-Ovoo** *var.* Erdenetsogt. Ömnögovĭ, S Mongolia 42°54′N 106°16′E
245 H2 **Bayan Qagan** Inner Mongolia, China 41°13′N 113°07′E
Bayansayr *see* Baatsagaan
239 I6 **Bayan Shan** ▲ C China 37°36′N 96°23′E
239 J2 **Bayanteeg** Övörhangay, C Mongolia 45°39′N 101°30′E
239 I1 **Bayantes** *var.* Altay. Dzavhan, N Mongolia 49°40′N 96°21′E
Bayantöhöm *see* Büren
239 L1 **Bayantsagaan** *var.* Dzogsool. Töv, C Mongolia 46°46′N 107°18′E
247 H4 **Bayantümen** *var.* Tsagaanders. Dornod, NE Mongolia 48°03′N 114°16′E
Bayan-Uhaa *see* Ih-Uul
247 I5 **Bayan Ul** *var.* Xi Ujimqin Qi. Nei Mongol Zizhiqu, N China 44°31′N 117°36′E
Bayan-Ulaan *see* Dzüünbayan-Ulaan
247 H3 **Bayan-Uul** *var.* Javarthushuu. Dornod, NE Mongolia 49°05′N 112°40′E
239 H2 **Bayan-Uul** *var.* Bayan. Govĭ-Altay, W Mongolia 47°05′N 95°13′E
239 L1 **Bayanuur** *var.* Tsul-Ulaan. Töv, C Mongolia 47°44′N 108°22′E
74 A7 **Bayard** Nebraska, C USA 41°45′N 103°19′W
79 K9 **Bayard** New Mexico, SW USA 32°45′N 108°07′W
169 L3 **Bayard, Col** *pass* SE France
Bayasgalant *see* Mönhhaan
214 E5 **Bayat** Çorum, N Turkey 40°34′N 34°07′E
114 A10 **Bayauca** Buenos Aires, Argentina 34°51′S 61°18′W
263 L8 **Bayawan** Negros, C Philippines 09°22′N 122°50′E
223 H6 **Bayāẕ** Kermān, C Iran 30°41′N 55°29′E
263 M7 **Baybay** Leyte, C Philippines 10°41′N 124°49′E
67 M7 **Bayboro** North Carolina, SE USA 35°08′N 76°49′W
215 I5 **Bayburt** Bayburt, NE Turkey 40°15′N 40°16′E
215 I5 **Bayburt** ◈ *province* NE Turkey
72 H7 **Bay City** Michigan, N USA 43°35′N 83°52′W
71 H8 **Bay City** Texas, SW USA 28°59′N 96°00′W
Baydarata Bay *see* Baydaratskaya Guba
195 L1 **Baydaratskaya Guba** *var.* Baydarata Bay. *bay* N Russian Federation
136 G6 **Baydhabo** *var.* Baydhowa, Isha Baydhabo, *It.* Baidoa. Bay, SW Somalia 03°08′N 43°39′E
Baydhowa *see* Baydhabo
133 J8 **Bayelsa** ◈ *state* S Nigeria
179 H11 **Bayerischer Wald** ▲▲ SE Germany
179 G11 **Bayern** *Eng.* Bavaria, *Fr.* Bavière. ◈ *state* SE Germany
229 L5 **Bayetovo** Narynskaya Oblast', C Kyrgyzstan 41°14′N 74°55′E
164 F3 **Bayeux** *anc.* Augustodurum. Calvados, N France 49°16′N 00°42′W
62 B5 **Bayfield** ≈ Ontario, S Canada
226 G7 **Baygekum** *Kaz.* Bäygequm. Kzylorda, S Kazakhstan 44°15′N 66°34′E
Bäygequm *see* Baygekum
114 G6 **Baygorria** Durazno, Uruguay 32°53′S 56°48′W
242 G5 **Bayiashan** Hubei, C China 28°00′N 112°39′E
214 B6 **Bayındır** Izmir, SW Turkey 38°12′N 27°40′E
216 C8 **Bāyir** *var.* Bā'ir. Ma'ān, S Jordan 30°46′N 36°40′E
Bay Islands *see* Bahía, Islas de la
217 I3 **Bayjī** *var.* Baiji. Ṣalāḥ ad Dīn, N Iraq 34°56′N 43°29′E
Baykadam *see* Saudakent
193 I8 **Baykal, Ozero** *Eng.* Lake Baikal. ◎ S Russian Federation
193 H8 **Baykal'sk** Irkutskaya Oblast', S Russian Federation 51°30′N 104°03′E
215 J7 **Baykan** Siirt, SE Turkey 38°08′N 41°43′E
193 H6 **Baykit** Evenkiyskiy Avtonomnyy Okrug, C Russian Federation 61°37′N 96°23′E
226 G5 **Baykonur** *var.* Baykonyr. Karaganda, C Kazakhstan 47°50′N 75°33′E
Baykonur *see* Baykonyr
226 F6 **Baykonyr** *var.* Baykonur, *Kaz.* Bayqongyr; *prev.* Leninsk. Kyzylorda, S Kazakhstan 45°38′N 63°20′E
Baykonyr *see* Baykonur
238 C4 **Baykurt** Xinjiang Uygur Zizhiqu, W China 39°56′N 75°33′E
62 E1 **Bay, Lac** ◎ Québec, SE Canada
263 K5 **Bay, Laguna de** ◎ Luzon, N Philippines
197 M3 **Baymak** Respublika Bashkortostan, W Russian Federation 52°34′N 58°20′E
68 G3 **Bay Minette** Alabama, S USA 30°52′N 87°46′W
222 F10 **Baynūnah** *desert* W United Arab Emirates
118 D8 **Bayo, Cerro** ▲ Neuquén, Argentina 37°09′S 70°30′W
278 I5 **Bay of Plenty** *off.* Bay of Plenty Region. ◈ *region* North Island, New Zealand
Bay of Plenty Region *see* Bay of Plenty
285 N2 **Bay of Wrecks** *bay* Kiritimati, E Kiribati
263 K4 **Bayombong** Luzon, N Philippines 16°29′N 121°08′E
167 L6 **Bayon** Lorraine, France 48°29′N 6°19′E
Bayonnaise Rocks *see* Beyonēsu-retsugan
164 F8 **Bayonne** *anc.* Lapurdum. Pyrénées-Atlantiques, SW France 43°30′N 01°28′W
68 C1 **Bayou D'Arbonne Lake** ▣ Louisiana, S USA
68 F4 **Bayou La Batre** Alabama, S USA 30°24′N 88°15′W
Bayou State *see* Mississippi
Bayqadam *see* Saudakent
Bayqongyr *see* Baykonyr
Bayram-Ali *see* Baýramaly
228 F8 **Baýramaly** *var.* Bayramaly; *prev.* Bayram-Ali. Mary Welaýaty, S Turkmenistan 37°33′N 62°08′E
187 K4 **Bayramiç** Çanakkale, Turkey 39°49′N 26°37′E
179 G10 **Bayreuth** *var.* Baireuth. Bayern, SE Germany 49°57′N 11°34′E
Bayrische Alpen *see* Bavarian Alps
Bayrūt *see* Beyrouth
68 F4 **Bay Saint Louis** Mississippi, S USA 30°18′N 89°19′W
Baysān *see* Bet She'an
Bayshint *see* Öndörshireet
65 I6 **Bay Shore** New York, USA 40°44′N 73°15′W
62 D3 **Bays, Lake of** ◎ Ontario, S Canada
68 F2 **Bay Springs** Mississippi, S USA 31°58′N 89°17′W
Bay State *see* Massachusetts
Baysun *see* Boysun
62 D3 **Baysville** Ontario, S Canada 45°10′N 79°03′W
220 F8 **Bayt al Faqīh** W Yemen 14°30′N 43°20′E
238 G3 **Baytik Shan** ▲▲ China/Mongolia
Bayt Laḥm *see* Bethlehem
71 I7 **Baytown** Texas, SW USA 29°43′N 94°59′W
259 L5 **Bayur, Tanjung** *headland* Borneo, N Indonesia 0°43′S 117°32′E
128 C3 **Bayy al Kabīr, Wādī** *dry watercourse* NW Libya
Bayyrqum *see* Bairkum
170 G8 **Baza** Andalucía, S Spain 37°30′N 02°45′W
215 M4 **Bazardüzü Dağı** *Rus.* Gora Bazardyuzyu. ▲ N Azerbaijan 41°13′N 47°50′E
Bazardyuzyu, Gora *see* Bazardüzü Dağı
Bazargic *see* Dobrich
139 J5 **Bazaruto, Ilha do** *island* SE Mozambique
164 G7 **Bazas** Gironde, SW France 44°27′N 00°11′W
170 G8 **Baza, Sierra de** ▲▲ S Spain
173 I8 **Baza, Sierra de** ▲▲ Spain
242 C1 **Bazhong** *var.* Bazhou. Sichuan, C China 31°55′N 106°44′E
Bazhong *see* Batang
245 J3 **Bazhou** Hebei, China 39°04′N 116°14′E
Bazhou *see* Bazhong
62 G1 **Bazin** ≈ Québec, SE Canada
Bazin *see* Pezinok
217 I5 **Bāzīyah** Al Anbār, C Iraq 33°50′N 42°41′E
166 E5 **Bazoches-au-Houlme** Basse-Normandie, France 48°49′N 0°14′W
218 J1 **Bcharré** *var.* Bcharreh, Bsharrī, Bsherri. NE Lebanon 34°16′N 36°01′E
218 G2 **Bcharré** Lebanon 34°15′N 36°00′E
Bcharreh *see* Bcharré
74 A3 **Beach** North Dakota, N USA 46°55′N 104°00′W
277 H7 **Beachport** South Australia 37°29′S 140°03′E
65 H8 **Beachwood** New Jersey, USA 39°56′N 74°12′W
161 L8 **Beachy Head** *headland* SE England, United Kingdom 50°44′N 00°16′E
65 H4 **Beacon** New York, NE USA 41°30′N 73°54′W
141 I9 **Beacon Bay** Eastern Cape, South Africa 32°58′S 27°57′E
160 G4 **Beacon Hill** ▲ United Kingdom 52°23′N 3°13′W
159 K4 **Beadnell** United Kingdom 55°33′N 1°38′W
160 E8 **Beaford** United Kingdom 50°55′N 4°03′W
117 D14 **Beagle Channel** *channel* Argentina/Chile
274 G2 **Beagle Gulf** *gulf* Northern Territory, N Australia
159 J4 **Beal** United Kingdom 55°40′N 1°54′W
Bealach an Doirín *see* Ballaghaderreen
Bealach Cláir *see* Ballyclare
Bealach Féich *see* Ballybofey
139 M5 **Bealanana** Mahajanga, NE Madagascar 14°33′S 48°44′E
Béal an Átha *see* Ballina
Béal an Átha Móir *see* Ballinamore
Béal an Mhuirhead *see* Belmullet
Béal Átha Beithe *see* Ballybay
Béal Átha Conaill *see* Ballyconnell
Beál Átha hAmhnais *see* Ballyhaunis
Béal Átha na Sluaighe *see* Ballinasloe
Béal Átha Seanaidh *see* Ballyshannon
Bealdovuopmi *see* Peltovuoma
Béal Feirste *see* Belfast
Béal Tairbirt *see* Belturbet
160 G8 **Beaminster** S England, United Kingdom
Beanna Boirche *see* Mourne Mountains
Beannchar *see* Banagher, Ireland
Beannchar *see* Bangor, Northern Ireland, UK
Beanntraí *see* Bantry
64 F8 **Bear** Delaware, USA 39°38′N 75°40′W
Bearalváhki *see* Berlevåg
53 I5 **Bear Bay** *coastal sea feature* Nunavut, N Canada
66 C7 **Bear Creek** ≈ Alabama/Mississippi, S USA
73 A10 **Bear Creek** ≈ Illinois, N USA
75 H13 **Bearden** Arkansas, C USA 33°43′N 92°37′W
72 E1 **Beardmore** Ontario, S Canada 49°36′N 87°57′W
293 I6 **Beardmore Glacier** *glacier* Antarctica
73 B10 **Beardstown** Illinois, N USA 40°01′N 90°25′W
74 B7 **Bear Hill** ▲ Nebraska, C USA 41°24′N 101°49′W
Bear Island *see* Bjørnøya
62 D3 **Bear Lake** Ontario, S Canada 45°28′N 79°31′W
79 I1 **Bear Lake** ◎ Idaho/Utah, NW USA
83 K6 **Bear, Mount** ▲ Alaska, USA 61°16′N 141°09′W
164 F9 **Béarn** *cultural region* SW France
292 F6 **Bear Peninsula** *peninsula* Antarctica
158 G3 **Bearsden** United Kingdom 55°55′N 4°21′W
80 E3 **Bear Valley** California, USA 38°28′N 120°02′W
80 D4 **Bear Valley** California, USA 37°34′N 120°07′W
232 E3 **Beās** ≈ India/Pakistan
171 H2 **Beasain** País Vasco, N Spain 43°03′N 02°11′W
170 G7 **Beas de Segura** Andalucía, S Spain 38°16′N 02°54′W
91 H6 **Beata, Cabo** *headland* SW Dominican Republic 17°34′N 71°25′W
91 H6 **Beata, Isla** *island* SW Dominican Republic
75 E8 **Beatrice** Nebraska, C USA 40°14′N 96°43′W
139 H3 **Beatrice** Mashonaland East, NE Zimbabwe 18°15′S 30°55′E
159 H5 **Beattock** United Kingdom 55°18′N 3°28′W
56 F1 **Beatton** ≈ British Columbia, W Canada
56 F1 **Beatton River** British Columbia, W Canada 57°35′N 121°45′W
80 H7 **Beatty** Nevada, W USA 36°53′N 116°44′W
66 G4 **Beattyville** Kentucky, S USA 37°33′N 83°44′W
137 G10 **Beau Bassin** W Mauritius 20°13′S 57°27′E
165 J8 **Beaucaire** Gard, S France 43°49′N 04°37′E
62 D2 **Beauchêne, Lac** ◎ Québec, SE Canada
277 M2 **Beaudesert** Queensland, E Australia 28°00′S 152°27′E
277 I7 **Beaufort** Victoria, SE Australia 37°27′S 143°24′E
67 M7 **Beaufort** North Carolina, SE USA 34°44′N 76°41′W
67 I10 **Beaufort** South Carolina, SE USA 32°23′N 80°40′W
166 E8 **Beaufort-en-Vallée** Pays de la Loire, France 47°26′N 0°13′W
83 J2 **Beaufort Sea** *sea* Arctic Ocean
Beaufort-Wes *see* Beaufort West
140 F8 **Beaufort West** *Afr.* Beaufort-Wes. Western Cape, SW South Africa 32°21′S 22°35′E
165 H4 **Beaugency** Loiret, C France 47°46′N 01°38′E
63 K1 **Beau Lake** ▣ Maine, NE USA
161 I8 **Beaulieu** United Kingdom 50°49′N 1°27′W
161 I8 **Beaulieu** ≈ United Kingdom
54 F4 **Beaulieu River** ≈ Northwest territories, N Canada
156 F5 **Beauly** N Scotland, United Kingdom 57°29′N 04°29′W
167 H3 **Beaumetz-lés-Loges** Nord-Pas-de-Calais, France 50°14′N 2°39′E
163 D12 **Beaumont** Hainaut, S Belgium 50°12′N 04°13′E
278 C12 **Beaumont** Otago, South Island, New Zealand 45°48′S 169°32′E
81 F11 **Beaumont** California, USA 33°56′N 116°59′W
68 F3 **Beaumont** Mississippi, S USA 31°10′N 88°55′W
71 J7 **Beaumont** Texas, SW USA 30°05′N 94°06′W
168 F5 **Beaumont-de-Lomagne** Tarn-et-Garonne, S France 43°54′N 01°00′E
164 G4 **Beaumont-sur-Sarthe** Sarthe, NW France 48°15′N 00°07′E
165 J5 **Beaune** Côte d'Or, C France 47°02′N 04°50′E
167 H7 **Beaune-la-Rolande** Centre, France 48°04′N 2°26′E
63 J1 **Beaupré** Québec, SE Canada 47°03′N 70°52′W
164 F5 **Beaupréau** Maine-et-Loire, NW France 47°13′N 00°57′W
163 F12 **Beauraing** Namur, SE Belgium 50°07′N 04°57′E
165 J7 **Beaurepaire** Isère, E France 45°20′N 05°03′E
167 K9 **Beaurepaire-en-Bresse** Bourgogne, France 46°40′N 5°23′E
55 J9 **Beausejour** Manitoba, S Canada 50°04′N 96°30′W
165 H2 **Beauvais** *anc.* Bellovacum, Caesaromagus. Oise, N France 49°27′N 02°04′E
57 L3 **Beauval** Saskatchewan, C Canada 55°10′N 107°37′W
167 H3 **Beauval** Picardie, France 50°06′N 2°20′E
164 E5 **Beauvoir-sur-Mer** Vendée, NW France 46°54′N 02°03′W
166 D10 **Beauvoir-sur-Niort** Poitou-Charentes, France 46°10′N 0°28′W
83 J4 **Beaver** Alaska, USA 66°22′N 147°31′W
75 C11 **Beaver** Oklahoma, C USA 36°48′N 100°32′W
62 C8 **Beaver** Pennsylvania, NE USA 40°39′N 80°19′W
79 H4 **Beaver** Utah, W USA 38°16′N 112°38′W
54 D4 **Beaver** ≈ British Columbia/Yukon Territory, W Canada
57 L4 **Beaver** ≈ Saskatchewan, C Canada
75 C8 **Beaver City** Nebraska, C USA 40°08′N 99°49′W
83 K5 **Beaver Creek** Yukon Territory, W Canada 62°20′N 140°45′W
73 G11 **Beavercreek** Ohio, N USA 39°42′N 83°58′W
83 J4 **Beaver Creek** ≈ Alaska, USA
75 C8 **Beaver Creek** ≈ Kansas/Nebraska, C USA
74 A3 **Beaver Creek** ≈ Montana/North Dakota, N USA
74 E7 **Beaver Creek** ≈ Nebraska, C USA
70 F3 **Beaver Creek** ≈ Texas, SW USA
72 D7 **Beaver Dam** Wisconsin, N USA 43°28′N 88°49′W
72 D7 **Beaver Dam Lake** ◎ Wisconsin, N USA
62 C8 **Beaver Falls** Pennsylvania, NE USA 40°45′N 80°20′W
77 H6 **Beaverhead Mountains** ▲▲ Idaho/Montana, NW USA
77 H6 **Beaverhead River** ≈ Montana, NW USA
55 J7 **Beaverhill Lake** ◎ Manitoba, C Canada
117 G11 **Beaver Island** *island* W Falkland Islands
72 F5 **Beaver Island** *island* Michigan, N USA
75 G11 **Beaver Lake** ▣ Arkansas, C USA
56 F3 **Beaverlodge** Alberta, W Canada 55°11′N 119°29′W
54 C2 **Beaver River** ≈ Yokon Territory, NW Canada
62 G5 **Beaver River** ≈ New York, NE USA
60 F6 **Beaver River** ≈ Oklahoma, C USA
73 J10 **Beaver River** ≈ Pennsylvania, NE USA
117 G11 **Beaver Settlement** Beaver Island, W Falkland Islands 51°30′S 61°15′W
Beaver State *see* Oregon
62 D4 **Beaverton** Ontario, S Canada 44°24′N 79°07′W
76 C5 **Beaverton** Oregon, NW USA 45°29′N 122°49′W
232 D6 **Beāwar** Rājasthān, N India 26°08′N 74°22′E
Bebas, Dasht-i *see* Bābūs, Dasht-e
110 A5 **Bebedouro** São Paulo, S Brazil 20°58′S 48°28′W
52 D8 **Bebensee Lake** ◎ Nunavut, NW Canada
159 I10 **Bebington** United Kingdom 53°21′N 3°01′W
181 H9 **Bebra** Hessen, C Germany 50°59′N 09°46′E
87 L5 **Becal** Campeche, SE Mexico 19°49′N 90°28′W
87 M6 **Becanchén** Yucatán, Mexico 19°53′N 89°14′W
63 I2 **Bécancour** ≈ Québec, SE Canada
161 M3 **Beccles** E England, United Kingdom 52°27′N 01°32′E
184 F2 **Bečej** *Ger.* Altbetsche, *Hung.* Óbecse, Rácz-Becse; *prev.* Magyar-Becse, Stari Bečej. Vojvodina, N Serbia 45°36′N 20°02′E
170 D2 **Becerréa** Galicia, NW Spain 42°51′N 07°10′W
130 G3 **Béchar** *prev.* Colomb-Béchar. W Algeria 31°38′N 02°11′W
83 H8 **Becharof Lake** ◎ Alaska, USA
166 C6 **Bécherel** Bretagne, France 48°18′N 1°57′W
188 C10 **Bechet** *var.* Bechetu. Dolj, SW Romania 43°45′N 23°57′E
Bechetu *see* Bechet
181 I14 **Bechhofen** Bayern, Germany 10°33′N 49°09′E
181 D13 **Bechhofen** Rheinland-Pfalz, Germany 7°24′N 49°21′E
171 M9 **Bechloul** Algeria
161 K6 **Beckenham** United Kingdom 51°23′N 0°02′W
159 H6 **Beckfoot** United Kingdom 54°49′N 3°24′W
161 J1 **Beckingham** E England, United Kingdom
161 J1 **Beckingham** C England, United Kingdom 53°24′N 5°00′E
159 L10 **Beckingham** C England, United Kingdom 53°24′N 5°00′E
67 I4 **Beckley** West Virginia, NE USA 37°46′N 81°12′W
180 E7 **Beckum** Nordrhein-Westfalen, W Germany 51°45′N 08°03′E
71 I5 **Beckville** Texas, SW USA 32°14′N 94°27′W
80 F1 **Beckwourth** California, USA 39°49′N 120°23′W
78 G3 **Becky Peak** ▲ Nevada, W USA 39°59′N 114°33′W
188 D6 **Beclean** *Hung.* Bethlen; *prev.* Betlen. Bistrița-Năsăud, N Romania 47°10′N 24°11′E
Bécs *see* Wien
183 E9 **Bečva** *Ger.* Betschau, *Pol.* Beczwa. ≈ E Czech Republic
Beczwa *see* Bečva
159 K7 **Bedale** United Kingdom 54°17′N 1°35′W
165 I8 **Bédarieux** Hérault, S France 43°37′N 03°10′E
180 B7 **Bedburg** Nordrhein-Westfalen, Germany 6°11′N 51°46′E
130 E3 **Beddouza, Cap** *headland* W Morocco 32°35′N 09°16′W
136 D4 **Bedelē** Oromīya, C Ethiopia 08°25′N 36°21′E
229 M5 **Bedel Pass** *Rus.* Pereval Bedel. *pass* China/Kyrgyzstan
Bedel, Pereval *see* Bedel Pass
155 D12 **Beder** Århus, C Denmark 56°03′N 10°13′E
161 J4 **Bedford** E England, United Kingdom 52°08′N 00°29′W
73 E12 **Bedford** Indiana, N USA 38°51′N 86°29′W
75 G8 **Bedford** Iowa, C USA 40°40′N 94°43′W
66 F3 **Bedford** Kentucky, S USA 38°36′N 85°18′W
65 L2 **Bedford** Massachusetts, USA 42°29′N 71°17′W
64 A7 **Bedford** Pennsylvania, NE USA 40°00′N 78°29′W
67 J4 **Bedford** Virginia, NE USA 37°20′N 79°31′W
161 K3 **Bedford Level** *physical region* E England, United Kingdom
161 K4 **Bedfordshire** *cultural region* E England, United Kingdom
159 K5 **Bedlington** United Kingdom 55°08′N 1°35′W
197 H3 **Bednodem'yanovsk** Penzenskaya Oblast', W Russian Federation 53°55′N 43°14′E
162 I3 **Bedum** Groningen, NE Netherlands 53°18′N 06°36′E
160 G6 **Bedwas** United Kingdom 51°36′N 3°12′W
161 I4 **Bedworth** United Kingdom 52°28′N 1°28′W
75 I12 **Beebe** Arkansas, C USA 35°04′N 91°52′W
64 D5 **Beech Glen** Pennsylvania, NE USA 41°19′N 76°35′W
Beechy Group *see* Chichijima-rettō
91 K5 **Beef Island** ✈ (Road Town)Tortola, E British Virgin Islands 18°25′N 64°31′W
Beehive State *see* Utah
163 G10 **Beek** Limburg, SE Netherlands 50°56′N 05°47′E
163 G10 **Beek** ✈ (Maastricht) Limburg, SE Netherlands 50°55′N 05°47′E
163 G8 **Beek-en-Donk** Noord-Brabant, S Netherlands 51°31′N 05°37′E
180 E7 **Beelen** Nordrhein-Westfalen, Germany 8°08′N 51°56′E
180 J6 **Beendorf** Sachsen-Anhalt, Germany 11°05′N 52°14′E
219 C9 **Beeri** Israel 31°25′N 34°29′E
219 E12 **Be'ér Menuḥa** Israel
219 E12 **Be'ér Menuḥa** Israel 30°17′N 35°06′E
219 E12 **Be'er Menuha** *prev.* Be'ér Menuḥa. Southern, S Israel 30°22′N 35°09′E
Be'ér Menuḥa *see* Be'er Menuha
163 C9 **Beernem** West-Vlaanderen, NW Belgium 51°09′N 03°18′E
163 F9 **Beerse** Antwerpen, N Belgium 51°20′N 04°52′E
Beersheba *see* Be'ér Sheva'
219 C10 **Be'ér Sheva'** Israel
219 D10 **Be'ér Sheva'** *var.* Beersheba, *Ar.* Bir es Saba; *prev.* Be'ér Sheva'. Southern, S Israel 31°15′N 34°47′E
219 D10 **Beér Sheva** Israel 31°14′N 34°47′E
Be'ér Sheva' *see* Be'ér Sheva'
162 F7 **Beesd** Gelderland, C Netherlands 51°52′N 05°12′E
163 H9 **Beesel** Limburg, SE Netherlands 51°16′N 06°02′E
140 F5 **Beeshoek** Northern Cape, South Africa 28°17′S 23°00′E
141 I3 **Beestekraal** North-West, N South Africa 25°21′S 27°40′E
180 D5 **Beesten** Niedersachsen, Germany 7°30′N 52°26′E
161 I2 **Beeston** United Kingdom 52°55′N 1°13′W
159 H6 **Beeswing** United Kingdom 55°00′N 3°44′W
159 I8 **Beetham** United Kingdom 54°12′N 2°46′W
292 E4 **Beethoven Peninsula** *peninsula* Alexander Island, Antarctica
Beetstersweach *see* Beetsterzwaag
162 H4 **Beetsterzwaag** *Fris.* Beetstersweach. Friesland, N Netherlands 53°03′N 06°04′E
180 J5 **Beetzendorf** Sachsen-Anhalt, Germany 11°06′N 52°42′E
70 G8 **Beeville** Texas, SW USA 28°25′N 97°47′W
134 F7 **Befale** Equateur, NW Dem. Rep. Congo 0°25′N 20°48′E
Befandriana *see* Befandriana Avaratra
139 M5 **Befandriana Avaratra** *var.* Befandriana, Befandriana Nord. Mahajanga, NW Madagascar 15°14′S 48°33′E
Befandriana Nord *see* Befandriana Avaratra
134 G7 **Befori** Equateur, N Dem. Rep. Congo 0°09′N 22°18′E
139 L9 **Befotaka** Fianarantsoa, S Madagascar 23°49′S 47°00′E
277 K7 **Bega** New South Wales, SE Australia 36°43′S 149°50′E
164 E3 **Bégard** Côtes d'Armor, NW France 48°37′N 03°18′W
184 G2 **Begejski Kanal** *canal* Vojvodina, NE Serbia
227 K3 **Begen'** Semipalatinsk, E Kazakhstan 51°11′N 79°03′E
Begoml' *see* Byahoml'
Begovat *see* Bekobod
160 G4 **Beguildy** United Kingdom 52°24′N 3°11′W
233 I7 **Begusarai** Bihār, NE India 25°25′N 86°08′E
223 H6 **Behābād** Yazd, C Iran 32°23′N 59°50′E
Behagle *see* Laï
103 N5 **Béhague, Pointe** *headland* E French Guiana 04°38′N 51°52′W
Behar *see* Bihār
222 E6 **Behbahān** *var.* Behbehān. Khūzestān, SW Iran 30°38′N 50°07′E
Behbehān *see* Behbahān
90 E2 **Behring Point** Andros Island, W Bahamas 24°28′N 77°44′W
222 G3 **Behshahr** *prev.* Ashraf. Māzandarān, N Iran 36°42′N 53°36′E
193 K9 **Bei'an** Heilongjiang, NE China 48°16′N 126°29′E
242 C3 **Beibei** Chongqing Shi, C China 29°55′N 106°47′E
Beibunar *see* Sredishte
Beibu Wan *see* Tongking, Gulf of
181 J8 **Beichlingen** Thüringen, Germany 11°15′N 51°14′E
Beida *see* Al Bayḍā'
245 L3 **Beidaihehaibin** Hebei, NE China 39°49′N 119°31′E
244 C7 **Beidao** Gansu, China 34°21′N 105°32′E
136 C4 **Beigi** Oromīya, C Ethiopia 09°13′N 34°48′E
236 G9 **Beihai** Guangxi Zhuangzu Zizhiqu, S China 21°29′N 109°10′E
239 I6 **Bei Hulsan Hu** ◎ C China
243 H8 **Bei Jiang** ≈ S China
245 J3 **Beijing** *var.* Pei-ching, *Eng.* Peking; *prev.* Pei-p'ing. ● (China) Beijing Shi, E China 39°58′N 116°23′E
245 J3 **Beijing** Beijing Shi, N China 39°48′N 116°33′E
245 J3 **Beijing** ✈ Beijing Shi, N China 39°54′N 116°22′E
Beijing *see* Beijing Shi, China
245 J2 **Beijing Shi** *var.* Beijing, Jing, Pei-ching, *Eng.* Peking; *prev.* Pei-p'ing. ◈ *municipality* E China
132 B2 **Beïla** Trarza, W Mauritania 18°07′N 15°56′W
162 I4 **Beilen** Drenthe, NE Netherlands 52°52′N 06°27′E
242 F9 **Beiliu** *var.* Lingcheng. Guangxi Zhuangzu Zizhiqu, S China 22°50′N 110°22′E
242 F9 **Beiliu Jiang** ▲▲ Guangxi, China
181 E10 **Beilstein** Hessen, Germany 8°15′N 50°36′E
239 H7 **Beilu He** ≈ W China
Beilul *see* Beylul
245 M1 **Beining** *prev.* Beizhen. Liaoning, NE China 41°34′N 121°51′E
156 E4 **Beinn Dearg** ▲ N Scotland, United Kingdom 57°47′N 04°52′W
Beinn MacDuibh *see* Ben Macdui
242 B7 **Beipan Jiang** ≈ S China
245 L1 **Beipiao** Liaoning, NE China 41°49′N 120°45′E
139 J4 **Beira** Sofala, C Mozambique 19°45′S 34°56′E
172 D4 **Beirã** Portalegre, Portugal 39°27′N 7°22′W
139 J4 **Beira** ✈ Sofala, C Mozambique 19°39′S 35°05′E
170 D4 **Beira Alta** *former province* N Portugal
170 D5 **Beira Baixa** *former province* C Portugal
170 C5 **Beira Litoral** *former province* N Portugal
Beirut *see* Beyrouth
Beisān *see* Bet She'an
57 I7 **Beiseker** Alberta, SW Canada 51°20′N 113°34′W
Beitai Ding *see* Wutai Shan
141 K1 **Beitbridge** Matabeleland South, S Zimbabwe 22°10′S 30°02′E
218 F3 **Beit Ed Dine** Lebanon 33°42′N 35°35′E
218 E7 **Beit Fūrik** West Bank 32°10′N 35°19′E
158 G4 **Beith** United Kingdom 55°44′N 4°38′W
219 C9 **Beit Ḥanūn** Gaza Strip 31°32′N 34°32′E
218 F6 **Beit HaShitta** Israel 32°33′N 35°26′E
219 E8 **Beitin** West Bank 31°56′N 35°14′E
219 E8 **Beit Jālā** West Bank
218 E5 **Beit Jann** Israel 32°57′N 35°22′E
219 C9 **Beit Lahiya** Gaza Strip 31°33′N 34°30′E
218 E6 **Beit Lehem HaGelilit** Israel 32°44′N 35°11′E
Beit Lekhem *see* Bethlehem
218 F3 **Beit Meri** Lebanon 33°51′N 35°35′E
219 E8 **Beit Sāhūr** West Bank 31°42′N 35°13′E
219 E8 **Beit Sirā** West Bank 31°53′N 35°03′E
188 B7 **Beiuș** *Hung.* Belényes. Bihor, NW Romania 46°40′N 22°21′E
Beizhen *see* Beining
172 C6 **Beja** *anc.* Pax Julia. Beja, SE Portugal 38°01′N 07°52′W
131 K1 **Béja** *var.* Bājah. N Tunisia 36°45′N 09°04′E
172 C7 **Beja** ◈ *district* S Portugal
131 J1 **Béjaïa** *var.* Bejaïa, *Fr.* Bougie; *anc.* Saldae. NE Algeria 36°49′N 05°03′E
Bejaïa *see* Béjaïa
170 E5 **Béjar** Castilla-León, N Spain 40°24′N 05°45′W
Bejraburi *see* Phetchaburi
87 K9 **Bejucal de Ocampo** Chiapas, Mexico 15°27′N 92°10′W
Bekaa Valley *see* El Beqaa
Bekabad *see* Bekobod
Békás *see* Bicaz
258 G8 **Bekasi** Jawa, C Indonesia 06°14′S 106°595′E
Bek-Budi *see* Qarshi
Bekdaş/Bekdash *see* Garabogaz
229 K6 **Bek-Dzhar** Oshskaya Oblast', SW Kyrgyzstan 40°22′N 73°08′E
183 H12 **Békés** *Rom.* Bichiș. Békés, SE Hungary 46°45′N 21°09′E
183 H12 **Békés** *off.* Békés Megye. ◈ *county* SE Hungary
183 H12 **Békéscsaba** *Rom.* Bichiș-Ciaba. Békés, SE Hungary 46°40′N 21°05′E
Békés Megye *see* Békés
217 J2 **Bēkhma** Arbīl, E Iraq 36°40′N 44°15′E
139 L9 **Bekily** Toliara, S Madagascar 24°12′S 45°20′E
252 H4 **Bekkai** *var.* Betsukai. Hokkaidō, NE Japan 43°23′N 145°07′E
229 I6 **Bekobod** *Rus.* Bekabad; *prev.* Begovat. Toshkent Viloyati, E Uzbekistan 40°17′N 69°11′E
197 H4 **Bekovo** Penzenskaya Oblast', W Russian Federation 52°27′N 43°41′E
Bel *see* Beliu
232 G7 **Bela** Uttar Pradesh, N India 25°55′N 82°00′E
230 F9 **Bela** Baluchistān, SW Pakistan 26°12′N 66°20′E
141 J3 **Bela Bela** Limpopo, South Africa 24°53′S 28°17′E
134 C5 **Bélabo** Est, C Cameroon 04°54′N 13°10′E
166 F10 **Bélâbre** Centre, France 46°33′N 1°10′E
184 G3 **Bela Crkva** *Ger.* Weisskirchen, *Hung.* Fehértemplom. Vojvodina, W Serbia 44°55′N 21°28′E
137 G10 **Bel Air** *var.* Rivière Sèche. E Mauritius
64 A8 **Bel Air** Maryland, USA 39°34′N 78°51′W
170 F7 **Belalcázar** Andalucía, S Spain 38°33′N 05°07′W
185 H5 **Bela Palanka** Serbia, SE Serbia 43°13′N 22°19′E
191 G10 **Belarus** *off.* Republic of Belarus, *var.* Belorussia, *Latv.* Baltkrievija; *prev.* Belorussian SSR, *Rus.* Belorusskaya SSR. ◆ *republic* E Europe
Belarus, Republic of *see* Belarus
Belau *see* Palau
113 H3 **Bela Vista** Mato Grosso do Sul, SW Brazil 22°04′S 56°25′W
141 L4 **Bela Vista** Maputo, S Mozambique 26°20′S 32°40′E
258 C3 **Belawan** Sumatera, W Indonesia 03°46′N 98°44′E
Běla Woda *see* Weisswasser
197 L2 **Belaya** ≈ W Russian Federation
193 K4 **Belaya Gora** Respublika Sakha (Yakutiya), NE Russian Federation 68°25′N 146°12′E
196 G6 **Belaya Kalitiva** Rostovskaya Oblast', SW Russian Federation 48°09′N 40°43′E
195 J9 **Belaya Kholunitsa** Kirovskaya Oblast', NW Russian Federation 58°54′N 50°52′E
Belaya Tserkov' *see* Bila Tserkva
133 K4 **Belbédji** Zinder, S Niger 14°35′N 08°00′E
168 G7 **Belcaire** Languedoc-Roussillon, France 42°49′N 1°58′E
168 G5 **Belcastel** Midi-Pyrénées, France 43°39′N 1°45′E
182 G7 **Bełchatów** *var.* Belchatow. Łódzski, C Poland 51°23′N 19°20′E
Belchatow *see* Bełchatów
53 H4 **Belcher Channel** *Sea waterway* Nunavut, NW Canada
Belcher, Îles *see* Belcher Islands
58 F4 **Belcher Islands** *Fr.* Îles Belcher. *island group* Nunavut, SE Canada
65 J2 **Belchertown** Massachusetts, USA 42°17′N 72°24′W
171 I4 **Belchite** Aragón, NE Spain 41°18′N 00°45′W
158 A9 **Belclare** Ireland 53°29′N 8°56′W
158 B7 **Belcoo** United Kingdom 54°17′N 7°52′W
74 D1 **Belcourt** North Dakota, N USA 48°50′N 99°44′W
64 F3 **Belden** New York, USA 42°12′N 75°41′W
72 F7 **Belding** Michigan, N USA 43°06′N 85°13′W
190 I5 **Belebelka** Novgorodskaya Oblast', Russian Federation
197 L3 **Belebey** Respublika Bashkortostan, W Russian Federation 54°04′N 54°13′E
136 H6 **Beledweyne** *var.* Belet Huen, *It.* Belet Uen. Hiiraan, C Somalia 04°39′N 45°12′E
228 B6 **Belek** Balkan Welaýaty, W Turkmenistan 39°57′N 53°51′E
107 M2 **Belém** *var.* Pará. *state capital* Pará, N Brazil 01°27′S 48°29′W
291 E8 **Belém Ridge** *undersea feature* C Atlantic Ocean
112 C6 **Belén** Catamarca, NW Argentina 27°36′N 67°00′W
102 D5 **Belén** Boyacá, C Colombia 06°01′N 72°55′W
88 G7 **Belén** Rivas, SW Nicaragua 11°30′N 85°55′W
112 G4 **Belén** Concepción, C Paraguay 23°25′S 57°14′W
114 F3 **Belén** Salto, N Uruguay 30°47′S 57°47′W
79 L7 **Belen** New Mexico, SW USA 34°37′N 106°46′W
114 E9 **Belén de Escobar** Buenos Aires, E Argentina 34°21′S 58°47′W
185 K5 **Belene** Pleven, N Bulgaria 43°39′N 25°09′E
185 J5 **Belene, Ostrov** *island* N Bulgaria
89 J9 **Belén, Río** ≈ C Panama
Belényes *see* Beiuș
280 A8 **Belep, Îles** *island group* W New Caledonia
Embalse de Belesar *see* Belesar, Encoro de
170 D2 **Belesar, Encoro de** *Sp.* Embalse de Belesar. ▣ NW Spain
168 G7 **Bélesta** Midi-Pyrénées, France 42°54′N 1°56′E
Belet Huen/Belet Uen *see* Beledweyne
196 F3 **Belëv** Tul'skaya Oblast', W Russian Federation 53°48′N 36°07′E
63 K4 **Belfast** Maine, NE USA 44°25′N 69°02′W
64 B2 **Belfast** New York, USA 42°21′N 78°07′W
158 E7 **Belfast** *Ir.* Béal Feirste. ◐ E Northern Ireland, United Kingdom 54°35′N 05°55′W
157 D8 **Belfast Aldergrove** ✈ E Northern Ireland, United Kingdom 54°37′N 06°11′W
158 E6 **Belfast City** ✈ Belfast City, E Northern Ireland, United Kingdom
157 E8 **Belfast Lough** *Ir.* Loch Lao. *inlet* E Northern Ireland, United Kingdom
74 B3 **Belfield** North Dakota, N USA 46°53′N 103°12′W
159 K4 **Belford** United Kingdom 55°36′N 1°50′W
111 I8 **Belford Roxo** Rio de Janeiro, Brazil 22°46′S 43°24′W
165 K4 **Belfort** Territoire-de-Belfort, E France 47°38′N 06°52′E
Belgard *see* Białogard
234 D6 **Belgaum** Karnātaka, W India 15°52′N 74°30′E
Belgian Congo *see* Congo (Democratic Republic of)
België/Belgique *see* Belgium
163 E11 **Belgium** *off.* Kingdom of Belgium, *Dut.* België, *Fr.* Belgique. ◆ *monarchy* NW Europe
Belgium, Kingdom of *see* Belgium
196 F5 **Belgorod** Belgorodskaya Oblast', W Russian Federation 50°38′N 36°37′E
Belgorod-Dnestrovskiy *see* Bilhorod-Dnistrovs'kyy
196 F5 **Belgorodskaya Oblast'** ◈ *province* W Russian Federation
Belgrad *see* Beograd
74 F4 **Belgrade** Minnesota, N USA 45°27′N 94°59′W
77 I5 **Belgrade** Montana, NW USA 45°46′N 111°10′W
Belgrade *see* Beograd
Belgrano, Cabo *see* Meredith, Cape
292 G3 **Belgrano II** *Argentinian research station* Antarctica 77°50′S 35°25′W
67 M6 **Belhaven** North Carolina, SE USA 35°36′N 76°50′W
168 F9 **Belianes** Cataluña, Spain 41°33′N 1°01′E
175 E12 **Belice** *anc.* Hypsas. ≈ Sicilia, Italy, C Mediterranean Sea
Belice *see* Belize/Belize City
172 C8 **Beliche** Faro, Portugal 37°16′N 7°30′W
184 G6 **Beli Drim** *Alb.* Drini i Bardhë. ≈ Albania/Serbia
Beligrad *see* Berat
282 B6 **Beliliou** *prev.* Peleliu. *island* S Palau
185 L5 **Beli Lom, Yazovir** ▣ NE Bulgaria
184 E2 **Beli Manastir** *Hung.* Pélmonostor; *prev.* Monostor. Osijek-Baranja, NE Croatia 45°46′N 16°38′E
164 F7 **Bélin-Béliet** Gironde, SW France 44°30′N 00°48′W
134 C7 **Bélinga** Ogooué-Ivindo, NE Gabon 01°05′N 13°12′E
67 J3 **Belington** West Virginia, NE USA 39°01′N 79°57′W
197 H3 **Belinskiy** Penzenskaya Oblast', W Russian Federation 52°58′N 43°25′E
258 F6 **Belinyu** Pulau Bangka, W Indonesia 01°37′S 105°45′E
111 J4 **Belisàrio** Minas Gerais, Brazil 20°55′S 42°28′W
258 G6 **Belitung, Pulau** *island* W Indonesia
188 B7 **Beliu** *Hung.* Bel. Arad, W Romania 46°31′N 21°57′E
185 J6 **Beli Vit** ≈ NW Bulgaria
88 E2 **Belize** *Sp.* Belice; *prev.* British Honduras, Colony of Belize. ◆ *commonwealth republic* Central America
88 E1 **Belize** *Sp.* Belice. ◈ *district* NE Belize
88 D2 **Belize** ≈ Belize/Guatemala
Belize *see* Belize City
88 E2 **Belize City** *var.* Belize, *Sp.* Belice. Belize, NE Belize 17°29′N 88°10′W
88 E2 **Belize City** ✈ Belize, NE Belize 17°31′N 88°15′W
Belize, Colony of *see* Belize
Beljak *see* Villach
82 G9 **Belkofski** Alaska, USA 55°07′N 162°04′W
193 J3 **Bel'kovskiy, Ostrov** *island* Novosibirskiye Ostrova, NE Russian Federation
141 I9 **Bell** Eastern Cape, South Africa 33°15′S 27°21′E
58 F7 **Bell** ≈ Québec, SE Canada
56 B6 **Bella Bella** British Columbia, SW Canada 52°04′N 128°07′W
164 G6 **Bellac** Haute-Vienne, C France 46°07′N 01°04′E
114 F6 **Bellaco** Rio Negro, Uruguay 32°36′S 57°54′W
56 C5 **Bella Coola** British Columbia, SW Canada 52°23′N 126°46′W
158 D6 **Bellaghy** United Kingdom 54°48′N 6°31′W
176 E6 **Bellagio** Lombardia, N Italy 45°58′N 09°15′E
72 G6 **Bellaire** Michigan, N USA 44°59′N 85°12′W
158 C8 **Bellananagh** Cavan, Ireland 53°56′N 7°25′W
158 B10 **Bellaneeny** Roscommon, C Ireland
176 E6 **Bellano** Lombardia, N Italy 46°06′N 09°21′E
234 E6 **Bellary** *var.* Ballari. Karnātaka, S India 15°11′N 76°54′E
277 L3 **Bellata** New South Wales, SE Australia 29°58′S 149°49′E
114 F2 **Bella Unión** Artigas, N Uruguay 30°18′S 57°35′W
116 H1 **Bella Vista** Corrientes, NE Argentina 28°30′S 59°03′W
112 D6 **Bella Vista** Tucumán, N Argentina 27°05′S 65°19′W
113 H3 **Bella Vista** Amambay, C Paraguay 22°08′S 56°20′W
104 C4 **Bellavista** Cajamarca, N Peru 05°43′S 78°48′W
104 D5 **Bellavista** San Martín, N Peru 07°04′S 76°35′W
81 E8 **Bella Vista** California, USA 35°39′N 118°19′W
277 M4 **Bellbrook** New South Wales, SE Australia 30°48′S 152°32′E
168 F9 **Bellcaire d'Urgell** Cataluña, Spain 41°45′N 0°55′E
75 I10 **Belle** Missouri, C USA 38°17′N 91°43′W
67 I3 **Belle** West Virginia, NE USA 38°13′N 81°32′W
158 B7 **Belleek** W Northern Ireland, United Kingdom 54°28′N 08°06′W
73 H10 **Bellefontaine** Ohio, N USA 40°22′N 83°45′W
64 B5 **Bellefonte** Pennsylvania, NE USA 40°54′N 77°43′W
74 A5 **Belle Fourche** South Dakota, N USA 44°40′N 103°50′W
77 L7 **Belle Fourche Reservoir** ▣ South Dakota, N USA
74 B5 **Belle Fourche River** ≈ South Dakota/Wyoming, N USA
169 J5 **Bellegarde** Languedoc-Roussillon, France 43°45′N 4°31′E
167 H7 **Bellegarde-du-Loiret** Centre, France 47°59′N 2°26′E
168 G1 **Bellegarde-en-Marche** Limousin, France 45°59′N 2°18′E
165 K6 **Bellegarde-sur-Valserine** Ain, E France 46°06′N 05°49′E
69 M8 **Belle Glade** Florida, SE USA 26°40′N 80°40′W
164 E4 **Belle Île** *island* NW France
59 L5 **Belle Isle** *island* Belle Isle, Newfoundland and Labrador, E Canada
166 A6 **Belle-Isle-en-Terre** Bretagne, France 48°33′N 3°24′W
59 L5 **Belle Isle, Strait of** *strait* Newfoundland and Labrador, E Canada
166 F6 **Bellème** Basse-Normandie, France 48°22′N 0°34′E
169 M2 **Bellentre** Rhône-Alpes, France 45°34′N 6°43′E
Bellenz *see* Bellinzona

◆ Country
● Country Capital
◇ Dependent Territory
○ Dependent Territory Capital
◈ Administrative Regions
✈ International Airport
▲ Mountain
▲▲ Mountain Range
Volcano
≈ River
◎ Lake
▣ Reservoir

Column 1

73 A8 **Belle Plaine** Iowa, C USA 41°54´N 92°16´W
74 G5 **Belle Plaine** Minnesota, N USA 44°39´N 93°47´W
62 D1 **Belleterre** Québec, SE Canada 47°24´N 78°40´W
82 E4 **Belleville** Ontario, SE Canada 44°10´N 77°22´W
165 J6 **Belleville** Rhône, E France 46°09´N 04°42´E
73 B12 **Belleville** Illinois, N USA 38°31´N 89°58´W
75 E9 **Belleville** Kansas, C USA 39°51´N 97°38´W
65 H6 **Belleville** New Jersey, USA 40°47´N 74°08´W
167 K10 **Belleville-sur-Saône** Rhône-Alpes, France 46°06´N 4°45´E
141 H9 **Bellevue** Eastern Cape, South Africa 33°22´S 25°57´E
75 F8 **Bellevue** Iowa, N USA 42°15´N 90°25´W
73 F8 **Bellevue** Nebraska, C USA 41°08´N 95°53´W
73 H3 **Bellevue** Ohio, N USA 41°16´N 82°50´W
70 G3 **Bellevue** Texas, SW USA 33°38´N 98°00´W
76 C3 **Bellevue** Washington, NW USA 47°36´N 122°12´W
103 M6 **Bellevue de l'Inini, Montagnes** ▲ S French Guiana
165 J6 **Belley** Ain, E France 45°46´N 05°41´E
Bellin see Kangirsuk
277 M3 **Bellingen** New South Wales, SE Australia 30°27´S 152°53´E
159 J5 **Bellingham** N England, United Kingdom 55°09´N 02°16´W
76 C2 **Bellingham** Washington, NW USA 48°46´N 122°29´W
Belling Hausen Mulde see Southeast Pacific Basin
292 D2 **Bellingshausen** Russian research station South Shetland Islands, Antarctica 61°57´S 58°23´W
Bellingshausen see Motu One
Bellingshausen Abyssal Plain see Bellingshausen Plain
287 K10 **Bellingshausen Plain** var. Bellingshausen Abyssal Plain. undersea feature SE Pacific Ocean 64°00´S 90°00´W
292 E5 **Bellingshausen Sea** sea Antarctica
162 J4 **Bellingwolde** Groningen, NE Netherlands 53°07´N 07°10´E
176 E5 **Bellinzona** Ger. Bellenz. Ticino, S Switzerland 46°12´N 09°02´E
54 B5 **Bellmead** Texas, SW USA 31°36´N 97°02´W
102 B5 **Bello** Antioquia, W Colombia 06°19´N 75°34´W
158 F4 **Bellochantuy** United Kingdom 55°31´N 5°42´W
112 F10 **Bellocq** Buenos Aires, E Argentina 35°55´S 61°32´W
Bello Horizonte see Belo Horizonte
281 J4 **Bellona** var. Mungiki. island S Solomon Islands
55 H8 **Bellona Strait** Sea waterway Nunavut, N Canada
Bellovacum see Beauvais
111 H4 **Bello Valle** Minas Gerais, Brazil 20°25´S 44°01´W
64 J1 **Bellows Falls** Vermont, NE USA 43°08´N 72°26´W
276 E4 **Bell, Point** headland South Australia 32°13´S 133°08´E
168 F9 **Bellpuig** Cataluña, Spain 41°37´N 1°01´E
71 H3 **Bells** Tennessee, S USA 35°42´N 89°05´W
71 H3 **Bells** Texas, SW USA 33°36´N 96°24´W
153 J3 **Bellshill** United Kingdom 55°49´N 4°01´W
152 A5 **Bellsund** inlet SW Svalbard
177 H5 **Belluno** Veneto, NE Italy 46°08´N 12°13´E
116 F3 **Bell Ville** Córdoba, C Argentina 32°35´S 62°41´W
138 D10 **Bellville** Western Cape, SW South Africa 33°30´S 18°43´E
71 H7 **Bellville** Texas, SW USA 29°57´N 96°15´W
65 H6 **Bellwood** Pennsylvania, NE USA 40°38´N 78°19´W
180 E6 **Belm** Niedersachsen, Germany 8°08´N 52°18´E
65 H7 **Belmar** New Jersey, USA 40°11´N 74°01´W
170 F7 **Belmez** Andalucía, S Spain 38°16´N 05°12´W
74 G6 **Belmond** Iowa, C USA 42°51´N 93°36´W
80 B3 **Belmont** California, USA 37°31´N 122°15´W
74 G3 **Belmont** New York, NE USA 42°14´N 78°02´W
67 I7 **Belmont** North Carolina, SE USA 35°13´N 81°01´W
109 H9 **Belmonte** Bahia, E Brazil 15°53´S 38°54´W
172 D2 **Belmonte** Castelo Branco, C Portugal 40°21´N 07°20´W
171 H6 **Belmonte** Castilla-La Mancha, C Spain 39°34´N 02°43´W
169 H5 **Belmont-sur-Rance** Midi-Pyrénées, France 43°49´N 2°46´E
88 C2 **Belmopan** ● (Belize) Cayo, C Belize 17°13´N 88°48´W
157 B8 **Belmullet** Ir. Béal an Mhuirhead. Mayo, W Ireland 54°14´N 09°59´W
163 C11 **Beloeil** Hainaut, SW Belgium 50°36´N 03°45´E
193 M4 **Belogorsk** Amurskaya Oblast', SE Russian Federation 50°55´N 128°24´E
Belogorsk see Bilohirs'k
185 H5 **Belogradchik** Vidin, NW Bulgaria 43°37´N 22°42´E
139 L10 **Beloha** Toliara, S Madagascar 25°10´S 45°03´E
111 H3 **Belo Horizonte** prev. Bello Horizonte. state capital Minas Gerais, SE Brazil 19°54´S 43°54´W
75 D9 **Beloit** Kansas, C USA 39°31´N 98°06´W
72 C3 **Beloit** Wisconsin, N USA 42°31´N 89°01´W
Belokorovichi see Bilokorovychi
192 F8 **Belokurikha** Altayskiy Kray, S Russian Federation 51°57´N 84°56´E
194 E3 **Belomorsk** Respublika Kareliya, NW Russian Federation 64°30´N 34°49´E
194 E3 **Belomorsko-Baltiyskiy Kanal** Eng. White Sea-Baltic Canal, White Sea Canal. canal NW Russian Federation 35°01´N 34°48´E
233 L8 **Belonia** Tripura, NE India 23°15´N 91°25´E
111 J2 **Belo Oriente** Minas Gerais, Brazil 19°14´S 42°28´W
Beloozersk see Byelaazyorsk
Belopol'ye see Bilopillya
170 G2 **Belorado** Castilla-León, N Spain 42°25´N 03°11´W
Belorechensk Krasnodarskiy Kray, SW Russian Federation 44°46´N 39°53´E
197 M2 **Beloretsk** Respublika Bashkortostan, W Russian Federation 53°58´N 58°22´E
Belorussia/Belorussian SSR see Belarus
Belorusskaya Gryada see Byelaruskaya Hrada
Belorusskaya SSR see Belarus
Beloshchel'ye see Nar'yan-Mar
185 M5 **Beloslav** Varna, E Bulgaria 43°13´N 27°42´E
Belostok see Białystok
Belo-sur-Tsiribihina see Belo Tsiribihina
52 L7 **Belot, Lac** ⊗ Northwest Territories, NW Canada
139 L8 **Belo Tsiribihina** var. Belo-sur-Tsiribihina. Toliara, W Madagascar 19°40´S 44°30´E
Belovar see Bjelovar
Belovezhskaya, Pushcha see Białowieża, Puszcza/Byelavyezhskaya, Pushcha
185 J7 **Belovo** Pazardzhik, C Bulgaria 42°10´N 24°01´E
227 M1 **Belovo** Kemerovskaya Oblast', S Russian Federation 54°25´N 86°13´E
Belovodsk see Bilovods'k
195 M3 **Beloyarsk** Taimal-Nenetskiy Avtonomnyy Okrug-Yugra, N Russian Federation 68°30´N 66°31´E
194 E3 **Beloye More** Eng. White Sea. sea NW Russian Federation
194 F3 **Beloye, Ozero** ⊗ NW Russian Federation
185 H7 **Belovo** Plovdiv, C Bulgaria 42°11´N 25°00´E
194 F3 **Belozërsk** Vologodskaya Oblast', NW Russian Federation 60°02´N 37°49´E
169 N9 **Belp** Bern, W Switzerland 46°54´N 07°31´E
174 B3 **Belp** ✈ (Bern) Bern, C Switzerland 46°55´N 07°29´E
175 G12 **Belpasso** Sicilia, Italy, C Mediterranean Sea 37°35´N 14°59´E
168 G6 **Belpech** Languedoc-Roussillon, France 43°12´N 1°45´E
161 I2 **Belper** United Kingdom 53°02´N 1°28´W
73 I11 **Belpre** Ohio, N USA 39°14´N 81°34´W
159 K3 **Belsay** United Kingdom 55°06´N 1°50´W
80 F7 **Belted Range** ▲ Nevada, USA
162 H5 **Beltervijde** ◇ N Netherlands
159 L9 **Belton** United Kingdom 53°33´N 0°49´W
75 G9 **Belton** Missouri, C USA 38°49´N 94°31´W
67 F7 **Belton** South Carolina, SE USA 34°31´N 82°29´W
69 H5 **Belton** Texas, SW USA 31°04´N 97°30´W
70 G6 **Belton Lake** ◙ Texas, SW USA
Bel'tsy see Bălţi
158 E8 **Belturbet** Ir. Béal Tairbirt. Cavan, N Ireland 54°06´N 07°26´W
227 M4 **Belukha, Gora** ▲ Kazakhstan/Russian Federation 49°50´N 86°44´E
175 H10 **Belvedere Marittimo** Calabria, SW Italy 39°37´N 15°52´E
73 D8 **Belvidere** Illinois, N USA 42°15´N 88°50´W
65 H4 **Belvidere** New Jersey, NE USA 40°49´N 75°05´W
277 J3 **Belvoir** United Kingdom 52°53´N 1°28´W
281 I1 **Belyando** seasonal river C Australia
Bely see Belyy
197 L4 **Belyayevka** Orenburgskaya Oblast', W Russian Federation 51°25´N 56°26´E
Belynichi see Byalynichy
194 D10 **Belyy, Bely, Beryj.** Tverskaya Oblast', W Russian Federation 55°51´N 32°57´E
196 F3 **Belyye Berega** Bryanskaya Oblast', W Russian Federation 53°08´N 34°28´E
192 F3 **Belyy, Ostrov** island N Russian Federation
192 F7 **Belyy Yar** Tomskaya Oblast', C Russian Federation 58°26´N 84°57´E
166 A7 **Belz** Bretagne, France 47°40´N 03°10´W
178 H7 **Belzig** Brandenburg, NE Germany 52°08´N 12°36´E
69 N3 **Belzoni** Mississippi, S USA 33°11´N 90°29´W
139 L7 **Bemaraha, Plateau du** see Bemaraha
135 C10 **Bembe** Uíge, NW Angola 07°03´S 14°25´E
172 D4 **Bembézar** ⊿ SW Spain
170 F7 **Bembézar, Embalse del** ⊙ SW Spain
161 J8 **Bembridge** S England, United Kingdom

Column 2

74 F3 **Bemidji** Minnesota, N USA 47°27´N 94°53´W
162 H7 **Bemmel** Gelderland, SE Netherlands 51°53´N 05°54´E
172 D3 **Bemposta** Castelo Branco, Portugal 40°04´N 7°13´W
172 C4 **Bemposta** Santarém, Portugal 39°21´N 8°08´W
159 M8 **Bempton** United Kingdom 54°08´N 0°10´W
261 H6 **Bemu** Pulau Seram, E Indonesia 03°21´S 129°58´E
Benàb see Bonàb
171 I3 **Benabarre** var. Benavarn. Aragón, NE Spain 42°06´N 00°28´E
Benaco see Garda, Lago di
135 G9 **Bena-Dibele** Kasai-Oriental, C Dem. Rep. Congo 04°01´S 22°50´E
171 I5 **Benagéber, Embalse de** ⊙ E Spain
173 J8 **Benahadux** Andalucía, Spain 36°56´N 2°27´W
173 N9 **Ben Ali** Algeria 36°13´N 00°41´E
277 I6 **Benalla** Victoria, SE Australia 36°33´S 146°00´E
173 I8 **Benalúa de las Villas** Andalucía, Spain 37°36´N 3°41´W
173 J7 **Benamaurel** Andalucía, Spain 37°36´N 2°42´W
170 F8 **Benamejí** Andalucía, S Spain 37°16´N 04°33´W
168 K7 **Benasque** var. Benabarre 169 G9 **Benasque** see Benabarre
172 B5 **Benavente** Santarém, C Portugal 38°59´N 08°49´W
171 G3 **Benavente** Castilla-León, N Spain 42°00´N 05°40´W
70 G9 **Benavides** Texas, SW USA 27°36´N 98°24´W
159 H2 **Benbecula** island NW Scotland, United Kingdom
55 H5 **Benbecula** Sea waterway Nunavut, N Canada
159 H2 **Ben Chonzie** ▲ C Scotland, United Kingdom
Benco see Benkovac
277 H4 **Bend** Oregon, NW USA 44°04´N 121°19´W
277 I8 **Benda Range** ▲ South Australia
277 L4 **Bendemeer** New South Wales, SE Australia 30°54´S 151°12´E
Bender see Tighina
Bender Beila/Bender Beyla see Bandarbeyla
Bender Cassim/Bender Qaasim see Boosaaso
158 F2 **Benderloch** United Kingdom 56°29´N 5°24´W
Bendery see Tighina
277 I6 **Bendigo** Victoria, SE Australia 36°46´S 144°19´E
181 D11 **Bendorf** Rheinland-Pfalz, Germany 7°34´N 50°26´E
190 C7 **Bēne** Dobele, SW Latvia 56°30´N 23°04´E
162 G7 **Beneden-Leeuwen** Gelderland, C Netherlands 51°52´N 05°32´E
179 G13 **Benedikfenwand** ▲ S Germany 47°39´N 11°28´E
132 F5 **Benemérita de San Cristóbal** see San Cristóbal
139 L9 **Benenitra** Toliara, S Madagascar 23°25´S 45°06´E
Beneschau see Benešov
Beneški Zaliv see Venice, Gulf of
183 C9 **Benešov** Ger. Beneschau. Středočeský Kraj, W Czech Republic 49°48´N 14°41´E
193 K2 **Benetta, Ostrov** island Novosibirskiye Ostrova, NE Russian Federation
166 G10 **Bénévent-l'Abbaye** Limousin, France 46°07´N 1°37´E
175 G9 **Benevento** anc. Beneventum, Malventum. Campania, S Italy 41°07´N 14°45´E
Beneventum see Benevento
N6 **Benfeld** Alsace, France 48°22´N 7°36´E
288 G6 **Bengal, Bay of** bay N Indian Ocean
Bengalooru see Bangalore
134 H7 **Bengamisa** Orientale, N Dem. Rep. Congo 0°58´N 25°11´E
Bengasi see Banghāzī
259 H8 **Bengawan, Sungai** ⊿ Jawa, S Indonesia
Bengazi see Banghāzī
241 I3 **Bengbu** var. Peng-pu. Anhui, E China 32°57´N 117°17´E
76 E4 **Benge** Washington, NW USA 46°55´N 118°01´W
Benghazi see Banghāzī
258 E4 **Bengkalis** Pulau Bengkalis, W Indonesia 01°27´N 102°10´E
258 E4 **Bengkalis, Pulau** island W Indonesia
259 H7 **Bengkayang** Borneo, C Indonesia 0°45´N 109°28´E
258 E7 **Bengkulu** prev. Bengkoeloe, Benkoelen, Benkulen. Sumatera, W Indonesia 03°46´S 102°16´E
258 E7 **Bengkulu** off. Propinsi Bengkulu; prev. Bengkoeloe, Benkoelen, Benkulen. ◆ province W Indonesia
Bengkulu, Propinsi see Bengkulu
135 C10 **Bengo** ◆ province W Angola
155 F8 **Bengtsfors** Västra Götaland, S Sweden 59°03´N 12°14´E
135 C12 **Benguela** var. Benguella. Benguela, W Angola 12°35´S 13°30´E
135 C12 **Benguela** ◆ province W Angola
Benguella see Benguela
219 D8 **Ben Gurion** ✈ Tel Aviv, C Israel 32°04´N 34°45´E
Bengweulu, Lake see Bangweulu, Lake
129 J3 **Benha** var. Banhā. N Egypt 30°28´N 31°11´E
286 B4 **Benham Seamount** undersea feature W Philippine Sea 15°48´N 124°15´E
156 H5 **Ben Hope** ▲ N Scotland, United Kingdom
134 H7 **Beni** Nord-Kivu, NE Dem. Congo 0°31´N 29°38´E
106 D9 **Beni** var. El Beni. ◇ department N Bolivia
130 D7 **Beni Abbès** W Algeria 30°07´N 02°09´W
171 J3 **Beni Abbès** W Algeria
171 J5 **Benicarló** País Valenciano, E Spain 40°25´N 00°25´E
171 I5 **Benicàssim** Cat. Benicàssim. País Valenciano, E Spain 40°03´N 00°03´E
Benicàssim see Benicàssim
173 N9 **Benicia** California, USA 38°03´N 122°10´W
171 I6 **Benidorm** País Valenciano, SE Spain 38°33´N 00°09´W
129 J4 **Beni Mazār** var. Beni Mazâr. C Egypt 28°29´N 30°44´E
130 D7 **Beni-Mellal** C Morocco 32°20´N 06°00´W
133 J8 **Benin** off. Republic of Benin; prev. Dahomey. ◆ republic W Africa
133 J8 **Benin, Bight of** gulf W Africa
133 J8 **Benin City** Edo, SW Nigeria 06°19´N 05°40´E
Benin, Republic of see Benin
106 D7 **Beni, Río** ⊿ N Bolivia
130 K2 **Beni-Saf** var. Beni-Saf. NW Algeria 35°19´N 01°23´W
Beni-Saf see Beni Saf
136 D4 **Benishangul** federal region W Ethiopia
171 J4 **Beni Slimane** Algeria
173 M5 **Benissa** País Valenciano, E Spain 38°43´N 00°03´E
129 J4 **Beni Suef** var. Banī Suwayf. N Egypt 29°09´N 31°04´E
Beni Suef see Beni Suef
55 J9 **Benito** Manitoba, S Canada 51°58´N 101°30´W
Benito see Uolo, Río
116 G3 **Benito Juárez** Buenos Aires, E Argentina 37°43´S 59°48´W
87 J8 **Benito Juárez** Chiapas, Mexico 16°53´N 93°11´W
85 J10 **Benito Juárez** Zacatecas, Mexico 21°29´N 103°33´W
86 F6 **Benito Juárez Internacional** ✈ (México) México. S Mexico 19°24´N 99°02´W
70 F3 **Benjamin** Texas, SW USA 33°35´N 99°49´W
106 D6 **Benjamin Constant** Amazonas, N Brazil 04°22´S 70°02´W
84 E3 **Benjamín Hill** Sonora, NW Mexico 30°13´N 111°08´W
117 B9 **Benjamín, Isla** island Archipiélago de los Chonos, S Chile
252 C5 **Benkei-misaki** headland Hokkaidō, NE Japan 42°49´N 140°10´E
74 D6 **Benkelman** Nebraska, C USA 40°04´N 101°30´W
156 F4 **Ben Klibreck** ▲ N Scotland, United Kingdom 58°15´N 04°23´W
184 B4 **Benkovac** It. Bencovazzo. Zadar, SW Croatia 44°02´N 15°36´E
Benkulen see Bengkulu
156 F6 **Ben Lawers** ▲ C Scotland, United Kingdom 56°33´N 04°13´W
156 F6 **Ben Lomond** California, USA 37°05´N 122°05´W
158 G2 **Ben Lomond** ▲ United Kingdom 56°11´N 4°38´W
158 G2 **Ben Lui** ▲ C Scotland, United Kingdom
156 F5 **Ben Macdui** var. Beinn MacDuibh. ▲ C Scotland, United Kingdom 57°02´N 03°42´W
175 D6 **Ben More** ▲ C Scotland, United Kingdom 56°26´N 06°00´W
156 F6 **Ben More** ▲ C Scotland, United Kingdom 56°22´N 04°31´W
156 F3 **Ben More Assynt** ▲ N Scotland, United Kingdom 58°09´N 04°51´W
281 D11 **Benmore, Lake** ⊗ South Island, New Zealand
180 G7 **Bennekenstein** Sachsen-Anhalt, Germany 10°48´N 51°40´E
162 G7 **Bennekom** Gelderland, SE Netherlands 51°59´N 05°40´E
67 I7 **Bennettsville** South Carolina, SE USA 34°36´N 79°40´W
156 F5 **Ben Nevis** ▲ N Scotland, United Kingdom 56°47´N 05°00´W
74 C4 **Bennett** South Dakota, N USA 43°56´N 96°45´W
279 H5 **Benneydale** Waikato, North Island, New Zealand 38°31´S 175°22´E
130 C4 **Bennichab** see Bennichchâb
175 D6 **Ben Mòre** ▲ C Scotland, United Kingdom 56°26´N 06°00´W
130 C4 **Bennichchâb** var. Bennichab. Inchiri, W Mauritania 19°26´N 15°21´W
65 M1 **Bennington** Vermont, NE USA 42°51´N 73°09´W
278 C10 **Ben Ohau Range** ▲ South Island, New Zealand
172 D2 **Benoni** Gauteng, NE South Africa 26°11´S 28°18´E
139 M4 **Be, Nosy** var. Nossi-Bé. island NW Madagascar
Bénoué see Benue

Column 3

171 I10 **Bensekrane** Algeria
181 F12 **Bensheim** Hessen, W Germany 49°41´N 08°38´E
79 J10 **Benson** Arizona, SW USA 31°55´N 110°16´W
74 F5 **Benson** Minnesota, N USA 45°19´N 95°36´W
67 K6 **Benson** North Carolina, SE USA 35°22´N 78°33´W
171 H10 **Benson** Algeria
260 D7 **Benteng** Pulau Selayar, C Indonesia 06°07´S 120°28´E
275 I3 **Bentinck Island** island Wellesley Islands, N Australia
136 A4 **Bentiu** Wahda, S Sudan 09°14´N 29°49´E
218 F5 **Bent Jbaïl** var. Bint Jubayl. S Lebanon 33°07´N 35°26´E
218 F5 **Bent Jbaïl** Lebanon 33°07´N 35°25´E
57 I6 **Bentley** Alberta, SW Canada 52°11´N 114°02´W
113 J7 **Bento Gonçalves** Rio Grande do Sul, S Brazil 29°12´S 51°34´W
75 H13 **Benton** Arkansas, C USA 34°34´N 92°35´W
80 B5 **Benton** California, USA 37°49´N 118°29´W
73 C12 **Benton** Illinois, S USA 38°00´N 88°55´W
71 I4 **Benton** Kentucky, S USA 36°51´N 88°21´W
75 H8 **Benton** Louisiana, S USA 32°41´N 93°44´W
73 H7 **Benton** Missouri, C USA 37°05´N 89°45´W
71 G2 **Benton** Tennessee, S USA 35°10´N 84°39´W
73 E8 **Benton Harbor** Michigan, N USA 42°06´N 86°27´W
75 G11 **Bentonville** Arkansas, C USA 36°23´N 94°13´W
170 G9 **Benza** Andalucía, S Spain
131 H2 **Ben Vorlich** ▲ C Scotland, United Kingdom
247 K7 **Benxi** prev. Pen-ch'i, Penhsihu, Penki. Liaoning, NE China 41°17´N 123°45´E
Benyakoni see Byenyakoni
184 F9 **Beòcin** Vojvodina, N Serbia 45°13´N 19°43´E
Beoderiesworth see Bury St Edmunds
184 D5 **Beograd** Eng. Belgrade, Ger. Belgrad; anc. Singidunum. ● (Serbia) Serbia, N Serbia 44°48´N 20°27´E
184 D5 **Beograd** Eng. Belgrade. ✈ Serbia, N Serbia 44°45´N 20°21´E
132 F3 **Béoumi** C Ivory Coast 07°40´N 05°34´W
78 F2 **Beowawe** Nevada, W USA 40°35´N 116°31´W
261 J4 **Bepondi, Pulau** island E Indonesia
250 B6 **Beppu** Oita, Kyūshū, SW Japan 33°18´N 131°30´E
250 D6 **Beppu-wan** bay SW Japan
280 E9 **Beqa** prev. Mbenga. island W Fiji
280 F9 **Beqa Barrier Reef** see Kavukavu Reef
103 I3 **Bequia** island S Saint Vincent and the Grenadines
184 F6 **Berane** prev. Ivangrad. E Montenegro 42°51´N 19°51´E
184 F9 **Berat** var. Berati, SCr. Beligrad. Berat, C Albania 40°43´N 19°46´E
184 F9 **Berat** ◇ district C Albania
Berätäu see Berettyó
Berati see Berat
Beraun see Berounka, Czech Republic
Beraun see Beroun, Czech Republic
259 J4 **Berau, Sungai** ⊿ Borneo, N Indonesia
261 I5 **Berau, Teluk** var. MacCluer Gulf. bay Papua, E Indonesia
136 C1 **Berber** River Nile, NE Sudan 18°01´N 34°00´E
136 I5 **Berbera** Sahil, N Somalia 10°24´N 45°02´E
134 D6 **Berbérati** Mambéré-Kadéi, SW Central African Republic 04°14´N 15°50´E
Berbería, Cabo de see Barbaria, Cap de
141 E4 **Berbice** Mpumalanga, South Africa 27°12´S 31°09´E
103 K5 **Berbice River** ⊿ NE Guyana
Berchid see Berrechid
188 H1 **Berck-Plage** Pas-de-Calais, N France 50°24´N 01°35´E
166 G2 **Berck-sur-Mer** Nord-Pas-de-Calais, France 50°24´N 1°36´E
70 G8 **Berclair** Texas, SW USA 28°33´N 97°32´W
189 L6 **Berda** ⊿ SE Ukraine
Berdichev see Berdychiv
114 C9 **Berdier** Buenos Aires, Argentina 34°24´S 60°16´W
193 I6 **Berdigestyakh** Respublika Sakha (Yakutiya), NE Russian Federation 62°02´N 127°03´E
193 J6 **Berdsk** Novosibirskaya Oblast', C Russian Federation 54°42´N 83°05´E
189 L7 **Berdyans'k** Rus. Berdyansk; prev. Osipenko. Zaporiz'ka Oblast', SE Ukraine 46°46´N 36°49´E
189 L7 **Berdyans'ka Kosa** spit SE Ukraine
189 L7 **Berdychiv** Rus. Berdichev. Zhytomyrs'ka Oblast', N Ukraine 49°54´N 28°39´E
66 F4 **Berea** Kentucky, S USA 37°34´N 84°18´W
Beregovo/Beregszász see Berehove
188 H5 **Berehove** Cz. Berehovo, Hung. Beregszász, Rus. Beregovo. Zakarpats'ka Oblast', W Ukraine 48°13´N 22°39´E
Berehovo see Berehove
280 D3 **Bereina** Central, S Papua New Guinea 08°29´S 146°30´E
228 C6 **Bereket** prev. Gazandzhyk, Kazandzhik, Turkm. Gazanjyk. Balkan Welaýaty, W Turkmenistan 39°17´N 55°27´E
65 G2 **Berekum** W Ghana 07°27´N 02°33´W
132 D5 **Berenda** California, USA 37°02´N 120°09´W
129 K6 **Berenice** var. Berenice, Minā Baranīs. SE Egypt 23°58´N 35°29´E
55 J8 **Berenice** see Berenice
Berens ⊿ Manitoba/Ontario, C Canada
55 J8 **Berens River** Manitoba, C Canada 52°22´N 97°00´W
74 C3 **Beresford** South Dakota, N USA 43°02´N 96°46´W
Berestechko L'vivs'ka Oblast', NW Ukraine 50°21´N 25°06´E
189 I7 **Bereslavka** Rus. Berdichev. 188 B4 **Beresteczko** Rus. Berdichev. ⊿ 189 H4 **Berettyó** Rom. Barcău; prev. Berătău, Berettó. ⊿ Hungary/Romania
183 H12 **Berettyóújfalu** Hajdú-Bihar, E Hungary 47°15´N 21°33´E
189 J8 **Bereza/Bereza Kartuska** see Byaroza
189 H7 **Berezanka** Mykolayivs'ka Oblast', S Ukraine 46°51´N 31°26´E
189 I7 **Berezanka** Mykolayivs'ka Oblast', N Ukraine 46°51´N 31°26´E
188 D4 **Berezhany** Pol. Brzeżany. Ternopil's'ka Oblast', W Ukraine 49°27´N 24°58´E
Berezina see Byerazino
Berezino see Byerazino
189 H7 **Bereznehuvate** Mykolayivs'ka Oblast', S Ukraine 47°18´N 32°51´E
194 G6 **Bereznik** Arkhangel'skaya Oblast', NW Russian Federation 62°50´N 42°45´E
195 K8 **Berezniki** Permskaya Oblast', NW Russian Federation 59°26´N 56°49´E
Berezovka see Berezivka, Ukraine
195 M5 **Berezovo** Khanty-Mansiyskiy Avtonomnyy Okrug-Yugra, N Russian Federation 63°58´N 64°38´E
197 M9 **Berezovskaya** Volgogradskaya Oblast', Russian Federation
193 L8 **Berezovyy** Khabarovskiy Kray, E Russian Federation 52°41´S 135°39´E
171 I9 **Berrouaghia** Algeria
159 I2 **Berrow** United Kingdom 51°16´N 3°01´W
171 I6 **Berry** cultural region C France
214 C7 **Berryessa, Lake** ◙ California, USA
61 M8 **Berry Islands** island group N Bahamas
173 N9 **Berryville** Arkansas, C USA 36°22´N 93°34´W
64 B9 **Berryville** Virginia, NE USA 39°09´N 77°59´W
140 C4 **Berseba** Karas, S Namibia 26°00´S 17°46´E
181 F10 **Berseenbrück** Niedersachsen, NW Germany 7°34´N 52°31´E
74 C2 **Berthold** North Dakota, USA 48°19´N 101°44´W
77 L4 **Berthoud** Colorado, C USA 40°18´N 105°04´W
103 H3 **Berti** Distrito Federal, N Venezuela 07°33´N 66°00´W
85 J5 **Bertioga** São Paulo, S Brazil 23°51´S 46°09´W
135 C8 **Bertoua** Est, E Cameroon 04°34´N 13°40´E
117 B13 **Bertrand, Cerro** ▲ S Argentina 50°00´S 73°21´E
277 H5 **Berri** South Australia 34°17´S 140°35´E
277 I7 **Berrigan** New South Wales, SE Australia 35°41´S 145°50´E

Column 4

155 H11 **Bergkvara** Kalmar, S Sweden 56°22´N 16°04´E
140 D9 **Bergland** Hardap, Namibia 22°59´S 17°00´E
181 D9 **Bergneustadt** Nordrhein-Westfalen, Germany 7°39´N 51°02´E
Bergomum see Bergamo
162 G7 **Bergse Maas** ⊿ S Netherlands
154 H5 **Bergsjö** Gävleborg, C Sweden 61°59´N 17°03´E
154 H5 **Bergsviken** Norrbotten, N Sweden 65°16´N 21°24´E
181 H12 **Bergtheim** Bayern, Germany 10°04´N 49°54´E
162 H3 **Bergum** Fris. Burgum. Friesland, N Netherlands 53°12´N 05°59´E
162 H3 **Bergumer Meer** ◙ N Netherlands
154 M4 **Bergviken** ◙ C Sweden
258 C5 **Berhala, Selat** strait Sumatera, W Indonesia
Berhampore see Baharampur
171 N10 **Berhoum** Algeria
193 N3 **Beringa, Ostrov** island E Russian Federation
163 F9 **Beringen** Limburg, NE Belgium 51°04´N 05°14´E
83 K8 **Bering Glacier** glacier Alaska, USA
Beringov Proliv see Bering Strait
193 N3 **Beringovskiy** Chukotskiy Avtonomnyy Okrug, NE Russian Federation 63°04´N 179°09´E
286 F7 **Bering Sea** sea N Pacific Ocean
73 H1 **Bering Strait** Rus. Beringov Proliv. strait Bering Sea/Chukchi Sea
Berislav see Beryslav
114 D9 **Berisso** Buenos Aires, Argentina 34°52´S 57°53´W
181 G8 **Berja** Thüringen, Germany 10°05´N 50°57´E
181 N9 **Berka** Thüringen, Germany 10°05´N 50°57´E
181 H7 **Berkel** ⊿ Germany/Netherlands
80 B8 **Berkeley** California, USA 37°52´N 122°16´W
64 B8 **Berkeley Springs** var. Bath. West Virginia, NE USA 39°38´N 78°14´W
180 J2 **Berkenthin** Schleswig-Holstein, Germany
161 J5 **Berkhampstead** United Kingdom 51°45´N 0°35´W
292 G4 **Berkner Island** island Antarctica
185 H5 **Berkovitsa** Montana, NW Bulgaria 43°15´N 23°05´E
157 H11 **Berkshire** former county S England, United Kingdom
163 D9 **Berlaar** Antwerpen, N Belgium 51°08´N 04°39´E
173 E11 **Berlanga** Extremadura, Spain 38°17´N 5°49´W
170 G2 **Berlanga de Duero** var. Berlanga. Castilla-León, N Spain 41°28´N 02°51´W
163 D8 **Berlare** Oost-Vlaanderen, NW Belgium 51°02´N 04°01´E
178 H3 **Berlin** ● (Germany) Berlin, NE Germany 52°31´N 13°26´E
N3 **Berlin** Maryland, NE USA 38°19´N 75°13´W
64 J4 **Berlin** New Hampshire, NE USA 44°27´N 71°13´W
64 H3 **Berlin** Pennsylvania, NE USA 39°54´N 78°55´W
72 C6 **Berlin** Wisconsin, N USA 43°57´N 88°59´W
178 H3 **Berlin** ◆ state NE Germany
Berlinchen see Barlinek
53 I7 **Berlinguet Inlet** coastal sea feature Nunavut, NE Canada
62 B8 **Berlin Lake** ◙ Ohio, N USA
277 L6 **Bermagui** New South Wales, SE Australia 36°26´S 150°04´E
84 H6 **Bermejillo** Durango, C Mexico 25°55´N 103°39´W
118 C10 **Bermejo** San Juan, Argentina 31°21´S 67°39´W
116 E4 **Bermejo, Río** ⊿ N Argentina
116 G2 **Bermejo, Río** ⊿ W Argentina
112 F5 **Bermejo, Río** ⊿ N Argentina
171 H2 **Bermeo** País Vasco, N Spain 43°25´N 02°44´W
170 E2 **Bermillo de Sayago** Castilla-León, N Spain 41°22´N 06°08´W
43 G4 **Bermuda** var. Bermuda Islands, Bermudas, Somers Islands. ◇ UK crown colony NW Atlantic Ocean
Bermuda Islands see Bermuda
43 H7 **Bermuda** var. Great Bermuda, Long Island, Main Island. island Bermuda
Bermudas see Bermuda
Bermuda-New England Seamount Arc see New England Seamounts
43 H7 **Bermuda Rise** undersea feature C Sargasso Sea 32°30´N 65°00´W
176 D4 **Bern Fr. Berne.** ● (Switzerland) Bern, W Switzerland 46°57´N 07°26´E
176 D4 **Bern Fr. Berne.** ◇ canton W Switzerland
79 M9 **Bernalillo** New Mexico, SW USA 35°18´N 106°33´W
52 D5 **Bernard Island** island Northwest Territories, N Canada
62 D9 **Bernard** Lake ◙ Ontario, S Canada
114 A5 **Bernardo de Irigoyen** Santa Fe, NE Argentina 34°15´N 61°07´W
65 H6 **Bernardsville** New Jersey, USA 40°43´N 74°34´W
118 H4 **Bernasconi** La Pampa, C Argentina 37°53´S 63°45´W
178 H2 **Bernau** Brandenburg, NE Germany 52°41´N 13°35´E
164 G3 **Bernay** Eure, N France 49°05´N 00°36´E
181 I9 **Bernburg** Sachsen-Anhalt, C Germany 51°47´N 11°45´E
176 D4 **Berner Alpen** var. Berner Oberland, Eng. Bernese Oberland. ▲ SW Switzerland
Berner Oberland/Bernese Oberland see Berner Alpen
166 H7 **Berneuil** Limousin, France 46°04´N 1°06´E
166 H3 **Berneville** Nord-Pas-de-Calais, France 50°16´N 2°40´E
177 M1 **Bernhardsthal** Niederösterreich, N Austria 48°41´N 16°51´E
68 C7 **Bernice** Louisiana, S USA 32°49´N 92°39´W
75 J11 **Bernie** Missouri, C USA 36°40´N 89°58´W
17 **Bernier Bay** coastal sea feature Nunavut, N Canada
274 C5 **Bernier Island** island Western Australia
174 D4 **Bernina, Passo del** pass SE Switzerland
174 D4 **Bernina, Piz It.** Pizzo Bernina. ▲ Italy/Switzerland 46°22´N 09°54´E see also Bernina, Pizzo
174 D4 **Bernina, Pizzo Rmsch.** Piz Bernina. ▲ Italy/Switzerland 46°22´N 9°54´E see also Bernina, Piz
163 C11 **Bérnissart** Hainaut, SW Belgium 50°29´N 03°37´E
183 C8 **Bernkastel-Kues** Rheinland-Pfalz, W Germany 49°55´N 07°04´E
139 L8 **Beroroha** Toliara, SW Madagascar 21°40´S 45°10´E
Bérounbouay see Gbéroubouay
183 B9 **Beroun** Ger. Beraun. Středočeský Kraj, W Czech Republic 49°58´N 14°05´E
183 B9 **Berounka** Ger. Beraun. ⊿ W Czech Republic
185 L6 **Berovo** E FYR Macedonia 41°45´N 22°52´E
218 G3 **Berqayl** var. Berchid. W Morocco 33°16´N 07°32´W
165 J7 **Berre, Étang de** ◙ SE France
277 H5 **Berri** South Australia 34°17´S 140°35´E

Column 5

171 K8 **Besalampy** Mahajanga, W Madagascar 16°43´S 44°29´E
169 H8 **Besalú** Cataluña, Spain 42°12´N 2°42´E
165 K5 **Besançon** anc. Besontium, Vesontio. Doubs, E France 47°14´N 06°01´E
175 I6 **Besbre** ⊿ C France
Bescanuova see Baška
181 B13 **Besch** Saarland, Germany 6°22´N 49°30´E
181 B8 **Besdan** see Bezdan
229 J6 **Beshariq** Rus. Besharyk; prev. Kirovo. Farg'ona Viloyati, E Uzbekistan 40°26´N 70°33´E
Besharyk see Beshariq
228 G5 **Beshbuloq** Rus. Beshulak. Navoiy Viloyati, N Uzbekistan 53°N 64°13´E
229 H5 **Beshkent** Qashqadaryo Viloyati, S Uzbekistan 38°47´N 65°42´E
Beshulak see Beshbuloq
261 H4 **Besir** Papua, E Indonesia 25°S 130°38´E
184 J3 **Beška** Vojvodina, N Serbia 45°09´N 20°04´E
218 F3 **Beskinta** Lebanon 33°56´N 35°47´E
Beskra see Biskra
197 I9 **Beslan** Respublika Severnaya Osetiya, SW Russian Federation 43°12´N 44°33´E
185 H6 **Besna Kobila** ▲ SE Serbia 42°31´N 22°16´E
214 D6 **Besni** Adıyaman, S Turkey 37°42´N 37°53´E
218 C2 **Besparmak Dağları** Eng. Kyrenia Mountains. ▲ N Cyprus
Bessarabia see Basarabeasca
158 J6 **Bessbrook** United Kingdom 54°12´N 6°25´W
181 D9 **Bessemer** Alabama, S USA 33°24´N 86°57´W
169 L2 **Bessèges** Languedoc-Roussillon, France 44°11´N 4°06´E
152 M5 **Bessels, Kapp** headland C Svalbard 78°36´N 21°43´E
66 D9 **Bessemer** Alabama, S USA
72 A3 **Bessemer** Michigan, N USA 46°28´N 90°03´W
67 I7 **Bessemer City** North Carolina, SE USA 35°16´N 81°16´W
181 B13 **Bessingen** Saarland, Germany 6°36´N 49°29´E
168 L6 **Besse-sur-Issole** Provence-Alpes-Côte d'Azur, France 43°21´N 6°10´E
165 H5 **Bessines-sur-Gartempe** Haute-Vienne, France 46°06´N 01°22´E
163 C8 **Best** Noord-Brabant, S Netherlands 51°31´N 05°24´E
155 D9 **Best** Västra Götaland, Sweden 57°28´N 14°06´E
191 H9 **Bestuzhevo** Arkhangel'skaya Oblast', NW Russian Federation 61°36´N 43°45´E
193 I6 **Bestyakh** Respublika Sakha (Yakutiya), NE Russian Federation 61°24´N 129°00´E
Beszterce see Bistriţa
Besztercebánya see Banská Bystrica
139 I3 **Betafo** Antananarivo, C Madagascar 19°50´S 46°50´E
170 D1 **Betanzos** Galicia, NW Spain 43°17´N 08°17´W
170 C1 **Betanzos, Ría de** estuary NW Spain
135 C8 **Bétaré Oya** Est, E Cameroon 05°34´N 14°09´E
114 C5 **Betbeder** Entre Ríos, Argentina 32°23´S 59°55´W
178 D8 **Bet Dagan** Israel
219 D8 **Bet Dagan** Israel 32°00´N 34°49´E
118 B8 **Betelu** Spain 43°01´N 1°59´W
133 I6 **Bétérou** País Valenciano, E Spain 39°35´N 00°28´E
133 J2 **Beteta** Castilla-La Mancha, Spain 40°34´N 2°04´W
219 L9 **Betera** Toliara, SW Madagascar 23°15´S 46°07´E
141 J3 **Bethal** Mpumalanga, NE South Africa 26°27´S 29°28´E
73 H3 **Bethany** Illinois, N USA 39°38´N 88°44´W
140 C4 **Bethanie** var. Bethanien, Bethany. Karas, S Namibia 26°32´S 17°11´E
Bethanien see Bethanie
75 F8 **Bethany** Missouri, C USA 40°15´N 94°01´W
75 F12 **Bethany** Oklahoma, C USA 35°31´N 97°37´W
Bethany see Bethanie
82 E8 **Bethel** Alaska, USA 60°47´N 161°45´W
65 H3 **Bethel** Connecticut, USA 41°22´N 73°25´W
64 J2 **Bethel** Maine, NE USA 44°24´N 70°47´W
16 **Bethel** North Carolina, SE USA 35°48´N 77°21´W
65 H5 **Bethel Park** Pennsylvania, USA 40°18´N 80°03´W
65 H4 **Bethesda** Maryland, NE USA 39°00´N 77°05´W
60 C10 **Bethesda** United Kingdom 53°10´N 4°05´W
65 H5 **Bethlehem** Pennsylvania, NE USA 40°37´N 75°22´W
45 J5 **Bethlehem** Free State, C South Africa 28°15´S 28°18´E
219 219 **Bethlehem** var. Beit Lehem, Ar. Bayt Laḥm, Heb. Bet Leḥem. C West Bank 31°43´N 35°12´E
Bethlen see Beclean
141 H7 **Bethulie** Free State, C South Africa 30°30´S 25°59´E
165 H1 **Béthune** Pas-de-Calais, N France 50°32´N 02°38´E
165 H2 **Béthune** ⊿ N France
Béthioua, Sistema var. Sistema Penibético, Eng. Baetic Cordillera, Baetic Mountains. ▲ S Spain
139 L6 **Betioky** prev. Betioky-Sud. Toliara, SW Madagascar 23°45´S 44°20´E
172 B3 **Betis** Spain
102 E3 **Betijoque** Trujillo, NW Venezuela 09°23´N 70°44´W
110 G3 **Betim** Minas Gerais, SE Brazil 19°56´S 44°10´W
284 C2 **Betio** Tarawa, W Kiribati 1°21´N 172°56´E
139 L9 **Betioky** Toliara, S Madagascar
181 D9 **Bet Kama** Israel 31°22´N 34°46´E
Betlen see Beclean
132 J9 **Bet Nir** Israel 31°39´N 34°52´E
219 D9 **Bet Nir** Israel
42 F9 **Betong** Yala, SW Thailand 05°45´N 101°05´E
132 H6 **Bétou** Likouala, N Congo 03°09´N 18°23´E
129 K8 **Betpak-Dala** Kaz. Betpaqdala. plateau S Kazakhstan
Betpaqdala see Betpak-Dala
139 L7 **Betroka** Toliara, S Madagascar 23°15´S 46°07´E
167 L8 **Betschdorf** Alsace, France 48°54´N 7°54´E
218 C9 **Bet Shean** Israel
218 E9 **Bet Shean** var. Beit She'an, Beisân; anc. Scythopolis, prev. Bet She'an. Northern, N Israel 32°30´N 35°30´E
219 E8 **Bet Shemesh** Israel
132 E9 **Bet Shemesh** Israel
141 H7 **Bettiesdam** Mpumalanga, South Africa 26°27´S 29°28´E
173 L10 **Bettioua** Algeria 35°48´N 00°16´W
82 F3 **Bettles** Alaska, USA 66°54´N 151°40´W
175 C8 **Bettola** Emilia-Romagna, C Italy 44°46´N 09°37´E
234 G4 **Bettiah** Bihar, N India 26°49´N 84°30´E
Bette, Picco see Bette, Pic
233 H6 **Bettiah** Bihar, N India 26°49´N 84°30´E
131 J4 **Bette, Pic** var. Bīkkū Bīttī, It. Picco Bette. ▲ S Libya 22°00´N 19°12´E
219 E9 **Bet Uzi'el** Israel
131 J4 **Bette, Picco** see Bette, Pic
72 F7 **Bettendorf** Iowa, C USA 41°31´N 90°31´W
180 C8 **Bettendorf** Luxembourg, NE Luxembourg 49°53´N 06°14´E
181 E8 **Bettrup** Nordrhein-Westfalen, Germany 7°53´N 51°43´E
162 H6 **Bettinge** ◇ Netherlands
181 B12 **Bétte, Pic var.** Bīkkū Bīttī, It. Picco Bette. ▲ S Libya
159 M4 **Betws-y-Coed** N Wales, United Kingdom 53°05´N 3°45´W
218 F7 **Bet Yizhaq-Shaar Hefer** Israel 32°19´N 34°53´E
181 H5 **Betzdorf** Rheinland-Pfalz, Germany
135 C9 **Beul** Uíge, NW Angola 06°15´S 15°32´E
181 F10 **Beuern** Hessen, Germany
72 F6 **Beulah** Michigan, N USA 44°37´N 86°05´W
74 B3 **Beulah** North Dakota, N USA 47°16´N 101°48´W
162 H3 **Beulakerwijde** ◙ N Netherlands
181 J9 **Beuningen** Gelderland, SE Netherlands
165 D9 **Beuvron** ⊿ C France
163 C8 **B. Everett Jordan Reservoir** var. Jordan Lake. ◙ North Carolina, USA
141 D9 **Beuvron** ⊿ C France
163 C9 **Beveren** Oost-Vlaanderen, N Belgium 51°13´N 04°15´E
159 M8 **Beverley** var. Beverly. E England, United Kingdom 53°51´N 00°26´W
75 K9 **Beverly** Massachusetts, USA 42°33´N 70°51´W
76 D5 **Beverly** Washington, NW USA 46°50´N 119°57´W
80 C10 **Beverly Hills** California, W USA 34°02´N 118°25´W
181 D8 **Beverungen** Nordrhein-Westfalen, Germany 9°22´N 51°40´E
162 E6 **Beverwijk** Noord-Holland, W Netherlands 52°28´N 04°40´E
159 L9 **Bewcastle** United Kingdom 55°04´N 2°41´W
161 J6 **Bexhill** United Kingdom 50°50´N 0°28´E
161 L7 **Bex** Vaud, SW Switzerland 46°15´N 7°00´E
181 L7 **Bexhill-on-Sea** var. Bexhill. SE England, United Kingdom 50°50´N 00°28´E
180 M7 **Bexhövede** Niedersachsen, Germany 8°41´N 53°29´E
215 I5 **Beyazit** var. Doğubayazıt. E Turkey
214 C8 **Beydağı** ▲ SW Turkey
Beyânu see Beya
215 M5 **Beyläqän** prev. Zhdanov. SW Azerbaijan

◆ Country	◇ Dependent Territory	✕ Administrative Regions	▲ Mountain	◣ Volcano	⊚ Lake
○ Country Capital	○ Dependent Territory Capital	✈ International Airport	▲ Mountain Range	✦ River	⊙ Reservoir

♦ Country
● Country Capital
◇ Dependent Territory
○ Dependent Territory Capital
◆ Administrative Regions
★ International Airport
▲ Mountain
▲ Mountain Range
♦ Volcano
♣ River
◎ Lake
⊠ Reservoir

◆ Country　◇ Dependent Territory　✕ Administrative Regions　▲ Mountain　☐ Lake
● Country Capital　○ Dependent Territory Capital　✈ International Airport　▲ Mountain Range　♒ River　☐ Reservoir　● Volcano

◆ Country   ◇ Dependent Territory   ◆ Administrative Regions   ▲ Mountain   ▲ Volcano   ○ Lake
● Country Capital   ○ Dependent Territory Capital   ✕ International Airport   ▲ Mountain Range   ≈ River   □ Reservoir

◆ Country   ◇ Dependent Territory   ◇ Administrative Regions   ▲ Mountain   ☒ Volcano   ☺ Lake
● Country Capital   ○ Dependent Territory Capital   × International Airport   ▲ Mountain Range   ↗ River   ☐ Reservoir

◆ Country ◇ Dependent Territory ◈ Administrative Regions ▲ Mountain ☒ Volcano ◎ Lake
● Country Capital ○ Dependent Territory Capital ✕ International Airport ▲ Mountain Range ♫ River ⊡ Reservoir

◆ Country ◇ Dependent Territory ● Administrative Regions ▲ Mountain ▼ Volcano ☉ Lake
◆ Country Capital ◇ Dependent Territory Capital ✕ International Airport ▲ Mountain Range ✍ River ☒ Reservoir

◆ Country
◆ Country Capital
⬦ Dependent Territory
○ Dependent Territory Capital
◇ Administrative Regions
✕ International Airport
▲ Mountain
▲ Mountain Range
⋇ Volcano
⊘ River
⊗ Lake
⊙ Reservoir

Fredericksburg - Ganderkesee

67 L3 **Fredericksburg** Virginia, NE USA 38°16′N 77°27′W
83 M7 **Frederick Sound** *sound* Alaska, USA
75 J10 **Fredericktown** Missouri, C USA 37°33′N 90°19′W
113 I6 **Frederico Westphalen** Rio Grande do Sul, S Brazil 27°22′S 53°20′W
63 M2 **Fredericton** *province capital* New Brunswick, SE Canada 45°57′N 66°40′W
155 E12 **Frederiksborg** *off.* Frederiksborgs Amt. ⬖ *county* E Denmark
Frederiksborgs Amt *see* Frederiksborg
Frederikshåb *see* Paamiut
155 D10 **Frederikshavn** *prev.* Fladstrand. Nordjylland, N Denmark 57°28′N 10°33′E
155 E12 **Frederikssund** Frederiksborg, E Denmark 55°51′N 12°05′E
91 K6 **Frederiksted** Saint Croix, S Virgin Islands (US) 17°41′N 64°51′W
155 E12 **Frederiksværk** *var.* Frederiksværk og Hanehoved. Frederiksborg, E Denmark 55°58′N 12°02′E
Frederiksværk og Hanehoved *see* Frederiksværk
102 B5 **Fredonia** Antioquia, W Colombia 05°57′N 75°42′W
79 H5 **Fredonia** Arizona, SW USA 36°57′N 112°31′W
75 F10 **Fredonia** Kansas, C USA 37°32′N 95°50′W
62 D6 **Fredonia** New York, NE USA 42°26′N 79°19′W
78 C2 **Fredonyer Pass** *pass* California, W USA
154 I2 **Fredrika** Västerbotten, N Sweden 64°03′N 18°25′E
154 G7 **Fredriksberg** Dalarna, C Sweden 60°07′N 14°23′E
Fredrikshald *see* Halden
Fredrikshamn *see* Hamina
155 E8 **Fredrikstad** Østfold, S Norway 59°12′N 10°57′E
289 C8 **Fred Seamount** *undersea feature* SW Indian Ocean 06°14′S 54°23′E
73 B12 **Freeburg** Illinois, N USA 38°25′N 89°54′W
80 B4 **Freedom** California, USA 36°56′N 121°46′W
65 H7 **Freehold** New Jersey, NE USA 40°14′N 74°14′W
64 E5 **Freeland** Pennsylvania, NE USA 41°01′N 75°54′W
276 G3 **Freeling Heights** ▲ South Australia 30°09′S 139°24′E
80 F2 **Freel Peak** ▲ California, W USA 38°52′N 119°52′W
59 M6 **Freels, Cape** *headland* Newfoundland and Labrador, E Canada 49°16′N 53°30′W
74 E6 **Freeman** South Dakota, N USA 43°21′N 97°26′W
61 L9 **Freeport** Grand Bahama Island, N Bahamas 26°28′N 78°43′W
73 C8 **Freeport** Illinois, N USA 42°18′N 89°37′W
71 I8 **Freeport** Texas, SW USA 28°57′N 95°21′W
61 L9 **Freeport** ✈ Grand Bahama Island, N Bahamas 26°31′N 78°48′W
70 G9 **Freer** Texas, SW USA 27°52′N 98°37′W
138 G7 **Free State** *off.* Free State Province; *prev.* Orange Free State, *Afr.* Oranje Vrystaat. ⬖ *province* C South Africa
Free State *see* Maryland
Free State Province *see* Free State
132 C7 **Freetown** ● (Sierra Leone) W Sierra Leone 08°27′N 13°16′W
137 J9 **Frégate** *island* Inner Islands, NE Seychelles
170 D7 **Fregenal de la Sierra** Extremadura, W Spain 38°10′N 06°39′W
276 D1 **Fregon** South Australia 26°44′S 132°03′E
166 B5 **Fréhel, Cap** *headland* NW France 48°41′N 02°21′W
154 C4 **Frei** Møre og Romsdal, S Norway 63°02′N 07°47′E
179 H9 **Freiberg** Sachsen, E Germany 50°55′N 13°21′E
180 G2 **Freiburg** Niedersachsen, Germany 9°17′N 53°50′E
Freiburg *see* Freiburg im Breisgau, Germany
Freiburg *see* Fribourg, Switzerland
179 C13 **Freiburg im Breisgau** *var.* Freiburg, *Fr.* Fribourg-en-Brisgau. Baden-Württemberg, SW Germany 48°N 07°52′E
Freiburg in Schlesien *see* Świebodzice
Freie Hansestadt Bremen *see* Bremen
181 E8 **Freienohl** Nordrhein-Westfalen, Germany 8°10′N 51°22′E
Freie und Hansestadt Hamburg *see* Brandenburg
172 D2 **Freineda** Guarda, Portugal 40°35′N 6°53′W
110 F1 **Frei Orlando** Minas Gerais, Brazil 18°48′S 45°12′W
181 C13 **Freisen** Saarland, Germany 7°15′N 49°33′E
179 G12 **Freising** Bayern, SE Germany 48°24′N 11°45′E
177 J2 **Freistadt** Oberösterreich, N Austria 48°31′N 14°31′E
Freistadtl *see* Hlohovec
179 I9 **Freital** Sachsen, E Germany 51°00′N 13°40′E
Freiwaldau *see* Jeseník
172 B3 **Freixianda** Santarém, Portugal 39°46′N 8°28′W
170 D4 **Freixo de Espada à Cinta** Bragança, N Portugal 41°05′N 06°49′W
172 D1 **Freixo de Espado a Cinta** Bragança, Portugal 41°05′N 6°49′W
165 K8 **Fréjus** *anc.* Forum Julii. Var, SE France 43°26′N 06°44′E
274 D7 **Fremantle** Western Australia 32°07′S 115°44′E
181 I14 **Fremdingen** Bayern, Germany 10°28′N 48°58′E
80 B3 **Fremont** California, W USA 37°34′N 122°01′W
73 G9 **Fremont** Indiana, N USA 41°43′N 84°54′W
74 H7 **Fremont** Iowa, C USA 41°12′N 92°26′W
72 F7 **Fremont** Michigan, N USA 43°28′N 85°56′W
74 E7 **Fremont** Nebraska, C USA 41°25′N 96°30′W
73 H9 **Fremont** Ohio, N USA 41°21′N 83°08′W
77 J7 **Fremont Peak** ▲ Wyoming, C USA 43°07′N 109°37′W
79 I4 **Fremont River** ≈ Utah, W USA
67 H6 **French Broad River** ≈ Tennessee, S USA
66 G4 **Frenchburg** Kentucky, S USA 37°58′N 83°37′W
80 C3 **French Camp** California, USA 37°53′N 121°16′W
62 C7 **French Creek** ≈ Pennsylvania, NE USA
76 E8 **Frenchglen** Oregon, NW USA 42°49′N 118°55′W
103 M6 **French Guiana** *var.* Guiana, Guyane. ◇ *French overseas department* N South America
French Guinea *see* Guinea
73 E12 **French Lick** Indiana, N USA 38°33′N 86°37′W
81 I8 **Frenchman Lake** ◎ Nevada, USA
158 A8 **Frenchpark** Roscommon, Ireland 53°52′N 8°24′W
278 F7 **French Pass** Marlborough, South Island, New Zealand 40°57′S 173°49′E
285 I7 **French Polynesia** ◇ *French overseas territory* S Pacific Ocean
French Republic *see* France
62 C2 **French River** ≈ Ontario, S Canada
French Somaliland *see* Djibouti
289 E12 **French Southern and Antarctic Territories** *Fr.* Terres Australes et Antarctiques Françaises. ◇ *French overseas territory* S Indian Ocean
French Sudan *see* Mali
French Territory of the Afars and Issas *see* Djibouti
French Togoland *see* Togo
64 G6 **Frenchtown** New Jersey, USA 40°32′N 75°04′W
131 H2 **Frenda** NW Algeria 35°04′N 01°03′E
181 J12 **Frensdorf** Bayern, Germany 10°52′N 49°49′E
161 J7 **Frensham** United Kingdom 51°09′N 0°48′W
183 F9 **Frenštát pod Radhoštěm** *Ger.* Frankstadt. Moravskoslezský Kraj, E Czech Republic 49°33′N 18°10′E
141 J6 **Frere** KwaZulu-Natal, South Africa 28°53′S 29°46′E
132 F8 **Fresco** S Ivory Coast 05°03′N 05°31′W
293 J9 **Freshfield, Cape** *headland* Antarctica
160 A3 **Freshford** Kilkenny, Ireland 52°44′N 7°24′W
167 L8 **Fresne-St-Mamés** Franche-Comté, France 47°33′N 5°52′E
85 J8 **Fresnillo** *var.* Fresnillo de González Echeverría. Zacatecas, C Mexico 23°11′N 102°53′W
Fresnillo de González Echeverría *see* Fresnillo
80 D5 **Fresno** California, W USA 36°45′N 119°48′W
172 F2 **Fresno-Alhàndiga** Castilla y León, Spain 40°43′N 5°37′W
166 G3 **Fressenneville** Picardie, France 50°04′N 1°34′E
Freu, Cabo del *see* Freu, Cap des
171 L5 **Freu, Cap des** *var.* Cabo del Freu. *cape* Mallorca, Spain, W Mediterranean Sea
181 G12 **Freudenberg** Baden-Württemberg, Germany 9°20′N 49°45′E
181 D9 **Freudenberg** Nordrhein-Westfalen, Germany 7°52′N 50°54′E
179 C12 **Freudenstadt** Baden-Württemberg, SW Germany 48°28′N 08°25′E
Freudenthal *see* Bruntál
167 H3 **Frévent** Nord-Pas-de-Calais, France 50°16′N 2°17′E
277 K10 **Freycinet Peninsula** *peninsula* Tasmania, SE Australia
132 C6 **Fria** W Guinea 10°27′N 13°38′W
138 A4 **Fria, Cape** *headland* NW Namibia 18°32′S 12°00′E
80 D5 **Friant** California, W USA 36°56′N 119°44′W
116 E1 **Frías** Catamarca, N Argentina 28°41′S 65°00′W
176 C4 **Fribourg** *Ger.* Freiburg. Fribourg, W Switzerland 46°50′N 07°10′E
174 A3 **Fribourg** *Ger.* Freiburg. ⬖ *canton* W Switzerland
Fribourg-en-Brisgau *see* Freiburg im Breisgau
76 C3 **Friday Harbor** San Juan Islands, Washington, NW USA 48°31′N 123°01′W
159 L8 **Fridaythorpe** United Kingdom 54°01′N 0°40′W
181 H9 **Frieda** Hessen, Germany 10°08′N 51°12′E
Friedau *see* Ormož
179 F12 **Friedberg** Bayern, S Germany 48°21′N 10°58′E
181 F11 **Friedberg** Hessen, W Germany 50°19′N 08°46′E
Friedeberg Neumark *see* Strzelce Krajeńskie
Friedek-Mistek *see* Frýdek-Místek
181 H9 **Friedewald** Hessen, Germany 9°52′N 50°53′E
181 H8 **Friedland** Niedersachsen, Germany 9°56′N 51°25′E
Friedland *see* Pravdinsk
180 J7 **Friedrichsbrunn** Sachsen-Anhalt, Germany 11°03′N 51°42′E
179 D13 **Friedrichshafen** Baden-Württemberg, S Germany 47°39′N 09°29′E
Friedrichstadt *see* Jaunjelgava
181 C13 **Friedrichsthal** Saarland, Germany 7°06′N 49°19′E
181 G9 **Frielendorf** Hessen, Germany 9°20′N 50°59′E
75 E8 **Friend** Nebraska, C USA 40°37′N 97°16′W
Friendly Islands *see* Tonga
103 L5 **Friendship** Coronie, N Suriname 05°50′N 56°16′W
72 C6 **Friendship** Wisconsin, N USA 43°58′N 89°48′W
177 J4 **Friesach** Kärnten, S Austria 46°58′N 14°24′E
Friesche Eilanden *see* Frisian Islands
179 C12 **Friesenheim** Baden-Württemberg, SW Germany 48°27′N 07°56′E
Friesische Inseln *see* Frisian Islands
162 G4 **Friesland** ⬖ *province* N Netherlands
180 E4 **Friesoythe** Niedersachsen, Germany 7°51′N 53°01′E
111 K8 **Frio, Cabo** *headland* SE Brazil 23°01′S 41°59′W
159 I1 **Friockheim** United Kingdom 56°38′N 2°38′W
70 D2 **Friona** Texas, SW USA 34°38′N 102°43′W
88 G7 **Frío, Río** ≈ N Costa Rica
70 F8 **Frio River** ≈ Texas, SW USA
158 E1 **Frisa, Loch** ◎ W Scotland, United Kingdom
163 H14 **Frisange** Luxembourg, S Luxembourg 49°31′N 06°12′E
Frisches Haff *see* Vistula Lagoon
79 H4 **Frisco Peak** ▲ Utah, W USA 38°31′N 113°17′W
144 C6 **Frisian Islands** *Dut.* Friesche Eilanden, *Ger.* Friesische Inseln. *island group* N Europe
65 I3 **Frissell, Mount** ▲ Connecticut, NE USA 42°01′N 73°25′W
155 F10 **Fristad** Västra Götaland, S Sweden 57°50′N 13°01′E
70 E2 **Fritch** Texas, SW USA 35°38′N 101°36′W
155 F10 **Fritsla** Västra Götaland, S Sweden 57°33′N 12°47′E
181 G9 **Fritzlar** Hessen, C Germany 51°09′N 09°16′E
174 F4 **Friuli-Venezia Giulia** ⬖ *region* NE Italy
Frjentsjer *see* Franeker
295 K9 **Frobisher Bay** *inlet* Baffin Island, Nunavut, NE Canada
Frobisher Bay *see* Iqaluit
57 L2 **Frobisher Lake** ◎ Saskatchewan, C Canada
159 I10 **Frodsham** United Kingdom 53°18′N 2°44′W
154 D3 **Frohavet** *sound* C Norway
Frohenbruck *see* Veselí nad Lužnicí
177 K4 **Frohnleiten** Steiermark, SE Austria 47°17′N 15°20′E
163 D12 **Froidchapelle** Hainaut, S Belgium 50°10′N 04°18′E
167 H4 **Froissy** Picardie, France 49°34′N 2°13′E
197 H5 **Frolovo** Volgogradskaya Oblast', SW Russian Federation 49°46′N 43°38′E
182 G3 **Frombork** *Ger.* Frauenburg. Warmińsko-Mazurkskie, NE Poland 54°21′N 19°40′E
161 H7 **Frome** SW England, United Kingdom 51°15′N 02°22′W
161 H8 **Frome** ≈ United Kingdom
276 G3 **Frome Creek** *seasonal river* South Australia
276 G4 **Frome Downs** South Australia 31°17′S 139°48′E
276 G3 **Frome, Lake** *salt lake* South Australia
166 B9 **Fromentine** Pays de la Loire, France 46°54′N 2°09′W
160 F2 **Frongoch** United Kingdom 52°56′N 3°38′W
181 F10 **Fronhausen** Hessen, Germany 8°42′N 50°42′E
Fronicken *see* Wronki
172 C5 **Fronteira** Portalegre, C Portugal 39°03′N 07°39′W
166 D10 **Frontenay-Rohan-Rohan** Poitou-Charentes, France 46°15′N 0°32′W
85 K5 **Frontera** Coahuila, NE Mexico 26°55′N 101°27′W
87 J7 **Frontera** Tabasco, SE Mexico 18°32′N 92°39′W
84 F2 **Fronteras** Sonora, NW Mexico 30°51′N 109°33′W
165 I8 **Frontignan** Hérault, S France 43°27′N 03°45′E
102 B4 **Frontino** Antioquia, NW Colombia 06°46′N 76°10′W
168 F5 **Fronton** Midi-Pyrénées, France 43°51′N 1°24′E
64 B10 **Front Royal** Virginia, NE USA 38°56′N 78°13′W
175 F8 **Frosinone** *anc.* Frusino. Lazio, C Italy 41°38′N 13°22′E
175 G8 **Frosolone** Molise, C Italy 41°34′N 14°25′E
71 H5 **Frost** Texas, SW USA 32°04′N 96°48′W
64 A8 **Frostburg** Maryland, NE USA 39°39′N 78°55′W
69 M7 **Frostproof** Florida, SE USA 27°45′N 81°31′W
Frostviken *see* Kvarnbergsvattnet
155 H8 **Frövi** Örebro, C Sweden 59°28′N 15°24′E
154 C3 **Frøya** *island* W Norway
55 K2 **Frozen Strait** *Sea waterway* Nunavut, N Canada
166 G2 **Fruges** Nord-Pas-de-Calais, France 50°31′N 2°08′E
79 J3 **Fruita** Colorado, C USA 39°10′N 108°42′W
74 A5 **Fruitdale** South Dakota, N USA 44°39′N 103°38′W
69 L6 **Fruitland Park** Florida, SE USA 28°51′N 81°54′W
Frumentum *see* Formentera
229 J6 **Frunze** Batkenskaya Oblast', SW Kyrgyzstan 40°07′N 71°40′E
Frunze *see* Bishkek
188 G6 **Frunzivka** Odes'ka Oblast', SW Ukraine 47°19′N 29°46′E
Frusino *see* Frosinone
167 N9 **Frutigen** Bern, W Switzerland 46°35′N 07°38′E
183 F9 **Frýdek-Místek** *Ger.* Friedek-Mistek. Moravskoslezský Kraj, E Czech Republic 49°40′N 18°22′E
284 E10 **Fua'amotu** Tongatapu, S Tonga 21°15′S 175°08′W
284 E1 **Fuafatu** *island* Funafuti Atoll, C Tuvalu
284 E2 **Fuagea** *island* Funafuti Atoll, C Tuvalu
284 E1 **Fualifeke** *atoll* C Tuvalu
284 E1 **Fualopa** *island* Funafuti Atoll, C Tuvalu
235 C14 **Fuammulah** *var.* Fuammulah, Gnaviyani. *atoll* S Maldives
Fuammulah *see* Fuammulah
243 L5 **Fu'an** Fujian, SE China 27°11′N 119°42′E
245 K9 **Fucheng** Anhui, E China 32°47′N 117°19′E
245 J5 **Fucheng** Hebei, E China 37°52′N 116°09′E
245 J6 **Fu-chia-chai** Shandong, E China 36°28′N 116°11′E
Fu-chien *see* Fujian
Fu-chou *see* Fuzhou
250 F5 **Fuchū** *var.* Hutyû. Hiroshima, Honshū, SW Japan 34°35′N 133°12′E
242 F8 **Fuchuan** *var.* Fuyang. Guangxi Zhuangzu Zizhiqu, S China 24°56′N 111°15′E
243 L3 **Fuchun-jiang Shuiku** ◎ S China
253 E8 **Fudai** Iwate, Honshū, C Japan 39°59′N 141°50′E
243 M5 **Fuding** *var.* Tongshan. Fujian, SE China 27°21′N 120°10′E
137 E9 **Fudua** *spring/well* S Kenya 02°13′S 39°43′E
172 G6 **Fuencaliente** Castilla-La Manacha, Spain 38°24′N 4°18′W
168 C10 **Fuendetodos** Aragón, Spain 41°21′N 0°57′W
170 F9 **Fuengirola** Andalucía, S Spain 36°32′N 04°38′W
168 A7 **Fuenmayor** La Rioja, Spain 42°28′N 2°33′W
172 G3 **Fuensalida** Castilla-La Manacha, Spain 40°03′N 4°12′W
173 K5 **Fuente-Álamo** Castilla-La Manacha, Spain 38°42′N 1°26′W
170 E7 **Fuente de Cantos** Extremadura, W Spain 38°15′N 06°18′W
170 E7 **Fuente del Maestre** Extremadura, W Spain 38°31′N 06°26′W
172 G8 **Fuente de Piedra** Andalucía, Spain 37°08′N 4°43′W
173 H4 **Fuente el Fresno** Castilla-La Manacha, Spain 39°14′N 3°46′W
170 E7 **Fuente Obejuna** Andalucía, S Spain 38°15′N 05°25′W
168 A9 **Fuentepinilla** Castilla y León, Spain 41°34′N 2°46′W
170 E4 **Fuentesaúco** Castilla-León, N Spain 41°14′N 05°30′W
173 L3 **Fuentes de Ayódar** Valenciana, Spain 40°02′N 0°25′W
173 I3 **Fuentidueña de Tajo** Madrid, Spain 40°07′N 3°09′W
118 D4 **Fuenzalida** Libertador General Bernardo O'Higgins, Chile 34°15′S 70°38′W
112 G2 **Fuerte Olimpo** *var.* Olimpo. Alto Paraguay, NE Paraguay 21°02′S 57°51′W
84 F6 **Fuerte, Río** ≈ C Mexico
170 C9 **Fuerteventura** *island* Islas Canarias, Spain, NE Atlantic Ocean
244 D8 **Fufeng** Shaanxi, China 34°13′N 107°31′E
221 H8 **Fughmah** *var.* Faghman, Fugma. C Yemen 16°08′N 49°23′E
152 A5 **Fuglehuken** *headland* W Svalbard 78°54′N 10°30′E
Fuglø *see* Fugloy
154 B1 **Fugloy** *Dan.* Fuglø. *island* NE Faeroe Islands
295 K3 **Fugløya Bank** *undersea feature* E Norwegian Sea 71°00′N 19°20′E
Fugma *see* Fughmah
136 E6 **Fugugo** *spring/well* NE Kenya 03°19′N 39°39′E
245 K5 **Fuguo** Shandong, E China 37°42′N 118°08′E
238 F2 **Fuhai** *var.* Burultokay. Xinjiang Uygur Zizhiqu, NW China 47°15′N 87°39′E
243 J4 **Fu He** ≈ S China
Fuhkien *see* Fujian
180 H2 **Fuhlsbüttel** ✈ (Hamburg) Hamburg, N Germany 53°37′N 09°57′E
179 G8 **Fuhne** ≈ C Germany
Fu-hsin *see* Fuxin
Fujairah *see* Al Fujayrah
251 K4 **Fuji** *var.* Huzi. Shizuoka, Honshū, S Japan 35°08′N 138°39′E
243 K6 **Fujian** *var.* Fu-chien, Fuhkien, Fukien, Min, Fujian Sheng. ⬖ *province* SE China
242 B2 **Fu Jiang** ≈ C China
Fujian Sheng *see* Fujian
251 K4 **Fujieda** *var.* Huzieda. Shizuoka, Honshū, S Japan 34°54′N 138°15′E
Fuji, Mount/Fujiyama *see* Fuji-san
247 M4 **Fujin** Heilongjiang, NE China 47°12′N 132°01′E
251 K4 **Fujinomiya** *var.* Huzinomiya. Shizuoka, Honshū, S Japan 35°16′N 138°33′E
251 L4 **Fuji-san** *var.* Fujiyama, *Eng.* Mount Fuji. ▲ Honshū, SE Japan 35°23′N 138°44′E
253 C14 **Fujisawa** *var.* Huzisawa. Kanagawa, Honshū, S Japan 35°22′N 139°29′E
253 B13 **Fuji-Yoshida** *var.* Huziyosida. Yamanashi, Honshū, S Japan 35°30′N 138°48′E
252 E4 **Fukagawa** *var.* Hukagawa. Hokkaidō, NE Japan 43°44′N 142°03′E
238 F3 **Fukang** Xinjiang Uygur Zizhiqu, W China 44°07′N 87°55′E
252 C7 **Fukaura** Aomori, Honshū, C Japan 40°38′N 139°55′E
284 E9 **Fukave** *island* Tongatapu Group, S Tonga
Fukien *see* Fujian
251 H4 **Fukuchiyama** *var.* Hukutiyama. Kyōto, Honshū, SW Japan 35°19′N 135°08′E
250 B7 **Fukue** *var.* Hukue. Nagasaki, Fukue-jima, SW Japan 32°41′N 128°52′E
250 A7 **Fukue-jima** *island* Gotō-rettō, SW Japan
251 I3 **Fukui** *var.* Hukui. Fukui, Honshū, SW Japan 36°03′N 136°12′E
251 I3 **Fukui** *off.* Fukui-ken, *var.* Hukui. ⬖ *prefecture* Honshū, SW Japan
Fukui-ken *see* Fukui
250 C6 **Fukuoka** *var.* Hukuoka, *hist.* Najima. Fukuoka, Kyūshū, SW Japan 33°36′N 130°24′E
250 D6 **Fukuoka** *off.* Fukuoka-ken, *var.* Hukuoka. ⬖ *prefecture* Kyūshū, SW Japan
Fukuoka-ken *see* Fukuoka
253 D11 **Fukushima** *var.* Hukusima. Fukushima, Honshū, C Japan 37°47′N 140°28′E
252 D6 **Fukushima** Hokkaidō, NE Japan 41°27′N 140°14′E
253 C11 **Fukushima** *off.* Fukushima-ken, *var.* Hukusima. ⬖ *prefecture* Honshū, C Japan
Fukushima-ken *see* Fukushima
250 F5 **Fukuyama** *var.* Hukuyama. Hiroshima, Honshū, SW Japan 34°29′N 133°21′E
132 B5 **Fulacunda** C Guinea-Bissau 11°44′N 15°03′W
205 I5 **Fūlādī, Kūh-e** ▲ E Afghanistan 34°38′N 67°32′E
280 G10 **Fulaga** *island* Lau Group, E Fiji
181 H10 **Fulda** Hessen, C Germany 50°33′N 09°41′E
74 F5 **Fulda** Minnesota, N USA 43°52′N 95°36′W
181 G8 **Fulda** ≈ C Germany
Fülek *see* Fil'akovo
159 L8 **Fulford** United Kingdom 53°56′N 1°04′W
243 K3 **Fuliang** Jiangxi, China 29°16′N 117°09′E
245 J8 **Fuliji** Anhui, E China 33°46′N 116°58′E
Fulin *see* Hanyuan
242 D3 **Fuling** Chongqing Shi, C China 29°45′N 107°23′E
81 D11 **Fullerton** California, SE USA 33°53′N 117°55′W
74 E7 **Fullerton** Nebraska, C USA 41°21′N 97°58′W
176 G4 **Fulpmes** Tirol, W Austria 47°11′N 11°22′E
80 B1 **Fulton** California, USA 38°30′N 122°46′W
66 C5 **Fulton** Kentucky, S USA 36°31′N 88°52′W
66 C8 **Fulton** Mississippi, S USA 34°16′N 88°24′W
75 I9 **Fulton** Missouri, C USA 38°50′N 91°57′W
62 F5 **Fulton** New York, NE USA 43°18′N 76°22′W
159 K10 **Fulwood** United Kingdom 53°21′N 1°33′W
Fuman/Fumen *see* Fowman
163 E12 **Fumay** Ardennes, N France 49°58′N 04°42′E
164 G7 **Fumel** Lot-et-Garonne, SW France 44°31′N 00°58′E
253 C13 **Funabashi** Chiba, Honshū, S Japan 35°42′N 139°59′E
284 E2 **Funafara** *atoll* C Tuvalu
284 F1 **Funafuti** ✈ Funafuti Atoll, C Tuvalu 08°30′S 179°12′E
Funafuti *see* Fongafale
284 F1 **Funafuti Atoll** *atoll* C Tuvalu
243 I1 **Funan** Anhui, China 32°23′N 115°21′E
Funan *see* Fusui
284 F2 **Funangongo** *atoll* C Tuvalu
154 F4 **Funäsdalen** Jämtland, C Sweden 62°33′N 12°33′E
170 A8 **Funchal** Madeira, Portugal, NE Atlantic Ocean 32°40′N 16°55′W
170 A8 **Funchal** ✈ Madeira, Portugal, NE Atlantic Ocean 32°38′N 16°53′W
102 C2 **Fundación** Magdalena, N Colombia 10°31′N 74°09′W
111 M3 **Fundao** Esperíto Santo, Brazil 19°54′S 40°24′W
172 C3 **Fundão** *var.* Fundáo. Castelo Branco, C Portugal 40°08′N 07°30′W
Fundáo *see* Fundão
84 F5 **Fundición** Sonora, Mexico 27°19′N 109°44′W
59 J9 **Fundy, Bay of** *bay* Canada/USA
Fünen *see* Fyn
114 B6 **Funes** Santa Fe, Argentina 32°55′S 60°49′W
102 A7 **Fúnes** Nariño, SW Colombia 0°59′N 77°27′W
Fünfkirchen *see* Pécs
139 I5 **Funhalouro** Inhambane, S Mozambique 23°04′S 34°24′E
111 H2 **Funilândia** Minas Gerais, Brazil 19°21′S 44°03′W
245 K3 **Funing** Hebei, China 39°32′N 119°08′E
245 L8 **Funing** Jiangsu, E China 33°43′N 119°47′E
242 B8 **Funing** *var.* Xinhua. Yunnan, SW China 23°39′N 105°41′E
244 G8 **Funiu Shan** ▲▲ C China
133 K5 **Funtua** Katsina, N Nigeria 11°31′N 07°19′E
244 E7 **Fuping** Shaanxi, China 34°27′N 109°06′E
243 L7 **Fuqing** Fujian, SE China 25°40′N 119°23′E
242 C6 **Fuquan** Guizhou, China 26°25′N 107°18′E
139 I2 **Furancungo** Tete, NW Mozambique 14°51′S 33°39′E
252 F4 **Furano** *var.* Hurano. Hokkaidō, NE Japan 43°23′N 142°24′E
188 D10 **Furculeşti** Teleorman, S Romania 43°51′N 25°07′E
Füred *see* Balatonfüred
218 D6 **Fureidis** Israel 32°36′N 34°57′E
218 D6 **FureidIsrael** Israel 32°36′N 34°57′E
252 H4 **Füren-ko** ◎ Hokkaidō, NE Japan
223 H8 **Fürg** *var.* Fürg. Fārs, S Iran 28°16′N 55°13′E
Fürg *see* Fürg
Furluk *see* Fârliug
Fūrmanov/Furmanovka *see* Moyynkum
Furmanovo *see* Zhalpaktal
158 F2 **Furnace** United Kingdom 56°09′N 5°10′W
110 E4 **Furnas, Represa de** ⊠ SE Brazil
172 C7 **Furnazinhas** Faro, Portugal 37°22′N 7°34′W
277 K8 **Furneaux Group** *island group* Tasmania, SE Australia
Furnes *see* Veurne
242 D4 **Furong Jiang** ≈ S China
218 I1 **Furqlus** Ḥimṣ, W Syria 34°40′N 37°02′E
180 D5 **Fürstenau** Niedersachsen, NW Germany 52°30′N 07°40′E
180 G7 **Fürstenau** Nordrhein-Westfalen, Germany 9°19′N 51°50′E
180 G7 **Fürstenberg** Niedersachsen, Germany 9°24′N 51°44′E
177 L4 **Fürstenfeld** Steiermark, SE Austria 47°03′N 16°05′E
179 F13 **Fürstenfeldbruck** Bayern, S Germany 48°10′N 11°16′E
178 I7 **Fürstenwalde** Brandenburg, NE Germany 52°22′N 14°04′E
181 J13 **Fürth** Bayern, S Germany 49°29′N 10°59′E
181 F13 **Fürth** Hessen, Germany 8°47′N 49°39′E
177 K2 **Furth bei Göttweig** Niederösterreich, NW Austria 48°22′N 15°33′E
252 D4 **Furubira** Hokkaidō, NE Japan 43°14′N 140°38′E
154 G6 **Furudal** Dalarna, C Sweden 61°10′N 15°07′E
251 J3 **Furukawa** *var.* Hida. Gifu, Honshū, SW Japan 36°13′N 137°11′E
253 D10 **Furukawa** *var.* Hurukawa, Ōsaki. Miyagi, Honshū, C Japan 38°36′N 140°57′E
53 J7 **Fury and Hecla Strait** *Sea waterway* Nunavut, N Canada
102 C6 **Fusagasugá** Cundinamarca, C Colombia 04°22′N 74°21′W
Fusan *see* Pusan
243 M1 **Fushan** Jiangsu, E China 31°48′N 120°45′E
245 M5 **Fushan** Shandong, E China 37°30′N 121°15′E
Fushë-Arëzi/Fushë-Arrësi *see* Fushë-Arrëz
184 F7 **Fushë-Arrëz** *var.* Fushë-Arëzi, Fushë-Arrësi. Shkodër, N Albania 42°05′N 20°01′E
Fushë-Kruja *see* Fushë-Krujë
184 F8 **Fushë-Krujë** *var.* Fushë-Kruja. Durrës, C Albania 41°30′N 19°43′E
245 N1 **Fushun** *var.* Fou-shan, Fu-shun. Liaoning, NE China 41°50′N 123°54′E
242 B3 **Fushun** Sichuan, C China 29°11′N 105°00′E
Fu-shun *see* Fushun
Fusin *see* Fuxin
248 C2 **Fusong** Jilin, NE China 42°20′N 127°17′E
179 F13 **Füssen** Bayern, S Germany 47°34′N 10°43′E
242 D9 **Fusui** *var.* Xinning; *prev.* Funan. Guangxi Zhuangzu Zizhiqu, S China 22°39′N 107°49′E
Futa Jallon *see* Fouta Djallon
117 B8 **Futaleufú** Los Lagos, S Chile 43°14′S 71°50′W
184 F3 **Futog** Vojvodina, NW Serbia 45°15′N 19°43′E
253 C14 **Futtsu** *var.* Huttu. Chiba, Honshū, S Japan 35°11′N 139°52′E
281 N5 **Futuna** *island* S Vanuatu
284 A10 **Futuna, Île** *island* S Wallis and Futuna
243 K5 **Futun Xi** ≈ SE China
243 M3 **Fuxi** Zhejiang, E China 29°29′N 121°22′E
244 E6 **Fuxian** *var.* Fu Xian. Shaanxi, C China 36°03′N 109°19′E
Fuxian *see* Wafangdian
Fu Xian *see* Fuxian
240 C7 **Fuxian Hu** ⊠ SW China
237 I4 **Fuxin** *var.* Fou-hsin, Fu-hsin, Fusin. Liaoning, NE China 41°59′N 121°40′E
245 M1 **Fuxin** Liaoning, China 42°02′N 121°26′E
Fuxing *see* Wangmo
241 H3 **Fuyang** Anhui, E China 32°52′N 115°51′E
243 L3 **Fuyang** Zhejiang, China 30°02′N 119°34′E
Fuyang *see* Fuchuan
245 I5 **Fuyang He** ≈ E China
193 K9 **Fuyu** Heilongjiang, NE China 47°48′N 124°26′E
247 N3 **Fuyuan** Heilongjiang, NE China 48°20′N 134°22′E
242 A6 **Fuyuan** Yunnan, China 25°25′N 104°09′E
Fuyu/Fu-yü *see* Songyuan
238 G2 **Fuyun** *var.* Koktokay. Xinjiang Uygur Zizhiqu, NW China 46°58′N 89°30′E
183 G11 **Füzesabony** Heves, E Hungary 47°46′N 20°25′E
243 L6 **Fuzhou** *var.* Foochow, Fu-chou. *province capital* Fujian, SE China 26°09′N 119°17′E
243 J5 **Fuzhou** Jiangxi, S China 27°58′N 116°20′E
245 M3 **Fuzhoucheng** Liaoning, NE China 39°44′N 121°44′E
215 L5 **Füzuli** *Rus.* Fizuli. SW Azerbaijan 39°33′N 47°09′E
191 F12 **Fyadory** *Rus.* Fëdory. Brestskaya Voblasts', SW Belarus 51°57′N 26°24′E
161 L5 **Fyfield** United Kingdom 51°44′N 0°16′E
155 D13 **Fyn** *off.* Fyns Amt, *var.* Fünen. ⬖ *county* C Denmark
155 D13 **Fyn** *Ger.* Fünen. *island* C Denmark
156 E6 **Fyne, Loch** *inlet* W Scotland, United Kingdom
Fyns Amt *see* Fyn
155 C8 **Fyresvatnet** ◎ S Norway
FYR Macedonia/FYROM *see* Macedonia, FYR
Fyzabad *see* Feyẓābād

G

175 B13 **Gaâfour** Tunisia
Gaafu Alifu Atoll *see* North Huvadhu Atoll
136 I5 **Gaalkacyo** *var.* Galka'yo, *It.* Galcaio. Mudug, C Somalia 06°42′N 47°24′E
228 F6 **Gabakly** *Rus.* Kabakly. Lebap Welaýaty, NE Turkmenistan 39°45′N 62°30′E
185 J5 **Gabare** Vratsa, NW Bulgaria 43°20′N 23°57′E
168 E5 **Gabarret** Aquitaine, France 43°59′N 0°01′E
171 I1 **Gabas** ≈ SW France
Gabasumdo *see* Tongde
80 H3 **Gabbs** Nevada, W USA 38°51′N 117°55′W
80 G4 **Gabbs Valley Range** ▲▲ Nevada, USA
135 C12 **Gabela** Cuanza Sul, W Angola 10°50′S 14°21′E
Gaberones *see* Gaborone
283 H9 **Gabert** *island* Caroline Islands, E Micronesia
131 K2 **Gabès** *var.* Qābis. E Tunisia 33°53′N 10°03′E
131 L2 **Gabès, Golfe de** *Ar.* Khalīj Qābis. *gulf* E Tunisia
Gablonz an der Neisse *see* Jablonec nad Nisou
Gablös *see* Cavalese
134 B7 **Gabon** *off.* Gabonese Republic. ◆ *republic* C Africa
Gabonese Republic *see* Gabon
141 H3 **Gaborone** *prev.* Gaberones. ● (Botswana) South East, SE Botswana 24°42′S 25°50′E
141 H3 **Gaborone** ✈ South East, SE Botswana 24°45′S 25°49′E
59 I1 **Gabriel Strait** *Sea waterway* Nunavut, NE Canada
170 E5 **Gabriel y Galán, Embalse de** ⊠ W Spain
223 I9 **Gābrīk, Rūd-e** ≈ SE Iran
185 K6 **Gabrovo** Gabrovo, N Bulgaria 42°54′N 25°19′E
185 J6 **Gabrovo** ⬖ *province* N Bulgaria
132 B5 **Gabú** *prev.* Nova Lamego. E Guinea-Bissau 12°16′N 14°09′W
169 N1 **Gaby** Piemonte, NW Italy 45°42′N 07°52′E
166 E5 **Gacé** Basse-Normandie, France 48°48′N 0°18′E
74 D3 **Gackle** North Dakota, N USA 46°34′N 99°07′W
184 E6 **Gacko** Repulika Srpska, S Bosnia and Herzegovina 43°08′N 18°29′E
234 D6 **Gadag** Karnātaka, W India 15°25′N 75°37′E
154 G2 **Gäddede** Jämtland, C Sweden 64°30′N 14°15′E
239 J7 **Gadê** *var.* Kequ; *prev.* Pagqên. Qinghai, C China 33°56′N 99°49′E
181 F12 **Gadernheim** Hessen, Germany 8°44′N 49°43′E
Gades/Gadier/Gadir/Gadire *see* Cádiz
173 J8 **Gàdor** Andalucía, Spain 36°57′N 2°29′W
171 H8 **Gádor, Sierra de** ▲▲ S Spain
231 H9 **Gadra** Sind, SE Pakistan 25°39′N 70°28′E
66 E8 **Gadsden** Alabama, S USA 34°00′N 86°00′W
81 H14 **Gadsden** Arizona, SW USA 32°33′N 114°45′W
Gadyach *see* Hadyach
134 D5 **Gadzi** Mambéré-Kadéï, SW Central African Republic 04°46′N 16°42′E
188 D9 **Găeşti** Dâmboviţa, S Romania 44°42′N 25°19′E
175 F9 **Gaeta** Lazio, C Italy 41°12′N 13°35′E
175 F9 **Gaeta, Golfo di** *var.* Gulf of Gaeta. *gulf* C Italy
Gaeta, Gulf of *see* Gaeta, Golfo di
282 E5 **Gaferut** *atoll* Caroline Islands, W Micronesia
172 C4 **Gàfete** Portalegre, Portugal 39°25′N 7°41′W
67 I7 **Gaffney** South Carolina, SE USA 35°03′N 81°40′W
Gäfle *see* Gävle
Gäfleborg *see* Gävleborg
131 K2 **Gafsa** *var.* Qafşah. W Tunisia 34°25′N 08°52′E
Gafurov *see* Ghafurov
229 I6 **Gagarin** Jizzax Viloyati, C Uzbekistan 40°40′N 68°04′E
179 C12 **Gaggenau** Baden-Württemberg, SW Germany 48°48′N 08°19′E
282 B4 **Gagil Tamil** *var.* Gagil-Tomil. *island* Caroline Islands, W Micronesia
Gagil-Tomil *see* Gagil Tamil
197 I2 **Gagino** Nizhegorodskaya Oblast', W Russian Federation 55°18′N 45°01′E
175 J10 **Gagliano del Capo** Puglia, SE Italy 39°49′N 18°22′E
154 G6 **Gagnef** Dalarna, C Sweden 60°34′N 15°04′E
132 F8 **Gagnoa** C Ivory Coast 06°11′N 05°56′W
59 I6 **Gagnon** Québec, E Canada 51°56′N 68°16′W
Gago Coutinho *see* Lumbala N'Guimbo
261 H4 **Gag, Pulau** *island* E Indonesia
215 I3 **Gagra** NW Georgia 43°17′N 40°18′E
73 H11 **Gahanna** Ohio, N USA 40°01′N 82°52′W
223 H8 **Gahkom** Hormozgān, S Iran 28°14′N 55°48′E
Gahnpa *see* Ganta
112 G1 **Gaíba, Laguna** ◎ E Bolivia
233 K7 **Gaibanda** *var.* Gaibanda. Rajshahi, NW Bangladesh 25°21′N 89°36′E
Gaibhlte, Cnoc Mór na n *see* Galtymore Mountain
177 I5 **Gail** ≈ S Austria
181 H14 **Gaildorf** Baden-Württemberg, S Germany 48°41′N 10°08′E
165 H8 **Gaillac** *var.* Gaillac-sur-Tarn. Tarn, S France 43°54′N 01°54′E
169 H4 **Gaillac-d'Avevron** Midi-Pyrénées, France 44°21′N 2°56′E
Gaillac-sur-Tarn *see* Gaillac
Gaillimh *see* Galway
Gaillimhe, Cuan na *see* Galway Bay
177 I5 **Gailtaler Alpen** ▲▲ S Austria
117 E8 **Gaimán** Chaco, S Argentina 43°15′S 65°30′W
66 E5 **Gainesboro** Tennessee, S USA 36°20′N 85°41′W
161 J1 **Gainesborough** United Kingdom 53°23′N 0°46′W
69 L5 **Gainesville** Florida, SE USA 29°39′N 82°19′W
66 G8 **Gainesville** Georgia, SE USA 34°18′N 83°49′W
75 H11 **Gainesville** Missouri, C USA 36°37′N 92°28′W
71 H3 **Gainesville** Texas, SW USA 33°39′N 97°08′W
177 L2 **Gainfarn** Niederösterreich, NE Austria 47°59′N 16°11′E
159 L10 **Gainsborough** E England, United Kingdom 53°24′N 00°48′W
219 A14 **Gain, Wâdi Abu el** Egypt
276 F4 **Gairdner, Lake** *salt lake* South Australia
Gaissane *see* Gáissát
152 H3 **Gáissát** *var.* Gaissane. ▲▲ N Norway
89 K9 **Gaital, Cerro** ▲ C Panama 08°37′N 80°04′W
64 C9 **Gaithersburg** Maryland, NE USA 39°08′N 77°13′W
245 M2 **Gaizhou** Liaoning, NE China 40°24′N 122°17′E
Gaizina Kalns *see* Gaiziņkalns
190 E6 **Gaiziņkalns** *var.* Gaizina Kalns. ▲ E Latvia 56°51′N 25°58′E
Gajac *see* Villeneuve-sur-Lot
83 J5 **Gakona** Alaska, USA 62°21′N 145°16′W
Galaassiya *see* Galaosiyo
Ğalāğıl *see* Jalājil
Galam, Pulau *see* Gelam, Pulau
168 E6 **Galan** Midi-Pyrénées, France 43°14′N 0°25′E
112 C5 **Galán, Cerro** ▲ NW Argentina 25°54′S 66°45′W
183 E10 **Galanta** *Hung.* Galánta. Trnavský Kraj, W Slovakia 48°12′N 17°45′E
228 G6 **Galaosiyo** *Rus.* Galaassiya. Buxoro Viloyati, C Uzbekistan 39°53′N 64°25′E
105 B9 **Galápagos** *off.* Provincia de Galápagos. ⬖ *province* W Ecuador, E Pacific Ocean
287 H5 **Galapagos Fracture Zone** *tectonic feature* E Pacific Ocean
Galapagos Islands *see* Colón, Archipiélago de
Galápagos, Islas de los *see* Colón, Archipiélago de
Galápagos, Provincia de *see* Galápagos
287 K6 **Galapagos Rise** *undersea feature* E Pacific Ocean 15°00′S 97°00′W
159 I4 **Galashiels** SE Scotland, United Kingdom 55°37′N 02°49′W
188 F8 **Galaţi** *Ger.* Galatz. Galaţi, E Romania 45°27′N 28°00′E
188 F8 **Galaţi** ⬖ *county* E Romania
175 J10 **Galatina** Puglia, SE Italy 40°10′N 18°10′E
175 J10 **Galatone** Puglia, SE Italy 40°09′N 18°05′E
Galatz *see* Galaţi
67 I5 **Galax** Virginia, NE USA 36°40′N 88°56′W
228 F9 **Galaýmor** *Rus.* Kala-i-Mor. Mary Welaýaty, S Turkmenistan 35°40′N 62°28′E
Galcaio *see* Gaalkacyo
170 B10 **Gáldar** Gran Canaria, Islas Canarias, NE Atlantic Ocean 28°09′N 15°40′W
154 C5 **Galdhøpiggen** ▲ S Norway 61°30′N 08°08′E
84 G3 **Galeana** Chihuahua, N Mexico 30°08′N 107°38′W
85 L7 **Galeana** Nuevo León, NE Mexico 24°45′N 99°59′W
86 E2 **Galeana** ✈ Nuevo León, Mexico 24°50′N 100°04′W
111 I8 **Galeão** ✈ (Rio de Janeiro) Rio de Janeiro, SE Brazil 22°48′S 43°16′W
260 G3 **Galela** Pulau Halmahera, E Indonesia 01°52′N 127°48′E
83 H5 **Galena** Alaska, USA 64°43′N 156°55′W
73 B8 **Galena** Illinois, N USA 42°25′N 90°25′W
75 G11 **Galena** Kansas, C USA 37°04′N 94°38′W
75 H11 **Galena** Missouri, C USA 36°45′N 93°30′W
91 L8 **Galeota Point** *headland* Trinidad, Trinidad and Tobago 10°07′N 60°59′W
171 H8 **Galera** Andalucía, S Spain 37°45′N 02°33′W
91 L7 **Galera Point** *headland* Trinidad, Trinidad and Tobago 10°49′N 60°54′W
104 B1 **Galera, Punta** *headland* NW Ecuador 0°49′N 80°03′W
73 B9 **Galesburg** Illinois, N USA 40°57′N 90°22′W
72 B6 **Galesville** Wisconsin, N USA 44°04′N 91°21′W
64 C4 **Galeton** Pennsylvania, NE USA 41°43′N 77°38′W
159 I8 **Galgate** United Kingdom 53°59′N 2°47′W
188 C6 **Gâlgău** *Hung.* Galgó; *prev.* Gîlgău. Sălaj, NW Romania 47°17′N 23°43′E
Galgó *see* Gâlgău
Galgóc *see* Hlohovec
136 H6 **Galguduud** *off.* Gobolka Galguduud. ⬖ *region* E Somalia
Galguduud, Gobolka *see* Galguduud
215 I3 **Gali** W Georgia 42°40′N 41°39′E
194 G9 **Galich** Kostromskaya Oblast', NW Russian Federation 58°21′N 42°21′E
185 I5 **Galiche** Vratsa, NW Bulgaria 43°36′N 23°53′E
170 D2 **Galicia** *anc.* Gallaecia. ⬖ *autonomous community* NW Spain
290 H4 **Galicia Bank** *undersea feature* E Atlantic Ocean 11°45′W 42°40′N
Galilee *see* HaGalil
275 J5 **Galilee, Lake** ◎ Queensland, NE Australia
Galilee, Sea of *see* Tiberias, Lake
111 K1 **Galiléia** Minas Gerais, Brazil 19°00′S 41°33′W
174 D6 **Galileo Galilei** ✈ (Pisa) Toscana, C Italy 43°40′N 10°22′E
73 H10 **Galion** Ohio, N USA 40°43′N 82°47′W
Galka'yo *see* Gaalkacyo
195 M10 **Galkino** Kurganskaya Oblast', Russian Federation
228 F7 **Galkynyş** *prev. Rus.* Deynau, Dyanev, *Turkm.* Dänew. Lebap Welaýaty, NE Turkmenistan 39°16′N 63°10′E
136 D3 **Gallabat** Gedaref, E Sudan 12°57′N 36°10′E
Gallaecia *see* Galicia
229 H6 **G'allaorol** Jizzax Viloyati, C Uzbekistan 40°01′N 67°30′E
176 E6 **Gallarate** Lombardia, NW Italy 45°39′N 08°47′E
166 G6 **Gallardon** Centre, France 48°32′N 1°42′E
75 G9 **Gallatin** Missouri, C USA 39°54′N 93°57′W
66 E5 **Gallatin** Tennessee, S USA 36°22′N 86°28′W
77 I6 **Gallatin Peak** ▲ Montana, NW USA 45°22′N 111°21′W
77 I6 **Gallatin River** ≈ Montana/Wyoming, NW USA
235 G11 **Galle** *prev.* Point de Galle. Southern Province, SW Sri Lanka 06°04′N 80°12′E
171 I3 **Gállego** ≈ NE Spain
168 C9 **Gàllego** ≈ Spain
287 J6 **Gallego Rise** *undersea feature* E Pacific Ocean 02°00′S 115°00′W
Gallegos *see* Río Gallegos
117 C12 **Gallegos, Río** ≈ Argentina/Chile
Gallia *see* France
68 E5 **Galliano** Louisiana, S USA 29°26′N 90°18′W
186 G2 **Gallikós** ≈ N Greece
79 L8 **Gallinas Peak** ▲ New Mexico, SW USA 34°14′N 105°47′W
102 D1 **Gallinas, Punta** *headland* NE Colombia 12°27′N 71°44′W
70 C2 **Gallinas River** ≈ New Mexico, SW USA
175 J10 **Gallipoli** Puglia, SE Italy 40°08′N 18°E
Gallipoli *see* Gelibolu
Gallipoli Peninsula *see* Gelibolu Yarımadası
73 I12 **Gallipolis** Ohio, N USA 38°49′N 82°14′W
152 F5 **Gällivare** *Lapp.* Váhtjer. Norrbotten, N Sweden 67°08′N 20°39′E
177 J2 **Gallneukirchen** Oberösterreich, N Austria 48°22′N 14°25′E
154 G4 **Gällö** Jämtland, C Sweden 62°57′N 15°15′E
171 H4 **Gallo** ≈ C Spain
175 F12 **Gallo, Capo** *headland* Sicilia, Italy, C Mediterranean Sea 38°13′N 13°18′E
79 K8 **Gallo Mountains** ▲▲ New Mexico, SW USA
62 F5 **Galloo Island** *island* New York, NE USA
158 F7 **Galloway, Mull of** *headland* S Scotland, United Kingdom 54°37′N 04°54′W
79 J7 **Gallup** New Mexico, SW USA 35°32′N 108°45′W
171 I3 **Gallur** Aragón, NE Spain 41°51′N 01°21′W
Gâlma *see* Guelma
239 I2 **Galshar** *var.* Buyant. Dzavhan, C Mongolia 47°14′N 97°14′E
239 M1 **Galshar** *var.* Buyant. Hentiy, C Mongolia 46°15′N 110°50′E
158 G4 **Galston** United Kingdom 55°35′N 4°23′W
239 J1 **Galt** *var.* Ider. Hövsgöl, C Mongolia 48°45′N 99°52′E
80 C2 **Galt** California, W USA 38°13′N 121°19′W
130 D6 **Galtat-Zemmour** C Western Sahara 25°07′N 12°21′W
155 D12 **Galten** Århus, C Denmark 56°09′N 09°54′E
157 C10 **Galtymore Mountain** *Ir.* Cnoc Mór na nGaibhlte. ▲ S Ireland 52°21′N 08°09′W
157 C10 **Galty Mountains** *Ir.* Na Gaibhlte. ▲▲ S Ireland
73 B9 **Galva** Illinois, N USA 41°10′N 90°02′W
71 I7 **Galveston** Texas, SW USA 29°17′N 94°48′W
71 I7 **Galveston Bay** *inlet* Texas, SW USA
71 I7 **Galveston Island** *island* Texas, SW USA
114 A5 **Gálvez** Santa Fe, C Argentina 32°03′S 61°14′W
157 B9 **Galway** *Ir.* Gaillimh. W Ireland 53°16′N 09°03′W
158 A9 **Galway** *Ir.* Gaillimh. *cultural region* W Ireland
157 B9 **Galway Bay** *Ir.* Cuan na Gaillimhe. *bay* W Ireland
138 D4 **Gam** Otjozondjupa, NE Namibia 20°10′S 20°51′E
261 N7 **Gama** ≈ SW Papua New Guinea
166 G3 **Gamaches** Picardie, France 49°59′N 1°33′E
251 J4 **Gamagōri** Aichi, Honshū, SW Japan 34°49′N 137°15′E
102 C4 **Gamarra** Cesar, N Colombia 08°21′N 73°46′W
Gámas *see* Kaamanen
141 K3 **GaMasemola** Limpopo, South Africa 24°30′S 29°46′E
238 F10 **Gamba** Xizang Zizhiqu, W China 28°13′N 88°32′E
Gamba *see* Zamtang
133 H6 **Gambaga** NE Ghana 10°32′N 00°28′W
136 C4 **Gambēla** Gambēla Hizboch, W Ethiopia 08°09′N 34°15′E
136 C5 **Gambēla** ⬖ *federal region* W Ethiopia
82 E5 **Gambell** Saint Lawrence Island, Alaska, USA 63°44′N 171°41′W
132 A4 **Gambia** *off.* Republic of The Gambia, The Gambia. ◆ *republic* W Africa
132 C5 **Gambia** *Fr.* Gambie. ≈ W Africa
290 G7 **Gambia Plain** *undersea feature* E Atlantic Ocean
Gambia, Republic of The *see* Gambia
Gambia, The *see* Gambia
Gambie *see* Gambia
73 I10 **Gambier** Ohio, N USA 40°22′N 82°24′W
285 L8 **Gambier, Îles** *island group* E French Polynesia
276 F6 **Gambier Islands** *island group* South Australia
159 J6 **Gamblesby** United Kingdom 54°44′N 2°36′W
135 D8 **Gamboma** Plateaux, E Congo 01°53′S 15°51′E
134 C6 **Gamboula** Mambéré-Kadéï, SW Central African Republic 04°09′N 15°12′E
79 J7 **Gamerco** New Mexico, SW USA 35°34′N 108°45′W
215 L5 **Gamış Dağı** ▲ W Azerbaijan 40°18′N 46°15′E
140 F9 **Gamka** ≈ Western Cape, South Africa
Gamlakarleby *see* Kokkola
155 H10 **Gamleby** Kalmar, S Sweden 57°54′N 16°25′E
Gammelstad *see* Gammelstaden
152 G6 **Gammelstaden** *var.* Gammelstad. Norrbotten, N Sweden 65°38′N 22°05′E
Gammouda *see* Sidi Bouzid
140 D7 **Gamoep** Northern Cape, South Africa 29°54′S 18°25′E
235 G10 **Gampola** Central Province, C Sri Lanka 07°10′N 80°34′E
261 H4 **Gam, Pulau** *island* E Indonesia
256 H4 **Gâm, Sông** ≈ N Vietnam
159 L10 **Gamston** United Kingdom 53°16′N 0°56′W
152 H3 **Gamvik** Finnmark, N Norway 71°04′N 28°08′E
235 B14 **Gan** Addu Atoll, C Maldives
Gan *see* Gansu, China
Gan *see* Jiangxi, China
Ganaane *see* Juba
79 J7 **Ganado** Arizona, SW USA 35°42′N 109°31′W
71 H8 **Ganado** Texas, SW USA 29°02′N 96°30′W
62 F4 **Gananoque** Ontario, SE Canada 44°21′N 76°11′W
Ganāveh *see* Bandar-e Gonāveh
215 L5 **Gäncä** *Rus.* Gyandzha; *prev.* Kirovabad, Yelisavetpol. W Azerbaijan 40°42′N 46°23′E
Ganchi *see* Ghonchí
Gand *see* Gent
135 C12 **Ganda** *var.* Mariano Machado, *Port.* Vila Mariano Machado. Benguela, W Angola 13°02′S 14°40′E
135 G10 **Gandajika** Kasai-Oriental, S Dem. Rep. Congo 06°42′S 24°01′E
233 H6 **Gandak** *Nep.* Nārāyāni. ≈ India/Nepal
59 M6 **Gander** Newfoundland and Labrador, SE Canada 48°56′N 54°33′W
59 M6 **Gander** ✈ Newfoundland and Labrador, E Canada 49°03′N 54°49′W
180 F4 **Ganderkesee** Niedersachsen, NW Germany 53°01′N 08°33′E

◆ Country
● Country Capital
◇ Dependent Territory
○ Dependent Territory Capital
⬖ Administrative Regions
✈ International Airport
▲ Mountain
▲▲ Mountain Range
Volcano
≈ River
◎ Lake
⊠ Reservoir

INDEX

◆ Country   ◇ Dependent Territory   ◈ Administrative Regions   ▲ Mountain   ⛰ Volcano   ⊚ Lake
● Country Capital   ○ Dependent Territory Capital   ✈ International Airport   ▲ Mountain Range   ← River   ⊚ Reservoir

◆ Country
● Country Capital
◇ Dependent Territory
◇ Dependent Territory Capital
◆ Administrative Regions
✈ International Airport
▲ Mountain
▲ Mountain Range
⛰ Volcano
♣ River
◎ Lake
◎ Reservoir

◆ Country
● Country Capital
◇ Dependent Territory
○ Dependent Territory Capital
◈ Administrative Regions
✕ International Airport
▲ Mountain
▲ Mountain Range
🌋 Volcano
➢ River
⊙ Lake
⊡ Reservoir

H

◆ Country ◇ Dependent Territory ⦿ Administrative Regions ▲ Mountain ☼ Volcano ☷ Lake
● Country Capital ○ Dependent Territory Capital ✈ International Airport ▲ Mountain Range ☂ River ☷ Reservoir

◆ Country ◇ Dependent Territory ◈ Administrative Regions ▲ Mountain ☒ Volcano ○ Lake
◉ Country Capital ○ Dependent Territory Capital ✕ International Airport ▲ Mountain Range ☒ River ☒ Reservoir

◆ Country   ◇ Dependent Territory   ◆ Administrative Regions   ▲ Mountain   ◣ Volcano   ◎ Lake
● Country Capital   ○ Dependent Territory Capital   ✈ International Airport   ▲ Mountain Range   ◆ River   ◎ Reservoir

◆ Country   ◆ Country Capital   ◇ Dependent Territory   ○ Dependent Territory Capital   ✕ Administrative Regions   ✕ International Airport   ▲ Mountain   ▲ Mountain Range   ▲ Volcano   ◈ River   ◙ Lake   ◙ Reservoir

◆ Country
● Country Capital
◇ Dependent Territory
○ Dependent Territory Capital
◇ Administrative Regions
✈ International Airport
▲ Mountain
▲ Mountain Range
🜨 Volcano
↗ River
© Lake
🌊 Reservoir

194 *E5* **Kepa** ***var.*** Kepe. Respublika Kareliya, NW Russian Federation *65°09′N 32°15′E*
Kepe *see* Kepa
283 *K2* **Kepirohi Falls** *waterfall* Pohnpei, E Micronesia
278 *B12* **Kepler Mountains** ▲▲ South Island, New Zealand
182 *E7* **Kępno** Wielkopolskie, C Poland *51°17′N 17°57′E*
190 *G3* **Kepor'e** Leningradskaya Oblast', Russian Federation
117 *H10* **Keppel Island** *island* N Falkland Islands
Keppel Island *see* Niuatoputapu
117 *H10* **Keppel Sound** *sound* N Falkland Islands
214 *B5* **Kepsut** Balıkesir, NW Turkey *39°41′N 28°09′E*
289 *H8* **Kepulauan** E Indian Ocean
258 *G4* **Kepulauan Riau** ***off.*** Propinsi Kepulauan Riau. ◐ *province* NW Indonesia
Kequ *see* Gadê
261 *J6* **Kerai** Papua, E Indonesia *03°53′S 134°30′E*
Kerak *see* Al Karak
235 *E9* **Kerala** ◐ *state* S India
261 *N6* **Keram** ≈ N Papua New Guinea
251 *H10* **Kerama-rettō** *island group* SW Japan
277 *I6* **Kerang** Victoria, SE Australia *35°46′S 144°01′E*
Kerasunt *see* Giresun
187 *H6* **Keratéa** ***var.*** Keratea. Attikí, C Greece *37°48′N 23°58′E*
Keratea *see* Keratéa
153 *H10* **Kerava** ***Swe.*** Kervo. Etelä-Suomi, S Finland *60°25′N 25°10′E*
Kerbala/Kerbela *see* Karbalā'
76 *B8* **Kerby** Oregon, NW USA *42°10′N 123°39′W*
189 *L8* **Kerch** ***Rus.*** Kerch'. Respublika Krym, SE Ukraine *45°22′N 36°30′E*
Kerch' *see* Kerch
Kerchens'ka Protska/Kerchenskiy Proliv *see* Kerch Strait
189 *L9* **Kerchens'kyy Pivostriv** *peninsula* S Ukraine
189 *L9* **Kerch Strait** ***var.*** Bosporus Cimmerius, Enikale Strait, ***Rus.*** Kerchenskiy Proliv, ***Ukr.*** Kerchens'ka Protska. *strait* Black Sea/Sea of Azov
Kerdilio *see* Kerdýlio
187 *H3* **Kerdýlio** ***var.*** Kerdilio. ▲ N Greece *40°46′N 23°37′E*
280 *B4* **Kerema** Gulf, S Papua New Guinea *07°59′S 145°46′E*
Keremitlik *see* Lyulyakovo
218 *D6* **Kerem Maharal** Israel *32°39′N 34°59′E*
214 *E4* **Kerempe Burnu** *headland* N Turkey *42°01′N 33°20′E*
219 *C10* **Kerem Shalom** Israel *31°12′N 34°17′E*
136 *E1* **Keren** ***var.*** Cheren. C Eritrea *15°45′N 38°22′E*
71 *H5* **Kerens** Texas, SW USA *32°07′N 96°13′W*
278 *H4* **Kerepehi** Waikato, North Island, New Zealand *37°18′S 175°33′E*
227 *H4* **Kerey, Ozero** ◎ C Kazakhstan
Kergel *see* Kärla
289 *E12* **Kerguelen** *island* C French Southern and Antarctic Territories
289 *F13* **Kerguelen Plateau** *undersea feature* S Indian Ocean
65 *H4* **Kerhonkson** New York, USA *41°46′N 74°18′W*
186 *E7* **Kerí** Zákynthos, Iónia Nisiá, Greece, C Mediterranean Sea *37°40′N 20°48′E*
137 *C8* **Kericho** Rift Valley, W Kenya *0°22′S 35°19′E*
278 *F2* **Kerikeri** Northland, North Island, New Zealand *35°14′S 173°58′E*
153 *J8* **Kerimäki** Itä-Suomi, E Finland *61°56′N 29°18′E*
258 *E6* **Kerinci, Danau** ◎ Sumatera, W Indonesia
258 *D6* **Kerinci, Gunung** ▲ Sumatera, W Indonesia *02°00′S 101°40′E*
Keriya *see* Yutian
238 *D5* **Keriya He** ≈ NW China
162 *F5* **Kerkbuurt** Noord-Holland, C Netherlands *52°29′N 05°08′E*
162 *F7* **Kerkdriel** Gelderland, C Netherlands *51°46′N 05°21′E*
131 *L2* **Kerkenah, Îles de** ***var.*** Kerkenna Islands, ***Ar.*** Juzur Qarqannah. *island group* E Tunisia
Kerkenna Islands *see* Kerkenah, Îles de
187 *K6* **Kerketévs** ▲ Sámos, Dodekánisa, Greece, Aegean Sea *37°44′N 26°39′E*
74 *F4* **Kerkhoven** Minnesota, N USA *45°12′N 95°18′W*
Kerki *see* Atamyrat
Kerkichi *see* Kerkiçi
228 *G7* **Kerkiçi** ***Rus.*** Kerkichi. Lebap Welaýaty, E Turkmenistan *37°46′N 65°18′E*
186 *G4* **Kerkíneo** *prehistoric site* Thessalía, C Greece
187 *H2* **Kerkíni, Límni** ***var.*** Límni Kerkinitis. ◎ N Greece
Kerkinitis Límni *see* Kerkíni, Límni
Kérkira *see* Kérkyra
163 *H10* **Kerkrade** Limburg, SE Netherlands *50°53′N 06°04′E*
Kerkuk *see* Kirkūk
186 *E4* **Kérkyra** ***var.*** Kérkira, ***Eng.*** Corfu. Kérkyra, Iónia Nisiá, Greece, C Mediterranean Sea *39°37′N 19°56′E*
186 *E4* **Kerkyra** ✈ Kérkyra, Iónia Nisiá, Greece, C Mediterranean Sea *39°36′N 19°55′E*
186 *D4* **Kérkyra** ***var.*** Kérkira, ***Eng.*** Corfu. *island* Iónia Nisiá, Greece, C Mediterranean Sea
286 *F7* **Kermadec Islands** *island group* New Zealand, SW Pacific Ocean
267 *J7* **Kermadec Ridge** *undersea feature* SW Pacific Ocean *30°30′S 178°30′W*
267 *J7* **Kermadec Trench** *undersea feature* SW Pacific Ocean
223 *I7* **Kermān** ***var.*** Kirman; ***anc.*** Carmana. Kermān, C Iran *30°18′N 57°05′E*
80 *D5* **Kerman** California, USA *36°43′N 120°04′W*
223 *H7* **Kermān** ***off.*** Ostān-e Kermān, ***var.*** Kirman; ***anc.*** Carmania. ◐ *province* SE Iran
223 *J8* **Kermān, Bīābān-e** *desert* SE Iran
Kermān, Ostān-e *see* Kermān
222 *G6* **Kermānshāh** ***var.*** Qahremānshahr; ***prev.*** Bākhtarān. Kermānshāhān, W Iran *34°19′N 47°04′E*
222 *D4* **Kermānshāh** Yazd, C Iran *34°19′N 47°04′E*
222 *D4* **Kermānshāh** ***off.*** Ostān-e Kermānshāhān; ***prev.*** Bākhtarān. ◐ *province* W Iran
Kermānshāhān, Ostān-e *see* Kermānshāh
185 *L6* **Kermen** Sliven, C Bulgaria *42°30′N 26°12′E*
70 *D5* **Kermit** Texas, SW USA *31°49′N 103°07′W*
67 *H4* **Kermit** West Virginia, NE USA *37°51′N 82°24′W*
80 *F7* **Kern Canyon** *valley* California, USA
67 *J6* **Kernersville** North Carolina, SE USA *36°12′N 80°13′W*
190 *G3* **Kernovo** Leningradskaya Oblast', Russian Federation
81 *E8* **Kern River** ≈ California, W USA
81 *E8* **Kernville** California, W USA *35°44′N 118°25′W*
187 *J8* **Kéros** *island* Kykládes, Greece, Aegean Sea
132 *D6* **Kérouané** SE Guinea *09°16′N 09°00′W*
181 *B9* **Kerpen** Nordrhein-Westfalen, W Germany *50°51′N 06°40′E*
228 *E6* **Kerpichli** Lebap Welaýaty, NE Turkmenistan *40°12′N 61°09′E*
158 *E2* **Kerrera** *island* United Kingdom
70 *D1* **Kerrick** Texas, SW USA *36°29′N 102°14′W*
Kerr Lake *see* John H. Kerr Reservoir
57 *L6* **Kerrobert** Saskatchewan, S Canada *51°56′N 109°09′W*
70 *F7* **Kerrville** Texas, SW USA *30°03′N 99°09′W*
67 *I7* **Kershaw** South Carolina, SE USA *34°33′N 80°34′W*
Kertel *see* Kärdla
155 *D12* **Kerteminde** Fyn, C Denmark *55°27′N 10°40′E*
237 *H3* **Kerulen** ***Chin.*** Herlen He, ***Mong.*** Herlen Gol. ≈ China/Mongolia
Kervo *see* Kerava
Kerýneia *see* Girne
58 *F6* **Kesagami Lake** ◎ Ontario, SE Canada
153 *J8* **Kesälahti** Itä-Suomi, SE Finland *61°54′N 29°49′E*
214 *B4* **Keşan** Edirne, NW Turkey *40°52′N 26°37′E*
253 *E9* **Kesennuma** Miyagi, Honshū, C Japan *38°55′N 141°35′E*
158 *B7* **Kesh** United Kingdom *54°32′N 7°43′W*
247 *L4* **Keshan** Heilongjiang, NE China *48°00′N 125°46′E*
72 *D6* **Keshena** Wisconsin, N USA *44°54′N 88°37′W*
214 *E5* **Keskin** Kırıkkale, C Turkey *39°41′N 33°36′E*
190 *J1* **Keskozero** Respublika Kareliya, Russian Federation
Késmárk *see* Kežmarok
175 *B14* **Kesra** Tunisia
161 *N3* **Kessingland** United Kingdom *52°25′N 1°43′E*
194 *E4* **Kesten'ga** ***var.*** Kest Enga. Respublika Kareliya, NW Russian Federation *65°53′N 31°47′E*
Kest Enga *see* Kesten'ga
162 *G7* **Kesteren** Gelderland, C Netherlands *51°55′N 05°34′E*
62 *D4* **Keswick** Ontario, S Canada *44°15′N 79°26′W*
159 *I7* **Keswick** NW England, United Kingdom *54°30′N 03°04′W*
183 *E12* **Keszthely** Zala, SW Hungary *46°47′N 17°16′E*
192 *F7* **Ket'** ≈ C Russian Federation
133 *H8* **Keta** SE Ghana *05°55′N 00°59′E*
259 *H6* **Ketapang** Borneo, C Indonesia *01°50′S 109°59′E*
197 *I7* **Ketchenery** ***prev.*** Sovetskoye. Respublika Kalmykiya, SW Russian Federation *47°18′N 44°31′E*
83 *N8* **Ketchikan** Revillagigedo Island, Alaska, USA *55°21′N 131°39′W*
76 *G7* **Ketchum** Idaho, NW USA *43°40′N 114°24′W*
Kete/Kete Krakye *see* Kete-Krachi
133 *H7* **Kete-Krachi** ***var.*** Kete, Kete Krakye. E Ghana *07°50′N 00°03′W*
162 *G5* **Ketelmeer** *channel* E Netherlands
230 *G10* **Keti Bandar** Sind, SE Pakistan *23°55′N 67°31′E*
227 *L7* **Ketmen', Khrebet** ▲▲ SE Kazakhstan
133 *I7* **Kétou** SE Benin *07°25′N 02°36′E*
182 *H4* **Kętrzyn** ***Ger.*** Rastenburg. Warmińsko-Mazurskie, NE Poland *54°05′N 21°24′E*
181 *F13* **Ketsch** Baden-Württemberg, Germany *8°32′N 49°22′E*
161 *J4* **Kettering** C England, United Kingdom *52°24′N 00°44′W*
73 *G11* **Kettering** Ohio, N USA *39°41′N 84°10′W*
64 *B4* **Kettle Creek** ≈ Pennsylvania, NE USA
76 *E3* **Kettle Falls** Washington, NW USA *48°36′N 118°03′W*
80 *C6* **Kettleman City** California, USA *36°01′N 119°58′W*
62 *B5* **Kettle Point** *headland* Ontario, S Canada *43°12′N 82°01′W*
74 *H4* **Kettle River** ≈ Minnesota, N USA
159 *J8* **Kettlewell** United Kingdom *54°08′N 2°03′W*
161 *J3* **Ketton** United Kingdom *52°37′N 0°33′W*
181 *C8* **Kettwig** Nordrhein-Westfalen, Germany *6°57′N 51°22′E*
280 *A3* **Ketu** ≈ W Papua New Guinea
64 *C2* **Keuka Lake** ◎ New York, NE USA
64 *D2* **Keuka Park** New York, USA *42°37′N 77°06′W*
181 *I8* **Keula** Thüringen, Germany *10°32′N 51°20′E*
Keupriya *see* Primorsko
153 *H8* **Keuruu** Länsi-Suomi, C Finland *62°15′N 24°34′E*
181 *B8* **Kevelaer** Nordrhein-Westfalen, Germany *6°15′N 51°35′E*
Kevevára *see* Kovin
152 *H3* **Kevo** ***Lapp.*** Geavvú. Lappi, N Finland *69°42′N 27°08′E*
91 *H4* **Kew** North Caicos, N Turks and Caicos Islands *21°52′N 71°57′W*
73 *C9* **Kewanee** Illinois, N USA *41°15′N 89°55′W*
72 *E6* **Kewaunee** Wisconsin, N USA *44°27′N 87°31′W*
72 *D4* **Keweenaw Bay** ◎ Michigan, N USA
72 *D3* **Keweenaw Peninsula** *peninsula* Michigan, N USA
72 *E3* **Keweenaw Point** *peninsula* Michigan, N USA
74 *C6* **Keya Paha River** ≈ Nebraska/South Dakota, N USA
Keyaygyr *see* Këk-Aygyr
69 *N9* **Key Biscayne** Florida, SE USA *25°41′N 80°09′W*
80 *C4* **Keyes** California, USA *37°33′N 120°55′W*
75 *A11* **Keyes** Oklahoma, C USA *36°48′N 102°15′W*
69 *N10* **Key Largo** Key Largo, Florida, SE USA *25°06′N 80°25′W*
158 *B8* **Key, Lough** ◎ C Ireland
161 *H6* **Keynsham** United Kingdom *51°25′N 2°30′W*
65 *H7* **Keyport** New Jersey, USA *40°26′N 74°12′W*
64 *A9* **Keyser** West Virginia, NE USA *39°25′N 78°59′W*
75 *E12* **Keystone Lake** ⊡ Oklahoma, C USA
79 *I10* **Keystone Peak** ▲ Arizona, SW USA *31°52′N 111°12′W*
Keystone State *see* Pennsylvania
67 *K5* **Keysville** Virginia, NE USA *37°02′N 78°28′W*
75 *H9* **Keytesville** Missouri, C USA *39°25′N 92°56′W*
69 *M10* **Key West** Florida Keys, Florida, SE USA *24°34′N 81°48′W*
195 *K9* **Kez** Udmurtskaya Respublika, NW Russian Federation *57°55′N 53°42′E*
Kezdivásárhely *see* Târgu Secuiesc
193 *H7* **Kezhma** Krasnoyarskiy Kray, C Russian Federation *58°57′N 101°00′E*
183 *G9* **Kežmarok** ***Ger.*** Käsmark, ***Hung.*** Késmárk. Prešovský Kraj, E Slovakia *49°09′N 20°25′E*
219 *D8* **Kfar Bin Nun** Israel *31°51′N 34°56′E*
218 *G2* **Kfar Habou** Lebanon *34°24′N 35°57′E*
219 *D8* **Kfar Menahem** Israel *31°44′N 34°50′E*
Kfar Saba *see* Kefar Sava
138 *E6* **Kgalagadi** ◐ *district* SW Botswana
141 *I2* **Kgatleng** ◐ *district* SE Botswana
282 *C9* **Kgkeklau** Babeldaob, N Palau
141 *I5* **Kgotsong** Free State, South Africa *27°23′S 26°37′E*
218 *H5* **Khabab** Syria
218 *H5* **Khabab** Syria *33°00′N 36°16′E*
195 *J4* **Khabarikha** ***var.*** Chabaricha. Respublika Komi, NW Russian Federation *65°52′N 52°19′E*
193 *L8* **Khabarovsk** Khabarovskiy Kray, SE Russian Federation *48°32′N 135°08′E*
193 *K6* **Khabarovskiy Kray** ◐ *territory* E Russian Federation
221 *J4* **Khabb** Abū Ẓaby, E United Arab Emirates *24°39′N 55°43′E*
Khabour, Nahr al *see* Khābūr, Nahr al
Khabura *see* Al Khābūrah
216 *G2* **Khābūr, Nahr al** ***var.*** Nahr al Khabour. ≈ Syria/Turkey
Khachmas *see* Xaçmaz
134 *H3* **Khadari** ≈ W Sudan
Khadera *see* Hadera
221 *K6* **Khādhil** ***var.*** Khudal. SE Oman *18°48′N 56°48′E*
234 *C5* **Khadki** ***prev.*** Kirkee. Mahārāshtra, W India *18°34′N 73°52′E*
171 *J9* **Khadra** Algeria
196 *G8* **Khadyzhensk** Krasnodarskiy Kray, SW Russian Federation *44°26′N 39°31′E*
185 *M6* **Khadzhiyska Reka** ≈ E Bulgaria
189 *H7* **Khadzhybeys'kyy Lyman** ◎ SW Ukraine
216 *E2* **Khafsah** Ḥalab, N Syria *36°16′N 38°03′E*
232 *G7* **Khāga** Uttar Pradesh, N India *25°47′N 81°05′E*
233 *I7* **Khagaria** Bihār, NE India *25°31′N 86°27′E*
230 *G8* **Khairpur** Sind, SE Pakistan *27°30′N 68°50′E*
192 *G8* **Khakasiya, Respublika** ***prev.*** Khakasskaya Avtonomnaya Oblast', ***Eng.*** Khakassia. ◐ *autonomous republic* C Russian Federation
Khakassia/Khakasskaya Avtonomnaya Oblast' *see* Khakasiya, Respublika
256 *E7* **Kha Khaeng, Khao** ▲ W Thailand *16°13′N 99°03′E*
140 *G3* **Khakhea** ***var.*** Kakia. Southern, S Botswana *24°41′S 23°29′E*
Khalach *see* Halaç
Khalándrion *see* Chalándri
197 *M4* **Khalilovo** Orenburgskaya Oblast', W Russian Federation *51°25′N 58°13′E*
Khalkabad *see* Xalqobod
222 *E2* **Khalkhāl** ***prev.*** Herowābād. Ardabīl, NW Iran *37°36′N 48°36′E*
Khalkidhikí *see* Chalkidikí
Khalkís *see* Chalkída
195 *L2* **Khal'mer-Yu** Respublika Komi, NW Russian Federation *68°00′N 64°45′E*
191 *G9* **Khalopyenichy** ***Rus.*** Kholopenichi. Minskaya Voblasts', NE Belarus *54°31′N 28°58′E*
Khalturin *see* Orlov
221 *K6* **Khalūf** ***var.*** Al Khaluf. E Oman *20°27′N 57°59′E*
232 *G8* **Khamaria** Madhya Pradesh, C India *23°07′N 80°54′E*
232 *C8* **Khambhāt** Gujarāt, W India *22°19′N 72°39′E*
232 *C9* **Khambhāt, Gulf of** ***Eng.*** Gulf of Cambay. *gulf* W India
256 *I7* **Khâm Đưc** ***var.*** Phước Sơn. Quang Nam-Đa Năng, C Vietnam *15°28′N 107°49′E*
234 *E4* **Khāmgaon** Mahārāshtra, C India *20°41′N 76°34′E*
220 *F8* **Khamir** ***var.*** Khamr. W Yemen *16°N 43°56′E*
220 *F7* **Khamīs Mushayt** ***var.*** Hamīs Musait. 'Asīr, SW Saudi Arabia *18°19′N 42°41′E*
193 *J6* **Khampa** Respublika Sakha (Yakutiya), NE Russian Federation *63°43′N 123°02′E*
Khamr *see* Khamir
140 *A1* **Khan** ≈ W Namibia
231 *H2* **Khānābād** Kunduz, NE Afghanistan *36°42′N 69°08′E*
Khân Abou Châmâte/Khan Abou Ech Cham *see* Khān Abū Shāmāt
218 *I4* **Khān Abū Shāmāt** ***var.*** Khân Abou Châmâte, Khan Abou Ech Cham. Dimashq, W Syria *33°43′N 36°56′E*
Khān al Baghdādī *see* Al Baghdādī
218 *J2* **Khan al Ḩayr** Syria *34°32′N 37°41′E*
Khān al Maḩāwīl *see* Al Maḩāwīl
217 *J5* **Khān al Mashāhidah** Baghdād, C Iraq *33°40′N 44°15′E*
217 *J6* **Khān al Muşallá** An Najaf, S Iraq *32°09′N 44°20′E*
217 *K4* **Khānaqīn** Diyālá, E Iraq *34°22′N 45°22′E*
218 *G5* **Khān Arnabah** Syria *33°10′N 35°53′E*
217 *J7* **Khān ar Ruḩbah** An Najaf, S Iraq *31°42′N 44°18′E*
217 *H2* **Khān as Sūr** Nīnawá, N Iraq *36°28′N 41°36′E*
217 *J5* **Khān Āzād** Baghdād, C Iraq *33°08′N 44°21′E*
218 *G4* **Khān Dannūn** Syria *33°20′N 36°14′E*
234 *I4* **Khandaparha** ***prev.*** Khandpara. Orissa, E India *20°15′N 85°11′E*
Khandpara *see* Khandaparha
231 *I2* **Khandūd** ***var.*** Khandud, Wakhan. Badakhshān, NE Afghanistan *36°57′N 72°19′E*
Khandud *see* Khandūd
232 *E9* **Khandwa** Madhya Pradesh, C India *21°49′N 76°23′E*
193 *K6* **Khandyga** Respublika Sakha (Yakutiya), NE Russian Federation *62°39′N 135°30′E*
218 *G1* **Khâne Hayât** Lebanon *34°35′N 36°01′E*
231 *I6* **Khānewāl** Punjab, NE Pakistan *30°18′N 71°56′E*
231 *I6* **Khāngarh** Punjab, E Pakistan *29°57′N 71°14′E*
Khanh Hung *see* Soc Trăng
Khaniá *see* Chaniá
Khanka *see* Xonqa
193 *L9* **Khanka, Lake** ***var.*** Hsing-K'ai Hu, Lake Hanka, ***Chin.*** Xingkai Hu, ***Rus.*** Ozero Khanka. ◎ China/Russian Federation
Khanka, Ozero *see* Khanka, Lake
Khankendi *see* Xankändi
Khanlar *see* Xanlar
193 *I5* **Khannya** ≈ NE Russian Federation
231 *H7* **Khānpur** Punjab, E Pakistan *28°31′N 70°30′E*
216 *D3* **Khān Shaykhūn** ***var.*** Khan Sheikhun. Idlib, NW Syria *35°27′N 36°38′E*
Khan Sheikhun *see* Khān Shaykhūn
227 *J7* **Khantau** Zhambyl, S Kazakhstan *44°13′N 73°47′E*
229 *N4* **Khan Tengri, Pik** ▲ SE Kazakhstan *42°17′N 80°11′E*
Khan-Tengri, Pik *see* Hantengri Feng
256 *G7* **Khanthabouli** ***prev.*** Savannakhét. Savannakhét, S Laos *16°38′N 104°49′E*
195 *N6* **Khanty-Mansiysk** ***prev.*** Ostyako-Voguls'k. Khanty-Mansiyskiy Avtonomnyy Okrug-Yugra, C Russian Federation *61°01′N 69°E*
192 *E5* **Khanty-Mansiyskiy Avtonomnyy Okrug** ◐ *autonomous district* C Russian Federation
217 *I3* **Khānūqah** Nīnawýé, C Iraq *35°25′N 43°15′E*
219 *C9* **Khān Yūnis** ***var.*** Khān Yūnus. S Gaza Strip *31°21′N 34°18′E*
219 *C9* **Khān YūnIsrael** Gaza Strip *31°20′N 34°18′E*
Khān Yūnus *see* Khān Yūnis
Khanzi *see* Ghanzi
217 *K3* **Khān Zūr** As Sulaymānīyah, E Iraq *35°03′N 45°08′E*
256 *E7* **Khao Laem Reservoir** ⊡ W Thailand
193 *I9* **Khapcheranga** Chitinskaya Oblast', S Russian Federation *49°46′N 112°21′E*
197 *J7* **Kharabali** Astrakhanskaya Oblast', SW Russian Federation *47°28′N 47°14′E*
233 *J8* **Kharagpur** West Bengal, NE India *22°30′N 87°19′E*
217 *K8* **Kharā'ib 'Abd al Karīm** Al Muthanná, S Iraq *31°07′N 45°33′E*
222 *G5* **Kharānaq** Yazd, C Iran *31°54′N 54°21′E*
219 *E9* **Khārās** West Bank
219 *E8* **Kharbata** West Bank *31°57′N 35°04′E*
Kharbin *see* Harbin
Kharchi *see* Mārwār
228 *E7* **Khardzhagaz** Ahal Welaýaty, C Turkmenistan *37°54′N 60°10′E*
Khārga Oasis *see* Great Oasis, The
232 *D9* **Khargon** Madhya Pradesh, C India *21°49′N 75°39′E*
231 *J4* **Khāriān** Punjab, NE Pakistan *32°52′N 73°52′E*
189 *M5* **Kharisyz'k** Donets'ka Oblast', E Ukraine *48°01′N 38°10′E*
189 *L3* **Kharkiv** ***Rus.*** Khar'kov. Kharkivs'ka Oblast', NE Ukraine *50°N 36°14′E*
189 *L3* **Kharkiv** ✈ Kharkivs'ka Oblast', E Ukraine *49°54′N 36°20′E*
Kharkiv *see* Kharkivs'ka Oblast'
189 *L4* **Kharkivs'ka Oblast'** ***var.*** Kharkiv, ***Rus.*** Khar'kovskaya Oblast'. ◐ *province* E Ukraine
Khar'kov *see* Kharkiv
Khar'kovskaya Oblast' *see* Kharkivs'ka Oblast'
194 *F3* **Kharlovka** Murmanskaya Oblast', NW Russian Federation *68°47′N 37°09′E*
185 *K7* **Kharmanli** Khaskovo, S Bulgaria *41°56′N 25°54′E*
185 *K7* **Kharmanliyska Reka** ≈ S Bulgaria
194 *G8* **Kharovsk** Vologodskaya Oblast', NW Russian Federation *59°57′N 40°05′E*
136 *B2* **Khartoum** ***var.*** El Khartûm, Khartum. ● (Sudan) Khartoum, C Sudan *15°33′N 32°32′E*
136 *B1* **Khartoum** ◐ *state* NE Sudan
136 *B1* **Khartoum** ✈ Khartoum, C Sudan *15°36′N 32°37′E*
136 *B2* **Khartoum North** Khartoum, C Sudan *15°38′N 32°33′E*
189 *M5* **Khartsyz'k** ***Rus.*** Khartsyzsk. Donets'ka Oblast', SE Ukraine *48°01′N 38°10′E*
Khartsyzsk *see* Khartsyz'k
Khartum *see* Khartoum
234 *E3* **Khās** Madhya Pradesh, C India *22°12′N 77°30′E*
Khasab *see* Al Khaşab
248 *E2* **Khasan** Primorskiy Kray, SE Russian Federation *42°24′N 130°45′E*
197 *I9* **Khasavyurt** Respublika Dagestan, SW Russian Federation *43°16′N 46°33′E*
223 *K8* **Khāsh** ***prev.*** Vāsht. Sīstān va Balūchestān, SE Iran *28°15′N 61°11′E*
230 *D5* **Khāsh, Dasht-e** ***Eng.*** Khash Desert. *desert* SW Afghanistan
Khash Desert *see* Khāsh, Dasht-e
Khashim Al Qirba/Khashm al Qirbah *see* Khashm el Girba
136 *D2* **Khashm el Girba** ***var.*** Khashim Al Qirba, Khashm al Qirbah. Kassala, E Sudan *15°00′N 35°59′E*
219 *F14* **Khashsh, Jabal al** ▲▲ S Jordan
215 *J4* **Khashuri** C Georgia *41°59′N 43°36′E*
233 *L7* **Khāsi Hills** *hill range* NE India
185 *K7* **Khaskovo** Khaskovo, S Bulgaria *41°56′N 25°35′E*
185 *K7* **Khaskovo** ◐ *province* S Bulgaria
193 *H4* **Khatanga** Taymyrskiy (Dolgano-Nenetskiy) Avtonomnyy Okrug, N Russian Federation *71°55′N 102°17′E*
193 *H4* **Khatanga** ≈ N Russian Federation
Khatanga, Gulf of *see* Khatangskiy Zaliv
193 *I4* **Khatangskiy Zaliv** ***var.*** Gulf of Khatanga. *bay* N Russian Federation
221 *K4* **Khatmat al Malāḩah** N Oman *24°58′N 56°22′E*
223 *H10* **Khaţmat al Malāḩah** Ash Shāriqah, E United Arab Emirates
193 *N4* **Khatyrka** Chukotskiy Avtonomnyy Okrug, NE Russian Federation *62°03′N 175°09′E*
Khauz-Khan *see* Hanhowuz
Khauzkhanskoye Vodoranilishche *see* Hanhowuz Suw Howdany
Khavaling *see* Khovaling
Khavast *see* Xovos
217 *L7* **Khawrah, Nahr al** ≈ S Iraq
Khawr Barakah *see* Baraka
221 *K4* **Khawr Fakkān** ***var.*** Khor Fakkan. Ash Shāriqah, NE United Arab Emirates *25°22′N 56°19′E*
220 *E3* **Khaybar** Al Madīnah, NW Saudi Arabia *25°53′N 39°16′E*
Khaybar, Kowtal-e *see* Khyber Pass
229 *J6* **Khaydarkan** ***var.*** Khaydarken. Batkenskaya Oblast', SW Kyrgyzstan *39°56′N 71°17′E*
Khaydarken *see* Khaydarkan
195 *K2* **Khaypudryskaya Guba** *headland* Nenetskiy Avtonomnyy okrug, Russian Federation *67°00′N 50°00′E*
195 *L1* **Khaypudyrskaya Guba** *bay* NW Russian Federation
217 *J1* **Khayrūzuk** Arbīl, E Iraq *36°58′N 44°19′E*
Khazar, Baḩr-e/Khazar, Daryā-ye *see* Caspian Sea
Khazarosp *see* Hazorasp
Khazretishi, Khrebet *see* Hazratishoh, Çatorkūhi
Khelat *see* Kālat
171 *K9* **Khemis Miliana** Algeria
130 *F2* **Khemisset** NW Morocco *33°52′N 06°04′W*
256 *H7* **Khemmarat** ***var.*** Kemarat. Ubon Ratchathani, E Thailand *16°03′N 105°11′E*
131 *J2* **Khenchela** ***var.*** Khenchla. NE Algeria *35°22′N 07°09′E*
Khenchla *see* Khenchela
130 *F3* **Khénifra** C Morocco *32°59′N 05°37′W*
171 *N9* **Kherrata** Algeria
Khersān, Rūd-e *see* Garm, Āb-e
189 *I7* **Kherson** Khersons'ka Oblast', S Ukraine *46°39′N 32°38′E*
Kherson *see* Khersons'ka Oblast'
189 *J9* **Khersones, Mys** ***Rus.*** Mys Khersonesskiy. *headland* S Ukraine *44°34′N 33°24′E*
Khersonesskiy, Mys *see* Khersones, Mys
189 *J7* **Khersons'ka Oblast'** ***var.*** Kherson, ***Rus.*** Khersonskaya Oblast'. ◐ *province* S Ukraine
Khersonskaya Oblast' *see* Khersons'ka Oblast'
193 *H4* **Kheta** Taymyrskiy (Dolgano-Nenetskiy) Avtonomnyy Okrug, N Russian Federation *71°33′N 99°40′E*
193 *H4* **Kheta** ≈ N Russian Federation
173 *M10* **Khettab** Algeria *35°54′N 00°30′E*
256 *H6* **Khe Ve** Quang Binh, C Vietnam *17°52′N 105°49′E*
231 *I4* **Khewra** Punjab, E Pakistan *32°41′N 73°04′E*
Khiam *see* El Khiyam
194 *E3* **Khibiny** ▲▲ NW Russian Federation
193 *I8* **Khilok** Chitinskaya Oblast', S Russian Federation *51°26′N 110°25′E*
193 *I8* **Khilok** ≈ S Russian Federation
196 *F2* **Khimki** Moskovskaya Oblast', W Russian Federation *55°57′N 37°48′E*
229 *J7* **Khingov** ***Rus.*** Obi-Khingou. ≈ C Tajikistan
Khíos *see* Chíos
231 *H9* **Khipro** Sind, SE Pakistan *25°50′N 69°24′E*
217 *I7* **Khirr, Wādī al** *dry watercourse* S Iraq
185 *J6* **Khisarya** Plovdiv, C Bulgaria *42°33′N 24°43′E*
219 *H14* **Khishshah, Wādī al** *dry watercourse* Jordan
Khiva/Khiwa *see* Xiva
256 *E7* **Khlong Khlung** Kamphaeng Phet, W Thailand *16°15′N 99°41′E*
257 *E11* **Khlong Thom** Krabi, SW Thailand *07°55′N 99°09′E*
257 *F8* **Khlung** Chantaburi, S Thailand *12°25′N 102°12′E*
Khmel'nik *see* Khmil'nyk
Khmel'nitskaya Oblast' *see* Khmel'nyts'ka Oblast'
Khmel'nitskiy *see* Khmel'nyts'kyy
188 *E4* **Khmel'nyts'ka Oblast'** ***var.*** Khmel'nyts'kyy, ***Rus.*** Khmel'nitskaya Oblast'; ***prev.*** Kamenets-Podol'skaya Oblast'. ◐ *province* NW Ukraine
188 *F4* **Khmel'nyts'kyy** ***Rus.*** Khmel'nitskiy; ***prev.*** Proskurov. Khmel'nyts'ka Oblast', W Ukraine *49°24′N 26°59′E*
Khmel'nyts'kyy *see* Khmel'nyts'ka Oblast'
188 *F4* **Khmil'nyk** ***Rus.*** Khmel'nik. Vinnyts'ka Oblast', C Ukraine *49°36′N 27°59′E*
226 *D4* **Khobda** ***prev.*** Novoalekseyevka. Aktyubinsk, W Kazakhstan *50°09′N 55°39′E*
215 *J3* **Khobi** W Georgia *42°20′N 41°54′E*
191 *I9* **Khodasy** ***Rus.*** Khodosy. Mahilyowskaya Voblasts', E Belarus *53°56′N 31°29′E*
188 *D4* **Khodoriv** ***Pol.*** Chodorów, ***Rus.*** Khodorov. L'vivs'ka Oblast', NW Ukraine *49°20′N 24°19′E*
Khodorov *see* Khodoriv
Khodosy *see* Khodasy
Khodzhakala *see* Hojagala
Khodzhambas *see* Hojambaz
Khodzhent *see* Khŭjand
Khodzheyli *see* Xo'jayli
Khoi *see* Khvoy
Khojend *see* Khŭjand
Khokand *see* Qo'qon
196 *G4* **Khokhol'skiy** Voronezhskaya Oblast', W Russian Federation *51°33′N 38°43′E*
256 *E7* **Khok Samrong** Lop Buri, C Thailand *15°03′N 100°44′E*
230 *G2* **Kholm** ***var.*** Tashqurghan, ***Pash.*** Khulm. Balkh, N Afghanistan *36°42′N 67°41′E*
194 *D10* **Kholm** Novgorodskaya Oblast', W Russian Federation *57°10′N 31°06′E*
Kholm *see* Chełm
Kholmech' *see* Kholmyech
193 *M8* **Kholmsk** Ostrov Sakhalin, Sakhalinskaya Oblast', SE Russian Federation *46°57′N 142°10′E*
191 *I11* **Kholmyech** ***Rus.*** Kholmech'. Homyel'skaya Voblasts', SE Belarus *52°09′N 30°37′E*
Kholon *see* Holon
Kholopenichi *see* Khalopyenichy
138 *C5* **Khomas** ◐ *district* C Namibia
140 *B1* **Khomas Hochland** ***var.*** Khomasplato. *plateau* C Namibia
Khomasplato *see* Khomas Hochland
Khomein *see* Khomeyn
222 *E5* **Khomeyn** ***var.*** Khomein, Khumain. Markazī, W Iran *33°38′N 50°03′E*
222 *F5* **Khomeynīshahr** ***prev.*** Homāyūnshahr. Eşfahān, C Iran *32°42′N 51°28′E*
Khoms *see* Al Khums
Khong Sedone *see* Muang Khôngxédôn
256 *F7* **Khon Kaen** ***var.*** Muang Khon Kaen. Khon Kaen, E Thailand *16°25′N 102°50′E*
Khonqa *see* Xonqa
256 *F7* **Khon San** Khon Kaen, E Thailand *16°40′N 101°51′E*
193 *K5* **Khonuu** Respublika Sakha (Yakutiya), NE Russian Federation *66°24′N 143°15′E*
197 *H5* **Khopër** ***var.*** Khoper. ≈ SW Russian Federation
Khoper *see* Khopër
193 *L8* **Khor** Khabarovskiy Kray, SE Russian Federation *47°44′N 134°48′E*
223 *J6* **Khorāsān-e Janūbī** ***off.*** Ostan-e Khorāsān-e Janūbī. ◐ *province* E Iran
223 *I4* **Khorāsān-e Razavī** ***off.*** Ostān-e Khorāsān, ***var.*** Khorassan, Khurasan. ◐ *province* NE Iran
223 *H2* **Khorāsān-e Shemālī** ***off.*** Ostan-e Khorāsān-e Shemālī. ◐ *province* NE Iran
Khorāsān, Ostān-e *see* Khorāsān-e Razavī
Khorassan *see* Khorāsān-e Razavī
Khorat *see* Nakhon Ratchasima
234 *I4* **Khordha** ***prev.*** Khurda. Orissa, E India *20°10′N 85°42′E*
195 *K3* **Khorey-Ver** Nenetskiy Avtonomnyy Okrug, NW Russian Federation *67°25′N 58°05′E*
Khorezmskaya Oblast' *see* Xorazm Viloyati
Khor Fakkan *see* Khawr Fakkān
227 *L7* **Khorgos** Almaty, SE Kazakhstan *44°13′N 80°22′E*
138 *B4* **Khorixas** Kunene, NW Namibia *20°23′S 14°55′E*
220 *F9* **Khormaksar** ***var.*** Aden. ✈ ('Adan) SW Yemen *12°56′N 45°00′E*
Khormal *see* Khurmāl
Khormuj *see* Khvormūj
Khorog *see* Khorugh
189 *J4* **Khorol** Poltavs'ka Oblast', NE Ukraine *49°49′N 33°17′E*
195 *L7* **Khorpiya** Sverdlovskaya Oblast', Russian Federation
222 *E5* **Khorramābād** ***var.*** Khurramabad. Lorestān, W Iran *33°29′N 48°21′E*
222 *D6* **Khorramshahr** ***var.*** Khurramshahr, Muhammerah; ***prev.*** Mohammerah. Khūzestān, SW Iran *30°30′N 48°09′E*
229 *J8* **Khorugh** ***Rus.*** Khorog. S Tajikistan *37°30′N 71°31′E*
Khorvot Khalutsa *see* Horvot Haluza
197 *J7* **Khosheutovo** Astrakhanskaya Oblast', SW Russian Federation *47°04′N 47°49′E*
Khotan *see* Hotan
Khotimsk *see* Khotsimsk
Khotin *see* Khotyn
191 *J10* **Khotsimsk** ***Rus.*** Khotimsk. Mahilyowskaya Voblasts', E Belarus *53°24′N 32°35′E*
188 *E5* **Khotyn** ***Rom.*** Hotin, ***Rus.*** Khotin. Chernivets'ka Oblast', W Ukraine *48°29′N 26°30′E*
130 *F3* **Khouribga** C Morocco *32°55′N 06°51′W*
229 *J7* **Khovaling** ***Rus.*** Khavaling. SW Tajikistan *38°22′N 69°54′E*
Khovd *see* Hovd
231 *H4* **Khowst** Khowst, E Afghanistan *33°22′N 69°57′E*
231 *H4* **Khowst** ◐ *province* E Afghanistan
Khoy *see* Khvoy
191 *H12* **Khoyniki** Homyel'skaya Voblasts', SE Belarus *51°54′N 29°58′E*
Khozretishi, Khrebet *see* Hazratishoh, Qatorkŭhi
Khrisoúpolis *see* Chrysoúpoli
193 *K4* **Khroma** ≈ NE Russian Federation
226 *E4* **Khromtau** ***Kaz.*** Khromtaū. Aktyubinsk, W Kazakhstan *50°14′N 58°22′E*
Khromtaū *see* Khromtau
Khrysokhou Bay *see* Chrysochoú, Kólpos
188 *G5* **Khrystynivka** Cherkas'ka Oblast', C Ukraine *48°49′N 29°55′E*
256 *G7* **Khuang Nai** Ubon Ratchathani, E Thailand *15°22′N 104°33′E*
Khudal *see* Khādhil
Khudat *see* Xudat
231 *J5* **Khudiān** Punjab, E Pakistan *30°59′N 74°19′E*
Khudzhand *see* Khŭjand
140 *F4* **Khuis** Kgalagadi, SW Botswana *26°37′S 21°50′E*
229 *I6* **Khŭjand** ***var.*** Khodzhent, Khojend, ***Rus.*** Khudzhand; ***prev.*** Leninabad, ***Taj.*** Leninobod. N Tajikistan *40°17′N 69°37′E*
228 *E4* **Khŭjayli** Qoraqalpog'iston Respublikasi, W Uzbekistan *42°23′N 59°27′E*
256 *G7* **Khukhan** Si Sa Ket, E Thailand *14°38′N 104°12′E*
195 *L4* **Khulga** ≈ Khanty-Mansiyskiy Avtonomnyy Okrug-Yugra, Russian Federation
Khulm *see* Kholm
233 *K8* **Khulna** Khulna, SW Bangladesh *22°48′N 89°32′E*
233 *K8* **Khulna** ◐ *division* SW Bangladesh
Khumain *see* Khomeyn
Khums *see* Al Khums
231 *J2* **Khunjerāb Pass** *pass* China/Pakistan
Khūnjerāb Pass *see* Kunjirap Daban
233 *I8* **Khunti** Jhārkhand, N India *23°02′N 85°19′E*
256 *D5* **Khun Yuam** Mae Hong Son, NW Thailand *18°54′N 97°54′E*
Khurais *see* Khurayş
Khurasan *see* Khorāsān-e Razavī
221 *H4* **Khurayş** ***var.*** Khurais. Ash Sharqīyah, C Saudi Arabia *25°06′N 48°03′E*
Khurda *see* Khordha
232 *F5* **Khurja** Uttar Pradesh, N India *28°15′N 77°51′E*
217 *K3* **Khurmāl** ***var.*** Khormal. As Sulaymānīyah, NE Iraq *35°19′N 46°06′E*
Khurramabad *see* Khorramābād
Khurramshahr *see* Khorramshahr
231 *I5* **Khushāb** Punjab, NE Pakistan *32°16′N 72°18′E*
188 *C5* **Khust** ***var.*** Husté, ***Cz.*** Chust, ***Hung.*** Huszt. Zakarpats'ka Oblast', W Ukraine *48°11′N 23°19′E*
140 *G2* **Khutse Game Reserve** Kweneng, Botswana
134 *I2* **Khuwei** Western Kordofan, C Sudan *13°02′N 29°13′E*
230 *F8* **Khuzdār** Baluchistān, SW Pakistan *27°49′N 66°39′E*
222 *E6* **Khūzestān** ***off.*** Ostān-e Khūzestān, ***var.*** Khuzistan, ***prev.*** Arabistan; ***anc.*** Susiana. ◐ *province* SW Iran
Khūzestān, Ostān-e *see* Khūzestān
Khuzistan *see* Khūzestān
231 *H2* **Khvājeh Ghār** ***var.*** Khwajaghar, Khwaja-i-Ghar. Takhār, NE Afghanistan *37°08′N 69°24′E*
197 *J4* **Khvalynsk** Saratovskaya Oblast', W Russian Federation *52°30′N 48°06′E*
222 *F8* **Khvormūj** ***var.*** Khormuj. Būshehr, S Iran *28°32′N 51°22′E*
222 *C2* **Khvoy** ***var.*** Khoi, Khoy. Āzarbāyjān-e Bākhtarī, NW Iran *38°36′N 45°04′E*
Khwajaghar/Khwaja-i-Ghar *see* Khvājeh Ghār
231 *H4* **Khyber Pass** ***var.*** Kowtal-e Khaybar. *pass* Afghanistan/Pakistan
281 *I1* **Kia** Santa Isabel, N Solomon Islands *07°34′S 158°31′E*
277 *L6* **Kiama** New South Wales, SE Australia *34°41′S 150°49′E*
263 *M10* **Kiamba** Mindanao, S Philippines *05°59′N 124°36′E*
135 *I10* **Kiambi** Katanga, SE Dem. Rep. Congo *07°15′S 28°01′E*
75 *F13* **Kiamichi Mountains** ▲▲ Oklahoma, C USA
75 *F13* **Kiamichi River** ≈ Oklahoma, C USA
62 *G2* **Kiamika, Réservoir** ⊡ Québec, SE Canada
Kiamusze *see* Jiamusi
82 *G4* **Kiana** Alaska, USA *66°58′N 160°25′W*
Kiangmai *see* Chiang Mai
Kiang-ning *see* Nanjing
Kiangsi *see* Jiangxi
Kiangsu *see* Jiangsu
152 *I6* **Kiantajärvi** ◎ E Finland
186 *G6* **Kiáto** ***prev.*** Kiáton. Pelopónnisos, S Greece *38°01′N 22°45′E*
Kiáton *see* Kiáto
Kiayi *see* Chiai
155 *C12* **Kibæk** Ringkøbing, W Denmark *56°03′N 08°52′E*
121 *K5* **Kibali** ***var.*** Uele (upper course). ≈ NE Dem. Rep. Congo
135 *B9* **Kibangou** Niari, SW Congo *03°27′S 12°21′E*
Kibarty *see* Kybartai
152 *I3* **Kiberg** Finnmark, N Norway *70°17′N 30°47′E*
135 *H9* **Kibombo** Maniema, E Dem. Rep. Congo *03°52′S 25°59′E*
137 *A9* **Kibondo** Kigoma, NW Tanzania *03°34′S 30°41′E*
136 *E5* **Kibre Mengist** ***var.*** Adola. Oromīya, C Ethiopia *05°50′N 39°06′E*
Kıbrıs *see* Cyprus
Kıbrıs/Kıbrıs Cumhuriyeti *see* Cyprus
137 *A9* **Kibungo** ***var.*** Kibungu. SE Rwanda *02°09′S 30°30′E*
Kibungu *see* Kibungo
184 *G8* **Kičevo** SW FYR Macedonia *41°31′N 20°57′E*
195 *H8* **Kichmengskiy Gorodok** Vologodskaya Oblast', NW Russian Federation *60°00′N 45°52′E*
72 *B7* **Kickapoo River** ≈ Wisconsin, N USA
57 *H7* **Kicking Horse Pass** *pass* Alberta/British Columbia, SW Canada
133 *H3* **Kidal** Kidal, C Mali *18°22′N 01°21′E*
133 *H2* **Kidal** ◐ *region* NE Mali
263 *M9* **Kidapawan** Mindanao, S Philippines *07°02′N 125°04′E*
161 *H4* **Kidderminster** C England, United Kingdom *52°23′N 02°14′W*
141 *I9* **Kidd's Beach** Eastern Cape, South Africa *33°09′S 27°41′E*
132 *C4* **Kidira** E Senegal *14°28′N 12°13′W*
161 *I5* **Kidlington** United Kingdom *51°49′N 1°17′W*
278 *I6* **Kidnappers, Cape** *headland* North Island, New Zealand *41°13′S 175°15′E*
159 *J10* **Kidsgrove** United Kingdom *53°05′N 2°14′W*
160 *E6* **Kidwelly** United Kingdom *51°44′N 4°18′W*
180 *H1* **Kiel** Schleswig-Holstein, N Germany *54°21′N 10°05′E*
182 *H7* **Kielce** ***Rus.*** Keltsy. Świętokrzyskie, C Poland *50°53′N 20°39′E*
159 *J5* **Kielder Water** ◎ N England, United Kingdom
155 *D13* **Kieler Bucht** *bay* N Germany
178 *E4* **Kieler Förde** *inlet* N Germany
257 *I9* **Kiên Đưc** ***var.*** Đak Lap. Đăc Lăc, S Vietnam *11°59′N 107°30′E*
135 *I11* **Kienge** Katanga, SE Dem. Rep. Congo *10°33′S 27°33′E*
180 *F5* **Kierchdorf** Niedersachsen, Germany *8°50′N 52°36′E*
181 *D9* **Kierspe** Nordrhein-Westfalen, Germany *7°35′N 51°08′E*
182 *C5* **Kietz** Brandenburg, NE Germany *52°33′N 14°36′E*
Kiev *see* Kyyiv
Kiev Reservoir *see* Kyyivs'ke Vodoskhovyshche
132 *D3* **Kiffa** Assaba, S Mauritania *16°38′N 11°23′W*
187 *H6* **Kifisiá** Attikí, C Greece *38°04′N 23°49′E*
186 *G5* **Kifisós** ≈ C Greece
217 *J4* **Kifrī** At Ta'mīn, N Iraq *34°44′N 44°58′E*
137 *A8* **Kigali** ● (Rwanda) C Rwanda *01°59′S 30°02′E*
137 *A8* **Kigali** ✈ C Rwanda *01°43′S 30°01′E*
215 *I6* **Kiğı** Bingöl, E Turkey *39°19′N 40°20′E*
59 *J3* **Kiglapait, Cape** *headland* Newfoundland and Labrador, NE Canada *57°14′N 61°24′W*
137 *A10* **Kigoma** Kigoma, W Tanzania *04°52′S 29°36′E*
137 *A9* **Kigoma** ◐ *region* W Tanzania
82 *C2* **Kīhei** ***var.*** Kihei. Maui, Hawaii, USA, C Pacific Ocean *20°47′N 156°28′W*
153 *G9* **Kihniö** Länsi-Suomi, W Finland *62°11′N 23°10′E*
190 *D5* **Kihnu** ***var.*** Kihnu Saar, ***Ger.*** Kühnö. *island* SW Estonia
Kihnu Saar *see* Kihnu
152 *H7* **Kiiminki** Oulu, C Finland *65°05′N 25°47′E*
251 *I5* **Kii-Nagashima** ***var.*** Nagashima. Mie, Honshū, SW Japan *34°10′N 136°18′E*
251 *I5* **Kii-sanchi** ▲▲ Honshū, SW Japan
152 *H5* **Kiistala** Lappi, N Finland *67°52′N 25°19′E*
251 *H6* **Kii-suidō** *strait* S Japan
250 *B4* **Kijang** *35°14′N 129°12′E*
251 *K9* **Kikai-shima** *island* Nansei-shotō, SW Japan
190 *H3* **Kikerino** Leningradskaya Oblast', Russian Federation
184 *G2* **Kikinda** ***Ger.*** Grosskikinda, ***Hung.*** Nagykikinda; ***prev.*** Velika Kikinda. Vojvodina, N Serbia *45°48′N 20°29′E*
Kikládhes *see* Kykládes
252 *D6* **Kikonai** Hokkaidō, NE Japan *41°40′N 140°25′E*
280 *B4* **Kikori** Gulf, S Papua New Guinea *07°25′S 144°13′E*
280 *B3* **Kikori** ≈ W Papua New Guinea
250 *D7* **Kikuchi** ***var.*** Kikuti. Kumamoto, Kyūshū, SW Japan *33°00′N 130°49′E*
Kikuti *see* Kikuchi
197 *H5* **Kikvidze** Volgogradskaya Oblast', SW Russian Federation *50°47′N 42°58′E*
62 *D1* **Kikwissi, Lac** ◎ Québec, SE Canada
135 *E9* **Kikwit** Bandundu, W Dem. Rep. Congo *05°S 18°53′E*
155 *F8* **Kil** Värmland, C Sweden *59°30′N 13°20′E*
154 *H6* **Kilafors** Gävleborg, C Sweden *61°13′N 16°34′E*
82 *B1* **Kīlauea** Kaua'i, Hawaii, USA, C Pacific Ocean *22°12′N 159°24′W*
82 *E3* **Kīlauea Caldera** ***var.*** Kilauea Caldera. *crater* Hawai'i, USA, C Pacific Ocean
Kilauea Caldera *see* Kīlauea Caldera
177 *K2* **Kilb** Niederösterreich, C Austria *48°06′N 15°21′E*
158 *G3* **Kilbarchan** United Kingdom *55°50′N 4°33′W*
158 *C10* **Kilbeggan** Westmeath, Ireland *53°22′N 7°30′W*
158 *E3* **Kilberry** W Scotland, United Kingdom
158 *G4* **Kilbirnie** United Kingdom *55°45′N 4°42′W*
158 *F4* **Kilbrannan Sound** *sound* W Scotland, United Kingdom
82 *G7* **Kilbuck Mountains** ▲▲ Alaska, USA
158 *F4* **Kilchattan** W Scotland, United Kingdom
158 *E4* **Kilchenzie** United Kingdom *55°28′N 5°40′W*
158 *E1* **Kilchoan** United Kingdom *56°42′N 6°06′W*
158 *D3* **Kilchoman** United Kingdom *55°47′N 6°26′W*
248 *D3* **Kilchu** NE North Korea *40°58′N 129°22′E*
158 *D10* **Kilcock** ***Ir.*** Cill Choca. Kildare, E Ireland *53°25′N 06°40′W*
158 *C8* **Kilcogy** Ireland *53°50′N 7°25′W*
158 *A10* **Kilcolgan** Galway, Ireland *53°12′N 8°52′W*
158 *A10* **Kilconnell** Galway, Ireland *53°20′N 8°24′W*
158 *B10* **Kilcormac** Offaly, Ireland *53°10′N 7°44′W*
277 *M2* **Kilcoy** Queensland, E Australia *26°58′S 152°30′E*
160 *A2* **Kilcullen** Kildare, Ireland *53°08′N 6°45′W*
158 *F4* **Kildalloig** United Kingdom *55°24′N 5°33′W*
158 *C10* **Kildare** ***Ir.*** Cill Dara. E Ireland *53°10′N 06°55′W*
158 *D10* **Kildare** ***Ir.*** Cill Dara. *cultural region* E Ireland
194 *F2* **Kil'din, Ostrov** *island* NW Russian Federation
158 *F4* **Kildonan** United Kingdom *55°26′N 5°06′W*
52 *C8* **Kilekale Lake** ◎ Northwets Territories, NW Canada
158 *F3* **Kilfinan** United Kingdom *55°58′N 5°20′W*
71 *I5* **Kilgore** Texas, SW USA *32°23′N 94°52′W*
Kilien Mountains *see* Qilian Shan
185 *K6* **Kilifarevo** Veliko Tŭrnovo, N Bulgaria *43°00′N 25°36′E*
137 *E9* **Kilifi** Coast, SE Kenya *03°37′S 39°50′E*
283 *L7* **Kili Island** ***var.*** Kōle. *island* Ralik Chain, S Marshall Islands
231 *J2* **Kilik Pass** *pass* Afghanistan/China
Kilimane *see* Quelimane
137 *E9* **Kilimanjaro** ◐ *region* E Tanzania
137 *D9* **Kilimanjaro** ***var.*** Uhuru Peak. Ѧ NE Tanzania *03°01′S 37°14′E*
Kilimbangara *see* Kolombangara
Kilinailau Islands *see* Tulun Islands
137 *E11* **Kilindoni** Pwani, E Tanzania *07°56′S 39°40′E*
194 *B9* **Kilingi-Nõmme** Estonia
190 *E5* **Kilingi-Nõmme** ***Ger.*** Kurkund. Pärnumaa, SW Estonia *58°07′N 24°00′E*
214 *G8* **Kilis** Kilis, S Turkey *36°43′N 37°07′E*
214 *G8* **Kilis** ◐ *province* S Turkey
187 *K3* **Kilitbahir** Çanakkale, Turkey *40°09′N 26°23′E*
188 *G8* **Kiliya** ***Rom.*** Chilia-Nouă. Odes'ka Oblast', SW Ukraine *45°30′N 29°16′E*
157 *B10* **Kilkee** ***Ir.*** Cill Chaoi. Clare, W Ireland *52°41′N 09°38′W*
158 *E8* **Kilkeel** United Kingdom *54°04′N 6°01′W*
158 *A8* **Kilkelly** Mayo, Ireland *53°52′N 8°51′W*
160 *A3* **Kilkenny** ***Ir.*** Cill Chainnigh. Kilkenny, S Ireland *52°39′N 07°15′W*
160 *A3* **Kilkenny** ***Ir.*** Cill Chainnigh. *cultural region* S Ireland
160 *E8* **Kilkhampton** United Kingdom *50°53′N 4°29′W*
157 *A9* **Kilkieran Bay** ***Ir.*** Cuan Chill Chiaráin. *bay* W Ireland
186 *G2* **Kilkís** Kentrikí Makedonía, N Greece *40°59′N 22°55′E*
157 *B8* **Killala Bay** ***Ir.*** Cuan Chill Ala. *inlet* NW Ireland
57 *J5* **Killam** Alberta, SW Canada *52°45′N 111°46′W*
277 *M2* **Killarney** Queensland, E Australia *28°18′S 152°15′E*
55 *I10* **Killarney** Manitoba, S Canada *49°12′N 99°40′W*
62 *B2* **Killarney** Ontario, S Canada *45°58′N 81°27′W*
157 *B11* **Killarney** ***Ir.*** Cill Airne. Kerry, SW Ireland *52°03′N 09°30′W*
74 *B3* **Killdeer** North Dakota, N USA *47°21′N 102°45′W*
74 *B2* **Killdeer Mountains** ▲▲ North Dakota, N USA
91 *L8* **Killdeer River** ≈ Trinidad, Trinidad and Tobago
158 *C5* **Killea** Donegal, Ireland *54°59′N 7°25′W*
158 *E4* **Killean** United Kingdom *55°38′N 5°39′W*
158 *G3* **Killearn** United Kingdom *56°02′N 4°22′W*
70 *G6* **Killeen** Texas, SW USA *31°07′N 97°44′W*
83 *H3* **Killik River** ≈ Alaska, USA
158 *B10* **Killimor** Galway, Ireland *53°10′N 8°17′W*
158 *G2* **Killin** United Kingdom *56°28′N 4°19′W*
59 *I2* **Killinek Island** *island* Nunavut, NE Canada
158 *E10* **Killiney Bay** *bay* Dublin, Ireland
Killini *see* Kyllíni
186 *F6* **Killínis, Akrotírio** *headland* S Greece *37°55′N 21°07′E*
158 *A6* **Killybegs** ***Ir.*** Na Ceala Beaga. NW Ireland *54°38′N 08°27′W*
160 *B2* **Kilmacanoge** Wicklow, Ireland *53°10′N 6°08′W*
158 *G3* **Kilmacolm** United Kingdom *55°53′N 4°37′W*
158 *B5* **Kilmacrenan** Donegal, Ireland *55°02′N 7°47′W*
160 *A4* **Kilmaganny** Kilkenny, Ireland *52°28′N 7°20′W*
Kilmain *see* Quelimane

◆ Country
● Country Capital
◇ Dependent Territory
○ Dependent Territory Capital
◐ Administrative Regions
✈ International Airport
▲ Mountain
▲▲ Mountain Range
Ѧ Volcano
≈ River
◎ Lake
⊡ Reservoir

◆ Country ◇ Dependent Territory ◈ Administrative Regions ▲ Mountain ℞ Volcano ◎ Lake
● Country Capital ○ Dependent Territory Capital ✈ International Airport ▲ Mountain Range ≈ River ◈ Reservoir

København - Kosi Bay

INDEX

361

Košice - Kuei Chou
INDEX
362

183 H10 **Košice** *Ger.* Kaschau, *Hung.* Kassa. Košický Kraj, E Slovakia 48°44′N 21°15′E
183 H10 **Košický Kraj** ◐ *region* E Slovakia
Kosigaya *see* Koshigaya
Kosikizima Rettô *see* Koshikijima-rettō
233 I6 **Kosi Reservoir** ⊠ E Nepal
188 D5 **Kosiv** Ivano-Frankivs'ka Oblast', W Ukraine 48°19′N 25°04′E
227 H4 **Koskol'** *Kaz.* Qosköl. Karaganda, C Kazakhstan 49°32′N 67°08′E
190 G3 **Koskolovo** Leningradskaya Oblast', Russian Federation
190 J2 **Kos'kovo** Leningradskaya Oblast', Russian Federation
195 I6 **Koslan** Respublika Komi, NW Russian Federation 63°27′N 48°52′E
Köslin *see* Koszalin
228 G7 **Koson** *Rus.* Kasan. Qashqadaryo Viloyati, S Uzbekistan 39°04′N 65°35′E
248 C4 **Kosŏng** SE North Korea 38°41′N 128°14′E
229 J5 **Kosonsoy** *Rus.* Kasansay. Namangan Viloyati, E Uzbekistan 41°15′N 71°28′E
184 G6 **Kosovo** *prev.* Autonomous Province of Kosovo and Metohija. ◆ *republic* SE Europe
Kosovo *see* Kosava
Kosovo and Metohija, Autonomous Province of *see* Kosovo
184 G6 **Kosovo Polje** *Serb.* Kosovo Polje. C Kosovo 42°40′N 21°07′E
Kosovo Polje *see* Kosovo Polje
184 G6 **Kosovska Kamenica** *Serb.* Kamenica; *prev.* Kosovska Kamenica. E Kosovo 42°37′N 21°33′E
Kosovska Kamenica *see* Kosovska Kamenica
184 G6 **Kosovska Mitrovica** *Serb.* Mitrovica, Kosovska Mitrovica, Titova Mitrovica. N Kosovo 42°54′N 20°52′E
Kosovska Mitrovica *see* Kosovska Mitrovica
283 H10 **Kosrae** ◐ *state* E Micronesia
283 J7 **Kosrae** *prev.* Kusaie. *island* Caroline Islands, E Micronesia
177 H3 **Kössen** Tirol, W Austria 47°40′N 12°24′E
132 F7 **Kossou, Lac de** ⊚ C Ivory Coast
Kossukavak *see* Krumovgrad
Kostajnica *see* Hrvatska Kostanjnica
Kostamus *see* Kostomuksha
226 G2 **Kostanay** *var.* Kustanay, *Kaz.* Qostanay. Kostanay, N Kazakhstan 53°16′N 63°34′E
226 G3 **Kostanay** *var.* Kostanayskaya Oblast', *Kaz.* Qostanay Oblysy. ◐ *province* N Kazakhstan
Kostanayskaya Oblast' *see* Kostanay
Kosten *see* Kościan
185 J7 **Kostenets** *prev.* Georgi Dimitrov. Sofiya, W Bulgaria 42°15′N 23°48′E
136 B2 **Kosti** White Nile, C Sudan 13°11′N 32°38′E
Kostnitz *see* Konstanz
194 D5 **Kostomuksha** *Fin.* Kostamus. Respublika Kareliya, NW Russian Federation 64°33′N 30°28′E
188 E2 **Kostopil'** *Rus.* Kostopol'. Rivnens'ka Oblast', NW Ukraine 50°20′N 26°29′E
Kostopol' *see* Kostopil'
194 G9 **Kostroma** Kostromskaya Oblast', NW Russian Federation 57°46′N 41°E
194 G9 **Kostroma** NW Russian Federation
195 H9 **Kostromskaya Oblast'** ◐ *province* NW Russian Federation
182 C5 **Kostrzyn** *Ger.* Cüstrin, Küstrin. Lubuskie, W Poland 52°35′N 14°40′E
182 E6 **Kostrzyn** Wielkopolskie, C Poland 52°23′N 17°13′E
189 M5 **Kostyantynivka** *Rus.* Konstantinovka. Donets'ka Oblast', SE Ukraine
Kostyukovichi *see* Kastsyukovichy
Kostyukovka *see* Kastsyukowka
Kôsyoku *see* Kōshoku
195 K4 **Kos'yu** Respublika Komi, NW Russian Federation 65°39′N 59°01′E
195 K4 **Kos'yu** NW Russian Federation
182 D4 **Koszalin** *Ger.* Köslin. Zachodnio-pomorskie, NW Poland 54°12′N 16°10′E
183 D11 **Kőszeg** *Ger.* Güns. Vas, W Hungary 47°23′N 16°33′E
232 E7 **Kota** *prev.* Kotah. Rājasthān, N India 25°14′N 75°52′E
Kota Baharu *see* Kota Bharu
Kota Bahru *see* Kota Bharu
259 K6 **Kotabaru** Pulau Laut, C Indonesia 03°15′S 116°15′E
258 E5 **Kota Baru** Sumatera, W Indonesia 01°07′S 101°43′E
Kotabaru *see* Jayapura
258 E2 **Kota Bharu** *var.* Kota Baharu, Kota Bahru. Kelantan, Peninsular Malaysia 06°07′N 102°15′E
Kotaboemi *see* Kotabumi
258 F7 **Kotabumi** *prev.* Kotaboemi. Sumatera, W Indonesia 04°50′S 104°54′E
231 H6 **Kot Addu** Punjab, E Pakistan 30°28′N 70°58′E
Kotah *see* Kota
259 K2 **Kota Kinabalu** *prev.* Jesselton. Sabah, East Malaysia 05°59′N 116°04′E
259 K2 **Kota Kinabalu** ✈ Sabah, East Malaysia 05°59′N 116°04′E
152 I5 **Kotala** Lappi, N Finland 67°01′N 29°00′E
Kotamobagoe *see* Kotamobagu
260 E3 **Kotamobagu** *prev.* Kotamobagoe. Sulawesi, C Indonesia 0°46′N 124°21′E
234 H5 **Kotapad** *var.* Kotapārh. Orissa, E India 19°10′N 82°23′E
Kotapārh *see* Kotapad
257 E11 **Ko Ta Ru Tao** *island* SW Thailand
258 I6 **Kotawaringin, Teluk** *bay* Borneo, C Indonesia
230 G8 **Kot Dīji** Sind, SE Pakistan 27°16′N 68°44′E
232 F5 **Kotdwāra** Uttarakhand, N India 29°44′N 78°33′E
195 I9 **Kotel'nich** Kirovskaya Oblast', NW Russian Federation 58°19′N 48°12′E
197 H6 **Kotel'nikovo** Volgogradskaya Oblast', SW Russian Federation 47°37′N 43°07′E
193 J3 **Kotel'nyy, Ostrov** *island* Novosibirskiye Ostrova, N Russian Federation
189 K3 **Kotel'va** Poltavs'ka Oblast', C Ukraine 50°04′N 34°46′E
181 H11 **Köthen** *var.* Cöthen. Sachsen-Anhalt, C Germany 51°46′N 11°59′E
Kôti *see* Kōchi
136 C6 **Kotido** NE Uganda 03°03′N 34°07′E
153 I10 **Kotka** Etelä-Suomi, S Finland 60°28′N 26°55′E
195 H7 **Kotlas** Arkhangel'skaya Oblast', NW Russian Federation 61°14′N 46°43′E
82 G5 **Kotlik** Alaska, USA 63°01′N 163°33′W
190 G3 **Kotly** Leningradskaya Oblast', Russian Federation
133 H8 **Kotoka** ✈ (Accra) S Ghana 05°41′N 00°10′W
Kotonu *see* Cotonou
184 E6 **Kotor** *It.* Cattaro. SW Montenegro 42°25′N 18°47′E
Kotor *see* Kotoriba
184 C1 **Kotoriba** *Hung.* Kotor. Medimurje, N Croatia 46°20′N 16°47′E
184 D7 **Kotorska, Boka** *It.* Bocche di Cattaro. *bay* SW Montenegro
184 D3 **Kotorsko** ◐ Republika Srpska, N Bosnia and Herzegovina
184 D4 **Kotor Varoš** ◐ Republika Srpska, N Bosnia and Herzegovina
Koto Sho/Kotosho *see* Lan Yü
197 H4 **Kotovsk** Tambovskaya Oblast', W Russian Federation 52°39′N 41°31′E
188 G6 **Kotovs'k** *Rus.* Kotovsk. Odes'ka Oblast', SW Ukraine 47°42′N 29°30′E
Kotovsk *see* Hînceşti
191 D10 **Kotra** W Belarus
230 G9 **Kotri** Sind, SE Pakistan 25°22′N 68°18′E
177 I5 **Kötschach** Kärnten, S Austria 46°41′N 12°57′E
234 G5 **Kottagūdem** Andhra Pradesh, E India 17°36′N 80°40′E
235 D8 **Kottappadi** Kerala, SW India 11°38′N 76°03′E
235 E9 **Kottayam** Kerala, SW India 09°34′N 76°31′E
Kottbus *see* Cottbus
134 F5 **Kotto** Central African Republic/Dem. Rep. Congo
284 D7 **Kotu Group** *island group* W Tonga
Koturdepe *see* Goturdepe
193 H5 **Kotuy** N Russian Federation
139 I2 **Kotwa** Mashonaland East, NE Zimbabwe 16°58′S 32°46′E
82 G4 **Kotzebue** Alaska, USA 66°54′N 162°36′W
82 G4 **Kotzebue Sound** *inlet* Alaska, USA
Kotzenan *see* Chocianów
140 C7 **Kotzesrus** Northern Cape, South Africa 30°58′S 17°50′E
Kotzman *see* Kitsman'
218 G1 **Kouaïkhât** Lebanon 34°34′N 36°05′E
133 I6 **Kouandé** NW Benin 10°20′N 01°42′E
134 F5 **Kouango** Ouaka, S Central African Republic 05°00′N 20°01′E
218 F2 **Koubba** Lebanon
132 G5 **Koudougou** C Burkina 12°15′N 02°23′W
162 G4 **Koudum** Friesland, N Netherlands 52°55′N 05°26′E
187 K10 **Koufonísi** *island* SE Greece
187 J7 **Koufonísi** *island* Kykládes, Greece, Aegean Sea
140 G9 **Kouga Dam** *dam* Eastern Cape, South Africa
82 F4 **Kougarok Mountain** ▲ Alaska, USA 65°41′N 165°29′W
135 B9 **Kouilou** S Congo
140 F9 **Kouka River** Eastern Cape, South Africa
53 K8 **Koukdjuak** Baffin Island, Nunavut, NE Canada
53 K8 **Koukdjuak River** Nunavut, NE Canada
218 B2 **Koúklia** SW Cyprus 34°42′N 32°35′E
135 B8 **Koulamoutou** Ogooué-Lolo, C Gabon 01°07′S 12°27′E
132 E5 **Koulikoro** Koulikoro, SW Mali 12°55′N 07°31′W
132 E4 **Koulikoro** ◐ *region* SW Mali
280 A8 **Koumac** Province Nord, W New Caledonia 20°34′S 164°18′E
251 K3 **Koumi** Nagano, Honshū, S Japan 36°06′N 138°27′E
134 D4 **Koumra** Moyen-Chari, S Chad 08°56′N 17°32′E
Kounadougou *see* Koundougou
132 F7 **Kounahiri** C Ivory Coast 07°47′N 05°51′W
132 C5 **Koundâra** Moyenne-Guinée, NW Guinea 12°28′N 13°15′W
132 F5 **Koundougou** *var.* Kounadougou. C Burkina 11°43′N 04°40′W
132 B4 **Koungheul** C Senegal 14°00′N 14°48′W
Kounradskiy *see* Konyrat
71 J6 **Kountze** Texas, SW USA 30°22′N 94°20′W
133 H5 **Koupéla** C Burkina 12°07′N 00°21′W
132 F5 **Kouri** Sikasso, SW Mali 12°09′N 04°46′W
103 M5 **Kourou** N French Guiana 05°08′N 52°37′W
187 I2 **Kouroú** NE Greece
132 D6 **Kouroussa** C Guinea 10°40′N 09°50′W
Kousseir *see* Al Quşayr
134 C2 **Kousséri** *prev.* Fort-Foureau. Extrême-Nord, NE Cameroon 12°05′N 14°56′E
Kouteifé *see* Al Quţayfah
132 F5 **Koutiala** Sikasso, S Mali 12°20′N 05°23′W
132 E6 **Kouto** NW Ivory Coast 09°51′N 06°25′W
153 I9 **Kouvola** Etelä-Suomi, S Finland 60°50′N 26°48′E
134 C7 **Kouyou** C Congo
245 K6 **Kouzhen** Shandong, E China 36°19′N 117°35′E
184 G3 **Kovačica** *Hung.* Antafalva; *prev.* Kovacsicza. Vojvodina, N Serbia 45°08′N 20°36′E
Kovacsicza *see* Kovačica
Kővárhosszúfalu *see* Satulung
Kovászna *see* Covasna
194 E3 **Kovdor** Murmanskaya Oblast', NW Russian Federation 67°32′N 30°27′E
194 E4 **Kovdozero, Ozero** ⊚ NW Russian Federation
188 D2 **Kovel'** *Pol.* Kowel. Volyns'ka Oblast', NW Ukraine 51°14′N 24°43′E
58 F1 **Kovic Bay** *coastal sea feature* Québec, NE Canada
58 G1 **Kovic River** Québec, E Canada
184 G3 **Kovin** *Hung.* Kevevára; *prev.* Temes-Kubin. Vojvodina, NE Serbia 44°45′N 20°59′E
Kovno *see* Kaunas
197 H1 **Kovrov** Vladimirskaya Oblast', W Russian Federation 56°24′N 41°21′E
197 H3 **Kovylkino** Respublika Mordoviya, W Russian Federation 54°03′N 43°52′E
182 F5 **Kowal** Kujawsko-pomorskie, C Poland 52°31′N 19°09′E
182 F5 **Kowalewo Pomorskie** *Ger.* Schönsee. Kujawsko-pomorskie, N Poland 53°07′N 18°48′E
Kowasna *see* Covasna
191 H10 **Kowbcha** *Rus.* Kolbcha. Mahilyowskaya Voblasts', E Belarus 53°39′N 29°14′E
Koweit *see* Kuwait
Kowel *see* Kovel'
279 D9 **Kowhitirangi** West Coast, South Island, New Zealand 42°54′S 171°01′E
243 H10 **Kowloon** Hong Kong, S China
Kowno *see* Kaunas
141 K3 **Kowyns Pass** *pass* Mpumalanga, South Africa
239 H5 **Kox Kuduk** *well* NW China
214 B7 **Köyceğiz** Muğla, SW Turkey 36°57′N 28°40′E
194 G4 **Koyda** Arkhangel'skaya Oblast', NW Russian Federation 66°22′N 42°42′E
Koymat *see* Goymat
Koymatdag, Gory *see* Goymatdag, Gory
234 D5 **Koyna Reservoir** ⊠ W India
253 C9 **Koyoshi-gawa** Honshū, C Japan
Koysanjaq *see* Koi Sanjaq
Koytash *see* Qo'ytosh
229 H8 **Köýtendag** *prev. Rus.* Charshanga, Charshangy, *Turkm.* Charshangngy. Lebap Welaýaty, E Turkmenistan 37°31′N 65°58′E
82 G5 **Koyuk** Alaska, USA 64°55′N 161°09′W
82 G4 **Koyuk River** Alaska, USA
83 H5 **Koyukuk** Alaska, USA 64°52′N 157°42′W
83 H4 **Koyukuk River** Alaska, USA
187 K4 **Kozak** İzmir, Turkey 39°15′N 27°06′E
214 F6 **Kozaklı** Nevşehir, C Turkey 39°12′N 34°48′E
250 F5 **Kōzan** Hiroshima, Honshū, SW Japan 34°35′N 133°02′E
214 F7 **Kozan** Adana, S Turkey 37°27′N 35°47′E
186 F3 **Kozáni** Dytikí Makedonía, N Greece 40°19′N 21°48′E
184 C3 **Kozara** ▲▲ NW Bosnia and Herzegovina
Kozarska Dubica *see* Bosanska Dubica
189 H2 **Kozelets'** *Rus.* Kozelets. Chernihivs'ka Oblast', NE Ukraine 50°54′N 31°09′E
Kozelets *see* Kozelets'
189 J4 **Kozel'shchyna** Poltavs'ka Oblast', C Ukraine 49°13′N 33°49′E
196 F3 **Kozel'sk** Kaluzhskaya Oblast', W Russian Federation 54°04′N 35°51′E
195 K4 **Kozhim** Respublika Komi, NW Russian Federation 65°43′N 59°25′E
195 K6 **Kozhimiz, Gora** ▲ NW Russian Federation 63°13′N 58°54′E
194 F6 **Kozhozero, Ozero** ⊚ NW Russian Federation
195 K5 **Kozhva** Respublika Komi, NW Russian Federation 65°06′N 57°00′E
195 K5 **Kozhva** NW Russian Federation
182 H6 **Kozienice** Mazowieckie, C Poland 51°35′N 21°31′E
177 J6 **Kozina** SW Slovenia 45°36′N 13°56′E
185 I5 **Kozloduy** Vratsa, NW Bulgaria 43°48′N 23°42′E
197 J2 **Kozlovka** Chuvashskaya Respublika, W Russian Federation 55°53′N 48°07′E
Kozlovshchina/Kozlowszczyzna *see* Kazlowshchyna
197 I1 **Koz'modem'yansk** Respublika Mariy El, W Russian Federation 56°19′N 46°33′E
188 D4 **Kozova** Ternopil's'ka Oblast', W Ukraine 49°25′N 25°09′E
185 H8 **Kožuf** ▲ S Macedonia 41°10′N 22°14′E
251 M7 **Kōzu-shima** *island* E Japan
Koz'yany *see* Kaz'yany
188 G4 **Kozyatyn** *Rus.* Kazatin. Vinnyts'ka Oblast', C Ukraine 49°41′N 28°49′E
133 H7 **Kpalimé** *var.* Palimé. SW Togo 06°54′N 00°38′E
133 H7 **Kpandu** E Ghana 07°00′N 00°18′E
140 G6 **Kraankuil** Northern Cape, South Africa 29°53′S 24°11′E
163 D8 **Krabbendijke** Zeeland, SW Netherlands 51°25′N 04°07′E
257 D11 **Krabi** *var.* Muang Krabi. Krabi, SW Thailand 08°04′N 98°52′E
257 D9 **Kra Buri** Ranong, SW Thailand 10°25′N 98°48′E
257 H8 **Krâchéh** *prev.* Kratie. Krâchéh, E Cambodia 12°29′N 106°01′E
155 D8 **Kragerø** Telemark, S Norway 58°54′N 09°25′E
184 G4 **Kragujevac** Serbia, C Serbia 44°01′N 20°55′E
Krainburg *see* Kranj
257 D9 **Kra, Isthmus of** *isthmus* Malaysia/Thailand
184 B4 **Krajina** *cultural region* SW Croatia
Krakatau, Pulau *see* Rakata, Pulau
Krakau *see* Kraków
183 G8 **Kraków** *Eng.* Cracow, *Ger.* Krakau; *anc.* Cracovia. Małopolskie, S Poland 50°03′N 19°58′E
178 G5 **Krakower See** ⊚ NE Germany
257 G8 **Krâlănh** Siĕmréab, NW Cambodia 13°35′N 103°27′E
102 F2 **Kralendijk** Bonaire, E Netherlands Antilles 12°07′N 68°13′W
184 B3 **Kraljevica** *It.* Porto Re. Primorje-Gorski Kotar, NW Croatia 45°15′N 14°36′E
184 G5 **Kraljevo** *prev.* Rankovićevo. Serbia, C Serbia 43°44′N 20°40′E
183 D8 **Královehradecký Kraj** *prev.* Hradecký Kraj. ◐ *region* N Czech Republic
Kralup an der Moldau *see* Kralupy nad Vltavou
183 B8 **Kralupy nad Vltavou** *Ger.* Kralup an der Moldau. Středočeský Kraj, NW Czech Republic 50°15′N 14°20′E
189 M5 **Kramators'k** *Rus.* Kramatorsk. Donets'ka Oblast', SE Ukraine 48°43′N 37°34′E
Kramatorsk *see* Kramators'k
154 I4 **Kramfors** Västernorrland, C Sweden 62°55′N 17°50′E
171 J9 **Kramis, Cap** *headland* Algeria
Kranéa *see* Kraniá
179 F14 **Kranebitten** ✈ (Innsbruck) Tirol, W Austria 47°18′N 11°21′E
186 F4 **Kraniá** *var.* Kranéa. Dytikí Makedonía, N Greece 39°54′N 21°21′E
181 J9 **Kranichfeld** Thüringen, Germany 11°12′N 50°51′E
187 H7 **Kranídi** Pelopónnisos, S Greece 37°21′N 23°09′E
177 J5 **Kranj** *Ger.* Krainburg. NW Slovenia 46°17′N 14°16′E
186 G4 **Krannón** *battleground* Thessalía, C Greece
141 J5 **Kransfontein** Free State, South Africa 28°08′S 28°34′E
141 K6 **Kranskop** KwaZulu-Natal, South Africa 28°58′S 30°52′E
Kranz *see* Zelenogradsk
184 C1 **Krapina** Krapina-Zagorje, N Croatia 46°12′N 15°52′E
184 C2 **Krapina** N Croatia
184 C2 **Krapina-Zagorje** *off.* Krapinsko-Zagorska Županija. ◐ *province* N Croatia
185 L4 **Krapinets** NE Bulgaria
Krapinsko-Zagorska Županija *see* Krapina-Zagorje
183 E8 **Krapkowice** *Ger.* Krappitz. Opolskie, SW Poland 50°29′N 17°56′E
Krappitz *see* Krapkowice
195 H8 **Krasavino** Vologodskaya Oblast', NW Russian Federation 60°56′N 46°27′E
190 J5 **Kraseya** Novgorodskaya Oblast', Russian Federation
195 J1 **Krasino** Novaya Zemlya, Arkhangel'skaya Oblast', N Russian Federation 70°45′N 54°16′E
195 J1 **Krasino** Novaya Zemlya, Russian Federation 71°34′N 52°19′E
248 E2 **Kraskino** Primorskiy Kray, SE Russian Federation 42°40′N 130°51′E
190 F7 **Krāslava** Krāslava, SE Latvia 55°56′N 27°08′E
191 G9 **Krasnaluki** *Rus.* Krasnoluki. Vitsyebskaya Voblasts', N Belarus 54°37′N 28°50′E
191 I10 **Krasnapollye** *Rus.* Krasnopol'ye. Mahilyowskaya Voblasts', E Belarus 53°20′N 31°24′E
215 I2 **Krasnaya Polyana** Krasnodarskiy Kray, SW Russian Federation 43°40′N 40°13′E
Krasnaya Slabada / Krasnaya Sloboda *see* Chyrvonaya Slabada
191 F9 **Krasnaye** *Rus.* Krasnoye. Minskaya Voblasts', C Belarus 54°14′N 27°05′E
182 I7 **Kraśnik** *Ger.* Kratznick. Lubelskie, E Poland 50°56′N 22°14′E
191 B13 **Kraśnik Fabryczny** Lublin, SE Poland 50°57′N 22°07′E
188 G6 **Krasni Okny** Odes'ka Oblast', SW Ukraine 47°33′N 29°28′E
197 I5 **Krasnoarmeysk** Saratovskaya Oblast', W Russian Federation 51°02′N 45°42′E
Krasnoarmeysk *see* Tayynsha
Krasnoarmeysk *see* Krasnoarmiys'k/Tayynsha
193 M3 **Krasnoarmeyskiy** Chukotskiy Avtonomnyy Okrug, NE Russian Federation 69°30′N 171°44′E
189 L5 **Krasnoarmiys'k** *Rus.* Krasnoarmeysk. Donets'ka Oblast', SE Ukraine 48°17′N 37°14′E
195 H7 **Krasnoborsk** Arkhangel'skaya Oblast', NW Russian Federation 61°31′N 45°57′E
196 G8 **Krasnodar** *prev.* Ekaterinodar, Yekaterinodar. Krasnodarskiy Kray, SW Russian Federation 45°06′N 39°01′E
196 G7 **Krasnodarskiy Kray** ◐ *territory* SW Russian Federation
189 N5 **Krasnodon** Luhans'ka Oblast', E Ukraine 48°17′N 39°44′E
190 I3 **Krasnofarfornyi** Novgorodskaya Oblast', Russian Federation
Krasnogor *see* Kallaste
190 G5 **Krasnogorodskoye** Pskovskaya Oblast', Russian Federation
195 J9 **Krasnogorskoye** *Latv.* Sarkaņi. Udmurtskaya Respublika, NW Russian Federation 57°42′N 52°29′E
Krasnograd *see* Krasnohrad
Krasnogvardeysk *see* Bulungh'ur
196 G8 **Krasnogvardeyskoye** Stavropol'skiy Kray, SW Russian Federation 45°49′N 41°31′E
Krasnogvardeyskoye *see* Krasnohvardiys'ke
189 K4 **Krasnohrad** *Rus.* Krasnograd. Kharkivs'ka Oblast', E Ukraine 49°22′N 35°28′E
189 K8 **Krasnohvardiys'ke** *Rus.* Krasnogvardeyskoye. Respublika Krym, S Ukraine 45°30′N 34°19′E
193 J8 **Krasnokamensk** Chitinskaya Oblast', S Russian Federation 50°03′N 118°01′E
195 K9 **Krasnokamsk** Permskaya Oblast', W Russian Federation 58°08′N 55°48′E
197 L4 **Krasnokholm** Orenburgskaya Oblast', W Russian Federation 51°34′N 54°11′E
189 K3 **Krasnokuts'k** *Rus.* Krasnokutsk. Kharkivs'ka Oblast', E Ukraine 50°01′N 35°03′E
Krasnokutsk *see* Krasnokuts'k
195 N6 **Krasnoleninskiy** Khanty-Mansiyskiy Avtonomnyy Okrug-Yugra, Russian Federation
196 G4 **Krasnolesnyy** Voronezhskaya Oblast', W Russian Federation 51°53′N 39°37′E
Krasnoluki *see* Krasnaluki
Krasnoosol'skoye Vodokhranilishche *see* Chervonooskil's'ke Vodoskhovyshche
189 J8 **Krasnoperekops'k** *Rus.* Krasnoperekopsk. Respublika Krym, S Ukraine 45°56′N 33°47′E
Krasnoperekopsk *see* Krasnoperekops'k
189 K3 **Krasnopillya** Sums'ka Oblast', NE Ukraine 50°46′N 35°17′E
Krasnopol'ye *see* Krasnapollye
192 G5 **Krasnosel'kup** Yamalo-Nenetskiy Avtonomnyy Okrug, N Russian Federation 65°46′N 82°11′E
190 G2 **Krasnosel'skpye** Leningradskaya Oblast', Russian Federation
194 F3 **Krasnoshchel'ye** Murmanskaya Oblast', NW Russian Federation 67°22′N 37°03′E
197 H3 **Krasnoslobodsk** Respublika Mordoviya, W Russian Federation 54°24′N 43°51′E
197 I6 **Krasnoslobodsk** Volgogradskaya Oblast', SW Russian Federation 48°41′N 44°34′E
Krasnostav *see* Krasnystaw
195 L8 **Krasnotur'insk** Sverdlovskaya Oblast', C Russian Federation 59°45′N 60°19′E
195 L10 **Krasnoufimsk** Sverdlovskaya Oblast', Russian Federation
195 L10 **Krasnoufimsk** Sverdlovskaya Oblast', C Russian Federation 56°43′N 57°39′E
195 L9 **Krasnoural'sk** Sverdlovskaya Oblast', C Russian Federation 58°24′N 59°44′E
197 L2 **Krasnousol'skiy** Respublika Bashkortostan, W Russian Federation 53°55′N 56°22′E
195 K8 **Krasnovishersk** Permskaya Oblast', NW Russian Federation 60°22′N 57°04′E
Krasnovodsk *see* Türkmenbaşy
Krasnovodskiy Zaliv *see* Türkmenbasy Aylagy
228 B5 **Krasnovodskoye Plato** *Turkm.* Krasnowodsk Platosy. *plateau* NW Turkmenistan
Krasnowodsk Aylagy *see* Türkmenbasy Aylagy
Krasnowodsk Platosy *see* Krasnovodskoye Plato
192 G7 **Krasnoyarsk** Krasnoyarskiy Kray, S Russian Federation 56°05′N 92°46′E
197 M3 **Krasnoyarskiy** Orenburgskaya Oblast', W Russian Federation 51°56′N 59°54′E
192 G6 **Krasnoyarskiy Kray** ◐ *territory* C Russian Federation
192 G7 **Krasnoyarskoye Vodokhranilishche** ⊠ S Russian Federation
Krasnoye *see* Krasnaye
Krasnoye Znamya *see* Gyzylbaydak
195 J7 **Krasnozatonskiy** Respublika Komi, NW Russian Federation 61°39′N 51°00′E
191 C8 **Krasnoznamensk** *prev.* Lasdehnen, *Ger.* Haselberg. Kaliningradskaya Oblast', W Russian Federation 54°57′N 22°28′E
189 I8 **Krasnoznam"yans'kyy Kanal** *canal* S Ukraine
182 J7 **Krasnystaw** *Rus.* Krasnostav. Lubelskie, SE Poland 51°N 23°10′E
196 D2 **Krasnyy** Smolenskaya Oblast', W Russian Federation 54°36′N 31°27′E
197 I1 **Krasnyye Baki** Nizhegorodskaya Oblast', W Russian Federation 57°07′N 45°12′E
197 J7 **Krasnyye Barrikady** Astrakhanskaya Oblast', SW Russian Federation 46°14′N 47°48′E
194 F9 **Krasnyy Kholm** Tverskaya Oblast', W Russian Federation 58°04′N 37°05′E
197 I5 **Krasnyy Kut** Saratovskaya Oblast', W Russian Federation 50°54′N 46°58′E
Krasnyy Liman *see* Krasnyy Lyman
189 M5 **Krasnyy Luch** *prev.* Krindachevka. Luhans'ka Oblast', E Ukraine 48°09′N 38°52′E
189 M4 **Krasnyy Lyman** *Rus.* Krasnyy Liman. Donets'ka Oblast', SE Ukraine 49°00′N 37°50′E
195 N10 **Krasnyy Oktyabr'** Kurganskaya Oblast', Russian Federation
197 J1 **Krasnyy Steklovar** Respublika Mariy El, W Russian Federation 56°14′N 48°49′E
197 I4 **Krasnyy Tekstil'shchik** Saratovskaya Oblast', W Russian Federation 51°35′N 45°49′E
197 J7 **Krasnyy Yar** Astrakhanskaya Oblast', SW Russian Federation 46°33′N 48°21′E
Krassóvár *see* Caraşova
188 F4 **Krasyliv** Khmel'nyts'ka Oblast', W Ukraine 49°38′N 26°59′E
Kratie *see* Krâchéh
185 H7 **Kratovo** NE FYR Macedonia 42°04′N 22°08′E
Kratznick *see* Kraśnik
261 L5 **Krau** Papua, E Indonesia 03°15′S 140°07′E
181 H13 **Krautheim** Baden-Württemberg, Germany 9°38′N 49°23′E
257 G9 **Krâvanh, Chuŏr Phnum** *Eng.* Cardamom Mountains, *Fr.* Chaîne des Cardamomes. ▲▲ W Cambodia
Kravasta Lagoon *see* Karavastasë, Laguna e
Krawang *see* Karawang
197 J9 **Kraynovka** Respublika Dagestan, SW Russian Federation 43°58′N 47°24′E
191 C8 **Kražiai** Šiaulai, C Lithuania 55°36′N 22°41′E
75 F13 **Krebs** Oklahoma, C USA 34°55′N 95°43′W
181 B8 **Krefeld** Nordrhein-Westfalen, W Germany 51°20′N 06°34′E
Kreisstadt *see* Krosno Odrzańskie
186 F5 **Kremastón, Technití Límni** ⊠ C Greece
Kremenchug *see* Kremenchuk
Kremenchugskoye Vodokhranilishche/ Kremenchuk Reservoir *see* Kremenchuts'ke Vodoskhovyshche
189 J4 **Kremenchuk** *Rus.* Kremenchug. Poltavs'ka Oblast', NE Ukraine 49°04′N 33°27′E
189 I4 **Kremenchuts'ke Vodoskhovyshche** *Eng.* Kremenchuk Reservoir, *Rus.* Kremenchugskoye Vodokhranilishche. ⊠ C Ukraine
188 E3 **Kremenets'** *Pol.* Krzemieniec, *Rus.* Kremenets. Ternopil's'ka Oblast', W Ukraine 50°06′N 25°43′E
Kremennaya *see* Kreminna
189 M4 **Kreminna** *Rus.* Kremennaya. Luhans'ka Oblast', E Ukraine 49°03′N 38°15′E
79 L3 **Kremmling** Colorado, C USA 40°03′N 106°23′W
177 K2 **Krems** NE Austria
Krems *see* Krems an der Donau
177 K2 **Krems an der Donau** *var.* Krems. Niederösterreich, N Austria 48°25′N 15°36′E
Kremsier *see* Kroměříž
177 J2 **Kremsmünster** Oberösterreich, N Austria 48°04′N 14°08′E
82 F9 **Krenitzin Islands** *island* Aleutian Islands, Alaska, USA
Kresena *see* Kresna
185 I7 **Kresna** *var.* Kresena. Blagoevgrad, SW Bulgaria 41°43′N 23°10′E
184 G4 **Krespoljin** Serbia, E Serbia 44°22′N 21°36′E
70 E3 **Kress** Texas, SW USA 34°21′N 101°43′W
193 N3 **Kresta, Zaliv** *bay* E Russian Federation
186 F7 **Kréstena** *prev.* Selinoús. Dytikí Ellás, S Greece 37°36′N 21°36′E
194 D9 **Kresttsy** Novgorodskaya Oblast', W Russian Federation 58°15′N 32°28′E
193 I6 **Krestyakh** Respublika Sakha (Yakutiya), NE Russian Federation 62°10′N 116°24′E
Kretikon Delagos *see* Kritikó Pélagos
190 B7 **Kretinga** *Ger.* Krottingen. Klaipėda, NW Lithuania 55°53′N 21°13′E
Kreutz *see* Cristuru Secuiesc
Kreuz *see* Križevci, Croatia
Kreuz *see* Risti, Estonia
181 B10 **Kreuzau** Nordrhein-Westfalen, Germany 6°29′N 50°45′E
Kreuzburg/Kreuzburg in Oberschlesien *see* Kluczbork
Kreuzingen *see* Bol'shakovo
176 E3 **Kreuzlingen** Thurgau, NE Switzerland 47°38′N 09°12′E
179 F13 **Kreuzspitze** ▲ S Germany 47°30′N 10°55′E
181 E9 **Kreuztal** Nordrhein-Westfalen, W Germany 50°58′N 08°00′E
191 E9 **Kreva** *Rus.* Krevo. Hrodzyenskaya Voblasts', W Belarus 54°19′N 26°17′E
Krevo *see* Kreva
Kría Vrísi *see* Krýa Vrýsi
134 A6 **Kribi** Sud, SW Cameroon 02°53′N 09°57′E
Krichëv *see* Krychaw
Krickerhäu/Kriegerhaj *see* Handlová
177 K3 **Krieglach** Steiermark, E Austria 47°33′N 15°37′E
181 E12 **Kriegsfeld** Rheinland-Pfalz, Germany 7°55′N 49°43′E
141 J4 **Kriel** Mpumalanga, South Africa 26°16′S 29°14′E
176 D4 **Kriens** Luzern, W Switzerland 47°03′N 08°17′E
Krievija *see* Russian Federation
252 G1 **Kril'on, Mys** *headland* Ostrov Sakhalin, SE Russian Federation 46°06′N 143°25′E
Krimmitschau *see* Crimmitschau
162 E7 **Krimpen aan den IJssel** Zuid-Holland, SW Netherlands 51°56′N 04°39′E
Krindachevka *see* Krasnyy Luch
187 H10 **Kríos, Akrotírio** *headland* Kríti, Greece, E Mediterranean Sea 35°17′N 23°31′E
234 F6 **Krishna** *prev.* Kistna. C India
235 F8 **Krishnagiri** Tamil Nādu, SE India 12°33′N 78°11′E
234 G6 **Krishna, Mouths of the** *delta* SE India
235 E8 **Krishnarājāsāgara Reservoir** ⊠ W India
155 H10 **Kristdala** Kalmar, S Sweden 57°24′N 16°12′E
Kristiania *see* Oslo
155 C9 **Kristiansand** *var.* Christiansand. Vest-Agder, S Norway 58°08′N 07°52′E
155 G12 **Kristianstad** Skåne, S Sweden 56°02′N 14°10′E
154 C3 **Kristiansund** *var.* Christiansund. Møre og Romsdal, S Norway 63°07′N 07°45′E
Kristiinankaupunki *see* Kristinestad
154 I1 **Kristineberg** Västerbotten, N Sweden 65°07′N 18°36′E
155 G8 **Kristinehamn** Värmland, C Sweden 59°17′N 14°09′E
153 G9 **Kristinestad** *Fin.* Kristiinankaupunki. Länsi-Suomi, W Finland 62°15′N 21°24′E
Kristyor *see* Crişcior
187 I10 **Kríti** *Eng.* Crete. ◐ *region* Greece, Aegean Sea
187 I9 **Kríti** *Eng.* Crete. *island* Greece, Aegean Sea
187 I9 **Kritikó Pélagos** *var.* Kretikon Delagos, *Eng.* Sea of Crete; *anc.* Mare Creticum. *sea* Greece, Aegean Sea
Kriulyany *see* Criuleni
184 E4 **Krivaja** NE Bosnia and Herzegovina
Krivaja *see* Mali Iđoš
185 H7 **Kriva Palanka** *Turk.* Eğri Palanka. NE Macedonia 42°13′N 22°19′E
Krivichi *see* Kryvychy
185 I5 **Krivodol** Vratsa, NW Bulgaria 43°23′N 23°30′E
196 G6 **Krivorozh'ye** Rostovskaya Oblast', SW Russian Federation 48°51′N 40°49′E
Krivoshin *see* Kryvoshyn
Krivoy Rog *see* Kryvyy Rih
184 C2 **Križevci** *Ger.* Kreuz, *Hung.* Kőrös. Varaždin, NE Croatia 46°02′N 16°32′E
184 B3 **Krk** *It.* Veglia. Primorje-Gorski Kotar, NW Croatia 45°01′N 14°36′E
184 A3 **Krk** *It.* Veglia; *anc.* Curieta. *island* NW Croatia
183 C13 **Krka** SE Slovenia
Krka *see* Gurk
174 F4 **Krn** ▲ NW Slovenia 46°15′N 13°37′E
183 E8 **Krnov** *Ger.* Jägerndorf. Moravskoslezský Kraj, E Czech Republic 50°05′N 17°40′E
Kroatien *see* Croatia
154 D7 **Krøderen** Buskerud, S Norway 60°06′N 09°48′E
154 D7 **Krøderen** ⊚ S Norway
Kroi *see* Krui
155 H9 **Krokek** Östergötland, S Sweden 58°40′N 16°25′E
Krokodil *see* Crocodile
154 G3 **Krokom** Jämtland, C Sweden 63°20′N 14°30′E
189 J2 **Krolevets'** *Rus.* Krolevets. Sums'ka Oblast', NE Ukraine 51°34′N 33°24′E
Krolevets *see* Krolevets'
Królewska Huta *see* Chorzów
183 E9 **Kroměříž** *Ger.* Kremsier. Zlínský Kraj, E Czech Republic 49°18′N 17°24′E
162 E5 **Krommenie** Noord-Holland, C Netherlands 52°30′N 04°46′E
196 F3 **Kromy** Orlovskaya Oblast', W Russian Federation 52°41′N 35°45′E
179 F10 **Kronach** Bayern, E Germany 50°14′N 11°19′E
181 F11 **Kronberg** Hessen, Germany 8°30′N 50°11′E
Krone an der Brahe *see* Koronowo
257 G9 **Krŏng Kaôh Kŏng** Kaôh Kông, SW Cambodia 11°37′N 102°59′E
155 G11 **Kronoberg** ◐ *county* S Sweden
193 N6 **Kronotskiy Zaliv** *bay* E Russian Federation
293 H2 **Kronprinsesse Märtha Kyst** *physical region* Antarctica
293 K2 **Kronprins Olav Kyst** *physical region* Antarctica
180 H1 **Kronshagen** Schleswig-Holstein, Germany 10°05′N 54°20′E
194 D8 **Kronshtadt** Leningradskaya Oblast', NW Russian Federation 60°01′N 29°42′E
Kronstadt *see* Braşov
141 I5 **Kroonstad** Free State, C South Africa 27°40′S 27°15′E
193 I7 **Kropotkin** Irkutskaya Oblast', C Russian Federation 58°30′N 115°21′E
196 G8 **Kropotkin** Krasnodarskiy Kray, SW Russian Federation 45°29′N 40°31′E
182 F6 **Krośniewice** Łódzskie, C Poland 52°14′N 19°10′E
183 I9 **Krosno** *Ger.* Krossen. Podkarpackie, SE Poland 49°40′N 21°46′E
182 C6 **Krosno Odrzańskie** *Ger.* Crossen, Kreisstadt. Lubuskie, W Poland 52°02′N 15°06′E
Krossen *see* Krosno
Krotoschin *see* Krotoszyn
182 E6 **Krotoszyn** *Ger.* Krotoschin. Wielkopolskie, C Poland 51°43′N 17°24′E
Krottingen *see* Kretinga
Krousón *see* Krousónas
187 I10 **Krousónas** *prev.* Krousón, Kroussón. Kríti, Greece, E Mediterranean Sea 35°14′N 24°59′E
Kroussón *see* Krousónas
181 C12 **Krov** Rheinland-Pfalz, Germany 7°05′N 49°59′E
Krraba *see* Krrabë
184 F8 **Krrabë** *var.* Krraba. Tiranë, C Albania 41°15′N 19°56′E
184 F7 **Krrabit, Mali i** ▲▲ N Albania
177 L6 **Krško** *Ger.* Gurkfeld; *prev.* Videm-Krško. E Slovenia 45°57′N 15°31′E
181 D11 **Kruft** Rheinland-Pfalz, Germany 7°20′N 50°23′E
139 H5 **Kruger National Park** *national park* Northern, N South Africa
141 H7 **Krugers** Free State, South Africa 29°56′S 25°49′E
141 I4 **Krugersdorp** Gauteng, NE South Africa 26°06′S 27°46′E
141 H6 **Krugersdriftdam** ⊠ Free State, South Africa
82 B9 **Krugloi Point** *headland* Agattu Island, Alaska, USA 52°30′N 173°46′E
Krugloye *see* Kruhlaye
191 H9 **Kruhlaye** *Rus.* Krugloye. Mahilyowskaya Voblasts', E Belarus 54°15′N 29°48′E
258 F7 **Krui** *var.* Kroi. Sumatera, SW Indonesia 05°11′S 103°55′E
163 D9 **Kruibeke** Oost-Vlaanderen, N Belgium 51°10′N 04°18′E
138 E9 **Kruidfontein** Western Cape, SW South Africa 32°50′S 21°59′E
163 D8 **Kruiningen** Zeeland, SW Netherlands 51°28′N 04°01′E
140 G10 **Kruisfontein** Eastern Cape, South Africa 34°00′S 24°44′E
Kruja *see* Krujë
184 F8 **Krujë** *var.* Kruja, *It.* Croia. Durrës, C Albania 41°30′N 19°48′E
Krulevshchina/Krulewshchyna *see* Krulyewshchyna
191 G8 **Krulyewshchyna** *Rus.* Krulevshchina, Krulewshchyna. Vitsyebskaya Voblasts', N Belarus 55°02′N 27°45′E
71 H4 **Krum** Texas, SW USA 33°15′N 97°14′W
179 E13 **Krumbach** Bayern, S Germany 48°12′N 10°21′E
184 F7 **Krumë** Kukës, NE Albania 42°11′N 20°25′E
Krummau *see* Český Krumlov
180 I2 **Krummesse** Schleswig-Holstein, Germany 10°39′N 53°47′E
162 J2 **Krummhorn-Greetsiel** Niedersachsen, Germany 7°03′N 53°42′E
185 K8 **Krumovgrad** *prev.* Kossukavak. Yambol, E Bulgaria 41°27′N 25°40′E
185 K8 **Krumovitsa** S Bulgaria
185 L7 **Krumovo** Yambol, E Bulgaria 42°16′N 26°25′E
257 E8 **Krung Thep, Ao** *var.* Bight of Bangkok. *bay* S Thailand
Krung Thep Mahanakhon *see* Ao Krung Thep
Krupa/Krupa na Uni *see* Bosanska Krupa
191 H9 **Krupki** Minskaya Voblasts', C Belarus 54°19′N 29°08′E
155 D13 **Kruså** *var.* Krusaa. Sønderjylland, SW Denmark 54°50′N 09°25′E
Krusaa *see* Kruså
52 E8 **Krusenstern, Cape** *headland* Northwest Territories, NW Canada 68°17′N 114°00′W
53 H7 **Krusenstern Lake** ⊚ Nunavut, N Canada
184 G5 **Kruševac** Serbia, C Serbia 43°37′N 21°20′E
184 G8 **Kruševo** SW FYR Macedonia 41°22′N 21°15′E
183 A8 **Krušné Hory** *Eng.* Ore Mountains, *Ger.* Erzgebirge. ▲ Czech Republic/Germany *see also* Erzgebirge
Krušné Hory *see* Erzgebirge
83 L7 **Kruzof Island** *island* Alexander Archipelago, Alaska, USA
186 G3 **Krýa Vrýsi** *var.* Kría Vrísi. Kentrikí Makedonía, N Greece 40°41′N 22°18′E
191 I10 **Krychaw** *Rus.* Krichëv. Mahilyowskaya Voblasts', E Belarus 53°42′N 31°43′E
Krym *see* Krym, Respublika
189 J9 **Krym, Respublika** *var.* Krym, *Eng.* Crimea, Crimean Oblast; *prev. Rus.* Krymskaya ASSR, Krymskaya Oblast'. ◐ *province* SE Ukraine
196 F8 **Krymsk** Krasnodarskiy Kray, SW Russian Federation 44°56′N 38°02′E
Krymskaya ASSR/Krymskaya Oblast' *see* Krym, Respublika
189 K9 **Kryms'ki Hory** ▲▲ S Ukraine
189 J9 **Kryms'kyy Pivostriv** *peninsula* S Ukraine
183 H9 **Krynica** *Ger.* Tannenhof. Małopolskie, S Poland 49°25′N 20°56′E
189 H6 **Kryve Ozero** Odes'ka Oblast', SW Ukraine 47°54′N 30°19′E
191 E11 **Kryvoshyn** *Rus.* Krivoshin. Brestskaya Voblasts', SW Belarus 52°52′N 26°08′E
191 F9 **Kryvychy** *Rus.* Krivichi. Minskaya Voblasts', C Belarus 54°43′N 27°17′E
189 J6 **Kryvyy Rih** *Rus.* Krivoy Rog. Dnipropetrovs'ka Oblast', SE Ukraine 47°53′N 33°24′E
188 G5 **Kryzhopil'** Vinnyts'ka Oblast', C Ukraine 48°22′N 28°51′E
Krzemieniec *see* Kremenets'
182 F7 **Krzepice** Śląskie, S Poland 50°58′N 18°42′E
182 D5 **Krzyż Wielkopolskie** Wielkopolskie, W Poland 52°52′N 16°03′E
Ksar al Kabir *see* Ksar-el-Kebir
Ksar al Soule *see* Er-Rachidia
171 L10 **Ksar Chellala** Algeria
131 I2 **Ksar El Boukhari** N Algeria 35°55′N 02°47′E
130 F2 **Ksar-el-Kebir** *var.* Alcázar, Ksar al Kabir, Ksar-el-Kébir, *Ar.* Al-Kasr al-Kebir, Al-Qsar al-Kbir, *Sp.* Alcazarquivir. NW Morocco 35°04′N 05°56′W
Ksar-el-Kébir *see* Ksar-el-Kebir
175 C14 **Ksar Hellal** Tunisia
182 E6 **Książ Wielkopolski** *Ger.* Xions. Weilkopolskie, W Poland 52°03′N 17°10′E
175 C14 **Ksour Essaf** Tunisia
197 H2 **Kstovo** Nizhegorodskaya Oblast', W Russian Federation 56°07′N 44°12′E
245 J8 **Kuai He** Anhui, China
259 J2 **Kuala Belait** W Brunei 04°48′N 114°12′E
Kuala Dungun *see* Dungun
259 J4 **Kualakeriau** Borneo, C Indonesia
258 I6 **Kualakuayan** Borneo, C Indonesia 02°01′S 112°35′E
258 E3 **Kuala Lipis** Pahang, Peninsular Malaysia 04°11′N 102°00′E
258 E3 **Kuala Lumpur** ● (Malaysia) Kuala Lumpur, Peninsular Malaysia 03°08′N 101°42′E
Kuala Pelabohan Kelang *see* Pelabuhan Klang
259 K2 **Kuala Penyu** Sabah, East Malaysia 05°37′N 115°36′E
258 D4 **Kuala, Sungai** Sumatera, W Indonesia
258 E2 **Kuala Terengganu** *var.* Kuala Trengganu. Terengganu, Peninsular Malaysia 05°20′N 103°07′E
258 E5 **Kualatungkal** Sumatera, W Indonesia 0°49′S 103°22′E
259 L2 **Kuamut, Sungai** East Malaysia
260 E3 **Kuandang** Sulawesi, N Indonesia 0°50′N 122°55′E
260 D3 **Kuandang, Teluk** *bay* Sulawesi, N Indonesia
248 B3 **Kuandian** *var.* Kuandian Manzu Zizhixian. Liaoning, NE China 40°41′N 124°46′E
Kuandian Manzu Zizhixian *see* Kuandian
Kuando-Kubango *see* Cuando Cubango
Kuang-chou *see* Guangzhou
Kuang-hsi *see* Guangxi Zhuangzu Zizhiqu
Kuang-tung *see* Guangdong
Kuang-yuan *see* Guangyuan
258 E3 **Kuantan** Pahang, Peninsular Malaysia 03°50′N 103°19′E
Kuantan, Batang *see* Indragiri, Sungai
Kuanza Norte *see* Cuanza Norte
Kuanza Sul *see* Cuanza Sul
Kuanzhou *see* Qingjian
Kuba *see* Quba
196 G8 **Kuban'** *var.* Hypanis. SW Russian Federation
Kubango *see* Cubango/Okavango
221 K5 **Kubārah** NW Oman 23°03′N 56°52′E
154 I3 **Kubbe** Västernorrland, C Sweden 63°31′N 18°04′E
134 G3 **Kubbum** Southern Darfur, W Sudan 11°47′N 23°47′E
194 G8 **Kubenskoye, Ozero** ⊚ NW Russian Federation
228 D3 **Kubla-Ustyurt** *Rus.* Komsomol'sk-na-Ustyurte. Qoraqalpog'iston Respublikasi, NW Uzbekistan 44°06′N 58°14′E
140 C6 **Kuboes** Northern Cape, South Africa 28°21′S 16°53′E
250 F6 **Kubokawa** Kōchi, Shikoku, SW Japan 33°22′N 133°14′E
185 L5 **Kubrat** *prev.* Balbunar. Razgrad, N Bulgaria 43°48′N 26°31′E
260 B8 **Kubu** Sumbawa, S Indonesia 08°15′S 115°30′E
185 H5 **Kučajske Planine** ▲▲ E Serbia
252 F2 **Kuccharo-ko** ⊚ Hokkaidō, N Japan
185 H4 **Kučevo** Serbia, NE Serbia 44°29′N 21°42′E
Kuchan *see* Qūchān
259 H4 **Kuching** *prev.* Sarawak. Sarawak, East Malaysia 01°32′N 110°20′E
259 H4 **Kuching** ✈ Sarawak, East Malaysia 01°32′N 110°20′E
250 C10 **Kuchinoerabu-jima** *island* Nansei-shotō, SW Japan
250 C7 **Kuchinotsu** Nagasaki, Kyūshū, SW Japan 32°36′N 130°11′E
177 I3 **Kuchl** Salzburg, NW Austria 47°37′N 13°12′E
230 E5 **Kūchnay Darweyshān** Helmand, S Afghanistan 31°02′N 64°10′E
Kuchurgan *see* Kuchurhan
188 G6 **Kuchurhan** *Rus.* Kuchurgan. NE Ukraine
Kuçova *see* Kuçovë
184 F9 **Kuçovë** *var.* Kuçova; *prev.* Qyteti Stalin. Berat, C Albania 40°48′N 19°55′E
187 K5 **Kucukbahce** İzmir, Turkey 38°34′N 26°23′E
214 C4 **Küçük Çekmece** İstanbul, NW Turkey 41°01′N 28°47′E
250 E5 **Kudamatsu** *var.* Kudamatu. Yamaguchi, Honshū, SW Japan 34°00′N 131°53′E
Kudamatu *see* Kudamatsu
Kudara *see* Ghŭdara
259 K1 **Kudat** Sabah, East Malaysia 06°54′N 116°47′E
Küddow *see* Gwda
190 H5 **Kudever'** Pskovskaya Oblast', Russian Federation
234 E7 **Kūdligi** Karnātaka, W India 14°58′N 76°24′E
Kudowa *see* Kudowa-Zdrój
183 D8 **Kudowa-Zdrój** *Ger.* Kudowa. Wałbrzych, SW Poland 50°27′N 16°20′E
189 H6 **Kudryavtsivka** Mykolayivs'ka Oblast', S Ukraine 47°18′N 31°02′E
259 I8 **Kudus** *prev.* Koedoes. Jawa, C Indonesia 06°46′S 110°48′E
195 K8 **Kudymkar** Komi-Permyatskiy Avtonomnyy Okrug, NW Russian Federation 59°01′N 54°40′E
Kudzsir *see* Cugir
Kuei-chou *see* Guizhou

◆ Country
● Country Capital
◇ Dependent Territory
○ Dependent Territory Capital
◐ Administrative Regions
✈ International Airport
▲ Mountain
▲▲ Mountain Range
Volcano
River
⊚ Lake
⊠ Reservoir

◆ Country ◇ Dependent Territory ◆ Administrative Regions ▲ Mountain ▲ Volcano ◎ Lake
● Country Capital ◎ Dependent Territory Capital ✈ International Airport ▲ Mountain Range ➧ River ◎ Reservoir

◆ Country	◇ Dependent Territory	○ Administrative Regions	▲ Mountain	☒ Volcano	◎ Lake
● Country Capital	○ Dependent Territory Capital	✕ International Airport	▲ Mountain Range	♒ River	◎ Reservoir

◆ Country   ◇ Dependent Territory   ◈ Administrative Regions   ▲ Mountain   ◊ Volcano   ◎ Lake
● Country Capital   ○ Dependent Territory Capital   ✕ International Airport   ▲ Mountain Range   ⟳ River   ▨ Reservoir

◆ Country	◇ Dependent Territory	◆ Administrative Regions	▲ Mountain	☒ Volcano	⊚ Lake
● Country Capital	○ Dependent Territory Capital	✈ International Airport	▲ Mountain Range	♣ River	⊞ Reservoir

Lumajang - Madzhalis

259 J9 **Lumajang** Jawa, C Indonesia 08°06′S 113°13′E
238 D7 **Lumajangdong Co** ◎ W China
135 G12 **Lumbala Kaquengue** Moxico, E Angola 12°40′S 22°34′E
135 F13 **Lumbala N'Guimbo** *var.* Nguimbo, Gago Coutinho, *Port.* Vila Gago Coutinho. Moxico, E Angola 14°08′S 21°25′E
67 J7 **Lumber River** ≈ North Carolina/South Carolina, SE USA
Lumber State *see* Maine
68 E3 **Lumberton** Mississippi, S USA 31°00′N 89°27′W
67 K7 **Lumberton** North Carolina, SE USA 34°37′N 79°00′W
171 I2 **Lumbier** Navarra, N Spain 42°39′N 01°19′W
139 L2 **Lumbo** Nampula, NE Mozambique 15°S 40°40′E
194 G3 **Lumbovka** Murmanskaya Oblast', NW Russian Federation 67°41′N 40°31′E
170 E4 **Lumbrales** Castilla-León, N Spain 40°57′N 06°43′W
233 L6 **Lumding** Assam, NE India 25°46′N 93°10′E
135 F12 **Lumege** *var.* Lumeje. Moxico, E Angola 11°30′S 20°57′E
Lumeje *see* Lumege
261 M5 **Lumi** Sandaun, NW Papua New Guinea 03°30′S 142°02′E
110 F5 **Luminàrias** Minas Gerais, Brazil 21°30′S 44°54′W
163 F10 **Lummen** Limburg, NE Belgium 50°58′N 05°12′E
153 G10 **Lumparland** Åland, SW Finland 60°06′N 20°15′E
257 I8 **Lumphăt** *prev.* Lomphat. Rôtânôkiri, NE Cambodia 13°30′N
57 N7 **Lumsden** Saskatchewan, S Canada 50°39′N 104°52′W
278 B12 **Lumsden** Southland, South Island, New Zealand 45°43′S 168°26′E
258 G7 **Lumut, Tanjung** *headland* Sumatera, W Indonesia 03°47′S 105°55′E
240 C7 **Lunan** Yunnan, SW China 24°47′N 103°17′E
159 J1 **Lunan Bay** *bay* United Kingdom
169 H5 **Lunas** Languedoc-Roussillon, France 43°42′N 3°12′E
188 D9 **Lunca Corbului** Argeş, S Romania 44°41′N 24°46′E
155 F12 **Lund** Skåne, S Sweden 55°42′N 13°10′E
78 F4 **Lund** Nevada, W USA 38°50′N 115°00′W
135 E11 **Lunda Norte** ◐ *province* NE Angola
135 F11 **Lunda Sul** ◐ *province* NE Angola
137 C13 **Lundazi** Eastern, NE Zambia 12°19′S 33°11′E
155 D8 **Lunde** Telemark, S Norway 61°31′N 06°38′E
180 F1 **Lunden** Schleswig-Holstein, Germany 9°01′N 54°20′E
Lundenburg *see* Břeclav
155 B9 **Lundevatnet** ◎ S Norway
Lundi *see* Runde
157 E12 **Lundy** *island* SW England, United Kingdom
160 D7 **Lundy Island** *island* United Kingdom
159 J8 **Lune** ≈ United Kingdom
141 K5 **Luneberg** Kwazulu Natal, South Africa 27°23′S 30°57′E
180 I3 **Lüneburg** Niedersachsen, N Germany 53°15′N 10°25′E
180 H4 **Lüneburger Heide** *heathland* NW Germany
165 I8 **Lunel** Hérault, S France 43°40′N 04°08′E
181 D8 **Lünen** Nordrhein-Westfalen, W Germany 51°37′N 07°31′E
59 J9 **Lunenburg** Nova Scotia, SE Canada 44°23′N 64°21′W
67 K5 **Lunenburg** Virginia, NE USA 36°56′N 78°15′W
180 F3 **Lunestedt** Niedersachsen, Germany 8°45′N 53°26′E
165 K3 **Lunéville** Meurthe-et-Moselle, NE France 48°35′N 06°30′E
138 F1 **Lunga** ≈ C Zambia
Lunga, Isola *see* Dugi Otok
238 D7 **Lungdo** Xizang Zizhiqu, W China 33°45′N 82°09′E
238 E8 **Lunggar** Xizang Zizhiqu, W China 31°10′N 84°01′E
132 C7 **Lungi** ✕ (Freetown) W Sierra Leone 08°36′N 13°10′W
Lungkiang *see* Qiqihar
Lungleh *see* Lunglei
233 L8 **Lunglei** *prev.* Lungleh. Mizoram, NE India 22°55′N 92°49′E
238 F9 **Lungsang** Xizang Zizhiqu, W China 29°50′N 88°27′E
135 F12 **Lungué-Bungo** *var.* Lungwebungu. ≈ Angola/Zambia *see also* Lungwebungu
Lungué-Bungo *see* Lungwebungu
135 G13 **Lungwebungu** *var.* Lungué-Bungo. ≈ Angola/Zambia *see also* Lungué-Bungo
Lungwebungu *see* Lungué-Bungo
232 C6 **Lūni** Rājasthān, N India 26°03′N 73°00′E
232 C7 **Lūni** ≈ N India
Luninets *see* Luninyets
80 G4 **Luning** Nevada, W USA 38°29′N 118°10′W
Łuniniec *see* Luninyets
197 I3 **Lunino** Penzenskaya Oblast', W Russian Federation 53°35′N 45°12′E
191 F11 **Luninyets** *Pol.* Łuniniec, *Rus.* Luninets. Brestskaya Voblasts', SW Belarus 52°15′N 26°48′E
232 D5 **Lūnkaransar** *var.* Lookransar, Lukransar. Rājasthān, NW India 28°32′N 73°50′E
191 D10 **Lunna** *Pol.* Łunna. Hrodzyenskaya Voblasts', W Belarus 53°27′N 24°16′E
132 C7 **Lunsar** W Sierra Leone 08°41′N 12°32′W
139 H2 **Lunsemfwa** ≈ C Zambia
238 E4 **Luntai** *var.* Bügür. Xinjiang Uygur Zizhiqu, NW China 41°48′N 84°14′E
162 G6 **Lunteren** Gelderland, C Netherlands 52°05′N 05°38′E
260 B8 **Lunyuk** Sumbawa, S Indonesia 08°56′S 117°15′E
177 K3 **Lunz am See** Niederösterreich, C Austria 47°54′N 15°01′E
247 M3 **Luobei** *var.* Fengxiang. Heilongjiang, NE China 47°35′N 130°51′E
242 D8 **Luocheng** Guangxi, China 24°28′N 108°32′E
Luocheng *see* Hui'an, Fujian, China
Luocheng *see* Luoding, Guangdong, China
244 E6 **Luochuan** Shaanxi, China 35°27′N 109°15′E
242 C7 **Luodian** *var.* Longping. Guizhou, S China 25°25′N 106°49′E
243 M1 **Luodian** Shanghai Shi, E China 31°25′N 121°20′E
242 F9 **Luoding** *var.* Luocheng. Guangdong, S China 22°44′N 111°28′E
243 I9 **Luofu Shan** ▲▲ Guangdong, China
245 H8 **Luohe** Henan, C China 33°37′N 114°00′E
244 G8 **Luo He** ≈ C China
244 E6 **Luo He** ≈ C China
242 B1 **Luojiang** Sichuan, C China 31°21′N 104°28′E
243 J7 **Luokou** Jiangxi, SE China 25°42′N 115°39′E
Luolajarvi *see* Kuoloyarvi
244 F8 **Luonan** Shaanxi, China 34°04′N 110°05′E
Luong Nam Tha *see* Louangnamtha
242 A7 **Luoping** Yunnan, China 24°32′N 104°11′E
242 E7 **Luoqing Jiang** ≈ S China
242 E8 **Luorong** Guang Zhuangzu Zizhiqu, S China 24°24′N 109°37′E
243 I1 **Luoshan** Henan, C China 32°12′N 114°30′E
243 I2 **Luotian** Hubei, China 30°28′N 115°13′E
243 H6 **Luoxiao Shan** ▲▲ S China
244 G7 **Luoyang** *var.* Honan, Lo-yang. Henan, C China 34°41′N 112°25′E
243 L6 **Luoyuan** *var.* Fengshan. Fujian, SE China 26°29′N 119°32′E
243 L6 **Luozhou** Fujian, SE China 25°59′N 119°21′E
135 C9 **Luozi** Bas-Congo, W Dem. Rep. Congo 04°57′S 14°08′E
138 G3 **Lupane** Matabeleland North, W Zimbabwe 18°54′S 27°44′E
242 B6 **Lupanshui** *prev.* Shuicheng. Guizhou, S China 26°38′N 104°49′E
258 I4 **Lupar, Batang** ≈ East Malaysia
Lupatia *see* Altamura
188 C8 **Lupeni** *Hung.* Lupény. Hunedoara, SW Romania 45°20′N 23°10′E
Lupény *see* Lupeni
137 C12 **Lupiliche** Niassa, N Mozambique 11°36′S 35°15′E
135 E13 **Lupire** Cuando Cubango, E Angola 14°39′S 19°39′E
263 N9 **Lupon** Mindanao, S Philippines 06°53′N 126°00′E
135 G10 **Luputa** Kasai-Oriental, S Dem. Rep. Congo 07°07′S 23°43′E
175 J14 **Luqa** ✕ (Valletta) S Malta 35°53′N 14°27′E
244 A7 **Luqu** *var.* Ma'ai. Gansu, C China 34°34′N 102°27′E
245 I4 **Luquan** Hebei, China 38°02′N 114°11′E
91 J8 **Luquillo, Sierra de** ▲▲ E Puerto Rico
75 D9 **Luray** Kansas, C USA 39°06′N 98°41′W
64 A10 **Luray** Virginia, NE USA 38°40′N 78°28′W
165 K4 **Lure** Haute-Saône, E France 47°42′N 06°30′E
135 E11 **Luremo** Lunda Norte, NE Angola 08°32′S 17°55′E
158 D7 **Lurgan** *Ir.* An Lorgain. S Northern Ireland, United Kingdom 54°28′N 06°20′W
106 D10 **Luribay** La Paz, W Bolivia 17°05′S 67°37′W
Luring *see* Gêrzê
139 L1 **Lúrio** Nampula, NE Mozambique 13°32′S 40°34′E
137 D13 **Lúrio, Rio** ≈ NE Mozambique
Luristan *see* Lorestān
Lurka *see* Lorca
138 G2 **Lusaka** ● (Zambia) Lusaka, SE Zambia 15°24′S 28°17′E
139 H2 **Lusaka** ◐ *province* C Zambia
138 G2 **Lusaka** ✕ Lusaka, C Zambia 15°10′S 28°22′E
135 G9 **Lusambo** Kasai-Oriental, C Dem. Rep. Congo 04°59′S 23°26′E
280 D4 **Lusancay Islands and Reefs** *island group* SE Papua New Guinea
135 E9 **Lusanga** Bandundu, SW Dem. Rep. Congo 04°55′S 18°40′E
135 I9 **Lusangi** Maniema, E Dem. Rep. Congo 04°39′S 27°10′E
Lusatian Mountains *see* Lausitzer Bergland
245 H8 **Lushan** Henan, C China 33°44′N 112°54′E
243 J3 **Lu Shan** ▲ Jiangxi, China 29°18′N 115°33′E
245 K6 **Lu Shan** ▲▲ Shandong, China
Lushar *see* Huangzhong
Lushnja *see* Lushnjë
184 F8 **Lushnjë** *var.* Lushnja. Fier, C Albania 40°54′N 19°43′E
137 E10 **Lushoto** Tanga, E Tanzania 04°48′S 38°20′E
245 M4 **Lushun** Liaoning, NE China 38°48′N 121°15′E
164 G5 **Lusignan** Vienne, W France 46°25′N 00°06′E
141 J8 **Lusikisiki** Eastern Cape, South Africa 31°21′S 29°35′E
158 E9 **Lusk** Dublin, Ireland 53°32′N 6°10′W
77 M8 **Lusk** Wyoming, C USA 42°45′N 104°27′W
Luso *see* Luena
158 G3 **Luss** United Kingdom 56°06′N 4°38′W
164 G5 **Lussac-les-Châteaux** Vienne, W France 46°23′N 00°44′E
169 J4 **Lussan** Languedoc-Roussillon, France 44°09′N 4°22′E
Lussin/Lussino *see* Lošinj
Lussinpiccolo *see* Mali Lošinj
176 F3 **Lustenau** Vorarlberg, W Austria 47°26′N 09°42′E
245 K3 **Lutai** Tianjin Shi, N China 39°19′N 117°49′E
243 M4 **Lutan** Zhejiang, SE China 29°00′N 120°13′E
243 N9 **Lü Tao** *var.* Huoshao Dao, Lütao, *Eng.* Green Island. *island* SE Taiwan
Lütao *see* Lü Tao
Lūt, Baḩrat/Lut, Bahret *see* Dead Sea
68 D4 **Lutcher** Louisiana, S USA 30°02′N 90°42′W
223 I6 **Lūt, Dasht-e** *var.* Kavīr-e Lūt. *desert* E Iran
135 F13 **Lutembo** Moxico, E Angola 13°30′S 21°21′E
Lutetia/Lutetia Parisiorum *see* Paris
Luteva *see* Lodève
62 C4 **Luther Lake** ◎ Ontario, S Canada
64 A5 **Luthersburg** Pennsylvania, USA 41°03′N 78°43′W
64 D9 **Lutherville** Maryland, USA 39°25′N 76°38′W
281 H1 **Luti** Choiseul Island, NW Solomon Islands 07°13′S 157°01′E
180 C2 **Lutje Horn** Niedersachsen, Germany
Lūt, Kavīr-e *see* Lūt, Dasht-e
161 K5 **Luton** E England, United Kingdom 51°53′N 00°25′W
157 I11 **Luton** ✕ (London) SE England, United Kingdom 51°54′N 00°24′W
176 C5 **Lutry** Vaud, SW Switzerland 46°31′N 06°32′E
54 G4 **Łutselk'e** *prev.* Snowdrift. Northwest Territories, W Canada 62°24′N 110°42′W
74 I2 **Lutsen** Minnesota, N USA 47°39′N 90°37′W
188 D3 **Luts'k** *Pol.* Łuck, *Rus.* Lutsk. Volyns'ka Oblast', NW Ukraine 50°45′N 25°23′E
Lutsk *see* Luts'k
Luttenberg *see* Ljutomer
181 H8 **Lutter** Thüringen, Germany 10°07′N 51°20′E
161 I4 **Lutterworth** United Kingdom 52°27′N 1°12′W
Lüttich *see* Liège
138 E9 **Luttig** Western Cape, SW South Africa 32°33′S 22°13′E
Lutto *see* Lotta
161 K3 **Lutton** United Kingdom 52°28′N 0°22′W
135 F12 **Lutuai** Moxico, E Angola 12°38′S 20°06′E
189 N5 **Lutuhyne** Luhans'ka Oblast', E Ukraine 48°24′N 39°12′E
261 J6 **Lutur, Pulau** *island* Kepulauan Aru, E Indonesia
69 L6 **Lutz** Florida, SE USA 28°09′N 82°27′W
Lutzow-Holm Bay *see* Lützow Holmbukta
293 K2 **Lützow Holmbukta** *var.* Lutzow-Holm Bay. *bay* Antarctica
140 E5 **Lutzputz** Northern Cape, South Africa 28°15′S 20°18′E
140 D8 **Lutzville** Western Cape, South Africa 31°33′S 18°21′E
136 G6 **Luuq** *It.* Lugh Ganana. Gedo, SW Somalia 03°42′N 42°34′E
152 H6 **Luusua** Lappi, NE Finland 66°28′N 27°16′E
69 H3 **Luverne** Alabama, S USA 31°43′N 86°15′W
74 F6 **Luverne** Minnesota, N USA 43°39′N 96°12′W
135 I10 **Luvua** ≈ SE Dem. Rep. Congo
135 F12 **Luvuei** Moxico, E Angola 13°08′S 21°09′E
141 K1 **Luvuvhu** ≈ Limpopo, South Africa
137 D12 **Luwego** ≈ S Tanzania
137 A12 **Luwingu** Northern, NE Zambia 10°13′S 29°58′E
260 E4 **Luwuk** *prev.* Loewoek. Sulawesi, C Indonesia 0°56′S 122°47′E
66 C8 **Luxapallila Creek** ≈ Alabama/Mississippi, S USA
163 H14 **Luxembourg** ● (Luxembourg) Luxembourg, S Luxembourg 49°37′N 06°08′E
163 H13 **Luxembourg** *off.* Grand Duchy of Luxembourg, *var.* Lëtzebuerg, Luxemburg. ◆ *monarchy* NW Europe
163 G13 **Luxembourg** ◐ *province* SE Belgium
163 H13 **Luxembourg** ◐ *district* S Luxembourg
72 E6 **Luxemburg** Wisconsin, N USA 44°32′N 87°42′W
Luxemburg *see* Luxembourg
165 K4 **Luxeuil-les-Bains** Haute-Saône, E France 47°49′N 06°22′E
242 E4 **Luxi** Hunan, S China 28°12′N 110°12′E
243 H5 **Luxi** Jiangxi, China 27°23′N 114°02′E
240 B7 **Luxi** *prev.* Mangshi. Yunnan, SW China 24°27′N 98°31′E
242 A7 **Luxi** Yunnan, China 24°19′N 103°28′E
135 E10 **Luxico** ≈ Angola/Dem. Rep. Congo
129 J5 **Luxor** *Ar.* Al Uqşur. E Egypt 25°39′N 32°39′E
129 J5 **Luxor** ✕ C Egypt 25°39′N 32°48′E
129 J5 **Luxor** *headland* Egypt
243 J5 **Luyang** Jiangxi, SE China 27°42′N 117°05′E
244 G4 **Luya Shan** ▲▲ C China
171 I1 **Luy de Béarn** ≈ SW France
164 F8 **Luy de France** ≈ SW France
245 I8 **Luyi** Henan, E China 33°52′N 115°28′E
243 M1 **Luyuan** Jiangsu, E China 31°51′N 120°38′E
245 K3 **Lu Yunhe** *canal* Shandong, China
172 C8 **Luz** Faro, Portugal 37°05′N 7°42′W
195 I8 **Luza** Kirovskaya Oblast', NW Russian Federation 60°38′N 47°13′E
195 I8 **Luza** ≈ NW Russian Federation
167 H5 **Luzarches** Île-de-France, France 49°06′N 2°25′E
170 D9 **Luz, Costa de la** *coastal region* SW Spain
182 C7 **Luže** *var.* Lausche. ▲ Czech Republic/Germany 50°51′N 14°40′E *see also* Lausche
Luže *see* Lausche
176 D4 **Luzern** *Fr.* Lucerne, *It.* Lucerna. Luzern, C Switzerland 47°03′N 08°17′E
174 B3 **Luzern** *Fr.* Lucerne. ◐ *canton* C Switzerland
242 E8 **Luzhai** Guangxi Zhuangzu Zizhiqu, S China 24°31′N 109°46′E
242 B6 **Luzhi** Guizhou, China 26°07′N 105°17′E
191 G8 **Luzhki** Vitsyebskaya Voblasts', N Belarus 55°21′N 27°52′E
242 B4 **Luzhou** Sichuan, C China 28°55′N 105°25′E
172 B7 **Luzianes** Beja, Portugal 37°35′N 8°29′W
Lužická Nisa *see* Neisse
Lužické Hory' *see* Lausitzer Bergland
Lužnice *see* Lainsitz
263 L4 **Luzon** *island* N Philippines
263 K2 **Luzon Strait** *strait* Philippines/Taiwan
167 J9 **Luzy** Bourgogne, France 46°47′N 3°58′E
Łużyckie, Gory *see* Lausitzer Bergland
188 D4 **L'viv** *Ger.* Lemberg, *Pol.* Lwów, *Rus.* L'vov. L'vivs'ka Oblast', W Ukraine 49°49′N 24°05′E
L'viv *see* L'vivs'ka Oblast'
188 D3 **L'vivs'ka Oblast'** *var.* L'viv, *Rus.* L'vovskaya Oblast'. ◐ *province* NW Ukraine
L'vov *see* L'viv
L'vovskaya Oblast' *see* L'vivs'ka Oblast'
Lwena *see* Luena
Lwów *see* L'viv
182 D6 **Lwówek** *Ger.* Neustadt bei Pinne. Wielkopolskie, C Poland 52°27′N 16°10′E
182 D7 **Lwówek Śląski** *Ger.* Löwenberg in Schlesien. Jelenia Góra, SW Poland 51°06′N 15°35′E
190 G3 **Lyady** Pskovskaya Oblast', Russian Federation
191 E10 **Lyakhavichy** *Rus.* Lyakhovichi. Brestskaya Voblasts', SW Belarus 53°02′N 26°16′E
Lyakhovichi *see* Lyakhavichy
278 B11 **Lyall, Mount** ▲ South Island, New Zealand 45°14′S 167°31′E
Lyallpur *see* Faisalābād
192 E6 **Lyamin** ≈ C Russian Federation
Lyangar *see* Langar
192 F6 **Lyantor** Khanty-Mansiyskiy Avtonomnyy Okrug-Yugra, C Russian Federation 61°40′N 72°21′E
195 L5 **Lyapin** ≈ Khanty-Mansiyskiy Avtonomnyy Okrug-Yugra, Russian Federation
194 D7 **Lyaskelya** Respublika Kareliya, NW Russian Federation 61°42′N 31°06′E
191 E11 **Lyasnaya** *Rus.* Lesnaya. Brestskaya Voblasts', SW Belarus 52°59′N 25°46′E
191 D11 **Lyasnaya** *Pol.* Leśna, *Rus.* Lesnaya. ≈ SW Belarus
194 D9 **Lychkovo** Novgorodskaya Oblast', W Russian Federation 57°55′N 32°24′E
Lyck *see* Ełk
154 I2 **Lycksele** Västerbotten, N Sweden 64°34′N 18°40′E
64 D4 **Lycoming Creek** ≈ Pennsylvania, NE USA
Lycopolis *see* Asyūţ
161 M7 **Lydd** United Kingdom 50°57′N 0°55′E
293 H2 **Lyddan Island** *island* Antarctica
139 H6 **Lydenburg** Mpumalanga, NE South Africa 25°10′S 30°29′E
160 E8 **Lydford** United Kingdom 50°38′N 4°06′W
160 G4 **Lydham** United Kingdom 52°30′N 2°55′W
160 G6 **Lydney** United Kingdom 51°44′N 2°32′W
191 G12 **Lyel'chytsy** *Rus.* Lel'chitsy. Homyel'skaya Voblasts', SE Belarus 51°47′N 28°20′E
191 I9 **Lyenina** *Rus.* Lenino. Mahilyowskaya Voblasts', E Belarus 54°25′N 31°08′E
191 G8 **Lyepyel'** *Rus.* Lepel'. Vitsyebskaya Voblasts', N Belarus 54°54′N 28°44′E
70 G10 **Lyford** Texas, SW USA 26°24′N 97°47′W
155 B9 **Lygna** ≈ S Norway
64 D6 **Lykens** Pennsylvania, NE USA 40°33′N 76°42′W
186 F8 **Lykódimo** ▲ S Greece 36°56′N 21°49′E
140 G4 **Lykso** North West, South Africa 27°13′S 24°05′E
160 G8 **Lyme Bay** *bay* United Kingdom
157 G12 **Lyme Bay** *bay* S England, United Kingdom
160 G8 **Lyme Regis** S England, United Kingdom 50°44′N 02°56′W
161 M7 **Lyminge** United Kingdom 51°07′N 1°05′E
161 I8 **Lymington** United Kingdom 50°45′N 1°33′W
159 J10 **Lymm** United Kingdom 53°22′N 2°26′W
161 M7 **Lympne** United Kingdom 51°04′N 1°02′E
182 G3 **Łyna** *Ger.* Alle. ≈ N Poland
65 I6 **Lynbrook** New York, USA 40°39′N 73°40′W
74 D6 **Lynch** Nebraska, C USA 42°49′N 98°27′W
66 E7 **Lynchburg** Tennessee, S USA 35°17′N 86°22′W
67 J4 **Lynchburg** Virginia, NE USA 37°24′N 79°09′W
67 J8 **Lynches River** ≈ South Carolina, SE USA
76 C2 **Lynden** Washington, NW USA 48°57′N 122°27′W
276 G3 **Lyndhurst** South Australia 30°19′S 138°20′E
75 F10 **Lyndon** Kansas, C USA 38°37′N 95°40′W
63 I4 **Lyndonville** Vermont, NE USA 44°31′N 71°58′W
161 M3 **Lyng** United Kingdom 52°43′N 1°04′E
155 B9 **Lyngdal** Vest-Agder, S Norway 58°10′N 07°08′E
152 F4 **Lyngen** *Lapp.* Ivgovuotna. *inlet* Arctic Ocean
155 D9 **Lyngør** Aust-Agder, S Norway 58°38′N 09°05′E
152 F4 **Lyngseidet** Troms, N Norway 69°36′N 20°07′E
160 F7 **Lynmouth** United Kingdom 51°13′N 3°49′W
65 M2 **Lynn** Massachusetts, NE USA 42°28′N 70°57′W
Lynn *see* King's Lynn
69 I4 **Lynn Haven** Florida, SE USA 30°15′N 85°39′W
55 I6 **Lynn Lake** Manitoba, C Canada 56°51′N 101°01′W
Lynn Regis *see* King's Lynn
160 F7 **Lynton** United Kingdom 51°13′N 3°50′W
191 F8 **Lyntupy** Vitsyebskaya Voblasts', NW Belarus 55°03′N 26°19′E
54 G4 **Lynx Lake** ◎ Northwest Territories, NW Canada
165 J6 **Lyon** *Eng.* Lyons; *anc.* Lugdunum. Rhône, E France 45°46′N 04°50′E
52 D7 **Lyon, Cape** *headland* Northwest Territories, NW Canada 69°47′N 123°10′W
53 J9 **Lyon Inlet** *coastal sea feature* Nunavut, N Canada
63 H4 **Lyon Mountain** ▲ New York, NE USA 44°42′N 73°52′W
165 J6 **Lyonnais, Monts du** ▲▲ C France
132 E10 **Lyon Point** *headland* SE Tristan da Cunha 37°06′S 12°13′W
276 E3 **Lyons** South Australia 30°40′S 133°50′E
79 L2 **Lyons** Colorado, C USA 40°13′N 105°16′W
69 L2 **Lyons** Georgia, SE USA 32°12′N 82°19′W
75 D10 **Lyons** Kansas, C USA 38°22′N 98°13′W
74 F7 **Lyons** Nebraska, C USA 41°56′N 96°28′W
64 D1 **Lyons** New York, NE USA 43°03′N 76°58′W
Lyons *see* Lyon
191 I8 **Lyozna** *Rus.* Liozno. Vitsyebskaya Voblasts', NE Belarus 55°02′N 30°48′E
189 J3 **Lypova Dolyna** Sums'ka Oblast', NE Ukraine 50°36′N 33°50′E
188 G4 **Lypovets'** *Rus.* Lipovets. Vinnyts'ka Oblast', C Ukraine 49°13′N 29°06′E
Lys *see* Leie
183 F9 **Lysá Hora** ▲ E Czech Republic 49°31′N 18°27′E
155 E9 **Lysekil** Västra Götaland, S Sweden 58°16′N 11°26′E
Lýsi *see* Akdoğan
77 K7 **Lysite** Wyoming, C USA 43°16′N 107°42′W
197 I2 **Lyskovo** Nizhegorodskaya Oblast', W Russian Federation 56°04′N 45°01′E
176 C4 **Lyss** Bern, W Switzerland 47°04′N 07°19′E
155 D11 **Lystrup** Århus, C Denmark 56°14′N 10°14′E
195 L9 **Lys'va** Permskaya Oblast', NW Russian Federation 58°04′N 57°48′E
189 H4 **Lysyanka** Cherkas'ka Oblast', C Ukraine 49°15′N 30°50′E
189 M4 **Lysychans'k** *Rus.* Lisichansk. Luhans'ka Oblast', E Ukraine 48°52′N 38°27′E
159 I9 **Lytham St Anne's** NW England, United Kingdom 53°45′N 03°01′W
159 L7 **Lythe** United Kingdom 54°30′N 0°41′W
278 E10 **Lyttelton** South Island, New Zealand 43°35′S 172°44′E
56 E8 **Lytton** British Columbia, SW Canada 50°12′N 121°34′W
191 G11 **Lyuban'** Minskaya Voblasts', S Belarus 52°48′N 28°00′E
191 G9 **Lyubanskaye Vodaskhovishcha** ⊠ C Belarus
188 F4 **Lyubar** Zhytomyrs'ka Oblast', N Ukraine 49°54′N 27°48′E
Lyubashëvka *see* Lyubashivka
189 H6 **Lyubashivka** *Rus.* Lyubashëvka. Odes'ka Oblast', SW Ukraine 47°49′N 30°18′E
191 E10 **Lyubcha** *Pol.* Lubcz. Hrodzyenskaya Voblasts', W Belarus 53°45′N 26°04′E
196 F2 **Lyubertsy** Moskovskaya Oblast', W Russian Federation 55°37′N 38°02′E
188 E1 **Lyubeshiv** Volyns'ka Oblast', NW Ukraine 51°46′N 25°33′E
194 G9 **Lyubim** Yaroslavskaya Oblast', NW Russian Federation 58°21′N 40°46′E
185 K7 **Lyubimets** Khaskovo, S Bulgaria 41°51′N 26°03′E
Lyublin *see* Lublin
188 D2 **Lyuboml'** *Pol.* Luboml. Volyns'ka Oblast', NW Ukraine 51°12′N 24°01′E
Lyubotin *see* Lyubotyn
189 K3 **Lyubotyn** *Rus.* Lyubotin. Kharkivs'ka Oblast', E Ukraine 49°57′N 35°57′E
196 E3 **Lyudinovo** Kaluzhskaya Oblast', W Russian Federation 53°52′N 34°28′E
195 J10 **Lyuk** Udmurtskaya Respublika, NW Russian Federation 56°55′N 52°45′E
185 L6 **Lyulyakovo** *prev.* Keremitlik. Burgas, E Bulgaria 42°53′N 27°05′E
191 F11 **Lyusina** *Rus.* Lyusino. Brestskaya Voblasts', SW Belarus 52°38′N 26°31′E
Lyusino *see* Lyusina

M

218 F6 **Maād** Jordan 32°36′N 35°37′E
218 F6 **Ma'ād** Irbid, N Jordan 32°37′N 35°36′E
Ma'ai *see* Luqu
Maalahti *see* Malax
Maale *see* Male'
218 E6 **Maale Gilboa** Israel 32°28′N 35°25′E
218 E6 **Maale GiLebanonoa** Israel 32°28′N 35°25′E
218 E5 **Maalot Tarshīḩa** Israel 33°01′N 35°16′E
129 K3 **Ma'ān** Jordan
219 F12 **Ma'ān** Ma'ān, SW Jordan 30°11′N 35°45′E
219 F12 **Maān** Jordan 30°12′N 35°44′E
216 C9 **Ma'ān** *off.* Muḩāfaz̧at Ma'ān, *var.* Ma'an, Ma'ān. ◐ *governorate* S Jordan
219 G10 **Ma'ān Ḩijāz, Wādī** *dry watercourse* Jordan
153 I8 **Maaninka** Itä-Suomi, C Finland 63°10′N 27°19′E
Maanĭt *see* Bayan, Töv, Mongolia
Maanĭt *see* Hishig Öndör, Bulgan, Mongolia
Ma'ān, Muḩāfaz̧at *see* Ma'ān
152 I7 **Maanselkä** Oulu, C Finland 63°54′N 28°28′E
243 K1 **Ma'anshan** Anhui, E China 31°45′N 118°32′E
243 H4 **Ma'ao** Jiangxi, SE China 29°03′N 114°19′E
282 B4 **Maap** *island* Caroline Islands, W Micronesia
218 E4 **Maaraké** Lebanon 33°16′N 35°18′E
190 E3 **Maardu** *Ger.* Maart. Harjumaa, NW Estonia 59°28′N 24°56′E
Ma'aret-en-Nu'man *see* Ma'arrat an Nu'mān
163 G9 **Maarheeze** Noord-Brabant, SE Netherlands 51°19′N 05°37′E
Maarianhamina *see* Mariehamn
216 D3 **Ma'arrat an Nu'mān** *var.* Ma'aret-en-Nu'man, *Fr.* Maarret enn Naamâne. Idlib, NW Syria 35°40′N 36°40′E
Maarret enn Naamâne *see* Ma'arrat an Nu'mān
162 F6 **Maarssen** Utrecht, C Netherlands 52°08′N 05°03′E
Maart *see* Maardu
158 B6 **Maas** Donegal, Ireland 54°50′N 8°22′W
163 G10 **Maas** *Fr.* Meuse. ≈ W Europe *see also* Meuse
Maas *see* Meuse
163 H9 **Maasbree** Limburg, SE Netherlands 51°22′N 06°03′E
163 G9 **Maaseik** *prev.* Maeseyck. Limburg, NE Belgium 51°05′N 05°48′E
263 M7 **Maasin** Leyte, C Philippines 10°10′N 124°55′E
163 G10 **Maasmechelen** Limburg, NE Belgium 50°58′N 05°42′E
218 F4 **Maâsser Ech Choûf** Lebanon 33°39′N 35°40′E
162 D7 **Maassluis** Zuid-Holland, SW Netherlands 51°55′N 04°15′E
141 J1 **Maasstroom** Limpopo, South Africa 22°45′S 28°27′E
163 G10 **Maastricht** *var.* Maestricht; *anc.* Traiectum ad Mosam, Traiectum Tungorum. Limburg, SE Netherlands 50°51′N 05°42′E
245 L9 **Maba** Jiangsu, E China 32°59′N 118°47′E
Maba *see* Qujiang
139 I5 **Mabalane** Gaza, S Mozambique 23°43′S 32°37′E
71 H5 **Mabank** Texas, SW USA 32°22′N 96°06′W
218 D7 **Mabarot** Israel 32°22′N 34°54′E
253 E8 **Mabechi-gawa** *var.* Mabuchi-gawa. ≈ Honshū, C Japan
243 L6 **Mabi** Fujian, SE China 26°22′N 119°40′E
242 A4 **Mabian** Sichuan, China 28°31′N 103°19′E
159 N10 **Mablethorpe** E England, United Kingdom 53°21′N 00°14′E
261 J4 **Maboi** Papua, E Indonesia 01°00′S 134°02′E
141 J3 **Mabopane** North West, South Africa 25°30′S 28°06′E
139 I5 **Mabote** Inhambane, S Mozambique 22°03′S 34°09′E
76 D5 **Mabton** Washington, NW USA 46°13′N 120°00′W
140 F3 **Mabuasehube Game Reserve** Kgalagadi, Botswana
Mabuchi-gawa *see* Mabechi-gawa
141 J3 **Mabula** Limpopo, South Africa 24°49′S 27°59′E
140 G2 **Mabutsane** Southern, S Botswana 24°24′S 23°34′E
117 B9 **Macá, Cerro** ▲ S Chile 45°07′S 73°11′W
111 K7 **Macaé** Rio de Janeiro, SE Brazil 22°21′S 41°48′W
277 L2 **Macalister** Queensland, Australia
137 D13 **Macaloge** Niassa, N Mozambique 12°27′S 35°25′E
52 G9 **MacAlpine Lake** ◎ Nunavut, N Canada
Macan *see* Bonerate, Kepulauan
259 M8 **Macan, Kepulauan** *island group* C Indonesia
241 H8 **Macao** *see* Macau
172 C4 **Mação** Santarém, C Portugal 39°33′N 08°00′W
107 L1 **Macapá** *state capital* Amapá, N Brazil 0°04′N 51°04′W
89 K10 **Macaracas** Los Santos, S Panama 07°46′N 80°31′W
103 I3 **Macare, Caño** ≈ NE Venezuela
91 M10 **Macare, Caño** ≈ NE Venezuela
103 I3 **Macareo, Caño** ≈ NE Venezuela
Macarsca *see* Makarska
277 H7 **Macarthur** Victoria, SE Australia 38°04′S 142°02′E
MacArthur *see* Ormoc
104 C3 **Macas** Morona Santiago, SE Ecuador 02°22′S 78°08′W
Macassar *see* Makassar
108 I4 **Macau** Rio Grande do Norte, E Brazil 05°05′S 36°37′W
241 H8 **Macau** *Chin.* Aomen, *Eng.* Macao. Guangdong, SE China 22°06′N 113°30′E
Macău *see* Makó, Hungary
117 J10 **Macbride Head** *headland* East Falkland, Falkland Islands 51°25′S 57°55′W
69 L4 **Macclenny** Florida, SE USA 30°16′N 82°07′W
159 J10 **Macclesfield** C England, United Kingdom 53°16′N 02°07′W
286 B4 **Macclesfield Bank** *undersea feature* N South China Sea 15°50′N 114°20′E
MacCluer Gulf *see* Berau, Teluk
274 F5 **Macdonald, Lake** *salt lake* Western Australia
275 H5 **Macdonnell Ranges** ▲▲ Northern Territory, C Australia
156 G4 **Macduff** NE Scotland, United Kingdom 57°40′N 02°29′W
170 D3 **Macedo de Cavaleiros** Bragança, N Portugal 41°31′N 06°57′W
Macedonia *see* Macedonia, FYR
Macedonia Central *see* Kentrikí Makedonía
Macedonia East and Thrace *see* Anatolikí Makedonía kai Thráki
185 H8 **Macedonia, FYR** *off.* the Former Yugoslav Republic of Macedonia, *var.* Macedonia, *Mac.* Makedonija, *abbrev.* FYR Macedonia, FYROM. ◆ *republic* SE Europe
Macedonia, the Former Yugoslav Republic of *see* Macedonia, FYR
Macedonia West *see* Dytikí Makedonía
108 I6 **Maceió** *state capital* Alagoas, E Brazil 09°40′S 35°44′W
132 D7 **Macenta** SE Guinea 08°31′N 09°32′W
177 J10 **Macerata** Marche, C Italy 43°18′N 13°27′E
54 G6 **MacFarlane** ≈ Saskatchewan, C Canada
276 F4 **Macfarlane, Lake** *var.* Lake Mcfarlane. ◎ South Australia
Macgillicuddy's Reeks Mountains *see* Macgillycuddy's Reeks
157 A11 **Macgillycuddy's Reeks** *var.* Macgillicuddy's Reeks Mountains, *Ir.* Na Cruacha Dubha. ▲▲ SW Ireland
55 I10 **MacGregor** Manitoba, S Canada 49°58′N 98°49′W
230 G6 **Mach** Baluchistān, SW Pakistan 29°52′N 67°20′E
104 C2 **Machachi** Pichincha, C Ecuador 0°33′S 78°34′W
110 E6 **Machado** Minas Gerais, Brazil 21°41′S 45°56′W
139 I5 **Machaila** Gaza, S Mozambique 22°15′S 32°57′E
Machaire Fíolta *see* Magherafelt
Machaire Rátha *see* Maghera
137 D8 **Machakos** Eastern, S Kenya 01°31′S 37°16′E
104 B3 **Machala** El Oro, SW Ecuador 03°20′S 79°57′W
141 I2 **Machaneng** Central, SE Botswana 23°12′S 27°30′E
139 J4 **Machanga** Sofala, E Mozambique 20°56′S 35°04′E
158 F4 **Macharioch** W Scotland, United Kingdom
136 B4 **Machar Marshes** *wetland* SE Sudan
167 J4 **Machault** Champagne-Ardenne, France 49°21′N 4°30′E
164 F5 **Machecoul** Loire-Atlantique, NW France 46°59′N 01°51′W
243 I2 **Macheng** Hubei, C China 31°10′N 115°00′E
234 F6 **Mācherla** Andhra Pradesh, C India 16°29′N 79°25′E
218 F4 **Machghara** Lebanon 33°31′N 35°39′E
233 H5 **Māchhāpuchhre** ▲ C Nepal 28°30′N 83°57′E
63 L4 **Machias** Maine, NE USA 44°44′N 67°28′W
63 K2 **Machias River** ≈ Maine, NE USA
170 A8 **Machico** Madeira, Portugal, NE Atlantic Ocean 32°43′N 16°47′W
163 B11 **Machiennes-Ville** Nord, N France 50°22′N 03°23′E
234 G6 **Machilīpatnam** *var.* Bandar Masulipatnam. Andhra Pradesh, E India 16°12′N 81°11′E
102 D3 **Machiques** Zulia, NW Venezuela 10°04′N 72°37′W
190 H5 **Machnovka** Pskovskaya Oblast', Russian Federation
158 E4 **Machrihanish** United Kingdom 55°26′N 5°45′W
218 H1 **Machta Hammoud** Lebanon
105 F8 **Machupicchu** Cusco, C Peru 13°08′S 72°30′W
160 F3 **Machynlleth** United Kingdom 52°36′N 3°51′W
114 D5 **Macià** Entre Ríos, Argentina 32°10′S 59°23′W
139 I6 **Macia** *var.* Vila de Macia. Gaza, S Mozambique 25°02′S 33°08′E
Macías Nguema Biyogo *see* Bioco, Isla de
114 B6 **Maciel** Santa Fe, Argentina 32°30′S 60°48′W
188 F9 **Măcin** Tulcea, SE Romania 45°15′N 28°09′E
277 L2 **Macintyre River** ≈ New South Wales/Queensland, SE Australia
275 K4 **Mackay** Queensland, NE Australia 21°10′S 149°10′E
274 G4 **Mackay, Lake** *salt lake* Northern Territory/Western Australia
54 G3 **MacKay Lake** ◎ Northwest Territories, NW Canada
54 F6 **MacKay River** ≈ Alberta, W Canada
56 E3 **Mackenzie** British Columbia, W Canada 55°18′N 123°09′W
52 B6 **Mackenzie** ≈ Northwest Territories, NW Canada
293 L4 **Mackenzie Bay** *bay* Antarctica
52 B6 **Mackenzie Bay** *bay* NW Canada
295 H7 **Mackenzie King Island** *island* Queen Elizabeth Islands, Northwest Territories, N Canada
54 C2 **Mackenzie Mountains** ▲▲ Northwest Territories, NW Canada
72 G5 **Mackinac, Straits of** ◎ Michigan, N USA
292 F3 **Mackintosh, Cape** *headland* Antarctica 72°52′S 60°00′W
57 K6 **Macklin** Saskatchewan, S Canada 52°19′N 109°51′W
277 M3 **Macksville** New South Wales, SE Australia 30°39′S 152°54′E
277 M3 **Maclean** New South Wales, SE Australia 29°30′S 153°15′E
52 G4 **Maclean Strait** *Sea waterway* Nunavut, N Canada
138 G9 **Maclear** Eastern Cape, SE South Africa 31°05′S 28°22′E
277 M4 **Macleay River** ≈ New South Wales, SE Australia
MacLeod *see* Fort Macleod
274 C5 **Macleod, Lake** ◎ Western Australia
54 B2 **Macmillan** ≈ Yukon Territory, NW Canada
73 B10 **Macomb** Illinois, N USA 40°27′N 90°40′W
175 B9 **Macomer** Sardegna, Italy, C Mediterranean Sea 40°15′N 08°47′E
137 E13 **Macomia** Cabo Delgado, NE Mozambique 12°15′S 40°06′E
165 J6 **Mâcon** *anc.* Matisco, Matisco Ædourum. Saône-et-Loire, C France 46°19′N 04°49′E
69 J1 **Macon** Georgia, SE USA 32°49′N 83°41′W
66 C9 **Macon** Mississippi, S USA 33°06′N 88°33′W
75 H9 **Macon** Missouri, C USA 39°44′N 92°27′W
68 D2 **Macon, Bayou** ≈ Arkansas/Louisiana, S USA
135 G12 **Macondo** Moxico, E Angola 12°31′S 23°45′E
139 I3 **Macossa** Manica, C Mozambique 17°51′S 33°54′E
172 F2 **Macotera** Castilla y León, Spain 40°50′N 5°17′W
57 N2 **Macoun Lake** ◎ Saskatchewan, C Canada
73 B11 **Macoupin Creek** ≈ Illinois, N USA
Macouria *see* Tonate
139 J4 **Macovane** Inhambane, SE Mozambique 21°30′S 35°07′E
277 I9 **Macquarie Harbour** *inlet* Tasmania, SE Australia
286 E10 **Macquarie Island** *island* New Zealand, SW Pacific Ocean
277 L5 **Macquarie, Lake** *lagoon* New South Wales, SE Australia
277 J3 **Macquarie Marshes** *wetland* New South Wales, SE Australia
267 H8 **Macquarie Ridge** *undersea feature* SW Pacific Ocean 57°00′S 159°00′E
277 K3 **Macquarie River** ≈ New South Wales, SE Australia
277 J9 **Macquarie River** ≈ Tasmania, SE Australia
293 K3 **Mac. Robertson Land** *physical region* Antarctica
157 B11 **Macroom** *Ir.* Maigh Chromtha. Cork, SW Ireland 51°54′N 08°57′W
86 B6 **Macuautitlàn** Jalisco, Mexico 19°57′N 104°58′W
88 E3 **Macuelizo** Santa Bárbara, NW Honduras 15°21′N 88°31′W
167 N10 **Macugnaga** Valle d'Aosta, NW Italy 45°58′N 07°58′E
276 F2 **Macumba River** ≈ South Australia
105 G8 **Macusani** Puno, S Peru 14°05′S 70°24′W
104 D3 **Macusari, Río** ≈ N Peru
87 J8 **Macuspana** Tabasco, SE Mexico 17°43′N 92°36′W
219 F8 **Ma'dabā** Jordan 31°43′N 35°48′E
219 F8 **Ma'dabā** *var.* Mādabā, Madeba; *anc.* Medeba. Ma'dabā, NW Jordan 31°44′N 35°48′E
Mādabā *see* Ma'dabā
139 L5 **Madagascar** *off.* Democratic Republic of Madagascar, *Malg.* Madagasikara; *prev.* Malagasy Republic. ◆ *republic* W Indian Ocean
139 M7 **Madagascar** *island* W Indian Ocean
204 G10 **Madagascar Basin** *undersea feature* W Indian Ocean 27°00′S 53°00′E
Madagascar, Democratic Republic of *see* Madagascar
204 G10 **Madagascar Plain** *undersea feature* W Indian Ocean 19°00′S 52°00′E
121 N8 **Madagascar Plateau** *var.* Madagascar Ridge, Madagascar Rise, *Rus.* Madagaskarskiy Khrebet. *undersea feature* W Indian Ocean 30°00′S 45°00′E
Madagascar Rise/Madagascar Ridge *see* Madagascar Plateau
Madagasikara *see* Madagascar
Madagaskarskiy Khrebet *see* Madagascar Plateau
172 B9 **Madalena** Pico, Azores, Portugal, NE Atlantic Ocean 38°32′N 28°15′W
133 M1 **Madama** Agadez, NE Niger 21°54′N 13°43′E
185 K8 **Madan** Smolyan, S Bulgaria 41°29′N 24°56′E
234 F7 **Madanapalle** Andhra Pradesh, E India 13°33′N 78°31′E
280 B3 **Madang** Madang, N Papua New Guinea 05°14′S 145°45′E
280 B3 **Madang** ◐ *province* N Papua New Guinea
228 D4 **Madaniyat** *Rus.* Madeniyet. Qoraqalpog'iston Respublikasi, W Uzbekistan 42°48′N 59°00′E
Madanīyīn *see* Médenine
133 J4 **Madaoua** Tahoua, SW Niger 14°06′N 06°01′E
Madaras *see* Vtáčnik
233 K8 **Madaripur** Dhaka, C Bangladesh 23°09′N 90°11′E
133 K5 **Madarounfa** Maradi, S Niger 13°16′N 07°07′E
Mađarska *see* Hungary
228 B7 **Madau** Balkan Welaýaty, W Turkmenistan 38°11′N 54°46′E
280 D4 **Madau Island** *island* SE Papua New Guinea
63 K1 **Madawaska** Maine, NE USA 47°19′N 68°19′W
62 E3 **Madawaska** ≈ Ontario, SE Canada
Madawaska Highlands *see* Haliburton Highlands
256 C4 **Madaya** Mandalay, C Myanmar (Burma) 22°12′N 96°05′E
175 G9 **Maddaloni** Campania, S Italy 41°03′N 14°23′E
74 D2 **Maddock** North Dakota, N USA 47°57′N 99°31′W
163 E8 **Made** Noord-Brabant, S Netherlands 51°41′N 04°48′E
Madeba *see* Ma'dabā
290 G5 **Madeira** *var.* Ilha de Madeira. *island* Madeira, Portugal, NE Atlantic Ocean
Madeira, Ilha de *see* Madeira
170 A8 **Madeira Islands** *Port.* Região Autoónoma da Madeira. ◐ *autonomous region* Madeira, Portugal, NE Atlantic Ocean
290 G5 **Madeira Plain** *undersea feature* E Atlantic Ocean
Madeira, Região Autoónoma da *see* Madeira Islands
290 G5 **Madeira Ridge** *undersea feature* E Atlantic Ocean 35°30′N 15°45′W
106 G4 **Madeira, Rio** *var.* Río Madera. ≈ Bolivia/Brazil *see also* Madera, Río
Madeira, Rio *see* Madera, Río
174 D3 **Mädelegabel** ▲ Austria/Germany 47°18′N 10°19′E
59 K7 **Madeleine, Îles de la** *Eng.* Magdalen Islands. *island group* Québec, E Canada
74 G5 **Madelia** Minnesota, N USA 44°03′N 94°26′W
78 C2 **Madeline** California, W USA 41°02′N 120°28′W
72 C4 **Madeline Island** *island* Apostle Islands, Wisconsin, N USA
215 H7 **Maden** Elazığ, SE Turkey 38°24′N 39°42′E
227 K5 **Madeniyet** Vostochnyy Kazakhstan, E Kazakhstan 47°51′N 78°37′E
Madeniyet *see* Madaniyat
84 G4 **Madera** Chihuahua, N Mexico 29°10′N 108°10′W
80 D5 **Madera** California, W USA 36°57′N 120°02′W
106 E7 **Madera, Río** *Port.* Rio Madeira. ≈ Bolivia/Brazil *see also* Madeira, Rio
Madera, Río *see* Madeira, Rio
176 E5 **Madesimo** Lombardia, N Italy 46°20′N 09°26′E
136 G1 **Madhāb, Wādī** *dry watercourse* NW Yemen
233 I7 **Madhepura** *prev.* Madhipure. Bihār, NE India 25°56′N 86°48′E
Madhipure *see* Madhepura
233 I6 **Madhubani** Bihār, N India 26°21′N 86°05′E
233 I7 **Madhupur** Jhārkhand, NE India 24°17′N 86°38′E
232 F8 **Madhya Pradesh** *prev.* Central Provinces and Berar. ◐ *state* C India
141 H4 **Madibogo** North-West, South Africa 26°25′S 25°12′E
106 D8 **Madidi, Río** ≈ W Bolivia
235 D8 **Madikeri** *prev.* Mercara. Karnātaka, W India 12°29′N 75°40′E
75 E13 **Madill** Oklahoma, C USA 34°06′N 96°46′W
135 C9 **Madimba** Bas-Congo, SW Dem. Rep. Congo 04°58′S 15°08′E
216 F3 **Ma'din** Ar Raqqah, C Syria 35°45′N 39°36′E
Madīnah, Minţaqat al *see* Al Madīnah
132 E6 **Madinani** NW Ivory Coast 09°37′N 06°57′W
220 F9 **Madīnat ash Sha'b** *prev.* Al Ittiḩād. SW Yemen 12°52′N 44°55′E
216 E3 **Madīnat ath Thawrah** *var.* Ath Thawrah. Ar Raqqah, N Syria 35°36′N 39°00′E
289 D8 **Madingley Rise** *undersea feature* W Indian Ocean
135 B9 **Madingo-Kayes** Kouilou, S Congo 04°27′S 11°43′E
135 C9 **Madingou** Bouenza, S Congo 04°10′S 13°33′E
Madioen *see* Madiun
80 C1 **Madison** California, USA 38°41′N 121°58′W
69 K4 **Madison** Florida, SE USA 30°27′N 83°24′W
66 G8 **Madison** Georgia, SE USA 33°37′N 83°28′W
66 F3 **Madison** Indiana, N USA 38°44′N 85°22′W
75 F10 **Madison** Kansas, C USA 45°01′N 96°11′W
63 K4 **Madison** Maine, NE USA 44°48′N 69°52′W
74 F5 **Madison** Minnesota, N USA 45°00′N 96°12′W
68 E2 **Madison** Mississippi, S USA 32°27′N 90°07′W
74 E7 **Madison** Nebraska, C USA 41°49′N 97°27′W
74 E5 **Madison** South Dakota, N USA 44°00′N 97°06′W
67 K3 **Madison** Virginia, NE USA 38°23′N 78°16′W
67 H4 **Madison** West Virginia, NE USA 38°03′N 81°50′W
72 C7 **Madison** *state capital* Wisconsin, N USA 43°04′N 89°22′W
67 K4 **Madison Heights** Virginia, NE USA 37°25′N 79°07′W
66 D4 **Madisonville** Kentucky, S USA 37°20′N 87°30′W
66 F6 **Madisonville** Tennessee, S USA 35°31′N 84°21′W
71 H6 **Madisonville** Texas, SW USA 30°58′N 95°56′W
Madisonville *see* Taiohae
259 I9 **Madiun** *prev.* Madioen. Jawa, C Indonesia 07°37′S 111°33′E
Madjene *see* Majene
62 E4 **Madoc** Ontario, SE Canada 44°31′N 77°27′W
Madoera *see* Madura, Pulau
136 E7 **Mado Gashi** North Eastern, E Kenya 0°40′N 39°09′E
239 J7 **Madoi** *var.* Huanghe; *prev.* Huangheyan. Qinghai, C China 34°53′N 98°07′E
283 K2 **Madolenihmw** Pohnpei, E Micronesia
190 E6 **Madona** *Ger.* Modohn. Madona, E Latvia 56°51′N 26°10′E
175 F12 **Madonie** ▲▲ Sicilia, Italy, C Mediterranean Sea
221 K6 **Madrakah, Ra's** *headland* E Oman 18°56′N 57°54′E
76 C6 **Madras** Oregon, NW USA 44°39′N 121°08′W
Madras *see* Tamil Nādu
Madras *see* Chennai
110 G5 **Madre de Deus de Minas** Minas Gerais, Brazil 21°29′S 44°20′W
104 G7 **Madre de Dios** *off.* Departamento de Madre de Dios. ◐ *department* E Peru
Madre de Dios, Departamento de *see* Madre de Dios
117 A12 **Madre de Dios, Isla** *island* S Chile
106 C8 **Madre de Dios, Río** ≈ Bolivia/Peru
42 E9 **Madre del Sur, Sierra** ▲▲ S Mexico
85 N6 **Madre, Laguna** *lagoon* NE Mexico
70 G10 **Madre, Laguna** *lagoon* Texas, SW USA
79 K8 **Madre Mount** ▲ New Mexico, SW USA 34°18′N 107°54′W
42 D8 **Madre Occidental, Sierra** *var.* Western Sierra Madre. ▲▲ C Mexico
42 E8 **Madre Oriental, Sierra** *var.* Eastern Sierra Madre. ▲▲ C Mexico
87 J9 **Madre, Sierra** *var.* Sierra de Soconusco. ▲▲ Guatemala/Mexico
263 L4 **Madre, Sierra** ▲▲ Luzon, N Philippines
79 K2 **Madre, Sierra** ▲▲ Colorado/Wyoming, C USA
170 G5 **Madrid** ● (Spain) Madrid, C Spain 40°25′N 03°43′W
74 G7 **Madrid** Iowa, C USA 41°52′N 93°49′W
170 G4 **Madrid** ◐ *autonomous community* C Spain
170 G6 **Madridejos** Castilla-La Mancha, C Spain 39°29′N 03°32′W
170 F4 **Madrigal de las Altas Torres** Castilla-León, N Spain 41°05′N 05°00′W
170 E6 **Madrigalejo** Extremadura, W Spain 39°08′N 05°36′W
78 A2 **Mad River** ≈ California, W USA
88 G5 **Madriz** ◐ *department* NW Nicaragua
173 H1 **Madrona** Castilla y León, Spain 40°54′N 4°10′W
170 E6 **Madroñera** Extremadura, W Spain 39°25′N 05°46′W
276 B4 **Madura** Western Australia 31°52′S 127°01′E
Madura *see* Madurai
235 E9 **Madurai** *prev.* Madura, Mathurai. Tamil Nādu, S India 09°55′N 78°07′E
259 J8 **Madura, Pulau** *prev.* Madoera. *island* C Indonesia
259 J8 **Madura, Selat** *strait* C Indonesia
197 J10 **Madzhalis** Respublika Dagestan, SW Russian Federation 42°12′N 47°46′E

◆ Country
● Country Capital
◇ Dependent Territory
○ Dependent Territory Capital
◐ Administrative Regions
✕ International Airport
▲ Mountain
▲▲ Mountain Range
Volcano
≈ River
◎ Lake
⊠ Reservoir

INDEX

◆ Country   ◇ Dependent Territory   ✕ Administrative Regions   ▲ Mountain   ☒ Volcano   ⊚ Lake
● Country Capital   ○ Dependent Territory Capital   ✈ International Airport   ▲ Mountain Range   ♣ River   ☒ Reservoir

Key
◆ Country ◇ Dependent Territory ◇ Administrative Regions ▲ Mountain ✖ Volcano ◎ Lake
● Country Capital ○ Dependent Territory Capital ✖ International Airport ▲ Mountain Range ✍ River ◻ Reservoir

◆ Country   ◇ Dependent Territory   ◈ Administrative Regions   ▲ Mountain   ⏣ Volcano   ⊚ Lake
● Country Capital   ○ Dependent Territory Capital   ✕ International Airport   ▲ Mountain Range   ᴪ River   ⊠ Reservoir

◆ Country   ◇ Dependent Territory   ⬠ Administrative Regions   ▲ Mountain   ⛰ Volcano   ⦿ Lake
● Country Capital   ○ Dependent Territory Capital   ✕ International Airport   ▲ Mountain Range   ॐ River   ◨ Reservoir

Mozambique - Mwenga

139 J3 **Mozambique** *off.* Republic of Mozambique; *prev.* People's Republic of Mozambique, Portuguese East Africa. ◆ *republic* S Africa
Mozambique Basin *see* Natal Basin
Mozambique, Canal de *see* Mozambique Channel
139 L2 **Mozambique Channel** *Fr.* Canal de Mozambique, *Mal.* Lakandranon' i Mozambika. *strait* W Indian Ocean
289 B11 **Mozambique Escarpment** *var.* Mozambique Scarp. *undersea feature* SW Indian Ocean 33°00′S 36°30′E
Mozambique, People's Republic of *see* Mozambique
289 B11 **Mozambique Plateau** *var.* Mozambique Rise. *undersea feature* SW Indian Ocean 32°00′S 35°00′E
Mozambique, Republic of *see* Mozambique
Mozambique Rise *see* Mozambique Plateau
Mozambique Scarp *see* Mozambique Escarpment
197 I9 **Mozdok** Respublika Severnaya Osetiya, SW Russian Federation 43°48′N 44°42′E
106 D10 **Mozetenes, Serranías de** ▲▲ C Bolivia
196 F2 **Mozhaysk** Moskovskaya Oblast', W Russian Federation 55°31′N 36°01′E
195 J10 **Mozhga** Udmurtskaya Respublika, NW Russian Federation 56°24′N 52°13′E
Mozyr' *see* Mazyr
135 J10 **Mpala** Katanga, E Dem. Rep. Congo 06°43′S 29°28′E
135 C8 **Mpama** ≈ C Congo
137 B10 **Mpanda** Rukwa, W Tanzania 06°21′S 31°01′E
137 B11 **Mpande** Northern, NE Zambia 09°13′S 31°42′E
141 K5 **Mpemvana** Kwazulu Natal, South Africa 27°35′S 30°42′E
141 I9 **Mpetu** Eastern Cape, South Africa 32°38′S 28°08′E
138 G4 **Mphoengs** Matabeleland South, SW Zimbabwe 21°04′S 27°56′E
137 B8 **Mpigi** S Uganda 0°14′N 32°19′E
137 B12 **Mpika** Northern, NE Zambia 11°50′S 31°30′E
138 G1 **Mpima** Central, C Zambia 14°25′S 28°34′E
138 G1 **Mpongwe** Copperbelt, C Zambia 13°25′S 28°13′E
137 A11 **Mporokoso** Northern, N Zambia 09°22′S 30°06′E
135 D8 **Mpouya** Plateaux, SE Congo 02°38′S 16°13′E
133 H8 **Mpraeso** C Ghana 06°36′N 00°43′W
137 B11 **Mpulungu** Northern, N Zambia 08°50′S 31°06′E
139 H6 **Mpumalanga** *prev.* Eastern Transvaal, *Afr.* Oos-Transvaal. ◈ *province* NE South Africa
138 C3 **Mpungu** Okavango, N Namibia 17°36′S 18°16′E
137 D10 **Mpwapwa** Dodoma, C Tanzania 06°21′S 36°29′E
Mqinvartsveri *see* Kazbek
182 H4 **Mrągowo** *Ger.* Sensburg. Warmińsko-Mazurskie, NE Poland 53°53′N 21°19′E
218 G2 **Mrâh en Naquâs** Lebanon 34°20′N 36°09′E
197 L3 **Mrakovo** Respublika Bashkortostan, W Russian Federation 52°43′N 56°36′E
139 I10 **Mramani** Anjouan, E Comoros 12°18′N 44°39′E
Mrauk U *see* Myohaung
184 D4 **Mrkonjić Grad** ◈ Republika Srpska, W Bosnia and Herzegovina
182 E5 **Mrocza** Kujawsko-pomorskie, C Poland 53°15′N 17°38′E
175 C14 **M'Saken** N Tunisia 35°44′N 10°34′E
141 H6 **Mselpoort** ≈ Free State, South Africa
190 H3 **Mshinskaya** Leningradskaya Oblast', Russian Federation
171 M10 **M'Sila** Algeria
194 E9 **Msta** ≈ NW Russian Federation
Mstislavl' *see* Mstsislaw
191 I9 **Mstsislaw** *Rus.* Mstislavl'. Mahilyowskaya Voblasts', E Belarus 54°01′N 31°43′E
218 F3 **Mtaïn** Lebanon
141 J7 **Mtamvuna** ≈ South Africa
141 J8 **Mtata** ≈ Eastern Cape, South Africa
141 J8 **Mtata Dam** ⊠ Eastern Cape, South Africa
Mtkvari *see* Kura
Mtoko *see* Mutoko
141 L6 **Mtonjaneni** Kwazulu Natal, South Africa 28°28′S 31°20′E
196 F3 **Mtsensk** Orlovskaya Oblast', W Russian Federation 53°17′N 36°34′E
141 L6 **Mtunzini** KwaZulu-Natal, South Africa 28°57′S 31°45′E
141 K7 **Mtwalume** KwaZulu-Natal, South Africa 30°29′S 30°38′E
137 F12 **Mtwara** Mtwara, SE Tanzania 10°17′S 40°11′E
137 E12 **Mtwara** ◈ *region* SE Tanzania
170 C8 **Mu** ▲ S Portugal 37°24′N 08°04′W
284 E9 **Mu'a** Tongatapu, S Tonga 21°11′S 175°07′W
Muai To *see* Mae Hong Son
139 K3 **Mualama** Zambézia, NE Mozambique 16°51′S 38°21′E
Mualo *see* Messalo, Rio
135 B10 **Muanda** Bas-Congo, SW Dem. Rep. Congo 05°53′S 12°17′E
Muang Chiang Rai *see* Chiang Rai
256 G5 **Muang Ham** Houaphan, N Laos 20°19′N 104°00′E
256 G6 **Muang Hinboun** Khammouan, C Laos 17°37′N 104°37′E
Muang Kalasin *see* Kalasin
Muang Khammouan *see* Thakhèk
257 H8 **Muang Không** Champasak, S Laos 14°08′N 105°48′E
256 H7 **Muang Khôngxédôn** *var.* Khong Sedone. Salavan, S Laos 15°34′N 105°46′E
Muang Khon Kaen *see* Khon Kaen
256 F4 **Muang Khoua** Phôngsali, N Laos 21°07′N 102°31′E
Muang Krabi *see* Krabi
Muang Lampang *see* Lampang
Muang Lamphun *see* Lamphun
Muang Loei *see* Loei
Muang Lom Sak *see* Lom Sak
Muang Nakhon Sawan *see* Nakhon Sawan
256 F5 **Muang Namo** Oudômxai, N Laos 20°58′N 101°46′E
Muang Nan *see* Nan
256 F5 **Muang Ngoy** Louangphabang, N Laos 20°43′N 102°42′E
256 F4 **Muang Ou Tai** Phôngsali, N Laos 22°06′N 101°59′E
Muang Pak Lay *see* Pak Lay
Muang Pakxan *see* Pakxan
256 H7 **Muang Pakxong** Champasak, S Laos 15°10′N 106°17′E
256 H6 **Muang Phalan** *var.* Muang Phalane. Savannakhét, S Laos 16°40′N 105°33′E
Muang Phalane *see* Muang Phalan
Muang Phan *see* Phan
Muang Phayao *see* Phayao
Muang Phichit *see* Phichit
256 H7 **Muang Phin** Savannakhét, S Laos 16°31′N 106°01′E
Muang Phitsanulok *see* Phitsanulok
Muang Phrae *see* Phrae
Muang Roi Et *see* Roi Et
Muang Sakon Nakhon *see* Sakon Nakhon
Muang Samut Prakan *see* Samut Prakan
256 F4 **Muang Sing** Louang Namtha, N Laos 21°12′N 101°09′E
Muang Ubon *see* Ubon Ratchathani
Muang Uthai Thani *see* Uthai Thani
256 F6 **Muang Vangviang** Viangchan, C Laos 18°53′N 102°27′E
Muang Xaignabouri *see* Xaignabouli
Muang Xay *see* Xai
256 H6 **Muang Xépôn** *var.* Sepone. Savannakhét, S Laos 16°40′N 106°15′E
258 E4 **Muar** *var.* Bandar Maharani. Johor, Peninsular Malaysia 02°01′N 102°35′E
258 C4 **Muara** Sumatera, W Indonesia 02°18′N 98°54′E
258 E6 **Muarabeliti** Sumatera, W Indonesia 03°13′S 103°00′E
258 E5 **Muarabungo** Sumatera, W Indonesia 01°28′S 102°06′E
258 E7 **Muaraenim** Sumatera, W Indonesia 03°40′S 103°48′E
259 J5 **Muarajuloi** Borneo, C Indonesia 0°12′S 114°03′E
259 K6 **Muarakaman** Borneo, C Indonesia 0°09′S 116°43′E
258 C5 **Muarasigep** Pulau Siberut, W Indonesia 01°01′S 98°48′E
258 E6 **Muaratembesi** Sumatera, W Indonesia 01°40′S 103°08′E
259 K5 **Muaratewe** *var.* Muarateweh; *prev.* Moearatewe. Borneo, C Indonesia 0°58′S 114°52′E
Muarateweh *see* Muaratewe
259 K4 **Muarawahau** Borneo, N Indonesia 01°03′N 116°48′E
158 E4 **Muasdale** Argyll and Bute, W Scotland, United Kingdom 55°36′N 05°41′W
220 C2 **Mubārak, Jabal** ▲ S Jordan 29°19′N 35°13′E
233 H7 **Mubārakpur** Uttar Pradesh, N India 26°05′N 83°19′E
Mubarek *see* Muborak
136 B7 **Mubende** SW Uganda 0°35′N 31°24′E
133 M6 **Mubi** Adamawa, NE Nigeria 10°15′N 13°18′E
228 G7 **Muborak** *Rus.* Mubarek. Qashqadaryo Viloyati, S Uzbekistan 39°17′N 65°10′E
261 I4 **Mubrani** Papua, E Indonesia 0°42′S 133°25′E
181 D9 **Much** Nordrhein-Westfalen, Germany 7°24′N 50°55′E
121 L7 **Muchinga Escarpment** *escarpment* NE Zambia
197 H4 **Muchkapskiy** Tambovskaya Oblast', W Russian Federation 51°51′N 42°25′E
242 A4 **Muchuan** Sichuan, C China 28°56′N 103°58′E
160 G3 **Much Wenlock** United Kingdom 52°36′N 2°33′W
158 D1 **Muck** *island* W Scotland, United Kingdom
277 K1 **Muckadilla** Queensland, Australia
158 D8 **Muckno Lough** ◎ NE Ireland
137 F12 **Mucojo** Cabo Delgado, N Mozambique 12°05′S 40°30′E
135 F11 **Muconda** Lunda Sul, NE Angola 10°37′S 21°19′E
102 E6 **Muco, Río** ≈ E Colombia
139 K3 **Mucubela** Zambézia, NE Mozambique 16°51′S 37°48′E
88 G4 **Mucupina, Monte** ▲ N Honduras 15°07′N 86°36′W
214 F6 **Mucur** Kirşehir, C Turkey 39°05′N 34°25′E
223 J5 **Mūd** Khorāsān-e Janūbī, E Iran 32°41′N 59°30′E
237 K3 **Mudanjiang** *var.* Mu-tan-chiang. Heilongjiang, NE China 44°33′N 129°40′E
248 E1 **Mudan Jiang** ≈ NE China
214 C5 **Mudanya** Bursa, NW Turkey 40°23′N 28°53′E
181 G13 **Mudau** Baden-Württemberg, Germany 9°12′N 49°32′E
74 B4 **Mud Butte** South Dakota, N USA 45°00′N 102°51′W
234 E6 **Muddebihāl** Karnātaka, C India 16°26′N 76°07′E
75 F13 **Muddy Boggy Creek** ≈ Oklahoma, C USA
79 I4 **Muddy Creek** ≈ Utah, W USA
79 N4 **Muddy Creek Reservoir** ⊠ Colorado, C USA
77 K8 **Muddy Gap** Wyoming, C USA 42°21′N 107°27′W
81 J9 **Muddy Peak** ▲ Nevada, W USA 36°17′N 114°40′W
180 I5 **Müden** Niedersachsen, Germany 10°22′N 52°32′E
141 K6 **Muden** KwaZulu-Natal, South Africa 28°58′S 30°23′E
277 K4 **Mudgee** New South Wales, SE Australia 32°37′S 149°36′E
74 F2 **Mud Lake** ◎ Minnesota, N USA
80 H5 **Mud Lake** ◎ Nevada, USA
74 E4 **Mud Lake Reservoir** ⊠ South Dakota, N USA
256 D7 **Mudon** Mon State, S Myanmar (Burma) 16°17′N 97°40′E
243 M2 **Mudu** Jiangsu, E China 31°15′N 120°31′E
136 I5 **Mudug** *off.* Gobolka Mudug. ◈ *region* NE Somalia
136 I5 **Mudug** *var.* Mudugh. *plain* N Somalia
Mudug, Gobolka *see* Mudug
Mudugh *see* Mudug
139 K2 **Muecate** Nampula, NE Mozambique 14°56′S 39°38′E
137 E12 **Mueda** Cabo Delgado, NE Mozambique 11°40′S 39°31′E
168 C9 **Muel** Aragón, Spain 41°28′N 1°05′W
88 G6 **Muelle de los Bueyes** Región Autónoma Atlántico Sur, SE Nicaragua 12°03′N 84°34′W
Muenchen *see* München
139 I1 **Muende** Tete, NW Mozambique 14°22′S 33°00′E
75 E14 **Muenster** Texas, SW USA 33°39′N 97°22′W
Muenster *see* Münster
89 I4 **Muerto, Cayo** *reef* NE Nicaragua
86 A2 **Muerto, Mar** *lagoon* SE Mexico
290 C6 **Muertos Trough** *undersea feature* N Caribbean Sea
138 F1 **Mufaya Kuta** Western, NW Zambia 14°30′S 24°18′E
138 G1 **Mufulira** Copperbelt, C Zambia 12°33′S 28°16′E
243 I3 **Mufu Shan** ▲▲ C China
Mugalla *see* Yutian
Mugalzhar Taūlary *see* Mugodzhary, Gory
215 M5 **Muğan Düzü** *Rus.* Muganskaya Ravnina, Muganskaya Step'. *physical region* S Azerbaijan
243 I3 **Mugang** Hubei, E China 29°43′N 115°16′E
Muganskaya Ravnina/Muganskaya Step' *see* Muğan Düzü
172 B4 **Muge, Ribeira de** ≈ Santarém, Portugal
177 J6 **Múggia** Friuli-Venezia Giulia, NE Italy 45°36′N 13°48′E
233 H7 **Mughal Sarāi** Uttar Pradesh, N India 25°18′N 83°07′E
Mughla *see* Muğla
221 J6 **Mughshin** *var.* Muqshin. S Oman 19°26′N 54°38′E
229 K7 **Mughsu** *Rus.* Muksu. ≈ C Tajikistan
250 G6 **Mugi** Tokushima, Shikoku, SW Japan 33°39′N 134°24′E
214 B7 **Muğla** *var.* Mughla. Muğla, SW Turkey 37°13′N 28°22′E
214 B7 **Muğla** *var.* Mughla. ◈ *province* SW Turkey
226 E4 **Mugodzhary, Gory** *Kaz.* Mugalzhar Taūlary. ▲▲ W Kazakhstan
168 D5 **Mugron** Aquitaine, France 43°45′N 0°45′W
139 K2 **Mugulama** Zambézia, NE Mozambique 16°01′S 37°33′E
Muḥāfazat Hims *see* Ḥimṣ
217 K6 **Muḥammad** Wāsiţ, E Iraq 32°46′N 45°14′E
217 I5 **Muḥammadīyah** Al Anbār, C Iraq 33°22′N 42°48′E
129 K7 **Muhammad Qol** Red Sea, NE Sudan 20°53′N 37°09′E
129 J4 **Muhammad, Râs** *headland* E Egypt 27°45′N 34°18′E
Muhammerah *see* Khorramshahr
Muḥātazat Al 'Aqabah *see* Al 'Aqabah
220 E7 **Muhāyil** *var.* Mahāil. 'Asīr, SW Saudi Arabia 18°34′N 42°01′E
219 F14 **Muhaysh, Wādī al** *dry watercourse* Jordan
216 G5 **Muḥaywīr** Al Anbār, W Iraq 33°35′N 41°06′E
219 G10 **Muhayy** Jordan 30°59′N 35°52′E
181 F14 **Mühlacker** Baden-Württemberg, SW Germany 48°57′N 08°51′E
Mühlbach *see* Sebeş
181 J9 **Mühlberg** Thüringen, Germany 10°49′N 50°52′E
Mühldorf *see* Mühldorf am Inn
179 H12 **Mühldorf am Inn** *var.* Mühldorf. Bayern, SE Germany 48°14′N 12°32′E
181 J12 **Mühlhausen** Bayern, Germany 10°47′N 49°45′E
181 I9 **Mühlhausen** *var.* Mühlhausen in Thüringen. Thüringen, C Germany 51°13′N 10°28′E
Mühlhausen in Thüringen *see* Mühlhausen
293 I2 **Mühlig-Hofmann Mountains** ▲▲ Antarctica
152 H7 **Muhos** Oulu, C Finland 64°48′N 26°00′E
181 J14 **Muhr** Bayern, Germany 10°42′N 49°09′E
216 E4 **Mūḩ, Sabkhat al** ◎ C Syria
190 D4 **Muhu** *Ger.* Mohn, Moon. *island* W Estonia
137 B8 **Muhutwe** Kagera, NW Tanzania 01°31′S 31°41′E
Muhu Väin *see* Väinameri
162 F6 **Muiden** Noord-Holland, C Netherlands 52°19′N 05°04′E
284 E9 **Mui Hopohoponga** *headland* Tongatapu, S Tonga 21°09′S 175°02′W
253 B11 **Muika** *var.* Muikamachi. Niigata, Honshū, C Japan 37°04′N 138°53′E
Muikamachi *see* Muika
Muinchille *see* Cootehill
Muineachán *see* Monaghan
160 A3 **Muine Bheag** *Eng.* Bagenalstown. Carlow, SE Ireland 52°42′N 06°57′W
159 I1 **Muirdrum** E Scotland, United Kingdom 56°32′N 02°39′W
159 I2 **Muirhead** United Kingdom 56°30′N 3°04′W
158 G4 **Muirkirk** United Kingdom 55°31′N 4°03′W
104 B1 **Muisne** Esmeraldas, NW Ecuador 0°35′N 79°58′W
139 K1 **Muite** Nampula, NE Mozambique 14°02′S 39°06′E
87 N4 **Mujeres, Isla** *island* E Mexico
219 F9 **Mūjib, Wādī al** *dry watercourse* Jordan
250 A2 **Muju** Chŏlla-bukto, South Korea 36°0′N 127°40′E
188 C5 **Mukacheve** *Hung.* Munkács, *Rus.* Mukachevo. Zakarpats'ka Oblast', W Ukraine 48°27′N 22°45′E
Mukachevo *see* Mukacheve
258 I3 **Mukah** Sarawak, East Malaysia 02°56′N 112°02′E
Mukalla *see* Al Mukallā
Mukama *see* Mokāma
Mukāshafa/Mukashshafah *see* Mukayshīfah
252 E5 **Mu-kawa** ≈ Hokkaidō, NE Japan
219 F9 **Mukāwir** Jordan 31°34′N 35°38′E
217 I4 **Mukayshīfah** *var.* Mukāshafa, Mukashshafah. Şalāḩ ad Dīn, N Iraq 34°24′N 43°44′E
256 G7 **Mukdahan** Mukdahan, E Thailand 16°31′N 104°43′E
Mukden *see* Shenyang
218 I1 **Mukharram al Fawqānī** Syria 34°49′N 37°05′E
219 E8 **Mukhmās** West Bank 31°52′N 35°17′E
251 N9 **Mukojima-rettō** *Eng.* Parry group. *island group* SE Japan
228 G8 **Mukry** Lebap Welaýaty, E Turkmenistan 37°39′N 65°37′E
Muksu *see* Mughsu
233 K7 **Muktagacha** *var.* Muktagacha. N Bangladesh 24°46′N 90°16′E
Muktagacha *see* Muktagacha
137 A12 **Mukuku** Central, C Zambia 12°10′S 29°50′E
137 A12 **Mukupa Kaoma** Northern, NE Zambia 09°55′S 30°19′E
136 D7 **Mukutan** Rift Valley, W Kenya 01°06′N 36°16′E
138 D3 **Mukwe** Caprivi, NE Namibia 18°01′S 21°24′E
171 I7 **Mula** Murcia, SE Spain 38°02′N 01°29′W
235 C13 **Mulaku Atoll** *var.* Meemu Atoll, Mulaku Atoll. *atoll* C Maldives
Mulaku Atoll *see* Mulaku Atoll
138 G2 **Mulalika** Lusaka, C Zambia 15°37′S 28°48′E
247 L4 **Mulan** Heilongjiang, NE China 45°57′N 128°00′E
137 D14 **Mulanje** *var.* Mlanje. Southern, S Malawi 16°05′S 35°29′E
84 G4 **Mulatos** Sonora, NW Mexico 28°42′N 108°44′W
66 D8 **Mulberry Fork** ≈ Alabama, S USA
83 H6 **Mulchatna River** ≈ Alaska, USA
195 L3 **Mul'da** Respublika Komi, NW Russian Federation 67°29′N 63°55′E
179 G8 **Mulde** ≈ E Germany
75 G12 **Muldrow** Oklahoma, C USA 35°25′N 94°34′W
84 D5 **Mulegé** Baja California Sur, NW Mexico 26°54′N 112°00′W
135 H9 **Mulenda** Kasai-Oriental, C Dem. Rep. Congo 04°19′S 24°55′E
70 D3 **Muleshoe** Texas, SW USA 34°13′N 102°43′W
139 K2 **Mulevala** Zambézia, NE Mozambique 16°25′S 37°35′E
181 H13 **Mulfingen** Baden-Württemberg, Germany 9°48′N 49°20′E
170 G8 **Mulhacén** *var.* Cerro de Mulhacén. ▲ S Spain 37°07′N 03°11′W
Mulhacén, Cerro de *see* Mulhacén
Mülhausen *see* Mulhouse
179 C13 **Mülheim** Baden-Württemberg, SW Germany 47°50′N 07°37′E
181 C8 **Mülheim** *var.* Mulheim an der Ruhr. Nordrhein-Westfalen, W Germany 51°25′N 06°50′E
Mulheim an der Ruhr *see* Mülheim
165 K4 **Mulhouse** *Ger.* Mülhausen. Haut-Rhin, NE France 47°45′N 07°20′E
240 C5 **Muli** *var.* Qiaowa, Muli Zangzu Zizhixian. Sichuan, C China 27°49′N 101°10′E
261 L7 **Muli** *channel* Papua, E Indonesia
248 E1 **Muling** Heilongjiang, NE China 44°54′N 130°35′E
Muli Zangzu Zizhixian *see* Muli
Mullach Íde *see* Malahide
160 B2 **Mullaghcleevaun** ▲ Wicklow, Ireland 53°06′N 6°25′W
158 A7 **Mullaghmore** Sligo, Ireland 54°28′N 8°27′W
Mullaitivu *see* Mullaittivu
235 G9 **Mullaittivu** *var.* Mullaitivu. Northern Province, N Sri Lanka 09°15′N 80°48′E
76 G4 **Mullan** Idaho, NW USA 47°28′N 115°48′W
74 C7 **Mullen** Nebraska, C USA 42°02′N 101°01′W
277 K4 **Mullengudgery** New South Wales, SE Australia 31°42′S 147°24′E
67 I4 **Mullens** West Virginia, NE USA 37°34′N 81°22′W
Müller-gerbergte *see* Muller, Pegunungan
259 J4 **Muller, Pegunungan** *Dut.* Müller-gerbergte ▲▲ Borneo, C Indonesia
261 M6 **Muller Range** ▲▲ W Papua New Guinea
141 K5 **Mullers Pass** *pass* KwaZulu-Natal, South Africa
72 G5 **Mullett Lake** ◎ Michigan, N USA
64 G8 **Mullica River** ≈ New Jersey, NE USA
70 G5 **Mullin** Texas, SW USA 31°33′N 98°40′W
160 A4 **Mullinavat** Kilkenny, Ireland 52°22′N 7°10′W
158 C9 **Mullingar** *Ir.* An Muileann gCearr. C Ireland 53°32′N 07°20′W
67 K8 **Mullins** South Carolina, SE USA 34°12′N 79°15′W
160 D10 **Mullion** United Kingdom 50°02′N 5°14′W
158 E2 **Mull, Isle of** *island* W Scotland, United Kingdom
197 J3 **Mullovka** Ul'yanovskaya Oblast', W Russian Federation 54°13′N 49°19′E
155 G10 **Mullsjö** Västra Götaland, S Sweden 57°56′N 13°55′E
158 E1 **Mull, Sound of** *strait* NW Scotland, United Kingdom
277 M2 **Mullumbimby** New South Wales, SE Australia 28°34′S 153°28′E
180 G4 **Mulmshorn** Niedersachsen, Germany 9°18′N 53°10′E
138 F2 **Mulobezi** Western, SW Zambia 16°48′S 25°11′E
135 D13 **Mulondo** Huíla, SW Angola 15°41′S 15°09′E
138 E2 **Mulonga Plain** *plain* W Zambia
135 I10 **Mulongo** Katanga, SE Dem. Rep. Congo 07°44′S 26°57′E
166 E7 **Mulsanne** Pays de la Loire, France 47°54′N 0°15′E
231 I6 **Multān** Punjab, E Pakistan 30°12′N 71°30′E
153 H8 **Multia** Länsi-Suomi, C Finland 62°27′N 24°49′E
Mulucha *see* Moulouya
138 G1 **Mulungushi** Central, C Zambia 14°15′S 28°27′E
139 H1 **Mulungwe** Central, C Zambia 13°57′S 29°51′E
Muluya *see* Moulouya
75 E11 **Mulvane** Kansas, C USA 37°28′N 97°14′W
277 J6 **Mulwala** New South Wales, SE Australia 35°59′S 146°00′E
Mulwiya *see* Moulouya
277 H4 **Mulyungarie** South Australia 31°29′S 140°45′E
225 E10 **Mumbai** *prev.* Bombay. *state capital* Mahārāshtra, W India 18°56′N 72°51′E
234 C4 **Mumbai** ✈ Mahārāshtra, W India 19°10′N 72°51′E
135 D13 **Mumbué** Bié, C Angola 13°52′S 17°15′E
280 B3 **Mumeng** Morobe, C Papua New Guinea 06°57′S 146°34′E
261 J4 **Mumi** Papua, E Indonesia 01°33′S 134°09′E
Muminabad/Mŭ'minobod *see* Leningrad
197 J8 **Mumra** Astrakhanskaya Oblast', SW Russian Federation 45°46′N 47°46′E
87 L5 **Muna** Yucatán, SE Mexico 20°29′N 89°41′W
193 I5 **Muna** ≈ NE Russian Federation
232 B6 **Munābāo** Rājasthān, NW India 25°46′N 70°19′E
Munamägi *see* Suur Munamägi
260 D6 **Muna, Pulau** *prev.* Moena. *island* C Indonesia
260 D6 **Muna, Selat** *strait* Sulawesi, C Indonesia
179 G10 **Münchberg** Bayern, E Germany 50°10′N 11°50′E
179 G13 **München** *var.* Muenchen, *Eng.* Munich, *It.* Monaco. Bayern, SE Germany 48°09′N 11°34′E
München-Gladbach *see* Mönchengladbach
176 D3 **Münchenstein** Basel-Land, NW Switzerland 47°31′N 07°38′E
181 F9 **Münchhausen** Hessen, Germany 8°43′N 50°57′E
54 C5 **Muncho Lake** British Columbia, W Canada 58°52′N 125°40′W
181 D14 **Münchweiler Rodalb** Rheinland-Pfalz, Germany 7°42′N 49°13′E
73 F10 **Muncie** Indiana, N USA 40°11′N 85°22′W
64 D5 **Muncy** Pennsylvania, NE USA 41°10′N 76°46′W
281 H2 **Munda** New Georgia, NW Solomon Islands 08°15′S 157°15′E
57 J5 **Mundare** Alberta, SW Canada 53°34′N 112°20′W
70 F4 **Munday** Texas, SW USA 33°27′N 99°37′W
73 D8 **Mundelein** Illinois, N USA 42°15′N 88°00′W
181 H8 **Münden** Niedersachsen, C Germany 52°16′N 08°54′E
161 M2 **Mundesley** United Kingdom 52°52′N 1°25′E
161 L3 **Mundford** E England, United Kingdom 52°30′N 00°39′E
171 H7 **Mundo** ≈ S Spain
277 L1 **Mundubbera** Queensland, Australia
135 C11 **Munenga** Cuanza Sul, NW Angola 10°03′S 14°40′E
171 H6 **Munera** Castilla-La Mancha, C Spain 39°03′N 02°29′W
66 B6 **Munford** Tennessee, S USA 35°27′N 89°49′W
66 E4 **Munfordville** Kentucky, S USA 37°17′N 85°55′W
276 E3 **Mungala** South Australia 30°36′S 132°57′E
277 K1 **Mungallala** Queensland, Australia
139 I3 **Mungári** Manica, C Mozambique 17°09′S 33°33′E
134 I6 **Mungbere** Orientale, NE Dem. Rep. Congo 02°38′N 28°30′E
233 I7 **Munger** *prev.* Monghyr. Bihār, NE India 25°23′N 86°28′E
276 G2 **Mungeranie** South Australia 28°02′S 138°42′E
Mu Nggava *see* Rennell
259 H4 **Mungguresak, Tanjung** *headland* Borneo, N Indonesia 01°57′N 109°19′E
Mungiki *see* Bellona
277 K2 **Mungindi** New South Wales, SE Australia 28°59′S 149°00′E
Mungkawn *see* Maingkwan
233 K8 **Mungla** *var.* Mungla. Khulna, S Bangladesh 22°18′N 89°34′E
Mungla *see* Mungla
135 D12 **Mungo** Huambo, W Angola 11°49′S 16°16′E
168 A6 **Munguia** Pais Vasco, Spain 43°21′N 2°50′W
282 B4 **Munguuy Bay** *bay* Yap, W Micronesia
135 E12 **Munhango** Bié, C Angola 12°12′S 18°34′E
110 D7 **Munhoz** Minas Gerais, Brazil 22°37′S 46°22′W
280 G8 **Munia** *island* Lau Group, E Fiji
Munich *see* München
172 F2 **Muñico** Castilla y León, Spain 40°42′N 5°01′W
171 I4 **Muniesa** Aragón, NE Spain 41°02′N 00°49′W
72 E4 **Munising** Michigan, N USA 46°24′N 86°39′W
111 K4 **Muniz Freire** Espírito Santo, Brazil 20°28′S 41°25′W
Munkács *see* Mukacheve
155 E9 **Munkedal** Västra Götaland, S Sweden 58°28′N 11°38′E
154 F7 **Munkfors** Värmland, C Sweden 59°50′N 13°35′E
163 C10 **Munkzwalm** Oost-Vlaanderen, NW Belgium 50°53′N 03°44′E
256 G7 **Mun, Mae Nam** ≈ E Thailand
233 K8 **Munshiganj** Dhaka, C Bangladesh 23°32′N 90°32′E
167 N9 **Münsingen** Bern, W Switzerland 46°53′N 07°34′E
165 K4 **Munster** Haut-Rhin, NE France 48°03′N 07°09′E
180 H4 **Munster** Niedersachsen, NW Germany 52°59′N 10°07′E
180 D7 **Münster** *var.* Muenster, Münster in Westfalen. Nordrhein-Westfalen, W Germany 51°58′N 07°38′E
176 D5 **Münster** Valais, S Switzerland 46°31′N 08°18′E
157 A10 **Munster** *Ir.* Cúige Mumhan. *cultural region* S Ireland
Münsterberg in Schlesien *see* Ziębice
Münster in Westfalen *see* Münster
180 D7 **Münsterland** *cultural region* NW Germany
181 D11 **Münstermaifeld** Rheinland-Pfalz, Germany 7°22′N 50°15′E
180 D6 **Münster-Osnabruck** ✈ Nordrhein-Westfalen, NW Germany 52°08′N 07°41′E
72 G4 **Munuscong Lake** ◎ Michigan, N USA
139 H3 **Munyati** ≈ C Zimbabwe
177 I2 **Münzkirchen** Oberösterreich, N Austria 48°29′N 13°37′E
152 G5 **Muodoslompolo** Norrbotten, N Sweden 67°57′N 23°31′E
152 I6 **Muojärvi** ◎ NE Finland
256 H5 **Mương Khến** Hoa Binh, N Vietnam 20°34′N 105°18′E
Muong Sai *see* Xai
256 F5 **Muong Xiang Ngeun** *var.* Xieng Ngeun. Louangphabang, N Laos 19°43′N 102°09′E
152 G5 **Muonio** Lappi, N Finland 67°58′N 23°40′E
Muonioälv/Muoniojoki *see* Muonionjoki
152 G5 **Muonionjoki** *var.* Muoniojoki, *Swe.* Muonioälv. ≈ Finland/Sweden
139 J3 **Mupa** ≈ C Mozambique
245 M5 **Muping** Shandong, E China 37°23′N 121°35′E
138 D3 **Mupini** Okavango, NE Namibia 17°55′S 19°34′E
136 B1 **Muqaddam, Wadi** ≈ N Sudan
216 E6 **Muqāţ** Al Mafraq, E Jordan 32°28′N 38°04′E
223 I10 **Muqaz** N Oman 24°13′N 56°48′E
136 H7 **Muqdisho** *Eng.* Mogadishu, *It.* Mogadiscio. ● (Somalia) Banaadir, S Somalia 02°06′N 45°27′E
136 H7 **Muqdisho** ✈ Banaadir, E Somalia 01°58′N 45°18′E
Muqshin *see* Mughshin
111 L5 **Muquy** Espírito Santo, Brazil 20°57′S 41°18′W
177 J4 **Mur** *SCr.* Mura. ≈ C Europe
Mura *see* Mur
215 K6 **Muradiye** Van, E Turkey 39°N 43°44′E
Muragarazi *see* Maragarazi
253 C10 **Murakami** Niigata, Honshū, C Japan 38°13′N 139°28′E
117 B12 **Murallón, Cerro** ▲ S Argentina 49°49′S 73°25′W
137 A9 **Muramvya** C Burundi 03°18′S 29°41′E
137 D8 **Murang'a** *prev.* Fort Hall. Central, SW Kenya 0°43′S 37°10′E
136 D6 **Murangering** Rift Valley, NW Kenya 03°48′N 35°29′E
Murapara *see* Murupara
220 E3 **Murār, Bi'r al** *well* NW Saudi Arabia
195 I8 **Murashi** Kirovskaya Oblast', NW Russian Federation 59°27′N 48°02′E
169 H3 **Murat** Cantal, C France 45°07′N 02°52′E
168 G2 **Murat** Limousin, France 45°29′N 2°15′E
195 M8 **Muratkovo** Sverdlovskaya Oblast', Russian Federation
215 I6 **Murat Nehri** *var.* Eastern Euphrates; *anc.* Arsanias. ≈ NE Turkey
169 H5 **Murat-sur-Vèbre** Midi-Pyrénées, France 43°42′N 2°52′E
175 C10 **Muravera** Sardegna, Italy, C Mediterranean Sea 39°24′N 09°34′E
253 D10 **Murayama** Yamagata, Honshū, C Japan 38°29′N 140°21′E
199 J8 **Muraysah, Ra's al** *headland* N Libya 31°58′N 25°00′E
172 D1 **Murça** Vila Real, N Portugal 41°24′N 07°28′W
136 J3 **Murcanyo** Bari, NE Somalia 11°39′N 50°27′E
222 F5 **Mūrcheh Khvort** *var.* Morcheh Khort. Eşfahān, C Iran 33°07′N 51°26′E
279 E8 **Murchison** Tasman, South Island, New Zealand 41°48′S 172°19′E
278 A11 **Murchison Mountains** ▲▲ South Island, New Zealand
274 D6 **Murchison River** ≈ Western Australia
171 I7 **Murcia** Murcia, SE Spain 37°59′N 01°08′W
171 H7 **Murcia** ◈ *autonomous community* SE Spain
165 H7 **Mur-de-Barrez** Aveyron, S France 44°48′N 02°39′E
166 G8 **Mur-de-Sologne** Centre, France 47°25′N 1°37′E
276 F5 **Murdinga** South Australia 33°46′S 135°46′E
74 C5 **Murdo** South Dakota, N USA 43°53′N 100°42′W
59 J7 **Murdochville** Québec, SE Canada 48°57′N 65°30′W
111 J5 **Mureai** Minas Gerais, Brazil 21°18′S 42°24′W
177 L4 **Mureck** Steiermark, SE Austria 46°42′N 15°46′E
187 K3 **Murefte** Turkey 40°40′N 27°15′E
185 J1 **Mureş** ◈ *county* N Romania
144 E7 **Mureş** ≈ Hungary/Romania
Mureş *see* Maros
Mureşul *see* Maros/Mureş
165 H8 **Muret** Haute-Garonne, S France 43°28′N 01°19′E
75 G13 **Murfreesboro** Arkansas, C USA 34°04′N 93°42′W
67 L5 **Murfreesboro** North Carolina, SE USA 36°26′N 77°06′W
66 E6 **Murfreesboro** Tennessee, S USA 35°50′N 86°25′W
Murgab *see* Morghāb, Daryā-ye/Murgap
Murgab *see* Murghob
228 F8 **Murgap** Mary Welaýaty, S Turkmenistan 37°19′N 61°48′E
228 F9 **Murgap** *var* Deryasy Murgap, Murghab, *Pash.* Daryā-ye Morghāb, *Rus.* Murgab. ≈ Afghanistan/Turkmenistan *see also* Morghāb, Daryā-ye
Murgap *see* Morghāb, Daryā-ye
Murgap, Deryasy *see* Morghāb, Daryā-ye/Murgap
185 J6 **Murgash** ▲ W Bulgaria 42°51′N 23°58′E
Murghab *see* Morghāb, Daryā-ye/Murgap
229 L7 **Murghob** *Rus.* Murgab. SE Tajikistan 38°11′N 74°E
229 K7 **Murghob** *Rus.* Murgab. ≈ SE Tajikistan
277 M1 **Murgon** Queensland, E Australia 26°08′S 152°04′E
284 G10 **Muri** Rarotonga, S Cook Islands 21°15′S 159°44′W
176 D4 **Muri** *var.* Muri bei Bern. Bern, W Switzerland 46°55′N 07°30′E
170 E2 **Murias de Paredes** Castilla-León, N Spain 42°51′N 06°11′W
Muri bei Bern *see* Muri
135 F11 **Muriege** Lunda Sul, NE Angola 09°55′S 21°12′E
282 G6 **Murilo Atoll** *atoll* Hall Islands, C Micronesia
Mūrītānīyah *see* Mauritania
178 H5 **Müritz** *var.* Müritzee. ◎ NE Germany
Müritzee *see* Müritz
178 G5 **Müritz-Elde-Kanal** *canal* N Germany
278 G3 **Muriwai Beach** Auckland, North Island, New Zealand 36°56′S 174°28′E
152 G6 **Murjek** Norrbotten, N Sweden 66°27′N 20°54′E
194 E2 **Murmansk** Murmanskaya Oblast', NW Russian Federation 68°59′N 33°08′E
194 E3 **Murmanskaya Oblast'** ◈ *province* NW Russian Federation
295 K2 **Murmansk Rise** *undersea feature* SW Barents Sea 71°00′N 37°00′E
194 E2 **Murmashi** Murmanskaya Oblast', NW Russian Federation 68°49′N 32°43′E
196 G2 **Murmino** Ryazanskaya Oblast', W Russian Federation 54°31′N 40°01′E
179 F13 **Murnau** Bayern, SE Germany 47°41′N 11°12′E
175 B8 **Muro, Capo di** *headland* Corse, France, C Mediterranean Sea 41°45′N 08°40′E
175 H9 **Muro Lucano** Basilicata, S Italy 40°48′N 15°33′E
197 H2 **Murom** Vladimirskaya Oblast', W Russian Federation 55°33′N 42°03′E
192 E7 **Muromtsevo** Omskaya Oblast', C Russian Federation 56°18′N 75°15′E
252 D5 **Muroran** Hokkaidō, NE Japan 42°20′N 140°58′E
170 C2 **Muros** Galicia, NW Spain 42°47′N 09°04′W
170 C2 **Muros e Noia, Ría de** *estuary* NW Spain
250 G6 **Muroto** Kōchi, Shikoku, SW Japan 33°16′N 134°10′E
250 G6 **Muroto-zaki** Shikoku, SW Japan
188 F5 **Murovani Kurylivtsi** Vinnyts'ka Oblast', C Ukraine 48°43′N 27°31′E
182 E5 **Murowana Goślina** Wielkolpolskie, W Poland 52°33′N 16°59′E
76 F7 **Murphy** Idaho, NW USA 43°14′N 116°36′W
66 G7 **Murphy** North Carolina, SE USA 35°05′N 84°02′W
80 D3 **Murphys** California, W USA 38°07′N 120°27′W
73 C13 **Murphysboro** Illinois, N USA 37°45′N 89°20′W
75 G8 **Murray** Iowa, C USA 41°03′N 93°56′W
66 C5 **Murray** Kentucky, S USA 36°35′N 88°20′W
276 G6 **Murray Bridge** South Australia 35°10′S 139°17′E
267 M1 **Murray Fracture Zone** *tectonic feature* NE Pacific Ocean
261 M7 **Murray, Lake** ◎ SW Papua New Guinea
67 I8 **Murray, Lake** ⊠ South Carolina, SE USA
53 J7 **Murray Maxwell Bay** *coastal sea feature* Nunavut, NE Canada
54 C4 **Murray, Mount** ▲ Yukon Territory, NW Canada 60°49′N 128°57′W
Murray Range *see* Murray Ridge
288 G5 **Murray Ridge** *var.* Murray Range. *undersea feature* N Arabian Sea 21°45′N 61°50′E
277 H5 **Murray River** ≈ SE Australia
140 G8 **Murraysburg** Western Cape, South Africa 31°57′S 23°45′E
277 H6 **Murrayville** Victoria, SE Australia 35°17′S 141°12′E
231 J4 **Murree** Punjab, E Pakistan 33°55′N 73°26′E
181 G14 **Murrhardt** Baden-Württemberg, S Germany 49°00′N 09°34′E
81 E12 **Murrieta** California, USA 33°33′N 117°13′W
81 E12 **Murrieta Hot Springs** California, USA 33°34′N 117°09′W
161 K3 **Murrow** United Kingdom 52°38′N 0°01′E
277 J5 **Murrumbidgee River** ≈ New South Wales, SE Australia
139 K2 **Murrupula** Nampula, NE Mozambique 15°26′S 38°46′E
277 L4 **Murrurundi** New South Wales, SE Australia 31°47′S 150°51′E
177 L4 **Murska Sobota** *Ger.* Olsnitz. NE Slovenia 46°41′N 16°09′E
234 E4 **Murtajāpur** *prev.* Murtazapur. Mahārāshtra, C India 20°43′N 77°28′E
133 I8 **Murtala Muhammed** ✈ (Lagos) Ogun, SW Nigeria 06°31′N 03°12′E
Murtazapur *see* Murtajāpur
176 C4 **Murten** Neuchâtel, W Switzerland 46°55′N 07°06′E
Murtensee *see* Morat, Lac de
277 I6 **Murtoa** Victoria, SE Australia 36°39′S 142°27′E
152 I6 **Murtovaara** Oulu, E Finland 65°40′N 29°25′E
Murua Island *see* Woodlark Island
234 C5 **Murud** Mahārāshtra, W India 18°27′N 72°56′E
278 I5 **Murupara** *var.* Murapara. Bay of Plenty, North Island, New Zealand 38°27′S 176°41′E
285 K8 **Mururoa** *var.* Moruroa. *atoll* Îles Tuamotu, SE French Polynesia
Murviedro *see* Sagunto
169 H6 **Murviel** Languedoc-Roussillon, France 43°26′N 3°08′E
232 G8 **Murwāra** Madhya Pradesh, N India 23°50′N 80°23′E
277 M2 **Murwillumbah** New South Wales, SE Australia 28°20′S 153°24′E
191 J9 **Murygino** Smolenskaya Oblast', Russian Federation
228 E6 **Murzechirla** *prev.* Mirzachirla. Ahal Welaýaty, C Turkmenistan 39°33′N 60°02′E
Murzuk *see* Murzuq
128 C5 **Murzuq** *var.* Marzūq, Murzuk. SW Libya 25°55′N 13°55′E
Murzuq, Edeyin *see* Murzuq, Idhān
128 B4 **Murzuq, Ḩamādat** *plateau* W Libya
128 C5 **Murzuq, Idhān** *var.* Edeyin Murzuq. *desert* SW Libya
177 L3 **Mürzzuschlag** Steiermark, E Austria 47°35′N 15°41′E
215 I6 **Muş** *var.* Mush. Muş, E Turkey 38°45′N 41°30′E
215 J6 **Muş** *var.* Mush. ◈ *province* E Turkey
190 D7 **Mūša** ≈ Latvia/Lithuania
280 C4 **Musa** ≈ S Papua New Guinea
129 J4 **Mûsa, Gebel** *var.* Gebel Mûsa. ▲ NE Egypt 28°33′N 33°51′E
Mûsa, Gebel *see* Mûsa, Gebel
Musaiyib *see* Al Musayyib
Musa Khel *see* Mūsa Khel Bāzār
231 H6 **Mūsa Khel Bāzār** *var.* Musa Khel. Baluchistān, SW Pakistan 30°53′N 69°52′E
185 I7 **Musala** ▲ W Bulgaria 42°12′N 23°36′E
258 C4 **Musala, Pulau** *island* W Indonesia
138 G2 **Musale** Southern, S Zambia 15°27′S 26°50′E
221 K5 **Muşalla** NE Oman 22°20′N 58°03′E
221 K3 **Musandam Peninsula** *Ar.* Masandam Peninsula. *peninsula* N Oman
Musay'īd *see* Umm Sa'īd
Muscat *see* Masqaţ
Muscat and Oman *see* Oman
74 I7 **Muscatine** Iowa, C USA 41°25′N 91°03′W
Muscat Sīb Airport *see* Seeb
73 E12 **Muscatuck River** ≈ Indiana, N USA
261 N5 **Muschu Island** *island* NW Papua New Guinea
72 B7 **Muscoda** Wisconsin, N USA 43°11′N 90°27′W
278 D10 **Musgrave, Mount** ▲ South Island, New Zealand 43°48′S 170°43′E
276 D1 **Musgrave Ranges** ▲▲ South Australia
Mush *see* Muş
219 F14 **Mushāsh al Kabid, Wādī** *dry watercourse* Jordan
216 C8 **Mushayyish, Qaşr al** *castle* Ma'ān, C Jordan
219 F14 **Mushayyish, Wādī al** *dry watercourse* Jordan
135 D8 **Mushie** Bandundu, W Dem. Rep. Congo 03°00′S 16°55′E
258 F6 **Musi, Air** *prev.* Moesi. ≈ Sumatera, W Indonesia
286 G3 **Musicians Seamounts** *undersea feature* N Pacific Ocean
141 K1 **Musina** Limpopo, South Africa 22°21′S 30°02′E
139 H5 **Musina** *prev.* Messina. Limpopo, NE South Africa 22°18′S 30°02′E
102 B4 **Musinga, Alto** ▲ NW Colombia 06°49′N 76°24′W
74 F1 **Muskeg Bay** *lake bay* Minnesota, N USA
72 F7 **Muskegon** Michigan, N USA 43°13′N 86°15′W
72 F7 **Muskegon Heights** Michigan, N USA 43°12′N 86°14′W
72 F7 **Muskegon River** ≈ Michigan, N USA
73 I11 **Muskingum River** ≈ Ohio, N USA
155 I8 **Muskö** Stockholm, C Sweden 58°58′N 18°10′E
Muskogean *see* Tallahassee
75 F12 **Muskogee** Oklahoma, C USA 35°45′N 95°21′W
62 D3 **Muskoka, Lake** ◎ Ontario, S Canada
136 D1 **Musmar** Red Sea, NE Sudan 18°13′N 35°40′E
218 E6 **Muşmuş** Israel 32°32′N 35°09′E
138 G1 **Musofu** Central, C Zambia 13°31′S 29°02′E
137 C8 **Musoma** Mara, N Tanzania 01°31′S 33°49′E
139 H1 **Musoro** Central, C Zambia 13°21′S 31°04′E
280 D1 **Mussau Island** *island* NE Papua New Guinea
159 I3 **Musselburgh** United Kingdom 55°56′N 3°03′W
162 J4 **Musselkanaal** Groningen, NE Netherlands 52°55′N 07°01′E
77 K4 **Musselshell River** ≈ Montana, NW USA
135 D11 **Mussende** Cuanza Sul, NW Angola 10°33′S 16°02′E
168 E3 **Mussidan** Dordogne, SW France 45°03′N 00°22′E
163 G14 **Musson** Luxembourg, SE Belgium 49°33′N 05°42′E
232 F4 **Mussoorie** Uttarakhand, N India 30°26′N 78°04′E
Musta *see* Mosta
232 G7 **Mustafābād** Uttar Pradesh, N India 25°54′N 81°17′E
214 B5 **Mustafakemalpaşa** Bursa, NW Turkey 40°03′N 28°25′E
Mustafa-Pasha *see* Svilengrad
136 G6 **Mustahīl** Sumalē, E Ethiopia 05°18′N 44°34′E
70 D4 **Mustang Draw** *valley* Texas, SW USA
71 H9 **Mustang Island** *island* Texas, SW USA
Mustasaari *see* Korsholm
Mustér *see* Disentis
117 C9 **Musters, Lago** ◎ S Argentina
103 I1 **Mustique** *island* C Saint Vincent and the Grenadines
190 E5 **Mustla** Viljandimaa, S Estonia 58°12′N 25°50′E
159 M7 **Muston** United Kingdom 54°13′N 0°19′W
194 C8 **Mustvee** Estonia
190 F4 **Mustvee** *Ger.* Tschorna. Jõgevamaa, E Estonia 58°51′N 26°59′E
88 G5 **Musún, Cerro** ▲ NE Nicaragua 13°01′N 85°02′W
277 L4 **Muswellbrook** New South Wales, SE Australia 32°17′S 150°55′E
183 H9 **Muszyna** Małopolskie, SE Poland 49°21′N 20°54′E
129 H5 **Mūţ** *var.* Mut. C Egypt 25°28′N 28°58′E
214 E8 **Mut** İçel, S Turkey 36°38′N 33°27′E
177 K5 **Muta** N Slovenia 46°37′N 15°09′E
285 I9 **Mutalau** N Niue 18°56′S 169°50′E
Mu-tan-chiang *see* Mudanjiang
138 F1 **Mutanda** North Western, NW Zambia 12°24′S 26°13′E
109 H8 **Mutá, Ponta do** *headland* E Brazil 13°54′S 38°54′W
139 I3 **Mutare** *var.* Mutari; *prev.* Umtali. Manicaland, E Zimbabwe 18°55′S 32°36′E
Mutari *see* Mutare
102 B4 **Mutatá** Antioquia, NW Colombia 07°16′N 76°32′W
159 H2 **Muthill** United Kingdom 56°19′N 3°50′W
Mutina *see* Modena
261 M7 **Muting** Papua, E Indonesia 07°10′S 140°41′E
139 I3 **Mutoko** *prev.* Mtoko. Mashonaland East, NE Zimbabwe 17°24′S 32°13′E
137 E9 **Mutomo** Eastern, S Kenya 01°50′S 38°13′E
193 H6 **Mutoray** Evenkiyskiy Avtonomnyy Okrug, C Russian Federation 61°30′N 101°00′E
Mutrah *see* Maţraḩ
Mutsamudu *see* Moutsamudou
135 G11 **Mutshatsha** Katanga, S Dem. Rep. Congo 10°40′S 24°26′E
252 D7 **Mutsu** *var.* Mutu. Aomori, Honshū, N Japan 41°18′N 141°11′E
252 D7 **Mutsu-wan** *bay* N Japan
167 N8 **Muttenz** Basel-Land, NW Switzerland 47°31′N 07°39′E
181 E13 **Mutterstadt** Rheinland-Pfalz, Germany 8°21′N 49°26′E
278 B13 **Muttonbird Islands** *island group* SW New Zealand
Muttra *see* Mathura
Mutu *see* Mutsu
139 J2 **Mutuáli** Nampula, N Mozambique 14°51′S 37°01′E
111 K3 **Mutum** Minas Gerais, Brazil 19°49′S 41°26′W
135 D12 **Mutumbo** Bié, C Angola 13°10′S 17°22′E
283 I9 **Mutunte, Mount** *var.* Mount Buache. ▲ Kosrae, E Micronesia 05°21′N 163°00′E
235 G10 **Mutur** Eastern Province, E Sri Lanka 08°27′N 81°15′E
140 G8 **Muuniksspoort pass** Eastern Cape, South Africa
152 H6 **Muurola** Lappi, NW Finland 66°22′N 25°20′E
244 E4 **Mu Us Shadi** *var.* Ordos Desert; *prev.* Mu Us Shamo. *desert* N China
Mu Us Shamo *see* Mu Us Shadi
135 C11 **Muxima** Bengo, NW Angola 09°33′S 13°58′E
194 E6 **Muyezerskiy** Respublika Kareliya, NW Russian Federation 63°54′N 32°00′E
87 N5 **Muyil** Quintana Roo, Mexico 20°04′N 87°37′W
137 A9 **Muyinga** NE Burundi 02°54′S 30°19′E
88 G6 **Muy Muy** Matagalpa, C Nicaragua 12°43′N 85°35′W
Muynak *see* Mo'ynoq
228 D3 **Mŭynoq** Qoraqalpog'iston Respublikasi, NW Uzbekistan 43°45′N 59°03′E
135 I10 **Muyumba** Katanga, SE Dem. Rep. Congo 07°13′S 27°02′E
231 J3 **Muzaffarābād** Jammu and Kashmir, NE Pakistan 34°23′N 73°34′E
231 I6 **Muzaffargarh** Punjab, E Pakistan 30°04′N 71°15′E
232 F5 **Muzaffarnagar** Uttar Pradesh, N India 29°28′N 77°42′E
233 I6 **Muzaffarpur** Bihār, N India 26°07′N 85°23′E
110 D5 **Muzambinho** Minas Gerais, Brazil 21°22′S 46°32′W
238 D4 **Muzat He** ≈ W China
139 H2 **Muze** Tete, NW Mozambique 15°05′S 31°16′E
195 M4 **Muzhi** Yamalo-Nenetskiy Avtonomnyy Okrug, N Russian Federation 65°25′N 64°28′E
164 E4 **Muzillac** Morbihan, NW France 47°34′N 02°30′W
Muzkol, Khrebet *see* Muzqŭl, Qatorkŭhi
184 G3 **Mužlja** *Hung.* Felsőmuzslya; *prev.* Gornja Mužlja. Vojvodina, N Serbia 45°21′N 20°25′E
102 C5 **Muzo** Boyacá, C Colombia 05°34′N 74°07′W
138 G2 **Muzoka** Southern, S Zambia 16°39′S 27°18′E
83 M8 **Muzon, Cape** *headland* Dall Island, Alaska, USA 54°39′N 132°41′W
85 K5 **Múzquiz** Coahuila, NE Mexico 27°54′N 101°30′W
229 K7 **Muzqŭl, Qatorkŭhi** *Rus.* Khrebet Muzkol. ▲▲ SE Tajikistan
238 D6 **Muz Tag** ▲ NW China 36°02′N 80°13′E
238 F6 **Muztag** ▲ W China 36°26′N 87°15′E
238 B5 **Muztagata** ▲ NW China 38°16′N 75°03′E
141 K6 **Mvoti** ≈ KwaZulu-Natal, South Africa
139 H3 **Mvuma** *prev.* Umvuma. Midlands, C Zimbabwe 19°17′S 30°32′E
139 I1 **Mwanya** Eastern, E Zambia 12°40′S 32°15′E
135 H10 **Mwanza** Katanga, SE Dem. Rep. Congo 07°49′S 26°49′E
137 B9 **Mwanza** Mwanza, NW Tanzania 02°31′S 32°56′E
137 B9 **Mwanza** ◈ *region* N Tanzania
139 I1 **Mwase Lundazi** Eastern, E Zambia 12°26′S 33°20′E
157 B9 **Mweelrea** *Ir.* Caoc Maol Réidh. ▲ W Ireland 53°37′N 09°47′W
135 F9 **Mweka** Kasai-Occidental, C Dem. Rep. Congo 04°52′S 21°38′E
137 A12 **Mwenda** Luapula, N Zambia 10°30′S 30°21′E
135 G10 **Mwene-Ditu** Kasai-Oriental, S Dem. Rep. Congo 07°06′S 23°34′E
141 L1 **Mwenezi** ≈ S Zimbabwe
135 I8 **Mwenga** Sud-Kivu, E Dem. Rep. Congo 03°00′S 28°28′E

◆ Country
● Country Capital
◇ Dependent Territory
○ Dependent Territory Capital
◈ Administrative Regions
✈ International Airport
▲ Mountain
▲▲ Mountain Range
Volcano
≈ River
◎ Lake
⊠ Reservoir

INDEX
379

Mweru, Lake - Nares Plain

135 I11 **Mweru, Lake** var. Lac Moero. ◎ Dem. Rep. Congo/ Zambia
135 G12 **Mwinilunga** North Western, NW Zambia 11°44′S 24°24′E
283 I6 **Mwokil Atoll** prev. Mokil Atoll. atoll Caroline Islands, E Micronesia
Myadel' see Myadzyel
191 F8 **Myadzyel** Pol. Miadzioł Nowy, Rus. Myadel'. Minskaya Voblasts', N Belarus 54°51′N 26°51′E
232 B6 **Myājlār** var. Miajlar. Rājasthān, NW India 26°16′N 70°21′E
190 G5 **Myakisevo** Pskovskaya Oblast', Russian Federation
193 L5 **Myakit** Magadanskaya Oblast', E Russian Federation 61°23′N 151°58′E
69 L7 **Myakka River** Florida, SE USA
194 F9 **Myaksa** Vologodskaya Oblast', NW Russian Federation 58°54′N 38°15′E
277 M4 **Myall Lake** ◎ New South Wales, SE Australia
256 C6 **Myanaung** Ayeyarwady, SW Myanmar (Burma) 18°17′N 95°19′E
256 D4 **Myanmar** off. Union of Myanmar, Myanmar. ◆ military dictatorship SE Asia
256 C6 **Myaungmya** Ayeyarwady, SW Myanmar (Burma) 16°33′N 94°55′E
Myaydo see Allanmyo
190 H7 **Myazha** Rus. Mezha. Vitsyebskaya Voblasts', NE Belarus 55°41′N 30°25′E
160 F5 **Myddfai** United Kingdom 51°57′N 3°47′W
160 G3 **Myddle** United Kingdom 52°49′N 2°47′W
160 E4 **Mydroilin** United Kingdom 52°10′N 4°15′W
160 E4 **Mydroilyn** W Wales, United Kingdom 51°09′N 04°14′W
191 I10 **Myerkulavichy** Rus. Merkulovichi. Homyel'skaya Voblasts', SE Belarus 52°58′N 30°36′E
64 E7 **Myerstown** Pennsylvania, NE USA 40°22′N 76°18′W
191 H9 **Myezhava** Rus. Mezhëvo. Vitsyebskaya Voblasts', NE Belarus 54°38′N 30°20′E
Myggenaes see Mykines
256 C4 **Myingyan** Mandalay, C Myanmar (Burma) 21°25′N 95°20′E
256 C4 **Myinmu** Sagaing, C Myanmar (Burma) 21°58′N 95°34′E
256 D3 **Myitkyina** Kachin State, N Myanmar (Burma) 25°24′N 97°25′E
256 C4 **Myittha** Mandalay, C Myanmar (Burma) 21°21′N 96°06′E
183 E10 **Myjava** Hung. Miava. Trenčiansky Kraj, W Slovakia 48°45′N 17°35′E
Myjeldino see Myyëldino
189 K6 **Mykhaylivka** Rus. Mikhaylovka. Zaporiz'ka Oblast', SE Ukraine 47°16′N 35°14′E
154 A1 **Mykines** Dan. Myggenaes. island W Faeroe Islands
188 D4 **Mykolayiv** L'vivs'ka Oblast', W Ukraine 49°34′N 23°58′E
189 I7 **Mykolayiv** Rus. Nikolayev. Mykolayivs'ka Oblast', S Ukraine 46°58′N 31°59′E
189 I7 **Mykolayiv** ✕ Mykolayivs'ka Oblast', S Ukraine 47°02′N 31°54′E
Mykolayiv see Mykolayivs'ka Oblast'
189 H6 **Mykolayivka** Odes'ka Oblast', SW Ukraine 47°34′N 30°48′E
189 J9 **Mykolayivka** Respublika Krym, S Ukraine 44°58′N 33°37′E
189 I6 **Mykolayivs'ka Oblast'** var. Mykolayiv, Rus. Nikolayevskaya Oblast'. ◐ province S Ukraine
187 J7 **Mýkonos** Mńykonos, Kykládes, Greece, Aegean Sea 37°27′N 25°20′E
187 J7 **Mýkonos** var. Míkonos. island Kykládes, Greece, Aegean Sea
195 I5 **Myla** Respublika Komi, NW Russian Federation 65°24′N 50°51′E
Mylae see Milazzo
153 I9 **Myllykoski** Etelä-Suomi, S Finland 60°45′N 26°52′E
233 K7 **Mymensingh** var. Mymensingh. Dhaka, N Bangladesh 24°45′N 90°23′E
Mymensingh see Mymensingh
153 G10 **Mynämäki** Länsi-Suomi, SW Finland 60°41′N 22°00′E
227 J6 **Mynaral** Kaz. Myngaral. Zhambyl, S Kazakhstan 45°25′N 73°37′E
Mynbulak see Mingbuloq
Mynbulak, Vpadina see Mingbuloq Botig'I
Myngaral see Mynaral
256 B5 **Myohaung** var. Mrauk U, Myohaung. Rakhine State, W Myanmar (Burma) 20°35′N 93°12′E
Myohaung see Myohaung
248 C4 **Myohyang-sanmaek** ▲▲ C North Korea
253 A12 **Myōkō-san** ▲ Honshū, S Japan 36°54′N 138°05′E
138 G2 **Myooye** Central, C Zambia 15°11′S 27°10′E
191 F8 **Myory** prev. Miyory. Vitsyebskaya Voblasts', N Belarus 55°39′N 27°39′E
152 C3 **Mýrdalsjökull** glacier S Iceland
152 E4 **Myre** Nordland, C Norway 68°54′N 15°04′E
189 J3 **Myrhorod** Rus. Mirgorod. Poltavs'ka Oblast', NE Ukraine 49°58′N 33°37′E
187 I4 **Mýrina** var. Mírina. Límnos, SE Greece 39°52′N 25°04′E
189 H4 **Myronivka** Rus. Mironovka. Kyyivs'ka Oblast', N Ukraine 49°40′N 30°59′E
67 K8 **Myrtle Beach** South Carolina, SE USA 33°41′N 78°53′W
76 B7 **Myrtle Creek** Oregon, NW USA 43°01′N 123°19′W
277 J6 **Myrtleford** Victoria, SE Australia 36°34′S 146°45′E
76 B7 **Myrtle Point** Oregon, NW USA 43°04′N 124°08′W
187 J10 **Mýrtos** Kríti, Greece, E Mediterranean Sea 35°00′N 25°34′E
Myrtoum Mare see Mirtóo Pélagos
154 G4 **Myrviken** Jämtland, C Sweden 62°59′N 14°19′E
155 E8 **Mysen** Østfold, S Norway 59°33′N 11°20′E
194 F9 **Myshkin** Yaroslavskaya Oblast', NW Russian Federation 57°47′N 38°28′E
195 N1 **Mys Kamennyy** headland Yamalo-Nenetskiy Avtonomnyy Okrug, Russian Federation
183 G9 **Myślenice** Malopolskie, S Poland 49°50′N 19°55′E
182 C5 **Myślibórz** Zachodnio-pomorskie, NW Poland 52°55′N 14°51′E
235 E8 **Mysore** var. Maisur. Karnātaka, W India 12°18′N 76°37′E
Mysore see Karnātaka
64 K4 **Mystic** Connecticut, NE USA 41°21′N 71°57′W
186 G7 **Mystrás** var. Mistras. Pelopónnisos, S Greece 37°03′N 22°22′E
195 J7 **Mysy** Komi-Permyatskiy Avtonomnyy Okrug, NW Russian Federation 60°40′N 53°59′E
183 F8 **Myszków** Śląskie, S Poland 50°36′N 19°20′E
257 H9 **My Tho** var. Mi Tho. Tiên Giang, S Vietnam 10°21′N 106°21′E
Mytilene see Mytilíni
187 K5 **Mytilíni** var. Mitilíni; anc. Mytilene. Lésvos, E Greece 39°06′N 26°33′E
196 F2 **Mytishchi** Moskovskaya Oblast', W Russian Federation 56°00′N 37°51′E
79 I3 **Myton** Utah, W USA 40°11′N 110°03′W
152 D2 **Mývatn** ◎ C Iceland
195 K7 **Myyëldino** var. Myjeldino. Respublika Komi, NW Russian Federation 61°46′N 54°48′E
137 C12 **Mzimba** Northern, NW Malawi 11°56′S 33°36′E
141 J7 **Mzimkhulu** Kwazulu Natal, South Africa
141 J8 **Mzimvubu** Eastern Cape, South Africa
141 K6 **Mzingazi** ◎ KwaZulu-Natal, South Africa
137 C12 **Mzuzu** Northern, N Malawi 11°23′S 34°03′E

N

179 G11 **Naab** SE Germany
162 D7 **Naaldwijk** Zuid-Holland, W Netherlands 52°00′N 04°13′E
82 D3 **Nā'ālehu** var. Naalehu. Hawaii, USA, C Pacific Ocean 19°04′N 155°36′W
219 D8 **Naan** Israel 31°52′N 34°51′E
153 G10 **Naantali** Swe. Nådendal. Länsi-Suomi, SW Finland 60°28′N 22°05′E
162 F6 **Naarden** Noord-Holland, C Netherlands 52°18′N 05°10′E
177 J2 **Naarn** N Austria
158 D10 **Naas** Ir. An Nás, Nás na Ríogh. Kildare, C Ireland 53°13′N 06°39′W
152 H3 **Näätämöjoki** Lapp. Njávdám. NE Finland
218 F3 **Nabaa es Safa** Lebanon 33°44′N 35°42′E
140 C6 **Nababeep** var. Nababiep. Northern Cape, W South Africa 29°36′S 17°46′E
Nababiep see Nababeep
Nabadwip see Navadwīp
172 C2 **Nabais** Guarda, Portugal 40°31′N 7°33′W
251 I5 **Nabari** Mie, Honshū, SW Japan 34°37′N 136°05′E
Nabatié see Nabatîyé
218 E4 **Nabatîyé** var. An Nabatīyah at Taḩtā, Nabatié, Nabatiyet et Tahta. SW Lebanon 33°18′N 35°36′E
218 F4 **Nabatîyé** Lebanon 33°21′N 35°29′E
218 E4 **Nabatîye** ◐ governorate Lebanon
Nabatiyet et Tahta see Nabatîyé
280 E8 **Nabavatu** Vanua Levu, N Fiji 16°35′S 178°55′E
284 D2 **Nabeina** island Tungaru, W Kiribati
197 K2 **Naberezhnyye Chelny** prev. Brezhnev. Respublika Tatarstan, W Russian Federation 55°43′N 52°21′E
83 K5 **Nabesna** Alaska, USA 62°22′N 143°00′W
83 K5 **Nabesna River** Alaska, USA
131 K1 **Nabeul** var. Nābul. NE Tunisia 36°32′N 10°45′E
232 E4 **Nābha** Punjab, NW India 30°22′N 76°12′E
140 E6 **Nabies** Northern Cape, South Africa 28°52′S 20°10′E
218 G3 **Nabi Rchâdé** Lebanon 34°00′N 36°02′E
261 J5 **Nabire** Papua, E Indonesia 03°23′S 135°31′E
220 F8 **Nabī Shu'ayb, Jabal an** ▲ W Yemen 15°24′N 44°04′E
280 E8 **Nabiti** Vanua Levu, N Fiji 16°37′S 178°54′E
218 E7 **Nablus** var. Nābulus, Heb. Shekhem; anc. Neapolis, Bibl. Shechem. N West Bank 32°13′N 35°16′E
141 J3 **Naboomspruit** Limpopo, South Africa 24°31′S 28°43′E
280 E8 **Nabouwalu** Vanua Levu, N Fiji 17°00′S 178°43′E
Nābul see Nabeul
Nābulus see Nablus
280 F8 **Nabuna** Vanua Levu, N Fiji 16°13′S 179°46′E
263 N9 **Nabunturan** Mindanao, S Philippines 07°34′N 125°54′E
159 L8 **Naburn** United Kingdom 53°54′N 1°05′W
139 L2 **Nacala** Nampula, NE Mozambique 14°30′S 40°37′E
88 E5 **Nacaome** Valle, S Honduras 13°30′N 87°31′W
Na Cealla Beaga see Killybegs
Na-Ch'ii see Nagqu
251 I6 **Nachikatsuura** var. Nachi-Katsuura. Wakayama, Honshū, SE Japan 33°37′N 135°54′E
Nachi-Katsuura see Nachikatsuura
137 E12 **Nachingwea** Lindi, SE Tanzania 10°21′S 38°46′E
183 D8 **Náchod** Královéhradecký Kraj, N Czech Republic 50°26′N 16°10′E
80 B6 **Nacimiento, Lake** California, USA
111 J2 **Nack** Minas Gerais, Brazil 19°14′S 42°19′W
63 L2 **Nackawic** New Brunswick, SE Canada 46°00′N 67°14′W
Na Clocha Liatha see Greystones
84 F2 **Naco** Sonora, NW Mexico 31°16′N 109°56′W
71 I5 **Nacogdoches** Texas, SW USA 31°36′N 94°40′W
84 F3 **Nàcori Chico** Sonora, Mexico 29°41′N 108°58′W
84 F3 **Nacozari de García** Sonora, NW Mexico 30°27′N 109°43′W
161 M5 **Nacton** United Kingdom 52°01′N 1°14′E
280 D8 **Nacula** prev. Nathula. island Yasawa Group, NW Fiji
118 G4 **Nacuñán** Mendoza, Argentina 34°03′S 67°58′W
Nada see Danzhou
184 G1 **Nădab** Arad, W Romania
85 K5 **Nadadores** Coahuila, Mexico 27°03′N 101°36′W
132 G6 **Nadawli** NW Ghana 10°30′N 02°40′W
170 D2 **Nadela** Galicia, NW Spain 42°58′N 07°33′W
Nådendal see Naantali
226 G2 **Nadezhdinka** prev. Nadezhdinskiy. Kostanay, N Kazakhstan 53°46′N 63°44′E
Nadezhdinskiy see Nadezhdinka
Nadgan see Nadqān, Qalamat
280 D9 **Nadi** prev. Nandi. Viti Levu, W Fiji 17°47′S 177°32′E
280 D9 **Nadi** prev. Nandi. ✕ Viti Levu, W Fiji 17°46′S 177°28′E
232 C8 **Nadiād** Gujarāt, W India 22°42′N 72°55′E
Nadikdik see Knox Atoll
218 G7 **Nādirah** Jordan 32°18′N 35°58′E
188 A7 **Nădlac** Ger. Nadlak, Hung. Nagylak. Arad, W Romania 46°10′N 20°47′E
Nadlak see Nădlac
130 G2 **Nador** prev. Villa Nador. NE Morocco 35°10′N 05°22′W
190 J2 **Nadporozhye** Leningradskaya Oblast', Russian Federation
221 I5 **Nadqān, Qalamat** var. Nadgan. well E Saudi Arabia
183 H11 **Nádudvar** Hajdú-Bihar, E Hungary 47°36′N 21°09′E
175 I13 **Nadur** Gozo, N Malta 36°03′N 14°18′E
280 F8 **Naduri** prev. Nanduri. Vanua Levu, N Fiji 16°26′S 179°08′E
188 D5 **Nadvirna** Pol. Nadwórna, Rus. Nadvornaya. Ivano-Frankivs'ka Oblast', W Ukraine 48°27′N 24°30′E
194 E6 **Nadvoitsy** Respublika Kareliya, NW Russian Federation 63°53′N 34°17′E
Nadvornaya/Nadwórna see Nadvirna
195 N3 **Nadym** Yamalo-Nenetskiy Avtonomnyy Okrug, N Russian Federation 65°25′N 72°40′E
192 F5 **Nadym** C Russian Federation
280 C3 **Nadzab** Morobe, C Papua New Guinea 06°36′S 146°46′E
155 A9 **Nærbø** Rogaland, S Norway 58°40′N 05°39′E
155 E13 **Næstved** Storstrøm, SE Denmark 55°12′N 11°47′E
133 L6 **Nafada** Gombe, E Nigeria 11°02′N 11°18′E
176 E4 **Näfels** Glarus, NE Switzerland 47°06′N 09°04′E
186 F6 **Náfpaktos** var. Návpaktos. Dytikí Ellás, C Greece 38°23′N 21°50′E
186 G7 **Náfplio** prev. Návplion. Pelopónnisos, S Greece 37°34′N 22°50′E
217 K4 **Naft Khāneh** Diyālá, E Iraq 34°01′N 45°26′E
230 F8 **Nāg** Baluchistān, SW Pakistan 27°43′N 65°31′E
263 L6 **Naga** off. Naga City; prev. Nueva Caceres. Luzon, N Philippines 13°36′N 123°10′E
Nagaarzê see Nagarzê
Naga City see Naga
58 D6 **Nagagami** Ontario, S Canada
250 E6 **Nagahama** Ehime, Shikoku, SW Japan 33°36′N 132°29′E
251 I4 **Nagahama** Shiga, Honshū, SW Japan 35°25′N 136°16′E
233 M6 **Nāga Hills** ▲▲ NE India
253 C10 **Nagai** Yamagata, Honshū, C Japan 38°08′N 140°00′E
Na Gaibhlte see Galty Mountains
82 G9 **Nagai Island** island Shumagin Islands, Alaska, USA
233 M6 **Nāgāland** ◐ state NE India
251 K2 **Nagano** Nagano, Honshū, S Japan 36°39′N 138°11′E
251 K3 **Nagano** off. Nagano-ken. ◐ prefecture Honshū, S Japan
Nagano-ken see Nagano
253 B11 **Nagaoka** Niigata, Honshū, C Japan 37°26′N 138°48′E
233 L6 **Nagaon** prev. Nowgong. Assam, NE India 26°21′N 92°41′E
235 F9 **Nāgappattinam** var. Negapatam, Negapattinam. Tamil Nādu, SE India 10°45′N 79°50′E
Nagara Nayok see Nakhon Nayok
Nagara Panom see Nakhon Phanom
Nagara Pathom see Nakhon Pathom
Nagara Sridharmaraj see Nakhon Si Thammarat
Nagara Svarga see Nakhon Sawan
234 F6 **Nāgārjuna Sāgar** E India
88 G6 **Nagarote** León, SW Nicaragua 12°15′N 86°35′W
238 G9 **Nagarzê** var. Nagaarzê. Xizang Zizhiqu, W China 28°57′N 90°26′E
250 C7 **Nagasaki** Nagasaki, Kyūshū, SW Japan 32°45′N 129°52′E
250 B6 **Nagasaki** off. Nagasaki-ken. ◐ prefecture Kyūshū, SW Japan
Nagasaki-ken see Nagasaki
250 C8 **Naga-shima** island SW Japan
250 E6 **Naga-shima** island SW Japan
Nagashima see Kii-Nagashima
250 D5 **Nagato** Yamaguchi, Honshū, SW Japan 34°22′N 131°10′E
232 D6 **Nāgaur** Rājasthān, NW India 27°12′N 73°48′E
232 D8 **Nāgda** Madhya Pradesh, C India 23°30′N 75°29′E
162 G5 **Nagele** Flevoland, N Netherlands 52°39′N 05°43′E
235 E10 **Nāgercoil** Tamil Nādu, SE India 08°11′N 77°30′E
233 M6 **Nāginimāra** Nāgāland, NE India 26°44′N 94°51′E
Na Gleannta see Glenties
251 I10 **Nago** Okinawa, Okinawa, SW Japan 26°36′N 127°59′E
232 G7 **Nāgod** Madhya Pradesh, C India 24°34′N 80°34′E
235 G11 **Nagoda** Southern Province, S Sri Lanka 06°13′N 80°13′E
179 D12 **Nagold** Baden-Württemberg, SW Germany 48°33′N 08°43′E
215 L5 **Nagorno-Karabakh** var. Nagorno- Karabakhskaya Avtonomnaya Oblast, Arm. Lerrnayin Gharabakh, Az. Dağliq Quarabağ, Rus. Nagornyy Karabakh. former autonomous region SW Azerbaijan
Nagorno- Karabakhskaya Avtonomnaya Oblast see Nagorno-Karabakh
193 J7 **Nagornyy** Respublika Sakha (Yakutiya), NE Russian Federation 55°53′N 124°58′E
Nagornyy Karabakh see Nagorno-Karabakh
195 J8 **Nagorsk** Kirovskaya Oblast', NW Russian Federation 59°18′N 50°49′E
237 L5 **Nagoya** Aichi, Honshū, SW Japan 35°10′N 136°53′E
234 F4 **Nāgpur** Mahārāshtra, C India 21°09′N 79°06′E
239 H8 **Nagqu** Chin. Na-Ch'ii; prev. Hei-ho. Xizang Zizhiqu, W China 31°30′N 91°57′E
232 F4 **Nāg Tibba Range** ▲▲ N India
91 I5 **Nagua** NE Dominican Republic 19°25′N 69°49′W
183 E13 **Nagyatád** Somogy, SW Hungary 46°15′N 17°25′E
Nagybánya see Baia Mare
Nagybecskerek see Zrenjanin
Nagydisznód see Cisnădie
Nagyenyed see Aiud
183 I11 **Nagykálló** Szabolcs-Szatmár-Bereg, E Hungary 47°50′N 21°47′E
183 E12 **Nagykanizsa** Ger. Grosskanizsa. Zala, SW Hungary 46°27′N 17°E
Nagykároly see Carei
183 G11 **Nagykáta** Pest, C Hungary 47°25′N 19°45′E
Nagykikinda see Kikinda
183 G12 **Nagykőrös** Pest, C Hungary 47°01′N 19°46′E
Nagy-Küküllő see Târnava Mare
Nagylak see Nădlac
Nagymihály see Michalovce
Nagyrőce see Revúca
Nagysomkút see Şomcuta Mare
Nagysurány see Šurany
Nagyszalonta see Salonta
Nagyszeben see Sibiu
Nagyszentmiklós see Sânnicolau Mare
Nagyszöllös see Vynohradiv
Nagyszombat see Trnava
Nagytapolcsány see Topoľčany
Nagyvárad see Oradea
251 I10 **Naha** Okinawa, Okinawa, SW Japan 26°10′N 127°40′E
219 D9 **Nahala** Israel
219 D9 **Nahala** Israel 31°40′N 34°48′E
218 E6 **Nahal Qishon** ▲▲ Israel
232 E4 **Nāhan** Himāchal Pradesh, NW India 30°33′N 77°18′E
Nahang, Rūd-e see Nihing
54 D4 **Nahanni Butte** hill range Northwest Territories, NW Canada
216 B5 **Nahariyya** prev. Nahariyya. Northern, N Israel 33°01′N 35°05′E
218 E5 **Nahariyya** Israel 33°00′N 35°05′E
Nahariyya see Nahariyya
222 E4 **Nahāvand** var. Nehavend. Hamadān, W Iran 34°13′N 48°21′E
181 D12 **Nahe** SW Germany
Na H-Iarmhidhe see Westmeath
218 G3 **Nahlé** Lebanon 34°02′N 36°20′E
283 J2 **Nahnalaud** ▲ Pohnpei, E Micronesia
Nahoi, Cape see Cumberland, Cape
218 F4 **Nahr al A waj** dry watercourse Syria
218 E4 **Nahr el Lītani** Lebanon
218 D6 **Nahsholim** Israel 32°37′N 34°55′E
Nahtavárr see Nattavaara
116 C7 **Nahuel Huapí, Lago** ◎ W Argentina
118 C7 **Nahueltoro** Bío-Bío, Chile 36°29′S 71°46′W
69 L3 **Nahunta** Georgia, SE USA 31°11′N 81°58′W
85 I5 **Naica** Chihuahua, N Mexico 27°53′N 105°30′W
57 N5 **Naicam** Saskatchewan, S Canada 52°26′N 104°30′W
168 G6 **Nailloux** Midi-Pyrénées, France 43°22′N 1°38′E
160 G6 **Nailsea** United Kingdom 51°26′N 2°46′W
161 H6 **Nailsworth** United Kingdom 51°42′N 2°13′W
Naiman Qi see Daqin Tal
238 G3 **Naimin Bulak** spring NW China
59 J3 **Nain** Newfoundland and Labrador, NE Canada 56°33′N 61°46′W
222 G5 **Nā'īn** Eşfahān, C Iran 32°52′N 53°05′E
232 F5 **Naini Tāl** Uttarakhand, N India 29°22′N 79°26′E
232 F8 **Nainpur** Madhya Pradesh, C India 22°26′N 80°10′E
280 F8 **Nairai** island C Fiji
156 F4 **Nairn** N Scotland, United Kingdom 57°36′N 03°51′W
156 F5 **Nairn** cultural region NE Scotland, United Kingdom
137 D8 **Nairobi** ● (Kenya) Nairobi Area, S Kenya 01°17′S 36°50′E
137 D8 **Nairobi** ✕ Nairobi Area, S Kenya 01°21′S 37°01′E
137 E13 **Nairoto** Cabo Delgado, NE Mozambique 12°22′S 39°05′E
190 D3 **Naissaar** island N Estonia
Naissus see Niš
280 G8 **Naitaba** var. Naitauba; prev. Naitamba. island Lau Group, E Fiji
Naitamba/Naitauba see Naitaba
137 D8 **Naivasha** Rift Valley, SW Kenya 0°44′S 36°26′E
137 D8 **Naivasha, Lake** ◎ SW Kenya
168 G4 **Najac** Midi-Pyrénées, France 44°13′N 1°59′E
Najaf see An Najaf
222 F5 **Najafābād** var. Nejafabad. Eşfahān, C Iran 32°38′N 51°23′E
220 F4 **Najd** var. Nejd. cultural region C Saudi Arabia
171 H2 **Nájera** La Rioja, N Spain 42°25′N 02°45′W
168 A8 **Najerilla** N Spain
247 K4 **Naji** var. Arun Qi. Nei Mongol Zizhiqu, N China 48°05′N 123°28′E
232 F5 **Najībābād** Uttar Pradesh, N India 29°37′N 78°19′E
Najima see Fukuoka
248 E2 **Najin** NE North Korea 42°13′N 130°16′E
217 J6 **Najm al Ḩassūn** Bābil, C Iraq 32°24′N 44°13′E
220 F7 **Najrān** var. Abā as Su'ūd. Najrān, S Saudi Arabia 17°31′N 44°09′E
220 G7 **Najrān** var. Minţaqat al Najrān. ◐ province S Saudi Arabia
Najrān, Minţaqat al see Najrān
250 B7 **Nakadōri-jima** island Gotō-rettō, SW Japan
252 E2 **Nakagawa** Hokkaidō, NE Japan 44°49′N 142°04′E
253 C12 **Naka-gawa** Honshū, S Japan
82 D2 **Nākālele Point** var. Nakalele Point. headland Maui, Hawai'i, USA 21°01′N 156°35′W
250 D6 **Nakama** Fukuoka, Kyūshū, SW Japan 33°53′N 130°48′E
Nakambé see White Volta
Nakamti see Nek'emtē
250 F7 **Nakamura** var. Shimanto. Kōchi, Shikoku, SW Japan 33°00′N 132°55′E
280 D3 **Nakanai Mountains** ▲▲ New Britain, E Papua New Guinea
251 K2 **Nakano** Nagano, Honshū, S Japan 36°43′N 138°23′E
250 F3 **Nakano-shima** island Oki-shotō, SW Japan
250 F4 **Nakano-umi** var. Naka-umi. ◎ Honshū, SW Japan
252 D7 **Nakasato** Aomori, Honshū, C Japan 40°58′N 140°26′E
252 F5 **Nakasatsunai** Hokkaidō, NE Japan 42°42′N 143°09′E
252 H4 **Nakashibetsu** Hokkaidō, NE Japan 43°31′N 144°58′E
136 B7 **Nakasongola** C Uganda 01°19′N 32°28′E
252 E2 **Nakatonbetsu** Hokkaidō, NE Japan 44°58′N 142°18′E
250 D6 **Nakatsu** var. Nakatu. Ōita, Kyūshū, SW Japan 33°37′N 131°11′E
251 J4 **Nakatsugawa** var. Nakatugawa. Gifu, Honshū, SW Japan 35°30′N 137°29′E
Nakatu see Nakatsu
Nakatugawa see Nakatsugawa
Naka-umi see Nakano-umi
252 D5 **Nakayama-tōge** pass Hokkaidō, NE Japan
Nakdong see Naktong-gang
Nakel see Nakło nad Notecią
136 E1 **Nakfa** var. Nakfa. N Eritrea 16°38′N 38°26′E
Nakfa see Nakfa
Nakhichevan' see Naxçıvan
219 A13 **Nakhl** Egypt 29°54′N 33°44′E
193 L9 **Nakhodka** Primorskiy Kray, SE Russian Federation 42°46′N 132°48′E
192 F5 **Nakhodka** Yamalo-Nenetskiy Avtonomnyy Okrug, N Russian Federation 67°48′N 77°48′E
Nakhon Navok see Nakhon Nayok
257 F8 **Nakhon Nayok** var. Nagara Nayok, Nakhon Navok. Nakhon Nayok, C Thailand 14°15′N 101°12′E
257 E8 **Nakhon Pathom** var. Nagara Pathom, Nakorn Pathom. Nakhon Pathom, W Thailand 13°49′N 100°06′E
256 G6 **Nakhon Phanom** var. Nagara Panom. Nakhon Phanom, E Thailand 17°22′N 104°46′E
256 F7 **Nakhon Ratchasima** var. Khorat, Korat. Nakhon Ratchasima, E Thailand 15°N 102°06′E
256 E7 **Nakhon Sawan** var. Muang Nakhon Sawan, Nagara Svarga. Nakhon Sawan, W Thailand 15°42′N 100°06′E
257 E10 **Nakhon Si Thammarat** var. Nagara Sridharmaraj, Nakhon Sithamnaraj. Nakhon Si Thammarat, SW Thailand 08°24′N 99°58′E
Nakhon Sithamnaraj see Nakhon Si Thammarat
217 M7 **Nakhrash** Al Başrah, SE Iraq 31°13′N 47°24′E
54 B4 **Nakina** British Columbia, W Canada 59°12′N 132°48′W
182 E5 **Nakło nad Notecią** Ger. Nakel. Kujawsko-pomorskie, C Poland 53°08′N 17°35′E
83 H7 **Naknek** Alaska, USA 58°45′N 157°01′W
232 E4 **Nakodar** Punjab, NW India 31°06′N 75°31′E
137 B11 **Nakonde** Northern, NE Zambia 09°22′S 42°47′E
140 E5 **Nakop** Northern Cape, South Africa 31°48′S 20°45′E
Nakorn Pathom see Nakhon Pathom
155 E13 **Nakskov** Storstrøm, SE Denmark 54°50′N 11°10′E
248 C6 **Naktong-gang** var. Nakdong, Jap. Rakutō-kō. C South Korea
137 D8 **Nakuru** Rift Valley, SW Kenya 0°16′S 36°04′E
56 G8 **Nakusp** British Columbia, SW Canada 50°14′N 117°48′W
230 F9 **Nāl** W Pakistan
239 K1 **Nalayh** Töv, C Mongolia 47°48′N 107°17′E
233 K6 **Nalbāri** Assam, NE India 26°36′N 91°49′E
117 B10 **Nalcayec, Isla** island Archipiélago de los Chonos, S Chile
197 H9 **Nal'chik** Kabardino-Balkarskaya Respublika, SW Russian Federation 43°30′N 43°39′E
234 F6 **Nalgonda** Andhra Pradesh, C India 17°04′N 79°15′E
233 J7 **Nalhāti** West Bengal, NE India 24°19′N 87°53′E
233 K7 **Nalitabari** Dhaka, N Bangladesh 25°06′N 90°11′E
234 F6 **Nallamala Hills** ▲▲ E India
214 D5 **Nallıhan** Ankara, NW Turkey 40°12′N 31°22′E
170 E1 **Nalón** NW Spain
256 D3 **Nalong** Kachin State, N Myanmar (Burma) 24°42′N 97°27′E
128 B2 **Nālūt** NW Libya 31°52′N 10°59′E
261 H6 **Nama** Pulau Manawoka, E Indonesia 04°07′S 131°22′E
282 G6 **Nama** island C Micronesia
141 L4 **Namaacha** Swaziland 25°59′S 32°01′E
139 J3 **Namacurra** Zambézia, NE Mozambique 17°31′S 37°03′E
282 C9 **Namai Bay** bay Babeldaob, N Palau
58 B7 **Namakan Lake** ◎ Canada/USA
222 F4 **Namak, Daryācheh-ye** marsh N Iran
141 K2 **Namakgale** Limpopo, South Africa 23°57′S 31°02′E
223 H4 **Namak, Kavīr-e** salt pan NE Iran
256 E5 **Namaklwe** Shan State, E Myanmar (Burma) 19°45′N 99°01′E
Namaksār, Kowl-e/Namakzār, Daryācheh-ye see Namakzar
230 D3 **Namakzar** Pash. Daryācheh-ye Namakzār, Kowl-e Namaksār. marsh Afghanistan/Iran
261 J7 **Namalau** Pulau Jursian, E Indonesia 05°50′S 134°43′E
137 D9 **Namanga** Rift Valley, S Kenya 02°33′S 36°48′E
229 J5 **Namangan** Namangan Viloyati, E Uzbekistan 40°59′N 71°34′E
Namanganskaya Oblast' see Namangan Viloyati
229 J5 **Namangan Viloyati** Rus. Namanganskaya Oblast'. ◐ province E Uzbekistan
139 L1 **Namapa** Nampula, NE Mozambique 13°43′S 39°48′E
140 C3 **Namaqualand** physical region S Namibia
136 B7 **Namasagali** C Uganda 01°02′N 32°58′E
280 D2 **Namatanai** New Ireland, NE Papua New Guinea 03°40′S 152°26′E
138 G2 **Nambala** Central, C Zambia 15°04′S 26°56′E
137 E11 **Nambanje** Lindi, SE Tanzania 08°37′S 38°21′E
261 J4 **Namber** Papua, E Indonesia 0°58′S 134°51′E
138 E3 **Nambiya** North West, N Botswana 18°09′S 23°08′E
181 C13 **Namborn** Saarland, Germany 7°08′N 49°31′E
277 M1 **Nambour** Queensland, E Australia 26°40′S 152°52′E
277 M3 **Nambucca Heads** New South Wales, SE Australia 30°37′S 153°00′E
238 G9 **Nam Co** ◎ W China
256 G4 **Nâm Cum** Lai Châu, N Vietnam 22°37′N 103°12′E
Namdik see Namorik Atoll
256 H5 **Nam Định** Nam Ha, N Vietnam 20°25′N 106°12′E
260 G5 **Namea, Tanjung** headland Pulau Seram, SE Indonesia
163 F11 **Namêche** Namur, SE Belgium 50°29′N 05°02′E
72 B4 **Namekagon Lake** ◎ Wisconsin, N USA
282 C10 **Namekakl Passage** passage Babeldaob, N Palau
Namen see Namur
139 K2 **Nametil** Nampula, NE Mozambique 15°46′S 39°21′E
55 H8 **Namew Lake** ◎ Saskatchewan/Manitoba, C Canada
248 C4 **Nam-gang** C North Korea
248 C6 **Nam-gang** S South Korea
250 A4 **Namhae** 34°50′N 127°53′E
248 C7 **Namhae-do** Jap. Nankai-tō. island S South Korea
Namhoi see Foshan
140 A2 **Namib Desert** desert W Namibia
135 B13 **Namibe** Port. Moçâmedes, Mossâmedes. Namibe, SW Angola 15°10′S 12°09′E
135 B14 **Namibe** ◐ province SE Angola
140 C3 **Namibia** off. Republic of Namibia, var. South West Africa, Afr. Suidwes-Afrika, Ger. Deutsch-Südwestafrika; prev. German Southwest Africa, South-West Africa. ◆ republic S Africa
291 I10 **Namibia Plain** undersea feature S Atlantic Ocean
Namibia, Republic of see Namibia
140 B2 **Namib-Naukluft Game Park** Hardap, Namibia
253 D11 **Namie** Fukushima, Honshū, C Japan 37°29′N 140°58′E
140 D6 **Namies** Northern Cape, South Africa 29°18′S 19°12′E
252 D7 **Namioka** Aomori, Honshū, C Japan 40°43′N 140°34′E
84 G4 **Namiquipa** Chihuahua, N Mexico 29°15′N 107°25′W
239 I9 **Namjagbarwa Feng** ▲ W China 29°39′N 95°00′E
Namka see Doilungdêqên
260 G5 **Namlea** Pulau Buru, E Indonesia 03°12′S 127°06′E
238 G9 **Namling** Xizang Zizhiqu, W China 29°40′N 88°58′E
Namnetes see Nantes
256 F6 **Nam Ngum** C Laos
Namo see Namu Atoll
277 L3 **Namoi River** New South Wales, SE Australia
283 H6 **Namoluk Atoll** atoll Mortlock Islands, C Micronesia
282 G6 **Namonuito Atoll** atoll Caroline Islands, C Micronesia
283 L7 **Namorik Atoll** var. Namdik. atoll Ralik Chain, S Marshall Islands
256 F5 **Nam Ou** N Laos
76 F7 **Nampa** Idaho, NW USA 43°32′N 116°33′W
132 F4 **Nampala** Ségou, W Mali 15°21′N 05°32′W
248 B4 **Namp'o** SW North Korea 38°46′N 125°25′E
139 K2 **Nampula** Nampula, NE Mozambique 15°09′S 39°14′E
139 K2 **Nampula** off. Província de Nampula. ◐ province NE Mozambique
Nampula, Província de see Nampula
248 B3 **Namsan-ni** NW North Korea 40°25′N 125°01′E
Namslau see Namysłów
154 E2 **Namsos** Nord-Trøndelag, C Norway 64°28′N 11°31′E
154 F1 **Namsskogan** Nord-Trøndelag, C Norway 64°57′N 13°04′E
256 D5 **Nam Teng** E Myanmar (Burma)
256 F5 **Nam Tha** N Laos
193 J6 **Namtsy** Respublika Sakha (Yakutiya), NE Russian Federation 62°42′N 129°30′E
256 D4 **Namtu** Shan State, E Myanmar (Burma) 23°04′N 97°26′E
56 B6 **Namu** British Columbia, SW Canada 51°46′N 127°49′W
283 L6 **Namu Atoll** var. Namo. atoll Ralik Chain, C Marshall Islands
280 G9 **Namuka-i-lau** island Lau Group, E Fiji
139 K2 **Namuli, Mont** ▲ NE Mozambique 15°15′S 37°33′E
137 E13 **Namuno** Cabo Delgado, N Mozambique 13°39′S 38°50′E
163 F11 **Namur** Dut. Namen. Namur, SE Belgium 50°28′N 04°52′E
163 F11 **Namur** Dut. Namen. ◐ province S Belgium
138 C3 **Namutoni** Kunene, N Namibia 18°49′S 16°55′E
248 B6 **Namwŏn** Jap. Nangen. S South Korea 35°24′N 127°20′E
263 H7 **Namyit Island** island S Spratly Islands
182 E7 **Namysłów** Ger. Namslau. Opole, SW Poland 51°03′N 17°41′E
256 E6 **Nan** var. Muang Nan. Nan, NW Thailand 18°47′N 100°50′E
134 D5 **Nana** W Central African Republic
252 D6 **Nanae** Hokkaidō, NE Japan 41°55′N 140°40′E
134 E4 **Nana-Grébizi** ◐ prefecture N Central African Republic
56 D9 **Nanaimo** Vancouver Island, British Columbia, SW Canada 49°08′N 123°58′W
134 D5 **Nana-Mambéré** ◐ prefecture W Central African Republic
243 L7 **Nan'an** Fujian, SE China 24°57′N 118°22′E
277 M1 **Nanango** Queensland, E Australia 26°42′S 151°58′E
251 J1 **Nanao** Ishikawa, Honshū, SW Japan 37°03′N 136°58′E
243 K9 **Nan'ao Dao** island S China
251 J1 **Nanatsu-shima** island SW Japan
104 E3 **Nanay, Río** NE Peru
242 C2 **Nanbu** Sichuan, C China 31°19′N 106°02′E
193 K9 **Nancha** Heilongjiang, NE China 47°09′N 129°17′E
243 J4 **Nanchang** var. Nan-ch'ang, Nanch'ang-hsien. province capital Jiangxi, S China 28°38′N 115°58′E
243 J4 **Nanchang** Jiangxi, China 28°20′N 115°34′E
Nan-ch'ang see Nanchang
Nanch'ang-hsien see Nanchang
245 M4 **Nanchangshan Dao** island Shandong, China
243 J5 **Nancheng** var. Jianchang. Jiangxi, S China 27°37′N 116°37′E
Nan-ching see Nanjing
242 C2 **Nanchong** Sichuan, C China 30°47′N 106°03′E
242 C4 **Nanchuan** Chongqing Shi, C China 29°06′N 107°13′E
245 L6 **Nancun** Shandong, E China 36°32′N 120°08′E
165 K3 **Nancy** Meurthe-et-Moselle, NE France 48°40′N 06°11′E
278 A11 **Nancy Sound** sound South Island, New Zealand
232 G4 **Nanda Devi** ▲ NW India 30°27′N 80°00′E
88 G6 **Nandaime** Granada, SW Nicaragua 11°45′N 86°02′W
242 C7 **Nandan** var. Minami-Awaji. Guangxi Zhuangzu Zizhiqu, S China 25°03′N 107°31′E
251 H5 **Nandan** Hyōgo, Awaji-shima, SW Japan 34°19′N 134°53′E
234 E5 **Nānded** Mahārāshtra, C India 19°11′N 77°21′E
277 L3 **Nandewar Range** ▲▲ New South Wales, SE Australia
Nandi see Nadi
240 B7 **Nanding He** China/Vietnam
Nándorhgy see Oţelu Roşu
114 A2 **Nanducita** Santa Fe, Argentina 30°22′S 61°09′W
234 D3 **Nandurbār** Mahārāshtra, W India 21°22′N 74°18′E
Nanduri see Naduri
234 F6 **Nandyāl** Andhra Pradesh, E India 15°30′N 78°28′E
243 J5 **Nanfeng** var. Qincheng. Jiangxi, S China 27°15′N 116°16′E
Nang see Nangxian
134 B5 **Nanga Eboko** Centre, C Cameroon 04°38′N 12°21′E
Nangah Serawai see Nangaserawai
231 J3 **Nanga Parbat** ▲ India/Pakistan 35°15′N 74°36′E
258 I5 **Nangapinoh** Borneo, C Indonesia 0°21′S 111°44′E
231 H4 **Nangarhār** ◐ province E Afghanistan
258 I5 **Nangaserawai** var. Nangah Serawai. Borneo, C Indonesia 0°20′S 112°26′E
258 I5 **Nangatayap** Borneo, C Indonesia 01°30′S 110°33′E
244 A6 **Nangdoi** Qinghai, China 36°07′N 102°01′E
Nangen see Namwŏn
165 I3 **Nangis** Seine-et-Marne, N France 48°36′N 03°02′E
248 C3 **Nangnim-sanmaek** ▲▲ C North Korea
245 I5 **Nangong** Hebei, E China 37°22′N 115°20′E
239 I8 **Nangqên** var. Xangda. Qinghai, C China 32°05′N 96°28′E
256 G7 **Nang Rong** Buri Ram, E Thailand 14°37′N 102°48′E
239 H9 **Nangxian** var. Nang. Xizang Zizhiqu, W China 29°04′N 93°03′E
Nan Hai see South China Sea
242 F1 **Nan He** C China
240 C6 **Nanhua** var. Longchuan. Yunnan, SW China 25°15′N 101°15′E
243 N2 **Nanhui** Shanghai Shi, China 31°02′N 121°27′E
Naniwa see Ōsaka
235 E8 **Nanjangūd** Karnātaka, W India 12°07′N 76°40′E
242 C1 **Nanjiang** Sichuan, China 32°13′N 106°29′E
243 K8 **Nanjing** Fujan, China 24°18′N 117°13′E
243 K1 **Nanjing** var. Nan-ching, Nanking; prev. Chianning, Chian-ning, Kiang-ning. Jiangsu. province capital Jiangsu, E China 32°03′N 118°47′E
Nankai-tō see Namhae-do
243 J3 **Nankang** Jiangxi, SE China 29°27′N 116°03′E
243 I7 **Nankang** var. Rongjiang. Jiangxi, S China 25°42′N 114°45′E
Nanking see Nanjing
250 F6 **Nankoku** Kōchi, Shikoku, SW Japan 33°33′N 133°37′E
245 J7 **Nan-kuan-chi** Shandong, E China 35°26′N 117°14′E
243 K2 **Nanling** Anhui, China 30°33′N 118°11′E
243 H7 **Nan Ling** ▲▲ S China
243 H3 **Nanlinqiao** Hubei, C China 29°34′N 114°21′E
242 E10 **Nanliu Jiang** S China
283 K2 **Nan Madol** ruins Temwen Island, E Micronesia
242 D9 **Nanning** var. Nan-ning; prev. Yung-ning. Guangxi Zhuangzu Zizhiqu, S China 22°50′N 108°19′E
Nan-ning see Nanning
52 F7 **Nanook River** Nunavut, N Canada
295 M8 **Nanortalik** Kitaa, S Greenland 60°12′N 44°53′W
Nanouki see Aranuka
242 C7 **Nanpan Jiang** ▲▲ Guangxi, China
242 A8 **Nanpan Jiang** S China
232 G6 **Nānpāra** Uttar Pradesh, N India 27°51′N 81°30′E
245 J4 **Nanpi** Hebei, E China 38°02′N 116°42′E
245 L2 **Nanpiao** Liaoning, China 41°05′N 120°26′E
243 K6 **Nanping** var. Nan-p'ing; prev. Yenping. Fujian, SE China 26°40′N 118°07′E
242 E3 **Nanping** Hubei, C China 30°25′N 108°47′E
Nan-p'ing see Nanping
Nanping see Jiuzhaigou
Nanpu see Pucheng
243 K5 **Nanpu Xi** Fujan, China
243 L7 **Nanri Dao** island SE China
243 L7 **Nanri Qundao** island group Fujan, China
251 I9 **Nansei-shotō** Eng. Ryukyu Islands. island group SW Japan
Nansei Syotō Trench see Ryukyu Trench
295 I4 **Nansen Basin** undersea feature Arctic Ocean
295 H4 **Nansen Cordillera** var. Arctic Mid Oceanic Ridge, Nansen Ridge. undersea feature Arctic Ocean 87°00′N 90°00′E
Nansen Ridge see Nansen Cordillera
53 H2 **Nansen Sound** Sound Nunavut, Canada
205 K5 **Nan Shan** ▲▲ C China
263 I7 **Nanshan Island** island E Spratly Islands
Nansha Qundao see Spratly Islands
58 G1 **Nantais, Lac** ◎ Québec, NE Canada
165 H3 **Nanterre** Hauts-de-Seine, N France 48°53′N 02°13′E
164 F5 **Nantes** Bret. Naoned; anc. Condivincum, Namnetes. Loire-Atlantique, NW France 47°12′N 01°32′W
167 H5 **Nanteuil-le-Haudouin** Picardie, France 49°08′N 2°48′E
168 F1 **Nantiat** Limousin, France 46°01′N 1°11′E
62 C6 **Nanticoke** Ontario, S Canada 42°49′N 80°04′W
64 E5 **Nanticoke** Pennsylvania, NE USA 41°12′N 76°00′W
62 F10 **Nanticoke River** Delaware/Maryland, NE USA
160 F4 **Nantmel** United Kingdom 52°17′N 3°25′W
57 I8 **Nanton** Alberta, SW Canada 50°21′N 113°47′W
243 M1 **Nantong** Jiangsu, E China 32°00′N 120°52′E
243 M8 **Nant'ou** W Taiwan 23°54′N 120°51′E
167 L10 **Nantua** Ain, E France 46°10′N 05°34′E
65 N4 **Nantucket** Nantucket Island, Massachusetts, NE USA 41°15′N 70°05′W
65 N4 **Nantucket Island** island Massachusetts, NE USA
65 N4 **Nantucket Sound** sound Massachusetts, NE USA
137 E13 **Nantulo** Cabo Delgado, N Mozambique 12°30′S 39°03′E
160 G2 **Nantwich** United Kingdom 53°04′N 2°31′W
64 A6 **Nanty Glo** Pennsylvania, USA 40°28′N 78°50′W
283 J1 **Nanuh** Pohnpei, E Micronesia
280 F8 **Nanuku Passage** channel NE Fiji
284 B4 **Nanumaga** var. Nanumanga. atoll NW Tuvalu
Nanumanga see Nanumaga
284 B4 **Nanumea Atoll** atoll NW Tuvalu
109 G10 **Nanuque** Minas Gerais, SE Brazil 17°49′S 40°21′W
260 F1 **Nanusa, Kepulauan** island group N Indonesia
247 K2 **Nanweng He** NE China
242 B4 **Nanxi** Sichuan, C China 28°54′N 104°59′E
242 G4 **Nanxian** var. Nan Xian, Nanzhou. Hunan, S China 29°23′N 112°18′E
Nan Xian see Nanxian
243 M2 **Nanxiang** Shanghai Shi, E China 31°18′N 121°18′E
243 H7 **Nanxiong** Guangdong, China 25°05′N 114°11′E
237 H6 **Nanyang** var. Nan-yang. Henan, C China 32°59′N 112°29′E
245 M8 **Nanyang** Jiangsu, E China 33°26′N 120°14′E
Nan-yang see Nanyang
245 J7 **Nanyang Hu** ◎ E China
253 C10 **Nan'yō** Yamagata, Honshū, C Japan 38°04′N 140°06′E
245 J3 **Nanyuan** Beijing Shi, N China 39°48′N 116°25′E
242 G5 **Nanyue** Hunan, S China 27°15′N 112°44′E
137 D8 **Nanyuki** Central, C Kenya 0°01′N 37°05′E
242 G1 **Nanzhang** Hubei, C China 31°47′N 111°48′E
244 G8 **Nanzhao** Henan, China 33°17′N 112°14′E
244 D9 **Nanzheng** Shaanxi, China 33°01′N 106°34′E
Nanzhou see Nanxian
173 M5 **Nao, Cabo de La** headland E Spain 38°43′N 00°13′E
59 H5 **Naococane, Lac** ◎ Québec, E Canada
233 J7 **Naogaon** Rajshahi, NW Bangladesh 24°49′N 88°59′E
245 I7 **Naokao** Henan, E China 34°56′N 115°05′E
Naokot see Naukot
86 G6 **Naolinco** Veracruz-Llave, Mexico 19°39′N 96°51′W
281 M2 **Naone** Maewo, C Vanuatu 15°03′S 168°06′E
Naoned see Nantes
186 G3 **Náousa** Kentrikí Makedonía, N Greece 40°38′N 22°04′E
80 B2 **Napa** California, W USA 38°15′N 122°17′W
83 H6 **Napaimiut** Alaska, USA 61°32′N 158°46′W
82 G6 **Napakiak** Alaska, USA 60°42′N 161°57′W
192 F4 **Napalkovo** Yamalo-Nenetskiy Avtonomnyy Okrug, N Russian Federation 70°06′N 73°43′E
62 F4 **Napanee** Ontario, SE Canada 44°13′N 76°57′W
261 K5 **Napanwainami** Papua, E Indonesia 03°01′S 135°51′E
261 J5 **Napan-Yaur** Papua, E Indonesia 02°55′S 134°50′E
82 G6 **Napaskiak** Alaska, USA 60°42′N 161°46′W
80 B2 **Napa Valley** valley California, USA
256 H4 **Na Phac** Cao Bằng, N Vietnam 22°24′N 105°54′E
261 J4 **Napido** Papua, E Indonesia 0°41′S 135°27′E
278 I6 **Napier** Hawke's Bay, North Island, New Zealand 39°30′S 176°55′E
293 L2 **Napier Mountains** ▲▲ Antarctica
63 H3 **Napierville** Québec, SE Canada 45°12′N 73°25′W
69 L9 **Naples** Florida, SE USA 26°08′N 81°48′W
71 I4 **Naples** Texas, SW USA 33°12′N 94°40′W
Naples see Napoli
242 B9 **Napo** Guangxi Zhuangzu Zizhiqu, S China 23°21′N 105°47′E
104 D2 **Napo** ◐ province NE Ecuador
74 D3 **Napoleon** North Dakota, N USA 46°30′N 99°46′W
73 G9 **Napoleon** Ohio, N USA 41°23′N 84°07′W
Napoléon-Vendée see la Roche-sur-Yon
68 D4 **Napoleonville** Louisiana, S USA 29°55′N 91°01′W
175 G9 **Napoli** Eng. Naples, Ger. Neapel; anc. Neapolis. Campania, S Italy 40°52′N 14°15′E
175 G9 **Napoli, Golfo di** gulf S Italy
104 E2 **Napo, Río** Ecuador/Peru
285 K6 **Napuka** island Îles Tuamotu, C French Polynesia
222 C3 **Naqadeh** Āžarbāyjān-e Bākhtarī, NW Iran 36°57′N 45°24′E
217 K4 **Naqnah** Diyālá, E Iraq 34°13′N 45°33′E
Nar see Nera
251 I5 **Nara** Nara, Honshū, SW Japan 34°41′N 135°49′E
132 E4 **Nara** Koulikoro, W Mali 15°04′N 07°19′W
251 I5 **Nara** off. Nara-ken. ◐ prefecture Honshū, SW Japan
230 G8 **Nāra Canal** irrigation canal S Pakistan
277 H7 **Naracoorte** South Australia 37°02′S 140°45′E
277 J5 **Naradhan** New South Wales, SE Australia 33°37′S 146°19′E
Naradhivas see Narathiwat
Nara-ken see Nara
104 B3 **Naranjal** Guayas, W Ecuador 02°43′S 79°38′W
87 M6 **Naranjal Poniente** Quintana Roo, Mexico 19°22′N 88°28′W
84 G6 **Naranjo** Sinaloa, Mexico 25°48′N 108°28′W
112 F1 **Naranjos** Santa Cruz, E Bolivia
86 G5 **Naranjos** Veracruz-Llave, E Mexico 21°21′N 97°41′W
239 I4 **Naran Sebstein Bulag** spring NW China
223 K8 **Narānū** Sīstān va Balūchestān, SE Iran
250 B7 **Narao** Nagasaki, Nakadōri-jima, SW Japan 32°40′N 129°03′E
234 F6 **Narasaraopet** Andhra Pradesh, E India 16°16′N 80°06′E
238 E3 **Narat** Xinjiang Uygur Zizhiqu, W China 43°20′N 84°02′E
257 F11 **Narathiwat** var. Naradhivas. Narathiwat, SW Thailand 06°25′N 101°48′E
79 N6 **Nara Visa** New Mexico, SW USA 35°35′N 103°06′W
Nārāyāni see Gandak
Narbada see Narmada
Narbo Martius see Narbonne
165 I9 **Narbonne** anc. Narbo Martius. Aude, S France 43°11′N 03°E
169 H6 **Narbonne-Plage** Languedoc-Roussillon, France 43°10′N 3°10′E
161 I3 **Narborough** United Kingdom 52°34′N 1°12′W
Narborough Island see Fernandina, Isla
170 E1 **Narcea** NW Spain
114 B3 **Naré** Santa Fe, Argentina 30°58′S 60°28′W
232 F4 **Narendranagar** Uttarakhand, N India 30°10′N 78°21′E
Nares Abyssal Plain see Nares Plain
290 D6 **Nares Plain** var. Nares Abyssal Plain. undersea feature NW Atlantic Ocean 23°30′N 63°00′W

◆ Country
● Country Capital
◇ Dependent Territory
○ Dependent Territory Capital
◐ Administrative Regions
✕ International Airport
▲ Mountain
▲▲ Mountain Range
Volcano
River
◎ Lake
Reservoir

INDEX

Legend (bottom):

♦ Country · ♦ Dependent Territory · ♦ Administrative Regions · ▲ Mountain · ▲ Volcano · ◎ Lake

● Country Capital · ◇ Dependent Territory Capital · ✕ International Airport · ▲ Mountain Range · ◈ River · ◎ Reservoir

Legend

◆ Country ◇ Dependent Territory ◈ Administrative Regions ▲ Mountain ▲ Volcano ◎ Lake
◆ Country Capital ○ Dependent Territory Capital ≈ Mountain Range ≈ River ⊞ Reservoir
✈ International Airport

◆ Country   ◇ Dependent Territory   ● Country Capital   ○ Dependent Territory Capital   ◆ Administrative Regions   ▲ Mountain   ▲ Mountain Range   ✗ International Airport   ☉ Volcano   ✦ River   ☉ Lake   ☉ Reservoir

◆ Country ◇ Dependent Territory ● Country Capital ○ Dependent Territory Capital
◆ Administrative Regions ▲ Mountain ▲ Volcano ◎ Lake
× International Airport ▲ Mountain Range ~ River ◙ Reservoir

INDEX

Qal'eh-ye Panjeh – Radoviště
INDEX
395

231 I2 **Qal'eh-ye Panjeh** *var.* Qala Panja. Badakhshān, NE Afghanistan *36°56′N 72°15′E*
Qalqaman *see* Kalkaman
Qalqiliya *see* Qalqīlya
218 D7 **Qalqīlya** *var.* Qalqiliya. Central, W West Bank Asia *32°11′N 34°58′E*
219 F8 **Qalya** West Bank *31°46′N 35°30′E*
Qalzhat *see* Kol'zhat
Qamar Bay *see* Qamar, Ghubbat al
221 I8 **Qamar, Ghubbat al** *Eng.* Qamar Bay. *bay* Oman/Yemen
221 J7 **Qamar, Jabal al** ▲▲ SW Oman
229 H7 **Qamashi** Qashqadaryo Viloyati, S Uzbekistan *38°52′N 66°30′E*
Qambar *see* Kambar
239 I8 **Qamdo** Xizang Zizhiqu, W China *31°09′N 97°09′E*
280 F8 **Qamea** *prev.* Nggamea. *island* N Fiji
128 E2 **Qamīnis** NE Libya *31°48′N 20°04′E*
Qamishly *see* Al Qāmishlī
218 E5 **Qâna** Lebanon *33°12′N 35°18′E*
Qânâq *see* Qaanaaq
218 H6 **Qanawāt** Syria *32°45′N 36°37′E*
Qandahār *see* Kandahār
136 J3 **Qandala** Bari, NE Somalia *11°30′N 50°00′E*
Qandyaghash *see* Kandyagash
219 F13 **Qannāsīyah, Jabal al** ▲▲ Jordan
216 F2 **Qanṭārī** Ar Raqqah, N Syria *36°24′N 39°16′E*
Qapiciğ Dağı *see* Qazangödağ
238 E3 **Qapqal** *var.* Qapqal Xibe Zizhixian. Xinjiang Uygur Zizhiqu, NW China *43°46′N 81°09′E*
Qapqal Xibe Zizhixian *see* Qapqal
Qapshagay Böyeni *see* Kapchagayskoye Vodokhranilishche
Qapshaghay *see* Kapchagay
Qapugtang *see* Zadoi
295 M8 **Qaqortoq** *Dan.* Julianehåb. ⬖ Kitaa, S Greenland
217 J3 **Qara Anjīr** At Ta'mīn, N Iraq *35°30′N 44°37′E*
Qarabāgh *see* Qarah Bāgh
Qarabaū *see* Karabau
Qaraböget *see* Karaboget
Qarabulaq *see* Karabulak
Qarabutaq *see* Karabutak
Qaraghandy/Qaraghandy Oblysy *see* Karaganda
Qaraghayly *see* Karagayly
217 K3 **Qara Gol** As Sulaymānīyah, NE Iraq *35°21′N 45°38′E*
128 G3 **Qārah** *var.* Qâra. NW Egypt *29°34′N 26°28′E*
218 H2 **Qārah** Syria *34°09′N 36°44′E*
Qârah *see* Qārah
230 D3 **Qarah Bāgh** *var.* Qarabāgh. Herāt, NW Afghanistan *35°06′N 61°33′E*
216 C5 **Qaraoun, Lac de** *var.* Buḩayrat al Qir'awn. ◎ S Lebanon
Qaraoy *see* Karaoy
Qaraqoyyn *see* Karakoyyn, Ozero
Qara Qum *see* Garagum
Qarasū *see* Karasu
Qaratal *see* Karatal
Qarataū *see* Karatau, Khrebet, Kazakhstan
Qarataū *see* Karatau, Zhambyl, Kazakhstan
Qaraton *see* Karaton
Qarazhal *see* Karazhal
136 J4 **Qardho** *var.* Kardh, *It.* Gardo. Bari, N Somalia *09°34′N 49°30′E*
222 D1 **Qareh Chāy** 〰 N Iran
222 E1 **Qareh Sū** 〰 NW Iran
Qariateïne *see* Al Qaryatayn
Qarkilik *see* Ruoqiang
229 H7 **Qarluq** *Rus.* Karluk. Surkhondaryo Viloyati, S Uzbekistan *38°17′N 67°39′E*
229 K7 **Qarokŭl** *Rus.* Karakul'. E Tajikistan *39°07′N 73°33′E*
229 K7 **Qarokŭl** *Rus.* Ozero Karakul'. ◎ E Tajikistan
Qarqan *see* Qiemo
238 F5 **Qarqan He** 〰 NW China
Qarqannah, Juzur *see* Kerkenah, Îles de
Qarqaraly *see* Karkaralinsk
230 F2 **Qarqīn** Jowzjān, N Afghanistan *37°25′N 66°03′E*
Qars *see* Kars
Qarsaqbay *see* Karsakpay
229 H7 **Qarshi** *Rus.* Karshi; *prev.* Bek-Budi. Qashqadaryo Viloyati, S Uzbekistan *38°54′N 65°48′E*
228 G7 **Qarshi Cho'li** *Rus.* Karshinskaya Step. *grassland* S Uzbekistan
228 G7 **Qarshi Kanali** *Rus.* Karshinskiy Kanal. *canal* Turkmenistan/Uzbekistan
218 F2 **Qartaba** Lebanon
218 F2 **Qartaba** Lebanon *34°06′N 35°51′E*
Qaryatayn *see* Al Qaryatayn
Qāsh, Nahr al *see* Gash
229 H7 **Qashqadaryo Viloyati** *Rus.* Kashkadar'inskaya Oblast'. ⬖ *province* S Uzbekistan
Qasigianguit *see* Qasigiannguit
295 K8 **Qasigiannguit** *var.* Qasigianguit, *Dan.* Christianshåb. ⬖ Kitaa, C Greenland
218 G5 **Qāsim** Syria *32°59′N 36°05′E*
Qaṣīm, Minṭaqat *see* Al Qaṣīm
218 E4 **Qâsmiyé** Lebanon *33°24′N 35°17′E*
244 F2 **Qasq** Inner Mongolia, China *40°26′N 111°04′E*
218 H7 **Qaṣr al Ḩallābāt** Jordan *32°04′N 36°22′E*
217 H5 **Qaṣr 'Amīj** Al Anbār, C Iraq *33°30′N 41°52′E*
219 H9 **Qaṣr aṭ Ṭūbah** Jordan
217 I6 **Qaṣr Darwīshāh** Karbalā', C Iraq *32°36′N 43°27′E*
222 C4 **Qaṣr-e Shīrīn** Kermānshāhān, W Iran *34°32′N 45°36′E*
129 H4 **Qasr Farâfra** *var.* Qasr Farâfra. W Egypt *27°00′N 27°59′E*
Qasr Farâfra *see* Qasr Farâfra
Qassim *see* Al Qaṣīm
220 F9 **Qa'ṭabah** SW Yemen *13°51′N 44°42′E*
218 G4 **Qaṭanā** *var.* Katana. Dimashq, S Syria *33°27′N 36°04′E*
218 G4 **Qaṭana** Syria *33°26′N 36°05′E*
221 H4 **Qatar** *off.* State of Qatar, *Ar.* Dawlat Qaṭar. ◆ *monarchy* SW Asia
Qatar, State of *see* Qatar
Qatrana *see* Al Qaṭrānah
222 G7 **Qaṭrūyeh** Fārs, S Iran *29°08′N 54°42′E*
Qattara Depression/Qaṭṭārah, Munkhafaḍ al *see* Qaṭṭâra, Monkhafad el
129 H3 **Qaṭṭâra, Monkhafad el** *var.* Munkhafaḍ al Qaṭṭārah *var.* Monkhafad el Qaṭṭâra, *Eng.* Qattara Depression. *desert* NW Egypt
Qaṭṭâra, Monkhafad el *see* Qaṭṭâra, Monkhafad el
Qattinah, Buhayrat *see* Ḩimṣ, Buḩayrat
Qausuittuq *see* Resolute
Qaydār *see* Qeydār
Qāyen *see* Qā'en
Qaynar *see* Kaynar
229 I6 **Qayroqqum** *Rus.* Kayrakkum. NW Tajikistan *40°16′N 69°46′E*
229 I6 **Qayroqqum, Obanbori** *Rus.* Kayrakkumskoye Vodokhranilishche. ⊠ NW Tajikistan
215 L6 **Qazangödağ** *Rus.* Gora Kapydzhik, *Turk.* Qapiciğ Dağı. ▲ SW Azerbaijan *39°18′N 46°00′E*
217 K5 **Qazānīyah** *var.* Dhū Shaykh. Diyālá, E Iraq *33°39′N 45°33′E*
Qazaqstan/Qazaqstan Respublikasy *see* Kazakhstan
215 K3 **Qazbegi** *Rus.* Kazbegi. NE Georgia *42°39′N 44°36′E*
230 G9 **Qāzi Ahmad** *var.* Kazi Ahmad. Sind, SE Pakistan *26°19′N 68°08′E*
215 M5 **Qazimämmäd** *Rus.* Kazi Magomed. SE Azerbaijan *40°03′N 48°56′E*
Qazris *see* Cáceres
222 E3 **Qazvīn** *var.* Kazvin. Qazvīn, N Iran *36°16′N 50°E*
222 E4 **Qazvīn** ⬖ *province* N Iran
280 F7 **Qelelevu Lagoon** *lagoon* NE Fiji
129 J5 **Qena** *var.* Qena; *anc.* Caene, Caenepolis. E Egypt *26°12′N 32°49′E*
Qena *see* Qena
184 F10 **Qeparo** Vlorë, S Albania *40°04′N 19°49′E*
Qeqertarssuaq *see* Qeqertarsuaq
295 K8 **Qeqertarsuaq** *var.* Qeqertarssuaq, *Dan.* Godhavn. ⬖ Kitaa, S Greenland
295 K8 **Qeqertarsuaq** *island* W Greenland
295 K8 **Qeqertarsuup Tunua** *Dan.* Disko Bugt. *inlet* W Greenland
Qerveh *see* Qorveh
223 H9 **Qeshm** Hormozgān, S Iran *26°58′N 56°17′E*
223 H9 **Qeshm** *var.* Jazīreh-ye Qeshm, Qeshm Island. *island* S Iran
Qeshm Island/Qeshm, Jazīreh-ye *see* Qeshm
Qey *see* Kīsh, Jazīreh-ye
222 E3 **Qeydār** *var.* Qaydār. Zanjān, NW Iran *36°50′N 47°40′E*
222 E3 **Qezel Owzan, Rūd-e** *var.* Ki Zil Uzen, Qi Zil Uzun. 〰 NW Iran
Qian *see* Guizhou
245 K3 **Qian'an** Hebei, E China *39°50′N 117°41′E*
243 M5 **Qiancang** Zhejiang, SE China *27°35′N 120°31′E*
242 E5 **Qiancheng** Hunan, S China *27°12′N 109°49′E*
Qiandaohu *see* Chun'an
Qiandao Hu *see* Xin'anjiang Shuiku
Qian Gorlo/Qian Gorlos/Qian Gorlos Mongolzu Zizhixian/Quianguozhen *see* Qianguo
247 K5 **Qianguo** *var.* Qian Gorlo, Qian Gorlos, Qian Gorlos Mongolzu Zizhixian, Quianguozhen. Jilin, NE China *45°05′N 124°52′E*
243 J7 **Qianjia** Fujian, SE China *25°12′N 116°09′E*
242 G3 **Qianjiang** Hubei, C China *30°23′N 112°58′E*
242 E3 **Qianjiang** Sichuan, C China *29°30′N 108°45′E*
242 E9 **Qian Jiang** 〰 S China
243 L3 **Qianli Gang** ▲▲ Zhejiang, China
240 C4 **Qianning** *var.* Gartar. Sichuan, C China *30°27′N 101°24′E*
243 M3 **Qianqing** Zhejiang, E China *30°08′N 120°24′E*
243 J2 **Qianshan** Anhui, China *30°22′N 116°20′E*
245 N2 **Qian Shan** ▲▲ NE China
243 N4 **Qiansuo** Zhejiang, SE China *28°42′N 121°27′E*
242 A3 **Qianwei** *var.* Yujin. Sichuan, C China *29°15′N 103°52′E*
242 B5 **Qianxi** Guizhou, S China *27°00′N 106°01′E*
244 E7 **Qianxian** Shaanxi, China *34°19′N 108°08′E*
242 E5 **Qianyang** Hunan, S China *27°19′N 110°06′E*
Qiaotou *see* Datong
Qiaowa *see* Muli
239 I4 **Qiaowan** Gansu, N China *40°37′N 96°40′E*
243 M4 **Qiaoxiajie** Zhejiang, SE China *28°10′N 120°33′E*
Qibilī *see* Kebili
242 G6 **Qidong** Hunan, S China *26°47′N 112°07′E*
243 M1 **Qidong** Jiangsu, China *31°29′N 121°23′E*
238 F6 **Qiemo** *var.* Qarqan. Xinjiang Uygur Zizhiqu, NW China *38°09′N 85°30′E*
245 J5 **Qihe** Shandong, China *36°28′N 116°28′E*
242 C4 **Qijiang** *var.* Gunan. Chongqing Shi, C China *29°01′N 106°40′E*
238 G3 **Qijiaojing** Xinjiang Uygur Zizhiqu, NW China *43°29′N 91°35′E*
Qike *see* Xunke
245 K1 **Qilaotu Shan** ▲▲ Hebei, China
230 G6 **Qila Saifullāh** Baluchistān, SW Pakistan *30°45′N 68°08′E*
239 J5 **Qilian** *var.* Babao. Qinghai, C China *38°09′N 100°08′E*
208 C4 **Qilian Shan** *var.* Kilien Mountains. ▲▲ N China
243 I8 **Qiling** Guangdong, SE China *24°05′N 115°27′E*
243 H6 **Qiling** Jiangxi, SE China *26°18′N 114°07′E*
295 J7 **Qimusseriarsuaq** *Dan.* Melville Bugt, *Eng.* Melville Bay. *bay* NW Greenland
244 C7 **Qin'an** Gansu, C China *34°49′N 105°50′E*
Qincheng *see* Nanfeng
Qing *see* Qinghai
247 L4 **Qing'an** Heilongjiang, NE China *46°53′N 127°29′E*
244 D6 **Qingcheng** Gansu, N China *36°01′N 107°53′E*
243 H9 **Qingcheng** Guangdong, SE China *23°42′N 113°02′E*
244 B9 **Qingchuan** Sichuan, C China *32°35′N 105°14′E*
245 L6 **Qingdao** *var.* Ching-Tao, Ch'ing-tao, Tsingtao, Tsintao, *Ger.* Tsingtau. Shandong, E China *36°31′N 120°55′E*
242 A4 **Qingfu** Sichuan, C China *28°27′N 104°33′E*
247 L4 **Qinggang** Heilongjiang, NE China *46°41′N 126°05′E*
Qinggil *see* Qinghe
245 J3 **Qingguang** Tianjin Shi, N China *39°12′N 117°02′E*
239 I6 **Qinghai** *var.* Chinghai, Koko Nor, Qing, Qinghai Sheng, Tsinghai. ⬖ *province* C China
239 J6 **Qinghai Hu** *var.* Ch'ing Hai, Tsing Hai, *Mong.* Koko Nor. ◎ C China
Qinghai Sheng *see* Qinghai
238 G2 **Qinghe** *var.* Qinggil. Xinjiang Uygur Zizhiqu, NW China *46°42′N 90°19′E*
244 F5 **Qingjian** *var.* Kuanzhou; *prev.* Xiuyan. Shaanxi, C China *37°10′N 110°09′E*
245 L8 **Qingjiang** Jiangsu, E China *33°35′N 119°01′E*
243 M4 **Qingjiang** Zhejiang, E China *28°17′N 121°06′E*
242 E3 **Qing Jiang** 〰 C China
Qingjiang *see* Huai'an
Qingkou *see* Ganyu
242 B6 **Qinglong** *var.* Liancheng. Guizhou, S China *25°49′N 105°10′E*
245 K2 **Qinglong** Hebei, E China *40°24′N 118°57′E*
245 I5 **Qingping** Shandong, E China *36°45′N 116°03′E*
243 M2 **Qingpu** Shanghai Shi, E China *31°05′N 121°00′E*
Qingshan *see* Wudalianchi
243 H4 **Qingshanshi** Hubei, C China *28°28′N 113°10′E*
242 A3 **Qingshen** Sichuan, C China *29°48′N 103°49′E*
244 C7 **Qingshui** Gansu, China *34°27′N 106°04′E*
244 G3 **Qingshuihe** Inner Mongolia, China *39°34′N 111°23′E*
239 I7 **Qingshuihe** Qinghai, C China *33°47′N 97°10′E*
244 C5 **Qingshui He** 〰 Ningxia, China
244 E6 **Qingshui Jiang** 〰 Guizhou, China
242 C5 **Qingshui Jiang** 〰 Guizhou, China
243 H8 **Qingtang** Guangdong, SE China *24°12′N 113°55′E*
243 M4 **Qingtian** Zhejiang, China *28°05′N 120°11′E*
244 C4 **Qingtongxia** Ningxia, China *37°31′N 106°00′E*
244 C4 **Qingtonxia Shuiku** ⊠ Ningxia, China
245 J4 **Qingxian** Hebei, China *38°20′N 116°29′E*
244 G5 **Qingxu** Shanxi, China *37°22′N 112°13′E*
244 D6 **Qingyang** *var.* Xifeng. Gansu, C China *35°46′N 107°35′E*
Qingyang *see* Jinjiang
248 B2 **Qingyuan** *var.* Qingyuan Manzu Zizhixian. Liaoning, NE China *42°08′N 124°55′E*
243 L5 **Qingyuan** Zhejiang, SE China *27°37′N 119°04′E*
Qingyuan *see* Weiyuan
Qingyuan *see* Shandan
Qingyuan Manzu Zizhixian *see* Qingyuan
245 J5 **Qingyun** Shandong, E China *37°47′N 117°23′E*
245 J3 **Qingyundian** Beijing Shi, N China *39°40′N 116°30′E*
243 H8 **Qingyun Shan** ▲▲ Guangdong, China
238 G7 **Qingzang Gaoyuan** *var.* Xizang Gaoyuan, *Eng.* Plateau of Tibet. *plateau* W China
242 C6 **Qingzhen** Guizhou, China *26°20′N 106°16′E*
245 K5 **Qingzhou** *prev.* Yidu. Shandong, E China *36°41′N 118°29′E*
244 G6 **Qin He** 〰 C China
245 L3 **Qinhuangdao** Hebei, E China *39°57′N 119°31′E*
242 D10 **Qin Jiang** ▲▲ Guangxi, China
244 E8 **Qin Ling** ▲▲ C China
244 G6 **Qinxian** *var.* Dingchang, Qin Xian. Shanxi, C China *36°46′N 112°42′E*
Qin Xian *see* Qinxian
245 H7 **Qinyang** Henan, C China *35°05′N 112°56′E*
242 D10 **Qinzhou** Guangxi Zhuangzu Zizhiqu, S China *22°09′N 108°36′E*
242 D10 **Qinzhou Wan** *bay* Guangxi, China
245 K3 **Qinzhuang** Hebei, N China *39°35′N 119°05′E*
Qiong *see* Hainan
240 F10 **Qionghai** *prev.* Jiaji. Hainan, S China *19°12′N 110°26′E*
242 A2 **Qionglai** Sichuan, C China *30°24′N 103°28′E*
240 C4 **Qionglai Shan** ▲▲ C China
Qiongxi *see* Hongyuan
240 F9 **Qiongzhou Haixia** *var.* Hainan Strait. *strait* S China
237 J3 **Qiqihar** *var.* Ch'i-ch'i-ha-erh, Tsitsihar; *prev.* Lungkiang. Heilongjiang, NE China *47°23′N 124°E*
Qir *see* Qīr-va-Kārzīn
238 D6 **Qira** Xinjiang Uygur Zizhiqu, NW China *37°05′N 80°45′E*
Qir'awn, Buḩayrat al *see* Qaraoun, Lac de
222 G8 **Qīr-va-Kārzīn** *var.* Qir. Fārs, S Iran *28°27′N 53°04′E*
218 E6 **Qiryat Ata** Israel *32°48′N 35°06′E*
218 E6 **Qiryat Bialik** Israel *32°49′N 35°05′E*
219 D9 **Qiryat Gat** *prev.* Qiryat Gat. Southern, C Israel *31°37′N 34°47′E*
219 D9 **Qiryat Gat** Israel *31°36′N 34°46′E*
Qiryat Gat *see* Qiryat Gat
219 D8 **Qiryat Mal'akhi** Israel *31°44′N 34°44′E*
219 D8 **Qiryat Ono** Israel *32°03′N 34°51′E*
218 F5 **Qiryat Shemona** Israel *33°12′N 35°34′E*
218 F5 **Qiryat Shemona** *prev.* Qiryat Shemona. Northern, N Israel *33°13′N 35°35′E*
Qiryat Shemona *see* Qiryat Shemona
218 E6 **Qiryat Tivon** Israel *32°43′N 35°07′E*
218 E6 **Qiryat Yam** Israel *32°51′N 35°04′E*
244 D7 **Qishan** Shaanxi, China *34°16′N 107°23′E*
Qishlaq *see* Garmsār
221 I8 **Qishn** SE Yemen *15°29′N 51°44′E*
218 **Qishon, Naḩal** *prev.* Naḩal Qishon. 〰 N Israel
Qishon, Naḩal *see* Qishon, Naḩal
Qita Ghazzah *see* Gaza Strip
238 G3 **Qitai** Xinjiang Uygur Zizhiqu, NW China *44°N 89°34′E*
247 M4 **Qitaihe** Heilongjiang, NE China *45°45′N 130°53′E*
221 J7 **Qitbīt, Wādī** *dry watercourse* S Oman
242 A8 **Qiubei** Yunnan, China *24°01′N 104°07′E*
245 M5 **Qixia** Shandong, China *37°10′N 120°30′E*
245 H7 **Qixian** *var.* Qi Xian, Zhaoge. Henan, C China *35°35′N 114°10′E*
245 I7 **Qixian** Henan, China *34°19′N 114°28′E*
244 G5 **Qixian** Shanxi, China *37°13′N 112°11′E*
Qi Xian *see* Qixian
242 G6 **Qiyang** Hunan, S China *26°35′N 111°52′E*
Qīzān *see* Jīzān
243 I3 **Qizhou** Anhui, E China *30°04′N 115°20′E*
Qizil Orda *see* Kzylorda
Qizil Qum/Qizilqum *see* Kyzyl Kum
229 L8 **Qizilrabot** *Rus.* Kyzylrabot. SE Tajikistan *37°29′N 74°44′E*
228 F6 **Qizilravote** *Rus.* Kyzylrabat. Buxoro Viloyati, C Uzbekistan *40°35′N 62°09′E*
Qi Zil Uzun *see* Qezel Owzan, Rūd-e
217 J3 **Qizil Yār** At Ta'mīn, N Iraq *35°26′N 44°12′E*
Qoghaly *see* Kugaly
Qogir Feng *see* K2
222 F4 **Qom** *var.* Kum, Qum. Qom, N Iran *34°43′N 50°54′E*
222 F4 **Qom** ⬖ *province* N Iran
Qomisheh *see* Shahreẓā
Qomolangma Feng *see* Everest, Mount
222 F5 **Qom, Rūd-e** 〰 C Iran
Qomsheh *see* Shahreẓā
Qomul *see* Hami
Qondūz *see* Kondoz
228 D4 **Qo'ng'irot** *Rus.* Kungrad. Qoraqalpog'iston Respublikasi, NW Uzbekistan *43°01′N 58°49′E*
Qongyrat *see* Konyrat
Qoqek *see* Tacheng
229 J6 **Qo'qon** *var.* Khokand, *Rus.* Kokand. Farg'ona Viloyati, E Uzbekistan *40°34′N 70°55′E*
Qorabowur Kirlari *see* Karabaur', Uval
Qoradaryo *see* Karadar'ya
228 D3 **Qorajar** *Rus.* Karadzhar. Qoraqalpog'iston Respublikasi, NW Uzbekistan *43°34′N 58°35′E*
228 G6 **Qorako'l** *Rus.* Karakul'. Buxoro Viloyati, C Uzbekistan *39°27′N 63°45′E*
141 J8 **Qora Mouth** Eastern Cape, South Africa *32°27′S 28°41′E*
228 E4 **Qorao'zak** *Rus.* Karauzyak. Qoraqalpog'iston Respublikasi, NW Uzbekistan *43°07′N 60°03′E*
228 C3 **Qoraqalpog'iston** *Rus.* Karakalpakya. Qoraqalpog'iston Respublikasi, NW Uzbekistan *44°45′N 56°06′E*
228 D4 **Qoraqalpog'iston Respublikasi** *Rus.* Respublika Karakalpakstan. ⬖ *autonomous republic* NW Uzbekistan
Qorghalzhyn *see* Korgalzhyn
218 F3 **Qornâyel** Lebanon *33°51′N 35°43′E*
216 B2 **Qornet es Saouda** ▲ NE Lebanon *36°06′N 34°06′E*
228 G6 **Qorowulbozor** *Rus.* Karaulbazar. Buxoro Viloyati, C Uzbekistan *39°28′N 64°49′E*
222 D4 **Qorveh** *var.* Qerveh, Qurveh. Kordestān, W Iran *35°09′N 47°48′E*
229 H6 **Qo'shrabot** *Rus.* Kushrabat. Samarqand Viloyati, C Uzbekistan *40°15′N 66°40′E*
Qosköl *see* Koskol'
Qosshaghyl *see* Koschagyl
Qostanay/Qostanay Oblysy *see* Kostanay
222 G8 **Qoṭbābād** Fārs, S Iran *28°52′N 53°40′E*
223 H8 **Qoṭbābād** Hormozgān, S Iran *27°49′N 56°00′E*
218 G1 **Qoubaïyât** *var.* Al Qubayyāt. N Lebanon *37°00′N 34°30′E*
218 G1 **Qoubaïyât** Lebanon *34°34′N 36°17′E*
Qoussantîna *see* Constantine
Qowowuyag *see* Cho Oyu
229 H6 **Qo'ytosh** *Rus.* Koytash. Jizzax Viloyati, C Uzbekistan *40°13′N 67°19′E*
228 E4 **Qozonketkan** *Rus.* Kazanketken. Qoraqalpog'iston Respublikasi, W Uzbekistan *42°59′N 59°21′E*
228 E4 **Qozoqdaryo** *Rus.* Kazakdar'ya. Qoraqalpog'iston Respublikasi, NW Uzbekistan *43°26′N 59°47′E*
65 K2 **Quabbin Reservoir** ⊠ Massachusetts, NE USA
140 E8 **Quaggasfontein pass** Northern Cape, South Africa
180 E5 **Quakenbrück** Niedersachsen, NW Germany *52°41′N 07°57′E*
64 F6 **Quakertown** Pennsylvania, NE USA *40°26′N 75°17′W*
277 I6 **Quambatook** Victoria, SE Australia *35°52′S 143°28′E*
70 F3 **Quanah** Texas, SW USA *34°17′N 99°46′W*
256 I7 **Quang Ngai** *var.* Quangngai, Quang Nghia. Quang Ngai, C Vietnam *15°09′N 108°50′E*
Quangngai *see* Quang Ngai
Quang Nghia *see* Quang Ngai
256 I6 **Quang Tri** *var.* Triệu Hai. Quang Tri, C Vietnam *16°46′N 107°11′E*
Quanjiang *see* Suichuan
243 K1 **Quanjiao** Anhui, E China *32°06′N 118°15′E*
Quan Long *see* Ca Mau
238 D6 **Quanshuigou** China/India *35°40′N 79°28′E*
160 G7 **Quantock Hills** ▲▲ United Kingdom
243 L7 **Quanzhou** *var.* Ch'uan-chou, Tsinkiang; *prev.* Chin-chiang. Fujian, SE China *24°56′N 118°31′E*
242 F7 **Quanzhou** Guangxi Zhuangzu Zizhiqu, S China *25°59′N 111°02′E*
243 L8 **Quanzhou Gang** *harbor* Fujan, China
55 I9 **Qu'Appelle** 〰 Saskatchewan, S Canada
59 H1 **Quaqtaq** *prev.* Koartac. Québec, NE Canada *60°50′N 69°30′W*
115 H2 **Quaraí** Rio Grande do Sul, S Brazil *30°38′S 56°25′W*
114 G1 **Quaraí, Rio** *Sp.* Río Cuareim. 〰 Brazil/Uruguay *see also* Cuareim, Río
Quaraí, Rio *see* Cuareim, Río
260 C5 **Quarles, Pegunungan** ▲▲ Sulawesi, C Indonesia
Quarnero *see* Kvarner
167 J8 **Quarré-les-Tombes** Bourgogne, France *47°22′N 3°59′E*
175 B10 **Quartu Sant' Elena** Sardegna, Italy, C Mediterranean Sea *39°15′N 09°12′E*
81 E9 **Quartz Hill** California, USA *34°39′N 118°13′W*
80 I6 **Quartzite Mountain** ▲ Nevada, USA *37°31′N 116°19′W*
81 I13 **Quartzsite** Nevada, USA *33°40′N 114°14′W*
74 I7 **Quasqueton** Iowa, C USA *42°23′N 91°45′W*
110 G7 **Quatis** Rio de Janeiro, Brazil *22°25′S 44°16′W*
137 G10 **Quatre Bornes** W Mauritius *20°15′S 57°28′E*
137 I9 **Quatre Bornes** Mahé, NE Seychelles
161 H4 **Quatt** United Kingdom *52°29′N 2°21′W*
215 M4 **Quba** *Rus.* Kuba. N Azerbaijan *41°22′N 48°30′E*
Qubba *see* Ba'qūbah
223 I3 **Qūchān** *var.* Kuchan. Khorāsān-Razavī, NE Iran *37°12′N 58°28′E*
141 K6 **Qudeni** KwaZulu-Natal, South Africa *28°36′S 30°52′E*
277 K6 **Queanbeyan** New South Wales, SE Australia *35°24′S 149°17′E*
63 J1 **Québec** *var.* Quebec. *province capital* Québec, SE Canada *46°50′N 71°15′W*
62 G1 **Québec** *var.* Quebec. ⬖ *province* SE Canada
114 F5 **Quebracho** Paysandú, W Uruguay *31°58′S 57°53′W*
118 D3 **Quebrada de Alvarado** Valparaíso, Chile *33°03′S 71°07′W*
180 J7 **Quedlinburg** Sachsen-Anhalt, C Germany *51°48′N 11°09′E*
218 G8 **Queen Alia** ✕ ('Ammān) 'Ammān, C Jordan
56 D7 **Queen Bess, Mount** ▲ British Columbia, SW Canada *51°15′N 124°29′W*
54 A7 **Queen Charlotte** British Columbia, SW Canada *53°18′N 132°04′W*
117 H11 **Queen Charlotte Bay** *bay* West Falkland, W Falkland Islands
54 A7 **Queen Charlotte Islands** *Fr.* Îles de la Reine-Charlotte. *island group* British Columbia, SW Canada
56 A6 **Queen Charlotte Sound** *sea area* British Columbia, W Canada
56 B7 **Queen Charlotte Strait** *strait* British Columbia, W Canada
75 H8 **Queen City** Missouri, C USA *40°24′N 92°34′W*
71 J4 **Queen City** Texas, SW USA *33°09′N 94°09′W*
295 H7 **Queen Elizabeth Islands** *Fr.* Îles de la Reine-Élisabeth. *island group* Nunavut, N Canada
293 L6 **Queen Mary Coast** *physical region* Antarctica
132 E10 **Queen Mary's Peak** ▲ C Tristan da Cunha
52 G8 **Queen Maud Gulf** *gulf* Arctic Ocean
293 H6 **Queen Maud Mountains** ▲▲ Antarctica
159 H5 **Queensberry** ▲ United Kingdom *55°16′N 3°37′W*
52 G4 **Queens Channel** *Sea waterway* Nunavut, N Canada
275 J5 **Queensland** ⬖ *state* N Australia
286 D7 **Queensland Plateau** *undersea feature* N Coral Sea
277 J9 **Queenstown** Tasmania, SE Australia *42°06′S 145°33′E*
278 B11 **Queenstown** Otago, South Island, New Zealand *45°01′S 168°44′E*
141 I8 **Queenstown** Eastern Cape, S South Africa *31°52′S 26°50′E*
64 D10 **Queenstown** Maryland, USA *38°57′N 76°58′W*
Queenstown *see* Cobh
76 B3 **Queets** Washington, NW USA *47°31′N 124°19′W*
114 F5 **Queguay** Paysandú, Uruguay *32°05′S 57°55′W*
114 F5 **Queguay Grande, Río** 〰 W Uruguay
108 G7 **Queimadas** Bahia, E Brazil *10°59′S 39°38′W*
111 H8 **Queimados** Rio de Janeiro, Brazil *22°43′S 43°34′W*
172 D2 **Queiriz** Guarda, Portugal *40°44′N 7°27′W*
135 D11 **Quela** Malanje, NW Angola *09°18′S 17°07′E*
118 C1 **Quelen, Punta** *point* Coquimbo, Chile
172 C8 **Quelfes** Faro, Portugal *37°03′N 7°49′W*
139 J3 **Quelimane** *var.* Kilimane, Kilmain, Quilimane. Zambézia, NE Mozambique *17°53′S 36°51′E*
118 C7 **Quella** Maule, Chile *36°04′S 72°05′W*
117 B8 **Quellón** *var.* Puerto Quellón. Los Lagos, S Chile *43°05′S 73°38′W*
Quelpart *see* Cheju-do
110 G7 **Queluz** São Paulo, Brazil *22°32′S 44°46′W*
79 K8 **Quemado** New Mexico, SW USA *34°18′N 108°29′W*
70 E8 **Quemado** Texas, SW USA *28°58′N 100°36′W*
90 G5 **Quemado, Punta de** *headland* E Cuba *20°13′N 74°07′W*
Quemoy *see* Chinmen Tao
112 E10 **Quemú Quemú** La Pampa, E Argentina *36°03′S 63°36′W*
118 B10 **Quepe** Araucanía, Chile *38°51′S 72°37′W*
234 C6 **Quepem** Goa, W India *15°13′N 74°03′E*
118 B10 **Quepe, Río** 〰 Araucanía, Chile
89 H8 **Quepos** Puntarenas, S Costa Rica *09°28′N 84°10′W*
Que Que *see* Kwekwe
116 G6 **Quequén Grande, Río** 〰 E Argentina
116 G6 **Quequén Salado, Río** 〰 E Argentina
Quera *see* Chur
86 E5 **Querétaro** Querétaro de Arteaga, C Mexico *20°36′N 100°24′W*
168 G7 **Quérigut** Midi-Pyrénées, France *42°42′N 2°06′E*
84 E3 **Querobabi** Sonora, NW Mexico *30°02′N 111°02′W*
89 H8 **Quesada** *var.* Ciudad Quesada, San Carlos. Alajuela, N Costa Rica *10°19′N 84°26′W*
170 G7 **Quesada** Andalucía, S Spain *37°52′N 03°05′W*
241 H3 **Queshan** Henan, C China *32°48′N 114°03′E*
56 E5 **Quesnel** British Columbia, SW Canada *52°59′N 122°30′W*
54 D8 **Quesnel Lake** ◎ British Columbia, SW Canada
79 L5 **Questa** New Mexico, SW USA *36°41′N 105°37′W*
164 E4 **Questembert** Morbihan, NW France *47°39′N 02°24′W*
291 D13 **Quest Fracture Zone** *tectonic feature* S Atlantic Ocean
112 C3 **Quetena, Río** 〰 SW Bolivia
230 F6 **Quetta** Baluchistān, SW Pakistan *30°15′N 67°E*
Quetzalcoalco *see* Coatzacoalcos
Quetzaltenango *see* Quezaltenango
104 B2 **Quevedo** Los Ríos, C Ecuador *01°02′S 79°27′W*
84 G8 **Quevedo, Península de** *peninsula* Sinaloa, Mexico
88 B4 **Quezaltenango** *var.* Quetzaltenango. Quezaltenango, W Guatemala *14°50′N 91°30′W*
87 K10 **Quezaltenango** *off.* Departamento de Quezaltenango, *var.* Quetzaltenango. ⬖ *department* SW Guatemala
Quezaltenango, Departamento de *see* Quezaltenango
88 D4 **Quezaltepeque** Chiquimula, SE Guatemala *14°38′N 89°25′W*
263 J8 **Quezon** Palawan, W Philippines *09°13′N 118°01′E*
263 K5 **Quezon City** Luzon, N Philippines *14°39′N 121°02′E*
245 J7 **Qufu** Shandong, E China *35°37′N 117°05′E*
172 B2 **Quiaios** Coimbra, Portugal *40°13′N 8°51′W*
135 C11 **Quibala** Cuanza Sul, NW Angola *10°44′S 14°58′E*
135 C11 **Quibaxe** *var.* Quibaxi. Cuanza Norte, NW Angola *08°30′S 14°36′E*
Quibaxi *see* Quibaxe
102 B5 **Quibdó** Chocó, W Colombia *05°40′N 76°38′W*
164 E4 **Quiberon** Morbihan, NW France *47°30′N 03°07′W*
164 E4 **Quiberon, Baie de** *bay* NW France
102 E3 **Quíbor** Lara, N Venezuela *09°55′N 69°35′W*
88 C3 **Quiché** *off.* Departamento del Quiché. ⬖ *department* W Guatemala
Quiché, Departamento del *see* Quiché
180 H2 **Quickborn** Schleswig-Holstein, Germany *9°54′N 53°44′E*
118 A10 **Quidico** Bío-Bío, Chile *38°15′S 73°30′W*
115 H4 **Quiebra Yugos** Uruguay *31°40′S 56°10′W*
87 H9 **Quiechapa** Oaxaca, Mexico *16°26′N 96°15′W*
181 C13 **Quierschied** Saarland, Germany *7°03′N 49°19′E*
163 D11 **Quiévrain** Hainaut, S Belgium *50°25′N 03°41′E*
84 G7 **Quila** Sinaloa, C Mexico *24°24′N 107°11′W*
135 C13 **Quilengues** Huíla, SW Angola *14°09′S 14°04′E*
Quilimane *see* Quelimane
118 C1 **Quilimarí** Coquimbo, Chile *32°07′S 71°30′W*
105 F8 **Quillabamba** Cusco, C Peru *12°49′S 72°41′W*
106 D10 **Quillacollo** Cochabamba, C Bolivia *17°26′S 66°16′W*
112 B3 **Quillagua** Antofagasta, N Chile *21°33′S 69°32′W*
165 H9 **Quillan** Aude, S France *42°52′N 02°11′E*
118 B10 **Quillen** Araucanía, Chile *38°28′S 72°24′W*
57 N6 **Quill Lakes** ◎ Saskatchewan, S Canada
116 B3 **Quillota** Valparaíso, C Chile *32°54′S 71°16′W*
114 E9 **Quilmes** Buenos Aires, Argentina *34°43′S 58°16′W*
115 M4 **Quilombo** Rio Grande do Sul, Brazil *31°32′S 52°28′W*
115 L5 **Quilombo** Rio Grande do Sul, Brazil *32°17′S 53°25′W*
235 E10 **Quilon** *var.* Kollam. Kerala, SW India *08°57′N 76°37′E* *see also* Kollam
277 I1 **Quilpie** Queensland, C Australia *26°39′S 144°15′E*
230 G3 **Quil-Qala** Bāmīān, N Afghanistan *35°13′N 67°02′E*
118 B9 **Quilquen** Araucanía, Chile *38°06′S 72°43′W*
243 K3 **Quimen** Anhui, E China *29°47′N 117°33′E*
112 E6 **Quimilí** Santiago del Estero, C Argentina *27°35′S 62°25′W*
106 G10 **Quimome** Santa Cruz, E Bolivia *17°45′S 61°15′W*
164 D4 **Quimper** *anc.* Quimper Corentin. Finistère, NW France *48°00′N 04°05′W*
Quimper Corentin *see* Quimper
164 E4 **Quimperlé** Finistère, NW France *47°52′N 03°33′W*
76 B3 **Quinault** Washington, NW USA *47°27′N 123°53′W*
76 B3 **Quinault River** 〰 Washington, NW USA
118 C7 **Quinchamávida** Maule, Chile *36°07′S 72°03′W*
78 C3 **Quincy** California, W USA *39°56′N 120°56′W*
69 J4 **Quincy** Florida, SE USA *30°35′N 84°34′W*
73 A10 **Quincy** Illinois, N USA *39°56′N 91°24′W*
65 L2 **Quincy** Massachusetts, NE USA *42°15′N 71°00′W*
76 D4 **Quincy** Washington, NW USA *47°13′N 119°51′W*
102 B6 **Quindío** *off.* Departamento del Quindío. ⬖ *province* C Colombia
102 B6 **Quindío, Nevado del** ▲ C Colombia *04°42′N 75°25′W*
112 D8 **Quines** San Luis, C Argentina *32°15′S 65°46′W*
167 L8 **Quingey** Franche-Comté, France *47°06′N 5°53′E*
82 G7 **Quinhagak** Alaska, USA *59°45′N 161°55′W*
132 B5 **Quinhámel** W Guinea-Bissau *11°52′N 15°52′W*
Qui Nhon/Quinhon *see* Quy Nhơn
Quinindé *see* Rosa Zárate
71 H4 **Quinlan** Texas, SW USA *32°54′N 96°08′W*
118 C2 **Quinquimo** Valparaíso, Chile *32°27′S 71°19′W*
115 M5 **Quinta** Rio Grande do Sul, S Brazil *32°05′S 52°18′W*
172 C3 **Quintã** Castelo Branco, Portugal *39°47′N 8°12′W*
115 H4 **Quintana** Salto, Uruguay *31°24′S 56°22′W*
170 G6 **Quintanar de la Orden** Castilla-La Mancha, C Spain *39°36′N 03°03′W*
87 M6 **Quintana Roo** ⬖ *state* SE Mexico
118 C3 **Quintay** Valparaíso, Chile *33°13′S 71°40′W*
118 C2 **Quintero, Bahía** *bay* Valparaíso, Chile
171 I4 **Quinto** Aragón, NE Spain *41°25′N 00°31′W*
176 E5 **Quinto** Ticino, S Switzerland *46°32′N 08°44′E*
75 F12 **Quinton** Oklahoma, C USA *35°07′N 95°22′W*
116 E4 **Quinto, Río** 〰 C Argentina
135 B10 **Quinzau** Dem. Rep. Congo, NW Angola *06°50′S 12°48′E*
62 D1 **Quinze, Lac des** ◎ Québec, SE Canada
87 H8 **Quiotepec** Oaxaca, Mexico *17°38′N 96°37′W*
173 K6 **Quipar** 〰 Murcia, Spain
135 C13 **Quipungo** Huíla, C Angola *14°49′S 14°29′E*
116 B5 **Quirihue** Bío Bío, C Chile *36°15′S 72°35′W*
110 E8 **Quirim** São Paulo, Brazil *23°02′S 45°38′W*
135 E12 **Quirima** Malanje, NW Angola *10°51′S 18°06′E*
277 L4 **Quirindi** New South Wales, SE Australia *31°29′S 150°40′E*
103 H3 **Quiriquire** Monagas, NE Venezuela *09°59′N 63°14′W*
62 B2 **Quirke Lake** ◎ Ontario, S Canada
112 F10 **Quiroga** Buenos Aires, E Argentina *35°18′S 61°22′W*
86 D6 **Quiroga** Michoacán, Mexico *19°40′N 101°32′W*
170 D2 **Quiroga** Galicia, NW Spain *42°28′N 07°15′W*
Quiróm, Salar *see* Pocitos, Salar
104 B4 **Quiroz, Río** 〰 NW Peru
63 M3 **Quispamsis** New Brunswick, SE Canada *45°24′N 65°57′W*
137 F13 **Quissanga** Cabo Delgado, NE Mozambique *12°24′S 40°33′E*
139 I6 **Quissico** Inhambane, S Mozambique *24°42′S 34°44′E*
70 E3 **Quitaque** Texas, SW USA *34°22′N 101°03′W*
137 F12 **Quiterajo** Cabo Delgado, NE Mozambique *11°37′S 40°22′E*
115 N2 **Quitéria** Rio Grande do Sul, Brazil *30°26′S 52°04′W*
69 K3 **Quitman** Georgia, SE USA *30°46′N 83°33′W*
68 F2 **Quitman** Mississippi, S USA *32°02′N 88°43′W*
71 I4 **Quitman** Texas, SW USA *32°37′N 95°26′W*
104 C1 **Quito** ● (Ecuador) Pichincha, N Ecuador *0°14′S 78°30′W*
Quito *see* Mariscal Sucre
84 D2 **Quitovac** Sonora, Mexico *31°31′N 112°45′W*
86 C6 **Quitupan** Jalisco, Mexico *19°55′N 102°52′W*
108 H4 **Quixadá** Ceará, E Brazil *04°57′S 39°04′W*
139 L2 **Quixaxe** Nampula, NE Mozambique *15°15′S 40°07′E*
243 H8 **Qujiang** *var.* Maba. Guangdong, S China *24°47′N 113°34′E*
242 C3 **Qu Jiang** 〰 C China
243 L4 **Qu Jiang** 〰 SE China
242 A7 **Qujing** Yunnan, SW China *25°39′N 103°52′E*
141 I9 **Quko** Eastern Cape, South Africa *32°41′S 28°10′E*
Qulan *see* Kulan
247 K4 **Qulin Gol** *prev.* Chaor He. 〰 NE China
228 G5 **QuljuqtovTog'lar** *Rus.* Gory Kul'dzhuktau. ▲▲ C Uzbekistan
Qulsary *see* Kul'sary
Qulyndy Zhazyghy *see* Kulunda Steppe
Qum *see* Qom
Qumälisch *see* Lubartów
239 H7 **Qumar He** 〰 C China
239 I7 **Qumarlêb** *var.* Yuegai; *prev.* Yuegaitan. Qinghai, C China *34°06′N 95°54′E*
Qumisheh *see* Shahreẓā
229 H8 **Qumqo'rg'on** *Rus.* Kumkurgan. Surkhondaryo Viloyati, S Uzbekistan *37°54′N 67°31′E*
Qunaytirah/Qunayṭirah, Muḩāfaẓat al *see* Al Qunayṭirah
228 D4 **Qŭnghirot** Qoraqalpog'iston Respublikasi, NW Uzbekistan *43°02′N 58°49′E*
282 F9 **Quoi** *island* Chuuk, C Micronesia
53 H8 **Quoich** 〰 Nunavut, NE Canada
140 E10 **Quoin Point** *headland* SW South Africa *34°48′S 19°39′E*
276 G4 **Quorn** South Australia *32°22′S 138°03′E*
229 J6 **Qŭqon** Farg'ona Viloyati, E Uzbekistan *40°34′N 70°55′E*
Qurein *see* Al Kuwayt
229 I8 **Qŭrghonteppa** *Rus.* Kurgan-Tyube. SW Tajikistan *37°51′N 68°42′E*
Qurlurtuuq *see* Kugluktuk
Qurveh *see* Qorveh
Quryq *see* Kuryk
Qusair *see* Al Quṣayr
215 M4 **Qusar** *Rus.* Kusary. NE Azerbaijan *41°26′N 48°27′E*
Quṣayr *see* Al Quṣayr
Quseir *see* Al Quṣayr
222 C2 **Qūshchī** Āzarbāyjān-e Gharbi, N Iran *37°59′N 45°05′E*
242 E6 **Qu Shui** 〰 Hunan, China
Qusmuryn *see* Kushmurun, Ozero
Qusmuryn *see* Kushmurun, Kostanay, Kazakhstan
Quṭayfah/Qutayfe/Quteife *see* Al Quṭayfah
Quthing *see* Moyeni
52 E7 **Quunnguq Lake** ◎ Northwest Territories, NW Canada
229 J6 **Quvasoy** *Rus.* Kuvasay. Farg'ona Viloyati, E Uzbekistan *40°17′N 71°53′E*
Quwair *see* Guwēr
244 G6 **Quwo** Shanxi, C China *35°38′N 111°28′E*
Quxar *see* Lhazê
Qu Xian *see* Quzhou
238 G9 **Qüxü** *var.* Xoi. Xizang Zizhiqu, W China *29°25′N 90°48′E*
245 I4 **Quyang** Hebei, China *38°22′N 114°25′E*
Quyang *see* Jingzhou
257 J9 **Quy Chanh** Ninh Thuân, S Vietnam *11°28′N 108°53′E*
257 J8 **Quy Nhơn** *var.* Quinhon, Qui Nhon. Binh Đinh, C Vietnam *13°47′N 109°11′E*
243 L4 **Quzhou** *var.* Qu Xian. Zhejiang, SE China *28°55′N 118°54′E*
Qyteti Stalin *see* Kuçovë
Qyzylaghash *see* Kyzylagash
Qyzylorda *see* Kzylorda
Qyzyltū *see* Kishkenekol'
Qyzylzhar *see* Kyzylzhar

R

Raa Atoll *see* North Maalhosmadulu Atoll
177 J2 **Raab** Oberösterreich, N Austria *48°19′N 13°40′E*
177 K4 **Raab** *Hung.* Rába. 〰 Austria/Hungary *see also* Rába
Raab *see* Rába
Raab *see* Győr
177 K1 **Raabs an der Thaya** Niederösterreich, E Austria *48°51′N 15°28′E*
152 H7 **Raahe** *Swe.* Brahestad. Oulu, W Finland *64°42′N 24°31′E*
162 H6 **Raalte** Overijssel, E Netherlands *52°23′N 06°16′E*
163 F8 **Raamsdonksveer** Noord-Brabant, S Netherlands *51°42′N 04°54′E*
218 D7 **Raananna** Israel *32°10′N 34°52′E*
53 H3 **Raanes Peninsula** *Peninsula* Nunavut, N Canada
152 H6 **Raanujärvi** Lappi, NW Finland *66°39′N 24°40′E*
156 D5 **Raasay** *island* NW Scotland, United Kingdom
136 J3 **Raas Caseyr** *headland* NE Somalia *11°51′N 51°16′E*
190 E3 **Raasiku** *Ger.* Rasik. Harjumaa, NW Estonia *59°22′N 25°11′E*
184 B3 **Rab** *It.* Arbe. Primorje-Gorski Kotar, NW Croatia *44°46′N 14°46′E*
184 B3 **Rab** *It.* Arbe. *island* NW Croatia
260 C8 **Raba** Sumbawa, S Indonesia *08°27′S 118°45′E*
218 F7 **Rābā** West Bank *32°23′N 35°22′E*
183 E11 **Rába** *Ger.* Raab. 〰 Austria/Hungary *see also* Raab
Rába *see* Raab
184 A3 **Rabac** Istra, NW Croatia *45°03′N 14°09′E*
170 D2 **Rábade** Galicia, NW Spain *43°07′N 07°37′W*
136 B2 **Rabak** White Nile, C Sudan *13°12′N 32°44′E*
280 D4 **Rabaraba** Milne Bay, SE Papua New Guinea *10°00′S 149°50′E*
168 G5 **Rabastens** Midi-Pyrénées, France *43°50′N 1°45′E*
164 G8 **Rabastens-de-Bigorre** Hautes-Pyrénées, S France *43°23′N 00°10′E*
175 I14 **Rabat** W Malta *35°51′N 14°25′E*
130 F2 **Rabat** *var.* al Dar al Baida. ● (Morocco) NW Morocco *34°02′N 06°51′W*
Rabat *see* Victoria
280 D2 **Rabaul** New Britain, E Papua New Guinea *04°13′S 152°11′E*
Rabbah Ammon/Rabbath Ammon *see* 'Ammān
74 B4 **Rabbit Creek** 〰 South Dakota, N USA
62 D1 **Rabbit Lake** ◎ Ontario, S Canada
280 F8 **Rabi** *prev.* Rambi. *island* N Fiji
220 D5 **Rābigh** Makkah, W Saudi Arabia *22°51′N 39°E*
88 C3 **Rabinal** Baja Verapaz, C Guatemala *15°05′N 90°26′W*
258 B4 **Rabi, Pulau** *island* NW Indonesia, East Indies
183 G9 **Rabka** Małopolskie, S Poland *49°38′N 20°E*
234 D6 **Rabkavi** Karnātaka, W India *16°40′N 75°03′E*
Râbniţa *see* Rîbniţa
177 L3 **Rabnitz** 〰 E Austria
194 E5 **Rabocheostrovsk** Respublika Kareliya, NW Russian Federation *64°58′N 34°46′E*
66 G7 **Rabun Bald** ▲ Georgia, SE USA *34°58′N 83°18′W*
128 F6 **Rabyānah** SE Libya *24°07′N 21°58′E*
128 E5 **Rabyānah, Ramlat** *var.* Rebiana Sand Sea, Şaḩrā' Rabyānah. *desert* SE Libya
Rabyānah, Şaḩrā' *see* Rabyānah, Ramlat
188 E7 **Răcăciuni** Bacău, E Romania *46°20′N 27°00′E*
Racaka *see* Riwoqê
175 F13 **Racalmuto** Sicilia, Italy, C Mediterranean Sea *37°25′N 13°44′E*
188 D9 **Răcari** Dâmboviţa, SE Romania *44°37′N 25°43′E*
Răcari *see* Durankulak
188 B9 **Răcăşdia** *Hung.* Rakasd. Caraş-Severin, SW Romania *44°58′N 21°36′E*
176 D8 **Racconigi** Piemonte, NE Italy *44°45′N 07°41′E*
73 I12 **Raccoon Creek** 〰 Ohio, N USA
51 N7 **Race, Cape** *headland* Newfoundland, Newfoundland and Labrador, E Canada *46°40′N 53°05′W*
68 D5 **Raceland** Louisiana, S USA *29°43′N 90°36′W*
65 N3 **Race Point** *headland* Massachusetts, NE USA *42°03′N 70°14′W*
218 G2 **Rachaaïne** Lebanon
218 G2 **Rachaaïne** Lebanon *34°23′N 35°55′E*
218 F4 **Rachaïya** Lebanon *33°30′N 35°50′E*
80 J6 **Rachel** Nevada, USA *37°39′N 115°45′W*
257 H10 **Rach Gia** Kiên Giang, S Vietnam *10°01′N 105°05′E*
257 G10 **Rach Gia, Vinh** *bay* S Vietnam
132 D2 **Rachid** Tagant, C Mauritania *18°48′N 11°41′W*
182 G5 **Raciąż** Mazowieckie, C Poland *52°46′N 20°04′E*
183 F8 **Racibórz** *Ger.* Ratibor. Śląskie, S Poland *50°05′N 18°10′E*
73 D8 **Racine** Wisconsin, N USA *42°42′N 87°50′W*
72 H2 **Racine Lake** ◎ Ontario, S Canada
160 F8 **Rackenford** United Kingdom *50°57′N 3°38′W*
80 D1 **Rackerby** California, USA *39°26′N 121°20′W*
183 F12 **Ráckeve** Pest, C Hungary *47°10′N 18°58′E*
Rácz-Becse *see* Bečej
220 F9 **Radā'** *var.* Ridā'. W Yemen *14°24′N 44°49′E*
184 G6 **Radan** ▲ SE Serbia *42°59′N 21°31′E*
117 D10 **Rada Tilly** Chubut, SE Argentina *45°54′S 67°33′W*
188 E6 **Rădăuţi** *Ger.* Radautz, *Hung.* Rádóc. Suceava, N Romania *47°49′N 25°58′E*
188 E5 **Rădăuţi-Prut** Botoşani, NE Romania *48°14′N 26°47′E*
Radautz *see* Rădăuţi
Radbusa *see* Radbuza
183 A9 **Radbuza** *Ger.* Radbusa. 〰 SE Czech Republic
66 E4 **Radcliff** Kentucky, S USA *37°50′N 85°57′W*
216 G2 **Radd, Wādī ar** *dry watercourse* N Syria
155 E8 **Råde** Østfold, S Norway *59°21′N 10°53′E*
179 H9 **Radebeul** Sachsen, E Germany *51°06′N 13°41′E*
177 K5 **Radeče** *Ger.* Ratschach. C Slovenia *46°01′N 15°10′E*
Radein *see* Radenci
188 D3 **Radekhiv** *Pol.* Radziechów, *Rus.* Radekhov. L'vivs'ka Oblast', W Ukraine *50°17′N 24°39′E*
Radekhov *see* Radekhiv
177 L4 **Radenci** *Ger.* Radein; *prev.* Radinci. NE Slovenia *46°36′N 16°02′E*
177 J4 **Radenthein** Kärnten, S Austria *46°48′N 13°42′E*
181 D9 **Radevormwald** Nordrhein-Westfalen, Germany *7°21′N 51°12′E*
Rádeyilikóé *see* Fort Good Hope
67 I5 **Radford** Virginia, NE USA *37°07′N 80°34′W*
232 C7 **Rādhanpur** Gujarāt, W India *23°52′N 71°49′E*
114 F8 **Radial Conchillas** Colonia, Uruguay *34°06′S 58°00′W*
Radinci *see* Radenci
197 J3 **Radishchevo** Ul'yanovskaya Oblast', W Russian Federation *52°49′N 47°54′E*
58 F5 **Radisson** Québec, E Canada *53°47′N 77°35′W*
141 J3 **Radium** Limpopo, South Africa *25°05′S 28°19′E*
57 H8 **Radium Hot Springs** British Columbia, SW Canada *50°39′N 116°09′W*
188 B7 **Radna** *Hung.* Máriaradna. Arad, W Romania *46°05′N 21°41′E*
185 K6 **Radnevo** Stara Zagora, C Bulgaria *42°17′N 25°58′E*
157 F10 **Radnor** *cultural region* E Wales, United Kingdom
Radnót *see* Iernut
Rádóc *see* Rădăuţi
179 D13 **Radolfzell am Bodensee** Baden-Württemberg, S Germany *47°43′N 08°58′E*
182 H7 **Radom** Mazowieckie, C Poland *51°23′N 21°08′E*
188 D10 **Radomireşti** Olt, S Romania *44°06′N 25°00′E*
182 G7 **Radomsko** *Rus.* Novoradomsk. Łódzkie, C Poland *51°04′N 19°25′E*
188 G3 **Radomyshl'** Zhytomyrs'ka Oblast', N Ukraine *50°30′N 29°16′E*
185 H7 **Radoviš** *prev.* Radovište. E Macedonia *41°39′N 22°26′E*
Radovište *see* Radoviš

◆ Country
● Country Capital
◇ Dependent Territory
○ Dependent Territory Capital
⬖ Administrative Regions
✕ International Airport
▲ Mountain
▲▲ Mountain Range
Volcano
〰 River
◎ Lake
⊠ Reservoir

◆ Country   ◇ Dependent Territory   ◆ Administrative Regions   ▲ Mountain   ⧫ Volcano   ☐ Lake
○ Country Capital   ○ Dependent Territory Capital   ✕ International Airport   ▲ Mountain Range   ♂ River   ☐ Reservoir

♦ Country	◇ Dependent Territory	✕ Administrative Regions	▲ Mountain	⛰ Volcano	◎ Lake
● Country Capital	○ Dependent Territory Capital	✈ International Airport	▲ Mountain Range	♒ River	☒ Reservoir

◆ Country	◇ Dependent Territory	✕ Administrative Regions	▲ Mountain	☁ Volcano	◎ Lake
● Country Capital	○ Dependent Territory Capital	✈ International Airport	▲ Mountain Range	✈ River	◙ Reservoir

INDEX

◆ Country
○ Country Capital
◇ Dependent Territory
○ Dependent Territory Capital
◈ Administrative Regions
✕ International Airport
▲ Mountain
▲ Mountain Range
⟷ River
☺ Lake
☑ Reservoir

Shëngjini - Sikanni Chief

Shëngjini *see* Shëngjin
Shengking *see* Liaoning
Shengsi Islands *see* Shengsi Liedao
243 *N2* **Shengsi Liedao** *Eng.* Shengsi Islands. *archipelago* Zhejiang Sheng, Shengsi Liedao, SE China Pacific Ocean East China Sea
Sheng Xian/Shengxian *see* Shengzhou
243 *M2* **Shengze** Jiangsu, E China *30°54′N 120°39′E*
243 *M3* **Shengzhou** *var.* Shengxian, Sheng Xian. Zhejiang, SE China *29°36′N 120°42′E*
244 *C6* **Shenjiahe Shuiku** ⊠ Ningxia, China
Shenking *see* Liaoning
194 *G7* **Shenkursk** Arkhangel'skaya Oblast', NW Russian Federation *62°10′N 42°58′E*
244 *F4* **Shenmu** Shaanxi, C China *38°49′N 110°27′E*
184 *F8* **Shën Noj i Madh** ▲ C Albania *41°23′N 20°07′E*
242 *F2* **Shennong Ding** ▲ C China *31°24′N 110°16′E*
242 *F1* **Shennongjia** Hubei, China *31°27′N 110°24′E*
Shenshi/Shensi *see* Shaanxi
245 *J5* **Shentou** Shandong, E China *37°22′N 116°42′E*
245 *I6* **Shenxian** Shandong, China *36°08′N 115°23′E*
245 *N1* **Shenyang** *Chin.* Shen-yang, *Eng.* Moukden, Mukden; *prev.* Fengtien. *province capital* Liaoning, NE China *41°50′N 123°26′E*
Shen-yang *see* Shenyang
243 *H10* **Shenzhen** Guangdong, S China *22°39′N 114°02′E*
245 *I4* **Shenzhou** Hebei, China *38°01′N 115°19′E*
232 *E7* **Sheopur** Madhya Pradesh, C India *25°41′N 76°42′E*
188 *F3* **Shepetivka** *Rus.* Shepetovka. Khmel'nyts'ka Oblast', NW Ukraine *50°12′N 27°01′E*
Shepetovka *see* Shepetivka
71 *I6* **Shepherd** Texas, SW USA *30°30′N 95°00′W*
281 *M4* **Shepherd Islands** *island group* C Vanuatu
66 *E4* **Shepherdsville** Kentucky, S USA *38°00′N 85°42′W*
54 *B5* **Sheppard Peak** ▲ Canada *57°41′N 132°37′W*
277 *J6* **Shepparton** Victoria, SE Australia *36°25′S 145°26′E*
161 *M6* **Sheppey, Isle of** *island* SE England, United Kingdom
161 *I3* **Shepshed** United Kingdom *52°45′N 1°17′W*
Sherabad *see* Sherobod
52 *F4* **Sherard Bay** *coastal sea feature* Nunavut, NW Canada
53 *I5* **Sherard, Cape** *headland* Nunavut, N Canada *74°36′N 80°10′W*
161 *H7* **Sherborne** S England, United Kingdom *50°58′N 02°30′W*
132 *C7* **Sherbro Island** *island* SW Sierra Leone
59 *K8* **Sherbrooke** Nova Scotia, SE Canada
63 *I3* **Sherbrooke** Québec, SE Canada *45°23′N 71°55′W*
74 *G6* **Sherburn** Minnesota, N USA *43°39′N 94°43′W*
64 *F2* **Sherburne** New York, USA *42°41′N 75°30′W*
158 *D8* **Shercock** Cavan, N Ireland
133 *N2* **Sherda** Borkou-Ennedi-Tibesti, N Chad *20°04′N 16°48′E*
129 *J8* **Shereik** River Nile, N Sudan *18°44′N 33°37′E*
196 *F2* **Sheremet'yevo** ✈ (Moskva) Moskovskaya Oblast', W Russian Federation *56°05′N 37°10′E*
233 *I7* **Shergāti** Bihār, N India *24°35′N 84°51′E*
75 *H13* **Sheridan** Arkansas, C USA *34°18′N 92°22′W*
80 *B1* **Sheridan** California, USA *38°28′N 123°02′W*
80 *D1* **Sheridan** California, USA *38°59′N 121°23′W*
77 *K6* **Sheridan** Wyoming, C USA *44°47′N 106°59′W*
276 *F5* **Sheringa** South Australia *33°51′S 135°13′E*
195 *M6* **Sherkaly** Khanty-Mansiyskiy Avtonomnyy Okrug-Yugra, Russian Federation
193 *J8* **Sherlovaya Gora** Chitinskaya Oblast', S Russian Federation *50°26′N 116°09′E*
71 *H3* **Sherman** Texas, SW USA *33°39′N 96°35′W*
292 *F6* **Sherman Island** *island* Antarctica
63 *L2* **Sherman Mills** Maine, NE USA *45°51′N 68°23′W*
74 *D7* **Sherman Reservoir** ⊠ Nebraska, C USA
229 *H8* **Sherobod** *Rus.* Sherabad. Surkhondaryo Viloyati, S Uzbekistan *37°43′N 66°59′E*
229 *H7* **Sherobod** *Rus.* Sherabad. 〰 S Uzbekistan
233 *K7* **Sherpur** Dhaka, N Bangladesh *25°00′N 90°01′E*
79 *M3* **Sherrelwood** Colorado, C USA *39°49′N 105°00′W*
161 *H6* **Sherston** United Kingdom *51°34′N 2°13′W*
163 *F8* **'s-Hertogenbosch** *Fr.* Bois-le-Duc, *Ger.* Herzogenbusch. Noord-Brabant, S Netherlands *51°41′N 05°19′E*
74 *C1* **Sherwood** North Dakota, N USA *48°55′N 101°36′W*
57 *J5* **Sherwood Park** Alberta, SW Canada *53°34′N 113°04′W*
104 *E6* **Sheshea, Río** 〰 E Peru
223 *I3* **Sheshtamad** Khorāsān-Razavī, NE Iran *36°03′N 57°45′E*
74 *F5* **Shetek, Lake** ◎ Minnesota, N USA
55 *I6* **Shethanei Lake** ◎ Manitoba, C Canada
156 *G1* **Shetland Islands** *island group* NE Scotland, United Kingdom
226 *B6* **Shetpe** Mangistau, SW Kazakhstan *44°06′N 52°03′E*
232 *B9* **Shetrunji** 〰 W India
Shevchenko *see* Aktau
189 *L4* **Shevchenkove** Kharkivs'ka Oblast', E Ukraine *49°40′N 37°13′E*
136 *D5* **Shewa Gīmīra** Southern Nationalities, S Ethiopia *07°12′N 35°49′E*
243 *K3* **Shexian** *var.* Huicheng, She Xian. Anhui, E China *29°53′N 118°27′E*
245 *H6* **Shexian** Hebei, China *36°20′N 113°24′E*
She Xian *see* Shexian
245 *M8* **Sheyang** *prev.* Hede. Jiangsu, E China *33°49′N 120°13′E*
74 *D2* **Sheyenne** North Dakota, N USA *47°49′N 99°08′W*
74 *E3* **Sheyenne River** 〰 North Dakota, N USA
156 *D4* **Shiant Islands** *island group* NW Scotland, United Kingdom
193 *N7* **Shiashkotan, Ostrov** *island* Kuril'skiye Ostrova, SE Russian Federation
73 *G8* **Shiawassee River** 〰 Michigan, N USA
221 *H8* **Shibām** C Yemen *15°49′N 48°24′E*
Shibarghān *see* Sheberghān
253 *B10* **Shibata** *var.* Sibata. Niigata, Honshū, C Japan *37°57′N 139°20′E*
252 *H4* **Shibecha** Hokkaidō, NE Japan *43°19′N 144°34′E*
Shiberghan/Shiberghān *see* Sheberghān
252 *F3* **Shibetsu** *var.* Sibetu. Hokkaidō, NE Japan *44°10′N 142°21′E*
252 *E4* **Shibetsu** *var.* Sibetu. Hokkaidō, NE Japan *43°57′N 142°13′E*
252 *H4* **Shibetsu** Hokkaidō, N Japan *43°40′N 145°10′E*
Shibh Jazirat Sīnā' *see* Sinai
129 *I3* **Shibîn el Kôm** *var.* Shibîn el Kôm. N Egypt *30°33′N 31°00′E*
Shibîn el Kôm *see* Shibîn el Kôm
242 *D5* **Shibing** Guizhou, S China *27°02′N 108°07′E*
222 *F8* **Shīb, Kūh-e** ▲▲ S Iran
58 *D4* **Shibogama Lake** ◎ Ontario, C Canada
Shibotsu-jima *see* Zelënyy, Ostrov
253 *B12* **Shibukawa** *var.* Sibukawa. Gunma, Honshū, S Japan *36°30′N 138°59′E*
250 *D9* **Shibushi** Kagoshima, Kyūshū, SW Japan *31°27′N 131°05′E*
250 *D9* **Shibushi-wan** *bay* SW Japan
245 *N3* **Shicheng Dao** *island* Liaoning, China
252 *D7* **Shichinohe** Aomori, Honshū, C Japan *40°40′N 141°07′E*
282 *E9* **Shichiyo Islands** *island group* Chuuk, C Micronesia
245 *N5* **Shidao** Shandong, E China *36°53′N 122°25′E*
227 *J3* **Shiderti** *var.* Shiderty. Pavlodar, NE Kazakhstan *51°40′N 74°50′E*
227 *J3* **Shiderti** 〰 N Kazakhstan
Shiderty *see* Shiderti
219 *F13* **Shīdīyah, Wādī ash** *dry watercourse* Jordan
Shīeli *see* Chiili
156 *E5* **Shiel, Loch** ◎ N Scotland, United Kingdom
251 *I4* **Shiga** *off.* Shiga-ken, *var.* Siga. ◈ *prefecture* Honshū, SW Japan
Shiga-ken *see* Shiga
Shigatse *see* Xigazê
221 *I7* **Shiḥan** *oasis* NE Yemen
Shih-chia-chuang/Shihmen *see* Shijiazhuang
242 *D5* **Shih-chien** Guizhou, S China *27°35′N 108°20′E*
238 *F3* **Shihezi** Xinjiang Uygur Zizhiqu, NW China *44°21′N 85°59′E*
242 *B3* **Shih-yang** Sichuan, C China *29°56′N 105°37′E*
Shiichi *see* Shyichy
184 *F8* **Shijak** *var.* Shijaku. Durrës, W Albania *41°21′N 19°34′E*
Shijaku *see* Shijak
245 *I4* **Shijiazhuang** Hebei, E China *39°04′N 114°52′E*
245 *I4* **Shijiazhuang** *var.* Shih-chia-chuang; *prev.* Shihmen. *province capital* Hebei, E China *38°04′N 114°28′E*
243 *L2* **Shijiedu** Anhui, E China *30°57′N 119°12′E*
245 *J3* **Shijingshan** Beijing Shi, N China *39°55′N 116°11′E*
245 *L7* **Shijiusuo** Shandong, E China *35°23′N 119°32′E*
252 *D6* **Shikabe** Hokkaidō, NE Japan *42°03′N 140°45′E*
230 *G7* **Shikārpur** Sind, S Pakistan *27°59′N 68°39′E*
197 *I4* **Shikhany** Saratovskaya Oblast', W Russian Federation *52°07′N 47°13′E*
282 *F9* **Shiki Islands** *island group* Chuuk, C Micronesia
250 *F6* **Shikoku** *var.* Sikoku. *island* SW Japan
286 *C4* **Shikoku Basin** *var.* Sikoku Basin. *undersea feature* N Philippine Sea *28°00′N 137°00′E*
Shikokuchūō *see* Kawanoe
250 *F6* **Shikoku-sanchi** ▲▲ Shikoku, SW Japan
M8 **Shikotan, Ostrov** *Jap.* Shikotan-tō. *island* NE Russian Federation
Shikotan-tō *see* Shikotan, Ostrov
252 *E5* **Shikotsu-ko** *var.* Sikotu Ko. ◎ Hokkaidō, NE Japan
136 *H5* **Shilabo** Sumalē, E Ethiopia *06°05′N 44°48′E*
197 *M4* **Shil'da** Orenburgskaya Oblast', W Russian Federation *51°46′N 59°48′E*
159 *K6* **Shildon** United Kingdom *54°38′N 1°39′W*
217 *K2* **Shilēr, Āw-e** 〰 E Iraq
233 *J6* **Shiliguri** *prev.* Siliguri. West Bengal, NE India *26°46′N 88°24′E*
243 *K8* **Shiliu** Fujian, SE China *24°09′N 117°32′E*
Shiliu *see* Changjiang
193 *I8* **Shilka** Chitinskaya Oblast', S Russian Federation *51°52′N 115°49′E*
205 *L4* **Shilka** 〰 S Russian Federation
160 *B3* **Shillelagh** Wicklow, Ireland *52°45′N 6°32′W*
161 *H8* **Shillingstone** United Kingdom *50°54′N 2°15′W*
64 *E7* **Shillington** Pennsylvania, NE USA *40°18′N 75°57′W*
233 *L7* **Shillong** *state capital* Meghālaya, NE India *25°37′N 91°54′E*
65 *F9* **Shiloh** New Jersey, NE USA *39°27′N 75°17′W*
242 *F10* **Shilong** Guangdong, S China *22°00′N 110°44′E*
196 *G3* **Shilovo** Ryazanskaya Oblast', W Russian Federation *54°18′N 40°53′E*
250 *C7* **Shimabara** *var.* Simabara. Nagasaki, Kyūshū, SW Japan *32°48′N 130°20′E*
250 *C7* **Shimabara-wan** *bay* SW Japan
251 *K4* **Shimada** *var.* Simada. Shizuoka, Honshū, S Japan *34°50′N 138°10′E*
250 *E4* **Shimane** *off.* Shimane-ken, *var.* Simane. ◈ *prefecture* Honshū, SW Japan
250 *F4* **Shimane-hantō** *peninsula* Honshū, SW Japan
Shimane-ken *see* Shimane
193 *K8* **Shimanovsk** Amurskaya Oblast', SE Russian Federation *52°00′N 127°36′E*
Shimanto *see* Nakamura
Shimbir Berris *see* Shimbiris
136 *I3* **Shimbiris** *var.* Shimbir Berris. ▲ N Somalia *10°43′N 47°10′E*
242 *F5* **Shimen** Hunan, S China *27°14′N 111°02′E*
252 *F4* **Shimizu** Hokkaidō, NE Japan *42°58′N 142°54′E*
251 *K4* **Shimizu** *var.* Simizu. Shizuoka, Honshū, S Japan *35°01′N 138°29′E*
232 *E4* **Shimla** *prev.* Simla. *state capital* Himāchal Pradesh, N India *31°07′N 77°09′E*
Shimminato *see* Shinminato
251 *L5* **Shimoda** *var.* Simoda. Shizuoka, Honshū, S Japan *34°40′N 138°55′E*
253 *C12* **Shimodate** *var.* Simodate. Ibaraki, Honshū, S Japan *36°20′N 140°00′E*
234 *D7* **Shimoga** Karnātaka, W India *13°56′N 75°31′E*
250 *C7* **Shimo-jima** *island* SW Japan
250 *B8* **Shimo-Koshiki-jima** *island* SW Japan
137 *E10* **Shimoni** Coast, S Kenya *04°40′S 39°22′E*
250 *D5* **Shimonoseki** *var.* Simonoseki, *hist.* Akamagaseki, Bakan. Yamaguchi, Honshū, SW Japan *33°57′N 130°54′E*
253 *C13* **Shimotsuma** *var.* Simotuma. Ibaraki, Honshū, S Japan *36°10′N 139°58′E*
194 *D9* **Shimsk** Novgorodskaya Oblast', NW Russian Federation *58°12′N 30°43′E*
218 *H1* **Shīn** Syria *34°47′N 36°26′E*
251 *K2* **Shinano-gawa** *var.* Sinano Gawa. 〰 Honshū, C Japan
221 *K4* **Shināṣ** N Oman *24°45′N 56°24′E*
230 *D4* **Shīndand** Herāt, W Afghanistan *33°19′N 62°09′E*
250 *B4* **Shin-dong** Kyŏngsang-namdo, South Korea *34°57′N 128°39′E*
Shinei *see* Hsinying
239 *J3* **Shinejinst** *var.* Dzalaa. Bayanhongor, C Mongolia *44°29′N 99°19′E*
71 *H7* **Shiner** Texas, SW USA *29°25′N 97°10′W*
256 *D2* **Shingbwiyang** Kachin State, N Myanmar (Burma) *26°40′N 96°14′E*
52 *B6* **Shingle Point** Yukon Territory, NW Canada
227 *L5* **Shingozha** Vostochnyy Kazakhstan, E Kazakhstan *47°46′N 80°38′E*
251 *I6* **Shingū** *var.* Singû. Wakayama, Honshū, SW Japan *33°41′N 135°57′E*
141 *L2* **Shingwedzi** 〰 Limpopo, South Africa
72 *I3* **Shining Tree** Ontario, S Canada *47°36′N 81°12′W*
250 *F4* **Shinji-ko** *var.* Sinzi-ko. ◎ Honshū, SW Japan
253 *C9* **Shinjō** *var.* Sinzyô. Yamagata, Honshū, C Japan *38°47′N 140°17′E*
156 *E4* **Shin, Loch** ◎ N Scotland, United Kingdom
251 *J2* **Shinminato** *var.* Shimminato, Sinminato. Toyama, Honshū, SW Japan *36°47′N 137°04′E*
250 *E5* **Shinnanyō** *var.* Shin-Nan'yō, Sinn'anyô. Yamaguchi, Honshū, SW Japan *34°05′N 131°41′E*
Shin-Nan'yō *see* Shinnanyō
67 *I2* **Shinnston** West Virginia, NE USA *39°22′N 80°19′W*
218 *H1* **Shinshār** *Fr.* Chinnchâr. Ḥimṣ, W Syria *34°36′N 36°45′E*
251 *J4* **Shinshiro** *var.* Sinsiro. Aichi, Honshū, SW Japan *34°53′N 137°29′E*
Shinshū *see* Chinju
252 *F4* **Shintoku** Hokkaidō, NE Japan *43°03′N 142°50′E*
137 *C9* **Shinyanga** Shinyanga, NW Tanzania *03°40′S 33°25′E*
137 *C9* **Shinyanga** ◈ *region* N Tanzania
253 *D10* **Shiogama** *var.* Siogama. Miyagi, Honshū, C Japan *38°19′N 141°00′E*
251 *K3* **Shiojiri** *var.* Sioziri. Nagano, Honshū, S Japan *36°08′N 137°58′E*
251 *I6* **Shiono-misaki** *headland* Honshū, SW Japan *33°25′N 135°45′E*
253 *D12* **Shioya-zaki** *headland* Honshū, C Japan *37°00′N 140°57′E*
185 *K6* **Shipchenski Prokhod** *pass* C Bulgaria
161 *L3* **Shipdham** United Kingdom *52°37′N 0°54′E*
240 *C7* **Shiping** Yunnan, SW China *23°45′N 102°23′E*
159 *K9* **Shipley** United Kingdom *53°50′N 1°46′W*
59 *J7* **Shippagan** *var.* Shippegan. New Brunswick, SE Canada *47°45′N 64°44′W*
Shippegan *see* Shippagan
64 *C7* **Shippensburg** Pennsylvania, NE USA *40°03′N 77°31′W*
79 *J6* **Shiprock** New Mexico, SW USA *36°47′N 108°41′W*
79 *J6* **Ship Rock** ▲ New Mexico, SW USA *36°41′N 108°50′W*
193 *N6* **Shipunskiy, Mys** *headland* E Russian Federation *53°04′N 159°57′E*
242 *D5* **Shiqian** Guizhou, China *27°19′N 108°08′E*
244 *D9* **Shiquan** Shaanxi, C China *33°05′N 108°15′E*
192 *G8* **Shira** Respublika Khakasiya, S Russian Federation *54°35′N 89°58′E*
251 *H6* **Shirahama** Wakayama, Honshū, SW Japan *33°40′N 135°21′E*
233 *K7* **Shirajganj Ghat** *var.* Shirajganj Ghat. Rajshahi, C Bangladesh *24°27′N 89°42′E*
Shirajganj Ghat *see* Shirajganj Ghat
252 *C6* **Shirakami-misaki** *headland* Hokkaidō, NE Japan *41°26′N 140°10′E*
253 *C11* **Shirakawa** *var.* Sirakawa. Fukushima, Honshū, C Japan *37°07′N 140°11′E*
251 *J2* **Shirakawa** Gifu, Honshū, SW Japan *36°17′N 136°52′E*
253 *B12* **Shirane-san** ▲ Honshū, S Japan *36°44′N 139°21′E*
251 *K3* **Shirane-san** ▲ Honshū, S Japan *35°39′N 138°13′E*
252 *G5* **Shiranuka** Hokkaidō, NE Japan *42°57′N 144°01′E*
252 *E5* **Shiraoi** Hokkaidō, NE Japan *42°34′N 141°24′E*
293 *H7* **Shirase Coast** *physical region* Antarctica
252 *F3* **Shirataki** Hokkaidō, NE Japan *43°55′N 143°14′E*
222 *F7* **Shīrāz** *var.* Shīrāz. Fārs, S Iran *29°38′N 52°34′E*
137 *C14* **Shire** *var.* Chire. 〰 Malawi/Mozambique
Shiree *see* Tsagaanhayrhan
Shireet *see* Bayandelger
252 *H3* **Shiretoko-hantō** *headland* Hokkaidō, NE Japan *44°06′N 145°07′E*
252 *H3* **Shiretoko-misaki** *headland* Hokkaidō, NE Japan *44°20′N 145°19′E*
197 *H3* **Shiringushi** Respublika Mordoviya, W Russian Federation *53°50′N 42°49′E*
230 *F2* **Shīrīn Tagāb** Fāryāb, N Afghanistan *36°49′N 65°01′E*
230 *F2* **Shīrīn Tagāb** 〰 N Afghanistan
252 *E6* **Shiriya-zaki** *headland* Honshū, C Japan *41°24′N 141°27′E*
226 *D5* **Shirkala, Gryada** *plain* W Kazakhstan
65 *J6* **Shirley** New York, USA *40°48′N 72°52′W*
253 *D10* **Shiroishi** *var.* Siroisi. Miyagi, Honshū, C Japan *38°00′N 140°38′E*
Shirokoye *see* Shyroke
253 *B11* **Shirone** *var.* Sirone. Niigata, Honshū, C Japan *37°46′N 139°00′E*
251 *J3* **Shirotori** Gifu, Honshū, SW Japan *35°53′N 136°52′E*
251 *K2* **Shirouma-dake** ▲ Honshū, S Japan *36°46′N 137°46′E*
294 *C5* **Shirshov Ridge** *undersea feature* W Bering Sea
Shirshütür/Shirshyutyur, Peski *see* Şirşütür Gumy
223 *I2* **Shīrvān** *var.* Shirwān. Khorāsān, NE Iran *37°25′N 57°55′E*
Shirwa, Lake *see* Chilwa, Lake
Shirwān *see* Shīrvān
238 *G3* **Shisanjianfang** Xinjiang Uygur Zizhiqu, W China *43°10′N 91°15′E*
82 *F9* **Shishaldin Volcano** ▲ Unimak Island, Alaska, USA *54°45′N 163°58′W*
243 *K7* **Shishan** Fujian, SE China *25°11′N 118°17′E*
Shishchitsy *see* Shyshchytsy
243 *L8* **Shishi** Fujian, China *24°26′N 118°23′E*
82 *F4* **Shishmaref** Alaska, USA *66°15′N 166°04′W*
242 *G3* **Shishou** Hubei, China *29°26′N 112°14′E*
158 *F4* **Shiskine** United Kingdom *55°31′N 5°18′W*
Shisur *see* Ash Shiṣar
244 *D3* **Shitanjing** Ningxia, China *39°08′N 106°13′E*
251 *J4* **Shitara** Aichi, Honshū, SW Japan *35°06′N 137°33′E*
232 *C6* **Shiv** Rājasthān, NW India *26°11′N 71°14′E*
235 *C5* **Shivāji Sāgar** *var.* Shivāji Sāgar. ⊠ W India
Shivāji Sāgar *see* Shivāji Sāgar
232 *E7* **Shivpuri** Madhya Pradesh, C India *25°28′N 77°41′E*
78 *G6* **Shivwits Plateau** *plain* Arizona, SW USA
Shiwalik Range *see* Siwalik Range
243 *H5* **Shiwan** Hunan, C China *28°10′N 113°49′E*
242 *C10* **Shiwan Dashan** ▲▲ Guangxi, China
242 *F1* **Shiyan** Hubei, C China *32°31′N 110°45′E*
245 *M9* **Shiyan** Jiangsu, E China *32°43′N 120°11′E*
244 *A4* **Shiyang He** 〰 C China
243 *J8* **Shizheng** Guangdong, SE China *24°31′N 115°49′E*
Shizilu *see* Junan
242 *A7* **Shizong** *var.* Danfeng. Yunnan, SW China *24°53′N 104′E*
242 *D3* **Shizu** Chongqing Shi, C China *29°35′N 108°05′E*
253 *E10* **Shizugawa** Miyagi, Honshū, NE Japan *38°40′N 141°26′E*
244 *D3* **Shizuishan** *var.* Dawukou. Ningxia, N China *39°04′N 106°22′E*
244 *D3* **Shizuishan** Ningxia, N China *39°32′N 107°05′E*
252 *F5* **Shizunai** Hokkaidō, NE Japan *42°20′N 142°24′E*
251 *K4* **Shizuoka** *var.* Sizuoka. Shizuoka, Honshū, S Japan *34°59′N 138°20′E*
251 *K4* **Shizuoka** *off.* Shizuoka-ken, *var.* Sizuoka. ◈ *prefecture* Honshū, S Japan
Shizuoka-ken *see* Shizuoka
Shklov *see* Shklow
191 *H9* **Shklow** *Rus.* Shklov. Mahilyowskaya Voblasts', E Belarus *54°13′N 30°18′E*
184 *F7* **Shkodër** *var.* Shkodra, *It.* Scutari, *SCr.* Skadar. Shkodër, NW Albania *42°03′N 19°31′E*
184 *F7* **Shkodër** ◈ *district* NW Albania
Shkodra *see* Shkodër
Shkodrës, Liqeni i *see* Scutari, Lake
184 *F8* **Shkumbinit, Lumi i** *var.* Shkumbî, Shkumbin. 〰 C Albania
Shkumbî/Shkumbin *see* Shkumbinit, Lumi i
Shligigh, Cuan *see* Sligo Bay
193 *H2* **Shmidta, Ostrov** *island* Severnaya Zemlya, N Russian Federation
277 *L6* **Shoalhaven River** 〰 New South Wales, SE Australia
55 *I9* **Shoal Lake** Manitoba, S Canada *50°28′N 100°36′W*
73 *E12* **Shoals** Indiana, N USA *38°40′N 86°47′W*
250 *F4* **Shōbara** *var.* Syôbara. Hiroshima, Honshū, SW Japan *34°52′N 133°00′E*
250 *G5* **Shōdo-shima** *island* SW Japan
161 *L6* **Shoeburyness** United Kingdom *51°32′N 0°48′E*
251 *J2* **Shō-gawa** 〰 Honshū, SW Japan
Shōka *see* Changhua
193 *H2* **Shokal'skogo, Proliv** *strait* N Russian Federation
65 *H3* **Shokan** New York, USA *41°58′N 74°13′W*
252 *E4* **Shokanbetsu-dake** ⛰ Hokkaidō, NE Japan *43°43′N 141°33′E*
229 *K8* **Shokhdara, Qatorkŭhi** *Rus.* Shakhdarinskiy Khrebet. ▲▲ SE Tajikistan
227 *H7* **Sholakkorgan** *var.* Chulakkurgan. Yuzhnyy Kazakhstan, S Kazakhstan *43°45′N 69°10′E*
226 *G3* **Sholaksay** Kostanay, N Kazakhstan *51°45′N 64°45′E*
Sholāpur *see* Solāpur
Sholdaneshty *see* Şoldăneşti
Shonzhy *see* Chundzha
Shoqpar *see* Chokpar
235 *D9* **Shoranūr** Kerala, SW India *10°53′N 76°06′E*
234 *E6* **Shorāpur** Karnātaka, C India *16°34′N 76°48′E*
229 *H7* **Sho'rchi** *Rus.* Shurchi. Surkhondaryo Viloyati, S Uzbekistan *37°58′N 67°40′E*
64 *L4* **Shore Acres** Rhode Island, NE USA *41°34′N 71°25′W*
161 *K8* **Shoreham-by-Sea** United Kingdom *50°50′N 0°14′W*
73 *D9* **Shorewood** Illinois, N USA *41°31′N 88°12′W*
Shorkazakhly, Solonchak *see* Kazakhlyshor, Solonchak
227 *I3* **Shortandy** Akmola, C Kazakhstan *51°45′N 71°01′E*
Shortepa/Shor Tepe *see* Shūr Tappeh
280 *F3* **Shortland Island** *var.* Alu. *island* Shortland Islands, NW Solomon Islands
275 *M1* **Shortland Islands** *island group* NW Solomon Islands
161 *I8* **Shorwell** United Kingdom *50°38′N 1°21′W*
Shosambetsu *see* Shosanbetsu
252 *E3* **Shosanbetsu** *var.* Shosambetsu. Hokkaidō, NE Japan *44°31′N 141°47′E*
81 *H9* **Shoshone** California, USA *35°58′N 116°16′W*
76 *G8* **Shoshone** Idaho, NW USA *42°56′N 114°24′W*
80 *I3* **Shoshone Mountains** ▲▲ Nevada, W USA
80 *I7* **Shoshone Peak** ▲ Nevada, USA *36°57′N 116°16′W*
77 *J6* **Shoshone River** 〰 Wyoming, C USA
141 *I1* **Shoshong** Central, SE Botswana *23°02′S 26°31′E*
77 *K7* **Shoshoni** Wyoming, C USA *43°13′N 108°06′W*
Shōshū *see* Sangju
189 *J1* **Shostka** Sums'ka Oblast', NE Ukraine *51°52′N 33°30′E*
159 *K6* **Shotley Bridge** United Kingdom *54°52′N 1°51′W*
278 *B11* **Shotover** 〰 South Island, New Zealand
159 *H3* **Shotts** United Kingdom *55°50′N 3°51′W*
243 *L3* **Shouchang** Zhejiang, E China *29°21′N 119°14′E*
245 *K5* **Shouguang** Shandong, China *36°32′N 118°26′E*
243 *L5* **Shouning** Fujian, China *27°16′N 119°18′E*
243 *J1* **Shouxian** Anhui, China *32°20′N 116°28′E*
244 *E8* **Shouyang Shan** ▲ Shaanxi, China *33°53′N 108°16′E*
228 *E5* **Shovot** *Rus.* Shavat. Xorazm Viloyati, W Uzbekistan *41°41′N 60°13′E*
79 *J8* **Show Low** Arizona, SW USA *34°15′N 110°01′W*
Show Me State *see* Missouri
195 *H3* **Shoyna** Nenetskiy Avtonomnyy Okrug, NW Russian Federation *67°50′N 44°09′E*
194 *G7* **Shozhma** Arkhangel'skaya Oblast', NW Russian Federation *61°57′N 40°10′E*
189 *H5* **Shpola** Cherkas'ka Oblast', N Ukraine *49°00′N 31°27′E*
Shqipëria/Shqipërisë, Republika e *see* Albania
68 *B1* **Shreveport** Louisiana, S USA *32°32′N 93°45′W*
160 *G3* **Shrewsbury** *hist.* Scrobesbyrig'. W England, United Kingdom *52°43′N 02°45′W*
65 *K2* **Shrewsbury** Massachusetts, USA *42°18′N 71°43′W*
64 *D8* **Shrewsbury** Pennsylvania, USA *39°46′N 76°41′W*
232 *C6* **Shri Mohangarh** *prev.* Sri Mohangorh. Rājasthān, NW India *27°17′N 71°18′E*
233 *J8* **Shrīrāmpur** *prev.* Serampore, Serampur. West Bengal, NE India *22°44′N 88°20′E*
160 *G4* **Shropshire** *cultural region* W England, United Kingdom
227 *J7* **Shu** *Kaz.* Shū. Zhambyl, SE Kazakhstan *43°34′N 73°41′E*
240 *C7* **Shuangbai** *var.* Tuodian. Yunnan, SW China *24°45′N 101°38′E*
247 *L5* **Shuangcheng** Heilongjiang, NE China *45°20′N 126°21′E*
Shuangcheng *see* Zherong
242 *G5* **Shuangfeng** Hunan, China *27°17′N 112°07′E*
242 *F5* **Shuangfeng** Hunan, S China *27°10′N 110°33′E*
240 *B7* **Shuangjiang** *var.* Weiyuan. Yunnan, SW China *23°28′N 99°43′E*
Shuangjiang *see* Jiangkou
Shuangjiang *see* Tongdao
248 *B1* **Shuangliao** *var.* Zhengjiatun. Jilin, NE China *43°31′N 123°32′E*
Shuang-liao *see* Liaoyuan
242 *C5* **Shuangliu** Guizhou, S China *27°04′N 106°51′E*
242 *A2* **Shuangliu** Sichuan, China *30°22′N 103°34′E*
Shuangshipu *see* Fengxian
242 *B4* **Shuang-tsao-fang** Sichuan, C China *28°55′N 105°45′E*
243 *I3* **Shuangxi** Hubei, E China *29°56′N 114°28′E*
193 *K9* **Shuangyashan** *var.* Shuang-ya-shan. Heilongjiang, NE China *46°37′N 131°10′E*
Shuang-ya-shan *see* Shuangyashan
Shu'aymiah *see* Shu'aymīyah
221 *K7* **Shu'aymīyah** *var.* Shu'aymiah. S Oman *17°55′N 55°39′E*
226 *D4* **Shubarkuduk** *Kaz.* Shubarqudyq. Aktyubinsk, W Kazakhstan *49°09′N 56°31′E*
Shubarqudyq *see* Shubarkuduk
226 *G5* **Shubar-Tengiz, Ozero** ◎ C Kazakhstan
52 *A5* **Shublik Mountains** ▲▲ Alaska, USA
243 *J2* **Shucheng** Anhui, China *31°16′N 116°34′E*
238 *C5* **Shufu** *var.* Tuokezhake. Xinjiang Uygur Zizhiqu, NW China *39°18′N 75°43′E*
229 *K8* **Shughnon, Qatorkŭhi** *Rus.* Shugnanskiy Khrebet. ▲▲ SE Tajikistan
Shugnanskiy Khrebet *see* Shughnon, Qatorkŭhi
245 *K7* **Shu He** 〰 E China
Shuicheng *see* Lupanshui
Shuiding *see* Huocheng
243 *K2* **Shuidong** Anhui, E China *30°29′N 118°09′E*
Shuidong *see* Dianbai
243 *K5* **Shuiji** Fujian, SE China *27°28′N 118°21′E*
Shuiji *see* Laixi
Shū-Ile Taūlary *see* Chu-Iliyskiye Gory
243 *N8* **Shuili** C Taiwan *23°49′N 120°50′E*
Shuilocheng *see* Zhuanglang
Shuiluo *see* Zhuanglang
231 *I6* **Shujāābād** Punjab, E Pakistan *29°53′N 71°23′E*
Shū, Kazakhstan *see* Shu
Shū, Kazakhstan/Kyrgyzstan *see* Chu
55 *M2* **Shukbuk Bay** *coastal sea feature* Nunavut, NE Canada
248 *D1* **Shulan** Jilin, NE China *44°28′N 126°57′E*
238 *C5* **Shule** Xinjiang Uygur Zizhiqu, NW China *39°19′N 76°06′E*
Shuleh *see* Shule He
239 *I5* **Shule He** *var.* Shuleh, Sulo. 〰 C China
244 *F2* **Shulinzhao** Inner Mongolia, China *40°15′N 110°01′E*
73 *B8* **Shullsburg** Wisconsin, N USA *42°37′N 90°12′W*
Shulu *see* Xinji
82 *G9* **Shumagin Islands** *island group* Alaska, USA
228 *D4* **Shumanay** Qoraqalpog'iston Respublikasi, W Uzbekistan *42°42′N 58°56′E*
185 *L5* **Shumen** Shumen, NE Bulgaria *43°17′N 26°57′E*
185 *L5* **Shumen** ◈ *province* NE Bulgaria
197 *I2* **Shumerlya** Chuvashskaya Respublika, W Russian Federation *55°31′N 46°24′E*
195 *N10* **Shumikha** Kurganskaya Oblast', C Russian Federation *55°12′N 63°09′E*
191 *H8* **Shumilina** *Rus.* Shumilino. Vitsyebskaya Voblasts', NE Belarus *55°18′N 29°37′E*
Shumilino *see* Shumilina
193 *N7* **Shumshu, Ostrov** *island* SE Russian Federation
188 *E3* **Shums'k** Ternopil's'ka Oblast', W Ukraine *50°06′N 26°04′E*
191 *J9* **Shumyachi** Smolenskaya Oblast', Russian Federation
Shūnan *see* Tokuyama
243 *K6* **Shunchang** Fujian, China *26°29′N 117°29′E*
83 *H4* **Shungnak** Alaska, USA *66°53′N 157°08′W*
Shunsen *see* Ch'unch'ŏn
Shuoxian *see* Shuozhou
245 *H3* **Shuozhou** *var* Shuoxian. Shanxi, C China *39°20′N 112°25′E*
220 *G9* **Shuqrah** *var.* Shaqrā. SW Yemen *13°26′N 45°44′E*
Shurab *see* Shŭrob
Shurchi *see* Sho'rchi
229 *J6* **Shŭrob** *Rus.* Shurab. NW Tajikistan *40°02′N 70°31′E*
223 *I6* **Shūr, Rūd-e** 〰 E Iran
230 *F2* **Shūr Tappeh** *var.* Shortepa, Shor Tepe. Balkh, N Afghanistan *37°22′N 66°49′E*
139 *H4* **Shurugwi** *prev.* Selukwe. Midlands, C Zimbabwe *19°40′S 30°00′E*
222 *D5* **Shūsh** *anc.* Susa, *Bibl.* Shushan. Khūzestān, SW Iran *32°12′N 48°20′E*
Shushan *see* Shūsh
222 *E6* **Shūshtar** *var.* Shustar, Shushter. Khūzestān, SW Iran *32°03′N 48°51′E*
Shushter/Shustar *see* Shūshtar
160 *G8* **Shute** United Kingdom *50°46′N 3°04′W*
221 *I5* **Shuṭfah, Qalamat** *well* E Saudi Arabia
217 *K6* **Shuwayjah, Hawr ash** *var.* Hawr as Suwayqiyah. ◎ E Iraq
194 *G10* **Shuya** Ivanovskaya Oblast', W Russian Federation *56°51′N 41°24′E*
83 *I7* **Shuyak Island** *island* Alaska, USA
245 *L8* **Shuyang** Shandong, E China *34°08′N 118°46′E*
256 *C4* **Shwebo** Sagaing, C Myanmar (Burma) *22°35′N 95°42′E*
256 *C6* **Shwedaung** Bago, W Myanmar (Burma) *18°44′N 95°12′E*
256 *D6* **Shwegyin** Bago, SW Myanmar (Burma) *17°56′N 96°59′E*
256 *D3* **Shweli** *Chin.* Longchuan Jiang. 〰 Myanmar (Burma)/China
256 *C5* **Shwemyo** Mandalay, C Myanmar (Burma) *20°04′N 96°13′E*
Shyghanaq *see* Chiganak
Shyghys Qazagastan Oblysy *see* Vostochnyy Kazakhstan
Shyghys Qongyrat *see* Shygys Konyrat
227 *J5* **Shygys Konyrat**, *Kaz.* Shyghys Qongyrat. Karaganda, C Kazakhstan *47°01′N 75°05′E*
191 *H11* **Shyichy** *Rus.* Shiichi. Homyel'skaya Voblasts', SE Belarus *52°15′N 29°14′E*
227 *H8* **Shymkent** *prev.* Chimkent. Yuzhnyy Kazakhstan, S Kazakhstan *42°19′N 69°36′E*
Shyngghyrlaū *see* Chingirlau
232 *F2* **Shyok** Jammu and Kashmir, NW India *34°13′N 78°12′E*
189 *J6* **Shyroke** *Rus.* Shirokoye. Dnipropetrovs'ka Oblast', E Ukraine *47°41′N 33°16′E*
189 *H6* **Shyryayeve** Odes'ka Oblast', SW Ukraine *47°21′N 30°11′E*
189 *J4* **Shyshaky** Poltavs'ka Oblast', C Ukraine *49°54′N 34°00′E*
191 *F10* **Shyshchytsy** *Rus.* Shishchitsy. Minskaya Voblasts', C Belarus *53°13′N 27°33′E*
231 *K3* **Siachen Muztāgh** ▲▲ NE Pakistan
Siadehan *see* Tākestān
230 *E8* **Siāhān Range** ▲▲ W Pakistan
222 *C1* **Siāh Chashmeh** *var.* Chālderān. Āžarbāyjān-e Gharbī, N Iran *39°02′N 44°22′E*
231 *J5* **Siālkot** Punjab, NE Pakistan *32°29′N 74°35′E*
280 *C3* **Sialum** Morobe, C Papua New Guinea *06°02′S 147°37′E*
Siam *see* Thailand
Siam, Gulf of *see* Thailand, Gulf of
243 *L2* **Sian** Anhui, E China *30°48′N 119°56′E*
Sian *see* Xi'an
Siang *see* Brahmaputra
Siangtan *see* Xiangtan
258 *G3* **Siantan, Pulau** *island* Kepulauan Anambas, W Indonesia
102 *D6* **Siare, Río** 〰 C Colombia
263 *N8* **Siargao Island** *island* S Philippines
280 *C3* **Siassi** Umboi Island, C Papua New Guinea *05°34′S 147°50′E*
186 *F3* **Siátista** Dytikí Makedonía, N Greece *40°16′N 21°34′E*
256 *B4* **Siatlai** Chin State, W Myanmar (Burma) *22°05′N 93°36′E*
263 *L8* **Siaton** Negros, C Philippines *09°03′N 123°03′E*
263 *L8* **Siaton Point** *headland* Negros, C Philippines *09°03′N 123°00′E*
190 *C7* **Šiauliai** *Ger.* Schaulen. Šiauliai, N Lithuania *55°55′N 23°21′E*
190 *D7* **Šiauliai** ◈ *province* N Lithuania
260 *F2* **Siau, Pulau** *island* N Indonesia
138 *G2* **Siavonga** Southern, SE Zambia *16°33′S 28°42′E*
Siazan' *see* Siyäzän
Sibah *see* As Sībah
175 *H10* **Sibari** Calabria, S Italy *39°45′N 16°26′E*
Sibata *see* Shibata
197 *M3* **Sibay** Respublika Bashkortostan, W Russian Federation *52°40′N 58°39′E*
141 *L5* **Sibayi, Lake** ◎ KwaZulu-Natal, South Africa
180 *H6* **Sibbesse** Niedersachsen, Germany *9°54′N 52°03′E*
153 *H10* **Sibbo** *Fin.* Sipoo. Etelä-Suomi, S Finland *60°22′N 25°20′E*
184 *C5* **Šibenik** *It.* Sebenico. Šibenik-Knin, S Croatia *43°43′N 15°54′E*
Sibenik *see* Šibenik-Knin
184 *C4* **Šibenik-Knin** *off.* Šibenska Županija, *var.* Sibenik. ◈ *province* S Croatia
Šibenik-Knin *see* Drniš
Šibenska Županija *see* Šibenik-Knin
Siberia *see* Sibir'
Siberoet *see* Siberut, Pulau
258 *C5* **Siberut, Pulau** *prev.* Siberoet. *island* Kepulauan Mentawai, W Indonesia
258 *C5* **Siberut, Selat** *strait* W Indonesia
Sibetu *see* Shibetsu
230 *G6* **Sibi** Baluchistān, SW Pakistan *29°31′N 67°54′E*
280 *A4* **Sibidiri** Western, SW Papua New Guinea *08°58′S 142°14′E*
193 *I5* **Sibir'** *var.* Siberia. *physical region* NE Russian Federation
195 *M5* **Sibirskiye Uvaly** *mountains* Khanty-Mansiyskiy Avtonomnyy Okrug-Yugra, Russian Federation
135 *C9* **Sibiti** Lékoumou, S Congo *03°41′S 13°20′E*
137 *C9* **Sibiti** 〰 C Tanzania
188 *C8* **Sibiu** *Ger.* Hermannstadt, *Hung.* Nagyszeben. Sibiu, C Romania *45°48′N 24°09′E*
188 *C8* **Sibiu** ◈ *county* C Romania
74 *F6* **Sibley** Iowa, C USA *43°24′N 95°45′W*
258 *C4* **Sibolga** Sumatera, W Indonesia *01°42′N 98°48′E*
258 *C4* **Sibolga, Teluk** *var.* Teluk Tapanuli. *bay* Sumatera, W Indonesia
159 *M10* **Sibsey** United Kingdom *53°02′N 0°01′E*
258 *I4* **Sibu** Sarawak, East Malaysia *02°18′N 111°49′E*
Sibukawa *see* Shibukawa
88 *E2* **Sibun** 〰 E Belize
134 *E5* **Sibut** *prev.* Fort-Sibut. Kémo, S Central African Republic *05°44′N 19°07′E*
263 *K10* **Sibutu** *island* SW Philippines
263 *K10* **Sibutu Passage** *passage* SW Philippines
263 *L6* **Sibuyan Island** *island* C Philippines
263 *L6* **Sibuyan Sea** *sea* W Pacific Ocean
283 *L4* **Sibylla Island** *island* N Marshall Islands
56 *G7* **Sicamous** British Columbia, SW Canada *50°49′N 118°52′W*
Sichelburger Gerbirge *see* Gorjanci
243 *J6* **Sicheng** Jiangxi, China *26°12′N 116°11′E*
257 *E10* **Sichon** *var.* Ban Sichon, Si Chon. Nakhon Si Thammarat, SW Thailand *09°03′N 99°51′E*
Si Chon *see* Sichon
240 *C3* **Sichuan** *var.* Chuan, Sichuan Sheng, Ssu-ch'uan, Szechuan, Szechwan. ◈ *province* C China
242 *B3* **Sichuan Pendi** *basin* C China
Sichuan Sheng *see* Sichuan
169 *L6* **Sicie, Cap** *headland* SE France *43°03′N 05°50′E*
175 *F12* **Sicilia** *Eng.* Sicily; *anc.* Trinacria. ◈ *region* Italy, C Mediterranean Sea
175 *F13* **Sicilia** *Eng.* Sicily; *anc.* Trinacria. *island* Italy, C Mediterranean Sea
Sicilian Channel *see* Sicily, Strait of
175 *E13* **Sicily, Strait of** *var.* Sicilian Channel. *strait* C Mediterranean Sea
88 *G3* **Sico Tinto, Río** *var.* Río Negro. 〰 NE Honduras
105 *G8* **Sicuani** Cusco, S Peru *14°21′S 71°13′W*
184 *F3* **Šid** Vojvodina, NW Serbia *45°07′N 19°13′E*
186 *D4* **Sidári** Kérkyra, Iónia Nisiá, Greece, C Mediterranean Sea *39°47′N 19°43′E*
259 *H5* **Sidas** Borneo, C Indonesia *0°24′N 109°46′E*
160 *G8* **Sidbury** United Kingdom *50°43′N 3°12′W*
161 *K6* **Sidcup** United Kingdom *51°25′N 0°07′E*
162 *I3* **Siddeburen** Groningen, NE Netherlands *53°15′N 06°52′E*
232 *C7* **Siddhapur** *prev.* Siddhpur, Sidhpur. Gujarāt, W India *23°57′N 72°28′E*
Siddhpur *see* Siddhapur
234 *F5* **Siddipet** Andhra Pradesh, C India *18°10′N 78°54′E*
260 *C6* **Sidenreng, Danau** ◎ Sulawesi, C Indonesia
132 *F6* **Sidéradougou** SW Burkina *10°39′N 04°16′W*
175 *H12* **Siderno** Calabria, SW Italy *38°18′N 16°19′E*
Siders *see* Sierre
232 *G7* **Sidhi** Madhya Pradesh, C India *24°24′N 81°54′E*
Sidhirókastron *see* Sidirókastro
Sidhpur *see* Siddhapur
171 *M9* **Sidi Aïssa** Algeria
Sīdī al Hānī', Sabkhat *see* Sidi el Hani, Sebkhet de
171 *J9* **Sidi Ali** Algeria
128 *G2* **Sīdi Barrâni** NW Egypt *31°38′N 25°58′E*
131 *H2* **Sidi Bel Abbès** *var.* Sidi bel Abbès, Sidi-Bel-Abbès. NW Algeria *35°12′N 00°43′W*
130 *E3* **Sidi-Bennour** W Morocco *32°39′N 08°28′W*
131 *K2* **Sidi Bouzid** *var.* Gammouda, Sīdī Bu Zayd. C Tunisia *35°05′N 09°20′E*
Sīdī Bu Zayd *see* Sidi Bouzid
131 *K2* **Sidi el Hani, Sebkhet de** *var.* Sabkhat Sīdī al Hānī'. *salt flat* NE Tunisia
171 *I10* **Sidi Hamadouche** Algeria
130 *D4* **Sidi-Ifni** SW Morocco *29°33′N 10°04′W*
130 *F2* **Sidi-Kacem** *prev.* Petitjean. N Morocco *34°21′N 05°46′W*
173 *M9* **Sidi Lakhdar** Algeria *36°12′N 00°28′E*
187 *H2* **Sidirókastro** *prev.* Sidhirókastron. Kentrikí Makedonía, NE Greece *41°14′N 23°23′E*
55 *H4* **Sid Lake** ◎ Northwest Territories, NW Canada
159 *I2* **Sidlaw Hills** ▲▲ United Kingdom
292 *G7* **Sidley, Mount** ▲ Antarctica *76°39′S 124°48′W*
160 *G8* **Sidmouth** United Kingdom *50°41′N 3°15′W*
77 *M3* **Sidney** Montana, NW USA *47°42′N 104°10′W*
74 *A7* **Sidney** Nebraska, C USA *41°09′N 102°57′W*
64 *F2* **Sidney** New York, NE USA *42°18′N 75°21′W*
73 *G10* **Sidney** Ohio, N USA *40°16′N 84°09′W*
66 *G8* **Sidney Lanier, Lake** ⊠ Georgia, SE USA
Sidon *see* Saïda
192 *G5* **Sidorovsk** Yamalo-Nenetskiy Avtonomnyy Okrug, N Russian Federation *66°34′N 82°12′E*
Sidra *see* Surt
Sidra/Sidra, Gulf of *see* Surt, Khalīj, N Libya
181 *E14* **Siebeldingen** Rheinland-Pfalz, Germany *8°03′N 49°13′E*
Siebenbürgen *see* Transylvania
Sieben Dörfer *see* Săcele
180 *F5* **Siedenburg** Niedersachsen, Germany *8°56′N 52°42′E*
182 *I6* **Siedlce** *Ger.* Sedlez, *Rus.* Sesdlets. Mazowieckie, C Poland *52°10′N 22°18′E*
181 *F8* **Siedlinghausen** Nordrhein-Westfalen, Germany *8°28′N 51°15′E*
181 *D10* **Sieg** 〰 W Germany
181 *C10* **Siegburg** Nordrhein-Westfalen, Germany *7°12′N 50°48′E*
181 *E9* **Siegen** Nordrhein-Westfalen, W Germany *50°53′N 08°02′E*
177 *L2* **Sieghartskirchen** Niederösterreich, E Austria *48°13′N 16°01′E*
182 *I5* **Siemiatycze** Podlaskie, NE Poland *52°27′N 22°52′E*
257 *H8* **Siěmpang** Stœng Trêng, NE Cambodia *14°07′N 106°24′E*
257 *G8* **Siěmréab** *prev.* Siemreap. Siěmréab, NW Cambodia *13°21′N 103°50′E*
Siemreap *see* Siěmréab
176 *G10* **Siena** *Fr.* Sienne; *anc.* Saena Julia. Toscana, C Italy *43°20′N 11°20′E*
Sienne *see* Siena
152 *G5* **Sieppijärvi** Lappi, NW Finland *67°09′N 23°58′E*
182 *F7* **Sieradz** Sieradz, C Poland *51°36′N 18°42′E*
167 *L4* **Sierck-les-Bains** Lorraine, France *49°26′N 6°21′E*
167 *N7* **Sierentz** Alsace, France *47°40′N 7°28′E*
182 *G5* **Sierpc** Mazowieckie, C Poland *52°51′N 19°44′E*
70 *B5* **Sierra Blanca** Texas, SW USA *31°10′N 105°22′W*
79 *M8* **Sierra Blanca Peak** ▲ New Mexico, SW USA *33°22′N 105°48′W*
80 *E1* **Sierra City** California, W USA *39°34′N 120°35′W*
116 *D7* **Sierra Colorada** Río Negro, S Argentina *40°37′S 67°48′W*
172 *E4* **Sierra de San Pedro** ▲▲ Spain
116 *E7* **Sierra Grande** Río Negro, E Argentina *41°34′S 65°21′W*
132 *B7* **Sierra Leone** *off.* Republic of Sierra Leone. ◆ *republic* W Africa
290 *H7* **Sierra Leone Basin** *undersea feature* E Atlantic Ocean *05°00′N 17°00′W*
120 *F5* **Sierra Leone Fracture Zone** *tectonic feature* E Atlantic Ocean
Sierra Leone, Republic of *see* Sierra Leone
Sierra Leone Ridge *see* Sierra Leone Rise
290 *G7* **Sierra Leone Rise** *var.* Sierra Leone Ridge, Sierra Leone Schwelle. *undersea feature* E Atlantic Ocean *05°30′N 21°00′W*
Sierra Leone Schwelle *see* Sierra Leone Rise
85 *J5* **Sierra Mojada** Coahuila, NE Mexico *27°13′N 103°42′W*
80 *F1* **Sierraville** California, USA *39°35′N 120°22′W*
79 *J10* **Sierra Vista** Arizona, SW USA *31°33′N 110°18′W*
176 *D5* **Sierre** *Ger.* Siders. Valais, SW Switzerland *46°18′N 07°33′E*
79 *I10* **Sierrita Mountains** ▲▲ Arizona, SW USA
Siete Moai *see* Ahu Akivi
242 *C10* **Sifang Ling** ▲▲ Guangxi, China
243 *H5* **Sifen** Hunan, C China *27°32′N 113°29′E*
132 *E7* **Sifié** W Ivory Coast *07°59′N 06°55′W*
187 *I8* **Sífnos** *anc.* Siphnos. *island* Kykládes, Greece, Aegean Sea
187 *I7* **Sífnou, Stenó** *strait* SE Greece
171 *J10* **Sig** Algeria
Siga *see* Shiga
280 *D9* **Sigatoka** *prev.* Singatoka. Viti Levu, W Fiji *18°10′S 177°30′E*
165 *I9* **Sigean** Aude, S France *43°02′N 02°58′E*
159 *M8* **Sigglesthorne** United Kingdom *53°54′N 0°14′W*
Sighet *see* Sighetu Marmaţiei
Sighetul Marmaţiei *see* Sighetu Marmaţiei
188 *C6* **Sighetu Marmaţiei** *var.* Sighet, Sighetul Marmaţiei, *Hung.* Máramarossziget. Maramureş, N Romania *47°56′N 23°53′E*
188 *D7* **Sighişoara** *Ger.* Schässburg, *Hung.* Segesvár. Mureş, C Romania *46°12′N 24°48′E*
258 *B2* **Sigli** Sumatera, W Indonesia *05°21′N 95°56′E*
171 *N8* **Sigli, Cap** *headland* Algeria
152 *C1* **Siglufjördhur** Nordhurland Vestra, N Iceland *66°09′N 18°56′W*
179 *D13* **Sigmaringen** Baden-Württemberg, S Germany *48°04′N 09°12′E*
179 *H11* **Signalberg** ▲ SE Germany *49°30′N 12°34′E*
81 *I14* **Signal Peak** ▲ Arizona, SW USA *33°20′N 114°03′W*
Signan *see* Xi'an
292 *E1* **Signy** *UK research station* South Orkney Islands, Antarctica *60°27′S 45°35′W*
167 *J4* **Signy-l'Abbaye** Champagne-Ardenne, France *49°42′N 4°25′E*
74 *H7* **Sigourney** Iowa, C USA *41°19′N 92°12′W*
187 *J5* **Sígri, Akrotírio** *headland* Lésvos, E Greece *39°12′N 25°49′E*
Sigsbee Deep *see* Mexico Basin
95 *H1* **Sigsbee Escarpment** *undersea feature* N Gulf of Mexico *26°00′N 92°30′W*
104 *C3* **Sigsig** Azuay, S Ecuador *03°04′S 78°50′W*
155 *I8* **Sigtuna** Stockholm, C Sweden *59°36′N 17°44′E*
88 *E4* **Siguatepeque** Comayagua, W Honduras *14°39′N 87°48′W*
171 *H4* **Sigüenza** Castilla-La Mancha, C Spain *41°04′N 02°38′W*
171 *I2* **Sigües** Aragón, NE Spain *42°39′N 01°00′W*
132 *D5* **Siguiri** NE Guinea *11°26′N 09°08′W*
190 *E6* **Sigulda** *Ger.* Segewold. Rīga, C Latvia *57°08′N 24°51′E*
Sihanoukville *see* Kâmpóng Saôm
242 *G10* **Sihe** Guangdong, S China *22°38′N 112°33′E*
179 *D14* **Sihlsee** ◎ NW Switzerland
87 *L6* **Sihochac** Campeche, Mexico
245 *K8* **Sihong** Jiangsu, China *33°17′N 118°07′E*
242 *G9* **Sihui** Guangdong, China *23°13′N 112°25′E*
153 *G9* **Siikainen** Länsi-Suomi, SW Finland *61°52′N 21°49′E*
153 *I8* **Siilinjärvi** Itä-Suomi, C Finland *63°05′N 27°40′E*
215 *J7* **Siirt** *var.* Sert; *anc.* Tigranocerta. Siirt, SE Turkey *37°56′N 41°56′E*
215 *J7* **Siirt** *var.* Sert. ◈ *province* SE Turkey
243 *M2* **Sijing** Shanghai Shi, E China *31°07′N 121°16′E*
281 *H4* **Sikaiana** *var.* Stewart Islands. *island group* W Solomon Islands
Sikandarabad *see* Secunderābād
232 *F6* **Sikandra Rao** Uttar Pradesh, N India *27°42′N 78°21′E*
56 *E1* **Sikanni Chief** British Columbia, W Canada *57°16′N 122°44′W*

INDEX

407

◆ Country ● Country Capital ◇ Dependent Territory ○ Dependent Territory Capital ◈ Administrative Regions ✈ International Airport ▲ Mountain ▲▲ Mountain Range ⛰ Volcano 〰 River ◎ Lake ⊠ Reservoir

◆ Country
● Country Capital
◇ Dependent Territory
○ Dependent Territory Capital
◇ Administrative Regions
✈ International Airport
▲ Mountain
▲ Mountain Range
▲ Volcano
➷ River
◎ Lake
⊟ Reservoir

Sleat, Sound of – Sort
INDEX
409

156 E5 **Sleat, Sound of** *strait* NW Scotland, United Kingdom
159 L8 **Sledmere** United Kingdom 54°04′N 0°34′W
Sledyuki *see* Slyedzyuki
58 F3 **Sleeper Islands** *island group* Nunavut, C Canada
72 F6 **Sleeping Bear Point** *headland* Michigan, N USA 44°54′N 86°02′W
74 G5 **Sleepy Eye** Minnesota, N USA 44°18′N 94°43′W
83 H6 **Sleetmute** Alaska, USA 61°42′N 157°10′W
Sléibhe, Ceann *see* Slea Head
159 L7 **Sleights** United Kingdom 54°27′N 0°40′W
Slēmānī *see* As Sulaymānīyah
293 H3 **Slessor Glacier** *glacier* Antarctica
158 F4 **Sliddery** United Kingdom 55°27′N 5°15′W
68 E4 **Slidell** Louisiana, S USA 30°16′N 89°46′W
65 H3 **Slide Mountain** ▲ New York, NE USA 42°00′N 74°23′W
162 E7 **Sliedrecht** Zuid-Holland, C Netherlands 51°50′N 04°46′E
175 J13 **Sliema** N Malta 35°54′N 14°31′E
158 A10 **Slieve Aughty Mountains** ▲▲ Galway, Ireland
158 C10 **Slieve Bloom Mountains** ▲▲ Ireland
157 D8 **Slieve Donard** ▲ SE Northern Ireland, United Kingdom 54°10′N 05°57′W
158 A8 **Slieve Gamph** ▲▲ N Ireland
158 C5 **Slieve Snaght** ▲ Donegal, Ireland 55°12′N 7°20′W
Sligeach *see* Sligo
158 A7 **Sligo** *Ir.* Sligeach. Sligo, NW Ireland 54°17′N 08°28′W
158 A8 **Sligo** *Ir.* Sligeach. *cultural region* NW Ireland
158 A7 **Sligo Bay** *bay* Ireland
157 B8 **Sligo Bay** *Ir.* Cuan Shligigh. *inlet* NW Ireland
159 L8 **Slingsby** United Kingdom 54°09′N 0°55′W
62 C8 **Slippery Rock** Pennsylvania, NE USA 41°02′N 80°02′W
155 J10 **Slite** Gotland, SE Sweden 57°37′N 18°46′E
185 L6 **Sliven** *var.* Slivno. Sliven, C Bulgaria 42°42′N 26°21′E
185 L6 **Sliven** ◈ *province* C Bulgaria
185 I6 **Slivnitsa** Sofiya, W Bulgaria 42°51′N 23°01′E
Slivno *see* Sliven
185 L4 **Slivo Pole** Ruse, N Bulgaria 43°57′N 26°15′E
74 F7 **Sloan** Iowa, C USA 42°13′N 96°13′W
81 I9 **Sloan** Nevada, W USA 35°56′N 115°13′W
80 E1 **Sloat** California, USA 39°52′N 120°44′W
Slobodka *see* Slabodka
195 I9 **Slobodskoy** Kirovskaya Oblast', NW Russian Federation 58°43′N 50°12′E
Slobodzeya *see* Slobozia
188 G7 **Slobozia** *Rus.* Slobodzeya. E Moldova 46°45′N 29°42′E
188 F9 **Slobozia** Ialomiţa, SE Romania 44°34′N 27°23′E
162 I3 **Slochteren** Groningen, NE Netherlands 53°13′N 06°48′E
191 E10 **Slonim** *Pol.* Słonim. Hrodzyenskaya Voblasts', W Belarus 53°06′N 25°19′E
Słonim *see* Slonim
162 G4 **Sloter Meer** ◎ N Netherlands
Slot, The *see* New Georgia Sound
161 J6 **Slough** S England, United Kingdom 51°31′N 00°36′W
183 G10 **Slovakia** *off.* Slovenská Republika, *Ger.* Slowakei, *Hung.* Szlovákia, *Slvk.* Slovensko. ◆ *republic* C Europe
Slovak Ore Mountains *see* Slovenské rudohorie
Slovechna *see* Slavyechna
174 G4 **Slovenia** *off.* Republic of Slovenia, *Ger.* Slowenien, *Slvn.* Slovenija. ◆ *republic* SE Europe
Slovenia, Republic of *see* Slovenia
Slovenija *see* Slovenia
177 K5 **Slovenj Gradec** *Ger.* Windischgraz. N Slovenia 46°29′N 15°05′E
177 L5 **Slovenska Bistrica** *Ger.* Windischfeistritz. NE Slovenia 46°21′N 15°27′E
Slovenská Republika *see* Slovakia
177 K5 **Slovenske Konjice** E Slovenia 46°21′N 15°28′E
183 G10 **Slovenské rudohorie** *Eng.* Slovak Ore Mountains, *Ger.* Slowakisches Erzgebirge, Ungarisches Erzgebirge. ▲▲ C Slovakia
Slovensko *see* Slovakia
189 M5 **Slov"yanoserbs'k** Luhans'ka Oblast', E Ukraine 48°41′N 39°00′E
189 M4 **Slov"yans'k** *Rus.* Slavyansk. Donets'ka Oblast', E Ukraine 48°51′N 37°38′E
Slowakei *see* Slovakia
Slowakisches Erzgebirge *see* Slovenské rudohorie
Slowenien *see* Slovenia
182 C6 **Słubice** *Ger.* Frankfurt. Lubuskie, W Poland 52°20′N 14°35′E
191 F11 **Sluch** *Rus.* Sluch'. ≈ C Belarus
188 F2 **Sluch** ≈ NW Ukraine
163 C9 **Sluis** Zeeland, SW Netherlands 51°18′N 03°22′E
184 B3 **Slunj** *Hung.* Szluin. Karlovac, C Croatia 45°06′N 15°35′E
182 E6 **Słupca** Wielkopolskie, C Poland 52°17′N 17°52′E
182 E3 **Słupia** *Ger.* Stolpe. ≈ NW Poland
182 E3 **Słupsk** *Ger.* Stolp. Pomorskie, N Poland 54°28′N 17°01′E
141 H3 **Slurry** North-West, South Africa 25°49′S 25°51′E
191 F10 **Slutsk** Minskaya Voblasts', S Belarus 53°02′N 27°32′E
191 H10 **Slyedzyuki** *Rus.* Sledyuki. Mahilyowskaya Voblasts', E Belarus 53°35′N 30°22′E
157 A9 **Slyne Head** *Ir.* Ceann Léime. *headland* W Ireland 53°25′N 10°11′W
193 H8 **Slyudyanka** Irkutskaya Oblast', S Russian Federation 51°36′N 103°28′E
75 H14 **Smackover** Arkansas, C USA 33°21′N 92°43′W
155 G10 **Småland** *cultural region* S Sweden
155 F10 **Smålandsstenar** Jönköping, S Sweden 57°10′N 13°24′E
161 M3 **Smallburgh** United Kingdom 52°46′N 1°27′E
Small Malaita *see* Maramasike
59 I4 **Smallwood Reservoir** ◎ Newfoundland and Labrador, S Canada
191 H9 **Smalyany** *Rus.* Smolyany. Vitsyebskaya Voblasts', NE Belarus 54°36′N 30°04′E
191 G9 **Smalyavichy** *Rus.* Smolevichi. Minskaya Voblasts', C Belarus 54°02′N 28°05′E
130 D5 **Smara** *var.* Es Semara. N Western Sahara 26°45′N 11°44′W
191 F9 **Smarhon'** *Pol.* Smorgonie, *Rus.* Smorgon'. Hrodzyenskaya Voblasts', W Belarus 54°29′N 26°24′E
140 G7 **Smartt Syndicate Dam** ▣ Northern Cape, South Africa
80 D1 **Smartville** California, USA 39°12′N 121°18′W
184 G4 **Smederevo** *Ger.* Semendria. Serbia, N Serbia 44°41′N 20°56′E
184 G4 **Smederevska Palanka** Serbia, C Serbia 44°24′N 20°56′E
154 H7 **Smedjebacken** Dalarna, C Sweden 60°08′N 15°25′E
188 E9 **Smeeni** Buzău, SE Romania 45°00′N 26°52′E
Smela *see* Smila
175 C9 **Smeralda, Costa** *cultural region* Sardegna, Italy, C Mediterranean Sea
161 H4 **Smethwick** United Kingdom 52°30′N 2°00′W
182 D6 **Śmigiel** *Ger.* Schmiegel. Wielkopolskie, C Poland 52°02′N 16°33′E
189 I4 **Smila** *Rus.* Smela. Cherkas'ka Oblast', C Ukraine 49°15′N 31°54′E
162 I4 **Smilde** Drenthe, NE Netherlands 52°57′N 06°28′E
57 L6 **Smiley** Saskatchewan, S Canada 51°40′N 109°24′W
70 G7 **Smiley** Texas, SW USA 29°16′N 97°38′W
Smilten *see* Smiltene
190 E6 **Smiltene** *Ger.* Smilten. Valka, N Latvia 57°25′N 25°53′E
193 L8 **Smirnykh** Ostrov Sakhalin, Sakhalinskaya Oblast', SE Russian Federation 49°43′N 142°48′E
57 I3 **Smith** Alberta, W Canada 55°06′N 113°57′W
80 F3 **Smith** Nevada, USA 38°48′N 119°20′W
52 C8 **Smith Arm** Northwest Territories, NW Canada
53 I4 **Smith Bay** *coastal sea feature* Nunavut, N Canada
83 H2 **Smith Bay** *bay* Alaska, NW USA
58 F1 **Smith, Cape** *headland* Québec, NE Canada 60°50′N 78°06′W
75 D9 **Smith Center** Kansas, C USA 39°46′N 98°46′W
56 C3 **Smithers** British Columbia, SW Canada 54°45′N 127°10′W
141 H7 **Smithfield** Free State, South Africa 30°13′S 26°32′E
67 K6 **Smithfield** North Carolina, SE USA 35°30′N 78°21′W
79 H1 **Smithfield** Utah, W USA 41°50′N 111°49′W
67 M5 **Smithfield** Virginia, NE USA 36°41′N 76°38′W
55 M4 **Smith Island** *island* Nunavut, C Canada
Smith Island *see* Sumisu-jima
73 D13 **Smithland** Kentucky, S USA 37°06′N 88°24′W
67 J5 **Smith Mountain Lake** *var.* Leesville Lake. ▣ Virginia, NE USA
78 A1 **Smith River** California, W USA 41°54′N 124°09′W
77 I4 **Smith River** ≈ Montana, NW USA
62 F4 **Smiths Falls** Ontario, SE Canada 44°54′N 76°01′W
76 F6 **Smiths Ferry** Idaho, NW USA 44°19′N 116°04′W
66 E5 **Smiths Grove** Kentucky, S USA 37°01′N 86°14′W
140 G9 **Smithskraal** Eastern Cape, South Africa 33°46′S 24°25′E
53 J3 **Smith Sound** *Sound* Nunavut, N Canada
277 J9 **Smithton** Tasmania, SE Australia 40°54′S 145°06′E
65 I6 **Smithtown** Long Island, New York, NE USA 40°52′N 73°13′W
66 E6 **Smithville** Tennessee, S USA 35°59′N 85°49′W
71 H7 **Smithville** Texas, SW USA 30°04′N 97°32′W
Šmohor *see* Hermagor
78 D2 **Smoke Creek Desert** *desert* Nevada, W USA
56 G4 **Smoky** ≈ Alberta, W Canada
276 E4 **Smoky Bay** South Australia 32°22′S 133°57′E
277 M4 **Smoky Cape** *headland* New South Wales, SE Australia 30°54′S 153°06′E
75 C9 **Smoky Hill River** ≈ Kansas, C USA
75 D9 **Smoky Hills** *hill range* Kansas, C USA
57 J4 **Smoky Lake** Alberta, SW Canada 54°08′N 112°26′W
154 C3 **Smøla** *island* W Norway
196 E2 **Smolensk** Smolenskaya Oblast', W Russian Federation 54°48′N 32°08′E
196 E2 **Smolenskaya Oblast'** ◈ *province* W Russian Federation
Smolensk-Moscow Upland *see* Smolensko-Moskovskaya Vozvyshennost'
196 E2 **Smolensko-Moskovskaya Vozvyshennost'** *var.* Smolensk-Moscow Upland. ▲▲ W Russian Federation
Smolevichi *see* Smalyavichy
186 F3 **Smólikas** *var.* Smolikás. ▲ W Greece 40°06′N 20°54′E
190 J3 **Smolino** Leningradskaya Oblast', Russian Federation
185 J8 **Smolyan** *prev.* Pashmakli. Smolyan, S Bulgaria 41°34′N 24°42′E
185 J8 **Smolyan** ◈ *province* S Bulgaria
Smolyany *see* Smalyany
77 I8 **Smoot** Wyoming, C USA 42°37′N 110°55′W
58 E7 **Smooth Rock Falls** Ontario, S Canada 49°17′N 81°37′W
54 G7 **Smoothstone Lake** ◎ Saskatchewan, C Canada
Smorgon'/Smorgonie *see* Smarhon'
190 G5 **Smoylovo** Pskovskaya Oblast', Russian Federation 57°34′N 28°57′E
155 F12 **Smygehamn** Skåne, S Sweden 55°19′N 13°25′E
292 F4 **Smyley Island** *island* Antarctica
64 F9 **Smyrna** Delaware, NE USA 39°18′N 75°36′W
66 F8 **Smyrna** Georgia, SE USA 33°52′N 84°30′W
66 E6 **Smyrna** Tennessee, S USA 36°00′N 86°30′W
Smyrna *see* İzmir
261 J5 **Snabai** Papua, E Indonesia 01°45′S 134°14′E
157 E8 **Snaefell** ▲ C Isle of Man 54°15′N 04°29′W
152 A2 **Snaefellsjökull** ▲ W Iceland 64°51′N 23°51′W
152 C2 **Snækollur** ▲ C Iceland 64°38′N 19°18′W
159 L9 **Snaith** United Kingdom 53°41′N 1°02′W
54 C1 **Snake** ≈ Yukon Territory, NW Canada
74 D5 **Snake Creek** ≈ South Dakota, N USA
277 J8 **Snake Island** *island* Victoria, SE Australia
78 G4 **Snake Range** ▲▲ Nevada, W USA
60 C2 **Snake River** ≈ NW USA
74 G4 **Snake River** ≈ Minnesota, N USA
74 B6 **Snake River** ≈ Nebraska, C USA
77 H7 **Snake River Plain** *plain* Idaho, NW USA
52 D10 **Snare** ≈ Northwest Territories, NW Canada
54 F3 **Snare Lakes** Northwest Territories, NW Canada
154 F2 **Snåsa** Nord-Trøndelag, C Norway 64°16′N 12°25′E
66 G5 **Sneedville** Tennessee, S USA 36°31′N 83°13′W
162 G4 **Sneek** Friesland, N Netherlands 53°02′N 05°40′E
140 G8 **Sneeuberge** ▲▲ Eastern Cape, South Africa
140 F8 **Sneeukraal** Western Cape, South Africa 31°54′S 22°40′E
Sneeuw-gebergte *see* Maoke, Pegunungan
155 C12 **Snejbjerg** Ringkøbing, C Denmark 56°08′N 08°55′E
80 D4 **Snelling** California, USA 37°31′N 120°26′W
161 L2 **Snettisham** United Kingdom 52°52′N 0°30′E
194 E2 **Snezhnogorsk** Murmanskaya Oblast', NW Russian Federation 69°12′N 33°20′E
192 G5 **Snezhnogorsk** Taymyrskiy (Dolgano-Nenetskiy) Avtonomnyy Okrug, N Russian Federation 68°06′N 87°37′E
Snezhnoye *see* Snizhne
174 G4 **Snežnik** ▲ SW Slovenia 45°36′N 14°25′E
182 H4 **Śniardwy, Jezioro** *Ger.* Spirdingsee. ◎ NE Poland
Sniečkus *see* Visaginas
189 I7 **Snihurivka** Mykolayivs'ka Oblast', S Ukraine 47°05′N 32°48′E
188 D4 **Snilov** ✈ (L'viv) L'vivs'ka Oblast', W Ukraine 49°45′N 23°59′E
183 I9 **Snina** *Hung.* Szinna. Prešovský Kraj, E Slovakia 49°N 22°10′E
189 M5 **Snizhne** *Rus.* Snezhnoye. Donets'ka Oblast', SE Ukraine 48°01′N 38°46′E
161 L6 **Snodland** SE England, United Kingdom 51°19′N 00°19′E
154 D4 **Snøhetta** *var.* Snohetta. ▲ S Norway 62°22′N 09°08′E
152 D6 **Snøtinden** ▲ C Norway 66°39′N 13°50′E
55 H5 **Snowbird Lake** ◎ Northwest Territories, C Canada
160 E2 **Snowdon** ▲ NW Wales, United Kingdom 53°04′N 04°04′W
157 F9 **Snowdonia** ▲▲ NW Wales, United Kingdom
54 G4 **Snowdrift** ≈ Northwest Territories, NW Canada
Snowdrift *see* Łutselk'e
79 J8 **Snowflake** Arizona, SW USA 34°30′N 110°04′W
67 M3 **Snow Hill** Maryland, NE USA 38°11′N 75°23′W
67 L6 **Snow Hill** North Carolina, SE USA 35°26′N 77°39′W
292 E3 **Snowhill Island** *island* Antarctica
55 I7 **Snow Lake** Manitoba, C Canada 54°56′N 100°02′W
79 K3 **Snowmass Mountain** ▲ Colorado, C USA 39°07′N 107°04′W
65 J1 **Snow, Mount** ▲ Vermont, NE USA 42°56′N 72°52′W
78 B3 **Snow Mountain** ▲ California, W USA 39°44′N 123°01′W
Snow Mountains *see* Maoke, Pegunungan
76 G3 **Snowshoe Peak** ▲ Montana, NW USA 48°15′N 115°44′W
276 G5 **Snowtown** South Australia 33°49′S 138°13′E
79 H1 **Snowville** Utah, W USA 41°59′N 112°42′W
78 F2 **Snow Water Lake** ◎ Nevada, W USA
277 K7 **Snowy Mountains** ▲▲ New South Wales/Victoria, SE Australia
277 K7 **Snowy River** ≈ New South Wales/Victoria, SE Australia
90 G4 **Snug Corner** Acklins Island, SE Bahamas 22°31′N 73°51′W
257 H9 **Snuŏl** Krâchéh, E Cambodia 12°04′N 106°26′E
188 E5 **Snyatyn** Ivano-Frankivs'ka Oblast', W Ukraine 48°30′N 25°50′E
75 D13 **Snyder** Oklahoma, C USA 34°37′N 98°56′W
70 E4 **Snyder** Texas, SW USA 32°43′N 100°54′W
140 E8 **Snyderspoort** *pass* Northern Cape, South Africa
139 L6 **Soalala** Mahajanga, W Madagascar 16°05′S 45°21′E
172 D3 **Soalheiras** Castelo Branco, Portugal 39°42′N 7°11′W
139 N6 **Soanierana-Ivongo** Toamasina, E Madagascar 16°53′S 49°35′E
161 I3 **Soar** ≈ United Kingdom
260 G3 **Soasiu** *var.* Tidore. Pulau Tidore, E Indonesia 0°40′N 127°25′E
102 D5 **Soatá** Boyacá, C Colombia 06°23′N 72°40′W
139 L7 **Soavinandriana** Antananarivo, C Madagascar 19°09′S 46°43′E
261 L6 **Soba** Papua, E Indonesia 04°18′S 139°11′E
133 K6 **Soba** Kaduna, C Nigeria 10°58′N 08°06′E
248 C6 **Sobaek-sanmaek** ▲▲ S South Korea
136 B4 **Sobat** ≈ E Sudan
261 M6 **Sobger, Sungai** ≈ Papua, E Indonesia
261 J5 **Sobiei** Papua, E Indonesia 02°31′S 134°30′E
196 G2 **Sobinka** Vladimirskaya Oblast', W Russian Federation 56°00′N 39°55′E
190 J5 **Soblago** Tverskaya Oblast', Russian Federation
197 K4 **Sobolevo** Orenburgskaya Oblast', W Russian Federation 51°57′N 51°42′E
Soborsin *see* Săvârşin
250 D7 **Sobo-san** ▲ Kyūshū, SW Japan 32°50′N 131°16′E
182 D7 **Sobótka** Dolnośląskie, SW Poland 50°53′N 16°48′E
108 G6 **Sobradinho** Bahia, E Brazil 09°33′S 40°56′W
Sobradinho, Barragem de *see* Sobradinho, Represa de
108 F7 **Sobradinho, Represa de** *var.* Barragem de Sobradinho. ▣ E Brazil
108 G3 **Sobral** Ceará, E Brazil 03°45′S 40°20′W
172 C3 **Sobral** Castelo Branco, Portugal 39°57′N 8°01′W
172 B4 **Sobral** Santarém, Portugal 39°22′N 8°37′W
172 D6 **Sobral da Adiça** Beja, Portugal 38°01′N 7°16′W
111 J2 **Sobràlia** Minas Gerais, Brazil 19°15′S 42°06′W
118 D2 **Sobrante, Río del** ≈ Valparaíso, Chile
171 I2 **Sobrarbe** *physical region* NE Spain
115 I9 **Soca** Canelones, Uruguay 34°41′S 55°41′W
184 A1 **Soča** *It.* Isonzo. ≈ Italy/Slovenia
182 G6 **Sochaczew** Mazowieckie, C Poland 52°15′N 20°15′E
167 M8 **Sochaux** Franche-Comté, France 47°31′N 6°50′E
196 G9 **Sochi** Krasnodarskiy Kray, SW Russian Federation 43°35′N 39°46′E
187 H3 **Sochós** *var.* Sohos, Sokhós. Kentrikí Makedonía, N Greece 40°49′N 23°23′E
285 I7 **Société, Archipel de la** *var.* Archipel de Tahiti, Îles de la Société, *Eng.* Society Islands. *island group* W French Polynesia
Société, Îles de la/Society Islands *see* Société, Archipel de la
67 J7 **Society Hill** South Carolina, SE USA 34°28′N 79°54′W
267 L6 **Society Ridge** *undersea feature* C Pacific Ocean
105 H13 **Socompa, Volcán** ⛰ N Chile 24°18′S 68°03′W
112 C4 **Socompa, Volcn** ⛰ Chile 24°18′S 68°06′W
Soconusco, Sierra de *see* Madre, Sierra
110 D7 **Socorro** São Paulo, Brazil 22°36′S 46°32′W
102 C5 **Socorro** Santander, C Colombia 06°30′N 73°16′W
79 L8 **Socorro** New Mexico, SW USA 33°58′N 106°55′W
Socotra *see* Suquţrā
173 J6 **Socovos** Castilla-La Manacha, Spain 38°20′N 1°58′W
257 H10 **Soc Trăng** *var.* Khanh Hung. Soc Trăng, S Vietnam 09°36′N 105°58′E
171 H6 **Socuéllamos** Castilla-La Mancha, C Spain 39°18′N 02°48′W
81 C8 **Soda Lake** *salt flat* California, W USA
152 H5 **Sodankylä** Lappi, N Finland 67°26′N 26°35′E
Sodari *see* Sodiri
80 E1 **Soda Springs** California, USA 39°19′N 120°23′W
80 E7 **Soda Springs** California, USA 36°02′N 118°45′W
77 I8 **Soda Springs** Idaho, NW USA 42°39′N 111°36′W
Soddo/Soddu *see* Sodo
66 F7 **Soddy Daisy** Tennessee, S USA 35°14′N 85°11′W
154 I7 **Söderfors** Uppsala, C Sweden 60°23′N 17°14′E
154 I6 **Söderhamn** Gävleborg, C Sweden 61°19′N 17°10′E
155 H9 **Söderköping** Östergötland, S Sweden 58°28′N 16°20′E
155 H8 **Södermanland** ◈ *county* C Sweden
155 I8 **Södertälje** Stockholm, C Sweden 59°11′N 17°39′E
136 A2 **Sodiri** *var.* Sawdirī, Sodari. Northern Kordofan, C Sudan 14°23′N 29°06′E
140 G7 **Sodium** Northern Cape, South Africa 30°10′S 23°07′E
136 D5 **Sodo** *var.* Soddo, Soddu. Southern Nationalities, S Ethiopia 06°49′N 37°43′E
154 H5 **Södra Dellen** ◎ C Sweden
155 H10 **Södra Vi** Kalmar, S Sweden 57°45′N 15°45′E
168 A6 **Sodupe** Pais Vasco, Spain 43°12′N 3°03′W
62 F5 **Sodus Point** *headland* New York, NE USA 43°16′N 76°59′W
260 E9 **Soe** *prev.* Soë. Timor, C Indonesia 09°51′S 124°29′E
Soebang *see* Subang
140 C7 **Soebatsfontein** Northern Cape, South Africa 30°07′S 17°35′E
Soekaboemi *see* Sukabumi
258 G8 **Soekarno-Hatta** ✈ (Jakarta) Jawa, S Indonesia
Soëla-Sund *see* Soela Väin
190 C4 **Soela Väin** *prev. Eng.* Sele Sound, *Ger.* Dagden-Sund, Soëla-Sund. *strait* W Estonia
Soemba *see* Sumba, Pulau
Soembawa *see* Sumbawa
Soemenep *see* Sumenep
Soengaipenoeh *see* Sungaipenuh
Soerabaja *see* Surabaya
Soerakarta *see* Surakarta
181 E8 **Soest** Nordrhein-Westfalen, W Germany 51°34′N 08°06′E
162 F6 **Soest** Utrecht, C Netherlands 52°10′N 05°20′E
180 E4 **Soeste** ≈ NW Germany
162 F6 **Soesterberg** Utrecht, C Netherlands 52°07′N 05°17′E
186 G4 **Sofádes** *var.* Sofádhes. Thessalía, C Greece 39°20′N 22°06′E
Sofádhes *see* Sofádes
139 I4 **Sofala** Sofala, C Mozambique 20°04′S 34°43′E
139 J3 **Sofala** ◈ *province* C Mozambique
139 J4 **Sofala, Baia de** *bay* C Mozambique
139 M5 **Sofia** *seasonal river* NW Madagascar
Sofia *see* Sofiya
187 H6 **Sofikó** Pelopónnisos, S Greece 37°46′N 23°04′E
Sofi-Kurgan *see* Sopu-Korgon
185 I6 **Sofiya** *var.* Sophia, *Eng.* Sofia, *Lat.* Serdica. ● (Bulgaria) Sofiya-Grad, W Bulgaria 42°42′N 23°20′E
185 I6 **Sofiya** ◈ *province* W Bulgaria
185 I6 **Sofiya** ✈ Sofiya-Grad, W Bulgaria 42°42′N 23°26′E
185 I6 **Sofiya, Grad** ◈ *municipality* W Bulgaria
Sofiyevka *see* Sofiyivka
189 J6 **Sofiyivka** *Rus.* Sofiyevka. Dnipropetrovs'ka Oblast', E Ukraine 48°04′N 33°55′E
193 L7 **Sofiysk** Khabarovskiy Kray, SE Russian Federation 51°32′N 139°46′E
193 K8 **Sofiysk** Khabarovskiy Kray, SE Russian Federation 52°20′N 133°37′E
194 E4 **Sofporog** Respublika Kareliya, NW Russian Federation 65°48′N 31°30′E
187 K9 **Sofraná** *prev.* Záfora. *island* Kykládes, Greece, Aegean Sea
251 N8 **Sōfu-gan** *island* Izu-shotō, SE Japan
239 H8 **Sog** Xizang Zizhiqu, W China 31°52′N 93°40′E
102 D5 **Sogamoso** Boyacá, C Colombia 05°43′N 72°56′W
214 E4 **Soğanlı Çayı** ≈ N Turkey
180 D4 **Sögel** Niedersachsen, Germany 7°31′N 52°51′E
154 B6 **Sogn** *physical region* S Norway
Sogndal *see* Sogndalsfjøra
154 B6 **Sogndalsfjøra** *var.* Sogndal. Sogn Og Fjordane, S Norway 61°13′N 07°05′E
155 C9 **Søgne** Vest-Agder, S Norway 58°05′N 07°49′E
154 B6 **Sognefjorden** *fjord* NE North Sea
154 B5 **Sogn Og Fjordane** ◈ *county* S Norway
263 M7 **Sogod** Leyte, C Philippines 10°25′N 125°00′E
239 J4 **Sogo Nur** ◎ N China
239 K7 **Sogruma** Qinghai, W China 32°32′N 100°52′E
248 B8 **Sŏgwip'o** S South Korea 33°14′N 126°33′E
129 I5 **Sohâg** *var.* Sohâg *var.* Sawhāj, Suliag. C Egypt 26°28′N 31°44′E
Sohâg *see* Sohâg
161 L4 **Soham** United Kingdom 52°20′N 0°21′E
Sohar *see* Şuḩār
290 E7 **Sohm Plain** *undersea feature* NW Atlantic Ocean
178 D3 **Soholmer Au** ≈ N Germany
Sohos *see* Sochós
Sohrau *see* Żory
181 C12 **Sohren** Rheinland-Pfalz, Germany 7°19′N 49°56′E
163 D11 **Soignies** Hainaut, SW Belgium 50°35′N 04°04′E
239 I9 **Soila** Xizang Zizhiqu, W China 30°40′N 97°07′E
165 I2 **Soissons** *anc.* Augusta Suessionum, Noviodunum. Aisne, N France 49°23′N 03°20′E
250 G5 **Sōja** Okayama, Honshū, SW Japan 34°40′N 133°42′E
232 D6 **Sojat** Rājasthān, N India 25°53′N 73°45′E
247 L8 **Sŏjosŏn-man** *inlet* W North Korea
188 D3 **Sokal'** *Rus.* Sokal. L'vivs'ka Oblast', NW Ukraine 50°29′N 24°17′E
248 C5 **Sokch'o** N South Korea 38°07′N 128°34′E
214 B7 **Söke** Aydın, SW Turkey 37°46′N 27°24′E
283 J1 **Sokehs Island** *island* E Micronesia
135 H11 **Sokele** Katanga, SE Dem. Rep. Congo 09°54′S 24°38′E
229 J6 **Sokh** *Uzb.* Sŭkh. ≈ Kyrgyzstan/Uzbekistan
Sokh *see* So'x
Sokhós *see* Sochós
215 I3 **Sokhumi** *Rus.* Sukhumi. NW Georgia 43°02′N 41°01′E
185 H5 **Sokobanja** Serbia, E Serbia 43°39′N 21°51′E
133 H7 **Sokodé** C Togo 08°58′N 01°10′E
193 L5 **Sokol** Magadanskaya Oblast', E Russian Federation 59°51′N 150°56′E
194 G8 **Sokol** Vologodskaya Oblast', NW Russian Federation 59°26′N 40°09′E
182 J4 **Sokółka** Podlaskie, NE Poland 53°24′N 23°31′E
132 F4 **Sokolo** Ségou, W Mali 14°43′N 06°02′W
183 A8 **Sokolov** *Ger.* Falkenau an der Eger; *prev.* Falknov nad Ohří. Karlovarský Kraj, W Czech Republic 50°10′N 12°38′E
183 I8 **Sokołów Małopolski** Podkarpackie, SE Poland 50°12′N 22°07′E
182 I5 **Sokołów Podlaski** Mazowieckie, C Poland 52°26′N 22°14′E
132 B4 **Sokone** W Senegal 13°53′N 16°22′W
133 J5 **Sokoto** Sokoto, NW Nigeria 13°05′N 05°16′E
133 J5 **Sokoto** ◈ *state* NW Nigeria
133 J5 **Sokoto** ≈ NW Nigeria
Sokotra *see* Suquţrā
229 K4 **Sokuluk** Chuyskaya Oblast', N Kyrgyzstan 42°53′N 74°19′E
188 F5 **Sokyryany** Chernivets'ka Oblast', W Ukraine 48°28′N 27°25′E
155 A8 **Sola** Rogaland, S Norway 58°53′N 05°36′E
281 M1 **Sola** Vanua Lava, N Vanuatu 13°51′S 167°34′E
155 A8 **Sola** ✈ (Stavanger) Rogaland, S Norway 58°54′N 05°36′E
86 G9 **Sola de Vega** Oaxaca, Mexico 16°31′N 96°58′W
137 D8 **Solai** Rift Valley, W Kenya 0°02′N 36°03′E
261 L8 **Solaka** Papua, E Indonesia 07°52′S 138°45′E
232 E4 **Solan** Himāchal Pradesh, N India 30°54′N 77°06′E
81 E12 **Solana Beach** California, USA 32°59′N 117°16′W
278 A13 **Solander Island** *island* SW New Zealand
Solano *see* Bahía Solano
234 D5 **Solāpur** *var.* Sholāpur. Mahārāshtra, W India 17°43′N 75°54′E
154 I3 **Solberg** Västernorrland, C Sweden 63°48′N 17°40′E
188 E6 **Solca** *Ger.* Solka. Suceava, N Romania 47°40′N 25°50′E
170 F9 **Sol, Costa del** *coastal region* S Spain
176 G5 **Solda** *Ger.* Sulden. Trentino-Alto Adige, N Italy 46°33′N 10°35′E
188 G6 **Şoldăneşti** *Rus.* Sholdaneshty. N Moldova 47°49′N 28°45′E
Soldau *see* Wkra
179 F14 **Sölden** Tirol, W Austria 46°58′N 11°01′E
75 F9 **Soldier Creek** ≈ Kansas, C USA
114 B7 **Soldini** Santa Fe, Argentina 33°02′S 60°45′W
83 I6 **Soldotna** Alaska, USA 60°29′N 151°03′W
182 F5 **Solec Kujawski** Kujawsko-pomorskie, C Poland 53°04′N 18°09′E
114 B2 **Soledad** Santa Fe, C Argentina 30°38′S 60°52′W
102 C2 **Soledad** Atlántico, N Colombia 10°54′N 74°48′W
80 B5 **Soledad** California, W USA 36°25′N 121°19′W
103 H4 **Soledad** Anzoátegui, NE Venezuela 08°10′N 63°36′W
113 I6 **Soledade** Rio Grande do Sul, S Brazil 28°50′S 52°30′W
Isla Soledad *see* East Falkland
161 I8 **Solent, The** *channel* S England, United Kingdom
175 C8 **Solenzara** Corse, France, C Mediterranean Sea 41°55′N 09°24′E
163 C12 **Solesmes** Nord-Pas-de-Calais, France 50°11′N 3°30′E
Soleure *see* Solothurn
154 A6 **Solheim** Hordaland, S Norway 60°54′N 05°30′E
194 G9 **Soligalich** Kostromskaya Oblast', NW Russian Federation 59°05′N 42°15′E
169 I3 **Solignac-sur-Loire** Auvergne, France 44°58′N 3°53′E
Soligorsk *see* Salihorsk
161 I4 **Solihull** C England, United Kingdom 52°25′N 01°45′W
195 K8 **Solikamsk** Permskaya Oblast', NW Russian Federation 59°37′N 56°46′E
197 L4 **Sol'-Iletsk** Orenburgskaya Oblast', W Russian Federation 51°09′N 55°05′E
175 C13 **Soliman** Tunisia
105 F9 **Solimana, Nevado** ▲ S Peru 15°24′S 72°49′W
106 E3 **Solimões, Rio** ≈ C Brazil
184 C5 **Solin** *It.* Salona; *anc.* Salonae. Split-Dalmacija, S Croatia 43°33′N 16°29′E
181 C9 **Solingen** Nordrhein-Westfalen, W Germany 51°10′N 07°05′E
114 D9 **Solís** Buenos Aires, Argentina 34°18′S 59°20′W
115 I9 **Solís** Lavalleja, Uruguay 34°20′S 55°27′W
115 I9 **Solis de Mataojo** Lavalleja, Uruguay 34°30′S 55°24′W
140 B2 **Solitaire** Hardap, Namibia 23°53′S 16°00′E
Solka *see* Solca
154 H3 **Sollefteå** Västernorrland, C Sweden 63°09′N 17°15′E
155 I8 **Sollentuna** Stockholm, C Sweden 59°26′N 17°56′E
171 L5 **Sóller** Mallorca, Spain, W Mediterranean Sea 39°46′N 02°42′E
154 G6 **Sollerön** Dalarna, C Sweden 60°55′N 14°34′E
169 L6 **Solliés-Pont** Provence-Alpes-Côte d'Azur, France 43°11′N 6°03′E
180 G7 **Solling** *hill range* C Germany
155 I8 **Solna** Stockholm, C Sweden 59°22′N 17°58′E
196 F1 **Solnechnogorsk** Moskovskaya Oblast', W Russian Federation 56°07′N 37°04′E
193 L8 **Solnechnyy** Khabarovskiy Kray, SE Russian Federation 50°41′N 136°42′E
193 K6 **Solnechnyy** Respublika Sakha (Yakutiya), NE Russian Federation 60°13′N 137°42′E
Solo *see* Surakarta
184 A8 **Solofra** Campania, S Italy 40°49′N 14°48′E
258 D5 **Solok** Sumatera, W Indonesia 0°45′S 100°42′E
88 C4 **Sololá** Sololá, W Guatemala 14°46′N 91°09′W
88 B4 **Sololá** *off.* Departamento de Sololá. ◈ *department* SW Guatemala
Sololá, Departamento de *see* Sololá
136 E6 **Sololo** Eastern, N Kenya 03°31′N 38°39′E
88 B3 **Soloma** Huehuetenango, W Guatemala 15°38′N 91°25′W
82 G5 **Solomon** Alaska, USA 64°33′N 164°26′W
75 E9 **Solomon** Kansas, C USA 38°55′N 97°22′W
281 H4 **Solomon Islands** *prev.* British Solomon Islands Protectorate. ◆ *commonwealth republic* W Solomon Islands N Melanesia W Pacific Ocean
281 J1 **Solomon Islands** *island group* Papua New Guinea/Solomon Islands
75 D9 **Solomon River** ≈ Kansas, C USA
286 D6 **Solomon Sea** *sea* W Pacific Ocean
73 J9 **Solon** Ohio, N USA 41°23′N 81°26′W
189 K5 **Solone** Dnipropetrovs'ka Oblast', E Ukraine 48°12′N 34°49′E
260 E8 **Solor, Kepulauan** *island group* S Indonesia
196 G2 **Solotcha** Ryazanskaya Oblast', W Russian Federation 54°43′N 39°50′E
176 D4 **Solothurn** *Fr.* Soleure. Solothurn, NW Switzerland 47°13′N 07°32′E
176 D4 **Solothurn** *Fr.* Soleure. ◈ *canton* NW Switzerland
194 F5 **Solovetskiye Ostrova** *island group* NW Russian Federation
191 J8 **Solov'yovo** Smolenskaya Oblast', Russian Federation
171 K3 **Solsona** Cataluña, NE Spain 42°00′N 01°31′E
184 C5 **Šolta** *It.* Solta. *island* S Croatia
Solţānābād *see* Kāshmar
222 E3 **Solţānīyeh** Zanjān, NW Iran 36°24′N 48°50′E
180 H4 **Soltau** Niedersachsen, NW Germany 52°59′N 09°50′E
180 I4 **Soltendieck** Niedersachsen, Germany 10°46′N 52°52′E
194 D9 **Sol'tsy** Novgorodskaya Oblast', W Russian Federation 58°09′N 30°23′E
Soltūstik Qazaqstan Oblysy *see* Severnyy Kazakhstan
Solun *see* Thessaloníki
184 G7 **Solunska Glava** ▲ C FYR Macedonia 41°43′N 21°24′E
160 D5 **Solva** United Kingdom 51°52′N 5°12′W
81 B8 **Solvang** California, USA 34°36′N 120°08′W
155 G12 **Sölvesborg** Blekinge, S Sweden 56°04′N 14°35′E
159 H6 **Solway Firth** *inlet* England/Scotland, United Kingdom
135 H12 **Solwezi** North Western, NW Zambia 12°11′S 26°23′E
253 D11 **Sōma** Fukushima, Honshū, C Japan 37°49′N 140°52′E
214 B6 **Soma** Manisa, W Turkey 39°10′N 27°36′E
136 G5 **Somali** ◈ *federal region* E Ethiopia
136 I4 **Somalia** *off.* Somali Democratic Republic, *Som.* Jamuuriyada Demuqraadiga Soomaaliyeed, Soomaaliya; *prev.* Italian Somaliland, Somaliland Protectorate. ◆ *republic* E Africa
288 D7 **Somali Basin** *undersea feature* W Indian Ocean 0°00′N 52°00′E
Somali Democratic Republic *see* Somalia
136 H4 **Somaliland** ◈ *disputed territory* N Somalia
Somaliland Protectorate *see* Somalia
121 N5 **Somali Plain** *undersea feature* W Indian Ocean 01°00′N 51°30′E
167 J8 **Sombernon** Bourgogne, France 47°18′N 4°42′E
184 E2 **Sombor** *Hung.* Zombor. Vojvodina, NW Serbia 45°46′N 19°07′E
163 E11 **Sombreffe** Namur, S Belgium 50°32′N 04°39′E
85 J8 **Sombrerete** Zacatecas, C Mexico 23°38′N 103°40′W
91 L5 **Sombrero** *island* N Anguilla
257 A10 **Sombrero Channel** *channel* Nicobar Islands, India
188 C6 **Şomcuta Mare** *Hung.* Nagysomkút; *prev.* Somcuţa Mare. Maramureş, N Romania 47°29′N 23°30′E
Somcuţa Mare *see* Şomcuta Mare
256 G6 **Somdet** Kalasin, E Thailand 16°41′N 103°44′E
163 G9 **Someren** Noord-Brabant, SE Netherlands 51°23′N 05°42′E
153 H10 **Somero** Länsi-Suomi, SW Finland 60°37′N 23°30′E
76 G3 **Somers** Montana, NW USA 48°04′N 114°16′W
67 M10 **Somerset** *var.* Somerset Village. W Bermuda 32°18′N 64°53′W
80 E2 **Somerset** California, USA 38°39′N 120°41′W
79 K4 **Somerset** Colorado, C USA 38°55′N 107°27′W
66 F5 **Somerset** Kentucky, S USA 37°05′N 84°36′W
65 L3 **Somerset** Massachusetts, NE USA 41°46′N 71°07′W
166 B1 **Somerset** *cultural region* SW England, United Kingdom
141 H9 **Somerset East** Eastern Cape, South Africa 32°43′S 25°35′E
Somerset East *see* Somerset-Oos
67 M10 **Somerset Island** *island* W Bermuda
295 I8 **Somerset Island** *island* Queen Elizabeth Islands, Nunavut, NW Canada
Somerset Nile *see* Victoria Nile
138 F9 **Somerset-Oos** *var.* Somerset East. Eastern Cape, S South Africa 32°44′S 25°35′E
Somerset Village *see* Somerset
138 D10 **Somerset-Wes** *var.* Somerset West. Western Cape, SW South Africa 34°05′S 18°51′E
140 D10 **Somerset-West** Western Cape, South Africa 34°06′S 18°51′E
Somerset West *see* Somerset-Wes
Somers Islands *see* Bermuda
64 G9 **Somers Point** New Jersey, NE USA 39°18′N 74°34′W
63 J5 **Somersworth** New Hampshire, NE USA 43°15′N 70°52′W
81 H14 **Somerton** Arizona, SW USA 32°36′N 114°42′W
65 L2 **Somerville** Massachusetts, USA 42°23′N 71°06′W
64 G6 **Somerville** New Jersey, NE USA 40°34′N 74°36′W
66 B6 **Somerville** Tennessee, S USA 35°14′N 89°24′W
71 H6 **Somerville** Texas, SW USA 30°21′N 96°31′W
71 H6 **Somerville Lake** ▣ Texas, SW USA
Someş/Somesch/Someşul *see* Szamos
165 H2 **Somme** ◈ *department* N France
165 H2 **Somme** ≈ N France
155 G9 **Sommen** Jönköping, S Sweden 58°07′N 14°58′E
155 H9 **Sommen** ◎ S Sweden
167 J4 **Sommepy-Tahure** Champagne-Ardenne, France 49°15′N 4°33′E
181 J9 **Sömmerda** Thüringen, C Germany 51°10′N 11°07′E
Sommerein *see* Šamorín
Sommerfeld *see* Lubsko
167 J5 **Sommesous** Champagne-Ardenne, France 48°44′N 4°12′E
103 M6 **Sommet Tabulaire** *var.* Mont Itoupé. ▲▲ S French Guiana
169 J5 **Sommières** Languedoc-Roussillon, France 43°47′N 4°05′E
183 E12 **Somogy** *off.* Somogy Megye. ◈ *county* SW Hungary
Somogy Megye *see* Somogy
173 I1 **Somolinos** Castilla-La Manacha, Spain 41°15′N 3°03′W
Somorja *see* Šamorín
173 H1 **Somosierra** ▲▲ Spain
170 G4 **Somosierra, Puerto de** *pass* N Spain
280 F8 **Somosomo** Taveuni, N Fiji 16°46′S 179°57′W
88 G5 **Somotillo** Chinandega, NW Nicaragua 13°01′N 86°53′W
88 G5 **Somoto** Madriz, NW Nicaragua 13°29′N 86°36′W
182 F6 **Sompolno** Wielkopolskie, C Poland 52°24′N 18°30′E
168 D7 **Somport, Col du** *var.* Puerto de Somport, *Sp.* Somport; *anc.* Summus Portus. *pass* France/Spain *see also* Somport
163 G8 **Son** Noord-Brabant, S Netherlands 51°32′N 05°34′E
155 E8 **Son** Akershus, S Norway 59°32′N 10°42′E
233 H7 **Son** *var.* Sone. ≈ C India
89 J10 **Soná** Veraguas, W Panama 08°00′N 81°20′W
Sonag *see* Zêkog
234 H4 **Sonapur** *prev.* Sonepur. Orissa, E India 20°50′N 83°58′E
261 I5 **Sonar** Papua, E Indonesia 02°31′S 133°01′E
155 D13 **Sønderborg** *Ger.* Sonderburg. Sønderjylland, SW Denmark 54°55′N 09°48′E
Sonderburg *see* Sønderborg
155 C13 **Sønderjylland** *var.* Sønderjyllands Amt. ◈ *county* SW Denmark
Sønderjyllands Amt *see* Sønderjylland
181 J8 **Sondershausen** Thüringen, C Germany 51°22′N 10°52′E
Sondre Strømfjord *see* Kangerlussuaq
176 F5 **Sondrio** Lombardia, N Italy 46°11′N 09°52′E
Sone *see* Son
Sonepur *see* Sonapur
112 C3 **Sonequera** ▲ S Bolivia 22°06′S 67°10′W
242 G6 **Songbai** Hunan, S China 26°35′N 112°35′E
243 I2 **Songbu** Hubei, E China 31°04′N 114°48′E
257 J8 **Sông Câu** Phu Yên, C Vietnam 13°26′N 109°12′E
257 H10 **Sông Đôc** Minh Hai, S Vietnam 09°03′N 104°51′E
137 D12 **Songea** Ruvuma, S Tanzania 10°42′S 35°39′E
166 G4 **Songeons** Picardie, France 49°33′N 1°52′E
261 M5 **Songgato, Sungai** ≈ Papua, E Indonesia
243 I4 **Songhu** Jiangxi, SE China 28°23′N 115°39′E
248 D1 **Songhua Hu** ◎ NE China
247 M4 **Songhua Jiang** *var.* Sungari. ≈ NE China
243 M2 **Songjiang** Shanghai Shi, E China 31°01′N 121°14′E
Sŏngjin *see* Kimch'aek
250 A3 **Sŏngju** 35°54′N 128°17′E
257 E11 **Songkhla** *var.* Songkla, *Mal.* Singora. Songkhla, SW Thailand 07°12′N 100°35′E
Songkla *see* Songkhla
243 J8 **Songkou** Guangdong, SE China 24°30′N 116°24′E
245 L2 **Song Ling** ▲▲ NE China
205 L7 **Sŏng Ma** *Laos* Ma, Nam. ≈ Laos/Vietnam
248 B4 **Songnim** SW North Korea 38°43′N 125°40′E
135 C10 **Songo** Uíge, NW Angola 07°30′S 14°56′E
139 I2 **Songo** Tete, NW Mozambique 15°36′S 32°45′E
135 C9 **Songololo** Bas-Congo, SW Dem. Rep. Congo 05°40′S 14°05′E
239 K7 **Songpan** *var.* Jin'an, *Tib.* Sungpu. Sichuan, C China 32°49′N 103°39′E
248 B8 **Sŏngsan** S South Korea
245 H8 **Song Shan** ▲ Henan, China 34°19′N 113°00′E
242 E4 **Songtao** Guizhou, China 28°06′N 109°07′E
243 L5 **Songxi** Fujian, SE China 27°33′N 118°46′E
244 G8 **Songxian** *var.* Song Xian. Henan, C China 34°11′N 112°04′E
Song Xian *see* Songxian
243 L4 **Songyang** *var.* Xiping; *prev.* Songyin. Zhejiang, SE China 28°29′N 119°27′E
Songyin *see* Songyang
247 L5 **Songyuan** *var.* Fu-yü, Petuna; *prev.* Fuyu. Jilin, NE China 45°10′N 124°52′E
242 G3 **Songzi** Hubei, China 30°06′N 111°28′E
Sonid Youqi *see* SaihanTal
Sonid Zuoqi *see* Mandalt
232 E5 **Sonīpat** Haryāna, N India 29°00′N 77°01′E
152 I7 **Sonkajärvi** Itä-Suomi, C Finland 63°40′N 27°30′E
256 G4 **Sơn La** Sơn La, N Vietnam 21°20′N 103°55′E
230 F9 **Sonmiāni** Baluchistān, S Pakistan 25°24′N 66°37′E
230 F9 **Sonmiāni Bay** *bay* S Pakistan
181 J11 **Sonneberg** Thüringen, C Germany 50°22′N 11°10′E
181 J11 **Sonnefeld** Bayern, Germany 11°08′N 50°13′E
174 F2 **Sonntagshorn** ▲ Austria/Germany 47°40′N 12°42′E
Sonoita *see* Sonoyta
84 D2 **Sonoita, Rio** *var.* Río Sonoyta. ≈ Mexico/USA
80 B2 **Sonoma** California, W USA 38°16′N 122°28′W
80 J1 **Sonoma Peak** ▲ Nevada, W USA 40°50′N 117°34′W
80 B2 **Sonoma Valley** *valley* California, USA
80 D3 **Sonora** California, W USA 37°58′N 120°22′W
70 E6 **Sonora** Texas, SW USA 30°34′N 100°39′W
60 C8 **Sonora** ◈ *state* NW Mexico
60 C7 **Sonoran Desert** *var.* Desierto de Altar. *desert* Mexico/USA *see also* Altar, Desierto de
84 E3 **Sonora, Río** ≈ NW Mexico
84 D2 **Sonoyta** *var.* Sonoita. Sonora, NW Mexico 31°49′N 112°50′W
Sonoyta, Río *see* Sonoita, Rio
222 D4 **Sonqor** *var.* Sunqur. Kermānshāhān, W Iran 34°45′N 47°39′E
250 A2 **Sŏnsan** 36°14′N 128°17′E
170 G5 **Sonseca** *var.* Sonseca con Casalgordo. Castilla-La Mancha, C Spain 39°40′N 03°59′W
Sonseca con Casalgordo *see* Sonseca
102 B5 **Sonsón** Antioquia, W Colombia 05°45′N 75°18′W
88 D5 **Sonsonate** Sonsonate, W El Salvador 13°44′N 89°43′W
88 C5 **Sonsonate** ◈ *department* SW El Salvador
282 A7 **Sonsorol Islands** *island group* S Palau
140 F4 **Sonstraal** Northern Cape, South Africa 27°07′S 22°28′E
184 E2 **Sonta** *Hung.* Szond; *prev.* Szonta. Vojvodina, NW Serbia 45°34′N 19°06′E
256 H4 **Sơn Tây** *var.* Sontay. Ha Tây, N Vietnam 21°06′N 105°32′E
Sontay *see* Sơn Tây
179 E13 **Sonthofen** Bayern, S Germany 47°31′N 10°16′E
Soochow *see* Suzhou
136 I4 **Sool** *off.* Gobolka Sool. ◈ *region* N Somalia
Soomaaliya/Soomaaliyeed, Jamuuriyada Demuqraadiga *see* Somalia
Soome Laht *see* Finland, Gulf of
69 K2 **Soperton** Georgia, SE USA 32°22′N 82°35′W
256 G5 **Sop Hao** Houaphan, N Laos 20°33′N 104°25′E
Sophia *see* Sofiya
260 G2 **Sopi** Pulau Morotai, E Indonesia 02°36′N 128°32′E
Sopianae *see* Pécs
261 I5 **Sopinusa** Papua, E Indonesia 03°31′S 132°55′E
260 G2 **Sopi, Tanjung** *headland* Pulau Morotai, N Indonesia 02°39′N 128°34′E
190 I5 **Sopki** Novgorodskaya Oblast', Russian Federation
134 H4 **Sopo** ≈ W Sudan
Sopockinie/Sopotskin/Sopotskino *see* Sapotskin
185 J6 **Sopot** Plovdiv, C Bulgaria 42°39′N 24°43′E
182 F3 **Sopot** *Ger.* Zoppot. Pomorskie, N Poland 54°26′N 18°33′E
256 E6 **Sop Prap** *var.* Ban Sop Prap. Lampang, NW Thailand 17°55′N 99°20′E
183 D11 **Sopron** *Ger.* Ödenburg. Győr-Moson-Sopron, NW Hungary 47°40′N 16°35′E
229 K6 **Sopu-Korgon** *var.* Sofi-Kurgan. Oshskaya Oblast', SW Kyrgyzstan 40°03′N 73°30′E
232 D2 **Sopur** Jammu and Kashmir, NW India 34°19′N 74°30′E
175 F8 **Sora** Lazio, C Italy 41°43′N 13°37′E
234 I4 **Sorada** Orissa, E India 19°46′N 84°29′E
154 I4 **Söråker** Västernorrland, C Sweden 62°32′N 17°32′E
105 H9 **Sorata** La Paz, W Bolivia 15°47′S 68°38′W
Sorau/Sorau in der Niederlausitz *see* Żary
171 H8 **Sorbas** Andalucía, S Spain 37°06′N 02°06′W
158 G6 **Sorbie** United Kingdom 54°47′N 4°26′W
Sord/Sórd Choluim Chille *see* Swords
141 L5 **Sordwana Bay** *bay* KwaZulu-Natal, South Africa
168 D4 **Sore** Aquitaine, France 44°19′N 0°35′W
63 H2 **Sorel** Québec, SE Canada 46°03′N 73°06′W
277 J10 **Sorell** Tasmania, SE Australia 42°49′S 147°34′E
277 J9 **Sorell, Lake** ◎ Tasmania, SE Australia
176 F7 **Soresina** Lombardia, N Italy 45°17′N 09°51′E
155 B7 **Sørfjorden** *fjord* S Norway
154 H5 **Sörforsa** Gävleborg, C Sweden 61°45′N 17°00′E
168 F2 **Sorges** Aquitaine, France 45°18′N 0°52′E
176 A9 **Sorgues** Vaucluse, SE France 44°N 04°52′E
214 F5 **Sorgun** Yozgat, C Turkey 39°49′N 35°10′E
171 H3 **Soria** Castilla-León, N Spain 41°47′N 02°26′W
171 H3 **Soria** ◈ *province* Castilla-León, N Spain
114 E7 **Soriano** Soriano, SW Uruguay 33°25′S 58°21′W
114 F7 **Soriano** ◈ *department* SW Uruguay
250 A5 **Sorido-do**
158 D1 **Sorisdale** United Kingdom 56°41′N 6°27′W
152 B6 **Sørkapp** *headland* SW Svalbard 76°34′N 16°33′E
223 I3 **Sorkh, Kūh-e** ▲▲ NE Iran
158 G4 **Sorn** United Kingdom 55°30′N 4°17′W
155 E12 **Sorø** Vestsjælland, E Denmark 55°26′N 11°34′E
Soro *see* Ghazal, Bahr el
188 F5 **Soroca** *Rus.* Soroki. N Moldova 48°10′N 28°18′E
110 C9 **Sorocaba** São Paulo, S Brazil 23°29′S 47°27′W
118 E1 **Sorocayense** San Juan, Argentina 31°33′S 69°26′W
Sorochino *see* Sarochyna
197 K3 **Sorochinsk** Orenburgskaya Oblast', W Russian Federation 52°26′N 53°10′E
Soroki *see* Soroca
190 H5 **Sorokino** Pskovskaya Oblast', Russian Federation
282 D6 **Sorol** *atoll* Caroline Islands, W Micronesia
261 H4 **Sorong** Papua, E Indonesia 0°49′S 131°16′E
136 C7 **Soroti** C Uganda 01°42′N 33°37′E
Sørøy *see* Sørøya
152 G3 **Sørøya** *var.* Sørøy, *Lapp.* Sállan. *island* N Norway
172 B5 **Sorraia, Rio** ≈ C Portugal
152 F4 **Sørreisa** Troms, N Norway 69°08′N 18°09′E
175 G9 **Sorrento** *anc.* Surrentum. Campania, S Italy 40°37′N 14°23′E
170 D6 **Sor, Ribeira de** *stream* C Portugal
293 J2 **Sør Rondane Mountains** ▲▲ Antarctica
154 H1 **Sorsele** Västerbotten, N Sweden 65°31′N 17°34′E
175 B9 **Sorso** Sardegna, Italy, C Mediterranean Sea 40°46′N 08°33′E
263 M6 **Sorsogon** Luzon, N Philippines 12°57′N 124°04′E
171 J2 **Sort** Cataluña, NE Spain 42°25′N 01°07′E

◆ Country
● Country Capital
◇ Dependent Territory
○ Dependent Territory Capital
◈ Administrative Regions
✈ International Airport
▲ Mountain
▲▲ Mountain Range
⛰ Volcano
≈ River
◎ Lake
▣ Reservoir

◆ Country   ◇ Dependent Territory   ◈ Administrative Regions   ▲ Mountain   ▲ Volcano   ◎ Lake
● Country Capital   ○ Dependent Territory Capital   ✕ International Airport   ▲ Mountain Range   ≈ River   ◎ Reservoir

Sua - Svintsovyy Rudnik
INDEX
412

Sua *see* Sowa
260 F8 **Suai** W East Timor 09°19′S 125°16′E
102 C5 **Suaita** Santander, C Colombia 06°07′N 73°30′W
129 K8 **Suakin** *var.* Sawakin. Red Sea, NE Sudan 19°06′N 37°17′E
243 N7 **Suao** *Jap.* Suō. N Taiwan 24°33′N 121°48′E
Suao *see* Suau
138 F4 **Sua Pan** *var.* Sua Pan. *salt lake* NE Botswana
Sua Pan *see* Sua Pan
84 F4 **Suaqui Grande** Sonora, NW Mexico 28°22′N 109°52′W
112 E7 **Suardi** Santa Fe, C Argentina 30°32′S 61°58′W
102 B6 **Suárez** Cauca, SW Colombia 02°55′N 76°41′W
280 D5 **Suau** *var.* Suao. Suaul Island, SE Papua New Guinea 10°39′S 150°03′E
190 D7 **Subačius** Panevėžys, NE Lithuania 55°46′N 24°45′E
258 G8 **Subang** *prev.* Soebang. Jawa, C Indonesia 06°32′S 107°45′E
258 D3 **Subang** ✈ (Kuala Lumpur) Pahang, Peninsular Malaysia
205 K6 **Subansiri** ≈ NE India
242 E6 **Subao Ding** ▲ Hunan, China 27°06′N 110°11′E
190 E7 **Subate** Daugvapils, SE Latvia 56°00′N 25°54′E
216 G4 **Subaykhān** Dayr az Zawr, E Syria 34°52′N 40°35′E
245 L8 **Subei Guangai Zongqu** *irrigation canal* Jiangsu, China
Subei/Subei Mongolzu Zizhixian *see* Dangchengwan
259 H3 **Subi Besar, Pulau** *island* Kepulauan Natuna, W Indonesia
Subiyah *see* Aş Şubayḩīyah
75 B10 **Sublette** Kansas, C USA 37°28′N 100°52′W
184 F2 **Subotica** *Ger.* Maria-Theresiopel, *Hung.* Szabadka. Vojvodina, N Serbia 46°06′N 19°41′E
188 E6 **Suceava** *Ger.* Suczawa, *Hung.* Szucsava. Suceava, NE Romania 47°41′N 26°16′E
188 E6 **Suceava** ◈ *county* NE Romania
188 E6 **Suceava** *Ger.* Suczawa. ≈ N Romania
184 C4 **Sučevići** Zadar, SW Croatia 44°13′N 16°04′E
183 G9 **Sucha Beskidzka** Małopolskie, S Poland 49°44′N 19°36′E
182 H7 **Suchedniów** Świętokrzyskie, C Poland 51°01′N 20°49′E
245 L7 **Sucheng** Jiangsu, E China 34°42′N 119°26′E
87 J8 **Suchiapa** Chiapas, Mexico 16°37′N 93°05′W
87 I8 **Suchilapan** Oaxaca, Mexico 17°24′N 94°59′W
88 B4 **Suchitepéquez** *off.* Departamento de Suchitepéquez. ◈ *department* SW Guatemala
Suchitepéquez, Departamento de *see* Suchitepéquez
Su-chou *see* Suzhou
Suchow *see* Xuzhou, Jiangsu, China
Suchow *see* Suzhou, Jiangsu, China
173 L7 **Sucina** Murcia, Spain 37°53′N 0°56′W
158 B10 **Suck** ≈ Ireland
157 C9 **Suck** ≈ C Ireland
Sucker State *see* Illinois
280 C4 **Suckling, Mount** ▲ S Papua New Guinea 09°36′S 149°00′E
112 D1 **Sucre** *hist.* Chuquisaca, La Plata. ● (Bolivia-legal capital) Chuquisaca, S Bolivia 18°53′S 65°25′W
102 C3 **Sucre** Santander, N Colombia 08°50′N 74°22′W
104 B2 **Sucre** Manabí, W Ecuador 01°21′S 80°27′W
102 B3 **Sucre** *off.* Departamento de Sucre. ◈ *province* N Colombia
103 H3 **Sucre** *off.* Estado Sucre. ◈ *state* NE Venezuela
Sucre, Departamento de *see* Sucre
Sucre, Estado *see* Sucre
104 D1 **Sucumbíos** ◈ *province* NE Ecuador
184 D5 **Sućuraj** Split-Dalmacija, S Croatia 43°07′N 17°10′E
108 B1 **Sucuriju** Amapá, NE Brazil 01°31′N 50°W
Suczawa *see* Suceava
134 B6 **Sud** *Eng.* South. ◈ *province* S Cameroon
194 F8 **Suda** ≈ NW Russian Federation
Suda *see* Soúda
189 K9 **Sudak** Respublika Krym, S Ukraine 44°52′N 34°57′E
70 D3 **Sudan** Texas, SW USA 34°04′N 102°32′W
134 I2 **Sudan** *off.* Republic of Sudan, *Ar.* Jumhuriyat as-Sudan; *prev.* Anglo-Egyptian Sudan. ◆ *republic* N Africa
Sudanese Republic *see* Mali
Sudan, Jumhuriyat as- *see* Sudan
Sudan, Republic of *see* Sudan
62 C2 **Sudbury** Ontario, S Canada 46°29′N 81°W
161 L5 **Sudbury** E England, United Kingdom 52°04′N 00°43′E
Sud, Canal de *see* Gonâve, Canal de la
136 A4 **Sudd** *swamp region* S Sudan
180 J3 **Sude** ≈ N Germany
180 I4 **Suderburg** Niedersachsen, Germany 10°28′N 52°54′E
Suderø *see* Sudhuroy
Sudest Island *see* Tagula Island
183 D8 **Sudeten** *var.* Sudetes, Sudetic Mountains, *Cz./Pol.* Sudety. ▲▲ Czech Republic/Poland
Sudetes/Sudetic Mountains/Sudety *see* Sudeten
180 H7 **Sudheim** Niedersachsen, Germany 9°59′N 51°40′E
152 A1 **Sudhureyri** Vestfirdhir, NW Iceland 66°08′N 23°31′W
152 C3 **Sudhurland** ◈ *region* S Iceland
154 B2 **Sudhuroy** *Dan.* Suderø. *island* S Faeroe Islands
261 K6 **Sudirman, Pegunungan** ▲▲ Papua, E Indonesia
194 G9 **Sudislavl'** Kostromskaya Oblast', NW Russian Federation 57°55′N 41°45′E
Südkarpaten *see* Carpaţii Meridionalii
135 I8 **Sud Kivu** *off.* Région Sud Kivu. ◈ *region* E Dem. Rep. Congo
Sud Kivu, Région *see* Sud Kivu
Südliche Morava *see* Južna Morava
180 C7 **Südlohn** Nordrhein-Westfalen, Germany 6°52′N 51°56′E
180 C5 **Süd-Nord-Kanal** *canal* NW Germany
196 G2 **Sudogda** Vladimirskaya Oblast', W Russian Federation 55°58′N 40°57′E
Sudostroy *see* Severodvinsk
134 A5 **Sud-Ouest** *Eng.* South-West. ◈ *province* W Cameroon
137 G11 **Sud Ouest, Pointe** *headland* SW Mauritius 20°27′S 57°18′E
280 B9 **Sud, Province** ◈ *province* S New Caledonia
196 E4 **Sudzha** Kurskaya Oblast', W Russian Federation 51°12′N 35°19′E
134 I5 **Sue** ≈ S Sudan
171 I6 **Sueca** País Valenciano, E Spain 39°13′N 00°19′W
185 J7 **Süedinenie** Plovdiv, C Bulgaria 42°14′N 24°36′E
Suero *see* Alzira
129 I3 **Suez** *Ar.* As Suways, El Suweis. NE Egypt 29°59′N 32°33′E
129 I3 **Suez Canal** *Ar.* Qanāt as Suways. *canal* NE Egypt
129 J4 **Suez, Gulf of** *var.* Suez, Gulf of. *gulf* NE Egypt
Suez, Gulf of *see* Suez, Gulf of
218 F7 **Sūf** Jordan 32°19′N 35°50′E
65 H5 **Suffern** New York, USA 41°07′N 74°09′W
57 K8 **Suffield** Alberta, SW Canada 50°15′N 111°05′W
67 M5 **Suffolk** Virginia, NE USA 36°44′N 76°37′W
161 L4 **Suffolk** *cultural region* E England, United Kingdom
222 D2 **Şūfiān** Āzarbāyjān-e Sharqī, N Iran 38°15′N 45°59′E
73 C10 **Sugar Creek** ≈ Illinois, N USA
72 G4 **Sugar Island** *island* Michigan, N USA
71 I7 **Sugar Land** Texas, SW USA 29°37′N 95°37′W
63 J3 **Sugarloaf Mountain** ▲ Maine, NE USA 45°01′N 70°18′W
132 G9 **Sugar Loaf Point** *headland* N Saint Helena 15°54′S 05°43′W
214 D7 **Suğla Gölü** ◎ SW Turkey
193 L4 **Sugoy** ≈ E Russian Federation
238 C4 **Sugun** Xinjiang Uygur Zizhiqu, W China 39°46′N 76°45′E
229 K6 **Sugut, Gora** ▲ SW Kyrgyzstan 39°52′N 73°36′E
259 L2 **Sugut, Sungai** ≈ East Malaysia
239 H5 **Suhai Hu** ◎ C China
244 C3 **Suhait** Nei Mongol Zizhiqu, N China 39°29′N 105°11′E
221 K4 **Şuḩār** *var.* Sohar. N Oman 24°20′N 56°43′E
236 G2 **Sühbaatar** Selenge, N Mongolia 50°12′N 106°14′E
239 M1 **Sühbaatar** *var.* Haylaastay. Sühbaatar, E Mongolia 46°44′N 113°51′E
239 M1 **Sühbaatar** ◈ *province* E Mongolia
181 I10 **Suhl** Thüringen, C Germany 50°37′N 10°43′E
180 I4 **Suhlendorf** Niedersachsen, Germany 10°46′N 52°56′E
176 D4 **Suhr** Aargau, N Switzerland 47°23′N 08°05′E
Sui'an *see* Zhangpu
243 L4 **Suichang** Zhejiang, SE China 28°35′N 119°16′E
242 B6 **Suicheng** Guizhou, China 26°19′N 105°01′E
Suicheng *see* Suixi
243 I6 **Suichuan** *var.* Quanjiang. Jiangxi, S China 26°26′N 114°34′E
Suid-Afrika *see* South Africa
244 F5 **Suide** *var.* Mingzhou. Shaanxi, C China 37°30′N 110°10′E
Suidwes-Afrika *see* Namibia
248 E1 **Suifenhe** Heilongjiang, NE China 44°22′N 131°12′E
Suigen *see* Suwŏn
237 J3 **Suihua** Heilongjiang, NE China 46°40′N 127°00′E
242 A4 **Suijiang** Sichuan, C China 28°40′N 104°14′E
Súilí, Loch *see* Swilly, Lough
242 E6 **Suining** Hunan, S China 26°35′N 110°09′E
245 K8 **Suining** Jiangsu, E China 33°54′N 117°58′E
242 B2 **Suining** Sichuan, C China 30°31′N 105°33′E
114 C10 **Suipacha** Buenos Aires, Argentina 34°47′S 59°41′W
167 J5 **Suippes** Marne, N France 49°08′N 04°31′E
157 C10 **Suir** *Ir.* An tSiúir. ≈ S Ireland
80 C2 **Suisun City** California, USA 38°14′N 122°02′W
251 H5 **Suita** Ōsaka, Honshū, SW Japan 34°39′N 135°27′E
64 D10 **Suitland** Maryland, USA 38°51′N 76°55′W
245 J8 **Suixi** Anhui, China 33°33′N 116°28′E
240 F8 **Suixi** *var.* Suicheng. Guangdong, S China 21°23′N 110°14′E
Sui Xian *see* Suizhou
242 C5 **Suiyang** Guizhou, China 27°35′N 107°07′E
245 L2 **Suizhong** Liaoning, NE China 40°19′N 120°22′E
243 H1 **Suizhou** *prev.* Sui Xian. Hubei, C China 31°46′N 113°20′E
230 G10 **Sujāwal** Sind, SE Pakistan 24°36′N 68°06′E
245 N1 **Sujiatun** Liaoning, NE China 41°40′N 123°20′E
258 G8 **Sukabumi** *prev.* Soekaboemi. Jawa, C Indonesia 06°55′S 106°56′E
259 H5 **Sukadana, Teluk** *bay* Borneo, W Indonesia
253 D11 **Sukagawa** Fukushima, Honshū, C Japan 37°16′N 140°20′E
Sukarnapura *see* Jayapura
Sukarno, Puntjak *see* Jaya, Puncak
Sükh *see* Sokh
185 M5 **Sukha Reka** ≈ NE Bulgaria
196 F3 **Sukhinichi** Kaluzhskaya Oblast', W Russian Federation 54°06′N 35°22′E
Sukhne *see* As Sukhnah
205 I2 **Sukhona** *var.* Tot'ma. ≈ NW Russian Federation
256 E6 **Sukhothai** *var.* Sukotai. Sukhothai, W Thailand 17°00′N 99°51′E
195 M9 **Sukhoy Log** Sverdlovskaya Oblast', Russian Federation
Sukhumi *see* Sokhumi
Sukkertoppen *see* Maniitsoq
230 G8 **Sukkur** Sind, SE Pakistan 27°45′N 68°46′E
Sukotai *see* Sukhothai
Sukra Bay *see* Şawqirah, Dawḩat
195 L9 **Suksun** Permskaya Oblast', NW Russian Federation 57°10′N 57°27′E
250 F7 **Sukumo** Kōchi, Shikoku, SW Japan 32°55′N 132°42′E
172 C1 **Sul** Viseu, Portugal 40°50′N 8°03′W
154 A5 **Sula** *island* S Norway
195 I4 **Sula** ≈ NW Russian Federation
189 J3 **Sula** ≈ N Ukraine
Sulaimaniya *see* As Sulaymānīyah
231 H5 **Sulaimān Range** ▲▲ C Pakistan
197 J9 **Sulak** Respublika Dagestan, SW Russian Federation 43°19′N 47°28′E
197 J9 **Sulak** ≈ SW Russian Federation
260 F5 **Sula, Kepulauan** *island group* C Indonesia
214 E5 **Sulakyurt** *var.* Konur. Kırıkkale, N Turkey 40°10′N 33°42′E
260 E9 **Sulamu** Timor, S Indonesia 09°57′S 123°33′E
156 D3 **Sula Sgeir** *island* NW Scotland, United Kingdom
260 C5 **Sulawesi** *Eng.* Celebes. *island* C Indonesia
259 M6 **Sulawesi Barat** *off.* Propinsi Sulawesi Barat. ◈ *province* C Indonesia
Sulawesi, Laut *see* Celebes Sea
260 C5 **Sulawesi Selatan** *off.* Propinsi Sulawesi Selatan, *Eng.* South Celebes, South Sulawesi. ◈ *province* C Indonesia
Sulawesi Selatan, Propinsi *see* Sulawesi Selatan
260 D4 **Sulawesi Tengah** *off.* Propinsi Sulawesi Tengah, *Eng.* Central Celebes, Central Sulawesi. ◈ *province* N Indonesia
Sulawesi Tengah, Propinsi *see* Sulawesi Tengah
260 D6 **Sulawesi Tenggara** *off.* Propinsi Sulawesi Tenggara, *Eng.* South-East Celebes, South-East Sulawesi. ◈ *province* C Indonesia
Sulawesi Tenggara, Propinsi *see* Sulawesi Tenggara
260 E3 **Sulawesi Utara** *off.* Propinsi Sulawesi Utara, *Eng.* North Celebes, North Sulawesi. ◈ *province* N Indonesia
Sulawesi Utara, Propinsi *see* Sulawesi Utara
217 J4 **Sulaymān Beg** At Ta'mīn, N Iraq
158 G7 **Sulby** N Isle of Man
155 B8 **Suldalsvatnet** ◎ S Norway
Sulden *see* Solda
182 D6 **Sulechów** *Ger.* Züllichau. Lubuskie, W Poland 52°05′N 15°37′E
182 C5 **Sulęcin** Lubuskie, W Poland 52°29′N 15°06′E
133 K6 **Suleja** Niger, C Nigeria 09°15′N 07°10′E
182 G7 **Sulejów** Łodzkie, S Poland 51°21′N 19°57′E
156 E3 **Sule Skerry** *island* N Scotland, United Kingdom
Suliag *see* Sohâg
132 C7 **Sulima** S Sierra Leone 06°59′N 11°34′W
188 G9 **Sulina** Tulcea, SE Romania 45°07′N 29°40′E
188 G9 **Sulina, Braţul** ≈ SE Romania
180 F5 **Sulingen** Niedersachsen, NW Germany 52°40′N 08°48′E
Sulisjielmmá *see* Sulitjelma
152 E5 **Suliskongen** ▲ C Norway 67°10′N 16°16′E
152 E5 **Sulitjelma** *Lapp.* Sulisjielmmá. Nordland, C Norway 67°10′N 16°05′E
104 B4 **Sullana** Piura, NW Peru 04°54′S 80°42′W
66 C8 **Sulligent** Alabama, S USA 33°54′N 88°07′W
73 D11 **Sullivan** Illinois, N USA 39°36′N 88°36′W
73 E11 **Sullivan** Indiana, N USA 39°05′N 87°24′W
75 I10 **Sullivan** Missouri, C USA 38°12′N 91°09′W
Sullivan Island *see* Lanbi Kyun
54 F9 **Sullivan Lake** ◎ Alberta, SW Canada
156 H1 **Sullom Voe** NE Scotland, United Kingdom 60°24′N 01°09′W
165 H4 **Sully-sur-Loire** Loiret, C France 47°46′N 02°21′E
Sulmo *see* Sulmona
175 F8 **Sulmona** *anc.* Sulmo. Abruzzo, C Italy 42°03′N 13°56′E
Sulo *see* Shule He
187 K1 **Suloglu** Edirne, Turkey 41°46′N 26°55′E
68 B4 **Sulphur** Louisiana, S USA 30°14′N 93°22′W
75 E13 **Sulphur** Oklahoma, C USA 34°31′N 96°58′W
74 B5 **Sulphur Creek** ≈ South Dakota, N USA
70 D4 **Sulphur Draw** ≈ Texas, SW USA
71 I4 **Sulphur River** ≈ Arkansas/Texas, SW USA
71 I4 **Sulphur Springs** Texas, SW USA 33°09′N 95°36′W
70 D4 **Sulphur Springs Draw** ≈ Texas, SW USA
72 H3 **Sultan** Ontario, S Canada 47°34′N 82°45′W
Sultānābād *see* Arāk
Sultan Alonto, Lake *see* Lanao, Lake
214 D6 **Sultan Dağları** ▲▲ C Turkey
187 K2 **Sultankoy** Edirne, Turkey 41°02′N 26°27′E
263 M9 **Sultan Kudarat** *var.* Nuling. Mindanao, S Philippines 07°20′N 124°16′E
232 G6 **Sultānpur** Uttar Pradesh, N India 26°15′N 82°04′E
86 E7 **Sultepec de Pedro Ascencio de Alquisiras** México, Mexico 18°52′N 99°57′W
263 K10 **Sulu Archipelago** *island group* SW Philippines
286 B5 **Sulu Basin** *undersea feature* SE South China Sea 08°00′N 121°30′E
Sülüktü *see* Sulyukta
Sulu, Laut *see* Sulu Sea
263 K8 **Sulu Sea** *var.* Laut Sulu. *sea* SW Philippines
226 G7 **Sulutobe** *Kaz.* Sulūtöbe. Kzylorda, S Kazakhstan 44°31′N 66°17′E
Sulūtöbe *see* Sulutobe
229 I6 **Sulyukta** *Kir.* Sülüktü. Batkenskaya Oblast', SW Kyrgyzstan 39°57′N 69°31′E
Sulz *see* Sulz am Neckar
179 D12 **Sulz am Neckar** *var.* Sulz. Baden-Württemberg, SW Germany 48°22′N 08°37′E
181 G12 **Sulzbach** Bayern, Germany 9°10′N 49°55′E
181 C13 **Sulzbach** Saarland, Germany 7°04′N 49°18′E
179 G11 **Sulzbach-Rosenberg** Bayern, SE Germany 49°30′N 11°43′E
292 G7 **Sulzberger Bay** *bay* Antarctica
180 H5 **Sülze** Niedersachsen, Germany 10°02′N 52°46′E
181 H12 **Sulzfeld am Main** Bayern, Germany 10°08′N 49°42′E
Sumail *see* Summēl
184 C5 **Sumartin** Split-Dalmacija, S Croatia 43°17′N 16°52′E
76 C2 **Sumas** Washington, NW USA 49°00′N 122°15′W
258 D5 **Sumatera** *Eng.* Sumatra. *island* W Indonesia
258 D5 **Sumatera Barat** *off.* Propinsi Sumatera Barat, *Eng.* West Sumatra. ◈ *province* W Indonesia
Sumatera Barat, Propinsi *see* Sumatera Barat
258 F6 **Sumatera Selatan** *off.* Propinsi Sumatera Selatan, *Eng.* South Sumatra. ◈ *province* W Indonesia
Sumatera Selatan, Propinsi *see* Sumatera Selatan
258 C4 **Sumatera Utara** *off.* Propinsi Sumatera Utara, *Eng.* North Sumatra. ◈ *province* W Indonesia
Sumatera Utara, Propinsi *see* Sumatera Utara
Sumatra *see* Sumatera
Šumava *see* Bohemian Forest
Sumayl *see* Summēl
217 K5 **Sumayr al Muḩammad** Diyālá, E Iraq 33°34′N 45°06′E
260 C8 **Sumba, Pulau** *Eng.* Sandalwood Island; *prev.* Soemba. *island* Nusa Tenggara, C Indonesia
228 C7 **Sumbar** ≈ W Turkmenistan
260 C8 **Sumba, Selat** *strait* Nusa Tenggara, S Indonesia
260 B8 **Sumbawa** *prev.* Soembawa. *island* Nusa Tenggara, C Indonesia
260 B8 **Sumbawabesar** Sumbawa, S Indonesia 08°30′S 117°25′E
137 B11 **Sumbawanga** Rukwa, W Tanzania 07°57′S 31°37′E
135 C12 **Sumbe** *var.* N'Gunza, *Port.* Novo Redondo. Cuanza Sul, W Angola 11°13′S 13°53′E
156 H2 **Sumburgh Head** *headland* NE Scotland, United Kingdom 59°51′N 01°16′W
183 E12 **Sümeg** Veszprém, W Hungary 47°01′N 17°13′E
134 I3 **Sumeih** Southern Darfur, S Sudan 09°50′N 27°39′E
259 J8 **Sumenep** *prev.* Soemenep. Pulau Madura, C Indonesia 07°01′S 113°51′E
Sumgait *see* Sumqayıt, Azerbaijan
Sumgait *see* Sumqayıtçay, Azerbaijan
111 J6 **Sumidouro** Rio de Janeiro, Brazil 22°03′S 42°41′W
251 M8 **Sumisu-jima** *Eng.* Smith Island. *island* SE Japan
217 I1 **Summēl** *var.* Sumail, Sumayl. Dahūk, N Iraq 36°52′N 42°51′E
159 K8 **Summer Bridge** United Kingdom 54°03′N 1°42′W
72 F5 **Summer Island** *island* Michigan, N USA
76 D8 **Summer Lake** ◎ Oregon, NW USA
56 F8 **Summerland** British Columbia, SW Canada 49°35′N 119°45′W
59 J8 **Summerside** Prince Edward Island, SE Canada 46°24′N 63°46′W
141 H10 **Summerstrand** Eastern Cape, South Africa 33°59′S 25°39′E
67 I3 **Summersville** West Virginia, NE USA 38°17′N 80°52′W
67 I3 **Summersville Lake** ▣ West Virginia, NE USA
67 J8 **Summerton** South Carolina, SE USA 33°36′N 80°21′W
66 F7 **Summerville** Georgia, SE USA 34°28′N 85°21′W
67 J9 **Summerville** South Carolina, SE USA 33°01′N 80°10′W
83 I5 **Summit** Alaska, USA 63°21′N 148°50′W
80 J3 **Summit Mountain** ▲ Nevada, W USA 39°23′N 116°25′W
79 L5 **Summit Peak** ▲ Colorado, C USA 37°21′N 106°42′W
Summus Portus *see* Somport, Col du
72 A7 **Sumner** Iowa, C USA 42°51′N 92°05′W
66 A8 **Sumner** Mississippi, S USA 33°58′N 90°22′W
279 E9 **Sumner, Lake** ◎ South Island, New Zealand
79 M7 **Sumner, Lake** ▣ New Mexico, SW USA
253 B11 **Sumon-dake** ▲ Honshū, C Japan 37°24′N 139°07′E
251 H5 **Sumoto** Hyōgo, Awaji-shima, SW Japan 34°28′N 134°52′E
183 E8 **Šumperk** *Ger.* Mährisch-Schönberg. Olomoucký Kraj, E Czech Republic 49°58′N 17°00′E
215 N4 **Sumqayıt** *Rus.* Sumgait. E Azerbaijan 40°33′N 49°41′E
215 M4 **Sumqayıtçay** *Rus.* Sumgait. ≈ E Azerbaijan
229 J5 **Sumsar** Dzhalal-Abadskaya Oblast', W Kyrgyzstan 41°12′N 71°16′E
189 J2 **Sums'ka Oblast'** *var.* Sumy, *Rus.* Sumskaya Oblast'. ◈ *province* NE Ukraine
Sumskaya Oblast' *see* Sums'ka Oblast'
194 F5 **Sumskiy Posad** Respublika Kareliya, NW Russian Federation 64°12′N 35°22′E
67 J8 **Sumter** South Carolina, SE USA 33°54′N 80°22′W
189 K2 **Sumy** Sums'ka Oblast', NE Ukraine 50°54′N 34°49′E
Sumy *see* Sums'ka Oblast'
239 I9 **Sumzom** Xizang Zizhiqu, W China 29°45′N 96°14′E
195 I9 **Suna** Kirovskaya Oblast', NW Russian Federation 57°53′N 50°04′E
194 E6 **Suna** ≈ NW Russian Federation
252 E4 **Sunagawa** Hokkaidō, NE Japan 43°30′N 141°55′E
233 L7 **Sunamganj** Sylhet, NE Bangladesh 25°04′N 91°24′E
247 L8 **Sunan** ✈ (P'yŏngyang) SW North Korea 39°12′N 125°40′E
Sunan/Sunan Yugurzu Zizhixian *see* Hongwansi
63 I5 **Sunapee Lake** ◎ New Hampshire, NE USA
158 E1 **Sunart, Loch** ◎ United Kingdom
219 I11 **Şunaynīrāt, Jibāl** *dry watercourse* Jordan
217 H3 **Sunaysilah** *salt marsh* N Iraq
66 F6 **Sunbright** Tennessee, S USA 36°12′N 84°39′W
77 I2 **Sunburst** Montana, NW USA 48°51′N 111°54′W
277 I7 **Sunbury** Victoria, SE Australia 37°36′S 114°45′E
67 M5 **Sunbury** North Carolina, SE USA 36°27′N 76°34′W
64 D6 **Sunbury** Pennsylvania, NE USA 40°51′N 76°47′W
114 A3 **Sunchales** Santa Fe, C Argentina 30°58′S 61°35′W
248 B4 **Sunch'ŏn** SW North Korea 39°28′N 125°58′E
248 B7 **Sunch'ŏn** *Jap.* Junten. S South Korea 34°56′N 127°29′E
141 I3 **Sun City** North-West, South Africa 25°20′S 27°06′E
79 H8 **Sun City** Arizona, SW USA 33°36′N 112°16′W
81 E11 **Sun City** California, USA 33°43′N 117°12′W
65 L1 **Suncook** New Hampshire, NE USA 43°07′N 71°25′W
245 K6 **Suncun** *prev.* Xinwen. Shandong, E China 35°49′N 117°36′E
Sunda Islands *see* Greater Sunda Islands
77 M6 **Sundance** Wyoming, C USA 44°24′N 104°22′W
233 K9 **Sundarbans** *wetland* Bangladesh/India
234 H3 **Sundargarh** Orissa, E India 22°07′N 84°02′E
258 F8 **Sunda, Selat** *strait* Jawa/Sumatera, SW Indonesia
205 L9 **Sunda Shelf** *undersea feature* S South China Sea 05°00′N 107°00′E
286 A5 **Sunda Trench** *undersea feature* E Indian Ocean
Sunda Trench *see* Java Trench
205 L10 **Sunda Trough** *undersea feature* E Indian Ocean 08°50′S 109°30′E
141 H9 **Sundays** ≈ Eastern Cape, South Africa
141 K6 **Sundays** ≈ KwaZulu-Natal, South Africa
155 I8 **Sundbyberg** Stockholm, C Sweden 59°22′N 17°58′E
159 K6 **Sunderland** *var.* Wearmouth. NE England, United Kingdom 54°55′N 01°23′W
181 E8 **Sundern** Nordrhein-Westfalen, W Germany 51°19′N 08°00′E
214 D5 **Sündiken Dağları** ▲▲ C Turkey
70 D3 **Sundown** Texas, SW USA 33°27′N 102°29′W
57 I6 **Sundre** Alberta, SW Canada 51°49′N 114°46′W
62 D3 **Sundridge** Ontario, S Canada 45°45′N 79°25′W
154 I4 **Sundsvall** Västernorrland, C Sweden 62°22′N 17°20′E
75 B9 **Sunflower, Mount** ▲ Kansas, C USA 39°01′N 102°02′W
Sunflower State *see* Kansas
258 D3 **Sungai Bernam** ≈ Peninsular Malaysia
258 F7 **Sungaibuntu** Sumatera, SW Indonesia 04°04′S 105°37′E
258 D5 **Sungaidareh** Sumatera, W Indonesia 0°58′S 101°30′E
257 F12 **Sungai Kolok** *var.* Sungai Ko-Lok. Narathiwat, SW Thailand 06°02′N 101°58′E
Sungai Ko-Lok *see* Sungai Kolok
258 D6 **Sungaipenuh** *prev.* Soengaipenoeh. Sumatera, W Indonesia 02°S 101°28′E
259 H5 **Sungaipinyuh** Borneo, C Indonesia 0°16′N 109°06′E
Sungari *see* Songhua Jiang
Sungaria *see* Dzungaria
Sungei Pahang *see* Pahang, Sungai
256 E6 **Sung Men** Phrae, NW Thailand 17°59′N 100°07′E
139 I2 **Sungo** Tete, NW Mozambique 16°31′S 33°58′E
Sungpu *see* Songpan
258 F6 **Sungsang** Sumatera, W Indonesia 02°22′S 104°50′E
185 L6 **Sungurlare** Burgas, E Bulgaria 42°47′N 26°46′E
214 F5 **Sungurlu** Çorum, N Turkey 40°10′N 34°23′E
184 C3 **Sunja** Sisak-Moslavina, C Croatia 45°21′N 16°33′E
243 L2 **Sunjiabu** Anhui, E China 30°54′N 118°53′E
159 M9 **Sunk Island** United Kingdom 53°39′N 0°05′W
233 I6 **Sun Koshī** ≈ E Nepal
141 H9 **Sunland** Eastern Cape, South Africa 33°31′S 25°37′E
154 C4 **Sunndalen** *valley* S Norway
154 C4 **Sunndalsøra** Møre og Romsdal, S Norway 62°39′N 08°37′E
154 I7 **Sunnersta** Uppsala, C Sweden 59°46′N 17°40′E
79 I3 **Sunnyside** Utah, W USA 39°33′N 110°23′W
76 D5 **Sunnyside** Washington, NW USA 46°01′N 119°58′W
80 B3 **Sunnyvale** California, W USA 37°22′N 122°02′W
72 C7 **Sun Prairie** Wisconsin, N USA 43°12′N 89°12′W
Sunqur *see* Sonqor
70 E1 **Sunray** Texas, SW USA 36°01′N 101°49′W
68 C4 **Sunset** Louisiana, S USA 30°24′N 92°04′W
70 G4 **Sunset** Texas, SW USA 33°24′N 97°45′W
Sunset State *see* Oregon
277 M1 **Sunshine Coast** *cultural region* Queensland, E Australia
Sunshine State *see* Florida
Sunshine State *see* New Mexico
Sunshine State *see* South Dakota
193 I6 **Suntar** Respublika Sakha (Yakutiya), NE Russian Federation 62°10′N 117°34′E
83 I5 **Suntrana** Alaska, USA 63°51′N 148°51′W
230 D9 **Suntsar** Baluchistān, SW Pakistan 25°30′N 62°03′E
248 B5 **Sunwi-do** *island* SW North Korea
247 L3 **Sunwu** Heilongjiang, NE China 49°29′N 127°15′E
132 G7 **Sunyani** W Ghana 07°22′N 02°18′W
245 I3 **Sunzhuang** Hebei, E China 39°26′N 115°47′E
Suō *see* Suao
153 H8 **Suolahti** Länsi-Suomi, C Finland 62°32′N 25°51′E
Suoločielgi *see* Saariselkä
Suomenlahti *see* Finland, Gulf of
Suomen Tasavalta/Suomi *see* Finland
152 I7 **Suomussalmi** Oulu, E Finland 64°54′N 29°05′E
250 D6 **Suō-nada** *sea* SW Japan
153 I8 **Suonenjoki** Itä-Suomi, C Finland 62°36′N 27°07′E
262 D7 **Suŏng** Kâmpóng Cham, C Cambodia 11°53′N 105°41′E
194 E7 **Suoyarvi** Respublika Kareliya, NW Russian Federation 62°02′N 32°24′E
Supanburi *see* Suphan Buri
104 C7 **Supe** Lima, W Peru 10°49′S 77°40′W
Supérieur, Lac *see* Superior, Lake
79 I9 **Superior** Arizona, SW USA 33°17′N 111°06′W
76 G4 **Superior** Montana, NW USA 47°11′N 114°53′W
75 D8 **Superior** Nebraska, C USA 40°01′N 98°04′W
72 A4 **Superior** Wisconsin, N USA 46°42′N 92°04′W
87 I9 **Superior, Laguna** *lagoon* S Mexico
72 D3 **Superior, Lake** *Fr.* Lac Supérieur. ◎ Canada/USA
79 I9 **Superstition Mountains** ▲▲ Arizona, SW USA
184 C5 **Supetar** *It.* San Pietro. Split-Dalmacija, S Croatia 43°22′N 16°34′E
257 E8 **Suphan Buri** *var.* Supanburi. Suphan Buri, W Thailand 14°29′N 100°10′E
261 J4 **Supiori, Pulau** *island* E Indonesia
180 J6 **Süplingen** Sachsen-Anhalt, Germany 11°20′N 52°17′E
180 J6 **Süpplingen** Niedersachsen, Germany 10°55′N 52°14′E
282 E2 **Supply Reef** *reef* N Northern Mariana Islands
293 H4 **Support Force Glacier** *glacier* Antarctica
215 J4 **Sup'sa** *var.* Supsa. ≈ W Georgia
Supsa *see* Sup'sa
Sūq 'Abs *see* 'Abs
217 L8 **Sūq ash Shuyūkh** Dhī Qār, SE Iraq 30°53′N 46°28′E
216 C3 **Şuqaylibīyah** Ḩamāh, W Syria 35°21′N 36°24′E
245 K8 **Suqian** Jiangsu, E China 33°57′N 118°18′E
Suqrah *see* Şawqirah
Suqrah Bay *see* Şawqirah, Dawḩat
221 J9 **Suquṭrā** *var.* Sokotra, *Eng.* Socotra. *island* SE Yemen
221 L5 **Şūr** NE Oman 22°32′N 59°33′E
Şūr *see* Soûr
197 I3 **Sura** Penzenskaya Oblast', W Russian Federation 53°23′N 45°03′E
197 I2 **Sura** ≈ W Russian Federation
230 F7 **Sūrāb** Baluchistān, SW Pakistan 28°28′N 66°15′E
Surabaja *see* Surabaya
259 J8 **Surabaya** *prev.* Surabaja, Soerabaja. Jawa, C Indonesia 07°14′S 112°45′E
154 H7 **Surahammar** Västmanland, C Sweden 59°43′N 16°13′E
259 I8 **Surakarta** *Eng.* Solo; *prev.* Soerakarta. Jawa, S Indonesia 07°32′S 110°50′E
Surakhany *see* Suraxanı
263 M9 **Surallah** Mindanao, S Philippines 06°16′N 124°46′E
215 J4 **Surami** C Georgia 41°59′N 43°36′E
223 K8 **Sūrān** Sīstān va Balūchestān, SE Iran 27°18′N 61°58′E
183 F11 **Šurany** *Hung.* Nagysurány. Nitriansky Kraj, SW Slovakia 48°05′N 18°10′E
277 K1 **Surat** Queensland, Australia
232 C9 **Sūrat** Gujarāt, W India 21°10′N 72°54′E
Suratdhani *see* Surat Thani
232 D5 **Sūratgarh** Rājasthān, NW India 29°20′N 73°59′E
257 E10 **Surat Thani** *var.* Suratdhani. Surat Thani, SW Thailand 09°09′N 99°20′E
191 J10 **Suraw** *Rus.* Surov. ≈ E Belarus
215 N5 **Suraxanı** *Rus.* Surakhany. E Azerbaijan 40°25′N 49°59′E
221 K6 **Surayr** E Oman 19°56′N 57°47′E
216 E2 **Suraysāt** Ḩalab, N Syria 36°42′N 38°01′E
191 I8 **Surazh** Vitsyebskaya Voblasts', NE Belarus 55°25′N 30°44′E
196 E3 **Surazh** Bryanskaya Oblast', W Russian Federation 53°04′N 32°29′E
118 A2 **Sur, Cabo** *headland* Easter Island, Chile, E Pacific Ocean 27°11′S 109°26′W
184 F3 **Surčin** Serbia, N Serbia 44°48′N 20°19′E
188 C6 **Surduc** *Hung.* Szurduk. Sălaj, NW Romania 47°13′N 23°20′E
185 H6 **Surdulica** Serbia, SE Serbia 42°43′N 22°10′E
163 I13 **Sûre** *var.* Sauer. ≈ W Europe *see also* Sauer
Sûre *see* Sauer
232 C8 **Surendranagar** Gujarāt, W India 22°44′N 71°43′E
81 A8 **Surf** California, USA 34°41′N 120°36′W
65 H8 **Surf City** New Jersey, NE USA 39°21′N 74°24′W
277 M2 **Surfers Paradise** Queensland, E Australia 27°54′S 153°18′E
67 K8 **Surfside Beach** South Carolina, SE USA 33°36′N 78°58′W
164 F6 **Surgères** Charente-Maritime, W France 46°07′N 00°44′W
192 F6 **Surgut** Khanty-Mansiyskiy Avtonomnyy Okrug-Yugra, C Russian Federation 61°13′N 73°28′E
192 G6 **Surgutikha** Krasnoyarskiy Kray, N Russian Federation 64°44′N 87°13′E
162 H3 **Surhuisterveen** Friesland, N Netherlands 53°11′N 06°10′E
171 K3 **Súria** Cataluña, NE Spain 41°50′N 01°45′E
222 G7 **Sūrīān** Fārs, S Iran
234 F6 **Suriāpet** Andhra Pradesh, C India 17°10′N 79°42′E
263 M8 **Surigao** Mindanao, S Philippines 09°43′N 125°31′E
256 G7 **Surin** Surin, E Thailand 14°53′N 103°29′E
Surinam *see* Suriname
103 L6 **Suriname** *off.* Republic of Suriname, *var.* Suriname; *prev.* Dutch Guiana, Netherlands Guiana. ◆ *republic* N South America
Suriname, Republic of *see* Suriname
Sūrīya/Sūrīyah, Al-Jumhūrīyah al-'Arabīyah as- *see* Syria
218 J3 **Suriyat, Wādī as** Syria
Surkhab, Darya-i- *see* Kahmard, Daryā-ye
Surkhandar'inskaya Oblast' *see* Surxondaryo Viloyati
Surkhandar'ya *see* Surxondaryo
Surkhet *see* Birendranagar
229 J7 **Surkhob** ≈ C Tajikistan
215 I5 **Sürmene** Trabzon, NE Turkey 40°56′N 40°03′E
Surov *see* Suraw
197 H6 **Surovikino** Volgogradskaya Oblast', SW Russian Federation 48°39′N 42°46′E
193 H7 **Surovo** Irkutskaya Oblast', S Russian Federation 55°45′N 105°31′E
80 A5 **Sur, Point** *headland* California, W USA 36°18′N 121°54′W
117 D12 **Sur, Punta** *headland* E Argentina 50°59′S 69°10′W
Surrentum *see* Sorrento
74 C2 **Surrey** North Dakota, N USA 48°13′N 101°05′W
166 D1 **Surrey** *cultural region* SE England, United Kingdom
67 L4 **Surry** Virginia, NE USA 37°08′N 81°34′W
167 N8 **Sursee** Luzern, W Switzerland 47°11′N 08°07′E
197 I3 **Sursk** Penzenskaya Oblast', W Russian Federation 53°06′N 45°46′E
197 I2 **Surskoye** Ul'yanovskaya Oblast', W Russian Federation 54°28′N 46°47′E
128 D2 **Surt** *var.* Sidra, Sirte. N Libya 31°13′N 16°35′E
155 E10 **Surte** Västra Götaland, S Sweden 57°49′N 12°01′E
128 C4 **Surt, Khalīj** *Eng.* Gulf of Sidra, Gulf of Sirti, Sidra. *gulf* N Libya
152 B3 **Surtsey** *island* S Iceland
215 H8 **Suruç** Şanlıurfa, S Turkey 36°58′N 38°24′E
251 K4 **Suruga-wan** *bay* SE Japan
258 E6 **Surulangun** Sumatera, W Indonesia 02°35′S 102°47′E
286 G2 **Surveyor Fracture Zone** *tectonic feature* N Pacific Ocean
180 D4 **Surwold** Niedersachsen, Germany 7°31′N 52°57′E
229 I7 **Surxondaryo** *Rus.* Surkhandar'ya. ≈ Tajikistan/Uzbekistan
229 H7 **Surxondaryo Viloyati** *Rus.* Surkhandar'inskaya Oblast'. ◈ *province* S Uzbekistan
Süs *see* Susch
176 C7 **Susa** Piemonte, NE Italy 45°10′N 07°01′E
250 D5 **Susa** Yamaguchi, Honshū, SW Japan 34°35′N 131°34′E
Susa *see* Shūsh
184 C6 **Sušac** *It.* Cazza. *island* SW Croatia
Sūsah *see* Sousse
250 F6 **Susaki** Kōchi, Shikoku, SW Japan 33°22′N 133°13′E
251 H6 **Susami** Wakayama, Honshū, SW Japan 33°32′N 135°32′E
114 A4 **Susana** Santa Fe, Argentina 31°22′S 61°31′W
222 D6 **Sūsangerd** *var.* Susangird. Khūzestān, SW Iran 31°40′N 48°06′E
Susangird *see* Sūsangerd
78 C2 **Susanville** California, W USA 40°25′N 120°39′W
176 F5 **Susch** *var.* Süs. Graubünden, SE Switzerland 46°45′N 10°04′E
215 H5 **Suşehri** Sivas, N Turkey 40°11′N 38°06′E
Susiana *see* Khūzestān
183 B9 **Sušice** *Ger.* Schüttenhofen. Plzeňský Kraj, W Czech Republic 49°14′N 13°32′E
83 I6 **Susitna** Alaska, USA 61°32′N 150°30′W
83 I5 **Susitna River** ≈ Alaska, USA
197 J1 **Suslonger** Respublika Mariy El, W Russian Federation 56°18′N 48°16′E
243 J3 **Susong** Anhui, China 30°05′N 116°05′E
170 G8 **Suspiro del Moro, Puerto del** *pass* S Spain
64 E4 **Susquehanna River** ≈ New York/Pennsylvania, NE USA
63 N2 **Sussex** New Brunswick, SE Canada 45°43′N 65°32′W
64 G5 **Sussex** New Jersey, NE USA 41°12′N 74°34′W
67 L5 **Sussex** Virginia, NE USA 36°54′N 77°16′W
157 I12 **Sussex** *cultural region* S England, United Kingdom
277 L6 **Sussex Inlet** New South Wales, SE Australia 35°10′S 150°35′E
163 G9 **Susteren** Limburg, SE Netherlands 51°04′N 05°50′E
180 D4 **Sustrum** Niedersachsen, Germany 7°17′N 52°55′E
56 C2 **Sustut Peak** ▲ British Columbia, W Canada 56°25′N 126°34′W
193 L5 **Susuman** Magadanskaya Oblast', E Russian Federation 62°46′N 148°08′E
283 H2 **Susupe** ● (Northern Mariana Islands-judicial capital) Saipan, S Northern Mariana Islands
86 E6 **Susupuato de Guenero** Michoacán, Mexico 19°13′N 100°24′W
214 B5 **Susurluk** Balıkesir, NW Turkey 39°55′N 28°10′E
80 G1 **Sutcliffe** Nevada, USA 39°57′N 119°36′W
214 D7 **Sütçüler** Isparta, SW Turkey 37°31′N 31°00′E
188 F9 **Şuţeşti** Brăila, SE Romania 45°13′N 27°27′E
140 E8 **Sutherland** Northern Cape, South Africa 32°24′S 20°40′E
138 E9 **Sutherland** Western Cape, SW South Africa 32°24′S 20°40′E
74 B7 **Sutherland** Nebraska, C USA 41°09′N 101°07′W
156 E4 **Sutherland** *cultural region* N Scotland, United Kingdom
278 B11 **Sutherland Falls** *waterfall* South Island, New Zealand
76 B7 **Sutherlin** Oregon, NW USA 43°23′N 123°18′W
231 J6 **Sutlej** ≈ India/Pakistan
Sutna *see* Satna
78 C4 **Sutter Creek** California, W USA 38°22′N 120°49′W
161 K2 **Sutterton** United Kingdom 52°54′N 0°05′W
140 F5 **Sutton** Northern Cape, South Africa 27°26′S 22°49′E
161 K6 **Sutton** United Kingdom 51°21′N 0°12′W
83 I6 **Sutton** Alaska, USA 61°42′N 148°53′W
67 I3 **Sutton** West Virginia, NE USA 38°41′N 80°43′W
58 E4 **Sutton** ≈ Ontario, C Canada
161 K3 **Sutton Bridge** E England, United Kingdom 52°47′N 00°11′E
161 H3 **Sutton Coldfield** C England, United Kingdom 52°34′N 01°48′W
159 L10 **Sutton in Ashfield** United Kingdom 53°07′N 1°16′W
67 I3 **Sutton Lake** ▣ West Virginia, NE USA
63 I3 **Sutton, Monts** *hill range* Québec, SE Canada
161 K1 **Sutton on Sea** E England, United Kingdom 53°19′N 00°17′W
159 N10 **Sutton on Sea** E England, United Kingdom 53°19′N 00°17′W
159 L8 **Sutton on the Forest** United Kingdom 54°05′N 1°07′W
58 E4 **Sutton Ridges** ▲▲ Ontario, C Canada
161 K3 **Sutton Saint James** United Kingdom 52°44′N 0°04′E
252 C5 **Suttsu** Hokkaidō, NE Japan 42°46′N 140°12′E
83 H8 **Sutwik Island** *island* Alaska, USA
Süüj *see* Dashinchilen
141 H8 **Suurberg** ▲▲ Eastern Cape, South Africa
190 E4 **Suure-Jaani** *Ger.* Gross-Sankt-Johannis. Viljandimaa, S Estonia 58°34′N 25°28′E
190 F5 **Suur Munamägi** *var.* Munamägi, *Ger.* Eier-Berg. ▲ SE Estonia 57°42′N 27°03′E
190 D4 **Suur Väin** *Ger.* Grosser Sund. *strait* W Estonia
229 K4 **Suusamyr** Chuyskaya Oblast', C Kyrgyzstan 42°07′N 73°55′E
280 E9 **Suva** ● (Fiji) Viti Levu, W Fiji 18°08′S 178°27′E
280 E9 **Suva** ✈ Viti Levu, C Fiji 18°01′S 178°30′E
184 G7 **Suva Gora** ▲▲ W FYR Macedonia
190 E7 **Suvainiškis** Panevėžys, NE Lithuania 56°09′N 25°15′E
Suvalkai/Suvalki *see* Suwałki
185 H6 **Suva Planina** ▲▲ SE Serbia
184 G7 **Suva Reka** *Serb.* Suva Reka. S Kosovo 42°23′N 20°50′E
Suva Reka *see* Suva Reka
196 F3 **Suvorov** Tul'skaya Oblast', W Russian Federation 54°08′N 36°33′E
188 G8 **Suvorove** Odes'ka Oblast', SW Ukraine 45°35′N 28°58′E
Suvorovo *see* Ştefan Vodă
251 K3 **Suwa** Nagano, Honshū, S Japan 36°01′N 138°07′E
Suwaik *see* As Suwayq
Suwaira *see* Aş Şuwayrah
182 I4 **Suwałki** *Lith.* Suvalkai, *Rus.* Suvalki. Podlaskie, NE Poland 54°06′N 22°56′E
256 G7 **Suwannaphum** Roi Et, E Thailand 15°36′N 103°46′E
69 K4 **Suwannee River** ≈ Florida/Georgia, SE USA
248 C10 **Suwanose-jima** *island group* Japan Asia Pacific Ocean
Şuwār *see* Aş Şuwār
284 F6 **Suwarrow** *atoll* N Cook Islands
221 J4 **Suwaydān** *var.* Sweiham. Abū Ẓaby, E United Arab Emirates 24°30′N 55°19′E
Suwaydá/Suwaydā', Muḩāfaẓat as *see* As Suwaydā'
219 G8 **Şuwaylih** Jordan 32°01′N 35°50′E
219 F8 **Suwaymah** Jordan 31°46′N 35°35′E
Suwayqiyah, Hawr as *see* Shuwayjah, Hawr ash
Suways, Qanāt as *see* Suez Canal
Suweida *see* As Suwaydā'
Suweon *see* Suwŏn
248 C5 **Suwŏn** *var.* Suweon, *Jap.* Suigen. NW South Korea 37°17′N 127°03′E
Su Xian *see* Suzhou
245 H9 **Suyahu Shuiku** ▣ Henan, China
195 L7 **Suyevatpaul'** Sverdlovskaya Oblast', Russian Federation
223 H9 **Sūzā** Hormozgān, S Iran 26°50′N 56°05′E
227 H7 **Suzak** *Kaz.* Sozaq. Yuzhnyy Kazakhstan, S Kazakhstan 44°09′N 68°28′E
Suzaka *see* Suzuka
196 G1 **Suzdal'** Vladimirskaya Oblast', W Russian Federation 56°27′N 40°29′E
169 J4 **Suze-la-Rousse** Rhône-Alpes, France 44°17′N 4°51′E
245 J8 **Suzhou** *var.* Su Xian. Anhui, E China 33°38′N 117°02′E
243 M2 **Suzhou** *var.* Soochow, Su-chou, Suchow; *prev.* Wuhsien. Jiangsu, E China 31°23′N 120°34′E
Suzhou *see* Jiuquan
248 B2 **Suzi He** ≈ NE China
Suz, Mys *see* Soye, Mys
251 J1 **Suzu** Ishikawa, Honshū, SW Japan 37°24′N 137°12′E
251 I4 **Suzuka** Mie, Honshū, SW Japan 34°52′N 136°37′E
251 K2 **Suzuka** *var.* Suzaka. Nagano, Honshū, S Japan 36°38′N 138°20′E
251 J1 **Suzu-misaki** *headland* Honshū, SW Japan 37°31′N 137°19′E
Svågälv *see* Svågan
154 H5 **Svågan** *var.* Svågälv. ≈ C Sweden
Svalava/Svaljava *see* Svalyava
152 B4 **Svalbard** ◇ *Norwegian dependency* Arctic Ocean
152 C2 **Svalbardhseyri** Nordhurland Eystra, N Iceland 65°43′N 18°03′W
155 F12 **Svalöv** Skåne, S Sweden 55°55′N 13°06′E
188 C5 **Svalyava** *Cz.* Svalava, Svaljava, *Hung.* Szolyva. Zakarpats'ka Oblast', W Ukraine 48°33′N 23°00′E
152 B5 **Svanbergfjellet** ▲ C Svalbard 78°40′N 18°10′E
178 J3 **Svaneke** Bornholm, E Denmark 55°07′N 15°08′E
155 G11 **Svängsta** Blekinge, S Sweden 56°16′N 14°46′E
155 F8 **Svanskog** Värmland, C Sweden 59°10′N 12°34′E
155 G8 **Svartå** Örebro, C Sweden 59°13′N 14°07′E
152 E6 **Svartisen** *glacier* C Norway
189 M4 **Svatove** *Rus.* Svatovo. Luhans'ka Oblast', E Ukraine 49°24′N 38°11′E
Svatovo *see* Svatove
Sväty Kríž nad Hronom *see* Žiar nad Hronom
257 G8 **Svay Chék, Stœng** ≈ Cambodia/Thailand
257 H9 **Svay Riĕng** Svay Riĕng, S Cambodia 11°05′N 105°48′E
152 B5 **Sveagruva** Spitsbergen, W Svalbard 77°53′N 16°42′E
155 F12 **Svedala** Skåne, S Sweden 55°30′N 13°15′E
190 E7 **Svėdesai** Utena, NE Lithuania 55°42′N 25°22′E
154 G5 **Sveg** Jämtland, C Sweden 62°02′N 14°20′E
191 B8 **Švėkšna** Klaipėda, W Lithuania 55°31′N 21°37′E
154 A5 **Svelgen** Sogn Og Fjordane, S Norway 61°47′N 05°18′E
155 D8 **Svelvik** Vestfold, S Norway 59°37′N 10°24′E
191 E8 **Švenčionėliai** *Pol.* Nowo-Święciany. Vilnius, SE Lithuania 55°10′N 26°00′E
191 E8 **Švenčionys** *Pol.* Swięciany. Vilnius, SE Lithuania 55°08′N 26°08′E
155 D13 **Svendborg** Fyn, C Denmark 55°04′N 10°38′E
155 F10 **Svenljunga** Västra Götaland, S Sweden 57°30′N 13°05′E
152 C5 **Svenskøya** *island* E Svalbard
154 G4 **Svenstavik** Jämtland, C Sweden 62°40′N 14°24′E
155 D11 **Svenstrup** Nordjylland, N Denmark 56°58′N 09°52′E
191 E8 **Šventoji** ≈ C Lithuania
189 N5 **Sverdlovs'k** *Rus.* Sverdlovsk; *prev.* Imeni Sverdlova Rudnik. Luhans'ka Oblast', E Ukraine 48°05′N 39°37′E
Sverdlovsk *see* Yekaterinburg
195 M8 **Sverdlovskaya Oblast'** ◈ *province* C Russian Federation
52 G3 **Sverdrup Channel** *Sea waterway* Nunavut, N Canada
52 G3 **Sverdrup Islands** *Island group* Nunavut, N Canada
192 G3 **Sverdrup, Ostrov** *island* N Russian Federation
Sverige *see* Sweden
184 B6 **Svetac** *prev.* Sveti Andrea, *It.* Sant'Andrea. *island* SW Croatia
Sveti Andrea *see* Svetac
Sveti Nikola *see* Sveti Nikole
185 H7 **Sveti Nikole** *prev.* Sveti Nikola. C FYR Macedonia 41°54′N 21°55′E
Sveti Vrach *see* Sandanski
193 L8 **Svetlaya** Primorskiy Kray, SE Russian Federation 46°33′N 138°20′E
191 A8 **Svetlogorsk** Kaliningradskaya Oblast', W Russian Federation 54°56′N 20°09′E
192 G5 **Svetlogorsk** Krasnoyarskiy Kray, N Russian Federation 66°51′N 88°29′E
Svetlogorsk *see* Svyetlahorsk
197 H8 **Svetlograd** Stavropol'skiy Kray, SW Russian Federation 45°20′N 42°53′E
Svetlovodsk *see* Svitlovods'k
191 A8 **Svetlyy** *Ger.* Zimmerbude. Kaliningradskaya Oblast', W Russian Federation 54°42′N 20°07′E
197 I4 **Svetlyy** Orenburgskaya Oblast', W Russian Federation 50°34′N 60°42′E
197 I4 **Svetlyy** Saratovskaya Oblast', W Russian Federation 51°42′N 45°40′E
194 D7 **Svetogorsk** *Fin.* Enso. Leningradskaya Oblast', NW Russian Federation 61°06′N 28°52′E
Svetozarevo *see* Jagodina
183 B9 **Švihov** *Ger.* Schwihau. Plzeňský Kraj, W Czech Republic 49°31′N 13°18′E
184 C5 **Svilaja** ▲▲ SE Croatia
184 G4 **Svilajnac** Serbia, C Serbia 44°15′N 21°12′E
185 L7 **Svilengrad** *prev.* Mustafa-Pasha. Khaskovo, S Bulgaria 41°45′N 26°14′E
Svinecea Mare, Munte *see* Svinecea Mare, Vârful
188 B9 **Svinecea Mare, Vârful** *var.* Munte Svinecea Mare. ▲ SW Romania 44°47′N 22°10′E
Svinø *see* Svínoy
154 B1 **Svínoy** *Dan.* Svinø. *island* NE Faeroe Islands
229 H8 **Svintsovyy Rudnik** *Turkm.* Swintsowyy Rudnik. Lebap Welaýaty, E Turkmenistan 37°54′N 66°25′E

◆ Country ● Country Capital ◇ Dependent Territory ○ Dependent Territory Capital ◈ Administrative Regions ✈ International Airport ▲ Mountain ▲▲ Mountain Range Volcano ≈ River ◎ Lake ▣ Reservoir

T

◆ Country
● Country Capital
◇ Dependent Territory
○ Dependent Territory Capital
◆ Administrative Regions
✗ International Airport
▲ Mountain
▲ Mountain Range
✗ Volcano
✗ River
○ Lake
○ Reservoir

◆ Country
◆ Country Capital
◇ Dependent Territory
○ Dependent Territory Capital
◈ Administrative Regions
✕ International Airport
▲ Mountain
▲ Mountain Range
▲ Volcano
∴ River
⊗ Lake
⊠ Reservoir

◆ Country
● Country Capital
◇ Dependent Territory
○ Dependent Territory Capital
✕ International Airport
▲ Mountain
▲ Mountain Range
⊙ Volcano
☞ River
◉ Administrative Regions
⊚ Lake
◎ Reservoir

◆ Country
● Country Capital
◇ Dependent Territory
○ Dependent Territory Capital
◆ Administrative Regions
✈ International Airport
▲ Mountain
▲ Mountain Range
▲ Volcano
☑ River
○ Lake
☑ Reservoir

Tymfristós - Urengoy

186 F5 **Tymfristós** *var.* Timfristos. ▲ C Greece 38°57′N 21°49′E
187 I10 **Tympáki** *var.* Timbaki; *prev.* Timbákion. Kriti, Greece, E Mediterranean Sea 35°04′N 24°47′E
193 J7 **Tynda** Amurskaya Oblast', SE Russian Federation 55°09′N 124°44′E
74 E6 **Tyndall** South Dakota, N USA 42°57′N 97°52′W
158 G2 **Tyndrum** United Kingdom 56°27′N 4°44′W
156 G7 **Tyne** ⚞ N England, United Kingdom
159 K5 **Tynemouth** NE England, United Kingdom 55°01′N 01°24′W
154 E4 **Tynset** Hedmark, S Norway 61°45′N 10°49′E
83 I6 **Tyonek** Alaska, USA 61°04′N 151°08′W
Tyôsi *see* Chôshi
Tyras *see* Dniester
Tyras *see* Bilhorod-Dnistrovs'kyy
Tyre *see* Soûr
154 D7 **Tyrifjorden** ◎ S Norway
155 G12 **Tyringe** Skåne, S Sweden 56°09′N 13°35′E
193 K8 **Tyrma** Khabarovskiy Kray, SE Russian Federation 50°00′N 132°04′E
Tyrnau *see* Trnava
186 G4 **Týrnavos** *var.* Tírnavos. Thessalía, C Greece 39°45′N 22°18′E
197 H9 **Tyrnyauz** Kabardino-Balkarskaya Respublika, SW Russian Federation 43°19′N 42°55′E
Tyrol *see* Tirol
64 B6 **Tyrone** Pennsylvania, NE USA 40°41′N 78°12′W
157 C8 **Tyrone** *cultural region* W Northern Ireland, United Kingdom
Tyros *see* Bahrain
277 I6 **Tyrrell, Lake** *salt lake* Victoria, SE Australia
144 E8 **Tyrrhenian Basin** *undersea feature* Tyrrhenian Sea, C Mediterranean Sea 39°30′N 13°00′E
175 D10 **Tyrrhenian Sea** *It.* Mare Tirreno. *sea* N Mediterranean Sea
Tysa *see* Tisa/Tisza
188 D5 **Tysmenytsya** Ivano-Frankivs'ka Oblast', W Ukraine 48°54′N 24°50′E
154 A7 **Tysnesøya** *island* S Norway
154 A7 **Tysse** Hordaland, S Norway 60°23′N 05°46′E
154 B7 **Tyssedal** Hordaland, S Norway 60°07′N 06°36′E
155 I8 **Tystberga** Södermanland, C Sweden 58°51′N 17°15′E
191 C8 **Tytuvėnai** Šiaulai, C Lithuania 55°36′N 23°14′E
226 B6 **Tyub-Karagan, Mys** *headland* SW Kazakhstan 44°40′N 50°19′E
229 L4 **Tyugel'-Say** Narynskaya Oblast', C Kyrgyzstan 41°57′N 74°40′E
227 I1 **Tyukalinsk** Omskaya Oblast', C Russian Federation 55°56′N 72°02′E
197 L3 **Tyul'gan** Orenburgskaya Oblast', W Russian Federation 52°27′N 56°08′E
195 N9 **Tyumen'** Tyumenskaya Oblast', C Russian Federation 57°11′N 65°29′E
192 E6 **Tyumenskaya Oblast'** ◆ *province* C Russian Federation
193 I6 **Tyung** ⚞ NE Russian Federation
229 M4 **Tyup** *Kir.* Tüp. Issyk-Kul'skaya Oblast', NE Kyrgyzstan 42°44′N 78°18′E
192 G8 **Tyva, Respublika** *prev.* Tannu-Tuva, Tuva, Tuvinskaya ASSR. ◆ *autonomous republic* C Russian Federation
188 F5 **Tyvriv** Vinnyts'ka Oblast', C Ukraine 49°01′N 28°28′E
157 F11 **Tywi** ⚞ S Wales, United Kingdom
160 E5 **Tywi, Afon** ⚞ United Kingdom
160 E3 **Tywyn** W Wales, United Kingdom 52°35′N 04°06′W
141 K2 **Tzaneen** Limpopo, NE South Africa 23°50′S 30°09′E
141 K2 **Tzaneen Dam** ◎ Limpopo, South Africa
Tzekung *see* Zigong
187 I7 **Tziá** *prev.* Kéa, Kéos; *anc.* Ceos. *island* Kykládes, Greece, Aegean Sea
87 K9 **Tzimol** Chiapas, Mexico 16°16′N 92°16′W
87 M5 **Tzucacab** Yucatán, SE Mexico 20°04′N 89°03′W

U

135 C12 **Uaco Cungo** *var.* Waku Kungo, *Port.* Santa Comba. Cuanza Sul, C Angola 11°21′S 15°04′E
UAE *see* United Arab Emirates
285 K5 **Ua Huka** *island* Îles Marquises, NE French Polynesia
103 H6 **Uaiacás** Roraima, N Brazil 03°28′N 63°13′W
Uamba *see* Wamba
Uanle Uen *see* Wanlaweyn
285 K5 **Ua Pu** *island* Îles Marquises, NE French Polynesia
136 F7 **Uar Garas** *spring/well* SW Somalia 01°19′N 41°22′E
107 H2 **Uatumã, Rio** ⚞ C Brazil
Ua Uíbh Fhailí *see* Offaly
102 F8 **Uaupés, Rio** *var.* Río Vaupés. ⚞ Brazil/Colombia *see also* Vaupés, Río
Uaupés, Rio *see* Vaupés, Río
111 I5 **Ubá** Minas Gerais, Brazil 21°07′S 42°56′W
227 L3 **Uba** ⚞ E Kazakhstan
226 G2 **Ubagan** *Kaz.* Obagan. ⚞ Kazakhstan/Russian Federation
280 D3 **Ubai** New Britain, E Papua New Guinea 05°38′S 150°45′E
114 E4 **Ubajay** Entre Ríos, Argentina 31°47′S 58°18′W
134 E5 **Ubangi** *Fr.* Oubangui. ⚞ C Africa
Ubangi-Shari *see* Central African Republic
111 J2 **Ubaporanga** Minas Gerais, Brazil 19°38′S 42°06′W
188 F2 **Ubarts'** *Ukr.* Ubort'. ⚞ Belarus/Ukraine *see also* Ubort'
Ubarts' *see* Ubort'
102 C5 **Ubaté** Cundinamarca, C Colombia 05°20′N 73°50′W
110 F9 **Ubatuba** São Paulo, S Brazil 23°26′S 45°04′W
231 H7 **Ubauro** Sind, SE Pakistan 28°08′N 69°43′E
263 M7 **Ubay** Bohol, C Philippines 10°02′N 124°29′E
165 K7 **Ubaye** ⚞ SE France
Ubayid, Wadi al *see* Ubayyiḑ, Wādī al
216 F5 **Ubaylah** Al Anbār, W Iraq 33°06′N 40°13′E
216 G7 **Ubayyiḑ, Wādī al** *var.* Wadi al Ubayid. *dry watercourse* SW Iraq
162 G7 **Ubbergen** Gelderland, E Netherlands 51°49′N 05°54′E
250 D5 **Ube** Yamaguchi, Honshū, SW Japan 33°57′N 131°15′E
170 G7 **Úbeda** Andalucía, S Spain 38°01′N 03°22′W
177 K4 **Übelbach** *var.* Markt-Übelbach. Steiermark, SE Austria 47°13′N 15°15′E
110 B3 **Uberaba** Minas Gerais, SE Brazil 19°47′S 47°57′W
107 H10 **Uberaba, Laguna** ◎ E Bolivia
110 A1 **Uberlândia** Minas Gerais, SE Brazil 18°17′S 48°17′W
179 D13 **Überlingen** Baden-Württemberg, S Germany 47°46′N 09°10′E
133 J8 **Ubiaja** Edo, S Nigeria 06°39′N 06°23′E
170 E2 **Ubiña, Peña** ▲ NW Spain 43°01′N 05°58′W
105 G9 **Ubinas, Volcán** ☒ S Peru 16°16′S 70°49′W
Ubol Rajadhani/Ubol Ratchathani *see* Ubon Ratchathani
256 F7 **Ubolratna Reservoir** ◙ C Thailand
141 L5 **Ubombo** KwaZulu-Natal, South Africa 27°34′S 32°05′E
256 H7 **Ubon Ratchathani** *var.* Muang Ubon, Ubol Rajadhani, Ubol Ratchathani, Udon Ratchathani. Ubon Ratchathani, E Thailand 15°15′N 104°50′E
191 G12 **Ubort'** *Bel.* Ubarts'. ⚞ Belarus/Ukraine *see also* Ubarts'
Ubort' *see* Ubarts'
170 E9 **Ubrique** Andalucía, S Spain 36°42′N 05°27′W
181 F14 **Ubstadt-Weiher** Baden-Württemberg, Germany 8°37′N 49°10′E
Ubsu-Nur, Ozero *see* Uvs Nuur
134 H7 **Ubundu** Orientale, C Dem. Rep. Congo 0°24′S 25°30′E
228 F7 **Üçajy** *var.* Üchajy, *Rus.* Uch-Adzhi. Mary Welaýaty, C Turkmenistan 38°06′N 62°44′E
215 M5 **Ucar** *Rus.* Udzhary. C Azerbaijan 40°31′N 47°40′E
104 F6 **Ucayali** *off.* Departamento de Ucayali. ◆ *department* E Peru
Ucayali, Departamento de *see* Ucayali
104 E4 **Ucayali, Río** ⚞ C Peru
Uccle *see* Ukkel
Uch-Adzhi/Üchajy *see* Üçajy
197 M2 **Uchaly** Respublika Bashkortostan, W Russian Federation 54°19′N 59°33′E
227 L5 **Ucharal** *Kaz.* Üsharal. Almaty, E Kazakhstan 46°08′N 80°55′E
250 D9 **Uchinoura** Kagoshima, Kyūshū, SW Japan 31°16′N 131°04′E
252 D5 **Uchiura-wan** *bay* NW Pacific Ocean
Uchkuduk *see* Uchquduq
229 K5 **Uchqo'rg'on** *Rus.* Uchkurghan. Namangan Viloyati, E Uzbekistan 41°06′N 72°04′E
229 K5 **Uchqo'rg'on** *Rus.* Uchkurghan. Namangan Viloyati, E Uzbekistan 41°06′N 72°04′E
228 G5 **Uchquduq** *Rus.* Uchkuduk. Navoiy Viloyati, N Uzbekistan 42°12′N 63°27′E
Uchsay *see* Uchsoy
228 D3 **Uchsoy** *Rus.* Uchsay. Qoraqalpog'iston Respublikasi, NW Uzbekistan 43°51′N 58°51′E
Uchtagan Gumy/Uchtagan, Peski *see* Uçtagan Gumy
193 K7 **Uchur** ⚞ E Russian Federation
181 D10 **Uckerath** Nordrhein-Westfalen, Germany 7°22′N 50°44′E
178 I5 **Uckermark** *cultural region* E Germany
161 K7 **Uckfield** United Kingdom 50°58′N 0°06′E
56 C9 **Ucluelet** Vancouver Island, British Columbia, SW Canada 48°55′N 123°34′W
228 C5 **Uçtagan Gumy** *var.* Uchtagan Gumy, *Rus.* Peski Uchtagan. *desert* NW Turkmenistan
193 K7 **Uda** ⚞ E Russian Federation
193 I5 **Udachnyy** Respublika Sakha (Yakutiya), NE Russian Federation 66°27′N 112°18′E
235 E8 **Udagamandalam** *var.* Ooty, Udhagamandalam; *prev.* Ootacamund. Tamil Nādu, SW India 11°28′N 76°42′E
232 D7 **Udaipur** *prev.* Oodeypore. Rājasthān, N India 24°35′N 73°41′E
Udayadhani *see* Uthai Thani
222 F10 **'Udayd, Khawr al** *var.* Khor al Udeid. *inlet* Qatar/Saudi Arabia
184 C4 **Udbina** Lika-Senj, W Croatia 44°33′N 15°46′E
155 E9 **Uddevalla** Västra Götaland, S Sweden 58°20′N 11°56′E
159 H4 **Uddington** C Scotland, United Kingdom
Uddjaur *see* Uddjaure
152 E6 **Uddjaure** *var.* Uddjaur. ◎ N Sweden
Udeid, Khor al *see* 'Udayd, Khawr al
163 G8 **Uden** Noord-Brabant, SE Netherlands 51°40′N 05°37′E
Uden *see* Udenhout
163 F8 **Udenhout** *var.* Uden. Noord-Brabant, S Netherlands 51°37′N 05°09′E
181 H8 **Uder** Thüringen, Germany 10°05′N 51°22′E
181 I9 **Udestedt** Thüringen, Germany 11°08′N 51°03′E
234 E5 **Udgīr** Mahārāshtra, C India 18°23′N 77°06′E
Udhagamandalam *see* Udagamandalam
232 E3 **Udhampur** Jammu and Kashmir, NW India 32°55′N 75°07′E
217 I9 **'Udhaybah, 'Uqlat al** *well* S Iraq
218 D7 **Udim** Israel 32°16′N 34°50′E
177 I6 **Udine** *anc.* Utina. Friuli-Venezia Giulia, NE Italy 46°05′N 13°10′E
267 K9 **Udintsev Fracture Zone** *tectonic feature* S Pacific Ocean
Udipi *see* Udupi
Udmurtia *see* Udmurtskaya Respublika
195 J10 **Udmurtskaya Respublika** *Eng.* Udmurtia. ◆ *autonomous republic* NW Russian Federation
194 E9 **Udomlya** Tverskaya Oblast', W Russian Federation 57°53′N 34°59′E
Udon Ratchathani *see* Ubon Ratchathani
256 F6 **Udon Thani** *var.* Ban Mak Khaeng, Udorndhani. Udon Thani, N Thailand 17°25′N 102°45′E
Udorndhani *see* Udon Thani
282 E9 **Udot** *atoll* Chuuk Islands, C Micronesia
193 L7 **Udskaya Guba** *bay* E Russian Federation
234 D7 **Udupi** *var.* Udipi. Karnātaka, SW India 13°18′N 74°46′E
Udzhary *see* Ucar
260 D4 **Uebonti, Teluk** *bay* Sulawesi, C Indonesia
178 I5 **Uecker** ⚞ NE Germany
178 I5 **Ueckermünde** Mecklenburg-Vorpommern, NE Germany 53°43′N 14°03′E
251 K2 **Ueda** *var.* Uyeda. Nagano, Honshū, S Japan 36°27′N 138°13′E
181 J12 **Uehlfeld** Bayern, Germany 10°44′N 49°40′E
134 G6 **Uele** *var.* Welle. ⚞ NE Dem. Rep. Congo
82 F4 **Uelen** Chukotskiy Avtonomnyy Okrug, Russian Federation 66°12′N 170°00′E
193 N2 **Uelen** Chukotskiy Avtonomnyy Okrug, NE Russian Federation 66°01′N 169°52′W
Uele (upper course) *see* Kibali, Dem. Rep. Congo
Uele (upper course) *see* Uolo, Río, Equatorial Guinea/Gabon
180 C5 **Uelsen** Niedersachsen, Germany 6°53′N 52°30′E
180 I4 **Uelzen** Niedersachsen, N Germany 52°58′N 10°34′E
251 I4 **Ueno** Mie, Honshū, SW Japan 34°45′N 136°08′E
180 H2 **Uetersen** Schleswig-Holstein, Germany 9°40′N 53°41′E
176 H5 **Uetze** Niedersachsen, Germany 10°12′N 52°28′E
197 L2 **Ufa** Respublika Bashkortostan, W Russian Federation 54°46′N 56°02′E
197 L2 **Ufa** ⚞ W Russian Federation
161 I6 **Uffington** United Kingdom 51°35′N 1°33′W
Ufra *see* Kenar
138 B4 **Ugab** ⚞ C Namibia
190 C6 **Ugāle** Ventspils, NW Latvia 57°16′N 21°58′E
136 B7 **Uganda** *off.* Republic of Uganda. ◆ *republic* E Africa
Uganda, Republic of *see* Uganda
216 C3 **Ugarit** *Ar.* Ra's Shamrah. *site of ancient city* Al Lādhiqīyah, NW Syria
118 F3 **Ugarteche** Mendoza, Argentina 33°13′S 68°53′W
83 H8 **Ugashik** Alaska, USA 57°30′N 157°24′W
175 J10 **Ugento** Puglia, SE Italy 39°53′N 18°09′E
141 J8 **Ugie** Eastern Cape, South Africa 31°12′S 28°14′E
170 G8 **Ugíjar** Andalucía, S Spain 36°58′N 03°03′W
165 L1 **Ugine** Savoie, E France 45°45′N 06°25′E
193 L8 **Uglegorsk** Ostrov Sakhalin, Sakhalinskaya Oblast', SE Russian Federation 49°05′N 142°06′E
Ugleural'sk *see* Ugleural'skiy
195 L8 **Ugleural'skiy** *var.* Ugleural'sk, *earlier* Polovinka. Permskaya Oblast', NW Russian Federation 58°57′N 57°37′E
194 F10 **Uglich** Yaroslavskaya Oblast', W Russian Federation 57°33′N 38°23′E
194 E9 **Uglovka** *var.* Okulovka. Novgorodskaya Oblast', W Russian Federation 58°24′N 33°16′E
193 N3 **Ugol'nyye Kopi** Chukotskiy Avtonomnyy Okrug, NE Russian Federation 64°43′N 177°46′E
196 E2 **Ugra** ⚞ W Russian Federation
167 I7 **Ugthorpe** United Kingdom 54°29′N 0°46′W
229 L5 **Ugyut** Narynskaya Oblast', C Kyrgyzstan 41°22′N 74°49′E
183 E9 **Uherské Hradiště** *Ger.* Ungarisch-Hradisch. Zlínský Kraj, E Czech Republic 49°05′N 17°26′E
183 E9 **Uherský Brod** *Ger.* Ungarisch-Brod. Zlínský Kraj, E Czech Republic 49°01′N 17°40′E
179 H11 **Uhlava** *Ger.* Angel. ⚞ W Czech Republic
Uhorshchyna *see* Hungary
73 J10 **Uhrichsville** Ohio, N USA 40°23′N 81°21′W
Uhuru Peak *see* Kilimanjaro
156 D4 **Uig** N Scotland, United Kingdom 57°35′N 06°22′W
135 C10 **Uíge** *Port.* Carmona, Vila Marechal Carmona. Uíge, NW Angola 07°37′S 15°02′E
135 D10 **Uíge** ◆ *province* N Angola
282 F10 **Uijec** *island* Chuuk, C Micronesia
248 C5 **Ŭijŏngbu** *Jap.* Giseifu. NW South Korea 37°42′N 127°02′E
226 D4 **Uil** *Kaz.* Oyyl. Aktyubinsk, W Kazakhstan 49°06′N 54°41′E
226 D4 **Uil** *Kaz.* Oyyl. ⚞ W Kazakhstan
79 I2 **Uinta Mountains** ▲ Utah, W USA
250 A3 **Ŭiryŏng** 35°18′N 128°17′E
138 B5 **Uis** Erongo, NW Namibia 21°08′S 14°49′E
141 H9 **Uitenhage** Eastern Cape, S South Africa 33°44′S 25°27′E
162 E5 **Uitgeest** Noord-Holland, W Netherlands 52°32′N 04°43′E
162 E6 **Uithoorn** Noord-Holland, C Netherlands 52°14′N 04°50′E
162 I3 **Uithuizen** Groningen, NE Netherlands 53°24′N 06°40′E
162 I3 **Uithuizermeeden** Groningen, NE Netherlands 53°25′N 06°43′E
140 D6 **Uitkyk** Northern Cape, South Africa 29°41′S 18°46′E
140 E5 **Uitsakpan** *salt lake* Northern Cape, South Africa
140 D8 **Uitspankraal** Western Cape, South Africa 32°03′S 19°24′E
283 K5 **Ujae Atoll** *var.* Wūjae. *atoll* Ralik Chain, W Marshall Islands
Ujain *see* Ujjain
183 F8 **Ujazd** Opolskie, S Poland 50°22′N 18°20′E
Uj-Becse *see* Novi Bečej
Újda *see* Oujda
283 J5 **Ujelang Atoll** *var.* Wujlān. *atoll* Ralik Chain, W Marshall Islands
183 J11 **Újfehértó** Szabolcs-Szatmár-Bereg, E Hungary 47°48′N 21°40′E
Újgradiska *see* Nova Gradiška
251 I4 **Uji** *var.* Uzi. Kyōto, Honshū, SW Japan 34°54′N 135°48′E
250 B9 **Uji-guntō** *island* Nansei-shotō, SW Japan
137 A10 **Ujiji** Kigoma, W Tanzania 04°55′S 29°39′E
232 D8 **Ujjain** *prev.* Ujain. Madhya Pradesh, C India 23°11′N 75°50′E
Újlak *see* Ilok
'Ujmān *see* 'Ajmān
Újmoldova *see* Moldova Nouă
Újszentanna *see* Sântana
Ujungpandang *see* Makassar
Ujung Salang *see* Phuket
Újvidék *see* Novi Sad
UK *see* United Kingdom
232 C9 **Ukāi Reservoir** ◙ W India
137 B8 **Ukara Island** *island* N Tanzania
'Ukash, Wādī *see* 'Akāsh, Wādī
137 C9 **Ukerewe Island** *island* N Tanzania
141 J6 **uKhahlamba Drakensberg Park** Kwazulu Natal, South Africa
217 H9 **Ukhayḑir, Wādī** Jordan
217 I6 **Ukhaydhir** Al Anbār, C Iraq 32°28′N 43°36′E
233 M7 **Ukhrul** Manipur, NE India 25°08′N 94°24′E
195 J6 **Ukhta** Respublika Komi, NW Russian Federation 63°31′N 53°48′E
78 A3 **Ukiah** California, W USA 39°07′N 123°14′W
76 E6 **Ukiah** Oregon, NW USA 45°06′N 118°57′W
163 E10 **Ukkel** *Fr.* Uccle. Brussels, C Belgium 50°47′N 04°19′E
191 D8 **Ukmergė** *Pol.* Wiłkomierz. Vilnius, C Lithuania 55°16′N 24°46′E
Ukraina *see* Ukraine
189 I5 **Ukraine** *off.* Ukraine, *Rus.* Ukraina, *Ukr.* Ukrayina; *prev.* Ukrainian Soviet Socialist Republic, Ukrainskay S.S.R. ◆ *republic* SE Europe
Ukraine *see* Ukraine
Ukrainian Soviet Socialist Republic *see* Ukraine
Ukrainskay S.S.R/Ukrayina *see* Ukraine
195 M10 **Uksyanskoye** Kurganskaya Oblast', Russian Federation
135 C12 **Uku** Cuanza Sul, NW Angola 11°25′S 14°18′E
250 B6 **Uku-jima** *island* Gotō-rettō, SW Japan
140 E2 **Ukwi** Kgalagadi, SW Botswana 23°41′S 20°26′E
191 H8 **Ula** *Rus.* Ulla. Vitsyebskaya Voblasts', N Belarus 55°14′N 29°15′E
214 B7 **Ula** Muğla, SW Turkey 37°08′N 28°25′E
191 H8 **Ula** *Rus.* Ulla. ⚞ N Belarus
236 G3 **Ulaanbaatar** *Eng.* Ulan Bator; *prev.* Urga. ● (Mongolia) Töv, C Mongolia 47°55′N 106°57′E
Ulaan-Ereg *see* Bayanmönh
236 E2 **Ulaangom** Uvs, NW Mongolia 49°56′N 92°06′E
238 G1 **Ulaanhus** *var.* Bilüü. Bayan-Ölgiy, W Mongolia 48°54′N 89°40′E
Ulaantolgoy *see* Möst
Ulaan-Uul *see* Öldziyt, Bayanhongor, Mongolia
Ulaan-Uul *see* Erdene, Dornogovĭ, Mongolia
244 E3 **Ulan** *var.* Otog Qi. Nei Mongol Zizhiqu, N China 39°05′N 107°58′E
239 J6 **Ulan** *var.* Xireg; *prev.* Xiligou. Qinghai, C China 36°59′N 98°21′E
Ulan Bator *see* Ulaanbaatar
244 C3 **Ulan Buh Shamo** *desert* N China
Ulanhad *see* Chifeng
237 I3 **Ulanhot** Nei Mongol Zizhiqu, N China 46°02′N 122°E
244 G1 **Ulan Hua** Inner Mongolia, China 41°19′N 111°25′E
197 I8 **Ulan Khol** Respublika Kalmykiya, SW Russian Federation 45°27′N 46°48′E
244 E2 **Ulansuhai Nur** ◎ N China
193 I8 **Ulan-Ude** *prev.* Verkhneudinsk. Respublika Buryatiya, S Russian Federation 51°55′N 107°40′E
238 G7 **Ulan Ul Hu** ◎ C China
281 K3 **Ulawa Island** *island* SE Solomon Islands
218 J3 **'Ulayyānīyah, Bi'r al** *var.* Al Hilbeh. *well* S Syria
193 L7 **Ul'banskiy Zaliv** *strait* E Russian Federation
Ulbo *see* Olib
159 M10 **Ulceby** United Kingdom 53°13′N 0°07′E
250 C1 **Ulchin** Kyŏngsang-bukto, South Korea 36°59′N 129°24′E
184 E7 **Ulcinj** S Montenegro 41°56′N 19°14′E
140 G5 **Ulco** Northern Cape, South Africa 28°19′S 24°13′E
Uldz *see* Norovlin
Uleåborg *see* Oulu
Uleälv *see* Oulujoki
155 D8 **Ulefoss** Telemark, S Norway 59°17′N 09°15′E
173 J8 **Uleila del Campo** Andalucía, Spain 37°11′N 2°12′W
Uleträsk *see* Oulujärvi
184 F7 **Ulëz** *var.* Ulëza. Dibër, C Albania 41°42′N 19°52′E
Ulëza *see* Ulëz
155 C11 **Ulfborg** Ringkøbing, W Denmark 56°16′N 08°21′E
162 H7 **Ulft** Gelderland, E Netherlands 51°53′N 06°23′E
159 K5 **Ulgham** United Kingdom 55°13′N 1°38′W
236 E3 **Uliastay** *prev.* Jibhalanta. Dzavhan, W Mongolia 47°47′N 96°53′E
282 C9 **Ulimang** Babeldaob, N Palau
121 K6 **Ulindi** ⚞ W Dem. Rep. Congo
282 D5 **Ulithi Atoll** *atoll* Caroline Islands, W Micronesia
184 G3 **Uljma** Vojvodina, NE Serbia 45°04′N 21°08′E
226 F4 **Ul'kayak** *Kaz.* Ölkeyek. ⚞ C Kazakhstan
227 I2 **Ul'ken-Karoy, Ozero** ◎ N Kazakhstan
Ülkenözen *see* Bol'shoy Uzen'
Ülkenqobda *see* Bol'shaya Khobda
170 C2 **Ulla** ⚞ NW Spain
Ulla *see* Ula
277 L6 **Ulladulla** New South Wales, SE Australia 35°21′S 150°25′E
233 K7 **Ullapara** Rajshahi, W Bangladesh 24°20′N 89°34′E
156 E4 **Ullapool** N Scotland, United Kingdom 57°54′N 05°10′W
155 F10 **Ullared** Halland, S Sweden 57°07′N 12°45′E
171 J4 **Ulldecona** Cataluña, NE Spain 40°36′N 00°27′E
159 K8 **Ulleskelf** United Kingdom 53°51′N 1°13′W
161 I4 **Ullesthorpe** United Kingdom 52°28′N 1°15′W
152 F3 **Ullsfjorden** *fjord* N Norway
159 I7 **Ullswater** ◎ NW England, United Kingdom
250 D1 **Ullŭng-do**
248 D6 **Ullŭng-do** *island* NE South Korea
179 E12 **Ulm** Baden-Württemberg, S Germany 48°24′N 09°59′E
77 I4 **Ulm** Montana, NW USA 47°27′N 111°32′W
277 M3 **Ulmarra** New South Wales, SE Australia 29°37′S 153°06′E
181 G11 **Ulmbach** Hessen, Germany 9°25′N 50°22′E
181 C11 **Ulmen** Rheinland-Pfalz, Germany 6°59′N 50°13′E
188 E9 **Ulmeni** Buzău, C Romania 45°08′N 26°43′E
188 E10 **Ulmeni** Călărași, S Romania 44°08′N 26°43′E
88 G4 **Ulmukhuás** Región Autónoma Atlántico Norte, NE Nicaragua 14°20′N 84°30′W
282 B6 **Ulong** *var.* Aulong. *island* Palau Islands, N Palau
139 I2 **Ulonguè** *var.* Ulongwé. Tete, NW Mozambique 14°34′S 34°21′E
Ulongwé *see* Ulonguè
159 I7 **Ulpha** United Kingdom 54°19′N 3°14′W
155 F10 **Ulricehamn** Västra Götaland, S Sweden 57°47′N 13°25′E
162 H3 **Ulrum** Groningen, NE Netherlands 53°24′N 06°20′E
248 C7 **Ulsan** *Jap.* Urusan. SE South Korea 35°33′N 129°19′E
154 B4 **Ulsteinvik** Møre og Romsdal, S Norway 62°21′N 05°53′E
157 C8 **Ulster** ◆ *province* Northern Ireland, United Kingdom/Ireland
158 C7 **Ulster Canal** *canal* Ireland/Northern Ireland, United Kingdom
260 F2 **Ulu** Pulau Siau, N Indonesia 02°46′N 125°22′E
193 J6 **Ulu** Respublika Sakha (Yakutiya), NE Russian Federation 60°18′N 127°27′E
88 D3 **Ulúa, Río** ⚞ NW Honduras
214 C5 **Ulubat Gölü** ◎ NW Turkey
187 M5 **Ulubey** Uşak, Turkey 38°25′N 29°17′E
214 C5 **Uludağ** ▲ NW Turkey 40°08′N 29°13′E
238 B4 **Uluggat** Xinjiang Uygur Zizhiqu, W China 39°45′N 74°10′E
214 F7 **Ulukışla** Niğde, S Turkey 37°33′N 34°29′E
282 F6 **Ulul** *island* Caroline Islands, C Micronesia
252 F6 **Ulumal** Campeche, Mexico 19°16′N 90°38′W
139 H7 **Ulundi** KwaZulu/Natal, E South Africa 28°18′S 31°26′E
238 F2 **Ulungur He** ⚞ NW China
238 F2 **Ulungur Hu** ◎ NW China
276 D1 **Uluru** *var.* Ayers Rock. *monolith* Northern Territory, C Australia
158 E2 **Ulva** *island* United Kingdom
Ulveah *see* Lopevi
159 I8 **Ulverston** NW England, United Kingdom 54°13′N 03°08′W
277 J9 **Ulverstone** Tasmania, SE Australia 41°09′S 146°10′E
154 B6 **Ulvik** Hordaland, S Norway 60°34′N 06°53′E
153 G9 **Ulvila** Länsi-Suomi, W Finland 61°26′N 21°55′E
189 H5 **Ul'yanivka** *Rus.* Ul'yanovka. Kirovohrads'ka Oblast', C Ukraine 48°18′N 30°15′E
190 H3 **Ul'yanovka** Leningradskaya Oblast', Russian Federation
Ul'yanovka *see* Ul'yanivka
197 J3 **Ul'yanovsk** *prev.* Simbirsk. Ul'yanovskaya Oblast', W Russian Federation 54°17′N 48°21′E
197 I3 **Ul'yanovskaya Oblast'** ◆ *province* W Russian Federation
227 J4 **Ul'yanovskiy** Karaganda, C Kazakhstan 50°05′N 73°45′E
Ul'yanovskiy Kanal *see* Ul'yanow Kanali
228 G7 **Ul'yanow Kanali** *Rus.* Ul'yanovskiy Kanal. *canal* Turkmenistan/Uzbekistan
Ulyshylanshyq *see* Uly-Zhylanshyk
75 B10 **Ulysses** Kansas, C USA 37°36′N 101°23′W
227 H4 **Ulytau, Gory** ▲ C Kazakhstan
193 I8 **Ulyunkhan** Respublika Buryatiya, S Russian Federation 54°48′N 111°01′E
226 G4 **Uly-Zhylanshyk** *Kaz.* Ulyshylanshyq. ⚞ C Kazakhstan
180 H2 **Ulzburg** Schleswig-Holstein, Germany 9°59′N 53°48′E
184 A2 **Umag** *It.* Umago. Istra, NW Croatia 45°25′N 13°32′E
Umago *see* Umag
87 L5 **Umán** Yucatán, SE Mexico 20°51′N 89°43′W
189 H5 **Uman'** *Rus.* Uman. Cherkas'ka Oblast', C Ukraine 48°45′N 30°10′E
282 F9 **Uman** *atoll* Chuuk Islands, C Micronesia
Uman *see* Uman'
Umanak/Umanaq *see* Uummannaq
'Umān, Khalīj *see* Oman, Gulf of
'Umān, Salṭanat *see* Oman
261 J6 **Umari** Papua, E Indonesia 04°18′S 135°22′E
232 G8 **Umaria** Madhya Pradesh, C India 23°34′N 80°49′E
231 H9 **Umar Kot** Sind, SE Pakistan 25°22′N 69°48′E
282 A2 **Umatac** SW Guam 13°17′N 144°40′E
282 A2 **Umatac Bay** *bay* SW Guam
217 I4 **Umayqah** Ṣalāḩ ad Dīn, C Iraq 34°32′N 43°45′E
194 E4 **Umba** Murmanskaya Oblast', NW Russian Federation 66°39′N 34°24′E
216 D5 **Umbāshī, Khirbat al** *ruins* As Suwaydā', S Syria
134 G3 **Umbelasha** ⚞ W Sudan
177 H10 **Umbertide** Umbria, C Italy 43°16′N 12°21′E
114 A3 **Umberto** *var.* Humberto. Santa Fe, C Argentina 30°52′S 61°19′W
141 K7 **Umbogintwini** KwaZulu-Natal, South Africa
280 C3 **Umboi Island** *var.* Rooke Island. *island* C Papua New Guinea
194 F3 **Umbozero, Ozero** ◎ NW Russian Federation
174 E7 **Umbria** ◆ *region* C Italy
Umbrian-Machigian Mountains *see* Umbro-Marchigiano, Appennino
172 D8 **Umbria, Punta** *headland* Andalucía, Spain
177 I10 **Umbro-Marchigiano, Appennino** *Eng.* Umbrian-Machigian Mountains. ▲ C Italy
154 J2 **Umeå** Västerbotten, N Sweden 63°50′N 20°15′E
154 I2 **Umeälven** ⚞ N Sweden
141 K6 **uMhali** KwaZulu-Natal, South Africa 29°28′S 31°13′E
141 K7 **Umhlanga Rocks** KwaZulu-Natal, South Africa 29°43′S 31°04′E
141 K7 **Umhlanga Rocks** Kwazulu Natal, South Africa 29°43′S 31°05′E
83 I2 **Umiat** Alaska, USA 69°22′N 152°09′W
141 K7 **Umkomaas** KwaZulu-Natal, South Africa 30°12′S 30°48′E
141 K7 **Umkomaas** ⚞ KwaZulu-Natal, South Africa
139 H8 **Umlazi** KwaZulu/Natal, E South Africa 29°58′S 30°50′E
141 K7 **Umlazi** KwaZulu-Natal, South Africa 29°58′S 30°53′E
217 L7 **Umm al Baqar, Hawr** *var.* Birkat ad Dawaymah. *spring* S Iraq
221 J7 **Umm al Ḩayt, Wādī** *var.* Wādī Amilḩayt. *seasonal river* SW Oman
Umm al Qaiwain *see* Umm al Qaywayn
221 J4 **Umm al Qaywayn** *var.* Umm al Qaiwain. Umm al Qaywayn, NE United Arab Emirates 25°43′N 55°55′E
217 I4 **Umm al Ṭūz** *var.* Umm al Tūz. Ṣalāḩ ad Dīn, C Iraq 34°53′N 42°42′E
Umm al Tūz *see* Umm al Ṭūz
216 D2 **Umm 'Āmūd** Ḩalab, N Syria 35°57′N 37°39′E
221 L6 **Umm ar Ruṣāṣ** *var.* Umm Ruṣayṣ. W Oman 20°26′N 58°48′E
136 A4 **Umm Samin** *salt flat* C Oman
218 H7 **Umm as Sirb** Jordan
221 J5 **Umm az Zumūl** *oasis* E Saudi Arabia
134 G1 **Umm Buru** Western Darfur, W Sudan 15°01′N 23°36′E
134 G3 **Umm Dafag** Southern Darfur, W Sudan 10°28′N 23°20′E
218 I6 **Umm Dat** Syria 32°46′N 36°46′E
Umm Durmān *see* Omdurman
218 E6 **Umm el Fahm** Haifa, N Israel 32°30′N 35°06′E
180 J6 **Ummendorf** Sachsen-Anhalt, Germany 11°11′N 52°09′E
219 F14 **Umm Ḩaraq, Wādī** *dry watercourse* Jordan
136 B2 **Umm Inderab** Northern Kordofan, C Sudan 15°12′N 31°54′E
134 H2 **Umm Keddada** Northern Darfur, W Sudan 13°36′N 26°42′E
220 D4 **Umm Lajj** Tabūk, W Saudi Arabia 25°02′N 37°19′E
216 E7 **Umm Maḩfur** ⚞ N Jordan
217 M9 **Umm Qaṣr** Al Baṣrah, SE Iraq 30°02′N 47°55′E
218 F6 **Umm Qays** Jordan 32°39′N 35°41′E
Umm Ruṣayṣ *see* Umm ar Ruṣāṣ
136 B3 **Umm Ruwaba** *var.* Umm Ruwābah, Um Ruwāba. Northern Kordofan, C Sudan 12°54′N 31°13′E
Umm Ruwābah *see* Umm Ruwaba
221 I4 **Umm Sa'id** *var.* Musay'īd. S Qatar 24°57′N 51°32′E
217 D9 **Umm Ṭuways, Wādī** *dry watercourse* N Jordan
82 E9 **Umnak Island** *island* Aleutian Islands, Alaska, USA
76 B7 **Umpqua River** ⚞ Oregon, NW USA
135 E12 **Umpulo** Bié, C Angola 12°43′S 17°42′E
234 F4 **Umred** Mahārāshtra, C India 20°54′N 79°19′E
217 M7 **Umr Sawān, Hawr** ◎ S Iraq
Um Ruwāba *see* Umm Ruwaba
250 A1 **Ŭmsŏng** 36°55′N 127°41′E
Umtali *see* Mutare
141 J8 **Umtata** Eastern Cape, South Africa 31°33′S 28°47′E
141 K8 **Umtentu** Eastern Cape, South Africa 31°08′S 30°09′E
141 K7 **Umtentweni** KwaZulu-Natal, South Africa
133 K8 **Umuahia** Abia, SW Nigeria 05°30′N 07°33′E
113 I4 **Umuarama** Paraná, S Brazil 23°45′S 53°20′W
Umvuma *see* Mvuma
141 K7 **Umzimkulu** Eastern Cape, South Africa 30°16′S 29°56′E
141 K1 **Umzingwani** ⚞ S Zimbabwe
141 K7 **Umzinto** KwaZulu-Natal, South Africa 30°19′S 30°40′E
173 J3 **Uña** Castilla-La Manacha, Spain 40°13′N 1°58′W
184 C3 **Una** ⚞ Bosnia and Herzegovina/Croatia
184 C4 **Unac** ⚞ W Bosnia and Herzegovina
69 J2 **Unadilla** Georgia, SE USA 32°15′N 83°44′W
64 F2 **Unadilla** New York, USA 42°20′N 75°19′W
64 F2 **Unadilla River** ⚞ New York, NE USA
109 D10 **Unaí** Minas Gerais, SE Brazil 16°24′S 46°49′W
82 G5 **Unalakleet** Alaska, USA 63°52′N 160°47′W
82 F9 **Unalaska Island** *island* Aleutian Islands, Alaska, USA
279 E8 **Una, Mount** ▲ South Island, New Zealand 42°12′S 172°34′E
137 D13 **Unango** Niassa, N Mozambique 12°45′S 35°28′E
Unao *see* Unnão
152 H5 **Unari** Lappi, N Finland 67°07′N 25°37′E
219 F12 **'Unayzah** Jordan
220 F3 **'Unayzah** *var.* Anaiza. Al Qaşim, C Saudi Arabia 26°03′N 44°00′E
216 F7 **'Unayzah, Jabal** ▲ Jordan/Saudi Arabia 32°09′N 39°11′E
Unci *see* Almería
112 C1 **Uncía** Potosí, C Bolivia 18°30′S 66°29′W
79 K4 **Uncompahgre Peak** ▲ Colorado, C USA 38°04′N 107°27′W
79 J4 **Uncompahgre Plateau** *plain* Colorado, C USA
155 G9 **Unden** ◎ S Sweden
141 J7 **Underberg** KwaZulu-Natal, South Africa 29°47′S 29°30′E
74 C3 **Underwood** North Dakota, N USA 47°25′N 101°09′W
261 H6 **Undur** Pulau Seram, E Indonesia 03°41′S 130°38′E
Undur Khan *see* Öndörhaan
196 E3 **Unecha** Bryanskaya Oblast', W Russian Federation 52°51′N 32°38′E
83 G9 **Unga** Unga Island, Alaska, USA 55°14′N 160°34′W
Ungaria *see* Hungary
277 J5 **Ungarie** New South Wales, SE Australia 33°39′S 146°54′E
Ungarisch-Brod *see* Uherský Brod
Ungarisches Erzgebirge *see* Slovenské rudohorie
Ungarisch-Hradisch *see* Uherské Hradiště
Ungarn *see* Hungary
59 I2 **Ungava Bay** *bay* Québec, E Canada
58 G2 **Ungava, Péninsule d'** *peninsula* Québec, SE Canada
Ungeny *see* Ungheni
188 F6 **Ungheni** *Rus.* Ungeny. W Moldova 47°13′N 27°48′E
Unguja *see* Zanzibar
228 E5 **Üngüz Angyrsyndaky Garagum** *Rus.* Zaunguzskiye Garagumy. *desert* N Turkmenistan
228 E6 **Unguz, Solonchakovyye Vpadiny** *salt marsh* C Turkmenistan
Ungvár *see* Uzhhorod
172 C2 **Unhais da Serra** Castelo Branco, Portugal 40°16′N 7°37′W
113 J5 **União da Vitória** Paraná, S Brazil 26°13′S 51°05′W
118 C7 **Unicavén** Maule, Chile 36°05′S 72°01′W
183 E9 **Uničov** *Ger.* Mährisch-Neustadt. Olomoucký Kraj, E Czech Republic 49°48′N 17°05′E
182 F6 **Uniejów** Łódzkie, C Poland 51°58′N 18°46′E
118 B8 **Unihue** Bío-Bío, Chile 37°07′S 72°55′W
184 A3 **Unije** *island* W Croatia
82 F9 **Unimak Island** *island* Aleutian Islands, Alaska, USA
82 F9 **Unimak Pass** *strait* Aleutian Islands, Alaska, USA
112 D10 **Unión** San Luis, C Argentina 35°09′S 65°55′W
75 I10 **Union** Missouri, C USA 38°27′N 91°01′W
64 G6 **Union** New Jersey, USA 40°40′N 74°55′W
76 E6 **Union** Oregon, NW USA 45°12′N 117°51′W
67 I7 **Union** South Carolina, SE USA 34°42′N 81°37′W
67 I4 **Union** West Virginia, NE USA 37°36′N 80°34′W
116 F7 **Unión, Bahía** *bay* E Argentina
65 H6 **Union Beach** New Jersey, USA 40°27′N 74°11′W
80 B3 **Union City** California, USA 37°36′N 122°01′W
73 G10 **Union City** Indiana, N USA 40°12′N 84°50′W
73 G8 **Union City** Michigan, N USA 42°03′N 85°06′W
65 H6 **Union City** New Jersey, USA 40°47′N 74°01′W
62 C7 **Union City** Pennsylvania, NE USA 41°54′N 79°51′W
66 C5 **Union City** Tennessee, S USA 36°26′N 89°03′W
76 C7 **Union Creek** Oregon, NW USA 42°54′N 122°26′W
138 E10 **Uniondale** Western Cape, SW South Africa 33°40′S 23°07′E
86 B6 **Unión de Tula** Jalisco, SW Mexico 19°58′N 104°16′W
73 D8 **Union Grove** Wisconsin, N USA 42°39′N 88°03′W
87 I9 **Unión Hidalgo** Oaxaca, Mexico 16°28′N 94°50′W
103 I1 **Union Island** *island* S Saint Vincent and the Grenadines
87 K10 **Unión Juárez** Chiapas, Mexico 15°04′N 92°05′W
Union of Myanmar *see* Burma
81 J11 **Union Pass** ▲ Nevada, USA 35°13′N 114°23′W
94 F3 **Union Reefs** *reef* SW Mexico
45 I2 **Union Seamount** *undersea feature* NE Pacific Ocean 49°35′N 132°45′W
69 I2 **Union Springs** Alabama, S USA 32°08′N 85°43′W
66 D4 **Uniontown** Kentucky, S USA 37°46′N 87°55′W
62 C9 **Uniontown** Pennsylvania, NE USA 39°54′N 79°44′W
75 H8 **Unionville** Missouri, C USA 40°28′N 93°00′W
80 I1 **Unionville** Nevada, USA 40°27′N 118°07′W
221 H5 **United Arab Emirates** *Ar.* Al Imārāt al 'Arabīyah al Muttaḩidah, *abbrev.* UAE; *prev.* Trucial States. ◆ *federation* SW Asia
United Arab Republic *see* Egypt
157 G10 **United Kingdom** *off.* United Kingdom of Great Britain and Northern Ireland, *abbrev.* UK. ◆ *monarchy* NW Europe
United Kingdom of Great Britain and Northern Ireland *see* United Kingdom
United Mexican States *see* Mexico
United Provinces *see* Uttar Pradesh
77 J3 **United States of America** *off.* United States of America, *var.* America, The States, *abbrev.* U.S., USA. ◆ *federal republic* North America
United States of America *see* United States of America
194 E6 **Unitsa** Respublika Kareliya, NW Russian Federation 62°31′N 34°31′E
57 L6 **Unity** Saskatchewan, S Canada 52°27′N 109°10′W
Unity State *see* Wahda
173 K2 **Universales, Montes** ▲ Aragón, Spain
171 I5 **Universales, Montes** ▲ C Spain
66 B3 **University City** Missouri, C USA 38°40′N 90°19′W
195 L10 **Unkurda** Chelyabinskaya Oblast, Russian Federation
281 M3 **Unmet** Malekula, C Vanuatu 16°09′S 167°16′E
181 D8 **Unna** Nordrhein-Westfalen, W Germany 51°32′N 07°41′E
Unnan *see* Kisuki
232 G6 **Unnão** *prev.* Unao. Uttar Pradesh, N India 26°32′N 80°30′E
281 N5 **Unpongkor** Erromango, S Vanuatu 18°48′S 169°01′E
Unruhstadt *see* Kargowa
156 H1 **Unst** *island* NE Scotland, United Kingdom
179 G8 **Unstrut** ⚞ C Germany
Unterdrauburg *see* Dravograd
181 H14 **Untergröningen** Baden-Württemberg, Germany 9°54′N 48°55′E
Unterlimbach *see* Lendava
180 I4 **Unterlüss** Niedersachsen, Germany 10°17′N 52°50′E
181 H14 **Untermünkheim** Baden-Württemberg, Germany 9°44′N 49°09′E
179 G12 **Unterschleissheim** Bayern, SE Germany 48°16′N 11°34′E
179 D14 **Untersee** ◎ Germany/Switzerland
181 J11 **Untersiemau** Bayern, Germany 10°58′N 50°12′E
178 H5 **Unterueckersee** ◎ NE Germany
174 B3 **Unterwalden** ◆ *canton* C Switzerland
181 H13 **Unterwittighausen** Baden-Württemberg, Germany 9°50′N 49°37′E
103 H7 **Uturán, Sierra de** ▲ Brazil/Venezuela
239 H7 **Unuli Horog** Qinghai, W China 35°10′N 91°50′E
214 G4 **Ünye** Ordu, W Turkey 41°08′N 37°14′E
Unza *see* Unzha
195 H9 **Unzha** *var.* Unza. ⚞ NW Russian Federation
134 A7 **Uolo, Río** *var.* Eyo (lower course), Mbini, Uele (upper course), Woleu; *prev.* Benito. ⚞ Equatorial Guinea/Gabon
103 I6 **Uonán** Bolívar, SE Venezuela 04°33′N 62°10′W
241 L6 **Uotsuri-shima** *island* China/Japan/Taiwan
251 J2 **Uozu** Toyama, Honshū, SW Japan 36°50′N 137°25′E
88 G7 **Upala** Alajuela, NW Costa Rica 10°52′N 85°W
103 I4 **Upata** Bolívar, E Venezuela 08°02′N 62°25′W
135 H11 **Upemba, Lac** ◎ SE Dem. Rep. Congo
118 D5 **Upeo** Maule, Chile 35°08′S 71°02′W
295 K7 **Upernavik** *var.* Upernivik. Kitaa, C Greenland 73°06′N 55°42′W
Upernivik *see* Upernavik
140 E5 **Upington** Northern Cape, W South Africa 28°28′S 21°14′E
Uplands *see* Ottawa
286 F6 **'Upolu** *island* SE Samoa
82 D3 **'Upolu Point** *var.* Upolu Point. *headland* Hawai'i, USA, C Pacific Ocean 20°15′N 155°51′W
160 G8 **Upottery** United Kingdom 50°52′N 3°08′W
Upper Austria *see* Oberösterreich
Upper Bann *see* Bann
62 G4 **Upper Canada Village** *tourist site* Ontario, SE Canada
160 F5 **Upper Chapel** United Kingdom 52°03′N 3°27′W
64 F8 **Upper Darby** Pennsylvania, NE USA 9°57′N 75°15′W
74 B7 **Upper Des Lacs Lake** ◙ North Dakota, N USA
278 G7 **Upper Hutt** Wellington, North Island, New Zealand 41°06′S 175°06′E
74 I6 **Upper Iowa River** ⚞ Iowa, C USA
76 C8 **Upper Klamath Lake** ◎ Oregon, NW USA
78 B3 **Upper Lake** California, W USA 39°07′N 122°53′W
78 C1 **Upper Lake** ◎ California, W USA
54 C4 **Upper Liard** Yukon Territory, W Canada 60°01′N 128°59′W
157 C8 **Upper Lough Erne** ◎ SW Northern Ireland, United Kingdom
158 C7 **Upper Lough Erne** ◎ United Kingdom
136 B4 **Upper Nile** ◆ *state* E Sudan
159 L8 **Upper Poppleton** United Kingdom 53°58′N 1°09′W
74 F2 **Upper Red Lake** ◎ Minnesota, N USA
73 H10 **Upper Sandusky** Ohio, N USA 40°49′N 83°16′W
Upper Volta *see* Burkina
161 J3 **Uppingham** United Kingdom 52°35′N 0°43′W
155 I8 **Upplandsväsby** *var.* Upplands Väsby. Stockholm, C Sweden 59°29′N 18°04′E
Upplands Väsby *see* Upplandsväsby
154 I7 **Uppsala** Uppsala, C Sweden 59°52′N 17°38′E
154 I7 **Uppsala** ◆ *county* C Sweden
82 E6 **Upright Cape** *headland* Saint Matthew Island, Alaska, USA 60°19′N 172°15′W
74 I1 **Upsala** Ontario, S Canada 49°01′N 90°27′W
66 E4 **Upton** Kentucky, S USA 37°25′N 85°53′W
77 M6 **Upton** Wyoming, C USA 44°06′N 104°37′W
220 F4 **'Uqlat aş Şuqūr** Al Qaşim, W Saudi Arabia 25°51′N 42°13′E
216 F5 **'Uqlat Şawāb** *well* W Iraq
Uqsuqtuuq *see* Gjoa Haven
Uqturpan *see* Wushi
102 B4 **Urabá, Golfo de** *gulf* NW Colombia
Uracas *see* Farallon de Pajaros
Uradar'ya *see* O'radaryo
Urad Qianqi *see* Xishanzui, N China
253 C14 **Uraga-suidō** *strait* SW Japan
252 G5 **Urahoro** Hokkaidō, NE Japan 42°47′N 143°41′E
252 F5 **Urakawa** Hokkaidō, NE Japan 42°11′N 142°42′E
226 D3 **Ural** *Kaz.* Zayyq. ⚞ Kazakhstan/Russian Federation
Ural Mountains *see* Ural'skiye Gory
226 C3 **Ural'sk** *Kaz.* Oral. Zapadnyy Kazakhstan, NW Kazakhstan 51°12′N 51°17′E
Ural'skaya Oblast' *see* Zapadnyy Kazakhstan
195 L8 **Ural'skiye Gory** *var.* Ural'skiy Khrebet, *Eng.* Ural Mountains. ▲ Kazakhstan/Russian Federation
195 L9 **Ural'skiye Gory** *mountains* Sverdlovskaya Oblast', Russian Federation
195 L4 **Ural'skiye Gory** *mountains* Yamalo-Nenetskiy Avtonomnyy Okrug, Russian Federation
Ural'skiy Khrebet *see* Ural'skiye Gory
216 D2 **Urām aş Şughrá** Ḩalab, N Syria 36°10′N 36°55′E
277 J6 **Urana** New South Wales, SE Australia 35°22′S 146°16′E
114 B7 **Uranga** Santa Fe, Argentina 33°16′S 60°42′W
54 G5 **Uranium City** Saskatchewan, C Canada 59°30′N 108°46′W
103 I6 **Uraricoera** Roraima, N Brazil 03°26′N 60°54′W
95 J3 **Uraricoera, Rio** ⚞ N Brazil
Ura-Tyube *see* Ŭroteppa
253 C13 **Urawa** *var.* Saitama. Saitama, Honshū, S Japan 35°52′N 139°40′E
195 M7 **Uray** Khanty-Mansiyskiy Avtonomnyy Okrug-Yugra, C Russian Federation 60°07′N 64°38′E
221 H4 **'Uray'irah** Ash Sharqīyah, E Saudi Arabia 25°59′N 48°52′E
73 D10 **Urbana** Illinois, N USA 40°06′N 88°12′W
73 H10 **Urbana** Ohio, N USA 40°04′N 83°46′W
74 G7 **Urbandale** Iowa, C USA 41°37′N 93°42′W
177 I9 **Urbania** Marche, C Italy 43°40′N 12°33′E
261 H4 **Urbinasopon** Papua, E Indonesia 0°19′S 131°12′E
177 I9 **Urbino** Marche, C Italy 43°45′N 12°38′E
161 H7 **Urchfont** United Kingdom 51°18′N 1°56′W
105 G8 **Urcos** Cusco, S Peru 13°40′S 71°38′W
226 A4 **Urda** Zapadnyy Kazakhstan, W Kazakhstan 48°52′N 47°31′E
170 G6 **Urda** Castilla-La Mancha, C Spain 39°25′N 03°43′W
Urdgol *see* Chandmanĭ
114 D6 **Urdinarrain** Entre Ríos, Argentina 32°41′S 58°53′W
170 G2 **Urduña** *var.* Orduña. País Vasco, N Spain 43°00′N 03°00′W
Urdunn *see* Jordan
227 L5 **Urdzhar** *Kaz.* Ürzhar. Vostochnyy Kazakhstan, E Kazakhstan 47°06′N 81°33′E
159 K8 **Ure** ⚞ United Kingdom
157 G8 **Ure** ⚞ N England, United Kingdom
191 G11 **Urechcha** *Rus.* Urech'ye. Minskaya Voblasts', S Belarus 52°57′N 27°54′E
Urech'ye *see* Urechcha
197 I1 **Uren'** Nizhegorodskaya Oblast', W Russian Federation 57°30′N 45°48′E
192 F5 **Urengoy** Yamalo-Nenetskiy Avtonomnyy Okrug, N Russian Federation 65°52′N 78°42′E

◆ Country
● Country Capital
◇ Dependent Territory
○ Dependent Territory Capital
◆ Administrative Regions
✈ International Airport
▲ Mountain
▲ Mountain Range
☒ Volcano
⚞ River
◎ Lake
◙ Reservoir

◆ Country   ○ Dependent Territory   ◇ Administrative Regions   ▲ Mountain   ▲ Volcano   ◎ Lake
● Country Capital   ○ Dependent Territory Capital   ✈ International Airport   ▲ Mountain Range   ❖ River   ◙ Reservoir

W

◆ Country
● Country Capital
◇ Dependent Territory
○ Dependent Territory Capital
◈ Administrative Regions
● International Airport
▲ Mountain
▲ Mountain Range
♒ Volcano
♒ River
◎ Lake
◎ Reservoir

◆ Country   ◇ Dependent Territory   ✶ Administrative Regions   ▲ Mountain   ▲ Volcano   ◉ Lake
● Country Capital ○ Dependent Territory Capital ✈ International Airport   ▲ Mountain Range   ♒ River   ▨ Reservoir

---

◆ Country   ◇ Dependent Territory   ◈ Administrative Regions   ▲ Mountain   ◣ Volcano   ◎ Lake
● Country Capital   ○ Dependent Territory Capital   ✕ International Airport   ▲ Mountain Range   ◢ River   ▢ Reservoir

Zhëltyye Vody - Zyryanovsk

Zhëltyye Vody *see* Zhovti Vody
Zheludok *see* Zhaludok
Zhem *see* Emba
244 *E8* **Zhen'an** Shaanxi, China 33°16′N 109°06′E
239 *M7* **Zhenba** Shaanxi, C China 32°42′N 107°55′E
242 *B7* **Zhenfeng** *var.* Mingu. Guizhou, S China 25°27′N 105°38′E
242 *D4* **Zheng'an** Guizhou, China 28°19′N 107°15′E
Zhengjiatun *see* Shuangliao
244 *E7* **Zhengning** *var.* Shanhe. Gansu, N China 35°29′N 108°21′E
Zhengxiangbai Qi *see* Qagan Nur
243 *H1* **Zhengyang** Henan, China 32°22′N 114°13′E
245 *H7* **Zhengzhou** *var.* Ch'eng-chou, Chengchow; *prev.* Chenghsien. *province capital* Henan, C China 34°45′N 113°38′E
243 *L1* **Zhenjiang** *var.* Chenkiang. Jiangsu, E China 32°08′N 119°30′E
247 *K5* **Zhenlai** Jilin, NE China 45°52′N 123°11′E
242 *B6* **Zhenning** Guizhou, China 26°02′N 105°27′E
244 *G9* **Zhenping** Henan, China 33°01′N 112°08′E
242 *E1* **Zhenping** Shaanxi, SE China 31°56′N 109°31′E
242 *B5* **Zhenxiong** Yunnan, SW China 27°31′N 104°52′E
242 *D5* **Zhenyuan** *var.* Wuyang. Guizhou, S China 27°07′N 108°33′E
243 *M2* **Zhenze** Jiangsu, E China 30°55′N 120°30′E
243 *M5* **Zherong** *var.* Shuangcheng. Fujian, SE China 27°16′N 119°54′E
227 *K7* **Zhetigen** *prev.* Nikolayevka. Almaty, SE Kazakhstan 43°39′N 77°10′E
Zhetiqara *see* Zhitikara
226 *B7* **Zhetybay** Mangistau, SW Kazakhstan 43°35′N 52°05′E
229 *I5* **Zhetysay** Yuzhnyy Kazakhstan, Kazakhstan 41°00′N 68°24′E
242 *B7* **Zhexiang** Guizhou, S China 25°33′N 105°39′E
242 *F5* **Zhexi Shuiku** ⊠ C China
227 *H5* **Zhezdy** Karaganda, C Kazakhstan 48°06′N 67°01′E
227 *H5* **Zhezkazgan** *Kaz.* Zhezqazghan; *prev.* Dzhezkazgan. Karaganda, C Kazakhstan 47°49′N 67°44′E
Zhezqazghan *see* Zhezkazgan
242 *F3* **Zhicheng** Hubei, C China 30°18′N 111°30′E
Zhicheng *see* Yidu
191 *I8* **Zhichitsy** Smolenskaya Oblast', Russian Federation
Zhidachov *see* Zhydachiv
239 *I7* **Zhidoi** *var.* Gyaijêpozhanggê. Qinghai, C China 33°55′N 95°39′E
245 *M4* **Zhifu Dao** *island* Shandong, China
193 *H8* **Zhigalovo** Irkutskaya Oblast', S Russian Federation 54°47′N 105°00′E
193 *J5* **Zhigansk** Respublika Sakha (Yakutiya), NE Russian Federation 66°45′N 123°20′E
197 *J3* **Zhigulevsk** Samarskaya Oblast', W Russian Federation 53°24′N 49°30′E
242 *B6* **Zhijin** Guizhou, China 26°23′N 105°28′E
191 *B8* **Zhilino** *Ger.* Schillen. Kaliningradskaya Oblast', W Russian Federation 54°55′N 21°54′E
Zhiloy, Ostrov *see* Çiloy Adası
197 *I5* **Zhirnovsk** Volgogradskaya Oblast', SW Russian Federation 51°01′N 44°49′E
240 *G6* **Zhishan** *prev.* Yongzhou. Hunan, S China 26°12′N 111°36′E
Zhitarovo *see* Vetren
226 *F3* **Zhitikara** *Kaz.* Zhetiqara; *prev.* Džetygara. Kostanay, NW Kazakhstan 52°14′N 61°12′E
Zhitkovichi *see* Zhytkavichy
197 *I6* **Zhitkur** Volgogradskaya Oblast', SW Russian Federation 48°58′N 46°14′E
Zhitomir *see* Zhytomyr
Zhitomirskaya Oblast' *see* Zhytomyrs'ka Oblast'
243 *J7* **Zhixi** Fujian, SE China 25°20′N 116°38′E
243 *I6* **Zhixia** Jiangxi, SE China 26°59′N 115°06′E
196 *E3* **Zhizdra** Kaluzhskaya Oblast', W Russian Federation 53°38′N 34°39′E
191 *H11* **Zhlobin** Homyel'skaya Voblasts', SE Belarus 52°53′N 30°01′E
Zhmerinka *see* Zhmerynka
188 *F5* **Zhmerynka** *Rus.* Zhmerinka. Vinnyts'ka Oblast', C Ukraine 49°00′N 28°02′E
231 *H5* **Zhob** *var.* Fort Sandeman. Baluchistān, SW Pakistan 31°21′N 69°31′E
231 *H5* **Zhob** ⇝ C Pakistan
Zhodino *see* Zhodzina
191 *G9* **Zhodzina** *Rus.* Zhodino. Minskaya Voblasts', C Belarus 54°06′N 28°21′E
193 *K2* **Zhokhova, Ostrov** *island* Novosibirskiye Ostrova, NE Russian Federation
Zholkev/Zholkva *see* Zhovkva
Zhondor *see* Jondor
238 *E9* **Zhongba** *var.* Tuoji. Xizang Zizhiqu, W China 29°37′N 84°11′E
Zhongba *see* Jiangyou
240 *B5* **Zhongdian** *var.* Larang. Yunnan, SW China 27°48′N 99°41′E
Zhongduo *see* Youyang
Zhonghe *see* Xiushan
Zhonghua Renmin Gongheguo *see* China
242 *B2* **Zhongjiang** Sichuan, China 31°01′N 104°25′E
245 *H7* **Zhongmou** Henan, E China 34°44′N 114°01′E
244 *C5* **Zhongning** Ningxia, N China 37°26′N 105°40′E
Zhongping *see* Huize
242 *F8* **Zhongsan** Guang Zhuangzu Zizhiqu, China 24°31′N 111°17′E
242 *C9* **Zhongshan** Guang Zhuangzu Zizhiqu, SE China 23°02′N 107°26′E
243 *H10* **Zhongshan** Guangdong, S China 22°30′N 113°20′E
293 *L4* **Zhongshan** *Chinese research station* Antarctica 69°23′S 76°34′E
239 *N6* **Zhongtiao Shan** ▲▲ C China
244 *C5* **Zhongwei** Ningxia, N China 37°31′N 105°10′E
242 *D3* **Zhongxian** *var.* Zhongzhou. Chongqing Shi, C China 30°16′N 108°03′E
242 *G2* **Zhongxiang** Hubei, C China 31°12′N 112°35′E
243 *I2* **Zhongyi** Hubei, E China 31°07′N 114°53′E
244 *B8* **Zhongzhai** Gansu, China 33°08′N 104°16′E
Zhongzhou *see* Zhongxian
Zhosaly *see* Dzhusaly
245 *K5* **Zhoucun** Shandong, E China 36°49′N 117°49′E
244 *A3* **Zhoujianjing** Gansu, China 38°34′N 102°14′E
245 *I8* **Zhoukou** *var.* Zhoukouzhen. Henan, C China 33°32′N 114°40′E
Zhoukouzhen *see* Zhoukou
243 *I5* **Zhouning** Fujan, China 27°04′N 119°13′E
243 *M2* **Zhoupu** Shanghai Shi, E China 31°07′N 121°34′E
243 *N3* **Zhoushan** Zhejiang, S China
Zhoushan Islands *see* Zhoushan Qundao
243 *N2* **Zhoushan Qundao** *Eng.* Zhoushan Islands. *island group* SE China
243 *J3* **Zhoutou** Anhui, E China 29°52′N 116°20′E
243 *H9* **Zhouxin** Guangdong, SE China 23°41′N 113°05′E
244 *E8* **Zhouzhi** Shaanxi, China 34°06′N 108°07′E
188 *D3* **Zhovkva** *Pol.* Zółkiew, *Rus.* Zholkev, Zholkva; *prev.* Nesterov. L'vivs'ka Oblast', NW Ukraine 50°04′N 24°E
189 *J5* **Zhovti Vody** *Rus.* Zhëltyye Vody. Dnipropetrovs'ka Oblast', E Ukraine 48°24′N 33°30′E
189 *I7* **Zhovtneve** *Rus.* Zhovtnevoye. Mykolayivs'ka Oblast', S Ukraine 46°50′N 32°00′E
Zhovtnevoye *see* Zhovtneve
185 *K6* **Zhrebchevo, Yazovir** ⊠ C Bulgaria
245 *N3* **Zhuanghe** Liaoning, NE China 39°42′N 123°00′E
244 *C7* **Zhuanglang** *var.* Shuiluo; *prev.* Shuilocheng. Gansu, C China 35°06′N 106°21′E
227 *H7* **Zhuantobe** *Kaz.* Zhūantöbe. Yuzhnyy Kazakhstan, S Kazakhstan 44°45′N 68°50′E
245 *L6* **Zhucheng** Shandong, E China 35°58′N 119°24′E
244 *B8* **Zhugqu** Gansu, C China 33°51′N 104°14′E
243 *H10* **Zhuhai** Guangdong, S China 22°16′N 113°30′E
243 *H3* **Zhuhe** Hebei, C China 29°44′N 113°07′E
Zhuizishan *see* Weichang
243 *M3* **Zhuji** Zhejiang, China 29°26′N 120°08′E
Zhuji *see* Shangqiu
243 *K1* **Zhujiang** Jiangsu, E China 32°03′N 118°37′E
243 *H10* **Zhujiang Kou** *estuary* Guangdong, China
243 *M2* **Zhujing** Shanghai Shi, E China 30°54′N 121°09′E
196 *E3* **Zhukovka** Bryanskaya Oblast', W Russian Federation 53°33′N 33°48′E
245 *H9* **Zhumadian** Henan, E China 32°59′N 114°02′E
245 *H9* **Zhumadian** Henan, C China 32°58′N 114°03′E
245 *I2* **Zhuolu** Hebei, China 40°13′N 115°08′E
Zhuo Xian *see* Zhuozhou
245 *H6* **Zhuozhang He** ⇝ Shanxi, China
245 *J3* **Zhuozhou** *prev.* Zhuo Xian. Hebei, E China 39°22′N 115°40′E
244 *G2* **Zhuozi** Inner Mongolia, China 40°34′N 112°20′E
244 *D3* **Zhuozi Shan** ▲ N China 39°28′N 106°58′E
Zhuravichi *see* Zhuravichy
191 *I10* **Zhuravichy** *Rus.* Zhuravichi. Homyel'skaya Voblasts', SE Belarus 53°15′N 30°33′E
227 *H3* **Zhuravlevka** Akmola, N Kazakhstan 52°00′N 69°59′E
189 *I3* **Zhurivka** Kyyivs'ka Oblast', N Ukraine 50°28′N 31°48′E
226 *E4* **Zhuryn** Aktyubinsk, W Kazakhstan 49°13′N 57°36′E
227 *J7* **Zhusandala, Step'** *grassland* SE Kazakhstan
242 *F1* **Zhushan** Hubei, C China 32°11′N 110°05′E
Zhushan *see* Xuan'en
242 *E1* **Zhuxi** Hubei, China 32°11′N 109°25′E
243 *L4* **Zhuxi** Zhejiang, SE China 28°11′N 118°54′E
243 *J1* **Zhuxiang** Anhui, E China 32°19′N 117°13′E
Zhuyang *see* Dazhu
243 *H5* **Zhuzhou** Hunan, S China 27°52′N 112°52′E
188 *D4* **Zhydachiv** *Pol.* Żydaczów, *Rus.* Zhidachov. L'vivs'ka Oblast', NW Ukraine 49°20′N 24°08′E
226 *C3* **Zhympity** *Kaz.* Zhympīty; *prev.* Dzhambeyty. Zapadnyy, W Kazakhstan 50°16′N 52°34′E
191 *G11* **Zhytkavichy** *Rus.* Zhitkovichi. Homyel'skaya Voblasts', SE Belarus 52°14′N 27°52′E
188 *G3* **Zhytomyr** *Rus.* Zhitomir. Zhytomyrs'ka Oblast', NW Ukraine 50°17′N 28°40′E
Zhytomyr *see* Zhytomyrs'ka Oblast'
188 *F2* **Zhytomyrs'ka Oblast'** *var.* Zhytomyr, *Rus.* Zhitomirskaya Oblast'. ◆ *province* N Ukraine
233 *K8* **Zia** ✈ (Dhaka) Dhaka, C Bangladesh
171 *N8* **Ziama Mansouria** Algeria
183 *F10* **Žiar nad Hronom** *var.* Sväty Kríž nad Hronom, *Ger.* Heiligenkreuz, *Hung.* Garamszentkereszt. Banskobystrický Kraj, C Slovakia 48°36′N 18°52′E
245 *K5* **Zibo** *var.* Zhangdian. Shandong, E China 36°51′N 118°01′E
244 *F5* **Zichang** *prev.* Wayaobu. Shaanxi, C China 37°08′N 109°40′E
Zichenau *see* Ciechanów
245 *K6* **Zichuan** Shandong, E China 36°39′N 117°56′E
183 *E8* **Ziębice** *Ger.* Münsterberg in Schlesien. Dolnośląskie, SW Poland 50°37′N 17°01′E
Ziebingen *see* Cybinka
Ziegenhais *see* Głuchołazy
182 *C6* **Zielona Góra** *Ger.* Grünberg, Grünberg in Schlesien, Grüneberg. Lubuskie, W Poland 51°56′N 15°31′E
163 *D8* **Zierikzee** Zeeland, SW Netherlands 51°39′N 03°55′E
242 *B3* **Zigong** *var.* Tzekung. Sichuan, C China 29°20′N 104°48′E
242 *F2* **Zigui** Hubei, C China 31°01′N 110°35′E
132 *B5* **Ziguinchor** SW Senegal 12°34′N 16°20′W
86 *D8* **Zihuatanejo** Guerrero, S Mexico 17°39′N 101°33′W
243 *I9* **Zijin** Guangdong, China 23°23′N 115°06′E
Ziketan *see* Xinghai
218 *D6* **Zikhron Yaakov** Israel 32°34′N 34°57′E
Zilah *see* Zalău
197 *M3* **Zilair** Respublika Bashkortostan, W Russian Federation 52°12′N 57°15′E
214 *F5* **Zile** Tokat, N Turkey 40°18′N 35°52′E
183 *F9* **Žilina** *Ger.* Sillein, *Hung.* Zsolna. Zlínský Kraj, N Slovakia 49°13′N 18°44′E
183 *F9* **Žilinský Kraj** ◆ *region* N Slovakia
128 *D4* **Zillah** *var.* Zallah. C Libya 28°30′N 17°33′E
Zillenmarkt *see* Zalău
177 *H4* **Ziller** ⇝ W Austria
Zillertal Alps *see* Zillertaler Alpen
177 *H4* **Zillertaler Alpen** *Eng.* Zillertal Alps, *It.* Alpi Aurine. ▲▲ Austria/Italy
180 *J7* **Zilly** Sachsen-Anhalt, Germany 50°49′N 51°57′E
190 *G7* **Zilupe** *Ger.* Rosenhof. Ludza, E Latvia 56°10′N 28°06′E
193 *H8* **Zima** Irkutskaya Oblast', S Russian Federation 53°57′N 101°57′E
86 *F5* **Zimapán** Hidalgo, C Mexico 20°45′N 99°21′W
86 *G8* **Zimatlán** Oaxaca, Mexico 16°52′N 96°47′W
138 *F3* **Zimba** Southern, S Zambia 17°20′S 26°11′E
139 *H3* **Zimbabwe** *off.* Republic of Zimbabwe; *prev.* Rhodesia. ◆ *republic* S Africa
Zimbabwe, Republic of *see* Zimbabwe
188 *C7* **Zimbor** *Hung.* Magyarzsombor. Sălaj, NW Romania 47°00′N 23°16′E
Zimmerbude *see* Svetlyy
188 *D10* **Zimnicea** Teleorman, S Romania 43°39′N 25°21′E
185 *L6* **Zimnitsa** Yambol, E Bulgaria 42°34′N 26°37′E
197 *H7* **Zimovniki** Rostovskaya Oblast', SW Russian Federation 47°07′N 42°29′E
86 *E6* **Zinapécuaro** Michoacán, Mexico 19°52′N 100°49′W
Zindajān *see* Zendeh Jan
133 *K4* **Zinder** Zinder, S Niger 13°47′N 09°02′E
133 *L4* **Zinder** ◆ *department* S Niger
132 *G5* **Ziniaré** C Burkina 12°35′N 01°18′W
Zinjan *see* Zanjān
220 *G9* **Zinjibār** SW Yemen 13°08′N 45°23′E
189 *J3* **Zin'kiv** *var.* Zen'kov. Poltavs'ka Oblast', NE Ukraine 50°11′N 34°22′E
Zinov'yevsk *see* Kirovohrad
Zintenhof *see* Sindi
73 *D8* **Zion** Illinois, N USA 42°27′N 87°49′W
102 *C5* **Zipaquirá** Cundinamarca, C Colombia 05°03′N 74°01′W
Zipser Neudorf *see* Spišská Nová Ves
219 *C9* **Ziqim** Israel
219 *C9* **Ziqim** Israel 31°36′N 34°31′E
86 *D7* **Zirándaro** Guerrero, Mexico 18°27′N 100°59′W
183 *E11* **Zirc** Veszprém, W Hungary 47°16′N 17°52′E
184 *B5* **Žirje** *It.* Zuri. *island* S Croatia
Zirknitz *see* Cerknica
176 *G4* **Zirl** Tirol, W Austria 47°17′N 11°16′E
181 *J13* **Zirndorf** Bayern, SE Germany 49°27′N 10°57′E
240 *F6* **Zi Shui** ⇝ C China
177 *L1* **Zistersdorf** Niederösterreich, NE Austria 48°32′N 16°45′E
86 *E6* **Zitácuaro** Michoacán, SW Mexico 19°28′N 100°21′W
Zito *see* Lhorong
242 *B1* **Zitong** Sichuan, C China 31°38′N 105°10′E
182 *C7* **Zittau** Sachsen, E Germany 50°53′N 14°48′E
141 *L4* **Zitundo** Mozambique 26°45′S 32°49′E
184 *E4* **Živinice** Federacija Bosna I Hercegovina, E Bosnia and Herzegovina 44°26′N 18°39′E
Ziwa Magharibi *see* Kagera
136 *E4* **Ziway Hāyk'** ◎ C Ethiopia
243 *H7* **Zixing** Hunan, S China 26°01′N 113°25′E
245 *J4* **Ziya He** ⇝ Hebei, China
197 *M4* **Ziyanchurino** Orenburgskaya Oblast', W Russian Federation 51°36′N 56°58′E
245 *K9* **Ziyang** Anhui, E China 33°03′N 118°04′E
242 *E1* **Ziyang** Shaanxi, C China 32°33′N 108°27′E
242 *B3* **Ziyang** Sichuan, China 30°05′N 104°23′E
242 *F6* **Ziyuan** Guangxi, China 26°01′N 110°23′E
242 *B6* **Ziyun** Guizhou, China 25°27′N 106°02′E
242 *C5* **Ziyun** Guizhou, S China 27°57′N 106°21′E
242 *B3* **Zizhong** Sichuan, C China 29°48′N 104°51′E
244 *F5* **Zizhou** Shaanxi, China 37°22′N 110°01′E
183 *F10* **Zlaté Moravce** *Hung.* Aranyosmarót. Nitriansky Kraj, SW Slovakia 48°24′N 18°20′E
184 *F5* **Zlatibor** ▲▲ W Serbia
185 *L6* **Zlati Voyvoda** Sliven, C Bulgaria 42°36′N 26°13′E
188 *C7* **Zlatna** *Ger.* Kleinschlatten, *Hung.* Zalatna; *prev.* *Ger.* Goldmarkt. Alba, C Romania 46°08′N 23°11′E
185 *J6* **Zlatna Panega** Lovech, N Bulgaria 43°07′N 24°09′E
185 *M5* **Zlatni Pyasŭtsi** Dobrich, NE Bulgaria 43°19′N 28°03′E
197 *M2* **Zlatoust** Chelyabinskaya Oblast', C Russian Federation 55°12′N 59°33′E
183 *H10* **Zlatý Stôl** *Ger.* Goldener Tisch, *Hung.* Aranycsasztal. ▲ C Slovakia 48°45′N 20°39′E
185 *H7* **Zletovo** NE FYR Macedonia 42°00′N 22°14′E
183 *E9* **Zlín** *prev.* Gottwaldov. Zlínský Kraj, E Czech Republic 49°14′N 17°40′E
183 *E9* **Zlínský Kraj** ◆ *region* E Czech Republic
128 *C2* **Zlīṭan** W Libya 32°28′N 14°34′E
182 *D4* **Złocieniec** *Ger.* Falkenburg in Pommern. Zachodnio-pomorskie, NW Poland 53°31′N 16°01′E
182 *F7* **Złoczew** Sieradz, S Poland 51°24′N 18°36′E
Złoczów *see* Zolochev
182 *D7* **Złotoryja** *Ger.* Goldberg. Dolnośląskie, W Poland 51°08′N 15°57′E
182 *E4* **Złotów** Wielkopolskie, C Poland 53°22′N 17°02′E
191 *J11* **Zlynka** Bryanskaya Oblast', Russian Federation
192 *F8* **Zmeinogorsk** Altayskiy Kray, S Russian Federation 51°07′N 82°16′E
182 *E7* **Żmigród** *Ger.* Trachenberg. Dolnośląskie, SW Poland 51°31′N 16°55′E
196 *F3* **Zmiyevka** Orlovskaya Oblast', W Russian Federation 52°39′N 36°20′E
189 *L4* **Zmiyiv** Kharkivs'ka Oblast', E Ukraine 49°40′N 36°22′E
Zna *see* Tsna
Znaim *see* Znojmo
196 *G4* **Znamenka** Tambovskaya Oblast', W Russian Federation 52°24′N 42°28′E
Znamenka *see* Znam"yanka
191 *B9* **Znamensk** Astrakhanskaya Oblast', W Russian Federation 54°37′N 21°13′E
192 *E7* **Znamenskoye** Omskaya Oblast', C Russian Federation 57°09′N 73°40′E
189 *I5* **Znam"yanka** *Rus.* Znamenka. Kirovohrads'ka Oblast', C Ukraine 48°41′N 32°40′E
182 *E5* **Żnin** Kujawsko-pomorskie, C Poland 52°50′N 17°41′E
183 *D10* **Znojmo** *Ger.* Znaim. Jihomoravský Kraj, SE Czech Republic 48°52′N 16°04′E
140 *F9* **Zoar** Western Cape, South Africa 33°29′S 21°26′E
134 *H6* **Zobia** Orientale, N Dem. Rep. Congo 02°57′N 25°55′E
139 *I2* **Zóbuè** Tete, NW Mozambique 15°36′S 34°26′E
162 *E7* **Zoetermeer** Zuid-Holland, W Netherlands 52°04′N 04°30′E
219 *E11* **Zofar** Israel
219 *E11* **Zofar** Israel 30°33′N 35°10′E
176 *D4* **Zofingen** Aargau, N Switzerland 47°18′N 07°57′E
239 *J9* **Zogang** *var.* Wangda. Xizang Zizhiqu, W China 29°41′N 97°54′E
176 *F6* **Zogno** Lombardia, N Italy 45°49′N 09°42′E
222 *E6* **Zohreh, Rūd-e** ⇝ SW Iran
244 *A8* **Zoigê** *var.* Dagcagoin. Sichuan, C China 33°44′N 102°57′E
Zółkiew *see* Zhovkva
176 *D4* **Zollikofen** Bern, W Switzerland 47°00′N 07°24′E
188 *D4* **Zolochev** *Pol.* Złoczów, *Rus.* Zolochiv. L'vivs'ka Oblast', W Ukraine 49°48′N 24°51′E
189 *K3* **Zolochiv** *Rus.* Zolochev. Kharkivs'ka Oblast', E Ukraine 50°16′N 35°58′E
Zolochiv *see* Zolochev
189 *M5* **Zolote** *Rus.* Zolotoye. Luhans'ka Oblast', E Ukraine 48°42′N 38°33′E
189 *I4* **Zolotonosha** Cherkas'ka Oblast', C Ukraine 49°39′N 32°05′E
Zolotoye *see* Zolote
Zólyom *see* Zvolen
137 *C14* **Zomba** Southern, S Malawi 15°22′S 35°23′E
Zombor *see* Sombor
163 *C9* **Zomergem** Oost-Vlaanderen, NW Belgium 51°07′N 03°31′E
229 *I6* **Zomin** *Rus.* Zaamin. Jizzax Viloyati, C Uzbekistan 39°56′N 68°16′E
134 *E6* **Zongo** Equateur, N Dem. Rep. Congo 04°18′N 18°42′E
86 *G7* **Zongolica** Veracruz-Llave, Mexico
214 *D4* **Zonguldak** Zonguldak, NW Turkey 41°26′N 31°47′E
214 *E4* **Zonguldak** ◆ *province* NW Turkey
163 *G10* **Zonhoven** Limburg, NE Belgium 50°59′N 05°22′E
222 *D2* **Zonūz** Āžarbāyjān-e Khāvarī, NW Iran 38°32′N 45°54′E
175 *B8* **Zonza** Corse, France, C Mediterranean Sea 41°49′N 09°13′E
Zoppot *see* Sopot
87 *H9* **Zoquitlan** Oaxaca, Mexico 16°33′N 96°23′W
Zorgho *see* Zorgo
133 *H5* **Zorgo** *var.* Zorgho. C Burkina 12°15′N 00°37′W
170 *E6* **Zorita** Extremadura, W Spain 39°18′N 05°42′W
231 *J1* **Zorkŭl** *Rus.* Ozero Zorkul'. ◎ SE Tajikistan
Zorkul', Ozero *see* Zorkŭl
104 *B3* **Zorritos** Tumbes, N Peru 03°43′S 80°42′W
183 *F8* **Żory** *var.* Zory, *Ger.* Sohrau. Śląskie, S Poland 50°04′N 18°42′E
132 *D7* **Zorzor** N Liberia 07°46′N 09°28′W
163 *C10* **Zottegem** Oost-Vlaanderen, NW Belgium 50°52′N 03°49′E
133 *I7* **Zou** ⇝ S Benin
133 *N1* **Zouar** Borkou-Ennedi-Tibesti, N Chad 20°25′N 16°28′E
245 *J7* **Zoucheng** Shandong, China 35°14′N 116°35′E
130 *C7* **Zouérat** *var.* Zouérate, Zouîrât. Tiris Zemmour, N Mauritania 22°44′N 12°29′W
Zouérate *see* Zouérat
Zoug *see* Zug
Zouîrât *see* Zouérat
132 *E7* **Zoukougbeu** C Ivory Coast 09°47′N 06°50′W
245 *K5* **Zouping** Shandong, China 36°32′N 117°26′E
162 *H3* **Zoutkamp** Groningen, NE Netherlands 53°22′N 06°17′E
163 *F10* **Zoutleeuw** *Fr.* Leau. Vlaams Brabant, C Belgium 50°49′N 05°06′E
190 *G3* **Zovka** Pskovskaya Oblast', Russian Federation
184 *F3* **Zrenjanin** *prev.* Petrovgrad, Veliki Bečkerek, *Ger.* Grossbetschkerek, *Hung.* Nagybecskerek. Vojvodina, N Serbia 45°23′N 20°24′E
184 *C3* **Zrinska Gora** ▲▲ C Croatia
Zsablya *see* Žabalj
179 *H8* **Zschopau** ⇝ E Germany
Zsebely *see* Jebel
Zsibó *see* Jibou
Zsilyvajdevulkán *see* Vulcan
Zsil/Zsily *see* Jiu
Zsolna *see* Žilina
Zsombolya *see* Jimbolia
Zsupanya *see* Županja
102 *G4* **Zuata** Anzoátegui, NE Venezuela 08°24′N 65°13′W
170 *G8* **Zubia** Andalucía, S Spain 37°10′N 03°36′W
291 *I9* **Zubov Seamount** *undersea feature* E Atlantic Ocean 20°45′S 08°45′E
194 *E10* **Zubtsov** Tverskaya Oblast', W Russian Federation 56°10′N 34°34′E
218 *E6* **Zububa** West Bank 32°32′N 35°13′E
173 *L3* **Zucaina** Valenciana, Spain 40°07′N 0°25′W
179 *F14* **Zuckerhütl** ▲ SW Austria 46°57′N 11°07′E
Zueila *see* Zawīlah
132 *F7* **Zuénoula** C Ivory Coast 07°26′N 06°03′W
171 *I3* **Zuera** Aragón, NE Spain 41°52′N 00°47′W
221 *J7* **Ẓufār** *Eng.* Dhofar. *physical region* SW Oman
176 *E4* **Zug** *Fr.* Zoug. Zug, C Switzerland 47°11′N 08°31′E
174 *C3* **Zug** *Fr.* Zoug. ◆ *canton* C Switzerland
215 *J3* **Zugdidi** W Georgia 42°30′N 41°52′E
179 *C14* **Zuger See** ◎ NW Switzerland
179 *F14* **Zugspitze** ▲ S Germany 47°25′N 10°58′E
163 *D8* **Zuid-Beveland** *var.* South Beveland. *island* SW Netherlands
162 *G6* **Zuidelijk-Flevoland** *polder* C Netherlands
Zuider Zee *see* IJsselmeer
162 *E7* **Zuid-Holland** *Eng.* South Holland. ◆ *province* W Netherlands
162 *H3* **Zuidhorn** Groningen, NE Netherlands 53°15′N 06°25′E
162 *I4* **Zuidlaardermeer** ◎ NE Netherlands
162 *I4* **Zuidlaren** Drenthe, NE Netherlands 53°06′N 06°41′E
163 *G8* **Zuid-Willemsvaart Kanaal** *canal* S Netherlands
162 *I5* **Zuidwolde** Drenthe, NE Netherlands 52°40′N 06°25′E
Zuitai/Zuitaizi *see* Kangxian
170 *G8* **Zújar** Andalucía, S Spain 37°33′N 02°52′W
170 *F7* **Zújar** ⇝ W Spain
170 *F6* **Zújar, Embalse del** ⊠ W Spain
136 *E2* **Zula** E Eritrea 15°19′N 39°40′E
102 *D3* **Zulia** *off.* Estado Zulia. ◆ *state* NW Venezuela
Zulia, Estado *see* Zulia
Zullapara *see* Sinchaingbyin
Züllichau *see* Sulechów
181 *B10* **Zulpich** Nordrhein-Westfalen, Germany 6°39′N 50°42′E
168 *B6* **Zumaia** Pais Vasco, Spain 43°18′N 2°15′W
171 *H2* **Zumárraga** País Vasco, N Spain 43°05′N 02°19′W
177 *K6* **Žumberačko Gorje** *var.* Gorjanči, Uskocke Planine, Žumberak, *Ger.* Uskokengebirge; *prev.* Sichelburger Gerbirge. ▲ Croatia/Slovenia *see also* Gorjanci
Žumberak *see* Gorjanci/Žumberačko Gorje
292 *F4* **Zumberge Coast** *coastal feature* Antarctica
Zumbo *see* Vila do Zumbo
74 *H5* **Zumbro Falls** Minnesota, N USA 44°15′N 92°25′W
74 *H5* **Zumbro River** ⇝ Minnesota, N USA
74 *H5* **Zumbrota** Minnesota, N USA 44°18′N 92°37′W
86 *E8* **Zumpango del Río** Guerrero, S Mexico 17°39′N 99°30′W
163 *E8* **Zundert** Noord-Brabant, S Netherlands 51°28′N 04°40′E
Zungaria *see* Dzungaria
133 *J6* **Zungeru** Niger, C Nigeria 09°49′N 06°10′E
79 *J7* **Zuni** New Mexico, SW USA 35°03′N 108°52′W
79 *K7* **Zuni Mountains** ▲▲ New Mexico, SW USA
242 *C5* **Zunyi** Guizhou, China 27°19′N 106°29′E
242 *C5* **Zunyi** Guizhou, S China 27°40′N 106°56′E
242 *C9* **Zuo Jiang** ⇝ China/Vietnam
176 *F5* **Zuoz** Graubünden, SE Switzerland 46°37′N 09°58′E
184 *E3* **Županja** *Hung.* Zsupanya. Vukovar-Srijem, E Croatia 45°03′N 18°42′E
184 *G7* **Žur** *Serb.* Žur. S Kosovo 42°10′N 20°37′E
Žur *see* Žur
195 *J9* **Zura** Udmurtskaya Respublika, NW Russian Federation 57°36′N 53°19′E
217 *K5* **Zurbāṭīyah** Wāsiṭ, E Iraq 33°13′N 46°07′E
Zuri *see* Žirje
176 *E4* **Zürich** *Eng./Fr.* Zurich, *It.* Zurigo. Zürich, N Switzerland 47°23′N 08°33′E
176 *E4* **Zürich** *Eng./Fr.* Zurich. ◆ *canton* N Switzerland
Zurich, Lake *see* Zürichsee
174 *C3* **Zürichsee** *Eng.* Lake Zurich. ◎ NE Switzerland
Zurigo *see* Zürich
229 *L8* **Zŭrkŭl** *Pash.* Sarī Qūl, *Rus.* Ozero Zurkul'. ◎ Afghanistan/Tajikistan *see also* Sarī Qūl
Zŭrkŭl *see* Sarī Qūl
Zurkul', Ozero *see* Sarī Qūl/Zŭrkŭl
182 *G5* **Żuromin** Mazowieckie, C Poland 53°00′N 19°54′E
176 *F4* **Zürs** Vorarlberg, W Austria 47°11′N 10°11′E
133 *J5* **Zuru** Kebbi, W Nigeria 11°28′N 05°13′E
176 *D3* **Zurzach** Aargau, N Switzerland 47°33′N 08°21′E
179 *F12* **Zusam** ⇝ S Germany
162 *H6* **Zutphen** Gelderland, E Netherlands 52°09′N 06°12′E
181 *G13* **Züttlingen** Baden-Württemberg, Germany 9°20′N 49°18′E
128 *C2* **Zuwārah** NW Libya 32°56′N 12°06′E
Zuwaylah *see* Zawīlah
195 *J9* **Zuyevka** Kirovskaya Oblast', NW Russian Federation 58°24′N 51°08′E
240 *G5* **Zuzhou** Hunan, S China 27°52′N 113°00′E
Zvenigorodka *see* Zvenyhorodka
189 *H4* **Zvenyhorodka** *Rus.* Zvenigorodka. Cherkas'ka Oblast', C Ukraine 49°05′N 30°58′E
193 *H7* **Zvezdnyy** Irkutskaya Oblast', C Russian Federation 56°43′N 106°22′E
195 *K9* **Zvëzdnyy** Permskaya Oblast', NW Russian Federation 57°45′N 56°20′E
139 *H4* **Zvishavane** *prev.* Shabani. Matabeleland South, S Zimbabwe 20°20′S 30°02′E
183 *F10* **Zvolen** *Ger.* Altsohl, *Hung.* Zólyom. Banskobystrický Kraj, C Slovakia 48°35′N 19°06′E
184 *E4* **Zvornik** E Bosnia and Herzegovina 44°24′N 19°07′E
162 *H3* **Zwaagwesteinde** *Fris.* De Westerein. Friesland, N Netherlands 53°16′N 06°08′E
162 *E6* **Zwanenburg** Noord-Holland, C Netherlands 52°22′N 04°44′E
140 *F9* **Zwars** Western Cape, South Africa 32°52′S 21°53′E
162 *H5* **Zwarte Meer** ◎ N Netherlands
162 *H5* **Zwarte Water** ⇝ N Netherlands
162 *H5* **Zwartsluis** Overijssel, E Netherlands 52°39′N 06°04′E
132 *E8* **Zwedru** *var.* Tchien. E Liberia 06°04′N 08°07′W
162 *I4* **Zweeloo** Drenthe, NE Netherlands 52°48′N 06°45′E
181 *D13* **Zweibrücken** *Fr.* Deux-Ponts, *Lat.* Bipontium. Rheinland-Pfalz, SW Germany 49°15′N 07°22′E
176 *C5* **Zweisimmen** Fribourg, W Switzerland 46°33′N 07°22′E
179 *G8* **Zwenkau** Sachsen, E Germany 51°11′N 12°19′E
181 *G9* **Zwesten** Hessen, Germany 9°11′N 51°03′E
177 *K1* **Zwettl** Wien, NE Austria 48°28′N 14°17′E
177 *J2* **Zwettl an der Rodl** Oberösterreich, N Austria 48°28′N 14°17′E
163 *C10* **Zwevegem** West-Vlaanderen, W Belgium 50°48′N 03°20′E
179 *H9* **Zwickau** Sachsen, E Germany 50°43′N 12°31′E
179 *H8* **Zwickauer Mulde** ⇝ E Germany
179 *H11* **Zwiesel** Bayern, SE Germany 49°02′N 13°14′E
162 *E7* **Zwijndrecht** Zuid-Holland, SW Netherlands 51°49′N 04°39′E
141 *H3* **Zwingli** North West, South Africa 24°52′S 26°09′E
180 *E3* **Zwischenahner Meer** ◎ Niedersachsen, Germany
Zwischenwässern *see* Medvode
Zwittau *see* Svitavy
182 *H7* **Zwoleń** Mazowieckie, SE Poland 51°21′N 21°37′E
162 *H5* **Zwolle** Overijssel, E Netherlands 52°31′N 06°06′E
68 *B2* **Zwolle** Louisiana, S USA 31°37′N 93°38′W
182 *G6* **Żychlin** Łódzkie, C Poland 52°15′N 19°38′E
Żydaczów *see* Zhydachiv
Zyembin *see* Zembin
Zyôetu *see* Jōetsu
182 *G6* **Żyrardów** Mazowieckie, C Poland 52°02′N 20°28′E
193 *L4* **Zyryanka** Respublika Sakha (Yakutiya), NE Russian Federation 65°45′N 150°43′E
227 *M3* **Zyryanovsk** Vostochnyy Kazakhstan, E Kazakhstan 49°45′N 84°16′E

◆ Country
● Country Capital
◇ Dependent Territory
○ Dependent Territory Capital
◆ Administrative Regions
✈ International Airport
▲ Mountain
▲▲ Mountain Range
⛰ Volcano
⇝ River
◎ Lake
⊠ Reservoir

INDEX

Picture credits

Data for the bathymetric maps provided by Planetary Visions Limited based on ETOPO2 global relief data, SRTM30 land elevation data and the Generalised Bathymetric
Chart of the Ocean.

ETOPO2 published by the U.S. Department of Commerce, National Oceanic and Atmospheric Administration, National Geophysical Data Center, 2001.

SRTM30 published by NASA and the National Geospatial Intelligence Agency, 2005, distributed by the U.S. Geological Survey.

GEBCO One Minute Grid reproduced from the GEBCO Digital Atlas published by the British Oceanographic Data Centre on behalf of the Intergovernmental Oceanographic
Commission of UNESCO and the International Hydrographic Organisation, 2003.

| ◆ Country | ◇ Dependent Territory | ◈ Administrative Regions | ▲ Mountain | ⛰ Volcano | ⊚ Lake |
| ● Country Capital | ○ Dependent Territory Capital | ✕ International Airport | ▲▲ Mountain Range | ⧗ River | ▣ Reservoir |

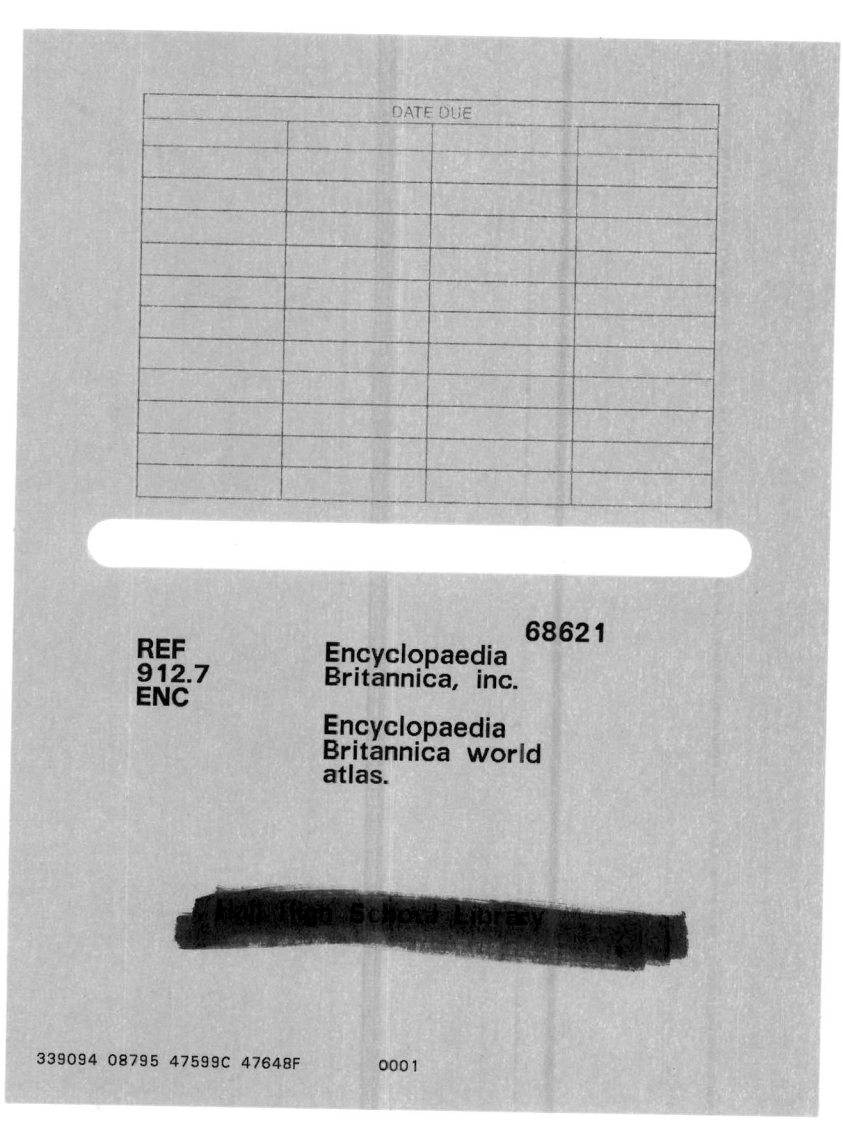

NORTH AMERICA

 CANADA
 UNITED STATES OF AMERICA
 MEXICO
 BELIZE
 COSTA RICA
 EL SALVADOR
 GUATEMALA
 HONDURAS

SOUTH AMERICA

 GRENADA
 HAITI
 JAMAICA
 ST KITTS & NEVIS
 ST LUCIA
 ST VINCENT & THE GRENADINES
 TRINIDAD & TOBAGO
 COLOMBIA

AFRICA

 URUGUAY
 CHILE
 PARAGUAY
 ALGERIA
 EGYPT
 LIBYA
 MOROCCO
 TUNISIA

 LIBERIA
 MALI
 MAURITANIA
 NIGER
 NIGERIA
 SENEGAL
 SIERRA LEONE
 TOGO

 BURUNDI
 DJIBOUTI
 ERITREA
 ETHIOPIA
 KENYA
 RWANDA
 SOMALIA
 SUDAN

EUROPE

 SOUTH AFRICA
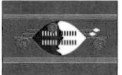 SWAZILAND
 ZAMBIA
 ZIMBABWE
 DENMARK
 FINLAND
 ICELAND
 NORWAY

 MONACO
  ANDORRA
 PORTUGAL
  SPAIN
 ITALY
 SAN MARINO
VATICAN CITY
 AUSTRIA

 BOSNIA & HERZEGOVINA
 CROATIA
 KOSOVO
 MACEDONIA
 MONTENEGRO
 SERBIA
 BULGARIA
 GREECE
MOLDOVA

ASIA

  ARMENIA
 AZERBAIJAN
 GEORGIA
 TURKEY
 IRAQ
 ISRAEL
 JORDAN
 LEBANON

 IRAN
 KAZAKHSTAN
 KYRGYZSTAN
 TAJIKISTAN
 TURKMENISTAN
 UZBEKISTAN
 AFGHANISTAN
 PAKISTAN

 TAIWAN
 JAPAN
 MYANMAR (BURMA)
 CAMBODIA
LAOS
PHILIPPINES
THAILAND
VIETNAM

AUSTRALASIA & OCEANIA

 MAURITIUS
 SEYCHELLES
 AUSTRALIA
NEW ZEALAND
PAPUA NEW GUINEA
FIJI
SOLOMON ISLANDS
VANUATU